# Advantage series

# Microsoft® Office Excel®

## Complete edition

Glen J. **Coulthard**

Sarah Hutchinson **Clifford**

McGraw Hill **Technology Education**

Boston   Burr Ridge, IL   Dubuque, IA   Madison, WI   New York   San Francisco   St. Louis
Bangkok   Bogotá   Caracas   Kuala Lumpur   Lisbon   London   Madrid   Mexico City
Milan   Montreal   New Delhi   Santiago   Seoul   Singapore   Sydney   Taipei   Toronto

# Technology Education

ADVANTAGE SERIES: MICROSOFT® OFFICE EXCEL 2003, COMPLETE EDITION
Published by McGraw-Hill Technology Education, an imprint of The McGraw-Hill Companies, Inc., 1221 Avenue
of the Americas, New York, NY, 10020. Copyright © 2005, by The McGraw-Hill Companies, Inc. All rights
reserved. No part of this publication may be reproduced or distributed in any form or by any means, or stored in a
data base or retrieval system, without the prior written consent of The McGraw-Hill Companies, Inc., including, but
not limited to, in any network or other electronic storage or transmission, or broadcast for distance learning.

Some ancillaries, including electronic and print components, may not be available to customers outside the United
States.

 This book is printed on acid-free paper.

1 2 3 4 5 6 7 8 9 0 WEB/WEB 0 9 8 7 6 5 4

ISBN  0-07-283418-8

Editor-in-chief: Bob Woodbury
Publisher: Brandon Nordin
Sponsoring editor: Marc Chernoff
Developmental editor: Lisa Chin-Johnson
Senior marketing manager: Andy Bernier
Senior project manager: Lori Koetters
Production supervisor: Debra R. Sylvester
Producer, media technology: Mark Molsky
Designer: Adam Rooke
Senior supplement producer: Rose M. Range
Senior digital content specialist: Brian Nacik
Cover design: Andrew Curtis
Cover image: © 2003 Getty Images
Typeface: 10/12 *Garamond*
Compositor: *GTS Graphics, Inc.*
Printer: *Webcrafters, Inc.*

Library of Congress Cataloging-in-Publication Data

Coulthard, Glen J.
    Microsoft Office Excel 2003 / Glen J. Coulthard, Sarah Hutchinson Clifford.—Complete ed.
        p. cm.—(Advantage series)
    Includes index.
    ISBN 0-07-283418-8
    1. Microsoft Excel (Computer file) 2. Business—Computer programs. 3. Electronic
spreadsheets. I. Clifford, Sarah Hutchinson. II. Title. III. Series.

HF5548.4.M523C6847 2005
005.54—dc22
                                                    2004049921

www.mhhe.com/it

# McGraw-Hill Technology Education

At MCGRAW-HILL TECHNOLOGY EDUCATION, we publish instructional materials for the technology education market, particularly computer instruction in post-secondary education—from introductory courses in traditional four-year universities to continuing education and proprietary schools. McGraw-Hill Technology Education presents a broad range of innovative products—texts, lab manuals, study guides, testing materials, and technology-based training and assessment tools.

We realize that technology has created and will continue to create new mediums for professors and students to use in managing resources and communicating information to one another. McGraw-Hill Technology Education provides the most flexible and complete teaching and learning tools available and offers solutions for the changing world of teaching and learning.

McGraw-Hill Technology Education is dedicated to providing today's instructors and students with the tools that will enable them to successfully navigate the world of Information Technology.

- **McGraw-Hill/Osborne**—This division of The McGraw-Hill Companies is known for its best-selling Internet titles Harley Hahn's *Internet & Web Yellow Pages* and the *Internet Complete Reference*. For more information, visit Osborne at www.osborne.com.

- **Digital Solutions**—Whether you want to teach a class online or merely to post your "bricks-and-mortar" class syllabus, McGraw-Hill Technology Education is committed to publishing digital solutions. Taking your course online does not have to be a solitary adventure, nor does it have to be a difficult one. We offer several solutions that will allow you to enjoy all the benefits of online course material.

- **Packaging Options**—For more information about our discount options, contact your McGraw-Hill sales representative at 1-800-338-3987 or visit our Web site at www.mhhe.com/it.

## What does this logo mean?

It means this courseware has been approved by the Microsoft® Office Specialist Program to be among the finest available for learning *Microsoft Office 2003, Microsoft Word 2003, Microsoft Excel 2003, Microsoft PowerPoint® 2003, and Microsoft Access 2003*. It also means that upon completion of this courseware, you may be prepared to take an exam for Microsoft Office Specialist qualification.

## What is a Microsoft Office Specialist?

A Microsoft Office Specialist is an individual who has passed exams for certifying his or her skills in one or more of the Microsoft Office desktop applications such as Microsoft Word, Microsoft Excel, Microsoft PowerPoint, Microsoft Outlook, Microsoft Access, or Microsoft Project. The Microsoft Office Specialist Program typically offers certification exams at the "Specialist" and "Expert" skill levels.* The Microsoft Office Specialist Program is the only program in the world approved by Microsoft for testing proficiency in Microsoft Office desktop applications and Microsoft Project. This testing program can be a valuable asset in any job search or career advancement.

## More Information:

To learn more about becoming a Microsoft Office Specialist, visit www.microsoft.com/officespecialist

To learn about other Microsoft Office Specialist approved courseware from McGraw-Hill/Technology Education, visit http://www.mhteched.com/catalogs/mous

---

* The availability of Microsoft Office Specialist certification exams varies by application, application version and language. Visit www.microsoft.com/office-specialist for exam availability.

Microsoft, the Microsoft Office Logo, PowerPoint, and Outlook are trademarks or registered trademarks of Microsoft Corporation in the United States and/or other countries, and the Microsoft Office Specialist Logo is used under license from owner.

# Preface

## The Advantage Series

# Goals/Philosophy

*The Advantage Series* presents the **What, Why,** and **How** of computer application skills to today's students. Each lab manual is based upon an efficient learning model that provides students and faculty with complete coverage of the most powerful software packages available today.

## Approach

*The Advantage Series* builds upon an efficient learning model that provides students and faculty with complete coverage and enhances critical thinking skills. The "**problem-solving**" approach teaches the What, Why, and How of computer application skills. This approach was further strengthened last year when the lead author of *the Advantage Series,* Glen Coulthard, met with members of the Microsoft Office Team to ensure that all the pedagogical features of the book are compatible with the requirements and standards of Microsoft.

    *The Advantage Series* introduces the "**Feature-Method-Practice**" layered approach. The *Feature* describes the command and tells the importance of that command. The *Method*

shows students how to perform the feature. The *Practice* allows students to apply the feature in a keystroke exercise.

**About the Series** *The Advantage Series* offers *three levels* of instruction. Each level builds upon the previous level. The following are the three levels of instructions:

> **Brief:** Covers the basics of the application, contains two to four chapters, and is typically 120–190 pages long.

> **Introductory:** Includes the Brief Lab manuals plus four additional chapters. The Introductory lab manuals are approximately 300 pages long and prepare students for the *Microsoft Office Specialist Exam.*

> **Complete:** Includes the Introductory lab manuals plus an additional four chapters of advanced level content. The Complete lab manuals are approximately 600–800 pages in length and prepare students to take the *Microsoft Office Specialist Expert Exam.*

> **Office 2003:** Includes the Brief lab manuals for Word, Excel, Access, and PowerPoint, plus three chapters of Integrating with Microsoft Office 2003.

# Features of This Book

*New and Improved Features:*

- A new design that makes it attractive and easier for students to follow and succeed with the material.

- An increase in the number of screenshots from previous editions enhances visual appeal and helps students successfully complete the hands-on exercises.

- More vigorous end-of-chapter contents available on the Web site.

- Updated Cases and hands-on exercises.

- Better implementation of design elements and shading for "Feature, Method, Practice" areas.

- Chapter Prerequisites

*Each lab manual features the following:*

- *Learning Objectives:* At the beginning of each chapter, a list of action-oriented objectives is presented detailing what is expected of the students.

- *Prerequisites:* Each chapter begins with a list of prerequisites that identify the skills necessary to complete the modules in that chapter.

- *Chapters:* Each lab manual is divided into chapters.

- *Modules:* Each chapter contains three to five independent modules, requiring approximately 30–45 minutes each to complete. Although we recommend you complete an entire chapter before proceeding, you may skip or rearrange the order of these modules to best suit your learning needs.

- *Case Studies:* Each chapter ends with a Case Study. The student is introduced to a fictitious person or company and their immediate problem or opportunity. Throughout the chapter, students obtain the knowledge and skills necessary to meet the challenges presented in the Case Study. At the end of each chapter, students are asked to solve problems directly related to the Case Study.

- *Feature-Method-Practice:* Each chapter highlights our unique "Feature-Method-Practice" layered approach.

The *Feature* layer describes the command or technique and persuades you of its importance and relevance. The *Method* layer shows you how to perform the procedure, and the *Practice* layer lets you apply the feature in a hands-on step-by-step exercise.

- *Instructions:* The numbered step-by-step progression for all hands-on examples and exercises are clearly identified. Students will find it surprisingly easy to follow the logical sequence of keystrokes and mouse clicks and will no longer worry about missing a step.

- *In Addition Boxes:* These content boxes are placed strategically throughout the chapter and provide information on advanced topics that are beyond the scope of the current discussion.

- *Self-Check Question Boxes:* At the end of each module, a brief self-check question appears for students to test their comprehension of the material. Answers to these questions appear in the Appendix.

- *Chapter Review:* The *Command Summary* and *Key Terms* provide an excellent review of the chapter content and prepare students for the short answer, true/false and multiple choice questions at the end of each chapter.

- *Hands-On Projects:* Each chapter concludes with hands-on projects that are divided into *Step-by-Step* and *On Your Own* which also reflect different levels of difficulty. In the *Step-by-Step* exercises, students are given step-by-step instructions and directions on how to complete a task. However, in the *On Your Own,* students are provided with instructions that allow for greater opportunities to apply the software to a variety of creative problem-solving situations.

- *Appendix: Microsoft Windows Quick Reference.* Each lab manual contains a *Microsoft Windows Quick Reference.* This quick reference teaches students the fundamentals of using a mouse and a keyboard, illustrates how to interact with a dialog box, and describes the fundamentals of how to use the Office 2003 Help System.

# preface

---

# Features of This Lab Manual

## Instructions

The numbered step-by-step progressions for all hands-on examples and exercises are clearly identified. Students will find it easy to follow the logical sequence of keystrokes and mouse clicks and will no longer worry about missing a step.

## In Addition Boxes

These content boxes are placed strategically throughout the chapter and provide information on topics that are beyond the scope of the current discussion.

## Self-Check Question Boxes

At the end of each module, a brief self-check question appears for students to test their comprehension of the material. Answers to these questions appear in the Appendix.

---

### Hands-On
#### exercises

step by step ▶

### 1. Creating and Using Range Names

In this exercise, you will practice working with named cell ranges in constructing formulas. To begin, you will use existing labels in the worksheet to define the range names automatically and then paste those names into the worksheet.

1. Open the data file named EX04HE01.

2. Save the workbook as "Departments" to your personal storage location.

3. To begin, name cell B8 "Total" using the Name Box in the Formula bar.

4. Use the existing worksheet labels in A2 through A7 to define range names for the data stored in cells B2 through B7. After choosing the Insert ➡ Name ➡ Create command, your screen should appear similar to the one shown in Figure 4.39.

**Figure 4.39**

Creating range names

---

### *In Addition* MAKING EFFICIENT USE OF RANGE NAMES

Range names facilitate the entry of formulas and functions in a worksheet. By using range names in place of cell references, you are less likely to make data-entry errors when constructing complex formulas. For those cells on a worksheet to which you must refer frequently, consider naming the cell ranges immediately. You can always delete, rename, or redefine these range names at a later date.

---

depending on the result, perform one of two calculations. Because the IF function is used in more complex problems, it is covered in Chapter 6 of the Advantage Series' Introductory and Complete editions.

 **SelfCheck**    **4.2** When might you use the Function Arguments dialog box or Insert Function dialog box to enter a function into the worksheet?

---

## 4.3 Creating an Embedded Chart

Since the earliest versions of spreadsheet software became available, users have been able to display their numerical data using graphs and charts. Although these graphics were acceptable for in-house business reports and school projects, they often lacked the depth and quality required by professional users. Until now! You can confidently use Excel 2003 to produce visually stunning worksheets and charts that are suitable for electronic business presentations, color print masters, published reports, and Web pages.

Many types of charts are available for presenting your worksheet data to engineers, statisticians, business professionals, and other audiences. Some popular business charts—line charts, column charts, pie

# Features of This Lab Manual

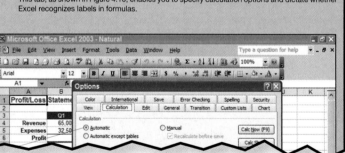

**4.1.4 Entering Natural Language Formulas**

→ **Feature**

Another alternative to cell references is a special type of expression called a **natural language formula**. Like a range name, a natural language formula allows you to build a formula using the row and column labels from the active worksheet. In effect, a natural language formula uses implicit range names. In order for natural language formulas to work effectively, however, the worksheet must be organized in a table format with distinctly labeled rows and columns.

→ **Method**

- SELECT: the cell where you want the result to appear
- TYPE: = (an equal sign)
- TYPE: an expression, such as Revenue-Expenses, using the actual row and column labels
- PRESS: ENTER

→ **Practice**

You will now use natural language formulas to calculate an expression in a worksheet. Ensure that no workbooks are open in the application window.

1. Open the data file named EX0414.

2. Save the workbook as "Natural" to your personal storage location.

3. Before you begin, you will need to review some configuration settings:
CHOOSE: Tools → Options
CLICK: *Calculation* tab
This tab, as shown in Figure 4.10, enables you to specify calculation options and dictate whether Excel recognizes labels in formulas.

**Figure 4.10**

Options dialog box, *Calculation* tab

## Feature-Method-Practice

Each chapter highlights our unique **"Feature-Method-Practice"** layered approach. The *Feature* layer describes the command or technique and persuades you of its importance and relevance. The *Method* layer shows you how to perform the procedure; while the *Practice* layer lets you apply the feature in a hands-on step-by-step exercise.

**CaseStudy** INTERIOR FOOTBALL LEAGUE (IFL)

The Interior Football League consists of eight elite football teams in as many communities. The IFL is run by a small group of dedicated volunteers who handle everything from coaching to administration. An ex-player himself, Doug Allen has volunteered for the organization for the past four years. In addition to fundraising, Doug is responsible for keeping records and tracking results for all of the teams in the league.

Shortly after the end of each season, the IFL publishes a newsletter that provides various statistics and other pertinent information about the season. In the past, this newsletter required weeks of effort, followed by days of typing results into a word processor. After enrolling in an Excel 2003 course, Doug now realizes that worksheets and charts can help him to complete his upcoming tasks. Specifically, he

## Case Studies

Each chapter ends with a Case Study. Throughout the chapter, students obtain the knowledge and skills necessary to meet the challenges presented in the Case Study. At the end of each chapter, students are asked to solve problems directly related to the Case Study.

preface

## Features of This Lab Manual

### Chapters

Each lab manual is divided into chapters. Each chapter is composed of three to five modules. Each module is composed of one or more lessons.

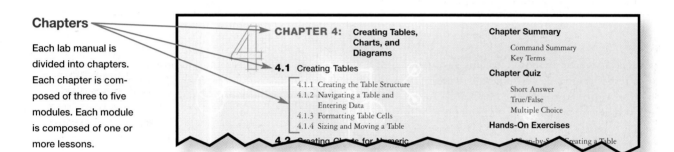

**CHAPTER 4:** Creating Tables, Charts, and Diagrams

**4.1** Creating Tables

4.1.1 Creating the Table Structure
4.1.2 Navigating a Table and Entering Data
4.1.3 Formatting Table Cells
4.1.4 Sizing and Moving a Table

4.2 Creating Charts for Numeric

**Chapter Summary**

Command Summary
Key Terms

**Chapter Quiz**

Short Answer
True/False
Multiple Choice

**Hands-On Exercises**

Step-by-Step: Creating a Table

### New Design

The new *Advantage Series* design offers a more vibrant colored environment overall, including a shaded area where the Feature-Method-Practice and numbered step-by-step instructions help maintain the focus.

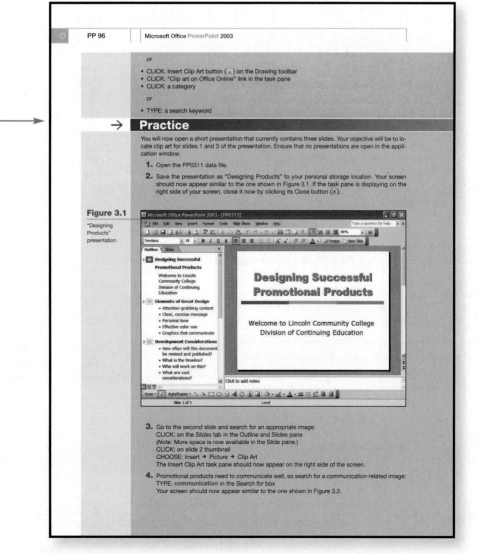

PP 96     Microsoft Office PowerPoint 2003

*or*

- CLICK: Insert Clip Art button ( ) on the Drawing toolbar
- CLICK: "Clip art on Office Online" link in the task pane
- CLICK: a category

*or*

- TYPE: a search keyword

→ **Practice**

You will now open a short presentation that currently contains three slides. Your objective will be to locate clip art for slides 1 and 3 of the presentation. Ensure that no presentations are open in the application window.

1. Open the PP0311 data file.

2. Save the presentation as "Designing Products" to your personal storage location. Your screen should now appear similar to the one shown in Figure 3.1. If the task pane is displaying on the right side of your screen, close it now by clicking its Close button ( ).

**Figure 3.1**

"Designing Products" presentation

3. Go to the second slide and search for an appropriate image:
   CLICK: on the *Slides* tab in the Outline and Slides pane
   (*Note:* More space is now available in the Slide pane.)
   CLICK: on slide 2 thumbnail
   CHOOSE: Insert → Picture → Clip Art
   The Insert Clip Art task pane should now appear on the right side of the screen.

4. Promotional products need to communicate well, so search for a communication-related image:
   TYPE: communication in the *Search for* box
   Your screen should now appear similar to the one shown in Figure 3.2.

# Teaching Resources

We understand that in today's teaching environment, offering a textbook alone is not sufficient to meet the needs of the many instructors who use our books. To teach effectively, instructors must have a full complement of supplemental resources to assist them in every facet of teaching, from preparing for class, to conducting a lecture, to assessing students' comprehension. *The Advantage Series* offers a fully integrated supplements package and Web site, as described below.

## Instructor's Resource Kit

- The **Instructor's Resource Kit** contains a computerized Test Bank, an Instructor's Manual, and PowerPoint Presentation Slides. Features of the Instructor's Resource Kit are described below.

- **Instructor's Manual:** The Instructor's Manual contains a chapter overview, lecture outlines, teaching tips, teaching strategies, pre-tests, post-tests, and additional case problems. Also included are answers to all end-of chapter material.

- **Computerized Test Bank:** The test bank contains more than 1,200 multiple choice, true/false, fill-in-the-blank, short answer, and essay questions. Each question will be accompanied by the correct answer, the level of learning difficulty, and corresponding page references. ExamView® ProTest Generating Software—ExamView is a testing tool that lets you create paper and online tests. This test generator is ideal for building tests, worksheets, and study guides (practice tests) in any subject. Using the online testing features, you can assess numerous reports that will help you focus on your students' learning needs.

- **PowerPoint Presentation Slides:** The presentation slides include lecture outlines, text figures, and speaker's notes. Also included are bullets to illustrate key terms and FAQ's.

## Online Learning Center/Web Site

Found at **www.mhhe.com/cit/advantage2003,** this site provides additional learning and instructional tools to enhance the comprehension of the text. The OLC/Web Site is divided into three areas:

*Information Center:* Contains core information about the text, supplements, and the authors.

*Instructor Center:* Offers instructional materials, downloads, additional exercises, and other relevant links for professors.

*Student Center:* Consists of fifty percent more end-of-chapter questions, hands-on projects, matching exercises, Internet exercises, learning objectives, prerequisites, chapter outlines, and more!

## Skills Assessment

*SimNet* is a simulated assessment and learning tool for either Microsoft® Office XP or Microsoft® Office 2003. SimNet allows students to study MS Office skills and computer concepts and allows professors to test and evaluate students' proficiency within MS Office applications and concepts. Students can practice and study their skills at home or in the school lab using SimNet, which does not require the purchase or installation of Office software.

SimNet includes:

**Structured Computer-Based Learning: SimNet** offers a complete computer-based learning side that presents each skill or topic in several different modes. *Teach Me* presents the skill or topic using text, graphics, and interactivity. *Show Me* presents the skill using an animation with audio narration to show how the skill is used or implemented. *Let Me Try* allows you to practice the skill in SimNet's robust simulated interface.

**Computer Concepts Coverage! SimNet** includes coverage of 60 computer concepts in both the Learning and the Assessment side.

**The Basics and More! SimNet** includes modules of content on:

| | |
|---|---|
| Word | Windows 2000 |
| Excel | Computer Concepts |
| Access | Windows XP Professional |
| PowerPoint | Internet Explorer 6 |
| Office XP Integration | FrontPage |
| Outlook | |

**More Assessment Questions! SimNet** includes more than **1,400** assessment questions.

**Practice or Pre-Tests Questions! SimNet** has a separate pool of more than **600** questions for Practice Tests or Pre-Tests.

**Comprehensive Exercises! SimNet** offers comprehensive exercises for each application. These exercises require the student to use multiple skills to solve one exercise in the simulated environment.

**Simulated Interface!** The simulated environment in **SimNet** has been substantially deepened to more realistically simulate the real applications. Students are no longer graded incorrectly just because they chose the wrong sub-menu or dialog box. The student is not graded until he or she does something that immediately invokes an action—just like the real applications!

## Digital Solutions to Help You Manage Your Course

* *PageOut:* PageOut is our Course Web Site Development Center, which offers a syllabus page, URL, McGraw-Hill Online Learning Center content, online exercises and quizzes, a grade book, discussion board, and an area for student Web pages.

  Available for free of charge with any McGraw-Hill/Irwin product, PageOut requires no prior knowledge of HTML or long hours of coding and serves as a way for course coordinators and professors to provide a full-course Web site. PageOut offers a series of templates—simply fill them with your course information and click on one of 16 designs. The process takes under an hour and leaves you with a **professionally designed Web site.** We will even get you started with sample Web sites or will enter your syllabus for you! PageOut is so straightforward and intuitive; it's little wonder why more than 12,000 college professors are using it.

  For more information, visit the PageOut web site at www.pageout.net.

* *Online Courses Available:* Online Learning Centers (OLCs) are the perfect solutions for your Internet-based content. Simply put, these Centers are "digital cartridges" that contain a book's pedagogy and supplements. As students read the book, they can go on line and take self-grading quizzes or work through interactive exercises. OLCs also provide students appropriate access to lecture materials and other key supplements.

# preface

Online Learning Centers can be delivered through any of these platforms:

- McGraw-Hill Learning Architecture (TopClass)
- Blackboard.com
- Ecollege.com (formally Real Education)
- WebCT (a product of Universal Learning Technology)

McGraw-Hill has partnerships with **WebCT** and **Blackboard** to make it even easier to take your course on line. Now you can have McGraw-Hill content delivered through the leading Internet-based learning tool for higher education.

## PowerWeb

PowerWeb is an exciting new online product available from McGraw-Hill. A nominally priced token grants students access through our website to a wealth of resources—all corresponding to computer literacy. Features include an interactive glossary; current events with quizzing, assessment, and measurement options; Web survey; links to related text content; and WWW searching capability via Northern Lights, an academic search engine. Visit the PowerWeb site at **www.dushkin.com/powerweb.**

# Acknowledgments

The success of *the Advantage Series* software tutorials is confirmation of the effort, teamwork, and dedication of many people. We sincerely thank the instructors, students, reviewers, and editors who have shared their comments and suggestions with us over the years. Our authors take pride in their work, and your comments help us to publish relevant learning materials with a sound pedagogical approach. The product you hold in your hands is a culmination of our best practices in writing and development, classroom testing, and your personal feedback.

McGraw-Hill Higher Education and, specifically, the Technology Education publishing group are comprised of caring and talented people. We are fortunate to have had Steve Schuetz manage the series into the new millennium. Marc Chernoff and Lisa Chin-Johnson deserve our sincere appreciation for their skillful handling of this edition. Special recognition also goes to the individuals who have helped author the Instructor's Resource Kits, specifically Rajiv Malkan (Montgomery College, TX), Alfred Zimermann (Hawaii Pacific University, HI) and Eileen Mullin (GenuineClass.com).

## Thanks to the Advantage Series Team

The following technical editors worked very hard to ensure the accuracy and integrity of every book in the series. Thank you for your efforts!

Maureen Ellis, Indiana University at Bloomington

Dominic Ligori, Seneca College, Canada

Wendy Hon Kam, Loyola University

Rajiv Malkan, Montgomery College

Randy Cullom, University of Northern Colorado

Jacob Phillips, Northern Virginia Community College

Jan Cady, Trinity Valley Community College

Ken Baker, Sinclair Community College

Ryan Murphy, Sinclair Community College

Rick Ingersoll, Appalachian State University

A special thank you goes to Ann Miller and Pat R. Graves for their invaluable contribution and commitment in getting the series published on time. Ann (co-author for Microsoft Word) and Pat (co-author for Microsoft PowerPoint) are extremely talented and conscientious writers. We are very fortunate to have them on *the Advantage Series* team! We are also very thankful to David Shank and other members of the Microsoft Office team for their valuable insight and contributions.

**Ann Miller, author of *the Advantage Series* Word Brief:** Thanks to Glen Coulthard for allowing me to be a part of such a wonderful writing team. His professionalism and sense of humor have added to my enjoyment of this project. I would also like to thank my family for their support and faith in me, my colleagues at Columbus State Community College for 30 years of friendship and learning, and finally, the editorial staff at McGraw-Hill for all their help and the opportunity to complete this project.

**Pat R. Graves, author of *the Advantage Series* PowerPoint Brief:** Many thanks go to Glen Coulthard for his guidance, the editors for their helpful suggestions, and to Lisa Chin-Johnson for managing the development process so effectively. I sincerely thank the many students who shared ideas and contributed resources, especially Kristen Goodman, Stephanie Nimmons, Mary Phelps, Ryan Gibson, and Jerry Rankin. Thanks also to William J. Gibbs for his technical assistance and to the management of Beaver Run Resort and EIU Booth Library for the resources shared. And to Brent Graves who has been continually supportive, I appreciate his encouragement.

## Write to Us

We welcome your comments and suggestions for books in *the Advantage Series.* On behalf of *the Advantage Series* team, please contact the lead author for the series at:

Glen J. Coulthard

glen@coulthard.com

www.coulthard.com

www.advantageseries.com

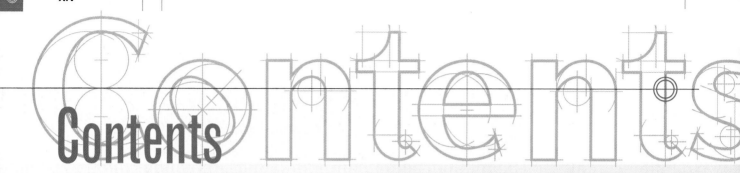

# Contents

**CHAPTER 7: Managing Worksheets and Workbooks 359**

**CHAPTER 12:** Introducing Visual Basic for Applications 785

# Microsoft® Office Excel®

## CHAPTER 1

### ⊕ Creating a Worksheet

**PREREQUISITES**

Although this chapter assumes no previous experience using Microsoft Office Excel 2003, you should be comfortable using a keyboard and mouse in the Microsoft Windows environment. You should be able to launch and exit programs and perform basic file management operations, such as opening and closing documents.

LEARNING
**OBJECTIVES**

After completing this chapter, you will be able to:

- Describe the different components of the application and workbook windows

- Select commands using the Menu bar, toolbars, and right-click menus

- Enter text, dates, numbers, and formulas in a worksheet

- Edit and erase cell data

- Use the Undo and Redo commands

- Start a new blank workbook

- Save, open, and close a workbook

# 1.1 Getting Started with Excel 2003

Microsoft Office Excel 2003 is an electronic spreadsheet program that enables you to store, manipulate, and chart numeric data. Researchers, statisticians, and businesspeople use spreadsheets to analyze and summarize mathematical, statistical, and financial data. Closer to home, you can use Excel to create a budget for your monthly living expenses, analyze returns in the stock market, develop a business plan, or calculate your student loan payments.

Excel 2003 enables you to create and modify worksheets—the electronic version of an accountant's ledger pad—and chart sheets. A **worksheet** (Figure 1.1) is divided into vertical columns and horizontal rows. The rows are numbered and the columns are labeled from A to Z, then AA to AZ, and so on to column IV. The intersection of a column and a row is called a **cell**. Each cell is given a **cell address,** like a post office box number, consisting of its column letter followed by its row number (for example, B4 or FX400). Excel 2003 allows you to open multiple worksheets and chart sheets within its application window.

**Figure 1.1**

An electronic worksheet

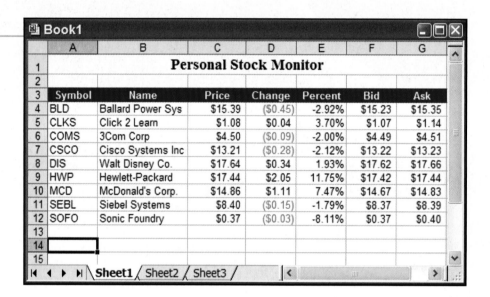

A **chart sheet** (Figure 1.2) displays a chart graphic that is typically linked to data stored in a worksheet. When the data is changed, the chart is updated automatically to reflect the new information. Charts may also appear alongside their data in a worksheet.

**Figure 1.2**

A chart sheet

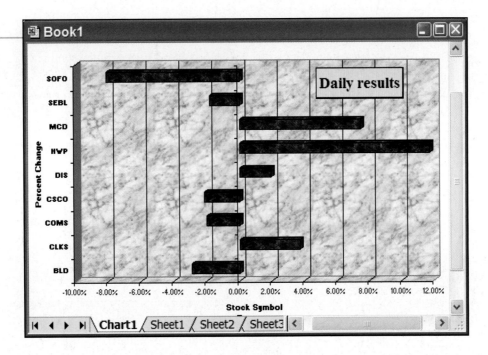

Related worksheets and chart sheets are stored together in a single disk file called a **workbook.** You can think of an Excel 2003 workbook file as a three-ring binder with tabs at the beginning of each new page or sheet. In this module, you will learn to load Microsoft Office Excel 2003 and will then proceed through a guided tour of its primary components.

## 1.1.1 Loading and Exiting Excel

→ # Feature

Microsoft Office Excel 2003 is an application software program that runs under the Microsoft Windows operating system. To load Excel 2003 in Windows XP, click the Start button ( *start* ) on the taskbar to display the Windows Start menu. Then, choose the All Programs menu option. In the menu that appears, choose Microsoft Office by either clicking or highlighting the menu option, and then click Microsoft Office Excel 2003. After a few moments, the Excel 2003 application window appears.

When you are finished doing your work, close the Excel 2003 application window so that your system's memory is freed for use by other Windows applications. To do so, choose the File, Exit command or click on the Close button ( × ) appearing in the top right-hand corner. These methods are used to close most Microsoft Windows applications.

→ # Method

To load Excel:

- CLICK: Start button ( *start* )
- CHOOSE: All Programs ➜ Microsoft Office
- CLICK: Microsoft Office Excel 2003

To exit Excel:

- CHOOSE: File ➜ Exit from Excel's Menu bar

  *or*

- CLICK: its Close button ( × )

→ **Practice**

You will load Microsoft Office Excel 2003 using the Windows Start menu and practice closing the application. Ensure that you have turned on your computer and that the Windows desktop appears.

**1.** Position the mouse pointer over the Start button ( *start* ) appearing in the bottom left-hand corner of the Windows taskbar and then click the left mouse button once. The Start menu appears.

**2.** Position the mouse pointer over the All Programs menu option. Notice that you do not need to click the left mouse button to display the list of programs in the fly-out or cascading menu. (*Note:* If you are using a version of Windows prior to XP, click the Programs menu option.)

**3.** Move the mouse pointer horizontally to the right until it highlights an option in the All Programs menu. You can now move the mouse pointer vertically within the menu to select an application.

**4.** Position the mouse pointer over the Microsoft Office program group and then move the highlight into the fly-out or cascading menu, similar to the graphic shown in Figure 1.3. (*Note:* Even if you are using Windows XP, the desktop theme, color scheme, and menu options may appear differently on your screen than in Figure 1.3.)

**Figure 1.3**

Highlighting an option in the Microsoft Office program group

**5.** Position the mouse pointer over the Microsoft Office Excel 2003 menu option and then click the left mouse button once. After a few seconds, the Excel 2003 application window appears (Figure 1.4).

**Figure 1.4**

Microsoft Office
Excel 2003
application
window

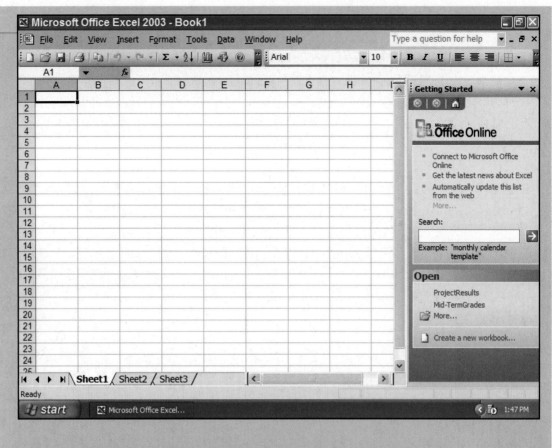

**6.** Depending on your system's configuration, an Office Assistant character, such as "Clippit" (shown at the right), may appear. You will learn how to hide this character in lesson 1.1.2.

**7.** To exit Excel:
CLICK: its Close button (✕) in the top right-hand corner
Assuming that no other applications are running and displayed, you are returned to the Windows desktop.

---

*In Addition* SWITCHING AMONG APPLICATIONS

A button appears on the Windows taskbar for each running application or open document. Switching among your open Microsoft Office System applications involves clicking on a taskbar button and is as easy as switching channels on a television set.

---

## 1.1.2 Touring Excel

→ **Feature**

The Excel 2003 **application window** acts as a container for your worksheet and chart windows. It also contains the primary components for working in Excel, including the *Windows icons*, *Menu bar*, *toolbars*, *task pane*, *Name Box*, *Formula bar*, and *Status bar*. The components of a worksheet **document window** include *scroll bars*, *sheet tabs*, *Tab Split bar*, and *Tab Scrolling bar*. Figures 1.5 and 1.6 identify several of these components.

# → Practice

In a guided tour, you will explore the features of the Excel application window and a worksheet window. Ensure that the Windows desktop appears before you begin.

**1.** Load Excel 2003, referring to the previous lesson if necessary.

**2.** Excel's application window is best kept maximized to fill the entire screen, as shown in Figure 1.5. As with most Microsoft Windows applications, you use the Windows Title bar icons—Minimize (▬), Maximize (□), Restore (⬓), and Close (✕)—to control the display of a window using the mouse. Figure 1.5 labels some of the components of Excel's application window.

**Figure 1.5**

Components of Excel's application window

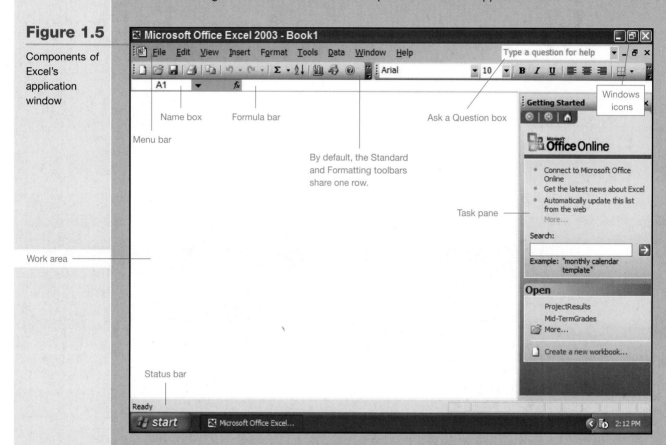

**3.** Below the Windows icons for the Excel application window, there are additional icons for minimizing, restoring, and closing the worksheet window. To display the worksheet as a window within the work area:
CLICK: its Restore button (⬓)
A worksheet window should now appear in the work area. Figure 1.6 labels the components found in a typical worksheet window.

## Figure 1.6

Components of Excel's worksheet window

Cell pointer

Row frame area

Mouse pointer

Worksheet cell

Tab Scrolling arrows

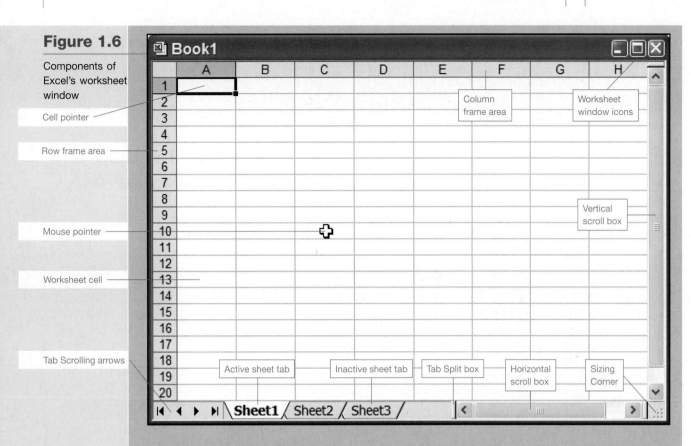

**4.** Let's return the worksheet window to its maximized state:
CLICK: its Maximize button (□)

**5.** The Menu bar groups Excel menu commands for easy access. To execute a command, click once on the desired Menu bar option and then click again on the command. (*Note:* Commands that appear dimmed are not available for selection. Commands that are followed by an ellipsis ( . . . ) will display a dialog box. If a pull-down menu displays a chevron ( ⊻ ) at the bottom, additional commands are displayed when it is selected.)

To practice using the Menu bar:
CHOOSE: Help
This instruction tells you to click the left mouse button once on the Help option appearing in the Menu bar. The Help menu appears, as shown here. (*Note:* All menu commands that you execute in this guide begin with the instruction "CHOOSE.")

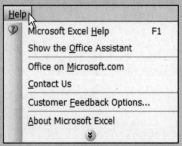

**6.** To display other pull-down menus, move the mouse to the left over other Menu bar options. As each option is highlighted, a menu appears with its associated commands.

**7.** To leave the Menu bar without making a command selection:
CLICK: in a blank area of the Title bar
(*Hint:* You can also click in a worksheet cell to leave the Menu bar.)

**8.** Excel provides context-sensitive *right-click menus* for quick access to relevant menu commands. Rather than searching for the appropriate command in the Menu bar, you can position the mouse pointer on any object, such as a cell, graphic, or toolbar button, and right-click the mouse to display a list of commonly selected commands.

To display a cell's right-click menu:
RIGHT-CLICK: cell A1
The pop-up menu shown in Figure 1.7 should appear.

**Figure 1.7**

Displaying the
right-click menu
for a cell

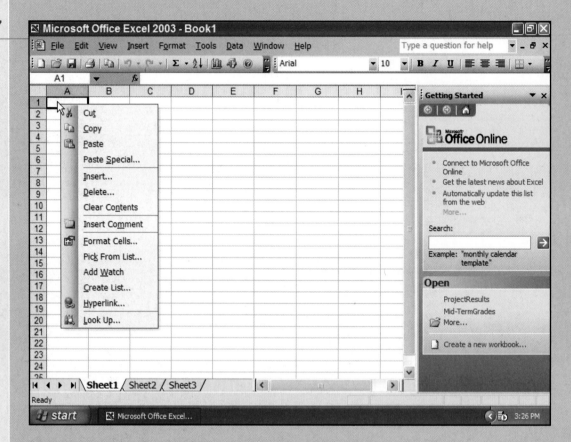

**9.** To remove the cell's right-click menu from the screen:
PRESS: ⌐ESC⌐ (or click on an empty portion of the Title bar)

**10.** If an Office Assistant character appears on your screen, do the following to hide it from view:
RIGHT-CLICK: *the character*
CHOOSE: Hide from the right-click menu
(*Note*: The character's name may appear in the command, such as "Hide Clippit.")

## 1.1.3 Displaying Menus, Toolbars, and the Task Pane

→ **Feature**

Software programs often become more difficult to learn with the addition of each new command or feature. In an attempt to reduce complexity, Microsoft incorporates **adaptive menus** that display only a subset of the most commonly used commands. Although the menus are shorter and less intimidating, this feature can sometimes frustrate novice users who cannot find desired commands by scanning the menus. Likewise, the Standard and Formatting toolbars share a single row under the Menu bar, displaying only a few of the many buttons available. However, you may find that learning to use Excel 2003 is greatly enhanced when the full menus and toolbars are displayed at all times. Finally, the **task pane** is positioned on the right side of your screen and provides convenient access to relevant commands and options. When you first start Excel 2003, the Getting Started task pane appears automatically, but you can choose to hide (and redisplay) the task pane using the View menu command.

→ **Method**

To disable the adaptive menus feature and display the Standard and Formatting toolbars on separate rows:

- CHOOSE: Tools → Customize
- CLICK: *Options* tab
- SELECT: *Show Standard and Formatting toolbars on two rows* check box
- SELECT: *Always show full menus* check box
- CLICK: Close command button

To display or hide a toolbar:

- CHOOSE: View → Toolbars
- CHOOSE: *a toolbar* from the menu

To display and hide the task pane:

- CHOOSE: View → Task Pane

  *or*

- CLICK: its Close button (⊠)

→ **Practice**

In this lesson, you will disable the adaptive menus feature, display the Standard and Formatting toolbars on separate rows, and toggle the display of the task pane. Ensure that you have completed the previous lesson.

**1.** To begin, display the Tools menu:
CHOOSE: Tools
You should now see the Tools pull-down menu. (*Hint:* When a desired command does not appear on a menu, you can extend the menu to view all of the available commands by waiting a short period or by clicking on the chevron ( ⥿ ) at the bottom of the pull-down menu.)

**2.** Let's turn off the adaptive menus feature and customize the Standard and Formatting toolbars. Do the following:
CHOOSE: Customize from the Tools pull-down menu
CLICK: *Options* tab
The Customize dialog box should now appear (Figure 1.8).

Excel

**Figure 1.8**

Customize dialog box: *Options* tab

**3.** On the *Options* tab of the Customize dialog box:
SELECT: *Show Standard and Formatting toolbars on two rows* check box
SELECT: *Always show full menus* check box
(*Note:* An option is activated when its check box is selected, as shown by a check mark (☑) displayed in the center of the box.)

**4.** To close the dialog box:
CLICK: Close command button
Figure 1.9 displays the Standard and Formatting toolbars as they should now appear on your screen. The Standard toolbar provides access to file management and editing commands, as well as special features such as wizards. The Formatting toolbar lets you access cell formatting commands.

**Figure 1.9**

Standard toolbar

Formatting toolbar

**5.** To hide the task pane:
CHOOSE: View → Task Pane
(*Note:* When a toolbar or the task pane is displayed, a check mark appears beside the option in the pull-down menu, as shown here.)

**6.** To redisplay the task pane:
CHOOSE: View → Task Pane
Your screen should now appear similar to the one shown in Figure 1.10.

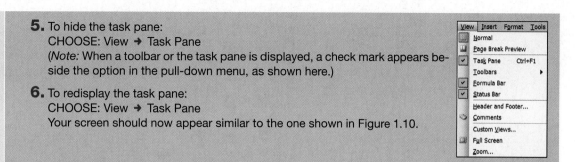

**Figure 1.10**

Customizing the application window

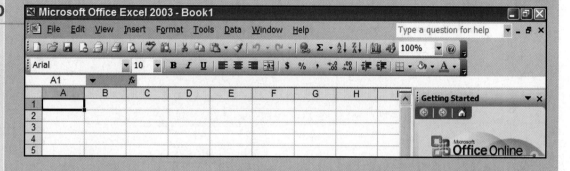

*Important: For the remainder of this learning guide, we assume that the adaptive menus feature has been disabled and that the Standard and Formatting toolbars are displayed on separate rows.*

## *In Addition* MOVING TOOLBARS

You can move toolbars around the Excel application window using the mouse. A *docked* toolbar appears attached to one of the window's borders. An *undocked* or *floating* toolbar appears in its own window, complete with a Title bar and Close button (⊠). To float a docked toolbar, drag its Move bar (┃) at the left-hand side toward the center of the window. To redock the toolbar, drag its Title bar toward the window's border until it attaches itself automatically.

**1.1**   How do you turn the adaptive menus feature on or off?

# 1.2 Creating Your First Worksheet

You create a worksheet by entering text labels, numbers, dates, and formulas into the individual cells. To begin entering data, first move the cell pointer to the desired cell in the worksheet. Then type the information that you want to appear in the cell. Complete the entry by pressing **ENTER** or by moving the cell pointer to another cell. In this module, you will learn how to navigate a worksheet, enter several types of data, and construct a simple formula expression.

## 1.2.1 Moving the Cell Pointer

### → Feature

The **cell pointer** is the cursor used to select a cell in the worksheet using either the mouse or keyboard. When you first open a new workbook, the *Sheet1* worksheet tab is active and the cell pointer is positioned in cell A1. As you move the cell pointer around the worksheet, Excel displays the current cell address in the **Name Box,** as shown here.

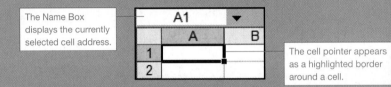

The Name Box displays the currently selected cell address.

The cell pointer appears as a highlighted border around a cell.

### → Method

Some common keystrokes for navigating a worksheet include:

- ⬆, ⬇, ⬅, and ➡
- **HOME**, **END**, **PgUp**, and **PgDn**
- **CTRL** + **HOME** to move to cell A1
- **CTRL** + **END** to move to the last cell in the active worksheet area
- **F5** (GoTo) key for moving to a specific cell address

### → Practice

You will now practice moving around an empty worksheet. Ensure that Excel is loaded and a blank worksheet appears.

**1.** With the cell pointer in cell A1, move to cell D4 using the following keystrokes:
PRESS: ➡ three times
PRESS: ⬇ three times
Notice that the cell address, D4, is displayed in the Name Box and that the column (D) and row (4) headings in the frame area appear highlighted.

**2.** To move to cell E12 using the mouse:
CLICK: cell E12
(*Hint:* Position the cross mouse pointer (⛶) over cell E12 and click the left mouse button once.)

**3.** To move to cell E124 using the keyboard:
PRESS: (PgDn) until row 124 is in view

PRESS: (↑) or (↓) to select cell E124
(*Hint:* The (PgUp) and (PgDn) keys are used to move up and down a worksheet by as many rows as fit in the current document window.)

**4.** To move to cell E24 using the mouse, position the mouse pointer on the vertical scroll box and then drag the scroll box upward to row 24, as shown in Figure 1.11. Then click cell E24 to select the cell.

**Figure 1.11**

Dragging the vertical scroll box

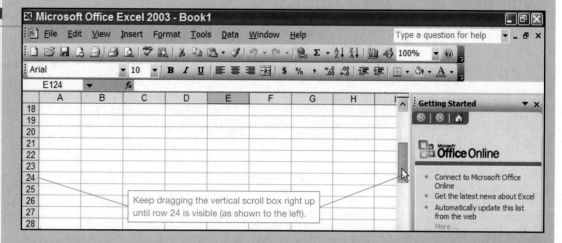

**5.** To move quickly to a specific cell address, such as cell AE24:
CLICK: once in the Name Box
TYPE: **ae24**
PRESS: (ENTER)
The cell pointer moves to cell AE24. (*Hint:* Because cell addresses are not case sensitive, you need not use capital letters when typing a cell address.)

**6.** To move the cell pointer in any direction until the cell contents change from empty to filled, from filled to empty, or until a border is encountered, press (CTRL) with an arrow key. For example:
PRESS: (CTRL)+(→) to move to column IV
PRESS: (CTRL)+(↓) to move to row 65536
The cell pointer now appears in the bottom right-hand corner of the worksheet. Notice, also, that "IV65536" appears in the Name Box.

**7.** To move back to cell A1:
PRESS: (CTRL)+(HOME)

### 1.2.2 Entering Text

→ **Feature**

Text labels are the titles, headings, and other descriptive information that you place in a worksheet to give it meaning and enhance its readability. Although a typical worksheet column displays fewer than nine characters, a single cell can store thousands of words. With longer entries, the text simply spills over the column border into the next cell, if it is empty. If the adjacent cell is not empty, the text will be truncated at its right border. Fortunately, you can also increase the cell's display or column width to view more of its information.

→ ## Method

To enter text into the selected cell:

- TYPE: **your text**
- PRESS: **ENTER**

→ ## Practice

In this lesson, you will create a worksheet by specifying text labels for the row and column headings.

**1.** Ensure that the cell pointer is positioned in cell A1 of the *Sheet1* worksheet.

**2.** Let's begin the worksheet by entering a title. As you type the following entry, watch the Formula bar:
TYPE: **Income Statement**
Your screen should appear similar to the one shown in Figure 1.12.

**Figure 1.12**

Typing text into the Formula bar

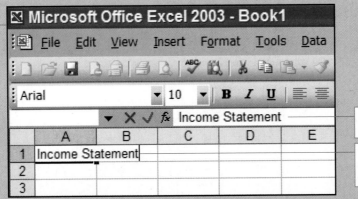

Your entry appears in the Formula bar as you type.

The cursor or insertion point shows where the next character typed will appear.

**3.** To enter the text into the cell, you press **ENTER** or click the Enter button (☑) in the Formula bar. To cancel an entry, you press **ESC** or click the Cancel (☒) button. Let's accept the entry:
PRESS: **ENTER**
Notice that the text entry is longer than the column's width and must spill over into column B. This is acceptable as long as you do not place anything in cell B1. You may also increase the width of column A.

After you press **ENTER**, the cell pointer moves down to the next row. If your pointer remains in cell A1, change this behavior using the Tools, Options command from the Menu bar. In the Options dialog box, click the *Edit* tab and ensure that the *Move selection after Enter* check box is selected with "Down" as the *Direction*, as shown in Figure 1.13.

**Figure 1.13**

Options dialog box: *Edit* tab

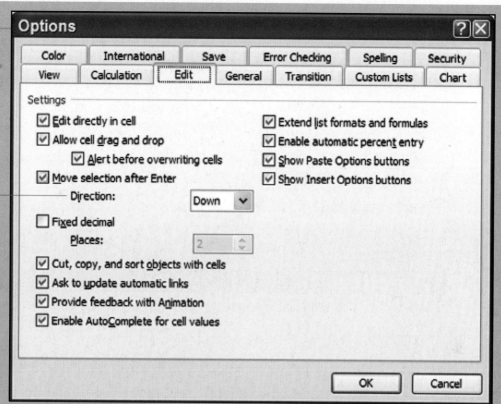

Select these options to change the behavior of the cell pointer after pressing the Enter key.

**4.** Move the cell pointer to cell B3.

**5.** Enter the following text label:
TYPE: **Revenue**
PRESS: ⬇
Notice that pressing ⬇ has the same result as pressing ENTER.

**6.** To finish entering the row labels:
TYPE: **Expenses**
PRESS: ⬇
TYPE: **Profit**
PRESS: ENTER
All of the textual information is now entered into the worksheet, as shown in Figure 1.14.

**Figure 1.14**

Entering text into a worksheet

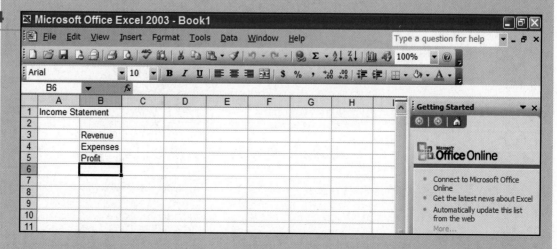

## 1.2.3 Entering Dates

 **Feature**

Date values are often used in worksheets as column headings, but they also appear in row entries such as invoice transactions and purchase orders. You enter date values into a cell using one of the common date formats recognized by Excel, such as mm/dd/yy (3/31/04) or dd-mmm-yy (31-Mar-04). Excel treats a date (or time) as a formatted number or value. Consequently, you can use date values to perform arithmetic calculations, such as finding out how many days have elapsed between two calendar dates.

**Method**

To enter a date value into the selected cell:

- TYPE: *a date,* such as 3/31/04
- PRESS: [ENTER]

**Practice**

You will now add date values into your worksheet as column headings. Ensure that you have completed the previous lesson.

**1.** Move to cell C2.

**2.** To enter a month and year combination as a date value, you can use the format mmm-yyyy. For example:
TYPE: **Mar-2004**
PRESS: ➡
Excel reformats the value to appear as "Mar-04." Why wouldn't you type "Mar-04" in the first place? The answer is that Excel must make certain assumptions about your entries. If you type "Mar-04," Excel assumes that you want March 4 of the current year, which may or may not be 2004. By entering a year value using all four digits, you avoid having Excel misinterpret your entry.

**3.** Starting in cell D2, do the following:
TYPE: **Apr-2004**
PRESS: ➡
TYPE: **May-2004**
PRESS: ➡
TYPE: **Jun-2004**
PRESS: [ENTER]

**4.** Move the cell pointer to cell C2 and compare your work with the worksheet shown in Figure 1.15. Looking in the Formula bar, notice that the date entry reads "3/1/2004" and not "Mar-04." As illustrated by this example, a cell's appearance on the worksheet can differ from its actual contents.

**Figure 1.15**

Entering date values into a worksheet

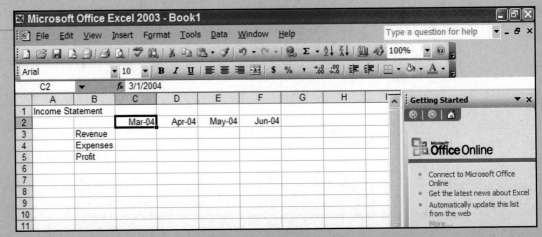

## 1.2.4 Entering Numbers

### → Feature

Numbers are entered into a worksheet for use in performing calculations, preparing reports, and creating charts. You can enter a raw or unformatted number, such as 3.141593, or a formatted number, such as 37.5% or $24,732.33. It is important to note that phone numbers, Social Security numbers, and zip codes are not treated as numeric values, because they are never used in performing mathematical calculations. Numbers and dates are right-aligned in a cell, as opposed to text, which aligns with the left border of a cell.

### → Method

To enter a number into the selected cell:

• TYPE: *a number,* such as $9,987.65 or 12.345%

• PRESS: ENTER

### → Practice

You will now add some numbers to the worksheet. Ensure that you have completed the previous lesson.

**1.** Move to cell C3.

**2.** To enter a value for March's revenue, do the following:
TYPE: 112,500
PRESS: →
Notice that you placed a comma (,) in the entry to separate the thousands from the hundreds. Excel recognizes symbols such as commas, dollar signs, and percentage symbols as numeric formatting.

**3.** Starting in cell D3, do the following:
TYPE: 115,800
PRESS: →
TYPE: 98,750
PRESS: →
TYPE: 112,830
PRESS: ENTER

**4.** Move the cell pointer to cell C3 and compare your work with the worksheet shown in Figure 1.16. Notice that the Formula bar reads "112500" without a comma separating the thousands. Similar to date values, numeric values may be formatted to display differently than the actual value stored.

**Figure 1.16**

Entering numbers into a worksheet

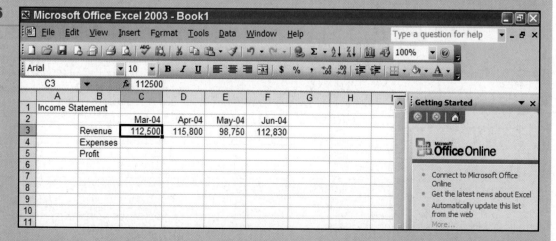

## 1.2.5 Entering Formulas

→ **Feature**

You use formulas to perform calculations, such as adding a column of numbers or calculating a mortgage payment. A **formula** is an expression, containing numbers, cell references, and/or mathematical operators, that is entered into a cell to display a calculated result. The basic mathematical operators ("+" for addition, "–" for subtraction, "/" for division, and "*" for multiplication) and rules of precedence from your high school algebra textbook also apply to an Excel formula. As a refresher, Excel calculates what appears in parentheses first, exponents second, multiplication and division operations (from left to right) third, and addition and subtraction (again from left to right) last.

→ **Method**

To enter a formula into the selected cell:

- TYPE: = (an equal sign)
- TYPE: *a formula*, such as **a4+b4**
- PRESS: ENTER

→ **Practice**

You will now enter formulas into the Income Statement worksheet. Ensure that you have completed the previous lesson.

**1.** Move to cell C4. Notice that the first step in entering a formula is to move to the cell where you want the result to display.

**2.** To tell Excel that what follows is a formula, first type an equal sign:
TYPE: =

**3.** In order to calculate March's expenses, you will now multiply the cell containing the monthly revenue (cell C3) by 60%. Do the following:
TYPE: **c3*60%**
Your screen should appear similar to the worksheet shown in Figure 1.17. Notice that the formula's cell address is color-coded and that this coding corresponds to the cell borders highlighted in the worksheet. This feature, called **Range Finder,** is especially useful when you need to identify whether a calculation is drawing data from the correct cells.

**Figure 1.17**

Typing a formula expression into the Formula bar

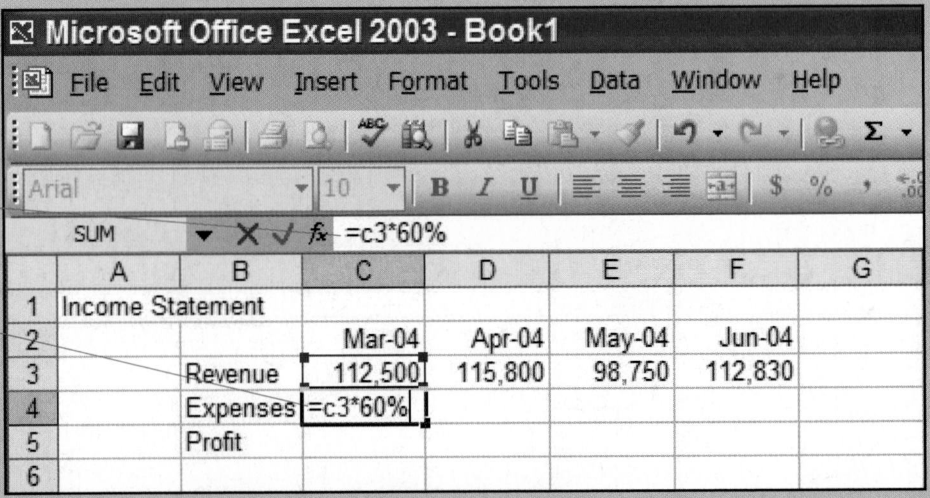

The expression is built in the Formula bar.

Notice that the blue-highlighted cell address "c3" in the formula expression corresponds with the cell outline immediately above.

**4.** To complete the entry and move to the next cell:
PRESS: ➡
The result, 67500, appears in the cell.

**5.** Let's use a method called *pointing* to enter the formula into cell D4. With pointing, you use the mouse or keyboard to point to the cell reference that you want to include in an expression. To illustrate:
TYPE: =
PRESS: ⬆
Notice that a dashed marquee appears around cell D3 and that the value "D3" appears in the Formula bar.

**6.** To finish entering the formula:
TYPE: *60%
PRESS: ➡
The result, 69480, appears in the cell.

**7.** For May's calculation, use the mouse to point to the desired cell reference. Do the following:
TYPE: =
CLICK: cell E3
Notice that a dashed marquee surrounds cell E3 to denote its selection.

**8.** To complete the formula:
TYPE: *60%
PRESS: ➡
The result, 59250, appears.

**9.** Last, enter the formula for December by typing:
TYPE: =f3*.6
PRESS: [ENTER]
The result, 67698, appears in cell F4. Notice that the value .6 may be used instead of 60% to yield the same result. Your worksheet should now appear similar to the one shown in Figure 1.18.

**Figure 1.18**

Entering formulas into a worksheet

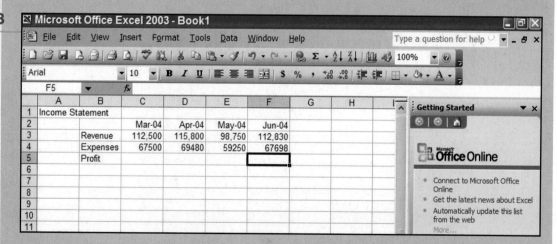

**10.** To finish the worksheet:
SELECT: cell C5

**11.** You will now enter a formula to calculate the profit by subtracting expenses from revenues for each month. Do the following:
TYPE: =c3−c4
Notice that "c3" appears in blue and "c4" appears in green, as shown below.

| | A | B | C |
|---|---|---|---|
| 1 | Income Statement | | |
| 2 | | | Mar-04 |
| 3 | | Revenue | 112,500 |
| 4 | | Expenses | 67500 |
| 5 | | Profit | =c3-c4 |
| 6 | | | |

Excel's color-coding of cell references in a formula makes it easier to spot potential errors.

**12.** On your own, enter formulas into cells D5, E5, and F5 using both the typing and pointing methods. (*Hint:* In the next chapter, you will learn easier methods for entering multiple formulas into your worksheet.) When completed, your worksheet should appear similar to the one shown in Figure 1.19.

**Figure 1.19**

Completing the worksheet

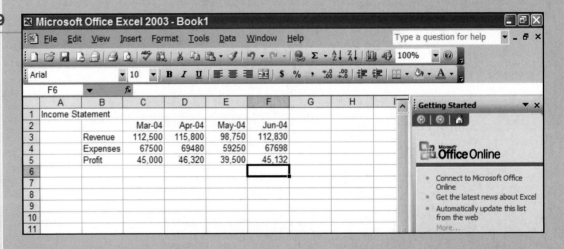

**13.** To illustrate the power of an electronic worksheet, let's change a cell's value and watch all the formulas that reference that cell recalculate their results automatically. Do the following:
SELECT: cell F3
TYPE: 100,000
PRESS: **ENTER**
Notice that the Expense calculation for Jun-04 (cell F4) is immediately updated to 60000 and the Profit cell now displays 40,000.

**14.** To conclude the module, you will close the worksheet without saving the changes. (*Note:* You will learn how to save a worksheet later in this chapter.) From the Menu bar:
CHOOSE: File ➔ Close
The following dialog box appears.

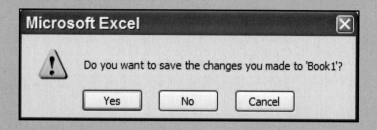

**15.** CLICK: No command button
There should be no workbooks open in the application window.

## *In Addition* REFERENCING CELLS IN A FORMULA

Two types of cell addresses (also called *cell references*) can be entered into formulas: *relative* and *absolute.* A relative cell address, such as B4, is one that is relative in position to other cells on the worksheet. When copied within a formula to the next column, for example, the relative cell address "B4" adjusts automatically to become "C4." An absolute cell address, on the other hand, refers to a specific cell in the worksheet and does not adjust when copied. Absolute cell addresses contain dollar signs, such as $B$4. It is important to note that Excel defaults to using relative cell addresses in formulas. Relative and absolute cell referencing is covered in Chapter 4.

 **1.2** Explain why a phone number is not considered a numeric value in an Excel worksheet.

# 1.3 Editing the Worksheet

What if you type a label, a number, or a formula into a cell and then decide it needs to be changed? Novices and experts alike make data entry errors when creating a worksheet. Fortunately, Excel provides several features for editing information that has already been entered. In this module, you will learn how to modify existing cell entries, erase the contents of a cell, and undo a command or typing error.

## 1.3.1 Editing a Cell's Contents

### → Feature

You can edit information either as you type or after you have entered data into a cell. Your ability to edit a worksheet effectively is an extremely valuable skill. In many occupations and businesses, you will be asked to modify and maintain existing worksheets, rather than create new ones from scratch. Indeed, most worksheets are prepared by revising standard or template-generated worksheets with up-to-date information. To this end, the editing methods presented in this lesson will benefit you as a relatively new user of Excel.

### → Method

To edit cell contents:

- To edit data as you type, press **BACKSPACE** and then correct the typographical error or spelling mistake.

- To replace a cell's contents entirely, select the cell and then type over the original data. When you press **ENTER** or select another cell, the new information overwrites the existing data.

- To edit a cell in which the text is too long or complicated to retype, double-click the cell to perform **in-cell editing.** In this mode, the flashing insertion point appears ready for editing inside the cell. Alternatively, you can press the **F2** (Edit) key or click in the Formula bar to enter Edit Mode, in which you edit the cell's contents in the Formula bar. Regardless, once the insertion point appears, you perform your edits using the arrow keys, **DELETE**, and **BACKSPACE**.

### → Practice

In this lesson, you will create a simple inventory worksheet and then practice modifying the data stored in the worksheet cells. Ensure that no workbooks are open in the application window.

**1.** To display a new workbook and worksheet:
CLICK: New button (▢) on the Standard toolbar
A new workbook, entitled "Book2," appears in the document area and the task pane is hidden. (*Note:* As an alternative to using the toolbar, you can start a new workbook by clicking the *Create a new workbook* option under the *Open* heading in the Getting Started task pane.)

**2.** SELECT: cell A1, if it is not already selected
Your screen should appear similar to the one shown in Figure 1.20. (*Note:* For the remainder of this guide, you may use either the keyboard or mouse to move the cell pointer.)

**Figure 1.20**

Displaying a new workbook

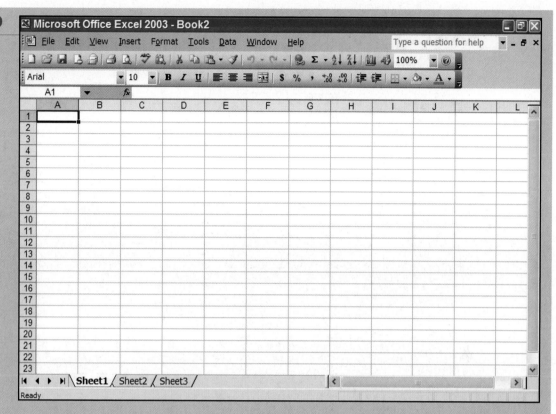

**3.** Let's enter a title for this worksheet:
   TYPE: **Otaga's Food Warehouse**
   PRESS: ⊕
   TYPE: **Inventory List**
   PRESS: **ENTER**

**4.** SELECT: cell A4

**5.** Now let's add some column headings:
   TYPE: **Code**
   PRESS: ➡
   TYPE: **Product**
   PRESS: ➡
   TYPE: **Quantity**
   PRESS: ➡
   TYPE: **Price**
   PRESS: **ENTER**

**6.** On your own, complete the worksheet as displayed in Figure 1.21. If you make a typing error, use **BACKSPACE** to correct your mistake prior to pressing **ENTER** or an arrow key.

**Figure 1.21**

Creating an
inventory
worksheet

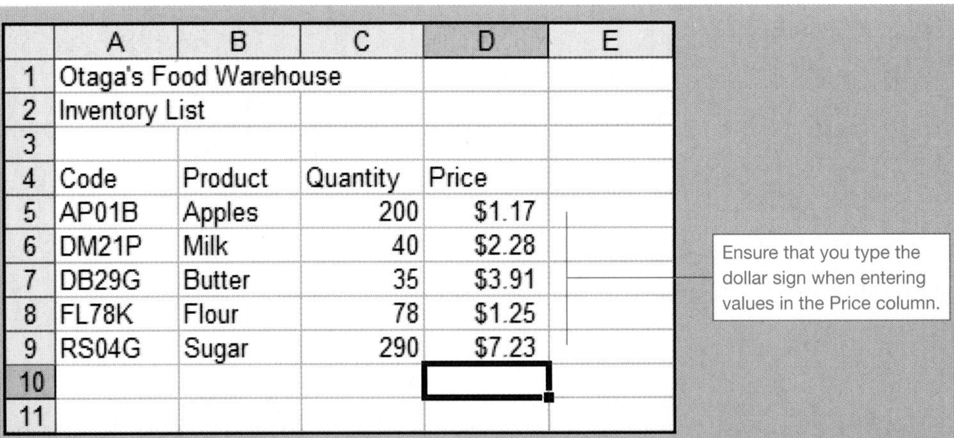

| | A | B | C | D | E |
|---|---|---|---|---|---|
| 1 | Otaga's Food Warehouse | | | | |
| 2 | Inventory List | | | | |
| 3 | | | | | |
| 4 | Code | Product | Quantity | Price | |
| 5 | AP01B | Apples | 200 | $1.17 | |
| 6 | DM21P | Milk | 40 | $2.28 | |
| 7 | DB29G | Butter | 35 | $3.91 | |
| 8 | FL78K | Flour | 78 | $1.25 | |
| 9 | RS04G | Sugar | 290 | $7.23 | |
| 10 | | | | | |
| 11 | | | | | |

> Ensure that you type the dollar sign when entering values in the Price column.

**7.** To begin editing this worksheet, let's change the column heading in cell D4 to read "Cost" instead of "Price." To replace the existing entry:
SELECT: cell D4

**8.** TYPE: **Cost**
PRESS: (ENTER)
Notice that the new entry overwrites the existing cell contents. (*Hint:* If you start typing an entry in the wrong cell, you can press ( ESC ) to exit Edit mode and restore the previous value.)

**9.** You activate in-cell editing by double-clicking a cell. To practice, let's change the quantity of butter from 35 to 350 packages:
DOUBLE-CLICK: cell C7
Notice that the Status bar now reads "Edit" in the bottom left-hand corner, instead of the word "Ready." A flashing insertion point also appears inside the cell, as shown in Figure 1.22.

**Figure 1.22**

Performing in-cell
editing

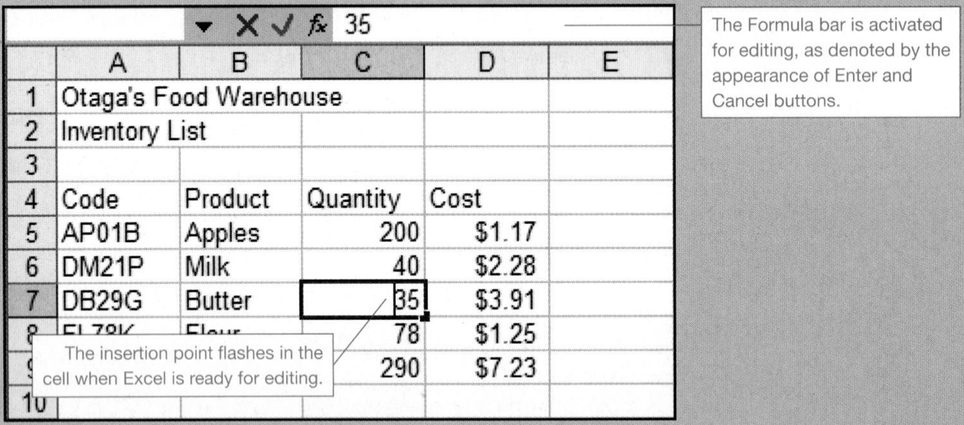

▼ ✕ ✓ ƒx  35

| | A | B | C | D | E |
|---|---|---|---|---|---|
| 1 | Otaga's Food Warehouse | | | | |
| 2 | Inventory List | | | | |
| 3 | | | | | |
| 4 | Code | Product | Quantity | Cost | |
| 5 | AP01B | Apples | 200 | $1.17 | |
| 6 | DM21P | Milk | 40 | $2.28 | |
| 7 | DB29G | Butter | 35 | $3.91 | |
| 8 | FL78K | Flour | 78 | $1.25 | |
| 9 | | | 290 | $7.23 | |
| 10 | | | | | |

> The Formula bar is activated for editing, as denoted by the appearance of Enter and Cancel buttons.

> The insertion point flashes in the cell when Excel is ready for editing.

**10.** To add a "0" to the end of the cell's contents:
PRESS: END to move the insertion point to the far right
TYPE: **0**
PRESS: ENTER
Notice that the Status bar once again reads "Ready" in the bottom left-hand corner.

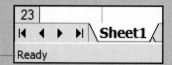

The current mode is displayed on the Status bar.

**11.** You can also activate Edit Mode by pressing the F2 (Edit) key or by clicking the I-beam mouse pointer inside the Formula bar. In this step, you edit one of the product codes. Do the following:
SELECT: cell A6
Notice that the text "DM21P" appears in the Formula bar.

**12.** To modify "DM" to read "DN," position the I-beam mouse pointer over the Formula bar entry, immediately to the left of the letter "M." Click the left mouse button and drag the mouse pointer to the right until the "M" is highlighted, as shown in Figure 1.23.

**Figure 1.23**

Editing an entry in the Formula bar

| A6 | ▼ X ✓ fx DM21P |
|---|---|

Drag the I-beam mouse pointer form left to right over the letter "M."

Formula Bar

| | A | B | C | D | E |
|---|---|---|---|---|---|
| 1 | Otaga's Food Warehouse | | | | |
| 2 | Inventory List | | | | |
| 3 | | | | | |
| 4 | Code | Product | Quantity | Cost | |
| 5 | AP01B | Apples | 200 | $1.17 | |
| 6 | DM21P | Milk | 40 | $2.28 | |
| 7 | DB29G | Butter | 350 | $3.91 | |
| 8 | FL78K | Flour | 78 | $1.25 | |
| 9 | RS04G | Sugar | 290 | $7.23 | |
| 10 | | | | | |
| 11 | | | | | |

**13.** Now that the desired letter is selected:
TYPE: **N**
PRESS: ENTER
The letter "N" replaces the selected letter in the Formula bar and cell.

## 1.3.2 Selecting and Erasing Cell Contents

→ ## Feature

You can quickly erase a single cell, a group of cells, or the entire worksheet with a few simple keystrokes. To erase the selected cell's contents, simply press the DELETE key. To erase the contents of more than one cell, use the mouse to drag over the desired area or cell range prior to pressing DELETE. Besides a cell's contents, you can delete specific characteristics of a cell, such as its formatting or attached comments. A **comment** is a special floating text box that you can attach to a worksheet cell. To display its text, you move the mouse pointer over the small red indicator that will appear in the upper right-hand corner of a cell containing a comment.

Excel

→ **Method**

To erase the contents of a cell or group of cells:

- SELECT: the cell or cell range
- PRESS: DELETE

To remove a cell's contents and/or its attributes:

- CHOOSE: Edit → Clear → *command*
- The *command* options include:
  All            Removes the cell contents and other attributes
  Formats       Removes the cell formatting only
  Contents      Removes the cell contents only (DELETE)
  Comments   Removes the cell comments only

→ **Practice**

You will now practice erasing information that is stored in the inventory worksheet. Ensure that you have completed the previous lesson.

**1.** SELECT: cell A2

**2.** To delete the subtitle:
PRESS: DELETE
Notice that you need not press ENTER or any other confirmation key. Pressing DELETE removes the contents of the cell immediately.

**3.** SELECT: cell A9

**4.** In order to delete more than one cell at a time, you first select the desired range of cells. In this step, you will select the cells from A9 to D9. Do the following:
PRESS: SHIFT and hold it down
CLICK: cell D9
RELEASE: SHIFT
The four cells should now appear highlighted, as shown in Figure 1.24.

**Figure 1.24**

Selecting a group of cells to erase

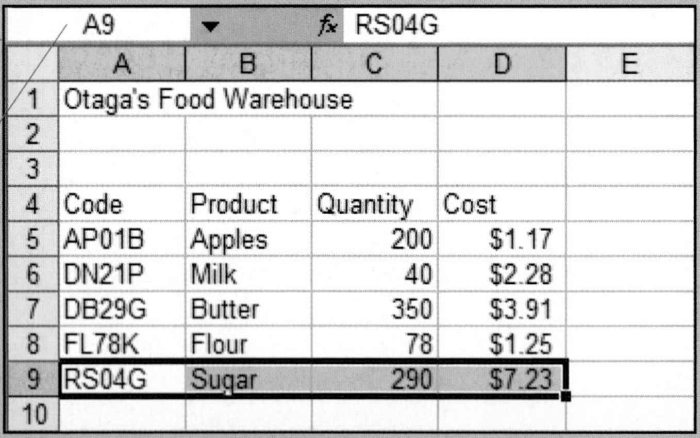

The Name box shows that the active cell is A9, displayed with a white background in the highlighted selection.

| | A | B | C | D | E |
|---|---|---|---|---|---|
| 1 | Otaga's Food Warehouse | | | | |
| 2 | | | | | |
| 3 | | | | | |
| 4 | Code | Product | Quantity | Cost | |
| 5 | AP01B | Apples | 200 | $1.17 | |
| 6 | DN21P | Milk | 40 | $2.28 | |
| 7 | DB29G | Butter | 350 | $3.91 | |
| 8 | FL78K | Flour | 78 | $1.25 | |
| 9 | RS04G | Sugar | 290 | $7.23 | |
| 10 | | | | | |

Name box: A9    *fx* RS04G

**5.** To erase all of the cell information, including contents and formatting:
CHOOSE: Edit → Clear → All
All of the entries in the selected cell range are deleted from the worksheet.

**6.** To erase the dollar values in the Cost column:
CLICK: cell D5 and keep the mouse button pressed down
DRAG: the mouse pointer downward to cell D8
Your screen should now appear similar to the one shown in Figure 1.25.

**Figure 1.25**

Selecting cells using the mouse

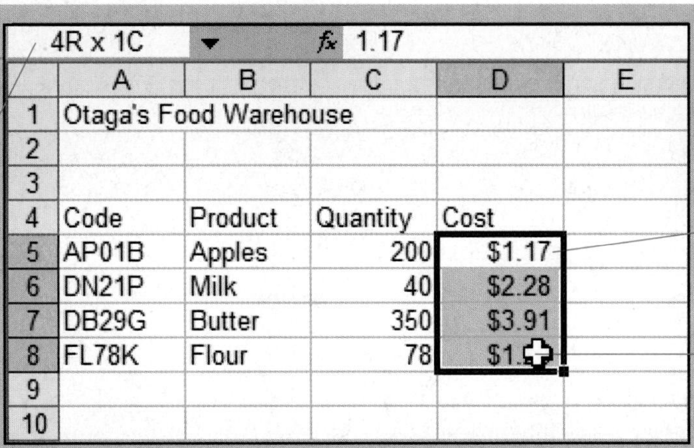

The Name box shows that four rows (4R) and one column (1C) are currently selected in the worksheet.

| 4R x 1C ▼ | | fx 1.17 | | |
|---|---|---|---|---|
| | A | B | C | D | E |

| | A | B | C | D | E |
|---|---|---|---|---|---|
| 1 | Otaga's Food Warehouse | | | | |
| 2 | | | | | |
| 3 | | | | | |
| 4 | Code | Product | Quantity | Cost | |
| 5 | AP01B | Apples | 200 | $1.17 | |
| 6 | DN21P | Milk | 40 | $2.28 | |
| 7 | DB29G | Butter | 350 | $3.91 | |
| 8 | FL78K | Flour | 78 | $1.⬛ | |
| 9 | | | | | |
| 10 | | | | | |

The active cell in this selection is D5, the first selected cell.

After clicking cell D5, keep the mouse button depressed and drag the mouse pointer down to cell D8. Once the desired cells are highlighted, you may release the mouse button.

**7.** Release the mouse button when the cells are highlighted.

**8.** PRESS: DELETE to remove the contents of the cell range

**9.** PRESS: CTRL + HOME to move the cell pointer to cell A1

### 1.3.3 Using Undo and Redo

→ **Feature**

The **Undo command** allows you to cancel up to your last 16 actions. The command is most useful for immediately reversing a command or modification that was mistakenly performed. If an error occurred several steps before, you can continue "undoing" commands until you return the worksheet to its original state prior to the mistake. Although it sounds somewhat confusing, you can use the Redo command to undo an Undo command. The **Redo command** allows you to reverse an Undo command that you performed accidentally.

→ **Method**

To reverse an action or command:

- CLICK: Undo button (↺▾)

  *or*

- CHOOSE: Edit → Undo

  *or*

- PRESS: CTRL + z

To reverse an Undo command:

- CLICK: Redo button (↻▾)

  *or*

- CHOOSE: Edit → Redo

Excel

→ **Practice**

Let's practice reversing some editing mistakes using the Undo command. Ensure that you have completed the previous lesson.

1. SELECT: cell A5
   Your worksheet should appear similar to the one shown in Figure 1.26.

**Figure 1.26**

Selecting cell A5

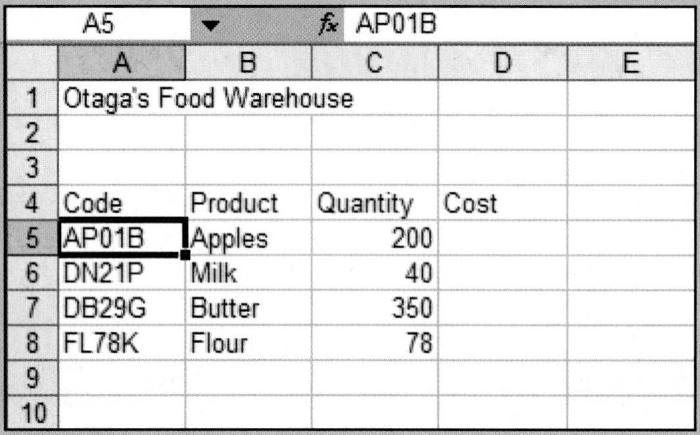

| A5 | ▼ | | *fx* | AP01B | |
|---|---|---|---|---|---|
| | A | B | C | D | E |
| 1 | Otaga's Food Warehouse | | | | |
| 2 | | | | | |
| 3 | | | | | |
| 4 | Code | Product | Quantity | Cost | |
| 5 | AP01B | Apples | 200 | | |
| 6 | DN21P | Milk | 40 | | |
| 7 | DB29G | Butter | 350 | | |
| 8 | FL78K | Flour | 78 | | |
| 9 | | | | | |
| 10 | | | | | |

2. In order to practice using the Undo command, let's delete the contents of the cell:
   PRESS: DELETE

3. To undo the last command or action performed:
   CLICK: Undo button (🔄▾) on the Standard toolbar
   (*Caution:* The tip of the mouse pointer should be placed over the curved arrow and not on the attached down arrow.)

4. SELECT: cell C5

5. To modify the quantity of apples:
   TYPE: 175
   PRESS: ENTER

6. To undo the last entry using a keyboard shortcut:
   PRESS: CTRL + z
   The value 175 is replaced with 200 in cell C5. (*Hint:* This shortcut keystroke is useful for quickly undoing a command or incorrect entry.)

7. Now let's make two modifications to the worksheet:
   SELECT: cell B5
   TYPE: Oranges
   PRESS: ⬇
   TYPE: Juice
   PRESS: ENTER

8. Let's view the history that Excel has been tracking for the Undo command. To begin, position the mouse pointer over the down arrow attached to the Undo button (🔄▾) on the Standard toolbar. Then click the down arrow once to display the drop-down list of "undoable" or reversible commands, as shown in Figure 1.27.

## Figure 1.27

Displaying
reversible
commands

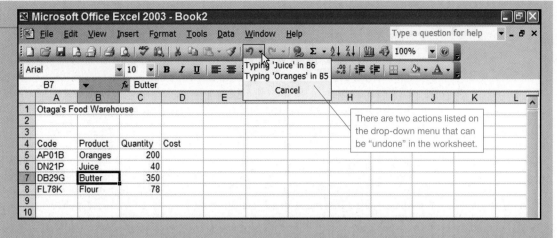

9. Move the mouse pointer slowly downward to select the two entries, as shown here.

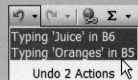

10. To perform the Undo operation, ensure that both items are highlighted and then do the following:
CLICK: "Typing 'Oranges' in B5" Undo option
(*Hint:* To remove the Undo drop-down menu, click the Title bar or the button's attached down arrow again.)

11. To conclude this module, close the worksheet without saving the changes. Do the following:
CHOOSE: File → Close

12. When the dialog box appears:
CLICK: No command button

**1.3**   Why is worksheet editing such a valuable skill?

_____

# 1.4 Managing Your Files

Managing the workbook files that you create is an important skill. The workbook you are using exists only in the computer's RAM (random access memory), which is highly volatile. If the power to your computer goes off, any changes that you have made to the workbook are lost. For this reason, you need to save your workbook permanently to the local hard disk, a network drive, or a removable disk. Creating, saving, opening, and closing workbooks are considered file management operations.

Saving your work to a named file on a disk is similar to placing it into a filing cabinet. For important workbooks (ones that you cannot risk losing), you should save your work every 15 minutes, or whenever you are interrupted, to protect against an unexpected power outage or other catastrophe. Saving a file without closing it is like placing a current copy in a filing cabinet. When naming workbook files, you can use up to 255 characters, including spaces, but it is wise to keep the length under 20 characters. You cannot, however, use the following characters or symbols:

$$\backslash \ / \ : \ ; \ * \ ? \ " < > |$$

In this module, you will practice creating a new workbook, saving and closing workbooks, creating workbook folders, and opening existing workbooks.

*Important: In this guide, we refer to the files that have been created for you as the **student data files**. Depending on your computer or lab setup, these files may be located on a removable diskette, in a folder on your hard disk, or on a network server. If necessary, ask your instructor or lab assistant where to find these data files. To download the Advantage Series' student data files from the Internet, visit our Web site at:*

**http://www.advantageseries.com**

*You will also need to identify a storage location, such as a removable disk or hard-drive subdirectory, for the files that you create, modify, and save.*

### 1.4.1 Beginning a New Workbook

→ **Feature**

There are three ways to create a new workbook. First, you can start with a blank workbook and enter all of the data from scratch. This is the method that you have used in the previous lessons. Next, you can select a workbook **template** that provides preexisting data and design elements. A template is a timesaving utility that promotes consistency in both design and function. Lastly, you can employ a **wizard** to help lead you step-by-step through the creation of a particular type of workbook.

→ **Method**

To display a new blank workbook:

• CLICK: New button ()

To begin a workbook using a template or wizard:

• CHOOSE: File → New

→ **Practice**

In this example, you will use a workbook template to create a new workbook for an invoicing application. Ensure that no workbooks are displayed in the application window.

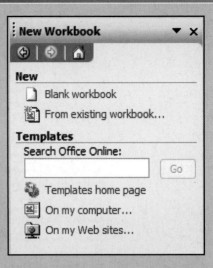

1. To create a workbook using a template, first display the New Workbook task pane:
CHOOSE: File → New
The New Workbook task pane appears, as shown here.

2. Using the hand mouse pointer (🖑):
CLICK: "On my computer. . ." under the *Templates* heading

3. The blank Workbook template icon appears on the *General* tab of the Templates dialog box. Excel uses this template when you click the New button (🗋) on the Standard toolbar. To view the custom templates that are shipped with Excel and stored locally on your computer, do the following:
CLICK: *Spreadsheet Solutions* tab
Your screen should now appear similar to the one shown in Figure 1.28. (*Note:* Depending on how Excel was installed and configured on your system, different template options may appear in your dialog box.)

**Figure 1.28**

Displaying solutions in the Templates dialog box

When you choose the "Complete Install" option during setup, Excel 2003 provides the *General* and *Spreadsheet Solutions* tabs for organizing your workbook templates.

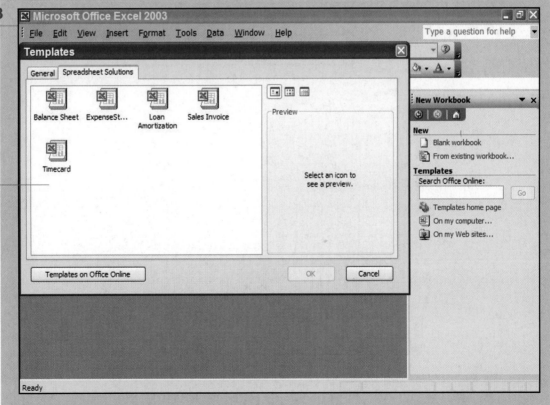

Excel

**4.** To create a new workbook based on the Sales Invoice template:
DOUBLE-CLICK: Sales Invoice template icon (⬜)
(*Note:* If you or your lab administrator has not installed the workbook templates, you must skip to step 6.)

**5.** Excel loads the template and displays the workbook shown in Figure 1.29. Scan the contents of the worksheet using the horizontal and vertical scroll bars. If the selected template cannot be found, Excel attempts to locate and install it. (*Note:* A dialog box may appear warning that the template may contain a **macro virus.** A virus is a hostile program that is secretly stored and shipped inside another program or document. As this template is from Microsoft and not from an unknown source, you can safely enable the macros.)

**Figure 1.29**

New workbook based on the Sales Invoice template

The Sales Invoice template contains a single worksheet tab named "Invoice."

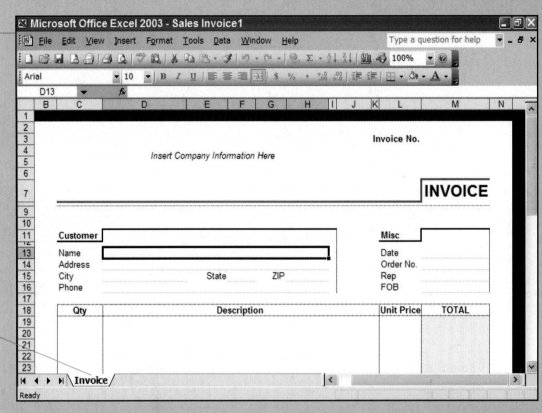

**6.** The workbook templates provided by Excel contain many advanced features. Rather than introducing these features now, let's close the workbook and continue our discussion of file management:
CHOOSE: File → Close
CLICK: No command button, if asked whether to save the changes

## *In Addition* ACCESSING OTHER WORKBOOK TEMPLATES

Besides the templates that ship with the Microsoft Office System, additional templates are available for free on the Internet. In the New Workbook task pane are two options that you may use to download such templates. First, the *On My Web sites . . .* option lets you retrieve workbook templates stored on Web servers around the world. This option is especially useful for retrieving shared templates from a company intranet. Second, the *Templates home page* option launches a Microsoft Web page dedicated to providing support and content for Microsoft Office users. Before creating a new workbook from scratch, you can peruse these templates to search for a possible starting point.

→ **1.4.2 Saving and Closing**

## Feature

Many options are available for saving a workbook to a permanent storage location. The File, Save command and the Save button ( ) on the toolbar allow you to overwrite an existing disk file with the latest version of a workbook. The File, Save As command enables you to save a workbook to a new filename or storage location. You can also specify a different file format for the workbook, such as an earlier version of Excel, using the Save As command. This is especially handy when you need to share a workbook with associates who haven't upgraded to the latest version. Once you have finished using a workbook, make sure you close the file to free up valuable system resources (RAM) in your computer.

## Method

To save a workbook:

- CLICK: Save button ( )

  *or*

- CHOOSE: File → Save

  *or*

- CHOOSE: File → Save As

To close a workbook:

- CLICK: its Close button ( )

  *or*

- CHOOSE: File → Close

## Practice

You will now practice saving and closing a workbook. Identify a storage location for your personal workbook files. If you want to use a diskette or other removable storage medium, insert the media into the drive now.

**1.** To create a new workbook from scratch:
CLICK: New button ( )
TYPE: **My First Workbook** into cell A1
PRESS: (ENTER)

**2.** To save the new workbook:
CLICK: Save button ( )
(*Note:* If the current workbook has not yet been saved, Excel displays the Save As dialog box regardless of the method you chose to save the file. The filenames and folder directories that appear in your Save As dialog box will differ from those shown in Figure 1.30.)

Excel

**Figure 1.30**

Save As dialog box

Lists the files that you have most recently worked with

Lists common desktop shortcuts

Excel's default working folder for storing files

Provides access to the resources on your computer

Lists files and folders stored on your intranet or Internet Web server

The currently selected folder is displayed in the *Save in* drop-down list box.

The "Advantage" folder is the default folder for storing the student data files.

Each folder item represents either a local folder or a shortcut to a remote storage folder.

Enter the workbook's filename in the drop-down text box.

Select a workbook file type from this drop-down list box.

**3.** The **Places bar,** located along the left border of the dialog box, provides convenient access to commonly used storage locations. To illustrate, let's view the resources available on your computer:
CLICK: My Computer button in the Places bar

**4.** Now let's display the available resources using the *Save in* drop-down list box. Do the following:
CLICK: down arrow attached to the *Save in* drop-down list box
Your screen will appear similar, but not identical, to the one shown in Figure 1.31.

**Figure 1.31**

Navigating the storage areas using the *Save in* drop-down list box

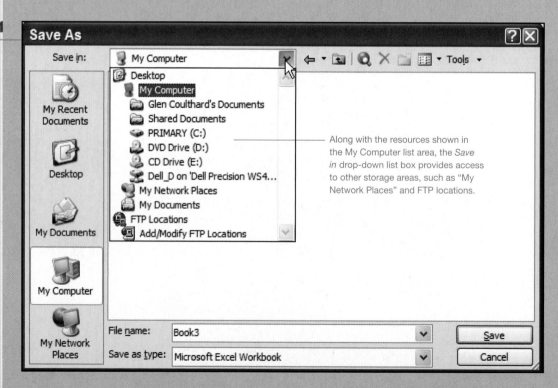

Along with the resources shown in the My Computer list area, the *Save in* drop-down list box provides access to other storage areas, such as "My Network Places" and FTP locations.

**5.** To browse the local hard drive:
SELECT: your local hard disk, usually labeled (C:)
The list area displays the folders and files stored in the root directory of your local hard disk.

**6.** To drill down and display the contents of a particular folder:
DOUBLE-CLICK: Program Files folder
This folder acts as a container for your application program folders and files. Figure 1.32 shows how full this folder can become.

**Figure 1.32**

The Program Files folder of the author's hard drive (C:)

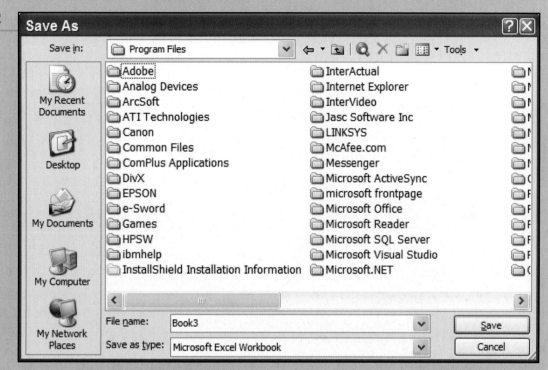

**7.** To return to the previous display:
CLICK: Back button (← ·) in the dialog box

**8.** Now, using either the Places bar or the *Save in* drop-down list box:
SELECT: *a storage location for your personal workbook files*
(*Note:* In this guide, we save files either to the My Documents folder or to a new folder you will create in lesson 1.4.4. However, your instructor or lab assistant may request that you save your workbook files to a removable disk or to a specified directory for your class work.)

**9.** Let's give the workbook file a unique name. Position the I-beam mouse pointer over the workbook name in the *File name* text box and then:
DOUBLE-CLICK: the *workbook name,* "Book3" in this example
The entire workbook name should appear highlighted.

**10.** To type over and replace the existing workbook name:
TYPE: **My First Workbook** as shown below

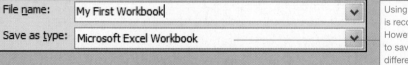

Using the default file type is recommended. However, you can choose to save a workbook in a different file format using this drop-down list box.

**11.** To complete the procedure:
CLICK: Save command button
When you are returned to the worksheet, notice that the workbook's name now appears in the Title bar.

**12.** Let's close the workbook:
CHOOSE: File → Close

There are times when you will need to save an existing workbook under a different filename. For example, you may want to create a backup copy or different version of the same workbook on your disk. You may instead want to use one workbook as a template for creating future workbooks that are similar in style and format. Rather than retyping an entirely new workbook, you can retrieve an old workbook, edit its content, and then save it under a different name using the Save As command on the File menu. Additionally, you can display the New Workbook task pane and select the "From existing workbook . . ." option to create a new workbook based on an existing file.

### 1.4.3 Opening an Existing Workbook

→ **Feature**

You use the Open dialog box to search for and retrieve existing workbooks that are stored on your local hard disk, a removable storage device, a network server, or on the Web. If you want to load an existing workbook when you first start Excel, click the Start button (*start*) and then choose the Open Office Document command on the All Programs menu. Or, if you have recently used the workbook, display the Start menu and then try the My Recent Documents command, which lists the most recently used files.

→ **Method**

To open an existing workbook:

• CLICK: Open button (🖾)

   *or*

• CHOOSE: File → Open

→ **Practice**

You will now retrieve a student data file named EX0143 that displays the market penetration for snowboard sales by Canadian province. To complete this exercise, you will need to know the storage location for the Advantage student data files.

**1.** Ensure that there are no workbooks displayed in the application window. Then, display the Open dialog box:
CLICK: Open button (🖾)

**2.** Using the Places bar or the *Look in* drop-down list box, locate the folder containing the Advantage student data files. (*Note:* In this guide, we retrieve the student data files from a folder named "Advantage.") Your screen should appear similar to the one shown in Figure 1.33 before proceeding.

**Figure 1.33**

Viewing the student data files for the Microsoft Office Excel 2003 tutorial

**3.** To view additional file information in the dialog box:
CLICK: down arrow beside the Views button (⊞ ▾)
The drop-down list shown at the right appears.

**4.** CHOOSE: Details
Each workbook is presented on a single line with additional file information, such as its size, type, and date. (*Hint:* You can sort the filenames in this list area by clicking on one of the column heading buttons.)

**5.** To return to a multicolumn list format:
CLICK: down arrow beside the Views button (⊞ ▾)
CHOOSE: List
Your screen should look like the one shown in Figure 1.33 once again.

**6.** Let's open one of the workbooks:
DOUBLE-CLICK: EX0143
The dialog box disappears and the workbook is loaded into the application window, as shown in Figure 1.34. (*Note:* The "EX0143" filename reflects that this workbook is used in lesson 1.4.3 of the Microsoft Office Excel 2003 learning guide.)

**Figure 1.34**

Opening the
EX0143
workbook

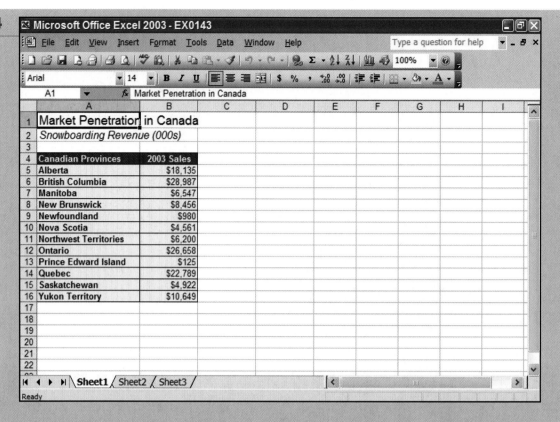

**7.** Let's prepare this worksheet for tracking sales in 2004:
SELECT: cell B4
TYPE: **2004 Sales**
PRESS: ENTER

**8.** To remove the existing 2003 data:
SELECT: cell B5
PRESS: SHIFT
CLICK: cell B16
The cell range from B5 through B16 should now appear highlighted.

**9.** PRESS: DELETE to remove the cell contents (but retain the formatting)
Your screen should now appear similar to the one shown in Figure 1.35. Notice that the selected range remains highlighted and that the only the data is removed. The cell's fill color and number formatting remain intact.

**Figure 1.35**

Modifying the
EX0143
workbook

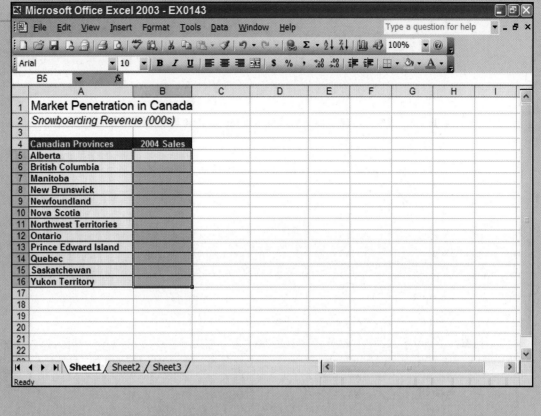

**10.** PRESS: `CTRL` + `HOME` to return to cell A1
Now proceed to the next lesson to learn how to create a new folder for saving and storing the modified workbook.

*In Addition* OPENING AND SAVING FILES OF DIFFERENT FORMATS

In the Open and Save As dialog boxes, you will notice a drop-down list box named *Files of type* and *Save as type* respectively. These list boxes allow you to select different file formats for opening and saving your files. For instance, you can save a workbook so that users with an earlier version of Excel are able to open and edit its contents. You can also open a file that was created using another spreadsheet software program, such as Lotus or Quattro Pro.

### 1.4.4 Creating a Workbook Folder

→ **Feature**

Storage folders help you organize your work. They also make it easier to find documents and back up your data. For example, you can use a folder to collect all of the workbooks related to a single fiscal period. You can also specify a folder to hold all of your personal documents, such as résumés and expense reports. Although Windows Explorer should be used for most folder management tasks, Excel enables you to create a new folder from within the Save As dialog box. After you navigate to where you want the folder to appear, click the Create New Folder button (▢) and then complete the steps presented below.

→ ## Method

To create a new workbook folder:

- CLICK: Create New Folder button ( ) in the Save As dialog box
- TYPE: *a name* for the new folder
- CLICK: OK command button

→ ## Practice

You will now create a folder for storing the workbooks that you will create in the remaining pages of this tutorial. Ensure that you have completed the previous lesson.

**1.** You may create a new folder for your workbooks using the Save As command on the File menu. To begin:
CHOOSE: File → Save As

**2.** This exercise assumes that you are able to create folders on your computer's local hard disk. If this is not the case, you may substitute a removable media drive for the My Documents folder. To begin, use the Places bar to select the desired location for the new folder:
CLICK: My Documents folder button in the Places bar

**3.** To create a subfolder in the My Documents folder:
CLICK: Create New Folder button ( )
Your screen should now appear similar to the one shown in Figure 1.36.

**Figure 1.36**

Creating a new folder in the Save As dialog box

**4.** In the New Folder dialog box:
TYPE: **My Workbooks**
CLICK: OK command button
You are immediately transferred into the new folder, as shown in the *Save in* drop-down list box.

**5.** Now you can save the workbook in the new folder. Let's choose a different filename for the workbook. If it is not already selected:
DOUBLE-CLICK: "EX0143" in the *File name* text box
The filename should appear highlighted before you proceed.

**6.** To replace the existing workbook name:
TYPE: **Snowboarding 2004** as shown below

| File name: | Snowboarding 2004 | ⌄ |
|---|---|---|
| Save as type: | Microsoft Excel Workbook | ⌄ |

**7.** To complete the procedure:
CLICK: Save command button

**8.** Let's close the workbook:
CHOOSE: File → Close

**9.** To exit Microsoft Office Excel 2003:
CHOOSE: File → Exit

## *In Addition* RENAMING AND DELETING A WORKBOOK FOLDER

Besides creating a workbook folder using the Open or Save As dialog boxes, you can rename and delete folders displayed in the list area. To rename a folder, right-click the folder and then choose Rename from the shortcut menu that appears. The folder's name will appear in Edit Mode within the list area. Type the new name and press `ENTER`. (*Hint:* You can also click on a folder twice slowly in order to edit a folder's name.) To delete a folder, right-click the desired folder and choose the Delete command. You will be asked to confirm the folder deletion in a dialog box. Make sure that you do not accidentally delete a folder containing files that you want to keep! To avoid this, you should open a folder and view its contents before performing the Delete command.

**1.4** In the Open and Save As dialog boxes, how do the List and Details views differ? Name two other views that are accessible from the Views button

# Chapter
## summary

Microsoft Office Excel 2003 is an electronic spreadsheet program. Spreadsheet software is used extensively in business for performing statistical analyses, summarizing numerical data, and publishing reports. Over the past two decades, spreadsheet software has proven to be the most robust and indispensable power tool for white-collar workers. You create a worksheet in Excel by typing text, numbers, dates, and formulas into cells. Editing the contents of a worksheet is also an important skill because of the frequency with which most worksheets are reused and modified. File management tasks—creating, saving, and opening workbook files, and creating a workbook folder for storing your work—are also key to your efficient and productive use of Excel 2003.

## Command Summary

Many of the commands and procedures appearing in this chapter are summarized in the following table.

| Skill Set | To Perform this Task... | Do the Following... |
|---|---|---|
| **Using Excel** | Launch Microsoft Office Excel 2003 | CLICK: Start button (*start*)<br>CHOOSE: All Programs → Microsoft Office<br>CLICK: Microsoft Office Excel 2003 |
| | Exit Microsoft Excel | CLICK: its Close button (☒)<br>*or*<br>CHOOSE: File → Exit |
| | Close a workbook | CLICK: its Close button (☒)<br>*or*<br>CHOOSE: File → Close |
| | Customize menus and toolbars | CHOOSE: Tools → Customize |
| **Managing Workbooks** | Create a new workbook | CLICK: New button (▯)<br>*or*<br>CHOOSE: File → New<br>SELECT: an option from the New Workbook task pane |
| | Use a template to create a new workbook | CHOOSE: File → New<br>CLICK: "On my computer . . ." under the *Templates* area of the New Workbook task pane<br>CLICK: *Spreadsheet Solutions* tab in the Templates dialog box<br>DOUBLE-CLICK: *a template* |
| | Locate and open an existing workbook | CLICK: Open button (▨)<br>*or*<br>CHOOSE: File → Open |
| | Open files of different formats | SELECT: a format from the *Files of type* drop-down list box in the Open dialog box |
| | Save a workbook | CLICK: Save button (▤)<br>*or*<br>CHOOSE: File → Save |
| | Save a workbook using a different filename, location, or format | CHOOSE: File → Save As |
| | Create a new folder while displaying the Save As dialog box | CLICK: Create New Folder button (▭) |
| **Working with Cells and Cell Data** | Navigate to a specific cell | CLICK: in the Name Box<br>TYPE: *cell address* |
| | Enter text labels, numbers, and dates | TYPE: *an entry* |
| | Enter a formula | TYPE: *=expression* |
| | Replace the current cell's contents with new data | TYPE: *new entry* |

| | |
|---|---|
| Activate Edit Mode to revise a cell's contents | DOUBLE-CLICK: in the desired cell<br>*or*<br>CLICK: in the Formula bar<br>*or*<br>PRESS: **F2** (Edit) key |
| Delete the current cell's contents | PRESS: **DELETE** |
| Delete all information (contents, formatting, and other attributes) associated with a cell | CHOOSE: Edit → Clear → All |
| Reverse or undo a command or series of commands | CLICK: Undo button (▾)<br>*or*<br>CHOOSE: Edit → Undo<br>*or*<br>PRESS: **CTRL** + **z** |
| Reverse or undo an Undo command | CLICK: Redo button (▾)<br>*or*<br>CHOOSE: Edit → Redo |

## Key Terms

This section specifies page references for the key terms identified in this chapter. For a complete list of definitions, refer to the Glossary at the back of this learning guide.

adaptive menus, *p. EX 9*                    Name Box, *p. EX 12*

application window, *p. EX 5*                Places bar, *p. EX 34*

cell, *p. EX 2*                              Range Finder, *p. EX 18*

cell address, *p. EX 2*                      Redo command, *p. EX 27*

cell pointer, *p. EX 12*                     task pane, *p. EX 9*

chart sheet, *p. EX 2*                       template, *p. EX 30*

comment, *p. EX 25*                          Undo command, *p. EX 27*

document window, *p. EX 5*                   wizard, *p. EX 30*

formula, *p. EX 18*                          workbook, *p. EX 2*

in-cell editing, *p. EX 22*                  worksheet, *p. EX 2*

macro virus, *p. EX 32*

## Chapter
quiz

## Short Answer

**1.** Explain the difference between an application window and a document or workbook window.

**2.** Where do toolbars appear in the application window?

**3.** What is the fastest method for moving to cell BE1762?

**4.** What is significant about how dates are entered into a worksheet?

**5.** How do you enter a formula into a cell? Provide an example.

**6.** What does it mean to use *pointing* to enter cell addresses in a formula?

**7.** How would you reverse the past three commands executed?

**8.** How do you create a new workbook based on a template?

**9.** How would you save a copy of the currently displayed workbook onto a diskette?

**10.** How would you save a workbook using Excel 2003 so that a person with Excel 95 is able to open and edit the file?

## True/False

**1.** _____ The cell reference "AX100" is an acceptable cell address.

**2.** _____ Pressing [CTRL]+[SHIFT] moves the cell pointer to cell A1.

**3.** _____ An Excel worksheet contains more than 68,000 rows.

**4.** _____ After a formula has been entered into a cell, you cannot edit the expression.

**5.** _____ A formula may contain both numbers and cell references, such as =A1*B7-500.

**6.** _____ Pressing [DELETE] erases the contents and formatting of the currently selected cell.

**7.** _____ Pressing [CTRL] + z will undo the last command executed.

**8.** _____ You can create a new folder from within the Save As dialog box.

**9.** _____ You access Excel's workbook templates using the Templates button (🗐) on the Standard toolbar.

**10.** _____ You can open workbook files that have been created using earlier versions of Excel.

## Multiple Choice

**1.** Which mouse shape is used to select cells in a worksheet?

 a. Arrow (↖)
 b. Cross (✛)
 c. Hand (🖑)
 d. Hourglass (⌛)

**2.** Excel displays the current cell address in the:

 a. Name Box
 b. Standard toolbar
 c. Status bar
 d. Title bar

**3.** Using a mouse, you move around a worksheet quickly using the:

 a. Scroll bars
 b. Status bar
 c. Tab Scrolling arrows
 d. Tab Split bar

**4.** When you enter a text label, Excel justifies the entry automatically between the cell borders as:

 a. Centered
 b. Fully justified
 c. Left-aligned
 d. Right-aligned

**5.** When you enter a date, Excel justifies the entry automatically between the cell borders as:

 a. Centered
 b. Fully justified
 c. Left-aligned
 d. Right-aligned

**6.** Which keyboard shortcut lets you modify the contents of a cell?

 a. [CTRL]
 b. [SHIFT]
 c. [F2]
 d. [F5]

**7.** Which is the correct formula for adding cells B4 and F7?

 a. =B4+F7
 b. @B4+F7
 c. $B4:F7
 d. =B4*F7

**8.** To save the current workbook using a different filename:

 a. CHOOSE: File, Save
 b. CHOOSE: File, Save As
 c. CLICK: Save button (🖫)
 d. CHOOSE: File, Rename

9. To open a new blank workbook:
   a. CLICK: New button (▯)
   b. CHOOSE: File, Open
   c. CHOOSE: File, Start
   d. CHOOSE: File, Template

10. To reverse an Undo command:
    a. CHOOSE: Edit, Go Back
    b. CHOOSE: File, Reverse Undo
    c. CLICK: Reverse button (↩▾)
    d. CLICK: Redo button (↪▾)

# Hands-On
### exercises

step by step

## 1. Creating a New Worksheet

This exercise lets you practice fundamental worksheet skills, including entering labels, numbers, dates, and formulas. You also practice saving your workbook.

1. Load Microsoft Office Excel 2003 and ensure that a blank worksheet is displayed.

2. To hide the task pane:
   CHOOSE: View ➜ Task Pane

3. Enter a title label for the worksheet in cell A1:
   TYPE: **Wally Burger's Fast Food**
   PRESS: ⬇

4. In cell A2, enter another label:
   TYPE: **Today is:**
   PRESS: ➡

5. In cell B2, enter today's date:
   TYPE: *your date* using the format dd-mmm-yy
   PRESS: (ENTER)
   (*Hint:* The date March 31, 2004 would be entered as 31-Mar-04.)

6. Complete the worksheet as it appears in Figure 1.37. (*Note:* Depending on how your computer is configured, the worksheet's date values may appear formatted differently on your screen.)

**Figure 1.37**

Wally Burger's
Fast Food
worksheet

These labels are
entered into column
A only, even though
their text spills over
into column B.

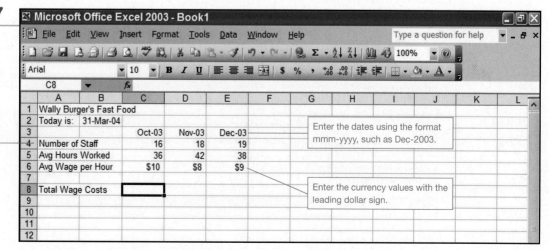

7. Now let's calculate the "Total Wage Costs" for October 2003.
   SELECT: cell C8, as shown in Figure 1.37
   TYPE: **=c4*c5*c6**
   PRESS: ➡
   The value $5,760 appears in cell C8.

**8.** Enter similar formulas into cells D8 and E8 using the pointing method. Which is the least costly month in terms of wages paid?

**9.** Modify the value in cell C4 to read "18" staff. Which month has the lowest wage cost now?

**10.** Let's save the workbook to your personal storage location:
CHOOSE: File ➜ Save As

**11.** On your own, navigate the Save As dialog box using the Places bar and *Save in* drop-down list box to locate your personal storage location for saving workbook files. When you are ready to proceed, name the workbook "**Wally Burger**" and compare the finished workbook to the one shown in Figure 1.38.

**Figure 1.38**

Completed "Wally Burger" workbook

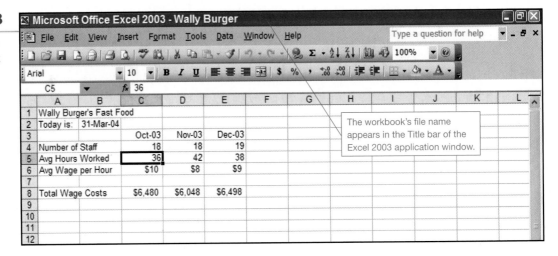

**12.** Close the workbook before proceeding.

step by step

## 2. Modifying a Worksheet

In this exercise, you enter and edit text labels in an existing worksheet, enter numbers and dates, select and delete a cell range, and use the Undo command.

**1.** Open the workbook named EX01HE02, located in the Advantage student data files location, to display the worksheet in Figure 1.39.

**Figure 1.39**

Opening the EX01HE02 workbook

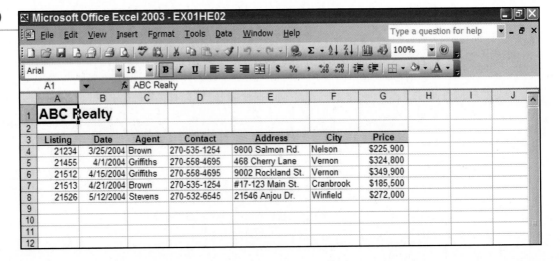

2. To save the workbook to your personal storage location:
   CHOOSE: File → Save As

3. On your own, navigate the Save As dialog box using the Places bar and *Save in* drop-down list box to locate your personal storage location for saving workbook files. When you are ready, name the workbook "**ABC Realty**" and proceed to the next step.

4. To change the "Contact" column heading to read "Phone":
   SELECT: cell D3
   TYPE: **Phone**
   PRESS: ENTER

5. To correct a spelling mistake that occurs in the "City" column:
   SELECT: cell F8
   PRESS: F2 to enter Edit mode

6. To change the name from "Winfield" to "Wimfield," do the following:
   PRESS: ◄ six times until the cursor appears to the left of the letter "n" in "Winfield"
   PRESS: DELETE
   TYPE: **m**
   PRESS: ENTER

7. To modify the address in a listing:
   SELECT: cell E7
   Notice that the cell contents now appear in the Formula bar.

8. To change the street name from "Main" to "Elm," position the I-beam mouse pointer over "Main" in the Formula bar and then double-click. Your screen should appear similar to Figure 1.40 before proceeding.

**Figure 1.40**

Modifying cell contents in the worksheet

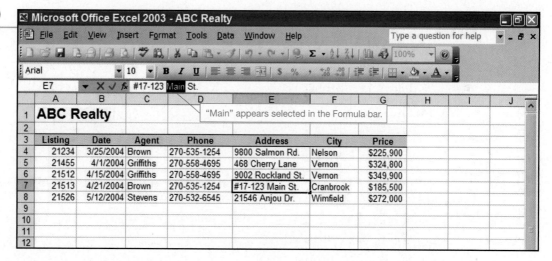

9. To replace the selected text:
   TYPE: **Elm**
   PRESS: ENTER
   (*Note:* Rather than pressing ENTER, you can also click the Enter button (✓) in the Formula bar.)

10. To erase both the contents and formatting in the "Price" column, do the following:
    SELECT: cell G3
    PRESS: SHIFT
    PRESS: ▼ five times to select the desired cell range
    RELEASE: SHIFT

**11.** To erase the cell range:
CHOOSE: Edit → Clear → All
Your screen should now appear similar to the one shown in Figure 1.41

**Figure 1.41**

Erasing a cell range in the worksheet

| | A | B | C | D | E | F | G | H | I | J |
|---|---|---|---|---|---|---|---|---|---|---|
| 1 | **ABC Realty** | | | | | | | | | |
| 2 | | | | | | | | | | |
| 3 | **Listing** | **Date** | **Agent** | **Phone** | **Address** | **City** | | | | |
| 4 | 21234 | 3/25/2004 | Brown | 270-535-1254 | 9800 Salmon Rd. | Nelson | | | | |
| 5 | 21455 | 4/1/2004 | Griffiths | 270-558-4695 | 468 Cherry Lane | Vernon | | | | |
| 6 | 21512 | 4/15/2004 | Griffiths | 270-558-4695 | 9002 Rockland St. | Vernon | | | | |
| 7 | 21513 | 4/21/2004 | Brown | 270-535-1254 | #17-123 Elm St. | Cranbrook | | | | |
| 8 | 21526 | 5/12/2004 | Stevens | 270-532-6545 | 21546 Anjou Dr. | Wimfield | | | | |
| 9 | | | | | | | | | | |
| 10 | | | | | | | | | | |
| 11 | | | | | | | | | | |
| 12 | | | | | | | | | | |

**12.** To undo this last command:
CLICK: Undo button ( ) on the Standard toolbar
The data and formatting reappear in the cell range.

**13.** Enter the following data for a new listing into row 9 of the worksheet, starting in cell A9:
Listing:     **21561**
Date:     **05/22/2004**
Agent:     **Kramer**
Phone:     **270-532-9764**
Address:     **1515 Michael Dr.**
City:     **Mission**
Price:     **$151,900**

**14.** Save and then close the workbook.

step by step

## 3. Entering Formulas

After creating a worksheet that includes text and values, you enter formulas to perform calculations and then save the workbook to your personal storage location.

**1.** To display a new workbook:
CLICK: New button ( )

**2.** Enter the company name in cell A1:
TYPE: **Johnson's Sport Mart**
PRESS: ⬇
TYPE: **Today is:**
PRESS: ➡

**3.** In cell B2, enter today's date:
TYPE: *your date* using the format dd-mmm-yy
PRESS: (ENTER)
(*Hint:* The date March 31, 2004 would be entered as 31-Mar-04.)

**4.** Complete the worksheet as it appears in Figure 1.42.

**Figure 1.42**

Johnson's Sport
Mart worksheet

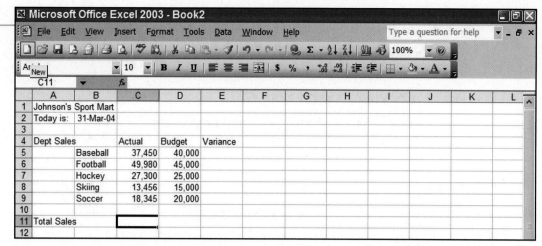

5. To begin, calculate the total sales for the "Actual" column:
   SELECT: cell C11
   TYPE: **=c5+c6+c7+c8+c9**
   PRESS: (ENTER)
   (*Hint:* There are easier methods for summing a column that you learn in the next chapter.)

6. Use a similar formula to display the sum of the "Budget" column in cell D11.

7. Now calculate the sales variance:
   SELECT: cell E5
   TYPE: **=c5–d5**
   PRESS: (ENTER)
   The value -2550 appears in the worksheet.

8. Using the same method, calculate the remaining variances for cells E6 through E9, and E11.

9. Let's save the workbook to your personal storage location:
   CHOOSE: File → Save As

10. On your own, navigate the Save As dialog box using the Places bar and *Save in* drop-down list box to locate your personal storage location for saving workbook files. When you are ready to proceed, name the workbook "**Johnson**" and compare the finished workbook to Figure 1.43.

**Figure 1.43**

Completed
"Johnson"
workbook

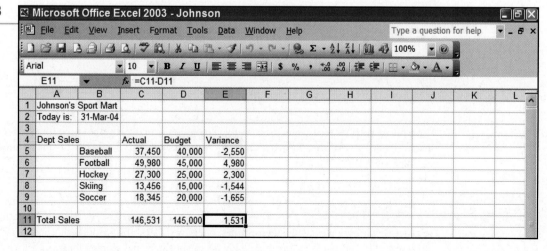

**11.** On your own, change some values in the "Actual" and "Budget" columns and view the calculated results.

**12.** Close the workbook without saving your changes.

on your own

## 4. Personal Monthly Budget

To practice working with text, values, and formulas, ensure that Excel is loaded and then display a blank workbook. You will now begin creating a personal budget. Enter a title that contains the words "My Monthly Budget." Under this title, include your name and the current month. Now enter the following expense categories and a reasonable amount for each:

- Rent/Mortgage
- Food
- Clothing
- Car expenses
- Utilities
- Education
- Entertainment

In the same column as the above labels, enter the words "Total Expenses." Then, beneath the column of numbers, enter a formula that sums the column. Now add a new column next to these budget figures that displays the percentage share for each budget category of the total expenses. For example, you would divide the value for Food by the Total Expenses value to calculate its share of the budget. (*Hint:* The division operator is specified using the forward slash symbol (/) on your keyboard.) Don't worry about formatting the results as percentages. Figure 1.44 provides an example of a completed worksheet.

**Figure 1.44**

Completing the "My Budget" workbook

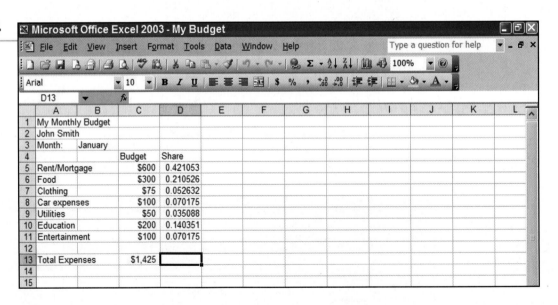

Experiment with increasing and decreasing the budget expense figures to see their effect on the percentage share calculations. When completed, save the workbook as "My Budget" to your personal storage location and then close the workbook.

on your own

## 5. My Grade Book

To practice working with data and formulas, open the EX01HE05 workbook (Figure 1.45). Before continuing, save the workbook as "My Grade Book" to your personal storage location. Enter sample marks into column D of the worksheet.

**Figure 1.45**

Opening the
EX01HE05
workbook

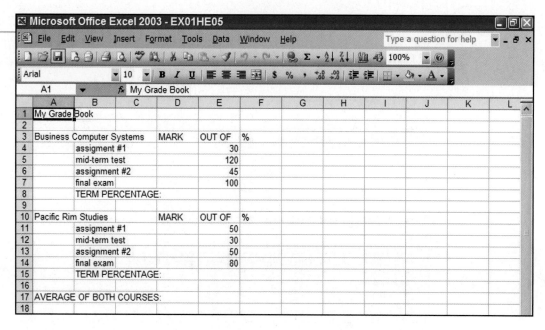

Enter formulas that calculate the percentage grade for each test or assignment by dividing the "MARK" column by the "OUT OF" column. Then, enter formulas that calculate the Term Percentages for each course. The results should display in cells F8 and F15. (*Hint:* You will need to use parentheses to group data in your formula equation. Specifically, you must divide the total course marks achieved by the total marks possible. This is a lengthy formula!) Finally, enter a formula that calculates the average percentage of both courses for display in cell F17. You will need to add together the two course percentages within parentheses and then divide the sum by 2. An example of the completed worksheet appears in Figure 1.46. Adjust some of the sample marks to check that the formulas are working correctly.

**Figure 1.46**

Completed "My
Grade Book"
workbook

Save the completed workbook to your personal storage location and then close the workbook.

on your own

## 6. My Questionnaire

You now assume the role of market researcher and finalize the analysis of a questionnaire using Excel 2003. To begin, open the EX01HE06 workbook (Figure 1.47). Save the workbook as "My Questionnaire" to your personal storage location. Review the contents of the worksheet.

**Figure 1.47**

Opening the
EX01HE06
workbook

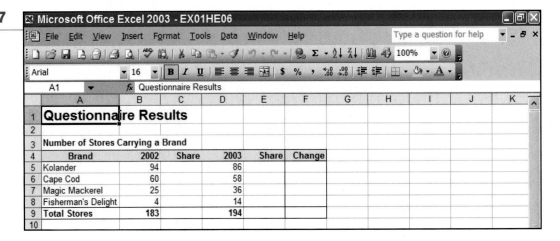

The "Kolander" brand of frozen fish has recently been renamed to "For the Halibut," and you immediately make this change in the worksheet. You also notice that the "Capetown Cod" brand is mistakenly entered as "Cape Cod," requiring you to edit another cell. You now calculate the market shares held by each brand in the years 2002 and 2003. For each brand in column C and E, enter a formula that divides a brand's results by the total number of stores in row 9. Don't worry about formatting the results as percentages. Lastly, calculate the percentage change that resulted for each brand between 2002 and 2003. The required formula may be described as: $(BrandResult2003 - BrandResult2002) / BrandResult2002$. (*Hint:* Do not enter this formula into the worksheet verbatim. You must replace these arguments with the appropriate cell addresses.) Check your work against the completed worksheet shown in Figure 1.48.

**Figure 1.48**

Completed "My
Questionnaire"
workbook

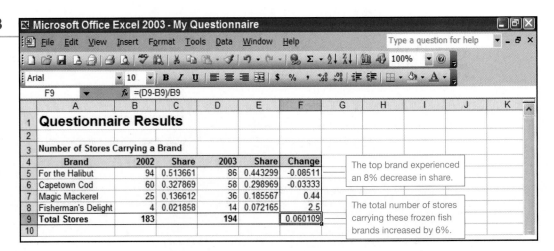

Save the workbook to your personal storage location. Close the workbook and exit Microsoft Office Excel 2003.

# CaseStudy  PACWEST TOURS

PacWest Tours is a small, privately owned bus charter company operating in the Pacific Northwest. The company's business consists primarily of local sightseeing tours and meeting destination-based transportation needs, such as airport and hotel transfers. Earlier this year, PacWest added a third luxury coach to their fleet of buses and retained two full-time and three part-time drivers. Besides the drivers, PacWest employs a full-time dispatcher and a mechanic. Samuel Wong, the general manager, started the company and oversees all aspects of its operation.

Administratively, PacWest operates with minimal paperwork and performs manual record keeping. All bookings are handwritten into a scheduling chart, and the drivers fill out travel logs at the end of each trip. Invoices and receipts are simply turned over to a bookkeeping service, as Samuel cannot afford a staff accountant. Recently, however, Samuel has been finding it increasingly difficult to obtain the information he needs to make key decisions. To remedy this problem, he has hired Renee Duvall, the daughter of one of his drivers, as an office assistant and computer operator. Samuel wants Renee to use Microsoft Office Excel 2003 to create a worksheet that will enable him to compare the monthly efficiency of his fleet of buses. You see, Samuel has an opportunity to purchase an additional luxury coach for well below market value. As a cost-conscious businessman, Samuel wants to have a clear understanding of how his current equipment is performing before spending any more money.

In the following case problems, assume the role of Renee and perform the same steps that she identifies. You may want to reread the chapter opening before proceeding.

1. Renee decides to create a new worksheet that she can use as a template for each month's report. She begins by loading Microsoft Office Excel 2003 and displaying a blank workbook. Her first step will be to enter the title and the row and column headings. Then, the workbook needs to be saved to disk so that it can be retrieved later as a starting point for the monthly reports.

   Renee creates the worksheet shown in Figure 1.49 and then saves it as "Fleet Stats" to her personal storage location.

**Figure 1.49**

Completing the "Fleet Stats" workbook

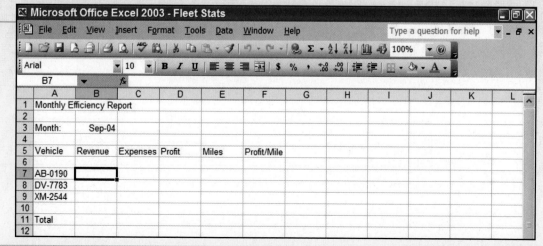

2. Satisfied that this format will provide Samuel with the information he needs, Renee begins to fill in the first month's figures. Most of the data she uses is taken directly from the monthly revenue and expense summaries prepared by the bookkeeping service. The driver's travel logs provide the rest of the data. After entering the information shown in Figure 1.50, Renee saves the workbook as "Sep-04 Stats" to her personal storage location.

**Figure 1.50**

Completing the "Sep-04 Stats" efficiency report

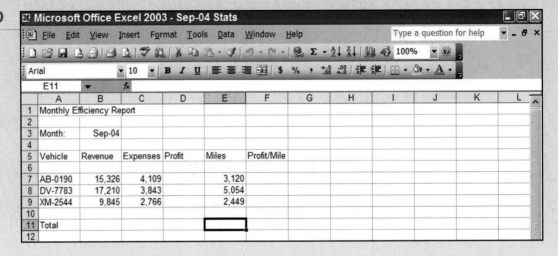

3. Now, Renee enters the formulas for the worksheet:

- She constructs formulas for display in row 11 that add the values appearing in the "Revenue," "Expenses," and "Miles" columns. The three formulas are entered into cells B11, C11, and E11.

- She enters formulas in cells D7, D8, and D9 that calculate the Profit by subtracting a bus's Expenses from the Revenue it generated. She then enters a sum formula for the column in cell D11.

- She calculates and displays the Profit per Mile in cells F7, F8, F9, and F11. The calculation she uses is simply the Profit from column D divided by the Miles in column E.

Unfortunately, Samuel has already left for the day. Renee decides to finish her work and go home; she saves the workbook as "Sep-04 Results" and then closes it. She is already looking forward to showing off her new creation (as shown in Figure 1.51) to Samuel in the morning.

**Figure 1.51**

Completing the "Sep-04 Results" workbook

| | A | B | C | D | E | F |
|---|---|---|---|---|---|---|
| 1 | Monthly Efficiency Report | | | | | |
| 2 | | | | | | |
| 3 | Month: | Sep-04 | | | | |
| 4 | | | | | | |
| 5 | Vehicle | Revenue | Expenses | Profit | Miles | Profit/Mile |
| 6 | | | | | | |
| 7 | AB-0190 | 15,326 | 4,109 | 11,217 | 3,120 | 3.595192 |
| 8 | DV-7783 | 17,210 | 3,843 | 13,367 | 5,054 | 2.644836 |
| 9 | XM-2544 | 9,845 | 2,766 | 7,079 | 2,449 | 2.890568 |
| 10 | | | | | | |
| 11 | Total | 42,381 | 10,718 | 31,663 | 10,623 | 3 |
| 12 | | | | | | |

F11 = =D11/E11

**4.** The next morning, Renee opens the "Sep-04 Results" workbook and asks Samuel to take a look at it. He is very pleased with the report and amazed at how quickly Excel can perform the calculations. Samuel asks Renee what it would take to produce this report for another month. She explains that all she needs to do is enter the month's revenues, expenses, and miles into the appropriate cells; Excel then recalculates the worksheet automatically. Samuel is impressed, realizing that he will finally have some decent information on which to base business decisions.

After mulling over the worksheet, Samuel decides it would be prudent to purchase the fourth luxury coach. With some minor modifications, he realizes that the workbook information would come in handy during his meeting with the bank's loan officer. Samuel asks Renee to make some revisions. First, the title of the report, explains Samuel, should read "PacWest Tours." The "Monthly Efficiency Report" title should be moved down to row 2. Furthermore, the buses should be identified by their names instead of their registration numbers. The bus names are Runner (AB-0190), Wanderer (DV-7783), and Zephyr (XM-2544). Samuel also asks Renee to change the column heading from "Vehicles" to "Fleet." The worksheet should now appear as shown in Figure 1.52.

**Figure 1.52**

Completing the "Sep-04 Summary" workbook

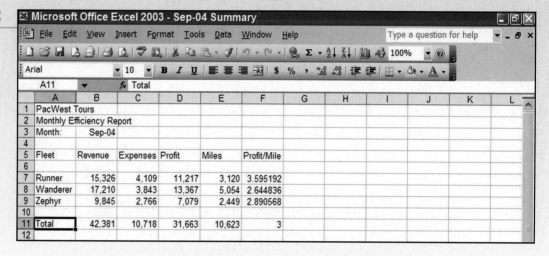

Renee makes the requested changes. She then saves the workbook as "Sep-04 Summary" and closes the workbook. As a last step, she exits Microsoft Office Excel 2003.

## Answers to Self-Check Questions

**SelfCheck**

**1.1** How do you turn the adaptive menus feature on or off? Choose the Tools, Customize command and then check the *Always show full menus* check box to turn the adaptive menus feature off. Remove the check to turn the feature back on.

**1.2** Explain why a phone number is not considered a numeric value in an Excel worksheet. Although it contains numbers, a phone number is never used to perform mathematical calculations.

**1.3** Why is worksheet editing such a valuable skill? Most worksheets in use today are revisions and updates of older worksheets. As a novice user, you often spend more time updating existing worksheets than constructing new ones.

**1.4** In the Open and Save As dialog boxes, how do the List and Details views differ? Name two other views that are accessible from the Views button. The List view uses a multicolumn format. The Details view displays one file per row. Furthermore, the Details view displays other information, including the file size, type, and modification date. The other views that appear on the drop-down menu include: Thumbnails, Tiles, Icons, Properties, Preview, and WebView.

# Microsoft® Office Excel®

## 2003

# CHAPTER 2

# Modifying a Worksheet

## PREREQUISITES

To successfully complete this chapter, you must be able to perform basic data entry and file management operations in Excel. Besides entering text, numbers, dates, and formulas into a worksheet, you will be asked to open, save, and close workbooks. You must also know how to use the toolbar, Menu bar, and right-click shortcut menus in Excel.

## LEARNING OBJECTIVES

After completing this chapter, you will be able to:

- Use several "Auto" features provided by Excel for entering and editing data and formulas

- Copy and move information using the Windows and Office Clipboards, and the drag and drop method

- Use the AutoFill feature and Fill commands to duplicate and extend data and formulas

- Insert and delete cells, rows, and columns

- Hide, unhide, and adjust rows and columns

# 2.1 Entering and Reviewing Data

Even new users can quickly learn to create workbooks and enter data using Microsoft Office Excel 2003. More experienced spreadsheet users know how to apply Excel's features efficiently and effectively in performing routine tasks. In this module, you are introduced to some popular Excel tools and methods that can help speed your learning and make you a more productive spreadsheet user. In addition to selecting and manipulating worksheet cells, you learn to use three of Excel's "Auto" features—*AutoComplete, AutoCalculate,* and *AutoSum.* These timesaving tools facilitate your entry of repetitive data in a worksheet and help you to construct and enter formulas for performing common calculations.

## 2.1.1 Selecting Cells and Ranges

### → Feature

A **cell range** is a single cell or rectangular block of cells. Each cell range has a beginning cell address in the top left-hand corner and an ending cell address in the bottom right-hand corner. To use a cell range in a formula, you separate the two cell addresses using a colon. For example, the cell range B4:C6 references the six shaded cells shown below. Notice that the current or active cell, B4, does not appear shaded in this graphic.

### → Method

To select a cell range using the mouse:

- CLICK: the cell in the top left-hand corner
- DRAG: the mouse pointer to the cell in the bottom right-hand corner

To select a cell range using the keyboard:

- SELECT: cell in the top left-hand corner
- PRESS: SHIFT and hold it down
- PRESS: *an arrow key* to extend the range highlighting
- RELEASE: SHIFT

### → Practice

In this exercise, you will open a workbook, save it to your personal storage location, and practice selecting single and multiple cell ranges. Ensure that Excel 2003 is loaded before proceeding.

**1.** Open the Advantage student data file named EX0210.

**2.** In the next two steps, you will save the workbook file as "My Gift List" to your personal storage location. Do the following:
CHOOSE: File → Save As
TYPE: **My Gift List** (but do not press [ENTER])

**3.** Using the *Save in* drop-down list box or the Places bar:
SELECT: *your personal storage location* (for example, the My Documents or My Workbooks folder, as shown in Figure 2.1)
CLICK: Save command button
(*Note:* Most lessons in this guide begin by opening an Advantage student data file and then saving it to your personal storage location using a new filename.)

**Figure 2.1**

Saving the
EX0210
workbook

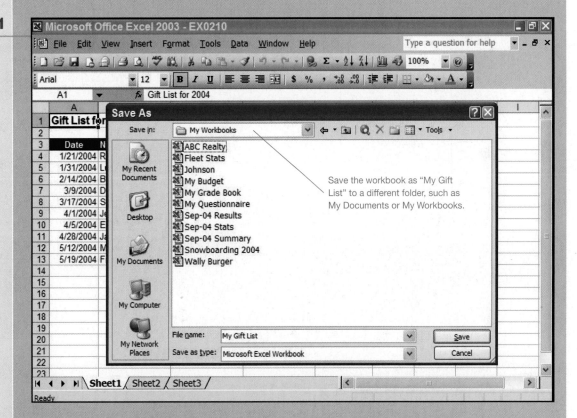

**4.** You will now practice selecting cell ranges. To begin:
SELECT: cell A3
(*Hint:* The word SELECT tells you to place the cell pointer at the identified cell address using either the keyboard or the mouse.)

**5.** To select the range from cell A3 to E3 using the keyboard:
PRESS: SHIFT and hold it down
PRESS: ➡ four times
Although it is not explicitly stated in the above instruction, you release the SHIFT key once the range is selected. Your screen should appear similar to the one shown in Figure 2.2.

**Figure 2.2**

Selecting the cell range A3:E3

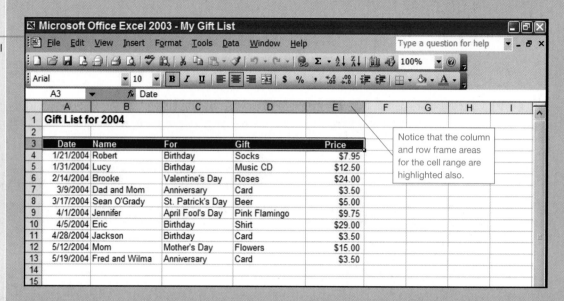

**6.** You learned in the previous chapter that the CTRL + HOME combination moves the cell pointer to cell A1. Pressing the HOME key by itself moves the cell pointer to column A within the same row. To illustrate, let's move the cell pointer back to cell A3:
PRESS: HOME

**7.** To select the same cell range, but more quickly and efficiently:
PRESS: SHIFT and hold it down
PRESS: CTRL + ➡ together
Notice that the entire cell range is selected. You may remember from the last chapter that the CTRL + arrow combination moves the cell pointer until the cell contents change from empty to filled or from filled to empty.

**8.** To select a cell range using the mouse:
CLICK: cell C6 and hold down the left mouse button
DRAG: the mouse pointer to E8 (and then release the mouse button)
Notice that the column letters and row numbers in the frame area appear highlighted for the selected cell range, as shown in Figure 2.3.

## Figure 2.3

Selecting a cell range using the mouse

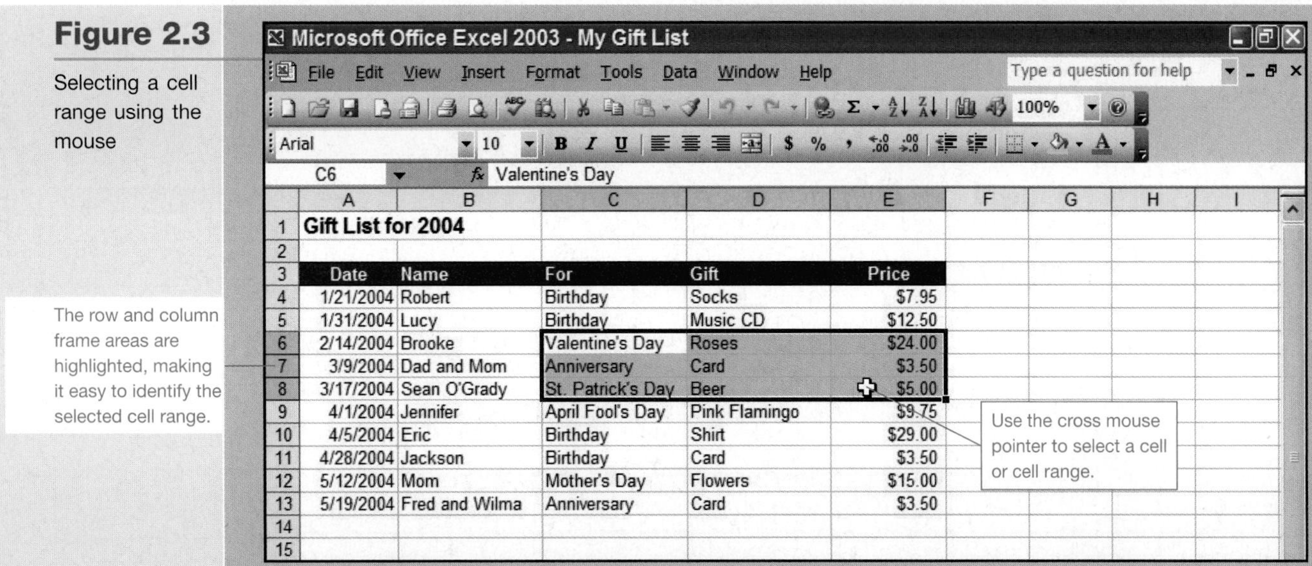

The row and column frame areas are highlighted, making it easy to identify the selected cell range.

**9.** For novice users, there is a mouse method easier than dragging a cell range for selection. To demonstrate, you will now select the cell range from B10 to D13:
CLICK: cell B10
PRESS: **SHIFT** and hold it down
CLICK: cell D13
The range between the two cells should now appear highlighted. (*Note:* Remember to release the **SHIFT** key after the last selection is made.)

**10.** You can also select multiple cell ranges on a worksheet. To begin:
DRAG: from cell A6 to cell E6
PRESS: **CTRL** and hold it down
DRAG: from cell A9 to cell E9
You should see two separate cell ranges highlighted on the worksheet. (*Note:* Release the **CTRL** key after making the cell range selection.)

**11.** To select a third cell range:
PRESS: **CTRL** and hold it down
DRAG: from cell A12 to cell E12
(*Note:* Release the **CTRL** key after making the selection.) Your screen should now look similar to the one shown in Figure 2.4.

**12.** To move the cell pointer to cell A1:
PRESS: **CTRL** + **HOME**

**Figure 2.4**

Selecting multiple
cell ranges using
the CTRL key

| | Microsoft Office Excel 2003 - My Gift List |
| --- | --- |

File   Edit   View   Insert   Format   Tools   Data   Window   Help          Type a question for help

Arial          ▼ 10 ▼   B  *I*  U   ≡ ≡ ≡ 国  $ % ,  ‰ .‰  ≝ ≝  国 ▾ ◇ ▾ A ▾

A12          ▼          fx  5/12/2004

| | A | B | C | D | E | F | G | H | I |
| --- | --- | --- | --- | --- | --- | --- | --- | --- | --- |
| 1 | **Gift List for 2004** | | | | | | | | |
| 2 | | | | | | | | | |
| 3 | Date | Name | For | Gift | Price | | | | |
| 4 | 1/21/2004 | Robert | Birthday | Socks | $7.95 | | | | |
| 5 | 1/31/2004 | Lucy | Birthday | Music CD | $12.50 | | | | |
| 6 | 2/14/2004 | Brooke | Valentine's Day | Roses | $24.00 | | | | |
| 7 | 3/9/2004 | Dad and Mom | Anniversary | Card | $3.50 | | | | |
| 8 | 3/17/2004 | Sean O'Grady | St. Patrick's Day | Beer | $5.00 | | | | |
| 9 | 4/1/2004 | Jennifer | April Fool's Day | Pink Flamingo | $9.75 | | | | |
| 10 | 4/5/2004 | Eric | Birthday | Shirt | $29.00 | | | | |
| 11 | 4/28/2004 | Jackson | Birthday | Card | $3.50 | | | | |
| 12 | 5/12/2004 | Mom | Mother's Day | Flowers | $15.00 | | | | |
| 13 | 5/19/2004 | Fred and Wilma | Anniversary | Card | $3.50 | | | | |
| 14 | | | | | | | | | |
| 15 | | | | | | | | | |
| 16 | | | | | | | | | |

The active cell, A12,
is the top left-hand
cell in the final cell
range selected.

## 2.1.2 Entering Data Using AutoComplete

→ **Feature**

The **AutoComplete** feature second-guesses what you are typing into a worksheet cell and suggests how to complete the entry. After analyzing your first few keystrokes and scanning the same column for similar entries, AutoComplete tacks on the remaining letters when it thinks it has found a match. You can accept the AutoComplete entry, or you can ignore its suggestion and continue typing. This feature can greatly reduce the number of repetitive entries you make in a worksheet.

→ **Method**

By default, the AutoComplete feature is turned on. If, however, you view its helpfulness as an intrusion, you can turn it off. To do so:

- CHOOSE: Tools → Options

- CLICK: *Edit* tab in the dialog box

- SELECT: *Enable AutoComplete for cell values* check box to toggle AutoComplete on (☑) or off (☐)

→ **Practice**

You now practice using Excel's AutoComplete feature to enter data. Ensure that the "My Gift List" workbook is displayed.

**1.** SELECT: cell A14

**2.** To add a new entry to the worksheet:
TYPE: 6/2/2004
PRESS: ➡
TYPE: **Anda**
PRESS: ➡

**3.** You will now enter the word "Birthday" into cell C14. After typing the first letter, Excel notices that there is only one other entry in the column that begins with the letter "B" and makes the assumption that this is the word you want to enter. To demonstrate:
TYPE: **B**
Notice that Excel completes the word "Birthday" automatically, as shown in Figure 2.5.

**Figure 2.5**

The AutoComplete feature completes the C14 cell entry for "Birthday"

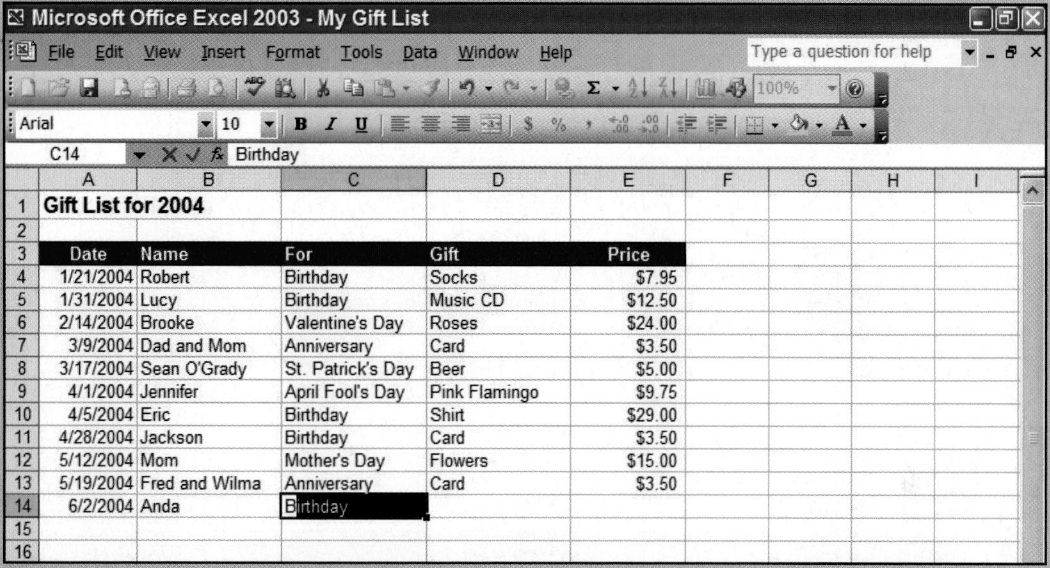

**4.** To accept the completed word:
PRESS: ➡

**5.** For the remaining cells in the row:
TYPE: **Shoes**
PRESS: ➡
TYPE: **$19.95**
PRESS: **ENTER** to move to the next row
PRESS: **HOME** to move to the first column (A)
Your cell pointer should now appear in cell A15.

**6.** Let's add another entry to the worksheet. Do the following:
TYPE: **6/5/2004**
PRESS: ➡
TYPE: **Trevor and Ann**
PRESS: ➡

**7.** You can also use Excel's AutoComplete feature to display a sorted list of all the unique entries in a column. To illustrate:
RIGHT-CLICK: cell C15 to display its shortcut menu
CHOOSE: Pick From List

AutoComplete generates the list and then displays its results in a pop-up list box, as shown in Figure 2.6.

**Figure 2.6**

Entering data using the AutoComplete pick list

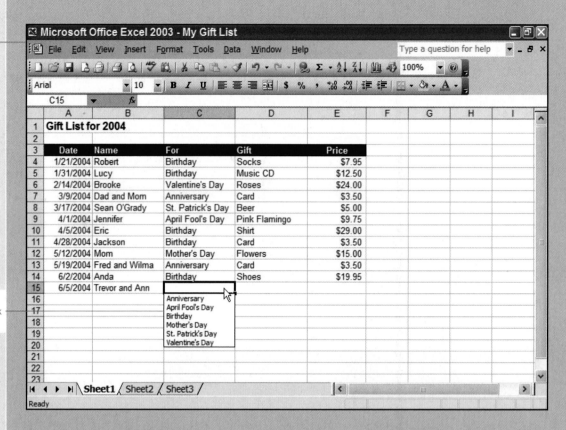

Displaying the AutoComplete "Pick From List" Feature

**8.** To make a selection:
CLICK: Anniversary in the pick list

**9.** As an alternative to choosing the Pick From List command in the right-click menu, Excel provides a shortcut key combination. To demonstrate:
CLICK: cell D15
PRESS: ALT + ↓ to display the column's pick list

**10.** To select an item:
CLICK: Flowers in the pick list

**11.** To complete the row:
PRESS: →
TYPE: $15.00
PRESS: ENTER

**12.** Save the workbook and keep it open for use in the next lesson. (*Hint:* The fastest methods for saving a workbook include clicking the Save button (🖫) or pressing CTRL + s.)

### 2.1.3 Using AutoCalculate and AutoSum

→ **Feature**

Using Excel's **AutoCalculate** feature, you can view the calculated result of a selected range of values in the Status bar. This feature is useful for checking the result of a calculation, such as summing a cell range, without actually having to store its value in the worksheet. If, on the other hand, you need to store the calculated result, click the **AutoSum** button ($\Sigma$ ·) on the Standard toolbar. With the AutoSum feature, Excel reviews the surrounding cells, guesses at the range you want to sum, and then places a SUM function (described in a later chapter) into the active cell.

→ **Method**

To use the AutoCalculate feature:

• SELECT: the range of values that you want to calculate

To use the AutoSum feature:

• SELECT: the cell where you want the result to appear

• CLICK: AutoSum button ($\Sigma$ ·)

→ **Practice**

Using the same worksheet, you will now practice viewing AutoCalculate results and entering an addition formula using AutoSum. Ensure that you have completed the previous lesson and that the "My Gift List" workbook is displayed.

**1.** Imagine that you want to know how much money to set aside for gifts in April. To find the answer quickly, do the following:
SELECT: cell range from E9 to E11
Notice that only the April values are selected in the Price column.

**2.** Review the Status bar. Notice that "Sum=$42.25" now appears near the right-hand side of the Status bar, as shown in Figure 2.7.

**Figure 2.7**

Using the AutoCalculate feature

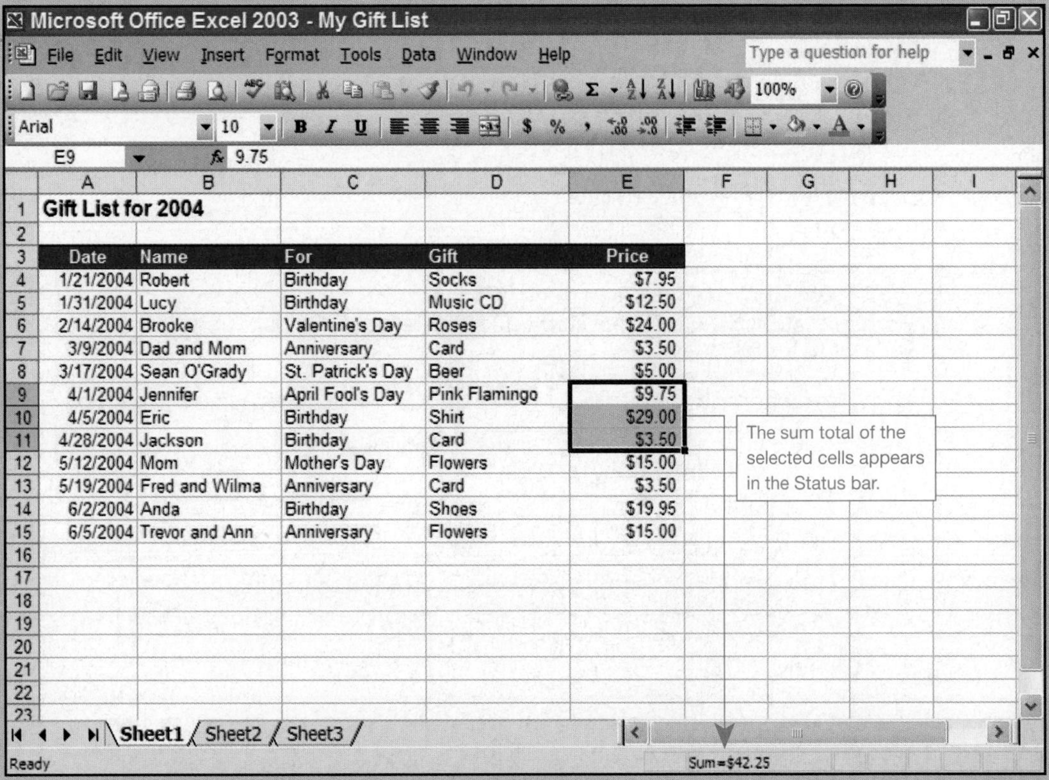

**3.** Let's perform another calculation:
SELECT: cell E4
PRESS: SHIFT and hold it down
PRESS: CTRL + ⬇
All of the cells under the Price column heading should now be selected. Assuming that you completed the previous lessons, the Status bar will now display "Sum=$148.65."

**4.** Using the AutoCalculate feature, you can also view the result of other calculations in the Status bar. To demonstrate, let's calculate the average value of gifts in the selected cell range:
RIGHT-CLICK: "Sum = $148.65" in the Status bar
Your screen should now appear similar to the one shown in Figure 2.8.

**Figure 2.8**

Displaying the right-click menu for the AutoCalculate feature

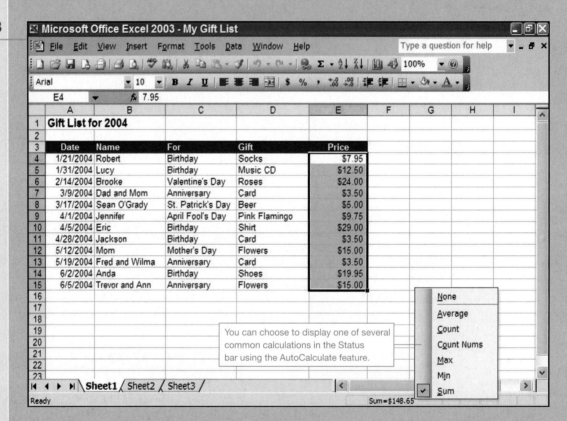

**5.** In the AutoCalculate right-click menu:
CHOOSE: Average
The Status bar now displays "Average=$12.39."

**6.** To make the Status bar display the sum of the selected cell range, do the following:
RIGHT-CLICK: "Average=$12.39" in the Status bar
CHOOSE: Sum

**7.** SELECT: cell D16

**8.** Let's enter a text label for the next calculation:
TYPE: **Total Cost**
PRESS: ➡

**9.** The quickest way to sum a row or column of values is using the AutoSum button (Σ▾) on the Standard toolbar. Make sure that you click the sigma (Σ) portion of the button, rather than the down arrow (▾). To demonstrate:

CLICK: AutoSum button (Σ ▼) once
A built-in function called SUM is entered into the cell, along with the range that Excel assumes you want to sum (Figure 2.9).

**Figure 2.9**

Using the AutoSum button (Σ ▼) to sum a cell range

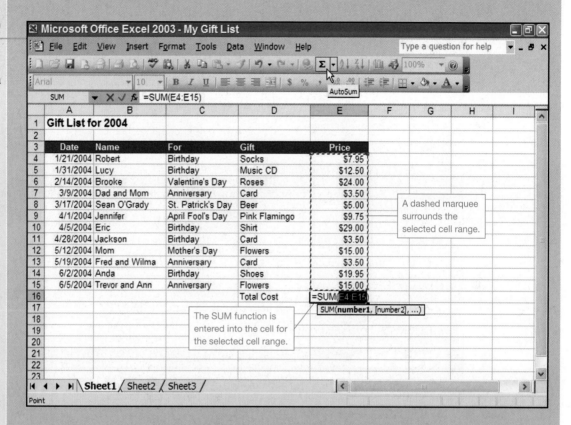

10. To accept the highlighted cells as the desired range:
CLICK: AutoSum button (Σ ▼) again
The result, $148.65, now appears in cell E16. (*Note:* You can also press **ENTER** or click the Enter button (☑) in the Formulas bar to accept the AutoSum entry.)

11. Let's change one of the column entries. Do the following:
SELECT: cell E14
TYPE: $119.95
PRESS: **ENTER**
Notice that the AutoSum result in cell E16 is recalculated automatically and now displays $248.65.

12. Save the workbook by clicking the Save button (🖫).

*In Addition* ACCESSING OTHER "AUTO"
CALCULATIONS USING THE AUTOSUM BUTTON (Σ ▼)

Similar to AutoCalculate's right-click menu that allowed you to display an average value, AutoSum provides alternative calculations from the drop-down arrow attached to its button (Σ ▼). Click the down arrow to display a list of possible functions, such as Average and Count. When you select one of these function commands, Excel inserts the function into the cell with the appropriate range parameters, similar to SUM.

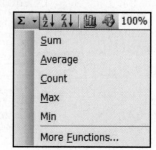

### 2.1.4 Inserting and Deleting Cells

→ ## Feature

You can insert a new, empty cell or cell range in the middle of existing data without destroying the data. Excel allows you to insert a cell range by pushing the existing range down or to the right. This feature is especially useful because it updates all the affected cell references used in formulas automatically. Similarly, Excel updates formulas when you delete a cell or cell range. Unlike clearing or erasing a cell's contents, deleting a cell or cell range does not leave a gap of empty cells behind.

→ ## Method

To insert a cell or cell range:

- SELECT: the desired cell or cell range
- CHOOSE: Insert → Cells
- SELECT: *Shift cells right* or *Shift cells down* option button
- CLICK: OK command button

To delete a cell or cell range:

- SELECT: the desired cell or cell range
- CHOOSE: Edit → Delete
- SELECT: *Shift cells left* or *Shift cells up* option button
- CLICK: OK command button

→ ## Practice

You will now practice inserting and deleting cells. Ensure that the "My Gift List" workbook is displayed.

**1.** Let's insert a new item into the worksheet in the proper ascending date order. To begin:
SELECT: cell range from A9 to E9

**2.** To insert a new range of cells:
CHOOSE: Insert → Cells
The Insert dialog box appears, as shown in Figure 2.10.

**Figure 2.10**

Inserting a range of cells using the Insert dialog box

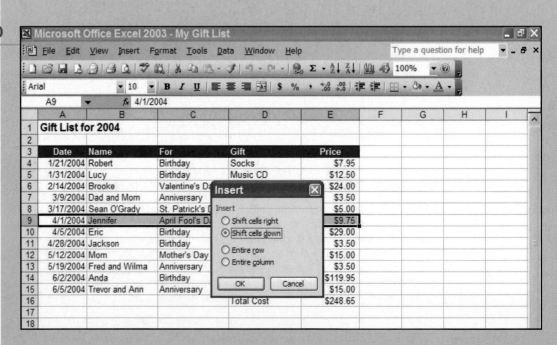

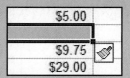

**3.** To complete the procedure:
SELECT: *Shift cells down* option button, if it is not already selected
CLICK: OK command button
The existing data is pushed down to make space for the new cells. Notice that the Insert Options icon ( ) appears attached to the right side of the cell range, as shown here. You can use this icon to choose formatting options for the newly inserted cells. Because we want to keep the default formatting for the new row, you may ignore the Insert Options icon ( ) for now.

**4.** Make sure that the cell range from A9 to E9 remains selected. Now let's enter a new item:
TYPE: **3/31/2004**
PRESS: [ENTER]
The cell pointer moves to the next available cell in the selected range, even though you pressed [ENTER] and not →. When you select a range for data entry, the cell pointer is confined to that range when you insert data using [ENTER].

**5.** To complete the row item with an Anniversary entry:
TYPE: **Tim and Starr**
PRESS: [ENTER]
TYPE: **An**
PRESS: [ENTER]
TYPE: **Mirror**
PRESS: [ENTER]
TYPE: **$37.00**
PRESS: [ENTER]
Notice that the cell pointer wraps around to the beginning of the selected range and that the "Total Cost" value in cell E17 is updated.

**6.** Now let's remove Jackson's birthday from the list:
SELECT: cell range from A12 to E12

**7.** To delete the selected cells:
CHOOSE: Edit → Delete
The Delete dialog box, similar to the Insert dialog box, is displayed, as shown in Figure 2.11.

**Figure 2.11**

Deleting a range
of cells using the
Delete dialog box

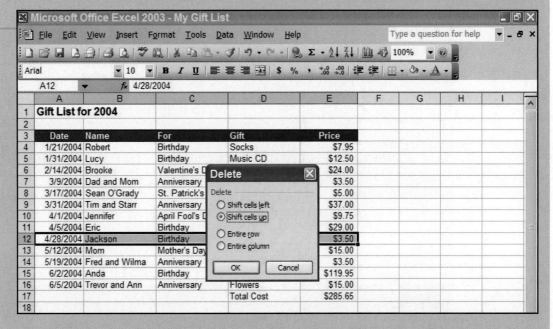

**8.** To complete the procedure
SELECT: *Shift cells up* option button, if it is not already selected
CLICK: OK command button
The remaining cells slide up one row to close the gap and the "Total Cost" value in cell E16 is updated to $282.15.

**9.** PRESS: CTRL + HOME to move to cell A1

**10.** Save and then close the workbook.

 **2.1** Which of the "Auto" features enables you to sum a range of values and display the result in the Status bar?

## 2.2 Copying and Moving Data

Excel 2003 provides several tools for copying, moving, and pasting data. Like the "Auto" features, these tools can help you reduce the number of repetitive entries you are required to make. For example, once you enter a formula to sum one column of values, you can duplicate that formula to sum the adjacent columns. There are three primary methods for copying and moving data. First, you can cut or copy a single piece of data from any application and store it on the **Windows Clipboard.** Then, you can paste the data into any other worksheet, workbook, or application. Second, you can choose the **Office Clipboard** to collect up to 24 items and then paste the stored data singularly or as a group into any other Office 2003 application. Last, you can use **drag and drop** to copy and move cell information short distances using the mouse. In this module, you will practice duplicating cell contents and extending data and formulas in a worksheet.

### 2.2.1 Using the Windows Clipboard

### → Feature

The Windows Clipboard is a software feature provided by the Windows operating system and is shared by the applications running on your computer. A limitation of this Clipboard is that it can hold only a single piece of data at any given time. Its advantage is that you can use it effectively to copy and move data among a variety of software programs. Once data exists on the Clipboard, it may be pasted multiple times and into multiple applications. The contents of the Clipboard are wiped clean, however, when the computer is turned off. When you perform a simple cut, copy, and paste operation in Excel, you are using the Windows Clipboard. Your alternatives are to use either the Office Clipboard (discussed in the next lesson) for copying multiple items at once or the mouse for quick drag and drop editing.

→  ## Method

| Task description | Menu command | Toolbar button | Keyboard shortcut |
| --- | --- | --- | --- |
| Move data from the worksheet to the Clipboard | Edit, Cut | ✂ | CTRL + X |
| Place a copy of the selected data on the Clipboard | Edit, Copy | 📋 | CTRL + C |
| Insert data stored on the Clipboard into the worksheet | Edit, Paste | 📋▾ | CTRL + V |

→  ## Practice

Using the Windows Clipboard, you will now practice copying and pasting data in a worksheet. The steps for moving data are identical to those for copying, except that you use the Cut command instead of Copy. Ensure that no workbooks are displayed in the application window.

**1.** Open the data file named EX0220 to display the workbook shown in Figure 2.12.

**Figure 2.12**

Opening the
EX0220 workbook

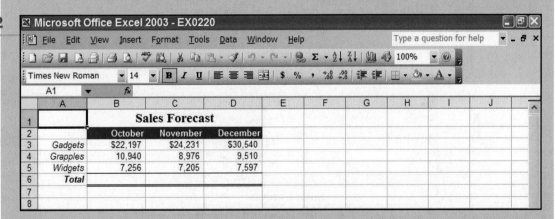

**2.** Save the file as "Sales Forecast" to your personal storage location.

**3.** To calculate totals for row 6 in the worksheet:
SELECT: cell range from B6 to D6
CLICK: AutoSum button ($\Sigma$ ·)
The results appear immediately in the selected range (Figure 2.13). Notice that you can fill an entire cell range using the AutoSum feature.

**Figure 2.13**

Entering totals using the AutoSum button ($\Sigma$ ·)

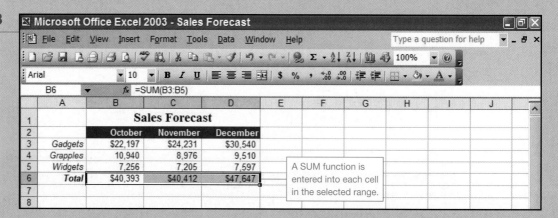

**4.** You will now use the Copy command to duplicate some cells in the worksheet. To begin:
SELECT: cell range from A2 to D6
Notice that all the data is selected, except for the title in row 1.

**5.** To copy the range selection to the Windows Clipboard:
CLICK: Copy button ( ) on the Standard toolbar
The range that you want to copy appears surrounded by a dashed marquee, or moving border, as shown in Figure 2.14.

**Figure 2.14**

Selecting and copying a range to the Clipboard

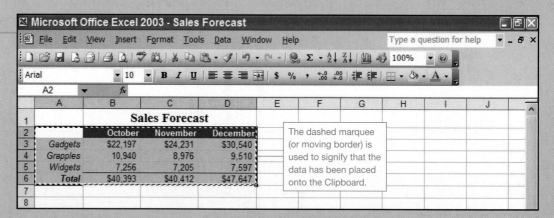

**6.** Now select the top left-hand corner of the worksheet location where you want to place the copied data. Do the following:
SELECT: cell A9

**7.** To paste the data from the Clipboard into the worksheet:
CLICK: Paste button ( ·)
Make sure that you click the clipboard portion of the Paste button ( ) and not the down arrow ( ). Once the data is pasted, notice that the Paste Options icon ( ) is displayed at the bottom right-hand corner of the new cell range. This icon allows you to select advanced formatting and paste options. For our purposes, you may ignore this icon and proceed to the next step.

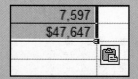

8. While the dashed marquee moves around the original cell range (A2:D6), the data on the Windows Clipboard remains available for pasting. Let's continue pasting the copied data into the worksheet using a shortcut keystroke:
   SELECT: cell A16
   PRESS: CTRL + v to paste the data
   Your screen should now appear similar to the one shown in Figure 2.15.

**Figure 2.15**

Copying and pasting data in a worksheet

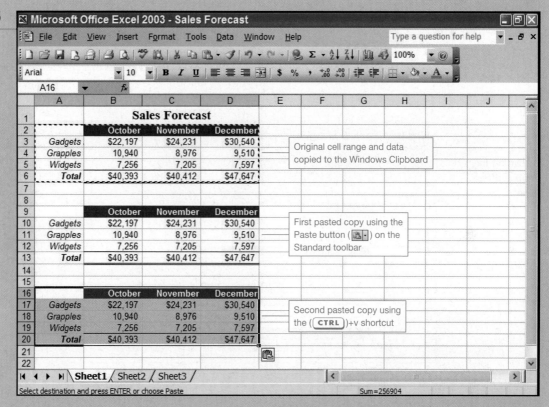

9. To remove the dashed marquee:
   PRESS: ESC
   Notice that the Paste button on the toolbar is now dimmed and unavailable for selection. In other words, the data is no longer available for pasting into the worksheet.

10. To return to cell A1:
    PRESS: CTRL + HOME

## 2.2.2 Using the Office Clipboard

→ # Feature

The Office Clipboard allows you to collect up to 24 data items and then paste them into Microsoft Office 2003 applications, such as Word, Excel, Access, and PowerPoint. For all intents and purposes, you work with the Office Clipboard in the same way you use the Windows Clipboard. In fact, the last item that you cut or copy to the Office Clipboard will be the one and only item stored on the Windows Clipboard. To copy an item to the Office Clipboard, first display the Clipboard task pane by choosing the Office Clipboard command on the Edit menu. Depending on your system's configuration, the Clipboard task pane may open automatically when you perform two copy operations in succession.

→ ## Method

To use the Office Clipboard:

- CHOOSE: Edit → Office Clipboard

→ ## Practice

You will now practice using the Office Clipboard and the Clipboard task pane. Ensure that you have completed the previous lesson and that the "Sales Forecast" workbook is displayed.

**1.** To demonstrate using the Office Clipboard:
CHOOSE: Edit → Office Clipboard
The Clipboard task pane appears docked at the right side of the application window, as shown in Figure 2.16. (*Hint:* Remember that, unlike the Windows Clipboard, the Office Clipboard can store up to 24 items and then paste them all at the same time.)

**Figure 2.16**

Displaying the Clipboard task pane

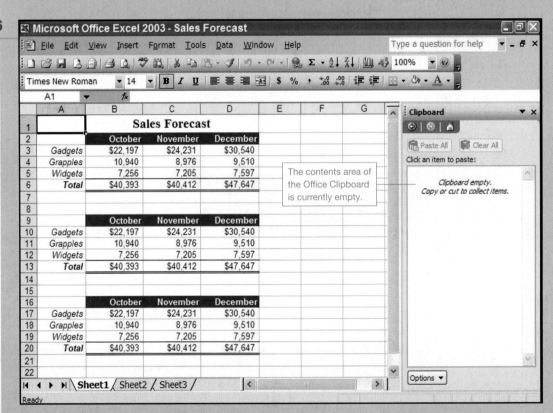

**2.** If the contents area of the Clipboard task pane is not empty:
CLICK: Clear All button (🔯 Clear All) in the task pane

**3.** Now let's add data items to the Office Clipboard:
SELECT: cell A3
CLICK: Copy button (📋)
Notice that the contents area of the Clipboard task pane now shows "Gadgets" and its title bar reads "1 of 24 –Clipboard."

4. To continue adding items:
SELECT: cell B3
CLICK: Copy button (⬚)
SELECT: cell C3
CLICK: Copy button (⬚)
SELECT: cell D3
CLICK: Copy button (⬚)
The task pane's title bar now reads "4 of 24," as shown in Figure 2.17. (*Note:* If you were to continue adding items, the first item ("Gadgets," in our example) would be overwritten by the 25th item collected.)

**Figure 2.17**

Clipboard task pane after collecting four items

Pastes all of the items appearing in the list box vertically into the worksheet

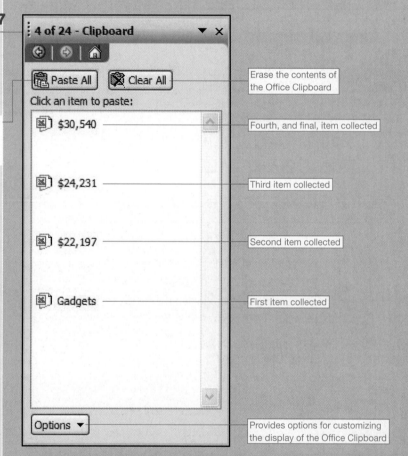

Erase the contents of the Office Clipboard

Fourth, and final, item collected

Third item collected

Second item collected

First item collected

Provides options for customizing the display of the Office Clipboard

5. Position the mouse pointer over one of the data items in the Clipboard task pane. The item will appear highlighted with a border and an attached down arrow at the right-hand side. On your own, click the down arrow to display the pop-up menu shown here. You use this menu to paste a single item from the list or to remove an item that you no longer need. To remove the pop-up menu, click the attached down arrow a second time.

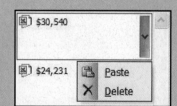

6. Now let's use the Paste All button (⬚ Paste All) to insert all of the collected data items into the worksheet. Do the following:
SELECT: cell F2
CLICK: Paste All button (⬚ Paste All) in the Clipboard task pane
The contents of the Office Clipboard are pasted vertically into a single column in the worksheet; each data item is placed into its own row, as shown in Figure 2.18. Notice that the first item added to the Office Clipboard appears in the first row of the pasted cell range.

**Figure 2.18**

Pasting items
from the Office
Clipboard into the
worksheet

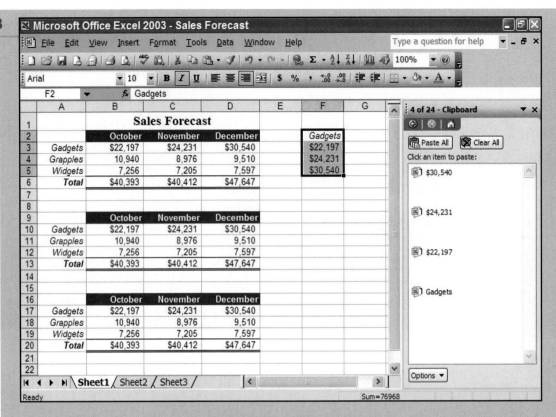

7. Let's prepare for another copy operation by clearing the Office Clipboard. Do the following:
CLICK: Clear All button (🗙 Clear All) in the Clipboard task pane

8. You will now collect, reorder, and then paste information from rows 3 through 5. The key to this step is to collect the data in the order that you want to paste it later. Therefore, to reorder the row data, do the following:
SELECT: cell range A5 through D5 ("Widgets")
PRESS: [CTRL] + c
SELECT: cell range A3 through D3 ("Gadgets")
PRESS: [CTRL] + c
SELECT: cell range A4 through D4 ("Grapples")
PRESS: [CTRL] + c
You should now see three items listed in the Clipboard task pane.

9. Now paste the results on top of an existing data area in the worksheet:
SELECT: A10
CLICK: Paste All button (📋 Paste All)
Notice that you need only select the top left-hand corner of the desired target range. Your screen should now appear similar to the one shown in Figure 2.19.

**Figure 2.19**

Pasting the row items into the worksheet

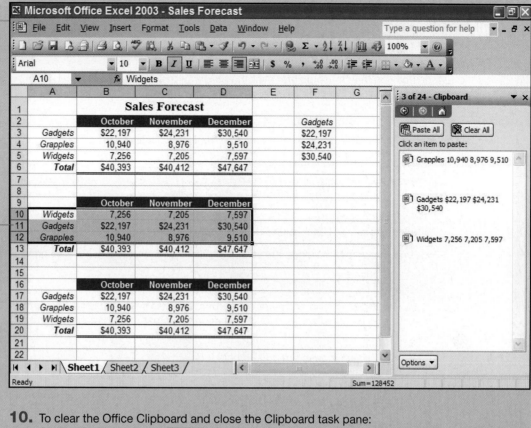

Notice that the rows are ordered differently than the original cell range in rows 3 through 5.

**10.** To clear the Office Clipboard and close the Clipboard task pane:

CLICK: Clear All button (🗙 Clear All)

CLICK: its Close button (☒)

**11.** Move the cell pointer to cell A1.

**12.** Save the workbook and keep it open for use in the next lesson.

### *In Addition* USING THE OFFICE CLIPBOARD TO EXCHANGE DATA IN OFFICE 2003

The Office Clipboard is an excellent tool for sharing data among the Office 2003 applications. You can copy worksheet data to the Office Clipboard and then paste the contents into a Word document or a PowerPoint presentation. You can also collect rows of data from an Access database and place them into your worksheet for analysis. When you need to transfer data, consider using the Office Clipboard instead of performing more complex linking and importing routines.

## 2.2.3 Using Drag and Drop

→ ## Feature

When you use the mouse to perform a drag and drop operation, you bypass the Windows and Office Clipboards altogether. The drag and drop method offers an efficient way to copy and move data from one location in your worksheet to another. Although you cannot perform multiple pastes or collect multiple items, the drag and drop method is the easiest and fastest way to copy and move a cell's contents short distances.

## → Method

To use drag and drop:

- SELECT: the cell range that you want to copy or move

- Position the mouse pointer over the border of the cell range until a white arrow over a four-pronged cross (⬚) appears.

- If you want to perform a copy operation, hold down the **CTRL** key.

- DRAG: the cell range by the border to the target destination

- Release the mouse button and, if necessary, the **CTRL** key.

## → Practice

Using the mouse, you will now practice dragging and dropping a cell range in the worksheet. Ensure that you have completed the previous lesson and that the "Sales Forecast" workbook is displayed.

**1.** Let's practice moving the data that was copied to column F in the previous lesson. Do the following:
SELECT: cell range from F2 to F5

**2.** Position the mouse pointer over a border of the selected cell range until a white diagonal arrow over a four-pronged cross (⬚) appears, as shown here.

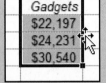

**3.** CLICK: left mouse button and hold it down
DRAG: mouse pointer downward until the ToolTip displays "F9:F12"
Before you release the mouse pointer to complete the drag and drop operation, your screen will appear similar to the one shown in Figure 2.20.

**4.** Release the mouse button to complete the drag and drop operation.

**Figure 2.20**

Using drag and drop to move cell data

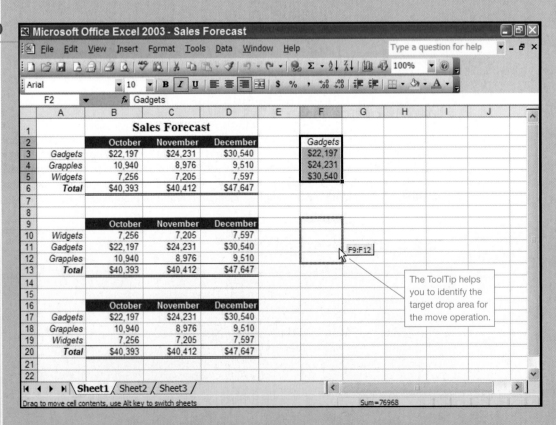

**5.** You will now copy the selected cell range back to its original location. To begin, ensure that the cell range from F9 to F12 is highlighted.

**6.** Position the mouse pointer (🔭) over a border of the cell range. Then:
PRESS: `CTRL` and hold it down
You should notice a plus sign added to the diagonal arrow mouse pointer (🔭).

**7.** CLICK: left mouse button and hold it down
DRAG: mouse pointer upward to F2:F5
The target cell range should appear as shown here.

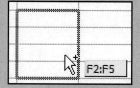

**8.** Release the mouse button and `CTRL` key to complete the copy operation. Your screen should appear similar to the one shown in Figure 2.21.

**9.** Save and then close the workbook.

**Figure 2.21**

Completing the "Sales Forecast" worksheet

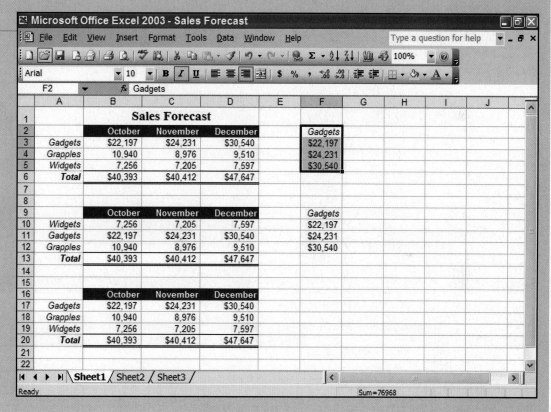

## 2.2.4 Creating a Series Using AutoFill

→ **Feature**

Excel's **AutoFill** feature allows you to enter a data series into a worksheet. Whether a mathematical progression of values (1, 2, 3, . . .) or a row of date headings (Jan, Feb, Mar, . . .), a **series** is a sequence of data that follows a pattern. This feature is a real time-saver and reduces the potential for making data entry errors.

→ # Method

To use AutoFill:

- SELECT: the cell range containing the data you want to extend

- DRAG: the **fill handle,** which is a black square that appears in the lower right-hand corner of the cell range, to extrapolate the series

- Release the mouse button to complete the operation.

→ # Practice

In this exercise, you create a new workbook and then extend the contents of cells using the fill handle and the AutoFill feature. Ensure that no workbooks appear in the application window.

1. To display a new workbook:
   CLICK: New button (🗋)

2. Let's enter some source data from which you will create a series:
   SELECT: cell A3
   TYPE: **Jan**
   PRESS: ⊙
   TYPE: **Period 1**
   PRESS: ⊙
   TYPE: **Quarter 1**
   PRESS: (ENTER)
   Each of these entries will become the starting point for creating three series that extend across their respective rows.

3. To extend the first entry in row 3:
   SELECT: cell A3

4. Position the mouse pointer over the small black square (the fill handle) in the bottom right-hand corner of the cell pointer. The mouse pointer will change to a black cross when positioned correctly. (*Hint:* Figure 2.22 identifies the fill handle and mouse pointer.)

**Figure 2.22**

Using a cell's fill handle

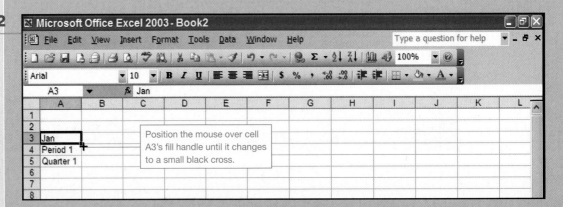

5. CLICK: left mouse button and hold it down
   DRAG: the mouse pointer to column F, until the ToolTip displays "Jun"

6. Release the mouse button to complete the AutoFill operation. The AutoFill Options icon (🖳) appears in the bottom right-hand corner of the range (shown here) to provide additional fill options. For our purposes, you may ignore this icon and proceed to the next step.

**7.** Let's extend the next two rows:
SELECT: cell A4
DRAG: fill handle for cell A4 to column F
SELECT: cell A5
DRAG: fill handle for cell A5 to column F
(*Note:* Always release the mouse button after dragging to the desired location.) Notice that Excel recognizes the word "quarter"; it resumes at Quarter 1 after entering Quarter 4, as shown in Figure 2.23.

**Figure 2.23**

Using AutoFill to complete cell ranges

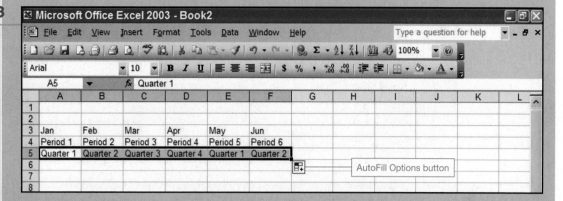

**8.** You can also extend a date series using the fill handle:
SELECT: cell A7
TYPE: **Sep-2003**
PRESS: ➡
TYPE: **Dec-2003**
PRESS: ENTER

**9.** To extend the range using the same increment (every three months), select both cells and then drag the range's fill handle:
SELECT: cell range from A7 to B7
DRAG: fill handle for the range to column F, as shown in Figure 2.24
When you release the mouse button, quarterly dates to Dec-2004 appear in the cell range.

**Figure 2.24**

Extending an incremental date series

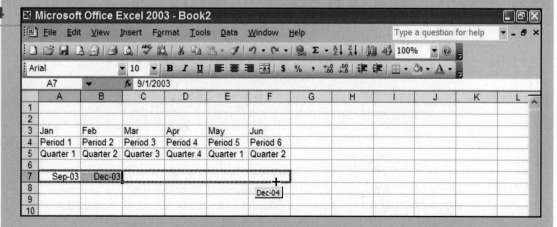

**10.** You can also extract a nonlinear series from a range of values:
SELECT: cell A9
TYPE: **12**
PRESS: ➡
TYPE: **15**
PRESS: ➡
TYPE: **17**
PRESS: **ENTER**
Notice that there is not a static incrementing value in this example.

**11.** To continue this range of values:
SELECT: cell range from A9 to C9
DRAG: fill handle for the range to column F
Excel calculates a "best guess" for the next few values. Your worksheet should now appear similar to the one shown in Figure 2.25.

**12.** Save the workbook as "My Series" to your personal storage location and then close the workbook.

## Figure 2.25

Completing the
"My Series"
workbook

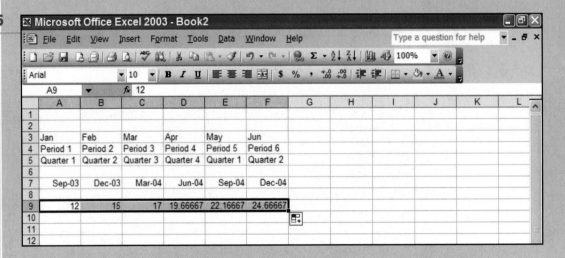

### 2.2.5 Extending a Cell's Contents

→ **Feature**

Another method for extending the contents of a cell is to use the Edit → Fill commands. These commands are especially useful for extending a formula across a row or down a column, saving you a tremendous amount of time compared to manual entry. If you prefer using the mouse, you can use a cell's fill handle to perform the same function, as covered in the previous lesson.

→ **Method**

To extend cell contents:

- SELECT: the desired cell range, ensuring that the data you want to copy is located in the top left-hand corner of the cell range (or in the bottom right-hand corner for filling up and to the left)

- CHOOSE: Edit → Fill → Right (or Left) to copy across a row

  *or*

- CHOOSE: Edit → Fill → Down (or Up) to copy down (or up) a column

→ **Practice**

In this exercise, you will open a cash flow worksheet and then copy and extend the formulas stored in it. Ensure that no workbooks appear in the application window.

**1.** Open the data file named EX0225 to display the workbook shown in Figure 2.26.

**Figure 2.26**

Opening the
EX0225 workbook

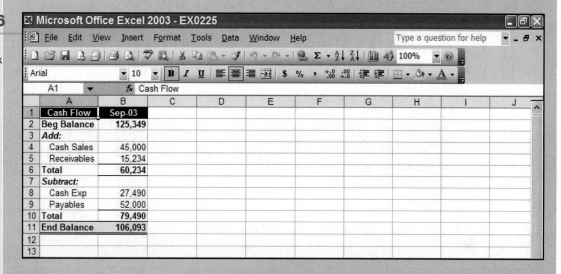

**2.** Save the file as "My Filled Cells" to your personal storage location.

**3.** To extend the date headings using the AutoFill feature:
SELECT: cell B1
DRAG: fill handle from cell B1 to column E
When you release the mouse button, the formatted date headings are entered into the columns up to Dec-03.

**4.** In this worksheet, the beginning balance for a new month is the ending balance from the previous month. To enter this formula into column C:
SELECT: cell C2
CLICK: Bold button (B) to apply boldface to the cell
TYPE: =b11
PRESS: (ENTER)
The result "106,093" from cell B11 appears in the C2.

**5.** To copy and extend this formula to the right:
SELECT: cell range from C2 to E2
Notice that the top left-hand cell in the selected range contains the formula and formatting that you want to copy.

6. CHOOSE: Edit → Fill → Right
   For the moment, only zeroes will appear in the remaining cells, as shown in Figure 2.27.

**Figure 2.27**

Extending cells
using the Edit,
Fill, Right
command

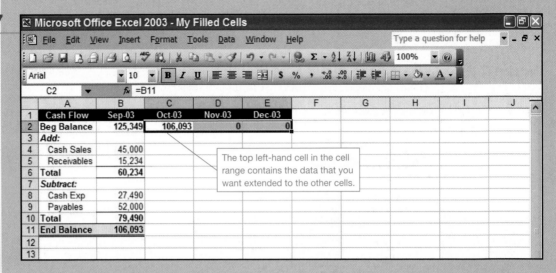

7. To extend the formulas for multiple ranges:
   SELECT: cell range from B6 to E6
   PRESS: CTRL and hold it down
   SELECT: cell range from B10 to E10
   SELECT: cell range from B11 to E11
   When all the ranges are highlighted, release the CTRL key.

8. To fill each row with formulas from column B:
   CHOOSE: Edit → Fill → Right
   Your worksheet should now appear similar to the one shown in Figure 2.28.

**Figure 2.28**

Filling multiple
ranges with
formulas stored
in the leftmost
column

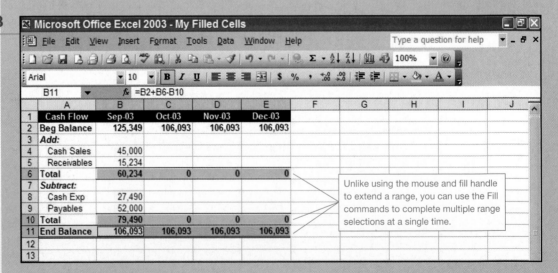

9. On your own, enter sample values into the worksheet (rows 4, 5, 8, and 9) and observe how the formulas recalculate the totals.

10. Save and then close the workbook.

**2.2** Which method would you use to copy several nonadjacent, or not beside one another, values for placement into a single worksheet column?

# 2.3 Modifying Rows and Columns

By adjusting the row heights and column widths in a worksheet, you can enhance the worksheet's appearance for both viewing and printing—in much the same way a textbook employs white space or a document uses double-spacing to make the text easier to read. You can also reorganize or modify the structure of a worksheet by inserting and deleting rows and columns. This module introduces you to the tools provided by Excel 2003 for revising and manipulating the appearance and structure of a worksheet.

## 2.3.1 Changing Column Widths

### → Feature

Previously, you were exposed to entering long text labels into a cell and watching as characters spilled over the cell borders into adjacent columns. For numeric entries, the data cannot extend beyond a column's borders. Instead, a series of number signs (#) fill the cell, informing you that the column is not wide enough to display the value. Fortunately, you can increase and decrease the width of your worksheet columns to allow for varying lengths of text labels, numbers, and dates. To speed the editing process, you can select and change more than one column width at a time. Excel can even calculate the best or **AutoFit** width for a column based on its existing entries. The maximum width for a column is 255 characters.

### → Method

To change a column's width using the mouse:

- DRAG: its right borderline in the frame area

To change a column's width using the menu:

- SELECT: a cell in the column that you want to format

- CHOOSE: Format → Column → Width

- TYPE: *value*, such as 12, for the desired width

To change a column's width to its best fit:

- DOUBLE-CLICK: its right borderline in the frame area

  *or*

- CHOOSE: Format → Column → AutoFit Selection

### → Practice

In this lesson, you open a workbook used to summarize the income earned by organizers of the Kettle Valley Craft Fair. You then change the worksheet's column widths to better view the data stored therein. Before proceeding, ensure that no workbooks are open in the application window.

**1.** Open the data file named EX0230 to display the workbook shown in Figure 2.29.

**Figure 2.29**

Opening the
EX0230 workbook

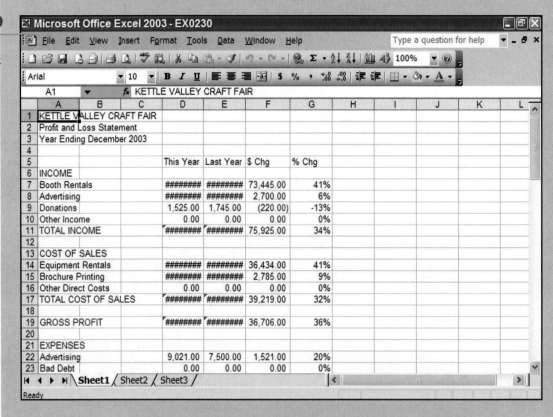

**2.** Save the file as "My Craft Fair" to your personal storage location.

**3.** In columns D and E of the worksheet, notice that some cells contain a series of "#" symbols. These symbols inform you that the columns are not wide enough to display the contents. To adjust the width of column D using a command from the Menu bar, first:
SELECT: cell D1
Notice that you need not select the entire column to change its width; in fact, you can choose any cell within the column.

**4.** CHOOSE: Format → Column → Width
The Column Width dialog box appears, as shown in Figure 2.30. Notice that 8.43 characters is the default column width.

**Figure 2.30**

Column Width
dialog box

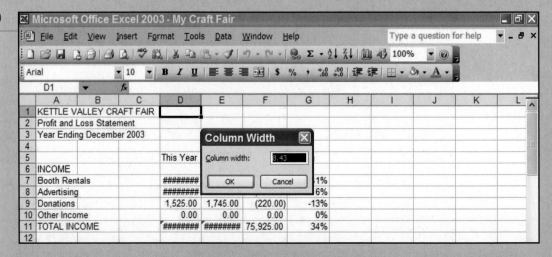

5. Enter the desired width as measured in characters:
   TYPE: 12
   PRESS: ENTER
   *or*
   CLICK: OK
   All of the values stored in column D should now be visible.

6. Now let's adjust the width for column E using the mouse. In the frame area, position the mouse pointer over the borderline between columns E and F. The mouse pointer changes shape (+) when positioned correctly, as shown in Figure 2.31.

7. CLICK: the borderline and hold down the mouse button
   DRAG: the mouse pointer to the right to increase the width to 12.00
   Notice that the width (in characters and pixels) is displayed in a ToolTip. Your screen should now appear similar to Figure 2.31.

**Figure 2.31**

Changing a column's width using the mouse

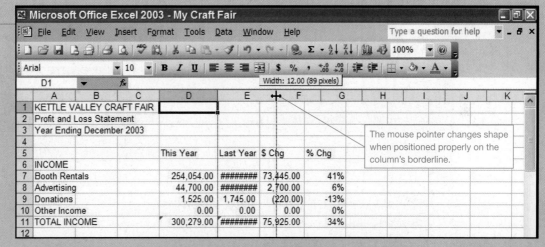

8. Release the mouse button to finalize the new column width setting.

9. The AutoFit feature enables you to find the best width for a column based on its existing cell entries. To demonstrate this feature, you must first select an entire column as the basis for the width calculation. Let's adjust column A to its best-fit width:
   SELECT: column A
   (*Hint:* This instruction tells you to move the mouse pointer over the "A" in the column frame area and click once. When done properly, the entire column appears highlighted, as shown in Figure 2.32.)

**Figure 2.32**

Selecting column A using the mouse

Use the black down arrow in the column frame area to select the entire column using the mouse.

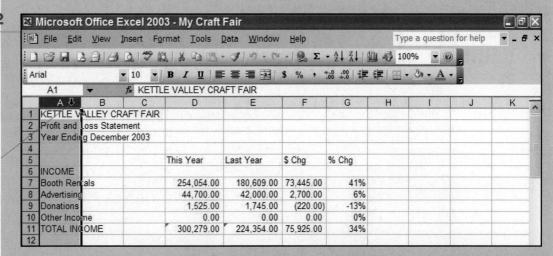

**10.** To calculate the best-fit width and make the change:
CHOOSE: Format → Column → AutoFit Selection
Notice that the column's width has been adjusted so that it can comfortably hold the longest cell entry.

**11.** PRESS: HOME to remove the column highlighting

**12.** Save the workbook and keep it open for use in the next lesson.

*In Addition* DOUBLE-CLICKING TO AUTOFIT A COLUMN'S WIDTH OR A ROW'S HEIGHT

After you become comfortable using the mouse to select the frame borderlines, try double-clicking the right frame borderline of a column or the bottom frame borderline of a row to AutoFit its width or height. You can select multiple columns or rows and change them all to their best-fit measurements by double-clicking any one of the selected cell's borderlines.

### 2.3.2 Changing Row Heights

## Feature

You can change the height of any worksheet row to customize the borders and line spacing in a worksheet. What's more, a row's height is adjusted automatically when you increase or decrease the font size of information appearing in the row. A row's height is measured in points, where 72 points is equal to one inch. The larger the font size that you select for a given cell, the larger its row height.

## Method

To change a row's height manually using the mouse:

• DRAG: its bottom borderline in the frame area

To change a row's height using the menu:

• SELECT: a cell in the row that you want to format

• CHOOSE: Format → Row → Height

• TYPE: *value*, such as 20, for the desired height in points

To change a row's height to its best fit:

• DOUBLE-CLICK: its bottom borderline in the frame area

  *or*

• CHOOSE: Format → Row → AutoFit

## Practice

You now change some row heights in the worksheet to improve the spacing between data. Ensure that you have completed the previous lesson and that the "My Craft Fair" workbook is displayed.

**1.** Ensure that cell A1 is selected in the worksheet. In the next two steps, you will change the line spacing for the entire worksheet. As with most formatting commands, you must first select the cell range for which you want to apply formatting. To select the entire worksheet:
CLICK: Select All button (■) in the top left-hand corner of the frame area (see Figure 2.33)

**2.** With the entire worksheet highlighted:
CHOOSE: Format → Row → Height
Your screen should now appear similar to the one shown in Figure 2.33.

**Figure 2.33**

Row Height dialog box

Click the Select All button to select the entire worksheet.

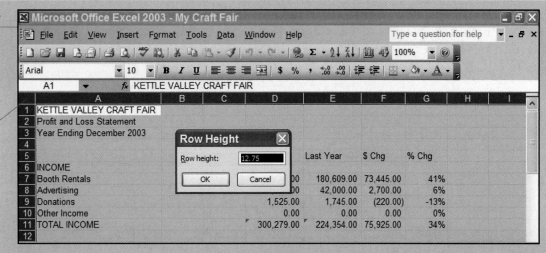

**3.** Enter the desired height as measured in points:
TYPE: **20**
PRESS: **ENTER**
*or*
CLICK: OK
Notice that the rows are enlarged, providing more white space.

**4.** To remove the selection highlighting:
CLICK: cell A1

**5.** Let's change the height of row 4 using the mouse. To begin, position the mouse pointer over the borderline between rows 4 and 5. Then:
CLICK: the borderline and hold down the mouse button
DRAG: the mouse pointer up to decrease the height to 9.00 points
As when you changed the column width, the mouse pointer changes shape and a yellow ToolTip appears with the current measurement, as shown in Figure 2.34.

**Figure 2.34**

Changing a column's width using the mouse

The mouse pointer changes shape when positioned properly on the row's borderline.

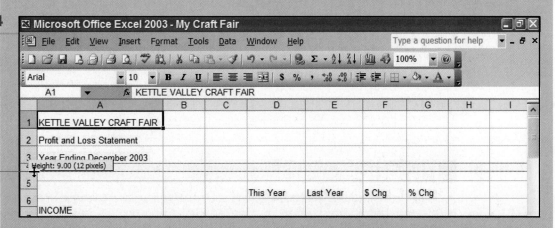

**6.** Release the mouse button to finalize the new row height setting.

**7.** Let's practice adjusting a row to its best-fit height:
SELECT: row 5
(*Hint*: This instruction tells you to move the mouse pointer over the "5" in the row frame area and click once. When this is done properly, the entire row will appear highlighted, as shown in Figure 2.35.)

**8.** CHOOSE: Format → Row → AutoFit
The row height is adjusted automatically, as shown in Figure 2.35.

**Figure 2.35**

Using AutoFit to change a row's height

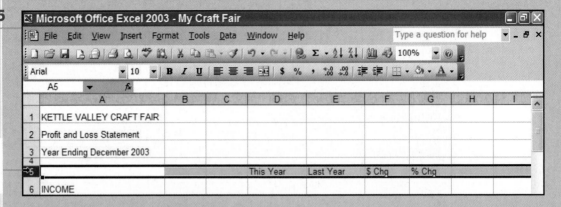

Use the black arrow in the row frame area to select the entire row.

**9.** PRESS: CTRL + HOME to move the cell pointer to cell A1

**10.** Save the workbook and keep it open for use in the next lesson.

### 2.3.3 Inserting and Deleting Rows and Columns

→ # Feature

You insert and delete rows and columns to affect the structure of a worksheet. In doing so, however, you must be careful not to change areas in your worksheet unintentionally. Deleting column B, for example, removes all of the data in the entire column, not just the cells that are currently visible on your screen.

→ # Method

To insert or delete a row:

• RIGHT-CLICK: *row number* in the row frame area

• CHOOSE: Insert or Delete

To insert or delete a column:

• RIGHT-CLICK: *column letter* in the column frame area

• CHOOSE: Insert or Delete

→ # Practice

In this lesson, you will practice inserting and deleting rows and columns. Ensure that you have completed the previous lessons and that the "My Craft Fair" workbook is displayed.

**1.** After adjusting the width for column A earlier in the module, you may have noticed that columns B and C do not contain any data. Before deleting rows or columns, however, it is always wise to check your assumptions. To do so:
CLICK: cell B1
PRESS: CTRL + ↓
The cell pointer scoots down to row 65536. If there were data in the column, the cell pointer would have stopped at the cell containing the data.

**2.** To check whether there is any data in column C:
PRESS: ➡
PRESS: CTRL + ⬆
The cell pointer scoots back up to row 1, not stopped by any cells containing data. You can now be certain that neither column B nor column C contains data.

**3.** Let's delete these two columns from the worksheet. To begin:
CLICK: column B in the frame area and hold down the mouse button
DRAG: the mouse pointer right to highlight column C as well, as shown in Figure 2.36

**Figure 2.36**

Selecting two columns in the worksheet

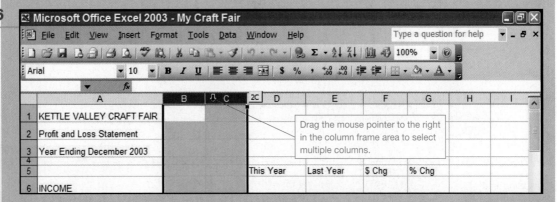

**4.** Release the mouse button after the two columns appear highlighted.

**5.** To delete these two columns:
RIGHT-CLICK: column C in the frame area
Notice that you need only right-click one of the selected column letters. Your screen should now appear similar to the one shown in Figure 2.37.

**Figure 2.37**

Displaying the right-click menu for the selected columns

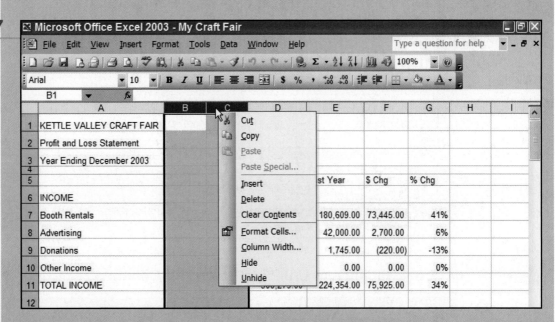

**6.** On the right-click menu:
CHOOSE: Delete
The blank columns are removed, but the column selection remains highlighted in case you want to apply additional formatting commands.

7. To insert a row:
   RIGHT-CLICK: row 8 in the frame area
   CHOOSE: Insert
   A new row is inserted at row 8, pushing down the existing rows. The Insert Options icon (⟨⟨⟩⟩) also appears below the newly inserted row.

8. To enter some new information:
   SELECT: cell A8
   TYPE: **Food Pavilion**
   PRESS: ➡
   TYPE: **55800**
   PRESS: ➡
   TYPE: **43750**
   PRESS: ENTER

9. To copy the formulas for calculating the annual increase:
   SELECT: cell range D7 to E8

10. CHOOSE: Edit → Fill → Down
    The results, 12,050.00 and 28%, now appear in row 8, as shown in Figure 2.38.

**Figure 2.38**

Inserting and deleting rows in the "My Craft Fair" workbook

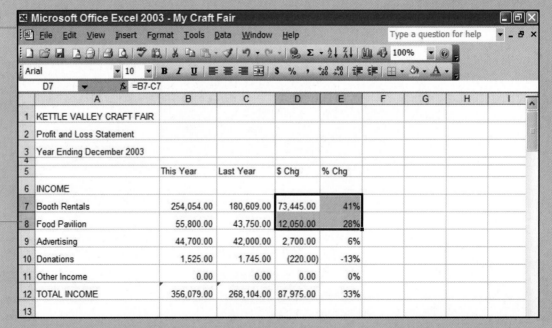

Entering data and extending formulas into the newly inserted row

11. PRESS: CTRL + HOME to move the cell pointer to cell A1

12. Save the workbook and keep it open for use in the next lesson.

### 2.3.4 Hiding and Unhiding Rows and Columns

→ **Feature**

Instead of deleting a row or column, you can modify a worksheet so that some of the data are not displayed. For example, you may want to hide rows and columns that contain sensitive data, such as salaries or commissions. You can also temporarily hide detailed information if you do not want it included in a particular report.

→ ## Method

To hide a row or column:

- RIGHT-CLICK: the frame area of the desired row or column
- CHOOSE: Hide

To unhide a row or column:

- SELECT: the rows or columns on both sides of the hidden row or column
- RIGHT-CLICK: the frame area of the selected rows or columns
- CHOOSE: Unhide

→ ## Practice

In this lesson, you will practice hiding and unhiding worksheet information. Ensure that you have completed the previous lessons and that the "My Craft Fair" workbook is displayed.

**1.** Let's hide columns D and E from displaying. Do the following:
CLICK: column D in the frame area
DRAG: the mouse pointer right to also highlight column E

**2.** To hide the selected columns:
RIGHT-CLICK: either column D or E in the frame area
CHOOSE: Hide
Notice that the column frame area in Figure 2.39 now shows A, B, C, and then F.

**Figure 2.39**

Hiding two columns in the worksheet

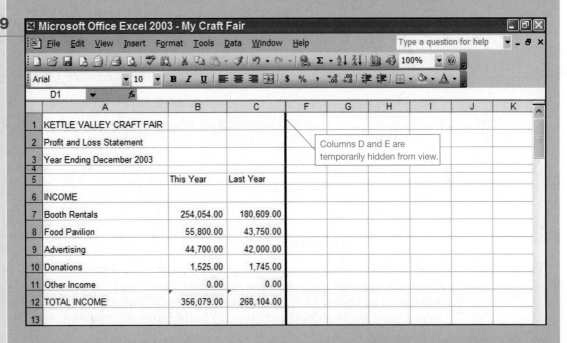

**3.** To hide several rows in the worksheet:
SELECT: rows 6 through 11 in the frame area
RIGHT-CLICK: any one of the selected rows (6 through 11) in the frame area
CHOOSE: Hide
The row frame area now displays a gap between row 5 and row 12.

**4.** To unhide columns D and E, you must select the columns on either side. For example:
CLICK: column C in the frame area
DRAG: the mouse pointer right to also highlight column F
Your screen should appear similar to the one shown in Figure 2.40.

**Figure 2.40**

Selecting columns in order to unhide the hidden columns

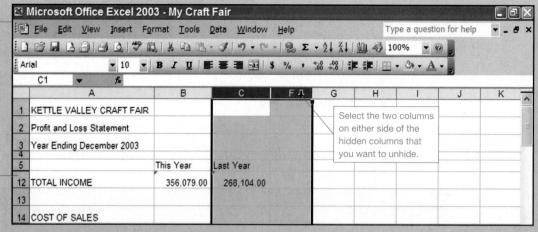

Notice the gap between rows 5 and 12 in the frame area. Rows 6 through 11 are temporarily hidden from view.

*Select the two columns on either side of the hidden columns that you want to unhide.*

**5.** Let's use the Menu bar to unhide the columns:
CHOOSE: Format → Column → Unhide
The columns reappear on the worksheet.

**6.** To unhide the rows:
SELECT: rows 5 through 12
CHOOSE: Format → Row → Unhide
The rows reappear on the worksheet. (*Hint:* Besides using the menu, you can right-click in the selected frame area and choose the Unhide command.)

**7.** PRESS: CTRL + HOME to move the cell pointer to cell A1

**8.** Save and then close the workbook.

**9.** Exit Microsoft Office Excel 2003.

 **2.3** Why must you be careful when deleting rows or columns?

## Chapter
### summary

Rarely will you begin and complete a worksheet without ever needing to correct an entry or modify its structure. Even professional spreadsheet users revisit their creations in order to adapt them to changing requirements or to make them more efficient. Fortunately, Excel provides several features and tools that make it easier for you to modify the contents and structure of a worksheet. One helpful set of "Auto" features includes AutoComplete for typing matching entries in a column and AutoSum and AutoCalculate for entering formulas. You also use the AutoFill feature to enter a series of data by dragging a cell range's fill handle. Like most Windows applications, Excel provides the standard Cut, Copy, and Paste commands for manipulating a worksheet's contents. The three approaches discussed in this chapter for copying and moving data include: the Windows Clipboard, the Office Clipboard, and the drag and drop method. You also learned to modify the structure of a worksheet by inserting and deleting cells, rows, and columns. Especially important for report presentation is your ability to adjust a worksheet's row heights and column widths and even hide (and unhide) rows and columns temporarily. You are well on your way to becoming a proficient spreadsheet user!

## Command Summary

Many of the commands and procedures appearing in this chapter are summarized in the following table.

| Skill Set | To Perform this Task... | Do the Following... |
|---|---|---|
| **Creating and Revising Formulas** | Enter the SUM function using the AutoSum button | SELECT: a cell to place the result<br>CLICK: AutoSum button (Σ ▾) |
| | Display the sum result of a calculation using AutoCalculate | SELECT: a cell range and view the result in the Status bar |
| **Working with Cells and Cell Data** | Insert a cell or cell range | SELECT: the desired cell range<br>CHOOSE: Insert → Cells |
| | Delete a cell or cell range | SELECT: the desired cell range<br>CHOOSE: Edit → Delete |
| | Insert data using AutoComplete | RIGHT-CLICK: the desired cell<br>CHOOSE: Pick From List<br>SELECT: the desired data |
| | Copy or move data using the toolbar | SELECT: the desired cell or range<br>CLICK: Copy (⧉) or Cut (✂)<br>SELECT: the target cell or range<br>CLICK: Paste button (⧉ ▾) |
| | Move data using drag and drop | SELECT: the desired cell or range<br>DRAG: the selection by its border |
| | Copy data using drag and drop | SELECT: the desired cell or range<br>PRESS: CTRL and hold it down<br>DRAG: the selection by its border |
| | Display the Clipboard task pane | CHOOSE: Edit → Office Clipboard |
| | Clear the Office Clipboard | CLICK: Clear All button (⧉ Clear All) |
| | Paste all of the contents from the Office Clipboard into the worksheet | CLICK: Paste All button (⧉ Paste All) |
| | Create a data series using the fill handle | SELECT: the desired range<br>DRAG: the fill handle |
| | Copy a formula across a row or down a column | SELECT: the range to fill, with the formula in the top left-hand corner<br>CHOOSE: Edit → Fill → Right (or Down) |
| **Formatting and Printing Worksheets** | Change a cell's column width | CHOOSE: Format → Column → Width<br>TYPE: *width* in characters |
| | Change a cell's row height | CHOOSE: Format → Row → Height<br>TYPE: *height* in points |
| | Insert and delete columns | RIGHT-CLICK: a column's frame area<br>CHOOSE: Insert or Delete |
| | Insert and delete rows | RIGHT-CLICK: a row's frame area<br>CHOOSE: Insert or Delete |
| | Hide a row or column | RIGHT-CLICK: in the frame area<br>CHOOSE: Hide |
| | Unhide a row or column | SELECT: rows or columns on either side of the hidden row or column<br>RIGHT-CLICK: the frame selection<br>CHOOSE: Unhide |

Excel

## Key Terms

This section specifies page references for the key terms identified in this chapter. For a complete list of definitions, refer to the Glossary at the back of this learning guide.

AutoCalculate, *p. EX 65*

AutoComplete, *p. EX 62*

AutoFill, *p. EX 79*

AutoFit, *p. EX 85*

AutoSum, *p. EX 65*

cell range, *p. EX 58*

drag and drop, *p. EX 70*

fill handle, *p. EX 80*

Office Clipboard, *p. EX 70*

series, *p. EX 79*

Windows Clipboard, *p. EX 70*

## Chapter

### q u i z

### Short Answer

**1.** What visible feature differentiates the active cell in a selected cell range?

**2.** How do you select more than one cell range at a time?

**3.** Where does Excel's AutoComplete feature get the values to display in a pick list?

**4.** What are the two choices for shifting existing data when you insert a new cell or cell range?

**5.** Name the two types of Clipboards and explain how they differ.

**6.** What is the primary difference between using the Clipboards and using the drag and drop method to copy information?

**7.** What is the fastest way to place five years' worth of quarterly headings at the top of your worksheet (that is, Jan-04, Mar-04, Jun-04, . . .)?

**8.** What does "########" in a cell indicate?

**9.** What is meant by a "best fit" or "AutoFit" column width?

**10.** In what circumstances might you want to hide a row or column?

### True/False

**1.** _____ You use ⌊ALT⌋ to select multiple cell ranges in a worksheet.

**2.** _____ Excel's AutoComplete feature allows you to sum a range of values and place the result into a worksheet cell.

**3.** _____ You use the Edit ➔ Clear command to delete the contents of a cell and the Edit ➔ Delete command to delete the actual cell.

**4.** _____ You can collect up to 32 items for pasting using the Office Clipboard.

**5.** _____ The Windows Clipboard can store only a single item for pasting.

**6.** _____ When you drag and drop a cell range using the ⌊CTRL⌋ key, a plus sign appears, indicating that you are using the copy feature.

**7.** _____ To copy and extend a formula to adjacent cells, you can use either the fill handle or the Edit ➔ Fill ➔ Right command.

**8.** _____ When you insert a column, the existing column is pushed to the left.

9.  _____  When you insert a row, the existing row is pushed down.

10.  _____  You unhide rows and columns using the Window ➜ Unhide All command.

## Multiple Choice

1. You hold down this key to select multiple cell ranges using the mouse:

   a.  `ALT`
   b.  `CTRL`
   c.  `SHIFT`
   d.  `PRTSCR`

2. This feature allows you to view the sum of a range of values without entering a formula into a worksheet cell:

   a. AutoCalculate
   b. AutoComplete
   c. AutoTotal
   d. AutoValue

3. The AutoSum feature enters this function into a cell to sum a range of values:

   a. ADD
   b. SUM
   c. TOTAL
   d. VALUE

4. If you want to delete cells from the worksheet, you select the desired range and then choose this command:

   a. Edit ➜ Clear ➜ All
   b. Edit ➜ Clear ➜ Cells
   c. Edit ➜ Cells ➜ Delete
   d. Edit ➜ Delete

5. To perform a drag and drop operation, you position the mouse pointer over the selected cell or cell range until it changes to this shape:

   a. ⬚
   b. ⬚
   c. ✛
   d. ✛

6. What menu command allows you to copy a formula in the active cell to a range of adjacent cells in a row?

   a. Edit ➜ Copy ➜ Right
   b. Edit ➜ Fill ➜ Down
   c. Edit ➜ Fill ➜ Right
   d. Edit ➜ Extend ➜ Fill

7. To select an entire column for editing, inserting, or deleting:

   a. PRESS: `ALT` + ⬇ with the cell pointer in the column
   b. DOUBLE-CLICK: a cell within the column
   c. CLICK: the column letter in the frame area
   d. CHOOSE: Edit ➜ Select Column

8. The height of a row is typically measured using these units:

   a. Characters
   b. Fonts
   c. Picas
   d. Points

9. To change a column's width using the mouse, you position the mouse pointer into the column frame area until it changes to this shape:

   a. ✛
   b. ⬚
   c. ⬚
   d. ✛

10. Row 5 is hidden on your worksheet. To unhide the row, you must make this selection before issuing the appropriate menu command:

   a. Rows 4 and 6
   b. Rows 1 through 4
   c. Row 4
   d. Row 6

## Hands-On
### exercises

step by step

## 1. Entering Data Using "Auto" Features

In this exercise, you practice using Excel's "Auto" features to enter information and calculate results. Specifically, you use AutoComplete to enter data into a column, AutoCalculate to display a calculated total, and then AutoSum to insert the calculated result into the worksheet.

**1.** Load Microsoft Office Excel 2003.

**2.** Open the data file named EX02HE01 to display the workbook shown in Figure 2.41.

**Figure 2.41**

Opening the
EX02HE01
workbook

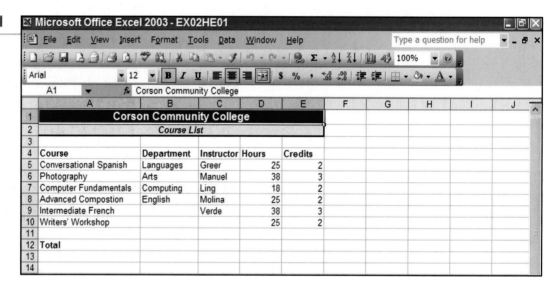

**3.** Save the workbook as "My Course List" to your personal storage location.

**4.** To complete this worksheet, you must enter some additional information for "Intermediate French." To begin:
SELECT: cell B9
TYPE: **L**
PRESS: (ENTER)
Notice that the word "Languages" is inserted automatically.

**5.** To enter some data for the "Writer's Workshop," do the following:
RIGHT-CLICK: cell B10
CHOOSE: Pick From List
A pick list appears with four options, as shown in Figure 2.42.

**Figure 2.42**

Displaying a cell's pick list

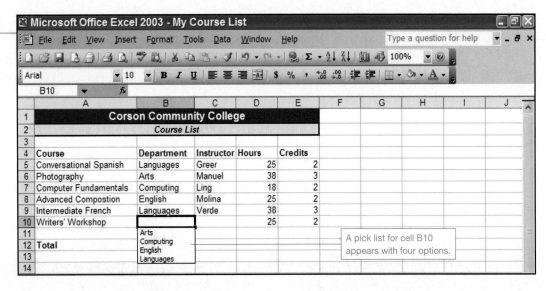

6. CLICK: English in the pick list

7. To access a column's AutoComplete pick list using the keyboard:
   SELECT: cell C10
   PRESS: [ALT] + [↓]
   PRESS: [↓] four more times to highlight "Molina"
   PRESS: [ENTER]

8. Now let's use the AutoCalculate feature to sum the total number of hours in column D without placing an entry into the worksheet. Do the following:
   SELECT: cell range from D5 to D10
   What result is displayed in the Status bar?

9. To enter a formula into the worksheet that sums the Hours column:
   SELECT: cell D12
   CLICK: AutoSum button ([Σ ▾])
   Excel reviews the worksheet and highlights its best guess of the range you want to sum, as shown in Figure 2.43.

**Figure 2.43**

Summing a column of values using the AutoSum button ([Σ ▾])

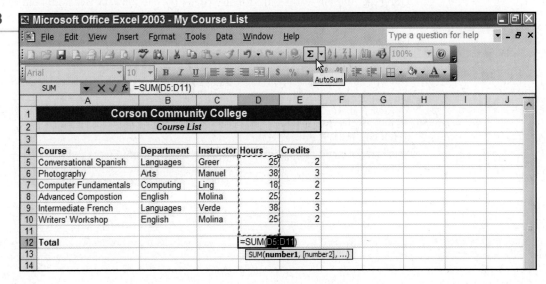

**10.** To accept the cell range:
CLICK: AutoSum button ($\Sigma$ ▾) again
The answer, 169, now appears in the cell.

**11.** On your own, total the values in column E and place the result in cell E12 using the AutoSum
button ($\Sigma$ ▾).

**12.** Save and then close the workbook.

step by step

## 2. Copying and Moving Data

You will now practice copying and moving data using Excel's AutoFill feature, drag and drop, and Edit
Fill commands.

**1.** Open the data file named EX02HE02 to display the workbook shown in Figure 2.44.

**Figure 2.44**

Opening the
EX02HE02
workbook

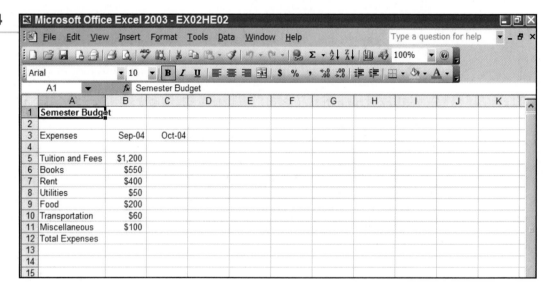

**2.** Save the workbook as "Semester Budget" to your personal storage location.

**3.** Using the AutoFill feature's fill handle, extend the dates in cells B3 and B4 out to December 2004
in the same row.

**4.** Using the drag and drop method, move the contents of cell A12 to cell A13. (*Hint:* Select cell A12
and then drag its cell border down one row.)

**5.** You will now extend several budget items to the new columns (Nov-04 and Dec-04). First, select the
cell range from cell B7 to E11.

**6.** To copy the budget values to the rest of the highlighted range:
CHOOSE: Edit ➔ Fill ➔ Right
Your screen should now appear similar to the one shown in Figure 2.45.

**Figure 2.45**

Moving and
extending data
ranges

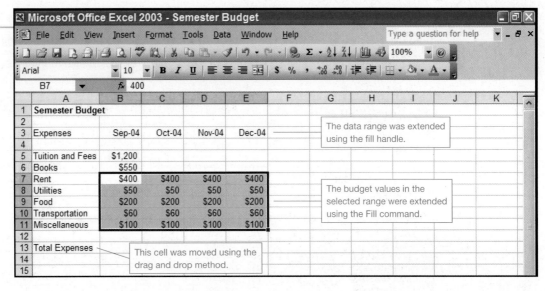

7. Using the AutoSum button ( Σ ▾ ), total the values in column B and display the result in cell B13. (*Hint:* Select cell B13 first and then click the AutoSum button ( Σ ▾ ) on the Standard toolbar.)

8. Copy the formula in cell B13 using the Copy button (🗐). The cell contents are placed onto the Windows Clipboard.

9. Select the cell range from C13 to E13.

10. Paste the contents of the Clipboard into the selected cells by clicking the Paste button (🗐▾).

11. PRESS: ESC to remove the dashed marquee
PRESS: CTRL + HOME to move to cell A1
Your screen should now appear similar to Figure 2.46.

**Figure 2.46**

Completed
"Semester Budget"
workbook

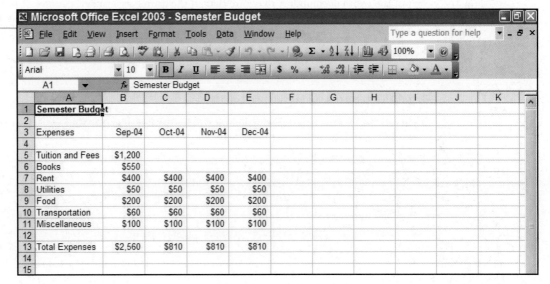

12. Save and then close the "Semester Budget" workbook.

step by step  ▶

## 3. Modifying a Worksheet's Structure

In this exercise, you will practice modifying the appearance and structure of an existing worksheet.

  **1.** Open the data file named EX02HE03 to display the workbook shown in Figure 2.47.

**Figure 2.47**

Opening the
EX02HE03
workbook

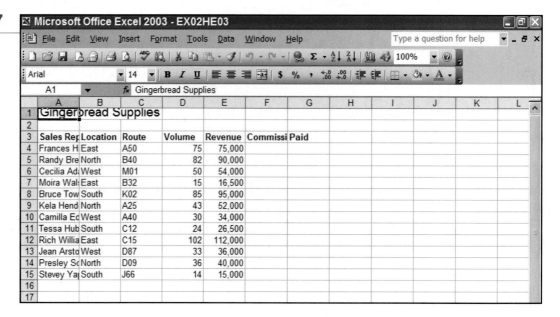

  **2.** Save the workbook as "Sales Force" to your personal storage location.

  **3.** You may have noticed that the title in cell A1 is difficult to read. Adjust the height for row 1 to its "best fit" or "AutoFit" height.

  **4.** The sales representatives' names are truncated by the "Location" entries in column B. Therefore, adjust the width of column A to ensure that all the names are visible.

  **5.** Change the column width for columns B through D to 8 characters.

  **6.** Change the column width for columns E through G to 10 characters.

  **7.** Change the height of rows 2 through 15 to 15.00.

  **8.** In cell F4, enter a commission rate of 5%.

  **9.** In cell G4, multiply the commission rate (F) by the Revenue (E). Your worksheet should now appear similar to the one shown in Figure 2.48.

| | A | B | C | D | E | F | G |
|---|---|---|---|---|---|---|---|
| 1 | Gingerbread Supplies | | | | | | |
| 2 | | | | | | | |
| 3 | Sales Rep | Location | Route | Volume | Revenue | Commissio | Paid |
| 4 | Frances Hillman | East | A50 | 75 | 75,000 | 5% | 3750 |
| 5 | Randy Brewski | North | B40 | 82 | 90,000 | | |
| 6 | Cecilia Adams | West | M01 | 50 | 54,000 | | |
| 7 | Moira Walsh | East | B32 | 15 | 16,500 | | |
| 8 | Bruce Towne | South | K02 | 85 | 95,000 | | |
| 9 | Kela Henderson | North | A25 | 43 | 52,000 | | |
| 10 | Camilla Edsell | West | A40 | 30 | 34,000 | | |
| 11 | Tessa Huberty | South | C12 | 24 | 26,500 | | |
| 12 | Rich Williams | East | C15 | 102 | 112,000 | | |
| 13 | Jean Arston | West | D87 | 33 | 36,000 | | |
| 14 | Presley Schuler | North | D09 | 36 | 40,000 | | |
| 15 | Stevey Yap | South | J66 | 14 | 15,000 | | |

## Figure 2.48

Adjusting rows and columns and entering a formula

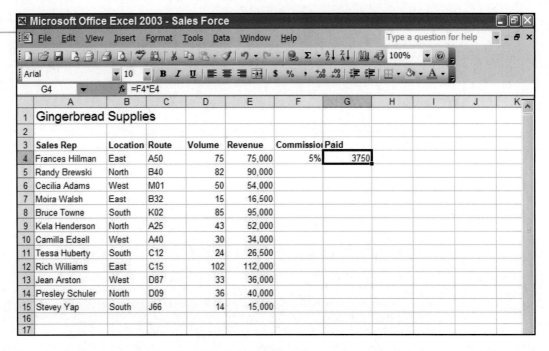

10. Using the Edit → Fill → Down command, copy the entries in cells F4 and G4 down their respective columns to row 15.
11. Remove the route information by deleting column C.
12. Remove the information for Bruce Towne by deleting the cell range A8 to F8 and then close up the gap.
13. Hide the Revenue column from displaying in the worksheet and then return the cell pointer to cell A1. Your worksheet should now appear similar to the one shown in Figure 2.49.

| | A | B | C | E | F |
|---|---|---|---|---|---|
| 1 | Gingerbread Supplies | | | | |
| 2 | | | | | |
| 3 | Sales Rep | Location | Volume | Commissio | Paid |
| 4 | Frances Hillman | East | 75 | 5% | 3750 |
| 5 | Randy Brewski | North | 82 | 5% | 4500 |
| 6 | Cecilia Adams | West | 50 | 5% | 2700 |
| 7 | Moira Walsh | East | 15 | 5% | 825 |
| 8 | Kela Henderson | North | 43 | 5% | 2600 |
| 9 | Camilla Edsell | West | 30 | 5% | 1700 |
| 10 | Tessa Huberty | South | 24 | 5% | 1325 |
| 11 | Rich Williams | East | 102 | 5% | 5600 |
| 12 | Jean Arston | West | 33 | 5% | 1800 |
| 13 | Presley Schuler | North | 36 | 5% | 2000 |
| 14 | Stevey Yap | South | 14 | 5% | 750 |

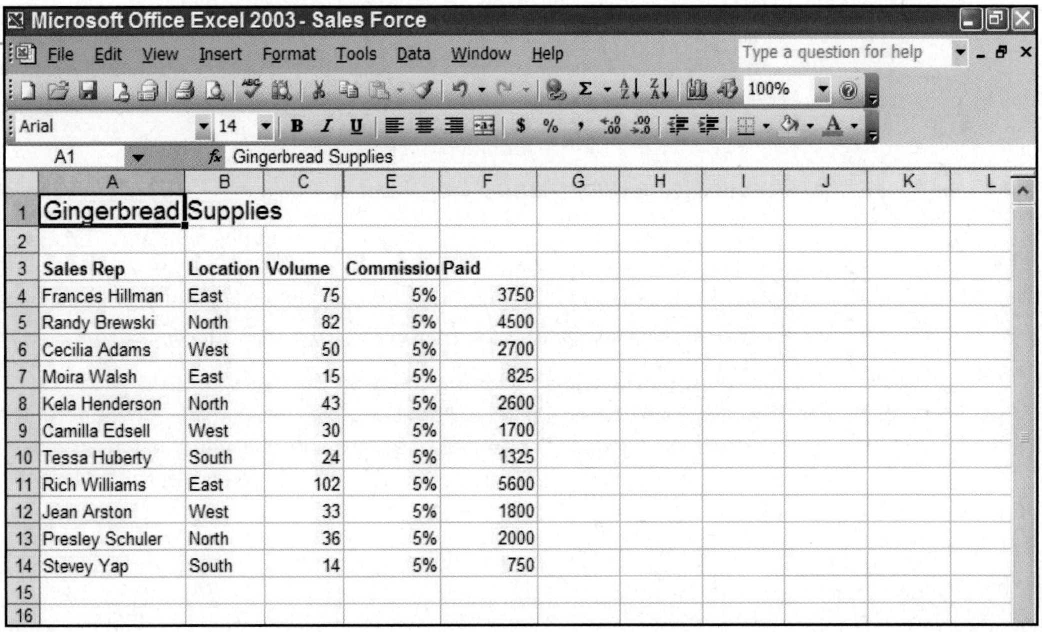

## Figure 2.49

Completed "Sales Force" workbook

**14.** Without placing a formula on the worksheet, calculate the total volume of sales generated by these sales reps. What is this value?

**15.** Save and then close the workbook.

on your own

## 4. Sparkle Ski-Free Manufacturing

Sparkle Ski-Free Manufacturing recently computerized the production scheduling for their four plants in Brookview, Cedar Hill, Newton, and Westside. The supervising foreman has entered in three years of results for each of the plants and has asked you to project the future production totals. You open the EX02HE04 workbook that he created and save it as "Sparkle Projection" to your personal storage location.

After expanding column A to 12 characters, you decide to use the AutoFill feature's fill handle to extend a row of data. Select each cell range individually, starting with B3 to D3, and drag the range's fill handle to column G in order to extrapolate the series. Using the AutoSum button (Σ ▾), total the units produced for each year and place the results into row 8, as shown in Figure 2.50.

**Figure 2.50**

Filling data ranges and calculating totals

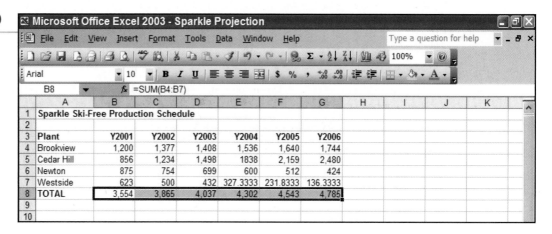

To display only the total results for the projected years, hide rows 4 through 7 and columns B through D. Only three values should now appear on the worksheet under their column headings. Save and then close the workbook.

on your own

## 5. Ouchi Office Assistance

A friend of yours has just accepted a position at Ouchi Office Assistance. In addition to her general administrative duties, she must help the accountant prepare monthly income statements. Because she seemed quite nervous about the new position, you offered to help her develop an Excel worksheet. You open the EX02HE05 workbook that she has been using and save it as "Ouchi OA" to her personal storage location.

After adjusting the column widths, you review the structure of the worksheet. To begin, you insert a row above Expenses and label it "Total Revenue." Then, you use the AutoSum feature to sum the revenues for September and October. Continuing in this manner, you adjust and insert rows, data, and formulas so that the worksheet appears similar to Figure 2.51. Then, you save and close the workbook.

**Figure 2.51**

Modifying a
worksheet's
structure and
appearance

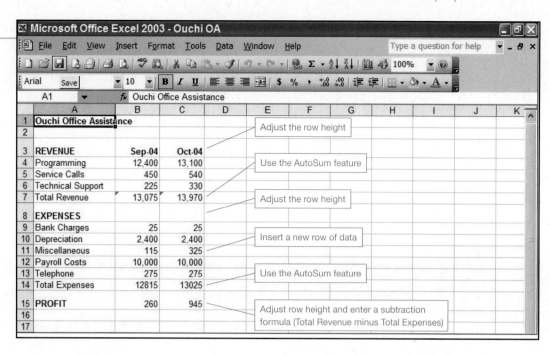

on your own

## 6. Running Diary

It is May and you are finally getting around to the New Year's resolution you made to get into shape. To motivate yourself, you decide to create a running diary using Microsoft Office Excel 2003. Open the data file named EX02HE06 (Figure 2.52) and then save it as "My Running Diary" to your personal storage location.

**Figure 2.52**

Opening the
EX02HE06
workbook

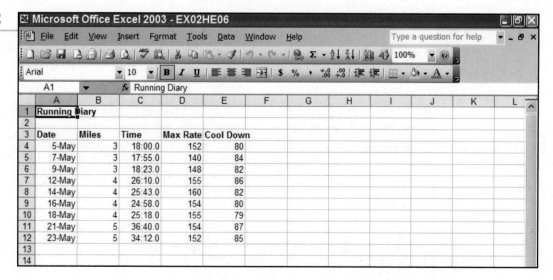

Given your current statistics, you would like to project how long it will take you to reach 10 miles. To do so, select the cell range from B4 through B12. Drag the fill handle for the range downward until the ToolTip displays a value over 10. Press CTRL + HOME to return to the top of the worksheet. To make it easier to count the number of runs, insert a new column A with the column heading "Run" and then move the title "Running Diary" back into cell A1 using drag and drop. Number each run in the column, using the fill handle to make the process faster. *How many runs will it take you to reach 10 miles?* Using Excel's AutoCalculate feature, find out how many miles you've run as of May 23. *How many miles have you run thus far?*

Impressed with your computer knowledge, your running partner asks you to track her running statistics also. Rather than create a new worksheet, you copy and paste the column headings beside your own, so that they begin in column H. Save and close the workbook and then exit Excel 2003.

# CaseProblems    BEAVERTON FINANCIAL SERVICES

Beaverton Financial Services, Inc., is the largest private insurance company in Oregon state. The company has always maintained a high profile in the community by sponsoring youth programs and providing assistance to local charities. This sense of community was one of the main attractions for James Wyndham, who recently joined the company as its internal business manager.

James recently assumed responsibility for generating the monthly profitability reports for one of Beaverton Financial's longest-standing clients, a local car dealership for whom the company tracks financing, insurance, and after-market sales results. With this increase in workload, James knows that he must streamline operations and find a more efficient method for summarizing the data he receives. Fortunately, his new computer just arrived with Microsoft Office Excel 2003 installed. Upon reviewing some of the car dealership's past data James identifies an opportunity to use Microsoft Office Excel 2003 for generating its reports.

In the following case problems, assume the role of James and perform the same steps that he identifies. You may want to reread the chapter opening before proceeding.

**1.** James decides to focus his attention on one report that is generated for the car dealership at the end of each month. He calls a good friend, whom he knows has several months' experience using Excel, and describes what he needs. He then sends his friend a fax of the actual report to help clarify the discussion. The next day, James receives an e-mail attachment from his friend that contains a workbook called EX02CP01. He opens the workbook (Figure 2.53) using Excel 2003 and then saves it as "PROFIT" to his personal storage location.

**Figure 2.53**

Opening the
EX02CP01
workbook

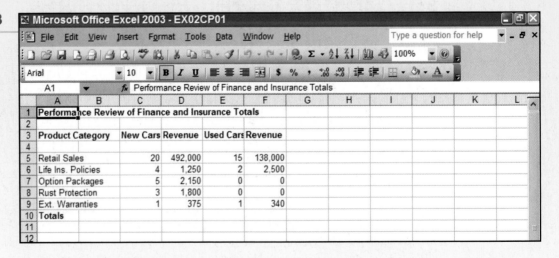

The PROFIT report, which is the car dealer's own abbreviation for a "Profitability Review of Finance and Insurance Totals," summarizes the number of new and used cars that are sold in a given month, including the number of financing, insurance, warranty, and rust protection packages. After reviewing the worksheet, James decides to make a few additions and modifications.

- In cell A1, edit the title to read "Profitability Review of Finance and Insurance Totals."

- In cells G3 and H3, enter the headings "Total Cars" and "Revenue," respectively.

- In cell G5, enter a formula that adds the number of new car sales to the number of used car sales.

- In cell H5, enter a formula that adds the revenue for new car sales to the revenue for used car sales.

- Using the fill handle, copy the formulas in cells G5 and H5 down their respective columns to row 9.

- Using the AutoSum feature, sum the values in columns C through H and place the results in row 10.

Save the workbook and keep it open for use in the next problem.

2. Wednesday morning does not start out well for James. The owner of the dealership calls to request that Beaverton Financial no longer track the sale of "Rust Protection" packages. He also asks James to hide the "Used Cars" columns in the report. Fortunately, James remembers how to remove and hide cells, rows, and columns. He also feels that this is a great opportunity to adjust some of the worksheet's column widths and row heights. Specifically, James performs the following steps:

- Select the "best fit" or "AutoFit" width for column A. Notice that the width is adjusted to handle the length of the title in cell A1.

- Specify a column width of 18 characters for column A.

- Specify a column width of 10 characters for columns C through H.

- Specify a row height of 7.50 points for row 4.

- Ensure that column B is empty, then delete the entire column.

- Select the cell range (A8:G8) for Rust Protection. Then choose the Edit → Delete command to remove the cells from the worksheet and shift the remaining cells upward.

- Select columns D and E for the Used Cars data, then hide the columns (i.e., keep them from displaying).

Move the cell pointer to cell A1. Your screen should appear similar to the one shown in Figure 2.54. Save the workbook and keep it open for use in the next problem.

**Figure 2.54**

Manipulating columns and rows in a worksheet

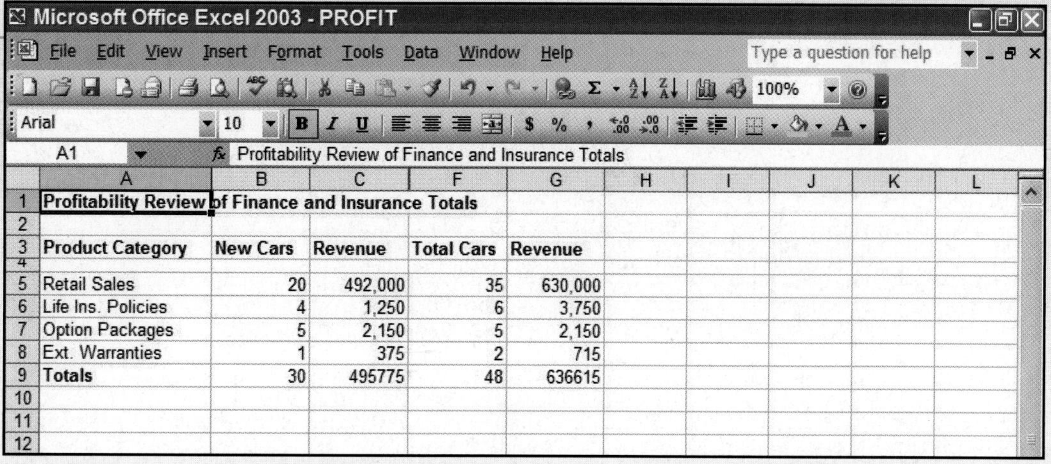

3. James decides that it would be helpful to develop a projection for next month's PROFIT report. Rather than create a new worksheet, he unhides columns D and E and then copies the data from cells A3 through G9 to the Windows Clipboard. He moves the cell pointer to cell A12, pastes the data, and then presses [ESC] to remove the dashed marquee. To complete the operation, James adjusts row 13 to match the height of row 4.

In order to start with a clean slate, James selects cells B14 through E17 and erases the cell contents in the range. Then he selects cell B14 and enters a formula that shows an increase of 20% over the value stored in cell B5. In other words, he multiplies the value in cell B5 by 1.2. Next, James copies the formula to the remaining cells in the range, as shown in Figure 2.55. To ensure that the projection area works properly, James changes some of the values in the original table area. Satisfied that the bottom projection table updates automatically, he saves and closes the workbook.

**Figure 2.55**

Creating a projection based on an existing range of cells

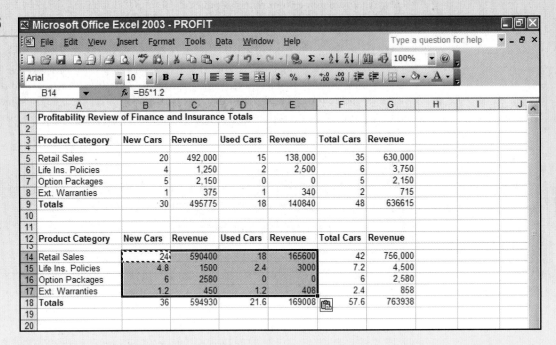

4. James opens a second workbook, EX02CP04, that he received from his friend. He then saves the workbook, shown in Figure 2.56, as "Car Buyers" to his personal storage location. This particular workbook stores customer information from each sale made in the month.

**Figure 2.56**

Opening the
EX02CP04
workbook

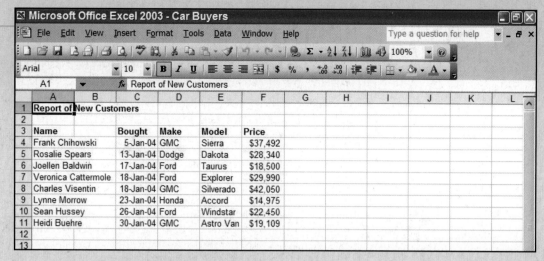

James reviews the worksheet and decides to make a few changes. First, he inserts a new column A and moves the title back into cell A1. He then enters 1 into cell A4 and 2 into cell A5. Using the mouse, James selects both cells and then drags the range's fill handle downward to continue numbering the customers. *What is the number of the last customer, Heidi Buehre?* He then moves to cell E12 and displays the AutoComplete pick list. *What vehicles are listed in the pick list and in what order do they appear?* To remove the pick list, James presses the `ESC` key. Finally, James uses Excel's AutoCalculate feature to sum the purchase price of all vehicles sold in January without having to enter a formula into the worksheet. *What is the total value of vehicles purchased?*

Ready to go home for the day, James saves and closes the workbook and then exits Microsoft Office Excel 2003.

## Answers to Self-Check Questions

**2.1** Which of the "Auto" features enables you to sum a range of values and display the result in the Status bar? AutoCalculate

**2.2** Which method would you use to copy several nonadjacent (not beside one another) values for placement into a single worksheet column? The Office Clipboard would provide the fastest method. After displaying the Clipboard task pane, clear the Clipboard and then collect up to 24 items in the desired sequence. You would then move to the target range and paste these items into a single column using the Paste All button ( Paste All ).

**2.3** Why must you be careful when deleting rows or columns? You must be careful because if you delete the entire row or column, you may inadvertently delete data that exists farther down a column or farther across a row. Ensure that a row or column is indeed empty before deleting it.

# Microsoft® Office Excel® 2003

## CHAPTER 3

# Formatting and Printing

### PREREQUISITES

To successfully complete this chapter, you must be comfortable performing basic data entry and editing tasks. You will be asked to modify worksheet information using toolbar buttons, Menu commands, and right-click shortcut menus. Web publishing is also introduced in this chapter, so you should know how to launch your Web browser software for viewing Web pages.

### LEARNING OBJECTIVES

After completing this chapter, you will be able to:

• Format cell entries to appear boldface or italic and with different typefaces and font sizes

• Format numeric and date values

• Format cells to appear with borders, shading, and color

• Preview and print a worksheet

• Publish a worksheet to the World Wide Web

• Define page layout options, such as margins, headers and footers, and paper orientation, for printing your worksheets

# 3.1 Enhancing a Worksheet's Appearance

Most people realize how important it is to create worksheets that are easy to read and pleasing to the eye. Clearly, a visually attractive worksheet will convey information better than an unformatted one. With Excel's formatting capabilities, you can enhance your worksheets for publishing online or for printing. In addition to choosing from a variety of fonts, styles, and cell alignments, you can specify decimal places and add currency and percentage symbols to values. The combination of these features enables you to produce professional-looking spreadsheet reports and presentations.

### 3.1.1 Applying Fonts, Font Styles, and Colors

→ **Feature**

Applying **fonts** to titles, headings, and other worksheet cells is often the most effective means for drawing a reader's attention to specific areas in your worksheet. You can also specify font styles, such as boldface and italic, adjust font sizes, and select colors. Do not feel obliged, however, to use every font that is available to you in a single worksheet. Above all, your worksheets must be easy to read— too many fonts, styles, and colors are distracting. As a rule, limit your font selection for a single worksheet to two or three common **typefaces,** such as Times New Roman and Arial.

→ **Method**

To apply character formatting to the contents of a cell, select the desired cell range and then use any of the following:

- CLICK: *Font* list box ( Arial ⏷ )
- CLICK: *Font Size* list box ( 10 ⏷ )
- CLICK: Bold button ( **B** )
- CLICK: Italic button ( *I* )
- CLICK: Underline button ( U )
- CLICK: Font Color button ( A ⏷ )

To display the *Font* formatting options:

- SELECT: cell range to format
- CHOOSE: Format → Cells
- CLICK: *Font* tab in the Format Cells dialog box
- SELECT: the desired font, font style, size, color, and effects

→ **Practice**

In this lesson, you will open and format a workbook that tracks a mutual fund portfolio. Before proceeding, ensure that Excel is loaded.

**1.** Open the data file named EX0310 to display the workbook shown in Figure 3.1.

**Figure 3.1**

Opening the
EX0310
workbook

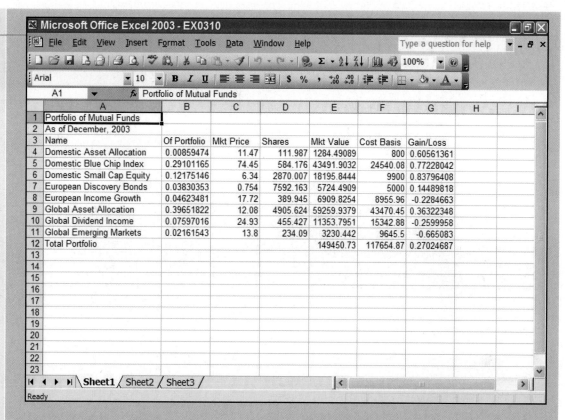

2. Save the file as "My Portfolio" to your personal storage location.

3. Your first step is to select the cell range to format. Do the following to begin formatting the column labels:
   SELECT: cell range from A3 to G3

4. Let's make these labels bold and underlined:
   CLICK: Bold button (**B**)
   CLICK: Underline button (U)

5. Now format the title labels in cells A1 and A2:
   SELECT: cell range from A1 to A2

6. To change the typeface used in the cells:
   CLICK: down arrow attached to the *Font* list box (Arial ▼)
   (*Note:* The fonts that appear in the list box are available for your use in Excel 2003. Some fonts are loaded with Windows and Microsoft Office, and a variety of other fonts may appear in the list from other application programs that you have installed.) Your screen will appear similar, but not identical, to the one shown in Figure 3.2.

Excel

## Figure 3.2

Selecting a typeface from the Font list box

The typeface names appearing in your *Font* drop-down list box will differ from the ones displayed here.

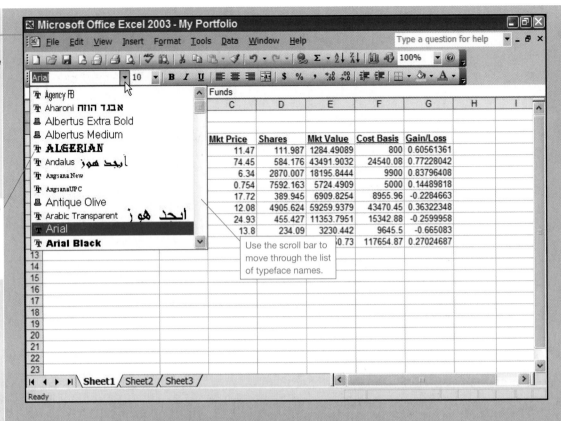

7. Using the scroll bars attached to the drop-down list box to move through the list of typeface names:
   SELECT: Times New Roman

8. To increase the font size:
   CLICK: down arrow attached to the *Font Size* list box (10 ▼)
   SELECT: 14
   The two cells now appear formatted using a 14-point, Times New Roman typeface; the row heights have also been adjusted automatically.

9. Besides the toolbar buttons, you can use the Format Cells dialog box to apply formatting to the selected cell range. To illustrate:
   SELECT: cell A1
   CHOOSE: Format → Cells
   CLICK: *Font* tab
   The Format Cells dialog box (Figure 3.3) displays the current formatting options for the active cell.

**Figure 3.3**

Format Cells
dialog box, *Font*
tab

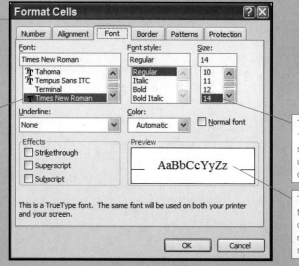

The font or typeface
is Times New
Roman, as you
selected previously
using the *Font* drop-
down list box.

The font size is
14 points, as you
selected previously
using the *Font Size*
drop-down list box.

The *Preview* area of
the dialog box
displays the visual
results of the
selections you make.

**10.** To add some additional flare to the title:
SELECT: *any typeface* from the *Font* list box
SELECT: Bold in the *Font style* list box
SELECT: 16 in the *Size* list box
SELECT: Blue from the *Color* drop-down list box
CLICK: OK command button
The title in cell A1 should now stand out from the rest of the data.

**11.** You can also use shortcut keys to apply formatting. To demonstrate:
SELECT: cell range from A12 to G12
PRESS: `CTRL` + **b** to apply boldface

**12.** Save the workbook and keep it open for use in the next lesson.

*In Addition*  COMMON SHORTCUT KEYS FOR FORMATTING YOUR
WORKSHEETS

To help speed up formatting operations, select the desired cell range and then use the following key
combinations:

- `CTRL` + **b** to apply boldface

- `CTRL` + **i** to apply italic

- `CTRL` + **u** to apply underlining

- `CTRL` + `SHIFT` + **f** to select a font typeface

- `CTRL` + `SHIFT` + **p** to select a font point size

### 3.1.2 Formatting Numbers and Dates

 **Feature**

Numeric formats improve the appearance and readability of numbers in a worksheet by inserting dollar signs, commas, percentage symbols, and decimal places. Although a number or date may appear
formatted on the worksheet, the underlying value that is stored in the cell (and seen in the Formula bar)
does not change. Excel stores date and time entries as values and, therefore, allows you to customize
their display as you do numbers.

→ ## Method

To apply number formatting, select the desired cell range and then use one of the following:

- CLICK: Currency Style button ($)
- CLICK: Percent Style button (%)
- CLICK: Comma Style button (,)
- CLICK: Increase Decimal button
- CLICK: Decrease Decimal button

To display the number formatting options:

- SELECT: cell range to format
- CHOOSE: Format → Cells
- CLICK: *Number* tab
- SELECT: a number or date format from the *Category* list box
- SELECT: formatting options for the selected category

→ ## Practice

You will now apply number, currency, percentage, decimal place, and date formatting to the worksheet. Ensure that you have completed the previous lesson and that the "My Portfolio" workbook is displayed.

**1.** In reviewing the worksheet, notice that the Of Portfolio and Gain/Loss columns in the worksheet contain data that is best represented using a percent number format. The Of Portfolio column (B) displays the proportional share of an investment compared to the total portfolio. The Gain/Loss column (G) calculates the performance gain or loss. To display these calculated results as percentages, do the following:
SELECT: cell range from B4 to B11
PRESS: **CTRL** and hold it down
SELECT: cell range from G4 to G12

**2.** Release the **CTRL** key after the last range is selected. Notice that these two ranges are highlighted independently—ready for formatting. (*Note:* You will no longer be reminded to release the **CTRL** key when dragging the cell pointer over a range.)

**3.** To apply a percent style:
CLICK: Percent Style button (%)

**4.** To display the percentages with two decimal places:
CLICK: Increase Decimal button twice
Your worksheet should now appear similar to the one shown in Figure 3.4.

**Figure 3.4**

Applying percent formatting to multiple cell ranges

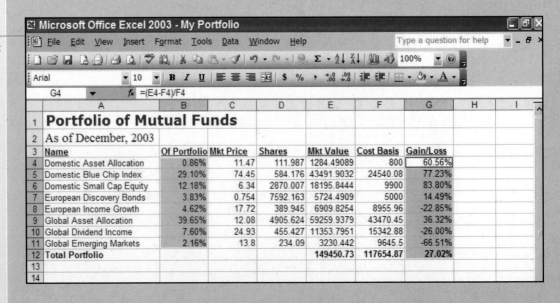

**5.** Let's apply some further number formatting:
SELECT: cell range from C4 to C11
CHOOSE: Format → Cells
CLICK: *Number* tab

**6.** In the Format Cells dialog box that appears:
SELECT: Currency in the *Category* list box
SELECT: 4 in the *Decimal places* spin box
SELECT: Black ($1,234.3210) in the *Negative numbers* list box
Your dialog box should now appear similar to the one shown in Figure 3.5.

**Figure 3.5**

Format Cells
dialog box,
*Number* tab

After selecting the
desired category for
numeric formatting,
customize the
display using the
other options in the
dialog box.

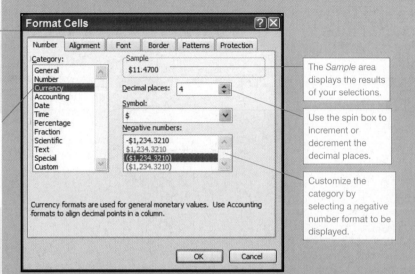

The *Sample* area
displays the results
of your selections.

Use the spin box to
increment or
decrement the
decimal places.

Customize the
category by
selecting a negative
number format to be
displayed.

**7.** To apply the formatting options:
CLICK: OK command button

**8.** To increase the decimal places in the Shares column:
SELECT: cell range from D4 to D11
CLICK: Increase Decimal button ($\begin{smallmatrix}+.0\\.00\end{smallmatrix}$)

**9.** To format the Currency style of remaining values:
SELECT: cell range from E4 to F12
CLICK: Currency Style button ($)

**10.** Depending on your system, the columns may not be wide enough to display the formatted values. With the cell range still selected:
CHOOSE: Format → Column → AutoFit Selection
You should now see all the data contained in the column, as shown in Figure 3.6.

**Figure 3.6**

Formatting values
in the worksheet

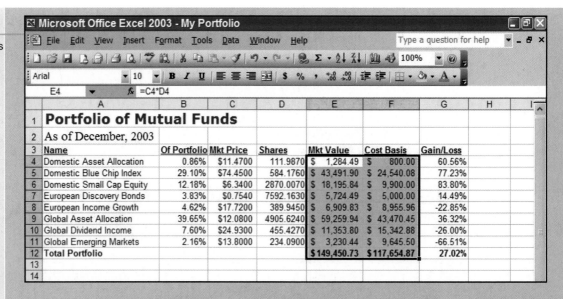

**11.** Now let's create a notes area:
SELECT: cell A14
TYPE: **Notes**
PRESS: ⬇

**12.** To enter the first note or comment:
TYPE: **31-Dec-2003**
PRESS: ➡
TYPE: **The market rebounded from a low of 7,200 in October.**
PRESS: **ENTER**

**13.** SELECT: cell A15
In the Formula bar, notice that the date reads 12/31/2003.

**14.** To format the date to appear differently on the worksheet:
CHOOSE: Format → Cells
SELECT: Date in the *Category* list box, if it is not already selected

**15.** To apply a new format, select one of the listed versions:
SELECT: "March 14, 2001" in the *Type* list box
CLICK: OK command button
(*Note:* The *Type* list box displays the date formats for March 14, 2001. Keep in mind that you are selecting a display format and not a date value to insert into the worksheet.) Your screen should now appear similar to the one shown in Figure 3.7.

**16.** Save the workbook and keep it open for use in the next lesson.

## Figure 3.7

Applying number and date formats

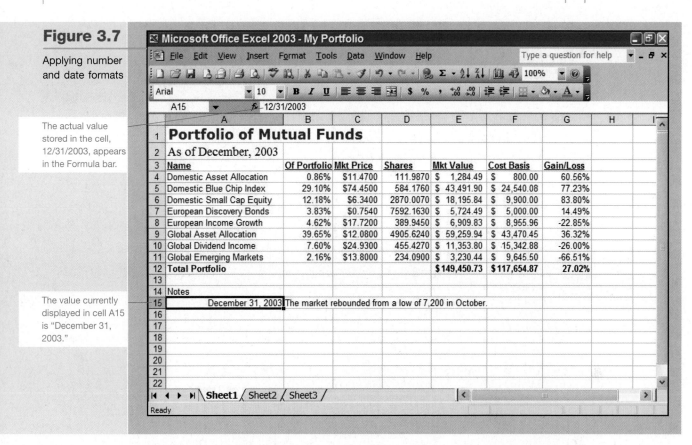

The actual value stored in the cell, 12/31/2003, appears in the Formula bar.

The value currently displayed in cell A15 is "December 31, 2003."

### 3.1.3 Aligning, Merging, and Rotating Cells

→ **Feature**

You can change the **cell alignment** for any type of data entered into a worksheet. By default, Excel aligns text against the left edge of a cell and values against the right edge. Not only can you change these default alignments, but you can also merge or combine data across cells. Rotating text within a cell allows you to fit longer text entries into a narrow column.

→ **Method**

To align and merge data, select the desired cell range and then use one of the following:

- CLICK: Align Left button (▤)
- CLICK: Center button (▤)
- CLICK: Align Right button (▤)
- CLICK: Merge and Center button (▦)

To display the alignment formatting options:

- SELECT: cell range to format
- CHOOSE: Format → Cells
- CLICK: *Alignment* tab
- SELECT: an option to align, merge, or rotate cells

→ **Practice**

You will now practice aligning, merging, and rotating text in cells. Ensure that you have completed the previous lessons in the module and that the "My Portfolio" workbook is displayed.

**1.** The easiest way to align a cell's contents is to use the buttons on the Formatting toolbar. To illustrate, let's manipulate the "Notes" title in cell A14:
SELECT: cell A14
CLICK: Bold button (**B**)
CLICK: Underline button (**U**)

**2.** To practice changing a cell's alignment:
CLICK: Align Right button (☰)
CLICK: Align Left button (☰)
CLICK: Center button (☰)
Notice the change in alignment that takes place with each mouse click.

**3.** You can change the cell alignment for number and date values also:
SELECT: cell A15
CLICK: Center button (☰)
The date appears centered under the column heading for "Notes."

**4.** Perhaps more interesting is your ability to merge cells together and then center their contents over a range. Do the following:
SELECT: cell range from A1 to G1
CLICK: Merge and Center button (☰)
Notice that the title is now centered over the table area, as shown in Figure 3.8. (*Note:* The merged cell is still considered to be cell A1. The next cell in the same row is cell H1.)

**Figure 3.8**

Aligning and merging cells

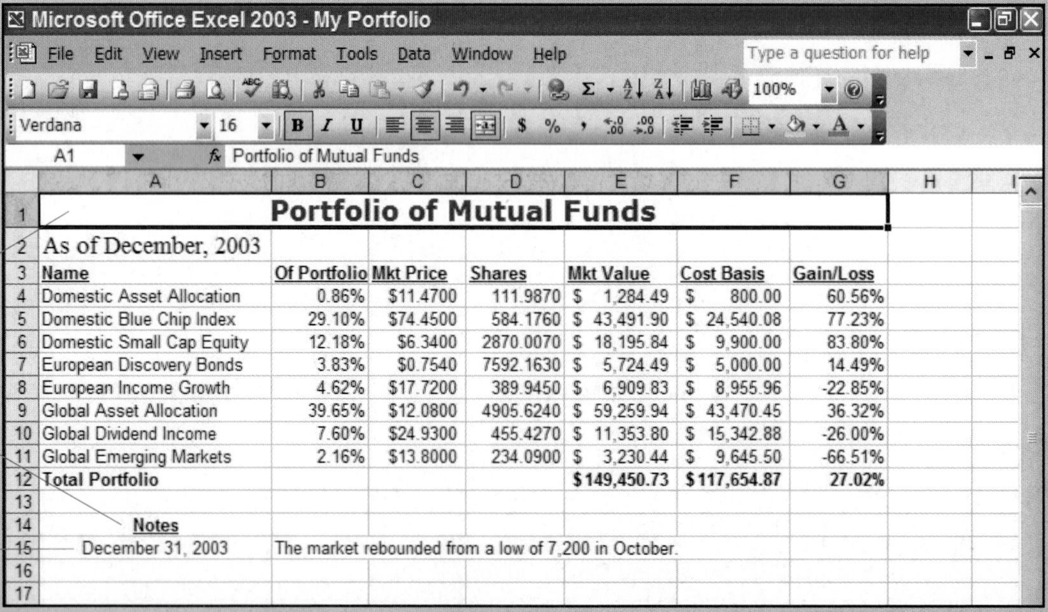

The title is centered in cell A1, which is a merged cell over the range A1:G1

The text is centered in cell A14.

The date value is centered in cell A15.

**5.** Let's merge and center the subtitle in cell A2 using the dialog box:
SELECT: cell range from A2 to G2
CHOOSE: Format → Cells
CLICK: *Alignment* tab
The Format Cells dialog box appears, as shown in Figure 3.9.

**Figure 3.9**

Format Cells
dialog box,
*Alignment* tab

Use controls in the
*Text alignment* area
to align text
horizontally and
vertically within a cell.

Use controls in the
*Text control* area to
change the way long
text entries are
displayed in a cell.

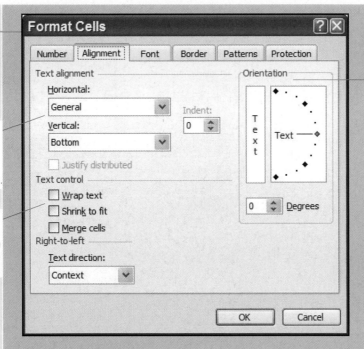

Use the dialog box
controls in the
*Orientation* area to
adjust the angle of
text displayed in a
cell.

**6.** In the Format Cells dialog box:
SELECT: Center from the *Horizontal* drop-down list box
SELECT: *Merge cells* check box
CLICK: OK command button

**7.** Let's practice splitting up a merged cell without using the Undo command. Ensure that cell A2 (which now covers the area to G2) is still selected and then do the following:
CHOOSE: Format → Cells
The last tab that was selected in the dialog box *(Alignment)* is displayed automatically.

**8.** To split the merged cell:
SELECT: *Merge cells* check box so that no (✓) appears
CLICK: OK command button
The entry remains centered but only between column A's borders.

**9.** Now let's practice rotating text. Do the following:
SELECT: cell range from B3 to G3
CHOOSE: Format → Cells

**10.** You set the rotation for text by clicking and dragging in the *Orientation* area of the dialog box. You can also specify a positive value in the *Degrees* spin box to angle text from bottom left to upper right. In this step, use the mouse to select an angle of 30 degrees:
DRAG: the "Text" line in the *Orientation* area to 30 degrees, as shown in Figure 3.10

**Figure 3.10**

Rotating text using the Format Cells dialog box

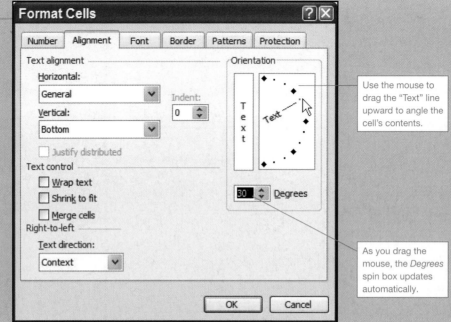

**11.** To apply the formatting change:
CLICK: OK command button
Your screen should now appear similar to the one shown in Figure 3.11.

**12.** Save the workbook and keep it open for use in the next lesson.

**Figure 3.11**

Changing the orientation or angle of text

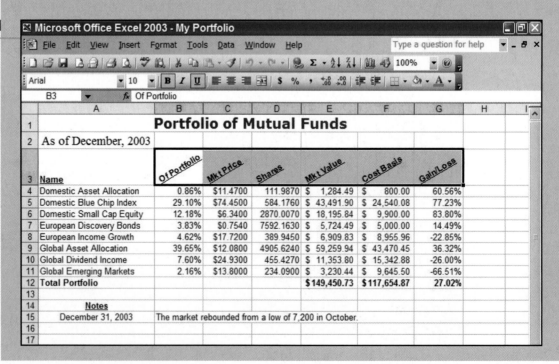

***In Addition*** DISPLAYING LONG TEXT ENTRIES IN A CELL

Excel provides several tools for working with long text entries. First, you can increase the row height of a cell and align its contents vertically between the top and bottom borders. You can then wrap the text to display in a single cell. Second, you can use the ALT + ENTER key combination to place a hard carriage return or line feed within a cell. Third, you can shrink an entry to fit between a column's borders.

### 3.1.4 Adding Borders and Shading

→ ## Feature

As with the other formatting options, you use borders, patterns, shading, and colors to enhance a worksheet's readability. The **gridlines** that appear in the worksheet window are nonprinting lines, provided only to help you line up information. Borders are used to place printed gridlines on a worksheet and to separate data into logical sections. These formatting options also enable you to create professional-looking invoice forms, memos, and tables.

→ ## Method

To apply borders or coloring, select the desired cell range and then:

• CLICK: Borders button (⊞▾)

• CLICK: Fill Color button (◔▾)

To display the border and patterns formatting options:

• SELECT: cell range to format

• CHOOSE: Format → Cells

• CLICK: border or patterns tab

• SELECT: borders or pattern, shading, and fill color options

→ ## Practice

In this exercise, you will format a worksheet by applying borders and fill coloring to selected cell ranges. Ensure that you have completed the previous lessons and that the "My Portfolio" workbook is displayed.

**1.** Move to cell A1.

**2.** In order to better see the borders that you will apply in this lesson, let's remove the gridlines from the worksheet display. To do so:
CHOOSE: Tools → Options
CLICK: *View* tab
Your dialog box should appear similar to the one shown in Figure 3.12.

**Figure 3.12**

Options dialog box, *View* tab

To remove the gridlines from displaying on the worksheet, deselect this check box option.

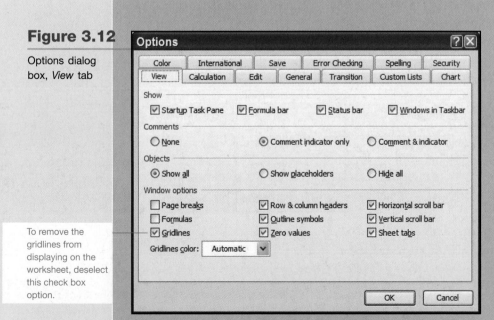

Excel

**3.** To proceed:
SELECT: *Gridlines* check box, so that no (☑) appears
CLICK: OK command button
Your worksheet should now appear similar to the one shown in Figure 3.13.

**Figure 3.13**

Removing the gridlines

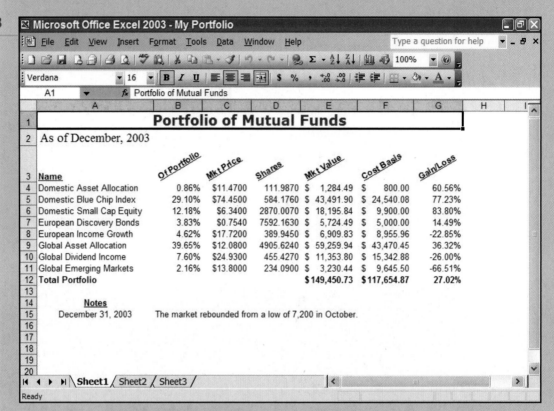

**4.** Now let's apply some borders:
SELECT: cell range from A12 to G12
(*Hint:* Use the column and row frame highlighting to help you line up the cell range.)

**5.** To display the border options available:
CLICK: down arrow attached to the Borders button (⊞▾)
A drop-down list of border options appears, as shown below.

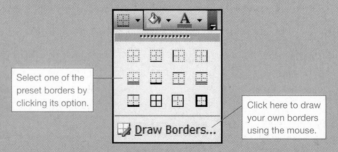

Select one of the preset borders by clicking its option.

Click here to draw your own borders using the mouse.

**6.** You can choose from a variety of preset border options or choose to draw your own borders. For this step, let's use the preset borders:
SELECT: Top and Double Bottom Border (▤) in the drop-down list
CLICK: cell A1 to remove the selection highlighting
A border now separates the data from the summary information in row 12. (*Note:* Clicking the Underline button (U̲) underlines only the words in a cell, whereas applying borders underlines the entire cell.)

**7.** To outline the "Notes" area:
SELECT: cell range from A14 to G18
CLICK: down arrow attached to the Borders button (⊞▾)
SELECT: Outside Borders button (⊡)

**8.** Now let's apply a new fill color (sometimes called *shading*) to the "Notes" area. Ensure that the cell range from A14 to G18 is still selected and then do the following:
CLICK: down arrow attached to the Fill Color button (🖌▾)
A drop-down list of colors appears, as shown below.

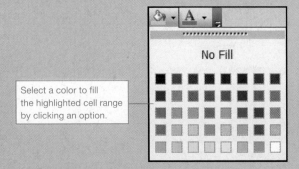

Select a color to fill the highlighted cell range by clicking an option.

**9.** SELECT: a light yellow color from the drop-down list
CLICK: cell A1 to remove the selection highlighting
The "Notes" area should now appear on a colored background.

**10.** To enhance the title in cell A1:
CLICK: down arrow attached to the Fill Color button (🖌▾)
SELECT: a dark blue color from the drop-down list

**11.** To better see the title, you will need to adjust the text color:
CLICK: down arrow attached to the Font Color button (A▾)
SELECT: white from the drop-down list
Your screen should now appear similar to the one shown in Figure 3.14.

**Figure 3.14**

Applying borders and colors to a worksheet

Formatted with a dark blue fill color and white font color

Formatted with a top and double bottom border

Formatted with an outline border and light yellow fill color

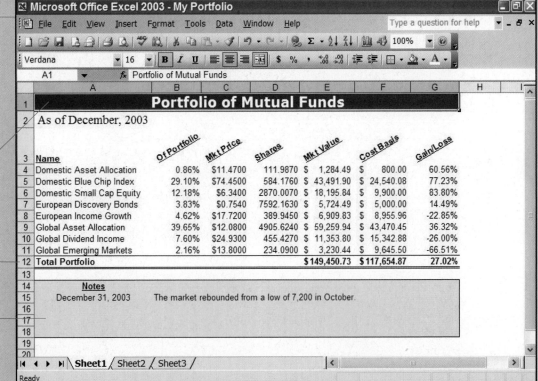

**12.** To turn the worksheet gridlines back on:
CHOOSE: Tools → Options
CLICK: *View* tab
SELECT: *Gridlines* check box, so that a check (☑) appears
CLICK: OK command button
Notice that the gridlines do not show through the cells that have been colored.

**13.** Let's practice drawing a border using the Borders toolbar:
CLICK: down arrow attached to the Borders button (⊞▾)
CHOOSE: Draw Borders
The Borders toolbar appears, as shown with labels below. (*Note:* The Borders button may appear differently than the graphic shown above, because it defaults to displaying the last border selection made.)

**14.** DRAG: the Borders toolbar by its Title bar so that cells E3 to E12 are visible (see Figure 3.15)

**15.** The Draw Borders button (▱▾) is set for "Draw Border," by default, which places an outline border around a cell range. Alternatively, you can choose the "Draw Border Grid" option (shown to the right) in order to place a border around each cell in a range.

Let's accept the default selection of "Draw Border" and use the pencil mouse pointer (✎) to draw an outline border:
CLICK: in the middle of cell E3
DRAG: downward to the middle of cell E11
The border extends as you move the mouse pointer down.

**16.** Release the mouse button to finish drawing the line. In addition to outlining the cell range, the border extends on an angle to follow the rotated text in cell E3. Your screen should now appear similar to the one shown in Figure 3.15.

## Figure 3.15

Drawing a border
around a cell
range

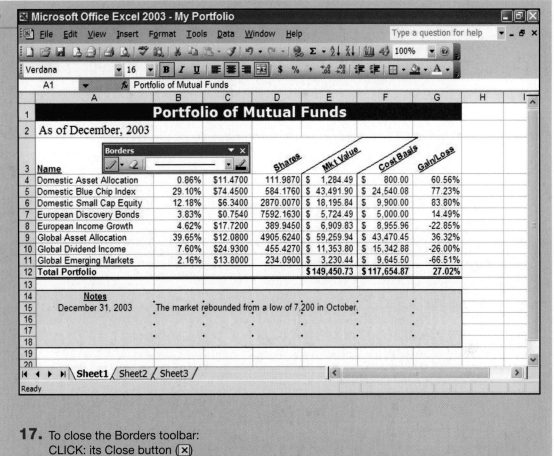

**17.** To close the Borders toolbar:
CLICK: its Close button (×)

**18.** Save and then close the workbook.

**3.1** What is the basic difference between using the Underline button
(U) and the Borders button (⊞·)?

## 3.2 Applying and Removing Formatting

Microsoft Excel provides a wealth of formatting commands for improving the appearance of a worksheet, its individual cells, and the contents within those cells. In addition to selecting formatting options individually, you can use the Format Painter button (🖌) and the Edit, Paste Special command to copy formatting characteristics. These tools, along with Excel's AutoFormat feature and Smart Tag button, can help you apply formatting commands to a worksheet consistently and more efficiently. In this module, you will work with these tools and also learn how to remove formatting characteristics from a worksheet.

### 3.2.1 Using Format Painter

→ ## Feature

Are you tired of selecting the same commands over and over? Excel 2003 understands these frustrations and provides an incredible time-saver for formatting your worksheets. With only a few clicks, the **Format Painter** feature allows you to copy the formatting styles and attributes from one area of your worksheet to another. Not only does Format Painter help speed up formatting procedures, but it also ensures formatting consistency within your workbooks. Now you can rest assured that all of your worksheet titles, headings, and data are formatted using the same fonts, sizes, colors, alignments, and numeric styles.

→ # Method

To copy formatting from one cell range to another:

- SELECT: the cell range with formatting you want to copy
- CLICK: Format Painter button (🖌) on the Standard toolbar
- SELECT: the cell range that you want to format

→ # Practice

You will now use Format Painter to copy formatting from one area of a worksheet to another. Ensure that no workbooks are open in the application window.

**1.** Open the data file named EX0320 to display the workbook shown in Figure 3.16.

**Figure 3.16**

Opening the EX0320 workbook

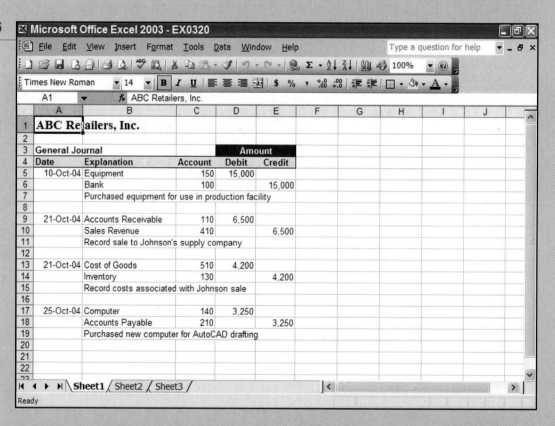

**2.** Save the file as "ABC Retailers" to your personal storage location.

**3.** You will now apply formatting commands to the first journal entry in the worksheet. After the formatting is completed, you will copy the set of formatting options to the other journal entries. To begin:
SELECT: cell A5

**4.** To change the date formatting:
CHOOSE: Format → Cells
CLICK: *Number* tab
SELECT: Date in the *Category* list box

SELECT: 3/14/2001 in the *Type* list box
CLICK: OK command button
(*Hint:* You may have to scroll down the *Type* list to find the date option. Do not select the first option in the list box, which appears as "*3/14/2001.") The cell entry now appears as 10/10/2004.

**5.** To emphasize the account numbers and explanation:
SELECT: cell range from C5 to C6
CLICK: Bold button (**B**)
SELECT: cell B7
CLICK: Italic button (*I*)

SELECT: Green from the Font Color button (A·)

**6.** To show the values in the Amount column as currency:
SELECT: cell range from D5 to E6
CLICK: Currency Style button (s)

**7.** To change the width of columns D and E, ensure that the cell range from D5 to E6 remains selected. Then, do the following:
CHOOSE: Format → Column → AutoFit Selection
The journal entry now appears formatted, as shown in Figure 3.17.

**Figure 3.17**

Formatting the
first journal entry

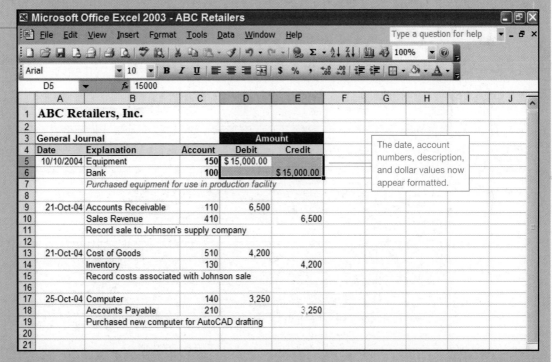

**8.** Using Format Painter, let's copy the formatting from this journal entry to another journal entry in the worksheet. Do the following:
SELECT: cell range from A5 to E7

**9.** To copy the formatting attributes:
CLICK: Format Painter button (☑) on the Standard toolbar
Notice that a dashed marquee, sometimes referred to as a moving border, appears around the selected range.

**10.** To apply the formatting to the next journal entry:
CLICK: cell A9 using the Format Painter mouse pointer (⊹▲)
(*Note:* You need only click the top left-hand cell in the target range.) Notice that the contents of the range remain the same, but the cells' formatting changes.

**11.** You can apply more than one coat to your worksheet using Format Painter. To demonstrate, ensure that the cell range A9 through E11 remains highlighted and then do the following:
DOUBLE-CLICK: Format Painter button (🖌)
Double-clicking the toolbar button locks it into active mode, even after you apply the first coat to a target cell range.

**12.** With the Format Painter button (🖌) toggled on, you can apply multiple formatting coats. Do the following:
CLICK: cell A13
CLICK: cell A17
The remaining journal entries have been formatted. Your screen should now appear similar to the one shown in Figure 3.18.

**Figure 3.18**

Applying a formatting coat using Format Painter

The dashed marquee surrounds the source cell range containing the formatting that was copied.

The Format Painter mouse pointer

| | A | B | C | D | E |
|---|---|---|---|---|---|
| 1 | **ABC Retailers, Inc.** | | | | |
| 2 | | | | | |
| 3 | General Journal | | | **Amount** | |
| 4 | **Date** | **Explanation** | **Account** | **Debit** | **Credit** |
| 5 | 10/10/2004 | Equipment | 150 | $ 15,000.00 | |
| 6 | | Bank | 100 | | $ 15,000.00 |
| 7 | | *Purchased equipment for use in production facility* | | | |
| 8 | | | | | |
| 9 | 10/21/2004 | Accounts Receivable | 110 | $ 6,500.00 | |
| 10 | | Sales Revenue | 410 | | $ 6,500.00 |
| 11 | | *Record sale to Johnson's supply company* | | | |
| 12 | | | | | |
| 13 | 10/21/2004 | Cost of Goods | 510 | $ 4,200.00 | |
| 14 | | Inventory | 130 | | $ 4,200.00 |
| 15 | | *Record costs associated with Johnson sale* | | | |
| 16 | | | | | |
| 17 | 10/25/2004 | Computer | 140 | $ 3,250.00 | |
| 18 | | Accounts Payable | 210 | | $ 3,250.00 |
| 19 | | *Purchased new computer for AutoCAD drafting* | | | |
| 20 | | | | | |
| 21 | | | | | |

**13.** To unlock or toggle this feature off:
CLICK: Format Painter button (🖌)

**14.** To better view your handiwork, do the following:
PRESS: CTRL + HOME

**15.** Save the workbook and keep it open for use in the next lesson.

*In Addition* PAINTING FORMATS USING THE INSERT OPTIONS ICON (🖌)

After inserting a new cell or cell range using the Insert → Cells command, you may notice that the Insert Options icon (🖌) appears near the bottom right-hand corner of the range. By clicking the down arrow attached to this icon, you display the pop-up menu shown here. Notice that you may copy and apply the formatting styles from either above or below the newly inserted cell range, or you may clear the formatting entirely.

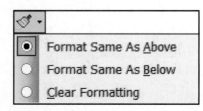

- ● Format Same As Above
- ○ Format Same As Below
- ○ Clear Formatting

### 3.2.2 Removing Formatting Attributes

→ ## Feature

Feel confident in formatting your worksheet to your heart's content. If you realize later that your font and color selections are less than desirable, you can safely remove the formatting without affecting the contents of your cells. The fastest and easiest method for removing formatting is to click the Undo button (🔄▾) immediately after choosing a formatting command. When the Undo command is inappropriate or unavailable, you can remove any cell's formatting by choosing the Edit → Clear → Formats command.

→ ## Method

To remove the formatting characteristics from a cell range while leaving its contents intact:

- SELECT: the desired cell range
- CHOOSE: Edit → Clear → Formats

→ ## Practice

You will now practice removing formatting characteristics from a cell range. Ensure that you have completed the previous lessons and that the "ABC Retailers" workbook is displayed.

**1.** Let's demonstrate the effects of entering data into a formatted cell. In this example, you will attempt to enter a value into a cell that is formatted to display a date. Do the following:
SELECT: cell A17
TYPE: 1000
PRESS: **ENTER**
The cell displays 9/26/1902. (*Note:* Excel 2003 stores dates as sequential numbers starting with "1" as January 1, 1900. The serial date value for January 1, 2004, for example, is 37,987.)

**2.** You will now remove the formatting from this cell:
SELECT: cell A17
CHOOSE: Edit → Clear → Formats
The cell now displays the correct value, 1000.

**3.** The Clear → Formats command on the Edit menu removes all formatting from a cell range. To remove a single formatting characteristic, you must modify that specific characteristic. To illustrate, let's remove the green color from the journal entry's explanatory note:
SELECT: cell B19
CLICK: down arrow attached to the Font Color button (A▾)
SELECT: Automatic from the drop-down list
The text retains the italic formatting but defaults to the black color.

**4.** To remove the italic formatting:
CLICK: Italic button (*I*) once
(*Note:* Several formatting commands are toggled on and off by clicking their respective toolbar buttons.)

**5.** To remove all of the formatting characteristics for the last two journal entries, do the following:
SELECT: cell range from A13 to E19
CHOOSE: Edit → Clear → Formats
Notice that the date in cell A13 is stored as a value, 38281, as shown in Figure 3.19. In the next lesson, you will use a new method to reapply formatting to the journal entries.

Excel

**Figure 3.19**

Removing
formatting using
the Clear →
Formats
command

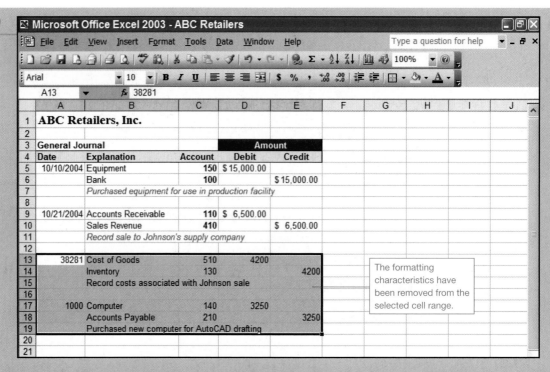

**6.** Save the workbook and keep it open for use in the next lesson.

### 3.2.3 Using the Paste Special Command

→ **Feature**

The Paste Special command on the Edit menu allows you to copy portions or characteristics of a cell or cell range to another area in your worksheet. Some of these characteristics include cell values, formulas, comments, and formats. Like the Format Painter feature, this command is useful for copying formatting options from one cell range to another. Additionally, you can use the Paste Special command to convert formulas into values, and transpose the orientation of values stored in a row or column.

→ **Method**

To copy and paste formatting characteristics:

• SELECT: the cell or range whose formatting you want to copy

• CLICK: Copy button (🗐)

• SELECT: the cells where you want to apply the formatting

• CHOOSE: Edit → Paste Special

• SELECT: *Formats* option button

• CLICK: OK command button

→ **Practice**

You will now practice copying and pasting formatting characteristics using the Paste Special command. Ensure that you have completed the previous lessons and that the "ABC Retailers" workbook is displayed.

**1.** In order to paste formatting characteristics, you must first copy them to the Clipboard. Do the following:
SELECT: cell range from A9 to E11
CLICK: Copy button (⊞)
A dashed marquee or moving border appears around the selected range. (*Note:* All information in the range is copied to the Clipboard, including the individual cell values and formatting characteristics.)

**2.** To paste only the formatting information back to the worksheet, select the target range and then display the Paste Special dialog box:
SELECT: cell A13
CHOOSE: Edit → Paste Special
The Paste Special dialog box, shown in Figure 3.20, provides several intermediate and advanced features. (*Hint:* You can also display this dialog box by clicking the down arrow attached to the Paste button (⊞▾) and choosing Paste Special from the drop-down menu.)

**Figure 3.20**

The Paste Special dialog box

Use the *Formats* option button to paste only the formatting characteristics from a cell range.

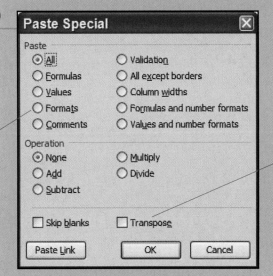

The *Transpose* check box allows you to change the column or row orientation of the selected cell range.

**3.** To paste the formatting from A9:E11 into cell A13:
SELECT: *Formats* option button
CLICK: OK command button
The formatting is applied.

**4.** To format the last journal entry:
SELECT: cell A17
CLICK: down arrow (▾) attached to the Paste button (⊞▾)
CHOOSE: Paste Special from the drop-down menu

**5.** In the Paste Special dialog box:
SELECT: *Formats* option button
CLICK: OK command button

**6.** To complete the copy and paste operation:
PRESS: ESC

**7.** SELECT: cell A17
TYPE: 10/25/2004
PRESS: ENTER
Your worksheet should now appear similar to the one shown in Figure 3.21.

Excel

**Figure 3.21**

Completing the
"ABC Retailers"
workbook

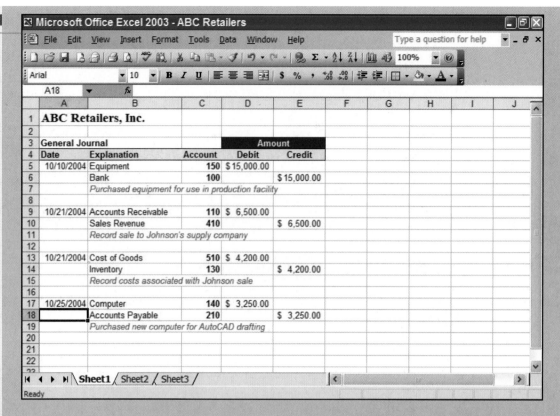

**8.** Save and then close the workbook.

*In Addition* PASTING FORMATS USING THE PASTE OPTIONS ICON (📋)

After completing a copy and paste operation using the Copy (📋) and Paste (📋) buttons on the toolbar, you may notice the Paste Options icon (📋) appear near the bottom right-hand corner of the pasted range. By clicking the down arrow attached to this icon, you display a pop-up menu with the options shown here. Notice that you may select the Formatting Only option button to paste only the formatting of the copied cell range, similar to making the selection from the Paste Special dialog box.

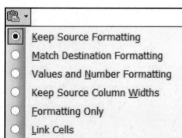

### 3.2.4 Using the AutoFormat Command

→ **Feature**

Rather than spend time selecting formatting options, you can use the **AutoFormat** feature to quickly apply an entire group of formatting commands to a cell range. The AutoFormat command works best when your worksheet data is organized using a table layout, with labels running down the left column and across the top row. After you specify one of the predefined table formats, Excel proceeds to apply fonts, number formats, alignments, borders, shading, and colors to the selected range. It is an excellent way to ensure consistent formatting across worksheets.

→ **Method**

- SELECT: cell range to format
- CHOOSE: Format → AutoFormat
- SELECT: an option from the list of samples

→ ## Practice

You will now apply a predefined table format to an appliance sales worksheet. Ensure that no workbooks are open in the application window.

**1.** Open the data file named EX0324 to display the worksheet shown in Figure 3.22.

**Figure 3.22**

Opening the
EX0324
workbook

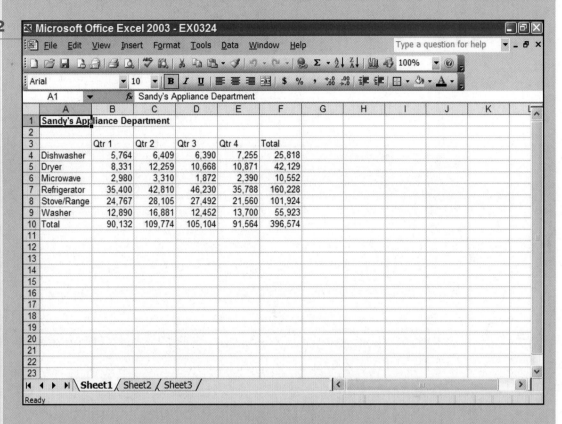

**2.** Save the workbook as "Sandy's Appliances" to your personal storage location.

**3.** To apply an AutoFormat style to specific cells in a worksheet, you first select the cell range that you want to format. Do the following:
SELECT: cell range from A3 to F10
(*Hint:* As long as the table layout does not contain blank rows or columns, you can place the cell pointer anywhere within the table. In this step, you select the entire range to make sure the formatting is applied to all cells.)

**4.** To display the AutoFormat options:
CHOOSE: Format → AutoFormat
The AutoFormat dialog box appears as shown in Figure 3.23.

**Figure 3.23**

AutoFormat dialog box

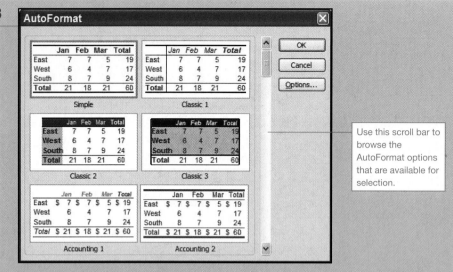

Use this scroll bar to browse the AutoFormat options that are available for selection.

**5.** After scrolling the list in the AutoFormat dialog box, do the following:
SELECT: Colorful 2 option
CLICK: OK command button

**6.** To remove the selection highlighting from the range:
CLICK: cell A1
Your worksheet should now appear similar to the one shown in Figure 3.24.

**Figure 3.24**

Applying an AutoFormat

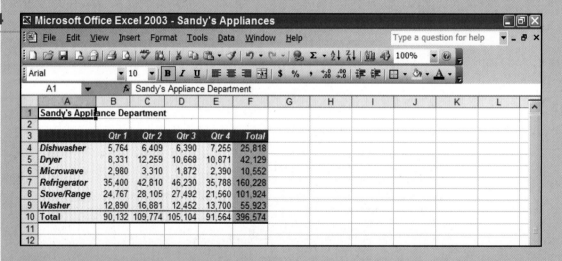

**7.** On your own, place the cell pointer within the table area and then apply some of the other Auto-Format options, such as Classic 2.

**8.** Save and then close the workbook.

*In Addition* SPECIFYING FORMATTING OPTIONS USING AUTOFORMAT

Using the AutoFormat dialog box, you can specify which formatting options to apply to a range. Click the Options command button to expand the dialog box. You can then select or deselect a variety of format check boxes, including *Number, Border, Font, Patterns, Alignment,* and *Width/Height.* Only those formatting options that are selected will be applied to the range.

**SelfCheck**  **3.2**   How might you ensure that related worksheets and workbooks are formatted consistently?

# 3.3 Printing and Web Publishing

There are several methods available for outputting your worksheet creations. Most commonly, you will print a worksheet to be inclusion in a report or other such document. However, the Internet is a strong publishing medium unto itself. With the proper access, anyone can become an author and publisher for a global audience. This module introduces you to previewing and printing workbooks using traditional tools, as well as to publishing workbooks electronically on the World Wide Web.

For those of you new to the online world, the **Internet** is a vast collection of computer networks that spans the entire planet. This worldwide infrastructure is made up of many smaller networks connected by standard telephone lines, fiber optics, cable, and satellites. The term **intranet** refers to a private and usually secure local or wide area network that uses Internet technologies to share information. To access the Internet, you need a network or modem connection that links your computer to your account on the university's network or an independent service provider (ISP).

Once you are connected to the Internet, you can use Web browser software, such as Microsoft Internet Explorer or Netscape Navigator, to access the **World Wide Web.** The Web provides a visual interface for the Internet and lets you search for information by clicking on highlighted words and images, known as **hyperlinks.** When you click a link, you are telling your computer's Web browser to retrieve a page from a Web site and display it on your screen. Not only can you publish your workbooks on the Web, but you can also incorporate hyperlinks directly within a worksheet to facilitate navigating between documents.

## 3.3.1 Previewing and Printing a Worksheet

→ **Feature**

Besides the **Normal view** that you have used thus far to view your worksheets, Excel provides two additional views for adjusting the appearance of your printed worksheet. In **Print Preview** mode, the worksheet is displayed in a full-page WYSIWYG (What You See Is What You Get) window with margins, page breaks, and headers and footers. You can use this view to move through the workbook pages, zoom in and out on desired areas, and modify layout options, such as print margins and column widths. When satisfied with its appearance, you can send the workbook to the printer directly from this window. Similar to Print Preview, **Page Break Preview** lets you view and adjust the layout of information on particular pages. In Page Break Preview mode, you set the print area and page breaks for a workbook. In this lesson, you use Print Preview and the Print command.

→ **Method**

To preview a workbook:

- CLICK: Print Preview button (🔍)
  *or*
- CHOOSE: File → Print Preview

To print a workbook:

- CLICK: Print button (🖨)
  *or*
- CHOOSE: File → Print

→ **Practice**

You will now open a relatively large workbook, preview it on the screen, and then send it to the printer. Ensure that no workbooks are displayed in the application window.

1. Open the data file named EX0330.

2. Save the workbook as "Published Titles" to your personal storage location.

3. To preview how the workbook will appear when printed:
   CLICK: Print Preview button (🔍)
   Your screen should now appear similar to the one shown in Figure 3.25.

**Figure 3.25**

Previewing a workbook

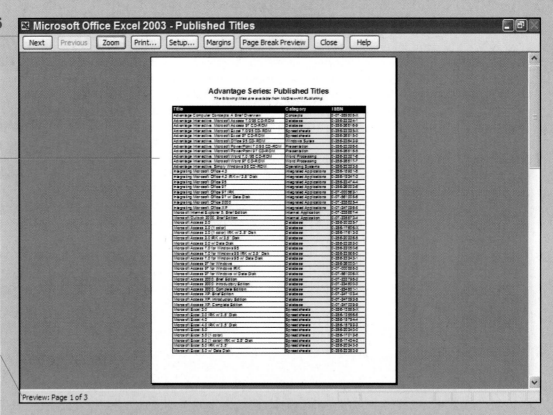

Print Preview mode displays the page as it will appear when printed. If your printer does not support color, the page appears with shades of gray, as shown here.

Identifies that you are in Preview mode and viewing "Page 1 of 3" total pages.

4. At the top of the Print Preview window, Excel provides a row of buttons for performing various functions. To display the next page in the Print Preview window:
   CLICK: Next button in the toolbar

5. To return to the first page:
   CLICK: Previous button in the toolbar

6. To zoom in on the worksheet, move the magnifying glass mouse pointer (🔍) over the worksheet area and then click once. Your screen should appear similar to the one shown in Figure 3.26.

**Figure 3.26**

Zooming in on
the worksheet

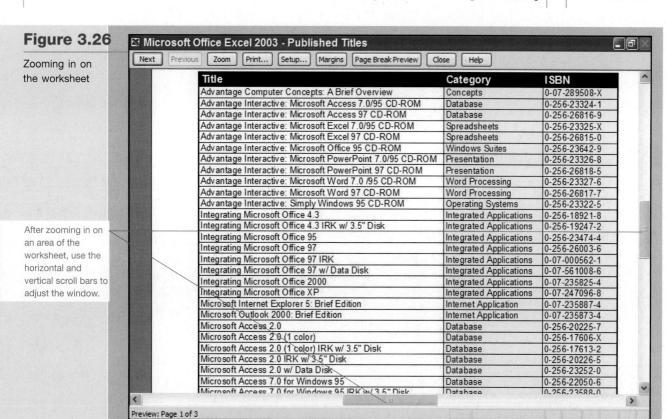

After zooming in on
an area of the
worksheet, use the
horizontal and
vertical scroll bars to
adjust the window.

**7.** To zoom out on the display, click the mouse pointer once again.

**8.** On your own, practice zooming in and out on different areas of the page and using the scroll bars
to position the window.

**9.** Assuming that you are satisfied with how the workbook appears, you can send it to the printer
from Print Preview. To demonstrate:
CLICK: Print button
You are returned to Normal view and the Print dialog box appears, as shown in Figure 3.27. You
can use this dialog box to select the desired printer, specify what pages to print, and input how
many copies to produce. (*Note:* The quickest method for sending the current worksheet to the
printer with the default options selected is to click the Print button ( ) in Normal view.)

**Figure 3.27**

Print dialog box

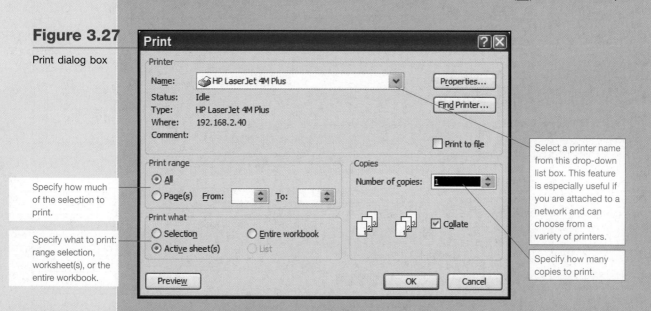

Specify how much
of the selection to
print.

Specify what to print:
range selection,
worksheet(s), or the
entire workbook.

Select a printer name
from this drop-down
list box. This feature
is especially useful if
you are attached to a
network and can
choose from a
variety of printers.

Specify how many
copies to print.

**10.** If you do not have access to a printer, click the Cancel command button and proceed to the next lesson. If you have a printer connected to your computer and want to print the worksheet, do the following:
CLICK: OK command button
After a few moments, the worksheet will appear at the printer.

### 3.3.2 Previewing and Publishing to the Web

→ **Feature**

Excel 2003 makes it easy to convert and publish a workbook for display on the World Wide Web. The process involves saving the workbook in HTML (Hypertext Markup Language) format for publishing to a Web server. You can choose to publish a single worksheet or an entire workbook, complete with graphics and hyperlink objects. After files have been saved using the proper format, you may upload them to your company's intranet or to a Web server. Excel's **Web Page Preview** mode allows you to see how your work will appear when displayed in a Web browser, prior to your saving and uploading it to the Web.

→ **Method**

To save a worksheet as a Web page:

- CHOOSE: File → Save as Web Page

To view a worksheet as a Web page:

- CHOOSE: File → Web Page Preview

→ **Practice**

You will now practice saving and viewing a worksheet as an HTML Web document. Ensure that you have completed the previous lesson and that the "Published Titles" workbook is displayed.

**1.** To save the current worksheet as a Web page:
CHOOSE: File → Save as Web Page
The Save As dialog box appears with some additional options, as shown in Figure 3.28. Notice that "Single File Web Page" appears as the file type in the *Save as type* drop-down list box.

**Figure 3.28**

Save As dialog box for a Web page

"Single File Web Page" is the default setting in the *Save as type* drop-down list box.

Use this button to save and "FTP" the Web page directly to a Web server connected to the Internet.

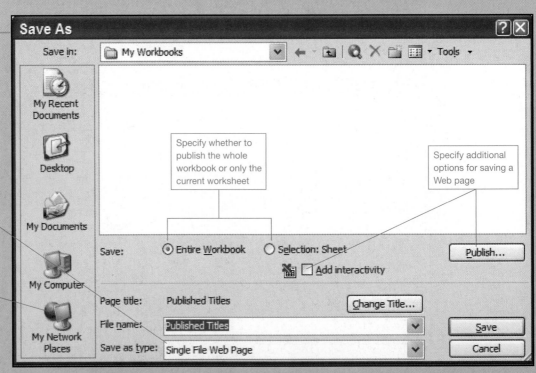

Excel

**2.** Using the *Save in* drop-down list box or the Places bar:
SELECT: *your personal storage location,* if not already selected (*Note:* To publish or post your workbook Web page directly to an intranet or to the Internet, you would click the My Network Places button shown in Figure 3.28 and then select your server location.)

**3.** In the *Save as type* drop-down list box:
SELECT: Web Page
(*Note:* If you choose "Single File Web Page," as shown in Figure 3.28, Excel 2003 creates an Internet Explorer archive file, which may not be accessible using other Web browsers. Therefore, we recommend that you create a standard HTML markup page for viewing in this lesson.)

**4.** To proceed with saving the workbook as a Web page:
CLICK: Save command button
The workbook document is saved as "Published Titles.htm" to your personal storage location.

**5.** To preview how the workbook will appear in a Web browser:
CHOOSE: File → Web Page Preview
After a few moments, the workbook appears displayed in your Web browser's window. Figure 3.29 shows how the worksheet Web page is displayed using Internet Explorer.

**Figure 3.29**

Viewing a worksheet as a Web page

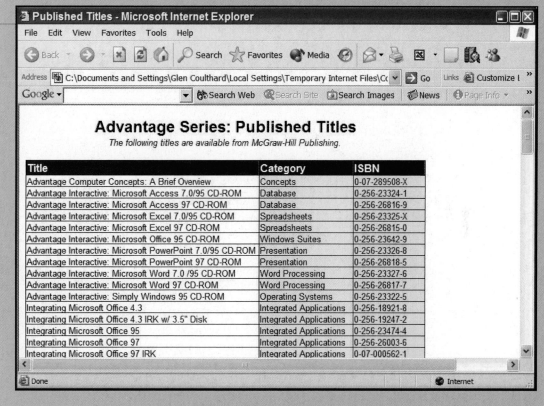

**6.** To close the Web browser window:
CLICK: its Close button (⊠)

**7.** Close the "Published Titles" workbook. If asked, you need not save the changes.

## *In Addition* PUBLISHING AN INTERACTIVE WEB PAGE

With Microsoft Internet Explorer and the Office Web Components, you can save a workbook as an interactive Web page, allowing users to enter, edit, and format data in your worksheet using their Web browsers. To create an interactive worksheet Web page, select the *Add interactivity* check box option in the Save As dialog box (see Figure 3.28) and then click the Publish command button to specify further options.

 **SelfCheck** | **3.3** How does the Print Preview display mode differ from the Web Page Preview display mode?

# 3.4 Customizing Print Options

For maximum control over the appearance of your printed worksheets, define the page layout settings using the File, Page Setup command. In the dialog box that appears, you can specify margins, headers, footers, and whether gridlines or row and column headings should appear on the final printed output. To make the process more manageable, Excel organizes the page layout settings into four tabs (*Page, Margins, Header/Footer,* and *Sheet*) in the Page Setup dialog box. The features and settings accessible from these tabs are discussed in the following lessons.

### 3.4.1 Adjusting Page and Margin Settings

→ **Feature**

You use the *Page* tab in the Page Setup dialog box to specify a worksheet's paper size, print scale, and print orientation, such as portrait or landscape. The *Margins* tab allows you to select the top, bottom, left, and right page **margins,** and to center the worksheet both horizontally and vertically on a page. You can also manipulate the page margins while viewing a worksheet in Print Preview mode.

→ **Method**

- CHOOSE: File → Page Setup
- CLICK: *Page* and/or *Margins* tabs
- SELECT: the desired page layout options

→ **Practice**

In this lesson, you will open and print a workbook that summarizes a company's amortization expense. Ensure that no workbooks are open in the application window.

**1.** Open the data file named EX0340 to display the workbook shown in Figure 3.30.

**Figure 3.30**

Opening the
EX0340
workbook

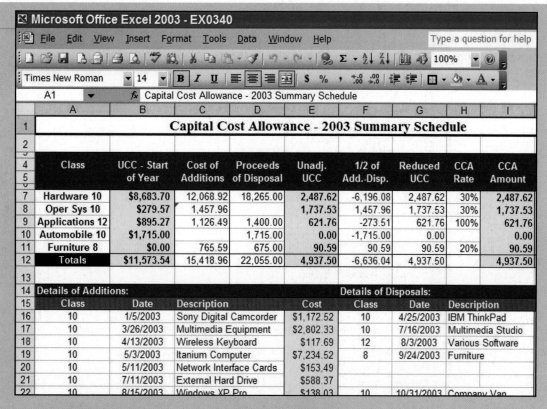

2. Save the file as "CCA Schedule" to your personal storage location.

3. To begin, let's display the worksheet using Print Preview mode:
   CLICK: Print Preview button ( )

4. Practice zooming in and out on the worksheet using the Zoom command button and the magnifying glass mouse pointer ( ).

5. To view the second page of the printout:
   CLICK: Next command button
   Notice that a portion of the worksheet's CCA table is truncated from printing on the first page and is displayed on the second page.

6. To exit from Print Preview mode:
   CLICK: Close button

7. In order to fit the worksheet on a single page, let's adjust the page layout settings. To begin:
   CHOOSE: File → Page Setup
   CLICK: *Page* tab, if it is not already selected
   Your screen should now appear similar to the one shown in Figure 3.31.

**Figure 3.31**

Page Setup
dialog box, *Page*
tab

Specify a portrait
(tall) or landscape
(wide) page
orientation.

Specify whether to
scale or shrink the
contents to fit the
page.

Specify printer
settings, such as
paper size and print
quality.

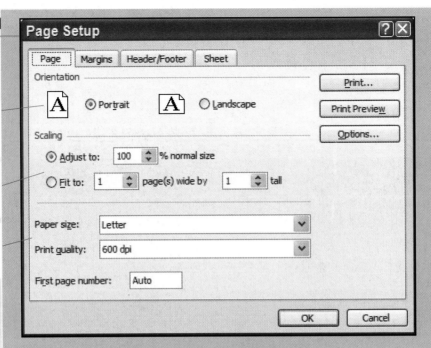

**8.** In the *Orientation* area:
SELECT: *Landscape* option button

**9.** To ensure that a worksheet prints on a single page, you specify scaling options in the Page
Setup dialog box. In the *Scaling* area:
SELECT: *Fit to* option button

**10.** Now specify "1" for *page(s) wide by* and then clear the *tall* spin box using **DELETE**. (*Hint:* You clear
the *tall* option in order to let Excel calculate the best height for the page.) The *Scaling* area now
appears as shown here.

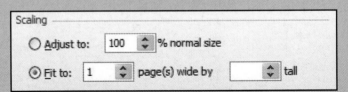

**11.** For narrower worksheets, you can center the printout between the left and right page margins.
To do so, you make a check box selection on the *Margins* tab. Do the following:
CLICK: *Margins* tab
Your screen should now appear similar to the one shown in Figure 3.32.

**Figure 3.32**

Page Setup
dialog box,
*Margins* tab

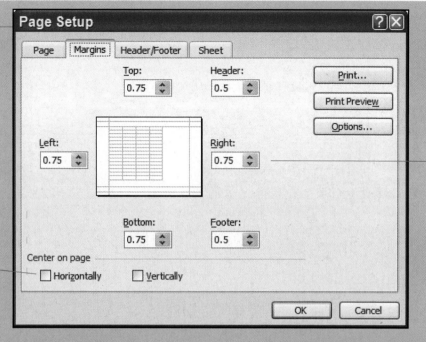

**Page Setup**

Page | Margins | Header/Footer | Sheet

Top: 0.75    Header: 0.5

Left: 0.75    Right: 0.75

Bottom: 0.75    Footer: 0.5

Print...
Print Preview
Options...

Center on page
☐ Horizontally    ☐ Vertically

OK    Cancel

You can specify the top, left, right, and bottom margins using the spin boxes in this area. You can also increase or decrease the space provided for the page header and page footer, discussed further in the next lesson.

Use these check boxes to center the worksheet vertically and/or horizontally on the printed page.

Excel

**12.** To proceed:
SELECT: *Horizontally* check box in the *Center on page* area

**13.** CLICK: Print Preview command button
As shown in Figure 3.33, the entire worksheet now appears centered between the margins on a single printed page.

**Figure 3.33**

Previewing a
worksheet after
setting page
options

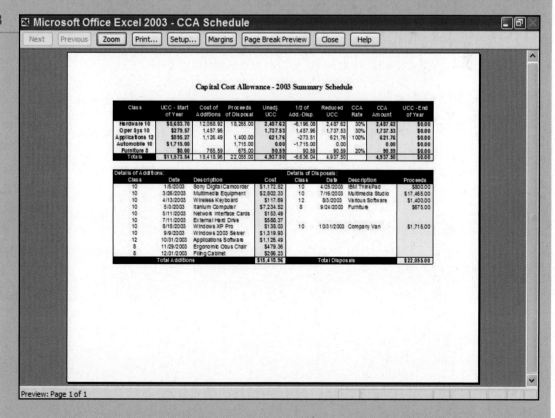

Microsoft Office Excel 2003 - CCA Schedule

Next | Previous | Zoom | Print... | Setup... | Margins | Page Break Preview | Close | Help

Capital Cost Allowance - 2003 Summary Schedule

Preview: Page 1 of 1

**14.** To exit from Print Preview mode and return to the worksheet:
CLICK: Close button

### 3.4.2 Inserting Headers and Footers

→ **Feature**

Descriptive information, such as the current date at the top or bottom of a page, can add a lot to your worksheet's presentation. The contents of a **header** (at the top of a page) or **footer** (at the bottom of a page) repeat automatically for each page that is printed. Some suggested uses for these areas include displaying your name, copyright information, the words "confidential" or "first draft," or page numbering. You may simply want to place the workbook's filename in the header so that you can easily find it again on your hard disk.

→ **Method**

- CHOOSE: File → Page Setup
- CLICK: *Header/Footer* tab
- SELECT: a predefined header or footer
    *or*
    CLICK: Custom Header button to design a new header
    *or*
    CLICK: Custom Footer button to design a new footer

→ **Practice**

You now add a custom header and footer to the worksheet. Ensure that you have completed the previous lesson and that the "CCA Schedule" workbook is displayed in Print Preview mode.

**1.** To display the Page Setup dialog box:
CHOOSE: File → Page Setup
The dialog box appears, displaying the last tab that was selected.

**2.** To add headers and footers to the printed page:
CLICK: *Header/Footer* tab

**3.** To select a footer for printing at the bottom of each page:
CLICK: down arrow attached to the *Footer* drop-down list
Your screen should now appear similar to the one shown in Figure 3.34.

**Figure 3.34**

Page Setup
dialog box,
*Header/Footer*
tab

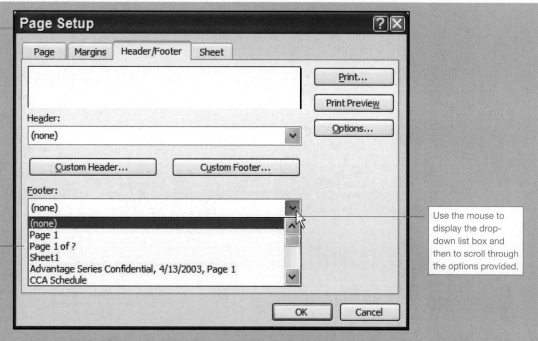

The Footer drop-
down list box
provides some
predefined options.

Use the mouse to
display the drop-
down list box and
then to scroll through
the options provided.

**4.** In the *Footer* drop-down list box:
SELECT: "CCA Schedule, Page 1" option
After you make the selection, you should see the workbook's filename "CCA Schedule" appear centered in the footer preview area, and the words "Page 1" should appear right-aligned, as shown below.

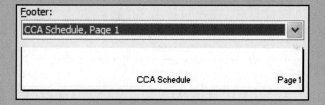

**5.** Now let's create a custom header:
CLICK: Custom Header command button
Figure 3.35 shows the Header dialog box and labels the buttons used for inserting information into the different sections.

**Figure 3.35**

Custom Header
dialog box

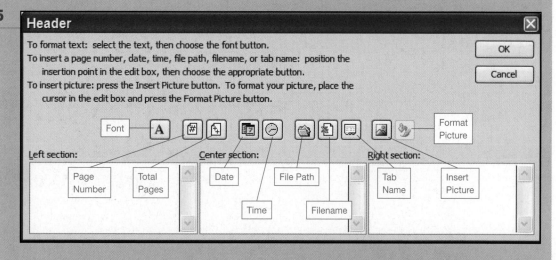

**6.** To create a header that prints your name at the left margin:
CLICK: the mouse pointer in the *Left section* area
TYPE: **Created by:** *your name*
(*Hint:* Enter your name rather than the text "your name.")

**7.** Now place the date against the right margin:
CLICK: the mouse pointer in the *Right section* area
TYPE: **Printed on:**
PRESS: Space Bar once
CLICK: Date button (⬛) as labeled in Figure 3.35

**8.** To complete the dialog box:
CLICK: OK command button
You will see the custom header appear in the preview area, as shown in Figure 3.36. (*Note:* Your name and the current date will appear in the *Header* preview area.)

### Figure 3.36

Page Setup dialog box, *Header/Footer* tab

The *Header* preview area displays the results of your custom selections.

The *Footer* preview area displays the results of your selection from the drop-down list box.

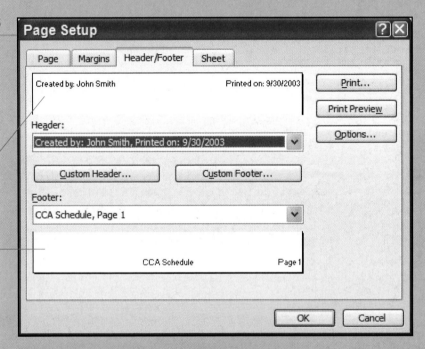

**9.** To display the worksheet in Print Preview mode:
CLICK: Print Preview command button
Notice the newly inserted header and footer in the Print Preview window shown in Figure 3.37.

**Figure 3.37**

Displaying the header and footer in Print Preview mode

The header appears at the top of the apage.

The footer appears at the bottom of the page.

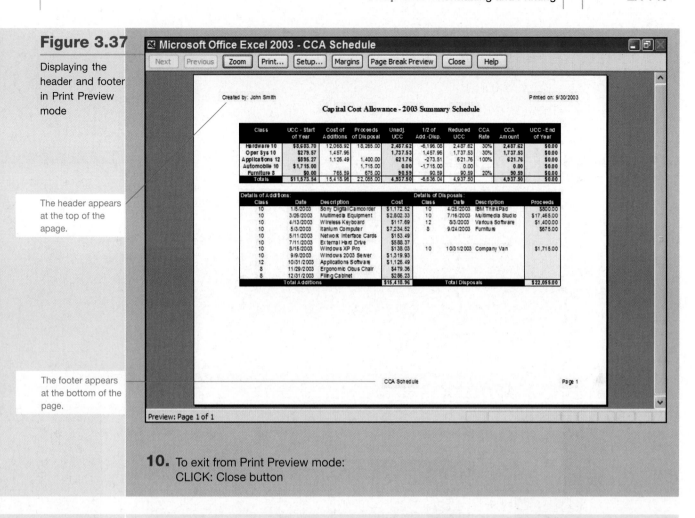

**10.** To exit from Print Preview mode:
CLICK: Close button

### 3.4.3 Selecting Worksheet Content to Print

→ **Feature**

From the Print dialog box, you can choose to print an entire workbook, a single worksheet, or a specified cell range. Alternatively, you can preselect a cell range to print by first specifying the print area. Other print options that are available from the Page Setup dialog box include printing the worksheet gridlines or row and column headings.

→ **Method**

To specify a print area:

• SELECT: *a cell range*

• CHOOSE: File → Print Area → Set Print Area

To clear a print area:

• CHOOSE: File → Print Area → Clear Print Area

To select from the general print options:

• CHOOSE: File → Print

• SELECT: one of the following *Print what* option buttons—*Selection, Active sheet(s)*, or *Entire workbook*

• SELECT: *Number of copies* to print

To specify whether to print gridlines or row and column headings:

- CHOOSE: File → Page Setup
- CLICK: *Sheet* tab
- SELECT: *Gridlines* check box to toggle the printing of gridlines
- SELECT: *Row and column headings* check box to print the frame area

→ ## Practice

In this lesson, you will practice selecting print options and setting print areas. You also have the opportunity to print the worksheet. Ensure that you have completed the previous lesson and that the "CCA Schedule" workbook is displayed.

**1.** You will often find the need to print specific ranges in a worksheet, rather than the entire workbook. This need is filled by first setting a print area. To practice selecting a cell range for printing:
SELECT: cell range from A1 (a merged cell) to J12
CHOOSE: File → Print Area → Set Print Area

**2.** Now that you have defined a specific cell range as the print area:
CLICK: Print Preview button (🔍)
Notice that only the selected range is previewed for printing, as shown in Figure 3.38.

**Figure 3.38**

Previewing a selected print area

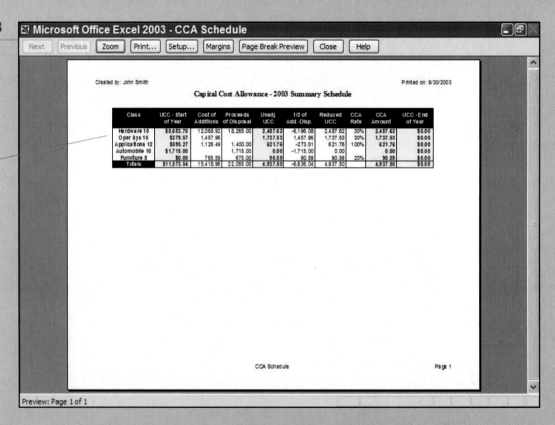

Only a portion of the worksheet now appears in the Print Preview window.

**3.** To return to the worksheet:
CLICK: Close button

**4.** To return to printing the entire worksheet:
CHOOSE: File → Print Area → Clear Print Area
This command removes the print area definition.

**5.** Let's view some other print options:
CHOOSE: File → Page Setup
CLICK: *Sheet* tab
Your screen should now appear similar to the one shown in Figure 3.39.

**Figure 3.39**

Page Setup dialog box, *Sheet* tab

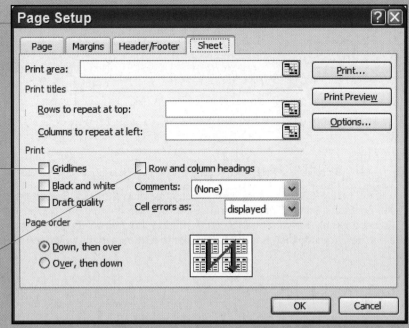

Select this check box to print gridlines for your worksheet.

Select this check box to print row and column frame headings.

Excel

**6.** Sometimes printing the gridlines or row and column headings is useful for reviewing a worksheet for errors. To demonstrate:
SELECT: *Gridlines* check box in the *Print* area
SELECT: *Row and column headings* check box
CLICK: Print Preview command button
Figure 3.40 shows that the printed worksheet now looks similar to the screen display, with the exception of the header and footer. (*Note:* All page setup options are saved along with the workbook file.)

**Figure 3.40**

Print previewing with gridlines and row and column headings

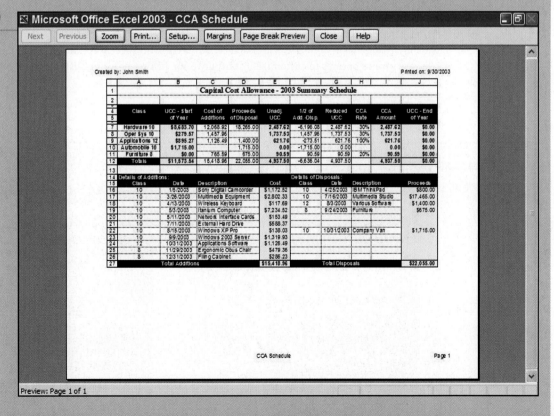

**7.** If you have a printer connected to your computer, perform the following actions. Otherwise, proceed to the next step.
CLICK: Print command button
CLICK: OK, when the Print dialog box appears

**8.** If necessary, close the Print Preview window.

**9.** Move to cell A1. Then save and close the "CCA Schedule" workbook.

**10.** Exit Microsoft Office Excel 2003.

### *In Addition* SENDING THE SCREEN TO THE PRINTER

Did you know that you can capture a screen image using the Print Screen key on your keyboard? When you press the Print Screen key, the current full-screen image is copied to the Windows Clipboard. To capture only the current application window, hold down CTRL + ALT and then press the Print Screen key. You can then paste this image into a document or workbook for printing.

**3.4** How would you create a custom footer that displayed your name against the left page border and your company's name against the right page border?

## Chapter summary

To enhance the appearance of worksheets, Excel 2003 offers many features and shortcuts that help you apply formatting to cells. You can select from various character formatting commands to change a cell's font typeface and size or to apply boldface, italic, and character underlining to its contents. The readability of numbers and dates is improved when you format values using currency and percent symbols, commas, and decimal places. Furthermore, you can change the appearance of a cell by aligning its contents, surrounding it with borders, or filling it with color. Lastly, you can apply professionally designed table formats to quickly change your worksheet's appearance. After the worksheet is formatted with your preferences, you can use various options to customize its output to the printer or for publishing to the World Wide Web.

### Command Summary

Many of the commands and procedures appearing in this chapter are summarized in the following table.

| Skill Set | To Perform this Task... | Do the Following... |
|---|---|---|
| **Formatting and Printing Worksheets** | Apply font typefaces, font sizes, and font styles | CHOOSE: Format → Cells<br>CLICK: *Font* tab |
| | Apply number formats | CHOOSE: Format → Cells<br>CLICK: *Number* tab |
| | Increase and decrease decimal places | CLICK: Increase Decimal button (⊞)<br>CLICK: Decrease Decimal button (⊞) |
| | Modify a cell's alignment | CHOOSE: Format → Cells<br>CLICK: *Alignment* tab |
| | Merge a range of cells | CHOOSE: Format → Cells<br>CLICK: *Alignment* tab<br>CLICK : *Merge cells* check box |

Excel

| Formatting and Printing Worksheets (con't) | Add borders, patterns, and shading using the menu | CHOOSE: Format → Cells<br>CLICK: *Border* or *Patterns* tab |
|---|---|---|
| | Add borders and fill colors using the Formatting toolbar | CLICK: Borders button (▦▾)<br>CLICK: Fill Color button (◇▾) |
| | Copy formatting from one range to another using the toolbar | SELECT: the desired range<br>CLICK: Format Painter button (🖌)<br>SELECT: the target range |
| | Copy formatting from one range to another using the Clipboard | SELECT: the desired range<br>CLICK: Copy button (▤)<br>SELECT: the target range<br>CHOOSE: Edit → Paste Special<br>SELECT: *Formats* option button |
| | Clear formatting that appears in a range | SELECT: the desired range<br>CHOOSE: Edit → Clear → Formats |
| | Use AutoFormat | CHOOSE: Format → AutoFormat<br>SELECT: *a predefined format* |
| | Preview a worksheet | CLICK: Print Preview button (🔍), or<br>CHOOSE: File → Print Preview |
| | Print a worksheet | CLICK: Print button (🖨), or<br>CHOOSE: File → Print |
| | Print the selected cell range, active worksheet, or the entire workbook | CHOOSE: File → Print<br>SELECT: *the desired option button* |
| | Set the worksheet area to print | SELECT: the desired range<br>CHOOSE: File → Print Area → Set Print Area |
| | Clear the selected print area | CHOOSE: File → Print Area → Clear Print Area |
| | Specify worksheet orientation and paper size | CHOOSE: File → Page Setup<br>CLICK: *Page* tab |
| | Specify print margins and placement on a page | CHOOSE: File → Page Setup<br>CLICK: *Margins* tab |
| | Define headers and footers for printing | CHOOSE: File → Page Setup<br>CLICK: *Header/Footer* tab |
| | Take a snapshot of the screen and store it on the Clipboard | PRESS: Print Screen key |
| Workgroup Collaboration | Save worksheet as an HTML document | CHOOSE: File → Save as Web Page |
| | Preview worksheet as a Web page | CHOOSE: File → Web Page Preview |

## Key Terms

This section specifies page references for the key terms identified in this chapter. For a complete list of definitions, refer to the Glossary at the back of this learning guide.

AutoFormat, *p. EX 134*

cell alignment, *p. EX 119*

fonts, *p. EX 112*

footer *p. EX 146*

Format Painter, *p. EX 127*

gridlines, *p. EX 123*

header, *p. EX 146*

HTML, *p. EX 140*

hyperlinks, *p. EX 137*

Internet, *p. EX 137*

intranet, *p. EX 137*

margins, *p. EX 142*

Normal view, *p. EX 137*

Print Preview, *p. EX 137*

Page Break Preview, *p. EX 137*

typefaces, *p. EX 112*

Web Page Preview, *p. EX 140*

World Wide Web, *p. EX 137*

## Chapter
### q u i z

### Short Answer

**1.** Why should you limit the number of typefaces used in a worksheet?

**2.** Name two methods for specifying decimal places in a worksheet.

**3.** How do you split a merged cell?

**4.** How do you apply multiple coats using the Format Painter tool?

**5.** Name two color settings that you can change in a worksheet.

**6.** How do you keep gridlines from displaying in a worksheet?

**7.** How do you make gridlines print in a worksheet?

**8.** What should you do prior to sending a worksheet to the printer?

**9.** Name the tabs in the Page Setup dialog box.

**10.** How do you create a Web page from a standard Excel worksheet?

### True/False

**1.** _____ The **B** button stands for bold. The **U** button stands for underline. The **I** button stands for incline.

**2.** _____ You use the *Number* tab in the Format Cells dialog box to select date and time formatting options.

**3.** _____ Whenever you merge cells, the contents must also be centered.

**4.** _____ You can remove formatting from a cell range by choosing the Edit ➔ Clear ➔ Formats command.

**5.** _____ The AutoFormat command works best when your data is organized using a table layout.

**6.** _____ You can only zoom in and out on a worksheet in Print Preview mode using the mouse.

**7.** _____ You can view a worksheet as it would appear in a Web browser, before or after saving it as a Web page.

8. \_\_\_\_ The two options for page orientation are *Picture* and *Landscape*.

9. \_\_\_\_ You can access the Page Setup dialog box directly from Print Preview mode.

10. \_\_\_\_ To convert a worksheet for display on the World Wide Web, you save the workbook as a "Web Page" in HTML format.

## Multiple Choice

1. To change the text color of a cell entry:
   a. CLICK: Fill Color button (⬛▾)
   b. CLICK: Font Color button (Ａ▾)
   c. CLICK: Text Color button (◀)
   d. You cannot change the text color of a cell entry.

2. Excel stores date and time entries as:
   a. Formats
   b. Formulas
   c. Labels
   d. Values

3. To merge a range of cells, select the *Merge cells* check box on this tab of the Format Cells dialog box:
   a. *Alignment* tab
   b. *Margins* tab
   c. *Merge* tab
   d. *Number* tab

4. To remove only a cell's formatting, you can:
   a. CHOOSE: Format ➜ Clear
   b. CHOOSE: Edit ➜ Clear ➜ Formats
   c. CHOOSE: Edit ➜ Formats ➜ Clear
   d. CHOOSE: Format ➜ Cells ➜ Clear

5. To copy a cell's formatting characteristics to another cell, you can:
   a. Use the AutoFormat feature
   b. Use the AutoPainter feature
   c. Use the Format Painter feature
   d. Use the Edit ➜ Paste Formats command

6. To select one of Excel's prebuilt table formats:
   a. CHOOSE: Format ➜ AutoFormat
   b. CHOOSE: Format ➜ AutoTable
   c. CHOOSE: Format ➜ TableFormat
   d. CHOOSE: Format ➜ Table

7. To produce gridlines on your printed worksheet:
   a. SELECT: *Gridlines* check box in the Page Setup dialog box
   b. CHOOSE: File ➜ Print ➜ Gridlines
   c. CLICK: Underline button (U) on the Formatting toolbar
   d. Both a and b above

8. To identify a specific cell range on the worksheet for printing:
   a. CHOOSE: File ➜ Print Range
   b. CHOOSE: File ➜ Print Area ➜ Set Print Area
   c. CHOOSE: File ➜ Set Print Area
   d. CHOOSE: File ➜ Set Print Range

9. To print data at the top of each page, you create the following:
   a. Footer
   b. Footnote
   c. Header
   d. Headline

10. To save the current worksheet as a Web page:
    a. CLICK: Save button (🖫)
    b. CHOOSE: File ➜ Save as Web Page
    c. CHOOSE: File ➜ Save as HTML
    d. CHOOSE: File ➜ Publish to Web

## Hands-On
### exercises

step by step

## 1. Performing Character and Numeric Formatting

In this exercise, you will use Excel's character and numeric formatting commands to enhance the appearance of a monthly bookstore report.

1. Load Microsoft Office Excel 2003.

2. Open the data file named EX03HE01 to display the worksheet shown in Figure 3.41.

**Figure 3.41**

Opening the
EX03HE01
workbook

| | A | B | C | D | E | F | G |
|---|---|---|---|---|---|---|---|
| 1 | University Bookstore | | | | | | |
| 2 | | | | | | | |
| 3 | ISBN | Title | Cost | Markup | Price | On Hand | Value |
| 4 | 0-201-06672-6 | Algorithms | 34 | 0.38 | 46.92 | 42 | 1970.64 |
| 5 | 0-02-395540-6 | Fiction 100 Anthology | 42.4 | 0.4 | 59.36 | 1039 | 61675.04 |
| 6 | 0-256-03331-5 | Intermediate Accounting | 44.95 | 0.4 | 62.93 | 430 | 27059.9 |
| 7 | 0-13-526293-3 | Law and Business Admin | 56.2 | 0.5 | 84.3 | 110 | 9273 |
| 8 | 0-201-40931-3 | Legal Guide to Multimedia | 44.95 | 0.63 | 73.2685 | 78 | 5714.943 |
| 9 | 0-07-034745-X | Marketing Research | 35.99 | 0.475 | 53.08525 | 339 | 17995.9 |
| 10 | Total Value | | | | | 2038 | 123689.4 |

3. Save the workbook as "Bookstore" to your personal storage location.

4. Make sure that cell A1 is selected and then display the Format Cells dialog box.

5. On the *Font* tab in the dialog box, select a font with a point size of 16.

6. Then, apply a dark red font color and boldface to the selection. When you are ready to proceed, click the OK command button.

7. Use the Merge and Center button (⊞) to center the title across the width of the worksheet (A1:G1).

8. Apply percentage formatting to the cell range from D4 to D9.

9. With the cell range still highlighted, increase the decimals in the percentage formatting to include two additional decimal places. Your worksheet should now appear similar to the one shown in Figure 3.42.

**Figure 3.42**

Applying cell
formatting

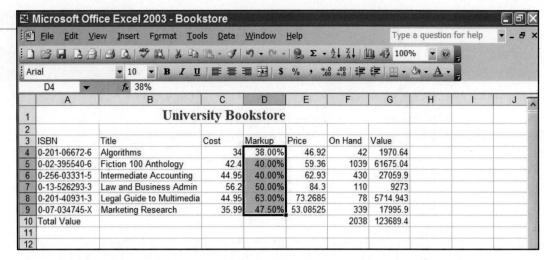

10. Apply currency formatting to the cell range from C4 to C10. (*Hint:* You include cell C10 in the range so that you can later copy this column's formatting to other ranges in the worksheet.)

11. Use the Format Painter button (🖋) to copy this range's formatting to columns E and G.

12. Use Format → Column → AutoFit Selection command to change the width of column G.

13. Use the Formatting toolbar to format the column headings in row 3, as shown in Figure 3.43.

**Figure 3.43**

Completing the
"Bookstore"
workbook

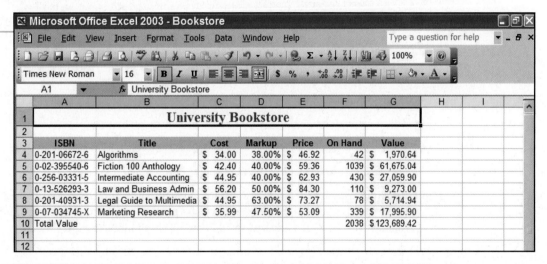

14. To better see the results of your formatting:
    CLICK: cell A1
    You now have a much nicer-looking report!

15. Save and then close the workbook.

tep by step

## 2. Enhancing a Worksheet's Readability

Incorporating some skills learned in Chapter 2, you will now practice modifying a worksheet and applying formatting commands in order to make it easier to read and understand.

1. Open the workbook named EX03HE02. This workbook contains quarterly inventory information, as shown in Figure 3.44.

**Figure 3.44**

Opening the
EX03HE02
workbook

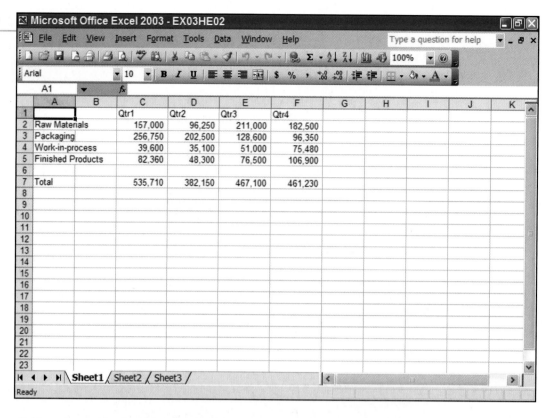

2. Save the workbook as "Cost Analysis" to your personal storage location.

3. Adjust the width of column A to 18 characters.

4. Delete column B.

5. Adjust columns B through E to their best-fit widths.

6. Format the headings in row 1 to appear boldface and centered in their respective columns.

7. Format the "Total" label in cell A7 to appear boldface and italic.

8. Insert two rows at the top of the worksheet for entering a title. (*Hint:* Rather than performing the Insert command twice to insert two rows, you can select rows 1 and 2 first and then perform the command once.) Your worksheet should now appear similar to Figure 3.45.

**Figure 3.45**

Inserting rows in
the worksheet

To insert two rows,
select rows 1 and 2
before choosing the
Insert → Rows
command from the
menu.

**9.** Enter a title for the worksheet:
SELECT: cell A1
TYPE: **Inventory Cost Analysis**
PRESS: ENTER

**10.** Merge and center the title in cell A1 between columns A and E.

**11.** Format the title to appear with a larger and more unique font. Apply boldface and a dark blue color to the font text on a light yellow background fill. Then, surround the merged cell with a Thick Box border.

**12.** To bring out the Total row, apply a Top and Double Bottom border to cells A9 through E9. With the cell range highlighted, assign a light gray background fill color.

**13.** To remove the selection highlighting and view the results, as shown in Figure 3.46:
CLICK: cell A3

**14.** Save and then close the workbook.

**Figure 3.46**

Completing the "Cost Analysis" workbook

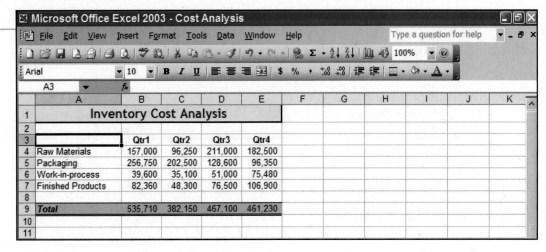

tep by step

### 3. Formatting and Printing a List

In this exercise, you will use the AutoFormat command, modify the formatting attributes selected, and then customize the page layout for printing.

**1.** Open the workbook named EX03HE03 to display the worksheet shown in Figure 3.47.

**Figure 3.47**

Opening the
EX03HE03
workbook

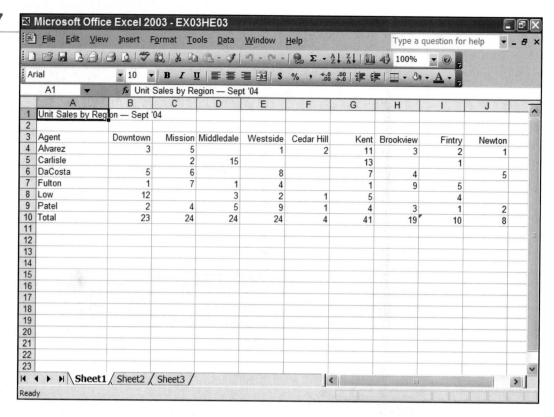

2. Save the workbook as "Unit Sales Summary" to your personal storage location.

3. Apply the "Classic 3" AutoFormat style to the cell range from A3 to K10.

4. Rotate the column headings from cell B3 to K3 so that they appear similar to those of the worksheet shown in Figure 3.48. Then, set the width of columns B through K to 8 characters.

5. Format the worksheet title in cell A1 to make it stand out from the table information. Your screen should appear similar to the one shown in Figure 3.48.

**Figure 3.48**

Applying the
"Classic 3"
AutoFormat

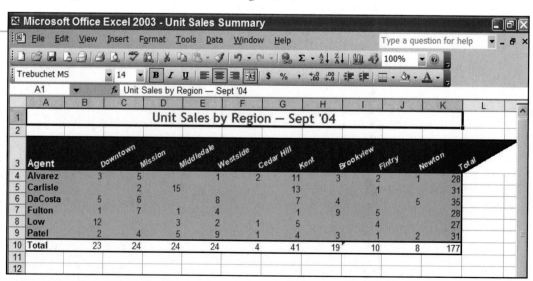

6. Display the Page Setup dialog box. Use the *Page* tab to change the page orientation to *Landscape* and to fit by "1" page wide.

7. Use the *Margins* tab in the Page Setup dialog box to center the worksheet horizontally on the page.

8. Use the *Header/Footer* tab to add a custom footer that prints the workbook's filename aligned left and the page number aligned right with the word "Page."

9. Add a custom header that shows the company name, "Detroit Distributions Inc.," aligned left and the current date aligned right.

10. Preview the worksheet. Your screen should now appear similar to the one shown in Figure 3.49.

**Figure 3.49**

Previewing the completed worksheet

The company name appears left-aligned in the header.

The workbook's file name appears left-aligned in the footer.

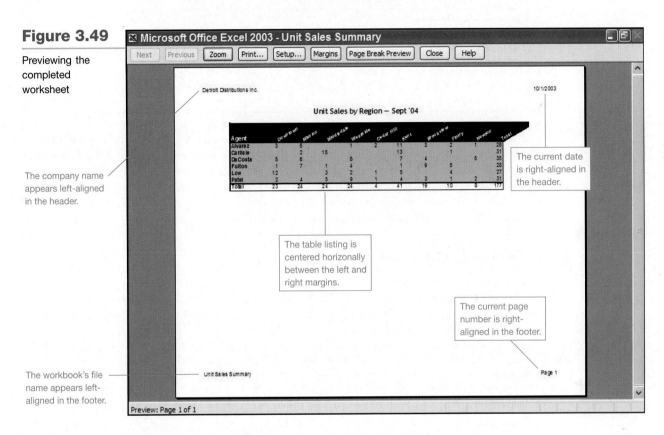

11. Print a copy of the worksheet.

12. Save and then close the workbook.

on your own

## 4. Financial Data Table

To practice formatting and manipulating data, open the workbook named EX03HE04 and make a copy of the file by saving the workbook as "Financial Data" to your personal storage location. On your own, resize all of the columns to ensure that the data is visible. Insert a new row at the beginning of the worksheet and enter the worksheet title "Boston Consolidated Group." Using fonts, colors, alignment, borders, and background fills, format the titles in rows 1 and 2 to stand out from the rest of the data. Figure 3.50 shows one possible solution.

**Figure 3.50**

Formatting the
title rows in a
worksheet

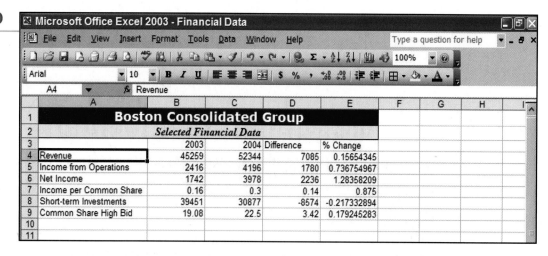

Format the data in columns B through D with currency formatting and two decimal places, except for the date headings. Format the data in column E with percent formatting and two decimal places. Center and apply boldface to the column headings in row 3. Apply boldface and italics to the cell range from A4 to A9. Before proceeding, adjust the column widths and row heights as required. Now use the Page Setup dialog box to center the worksheet between the page margins for printing. Preview and then print the worksheet. When you are ready to proceed, save and then close the workbook.

on your own

## 5. Personal Expense Comparison

To practice working with formatting and page layout options, use Excel 2003 to create a monthly expense comparison worksheet. After displaying a blank workbook, enter the following column headings in a single row: **Expense, January, February,** and **Change**. Then enter the following expense categories in a single column under the "Expense" heading.

- Rent/Mortgage

- Food

- Clothing

- Transportation

- Utilities

- Education

- Entertainment

For both the January and February columns, enter some reasonable data. Add the label "Total" below the last expense category and then use AutoSum to calculate totals for the monthly columns. Create formulas to calculate the difference for each expense category. Use the AutoFormat "Accounting 2" option to format the worksheet to appear similar to the one shown in Figure 3.51. Save the workbook as "My Expenses" to your personal storage location.

**Figure 3.51**

Creating an expense worksheet

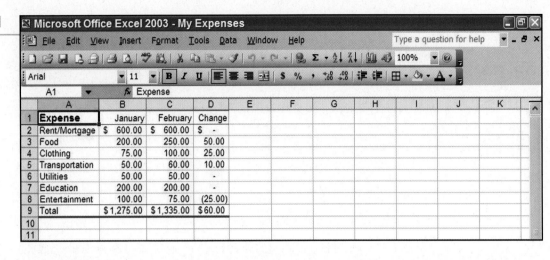

For printing purposes, add a custom footer that prints the current date, your name, and the page number at the bottom of each page. When you are finished, preview and print the worksheet with gridlines and row and column headings. Then, save and close the workbook.

on your own

## 6. Reproducing a Formatted Worksheet

In this exercise, place yourself in the position of a new employee for an accounting firm. Your manager calls you into her office, hands you a color-printed page, and asks you to reproduce its contents in a worksheet. The page appears as it would in Print Preview mode in Figure 3.52. (*Note:* Do not worry if the screen graphic is not clear enough to copy its contents accurately. This exercise requires that you focus on formatting cells and selecting page layout options.)

**Figure 3.52**

Original worksheet to reproduce in Excel 2003

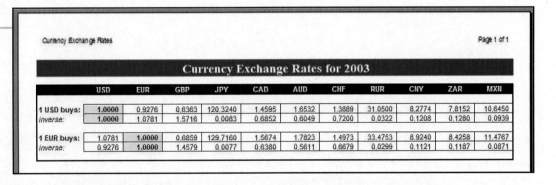

After entering data, adjusting column widths, applying borders and fill colors, and formatting cells, you prepare the worksheet for printing. Ensure that you add a header "Currency Exchange Rates," as shown in Figure 3.52, and center the worksheet between the left and right margins of a landscape page. Then, send the worksheet to your printer. When you are finished, save the workbook as "My Reproduction" to your personal storage location and then close it. Lastly, exit Microsoft Office Excel 2003.

Excel

# CaseStudy　SPINNERS!

Spinners! is an independently owned sidewalk store that is located in the downtown core of Randall, West Virginia. Established in 1974, Spinners! has successfully sold record albums, eight-track tapes, cassettes, and audio CDs. Recently, the store began stocking movie videos and DVDs. For the past 25 years, the company's most prominent business strategy has been a commitment to stocking a music selection with broad audience appeal. Spinners! has always taken pride in their large inventory and in providing personalized customer service.

With the recent announcement that a discount superstore chain is moving into the area, Spinners! is facing increased competitive pressures. Stacy Marvin, the store's owner and general manager, realizes that in order to stay competitive, she needs to be able to track and analyze her inventory costs, stock levels, and sales trends quickly and accurately. In a meeting with Justin Lee, her senior sales associate, she discusses some possible ideas for combating the new competitor. In addition to handling many of the purchasing and receiving duties, Justin is also the primary contact person for suppliers. As Stacy's most trusted employee, Justin has complete access to the company's accounting software and Microsoft Office Excel 2003, both of which are loaded on the office's personal computer.

In the following case problems, assume the role of Justin and perform the same steps that he identifies.

1. Stacy asks Justin to prepare a worksheet that will summarize the company's current stock levels. He begins by launching Microsoft Office Excel 2003 so that a new blank workbook is displayed. As shown in Figure 3.53, he enters the worksheet title, row and column labels, and inventory values for each category. (*Note:* Column A's width has been adjusted slightly so that you can see the text label entries.)

**Figure 3.53**

Creating an inventory worksheet

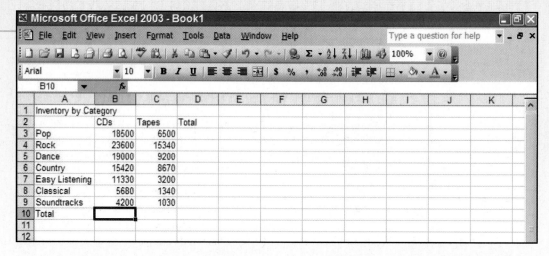

Using the AutoSum feature, Justin has Excel 2003 calculate totals for both the row and column values. He then selects the cell range from A2 to D10 and applies the "Classic 2" AutoFormat style. Not yet satisfied, he merges and centers the title in row 1 between columns A and D and then applies formatting to make it stand out from the rest of the worksheet. Justin saves the workbook as "Spinners Inventory1" to his personal storage location and prints a copy to show to Stacy.

**2.** After reviewing the worksheet, Stacy asks Justin to make the following adjustments:

- Insert a new row for "World Music" at row 9, enter 4100 for CDs and 3500 for Tapes, and ensure the totals are updated.

- Adjust the width of column A to 15 characters and then change the height of row 1 to 24 points. Increase the title's font size to fit snugly within the new row height.

- Make the values appear with dollar signs and commas, but with no decimal places.

- Adjust the width of columns B, C, and D to at least 10 characters wide.

After Justin finishes customizing the worksheet (Figure 3.54), he saves the workbook as "Spinners Inventory2" and then closes it.

**Figure 3.54**

Customizing the inventory worksheet

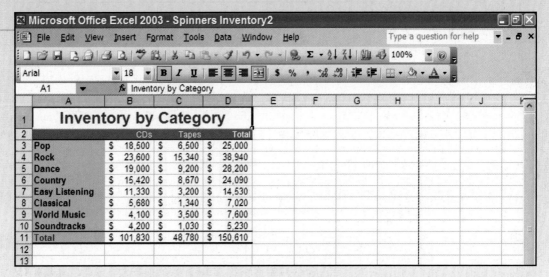

**3.** The next day, Stacy assigns Justin the task of completing the company's Advertising Schedule worksheet that she started a few days earlier. Justin opens the workbook named EX03CP03 and then saves it as "Spinners Advertising" to his personal storage location. According to the sticky notes attached to Stacy's printout of the worksheet, Justin needs to enter the following three new promotions:

- Back-to-School: 1 newspaper ad on August 27 for $500

- Rocktober Blitz: 6 radio spots on October 11 for $2,900

- Christmas: 3 TV ads starting December 1 for $9,000

After entering the new data, Justin formats the worksheet by applying the Currency style to the "Cost" column and increasing the width of the column. He then decreases the decimal places shown to 0. Using the Format Cells dialog box, Justin changes the date values in column C to appear in a "dd-mmm-yy" format and then adjusts the column's width to 10 characters.

Noticing that Stacy placed an extra column between the "Theme" and "Date" columns, Justin deletes column B and then resizes column A to display using its best-fit width. He also selects a new typeface, font size, and alignment for the column headings and title, as shown in Figure 3.55. Justin prints, saves, and then closes the workbook.

**Figure 3.55**

Formatting the "Spinners Advertising" workbook

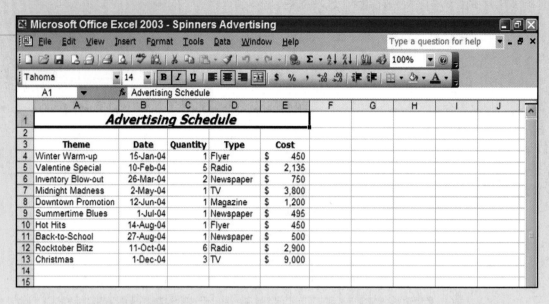

4. Having completed his work for Stacy, Justin opens one of his pet worksheet projects named EX03CP04. This workbook contains a sales transaction analysis that summarizes information from the store's point-of-sale equipment. He immediately saves the workbook as "Spinners Daily Sales" to his personal storage location.

To speed the formatting process, Justin uses the AutoFormat feature to apply a combination of table formatting attributes to the worksheet. Then, to distinguish the cells containing the times of day from the rest of the worksheet area, Justin applies a dark red fill color to the background of Row 1 and makes the font color white. Next he increases the width for all of the columns to give the worksheet a roomier look. He then adds some column borders to separate the data. At the top of the worksheet, Justin inserts a new row and then enters the title "Sales Transactions by Time Period." He merges and centers the title over the columns and then applies formatting to make the title stand out from the data, as in the worksheet shown in Figure 3.56.

**Figure 3.56**

Formatting the "Spinners Daily Sales" workbook

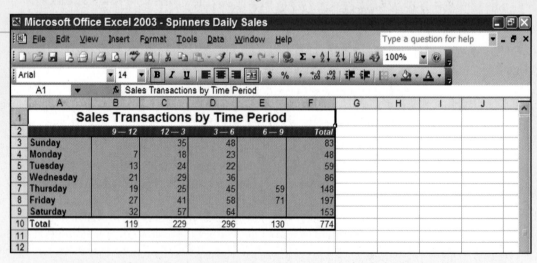

To prepare for printing, Justin adds a custom header that places the company name at the center of the page. He then adds a custom footer that contains the words "Prepared by *your name*" on the left, the date in the center, and the page number on the right-hand side. Next, he adjusts the page setup so the worksheet is centered horizontally on the page. After printing the worksheet, Justin saves it as a Web page (but not as a Single File Web Page archive) and views it using his Web browser. He closes the Web browser when he is ready to proceed. Satisfied that he has put in a full day, Justin saves and closes the workbook and exits Microsoft Office Excel 2003.

# Answers to Self-Check Questions

**SelfCheck**

**3.1** What is the basic difference between using the Underline button ( 🖳 ) and the Borders button ( 🖳▾ )? When you apply an underline to a cell, only the words in the cell appear underlined. When you apply a border underline to a cell, the entire cell is underlined. Also, borders may be applied to each side of a cell, such as top, bottom, left, and right.

**3.2** How might you ensure that related worksheets and workbooks are formatted consistently? Use the same predefined AutoFormat style to format data in all of the worksheets.

**3.3** How does the Print Preview display mode differ from the Web Page Preview display mode? Print Preview appears in the Excel application window and displays the workbook as it will appear when printed. Web Page Preview uses the computer's default Web browser to display an HTML rendering of the current worksheet.

**3.4** How would you create a custom footer that displayed your name against the left page border and your company's name against the right page border? In the Page Setup dialog box, click the Custom Footer command button on the *Header/Footer* tab. Then, enter your name into the left text box and your company's name into the right text box of the Footer dialog box.

Excel

# Notes

# Microsoft®Office**Excel**®

## 2003

## CHAPTER 4

## Analyzing Your Data

## PREREQUISITES

To successfully complete
this chapter, you must be
able to enter values, dates,
and simple formulas into a
worksheet. You will be
asked to select multiple
cell ranges, modify work-
sheet information, and access Excel 2003 features
using the toolbar and
menus. The final module
on creating embedded
charts assumes no prior
charting knowledge, but
you do need to know how
to preview and print a
worksheet.

## LEARNING OBJECTIVES

After completing this chapter,
you will be able to:

- Create, modify, remove, and
  apply range names

- Understand absolute and
  relative cell addresses

- Use natural language
  formulas in a worksheet

- Use mathematical and sta-
  tistical functions, such as
  SUM, AVERAGE, COUNT,
  MIN, and MAX

- Use date functions, such as
  NOW and TODAY

- Embed, move, and size a
  chart on a worksheet

- Preview and print a chart

# 4.1 Working with Named Ranges

In its simplest form, a cell range can be defined as a single cell, such as B4. Still, the term "cell range" is more commonly used to describe a "from here to there" area on a worksheet. A range can also cover a three-dimensional area, crossing more than one worksheet within a workbook. In a new workbook, Excel provides three worksheets named *Sheet1, Sheet2,* and *Sheet3.* It may help you to think of a worksheet as a tear-off page on a notepad, with the notepad representing the workbook. You access the worksheets in a workbook by clicking on the tabs appearing along the bottom of the document window.

A cell range can also be given a nickname, or **range name,** that can later be used in constructing formulas. For example, the formula expression **=Revenue-Expenses** is far easier to understand than **=C5-C6**. Working with cell references from more than one worksheet adds another level of complexity. For example, if the value for Revenue is stored on *Sheet1* and the value for Expenses is stored on *Sheet2,* the formula would read **=Sheet1!C5-Sheet2!C6**. Notice that the worksheet name is separated from the cell address using an exclamation point (!). By default, range names already contain this information, making them far easier to remember than these cryptic expressions. In this module, you will learn how to name ranges and how to work with different types of cell references.

## 4.1.1 Naming Cell Ranges

→ **Feature**

By naming individual cells and groups of cells in a worksheet, you make the worksheet, and the formulas contained therein, much easier to read and construct. There are two ways to name a cell range. One way is to click in the Name Box, located at the far left of the Formula bar, and then type a unique name with no spaces. The second way is to use a menu command to create names automatically from the row and column headings appearing in a worksheet. Once a range is named, you may select the cells that it represents in the worksheet by choosing its entry in the Name Box.

→ **Method**

To name a cell range using the Name Box:

- SELECT: the desired range
- CLICK: in the Name Box
- TYPE: range_name, such as "**Profit**," without spaces

To name a cell range using the Menu bar:

- SELECT: the desired range, including the row and column headings
- CHOOSE: Insert → Name → Create

→ **Practice**

You will now name several cell ranges appearing in an existing worksheet using the methods described above. Before proceeding, ensure that Microsoft Office Excel 2003 is loaded.

**1.** Open the data file named EX0410 to display the worksheet shown in Figure 4.1.

**Figure 4.1**

Opening the
EX0410 workbook

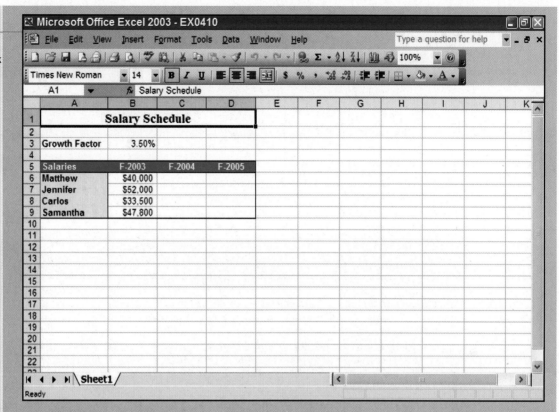

**2.** Save the workbook as "Salaries" to your personal storage location.

**3.** To increase Matthew's salary by the growth factor appearing in cell B3, perform the following steps:
SELECT: cell C6
TYPE: =b6*(1+b3)
PRESS: ENTER
The answer, 41400, appears in cell C6.

**4.** Now put yourself in the place of another user who needed to review this worksheet. To understand the calculation in cell C6, that person would first have to track down each cell address referenced by the formula. A better approach is to name the cells that are commonly referred to in formulas. Let's name the cell containing the growth factor before entering a formula to increase Jennifer's salary:
SELECT: cell B3
CLICK: in the Name Box with the I-beam mouse pointer
TYPE: Growth (as shown in Figure 4.2)

**Figure 4.2**

Naming a cell range

Define a range name using the Name Box.

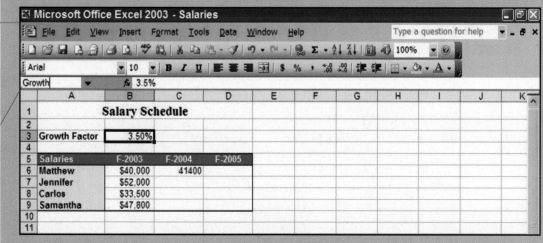

**5.** PRESS: [ENTER]
You have now created a named range called "Growth" that you can use in place of the cell address when entering formulas.

**6.** To use the range name:
SELECT: cell C7
TYPE: =b7*(1+Growth)
PRESS: [ENTER]
The answer, 53820, appears. A new user reading this formula would be better able to decipher its objective.

**7.** You can also use range names to navigate within your worksheet:
CLICK: down arrow attached to the Name Box
SELECT: Growth in the drop-down list that appears
The cell pointer moves immediately to cell B3.

**8.** Now update the growth factor:
TYPE: 5%
PRESS: [ENTER]
The worksheet cells containing formulas are updated.

**9.** Another method for creating range names uses the existing heading labels in your worksheet. You can use this method effectively when the data is organized in a table layout. To demonstrate:
SELECT: cell range from A5 to D9
Notice that the selected range includes the fiscal years across the top row and the employee names down the leftmost column.

**10.** To specify that the heading labels be used in naming the ranges:
CHOOSE: Insert → Name → Create

**11.** In the Create Name dialog box, ensure that the *Top row* and *Left column* check boxes appear selected as shown in Figure 4.3.

**Figure 4.3**

Creating range names from worksheet values

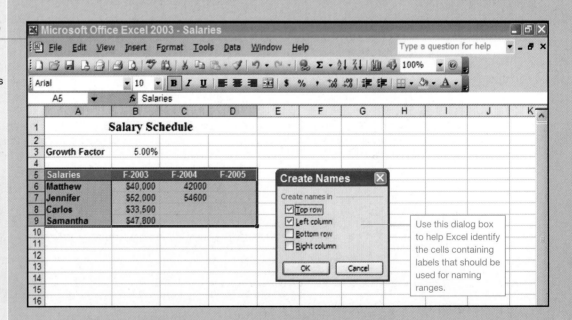

**12.** To complete the operation:
CLICK: OK command button

**13.** Now let's practice selecting named ranges:
CLICK: down arrow attached to the Name Box
Many range names now appear in the drop-down list, as shown in Figure 4.4.

**Figure 4.4**

Displaying range
names in the
Name Box

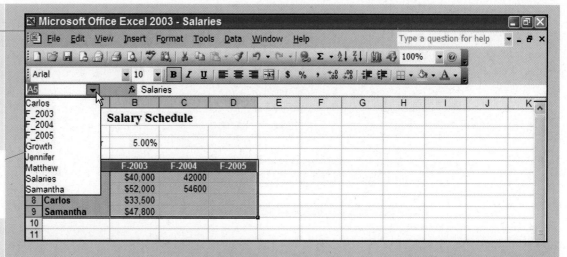

Excel 2003 creates
these range names
using the column
and row heading
labels.

Excel

**14.** To move the cell pointer to one of the row ranges:
CLICK: Jennifer in the drop-down list
The cell range from B7 to D7 appears selected.

**15.** To display one of the column ranges:
CLICK: down arrow attached to the Name Box
CLICK: F_2004 in the drop-down list
(*Note:* The label "F_2004" is used as the column heading instead of the value 2004, because
Excel can create range names only from labels, not values. You must also beware of conflicts
with cell addresses. For example, the range name "F2004" is unacceptable because it refers to
an actual cell address on the worksheet.)

**16.** Finally, let's select the entire data area in the table:
CLICK: down arrow attached to the Name Box
CLICK: Salaries in the drop-down list
The range from cell B6 to D9 is highlighted.

**17.** PRESS: CTRL + HOME to remove the selection highlighting

**18.** Save the workbook and keep it open for use in the next lesson.

## 4.1.2 Managing Range Names

→ **Feature**

Once you have created range names, you can easily modify and delete them using the Define Name
dialog box. Another useful Excel feature is the ability to paste a list of range names into your worksheet. You can then refer to this list, as you would a legend on a road map, when you are building formula expressions or when you need to jump to a particular spot in the worksheet.

→ **Method**

To display the Define Name dialog box:

• CHOOSE: Insert → Name → Define

To paste range names into the worksheet:

• CHOOSE: Insert → Name → Paste

→ **Practice**

You will now practice deleting and pasting range names. Ensure that you have completed the previous lesson and that the "Salaries" workbook is displayed.

**1.** You manipulate range names using the Define Name dialog box. To illustrate, let's delete the yearly range names that were created in the last lesson. Do the following:
CHOOSE: Insert → Name → Define
The dialog box shown in Figure 4.5 should now appear on the screen

**Figure 4.5**

The Define Name dialog box

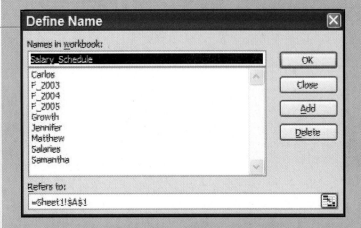

**2.** To remove the "F_2003" range name:
SELECT: F_2003 in the *Names in workbook* list box
Notice that the range address "=Sheet1!$B$6:$B$9" appears in the *Refers to* text box. (*Note:* If necessary, you can edit the cell references appearing in this text box. The significance of dollar signs in the range address is discussed in the next lesson.)

**3.** CLICK: Delete command button

**4.** To remove the remaining yearly range names:
SELECT: F_2004 in the list box
CLICK: Delete command button
SELECT: F_2005 in the list box
CLICK: Delete command button

**5.** To dismiss the dialog box:
CLICK: Close command button

**6.** To help you document and double-check the cell references in a worksheet, Excel 2003 enables you to paste a list of all named ranges into the worksheet. To demonstrate this technique:
SELECT: cell A12
CHOOSE: Insert → Name → Paste
CLICK: Paste List command button

**7.** To remove the selection highlighting:
PRESS: CTRL + HOME
Your screen should now appear similar to the one shown in Figure 4.6.

## Figure 4.6

Pasting a list of range names into the worksheet

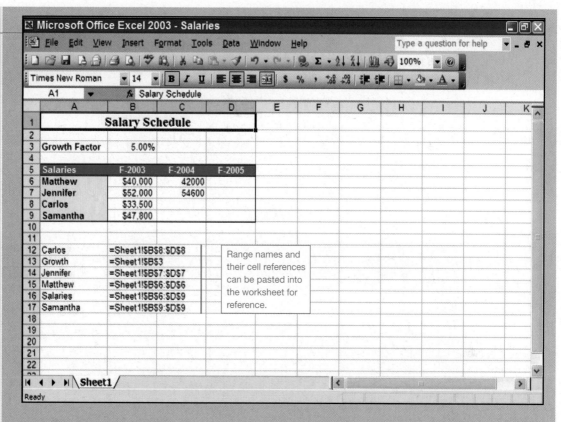

**8.** Save the workbook and keep it open for use in the next lesson.

### *In Addition* MAKING EFFICIENT USE OF RANGE NAMES

Range names facilitate the entry of formulas and functions in a worksheet. By using range names in place of cell references, you are less likely to make data-entry errors when constructing complex formulas. For those cells on a worksheet to which you must refer frequently, consider naming the cell ranges immediately. You can always delete, rename, or redefine these range names at a later date.

## 4.1.3 Using References in Formulas

### → Feature

There are two types of cell references that you can enter into formulas: *relative* and *absolute*. The difference between the two types becomes especially important when you start copying and moving formulas in your worksheet. A **relative cell address** in a formula adjusts itself automatically when copied, because the cell reference is relative to where it sits in the worksheet. An **absolute cell address** always refers to an exact cell location in the worksheet.

### → Method

The formulas that you have entered so far have all used relative cell references—Excel's default. To specify an absolute reference, you precede each column letter and row number in a cell address with a dollar sign. For example, to make cell B5 an absolute cell reference, you type $B$5. A **mixed cell address,** on the other hand, locks only a portion of a cell address by placing the dollar sign ($) before either the address's column letter or row number, such as B$5. Sometimes it helps to vocalize the word "absolutely" as you read a cell address, so you would read $B$5 as "absolutely column B and absolutely row 5."

## → Practice

In this lesson, you will practice using relative and absolute cell addressing in performing simple copy and paste operations. Ensure that you have completed the previous lesson and that the "Salaries" workbook is displayed.

**1.** Let's begin by reviewing the formula in cell C6:
SELECT: cell C6
Review the expression "=B6*(1+B3)" in the Formula bar. You can vocalize the formula in cell C6 as "take the value appearing one cell to my left and then multiply it by 1 plus the value appearing three rows up and one column to the left." Notice that you need to use cell C6 as a point of reference for this formula to make any sense. This is an example of a relative cell reference.

**2.** Let's copy the formula in cell C6 to cell D6:
CLICK: Copy button (⧉) on the Standard toolbar
SELECT: cell D6
CLICK: Paste button (⧉)
PRESS: ESC to remove the dashed marquee, or moving border
The result, 42000, appears in cell D6, as shown in Figure 4.7. This, however, is not the desired result. The value has not been incremented by the growth factor of 5% in cell B3.

**Figure 4.7**

Copying a formula with relative cell addresses

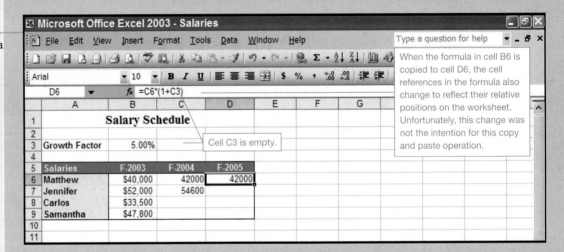

**3.** In the Formula bar, notice that the formula "=C6*(1+C3)" does not perform the correct calculation. Copying and pasting has modified the cell addresses by automatically adjusting the column letters. To ensure that Excel does not change a cell address during a copy operation, you need to make it absolute. Let's begin again:
PRESS: DELETE to remove the formula in cell D6

**4.** Move the cell pointer to cell C6. Now position the I-beam mouse pointer over the cell address B3 in the Formula bar and then click the left mouse button once.

**5.** To change the growth factor reference into an absolute address, you type dollar signs in front of the column letter and row number. You may also use the following shortcut method:
PRESS: F4 (ABS key; ABS stands for absolute)
Notice that B3 now appears as $B$3, as shown in Figure 4.8.

**Figure 4.8**

Changing a cell
address from
relative to
absolute

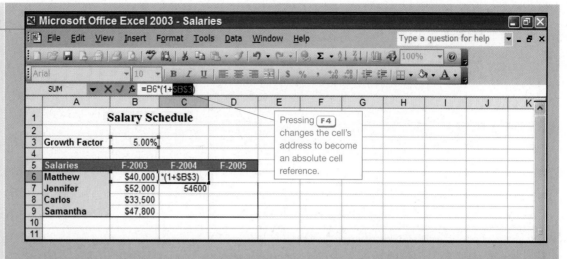

6. Continue pressing F4 to see how Excel cycles through possible combinations of relative, absolute, and mixed cell addressing.

7. Before proceeding, ensure that $B$3 appears in the Formula bar and then press ENTER or click the Enter button (✓).

8. Copy and paste the formula stored in cell C6 back into cell D6. Remember to press ESC to remove the dashed marquee. The correct result, 44100, now appears in the cell.

9. Range names are defined using absolute cell addresses. To illustrate, remember that you used a range name, Growth, in constructing the formula for cell C7. On your own, copy the formula in cell C7 to cell D7, as shown in Figure 4.9. The formula calculates correctly.

**Figure 4.9**

Copying and
pasting a formula
with a range
name

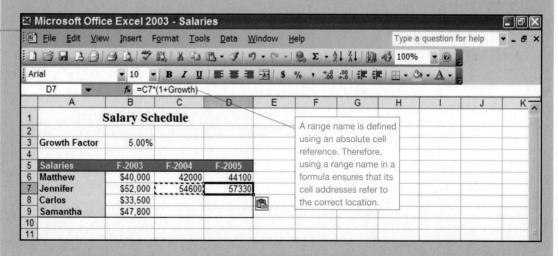

10. To continue:
    PRESS: ESC to remove the dashed marquee

11. PRESS: CTRL+HOME to move to cell A1

12. Save and then close the worksheet.

### 4.1.4 Entering Natural Language Formulas

→ ## Feature

Another alternative to cell references is a special type of expression called a **natural language formula**. Like a range name, a natural language formula allows you to build a formula using the row and column labels from the active worksheet. In effect, a natural language formula uses implicit range names. In order for natural language formulas to work effectively, however, the worksheet must be organized in a table format with distinctly labeled rows and columns.

→ ## Method

- SELECT: the cell where you want the result to appear
- TYPE: = (an equal sign)
- TYPE: an expression, such as Revenue-Expenses, using the actual row and column labels
- PRESS: ENTER

→ ## Practice

You will now use natural language formulas to calculate an expression in a worksheet. Ensure that no workbooks are open in the application window.

1. Open the data file named EX0414.

2. Save the workbook as "Natural" to your personal storage location.

3. Before you begin, you will need to review some configuration settings:
   CHOOSE: Tools → Options
   CLICK: *Calculation* tab
   This tab, as shown in Figure 4.10, enables you to specify calculation options and dictate whether Excel recognizes labels in formulas.

**Figure 4.10**

Options dialog box, *Calculation* tab

Select this option to have Excel recalculate the formulas in your worksheet whenever you change a value.

Ensure that this check box is selected before attempting to enter a natural language formula.

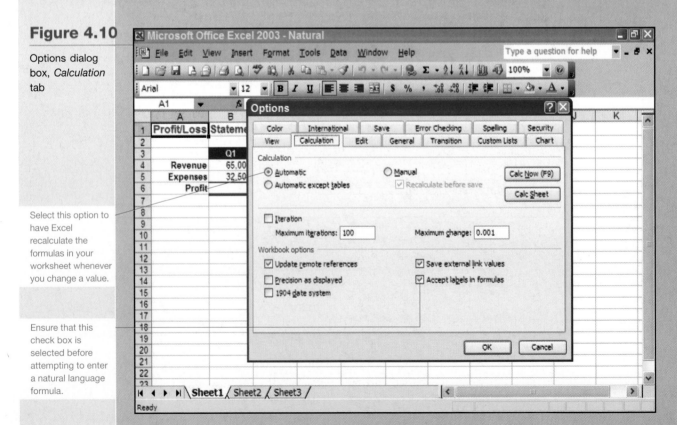

**4.** On the *Calculation* tab of the Options dialog box:
CLICK: *Automatic* option button, if it is not already selected
CLICK: *Accept labels in formulas* check box so that a ✔ appears
CLICK: OK command button

**5.** This worksheet does not contain any named ranges. You will, however, calculate the profit for Q1 using a natural language formula. To proceed:
SELECT: cell B6
TYPE: **=Revenue-Expenses**
PRESS: ➡
The result, 32500, appears in the cell.

**6.** To proceed, enter the same natural language formula into cell C6. Excel again calculates the result correctly.

**7.** Now try copying the formula in cell C6 to cells D6 and E6. As illustrated, you can copy and paste natural language formulas as well. Your worksheet should now appear similar to the one shown in Figure 4.11.

**Figure 4.11**

Entering and copying natural language formulas

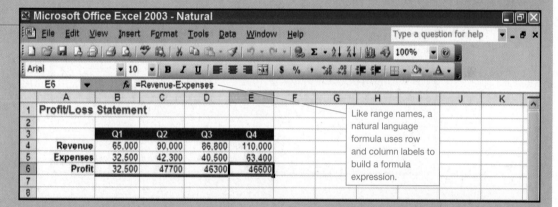

**8.** To confirm that "Revenue" and "Expenses" are not range names:
CHOOSE: Insert ➜ Name ➜ Define
Notice that there are no range names defined in the dialog box.

**9.** CLICK: Close command button

**10.** Save and then close the workbook.

**4.1** Why is "AD2002" an unacceptable name for a cell range?

# 4.2 Using Built-In Functions

This module introduces you to Excel's built-in **functions.** Do not let the word "function" conjure up visions of your last calculus class; functions are merely shortcuts that you use in place of entering lengthy and complicated formulas. Functions are incredible time-savers that can increase your productivity in creating worksheets.

There are several methods for entering a function into a worksheet cell. To begin with, you can type a function name, preceded by an equal sign (=), and then enter its **arguments** (labels, values, or cell references). Many functions are quite complex, however, and all require that you remember the precise order, called **syntax,** in which to enter arguments. An easier method is to search for and select a function from the Insert Function dialog box shown in Figure 4.12. You access this dialog box by choosing the Insert → Function command or by clicking the Insert Function button (*ƒ*). In addition to organizing Excel's functions into tidy categories (further described in Table 4.1), the Insert Function dialog box lets you view a function's syntax, along with a brief description.

**Figure 4.12**

Insert Function
dialog box

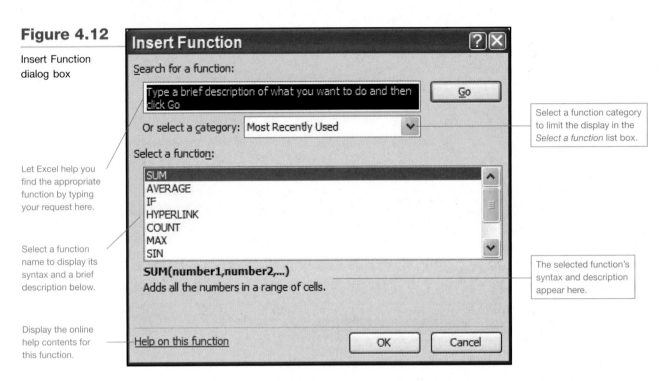

Let Excel help you
find the appropriate
function by typing
your request here.

Select a function
name to display its
syntax and a brief
description below.

Display the online
help contents for
this function.

Select a function category
to limit the display in the
*Select a function* list box.

The selected function's
syntax and description
appear here.

**Table 4.1**

Function
Categories

| Category | Description |
|---|---|
| Financial | Determine loan payments, present and future values, depreciation schedules, and rates of return |
| Date & Time | Perform date and time calculations; input the current date and/or time into a cell |
| Math & Trig | Sum a range of values; perform trigonometric calculations; determine absolute and rounded values |
| Statistical | Determine the average, median, minimum, and maximum values for a range; calculate statistical measures, such as variance and standard deviation |
| Lookup & Reference | Look up and select values from a range; return the active cell's column letter and row number |
| Database | Perform mathematical and statistical calculations on worksheet values in a table or list format |
| Text | Manipulate, compare, format, and extract textual information; convert values to text (and vice versa) |
| Logical | Perform conditional calculations using IF statements; compare and evaluate values |
| Information | Return information about the current environment; perform error-checking and troubleshooting |

### 4.2.1 Adding Values (SUM)

→ # Feature

You use the SUM function to add the values appearing in a range of cells. SUM is the most frequently used function in Excel 2003, saving you from having to enter long addition formulas such as "=A1+A2+A3...+A99." As you have already seen, the AutoSum button (Σ ·) inserts the SUM function into a worksheet cell automatically, guessing at the range argument to use. If entering the function manually, you can use a block of cells, such as A3:A8, as the range argument, or enter individual cell addresses separated by commas, as in A3,A5,A7.

→ # Method

=SUM(*range*)

→ # Practice

You now practice entering the SUM function. Ensure that no workbooks appear in the application window.

**1.** Open the data file named EX0420 to display the worksheet shown in Figure 4.13.

**Figure 4.13**

Opening the EX0420 workbook

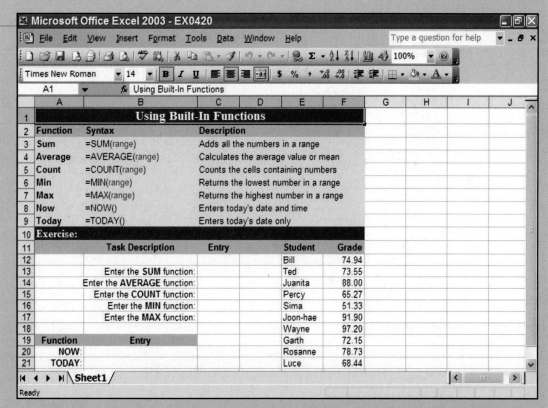

**2.** Save the workbook as "Functions" to your personal storage location.

**3.** Let's total the grade values in column F. Do the following:
SELECT: cell C13

**4.** To enter the SUM function:
TYPE: =sum(f12:f21
Notice that the cell range is highlighted with Excel's Range Finder feature (shown in Figure 4.14) as you enter the function arguments.

**Figure 4.14**

Entering the SUM function

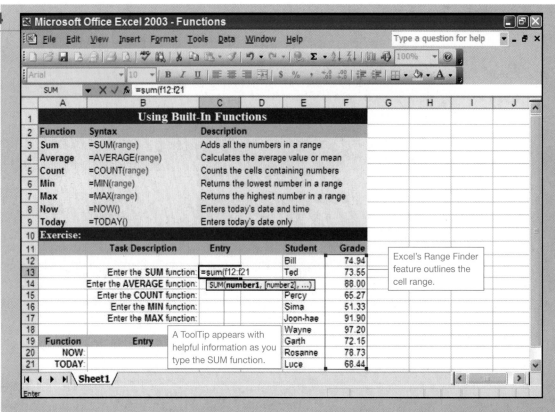

**5.** To complete the function:
PRESS: ENTER
If you forget to add the right-hand parenthesis for a function (as we did here on purpose), Excel 2003 will automatically add the parenthesis and complete your entry. The result, 761.51, should now appear in the cell. (*Note:* You can enter a function's name and arguments using either lowercase or uppercase letters.)

**6.** Let's change Percy's grade from 65.27:
SELECT: cell F15

**7.** To enter the revised grade:
TYPE: 75.27
PRESS: ENTER
The new SUM result displays 771.51 in cell C13.

**8.** Save the workbook and keep it open for use in the next lesson.

### 4.2.2 Calculating Averages (AVERAGE)

→ **Feature**

You use the AVERAGE function to compute the average value, sometimes called the arithmetic mean, for a range of cells. This function adds together all of the numeric values in a range and then divides the sum by the number of cells used in the calculation. You can use a block of cells, such as A3:A8, as the range argument or enter individual cell addresses separated by commas, as in A3,A5,A7.

→ **Method**

=AVERAGE(*range*)

→ **Practice**

In this exercise, you will calculate the average value for a named range in a worksheet. Ensure that you have completed the previous lesson and that the "Functions" workbook is displayed.

**1.** To make it easier to enter functions, let's name the cell ranges on your worksheet. First, name the range that contains the grade values:
SELECT: cell range from E11 to F21
Noticed that you include the column headings, Student and Grade, in the selection.

**2.** CHOOSE: Insert → Name → Create
Your screen should now appear similar to the one shown in Figure 4.15.

**Figure 4.15**

Naming a cell range on the worksheet

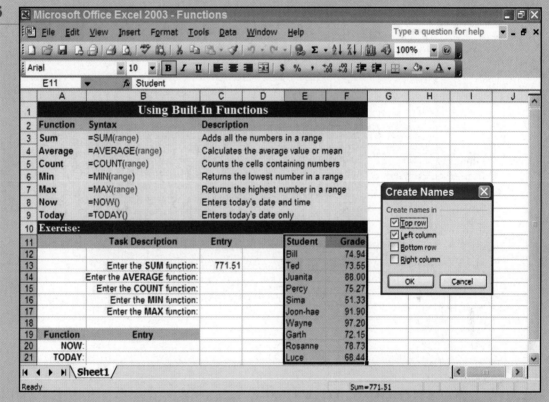

**3.** In the Create Names dialog box:
CLICK: *Top row* check box, if it is not already selected
CLICK: *Left column* check box, if it is not already selected
CLICK: OK command button

**4.** To view the range names that have been created:
CLICK: down arrow attached to the Name Box
The Name Box appears with each of the students' names, along with Grade and Student, as shown here.

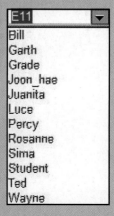

**5.** In the *Name* drop-down list box:
SELECT: Garth
Your cell pointer should now be positioned in cell F19. Notice also that the Name Box displays the name "Garth"

**6.** To select the entire "Grade" range:
CLICK: down arrow attached to the Name Box
SELECT: Grade in the drop-down list
The cell range from F12 to F21 is selected.

**7.** Let's use the range name to calculate the average grade:
SELECT: cell C14
TYPE: =average(grade)
Notice again how the Range Finder feature highlights the cell range.

**8.** PRESS: [ENTER]
The result, 77.151, appears in the cell.

**9.** To determine the average of a list of nonadjacent values, separate the items in the list using commas. To illustrate:
SELECT: cell D14
TYPE: =average(Bill,Ted,Sima,Rosanne)
Your worksheet should appear similar to the one shown in Figure 4.16.

**Figure 4.16**

Averaging a list of nonadjacent cells

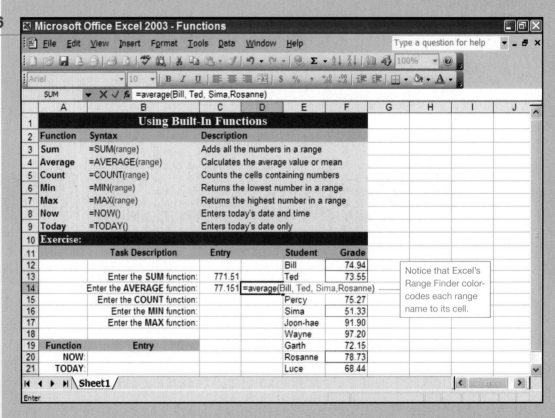

**10.** PRESS: [ENTER] to enter the function into cell D14
The average of these students' grades is 69.6375.

## 4.2.3 Counting Values (COUNT)

→ **Feature**

The COUNT function counts the number of cells in a range that contain numeric or date values. This function ignores cells containing text labels. You can use this function to determine how many entries are present in a worksheet column. As with SUM and AVERAGE, you can use a block of cells, such as A3:A8, as the range argument or enter individual cell addresses separated by commas, as in A3,A5,A7.

→ ## Method

=COUNT(*range*)

→ ## Practice

You will now enter the COUNT function in the "Functions" workbook. Ensure that you have completed the previous lessons and that the "Functions" workbook is displayed.

**1.** Now move the cell pointer to where you want the COUNT function's result to appear. Do the following:
SELECT: cell C15

**2.** Let's use the mouse to help count the number of entries in a range:
TYPE: =count(

**3.** Using the mouse, position the cell pointer over cell F12. Then:
CLICK: cell F12 and hold down the left mouse button
DRAG: mouse pointer to cell F21
Notice that as you drag the mouse pointer, the range is entered into the function as an argument. When you reach cell F21, the argument displays the range name "Grade," as shown in Figure 4.17.

**Figure 4.17**

Using the mouse to select a cell range

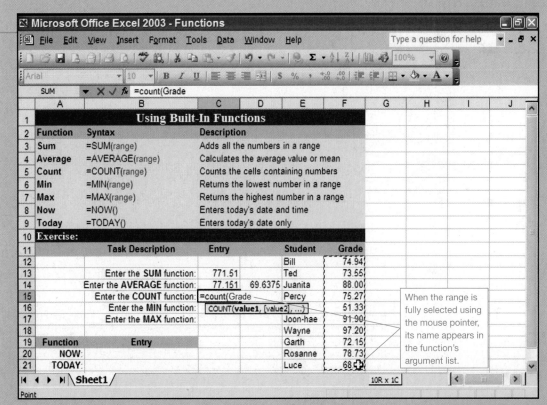

**4.** Release the mouse button.

**5.** To complete the function entry:
TYPE: )
PRESS: ENTER
The result, 10, appears in cell C15.

**6.** Save the workbook and keep it open for use in the next lesson.

## *In Addition* THE DIFFERENCE BETWEEN COUNT AND COUNTA

The COUNT function has a second cousin named the COUNTA function. Whereas COUNT tallies the cells containing numbers and dates, COUNTA counts all nonblank cells. The primary difference, therefore, is that the COUNTA function includes text labels in its calculations.

### 4.2.4 Analyzing Values (MIN and MAX)

→ ## Feature

You use the MIN and MAX functions to determine the minimum (lowest) and maximum (highest) values in a range of cells. These functions are useful in pulling information from your worksheet, such as the highest mark appearing in a teacher's grade book. You can use a block of cells as the range argument, such as A3:A8, or enter individual cell addresses separated by commas, as in A3,A5,A7.

→ ## Method

=MIN(*range*)
=MAX(*range*)

→ ## Practice

In this lesson, you will use the Function Arguments dialog box to calculate the minimum and maximum grades in a range. Ensure that you have completed the previous lessons in this module and that the "Functions" workbook is displayed.

**1.** To calculate the lowest grade achieved:
SELECT: cell C16
TYPE: =min(grade)
PRESS: ➡
The result, 51.33, appears.

**2.** To find the lowest grade achieved among three students:
TYPE: =min(Wayne,Garth,Luce)
PRESS: **ENTER**
The result, 68.44, appears.

**3.** Now let's use Excel's Function Arguments dialog box to calculate the maximum value in a range. Do the following:
SELECT: cell C17
TYPE: =max(
Ensure that you include the open parenthesis "(" at the end of the function name.

**4.** To display the Function Arguments dialog box:
CLICK: Insert Function button (*fx*) in the Formula bar
The Function Arguments dialog box appears, as shown in Figure 4.18.

**Figure 4.18**

Function
Arguments dialog
box

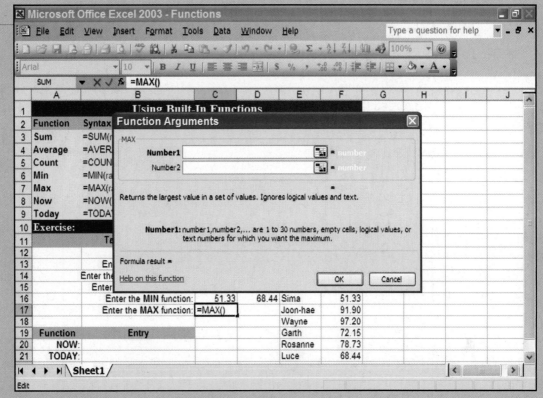

**5.** In the *Number1* argument text box:
TYPE: **grade**
Notice that the actual cell contents appear at the right of the text box and that the result is calculated immediately, as shown in Figure 4.19.

**Figure 4.19**

Entering
arguments for the
MAX function

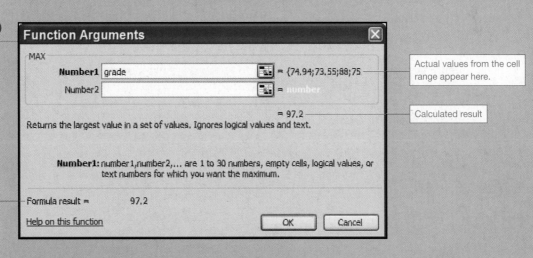

Actual values from the cell range appear here.

Calculated result

The calculated formula result appears here.

**6.** To complete the entry:
CLICK: OK command button
The result, 97.2, is placed into the cell.

**7.** To find the maximum grade achieved among three students:
SELECT: cell D17
TYPE: **=max(**
CLICK: Insert Function button ()

**8.** In the Function Arguments dialog box:
   TYPE: **Juanita**
   PRESS: [ TAB ]
   TYPE: **Ted**
   PRESS: [ TAB ]
   TYPE: **Luce**
   Notice that the Formula bar displays the function as you build it in the Function Arguments dialog box (shown in Figure 4.20).

**Figure 4.20**

Entering arguments into the Function Arguments dialog box

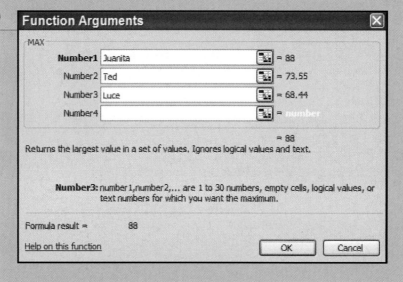

**Function Arguments** ☒

MAX

| **Number1** | Juanita | 🔢 | = 88 |
| Number2 | Ted | 🔢 | = 73.55 |
| Number3 | Luce | 🔢 | = 68.44 |
| Number4 | | 🔢 | = number |

= 88

Returns the largest value in a set of values. Ignores logical values and text.

**Number3:** number1,number2,... are 1 to 30 numbers, empty cells, logical values, or text numbers for which you want the maximum.

Formula result =          88

Help on this function                                    [ OK ]    [ Cancel ]

**9.** To complete the entry:
   CLICK: OK command button
   The result, 88, appears in the cell.

### 4.2.5 Calculating Dates (NOW and TODAY)

→ **Feature**

You use the NOW and TODAY functions to display the date and time in your worksheets. The NOW function returns the current date and time as provided by your computer's internal clock. The way the function's result appears in a worksheet cell is determined by the date and time formatting selected. Unlike the NOW function, the TODAY function provides only the current date. Neither of these functions requires an argument.

→ **Method**

=NOW( )
=TODAY( )

→ **Practice**

In this exercise, you will insert the NOW and TODAY functions into the worksheet. Ensure that you have completed the previous lessons in this module and that the "Functions" workbook is displayed.

**1.** To start this lesson, let's practice using the Insert Function dialog box to search for a function. First, position the cell pointer where you want the result to appear:
   SELECT: cell B20

2. Now display the Insert Function dialog box:
CLICK: Insert Function button ( $f_x$ )
(*Hint:* You can also choose the Insert → Function command on the menu.)

3. In the *Search for a function* text box:
TYPE: **to display the current time**
CLICK: Go command button

4. In the *Select a function* list box:
CLICK: NOW function
The dialog box should now appear similar to Figure 4.21.

**Figure 4.21**

Searching for a function "to display the current time"

Type your request for a function here and then click the Go command button to perform the search.

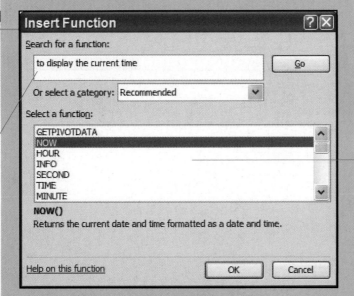

The results of the function search appear in this list box. Click on a function to display its description below the list box.

5. With the NOW function selected in the *Select a function* list box, read the description that starts with "Returns the current date and time."

6. To insert the NOW function into cell B20:
CLICK: OK command button

7. The Function Arguments dialog box appears, as shown in Figure 4.22, asking for confirmation:
CLICK: OK command button
The date is displayed in cell B20 using the "mm/dd/yyyy" format, depending on your default settings. The time is typically displayed using the "hh:mm" 24-hour clock format.

Excel

**Figure 4.22**

Function Arguments dialog box for the NOW function

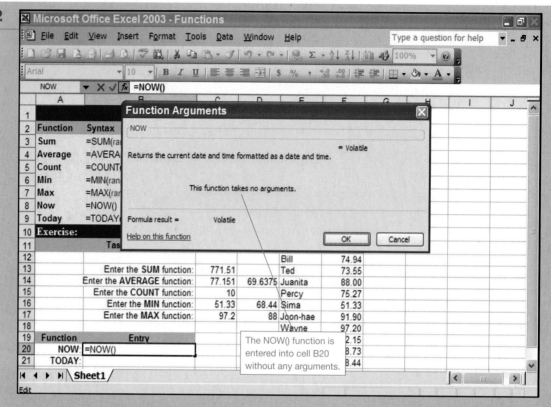

**8.** To display only the time in the cell, you must reformat the entry:
SELECT: cell B20, if it is not already selected
CHOOSE: Format → Cells
CLICK: *Number* tab

**9.** Now select a time format:
SELECT: Time in the *Category* list box
SELECT: 1:30:55 PM in the *Type* list box
Figure 4.23 shows the selections in the Format Cells dialog box.

**Figure 4.23**

Formatting the display of the current time

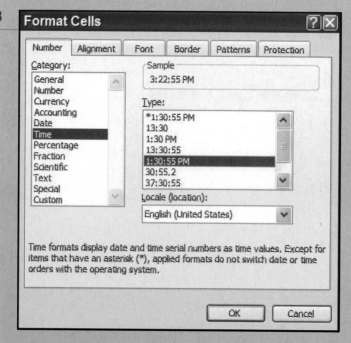

**10.** CLICK: OK command button

**11.** To recalculate the NOW function:
PRESS: **F9** (CALC key)
You should see the cell value change to the current time. (*Hint:* You can use **F9** to recalculate all formulas and functions in a worksheet.)

**12.** To select a function for entering the current date:
SELECT: B21
CLICK: Insert Function button ( 𝑓ₓ )

**13.** To display a list of the available function categories, as shown in Figure 4.24, do the following:
CLICK: down arrow attached to the *Or select a category* drop-down list box

**Figure 4.24**

Displaying the
function
categories

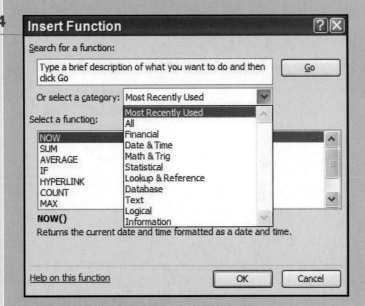

**14.** In the category drop-down list box:
SELECT: Date & Time

**15.** Scroll through the *Select a function* list box and then:
SELECT: TODAY
CLICK: OK command button

**16.** The Function Arguments dialog box asks for confirmation:
CLICK: OK command button
The current date now appears in cell B21.

**17.** As you did in formatting the time, use the Format Cells dialog box to select a "dd-mmm-yy" date format. Your worksheet should now appear similar to the one shown in Figure 4.25.

**18.** Save and then close the workbook.

## Figure 4.25

Completing the "Functions" workbook

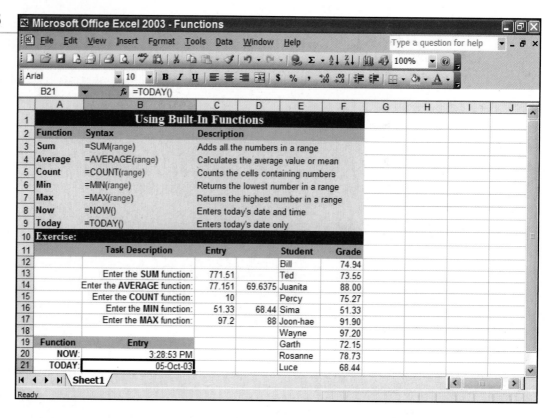

### In Addition   THE IF FUNCTION

The IF function is arguably one of the most useful of Excel's functions. Using the IF function allows you to employ conditional logic in your worksheets. Specifically, you can test for a condition and then, depending on the result, perform one of two calculations. Because the IF function is used to solve more complex problems, it is covered in Chapter 6 of the Advantage Series' Introductory and Complete editions.

**4.2** When might you use the Function Arguments dialog box or Insert Function dialog box to enter a function into the worksheet?

## 4.3 Creating an Embedded Chart

Since the earliest versions of spreadsheet software became available, users have been able to display their numerical data using graphs and charts. Although these graphics were acceptable for in-house business reports and school projects, they often lacked the depth and quality required by professional users. Until now! You can confidently use Excel 2003 to produce visually stunning worksheets and charts that are suitable for electronic business presentations, color print masters, published reports, and Web pages.

Many types of charts are available for presenting your worksheet data to engineers, statisticians, business professionals, and other audiences. Some popular business charts—line charts, column charts, pie charts, and XY scatter plot diagrams—are described below.

• *Line Charts*   When you need to plot trends or show changes over a period of time, the **line chart** is the perfect tool. The angles of the line reflect the degree of variation, and the distance of the line from the horizontal axis represents the amount of the variation. An example of a line chart appears in Figure 4.26, along with some basic terminology.

**Figure 4.26**

A line chart

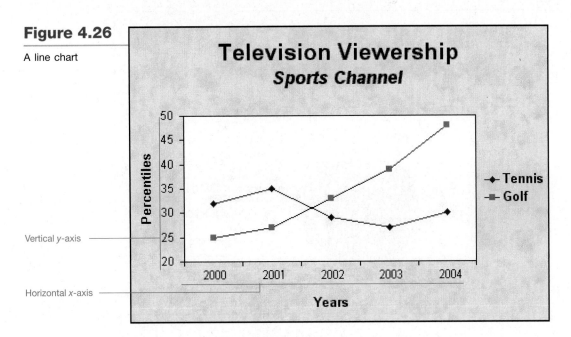

Vertical *y*-axis

Horizontal *x*-axis

• *Bar or Column Charts*   When the purpose of the chart is to compare one data element with another data element, a **column chart** is the appropriate form to use. Like a line chart, a column chart (Figure 4.27) shows variations over a period of time. A **bar chart** also uses rectangular images, but the images run horizontally rather than vertically.

**Figure 4.27**

A column chart

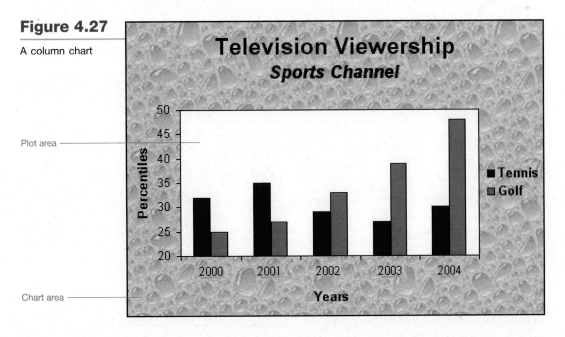

Plot area

Chart area

- *Pie Charts*   A **pie chart** shows the proportions of individual components compared to the total. Like a real pie (the baked variety), a pie chart is divided into slices or wedges. (In Excel 2003, you can even pull out the slices from the rest of the pie.) An example of a pie chart appears in Figure 4.28.

**Figure 4.28**

A pie chart

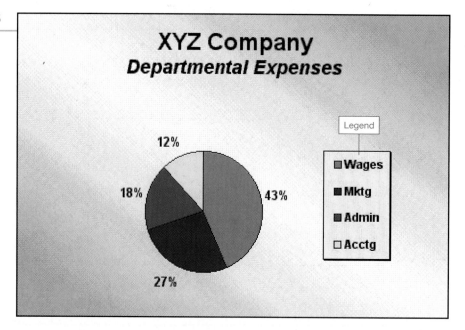

- *Scatter Plot Diagrams*   **XY charts,** which are commonly referred to as **scatter plot diagrams,** show how one or more data elements relate to another data element. Although they look much like line charts, XY charts show the correlation between elements and include a numeric scale along both the x- and y-axes. The XY chart in Figure 4.29 shows that worker productivity diminishes as stress levels increase.

**Figure 4.29**

An XY chart

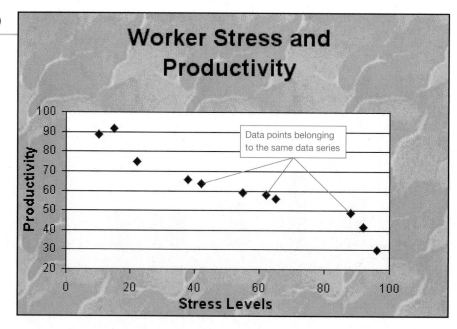

There are two methods for creating a chart in Excel 2003, differing primarily in the way the chart is stored and printed. First, you can create a new chart as a separate sheet in a workbook. This method works well for printing full-page charts and for creating computer-based presentations or electronic slide shows. Second, you can create an **embedded chart** that is stored on the worksheet. Embed a chart when you want to view or print the chart alongside the worksheet data. Whichever approach you choose, you can use the step-by-step features in Excel's **Chart Wizard** to construct the chart from existing worksheet data.

In this module, you will learn how to create and print an embedded chart.

### 4.3.1  Creating a Chart Using the Chart Wizard

→ **Feature**

Creating an impressive chart in Excel 2003 is surprisingly easy. To begin, select a range of cells that you want to plot and then launch the Chart Wizard. The wizard examines the selected range and then displays its dialog box. You make selections, such as choosing a chart type, and proceed through the steps to embed the chart on the worksheet. An embedded chart is actually placed over—not entered into—a cell range. Once it is embedded, you can move, size, and delete the chart at any time.

→ **Method**

- SELECT: the cell range to plot in a chart
- CLICK: Chart Wizard button (📊)
- Complete the steps in the Chart Wizard.

→ **Practice**

You will now create and embed a new chart onto a worksheet.

**1.** Open the data file named EX0430 to display the worksheet in Figure 4.30.

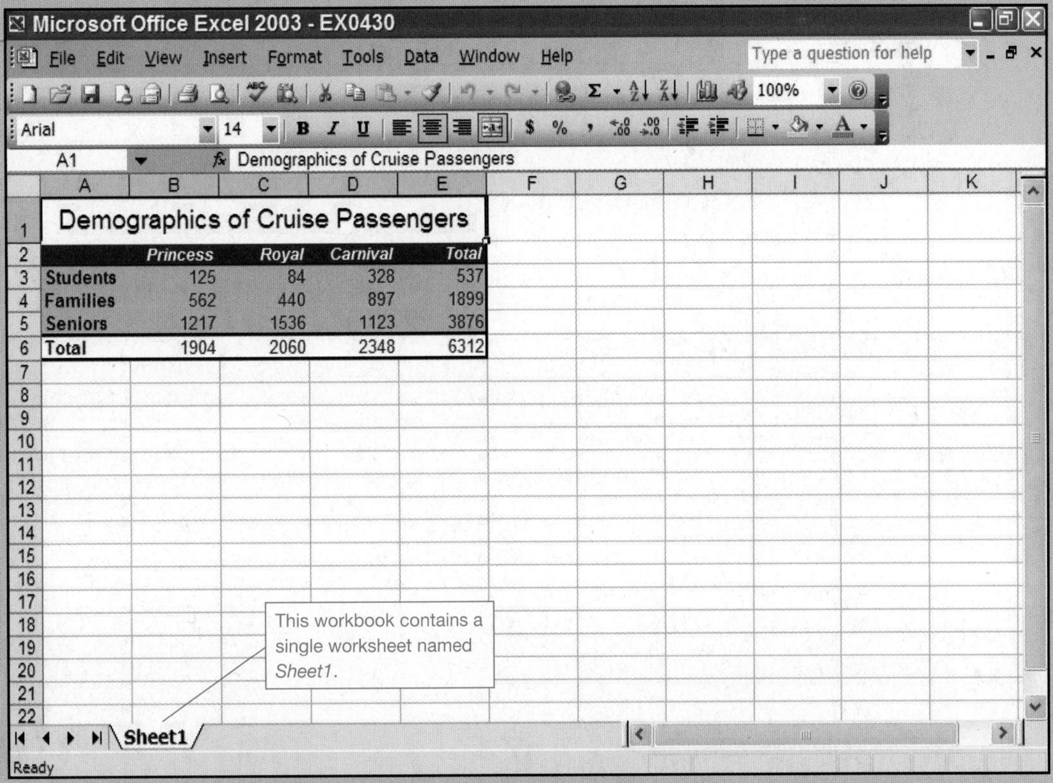

**Figure 4.30**

Opening the EX0430 workbook

This workbook contains a single worksheet named *Sheet1*.

**2.** Save the workbook as "Cruising" to your personal storage location.

**3.** Let's plot the worksheet's demographic data. To begin, select both the column headings and the data area:
SELECT: cell range from A2 to D5
(**Caution:** Do not include the title in cell A1 or the "Total" cells in row 6 or column E in the range selection.)

**4.** To start the Chart Wizard:
CLICK: Chart Wizard button (⊞) on the Standard toolbar
The Chart Wizard dialog box appears, as shown in Figure 4.31.

**Figure 4.31**

Chart Wizard:
Step 1 of 4

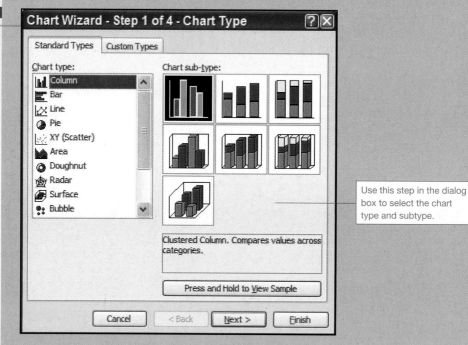

Use this step in the dialog box to select the chart type and subtype.

**5.** To see a sample of how Excel will plot this data:
CLICK: "Press and Hold to View Sample" command button
(*Note:* You must hold down the left mouse button to see the chart inside the *Sample* preview window. When you are finished viewing, release the mouse button.)

**6.** Let's select a different chart sub-type that amalgamates (adds together) the data series in a column. Do the following:
SELECT: Stacked Column in the *Chart sub-type area,* as shown here
(*Hint:* When you click on a chart sub-type, the chart's name and description appear above the "Press and Hold to View Sample" command button.)

**7.** Once again, preview a sample of the chart:
CLICK: "Press and Hold to View Sample" command button

**8.** To continue creating the chart:
CLICK: [ Next> ] to proceed to Step 2 of 4
Your screen should now appear similar to the one shown in Figure 4.32.

**Figure 4.32**

Chart Wizard:
Step 2 of 4

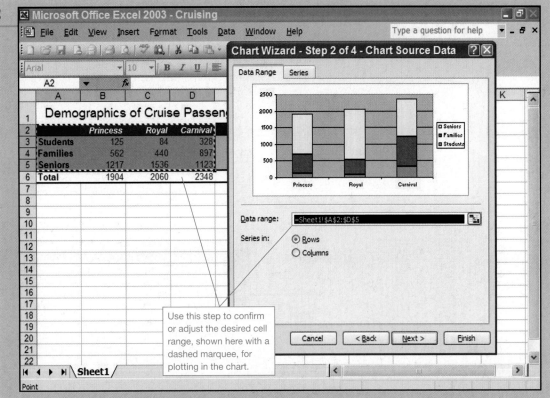

Use this step to confirm or adjust the desired cell range, shown here with a dashed marquee, for plotting in the chart.

**9.** Because you selected the data range prior to launching the Chart Wizard, you can accept the default entry in Step 2 and proceed:
CLICK: Next> to proceed to Step 3 of 4

**10.** In Step 3 of 4 of the Chart Wizard:
TYPE: **Cruise Lines** into the *Category (X) axis* text box
TYPE: **Passengers** into the *Value (Y) axis* text box
(*Hint:* Click the I-beam mouse pointer into a text box and then type the appropriate text. You can also press TAB to move forward through the text boxes.) Notice that the preview area is immediately updated to display the new titles, as shown in Figure 4.33.

**Figure 4.33**

Chart Wizard:
Step 3 of 4

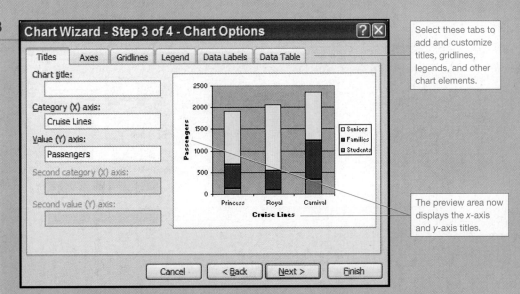

Select these tabs to add and customize titles, gridlines, legends, and other chart elements.

The preview area now displays the x-axis and y-axis titles.

**11.** To proceed to the final step:
CLICK: Next>

**12.** In Step 4 of 4, you specify where you want to store the chart. To create an embedded chart:
CLICK: *As object in* option button, as shown in Figure 4.34
Notice that the current worksheet's name, *Sheet1,* already appears in the drop-down list box next to the option button.

**Figure 4.34**

Chart Wizard:
Step 4 of 4

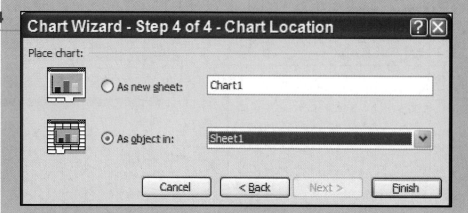

**13.** To complete the Chart Wizard:
CLICK: Finish
The embedded chart appears in the application window, as shown in Figure 4.35. (*Note:* You may also see Excel's Chart toolbar appear.)

**Figure 4.35**

Adding a chart as an embedded object to the worksheet

Excel's Range Finder feature displays the range plotted in the selected chart.

The Chart toolbar will appear when the chart object is selected.

The embedded chart object floats above the cells in the worksheet.

Size a chart by dragging one of the selection boxes that appear around the selected chart object.

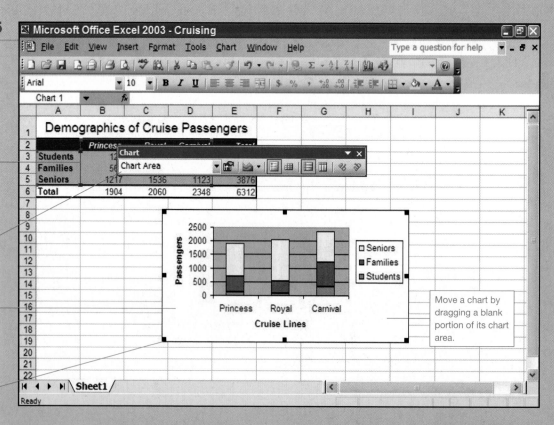

Move a chart by dragging a blank portion of its chart area.

**14.** The black selection boxes (sometimes called "sizing handles") that surround the chart indicate that the chart is currently selected. Using the mouse, you can size the embedded chart by dragging these boxes. On your own, practice sizing the chart.

**15.** You can move the chart by dragging the object with the mouse. Position the white mouse arrow over a blank portion of the chart's background area. Then, drag the chart into position. Practice moving and sizing the chart to cover the range from cell A8 to E20, immediately beneath the data area.

**16.** To return focus to the worksheet:
CLICK: any cell visible in the worksheet area, such as cell A1
Notice that the selection boxes around the chart disappear, as shown in Figure 4.36.

**Figure 4.36**

Returning focus
to the worksheet

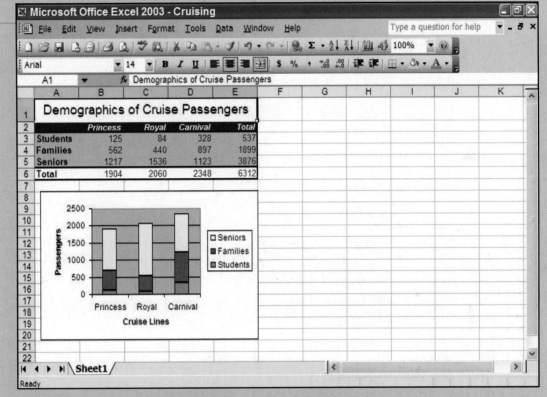

**17.** One of the most significant features of an Excel chart is that it remains dynamically linked to the data stored in the worksheet. To illustrate, let's update the "Carnival" column in the embedded chart:
SELECT: cell D5
TYPE: 400
PRESS: ENTER
The chart is updated immediately to reflect the new data.

**18.** Save the workbook and keep it open for use in the next lesson.

### 4.3.2 Previewing and Printing an Embedded Chart

→ ## Feature

One of the primary reasons for embedding a chart on a worksheet is to view and print it alongside its worksheet data. You must ensure, however, that the print area (or worksheet range) includes the entire chart object. As you learned in the previous chapter, you can manipulate various page setup options, including margins, headers, and footers. Remember also to preview your worksheet and chart before sending it to the printer.

→ ## Method

- SELECT: a cell range that includes the chart

- CHOOSE: File → Print Area → Set Print Area

- CHOOSE: File → Print Preview

    *or*

- CHOOSE: File → Print

→ ## Practice

You will now preview and print an embedded chart along with its worksheet data. Ensure that you have completed the previous lesson and that the "Cruising" workbook is displayed.

**1.** To print the worksheet and embedded chart on the same page:
SELECT: cell range from A1 to F21
(*Note:* Depending on the size and placement of your chart object, you may need to increase or decrease this print range. Make sure that the entire object is covered in the highlighted range.)

**2.** CHOOSE: File → Print Area → Set Print Area
Your screen should appear similar to the one shown in Figure 4.37.

**Figure 4.37**

Specifying the worksheet range to be printed

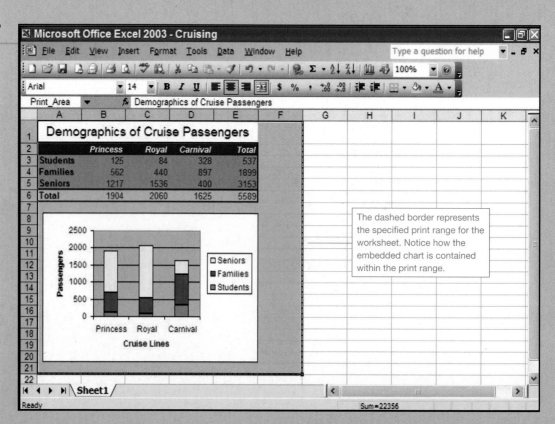

The dashed border represents the specified print range for the worksheet. Notice how the embedded chart is contained within the print range.

**3.** To preview the worksheet and chart:
CLICK: Print Preview button (🔍)

**4.** To zoom in on the preview window:
CLICK: Zoom command button

**5.** On your own, scroll the preview window so that it appears similar to the one shown in Figure 4.38. Notice that the chart is printed immediately and seamlessly below the worksheet data. (*Note:* If you do not have a color printer specified as your default, the worksheet and chart will not appear in color as shown here.)

**Figure 4.38**

Previewing an embedded chart

Worksheet data area

Embedded chart object

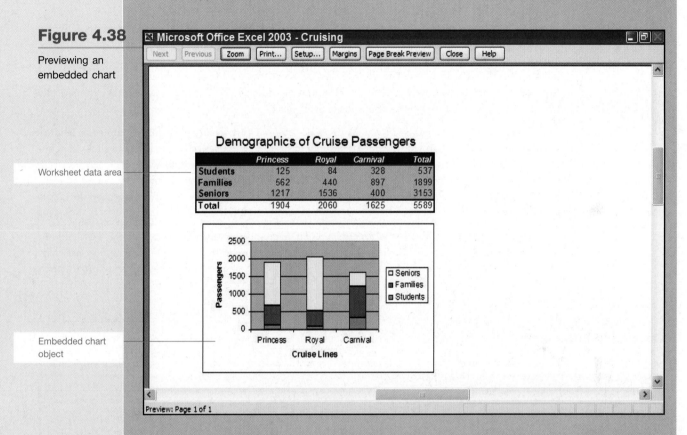

**6.** To print the chart from the Preview window:
CLICK: Print command button

**7.** If you do not have access to a printer, click the Cancel command button and proceed to the next step. If you have a printer attached to your computer and want to print this chart, do the following:
CLICK: OK command button

**8.** To remove the selection highlighting from the worksheet area:
CLICK: cell A1
(*Hint:* You may have noticed that we often select cell A1 prior to saving the workbook. The reason is that Excel saves and restores the cell pointer's position for the next time you open the workbook.)

**9.** Save and then close the workbook.

**10.** Exit Microsoft Office Excel 2003.

 **4.3** What must you ensure when selecting the print range for a worksheet that contains an embedded chart?

# Chapter
## summary

Excel 2003 provides powerful tools for analyzing and summarizing data. The ability to name cells and ranges for use in constructing expressions and navigating the worksheet increases accuracy and efficiency. You can also create formula expressions using either relative or absolute cell references. Specifying an absolute cell address by adding dollar signs ($) serves to anchor a cell reference to an exact location on the worksheet. The default, however, is to use relative cell addresses, which Excel can adjust automatically when you copy formulas to new locations in the worksheet.

Built-in functions, such as SUM and AVERAGE, are used as shortcuts to perform complex or lengthy calculations. Excel 2003 provides hundreds of functions, sorted alphabetically into categories for your convenience. You enter a function by typing directly into a worksheet cell or by displaying the Insert Function dialog box and then selecting the desired function. Another helpful productivity feature provided by Excel is the Function Arguments dialog box, which prompts you in entering the required arguments for a particular function.

Charts and graphics help to organize and present data and to convey meaning for the users of your worksheets. Most people agree that it is easier to infer trends and patterns from a line graph or bar chart than from a table of numerical data. Fortunately, Excel 2003's Chart Wizard makes it easy to produce and format a variety of chart types. You can even embed and print your charts alongside the data stored in a worksheet.

## Command Summary

Many of the commands and procedures appearing in this chapter are summarized in the following table:.

| Skill Set | To Perform this Task... | Do the Following... |
|---|---|---|
| **Working with Cells and Cell Data** | Name a cell range | SELECT: the desired range<br>CLICK: in the Name Box<br>TYPE: *range name* |
| | Create range names from labels appearing on the worksheet | SELECT: the desired range<br>CHOOSE: Insert → Name → Create |
| | Modify and delete range names | CHOOSE: Insert → Name → Define |
| | Paste a list of range names onto the worksheet | CHOOSE: Insert → Name → Paste |
| **Creating and Revising Formulas** | Modify and use cell references (absolute, relative, and mixed) | SELECT: the desired cell<br>CLICK: in the cell address in the Formula bar<br>PRESS: F4 (ABS key) to apply reference type |
| | Recalculate formulas in a worksheet | PRESS: F9 (CALC key) |
| | Use the Insert Function dialog box to enter a function and its arguments | CLICK: Insert Function button (fx)<br>SELECT: a category and function |

| | Use basic functions:<br>• Sum a range of values<br>• Average a range of values<br>• Count the numeric and date values in a range<br>• Find the lowest value in a range<br>• Find the highest value in a range | =SUM(*range*)<br>=AVERAGE(*range*)<br>=COUNT(*range*)<br><br>=MIN(*range*)<br>=MAX(*range*) |
| | Use date functions:<br>• Enter the current date and time<br>• Enter today's date | =NOW( )<br>=TODAY( ) |
| **Creating and Modifying Graphics** | Use the Chart Wizard to create a chart | SELECT: the cell range to plot<br>CLICK: Chart Wizard button ( ) |
| | Preview and print an embedded chart | SELECT: the desired range<br>CHOOSE: File → Print Area → Set Print Area<br>CLICK: Print Preview ( ) or Print ( ) |

## Key Terms

This section specifies page references for the key terms identified in this chapter. For a complete list of definitions, refer to the Glossary at the back of this learning guide.

absolute cell address, *p. EX 175*          mixed cell address, *p. EX 175*

arguments, *p. EX 179*          pie chart, *p. EX 194*

bar chart, *p. EX 193*          natural language formula, *p. EX 178*

Chart Wizard, *p. EX 195*          range name, *p. EX 170*

column chart, *p. EX 193*          relative cell address, *p. EX 175*

embedded chart, *p. EX 195*          scatter plot diagrams, *p. EX 194*

functions, *p. EX 180*          syntax, *p. EX 180*

line chart, *p. EX 193*          XY charts, *p. EX 194*

# Chapter
### q u i z

## Short Answer

1. Why would you want to name a range of cells?

2. How do you place a list of range names into the worksheet?

3. Name the two primary types of cell references and explain how they differ.

4. In order for natural language formulas to work effectively, how should the worksheet be organized?

5. Which function would you use to extract the highest value from a range named "salary"? How would you enter the function?

6. Which function would you use to place only the current time in your worksheet? What else might you want to do after entering the function?

7. What is the name of the dialog box that you can use to select functions from categories? How do you access this dialog box?

**8.** What is the name of the dialog box that can help you to enter a function's arguments correctly? How do you access this dialog box?

**9.** Describe the four steps in creating a chart using the Chart Wizard dialog boxes.

**10.** What are the black boxes called that surround an embedded chart? For what are they used?

## True/False

**1.** _____ Range names that you create use relative cell references.

**2.** _____ Cell addresses that you enter into formulas use, by default, absolute cell references.

**3.** _____ The "$s" in the cell reference $D$5 indicate an absolute cell reference.

**4.** _____ To ensure that a cell address appears in formulas as an absolute cell reference, move the cell pointer to the cell location and press `F4`.

**5.** _____ You enter a function using parentheses instead of the equal sign.

**6.** _____ The SUM function appears in the Math & Trig function category of the Insert Function dialog box.

**7.** _____ The TODAY function updates the computer's internal clock to the current date and time.

**8.** _____ A pie chart shows the proportions of individual components compared to the total.

**9.** _____ The Chart Wizard allows you to place a chart on a separate sheet in the workbook or as an embedded object on a worksheet.

**10.** _____ You can move and size a chart object once it is embedded on the worksheet.

## Multiple Choice

**1.** What menu command allows you to create range names using the labels that already appear in the worksheet?

a. Edit → Name → Create
b. Insert → Name → Create
c. Insert → Name → Define
d. Range → Name → Create

**2.** Which of the following symbols precedes an absolute cell reference?

a. &
b. @
c. $
d. #

**3.** In Edit mode, which key do you press to change a cell address to being absolute, relative, or mixed?

a. `F2`
b. `F3`
c. `F4`
d. `F9`

**4.** Which key do you press to recalculate or update a worksheet?

a. `F2`
b. `F3`
c. `F4`
d. `F9`

**5.** Which is the correct expression for adding the values stored in the cell range from A1 to A20?

a. =ADD(A1+A20)
b. =AutoSUM(A1,A20)
c. =SUM(A1+A20)
d. =SUM(A1:A20)

**6.** Which is the correct expression for determining the average of a range named "Units"?

a. =AVERAGE(Units)
b. =AVG(Units)
c. =SUM(Units/Average)
d. =UNITS(Average)

7. What does the COUNT function actually count?

   a. All of the cells in a range

   b. All of the cells containing data in a range

   c. Only those cells containing text and numbers

   d. Only those cells containing numeric or date values

8. Which button do you click to display the Insert Function dialog box?

   a. [ *fx* ]

   b. [ 📋 ]

   c. [ ⤺ ▾ ]

   d. [ Σ ▾ ]

9. What is the name of the step-by-step charting tool provided by Excel?

   a. Chart Master

   b. Chart Wizard

   c. Plot Master

   d. Plot Wizard

10. A chart may be created as a separate chart sheet or as an embedded object. In which step of the Chart Wizard do you specify how a chart is created and stored?

   a. Step 1

   b. Step 2

   c. Step 3

   d. Step 4

# Hands-On
### exercises

step by step

## 1. Creating and Using Range Names

In this exercise, you will practice working with named cell ranges in constructing formulas. To begin, you will use existing labels in the worksheet to define the range names automatically and then paste those names into the worksheet.

1. Open the data file named EX04HE01.

2. Save the workbook as "Departments" to your personal storage location.

3. To begin, name cell B8 "Total" using the Name Box in the Formula bar.

4. Use the existing worksheet labels in A2 through A7 to define range names for the data stored in cells B2 through B7. After choosing the Insert ➡ Name ➡ Create command, your screen should appear similar to the one shown in Figure 4.39.

**Figure 4.39**

Creating range names

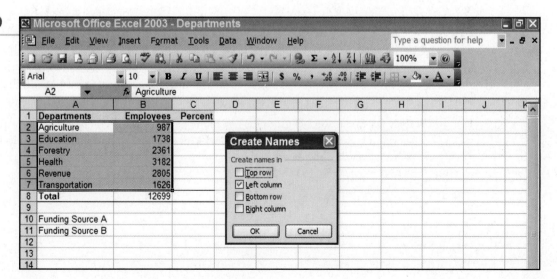

5. Starting in cell E2, paste a complete list of the range names that you just created into the worksheet.

**6.** Move to cell B10 in order to prepare for entering the first formula.

**7.** To enter a formula using the named cell ranges:
TYPE: =
CLICK: cell B3
Notice that "Education" appears in the Formula bar in place of the cell B3 reference.

**8.** To continue the formula:
TYPE: +
CLICK: cell B5
CLICK: Enter button (☑)
The expression now reads "=Education+Health" in the Formula bar.

**9.** Move to cell B11 to enter the next formula.

**10.** Using the typing or pointing method, enter an expression that totals the remaining departments not included in the previous formula. Before pressing (**ENTER**), your screen should appear similar to the one shown in Figure 4.40.

**Figure 4.40**

Entering a formula using named ranges

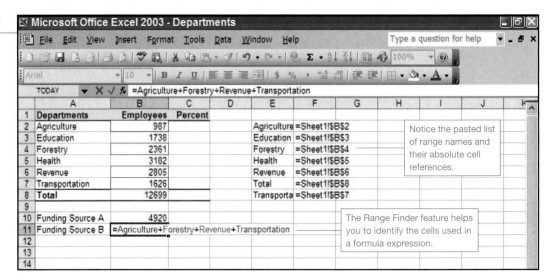

**11.** Ensure that you complete the formula entry by pressing (**ENTER**).

**12.** Now calculate the employment percentage for each department. Starting in cell C2, enter a formula that can be later used for copying. To do so, specify an absolute cell reference for the Total value and a relative cell reference for the Department value. (*Hint:* A range name provides an absolute cell reference. Therefore, you cannot use the range name "Agriculture" in the formula expression.)

**13.** Copy the formula in cell C2 to the remaining departments in column C using the fill handle, as shown in Figure 4.41. (*Hint:* The fill handle for a cell or cell range is the small black box in the bottom right-hand corner of the range selection.)

**Figure 4.41**

Using the fill
handle to copy a
formula

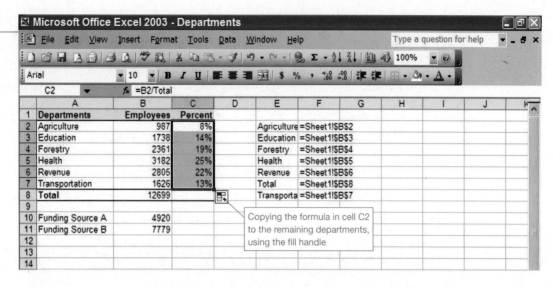

**14.** On your own, select the cells in the range C2:C8 and view the contents in the Formula bar. Notice
that the relative cell references (B2, B3, . . . B8) adjust automatically. The range name "Total"
remains absolute.

**15.** Save and then close the "Departments" workbook.

step by step

## 2. Entering Functions

You will now practice using some of Excel 2003's built-in functions to complete an existing worksheet.
You also use the AutoFill feature to create a series and then the Fill command to copy formulas.

**1.** Open the data file named EX04HE02 to display the worksheet shown in Figure 4.42.

**Figure 4.42**

Opening the
EX04HE02
workbook

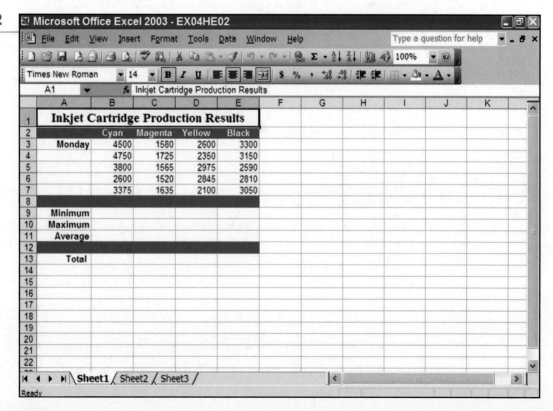

**2.** Save the workbook as "Inkjet Results" in your personal storage location.

**3.** Use the fill handle to complete a series listing the days of the week (Monday through Friday) in cells A3 to A7.

**4.** In cell B9, enter the following function to calculate the minimum production amount for cyan cartridges:
TYPE: **=min(b3:b7)**
PRESS: (ENTER)

**5.** Using the same approach, enter formulas in cells B10 and B11 to calculate the maximum and average production for cyan.

**6.** Select the cell range from B9 to E11 and then use the Edit → Fill → Right command to copy the formulas to columns C, D, and E.

**7.** Select the cell range from A2 to E7 and then use the Insert → Name → Create command to assign range names using the existing row and column labels, as shown in Figure 4.43.

**Figure 4.43**

Creating range names

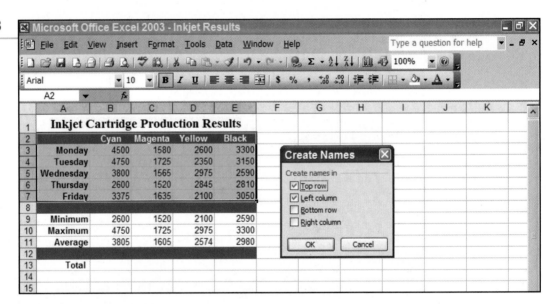

**8.** Paste a list of the range names starting in cell G2.

**9.** Adjust the widths for columns G and H to their best fit.

**10.** To calculate the total production for cyan cartridges:
SELECT: cell B13
TYPE: **=sum(cyan)**
PRESS: (ENTER)

**11.** Using the same technique, calculate the totals for the Magenta, Yellow, and Black columns. (*Note:* You cannot use the Edit, Fill, Right command, because the named range "Cyan" uses an absolute cell reference.)

**12.** Figure 4.44 shows the completed worksheet. Save and then close the workbook.

**Figure 4.44**

Completing the
"Inkjet Results"
workbook

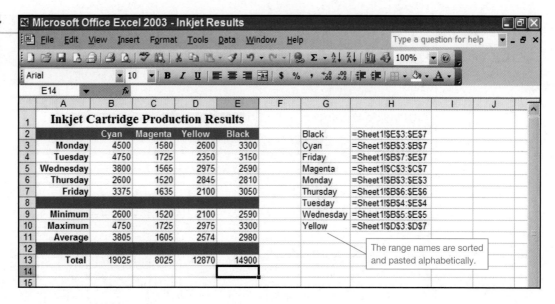

step by step

## 3. Creating an Embedded Chart

You will now practice creating an embedded column chart using Excel 2003's Chart Wizard. You will then print out this chart alongside its worksheet data.

1. Open the data file named EX04HE03.

2. Save the workbook as "Citywide Employment" to your personal storage location.

3. As shown in Figure 4.45, select the cell range from A3 to G5 for plotting the data in a chart. (*Note:* You do not include the "Total" row or "Total" column in the range selection.)

**Figure 4.45**

Selecting the
data to plot in a
chart

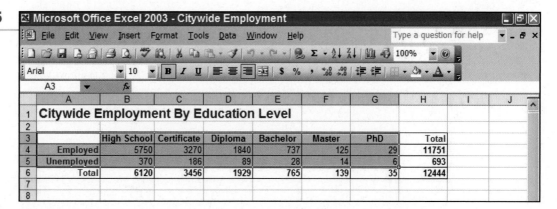

4. Launch the Chart Wizard by clicking its button (📊) on the Standard toolbar.

5. To display the two categories, Employed and Unemployed, side by side in a chart, select a "Column" chart type with a "Stacked Column" sub-type; then proceed to Step 2 of 4.

6. Accept the default range selection and then proceed to Step 3 of 4.

7. On the *Titles* tab of Step 3 in the Chart Wizard:
TYPE: **Education Level** into the *Category (X) axis* text box
TYPE: **Population** into the *Value (Y) axis* text box
Your screen should now appear similar to the one shown in Figure 4.46.

**Figure 4.46**

Completing Step
3 of the Chart
Wizard dialog
box

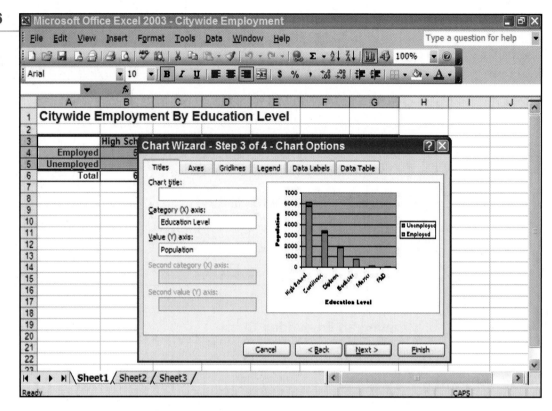

8. Proceed to the last step in the Chart Wizard dialog box.

9. In the last step of the dialog box, click the *As object in* option button and then click ⌐ Finish ⌐. The chart object appears in the middle of the application window.

10. Move the embedded chart below the data area using the mouse pointer.

11. Enlarge the size of the embedded chart by dragging its selection boxes, so that it appears similar to the one shown in Figure 4.47. (*Note:* Because of their small values, categories such as "Master" and "PhD" do not show up well in this chart. Fortunately, Excel 2003 allows you to modify a chart's type and formatting at any time in order to improve its appearance.)

**Figure 4.47**

Sizing and
moving an
embedded chart

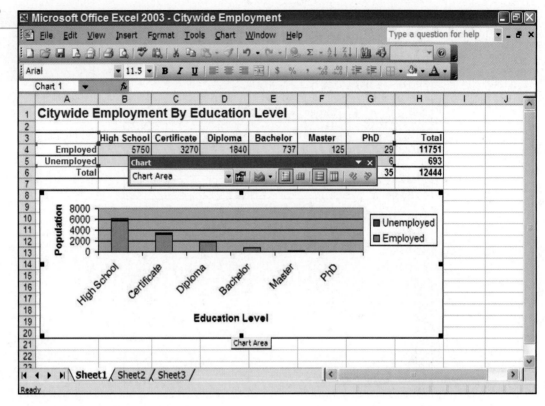

**12.** Save and then print the worksheet data and chart. When you are finished, close the "Citywide
Employment" workbook.

on your own

## 4. Creating a Mortgage Rate Chart

In this exercise, your business associate has created a worksheet for you compiling mortgage rates from the
previous six quarters. Your objective is to enhance the worksheet's presentation by embedding a line chart
alongside or below the data. To begin, open the EX04HE04 workbook (Figure 4.48) and then save it as
"Mortgage Rates" to your personal storage location.

**Figure 4.48**

Opening the
EX04HE04
workbook

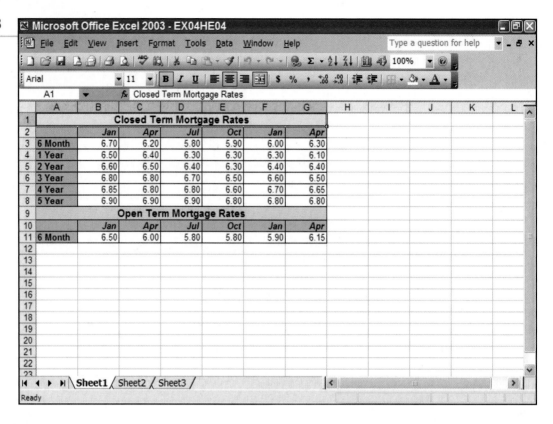

Using the data for closed term mortgage rates only, select the cell range from A2 to G8 and then launch the Chart Wizard. In the Chart Wizard dialog boxes, select a line chart with markers displayed at each data value and then add the title "Average Mortgage Rates" to the top of the chart. Embed the chart as an object and then move and size it to appear similar to the chart shown in Figure 4.49.

**Figure 4.49**

Embedding a line
chart into the
worksheet

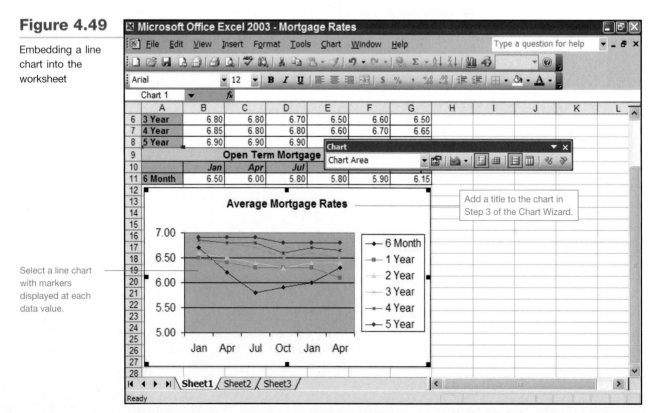

Select a line chart
with markers
displayed at each
data value.

When you are satisfied with the results, set the print area to include both the data and the embedded chart object. Preview and then print the worksheet. Finally, save and then close the "Mortgage Rates" workbook.

on your own

## 5. Calculating Auto Fuel Statistics

In this exercise, you will practice naming ranges and entering functions. To begin, open the EX04HE05 workbook and then save it as "Auto Fuel" to your personal storage location.

Let's create some range names. Assign the name "Capacity" to the cell range B2:B7. Assign the name "City" to the cell range C2:C7. Assign the name "Hwy" to the cell range D2:D7. Paste a list of the range names in column F. In row 8, calculate the average for each column using their respective range names and the AVERAGE function. Format the new values to appear with two decimal places only. For more practice, enter a function in cell B10 that returns a count of the number of numerical entries in the "Capacity" range. In cell C10, display the minimum miles per gallon city rating. In cell D10, display the maximum miles per gallon highway rating. Then, place formatted descriptive labels above each calculation in row 9. Your worksheet should appear similar to the one shown in Figure 4.50.

**Figure 4.50**

Completing the "Auto Fuel" workbook

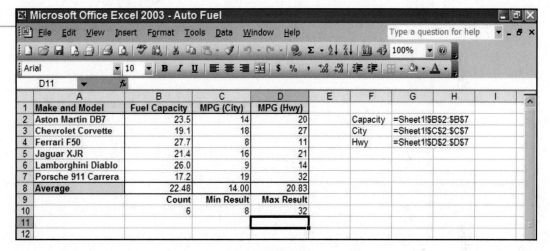

Preview and then print the worksheet using a landscape page orientation. When you are finished, save and then close the "Auto Fuel" workbook.

on your own

## 6. Displaying Expenses in a Pie Chart

For additional practice creating charts, open the EX04HE06 data file. Before continuing, save the workbook as "Expense Chart" to your personal storage location. Then, complete the worksheet by inputting your monthly expenses into the appropriate cells.

Using the Chart Wizard, create a pie chart of these expenses. Do not add a title to the chart. Save it as an embedded object in the worksheet. Once it appears on the worksheet, size the chart so that the information is easily read. Position the chart to the right of the worksheet data. Print the worksheet data and the chart on the same page, as shown in Figure 4.51. Remember to use the Set Print Area command and Print Preview to ensure that your settings are correct.

**Figure 4.51**

Plotting expenses using a pie chart

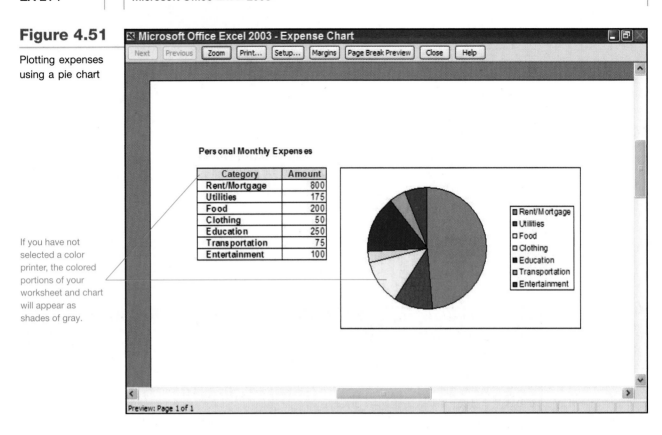

If you have not selected a color printer, the colored portions of your worksheet and chart will appear as shades of gray.

When you are satisfied with the results, send the worksheet and embedded chart to the printer. Save and then close the "Expense Chart" workbook. Then exit Microsoft Office Excel 2003.

# CaseStudy     INTERIOR FOOTBALL LEAGUE (IFL)

The Interior Football League consists of eight elite football teams in as many communities. The IFL is run by a small group of dedicated volunteers who handle everything from coaching to administration. An ex-player himself, Doug Allen has volunteered for the organization for the past four years. In addition to fundraising, Doug is responsible for keeping records and tracking results for all of the teams in the league.

Shortly after the end of each season, the IFL publishes a newsletter that provides various statistics and other pertinent information about the season. In the past, this newsletter required weeks of effort, followed by days of typing results into a word processor. After enrolling in an Excel 2003 course, Doug now realizes that worksheets and charts can help him to complete his upcoming tasks. Specifically, he has recently learned how to use ranges and functions in Excel and now wants to use them to produce worksheets that can be incorporated into the newsletter.

In the following case problems, assume the role of Doug and perform the same steps that he identifies.

1. It is 8:00 on a Sunday evening when Doug decides to sit down at his home computer and spend some time working on the IFL newsletter. After loading Excel, he opens the EX04CP01 workbook that he has been using to project next year's attendance levels. Doug wants to communicate the fine growth in attendance that the IFL has been experiencing. Before continuing, he saves the workbook as "IFL Attendance" to his personal storage location.

   Having learned about range names, Doug's first step is to use the Name Box and apply a range name of "Factor" to cell C12. Then, he selects the cell range A2:B10 and uses the Insert → Name → Create command to create range names from the selection's row and column labels. To verify that the range names are correct, Doug selects cell E3 in the worksheet and then pastes a list of all existing named ranges. After returning to cell A1, Doug's worksheet appears similar to Figure 4.52.

**Figure 4.52**

Pasting range names into the worksheet

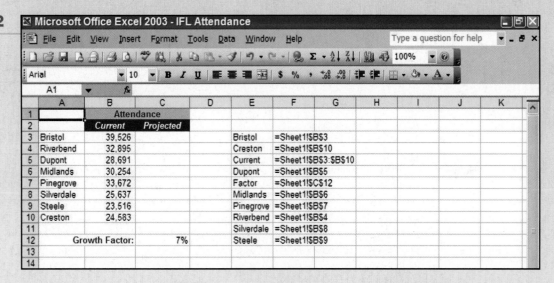

Doug remembers that to calculate next year's attendance using a growth factor formula, he will have to use both relative and absolute cell addresses. Otherwise, when he performs a copy operation, the formula's cell addresses will not be adjusted automatically. Doug wants to ensure that the formulas always use the value in cell C12 as the growth factor. Fortunately, he also remembers that a named range is, by default, an absolute reference. Therefore, using a relative cell address and the "Factor" range name, Doug can complete his task. To begin, he enters the formula **=b3*(1+Factor)** into cell C3. Notice that Doug typed "b3" and not "Bristol" into the cell. (*Hint:* The range name "Bristol" refers to the absolute cell address $B$3 and not to the relative cell address that is required for this calculation.) This formula calculates next year's projected attendance for Bristol.

Doug uses Excel's AutoFill feature to extend the formula in cell C3 for the rest of the teams. As shown in Figure 4.53, he uses the Format Painter to copy the numbering formats from column B to the new results in column C. Doug saves and then closes the workbook.

**Figure 4.53**

Formatting the
worksheet results

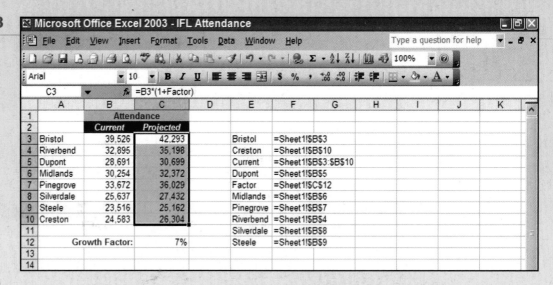

2. Last week, Doug began constructing a worksheet that shows the team standings at the end of the
   IFL's regular season play. To review the worksheet, he opens the EX04CP02 file and then saves it as
   "IFL Standings" to his personal storage location.

   With the teams already in the proper order, Doug wants to chart their results. He selects the cell
   range B2:C10 and then launches the Chart Wizard. In the first step, Doug selects a "Clustered bar
   with a 3-D visual effect" chart. In Step 3, Doug removes the chart title that appears in the dialog box.
   He then clicks the Finish command button. When the embedded chart appears in the application
   window, Doug sizes it so that all the team names are visible on the vertical axis. He then moves the
   chart so that it appears as shown in Figure 4.54.

**Figure 4.54**

Analyzing data
using an
embedded chart

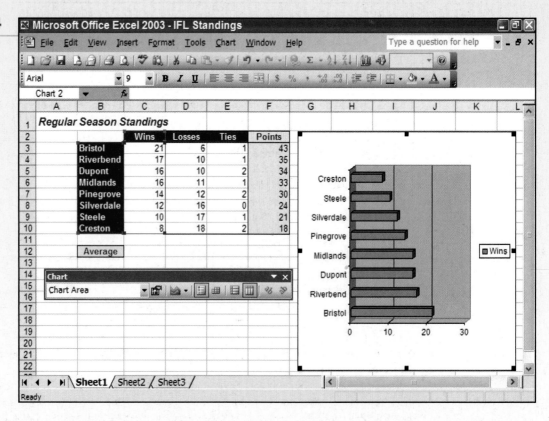

Continuing his work, Doug enters a formula into cell C12 that averages the values in that column. He uses the Edit → Fill → Right command to extend the formula across to column F. Finally, Doug prints the worksheet and chart using the landscape page orientation. He then saves and closes the workbook.

3. With the deadline for the season-end newsletter fast approaching, Doug is determined to finish the Team Statistics worksheet. He opens the EX04CP03 data file and then saves it as "IFL Team Stats" to his personal storage location.

After double-checking to make sure that the formulas in column D are correct, Doug copies the formula from cell D3 to the cell range D14:D21. He then uses the AutoSum button (Σ ▾) to enter SUM functions into cells C11 and C22 that sum the points for Offense and Defense, respectively. He applies boldface to the new results. In column G, Doug uses Excel's built-in functions to find the highest, lowest, and average number of points for both Offense and Defense. He names the two data ranges in column C (C3:C10 and C14:C21) and then enters the functions into the appropriate cells, as shown in Figure 4.55. When he is finished, Doug saves and then closes the workbook.

**Figure 4.55**

Completing the "IFL Team Stats" worksheet

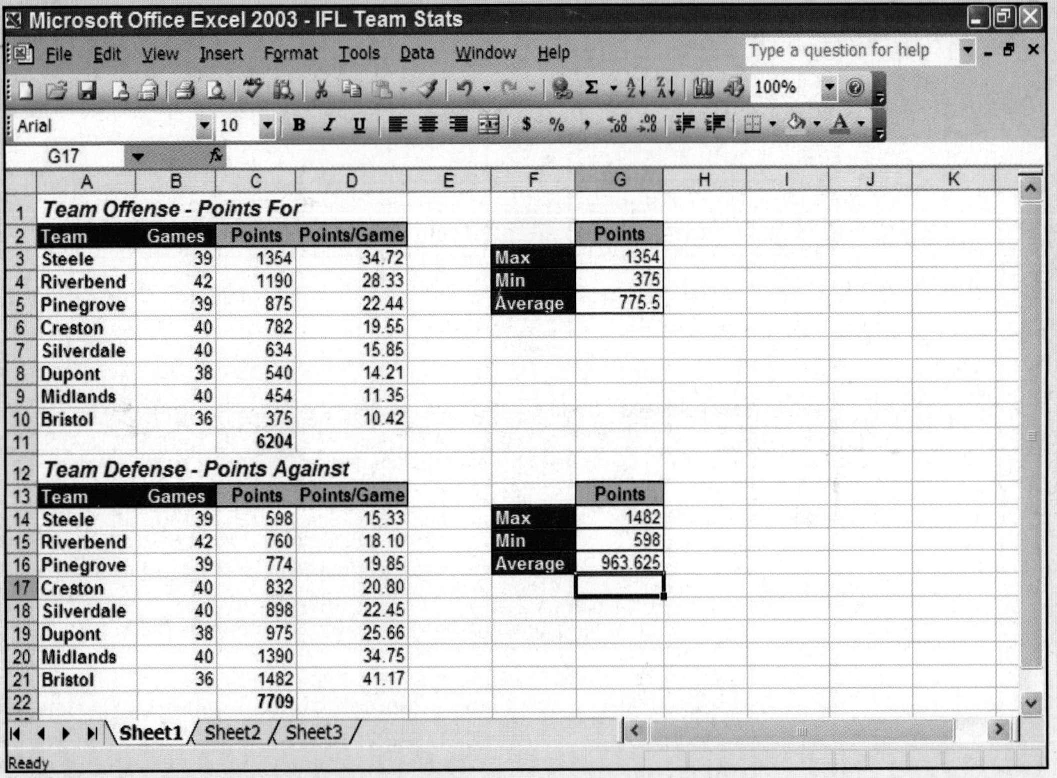


| | A | B | C | D | E | F | G |
|---|---|---|---|---|---|---|---|
| 1 | Team Offense - Points For | | | | | | |
| 2 | Team | Games | Points | Points/Game | | | Points |
| 3 | Steele | 39 | 1354 | 34.72 | | Max | 1354 |
| 4 | Riverbend | 42 | 1190 | 28.33 | | Min | 375 |
| 5 | Pinegrove | 39 | 875 | 22.44 | | Average | 775.5 |
| 6 | Creston | 40 | 782 | 19.55 | | | |
| 7 | Silverdale | 40 | 634 | 15.85 | | | |
| 8 | Dupont | 38 | 540 | 14.21 | | | |
| 9 | Midlands | 40 | 454 | 11.35 | | | |
| 10 | Bristol | 36 | 375 | 10.42 | | | |
| 11 | | | 6204 | | | | |
| 12 | Team Defense - Points Against | | | | | | |
| 13 | Team | Games | Points | Points/Game | | | Points |
| 14 | Steele | 39 | 598 | 15.33 | | Max | 1482 |
| 15 | Riverbend | 42 | 760 | 18.10 | | Min | 598 |
| 16 | Pinegrove | 39 | 774 | 19.85 | | Average | 963.625 |
| 17 | Creston | 40 | 832 | 20.80 | | | |
| 18 | Silverdale | 40 | 898 | 22.45 | | | |
| 19 | Dupont | 38 | 975 | 25.66 | | | |
| 20 | Midlands | 40 | 1390 | 34.75 | | | |
| 21 | Bristol | 36 | 1482 | 41.17 | | | |
| 22 | | | 7709 | | | | |

4. The final worksheet that Doug needs to compile is for the "Points Per Quarter" statistics. Doug opens the EX04CP04 data file and saves it as "IFL Scoring" in his personal storage location.

Using one of Excel's built-in functions, Doug calculates and displays the total points scored by the first team in column F. After entering the function, he uses the cell's fill handle to extend the formula to the rest of the teams. Next, he uses the appropriate function in row 11 to calculate the average for the first quarter. He formats the result to display with no decimal places and then extends the formula to cover columns C through F. Doug completes the worksheet using the MIN and MAX functions to calculate the high and low scores for each period. As before, he extends these functions to cover the remaining columns.

Satisfied with the results thus far, Doug decides to place an embedded stacked column chart under the data table. He sizes and positions the chart to appear similar to Figure 4.56. Doug then previews and prints the worksheet and chart on the same page. He saves and closes the workbook and then exits Microsoft Office Excel 2003.

**Figure 4.56**

Completing the
"IFL Scoring"
worksheet

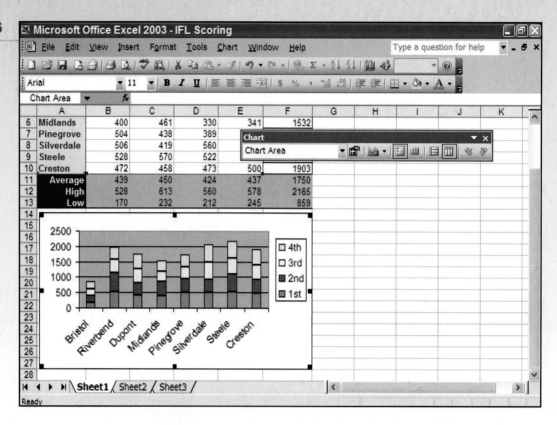

## Answers to Self-Check Questions

**4.1**   Why is "AD2002" an unacceptable name for a cell range? You cannot
name a cell range using an actual cell reference on the worksheet.

**4.2**   When might you use the Function Arguments dialog box or Insert
Function dialog box to enter a function into the worksheet? If you need
help entering the arguments in the correct order or if you cannot remember
a function's name or proper syntax, you can use these tools to refresh your
memory or to assist you in completing the task.

**4.3**   What must you do when selecting the print range for a worksheet that
contains an embedded chart? Because charts do not appear in cells on a
worksheet, you must be sure to select the print range to include these
graphic objects. For example, select the cells that appear underneath the
embedded chart that you want to print.

# Notes

# Notes

# Notes

# Notes

# Notes

# Notes

# Microsoft®Office**Excel**®

## 2003

## CHAPTER 5

 # Presenting Your Data

### PREREQUISITES

This chapter presumes that you are familiar with Excel's basic editing and formatting commands. You also build upon your knowledge of plotting data in a chart, first introduced near the end of Chapter 4. The remainder of the chapter focuses on enhancing worksheets with embedded objects, drawing tools, and graphic files.

### LEARNING OBJECTIVES

After reading this chapter, you will be able to:

- Indent, align, wrap, and shrink a cell entry

- Create and apply number formats and styles to maintain consistency and to speed worksheet formatting

- Use drawing tools to create and format lines and shapes for enhancing a worksheet's appearance

- Insert WordArt objects, clip art, photographs, and other embedded objects into a worksheet

- Create, modify, and format chart sheets and elements

# 5.1 Formatting Cells

Microsoft Office Excel 2003 provides a wealth of formatting options to improve the appearance of a worksheet, its individual cells, and the contents within those cells. While the more popular formatting commands such as changing a cell's font and fill color were described in previous chapters, this module introduces additional features to help round out your formatting toolkit. As with other computer programs, knowing what you can do with the software is as important as remembering how to do it. In the first module, you learn how to manipulate text within a cell. You also apply formatting options using the AutoFormat command and implement conditional formatting in a cell range.

### 5.1.1 Indenting and Aligning Text

→ ## Feature

Just as you may indent a paragraph in Microsoft Word to make it stand out from the rest of the document, you can indent a text label, date, or numeric value within a cell. Indenting has the effect of aligning a cell's contents to either the left or right borders and then moving the entire entry one or more character spaces in from the border. Apart from indenting text, you can align a cell's contents vertically between a row's top and bottom borders. This feature is especially useful when you increase a cell's height and add a background fill color.

→ ## Method

Using the Menu bar to indent a cell's contents:

- CHOOSE: Format → Cells
- CLICK: *Alignment* tab
- SELECT: Left (Indent) or Right (Indent) from the *Horizontal* drop-down list box
- SELECT: a value in the *Indent* spin box to indent the cell contents
- CLICK: OK command button

Using the Menu bar to align a cell's contents vertically:

- CHOOSE: Format → Cells
- CLICK: *Alignment* tab
- SELECT: an option from the *Vertical* drop-down list box
- CLICK: OK command button

Using the Formatting toolbar:

- CLICK: Increase Indent (⊞),

  *or*

- CLICK: Decrease Indent (⊞)

→ ## Practice

You will now practice indenting and aligning text in an existing worksheet. Before proceeding, ensure that Microsoft Office Excel 2003 is loaded.

**1.** Open the data file named EX0510 to display the workbook shown in Figure 5.1.

**Figure 5.1**

Opening the
EX0510
workbook

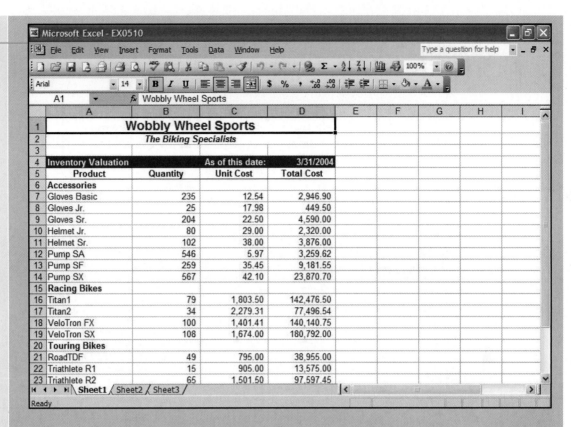

**2.** Save the workbook as "Wobbly Inventory" to your personal storage location.

**3.** In the Product column (A), indenting the product names will set them apart from their categories. To do so:
SELECT: cell range from A7 to A14

**4.** To indent the selection to the right:
CLICK: Increase Indent button ( ) twice

**5.** To indent the other categories' product entries:
SELECT: cell range from A16 to A19
PRESS: **CTRL** and hold it down
SELECT: cell range from A21 to A25
Two cell ranges should now be highlighted on the worksheet. (*Note:* Remember to release the **CTRL** key after selecting the last range.)

**6.** This time, let's use the Format Cells dialog box to indent the selection:
CHOOSE: Format → Cells
CLICK: *Alignment* tab

**7.** By clicking the up arrow attached to the spin box:
SELECT: 2 in the *Indent* spin box
Your screen should now appear similar to the one shown in Figure 5.2.

**Figure 5.2**

Indenting the contents of the selected range

Specify the number of character spaces to indent to the right

Two separate ranges selected at the same time

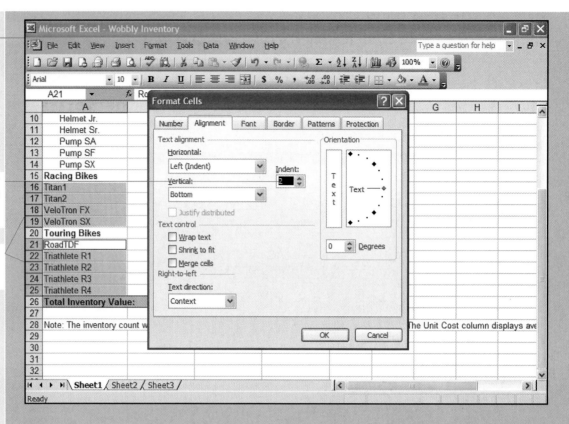

8. To accept the dialog box and continue:
   CLICK: OK command button
   The cell entries in the selected ranges should now appear indented.

9. To demonstrate how you can align the contents of a cell range vertically, do the following:
   SELECT: cell range from A4 to D4

10. Let's start by increasing the cell height in this row:
    CHOOSE: Format → Row → Height
    TYPE: 24 into the *Row height* text box
    CLICK: OK command button
    Your worksheet should now appear similar to the one shown in Figure 5.3. Notice that the cell contents remain aligned to the bottom border.

**Figure 5.3**

Increasing the cell height in a row

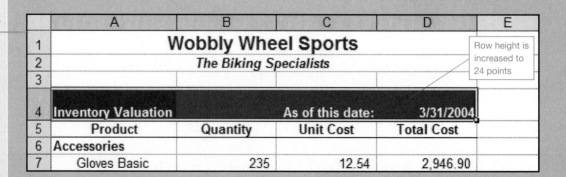

11. To center the cell contents vertically:
    CHOOSE: Format → Cells

**12.** On the *Alignment* tab of the dialog box:
SELECT: Center from the *Vertical* drop-down list box
CLICK: OK command button
The row now appears as shown below.

| 4 | **Inventory Valuation** | **As of this date:** | **3/31/2004** |

**13.** PRESS: CTRL + HOME to cancel the selection

**14.** Save the workbook, and keep it open for use in the next lesson.

## 5.1.2 Wrapping and Shrinking Text

### → Feature

In addition to indenting text, you can wrap a longer text entry within a cell, enter line breaks, and shrink an entry to fit within a column. These formatting features, along with aligning, merging, and splitting cells, are especially useful for enhancing titles, headings, comments, and larger blocks of text.

### → Method

- CHOOSE: Format → Cells

- CLICK: *Alignment* tab

- SELECT: *Wrap text* check box in the *Text control* area,

  *or*

- SELECT: *Shrink to fit* check box in the *Text control* area

- CLICK: OK command button

### → Practice

You will now practice wrapping a short sentence within a cell and shrinking a text entry to fit in its respective column. Ensure that you've completed the previous lesson and that the "Wobbly Inventory" workbook is displayed.

**1.** To format the appearance of a sentence or paragraph that appears in a single cell, do the following:
SELECT: cell range from A28 to D28
(*Note:* The text entry is stored entirely in the leftmost cell (A28) of the selected range.)

**2.** You will now merge the selected cells to form a single cell and then wrap the entry to appear between its column borders. To do so:
CHOOSE: Format → Cells
SELECT: Center in the *Vertical* drop-down list box
SELECT: *Wrap text* check box so that a ✓ appears
SELECT: *Merge cells* check box so that a ✓ appears
CLICK: OK command button
(*Note:* Remember that you can split a merged cell by removing the check mark from the *Merge cells* check box.)

**3.** Now, increase the height of the row:
CHOOSE: Format → Row → Height
TYPE: **50**
CLICK: OK command button
All of the text in the cell entry should now be visible, as shown in Figure 5.4.

## Figure 5.4

Formatting the display of a long text entry

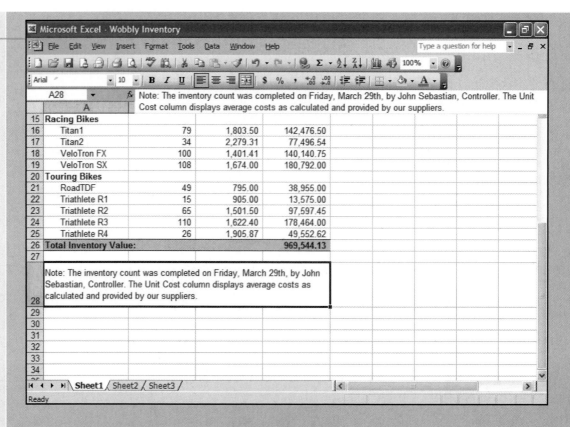

4. If you want to specify where Excel inserts line breaks in a longer text entry, use the **ALT** + **ENTER** keystroke combination. To illustrate, let's enter Edit mode:
   PRESS: **F2** (Edit key)

5. Position the I-beam mouse pointer to the left of the word "by" in the first line, as shown below, and then click the left mouse button once to place the insertion point in the cell.

|     | Note: The inventory count was completed on Friday, March 29th, by John Sebastian, Controller. The Unit Cost column displays average costs as calculated and provided by our suppliers. |
| 28  | |

I-beam mouse pointer

6. To insert a line break:
   PRESS: **ALT** + **ENTER**
   Notice that the second line now starts with the word "by."

7. Insert another line break so that the third line begins with the word "average," as shown below.

The insertion point now appears at the beginning of the third line

|     | Note: The inventory count was completed on Friday, March 29th, by John Sebastian, Controller. The Unit Cost column displays average costs as calculated and provided by our suppliers. |
| 28  | |

8. To complete the editing process:
PRESS: ENTER

9. To shrink an entry to fit within its cell borders:
SELECT: cell A26
CHOOSE: Format → Cells
SELECT: *Shrink to fit* check box so that a ✓ appears
CLICK: OK command button
Excel will adjust this cell entry automatically if you reduce the width of the column. Your screen should appear similar to the one shown in Figure 5.5.

10. Save the workbook, and keep it open for use in the next lesson.

**Figure 5.5**

Manipulating text entries in a worksheet

| | A | B | C | D | E | F | G | H | I |
|---|---|---|---|---|---|---|---|---|---|
| 15 | **Racing Bikes** | | | | | | | | |
| 16 | Titan1 | 79 | 1,803.50 | 142,476.50 | | | | | |
| 17 | Titan2 | 34 | 2,279.31 | 77,496.54 | | | | | |
| 18 | VeloTron FX | 100 | 1,401.41 | 140,140.75 | | | | | |
| 19 | VeloTron SX | 108 | 1,674.00 | 180,792.00 | | | | | |
| 20 | **Touring Bikes** | | | | | | | | |
| 21 | RoadTDF | 49 | 795.00 | 38,955.00 | | | | | |
| 22 | Triathlete R1 | 15 | 905.00 | 13,575.00 | | | | | |
| 23 | Triathlete R2 | 65 | 1,501.50 | 97,597.45 | | | | | |
| 24 | Triathlete R3 | 110 | 1,622.40 | 178,464.00 | | | | | |
| 25 | Triathlete R4 | 26 | 1,905.87 | 49,552.62 | | | | | |
| 26 | Total Inventory Value: | | | 969,544.13 | | | | | |
| 27 | | | | | | | | | |
| 28 | Note: The inventory count was completed on Friday, March 29th, by John Sebastian, Controller. The Unit Cost column displays average costs as calculated and provided by our suppliers. | | | | | | | | |
| 29 | | | | | | | | | |
| 30 | | | | | | | | | |
| 31 | | | | | | | | | |
| 32 | | | | | | | | | |
| 33 | | | | | | | | | |
| 34 | | | | | | | | | |

Shrinking an entry to fit within a cell

Merging and wrapping a text entry across four columns

### 5.1.3 Selecting AutoFormat Options

→ **Feature**

The AutoFormat command lets you select a predefined table format for a cell range, complete with numeric formats, alignments, borders, shading, and colors. By default, all of the formatting elements for the chosen AutoFormat option are applied to the worksheet selection. If this is not the desired effect, Excel 2003 allows you to limit the application of formatting commands to a selection of elements. You may, for example, want to format a range using an AutoFormat's color and font selections without adjusting the existing column widths.

→ **Method**

- SELECT: cell range to format
- CHOOSE: Format → AutoFormat
- CLICK: Options command button
- SELECT: an option from the *Table format* list box
- SELECT: the desired options in the *Formats to apply* area
- CLICK: OK command button

→ **Practice**

Let's practice using the AutoFormat command to apply selected formatting options to a cell range. Ensure that you've completed the previous lesson and that the "Wobbly Inventory" worksheet is displayed.

**1.** Before choosing the AutoFormat command, select the cell range that you want formatted. If you do not preselect a range, Excel tries to determine the range for you. To illustrate:
SELECT: cell A4
CHOOSE: Format → AutoFormat
Notice that the table area in the worksheet is selected behind the AutoFormat dialog box. (*Hint:* To better view the selected area, move the AutoFormat dialog box out of the way by dragging its Title bar.)

**2.** Each table format includes six formatting elements: *Number, Font, Alignment, Border, Patterns,* and *Width/Height*. You can specify which portions of an AutoFormat style you want to apply to the selected range. To make your selections:
CLICK: Options command button
Your screen should now appear similar to the one shown in Figure 5.6.

**Figure 5.6**

AutoFormat
dialog box

Select a table
format to apply in
this list area

Excel selects a
range to format
based on a "best
guess"

Select the
formatting elements
to apply

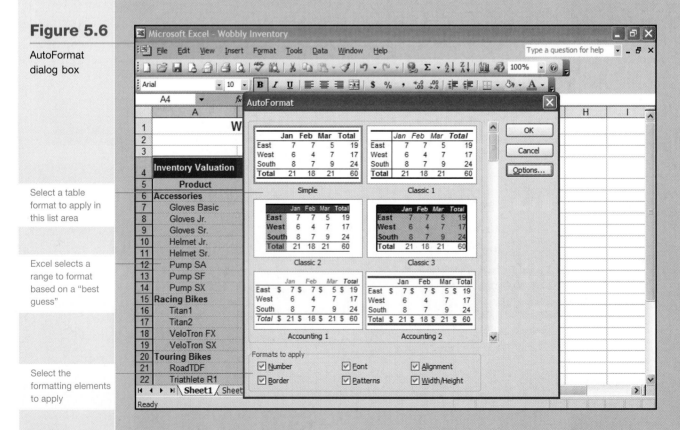

**3.** To apply only the *Font* and *Patterns* selections:
CLICK: *Number* check box so that no ✓ appears
CLICK: *Border* check box so that no ✓ appears
CLICK: *Alignment* check box so that no ✓ appears
CLICK: *Width/Height* check box so that no ✓ appears
Notice that the table previews in the list area are updated dynamically.

**4.** To complete the AutoFormat selection, scroll down the list box and then:
SELECT: List 2
CLICK: OK command button
Notice that the worksheet is formatted using font selections and colors, but that the indentation and number formatting remains the same.

**5.** On your own, apply only the *Font* and *Patterns* selections for the "Colorful 2" AutoFormat option. (*Hint:* Excel does not remember the last selections you made in the AutoFormat dialog box.)

**6.** Move your cell pointer to A1. Your screen should now appear similar to the one shown in Figure 5.7.

**7.** Save the changes, and then close the workbook.

**Figure 5.7**

Applying selected elements of an AutoFormat option

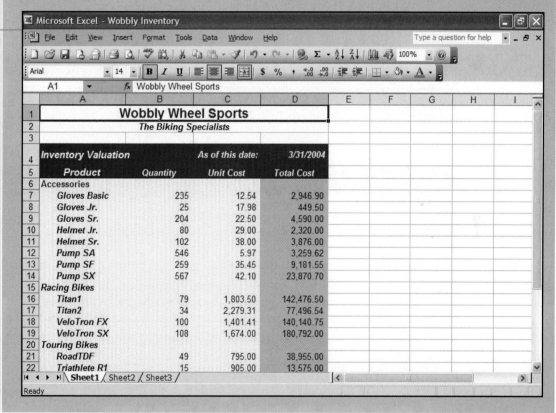

   **5.1**   What are the two ways that you can indent a cell entry?

# 5.2 Using Number Formats and Styles

Excel 2003 provides several built-in number formats and styles for improving the readability and display of your worksheet data. Number formats change the appearance of values by adding standard symbols, such as dollar signs, commas, and percentage symbols. Styles, which are most commonly associated with word processing, ensure formatting consistency and reduce repetitive procedures. Similar in function to an AutoFormat option, a **style** is a set of formatting characteristics that has been assigned a name. In addition to applying these formatting options, you learn how to create and define your own custom formats and styles in this module.

### 5.2.1 Using Number Formats

→ ## Feature

You can enter a formatted number (for example, 87.5%) into a worksheet by typing the number along with the desired symbols. To apply formatting to an existing value, choose a format from the *Number* tab in the Format Cells dialog box. Regardless of how a value is displayed, Excel stores values (numbers and dates) internally in their raw or unformatted form. In other words, the value appearing in a cell may not be equal to the raw value used by Excel in performing a calculation.

Let's look at an example. Take two values, 2.3 and 2.4, that are stored in cells A1 and A2. These values are then formatted to display without decimal places, leaving the number 2 displayed in each cell. In cell A3, you enter the formula =A1+A2 and then format the cell similarly. You will find that Excel correctly calculates 2.3+2.4 to equal 4.7, and then rounds the answer to display 5 in cell A3. So now, due to number formatting, your worksheet displays 2+2=5. Be aware of this formatting paradox when evaluating a worksheet's results!

→ ## Method

To view a cell's actual value:

- SELECT: the desired cell

- View the value that appears in the Formula bar.

To remove a cell's formatting characteristics:

- SELECT: the desired cell

- CHOOSE: Edit → Clear → Formats

→ ## Practice

You will now practice applying and removing number and date formatting. Ensure that no workbooks appear in the Excel 2003 application window.

**1.** To display a new workbook:
CLICK: New button ([ ]) on the Standard toolbar

**2.** Enter the following data, starting in cell A1, exactly as shown:
TYPE: 1000
PRESS: ⬇
TYPE: $5,000.00
PRESS: ⬇
TYPE: 5/10/2004
PRESS: [ENTER]
Your worksheet should now contain the following information. (*Note:* In Windows, the computer's default display format for date values is set using the Regional Settings option in the Control Panel. Based on this setting, you may see "5/10/04" appear in cell A3.)

| | A |
|---|---|
| 1 | 1000 |
| 2 | $5,000.00 |
| 3 | 5/10/2004 |

- No number format applied to data
- Currency number format with two decimal places
- Date format using month/day/year order

**3.** To view the actual value in a cell:
SELECT: cell A2 and then look in the Formula bar
Notice that the $5,000.00 entry appears as 5000 in the Formula bar.

**4.** The **cell layer** in a worksheet holds both the data and formatting (number formats, borders, and font attributes) for a particular cell address. Each of these elements can be changed without affecting the other. For example, you can apply formatting to a cell without affecting its contents. It's also important to understand that a cell without data may still have formats associated with it. These formats remain until they, too, are cleared from the cell. To illustrate:
SELECT: cell range from A1 to A3
PRESS: `DELETE`
Notice that the worksheet once again appears empty.

**5.** Although the cells are now cleared of data, you will see that the formats are retained. Do the following:
TYPE: 12345
PRESS: ⬇
TYPE: 12345
PRESS: ⬇
TYPE: 12345
PRESS: `ENTER`

**6.** Move the cell pointer to cell A5. Your worksheet should now display the values shown here. Notice that pressing `DELETE` removes only the contents of the selected cell range and not its formatting.

| | A |
|---|---|
| 1 | 12345 |
| 2 | $12,345.00 |
| 3 | 10/18/1933 |

**7.** To remove the formatting information that is stored in the cell layer:
SELECT: cell range from A1 to A3
CHOOSE: Edit → Clear → Formats
Notice that the value "12345" appears in all of the cells.

**8.** Close the workbook without saving the changes.

## In Addition UNDERSTANDING HOW EXCEL 2003 STORES DATES AND TIMES

Excel stores dates as serial values equal to the number of days that have elapsed since January 1, 1900. For example, Excel stores the date January 1, 2000 as 36526. Times (hours, minutes, and seconds) are stored as decimal fractions equal to a portion of a day. Because dates and times are values, they can be used in performing calculations.

### *In Addition* EXCEL 2003 AND THE MILLENNIUM ISSUE

In the process of converting formatted dates into serial values, Excel applies some general rules. For entries using a two-digit year of 00 to 29 (e.g., 3/31/05), Excel converts the year to 2000 to 2029. For year entries using 30 to 99, Excel converts the year to 1930 to 1999. You can avoid these conversion issues altogether by always using a four-digit year when entering dates, such as 3/31/2005 or 31-Mar-2005.

## 5.2.2 Creating a Custom Number Format

### → Feature

If one of Excel's built-in number or date formats is not suitable, you can select from a variety of formatting codes to create your own **custom format.** All number formats, built-in and custom, consist of four sections separated by semicolons. If you were to apply the number format shown below, for example, a positive, negative, or zero value entered into the formatted cell would appear with two decimal places, while any text entry would display "N/A." Note that the "N/A" will not appear in the Formula bar since it is part of the number formatting construct and not part of the cell contents.

$$\#,\#\#0.00;[Red](\#,\#00.00);0.00;"N/A"$$

| Display format for positive values | Display format for negative values | Display format when zero | Display format for text entries |

### → Method

To create a custom number format:

- CHOOSE: Format → Cells
- CLICK: *Number* tab
- SELECT: Custom in the *Category* list box
- TYPE: *format codes* (Table 5.1) in the *Type* text box
- CLICK: OK command button

### → Practice

Let's practice creating a custom date format. Ensure that no workbooks appear in the Excel 2003 application window.

**1.** Open the data file named EX0520 to display the workbook shown in Figure 5.8.

## Figure 5.8

Opening the
EX0520
workbook

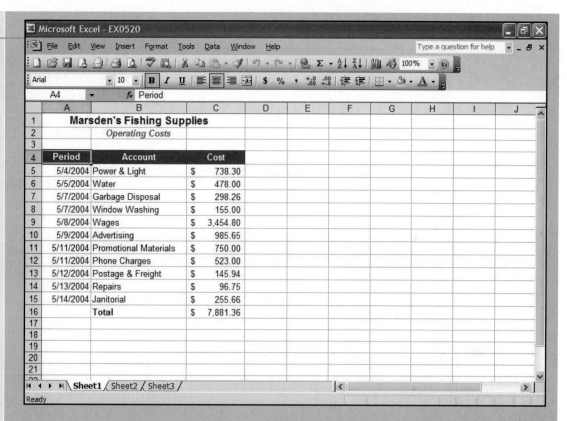

**2.** Save the workbook as "Marsden" to your personal storage location.

**3.** In column A the date values under the heading "Period" are displayed in a typical "month/day/year" fashion. Since this worksheet contains operating results limited to May, 2004, you can remove the month and year from the display format. Do the following:
SELECT: cell range from A5 to A15
CHOOSE: Format → Cells
CLICK: *Number* tab in the dialog box

**4.** The currently selected format appears, "Date" in the *Category* list box and "3/14/2001" in the *Type* list box. To change the display to appear with the day of the week and then the day number, you need to apply a custom format. To create the new format:
SELECT: Custom in the *Category* list box

**5.** To remove the contents of the *Type* text box:
DOUBLE-CLICK: "m/d/yyyy" in the *Type* text box to select it
PRESS: DELETE

**6.** To enter the desired format:
TYPE: **ddd, d**
Notice that the *Sample* area in the Format Cells dialog box shows how the newly formatted value will appear (Figure 5.9.)

**Figure 5.9**

Creating a
custom date
format

Select the
"Custom" option in
the *Category* list
box to create your
own custom format

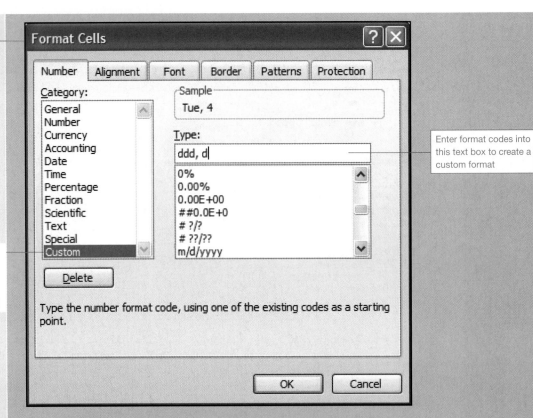

Enter format codes into
this text box to create a
custom format

**7.** CLICK: OK command button
The selected cells in the worksheet now appear formatted. (*Hint:* Refer to Table 5.1 for a listing
of commonly used custom format codes.)

**Table 5.1**

Format Codes

| Code... | Description... |
|---|---|
| # | Digit placeholder; displays a number, if available |
| 0 | Digit placeholder; displays a number or, if no number is available, a zero |
| ? | Alignment placeholder; adds a space to align the decimal point; displays fractions |
| , | Comma; displays a comma as the thousands separator (or as a multiple of a thousand) |
| @ | Entered in the text portion of a format, concatenates the format with the cell's text entry |
| [*color*] | Color indicator; assigns a color to a display format |
| **d and dd** | Day; displays as 1–31 and 01–31 |
| **ddd and dddd** | Day; displays as Sun–Sat and Sunday–Saturday |
| **m and mm** | Month; displays as 1–12 and 01–12 |
| **mmm and mmmm** | Month; displays as Jan–Dec and January–December |
| **yy and yyyy** | Year; displays as 00–99 and 1900–9999 |
| **h, m, and s** | Similar to date codes; "h" for hours, "m" for minutes, and "s" for seconds. Use "AM/PM" for a 12-hour clock. |

8. A custom number format is always saved with the workbook. To view the new format:
   CHOOSE: Format → Cells
   SELECT: Custom in the *Category* list box, if it isn't already selected

9. Scroll through the *Type* list box to view the custom formats. Some additional custom formats that you can create are provided in Table 5.2. For now, close the dialog box without making a selection:
   CLICK: Cancel command button

**Table 5.2**

Examples of
Custom Formats

| Custom Format... | Value Entered... | Value Displayed... |
|---|---|---|
| $#,##0.00 | 1234.5678 | $1,234.57 |
| 0.000% | .07925469 | 7.925% |
| # ?/? | 5.25 | 5 1/4 |
| (###) ###-#### | 6307894000 | (630) 789-4000 |
| ;;;"Part #"@ | xyz123 | Part # xyz123 |

10. Save the workbook (Figure 5.10), and keep it open for use in the next lesson.

**Figure 5.10**

Applying a
Custom Format

| | A | B | C | D |
|---|---|---|---|---|
| 1 | **Marsden's Fishing Supplies** | | | |
| 2 | *Operating Costs* | | | |
| 3 | | | | |
| 4 | **Period** | **Account** | **Cost** | |
| 5 | Tue, 4 | Power & Light | $ 738.30 | |
| 6 | Wed, 5 | Water | $ 478.00 | |
| 7 | Fri, 7 | Garbage Disposal | $ 298.26 | |
| 8 | Fri, 7 | Window Washing | $ 155.00 | |
| 9 | Sat, 8 | Wages | $ 3,454.80 | |
| 10 | Sun, 9 | Advertising | $ 985.65 | |
| 11 | Tue, 11 | Promotional Materials | $ 750.00 | |
| 12 | Tue, 11 | Phone Charges | $ 523.00 | |
| 13 | Wed, 12 | Postage & Freight | $ 145.94 | |
| 14 | Thu, 13 | Repairs | $ 96.75 | |
| 15 | Fri, 14 | Janitorial | $ 255.66 | |
| 16 | | Total | $ 7,881.36 | |
| 17 | | | | |

Excel

### 5.2.3 Applying and Modifying Styles

→ ## Feature

Using styles to enhance cells ensures that you are formatting your workbooks consistently and efficiently. Also, when you change the formatting specifications stored in a style, all cells based on that style are updated automatically. Consequently, it is much easier to make global changes to a worksheet's appearance when styles are used throughout. Excel provides five predefined or built-in styles (Comma, Comma [0], Currency, Currency [0], and Percent) for number formatting and one default style called Normal. You apply a style to a selected cell range using the Style dialog box or by clicking the Formatting toolbar buttons ($, %, •).

→ ## Method

- SELECT: the desired cell range
- CHOOSE: Format → Style
- SELECT: an option from the *Style name* drop-down list box
- CLICK: OK command button

→ ## Practice

You will now practice applying and modifying styles. Ensure that you've completed the previous lesson and that the "Marsden" workbook is displayed.

**1.** To begin, remove the cell formatting for the Cost values in column C:
SELECT: cell range from C5 to C16
CHOOSE: Edit → Clear → Formats
Notice that the raw and unformatted values now appear in the column.

**2.** With the range still highlighted, let's apply an existing style to the Cost values using the menu:
CHOOSE: Format → Style
The dialog box shown in Figure 5.11 appears.

**Figure 5.11**

Style dialog box

Styles are composed of these six elements

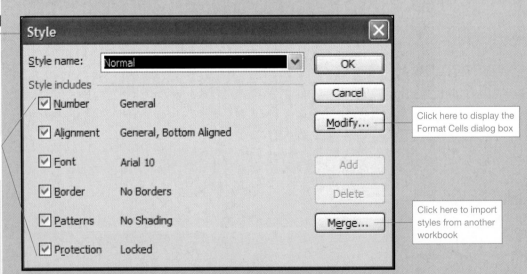

**3.** To choose an existing style that displays no decimal places:
SELECT: Currency [0] from the *Style name* drop-down list box
Notice that the only selected formatting option for this style is the *Number* check box.

4. To apply the style and continue:
CLICK: OK command button
The column values are formatted.

5. Let's apply the Currency style (not Currency [0]) to the range:
CLICK: Currency Style button ( $ )

6. You will now modify the style so that the dollar sign displays next to the number, rather than left-aligned to the cell border. To begin:
CHOOSE: Format → Style
CLICK: Modify command button
The Format Cells dialog box appears.

7. To adjust the positioning of the dollar sign:
SELECT: Currency from the *Category* list box
SELECT: 2 in the *Decimal places* spin box, if not already selected
SELECT: red-colored ($1,234.10) in the *Negative numbers* list box
CLICK: OK command button

8. To apply the modified style and continue:
CLICK: OK command button
For this workbook only, this is the new formatting specification for the Currency style. Any cells in this workbook that have been previously formatted using the Currency style will be updated automatically.

9. To demonstrate the style:
CLICK: Comma Style button ( , )
CLICK: Currency Style button ( $ )
Notice that the Currency style no longer uses the Accounting number format, which displays the dollar sign left-aligned with the cell border. Your worksheet should appear similar to the one shown in Figure 5.12.

10. Save the workbook, and keep it open for use in the next lesson.

**Figure 5.12**

Modifying and
applying the
Currency style

| | A | B | C | D |
|---|---|---|---|---|
| 1 | **Marsden's Fishing Supplies** | | | |
| 2 | | *Operating Costs* | | |
| 3 | | | | |
| 4 | **Period** | **Account** | **Cost** | |
| 5 | Tue, 4 | Power & Light | $738.30 | |
| 6 | Wed, 5 | Water | $478.00 | |
| 7 | Fri, 7 | Garbage Disposal | $298.26 | |
| 8 | Fri, 7 | Window Washing | $155.00 | |
| 9 | Sat, 8 | Wages | $3,454.80 | |
| 10 | Sun, 9 | Advertising | $985.65 | |
| 11 | Tue, 11 | Promotional Materials | $750.00 | |
| 12 | Tue, 11 | Phone Charges | $523.00 | |
| 13 | Wed, 12 | Postage & Freight | $145.94 | |
| 14 | Thu, 13 | Repairs | $96.75 | |
| 15 | Fri, 14 | Janitorial | $255.66 | |
| 16 | | Total | $7,881.36 | |
| 17 | | | | |

### 5.2.4 Creating and Removing Styles

→ **Feature**

To increase your formatting productivity, Excel allows you to create and name your own styles. You can specify up to six formatting elements for each style, including *Number, Alignment, Font, Border, Patterns,* and *Protection.* You do not, however, need to use all six elements. As with custom number formats, custom styles are stored within the workbook in which they are created.

→ **Method**

- SELECT: a cell on which to base the formatting specification
- CHOOSE: Format → Style
- TYPE: *style name* in the *Style name* drop-down list box
- CLICK: Add command button

→ **Practice**

Let's practice creating and removing styles in the "Marsden" workbook. Ensure that you've completed the previous lesson and that the "Marsden" workbook is displayed.

**1.** To create a new style based on the appearance of an existing cell, select the desired cell and then display the Style dialog box:
SELECT: cell C4
CHOOSE: Format → Style

**2.** To name the new style, begin typing to overwrite the current style's name in the *Style name* drop-down box:
TYPE: **ColumnHead**
(*CAUTION:* Do not press (ENTER) after typing this entry.) The Style dialog box should now appear similar to the one shown in Figure 5.13.

**Figure 5.13**

Defining a new style

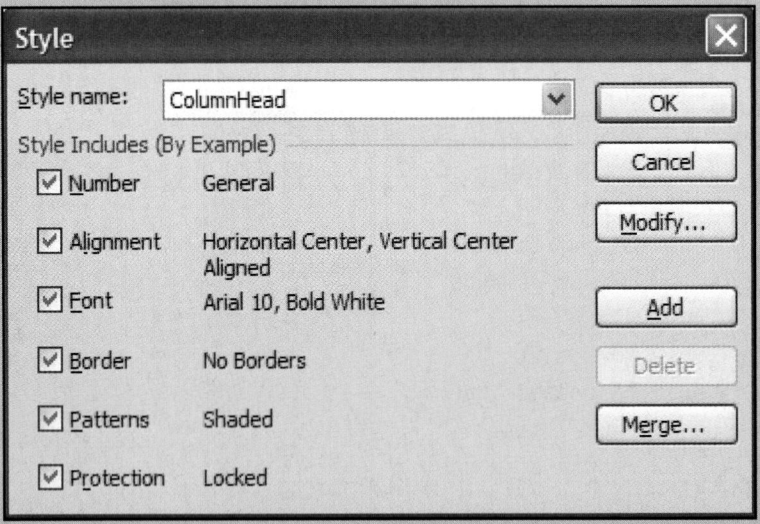

**3.** Notice that the Style dialog box inherits and displays the formatting attributes of the currently selected cell, as shown in Figure 5.13. The frame border for the *Style Includes* area also displays "By Example." Let's remove some of the formatting elements that you will not use:
CLICK: *Number* check box to remove the ✓
CLICK: *Protection* check box to remove the ✓
(*Hint:* At this point, you can modify any of the formatting attributes by clicking the Modify command button. If desired, make your changes using the Format Cells dialog box, and then click the OK command button to return.)

**4.** To add the current formatting as a style to the workbook:
CLICK: Add command button
CLICK: OK command button

**5.** To apply the new style:
SELECT: cell D4
CHOOSE: Format → Style
SELECT: ColumnHead from the *Style name* drop-down list box
CLICK: OK command button
The style has now been applied to the cell.

**6.** TYPE: **Paid**
PRESS: ENTER
The entry should appear formatted as the other column headings, as shown in Figure 5.14.

**Figure 5.14**

Applying a new style

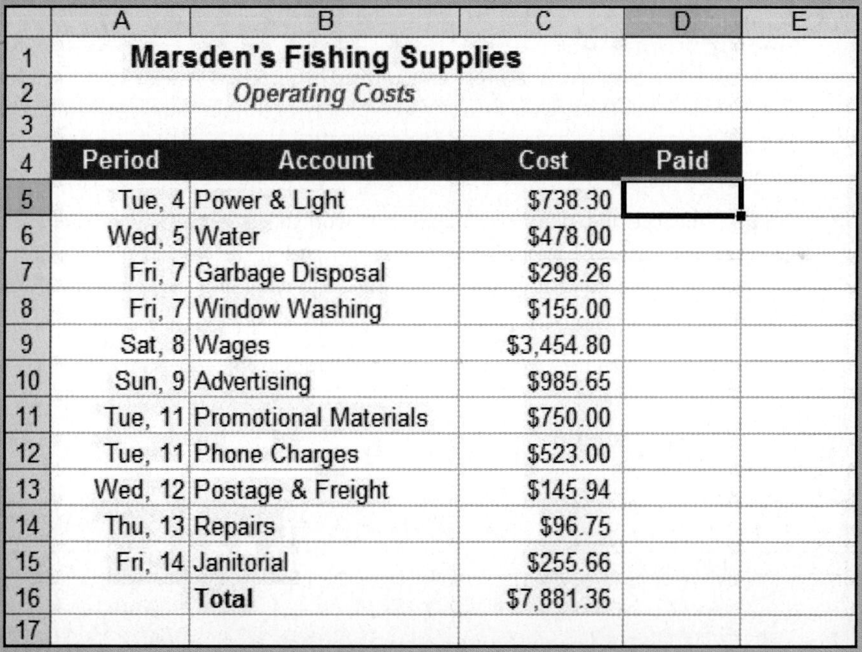

| | A | B | C | D | E |
|---|---|---|---|---|---|
| 1 | **Marsden's Fishing Supplies** | | | | |
| 2 | | *Operating Costs* | | | |
| 3 | | | | | |
| 4 | **Period** | **Account** | **Cost** | **Paid** | |
| 5 | Tue, 4 | Power & Light | $738.30 | | |
| 6 | Wed, 5 | Water | $478.00 | | |
| 7 | Fri, 7 | Garbage Disposal | $298.26 | | |
| 8 | Fri, 7 | Window Washing | $155.00 | | |
| 9 | Sat, 8 | Wages | $3,454.80 | | |
| 10 | Sun, 9 | Advertising | $985.65 | | |
| 11 | Tue, 11 | Promotional Materials | $750.00 | | |
| 12 | Tue, 11 | Phone Charges | $523.00 | | |
| 13 | Wed, 12 | Postage & Freight | $145.94 | | |
| 14 | Thu, 13 | Repairs | $96.75 | | |
| 15 | Fri, 14 | Janitorial | $255.66 | | |
| 16 | | Total | $7,881.36 | | |
| 17 | | | | | |

**7.** Save the workbook before proceeding to the next step.

**8.** Now let's practice removing a style from the workbook:
CHOOSE: Format → Style
SELECT: ColumnHead from the *Style name* drop-down list box
CLICK: Delete command button
CLICK: OK command button
Notice that the style formatting is removed from cells C4 and D4.

**9.** Close the workbook without saving the changes.

 **5.2** Using the Style dialog box, how would you change the default font for an entire workbook to be 12-point, Times New Roman?

# 5.3 Working with Draw Objects

Think of your worksheet as a single piece of paper composed of two layers. On the first layer, called the *cell layer,* you enter labels, values, and formulas into a worksheet grid of rows and columns. The second layer, known as the **draw layer,** exists as an invisible surface floating above (and mostly independent of) the worksheet cells. This transparent layer holds **objects,** such as lines, arrows, clip art images, pictures, and embedded charts. You can size, move, and delete objects on the draw layer without affecting the data stored in the underlying cells.

Even though you can format a worksheet in many different ways, you should practice restraint and follow these basic visual design principles.

- *Simplicity*    Do not clutter your worksheet with too many graphics. If you incorporate too many draw objects, the worksheet data becomes muddled and difficult to understand. As a general rule, include only those graphics that help clarify or draw the reader's attention to specific worksheet information.

- *Unity*    Although white space is important, too much space between worksheet data and graphic objects can destroy the unity of your visual presentation. The graphics that you use must clearly relate to the data.

- *Emphasis*    Use emphasis sparingly and correctly. Emphasis is used to draw one's attention to certain areas or trends through highlighting. You typically highlight data by adding draw objects, such as arrows, or by using colors, patterns, and textures. Too much highlighting tends to confuse and frustrate the reader.

- *Balance*    Balance and symmetry make your worksheets visually attractive and enjoyable to read. A worksheet must appear balanced—both as a unit and in the context of the printed page. Changing the position of draw objects, emphasizing headings, and changing the thickness of lines and borders can all affect balance.

In this module you learn how to insert and manipulate graphic objects on the draw layer of a worksheet.

### 5.3.1 Inserting Objects on the Draw Layer

→ **Feature**

You place lines, arrows, rectangles, ovals, and other shapes (collectively known as **AutoShapes**) onto the draw layer of a worksheet. AutoShapes can serve to draw the viewer's attention to specific areas or to simply enhance a worksheet's visual appearance. While working on the draw layer, you may find it useful to increase and decrease the zoom setting, as you would in previewing a page to print.

→ **Method**

To insert objects onto the draw layer:

- CLICK: an object button on the Drawing toolbar
- CLICK: in the worksheet to insert the object
- DRAG: the object's selection handles to size the object
- DRAG: the center of the object to move it

→ ## Practice

You will now insert and manipulate AutoShape objects on the worksheet's draw layer. Ensure that no workbooks appear in the Excel 2003 application window.

**1.** Open the data file named EX0530 to display the workbook shown in Figure 5.15.

**Figure 5.15**

Opening the
EX0530
workbook

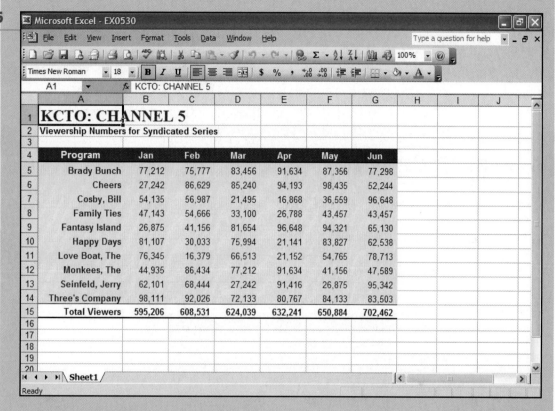

**2.** Save the workbook as "KCTO Ch5" to your personal storage location.

**3.** You use the Drawing toolbar to add graphics to a worksheet. To display the Drawing toolbar:
CLICK: Drawing button ( ) on the Standard toolbar

**4.** If the Drawing toolbar does not appear docked along the bottom of the window (as shown labeled in Figure 5.16), drag the toolbar into position by its Move handle ( ) or by its Title bar.

**Figure 5.16**

Drawing toolbar

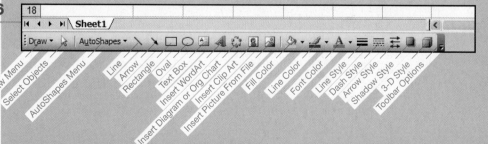

**5.** When working on the draw layer, it's sometimes easier to zoom in and out on specific areas of the worksheet. To practice zooming:
SELECT: cell range from A1 to G1
CHOOSE: View → Zoom

**6.** In the Zoom dialog box (shown here):
SELECT: *Fit selection* option button
CLICK: OK command button
The columns from A through G should now be visible.

**7.** To display a few additional columns:
SELECT: cell range from A1 to K1
CLICK: down arrow attached to the Zoom button ([100% ▾])
CLICK: Selection in the drop-down menu, as shown in Figure 5.17

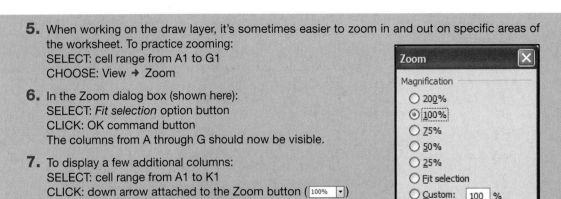

**Figure 5.17**

Zooming in and out on a worksheet

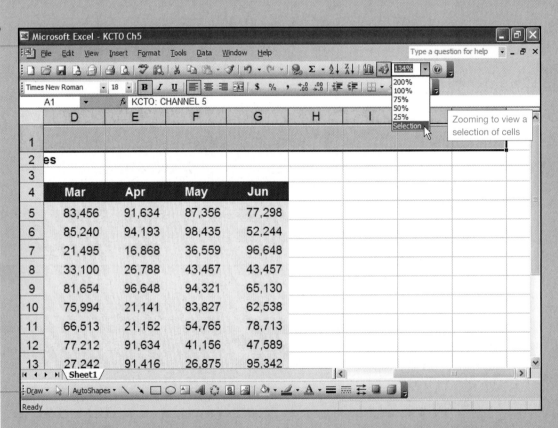

Drawing toolbar

**8.** To add some excitement and impact, let's place an explosion graphic containing the words "Great Results!" in the top right-hand corner of the worksheet. Do the following:
CLICK: AutoShapes button ([AutoShapes ▾]) on the Drawing toolbar
CHOOSE: Stars and Banners
The menu shown in Figure 5.18 appears.

**Figure 5.18**

AutoShapes
menu

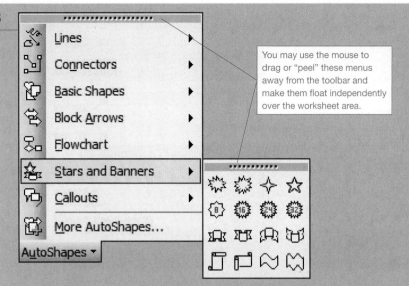

You may use the mouse to drag or "peel" these menus away from the toolbar and make them float independently over the worksheet area.

9. On the Stars and Banners submenu:
SELECT: Explosion 1 (⚙)
The shortcut menu closes, and your mouse pointer changes into a small crosshair as you move it over the worksheet cells.

10. There are two methods for placing an object onto the draw layer. For most objects, you simply click the crosshair mouse pointer anywhere on the worksheet to create a default-sized graphic. For more precision, you drag the mouse pointer and size the object as you place it. Let's insert a default-sized Explosion graphic object:
CLICK: in the middle of cell H2
(*Note:* Although cell H2 is used as a reference point in the above step, the object is not attached or *anchored* to the cell in any way.)

11. The Explosion object appears surrounded by eight white circles, as shown to the right. These circles are called **sizing handles** and only appear when the object is selected. The green circle in the graphic is the **rotating handle,** which is used to rotate the image. Some AutoShapes also have a diamond-shaped **adjustment handle,** which you drag to change the appearance but not the shape of the object. To cancel your selection of the AutoShape object:
CLICK: cell D1 *(or any other cell)*
The rotating and sizing handles do not display when the graphic is no longer selected.

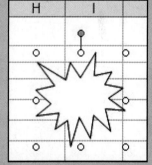

12. Position the mouse pointer over the Explosion object until the mouse pointer changes shape to a four-pronged cross and arrow. To move a graphic, drag the object's border using this mouse pointer. To size a graphic, select the object and drag its sizing handles. To begin:
CLICK: Explosion object once to select it
Notice that the sizing handles are displayed. You will also see the name of the object, AutoShape 1, appear in the Name box.

13. On your own, practice moving and sizing the Explosion object. Before proceeding, size and position the AutoShape to appear similar to the one shown in Figure 5.19.

## Figure 5.19

Moving and
sizing an
AutoShape
graphic object

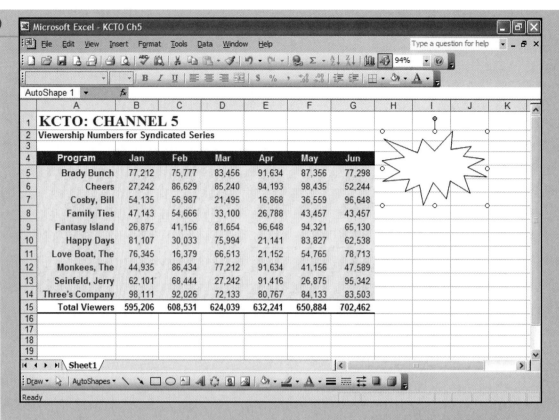

**14.** To display text within the Explosion object:
RIGHT-CLICK: Explosion object
CHOOSE: Add Text
You should now see a flashing I-beam cursor inside of the object.

**15.** On the Formatting toolbar, set the display format for the text:
SELECT: 12 points from the Font Size button ( 10 ▾ )
CLICK: Center button ( ▤ )
CLICK: Bold button ( B )
(*Note:* You can also apply formatting after you have typed the text.)

**16.** You are now ready to enter some text:
TYPE: Great
PRESS: **ENTER**
TYPE: Results!
CLICK: cell D1 to cancel the selection
The Explosion object now displays the comment, as shown
here.

**17.** If necessary, adjust the size of the Explosion object so that all of the text is visible. (*Hint:* When
you move the mouse over the text portion of an object, the pointer changes shape to an I-beam.
To start editing the text, you click once on the text portion. To select the object, position the
mouse pointer over one of its borders and click once.)

**18.** Save the workbook and keep it open for use in the next lesson.

## 5.3.2 Sizing, Moving, and Formatting Draw Objects

→ **Feature**

Besides sizing an object, you can enhance an AutoShape's appearance and visibility by selecting line styles and fill colors. You can also move and copy objects using standard drag-and-drop techniques or the Clipboard. To remove an object from the draw layer, select the object and press the (DELETE) key.

→ **Method**

To display the Format AutoShape dialog box:

• DOUBLE-CLICK: an AutoShape object,

  *or*

• RIGHT-CLICK: an AutoShape object

• SELECT: Format AutoShape

→ **Practice**

You will now practice inserting, copying, removing, and formatting draw objects. Ensure that you have completed the previous lesson and that the "KCTO Ch5" workbook is displayed.

**1.** Using the Drawing toolbar, let's format the "Great Results!" Explosion object by selecting a new background fill color:
SELECT: Explosion object by clicking once on its border
CLICK: down arrow attached to the Fill Color button ([🖌▾])
Your screen should appear similar to the one shown in Figure 5.20.

**Figure 5.20**

Changing the
color of an
AutoShape object

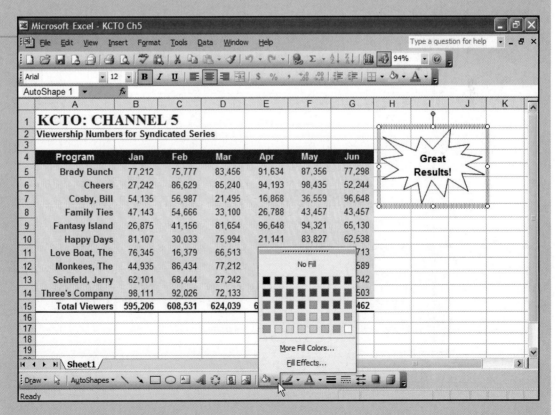

2. SELECT: Blue from the color palette
(*Note:* When you position the mouse pointer over a color, look for the ScreenTip color name.)

3. To make the object's text easier to read, drag the I-beam mouse pointer over the text "Great Results!" until the two words are selected. Then, change the text color:
CLICK: down arrow attached to the Font Color button (![A▾])
SELECT: White from the color palette

4. To cancel the selection:
CLICK: cell D1
The Explosion object should now appear similar to the one shown here.

5. Let's use some more draw objects to highlight information on the worksheet. Do the following:
CLICK: Oval button (![○]) on the Drawing toolbar

6. Rather than clicking on the worksheet to place a default-sized oval, position the mouse pointer above and to the left of the value in cell G13. Then, click the mouse button and drag the crosshair pointer to the bottom right-hand corner of the cell. When finished dragging the pointer, release the mouse button. You should now see a white oval appear over top of the cell, as shown here.

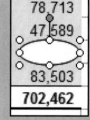

7. To change the oval's formatting characteristics:
RIGHT-CLICK: Oval object
SELECT: Format AutoShape
The Format AutoShape dialog box appears, as shown in Figure 5.21. (*Hint:* You can also double-click on the border of an object to display the dialog box shown in Figure 5.21.)

**Figure 5.21**

Format AutoShape dialog box: *Colors and Lines* tab

**8.** In the *Fill* area of the dialog box:
SELECT: "No Fill" from the *Color* drop-down list box

**9.** In the *Line* area of the dialog box:
SELECT: Red from the *Color* drop-down list box
SELECT: 2¼ pt from the *Style* drop-down list box

**10.** Before closing this dialog box:
CLICK: *Size* tab to view options for sizing and rotating the object
CLICK: *Protection* tab to view the object's "locked" status
CLICK: *Properties* tab to view options for positioning and printing
CLICK: *Web* tab to specify the text property of a Web graphic
CLICK: *Colors and Lines* tab to return to the first tab
CLICK: OK command button
The object should now appear as shown here.

**11.** Let's add an arrow to the worksheet to direct the reader's attention:
CLICK: Arrow button (⬎) on the Drawing toolbar
DRAG: from the bottom of the Explosion object to the top right-hand corner of the Oval object (and then release the mouse button)
(*Note:* When inserting an arrow, notice that the arrowhead points in the direction you dragged.)

**12.** To format this arrow using the Drawing toolbar:
CLICK: Line Style button (≡)
SELECT: 1½ pt from the pop-up menu
SELECT: cell D1 to cancel the selection
The arrow line appears darker and more distinguishable. Your worksheet should now appear similar to the one shown in Figure 5.22.

**Figure 5.22**

Placing and formatting draw objects

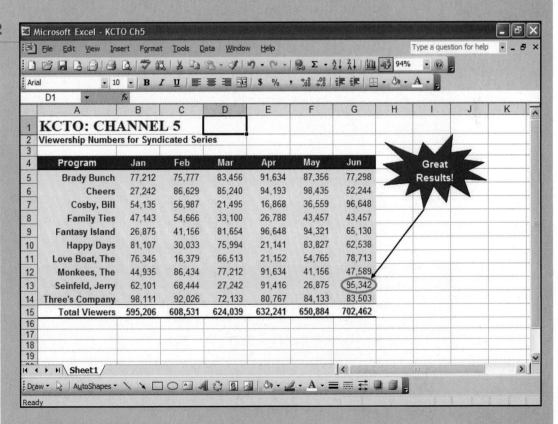

**13.** In addition to sizing and moving objects, you can also copy and delete objects that you place onto a worksheet. You will now place a copy of the red Oval object over cell G8. To do so, position the mouse pointer over the border of the red Oval object until the mouse pointer changes. Then do the following to copy the object:
PRESS: CTRL and hold it down
CLICK: the left mouse button and hold it down
DRAG: the red Oval object over cell G8

**14.** Release the mouse button when the new object is positioned correctly. Then release the CTRL key to complete the operation. You should now see a second red Oval object appear on the worksheet. (*Note:* When you press the CTRL key, the mouse pointer changes to an arrow with a plus sign attached.)

**15.** To delete the copied Oval object appearing over cell G8, ensure that it is selected and do the following:
PRESS: DELETE

**16.** Save the workbook, and keep it open for use in the next lesson.

*In Addition* ORDERING THE DISPLAY OF OBJECTS ON THE DRAW LAYER

The last object that you add to the draw layer is displayed in front of or overlapping all other objects. To change the display order of an object, right-click the object and select the Order command. You can then manipulate the object using the Bring to Front, Send to Back, Bring Forward, and Send Backward commands. Layering objects becomes especially important when you add multiple objects, such as WordArt, clip art, diagrams, and embedded charts, to a worksheet's draw layer.

### 5.3.3 Applying Shadows and 3-D Effects

→ **Feature**

Excel provides two special formatting commands for enhancing draw objects. First, you can make a graphic appear with a shadowed background. Second, you can modify (also known as extrude) an object to appear three-dimensional. These formatting enhancements provide you with several ways to enhance and customize the look of AutoShape objects in your worksheets.

→ **Method**

To apply Shadow or 3-D Effects, select an object and then:

• CLICK: Shadow Style button (▣) on the Drawing toolbar,

  *or*

• CLICK: 3-D Style button (▣) on the Drawing toolbar

→ **Practice**

You will now practice applying special effects to the Explosion object. Ensure that you have completed the previous lesson and that the "KCTO Ch5" workbook is displayed.

**1.** To begin, select the object that you want to format:
SELECT: Explosion object
Ensure that the object appears surrounded by sizing handles.

**2.** To apply a shadowed background:
CLICK: Shadow Style button (▣) on the Drawing toolbar
The pop-up menu shown at the right will appear. When you move the mouse pointer over a menu option, you will see the button's name displayed in a ScreenTip.

**3.** SELECT: Shadow Style 2 (⬛)
The object now appears with a slight shadow.

**4.** Let's apply a more pronounced shadow:
CLICK: Shadow Style button (⬛)
SELECT: Shadow Style 4 (⬛)
Your worksheet should appear similar to the one shown in Figure 5.23.

**Figure 5.23**

Applying a shadow style effect

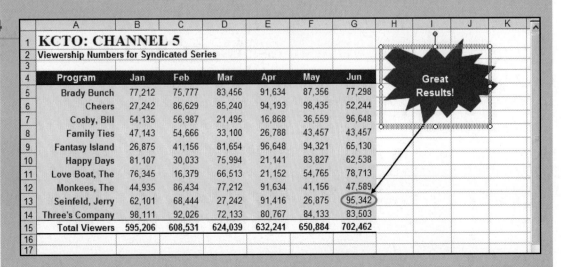

| | A | B | C | D | E | F | G | H | I | J | K |
|---|---|---|---|---|---|---|---|---|---|---|---|
| 1 | KCTO: CHANNEL 5 | | | | | | | | | | |
| 2 | Viewership Numbers for Syndicated Series | | | | | | | | | | |
| 3 | | | | | | | | | | | |
| 4 | **Program** | **Jan** | **Feb** | **Mar** | **Apr** | **May** | **Jun** | | | | |
| 5 | Brady Bunch | 77,212 | 75,777 | 83,456 | 91,634 | 87,356 | 77,298 | | | | |
| 6 | Cheers | 27,242 | 86,629 | 85,240 | 94,193 | 98,435 | 52,244 | | | | |
| 7 | Cosby, Bill | 54,135 | 56,987 | 21,495 | 16,868 | 36,559 | 96,648 | | | | |
| 8 | Family Ties | 47,143 | 54,666 | 33,100 | 26,788 | 43,457 | 43,457 | | | | |
| 9 | Fantasy Island | 26,875 | 41,156 | 81,654 | 96,648 | 94,321 | 65,130 | | | | |
| 10 | Happy Days | 81,107 | 30,033 | 75,994 | 21,141 | 83,827 | 62,538 | | | | |
| 11 | Love Boat, The | 76,345 | 16,379 | 66,513 | 21,152 | 54,765 | 78,713 | | | | |
| 12 | Monkees, The | 44,935 | 86,434 | 77,212 | 91,634 | 41,156 | 47,589 | | | | |
| 13 | Seinfeld, Jerry | 62,101 | 68,444 | 27,242 | 91,416 | 26,875 | 95,342 | | | | |
| 14 | Three's Company | 98,111 | 92,026 | 72,133 | 80,767 | 84,133 | 83,503 | | | | |
| 15 | **Total Viewers** | 595,206 | 608,531 | 624,039 | 632,241 | 650,884 | 702,462 | | | | |
| 16 | | | | | | | | | | | |
| 17 | | | | | | | | | | | |

**5.** To replace the shadow with a 3-D effect:
CLICK: 3-D Style button (⬛) on the Drawing toolbar
A pop-up menu will appear. (*Note:* An object cannot display both a shadowed background and a 3-D effect at the same time.)

**6.** SELECT: 3-D Style 15 (⬛)
(*Note:* This 3-D style is obviously overwhelming for this worksheet and is used for demonstrative purposes only. Remember to think about *simplicity, emphasis, unity,* and *balance* when inserting and formatting graphics.)

**7.** To select a more subtle 3-D style:
CLICK: 3-D Style button (⬛) on the Drawing toolbar
SELECT: 3-D Style 1 (⬛)
Your worksheet should appear similar to the one shown in Figure 5.24.

**8.** Save and close the workbook.

**Figure 5.24**

Applying a 3-D style effect

| | A | B | C | D | E | F | G | H | I | J | K |
|---|---|---|---|---|---|---|---|---|---|---|---|
| 1 | KCTO: CHANNEL 5 | | | | | | | | | | |
| 2 | Viewership Numbers for Syndicated Series | | | | | | | | | | |
| 3 | | | | | | | | | | | |
| 4 | **Program** | **Jan** | **Feb** | **Mar** | **Apr** | **May** | **Jun** | | | | |
| 5 | Brady Bunch | 77,212 | 75,777 | 83,456 | 91,634 | 87,356 | 77,298 | | | | |
| 6 | Cheers | 27,242 | 86,629 | 85,240 | 94,193 | 98,435 | 52,244 | | | | |
| 7 | Cosby, Bill | 54,135 | 56,987 | 21,495 | 16,868 | 36,559 | 96,648 | | | | |
| 8 | Family Ties | 47,143 | 54,666 | 33,100 | 26,788 | 43,457 | 43,457 | | | | |
| 9 | Fantasy Island | 26,875 | 41,156 | 81,654 | 96,648 | 94,321 | 65,130 | | | | |
| 10 | Happy Days | 81,107 | 30,033 | 75,994 | 21,141 | 83,827 | 62,538 | | | | |
| 11 | Love Boat, The | 76,345 | 16,379 | 66,513 | 21,152 | 54,765 | 78,713 | | | | |
| 12 | Monkees, The | 44,935 | 86,434 | 77,212 | 91,634 | 41,156 | 47,589 | | | | |
| 13 | Seinfeld, Jerry | 62,101 | 68,444 | 27,242 | 91,416 | 26,875 | 95,342 | | | | |
| 14 | Three's Company | 98,111 | 92,026 | 72,133 | 80,767 | 84,133 | 83,503 | | | | |
| 15 | **Total Viewers** | 595,206 | 608,531 | 624,039 | 632,241 | 650,884 | 702,462 | | | | |
| 16 | | | | | | | | | | | |
| 17 | | | | | | | | | | | |

**SelfCheck**

**5.3** How would you place a "STOP" sign on a worksheet using the techniques described in this module?

# 5.4 Working with Other Media

In addition to lines, ovals, and other AutoShapes, Excel 2003 allows you to insert WordArt objects, clip art images, organization charts, digital photographs, sounds, and other media elements into your worksheets. Imagine, for a moment, attaching a sound clip to a cell that explains how its result is calculated; or, in an inventory worksheet, providing an item's picture beside its numerical data. Used in this manner, media helps reduce ambiguity and enhances a worksheet's appearance and ease of use. Used incorrectly, however, media can jumble the message you are trying to convey and quickly distract the user. In this module you learn how to enhance your worksheets using common media elements.

### 5.4.1 Inserting WordArt

→ **Feature**

**WordArt** is a shared application provided in Microsoft Office System 2003 that you use to insert text objects formatted with special effects. WordArt objects attract your reader's attention by emphasizing text beyond basic formatting techniques. WordArt is used primarily for worksheet headings and titles.

→ **Method**

To insert a WordArt object into your worksheet:

• CHOOSE: Insert → Picture → WordArt,

  *or*

• CLICK: Insert WordArt button (⊿) on the Drawing toolbar

• SELECT: a style from the WordArt Gallery dialog box

• TYPE: *your text* into the Edit WordArt Text dialog box

→ **Practice**

In this lesson you use WordArt to create a worksheet title heading. Ensure that no workbooks appear in the Excel 2003 application window.

**1.** Open the data file named EX0540. Although similar to the workbook used in the previous module, this worksheet provides some extra white space at the top for inserting media elements.

**2.** Save the workbook as "KCTO Media" to your personal storage location.

**3.** To insert a WordArt object:
CLICK: Insert WordArt button (⊿) on the Drawing toolbar
(*Note:* If the Drawing toolbar is not visible, choose the Insert → Picture → WordArt command from the menu.) The WordArt Gallery dialog box, shown in Figure 5.25, will appear.

**Figure 5.25**

WordArt Gallery
dialog box

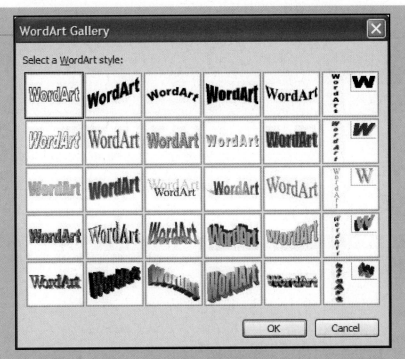

4. SELECT: *a horizontal WordArt style*, such as the one shown here
   CLICK: OK command button

5. In the Edit WordArt Text dialog box (Figure 5.26):
   TYPE: **KCTO**
   CLICK: OK command button
   The WordArt object appears, along with the WordArt toolbar, on the draw layer. (*Hint:* Ensure that you keep your text concise—do not enter long sentences for display using WordArt.)

**Figure 5.26**

Entering the
WordArt text

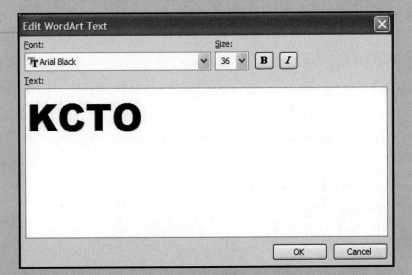

6. To position the title at the top of the worksheet:
   DRAG: WordArt object to row 1

**7.** On your own, size and position the WordArt object as you would any graphic object. (*Hint:* Refer to Figure 5.27 for an example.)

**8.** Save the workbook, and keep it open for use in the next lesson.

**Figure 5.27**

Positioning a WordArt object

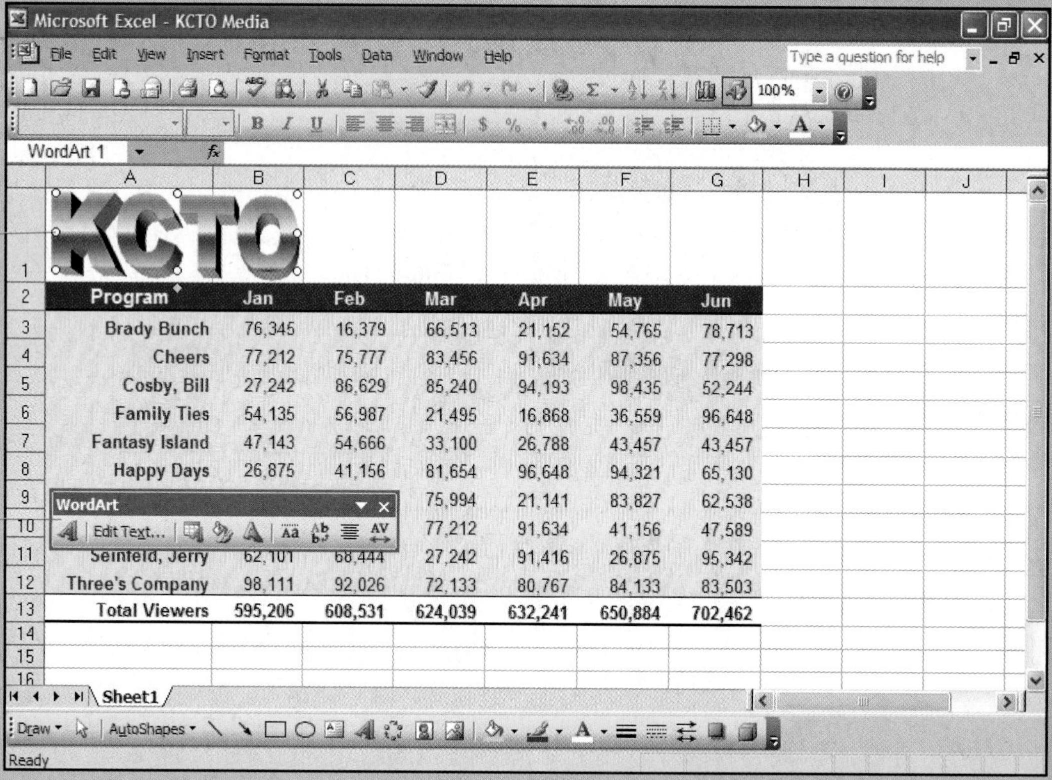

When selected, the WordArt object appears with sizing handles

Use the WordArt toolbar to redisplay the WordArt Gallery, edit the WordArt text, or apply formatting to the object

### 5.4.2 Inserting Clip Art

→ **Feature**

The **Clip Organizer,** another shared application, enables you to search for and insert pictures, sound, animation, and video into your worksheets. Media clips may be stored on your local hard disk, on a local area network (LAN), or on the World Wide Web. If you fully installed Excel 2003 or Microsoft Office System 2003, the Organizer will already contain many media clips sorted into a variety of categories.

→ **Method**

To insert clip art into your worksheet:

• CHOOSE: Insert → Picture → Clip Art,

  *or*

• CLICK: Insert Clip Art button (🖼) on the Drawing toolbar

• Search for a desired clip using the Clip Art task pane,

  *or*

• CLICK: "Organize clips" at the bottom of the task pane

→ **Practice**

Let's add one of the standard clip art images to the worksheet. Ensure that you've completed the previous lesson and that the "KCTO Media" workbook is displayed.

**1.** To begin, let's display the Clip Art task pane:
SELECT: cell G1
CLICK: Insert Clip Art button () on the Drawing toolbar
The Clip Art task pane, shown in Figure 5.28, appears to the right of the worksheet area. (*Hint:* If this is the first time that the Clip Art feature has been run on your computer, the Add Clips to Organizer dialog box may display. Click the Now command button to have Excel gather and categorize the available media elements.)

**Figure 5.28**

Displaying the Clip Art task pane

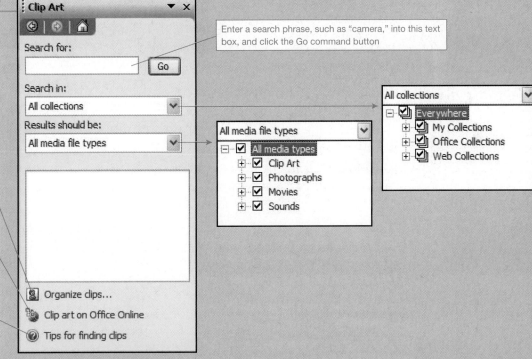

Display the Clip Organizer dialog box

Go to the Microsoft Design Gallery on the World Wide Web

Access helpful tips for searching for clips

**2.** Let's search for an image of a movie camera:
TYPE: **movie** in the *Search for* box
CLICK: Go command button
The task pane displays some initial results. (*Note:* If there are no clips found for "movie," use the search phrase "camera" or some other phrase to ensure that you find some clip art.)

**3.** Use the scroll bar to scroll through the clip art options until you find a picture of a movie camera, as shown in Figure 5.29.

**Figure 5.29**

Viewing the results of a clip art search

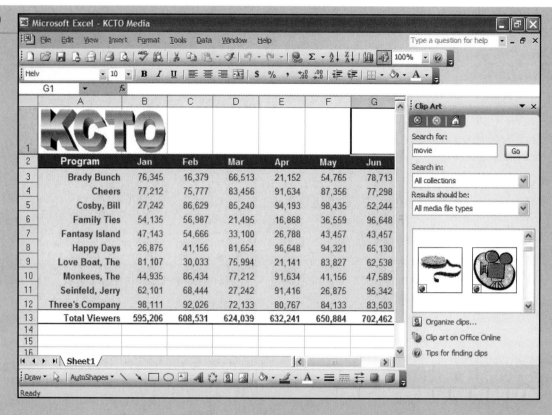

4. Position the mouse over the image (not over the down arrow attached to the image) and then click once to insert it into the worksheet. (*Note:* If this image is not available, select an alternative clip art image to work with.)

5. To hide the task pane, you can click its Close button or do the following:
CHOOSE: View → Task Pane
You should now see a large clip art image of the movie camera appear on your worksheet.

6. On your own, move and size the clip art image to appear similar to the one shown in Figure 5.30. When ready to proceed:
SELECT: cell A2

7. Save the workbook, and keep it open for use in the next lesson.

**Figure 5.30**

Moving and sizing a clip art image

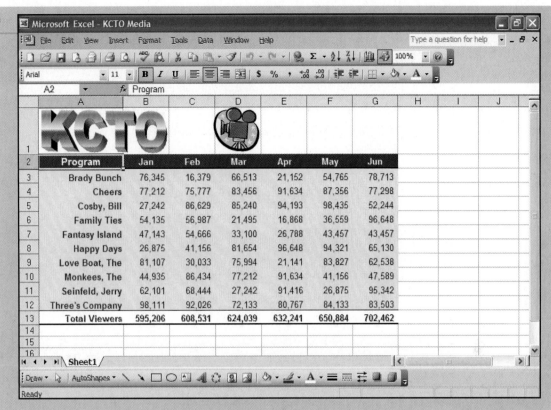

### 5.4.3 Inserting and Manipulating Pictures

→ ## Feature

In addition to clip art images, you can add other graphic files to your worksheets. A computer **graphic file,** such as a business logo, is typically created by a professional illustrator. However, you can easily create your own graphic files using a digital camera or a scanner. A **scanner** is a hardware device that converts photographs and other paper-based material into computer images. Besides moving and sizing these images, you can use Excel's Drawing and Picture toolbars to manipulate and format their appearance in order to get the look you desire.

→ ## Method

To insert a graphic or picture file:

• CHOOSE: Insert → Picture → From File,

  *or*

• CLICK: Insert Picture From File button (⬚) on the Drawing toolbar

• Use the Places bar and *Look in* drop-down list box to select the folder location of the graphic or picture file you want to insert.

• SELECT: the graphic or picture file

• CLICK: Insert command button

To manipulate a graphic or picture file's appearance using the Format Picture dialog box:

- RIGHT-CLICK: the desired object
- CHOOSE: Format → Picture
- CLICK: *Size* tab to change the size, rotation, and scale of an object
- CLICK: *Picture* tab to crop the image and change its color, brightness, and contrast

To manipulate a graphic or picture file, select the object and then click the desired button on the Picture toolbar:

- CLICK: Crop button ([_]) to crop a particular section
- CLICK: Rotate Left 90 Degrees button ([_]) to rotate the object
- CLICK: Color button ([_]) to convert a color image to grayscale or black and white, or to give it a washed-out appearance
- CLICK: More Contrast button ([_]) to sharpen an image
- CLICK: Less Contrast button ([_]) to soften an image
- CLICK: More Brightness button ([_]) to lighten an image
- CLICK: Less Brightness button ([_]) to darken an image

## → Practice

In this lesson you will manipulate the existing clip art image and then insert and format a new graphic image. Ensure that you've completed the previous lesson and that the "KCTO Media" workbook is displayed.

1. SELECT: the movie camera clip art image
   The Picture toolbar should appear.

2. To demonstrate the rotate left feature:
   CLICK: Rotate Left 90 Degrees button ([_])
   Notice that the camera lens is now pointing down.

3. To return the image to its original view:
   CLICK: Rotate Left 90 Degrees button ([_]) three more times

4. You can also mirror an object horizontally or vertically. To illustrate:
   CLICK: Draw menu button on the Drawing toolbar
   CHOOSE: Rotate or Flip → Flip Horizontal
   Notice that the camera lens is now facing in the opposite direction, as shown here.

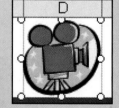

5. Now let's insert a picture file:
   SELECT: cell A2 in the worksheet
   CLICK: Insert Picture From File button ([_]) on the Drawing toolbar
   The Insert Picture dialog box appears.

6. Using the Places bar and the *Look in* drop-down list box, display the contents of the Advantage student data folder.

7. DOUBLE-CLICK: EX0543.jpg to insert the graphic
   (*Note:* You can import various types of graphic and picture files for use in a worksheet.) You should now see a small image of a brick wall appear near the cell pointer.

8. Size the image to cover the worksheet data area by dragging its bottom-right selection handle. Use Figure 5.31 to guide your sizing.

**Figure 5.31**

Sizing the inserted graphic file

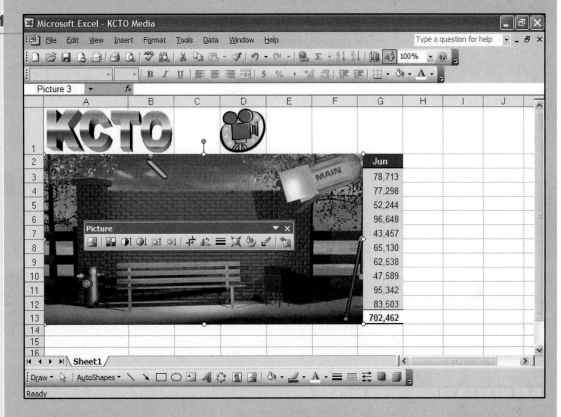

9. Now drag the entire image to the right, so that its right border touches the borderline between columns I and J.

10. You will now crop this picture so that only the right side of the image (near the "Main" light) is displayed. Before proceeding, ensure that the image remains selected and then:
CLICK: Crop button (⬚) on the Picture tool
Notice that black handles appear around the image.

11. On your own, drag the handle appearing on the left vertical edge of the image to the right, so the image covers only columns H and I. Use Figure 5.32 to help guide you in this task.

**Figure 5.32**

Cropping an image

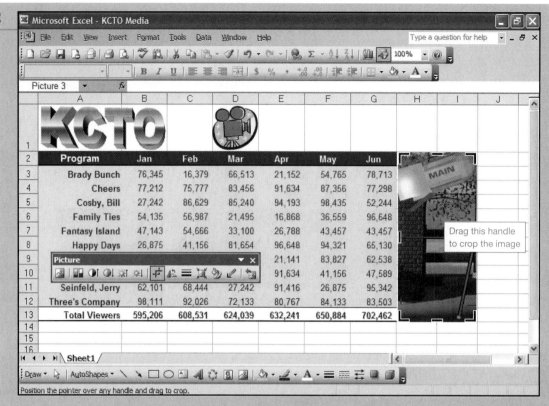

12. To return the image to having the default sizing handles:
CLICK: Crop button (⊞) on the Picture tool

13. You can also adjust the intensity and sharpness of an image file using the Picture toolbar. To demonstrate, ensure that the image remains selected and then:
CLICK: More Contrast button (▣) twice to sharpen the image
CLICK: Less Brightness button (▣) twice to darken the image

14. To reverse the effects:
CLICK: More Brightness button (▣) twice to lighten the image
CLICK: Less Contrast button (▣) twice to soften the image

15. To give the image less emphasis, let's change its color to appear faded:
CLICK: Color button (▣) on the Picture toolbar to display a menu
CLICK: Washout menu option
The image should now appear faded.

16. You will now preview how this worksheet will look when printed. To begin, let's set some page parameters:
CHOOSE: File → Page Setup
CLICK: *Page* tab in the Page Setup dialog box
CLICK: *Landscape* option button in the *Orientation* area

17. To preview the worksheet from the Page Setup dialog box:
CLICK: Print Preview command button
If you have a color printer specified, your screen will appear similar to the one shown in Figure 5.33. Otherwise, the worksheet will appear in black and white.

**Figure 5.33**

Previewing the worksheet

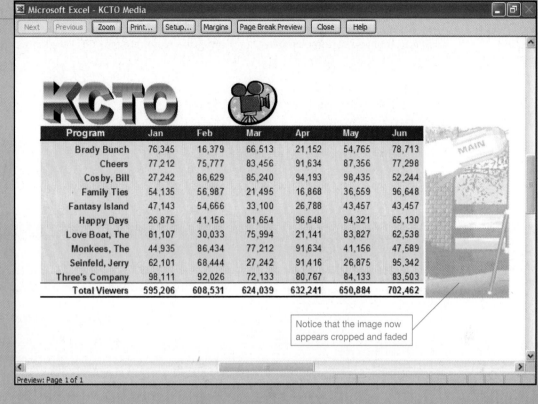

Notice that the image now appears cropped and faded

**18.** To return to the worksheet:
CLICK: Close button to close the Preview window

**19.** Save the workbook, and keep it open for use in the next lesson.

## 5.4.4 Displaying a Background Bitmap

### → Feature

You can apply a textured background to your worksheet by selecting a bitmap for display. The bitmap is tiled (repeated ad infinitum) across the entire worksheet area. This feature is especially useful for displaying a light watermark containing the word "DRAFT" or "CONFIDENTIAL," or for specifying a company's logo as the background for a page. However, you should note that a background bitmap can increase a workbook's file size dramatically. Also, because you cannot print a background image, this feature should only be used to enhance a worksheet for on-screen viewing.

### → Method

To select a background bitmap for display:

- CHOOSE: Format → Sheet
- CHOOSE: Background
- SELECT: a background bitmap

→ ## Practice

In this lesson you tile the worksheet's background with graphic images that have been created for you. Ensure that you've completed the previous lesson and that the "KCTO Media" worksheet is displayed.

**1.** SELECT: cell A2

**2.** To display a bitmap for the sheet background:
CHOOSE: Format → Sheet → Background

**3.** Using the *Look in* drop-down list, navigate to the folder containing the student data files and then do the following:
SELECT: EX0543A from the file list area
CLICK: Insert command button
The worksheet window will appear covered by the selected graphic, as shown in Figure 5.34.

**Figure 5.34**

Displaying a brightly colored background

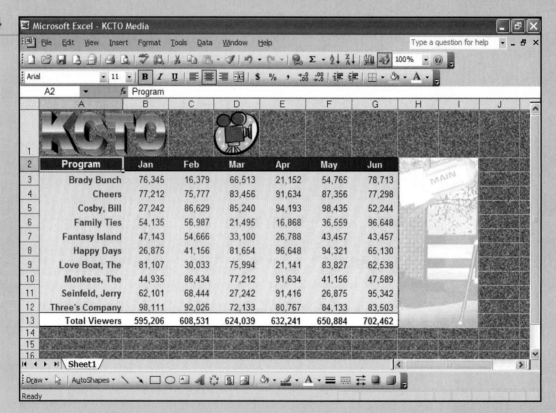

**4.** Let's choose a more subtle background:
CHOOSE: Format → Sheet → Delete Background
CHOOSE: Format → Sheet → Background
(*Note:* You must remove the existing background image prior to selecting a new bitmap for display.)

**5.** To select a new graphic:
SELECT: EX0543B from the file list area
CLICK: Insert command button

**6.** To remove the Drawing toolbar from the display:
RIGHT-CLICK: any button on the Drawing toolbar
SELECT: Drawing
The toolbar is removed from the Excel 2003 application window. Your screen should now appear similar to the one shown in Figure 5.35.

**7.** Save and close the workbook.

**Figure 5.35**

Selecting a subtle image for the sheet background

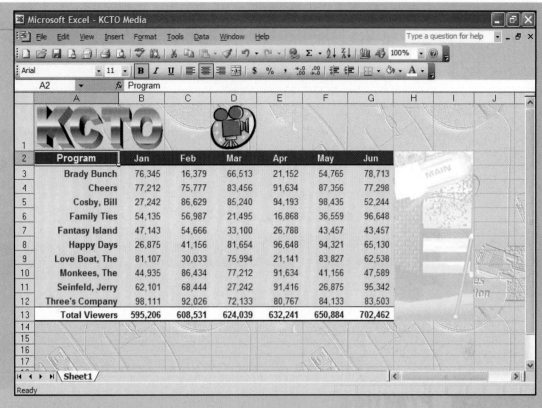

## In Addition INSERTING A DIAGRAM OR ORGANIZATION CHART

WordArt, clip art, and other graphic files are used to enhance the presentation of worksheet information. Diagrams and organization charts, on the other hand, often contain the information themselves. To insert a diagram or organization chart, click the appropriate button ( ) on the Drawing toolbar or choose the Insert → Diagram command. You can then make a selection from the Diagram Gallery dialog box shown here. For more information, access the Microsoft Office Excel 2003 Help system.

**5.4** Name four types of media files that you can search for using the Clip Art task pane.

## 5.5 Creating a Chart Sheet

Although the Chart Wizard does a satisfactory job of creating a chart, you will want to explore Excel 2003's customizing and formatting options for more demanding jobs. For instance, you can easily change a chart's entire appearance by simply applying a new chart type. You can also update a chart by adding and deleting data series in its plot area. In this module you create a separate chart sheet and perform some basic editing tasks.

### 5.5.1 Plotting Your Worksheet Data

→ **Feature**

When your data doesn't fall neatly into a table layout, you must manually select the individual ranges that you want to plot. One of the key points to remember is that the selected ranges should be the same shape and size (that is, they must contain the same number of data elements). Using this method, you can also select the headings and labels that you want to include as the legend for the data series and as the titles for the axes.

→ **Method**

To plot your worksheet data in a chart:

- SELECT: the first cell range to plot
- PRESS: CTRL and hold it down
- SELECT: the additional ranges to plot in the chart
- Release: CTRL
- CHOOSE: Insert → Chart,

    *or*

- CLICK: Chart Wizard button (📊)
- Complete the steps in the Chart Wizard.

→ **Practice**

You will now create a chart from a worksheet that uses a number of nonadjacent rows and columns to store survey information. Ensure that no workbooks are open in the Excel 2003 application window.

**1.** Open the data file named EX0550 to display the workbook shown in Figure 5.36.

**Figure 5.36**

Opening the EX0550 workbook

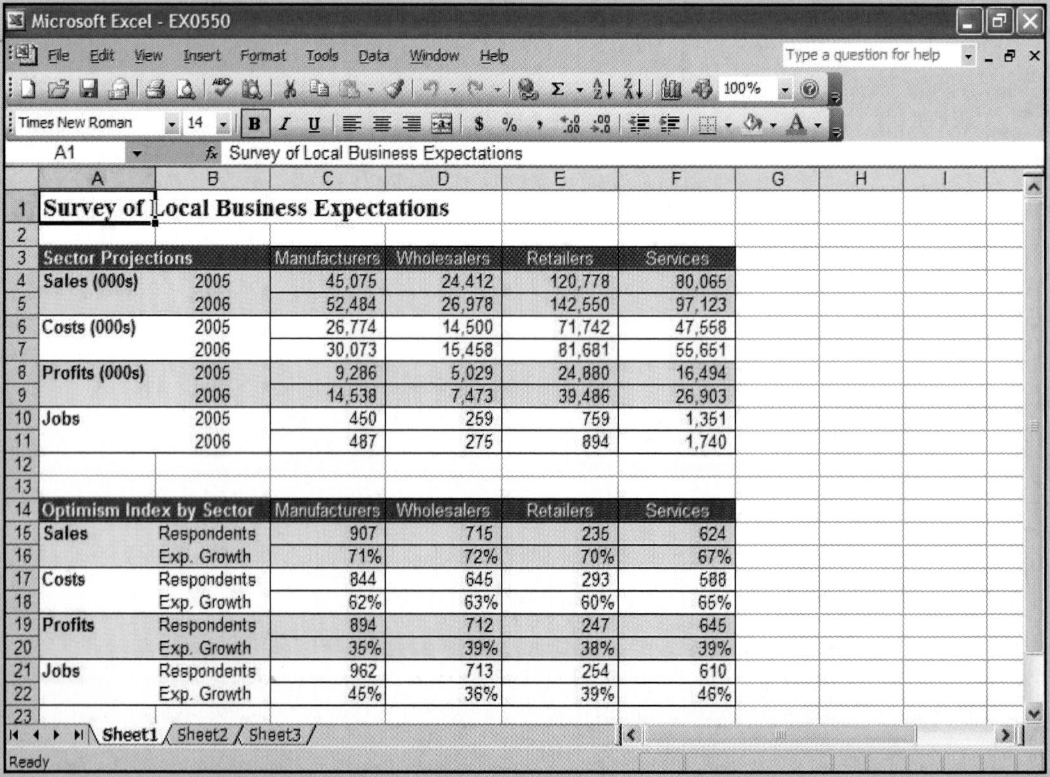

Excel

**2.** Save the workbook as "Local Survey" to your personal storage location.

**3.** Your objective is to create a pie chart that displays the proportion of total jobs represented by each sector. To begin, locate the 2005 "Jobs" data in row 10 and then do the following:
SELECT: cell range from B10 to F10

**4.** To select the sector names for display as the legend:
PRESS: CTRL and hold it down
SELECT: cell range from B3 to F3
Notice that you included cell B3 in the selection, because the Chart Wizard prefers that all ranges be an identical shape. (*Note:* Remember to release the CTRL key when you have finished selecting ranges.)

**5.** To start the Chart Wizard:
CLICK: Chart Wizard button (⊞)

**6.** In Step 1 of 4 in the Chart Wizard:
SELECT: Pie in the *Chart type* list box
SELECT: "Pie with a 3-D visual effect" in the *Chart sub-type* area
(*Hint:* Remember that you can click on a subtype to view its name.)

**7.** Preview the chart using the "Click and Hold to View Sample" command button and then:
CLICK: Next to proceed
Your screen should now appear similar to the one shown in Figure 5.37. Notice that each sector is shown as a wedge of the pie. The larger the wedge, the larger the proportional share of the total that that sector comprises.

**Figure 5.37**

Chart Wizard:
Step 2 of 4

The ranges being plotted in the chart appear in the worksheet surrounded by a bounding outline or moving border

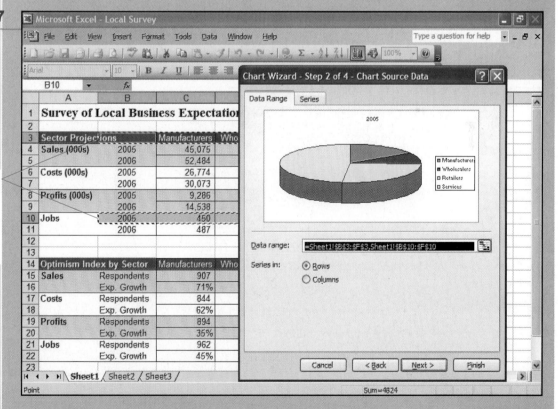

**8.** To remove the chart's title:
CLICK: Next to proceed to Step 3 of 4
DOUBLE-CLICK: "2005" in the *Chart title* text box
PRESS: DELETE

**9.** To finish creating the chart:
CLICK: [Next] to proceed to Step 4 of 4

**10.** To store the pie chart in a separate chart sheet:
SELECT: *As new sheet* option button
TYPE: **Jobs Chart** in the *As new sheet* text box
Your screen should now appear similar to the one shown in Figure 5.38.

**Figure 5.38**

Chart Wizard:
Step 4 of 4

**11.** CLICK: [Finish]
The chart appears in the Excel 2003 application window. Notice the chart and sheet tabs that appear along the bottom of the window.

**12.** Save the workbook and keep it open for use in the next lesson.

### 5.5.2 Applying Chart Types

→ **Feature**

Using the Chart Wizard, you can specify an initial chart type for plotting your data. There are many different chart types and subtypes from which to choose. And you can change the current chart type at any time to provide a different view of your data. Table 5.3 describes the fourteen standard chart types that are available in Excel's gallery. (*Note:* There are also twenty additional custom chart types.)

→ **Method**

To apply a different chart type:

• CHOOSE: Chart → Chart Type

• SELECT: a type from the *Chart type* list box

• SELECT: a subtype from the *Chart sub-type* area

• CLICK: OK command button

→ **Practice**

Let's change the chart type of the recently created pie chart. Ensure that you've completed the previous lesson and that the *Jobs Chart* sheet is displayed in the "Local Survey" workbook.

**Table 5.3**

Standard Chart Types

| Chart Type... | Description... |
|---|---|
| Area | Compares the amount or magnitude of change in data elements over a period of time. |
| Bar | Compares data elements by value or time. |
| Bubble | Plots the relationship between different sets of data; like an XY chart, but includes a third variable whose value is shown by the size of the bubble. |
| Column | Compares data elements over a period of time. |
| Cylinder, Cone, and Pyramid | Uses a cylinder, cone, or pyramid shape in place of a rectangle for a bar or column chart. |
| Doughnut | Shows the proportion of individual elements when compared to a total. |
| Line | Shows trends in data over equal intervals of time. |
| Pie | Shows the proportion of each individual element when compared to the total. |
| Radar | Shows each category as an axis or spoke from the center point, with lines connecting values in the same series. |
| Stock | Shows value ranges in a high-low-close chart format; typically used for quoting stocks. |
| Surface | Shows various combinations between two sets of data. |
| XY (Scatter Plot) | Plots the relationships between different sets of data, usually for scientific numerical analysis. |

**1.** Let's view the available chart types:
CHOOSE: Chart ➔ Chart Type
The Chart Type dialog box, which is identical to Step 1 of the Chart Wizard dialog box, appears on the screen. (*Note:* The Chart command appears on the Menu bar when you are working in a Chart sheet tab or when you've selected an embedded chart object.)

**2.** To display a horizontal 3-D bar chart:
SELECT: Bar in the *Chart type* list box
SELECT: "Clustered bar with a 3-D visual effect" in the *Chart sub-type* area
CLICK: OK command button
Your screen should now appear similar to the one shown in Figure 5.39.

## Figure 5.39

Selecting a
different chart
type

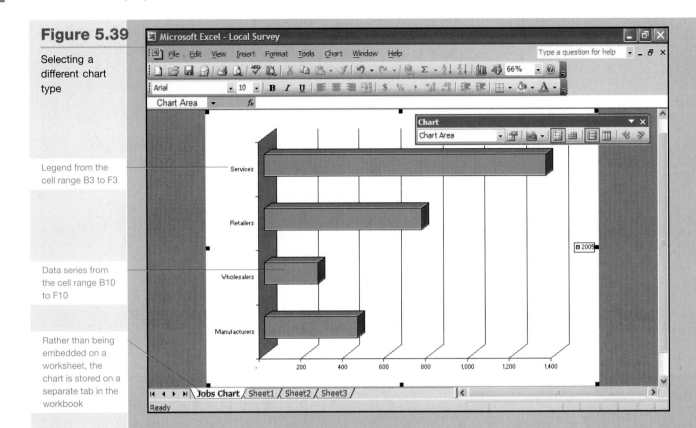

Legend from the
cell range B3 to F3

Data series from
the cell range B10
to F10

Rather than being
embedded on a
worksheet, the
chart is stored on a
separate tab in the
workbook

**3.** To ensure that you are viewing as much of the chart as possible:
SELECT: Selection from the Zoom button ( 100% ▾ )

**4.** On your own, apply some of the other chart types. When you are ready to proceed, perform steps 2
and 3 to reselect the horizontal bar chart prior to moving on to the next lesson.

**5.** Save the workbook, and keep it open for use in the next lesson.

### 5.5.3 Adding and Deleting Data Series

→ **Feature**

Imagine that you have created a chart only to find that you forgot to include an important set of data.
Rather than creating a completely new chart, you can add and delete data series to and from the
existing chart. When working in a separate chart sheet, you can use the Menu bar or the Copy and
Paste commands to add a new data series to an existing chart.

→ **Method**

To add a new data series:

- CHOOSE: Chart → Add Data
- SELECT: the cell range in the worksheet

To delete an existing data series:

- RIGHT-CLICK: the data series in the plot area
- SELECT: Clear

→ # Practice

In this lesson you practice adding a comparative data series for the year 2006 to the *Jobs Chart* sheet. Ensure that you've completed the previous lesson and that the *Jobs Chart* sheet is displayed in the "Local Survey" workbook.

**1.** To add a new data series to the horizontal bar chart:
CHOOSE: Chart → Add Data
A dialog box appears allowing you to enter the desired cell range.

**2.** Let's collapse the Add Data dialog box in order to make it easier to see the worksheet data that we need to select:
CLICK: Dialog Collapse button (🔲) for the *Range* text box
The dialog box withdraws so that only its text box appears.

**3.** To display the worksheet data:
CLICK: *Sheet1* tab at the bottom of the worksheet window
Notice that the Add Data – Range dialog box remains visible.

**4.** With the worksheet displayed in the Excel 2003 application window:
SELECT: cell range from B11 to F11 using the mouse
Notice that the absolute addresses of the cell range appear in the dialog box, as shown in Figure 5.40.

**Figure 5.40**

Adding a range to the plot area

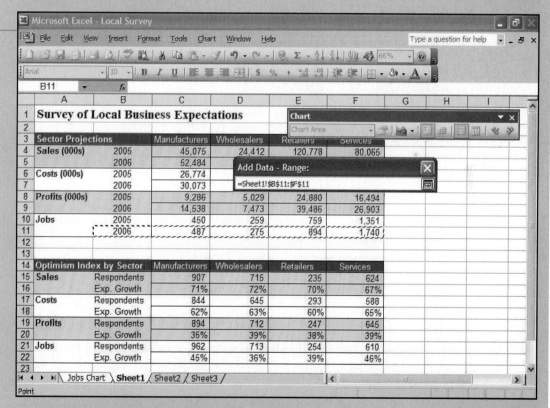

**5.** To expand the Add Data dialog box:
CLICK: Dialog Expand button (🔲)

**6.** To complete the process:
CLICK: OK command button

The *Jobs Chart* sheet is immediately displayed, as shown in Figure 5.41, showing the new data series as another horizontal bar. (*Note:* If you make a mistake and need to delete a data series from a chart, you right-click the series and then select the Clear command.)

7. Save and close the workbook.

**Figure 5.41**

Adding a data series to a chart sheet

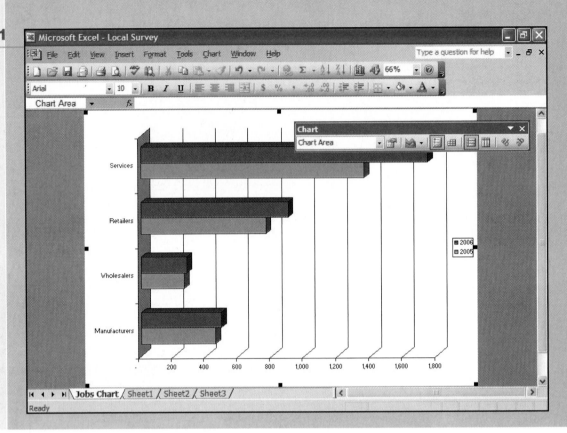

    **5.5** What must you remember when selecting nonadjacent ranges in preparation for the Chart Wizard or to add to a chart's plot area?

# 5.6 Customizing Charts

Customizing a chart involves adding titles, legends, and annotations. You can also use arrows and AutoShapes to emphasize certain aspects of the chart. Formatting a chart refers to setting the display options for each chart element. For example, Excel differentiates each data series in a chart by assigning them different colors. When you print the chart to a noncolor printer, however, the various colors appear as shades of gray. Therefore, you may need to format the columns to display patterns instead of colors. Modifying font typefaces and sizes can also improve a chart's readability.

As you may have noticed, Excel modifies the work area when a chart sheet is active. Additional menu commands and the Chart toolbar appear for formatting and manipulating the parts of a chart. Take a few moments to study the parts of a chart labeled in Figure 5.42 and described in Table 5.4.

**Figure 5.42**

Parts of a Chart

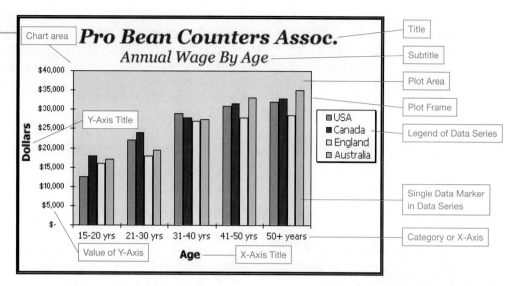

**Table 5.4**

Parts of a Chart

| Chart Element... | Description... |
| --- | --- |
| Chart and Chart Frame | The area inside a chart, including the **plot area,** titles, **legend,** and other objects. |
| Plot Area and Plot Frame | The area for plotting values from the worksheet. The plot area contains the axes and data series. |
| Axes (X and Y) and Axes Titles | The area bounding the plot area on the bottom (horizontal category **X-axis**) and on the side (vertical value **Y-axis**). |
| Data Marker | A single dot, bar, or symbol that represents one number from the worksheet. |
| Data Series | A series of related values from the worksheet. A data series consists of related data markers. |
| Legend | A key for deciphering the different data series and markers appearing in the plot area. |

## 5.6.1 Formatting Chart Elements

### → Feature

To differentiate your charts, employ some of Excel's chart formatting tools. Like formatting a worksheet, you can specify fonts (also called typefaces) and style attributes, text and fill colors, and even rotate text on angles. Used with good taste and judgment, these commands can produce effective results.

### → Method

To display the Format dialog box for a chart element:

- DOUBLE-CLICK: a chart element

  *or*

- RIGHT-CLICK: a chart element
- SELECT: Format command

→ ## Practice

You will now practice formatting an existing chart. The workbook displays a quarterly summary of the hospital beds required in a small community. Ensure that no workbooks are open in the Excel 2003 application window.

**1.** Open the data file named EX0560 to display the workbook shown in Figure 5.43.

**Figure 5.43**

Opening the
EX0560
workbook

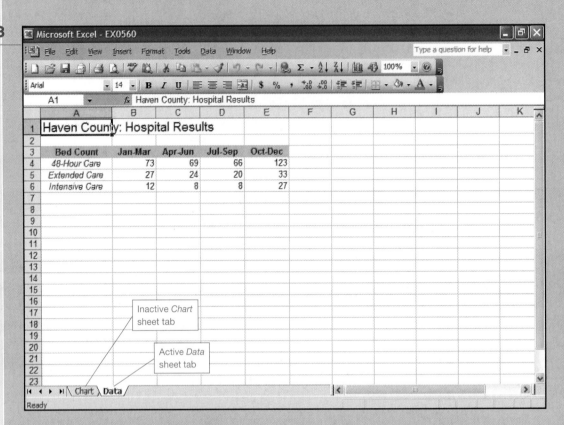

**2.** Save the workbook as "Haven County" to your personal storage location.

**3.** To display the chart sheet:
CLICK: *Chart* sheet tab
A 3-D column chart has been created using the Chart Wizard. Each quarter is displayed along the horizontal or X-axis and the number of beds is displayed on the vertical or Y-axis. A simple legend is also provided to differentiate the three data series that are plotted.

**4.** Ensure that the Chart toolbar appears in the Excel 2003 application window. (*Hint:* If the Chart toolbar is not visible, right-click an existing toolbar and select Chart from the menu.) You may dock the toolbar against one of the borders or float the toolbar, as shown in Figure 5.44. If your screen does not look similar to the one shown in Figure 5.44, click the Selection option from the Zoom button ( 100% ▾ ) on the Standard toolbar.

**Figure 5.44**

*Chart* sheet tab for "Haven County"

Chart toolbar

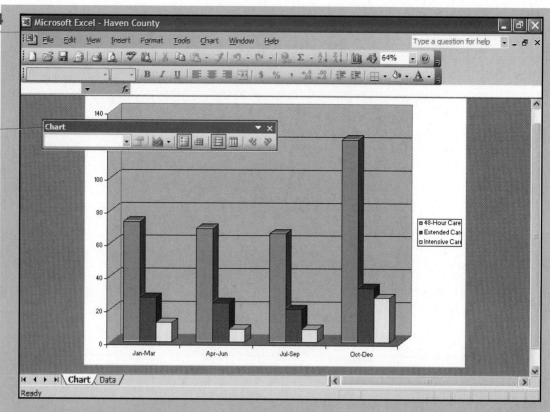

5. Let's format the legend so that it stands apart from the other chart elements. Position the mouse pointer over the legend and then:
RIGHT-CLICK: the legend
SELECT: Format Legend
A dialog box appears with a variety of formatting options.

6. To reposition the legend in the chart area:
CLICK: *Placement* tab
SELECT: *Bottom* option button
CLICK: OK command button
The legend now appears at the bottom of the chart, as shown below.

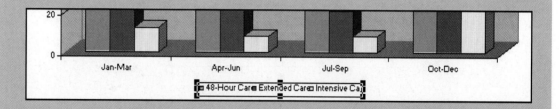

7. To continue formatting the legend:
DOUBLE-CLICK: the border of the legend
The Format Legend dialog box displays immediately.

8. Let's return the legend to its original position using the *Placement* tab:
SELECT: *Right* option button

**9.** To change the legend's typeface and font size:
CLICK: *Font* tab
SELECT: Times New Roman from the *Font* list box
SELECT: Bold from the *Font style* list box
SELECT: 12 from the *Size* list box

**10.** To change the legend's background color and appearance:
CLICK: *Patterns* tab
SELECT: *Shadow* check box in the *Border* area
SELECT: a pale yellow color in the *Area* area

**11.** To complete the legend formatting:
CLICK: OK command button

**12.** You can move and size certain chart objects using the mouse. On your own, position the mouse pointer over one of the black selection boxes surrounding the legend. Then drag the box in order to size the legend as shown in Figure 5.45. For all of the text to be visible, the legend may need to overlap the plot area. Release the mouse button when you are finished.

**Figure 5.45**

Formatting the legend

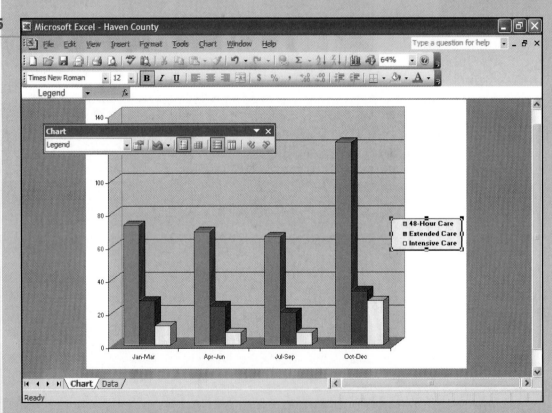

**13.** To format a data series, double-click one of its columns:
DOUBLE-CLICK: the 48-Hour Care column for Apr-Jun
Notice that the Format Data Series dialog box (Figure 5.46) that appears is similar to the Format Legend dialog box.

**Figure 5.46**

Format Data
Series dialog box:
*Patterns* tab

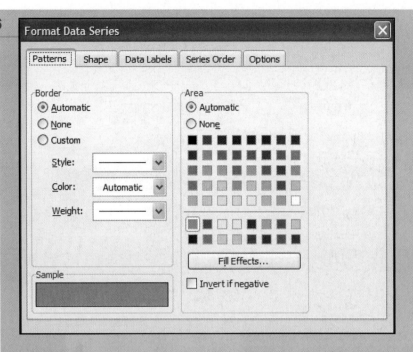

**14.** On your own, click on each tab in the Format Data Series dialog box. You use the *Shape* tab to control the column shape, the *Data Labels* tab to add labels and values to the chart, the *Series Order* tab to adjust the column ordering, and the *Options* tab to adjust a few additional display particulars. Return to the *Patterns* tab once you have finished.

**15.** Let's change the color of the data series:
SELECT: a teal green color from the *Area* area
CLICK: OK command button
Notice that the legend and the entire data series are modified.

**16.** Save the workbook, and keep it open for use in the next lesson.

## 5.6.2 Adding and Deleting Chart Elements

### → Feature

You can easily add and delete elements, such as titles, headings, data labels, and legend text, for an existing chart. Titles are used to state the purpose of the chart and to explain the scales used for the axes. Data labels appear inside the plot area and display the actual values plotted by each data symbol. A legend provides a visual key for the data series plotted in the chart. Finally, you can display a data grid containing the actual values that you've plotted on the chart. To remove any element appearing in a chart, you right-click the element and then select the Clear command.

### → Method

To modify common chart elements:

- SELECT: the chart

- CHOOSE: Chart → Chart Options

→ **Practice**

You will now practice adding titles and a data table to the chart. Ensure that you've completed the previous lesson and that the "Haven County" workbook is displayed.

**1.** To add and delete chart elements:
CHOOSE: Chart → Chart Options
As in Step 3 in the Chart Wizard, you use the Chart Options dialog box (Figure 5.47) to modify titles, axes, gridlines, legends, data labels, and a data table.

**Figure 5.47**

Chart Options dialog box: *Titles* tab

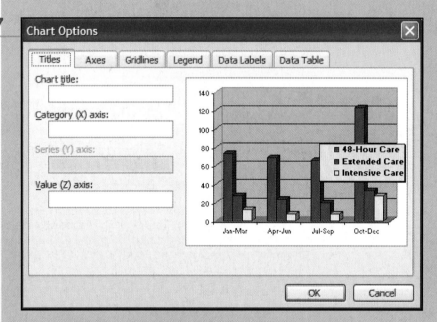

**2.** Let's add two titles to the chart:
CLICK: *Titles* tab, if it isn't already selected
TYPE: **Haven County Hospital** in the *Chart title* text box
TYPE: **Bed Count** in the *Value (Z) axis* text box
Notice that the preview area is updated to show the titles.

**3.** A data table displays a grid of the plotted values beneath the X-axis. To add a data table to the chart:
CLICK: *Data Table* tab
SELECT: *Show data table* check box
CLICK: OK command button

**4.** To remove any object selection:
CLICK: on the gray matting around the chart
Your screen should now appear similar to the one shown in Figure 5.48.

**Figure 5.48**

Adding titles and
a data table

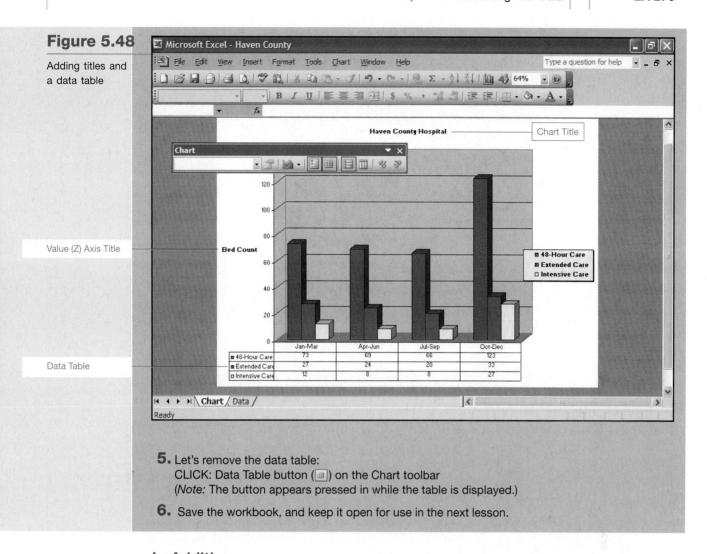

5. Let's remove the data table:
   CLICK: Data Table button (▦) on the Chart toolbar
   (*Note:* The button appears pressed in while the table is displayed.)

6. Save the workbook, and keep it open for use in the next lesson.

*In Addition* MANIPULATING CHART ELEMENTS USING THE CHART TOOLBAR

You can also use the buttons on the Chart toolbar to select a chart element ( [Chart Area ▾] ), display
the Format dialog box (🖾), change the chart type (📊▾), display and hide the legend (▤), and rotate
text (�℣, ℣).

### 5.6.3 Adding Draw Objects to a Chart

→ **Feature**

Similar to adding draw objects to a worksheet, you can insert arrows and other AutoShape graphics
onto a chart sheet. In the previous lesson, you attached text to specific regions on a chart, such as
titles and axes. By adding a text box, you can display free-form text anywhere on a chart.

→ **Method**

To add draw objects to a chart:

• CLICK: an object button on the Drawing toolbar

• CLICK: on the chart sheet to insert the object

• Size and move the object as desired.

→ **Practice**

You will now enhance the chart by adding a text box and an arrow. Ensure that you've completed the previous lesson and that the "Haven County" workbook is displayed.

**1.** To add draw objects to the chart:
CLICK: Drawing button (⊞) on the Standard toolbar
SELECT: 100% from the Zoom button (100% ▾)

**2.** Using Figure 5.49 as your guide, scroll the window to view the appropriate area of the chart. To add an arrow to the chart:
CLICK: Arrow button (◥) on the Drawing toolbar

**3.** You can use the keyboard to help you draw a straight arrow:
PRESS: SHIFT and hold it down

**4.** On your own, position the mouse pointer above the Jul-Sep columns and then drag the pointer toward the 48-Hour Care column for Oct-Dec. When satisfied, release the mouse button and the SHIFT key. A straight arrow will appear in the plot area. (*Hint:* If you make a mistake, select the object and press DELETE.)

**5.** To add a text box to the chart:
CLICK: Text Box button (⊞) on the Drawing toolbar
CLICK: the I-beam mouse pointer above the Apr-Jun columns
TYPE: October Flooding
PRESS: ENTER
TYPE: and Cold Winter

**6.** Position the mouse pointer over one of the borders (not selection handles) of the text box and drag the box into place, as shown in Figure 5.49. (*Hint:* You can also format the text to appear with a different typeface and font size.)

**Figure 5.49**

Adding draw objects to a chart

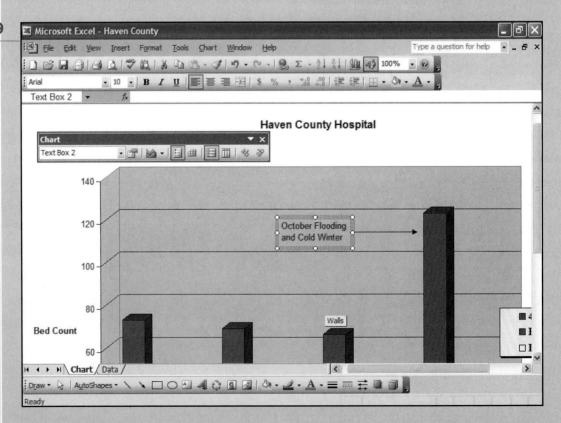

7. Remove the Drawing toolbar from the Excel 2003 application window.

8. Save the workbook, and keep it open for use in the next lesson.

### 5.6.4 Printing a Separate Chart Sheet

→ ## Feature

For the most part, a chart sheet is printed using the same process you use in printing a worksheet. There are some subtle differences, however, in how you choose to fit the chart to the printed page. For example, using the Page Setup dialog box, you can specify that the chart be expanded to fit the full page or scaled proportionally. For review purposes, you may also choose to print the chart using draft quality or in black and white. In addition to saving ink, these print options take much less time to produce output than if you used your printer's best quality.

→ ## Method

To display the Page Setup dialog box for a chart sheet:

- CHOOSE: File → Page Setup
- CLICK: *Chart* tab in the dialog box

→ ## Practice

You will now practice printing a chart sheet. Ensure that you've completed the previous lesson and that the "Haven County" workbook is displayed.

1. To specify page setup options for a chart:
   CHOOSE: File → Page Setup
   CLICK: *Chart* tab in the dialog box
   You should see the dialog box shown in Figure 5.50.

**Figure 5.50**

Page Setup dialog box: *Chart* tab

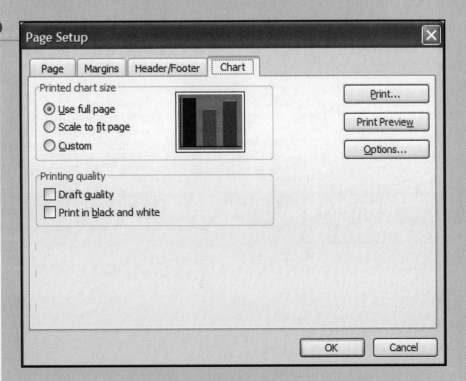

**2.** In the *Printed chart size* area:
SELECT: *Scale to fit page* option button

**3.** To preview how the chart sheet will appear when printed:
CLICK: Print Preview command button
If you have a color printer set as your default printer, your screen will appear similar to that shown in Figure 5.51. A black-and-white printer set as the default will cause the Print Preview window to display the chart elements using shades of gray.

**Figure 5.51**

Print previewing a chart sheet

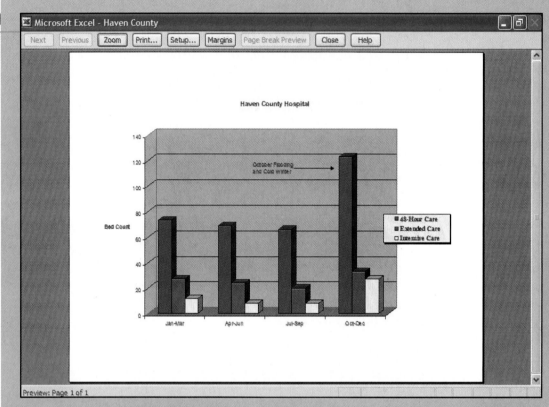

**4.** If you have a printer connected to your computer, click the Print command button in the toolbar area, and then click the OK command button in the Print dialog box to continue. If you do not have a printer, click the Close command button in the Print Preview window.

**5.** Save and then close the workbook.

**5.6** What might you do differently in formatting a chart for printing as opposed to formatting a chart for displaying online?

# Chapter
### s u m m a r y

Most people recognize the benefit of using formatting styles, graphics, and charts to improve the effectiveness of their presentations. Once the domain of desktop publishing and graphics software, Excel now enables you to indent, rotate, wrap, and shrink text entries, insert graphics and pictures, and plot data using a variety of chart formats. If used properly, a worksheet's formatting can help you direct the reader's attention and emphasize key areas. Yet sometimes a simple graphic representation of data is all that is needed, especially for conveying information from rows and columns of tiny numbers. For the same reason that road maps are easier to follow than written directions, a visual display is far more appealing and effective than numbers alone. Charts can help you summarize and present data, and predict or forecast trends. In this chapter you learned several principles and commands for successfully formatting and incorporating graphics in a worksheet.

## Command Summary

Many of the commands and procedures appearing in this chapter are summarized in the following table.

| Skill Set | To Perform This Task . . . | Do the Following . . . |
|---|---|---|
| **Formatting and Printing Worksheets** | Indent and rotate text in a cell | CHOOSE: Format → Cells<br>CLICK: *Alignment* tab |
| | Wrap, merge, and shrink text entries appearing in a cell(s) | CHOOSE: Format → Cells<br>CLICK: *Alignment* tab |
| | Apply select formatting elements from an AutoFormat option | CHOOSE: Format → AutoFormat<br>CLICK: Options command button |
| | Apply, modify, and remove styles | CHOOSE: Format → Style<br>SELECT: the desired style<br>CLICK: OK, Modify, or Delete command button |
| | Create a new style | SELECT: a cell with the desired formatting<br>CHOOSE: Format → Style<br>TYPE: *style name*<br>CLICK: Add command button |
| | Display a background bitmap | CHOOSE: Format → Sheet → Background<br>SELECT: a bitmap file |
| **Working with Cells and Cell Data** | Apply number formats | CHOOSE: Format → Cells<br>CLICK: *Number* tab<br>SELECT: the desired number format |
| **Formatting Numbers** | Create custom number formats | CHOOSE: Format → Cells<br>CLICK: *Number* tab<br>SELECT: Custom in the *Category* list box<br>TYPE: *custom format* |
| **Creating and Modifying Graphics** | Create and modify lines and AutoShape objects | CLICK: an object button on the Drawing toolbar<br>CLICK: in the worksheet |
| | Size and move objects on the draw layer | DRAG: object's handles to size, *or*<br>DRAG: object's borders to move |

| | |
|---|---|
| Delete an object on the draw layer | SELECT: an object<br>PRESS: DELETE |
| Create and modify 3-D shapes and apply shadows to objects | SELECT: an object<br>CLICK: 3-D Style button (⬛), or<br>CLICK: Shadow Style button (⬛) |
| Format an AutoShape object | RIGHT-CLICK: an AutoShape object<br>SELECT: Format command |
| Insert a WordArt object | CLICK: Insert WordArt button (⬛), or<br>CHOOSE: Insert → Picture → WordArt |
| Insert a Clip Art object | CLICK: Insert Clip Art button (⬛), or<br>CHOOSE: Insert → Picture → Clip Art |
| Insert a graphic or picture file | CLICK: Insert Picture From File button (⬛), or<br>CHOOSE: Insert → Picture → From File |
| Modify charts; change the chart type | CHOOSE: Chart → Chart Type<br>SELECT: a type and subtype |
| Modify charts; add data series | CHOOSE: Chart → Add Data<br>SELECT: the additional range to plot |
| Modify charts; add chart elements, such as titles | SELECT: the chart<br>CHOOSE: Chart → Chart Options |
| Format a chart element | RIGHT-CLICK: a chart element<br>CHOOSE: Format command |
| Change the page setup for charts | CHOOSE: File → Page Setup<br>CLICK: *Chart* tab |

## Key Terms

This section specifies page references for the key terms identified in this chapter. For a complete list of definitions, refer to the Glossary provided at the end of this learning guide.

AutoShapes, *p. EX 244*

cell layer, *p. EX 235*

Clip Organizer, *p. EX 256*

custom format, *p. EX 236*

draw layer, *p. EX 244*

graphic file, *p. EX 259*

legend, *p. EX 273*

objects, *p. EX 244*

plot area, *p. EX 273*

scanner, *p. EX 259*

sizing handles, *p. EX 247*

style, *p. EX 234*

WordArt, *p. EX 254*

X-axis, *p. EX 273*

Y-axis, *p. EX 273*

## Chapter
### quiz

## Short Answer

**1.** Which six formatting elements are included in the AutoFormat feature?

**2.** What is the difference between a custom format and a style?

3. How would you change the function of a style button ($\boxed{\$}$, $\boxed{\%}$, or $\boxed{,}$) on the Formatting toolbar?

4. Name the four visual design principles described in this chapter.

5. Describe the two primary layers that exist in a worksheet.

6. How do you format a draw object?

7. Name some ways that you can format a graphic or picture file.

8. What are some placement options for a chart's legend?

9. How do you add an arrow to a chart?

10. How do you add free-form text to a chart?

## True/False

1. _____ Custom number formats can be used to enhance the display of date and time values.

2. _____ You can create and apply styles to format values in a worksheet but not text labels.

3. _____ Excel's library of lines, arrows, and other draw objects that you can add to a worksheet are collectively known as *AutoShapes*.

4. _____ You can only place text in the cell layer of a worksheet.

5. _____ To size a graphic object, such as a circle or rectangle, drag its selection or sizing handles.

6. _____ Because a WordArt object usually replaces a worksheet title, it is stored in the cell layer of a worksheet.

7. _____ If you forget to enter a chart title using the Chart Wizard, you can always add one later.

8. _____ You double-click a chart element to display its Format dialog box.

9. _____ You cannot print a chart unless it is embedded on a worksheet.

10. _____ Excel provides special page setup options for printing a chart.

## Multiple Choice

1. Which of the following statements about the AutoFormat command is <u>false</u>?

   a. You can format an area using fonts, shading, and border attributes.
   b. You can format an area by applying only column width and row height attributes.
   c. By your selecting one cell, the AutoFormat command can identify a surrounding table area for formatting.
   d. The AutoFormat command will not work on a worksheet area that already contains formatting.

2. When creating a custom number format, you place codes in the following order, separated by semicolons:

   a. positive; negative; text
   b. zero; positive; negative; text
   c. positive; negative; zero; text
   d. positive; zero; negative; text

3. Excel provides the following built-in styles, accessible from the Formatting toolbar:

   a. Comma, Percent, Currency
   b. Comma, Normal, Percent
   c. Comma [0], Percent, Accounting
   d. Number, Currency [2], Font

4. Which of the following is <u>not</u> one of the visual design principles mentioned in this chapter?

   a. Emphasis
   b. Unity
   c. Artistry
   d. Balance

5. Which of the following statements about graphic objects is <u>true</u>?

   a. Graphic objects float above the cell layer of a worksheet.

   b. Graphic objects float below the cell layer of a worksheet.

   c. Once inserted, you can size but not move a graphic object.

   d. You must select an object's color before placing it onto a worksheet.

6. To copy an AutoShape object using drag and drop, hold down this key as you drag the object using the mouse.

   a. ( ALT )

   b. ( CTRL )

   c. ( SHIFT )

   d. ( HOME )

7. Two special effects that you can apply to draw objects include:

   a. Shadow and Extrude

   b. Extrude and 3-D

   c. Implode and Explode

   d. Shadow and 3-D

8. Which of the following media types is <u>not</u> available for limiting a search in the Clip Art task pane?

   a. Animation

   b. Movies

   c. Photographs

   d. Sounds

9. To add a new data series to an existing chart:

   a. DOUBLE-CLICK: the desired data series

   b. CHOOSE: Chart ➜ Add Data

   c. CHOOSE: Chart ➜ Chart Options

   d. You cannot add a data series to an existing chart.

10. When defining the page setup for a separate chart sheet, you will notice the addition of a new tab in the dialog box called:

   a. Draw

   b. Graph

   c. Chart

   d. Object

## Hands-On

### exercises

step by step

### 1. Adding Draw Objects to a Worksheet

Draw objects are used to emphasize particular areas in your worksheet and to enhance its overall appearance. In this exercise you practice inserting AutoShape objects onto the draw layer of an existing worksheet.

1. Open the data file named EX05HE01.

2. Save the workbook as "IT Courses" to your personal storage location.

3. Display the Drawing toolbar, if it is not already displayed.

4. In order to emphasize a new course called "Advanced HTML/XML," let's add an AutoShape object to the worksheet. Do the following:
CLICK: AutoShapes button ( AutoShapes▾ ) on the Drawing toolbar
CHOOSE: Stars and Banners

5. On the Stars and Banners cascading menu:
CHOOSE: Horizontal Scroll ( ▭ )

6. To place a default-sized graphic object on the draw layer:
CLICK: in the middle of cell E2
Your screen should now appear similar to the one shown in Figure 5.52.

**Figure 5.52**

Inserting the
Horizontal Scroll
AutoShape

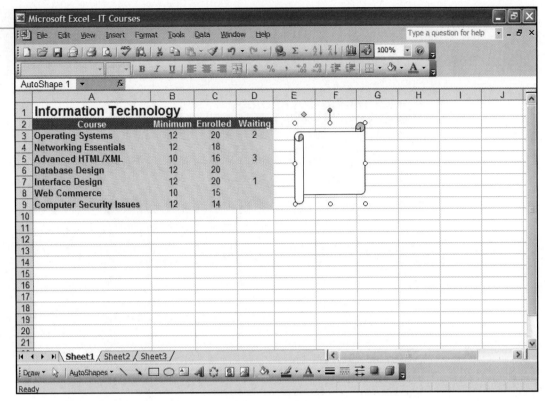

7. To place a text comment in the Horizontal Scroll object:
   RIGHT-CLICK: inside the Horizontal Scroll object
   SELECT: Add Text

8. To complete the entry:
   CLICK: Center button (▤)
   TYPE: **New**
   PRESS: (ENTER)
   TYPE: **Course**

9. Using the sizing handles, make the Horizontal Scroll object smaller as shown to the right.

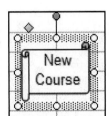

10. Using the Shadow Style button (▣) on the Drawing toolbar, apply Shadow Style 6 (▣) to the object.

11. Using the Zoom button (100% ▾), zoom the window to display only the worksheet columns from A to F.

12. Add an Oval object to highlight the value in cell D5 of the "Waiting" column. Format the oval object to appear with no fill color and a 1½ pt dark red line, as shown in Figure 5.53.

**Figure 5.53**

Placing an Oval object on the worksheet

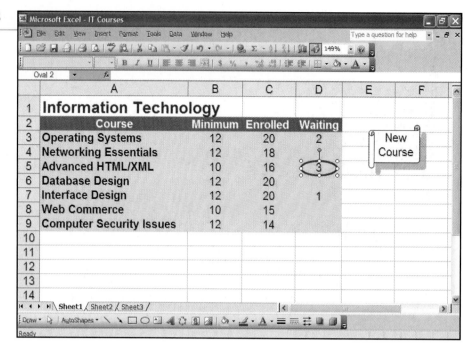

**13.** Finally, add an arrow to point from the Scroll object to the Oval object.

**14.** SELECT: cell A2 to cancel the selection.

**15.** Save and then close the "IT Courses" workbook.

step by step

## 2. Formatting Cells and Creating Styles

You will now practice manipulating and formatting text in a worksheet. In addition, you are given the opportunity to define a new formatting style.

**1.** Open the data file named EX05HE02 to display the workbook shown in Figure 5.54.

**Figure 5.54**

Opening the EX05HE02 workbook

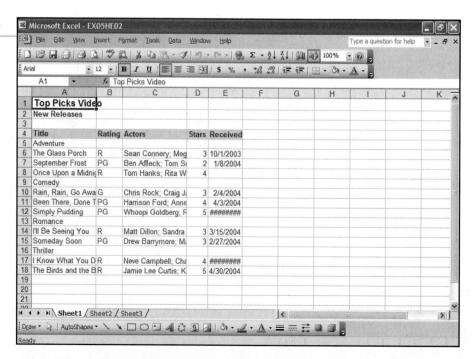

2. Save the workbook as "New Releases" to your personal storage location.

3. Your objective in this exercise is to format the worksheet to display all of the text information without changing any column widths. To begin, rotate the headings in cells A4 through E4 by 20 degrees.

4. Wrap the text appearing in the cell range A5 through A18 (Title column) and for the cell range C6 through C18 (Actors column).

5. Because you may want to change their formatting characteristics later, you decide to highlight the category headings (Adventure, Comedy, Romance, and Thriller) in column A using a style. Do the following:
   SELECT: cell A5
   CLICK: Bold button ( B )
   SELECT: Dark Red color from the Fill Color button (  )
   SELECT: White color from the Font Color button ( A )

6. To define a new style based on this newly formatted cell:
   CHOOSE: Format ➜ Style
   TYPE: **Category**
   Notice that the *Style Includes* area now displays *(By Example)* and lists the formatting attributes for the selected cell.

7. Remove the formatting attributes that are not part of the style:
   CLICK: *Number* check box to remove the ✓
   CLICK: *Protection* check box to remove the ✓
   The dialog box should appear similar to the one shown in Figure 5.55.

**Figure 5.55**

Creating a
custom style
definition

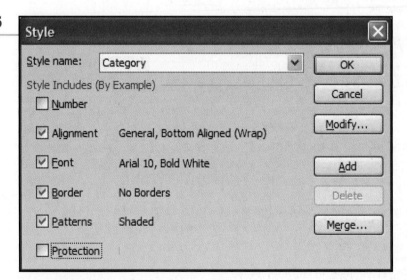

8. To add the new style:
   CLICK: Add command button
   CLICK: OK command button

9. Select cells A9, A13, and A16 and then apply the Category style using the Format ➜ Style command.

10. Shrink the contents of the Received column (E6:E18) to fit inside the worksheet cells.

11. Change the text's vertical alignment to appear centered vertically in the cell range from A5 to E18.

**12.** To help differentiate the category headings from the movie titles, indent the individual movie titles appearing in column A.

**13.** PRESS: CTRL + HOME to return to the top of the worksheet
Your worksheet should now appear similar to the one shown in Figure 5.56.

**14.** Save and then close the workbook.

**Figure 5.56**

Formatting cells
using alignments
and styles

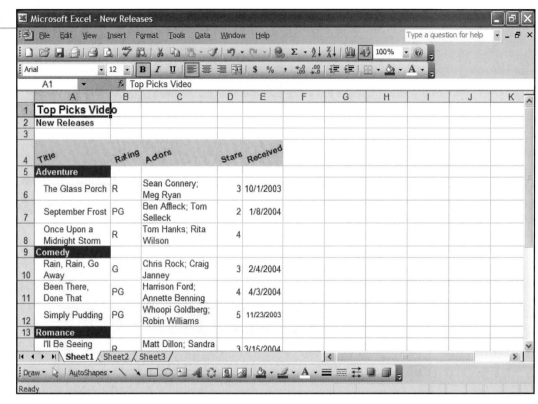

step by step

## 3. Inserting WordArt and Clip Art

In this exercise you insert WordArt and clip art objects to enhance the attractiveness of a worksheet. You also use AutoShapes to direct the reader's attention to specific information.

**1.** Open the data file named EX05HE03.

**2.** Save the workbook as "Dept Expenses" to your personal storage location.

**3.** In the next few steps, you improve the worksheet title using WordArt. To begin, delete the existing title that appears in cell A1.

**4.** Using the Insert WordArt button ( ) on the Drawing toolbar, add a worksheet title that includes the text "Genius Electronics." You may select any style and formatting (font, font size, and font style) that you desire.

**5.** Adjust the height of row 1 and then size and move the WordArt object into position at the top of the worksheet, as shown in Figure 5.57.

**Figure 5.57**

Inserting a
WordArt object
as a title

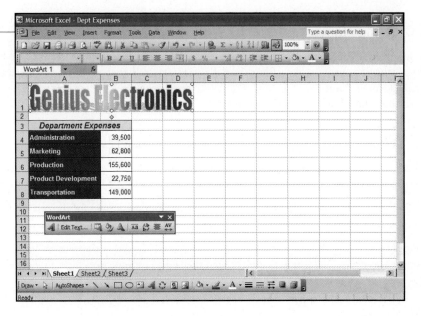

6. Using the Insert Clip Art button (🖼) on the Drawing toolbar, search for a "computer" graphic to appear beside the table of expenses.

7. Size and move the clip art graphic so that it is roughly the same height as the table of expenses. Close the Clip Art task pane.

8. Using the Oval button (◯) on the Drawing toolbar, draw an oval over the value appearing in cell B8. Then format the object to display using no fill color and to have a bright blue 3-point line.

9. Insert an Explosion AutoShape object a few rows below cell B8 and include the text "Capital Expense."

10. Size and move the Explosion object to ensure that all of the text is visible. Format the object to appear with a short shadow.

11. Draw an arrow to point from the Explosion object to the Oval object. Select cell A3 to remove the sizing handles. Your screen should now appear similar to the one shown in Figure 5.58.

12. Save and then close the "Dept Expense" workbook.

**Figure 5.58**

Enhancing a
worksheet with
graphic objects

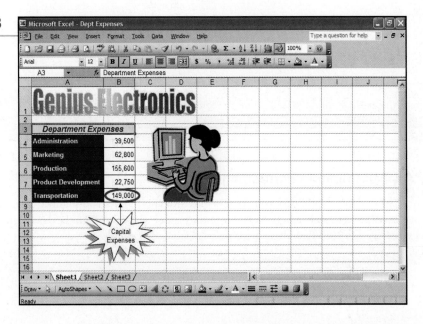

on your own

## 4. Creating Number Formats

In this exercise you practice formatting a worksheet using various features found in the Format Cells dialog box. To begin, open the data file named EX05HE04, and then save it as "Purchase Results" to your personal storage location.

Perform the following formatting steps:

- Make the column headings in row 4 easier to read by centering the contents both horizontally and vertically. Then wrap the text contained in the column headings.

- Use the Format Cells dialog box to apply a currency number format, with no decimal places, to the cell range from C5 to D10.

- Use the Format Cells dialog box to create a custom number format for the cell range from A5 to A15. Enter **2004 - #####** into the *Type* box of the *Number* tab.

- Apply a custom format to the date range from E5 to E15 so that the date "5/7/2004" in cell E5 appears as "Fri-05/07." Select cell E11, and then compare your worksheet to Figure 5.59.

When you are ready to proceed, save and then close the workbook.

**Figure 5.59**

Formatting a worksheet using custom formats

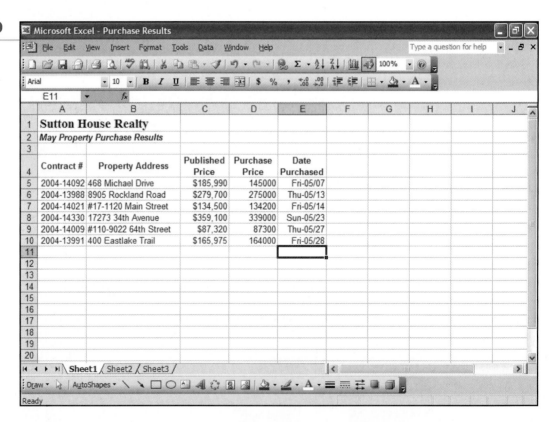

on your own

## 5. Applying Custom Formatting

Toward enhancing a workbook, you are now asked to apply styles and number formats, insert a clip art image, save the workbook, and then send it to the printer. To begin, open the data file named EX05HE05, and save it as "OffRoad Rentals" to your personal storage location.

Perform the following steps to enhance the worksheet:

• Replace the title in cell A1 with a WordArt object that is centered above the monthly columns.

• Apply a currency number format, with no decimal places, to the values appearing in rows 5 and 8.

• Apply a comma number format, with the thousands separator but no decimal places, to the values appearing in rows 6 and 7.

• Apply the "Classic 3" AutoFormat option to the worksheet's table area, but do not alter the existing number formats, alignment, or width and height of columns and rows.

• Adjust the WordArt object as required.

• Insert a related clip art graphic to appear to the right of the table area. (*Note:* If you cannot find the graphic shown in Figure 5.60, select any graphic that you feel is appropriate.)

Save the workbook, and then send it to the printer using a landscape orientation. Figure 5.60 shows one example of a completed worksheet. When satisfied with the printed output, close the workbook.

**Figure 5.60**

Enhancing a worksheet with images

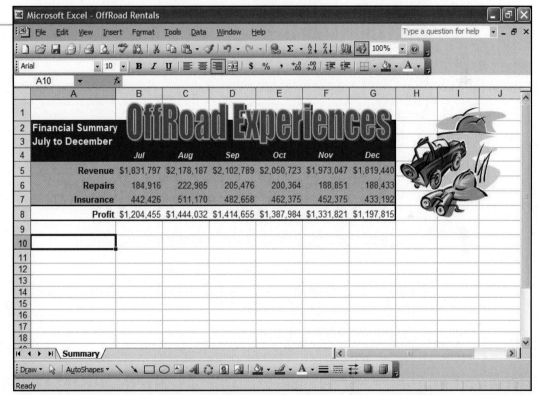

 on your own

## 6. Formatting a Chart

An associate has asked that you review and modify a departmental Excel chart. After opening the EX05HE06 data file, you review and save the friend's workbook as "Comm Survey" to your personal storage location. To display the chart, you click on the *Chart1* tab appearing at the bottom of the worksheet window. Before proceeding, click on a blank part of the chart area, and then use the Zoom button ( 100% ▾ ) to fit to selection (Figure 5.61).

**Figure 5.61**

Fitting a chart
sheet to its
best fit

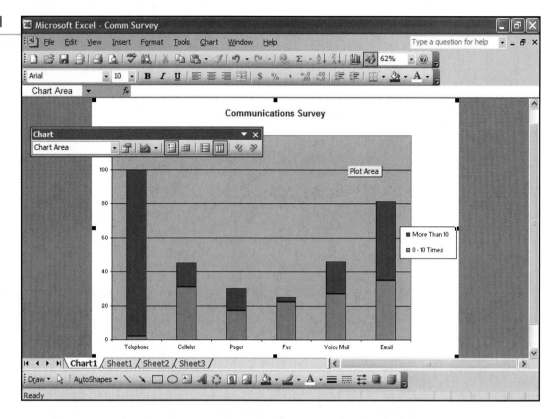

Immediately, you notice some features that you'd like to change. In particular, you perform the following steps:

- Change the chart type to a clustered column with a 3-D visual effect.
- Change the title to "Weekly Usage of Communications Technology."
- Format the title to appear in an 18-point font size, boldface, and italic.
- Move the legend to the bottom of the chart.
- Format the legend to appear in a larger font and with a shadow and fill color. (*Note:* You may have to size the legend to view its contents.)

When you are finished, save and print the chart sheet. Then close the "Comm Survey" workbook.

# CaseStudy　WHITE DOVE PLAINS

White Dove Plains is a small Western city with a frontier heritage. By encouraging its downtown store-fronts to adopt a Western theme and by holding several frontier-oriented events, the White Dove Plains business community has succeeded in developing and promoting a thriving tourist destination. The two most popular events, sponsored by local businesspeople, are the annual Cattle Drive and the Gold Rush Fair.

White Dove Plains's Chamber of Commerce is busily working on an information package to further promote the area's attractions. Specifically, an internal committee has appointed Wendy Manuel, owner of the Prairie Schooner Gift Shop, to take charge of developing the promotional package. After many discussions with other business owners, Wendy feels that a strong visual presentation will provide the most impact. She also wants to highlight some census data that is stored in an Excel worksheet.

In the following case problems, assume the role of Wendy and perform the same steps that she identifies.

**1.** Wendy is taking her newfound responsibility very seriously. She has garnered input from small-business owners and from members of several community service groups. With the help of a friend at the local college, she has also finished compiling a workbook of key statistics for the area. Now she wants to improve the appearance of the worksheet for inclusion in the information package.

To begin, Wendy opens the EX05CP01 data file and saves the workbook as "Fast Facts" to her personal storage location. For her initial objective, Wendy wants to insert a few labels on the worksheet. She clicks the AutoShapes button on the Drawing toolbar and then chooses the Callouts menu. After selecting and inserting the AutoShape object named "Rounded Rectangular Callout" to the right of the "Schools" area, Wendy types "Regional College" and watches as the callout expands automatically. She sizes and formats the object so that each word appears centered on its own line. Then she drags the object's yellow diamond-shaped selection handle to point its stem toward cell B12. Finally, she applies formatting to emphasize the callout.

On the same worksheet, Wendy uses WordArt to insert a title at the top of the page. After selecting a suitable style in the WordArt Gallery dialog box, she enters the words "Fast Facts" and selects an interesting typeface and font size. Wendy finds that she must increase the height of row 1 in order to place the object neatly in the row. She also fine-tunes the title by sizing the WordArt object. Satisfied with the visual balance of the worksheet (Figure 5.62), Wendy saves and then closes the workbook.

**Figure 5.62**

Inserting an AutoShape and a WordArt object

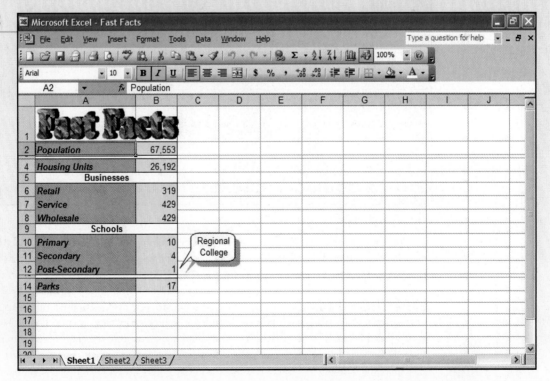

2. Last year, the Tourist Information Center displayed a guest book and welcomed visitors to sign in and provide comments or suggestions. Using this guest book, Wendy was able to identify the number and origin of visitors. Having entered this information into a worksheet, Wendy now wants to create a visual representation of the data using Excel's charting capabilities. She opens the EX05CP02 data file and then saves the workbook as "Visitors" to her personal storage location.

Wendy begins by selecting the cell range (A3:B7) containing the visitor information and then launches the Chart Wizard. After viewing several different chart types, Wendy decides on using the "Exploded Pie" style and proceeds through the wizard. She entitles the chart "Visitor Origins" and makes sure to create it as a new sheet.

Wendy feels that the chart needs to be enhanced before including it with the other promotional material. She decides to apply some basic formatting. First, she sizes the Chart toolbar to display its buttons on two rows (refer to Figure 5.63) and moves it off to one side. Then she specifies a fill color for the Chart area and increases the title's font size to 36 points. She formats the legend to display using an 18-point font size, sizes the legend using the mouse, and then chooses the same fill color as the Chart area with no border lines. Stepping away from her monitor to view the chart from another perspective, Wendy decides to apply even further formatting to the legend. Once completed, the chart sheet appears similar to Figure 5.63. Wendy saves and then closes the "Visitors" workbook.

**Figure 5.63**

Creating an exploded pie chart

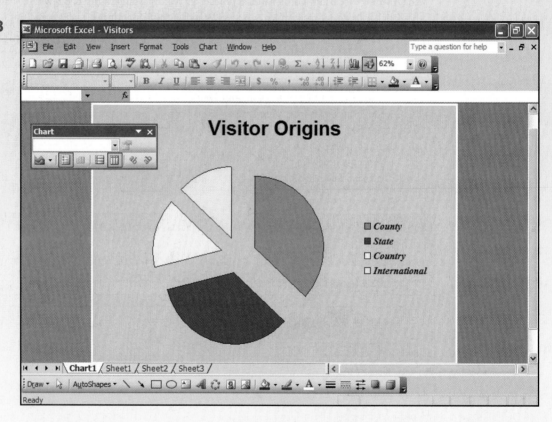

3. After she comes back from lunch, Wendy notices that a new diskette has been placed on her desk. The diskette label reads "Market Occupancy Levels," and the attached note tells her that it is from the Tourism Information Center. She opens the EX05CP03 workbook that is stored on the diskette and saves it as "Occupancy" to her personal storage location. After reviewing the table of numbers, Wendy selects the data range and launches the Chart Wizard. She decides to use a line chart to show how the occupancy levels progressed over the season for each category. She accepts all the Chart Wizard's suggested defaults for the first three steps, but chooses to store the chart on a separate chart sheet.

Although the line chart is practical, Wendy believes that a stacked column chart will better display the cumulative occupancies for the entire region. After changing the chart's type, she moves the legend to the bottom of the chart and then selects the plot area by clicking on its gray background. She reduces the height of the plot area by grabbing the center sizing handle at the top of the plot area and dragging it downward. Then she applies formatting to the axes using an Arial 12-point font and to the legend using a Times New Roman 14-point font. To finish off the chart, she adds a WordArt title of "Occupancy Levels" to the top. She then saves and closes the workbook.

4. During last year's Cattle Drive, the Chamber of Commerce conducted a survey to gauge the effectiveness of their advertising efforts. Visitors were asked to fill in a form indicating how they had heard of the event. Wendy has created a chart to summarize the results, but feels that it needs some changes. She opens the EX05CP04 workbook and saves it as "Survey" to her personal storage location.

   After sizing the chart to fill the window, Wendy sees that the information for Radio advertising is missing. She displays the *Data* worksheet by clicking its sheet tab, adds a new row category for "Radio," and enters a value of 633. Once completed, she switches back to the *Chart* sheet and adds this new data series to the chart. The chart is updated automatically. She then replaces the title with the WordArt object shown in Figure 5.64.

**Figure 5.64**

Modifying a pie chart

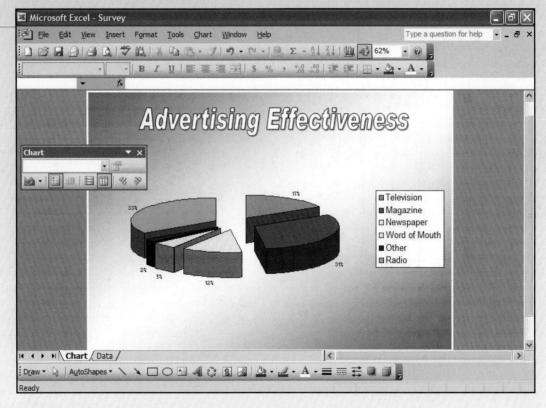

Wendy determines that the chart might be more effective as a three-dimensional bar chart. After converting it, Wendy deletes the legend, removes the data labels, and formats the axes to use a larger font. She then selects and increases the size of the chart's plot area. Satisfied with the chart's new appearance, she prints the chart sheet and then saves and closes the workbook. The information package is shaping up nicely! Wendy exits Excel and decides to take the rest of the day off.

## Answers to Self-Check Questions

**5.1** What are the two ways that you can indent a cell entry? To indent a cell's contents, (1) use the *Alignment* tab of the Format Cells dialog box or (2) click the Increase Indent ( ) button on the toolbar.

**5.2** Using the Style dialog box, how would you change the default font for an entire workbook to be 12-point, Times New Roman? You can modify the Normal style for the workbook using the Format, Style command. Click the Modify command button in the Style dialog box and then make the required changes in the Format Cells dialog box. After you return to the worksheet, all cells based on the Normal style will appear formatted.

**5.3** How would you place a "STOP" sign on a worksheet using the techniques described in this module? Click the AutoShapes button on the Drawing toolbar and then select an Octagon shape from the Basic Shapes menu. After placing the object onto the draw layer, apply a red fill color. Then add and center the text "STOP" inside the object and format the word to appear white and boldface.

**5.4** Name four types of media files that you can search for using the Clip Art task pane. The four media types shown in Figure 5.28 are Clip Art, Photographs, Movies, and Sounds.

**5.5** What must you remember when selecting nonadjacent ranges in preparation for the Chart Wizard or to add to a chart's plot area? You must ensure that the ranges are the same shape and size.

**5.6** What might you do differently in formatting a chart for printing as opposed to formatting a chart for displaying online? When formatting a chart for printing, you must concern yourself with the quality of output the printer is capable of. Therefore, you may use patterns and shading levels instead of colors. For online or computer-based presentations, the use of colors in charts works well to differentiate the various elements.

# Microsoft®Office**Excel**®

2003

CHAPTER 6

# Performing Calculations

## PREREQUISITES

This chapter focuses on analyzing and manipulating worksheet information using Excel's built-in functions. Successful completion of the content depends on your ability to enter and edit formulas and your ability to grasp analytical concepts. You should possess a basic understanding of calculations involving date, time, mathematical, statistical, and financial concepts.

## LEARNING OBJECTIVES

After reading this chapter, you will be able to:

• Construct nested formula expressions

• Use the logical IF function to make decisions

• Use Goal Seek to perform basic what-if analysis

• Use date and time functions, including DATE, DAY, MONTH, YEAR, WEEKDAY, and TIME

• Use mathematical and statistical functions, including ROUND, RAND, ABS, and INT

• Use text functions to convert, extract, manipulate, and join labels and other character strings

• Use financial functions, including PV, FV, and PMT

# 6.1 Working with Formulas and Functions

Early on in your discovery of Microsoft Office Excel, you learned that entering a formula required typing an equal sign (=) followed by the expression you wanted to evaluate. As you may have already guessed, there is a little more to performing calculations than simply adding and subtracting cell addresses in a worksheet. In this chapter you practice constructing formulas and implementing Excel's many built-in functions.

A formula is composed of *operands* and *operators*. An **operand** is an element that you want included in the calculation and may either be a **constant** value (i.e., any number, date, or text entry), a range name, or a cell address. An **operator** is the symbol used to determine what type of calculation to perform on the operand(s). Excel provides four categories of calculation operators—*arithmetic* (+, −, *, /, %, and ^), *comparison* (=, >, <, >=, <=, <>), *text* (&), and *reference* (for example, the colon [:], comma [,], and space [ ] characters).

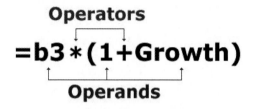

When you combine two or more operators in the same expression, Excel performs the calculation according to the operator **order of precedence** shown in Table 6.1. For those instances where an expression contains operators of the same precedence (multiplication and division or addition and subtraction), Excel evaluates the expression from left to right. You can force a portion of an expression to evaluate first, superseding the order of precedence, by placing it within parentheses (as shown above). This process, called *nesting*, is discussed in the first lesson.

**Table 6.1**

Operators in Order of Precedence

| Calculated... | Symbols... | Description... |
|---|---|---|
| First | % | Percent operator; converts a value to a percentage by dividing it by 100 (e.g., 20% is equal to 0.20.) |
| Second | ^ | Exponentiation operator; raises the base value to the power specified (e.g., 3^2 is 3*3 and equal to 9; 4^3 is 4*4*4 and equal to 64.) |
| Third | * and / | Multiplication and Division operators; performs a calculation using operands on either side of the operator |
| Fourth | + and − | Addition and Subtraction operators; performs a calculation using operands on either side of the operator |
| Fifth | & | Concatenation (link) operator for text; joins two character strings together |

The most common methods for entering a formula are *typing* and *pointing*. In typing a formula, the entire expression is typed on the keyboard, including the equal sign, operands, and operators. For entering functions, type the function name and then place its arguments within parentheses. (*Hint:* A useful rule of thumb is to never insert spaces when entering a formula expression.) The pointing method uses both the keyboard and the mouse. After typing the equal sign, the expression is constructed by clicking on the desired cells (operands) and typing the required operators. You can also type a function's name, followed by a left parenthesis, and then use pointing to select the cells or ranges to include as the function's arguments. When finished, remember to place a right closing parenthesis at the end of the function's argument list.

Because entering a function correctly requires that you adhere to its syntax rules, most people prefer to engage the Insert Function dialog box or the Function Arguments dialog box for assistance. These two tools are especially helpful when you can't remember the name of a particular function or when you need to be reminded of its argument list. Another technique that can help you enter functions is to use range names in place of cell addresses in the argument list. To illustrate, the expression =SUM(Donations) is much easier to read and understand than =SUM(AC12:DC239). In this module you practice creating, nesting, displaying, and printing formulas and functions. You also learn to use the logical IF function for conducting conditional tests on worksheet values and formula expressions.

## 6.1.1 Nesting Formulas and Functions

→ ## Feature

Parentheses enable you to control the order by which portions of an expression are evaluated. For example, the formula =4+3*2 is equal to 10, because the order of precedence states that multiplication (3*2) is performed before addition. To force the addition to take place first, insert parentheses into the formula so that it reads =(4+3)*2. The new result is 14. The process of using parentheses to force the order of calculation within an expression is called **nesting**. In addition to affecting the calculation order, parentheses also offer the benefit of making your formula expressions easier to read and understand.

→ ## Practice

In addition to nesting calculations, you will use Excel's *Range Finder* feature to help identify a formula's operands. Before proceeding, ensure that Microsoft Office Excel 2003 is loaded.

**1.** Open the data file named EX0610 to display the worksheet shown in Figure 6.1.

**Figure 6.1**

Opening the
EX0610
workbook

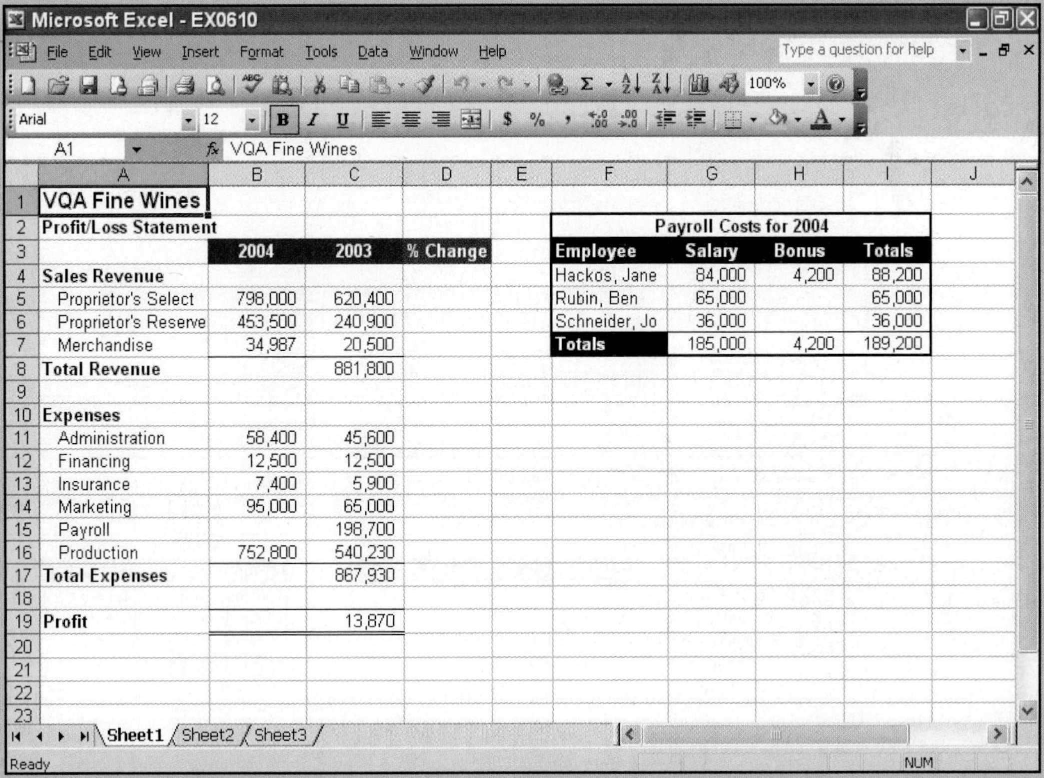

**2.** Save the workbook as "VQA Wines" to your personal storage location.

**3.** For review, let's use the typing method to enter a function:
SELECT: cell B8
TYPE: =sum(b5:b7)
PRESS: ENTER
The result, 1,286,487, appears in cell B8.

**4.** You will now use the pointing method to enter a formula that references the "Payroll Costs for 2004" table:
SELECT: cell B15
TYPE: =
CLICK: cell I7
Notice that the expression is built dynamically in Excel's Formula bar as you type and click on cells.

**5.** PRESS: ENTER to complete the entry

**6.** To add together the expenses, use the SUM function:
SELECT: cell B17
TYPE: =sum(

**7.** You may now specify the function's arguments by pointing:
SELECT: cell range from B11 to B16 using the mouse
TYPE: )
PRESS: ENTER
The result, 1,128,165, now appears in cell B17.

**8.** To finish the column entries:
SELECT: cell B19
TYPE: =
CLICK: cell B8 (Total Revenue)
TYPE: –
CLICK: cell B17 (Total Expenses)
PRESS: ENTER
The total profit for 2004, as shown in cell B19, is 158,322.

**9.** Nesting allows you to construct more complex expressions. To begin, let's review a cell that contains a nested formula:
SELECT: cell H4
PRESS: F2 (Edit key)
Your screen should now appear similar to the one shown in Figure 6.2. Notice that the formula's operands are color-coded by Excel's Range Finder feature and that these colors correspond to the highlighted cells. In this formula an employee's bonus is calculated by adding five percent of his or her salary to one percent of the total revenue for the year.

**Figure 6.2**

Viewing operands and operators in a formula expression

| | A | B | C | D | E | F | G | H | I | J |
|---|---|---|---|---|---|---|---|---|---|---|
| | SUM ▼ X ✓ ƒ𝑥 =(5%*G4)+(1%*B8) | | | | | | | | | |
| 1 | VQA Fine Wines | | | | | | | | | |
| 2 | Profit/Loss Statement | | | | | Payroll Costs for 2004 | | | | |
| 3 | | 2004 | 2003 | % Change | | Employee | Salary | Bonus | Totals | |
| 4 | Sales Revenue | | | | | Hackos, Jane | 84,000 | =(5%*G4)+(1%*B8) | | |
| 5 | Proprietor's Select | 798,000 | 620,400 | | | Rubin, Ben | 65,000 | | 65,000 | |
| 6 | Proprietor's Reserve | 453,500 | 240,900 | | | Schneider, Jo | 36,000 | | 36,000 | |
| 7 | Merchandise | 34,987 | 20,500 | | | Totals | 185,000 | 17,065 | 202,065 | |
| 8 | Total Revenue | 1,286,487 | 881,800 | | | | | | | |
| 9 | | | | | | | | | | |

Two nested calculations in one formula expression

Excel's Range Finder feature highlights the expression's operands in the worksheet

**10.** Let's practice entering this nested bonus calculation by typing:
PRESS: ESC to exit the Edit mode for cell H4
SELECT: cell H5
TYPE: =(5%*g5)+(1%*b8)
PRESS: ENTER
The result, 16,115, is displayed. Notice that the parentheses group the calculations, making the formula easier to read.

**11.** Now enter the same formula by pointing:
SELECT: cell H6
TYPE: =(5%*
CLICK: cell G6
TYPE: )+(1%*
CLICK: cell B8
TYPE: )
PRESS: ENTER
The result, 14,665, appears. You may agree that it is easier to type this formula than to keep reaching for the mouse to click on cells.

**12.** For additional practice in using nesting, calculate the percentage change that occurs between the two years displayed in the income statement:
SELECT: cell D5
TYPE: =(
PRESS: ◄ twice to select cell B5
TYPE: –
PRESS: ◄ once to select cell C5
TYPE: )/
PRESS: ◄ once to select cell C5
PRESS: ENTER
As demonstrated, it is sometimes easier to point to cells using the keyboard than using the mouse.

**13.** To copy this formula to the remaining cells:
SELECT: cell D5
CLICK: Copy button (⧉) on the Standard toolbar
SELECT: cell range from D6 to D8
PRESS: CTRL and hold it down
SELECT: cell range from D11 to D17

**14.** Keep the CTRL key pressed down to select the last cell:
CLICK: cell D19
Multiple ranges should now be highlighted. (*Hint:* Remember to release the CTRL key before proceeding.)

**15.** To complete the copy operation:
CLICK: Paste button (⧉▾) on the Standard toolbar
Your screen should now appear similar to the one shown in Figure 6.3.

**Figure 6.3**

Copying a formula to several cell ranges

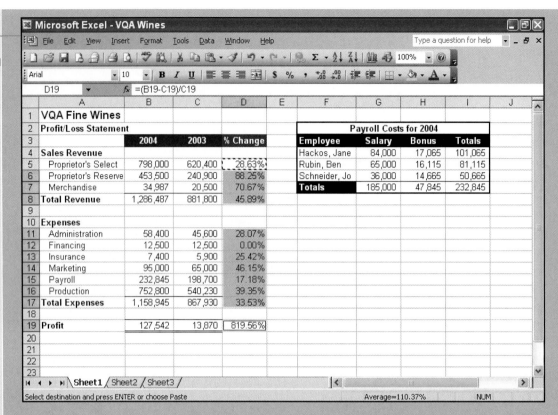

**16.** PRESS: [ESC] to remove the bounding outline

**17.** PRESS: [CTRL]+[HOME] to move the cell pointer

**18.** Save the workbook, and keep it open for use in the next lesson.

### 6.1.2 Making Decisions (IF)

→ **Feature**

You use the IF function when you need to employ conditional logic in your worksheets. The IF function lets you test for a condition and then, depending on the result, perform one of two calculations. By using nesting and IF statements together, you can perform numerous tests and branch to more than two calculations, if necessary. Conditional expressions make use of the following comparison operators: equal (=), not equal (<>), less than (<), less than or equal to (<=), greater than (>), and greater than or equal to (>=).

→ **Method**

To test for one condition:

• =IF(*condition,true,false*)

To test for two conditions using nesting:

• =IF(*condition,true,IF(condition,true,false*))

→ **Practice**

You will now practice using the IF function. Ensure that you've completed the previous lesson and that the "VQA Wines" workbook is displayed.

**1.** Let's change the method for calculating the employee bonuses. Instead of granting an automatic 1% bonus of the "Total Revenue" value in cell B8, you will use an IF function to specify a conditional expression. To begin:
SELECT: cell F9

**2.** In cell F9 you will use an IF function to print the words "Bonus Paid" or "No Bonus," depending on whether the value in the "Total Revenue" cell is $1,000,000 or more. Do the following:
TYPE: =if(
CLICK: Insert Function button ($f_x$) in the Formula bar
The dialog box shown in Figure 6.4 appears.

**Figure 6.4**

Constructing an IF function

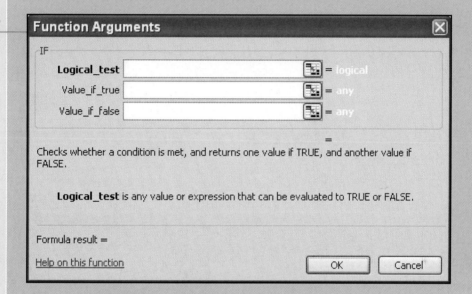

**3.** In the *Logical_test* text box, enter a condition to test whether the "Total Revenue" is greater than or equal to $1,000,000:
TYPE: **b8>=1000000**
PRESS: TAB
Notice that the condition evaluates to "TRUE" in the dialog box.

**4.** In the *Value_if_true* text box, specify the entry or the calculation to perform if the logical test is true:
TYPE: **"Bonus Paid"**
PRESS: TAB
Notice the use of quotation marks to specify a text entry into the cell.

**5.** In the *Value_if_false* text box, specify the entry to perform if the "Total Revenue" is less than $1,000,000:
TYPE: **"No Bonus"**
CLICK: OK command button
The result, "Bonus Paid," is displayed in cell F9.

**6.** To test the conditional expression:
SELECT: cell B5
TYPE: 400000
PRESS: ENTER
Because the "Total Revenue" value of 888,487 is less than $1,000,000, cell F9 now displays the words "No Bonus."

**7.** To facilitate adjustments to the bonus calculations in column H, let's compute and place the bonus percentage in cell G9. Do the following:
SELECT: cell G9

**8.** Your objective is to construct an IF function that places a percent factor in cell G9 for use in calculating the employee bonuses:
TYPE: =if(b8>=1000000, 1%, 0%)
PRESS: **ENTER**
Since the "Total Revenue" value is less than $1,000,000, a zero (0) is displayed in cell G9.

**9.** Using the Formatting toolbar, apply the Percent format to the entry in cell G9 and increase the decimal places to two.

**10.** You must now adjust the bonus calculation in cell H4. Do the following:
SELECT: cell H4
PRESS: **F2** (EDIT key)

**11.** In the Formula bar:
DRAG: the I-beam mouse pointer over "1%" in the expression
Your screen should appear similar to the one shown in Figure 6.5.

**Figure 6.5**

Editing the "Bonus" formula expression

| SUM | ▼ | X ✓ | $f_x$ | =(5%*G4)+(1%*B8) | | | H | I | J |
|---|---|---|---|---|---|---|---|---|---|
| | A | B | C | | | | | | |
| 1 | VQA Fine Wines | | | | | | | | |
| 2 | Profit/Loss Statement | | | | | Payroll Costs for 2004 | | | |
| 3 | | 2004 | 2003 | % Change | Employee | Salary | Bonus | Totals | |
| 4 | Sales Revenue | | | | Hackos, Jane | 84,000 | =(5%*G4)+(1%*B8) | | |
| 5 | Proprietor's Select | 400,000 | 620,400 | -35.53% | Rubin, Ben | 65,000 | 12,135 | 77,135 | |
| 6 | Proprietor's Reserve | 453,500 | 240,900 | 88.25% | Schneider, Jo | 36,000 | 10,685 | 46,685 | |
| 7 | Merchandise | 34,987 | 20,500 | 70.67% | Totals | 185,000 | 35,905 | 220,905 | |
| 8 | Total Revenue | 888,487 | 881,800 | 0.76% | | | | | |
| 9 | | | | | No Bonus | 0.00% | | | |

Drag the I-beam mouse pointer over the "1%" operand to edit the formula

These "IF" statements provide dynamic results

**12.** To replace the "1%" with the factor appearing in cell G9:
TYPE: $G$9
You specify an absolute cell reference in order to facilitate copying the formula in a later step.

**13.** You must also make the cell reference for the "Total Revenue" value absolute. To do so, position the insertion point between the "B" and the "8" in the cell address B8, as shown below.

=(5%*G4)+($G$9*B8)

Ensure that the flashing insertion point appears in the cell address for the "Total Revenue" value

**14.** To make the cell reference absolute:
PRESS: **F4** (ABS key)
The cell address should now read "$B$8." (*Hint:* ABS stands for Absolute in this instruction.)

**15.** To finish editing the formula:
PRESS: **ENTER**
The value, 4,200, appears in cell H4.

**16.** Now copy the formula expression in cell H4 to cells H5 and H6.

**17.** To conclude the exercise, let's test the results:
SELECT: cell B5
TYPE: 800000
PRESS: **ENTER**
Because "Total Revenue" is greater than $1,000,000, the "Bonus Paid" is "1.00%" and the bonus values in column H are recalculated, as shown in Figure 6.6.

**18.** Save the workbook, and keep it open for use in the next lesson.

**Figure 6.6**

Completing the
VQA Wines
workbook

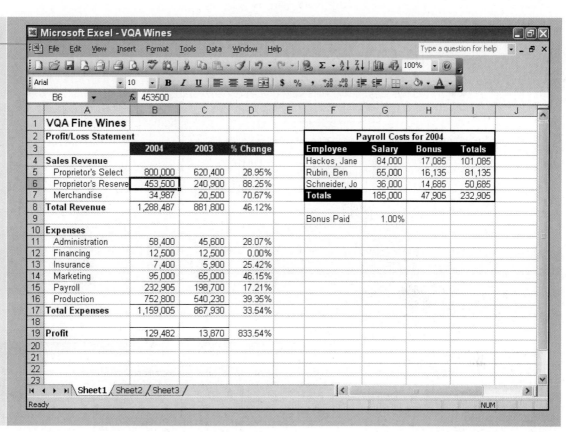

## 6.1.3 Finding Answers Using Goal Seek

→ **Feature**

**Goal seeking,** also called *backward solving,* lets you begin at the finish line and then work backward to solve a problem. When you know the desired result for a formula, you can use goal seeking to calculate the input value. For example, goal seeking can determine the number of units that must be sold to generate $30,000 of net income. Through an iterative (trial and error) process, Excel repeatedly substitutes values into the input cell (units sold) until the formula that calculates net income displays $30,000. One limitation of goal seek, however, is that while it is extremely fast and easy to use, it allows only one input cell to be manipulated in order to satisfy the target value.

→ **Method**

To perform a goal seek operation:

- CHOOSE: Tools → Goal Seek

- In the *Set cell* text box, enter the cell containing the outcome formula.

- In the *To value* text box, enter the desired target value.

- In the *By changing cell* text box, enter the input cell that Excel may change to achieve the target value.

- CLICK: OK command button

→ **Practice**

You will now use goal seeking to backward solve a formula in the worksheet. Ensure that you've completed the previous lesson and that the "VQA Wines" workbook is displayed.

**1.** In this lesson you will use the VQA Wines workbook as a what-if analysis tool. Your objective is to find the Proprietor's Reserve sales revenue required to earn $1,000,000 of Total Revenue. To begin, position the cell pointer on the cell containing the target outcome formula:
SELECT: cell B8

**2.** Now issue the Goal Seek command:
CHOOSE: Tools → Goal Seek
Your screen should appear similar to the one shown in Figure 6.7.

**Figure 6.7**

Goal Seek dialog box

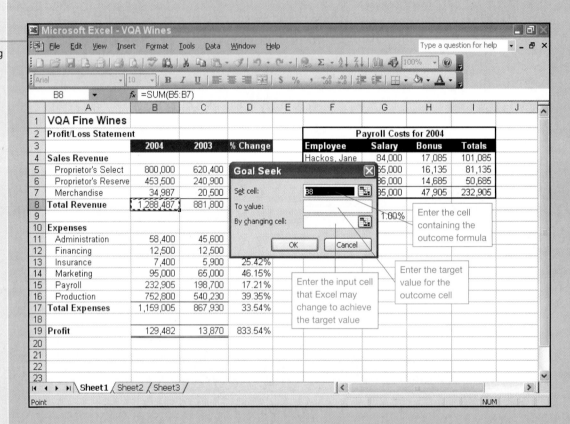

**3.** In the Goal Seek dialog box, ensure that the *Set cell* text box contains a reference to cell B8 and then do the following:
PRESS: TAB to select the *To value* text box
TYPE: 1000000
(*Hint:* You are telling Excel what value you want to appear in cell B8.)

**4.** Now select the cell that Excel is allowed to manipulate to achieve the results specified in the *To value* text box:
PRESS: TAB to select the *By changing cell* text box
TYPE: b6
Cell B6 contains the sales revenue value for the Proprietor's Reserve.

**5.** To proceed with goal seeking:
CLICK: OK command button
When Excel finds an answer, the worksheet is updated with a new value in cell B6 (165,013) and a confirmation dialog box is displayed (Figure 6.8).

## Figure 6.8

Successful goal seeking operation

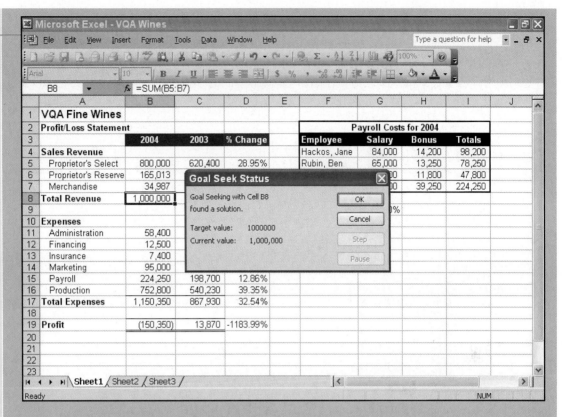

**6.** CLICK: OK command button to accept the solution

**7.** In a real-world application, you would save this modified workbook under a new file name. To save disk space, let's save the workbook under the same name and keep it open for use in the next lesson.

## 6.1.4 Displaying and Printing Formulas and Functions

### → Feature

By default, Excel displays only the results of a formula or function in a worksheet cell. But for documentation purposes, you may want to display and print the actual formula expressions. This feature is also helpful when auditing and testing a worksheet for accuracy and validity. Fortunately, Excel allows you to display and print a hard copy of worksheet formulas. You can then annotate the printout with handwritten notes and store it away as a paper backup for the original workbook.

### → Method

To display worksheet formulas for printing:

- CHOOSE: Tools → Options
- CLICK: *View* tab
- SELECT: *Formulas* check box in the *Window options* area
- CLICK: OK command button
- CLICK: Print button (🖼) on the Standard toolbar, if desired

→ **Practice**

In this lesson you will display formulas in a worksheet and then print the results. Ensure that you've completed the previous lesson and that the "VQA Wines" workbook is displayed.

**1.** To display the Options dialog box (Figure 6.9):
CHOOSE: Tools → Options
CLICK: *View* tab

**Figure 6.9**

Options dialog box: *View* tab

Select this check box to display formulas in your worksheet

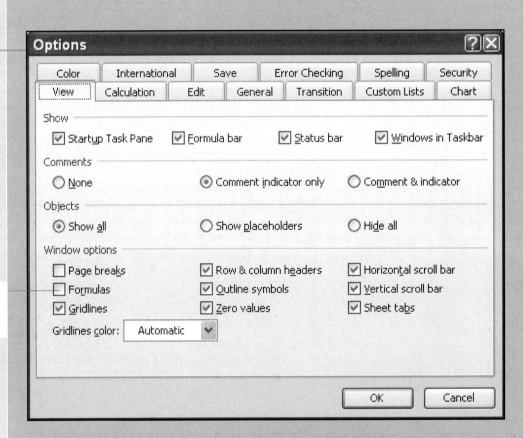

**2.** To display the formula expressions appearing in cells:
SELECT: *Formulas* check box so that a ✓ appears
CLICK: OK command button
The worksheet should now appear with formulas displayed.

**3.** If the Formula Auditing toolbar appears (as shown below):
CLICK: its Close button ([×])

**4.** Now let's change the width of the first column:
SELECT: cell A1
CHOOSE: Format → Column → AutoFit Selection

**5.** On your own, reduce the widths for columns B, C, and D to eight characters. Then, scroll through the worksheet and review the cell entries.

**6.** To help you reference cells and formulas in a hardcopy printout, you can add gridlines and frame headers to the page. To illustrate:
CHOOSE: File → Page Setup
CLICK: *Sheet* tab

**7.** Make the desired selections in the dialog box:
SELECT: *Gridlines* check box in the *Print* area
SELECT: *Row and column headings* check box in the *Print* area
CLICK: Print Preview command button
The worksheet appears in the Preview window.

**8.** Zoom in on the worksheet to view the printed formulas. Your screen should now appear similar to the one shown in Figure 6.10.

**Figure 6.10**

Previewing worksheet formulas

You can include the column and row frame borders, along with gridlines, to help you line up information in the worksheet printout

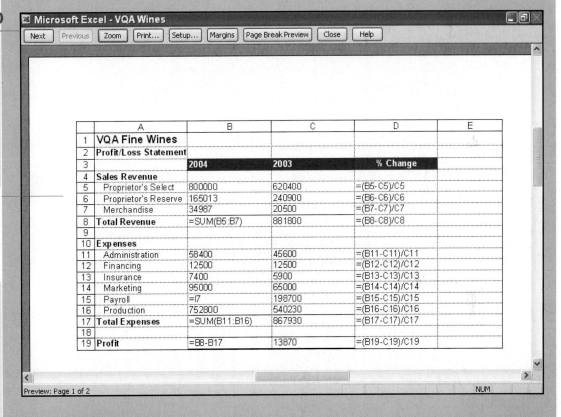

**9.** If you have a printer connected to your computer, perform the following instruction. Otherwise, click the Close command button in the toolbar and proceed to the next step:
CLICK: Print command button in the toolbar
CLICK: OK command button

**10.** To reset the worksheet window:
CHOOSE: Tools → Options
SELECT: *Formulas* check box so that no ✓ appears
CLICK: OK command button

**11.** On your own, change the widths for columns A through D to their best fit and select cell A1.

**12.** Close the workbook and save the changes.

**6.1** Provide two reasons for nesting a calculation in a formula expression.

# 6.2 Using Date and Time Functions

Besides the TODAY and NOW functions provided by Excel to dynamically display the current date and time, there are several additional date and time functions that enable you to perform calculations. These functions also allow you to format, present, and convert date and time values in a worksheet. In this module you learn to use functions in order to enter a date value using Excel's proper format, and also to extract the year, month, day, and weekday from a particular date value. You also learn to evaluate date and time expressions.

## 6.2.1 Entering a Date (DATE)

### → Feature

Did you know that Excel stores a date value as a serial number, beginning with January 1, 1900, as number 1? The number of days that have elapsed since this first date yields all other date values. For example, January 1, 2005, is stored by Excel as 38,353, regardless of how it may be formatted to display in the worksheet. Excel's DATE function provides one method for returning a serial date value given three separate arguments for the year, month, and day. Once calculated, you can format the result to appear as a date rather than a serial number. The DATE function is especially useful for calculating the difference between two dates and for constructing date values from worksheet entries.

### → Method

• =DATE(*year,month,day*)

### → Practice

You will now practice entering the DATE function. Ensure that no workbooks appear in the application window.

**1.** Open the data file named EX0620 to display the workbook shown in Figure 6.11. This workbook provides a summary area for function syntax, sorted alphabetically, followed by an exercise area starting at row 10.

**Figure 6.11**

Opening the
EX0620
workbook

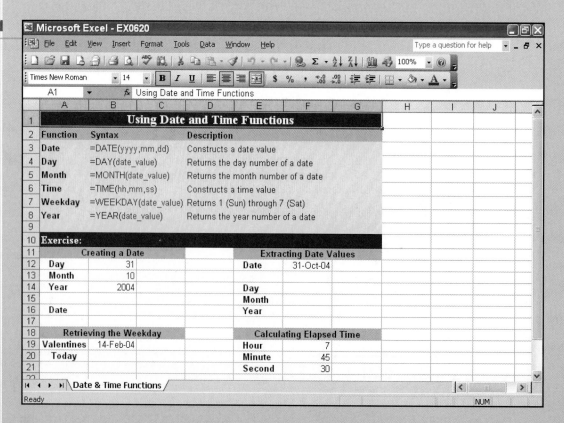

**2.** Save the workbook as "Functions 620" to your personal storage location.

**3.** After reviewing the function names and descriptions:
SELECT: cell A10, which is a merged cell

**4.** As shown below, use the vertical scroll bar to scroll the window downward, so that row 10 appears as the first row at the top of the worksheet.

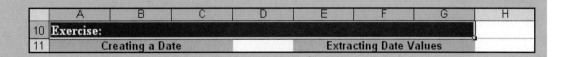

**5.** You will now construct a date value from three separate arguments in the worksheet. To begin:
SELECT: cell B16
TYPE: =date(

**6.** Let's display the Function Arguments dialog box:
CLICK: Insert Function button (fx)

**7.** Move the Function Arguments dialog box by dragging its Title bar, so that you can see the values in columns A and B.

**8.** In the *Year* text box:
TYPE: b14
PRESS: TAB

**9.** In the *Month* text box:
TYPE: b13
PRESS: TAB

**10.** In the *Day* text box:
TYPE: b12
Your screen should now appear similar to the one shown in Figure 6.12. Notice that Excel retrieves the cell values for display in the Function Arguments dialog box.

**Figure 6.12**

Entering the DATE function

The function expression is built as you enter arguments into the dialog box

The calculated result is displayed as both a serial value and as a formatted date value

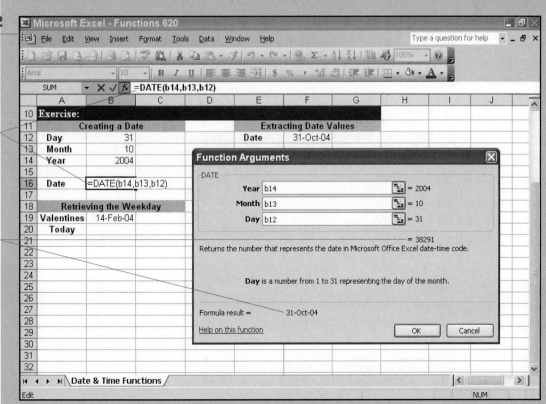

**11.** To complete the function:
CLICK: OK command button
The formatted date value, 31-Oct-04, is displayed.

**12.** To change the date value:
SELECT: cell B13
TYPE: 12
PRESS: ENTER
The date in cell B16 changes to 31-Dec-04. You now have a dynamic date value that you can adjust by changing its individual arguments.

**13.** Let's do some date arithmetic. To display the number of days between the date appearing in cell B16 and today, do the following:
SELECT: cell C16
TYPE: =
PRESS: ← once
TYPE: -today()
PRESS: ENTER
Unfortunately, the desired numeric result is incorrectly formatted as a date value. Also, notice that you used the TODAY function as an operand in the expression.

**14.** To adjust the cell formatting:
SELECT: C16
CLICK: Comma Style button ( ⸳ )
The correct number of days now appears in cell C16.

**15.** Save the workbook, and keep it open for use in the next lesson.

### 6.2.2 Extracting Date Values (DAY, MONTH, and YEAR)

→ # Feature

Excel provides three functions that you may use to extract the day, month, and year values from a particular date. These functions are used to display a date's component values separately in a worksheet or to calculate operands for use in other formulas or functions.

→ # Method

- =DAY(*date_value*)

- =MONTH(*date_value*)

- =YEAR(*date_value*)

→ # Practice

You will now extract the day, month, and year for a given date value. Ensure that the "Functions 620" workbook is displayed.

**1.** Let's name the source cell to use in the following functions:
SELECT: cell F12
CLICK: in the Name box using the I-beam mouse pointer
TYPE: myDate
PRESS: ENTER

**2.** To return the day number from the date value stored in myDate:
SELECT: cell F14
TYPE: =day(myDate)
PRESS: ↓

**3.** To return the month number:
TYPE: =month(myDate)
PRESS: ⬇

**4.** To return the year number:
TYPE: =year(myDate)
PRESS: ENTER

**5.** SELECT: cell F12
Your screen should now appear similar to the one shown in Figure 6.13.

**Figure 6.13**

Entering the DAY, MONTH, and YEAR functions

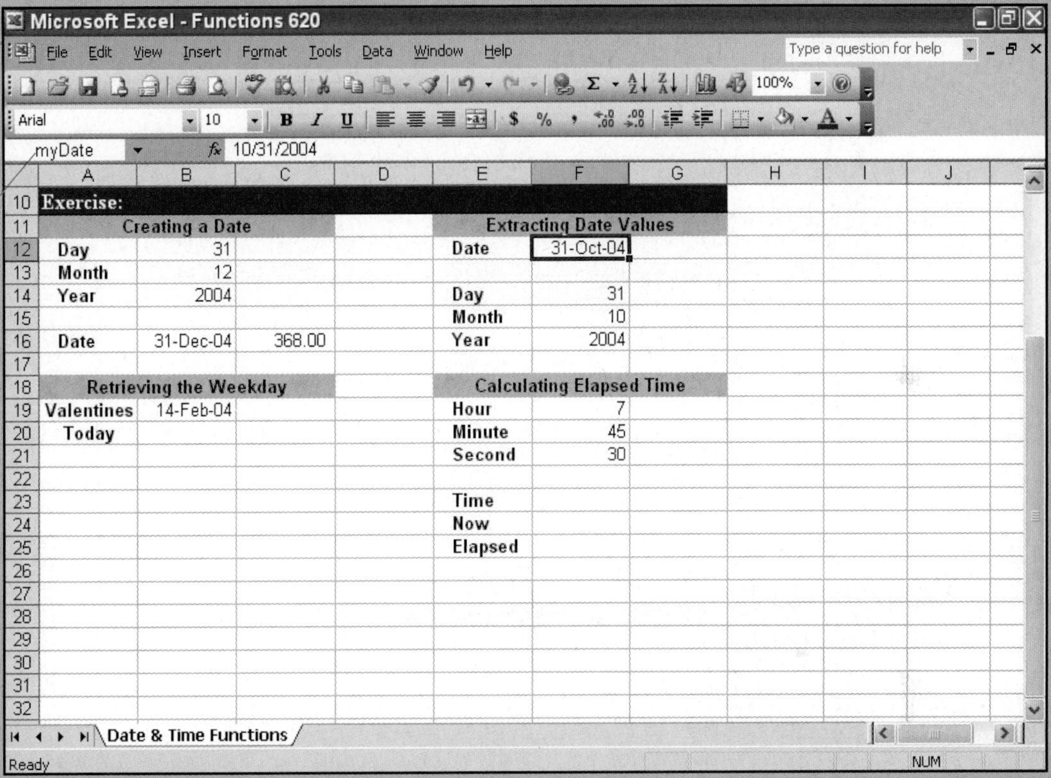

The active cell, F12, is named "myDate," as shown in the Name box

**6.** Let's change the original myDate value. To insert the current date into cell F12 using a keyboard shortcut:
PRESS: CTRL +;
PRESS: ENTER
Notice that the day, month, and year values are updated as soon as the new value is entered.

**7.** Save the workbook, and keep it open for use in the next lesson.

### 6.2.3 Calculating the Day of the Week (WEEKDAY)

→ **Feature**

The WEEKDAY function calculates the day of the week by returning a number between 1 (Sunday) and 7 (Saturday). For example, the function returns the number 4 if the date argument falls on a Wednesday. Rather than using the WEEKDAY function, another way of displaying the weekday is to apply the "ddd" or "dddd" custom format option to a standard date value.

→ ## Method

- =WEEKDAY(*date_value*)

→ ## Practice

You will now calculate the day of the week for two date values. Ensure that the "Functions 620" workbook is displayed.

**1.** Let's use the Insert Function dialog box to insert the WEEKDAY function for the date appearing in cell B19. Do the following:
SELECT: cell C19
CHOOSE: Insert → Function
The Insert Function dialog box appears.

**2.** To pick the desired function:
SELECT: Date & Time in the *Or select a category* drop-down list box
SELECT: Weekday in the *Select a function* list box
Your dialog box should now appear similar to the one shown in Figure 6.14.

**Figure 6.14**

Selecting the
WEEKDAY
function

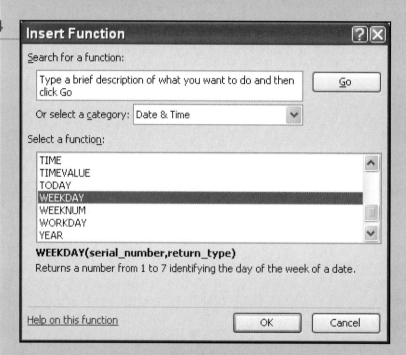

**3.** CLICK: OK command button to proceed
The Function Arguments dialog box now replaces the Insert Function dialog box.

**4.** With the insertion point in the *Serial_number* text box:
CLICK: cell B19
Notice that the date's serial value, 38031, appears to the right of the text box and the result, 7, appears near the bottom of the Function Arguments dialog box.

**5.** To complete the Function Arguments dialog box:
CLICK: OK command button
The answer, 7 (for Saturday), appears in the cell.

**6.** To demonstrate another method for displaying the weekday, let's insert the current date:
SELECT: cell B20
PRESS: CTRL +;
PRESS: ENTER

7. You will now format the cell to display the weekday:
SELECT: cell B20
CHOOSE: Format → Cells
CLICK: *Number* tab
SELECT: Custom in the *Category* list box

8. To begin creating a new custom format:
SELECT: the contents of the *Type* text box using the mouse
PRESS: DELETE to remove the existing entry

9. Now enter the desired custom format symbols:
TYPE: **dddd**
CLICK: OK command button
The long name for the current day of the week should appear. (*Hint:* To display the three-letter abbreviation for the weekday name, use the "ddd" custom format option instead.) Your worksheet should appear somewhat similar to the one shown in Figure 6.15.

10. Save the workbook, and keep it open for use in the next lesson.

**Figure 6.15**

Displaying the weekday of a date value

Using a custom number format to display the weekday name

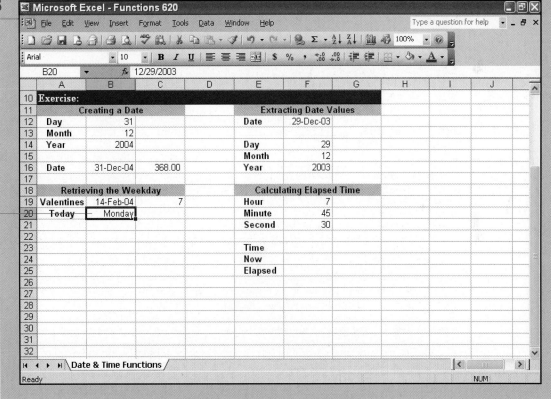

## 6.2.4 Calculating Elapsed Time (TIME)

 **Feature**

Similar to the DATE function, the TIME function returns a time value given three separate arguments for hour, minute, and second. You specify the hour argument using the range 0 to 23, the minute argument using 0 to 59, and the second argument using 0 to 59. You can use this function to calculate the elapsed time between two time values.

→ ## Method

• =TIME*(hour,minute,second)*

→ ## Practice

In this lesson you will create an expression that calculates the amount of time to elapse between two values. Ensure that the "Functions 620" workbook is displayed.

**1.** Enter the TIME function by typing:
SELECT: cell F23
TYPE: =time(
A ScreenTip appears, as shown below, to help you enter the function.

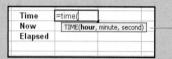

The ScreenTip provides an ordered list of the required function arguments. The argument appearing in boldface is the next argument to be entered.

**2.** To finish entering the arguments:
TYPE: f19,f20,f21)
The ScreenTip disappears when you type the closing parenthesis.

| Calculating Elapsed Time | |
|---|---|
| Hour | 7 |
| Minute | 45 |
| Second | 30 |
| | |
| Time | =time(f19,f20,f21) |

**3.** PRESS: ENTER to complete the entry
The time, 7:45 AM, appears in the formatted cell.

**4.** You can insert the current time into a cell using a keyboard shortcut:
SELECT: cell F24
PRESS: CTRL +:
(*Hint:* This instruction can also be written CTRL + SHIFT +;.)

**5.** PRESS: ENTER to complete the entry

**6.** To calculate the amount of time that has elapsed between these two time values:
SELECT: cell F25
TYPE: =f24–f23
PRESS: ENTER
Notice that the result inherits the source cells' time formatting.

**7.** To format the cell to display a more appropriate measuring unit:
SELECT: cell F25
CHOOSE: Format → Cells

**8.** On the *Number* tab of the dialog box:
SELECT: Time in the *Category* list box, if not already selected
SELECT: 37:30:55 in the *Type* list box
CLICK: OK command button
The number of hours, minutes, and seconds to elapse are now displayed. Your worksheet should appear similar, but not identical, to the one shown in Figure 6.16.

**9.** Save and then close the workbook.

**Figure 6.16**

Completing the
Functions 620
workbook

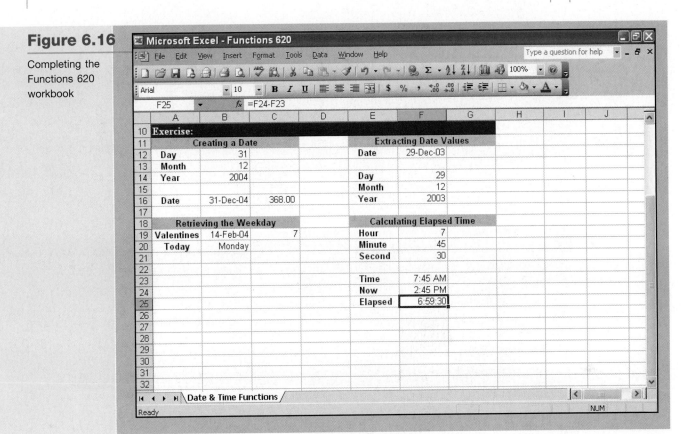

## In Addition CALCULATING THE ELAPSED NUMBER OF DAYS, MONTHS, AND YEARS

Rather than using a formula, you can use Excel's DATEDIF function to calculate the difference between two dates. The function syntax is **DATEDIF(*start_date,end_date,unit*["Y","M","D"])**. Using the last argument, you can choose to display the result in terms of the number of years, months, or days to elapse. For example, the function **=DATEDIF(a1,a2,"D")** would return the number of days between the date entries in cells A1 and A2. Unfortunately, there exists no such function for calculating the difference between two times.

**6.2** Name two methods for calculating and displaying the day of the week (e.g., Wednesday).

# 6.3 Using Mathematical and Statistical Functions

Excel provides a collection of mathematical, trigonometric, and statistical functions, extending beyond the SUM, AVERAGE, MIN, MAX, and COUNT functions introduced in module 4.2. Whether you need to calculate the sides of a triangle, generate a list of random numbers, or calculate the standard deviations for an experimental research study, these functions can save you tremendous amounts of time and complexity. In this module you are introduced to four of these functions: ROUND, RAND, ABS, and INT. You also use the Paste Special feature to convert a formula expression into its resulting value.

### 6.3.1 Rounding Values (ROUND)

→ ## Feature

The ROUND function returns the **rounded value** of a cell to the number of digits specified. If the number of digits is greater than 0, the value is rounded to the number of decimal places. For example, the function ROUND(3.147,2) would return the value 3.15. If the number of digits is 0, the value is rounded to the nearest integer. If the number of digits is less than 0, the value is rounded to the left of the decimal point.

→ ## Method

• =ROUND(*number,digits*)

→ ## Practice

You will now practice entering the ROUND function using the Insert Function dialog box. Ensure that no workbooks appear in the application window.

1. Open the data file named EX0630 to display the workbook shown in Figure 6.17. This workbook provides a summary area for function syntax, in rows 1 through 7, followed by an exercise area starting at row 8.

**Figure 6.17**

Opening the EX0630 workbook

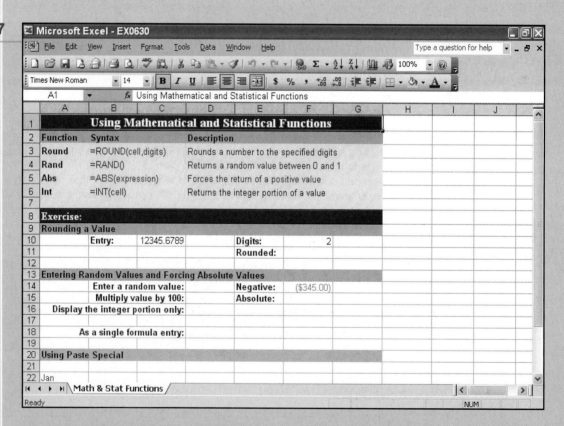

2. Save the workbook as "Functions 630" to your personal storage location.

3. After reviewing the function names and descriptions:
SELECT: cell A8, which is a merged cell

**4.** As shown below, use the vertical scroll bar to scroll the window downward, so that row 8 appears as the first row at the top of the worksheet.

| | A | B | C | D | E | F | G | H |
|---|---|---|---|---|---|---|---|---|
| 8 | Exercise: | | | | | | | |
| 9 | Rounding a Value | | | | | | | |

**5.** Your objective in the next few steps is to round the value appearing in cell C10 to the number of digits displayed in cell F10. Let's use the Insert Function dialog box to enter the ROUND function:
SELECT: cell F11
CLICK: Insert Function button ($f_x$)

**6.** In the Insert Function dialog box:
TYPE: **Rounding a value** in the *Search for a function* text box
CLICK: Go command button
Your dialog box should appear similar to the one shown in Figure 6.18.

**Figure 6.18**

Searching for the ROUND function

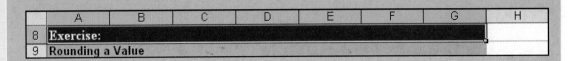

Enter your search query for a function in this text box

Select the desired function in this list box

**Insert Function** [?][X]

Search for a function:

| Rounding a value | Go |

Or select a category: Recommended ▼

Select a function:

| ROUND |
| ODD |
| INT |
| MROUND |
| ROUNDUP |
| ROUNDDOWN |
| FIXED |

**ROUND(number,num_digits)**
Rounds a number to a specified number of digits.

Help on this function          OK          Cancel

**7.** To proceed, ensure that ROUND appears selected in the *Select a function* list box (as shown in Figure 6.18) and then:
CLICK: OK command button
The Function Arguments dialog box for the ROUND function replaces the Insert Function dialog box.

**8.** In the *Number* text box, you can type a cell address, select a cell from the visible portion of the worksheet, or input a numeric value to round. You can also collapse the dialog box and then select a cell, as illustrated in this step:
CLICK: Collapse Dialog button (🔲) for the *Number* text box
CLICK: cell C10
Your screen should now appear similar to the one shown in Figure 6.19.

**Figure 6.19**

Selecting a
function argument

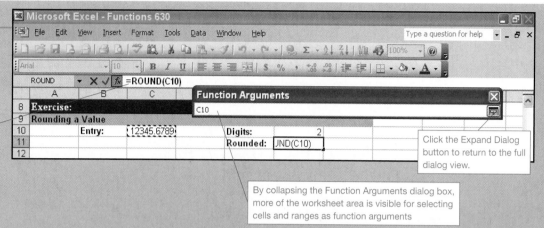

This ROUND
function is built as
you select the
function arguments

By collapsing the Function Arguments dialog box,
more of the worksheet area is visible for selecting
cells and ranges as function arguments

Click the Expand Dialog
button to return to the full
dialog view.

**9.** To expand the Function Arguments dialog box:
CLICK: Expand Dialog button (📼)
PRESS: **TAB** to move to the next text box
Notice that the function being built also appears in the Formula bar.

**10.** For the *Num_digits* text box, enter the cell address containing the number of digits to display:
TYPE: **F10**
The Function Arguments dialog box should now appear as shown in Figure 6.20.

**Figure 6.20**

Function
Arguments dialog
box for the
ROUND function

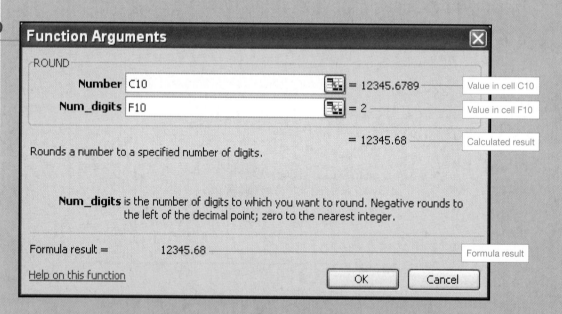

Value in cell C10

Value in cell F10

Calculated result

Formula result

**11.** To complete the Function Arguments dialog box:
CLICK: OK command button
The result, 12345.68, is entered into cell F11.

**12.** To demonstrate how changing the rounding digit affects the result:
SELECT: cell F10
TYPE: **0**
PRESS: **ENTER**
The result in cell F11 is updated to display 12346.

**13.** Now let's enter a negative value for the rounding digit:
SELECT: cell F10
TYPE: –2
PRESS: ⎡ENTER⎤
The result in cell F11 is updated to display 12300.

**14.** Save the workbook, and keep it open for use in the next lesson.

### 6.3.2 Finding Random Values (RAND and INT)

→ ## Feature

The RAND function is used to calculate a **random number** between 0 and 1. Each time the worksheet is recalculated, the RAND function will calculate a new random value. To manually force the worksheet to recalculate, press the ⎡F9⎤ (Calc key).

   The INT function returns the **integer value** of a number or cell. The integer portion of a number is the value appearing to the left of the decimal point. For example, the integer portion of 123.99 is 123. You use the INT function to extract the integer value of a number.

→ ## Method

- =RAND()

- =INT(*cell*)

→ ## Practice

In this lesson you calculate a random value between 0 and 100 and then return the integer portion of the value. Ensure that the "Functions 630" workbook is displayed.

**1.** The RAND function enables you to generate random data. You might use this function to provide test data for analyzing share prices or evaluating statistical hypotheses. To enter the function:
SELECT: cell D14
TYPE: =rand()
PRESS: ⬇
A value between 0 and 1 should now appear in the cell.

**2.** To display the random value as a number between 0 and 100:
TYPE: =
PRESS: ⬆
TYPE: *100
PRESS: ⬇
Notice that Excel updates the random value when you press ⬇.

**3.** The INT function, unlike ROUND, simply truncates the decimal portion of a value—no rounding takes place. To extract only the integer portion of cell D15, do the following:
TYPE: =int(
PRESS: ⬆
TYPE: )
PRESS: ⎡ENTER⎤
Only the value to the left of the decimal point appears in cell D16.

**4.** Using a single formula, you can calculate a random value between 0 and 10 that displays to two decimal places only. To illustrate:
SELECT: cell D18
TYPE: =round(rand()*10,2)
PRESS: ⎡ENTER⎤
A value between 0 and 10 should now appear. Notice that you nest the RAND function as an argument in the ROUND function. Your worksheet should appear similar, but not identical, to the one shown in Figure 6.21.

Excel

**Figure 6.21**

Using the RAND, INT, and ROUND functions

| | A | B | C | D | E | F | G | H |
|---|---|---|---|---|---|---|---|---|
| 8 | Exercise: | | | | | | | |
| 9 | Rounding a Value | | | | | | | |
| 10 | | Entry: | 12345.6789 | | Digits: | -2 | | |
| 11 | | | | | Rounded: | 12300 | | |
| 12 | | | | | | | | |
| 13 | Entering Random Values and Forcing Absolute Values | | | | | | | |
| 14 | | Enter a random value: | 0.612921 | Negative: | | ($345.00) | | |
| 15 | | Multiply value by 100: | 61.2921004 | Absolute: | | | | |
| 16 | Display the integer portion only: | | 61 | | | | | |
| 17 | | | | | | | | |
| 18 | As a single formula entry: | | 8.65 | | | | | |
| 19 | | | | | | | | |

Integer portion of cell D15

Nesting RAND within ROUND

**5.** To generate new values, do the following:
PRESS: [F9] (Calc key) repeatedly
With each key press, new random values appear in the cells.

**6.** Save the workbook, and keep it open for use in the next lesson.

*In Addition* DISPLAYING A RANDOM NUMBER WITHIN A RANGE

The RANDBETWEEN function, provided with the Analysis Tookpak add-in, returns a random number that falls between a predetermined integer range. You specify a low integer and an upper integer using the following syntax: **RANDBETWEEN(*lower,upper*)**. RANDBETWEEN is especially useful for entering sample or test data into your worksheets.

### 6.3.3 Displaying a Number's Absolute Value (ABS)

→ **Feature**

The ABS function is used to display a number without its sign. In other words, the function returns the absolute or positive value for a cell, value, or expression. For example, the entry =ABS(-4) returns 4. Most often, you nest another formula or function within the ABS function to force a positive result.

→ **Method**

• =ABS(*expression*)

→ **Practice**

In this lesson you use the ABS function to strip a number of its sign. Ensure that the "Functions 630" workbook is displayed.

**1.** The ABS function is very easy to use. You simply nest a value or result of a formula within the ABS parentheses. To illustrate:
SELECT: cell F15

**2.** You will now display the absolute value of the number appearing in cell F14. Do the following:
TYPE: =abs(f14)
PRESS: [ENTER]
The value $345.00 now appears in cell F15.

**3.** Save the workbook, and keep it open for use in the next lesson.

### 6.3.4 Using Paste Special to Convert Data

→ ## Feature

After populating cells using the RAND or RANDBETWEEN functions, you may wish to convert the results into values that no longer change with each recalculation. The Paste Special command enables you to paste a formula back into the worksheet as a static value. You can also use the Paste Special command to transpose values from a column to row orientation or vice versa. After a paste operation, you can access additional features by clicking the Paste Options button (🖹) attached to the destination range.

→ ## Method

To convert data from formula expressions to static values:

- SELECT: the desired cell or cell range
- CLICK: Copy button (🖹)
- SELECT: the desired target cell
- CHOOSE: Edit → Paste Special
- SELECT: *Values* option button to convert formulas to values
- SELECT: *Transpose* check box to change the orientation of data

→ ## Practice

In this lesson you practice transposing values in the worksheet and converting the results of a RAND function to static worksheet values. Ensure that the "Functions 630" worksheet is displayed.

**1.** In the cell range from A22 to A27, the worksheet stores a list of month names. You can use the Paste Special command to transpose this columnar list to display on a single row. Do the following:
SELECT: cell range from A22 to A27

**2.** To copy the cell contents to the Clipboard:
CLICK: Copy button (🖹) on the toolbar

**3.** Now let's transpose the orientation of the selected cell range:
SELECT: cell B21
CHOOSE: Edit → Paste Special
SELECT: *Transpose* check box so that a ✓ appears
The dialog box should now appear similar to the one shown in Figure 6.22.

**Figure 6.22**

Using the Paste Special command

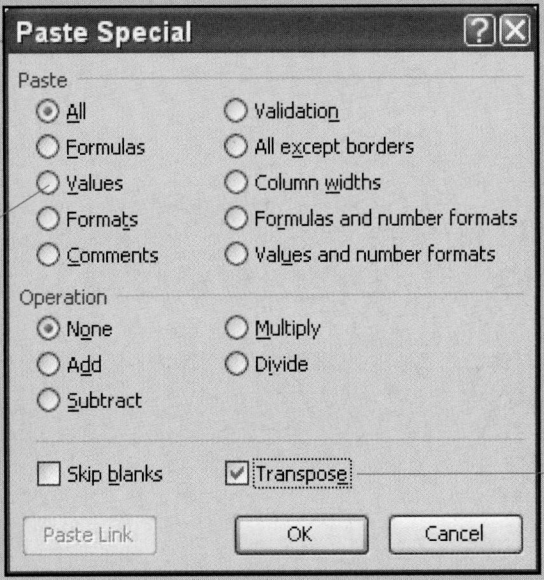

Select the *Values* option button to convert data copied to the Clipboard to their static values

Select the *Transpose* check box to change the row and column orientation of data stored on the Clipoard

**4.** To complete the operation:
CLICK: OK command button
The month names now appear in the range from cell B21 to G21.

**5.** PRESS: `ESC` to remove the bounding outline

**6.** Let's fill a cell range with a table of random numbers. To do so, you will learn a shortcut for entering similar entries. Do the following:
SELECT: cell range from B22 to G27
TYPE: =int(rand()*100)
Although the entire range is selected, you enter a formula into the top left-hand cell only (Figure 6.23).

**Figure 6.23**

Filling a range with a single entry

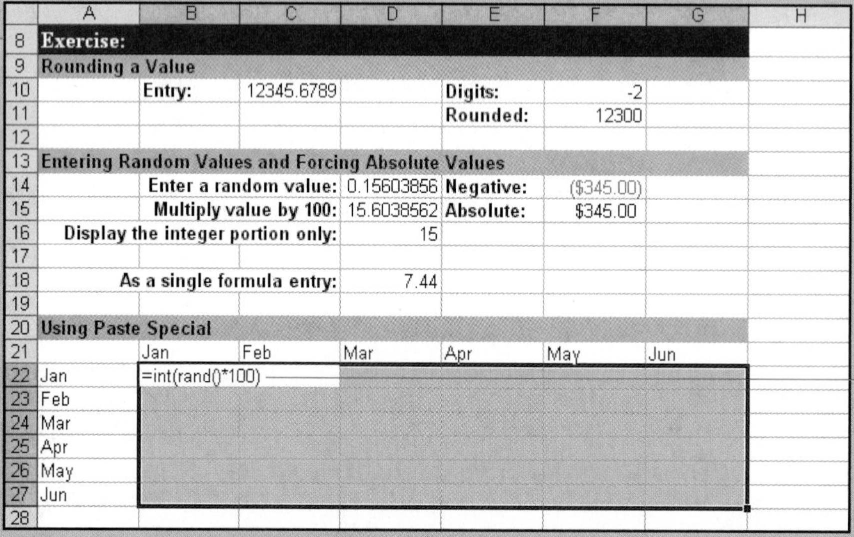

| | A | B | C | D | E | F | G | H |
|---|---|---|---|---|---|---|---|---|
| 8 | Exercise: | | | | | | | |
| 9 | Rounding a Value | | | | | | | |
| 10 | | Entry: | 12345.6789 | | Digits: | -2 | | |
| 11 | | | | | Rounded: | 12300 | | |
| 12 | | | | | | | | |
| 13 | Entering Random Values and Forcing Absolute Values | | | | | | | |
| 14 | | Enter a random value: | 0.15603856 | Negative: | ($345.00) | | | |
| 15 | | Multiply value by 100: | 15.6038562 | Absolute: | $345.00 | | | |
| 16 | Display the integer portion only: | | 15 | | | | | |
| 17 | | | | | | | | |
| 18 | As a single formula entry: | | 7.44 | | | | | |
| 19 | | | | | | | | |
| 20 | Using Paste Special | | | | | | | |
| 21 | | Jan | Feb | Mar | Apr | May | Jun | |
| 22 | Jan | =int(rand()*100) | | | | | | |
| 23 | Feb | | | | | | | |
| 24 | Mar | | | | | | | |
| 25 | Apr | | | | | | | |
| 26 | May | | | | | | | |
| 27 | Jun | | | | | | | |
| 28 | | | | | | | | |

Entering a formula into the top left-hand corner of the selected cell range

**7.** PRESS: `CTRL`+`ENTER`
The selected range is filled with the same formula expression.

**8.** With the range still selected:
PRESS: `F9` (Calc key) repeatedly
Notice that the values are updated in the table.

**9.** To copy the selected table to the Clipboard:
CLICK: Copy button ( 📋 )

**10.** Now let's convert the copied formulas to their static values:
CLICK: down arrow attached to the Paste button ( 📋▾ )
Your screen should now appear similar to the one shown in Figure 6.24.

**Figure 6.24**

Displaying the
Paste options

Menu of paste
options accessed by
clicking the down
arrow attached to
the Paste button
(⌐•)

Selected cell range
copied to the
Clipboard

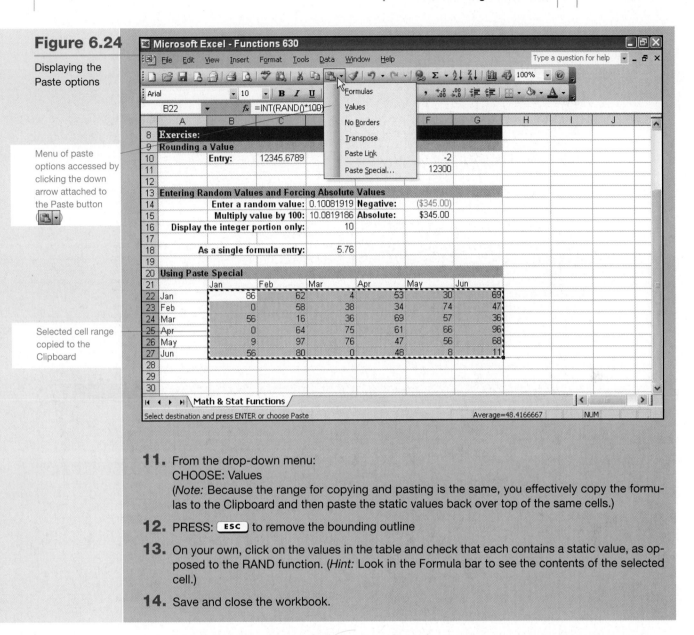

11. From the drop-down menu:
    CHOOSE: Values
    (*Note:* Because the range for copying and pasting is the same, you effectively copy the formulas to the Clipboard and then paste the static values back over top of the same cells.)

12. PRESS: [ ESC ] to remove the bounding outline

13. On your own, click on the values in the table and check that each contains a static value, as opposed to the RAND function. (*Hint:* Look in the Formula bar to see the contents of the selected cell.)

14. Save and close the workbook.

   **6.3** What are the results of the functions INT(4.55) and ROUND(4.55,0)?

# 6.4 Using Text Manipulation Functions

As a competent Excel user, you will most certainly be asked at some point to summarize information that has been entered by less experienced users or has been imported from different applications. Frequently, data from these sources requires "cleaning up" to make it presentable in reports. It is in these circumstances that you will find Excel's text functions to be extremely useful. These functions enable you to compare, convert, format, extract, and combine textual data. In this module you learn how to manipulate text labels, also called **character strings,** in your worksheet.

## 6.4.1 Analyzing a String (LEN and SEARCH)

→ **Feature**

The LEN function returns the number of characters, including spaces, in a string. For example, the expression LEN("ABC") is equal to 3 and LEN("A B C") is equal to 5. While not used by itself very often, the LEN function helps you in calculating character positions and extracting text using other functions. The SEARCH function is also used for locating character positions in a string.

→ **Method**

- =LEN*(text)*

- =SEARCH*(find_text,text,start)*

→ **Practice**

You will now practice entering the LEN and SEARCH text functions. Ensure that no workbooks appear in the application window.

**1.** Open the data file named EX0640 to display the workbook shown in Figure 6.25. This workbook provides a summary area for function syntax, in rows 1 through 14, followed by an exercise area starting at row 15.

**Figure 6.25**

Opening the
EX0640
workbook

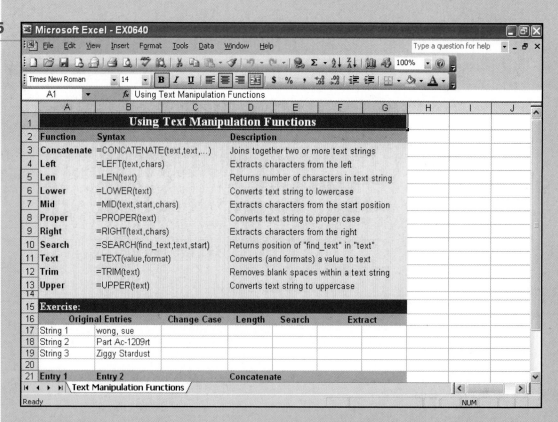

**2.** Save the workbook as "Functions 640" to your personal storage location.

**3.** After reviewing the function names and descriptions:
SELECT: cell A15, which is a merged cell

**4.** As shown below, use the vertical scroll bar to scroll the window downward, so that row 15 appears as the first row at the top of the worksheet.

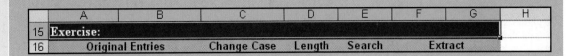

**5.** To calculate the length of the text label in cell B17, do the following:
SELECT: cell D17
TYPE: =len(b17)
PRESS: ENTER
The result, 9, appears in the cell. Notice that the calculation included the comma and space in addition to the characters stored in cell B17.

**6.** To copy this formula to the other two rows:
SELECT: cell range from D17 to D19
CHOOSE: Edit → Fill → Down

**7.** To find the character position of the comma in cell B17:
SELECT: cell E17
TYPE: =search(
CLICK: Insert Function button ($f_x$)
The Function Arguments dialog box appears with the required prompts appearing in boldface lettering.

**8.** By dragging its Title bar, position the Function Arguments dialog box below row 18, as shown in Figure 6.26.

**Figure 6.26**

Functions Arguments dialog box for the Search function

Argument names appearing in boldface are required entries

Argument names appearing in regular style are optional

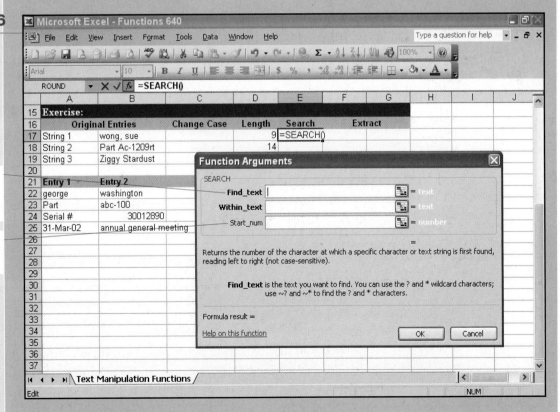

9. In the *Find_text* text box, enter the text surrounded by quotation marks that you want to search for in the cell:
TYPE: ","
PRESS: TAB

10. In the *Within_text* text box, enter the cell address containing the text label that you want to search:
CLICK: cell B17
Notice that the result, 5, already appears in the dialog box. In other words, a comma appears at the fifth character position in the cell.

11. You do not need to enter the *Start_num* argument, since Excel defaults to beginning the search at the first character position. To complete the Function Arguments dialog box:
CLICK: OK command button

12. In the next few steps, you enter the identical SEARCH function into cells E18 and E19 using the CTRL + ENTER keystroke. To begin, select the cell range that will accept the SEARCH function:
SELECT: cell range from E18 to E19

13. To find the character position of the first empty space, enter a space between quotation marks for the *Find_text* argument:
TYPE: =search(" ",b18)
Notice that you entered the relative cell address (B18) in order to calculate the search function for the active cell (E18). Excel will automatically adjust the relative address, B18 to B19, when it fills the remaining cell in the range.

14. To complete the operation:
PRESS: CTRL + ENTER
Your worksheet should now appear similar to the one shown in Figure 6.27.

15. Save the workbook, and keep it open for use in the next lesson.

**Figure 6.27**

Calculating string lengths and character positions

| | A | B | C | D | E | F | G | H |
|---|---|---|---|---|---|---|---|---|
| 15 | **Exercise:** | | | | | | | |
| 16 | | **Original Entries** | **Change Case** | **Length** | **Search** | **Extract** | | |
| 17 | String 1 | wong, sue | | 9 | 5 | | | |
| 18 | String 2 | Part Ac-1209rt | | 14 | 5 | | | |
| 19 | String 3 | Ziggy Stardust | | 14 | 6 | | | |
| 20 | | | | | | | | |
| 21 | **Entry 1** | **Entry 2** | | **Concatenate** | | | | |
| 22 | george | washington | | | | | | |
| 23 | Part | abc-100 | | | | | | |
| 24 | Serial # | 30012890 | | | | | | |
| 25 | 31-Mar-02 | annual general meeting | | | | | | |
| 26 | | | | | | | | |

## 6.4.2 Changing the Case (LOWER, PROPER, and UPPER)

→ **Feature**

Excel provides three functions for changing the case of text labels. The LOWER and UPPER functions return character strings in lowercase and uppercase, respectively. The PROPER function capitalizes the first character in each word of a character string. Once displayed in the desired case, you may use the Paste Special command to permanently convert the calculated results to static values.

→ ## Method

- =LOWER(*text*)
- =PROPER(*text*)
- =UPPER(*text*)

→ ## Practice

Using these three functions, you will now change the case of text labels in a worksheet. Ensure that the "Functions 640" workbook is displayed.

**1.** To convert the text label in cell B16 to proper case:
SELECT: cell C17
TYPE: **=proper(b17)**
PRESS: ⬇
The result, "Wong, Sue," appears in cell C17.

**2.** To convert the text label in cell B18 to uppercase:
SELECT: cell C18
TYPE: **=upper(b18)**
PRESS: ⬇
The result, "PART AC-1209RT," appears in cell C18. (*Note:* If the entry does not fit within the column, increase the column's display width.)

**3.** To convert the text label in cell B19 to lowercase:
TYPE: **=lower(b19)**
PRESS: ENTER
The result, "ziggy stardust," appears in cell C19.

**4.** Let's replace the text labels in column B with the newly calculated results. Do the following:
SELECT: cell range from C17 to C19
CLICK: Copy button (⬚)

**5.** To paste the result of the copied formulas into column B:
SELECT: cell B17
CLICK: down arrow attached to the Paste button (⬚▾)
SELECT: Values

**6.** PRESS: ESC to remove the bounding outline

**7.** On your own, adjust the display width of column B to appear similar to the one shown in Figure 6.28.

**8.** Save the workbook, and keep it open for use in the next lesson.

**Figure 6.28**

Changing the case of character strings

| | A | B | C | D | E | F | G | H |
|---|---|---|---|---|---|---|---|---|
| 15 | **Exercise:** | | | | | | | |
| 16 | **Original Entries** | | **Change Case** | **Length** | **Search** | **Extract** | | |
| 17 | String 1 | Wong, Sue | Wong, Sue | 9 | 5 | | | |
| 18 | String 2 | PART AC-1209RT | PART AC-1209RT | 14 | 5 | | | |
| 19 | String 3 | ziggy stardust | ziggy stardust | 14 | 6 | | | |
| 20 | | | | | | | | |
| 21 | **Entry 1** | **Entry 2** | | **Concatenate** | | | | |
| 22 | george | washington | | | | | | |
| 23 | Part | abc-100 | | | | | | |
| 24 | Serial # | 30012890 | | | | | | |
| 25 | 31-Mar-02 | annual general meeting | | | | | | |
| 26 | | | | | | | | |

Excel

### 6.4.3 Extracting Characters (LEFT, MID, and RIGHT)

→ ## Feature

Imagine that you've received a worksheet that needs to be sorted by surname. Unfortunately, all of the data has been entered as "Firstname, Lastname." To perform a sort, you must first extract the surname from each cell using a process called **parsing**. Excel provides three functions—LEFT, MID, and RIGHT—for use in parsing or extracting character strings in text labels.

→ ## Method

- =LEFT*(text,characters)*

- =MID*(text,start,characters)*

- =RIGHT*(text,characters)*

→ ## Practice

In addition to applying Excel's LEFT and RIGHT functions for extracting characters, you practice nesting functions in this lesson. Although not used in this practice exercise, the MID function differs only in that you provide a starting position for where to begin extracting characters. Ensure that the "Functions 640" workbook is displayed.

**1.** Your objective is to parse or separate the entry in cell B17 into two cells, F17 and G17. To begin:
SELECT: cell F17

**2.** To extract the person's surname into cell F17:
TYPE: =left(
CLICK: Insert Function button (📻)
The Function Arguments dialog box appears for the LEFT function.

**3.** In the *Text* text box, specify the text that you want to parse:
CLICK: cell B17
PRESS: [ TAB ]

**4.** In the *Num_chars* text box, you enter the number of characters to extract from the first character position. Because you wouldn't know the exact length of each person's last name, you need to nest the SEARCH function within the LEFT function to find the character position of the comma. Do the following:
TYPE: search(",",b17)
Notice that the result, 5, appears to the right of the text box.

**5.** With the comma appearing at the fifth position, you need to tell the LEFT function to extract one less than this value:
TYPE: −1
Your screen should now appear similar to the one shown in Figure 6.29.

**Figure 6.29**

Function
Arguments dialog
box for the LEFT
function

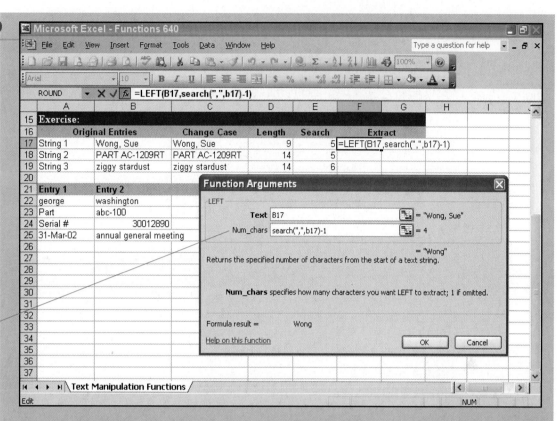

Nesting the
SEARCH function
in the *Num_chars*
argument text box

6. To complete the Function Arguments dialog box:
   CLICK: OK command button

7. To demonstrate the dynamic nature of this function:
   SELECT: cell B17
   TYPE: **Yashin, Steve**
   PRESS: (ENTER)
   Notice that the function in cell F17 extracts the new last name.

8. To return the first name, you use the RIGHT function and then calculate how many characters to
   extract from right to left:
   SELECT: cell G17

9. To extract the person's first name into cell G17.
   TYPE: **=right(**
   CLICK: Insert Function button (*fx*)
   The Function Arguments dialog box appears for the RIGHT function.

10. In the *Text* text box:
    CLICK: cell B17
    PRESS: (TAB)

11. In the *Num_chars* text box, enter the number of characters to extract from the last character po-
    sition and moving left. To calculate this value, you must subtract the character position of the
    space from the length of the string. Do the following:
    TYPE: **len(b17)-search(" ",b17)**
    Your screen should now appear similar to the one shown in Figure 6.30.

**Figure 6.30**

Function
Arguments dialog
box for the
RIGHT function

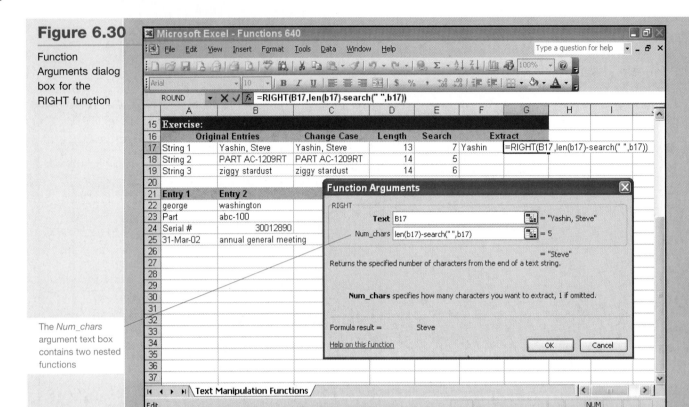

The *Num_chars*
argument text box
contains two nested
functions

**12.** To complete the Function Arguments dialog box:
CLICK: OK command button
Looking in the Formula bar, notice that there are three functions—RIGHT, LEN, and SEARCH—
nested in this one expression!

**13.** Using the previous steps as your guide, separate the word "Part" from the part number in cell
B18 and place the results in cells F18 and G18. Then, parse the name entry in cell B19 so that
the first and last names appear separately in cells F19 and G19. Your worksheet should appear
similar to the one shown in Figure 6.31 before proceeding.

**Figure 6.31**

Parsing text
labels

|    | A | B | C | D | E | F | G | H |
|----|---|---|---|---|---|---|---|---|
| 15 | **Exercise:** | | | | | | | |
| 16 | | **Original Entries** | **Change Case** | **Length** | **Search** | **Extract** | | |
| 17 | String 1 | Yashin, Steve | Yashin, Steve | 13 | 7 | Yashin | Steve | |
| 18 | String 2 | PART AC-1209RT | PART AC-1209RT | 14 | 5 | PART | AC-1209RT | |
| 19 | String 3 | ziggy stardust | ziggy stardust | 14 | 6 | ziggy | stardust | |
| 20 | | | | | | | | |
| 21 | **Entry 1** | **Entry 2** | | | **Concatenate** | | | |
| 22 | george | washington | | | | | | |
| 23 | Part | abc-100 | | | | | | |
| 24 | Serial # | 30012890 | | | | | | |
| 25 | 31-Mar-02 | annual general meeting | | | | | | |
| 26 | | | | | | | | |

**14.** On your own, enter new values into cells B17, B18, and B19 to see the results of your function
entries.

**15.** Save the workbook, and keep it open for use in the next lesson.

### 6.4.4 Concatenating Strings (&, CONCATENATE, TEXT, and TRIM)

→ ## Feature

In a process opposite to parsing, you can **concatenate,** or join, two text strings using the ampersand "&" operator or the CONCATENATE function. The ampersand is commonly used to join text entries with numeric values in a sentence-like structure. To do so, however, requires that you use the TEXT function to convert the value to a character string. You cannot, in other words, combine a text label with a numeric value directly. The TRIM function is used to remove any trailing blank spaces that may exist at the end of a text label.

→ ## Method

- &

- =CONCATENTATE*(text1,text2, . . .)*

- =TEXT*(value,format)*

- =TRIM*(text)*

→ ## Practice

In this lesson you will join labels and values using some of these functions. Ensure that the "Functions 640" workbook is displayed.

**1.** Joining two text labels together is an easy task. To illustrate:
SELECT: cell D22
TYPE: =a22&b22
PRESS: (ENTER)
Although the two cell entries are combined, notice that there is no space inserted between the first and last names.

**2.** Let's edit the expression to insert a space:
SELECT: cell D22
PRESS: (F2) (Edit key)
PRESS: ◀ three times
The flashing insertion point should be positioned to the immediate right of the ampersand, as shown below.

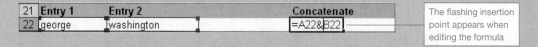

| 21 | Entry 1 | Entry 2 | | Concatenate | |
|----|---------|---------|--|-------------|--|
| 22 | george | washington | | =A22&B22 | |

The flashing insertion point appears when editing the formula

**3.** To add a character space, you must insert another join:
TYPE: " "&
PRESS: (ENTER)
In the Formula bar, the expression =A22&" "&B22 returns "george washington" in cell D22.

**4.** You can also nest functions when joining the cell entries:
SELECT: cell D23
TYPE: =a23&" "&upper(b23)
PRESS: (ENTER)
The UPPER function converts the part number to uppercase before joining it with the contents of cell A23.

**5.** You can also use the CONCATENATE function to join strings. To illustrate:
TYPE: =concatenate(
CLICK: Insert Function button ([ƒₓ])
The Function Arguments dialog box appears for the CONCATENATE function.

**6.** In the *Text1* text box:
CLICK: cell A24
PRESS: TAB
Notice that a new *Text* box appears in the Function Arguments dialog box.

**7.** The CONCATENATE function also accepts numeric values as text strings, so you do not need to use the TEXT function to convert the value in cell B24. To proceed:
CLICK: cell B24
Your dialog box should now appear similar to the one shown in Figure 6.32.

**Figure 6.32**

Joining cell contents using the CONCATENATE function

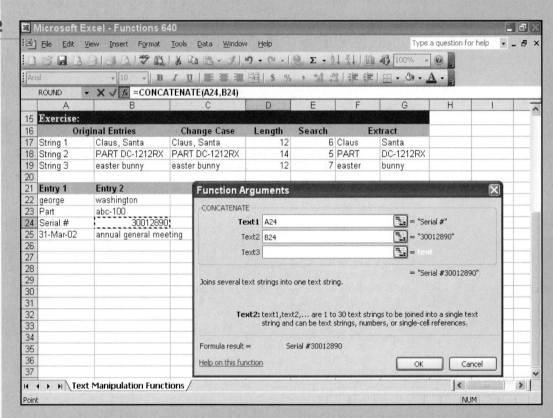

**8.** To enter the result into cell D24:
CLICK: OK command button

**9.** In order to join a date value (cell A25) with a text label (cell B25) using the ampersand (&), you must use the TEXT function to first convert the date to a character string:
SELECT: cell D25
TYPE: =proper(b25)&" is on "&text(a25,"mmmm dd, yyyy")
Your formula expression should appear as shown below.

| 25 | 31-Mar-02 | annual general meeting | =proper(B25)&" is on "&text(A25,"mmmm dd, yyyy") |

**10.** To complete the entry:
PRESS: ENTER
Notice that the TEXT function uses the same designators for formatting the date value as you would use in creating a custom number format.

**11.** Let's demonstrate the dynamic nature of the last entry:
SELECT: cell A25
TYPE: **14-Feb-04**
PRESS: **ENTER**
The text string in cell D25 is updated automatically, as shown in Figure 6.33.

**12.** Save and then close the workbook.

**Figure 6.33**

Joining cell contents using the & operator

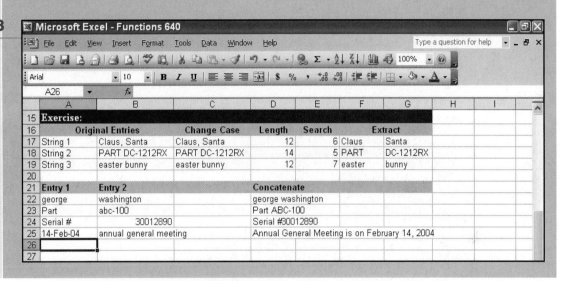

**6.4**  Cell A1 contains a person's area code and phone number in the form (789)555-1234. What expression would you enter in cell A2 to extract only the phone number for display?

# 6.5 Using Financial Functions

Excel's financial functions enable you to confidently use complex financial formulas in your worksheets. And the best part is that you don't even need to understand the difference between a stock and a bond! Some of the more popular functions are devoted to making investment decisions and working with annuity scenarios. Although it sounds technical, an **annuity** is simply a series of equal cash payments that are made over a given period of time, such as an investment contribution or mortgage payment. In this module you learn to solve annuity problems using the present value (PV), future value (FV), and loan payment (PMT) functions.

## 6.5.1 Calculating Present and Future Values (PV and FV)

→ **Feature**

The PV function calculates how much a series of investment contributions is worth in today's dollars. In other words, the PV function returns the **present value** of an annuity given a constant interest rate. The FV function calculates the **future value** of an annuity, such as an investment contribution for retirement. The FV function returns the total future value of a series of equal payments made periodically at a constant interest rate.

→ ## Method

- =PV*(rate,periods,payment)*

- =FV*(rate,periods,payment)*

→ ## Practice

In this lesson you will practice using the PV and FV functions in realistic scenarios. Ensure that no workbooks appear in the application window.

**1.** Open the data file named EX0650 to display the workbook shown in Figure 6.34. This workbook provides a summary area for function syntax, in rows 1 through 6, followed by an exercise area starting at row 7.

**Figure 6.34**

Opening the EX0650 workbook

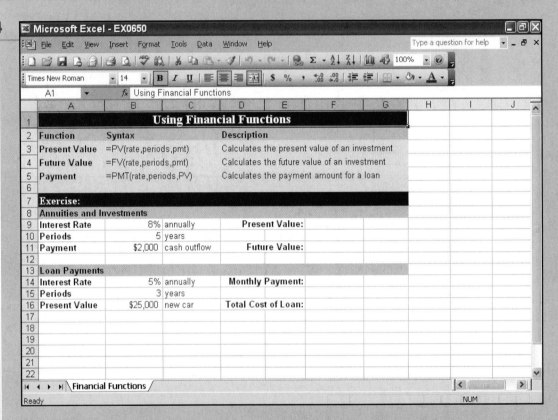

**2.** Save the workbook as "Functions 650" to your personal storage location.

**3.** After reviewing the function names and descriptions:
SELECT: cell A7, which is a merged cell

**4.** As shown below, use the vertical scroll bar to scroll the window downward, so that row 7 appears as the first row at the top of the worksheet.

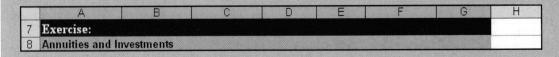

**5.** Constructing expressions that use several functions or arguments is much easier when you name the required cell ranges. To name the cell containing the interest or discount rate:
SELECT: cell B9
CLICK: in the Name box
TYPE: **Rate**
PRESS: ENTER

6. To name the cell containing the number of periods for which payments are made:
SELECT: cell B10
CLICK: in the Name box
TYPE: **Periods**
PRESS: [ENTER]

7. To name the cell containing the payment amount:
SELECT: cell B11
CLICK: in the Name box
TYPE: **Payment**
PRESS: [ENTER]

8. To view the range names:
CLICK: down arrow attached to the Name box
You should now see the following list of range names.

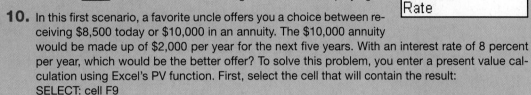

9. PRESS: [ESC] to remove the list of range names from displaying

10. In this first scenario, a favorite uncle offers you a choice between re-ceiving $8,500 today or $10,000 in an annuity. The $10,000 annuity would be made up of $2,000 per year for the next five years. With an interest rate of 8 percent per year, which would be the better offer? To solve this problem, you enter a present value cal-culation using Excel's PV function. First, select the cell that will contain the result:
SELECT: cell F9

11. Let's use the Function Arguments dialog box to enter the PV function:
TYPE: **=pv(**
CLICK: Insert Function button ([fx])

12. In the Function Arguments dialog box, enter the required range names:
TYPE: **Rate** in the *Rate* text box
PRESS: [TAB]
TYPE: **Periods** in the *Nper* text box
PRESS: [TAB]
TYPE: **Payment** in the *Pmt* text box
Your screen should now appear similar to the one shown in Figure 6.35. Notice that the formula result shows a negative value, representing a cash outflow.

**Figure 6.35**

Function Arguments dialog box for the PV function

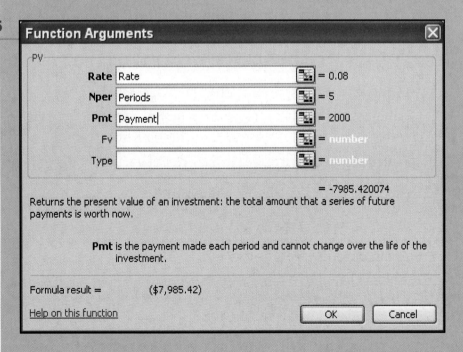

**13.** To complete the entry:
CLICK: OK command button
The better offer is receiving $8,500 today, compared to receiving $7,985.42 in today's dollars over the next five years.

**14.** With the majority of these types of calculations, you are concerned with the result's absolute or positive value. Negative values are typically evaluated as cash outflows, while positive values are cash inflows. Therefore, edit the formula so that it is enclosed within the ABS function (i.e., =ABS(PV(Rate,Periods,Payment))).

**15.** Let's change the scenario slightly. The same uncle offers you a choice between receiving a flat $11,500 five years from now or an annuity of $2,000 per year for the next five years. Which offer is better given an 8 percent interest rate? This problem requires that you enter a future value calculation. To begin, select the cell that will contain the result:
SELECT: cell F11

**16.** Enter the FV function within an ABS function to begin:
TYPE: =abs(fv(
Notice the ScreenTip that appears, as shown here.

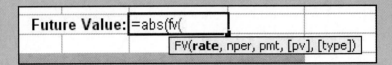

**17.** To complete the function:
TYPE: Rate,Periods,Payment))
PRESS: ENTER
The better offer is receiving the $2,000 annuity, since its future value is worth $233.20 more than the flat $11,500.

**18.** On your own, change the Interest Rate value in cell B9 to 5%. Do your decisions change for the previous scenarios? Your workbook should now appear similar to the one shown in Figure 6.36.

**19.** Save the workbook, and keep it open for use in the next lesson.

**Figure 6.36**

Entering the PV and FV functions

|    | A | B | C | D | E | F | G | H |
|----|---|---|---|---|---|---|---|---|
| 7 | **Exercise:** | | | | | | | |
| 8 | **Annuities and Investments** | | | | | | | |
| 9 | Interest Rate | 5% | annually | | Present Value: | $8,658.95 | | |
| 10 | Periods | 5 | years | | | | | |
| 11 | Payment | $2,000 | cash outflow | | Future Value: | $11,051.26 | | |
| 12 | | | | | | | | |
| 13 | **Loan Payments** | | | | | | | |
| 14 | Interest Rate | 5% | annually | | Monthly Payment: | | | |
| 15 | Periods | 3 | years | | | | | |
| 16 | Present Value | $25,000 | new car | | Total Cost of Loan: | | | |
| 17 | | | | | | | | |
| 18 | | | | | | | | |

### 6.5.2 Calculating Payments (PMT)

## → Feature

The PMT function calculates the payment amount for a loan or mortgage, given a constant interest rate and number of periods. The *rate* argument is the interest rate charged, *periods* is the amortization length, and *pv* is the present value or loan amount. To find the annual payments required for a

$100,000 mortgage at 7% over 25 years, you enter the function =PMT(.07,25,100000). Notice that you can use either 7% or .07 in this calculation. To calculate the monthly payments, you can divide the annual interest rate by 12 months and then multiply the number of periods by 12. Thus, the entry becomes =PMT(.07/12,25*12,100000). You can also determine the total amount of money paid over the term of the loan by multiplying the PMT result by the number of periods used in the calculation.

→ ## Method

• =PMT(*rate,periods,pv*)

→ ## Practice

In this lesson you learn how to calculate a payment for a car loan. Ensure that the "Functions 650" workbook is displayed.

**1.** Your objective in this lesson is to calculate the payment required to purchase a $25,000 car. To begin:
SELECT: cell F14

**2.** Let's use the Function Arguments dialog box to enter the PMT function:
TYPE: =pmt(
CLICK: Insert Function button ( 𝑓𝑥 )

**3.** In the Function Arguments dialog box, specify the required arguments:
TYPE: **b14/12** in the *Rate* text box
PRESS: TAB
TYPE: **b15*12** in the *Nper* text box
PRESS: TAB
Notice that you divide the annual interest rate by 12 to calculate the monthly rate and multiply the periods (years) by 12 to get the number of months.

**4.** To enter the principal loan amount:
TYPE: **b16** in the *Pv* text box
Your screen should now appear as shown in Figure 6.37.

**Figure 6.37**

Function Arguments dialog box for the PMT function

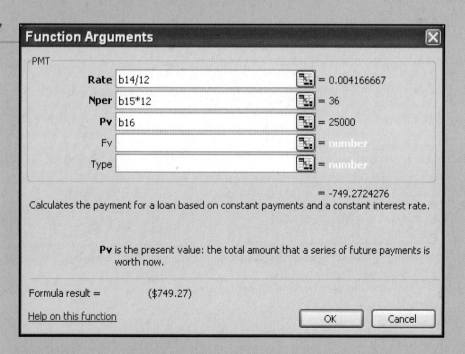

| Function Arguments | | |
|---|---|---|
| PMT | | |
| **Rate** b14/12 | 📊 | = 0.004166667 |
| **Nper** b15*12 | 📊 | = 36 |
| **Pv** b16 | 📊 | = 25000 |
| Fv | 📊 | = number |
| Type | 📊 | = number |

= -749.2724276

Calculates the payment for a loan based on constant payments and a constant interest rate.

**Pv** is the present value: the total amount that a series of future payments is worth now.

Formula result = ($749.27)

Help on this function         OK      Cancel

**5.** To complete the entry:
CLICK: OK command button
The answer ($749.27) appears in cell F15. The payment appears in parentheses to indicate it is a negative number, since it is a cash outflow from yourself to the bank.

**6.** On your own, edit the formula so that it is enclosed within the ABS function.

**7.** Now calculate the total payment amount:
SELECT: cell F16
TYPE: =f14*(b15*12)
PRESS: ⟨ENTER⟩
The total cost of the financed car will be $26,973.81.

**8.** On your own, change the values in cells B14, B15, and B16. For example, calculate the monthly payment for a $30,000 car loan given an interest rate of 6%. Your worksheet should appear similar to the one shown in Figure 6.38.

**9.** Save and then close the workbook.

**Figure 6.38**

Completing the "Functions 650" workbook

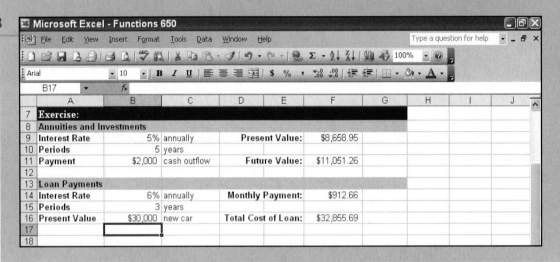

## *In Addition* USING OTHER FINANCIAL FUNCTIONS

Excel provides two variations on the PMT function for calculating the principal and interest portions of a PMT result. The PPMT function returns the principal payments and the IPMT function returns the interest payments. There are several other useful functions for evaluating investment decisions, such as NPV for finding the net present value of cash flows and IRR for calculating the internal rate of return. For more information, access the Microsoft Office Excel 2003 Help system.

**6.5** How might you incorporate the IF function to calculate a mortgage payment in which the interest rate changed depending on the term chosen?

# Chapter
## summary

Microsoft Office Excel 2003 provides many built-in functions and tools, such as Goal Seek, to help you perform complex calculations and analyze or extract information. When building formula expressions, remember that Excel follows the operator order of precedence, and provides a variety of arithmetic, comparison, text, and reference operators. To control or force a particular order of calculation, you must nest portions of a formula expression within parentheses.

Some of the more commonly used functions are contained in the *Logical, Date & Time, Math & Trig, Statistical, Text,* and *Financial* categories. The Logical category contains the IF function for creating a conditional expression and then performing calculations based on its result. From the Date & Time category, the DATE, DAY, MONTH, NOW, TIME, TODAY, WEEKDAY, and YEAR are particularly useful. Mathematical and statistical functions, such as ABS, INT, RAND, and ROUND, can help generate test data and summarize your worksheet. Text functions are used to extract, convert, and manipulate character strings. Finally, the Financial category provides some easy-to-use functions for evaluating complex investment decisions (PV and FV), solving annuity problems, and calculating loan payments (PMT). For help creating formula expressions containing functions, use the Insert Function dialog box and the Function Arguments dialog box, accessed by clicking the Insert Function button ( fx ) in the Formula bar.

## Command Summary

Many of the commands and procedures appearing in this chapter are summarized in the following table.

| Skill Set | To Perform This Task . . . | Do the Following . . . |
|---|---|---|
| **Working with Cells and Cell Data** | Convert formula results to static values | SELECT: formula to copy<br>CLICK: Copy button ( )<br>SELECT: target location<br>CLICK: down arrow attached to the Paste button ( )<br>SELECT: Values |
| | Transpose worksheet values from a column or row orientation | SELECT: cells to transpose<br>CLICK: Copy button ( )<br>SELECT: target location<br>CHOOSE: Edit → Paste Special<br>SELECT: *Transpose* check box |
| **Analyzing Data** | Use goal seeking to find the input value required to produce an outcome | CHOOSE: Tools → Goal Seek |
| **Formatting and Printing Worksheets** | Display and print formulas in a worksheet | CHOOSE: Tools → Options<br>CLICK: *View* tab<br>SELECT: *Formulas* check box<br>CLICK: OK command button<br>CLICK: Print button ( ) |
| **Creating and Revising Formulas** | Use the IF logical function:<br>• Evaluate a condition to true or false | =IF(condition,true,false) |
| | Use date and time functions:<br>• Enter a date value<br>• Return the day number<br>• Return the month number<br>• Enter a time value<br>• Calculate the weekday<br>• Return the year number | =DATE(year,month,day)<br>=DAY(date_value)<br>=MONTH(date_value)<br>=TIME(hour,minute,second)<br>=WEEKDAY(date_value)<br>=YEAR(date_value) |

Use mathematical and statistical functions:
- Force an absolute or positive value      =ABS*(expression)*
- Extract a value's integer portion      =INT*(cell)*
- Return a number between 0 and 1      =RAND()
- Round a value to specific digits      =ROUND*(number,digits)*

Use text manipulation functions:
- Joins together two or more strings      =CONCATENATE*(text1,text2. . .)*
- Extract text from the left      =LEFT*(text,chars)*
- Return the length of a string      =LEN*(text)*
- Convert a string to lowercase      =LOWER*(text)*
- Extract text from the middle      =MID*(text,start,chars)*
- Convert a string to proper case      =PROPER*(text)*
- Extract text from the right      =RIGHT*(text,chars)*
- Return a string's position      =SEARCH*(find,text,start)*
- Convert a value to a string      =TEXT*(value,format)*
- Remove trailing spaces in a string      =TRIM*(text)*
- Convert a string to uppercase      =UPPER*(text)*

Use financial functions:
- Calculate a loan payment      =PMT*(rate,periods,pv)*
- Calculate the present value of an annuity      =PV*(rate,periods,payment)*
- Calculate the future value of an annuity      =FV*(rate,periods,payment)*

## Key Terms

This section specifies page references for the key terms identified in this chapter. For a complete list of definitions, refer to the Glossary provided at the end of this learning guide.

annuity, *p. EX 337*

character strings, *p. EX 327*

concatenate, *p. EX 335*

constant, *p. EX 300*

future value, *p. EX 337*

goal seeking, *p. EX 307*

integer value, *p. EX 323*

nesting, *p. EX 301*

operand, *p. EX 300*

operator, *p. EX 300*

order of precedence, *p. EX 300*

parsing, *p. EX 332*

present value, *p. EX 337*

random number, *p. EX 323*

rounded value, *p. EX 320*

## Chapter
### quiz

## Short Answer

**1.** Explain the difference between an *operand* and an *operator*.

**2.** How do you overrule the operator order of precedence?

**3.** What does the "outcome cell" refer to in goal seeking?

**4.** What two dialog boxes help you to find and insert Excel's built-in functions?

**5.** Name one method for documenting the formulas in a worksheet.

**6.** How do the ROUND and INT functions differ?

7. What does it mean to *transpose* a cell range?

8. Explain the difference between *parsing* and *concatenating*.

9. How might you use the IF function to test more than one condition?

10. List some of the comparison operators used to create conditional expressions in an IF function.

## True/False

1. _____ Nesting is the process of placing operators between operands.

2. _____ The Paste Special command can paste values, formulas, and even transpose the contents of a row or column.

3. _____ To display formulas in your worksheet, choose the View ➔ Options command and then select the *Formulas* check box.

4. _____ For goal seeking, an outcome cell can contain a formula expression but not a function.

5. _____ The RAND function only works when nested within a ROUND or INT function.

6. _____ The PROPER function returns the correct syntax for a function.

7. _____ You can concatenate text strings using the ampersand, "&."

8. _____ The PV and FV functions are used to evaluate annuity problems.

9. _____ You must use the Function Arguments dialog box to enter the PMT function.

10. _____ The IF function is categorized as a "Logical" function.

## Multiple Choice

1. The following expression evaluates to 12.
   a. =3+3*2
   b. =(3+3)*2
   c. =3+(3*2)
   d. Both a and b

2. The Excel feature that color-codes an expression's cell references during Edit mode is called:
   a. Range Filter
   b. Cell Finder
   c. Range Finder
   d. Edit Formula

3. Which of the following is not a function in the Date & Time category?
   a. DAYS360
   b. MINUTE
   c. WEEKDAY
   d. WEEKEND

4. The following function displays the number of days remaining until the end of the year:
   a. =date(year(now(),12,31)-today())
   b. =date(year(now(),12,31)-then())
   c. =today()-(month(12)+day(31))
   d. =date(12,31)-today()

5. Which is the correct expression for extracting the integer portion of a random number between 0 and 100?
   a. =INTEGER(RAND*10)
   b. =INT(RAND()*100)
   c. =RAND(INT()*100)
   d. =RAND(ROUND()*100

6. Which key do you press to recalculate or update a worksheet?
   a. F2
   b. F3
   c. F4
   d. F9

**7.** The following function returns the number 9 in a worksheet cell:

    a. =extract(",","Tampa Bay, FL")
    b. =search(",","Spokane, WA")
    c. =len("New York, NY")
    d. =search(",","Stockton, CA")

**8.** Which of the following best describes the FV function?

    a. Calculates the future value of an annuity.
    b. Evaluates the lump sum payment of a mortgage.
    c. Calculates the discounted present value of an annuity.
    d. Calculates the value of a series of unequal payments.

**9.** Which of the following is the correct syntax for the IF function?

    a. =IF(condition,false,true)
    b. =IF(condition,true,false)
    c. =IF(true,false,condition)
    d. =IF(false,true,condition)

**10.** Which of the following is not a comparison operator?

    a. >
    b. <=
    c. =
    d. \

# Hands-On
## exercises

step by step  

### 1. Building Formula Expressions

In this exercise you practice modifying and enhancing a gradebook worksheet using Excel's built-in functions. You also use parentheses within a formula expression to force the order of calculation and to make it more readable.

    **1.** Open the data file named EX06HE01 to display the workbook shown in Figure 6.39.

**Figure 6.39**

Opening the
EX06HE01
workbook

Microsoft Excel - EX06HE01

File   Edit   View   Insert   Format   Tools   Data   Window   Help     Type a question for help

A1    COMP102: Computers for Business

| | A | B | C | D | E | F | G | H | I | J |
|---|---|---|---|---|---|---|---|---|---|---|
| 1 | COMP102: Computers for Business | | | | | | | | | |
| 2 | Student Gradebook | | | | | | | | | |
| 3 | | | | | | | | | | |
| 4 | Weighting | 15% | 35% | 50% | 100% | | | | | |
| 5 | Student Name | Quizzes | Mid-Term | Final | GRADE | | | | | |
| 6 | Marjorie Blackwood | 70.89 | 70.12 | 54.91 | | | | | | |
| 7 | Caitlan Davidson | 79.23 | 75.70 | 62.39 | | | | | | |
| 8 | Dave Guidroz | 88.13 | 82.14 | 80.79 | | | | | | |
| 9 | Andrew Harms | 97.01 | 91.07 | 84.13 | | | | | | |
| 10 | George Alander | 85.09 | 80.01 | 89.33 | | | | | | |
| 11 | Rolf Petrov | 51.33 | 62.38 | 63.89 | | | | | | |
| 12 | Dana Winnett | 66.67 | 69.10 | 55.14 | | | | | | |
| 13 | Sandra Kumar | 56.70 | 63.32 | 46.24 | | | | | | |
| 14 | Sean Inglis | 52.88 | 97.35 | 68.76 | | | | | | |
| 15 | Jane Dupres | 92.69 | 96.79 | 81.36 | | | | | | |
| 16 | Tony Truong | 92.84 | 90.54 | 89.96 | | | | | | |
| 17 | Paul Pavloff | 83.33 | 97.19 | 77.81 | | | | | | |
| 18 | Average Results | | | | | | | | | |
| 19 | | | | | | | | | | |
| 20 | | | | | | | | | | |
| 21 | | | | | | | | | | |
| 22 | | | | | | | | | | |
| 23 | | | | | | | | | | |

Sheet1 / Sheet2 / Sheet3 /

Ready        NUM

2. Save the workbook as "Grade Calculations" to your personal storage location.

3. Your objective is to create a nested formula that calculates each student's final grade given the weighting factors entered on row 4. To facilitate entering the formula, let's name the required cell ranges:
SELECT: cell B4
CLICK: in the Name box
TYPE: **Quizzes**
PRESS: ⏎

4. Using the same method, name cell C4 **MidTerm** and cell D4 **Final**. Then, do the following:
SELECT: cell E6

5. To calculate the weighted course grade for Marjorie Blackwood:
TYPE: **=(b6\*Quizzes)+(c6\*MidTerm)+(d6\*Final)**
Your worksheet should appear as shown in Figure 6.40. Notice that you placed each weight calculation in parentheses to improve the formula's readability.

**Figure 6.40**

Entering nested calculations in a formula expression

| | A | B | C | D | E | F | G | H | I | J |
|---|---|---|---|---|---|---|---|---|---|---|
| 1 | COMP102: Computers for Business | | | | | | | | | |
| 2 | Student Gradebook | | | | | | | | | |
| 3 | | | | | | | | | | |
| 4 | Weighting | 15% | 35% | 50% | 100% | | | | | |
| 5 | Student Name | Quizzes | Mid-Term | Final | GRADE | | | | | |
| 6 | Marjorie Blackwood | 70.89 | 70.12 | 54.91 | =(b6\*Quizzes)+(c6\*MidTerm)+(d6\*Final) | | | | | |
| 7 | Caitlan Davidson | 79.23 | 75.70 | 62.39 | | | | | | |
| 8 | Dave Guidroz | 88.13 | 82.14 | 80.79 | | | | | | |
| 9 | Andrew Harms | 97.01 | 91.07 | 84.13 | | | | | | |
| 10 | George Alander | 85.09 | 80.01 | 89.33 | | | | | | |
| 11 | Rolf Petrov | 51.33 | 62.38 | 63.89 | | | | | | |
| 12 | Dana Winnett | 66.67 | 69.10 | 55.14 | | | | | | |
| 13 | Sandra Kumar | 56.70 | 63.32 | 46.24 | | | | | | |
| 14 | Sean Inglis | 52.88 | 97.35 | 68.76 | | | | | | |
| 15 | Jane Dupres | 92.69 | 96.79 | 81.36 | | | | | | |
| 16 | Tony Truong | 92.84 | 90.54 | 89.96 | | | | | | |
| 17 | Paul Pavloff | 83.33 | 97.19 | 77.81 | | | | | | |
| 18 | Average Results | | | | | | | | | |
| 19 | | | | | | | | | | |

6. To complete the formula entry:
PRESS: ⏎
The result, 62.63, appears.

7. To copy this formula for the remaining students:
SELECT: cell range from E6 to E17
CHOOSE: Edit → Fill → Down

8. Now let's calculate the average results for each course component:
SELECT: cell range from B18 to E18
TYPE: **=average(b6:b17)**
PRESS: CTRL + ENTER
The correct function is entered into each cell of the selected range.

9. To display the formulas in the worksheet:
CHOOSE: Tools → Options
CLICK: *View* tab
SELECT: *Formulas* check box
CLICK: OK command button

**10.** On your own, move the pointer to cell A1, and then adjust the column widths to better display their contents. Finally, print the worksheet using a landscape orientation so that it fits on a single page, as shown in the Print Preview window of Figure 6.41.

**Figure 6.41**

Previewing the formulas that appear in a worksheet

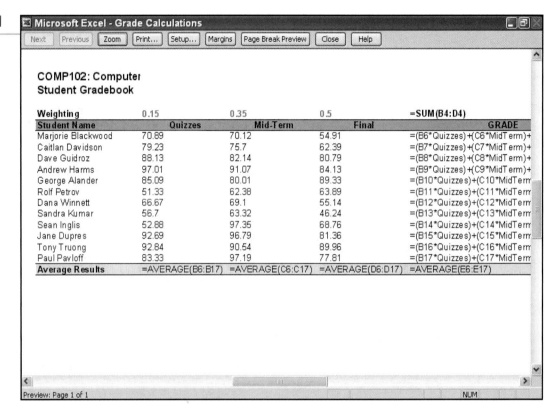

**11.** Return to the worksheet and change the display to view the worksheet values, instead of formulas. Adjust the column widths to their "best fit" before proceeding.

**12.** Save and close the workbook.

step by step

## 2. Using Random Numbers

In this exercise you create a worksheet that uses Excel's mathematical and statistical functions to generate a value for use in a sweepstakes contest. You then use the logical IF function to test whether a value meets a predetermined condition.

**1.** Open the data file named EX06HE02.

**2.** Save the workbook as "Sweepstakes" to your personal storage location.

**3.** Your first step is to populate the worksheet with a list of 10 random integer values between 0 and 100. To begin:
SELECT: cell range from A5 to A14
TYPE: =int(rand()*100)
PRESS: CTRL + ENTER
Random integer values between 0 and 100 should now appear in the cell range.

**4.** To calculate the average value of this range:
SELECT: cell D6
TYPE: =average(a5:a14)
PRESS: ENTER

5. Each person pays one dollar for a chance to press the **F9** (Calc key). To win the jackpot, the value in cell D6 must be greater than the value appearing in cell D5. To demonstrate:
PRESS: **F9** (Calc key) repeatedly
Did you best the value in cell D5?

6. You will now add an IF function that more clearly informs the participant about how they've done. To begin:
SELECT: cell D8

7. Let's use the Function Arguments dialog box to enter the IF function:
TYPE: **=if(**
PRESS: Insert Function button (**fx**)
The Function Arguments dialog box appears.

8. In the *Logical_test* text box, you enter the condition to test for. In this case the winner must achieve an average random value that is greater than the value specified in cell D5. To enter this condition:
TYPE: **d6>d5**
PRESS: **TAB**

9. Now enter the text messages to display:
TYPE: **"Winner!"** in the *Value_if_true* text box
PRESS: **TAB**
TYPE: **"Try Again!"** in the *Value_if_false* text box
Your screen should appear similar to the one shown in Figure 6.42.

**Figure 6.42**

Function Arguments dialog box for the IF function

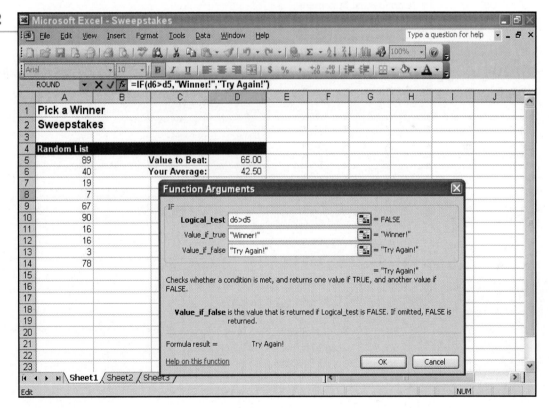

10. To complete the entry:
CLICK: OK command button

11. On your own, press the **F9** (Calc key) repeatedly to test the function.

12. Save and then close the workbook.

step by step

## 3. Nesting Formulas and Functions

Using a retirement plan worksheet, you now practice entering logical IF functions and calculating future investment values. This exercise is especially useful for learning how to nest formulas and functions.

1. Open the data file named EX06HE03.

2. Save the workbook as "Retirement Plan" to your personal storage location.

3. For this retirement package, the company has agreed to match each employee's annual contribution up to a maximum of 5% of their salary. To calculate the company's contribution, do the following:
   SELECT: cell D5

4. Now enter an IF function using the Function Arguments dialog box that determines whether the employee's contribution is greater than 5% of their salary. If it is, input the 5% contribution limit for Staples. If the contribution isn't greater than 5% of their salary, match the employee's contribution. (*Hint:* Try to figure out the IF function's arguments before looking at the answer in Figure 6.43!)

**Figure 6.43**

Calculating the employer contribution using an IF function

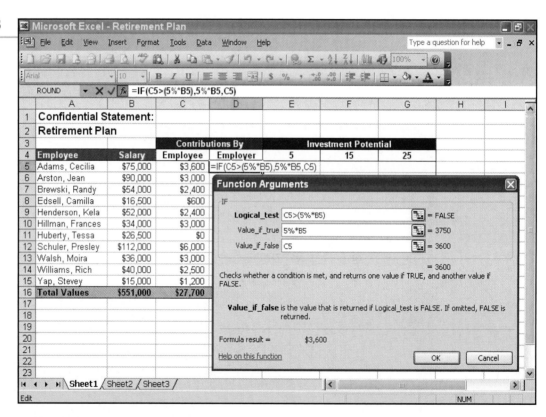

5. Copy the function that you entered in cell D5 to the remainder of the employee cells in column D.

6. Now let's calculate each employee's retirement nest egg. To begin, enter an annual return rate of 8% for the company's investments:
   SELECT: cell B3
   TYPE: **8.00%**
   PRESS: (**ENTER**)

7. To make calculating the future values easier, name the required cells. First, name cell B3 **ReturnRate**. Then name cells E4 **ShortTerm**, F4 **MidTerm**, and G4 **LongTerm**.

**8.** You use the FV function to determine the investment's growth potential in the timeframe specified in cells E4, F4, and G4. To begin:
SELECT: cell E5

**9.** For the total annuity amount, you must add together the employee and employer contributions. Also, remember that the FV function calculates the future value of contributions made each year for the number of years specified. To proceed:
TYPE: **=fv(**
CLICK: Insert Function button (fx)

**10.** Complete the Function Arguments dialog box as follows:
TYPE: **ReturnRate** in the *Rate* text box
PRESS: TAB
TYPE: **ShortTerm** in the *Nper* text box
PRESS: TAB
TYPE: **c5+d5** in the *Pmt* text box
CLICK: OK command button

**11.** In the Information dialog box that appears:
CLICK: Yes command button to have Excel add the closing parenthesis

**12.** On your own, enter the FV functions for the MidTerm and LongTerm periods in cells F5 and G5, respectively. Format and then copy these three FV functions to the remaining employee rows in the table. Your screen should appear similar to the one shown in Figure 6.44.

**Figure 6.44**

Completing the Retirement Plan workbook

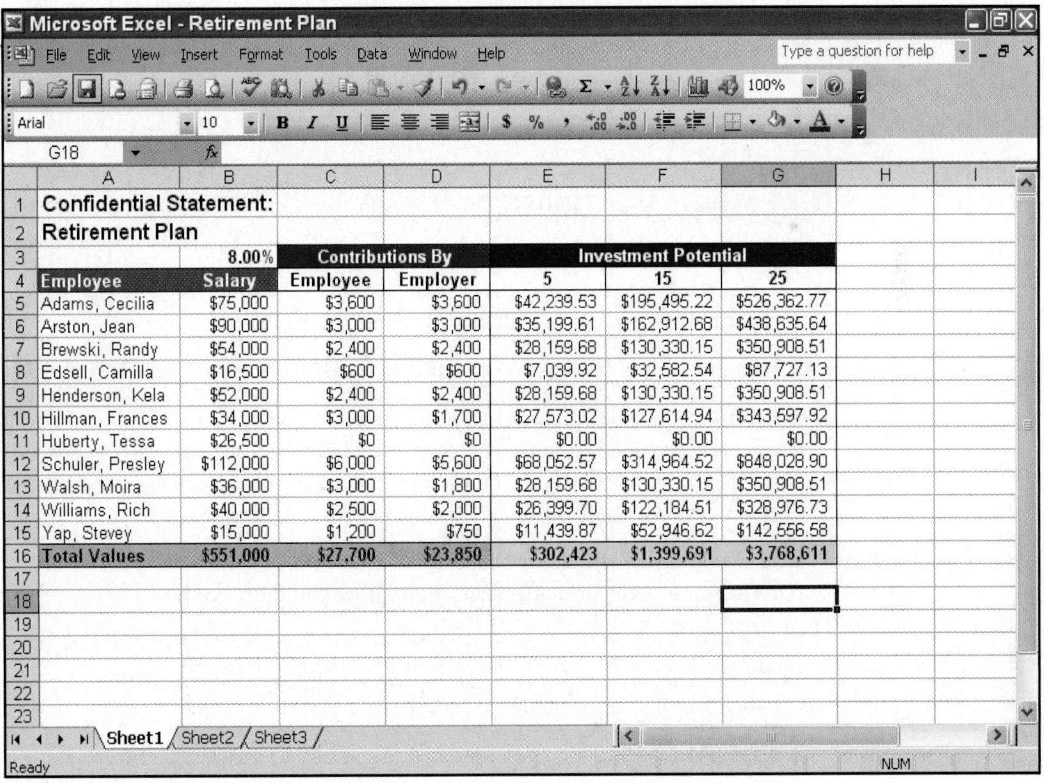

| | A | B | C | D | E | F | G |
|---|---|---|---|---|---|---|---|
| 1 | Confidential Statement: | | | | | | |
| 2 | Retirement Plan | | | | | | |
| 3 | | 8.00% | Contributions By | | Investment Potential | | |
| 4 | Employee | Salary | Employee | Employer | 5 | 15 | 25 |
| 5 | Adams, Cecilia | $75,000 | $3,600 | $3,600 | $42,239.53 | $195,495.22 | $526,362.77 |
| 6 | Arston, Jean | $90,000 | $3,000 | $3,000 | $35,199.61 | $162,912.68 | $438,635.64 |
| 7 | Brewski, Randy | $54,000 | $2,400 | $2,400 | $28,159.68 | $130,330.15 | $350,908.51 |
| 8 | Edsell, Camilla | $16,500 | $600 | $600 | $7,039.92 | $32,582.54 | $87,727.13 |
| 9 | Henderson, Kela | $52,000 | $2,400 | $2,400 | $28,159.68 | $130,330.15 | $350,908.51 |
| 10 | Hillman, Frances | $34,000 | $3,000 | $1,700 | $27,573.02 | $127,614.94 | $343,597.92 |
| 11 | Huberty, Tessa | $26,500 | $0 | $0 | $0.00 | $0.00 | $0.00 |
| 12 | Schuler, Presley | $112,000 | $6,000 | $5,600 | $68,052.57 | $314,964.52 | $848,028.90 |
| 13 | Walsh, Moira | $36,000 | $3,000 | $1,800 | $28,159.68 | $130,330.15 | $350,908.51 |
| 14 | Williams, Rich | $40,000 | $2,500 | $2,000 | $26,399.70 | $122,184.51 | $328,976.73 |
| 15 | Yap, Stevey | $15,000 | $1,200 | $750 | $11,439.87 | $52,946.62 | $142,556.58 |
| 16 | Total Values | $551,000 | $27,700 | $23,850 | $302,423 | $1,399,691 | $3,768,611 |

**13.** Using Excel's Goal Seek command, find the return rate required for Cecilia Adams to earn $200,000 on 15 years of her investment.

**14.** Save and then close the workbook.

on your own

## 4. Creating a Mortgage Table

In this exercise you complete a simple mortgage table that determines the monthly payments for a home purchase, given a variety of interest rates and amortization periods. To begin, open the EX06HE04 workbook (Figure 6.45), and save it as "Mortgage Table" to your personal storage location.

**Figure 6.45**

Opening the
EX06HE04
workbook

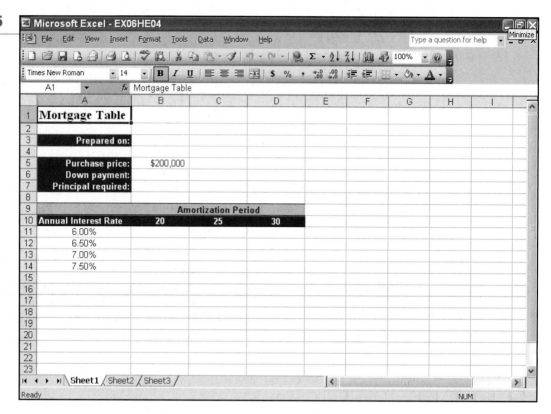

Perform the following steps to complete the mortgage table:

- Enter a function to display the current date in cell B3. Format the date to display as "dd-mmm-yyyy."

- In cell B6 enter an IF function using the Function Arguments dialog box that calculates the down payment. If the purchase price is greater than $150,000, the down payment required is 10% of the purchase price. Otherwise, the down payment is 15% of the purchase price. Remember to use the cell reference "B5" in the function rather than the static value of $200,000.

- Enter a formula in cell B7 that subtracts the down payment in cell B6 from the purchase price in cell B5. The result is the principal loan amount that you must borrow.

- In cell B11 use the PMT function (nested within an ABS function) to calculate the monthly payment for the principal loan amount, given the periods in cell B10 and the interest rate in cell A11. Because you want to copy this formula, you must make some of the cell references absolute, as shown below.

| 9 | | Amortization Period | | |
| --- | --- | --- | --- | --- |
| 10 | **Annual Interest Rate** | **20** | **25** | **30** |
| 11 | 6.00% | =ABS(PMT($A11/12,B$10*12,$B$7)) | | |
| 12 | 6.50% | | | |

- Copy the formula in cell B11 to the cell range from B11 to D14. The entire range should now appear filled with payment results.

Once you have finished constructing the mortgage table, adjust the purchase price value to $300,000. Notice the effect that this variable has on the monthly payment and the required down payment. When you are ready to proceed, print, save, and then close the workbook.

on your own

## 5. Air Quality Measurements

You will now practice working with named cell ranges and entering built-in functions. To begin, open the EX06HE05 workbook, and save it as "Air Quality" to your personal storage location.

Using the Name box, review the list of existing named ranges in the worksheet. Experiment by selecting range names to see which cells are referenced. Then use the Insert → Name → Paste command to create a list of names beginning in cell F1. Adjust the width of columns F and G to view the contents. After moving the pointer to cell A1, your screen should appear similar to that shown in Figure 6.46.

**Figure 6.46**

Pasting range names into the worksheet

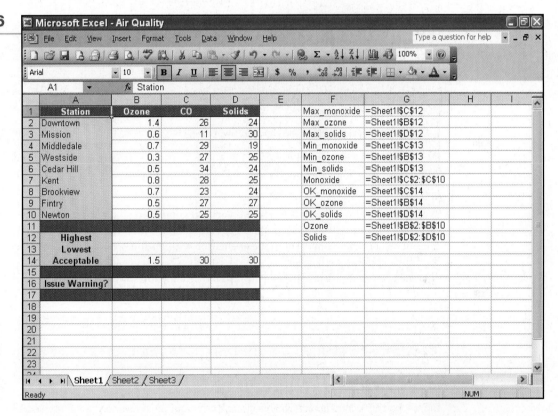

Using the range names and appropriate functions, calculate the highest and lowest measurements for each of the three types of air pollution. Then use the IF function and range names to determine whether a warning needs to be issued for any of the three categories. If the "Highest" value is greater than the "Acceptable" amount, display "YES" in the corresponding "Issue Warning?" cell, otherwise display "NO." (*Hint:* In the IF function, use double quotes around text values that you want to enter into a cell.)

When you are finished, save and then close the "Air Quality" workbook.

on your own

## 6. Functions-R-Great!

To practice working with date, time, mathematical, statistical, text, financial, and logical functions, open the data file named EX06HE06 to display the workbook shown in Figure 6.47. This workbook provides a series of exercises for calculating, parsing, and concatenating data. Save it as "Functions-R-Great" to your personal storage location.

**Figure 6.47**

Opening the
EX06HE06
workbook

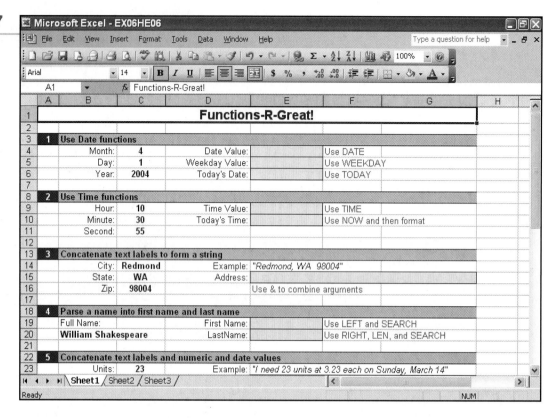

Work your way down the worksheet until you have completed all ten of the examples. When finished, display the formulas in the worksheet and adjust the column widths as desired. Modify the page setup options to print on one page using a landscape orientation with gridlines and row and column headings displayed. Send the worksheet to the printer.

When you are finished, save and then close the "Functions-R-Great" workbook.

# CaseStudy    EVERMAX SYSTEMS LTD.

Jackson White graduated with honors from St. John's College in the spring of 2004. It wasn't until last month, however, that he received his first job offer and began working for Evermax Systems in Baltimore. In the months prior to accepting the position, Jackson studied vigorously to update his skills in Microsoft Office Excel 2003. Not surprisingly, his dedication and commitment paid off with an offer to become the assistant controller for Evermax.

Evermax's growth has exceeded even the company founder's expectations. However, the administrative system hasn't kept up with the increased transactions and paper flow in the office. One of Jackson's first duties will be to automate some of the more common procedures being performed by the sales staff. Having just finished an Excel refresher course, Jackson is ready to put the electronic spreadsheet to work for Evermax's staff. He recommends to his boss that they convert their in-house sales team from a one-write paper-based system to an Excel workbook application. To illustrate his point, he develops a sample workbook and shows how they can create and print invoices. Impressed with the initial demonstration, the president has asked him to make some minor modifications and then provide the workbook to two staff members for testing. Jackson is eager to implement his newly learned skills. He is certain that he can make the workbook even faster and easier to use!

In the following case problems, assume the role of Jackson and perform the same steps that he identifies.

**1.** Jackson arrives early at the office with his notebook computer in tow. Even before his customary morning coffee, he docks the computer at his workstation, turns on the power, and then launches Excel 2003. Unfortunately, Jackson's accounting duties have kept him occupied over the past few days, so he decides to perform a quick review of his sample workbook. He loads the file named EX06CP01 and then saves it as "Evermax" to his personal storage location.

Reviewing the sample workbook (Figure 6.48), Jackson remembers that he has already entered a fictitious customer and some invoice details. However, he hasn't yet entered formulas to calculate the total amounts in column E. To complete the detail area, Jackson selects the cell range from E8 through E11 and then types a formula to multiply the values in the Quantity and Price columns. Instead of pressing ENTER, he uses the CTRL+ENTER keystroke to complete the entry for all of the selected cells. In cell E12, Jackson enters a SUM function that adds together the results in the Total column. He enters the TODAY function in cell B3 and then formats the result to display using the "March 14, 2001" format. Jackson saves the workbook before proceeding.

**Figure 6.48**

The "Evermax" workbook

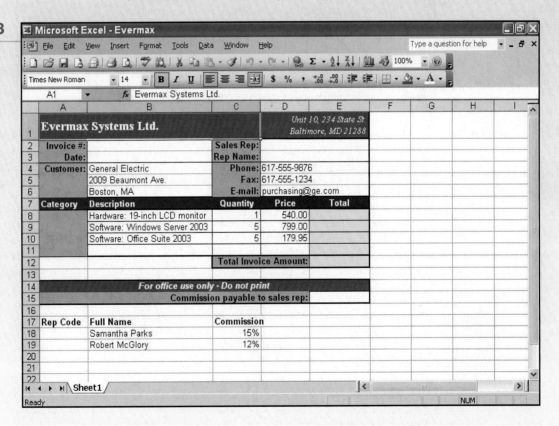

**2.** Jackson wants to complete the workbook so that two of the sales staff can test it. Before handing it off to them, he ensures that their names appear in cells B18 and B19, next to their commission rates in column C. Although he has only used the LEFT and RIGHT functions in the past, Jackson determines that the MID function can help him create a "Rep Code" automatically for each entry. The function extracts the first three letters of the person's last name and then converts it to display in uppercase letters. For example, Samantha Park's rep code will read "PAR" in cell A18 and Robert McGlory's rep code will read "MCG" in cell A19.

Jackson realizes that he needs to nest three functions in one formula expression. The MID function must appear inside the UPPER function in order to return uppercase letters. Furthermore, the SEARCH function is required to calculate the starting point argument for the MID function. (*Hint:* Start the formula with **=upper(mid(** and then click the Insert Function button ([*fx*]).) If you need assistance, refer to the Function Arguments dialog box shown in Figure 6.49.

**Figure 6.49**

Function
Arguments dialog
box for the MID
function

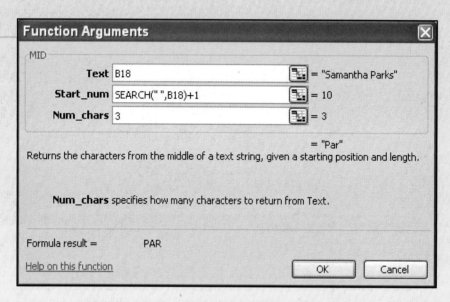

Once finished, Jackson selects cell D2 and enters "PAR" as the Sales Rep in this example. In cell D3, he uses an IF function to see whether the value in cell D2 equals the value in cell A18. If a match is found, Jackson places the name appearing in cell B18 into cell D3. If no match is found, the rep is assumed to be the name entered into cell B19. Jackson then saves the workbook.

**3.** According to the sales reps' compensation agreements, they earn a commission on every invoice that they generate. Each sales rep is assigned a commission rate between 10 and 15 percent, depending on his or her seniority with the company. To prepare for entering the commission calculation, Jackson selects cell E15. He realizes that he must multiply a commission rate from cell C18 or cell C19 by the total invoice amount shown in cell E12. First, Jackson determines which commission rate to use in the calculation using an IF function. If neither of the existing rep codes appears in cell D2, a "0" is entered in cell E15. After entering the expression, Jackson checks his work and then saves the workbook.

**4.** To further enhance the worksheet, Jackson decides to have Excel generate the invoice number automatically. Each invoice is numbered by combining the current date with the first three characters of the customer's name in uppercase letters. For example, the invoice number in the "Evermax" worksheet should read "yyyymm-CUS-dd." If the date were December 31, 2004, the invoice number would be "200412-GEN-31." With the current date already displayed in cell B3, Jackson proceeds to enter a concatenation formula that combines the date values (using the TEXT function) with the first three characters of the customer's name. Figure 6.50 shows the completed worksheet given a current date of December 30, 2003.

**Figure 6.50**

Completing the "Evermax" workbook

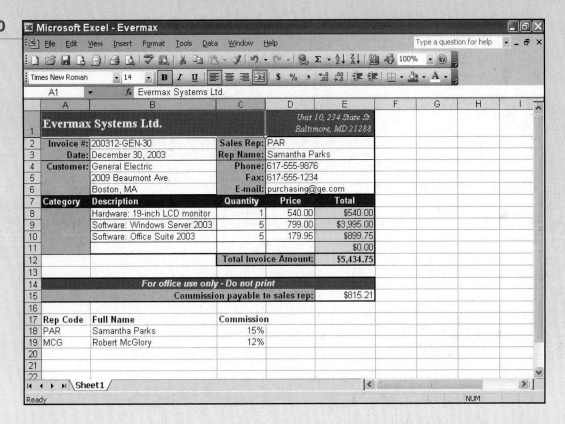

Pleased with his latest results, Jackson displays the formulas he has entered and then adjusts the column widths in the worksheet. (*Note:* There are some long formulas in this worksheet!) In preparation for printing, he specifies page setup options to print the worksheet using landscape orientation and with gridlines and row and column headings. After sending the worksheet to the printer, Jackson saves and then closes the workbook. Finally, he exits Excel 2003 and calls it a day. And what a day it was!

# Answers to Self-Check Questions

**SelfCheck**

**6.1** Provide two reasons for nesting a calculation in a formula expression.
1. to force the calculation to perform before another calculation, as dictated by the operator order of precedence
2. to make a formula expression easier to read and understand

**6.2** Name two methods for calculating and displaying the day of the week (e.g., Wednesday).
1. Use the WEEKDAY function, and then translate the return value (1 to 7) to the appropriate weekday value.
2. Use the Format command to apply a custom number format using either the "ddd" or "dddd" option.

**6.3** What are the results of the functions INT(4.55) and ROUND(4.55,0)?
- INT(4.55) returns the number 4.
- ROUND(4.55,0) returns the number 5.

**6.4** Cell A1 contains a person's area code and phone number in the form (789)555-1234. What expression would you enter in cell A2 to extract only the phone number for display? Here is one formula expression that solves the stated problem:
**=RIGHT(A1,LEN(A1)-SEARCH(")",A1))**

**6.5** How might you incorporate the IF function to calculate a mortgage payment in which the interest rate changed depending on the term chosen? You would use a nested IF function, with a logical test on the term period, to calculate the *Rate* argument for the PMT function.

# Microsoft®Office**Excel**®

## CHAPTER **7**

# Managing Worksheets and Workbooks

## **PREREQUISITES**

To successfully complete this chapter, you must know how to choose menu commands and how to navigate a worksheet. You will be asked to perform basic formatting commands and to print and preview worksheets. You should have some previous experience constructing and editing long formula expressions.

## LEARNING **OBJECTIVES**

After reading this chapter, you will be able to:

- Freeze titles for viewing large worksheets

- Divide the worksheet window into panes

- Outline a worksheet for reporting purposes

- Perform global workbook editing operations

- Navigate, rename, insert, delete, move, and copy worksheets in a workbook

- Consolidate multiple-sheet workbooks and multiple workbook files

- Insert, edit, and format cell comments

- Use the Research Pane to look up information

# 7.1 Viewing and Printing Large Worksheets

The workbooks created and used in this learning guide are kept small in order to limit their file sizes and download times from the Internet. Conversely, workbooks used in industry are typically quite expansive, containing multiple worksheets and storing hundreds of rows of data. Furthermore, these worksheets seem to grow larger with each passing year and with each new user. Knowing how to efficiently manage and work with large worksheets directly impacts your productivity.

Most worksheets display row and column titles to serve as a frame of reference for the data contained therein. For example, a worksheet that stores address information might provide column headings labeled surname, address, city, and phone. As you move the cell pointer around the worksheet, these headings can scroll out of view. Excel 2003 provides two solutions that make it easier to use large worksheets. First, you can freeze the titles of a worksheet so that certain columns and rows are always visible. Second, for those worksheets that do not group data neatly under headings, you can divide a worksheet window into two or four independent **panes.** This module shows you how to use these two features to navigate and work within a large worksheet.

You also learn about **outlining** a worksheet in this module. Outlining lets you view your data differently by displaying or hiding worksheet details. For example, a company president might prefer to review the sales results for the organization by region, while the regional managers require a more detailed analysis broken down by salesperson. Using outlines, the worksheets used to generate these reports can be one and the same. Outlining lets you report the same information using different views for different needs. Also in this module you learn to set print titles and other options for printing large worksheets.

## 7.1.1 Freezing and Unfreezing Panes

→ **Feature**

You can freeze specific rows and columns within a worksheet window so they appear at all times, regardless of where you move the cell pointer. This command is especially useful for those worksheets where the data is arranged in a table layout with row and column headings.

→ **Method**

To freeze and unfreeze panes:

- Position the cell pointer below and to the right of the row(s) and column(s) that you want to freeze.

- CHOOSE: Window → Freeze Panes to freeze the rows and columns

- CHOOSE: Window → Unfreeze Panes to unfreeze the panes

→ **Practice**

In this lesson you open an existing worksheet and practice freezing and unfreezing titles. Before proceeding, ensure that Excel 2003 is loaded.

**1.** Open the data file named EX0710 to display the worksheet shown in Figure 7.1.

**Figure 7.1**

Opening the
EX0710
workbook

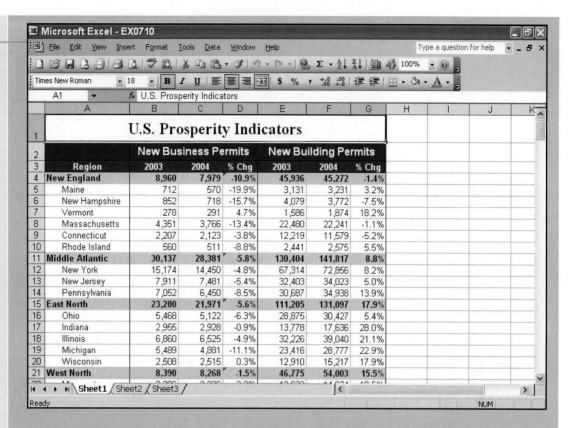

2. Save the workbook as "Indicators" to your personal storage location.

3. SELECT: cell A3

4. To move to the bottom of the worksheet's active area:
   PRESS: CTRL+⬇
   The cell pointer moves down to row 64. Notice that the column headings have moved out of view at the top of the worksheet window. Do you remember what data is stored in each column? Probably not.

5. Let's return to the top of the worksheet:
   PRESS: CTRL+HOME

6. The column headings for the worksheet are stored in rows 1, 2, and 3. Using panes, Excel enables you to freeze these rows on the screen for display at all times. To illustrate:
   SELECT: cell B4
   Notice that you selected a cell immediately below the row that you want to freeze (row 3) and to the right of the "Region" column.

7. CHOOSE: Window → Freeze Panes

8. Once again, let's move down to the last row in the worksheet:
   PRESS: CTRL+⬇
   Notice that the column headings do not move out of view this time, as shown in Figure 7.2.

**Figure 7.2**

Freezing titles

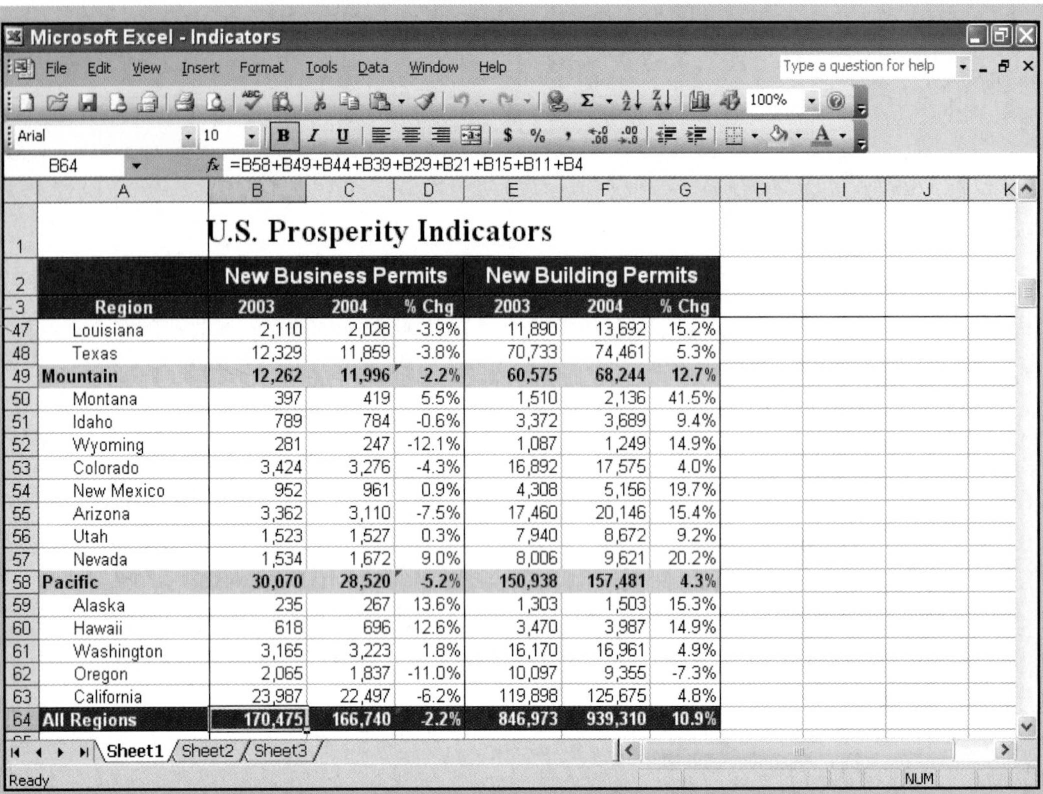

The row numbering skips from row 3 to 47

| | A | B | C | D | E | F | G |
|---|---|---|---|---|---|---|---|
| 1 | | U.S. Prosperity Indicators | | | | | |
| 2 | | New Business Permits | | | New Building Permits | | |
| 3 | Region | 2003 | 2004 | % Chg | 2003 | 2004 | % Chg |
| 47 | Louisiana | 2,110 | 2,028 | -3.9% | 11,890 | 13,692 | 15.2% |
| 48 | Texas | 12,329 | 11,859 | -3.8% | 70,733 | 74,461 | 5.3% |
| 49 | **Mountain** | 12,262 | 11,996 | -2.2% | 60,575 | 68,244 | 12.7% |
| 50 | Montana | 397 | 419 | 5.5% | 1,510 | 2,136 | 41.5% |
| 51 | Idaho | 789 | 784 | -0.6% | 3,372 | 3,689 | 9.4% |
| 52 | Wyoming | 281 | 247 | -12.1% | 1,087 | 1,249 | 14.9% |
| 53 | Colorado | 3,424 | 3,276 | -4.3% | 16,892 | 17,575 | 4.0% |
| 54 | New Mexico | 952 | 961 | 0.9% | 4,308 | 5,156 | 19.7% |
| 55 | Arizona | 3,362 | 3,110 | -7.5% | 17,460 | 20,146 | 15.4% |
| 56 | Utah | 1,523 | 1,527 | 0.3% | 7,940 | 8,672 | 9.2% |
| 57 | Nevada | 1,534 | 1,672 | 9.0% | 8,006 | 9,621 | 20.2% |
| 58 | **Pacific** | 30,070 | 28,520 | -5.2% | 150,938 | 157,481 | 4.3% |
| 59 | Alaska | 235 | 267 | 13.6% | 1,303 | 1,503 | 15.3% |
| 60 | Hawaii | 618 | 696 | 12.6% | 3,470 | 3,987 | 14.9% |
| 61 | Washington | 3,165 | 3,223 | 1.8% | 16,170 | 16,961 | 4.9% |
| 62 | Oregon | 2,065 | 1,837 | -11.0% | 10,097 | 9,355 | -7.3% |
| 63 | California | 23,987 | 22,497 | -6.2% | 119,898 | 125,675 | 4.8% |
| 64 | **All Regions** | 170,475 | 166,740 | -2.2% | 846,973 | 939,310 | 10.9% |

B64 ▼  ƒx =B58+B49+B44+B39+B29+B21+B15+B11+B4

9. PRESS: ➡ and hold it down until the columns begin to scroll
   You will notice that column A is also frozen in place.

10. PRESS: CTRL + HOME
    Because the titles above row 3 and to the left of column A are frozen, the cell pointer moves to cell B4, instead of cell A1.

11. To unfreeze the panes and move the pointer to cell A1:
    CHOOSE: Window ➔ Unfreeze Panes
    PRESS: CTRL + HOME
    The cell pointer now moves freely in the titles area.

12. Save the workbook, and keep it open for use in the next lesson.

## 7.1.2 Splitting the Worksheet Window

### → Feature

You can split the worksheet's window into two or four independent panes. To move among the panes, click the mouse pointer on a cell within the desired pane. This feature makes it easier to view and manage worksheet data that does not fit in a single window.

### → Method

Using the Menu bar:

• Position the cell pointer below or to the right of the row or column where you want the split to occur.

• CHOOSE: Window ➔ Split to divide the window into panes

• CHOOSE: Window ➔ Remove Split to remove the panes

Excel

Using the mouse:

- DRAG: the horizontal split box and the vertical split box, appearing at the end of each scroll bar, to divide the window into panes

- Finalize positioning of the panes by dragging the actual pane border that appears inside the worksheet window.

- Remove a pane by double-clicking its split box.

Horizontal Split Box

Vertical Split Box

## → Practice

You now use two independent window panes to display different areas in the worksheet. Ensure that you have completed the previous lesson and the "Indicators" workbook is displayed.

**1.** Let's split the worksheet window into two horizontal panes. Position the mouse pointer over the horizontal split box (above the vertical scroll bar). When positioned correctly, the pointer changes shape (⬍).

**2.** CLICK: left mouse button and hold it down
DRAG: the split box downward to split the window in half

**3.** Release the mouse button. You now have two vertical scroll bars for controlling the two panes independently, as shown in Figure 7.3.

**Figure 7.3**

Splitting a worksheet window into panes

Top or upper window pane

Bottom or lower window pane

Microsoft Excel - Indicators

| | A | B | C | D | E | F | G |
|---|---|---|---|---|---|---|---|
| 1 | | | U.S. Prosperity Indicators | | | | |
| 2 | | New Business Permits | | | New Building Permits | | |
| 3 | Region | 2003 | 2004 | % Chg | 2003 | 2004 | % Chg |
| 4 | New England | 8,960 | 7,979 | -10.9% | 45,936 | 45,272 | -1.4% |
| 5 | Maine | 712 | 570 | -19.9% | 3,131 | 3,231 | 3.2% |
| 6 | New Hampshire | 852 | 718 | -15.7% | 4,079 | 3,772 | -7.5% |
| 7 | Vermont | 278 | 291 | 4.7% | 1,586 | 1,874 | 18.2% |
| 8 | Massachusetts | 4,351 | 3,766 | -13.4% | 22,480 | 22,241 | -1.1% |
| 9 | Connecticut | 2,207 | 2,123 | -3.8% | 12,219 | 11,579 | -5.2% |
| 10 | Rhode Island | 560 | 511 | -8.8% | 2,441 | 2,575 | 5.5% |
| 11 | Middle Atlantic | 30,137 | 28,381 | -5.8% | 130,404 | 141,817 | 8.8% |
| 12 | New York | 15,174 | 14,450 | -4.8% | 67,314 | 72,856 | 8.2% |
| 13 | New Jersey | 7,911 | 7,481 | -5.4% | 32,403 | 34,023 | 5.0% |
| 14 | Pennsylvania | 7,052 | 6,450 | -8.5% | 30,687 | 34,938 | 13.9% |
| 15 | East North | 23,280 | 21,971 | -5.6% | 111,205 | 131,097 | 17.9% |
| 16 | Ohio | 5,468 | 5,122 | -6.3% | 28,875 | 30,427 | 5.4% |
| 17 | Indiana | 2,955 | 2,928 | -0.9% | 13,778 | 17,636 | 28.0% |
| 18 | Illinois | 6,860 | 6,525 | -4.9% | 32,226 | 39,040 | 21.1% |
| 19 | Michigan | 5,489 | 4,881 | -11.1% | 23,416 | 28,777 | 22.9% |
| 20 | Wisconsin | 2,508 | 2,515 | 0.3% | 12,910 | 15,217 | 17.9% |
| 21 | West North | 8,390 | 8,268 | -1.5% | 46,775 | 54,003 | 15.5% |

Vertical scroll bar for the top pane

Vertical scroll bar for the bottom pane

Sheet1 / Sheet2 / Sheet3 /

Ready     NUM

**4.** Clicking a cell that is displayed in a window pane makes that pane active. To move the cell pointer to row 64 in the bottom window pane:
CLICK: on any cell in column A of the lower window pane
PRESS: CTRL + ⬇

**5.** Let's enter a new value for Vermont in the top window pane:
SELECT: cell C7

**6.** As you press ENTER, watch the total formula in row 64.
TYPE: 2910
PRESS: ENTER
The value in cell C64 changes to 169,359, as shown in Figure 7.4. The ability to separate a worksheet into window panes enables you to view the most relevant areas in your worksheet at all times.

**Figure 7.4**

Updating data in a multipaned worksheet

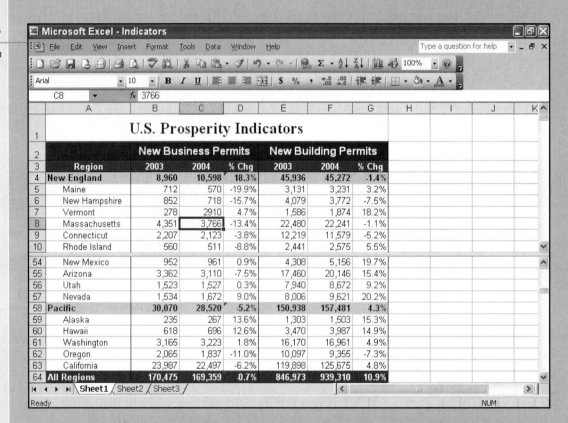

**7.** To remove all panes from the worksheet window:
CHOOSE: Window → Remove Split

**8.** Save the workbook, and keep it open for use in the next lesson.

### 7.1.3 Outlining a Worksheet

→ **Feature**

The process of outlining a worksheet groups related data together and allows you to display or hide the data as a single unit. Excel 2003 can automatically outline a worksheet based on the existence of summary formulas, such as the SUM function. When you select a range and issue the Auto Outline command, Excel inserts outline levels at each subtotal formula and for the grand total. Once outlined, you can print a worksheet or plot a chart using only the visible data at a specific level in the outline.

→ ## Method

To outline a worksheet automatically:

- SELECT: a cell within the worksheet area that you want to outline
- CHOOSE: Data → Group and Outline → Auto Outline to create an outline
- CHOOSE: Data → Group and Outline → Clear Outline to remove an outline

→ ## Practice

You will now practice outlining the contents of an existing worksheet. Ensure that you have completed the previous lesson and the "Indicators" workbook is displayed.

**1.** To begin, review the contents of this worksheet:
SELECT: cell B4
Looking in the Formula bar, notice that this cell contains a SUM function. In fact, all rows formatted similarly to row 4 provide summary formulas.

**2.** PRESS: CTRL + ↓
Notice that cell B64 contains a formula that adds together all of the subtotal formulas.

**3.** PRESS: CTRL + HOME

**4.** Excel uses the existing formulas in a worksheet to determine the best approach for outlining. To begin, you place the cell pointer within the data area that you want to outline:
SELECT: cell A4

**5.** To outline the worksheet automatically:
CHOOSE: Data → Group and Outline → Auto Outline
Your screen should now appear similar to the one shown in Figure 7.5. The outlining symbols are described further in Table 7.1.

### Figure 7.5

Outlining a worksheet

Column-Level buttons

Row-Level buttons

Row-Level bar shows the detail rows for a specific group; click the bar to hide the detail

Hide Detail button

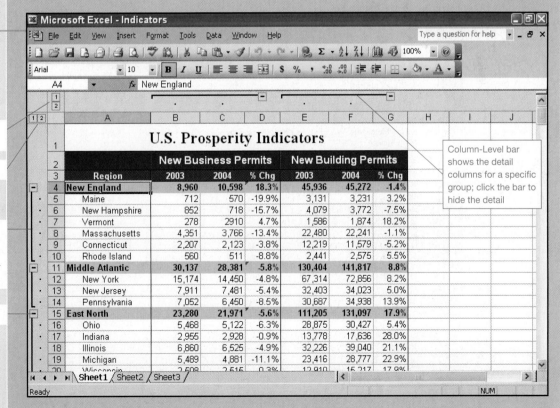

Column-Level bar shows the detail columns for a specific group; click the bar to hide the detail

**Table 7.1**

Outline Symbols

| Symbol... | Description... |
|---|---|
| 1, 2, 3, ... | Column- and Row-Level buttons let you change the display summary level for the entire worksheet; an outline can have up to eight levels of detail. |
| ➕ | Show Detail button lets you expand and display all detail rows and columns for a specific group. |
| ➖ | Hide Detail button lets you collapse and hide all detail rows and columns for a specific group. |

**6.** To collapse some of the detail in the worksheet:
CLICK: Row-Level 1 button ( 1 )
All rows containing data for the individual states are hidden; only the Region subtotals remain.

**7.** To display the detailed information for West North:
CLICK: Show Detail button ( ➕ ) to the left of row 21
Notice that only those states in the West North region are displayed, as shown in Figure 7.6.

**Figure 7.6**

Collapsing and expanding an outlined worksheet

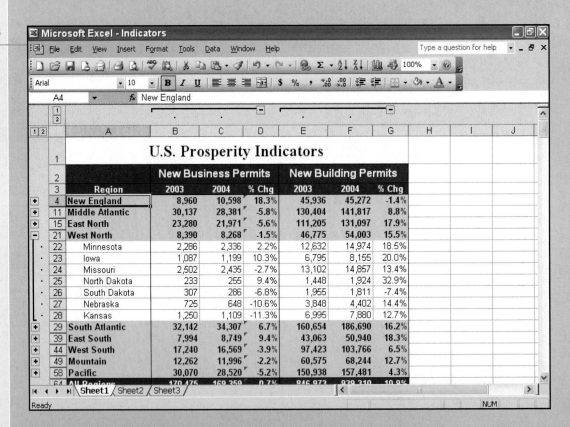

**8.** To preview how the worksheet will print:
CLICK: Print Preview button ( )
Notice that the preview appears identical to the worksheet display.

**9.** CLICK: Close command button to return to the worksheet

**10.** On your own, practice collapsing and expanding the outline symbols in the worksheet. (*Hint:* You can collapse a detail level by selecting the row- or column-level bars.)

**11.** To remove the outline (and all of the associated symbols) from the worksheet, do the following:
CHOOSE: Data → Group and Outline → Clear Outline

**12.** Save the workbook, and keep it open for use in the next lesson.

### *In Addition* OUTLINING A WORKSHEET MANUALLY

If your worksheet does not contain summary formulas, you need to manually group the detail sections that you want outlined. Select the desired rows or columns and then use the Group and Ungroup commands under the Data → Group and Outline menu option.

## 7.1.4 Specifying Print Titles and Options

→ # Feature

Similar to freezing panes to keep column and row headings in view, you can set **print titles** to appear at the top of each printed page. Using data stored in the worksheet, Excel repeats the specified row information whenever a page break is encountered. This feature makes the printouts for larger worksheets easier to read.

→ # Method

To specify print titles for a large worksheet:

• CHOOSE: File → Page Setup

• CLICK: *Sheet* tab

• Specify the desired rows in the *Print titles* area.

→ # Practice

Let's practice setting print titles and printing a large worksheet. Ensure that the "Indicators" workbook is displayed.

**1.** To select the worksheet area to print:
SELECT: cell A4
PRESS: CTRL +*
This keystroke shortcut selects the worksheet's active area. (*Hint:* To access the asterisk, you need to press the key combination of SHIFT +8.)

**2.** Now define the current selection as the worksheet area to print:
CHOOSE: File → Print Area → Set Print Area
(*Note:* Use the Set Print Area command when you need to specify a limited range in the worksheet for printing. In this example, choosing the command was not necessary since you want to print the entire worksheet.)

**3.** To specify a landscape orientation:
CHOOSE: File → Page Setup
CLICK: *Page* tab
SELECT: *Landscape* option button in the *Orientation* area

**4.** To make the font size appear larger than normal in the printout:
SELECT: 125 in the spin box for the *Adjust to* option button
CLICK: Print Preview command button
(*Note:* You use Excel's scaling feature to reduce a worksheet's print area to fit on a specified number of pages or to increase a printout's font size for easier reading.) Your screen should now appear similar to the one shown in Figure 7.7.

## Figure 7.7

Previewing a
large worksheet

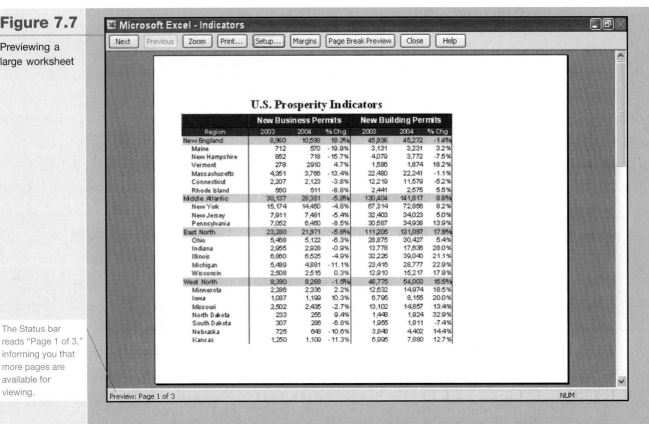

The Status bar
reads "Page 1 of 3,"
informing you that
more pages are
available for
viewing.

**5.** In the bottom left-hand corner of the Preview window, notice that the Status bar reads "Page 1 of 3." (*Note:* Your screen may read "Page 1 of 2" or "Page 1 of 4" for this step, depending on the resolution of your monitor and printer.) To view the next page:
CLICK: Next command button in the top left-hand corner

**6.** Notice that there are no column headings on page 2 from the title rows in the worksheet. By specifying print titles, you can make your printout more attractive and easier to read. To begin:
CLICK: Close command button
PRESS: CTRL + HOME

**7.** CHOOSE: File → Page Setup
CLICK: *Sheet* tab

**8.** In the *Print titles* area of the Page Setup dialog box:
CLICK: Dialog Collapse button ( ) beside the *Rows to repeat at top* text box
SELECT: cell range from A2 to A3
Notice that only the absolute row numbers "$2:$3" are entered for the range, as shown in Figure 7.8.

## Figure 7.8

Selecting print
titles

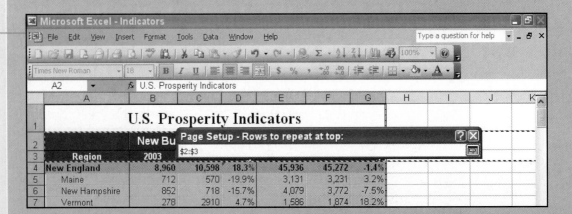

9. CLICK: Dialog Expand button (▣) in the floating range window

10. To preview the worksheet:
CLICK: Print Preview command button
CLICK: Next command button
Notice that rows 2 and 3 are repeated on the second page.

11. To print the worksheet:
CLICK: Print command button to display the Print dialog box
CLICK: OK command button
(*Note:* If you do not want to print the worksheet, click the Cancel command button in the Print dialog box.)

12. Save the workbook, and keep it open for use in the next lesson.

### 7.1.5 Using the Page Break Preview Mode

→ **Feature**

After formatting a worksheet and specifying its print options, you can switch display modes to adjust where page breaks occur. In the Page Break Preview mode, you manipulate the location of page breaks by dragging them using the mouse.

→ **Method**

To modify a worksheet's printout using Page Break Preview mode:

• CHOOSE: View → Page Break Preview

• DRAG: page break lines using the mouse

• CHOOSE: View → Normal to return to normal viewing

→ **Practice**

You now practice adjusting page breaks for the worksheet printout. Ensure that the "Indicators" workbook is displayed.

1. To view the worksheet using Page Break Preview mode:
CHOOSE: View → Page Break Preview
(*Note:* If the Welcome to Page Break Preview dialog box appears as shown below, click the OK command button to close it.)

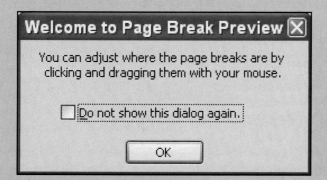

2. The right margin and page break borders appear in blue. Position the mouse pointer over the dashed page break line (somewhere near row 28) until the pointer changes shape (↕). (*Hint:* You may have to scroll the window down to see the dashed page break line.)

**3.** DRAG: page break line upward to between rows 20 and 21
When you release the mouse, the new page break is set in the window, as shown in Figure 7.9.

**Figure 7.9**

Setting a page break in Page Break Preview

Watermarking for Page 1

Watermarking for Page 2

Drag the right blue margin line to set the page border

Drag the blue page break line to set the page break

### U.S. Prosperity Indicators

| | Region | New Business Permits | | | New Building Permits | | |
|---|---|---|---|---|---|---|---|
| | | 2003 | 2004 | % Chg | 2003 | 2004 | % Chg |
| 4 | New England | 8,960 | 10,598 | 18.3% | 45,936 | 45,272 | -1.4% |
| 5 | Maine | 712 | 570 | -19.9% | 3,131 | 3,231 | 3.2% |
| 6 | New Hampshire | 852 | 718 | -15.7% | 4,079 | 3,772 | -7.5% |
| 7 | Vermont | 278 | 2910 | 4.7% | 1,586 | 1,874 | 18.2% |
| 8 | Massachusetts | 4,351 | 3,766 | -13.4% | 22,480 | 22,241 | -1.1% |
| 9 | Connecticut | 2,207 | 2,123 | -3.8% | 12,219 | 11,579 | -5.2% |
| 10 | Rhode Island | 560 | 511 | -8.8% | 2,441 | 2,575 | 5.5% |
| 11 | Middle Atlantic | 30,137 | 28,381 | -5.8% | 130,404 | 141,817 | 8.8% |
| 12 | New York | 15,174 | 14,450 | -4.8% | 67,314 | 72,856 | 8.2% |
| 13 | New Jersey | 7,911 | 7,481 | -5.4% | 32,403 | 34,023 | 5.0% |
| 14 | Pennsylvania | 7,052 | 6,450 | -8.5% | 30,687 | 34,938 | 13.9% |
| 15 | East North | 23,280 | 21,971 | -5.6% | 111,205 | 131,097 | 17.9% |
| 16 | Ohio | 5,468 | 5,122 | -6.3% | 28,875 | 30,427 | 5.4% |
| 17 | Indiana | 2,955 | 2,928 | -0.9% | 13,778 | 17,636 | 28.0% |
| 18 | Illinois | 6,860 | 6,525 | -4.9% | 32,226 | 39,040 | 21.1% |
| 19 | Michigan | 5,489 | 4,881 | -11.1% | 23,416 | 28,777 | 22.9% |
| 20 | Wisconsin | 2,508 | 2,515 | 0.3% | 12,910 | 15,217 | 17.9% |
| 21 | West North | 8,390 | 8,268 | -1.5% | 46,775 | 54,003 | 15.5% |
| 22 | Minnesota | 2,286 | 2,336 | 2.2% | 12,632 | 14,974 | 18.5% |
| 23 | Iowa | 1,087 | 1,199 | 10.3% | 6,795 | 8,155 | 20.0% |
| 24 | Missouri | 2,502 | 2,435 | -2.7% | 13,102 | 14,857 | 13.4% |
| 25 | North Dakota | 233 | 255 | 9.4% | 1,448 | 1,924 | 32.9% |
| 26 | South Dakota | 307 | 286 | -6.8% | 1,955 | 1,811 | -7.4% |
| 27 | Nebraska | 725 | 648 | -10.6% | 3,848 | 4,402 | 14.4% |
| 28 | Kansas | 1,250 | 1,109 | -11.3% | 6,995 | 7,880 | 12.7% |
| 29 | South Atlantic | 32,142 | 34,307 | 6.7% | 160,654 | ##### | 16.2% |
| 30 | Maryland | 3,310 | 3,668 | 10.8% | 15,668 | 18,534 | 18.3% |
| 31 | Delaware | 534 | 602 | 12.7% | 2,675 | 2,661 | -0.5% |
| 32 | District of Col | 535 | 636 | 17.0% | 2,757 | 3,457 | 25.4% |
| 33 | Virginia | 3,591 | 3,779 | 5.2% | 18,557 | 21,852 | 17.8% |
| 34 | West Virginia | 563 | 555 | -2.5% | 2,682 | 4,239 | 58.1% |
| 35 | North Carolina | 4,007 | 4,578 | 14.3% | 19,504 | 25,464 | 30.6% |
| 36 | South Carolina | 1,903 | 2,014 | 5.8% | 10,175 | 11,236 | 10.4% |
| 37 | Georgia | 5,334 | 5,383 | 0.9% | 28,627 | 29,853 | 4.3% |
| 38 | Florida | 12,299 | 13,032 | 6.0% | 60,009 | 69,388 | 15.6% |

Sheet1 / Sheet2 / Sheet3

**4.** Everything above the page break line appears on the first page and everything below the line appears on the following pages. After using the vertical scroll bar to move the window downward, set the next page break to occur between rows 43 and 44.

**5.** To preview the worksheet's new settings:
CLICK: Print Preview button ( )

**6.** Move among the pages using the Next and Previous command buttons.

**7.** To return to the normal display:
CLICK: Close command button on the toolbar

**8.** Let's return to the Normal viewing mode:
CHOOSE: View → Normal
Notice that there are dashed lines in the worksheet representing the page breaks.

**9.** Save and then close the workbook.

### *In Addition* INSERTING AND REMOVING A PAGE BREAK

To insert a manual page break, position the cell pointer below the row where you wish the page break to occur and then choose the Insert → Page Break command. To remove a manually inserted page break, position the cell pointer in the same location and then issue the Insert → Remove Page Break command.

**7.1**   How would you divide a worksheet window into four panes?

## 7.2   Working with Data in Large Worksheets

When all the data for a worksheet fits on a single screen, the editing tasks are relatively simple. The larger and more complex the worksheet is, the more difficult it is to edit. In this module you learn how to find and replace data and cell formats in a large worksheet and how to check a worksheet for spelling errors.

### 7.2.1  Finding Data and Cell Formats

→ ## Feature

The Find command in Excel lets you search an entire workbook for the existence of a few characters, a word, or a phrase. You can also search a workbook for the existence of a particular formatting specification. Within large worksheets, this command is especially useful for moving the cell pointer to a particular cell for editing. Most commonly, the Find command is used to locate a record in a worksheet list. If you've ever used word processing or database management software, you're most likely familiar with this command already.

→ ## Method

To find data in a worksheet:

• CHOOSE: Edit → Find,

   *or*

• PRESS: CTRL+f

→ ## Practice

In this lesson you practice finding data and cell formats in a worksheet. Ensure that no workbooks appear in the Excel application window.

**1.** Open the data file named EX0720 to display the workbook shown in Figure 7.10.

**Figure 7.10**

Opening the
EX0720
workbook

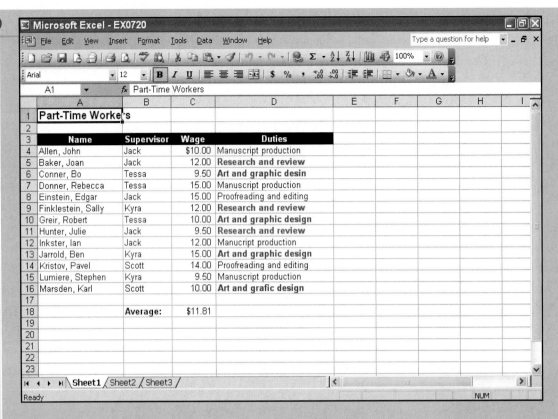

**Figure 7.11**

Find and Replace
dialog box: *Find*
tab

Enter the search
parameter that you
want to find

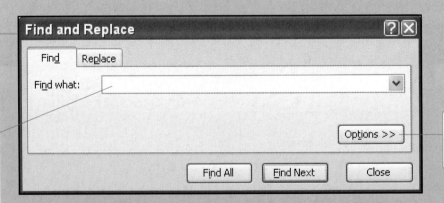

**2.** Save the workbook as "Part-Timers" to your personal storage location.

**3.** Let's use the Find command to search the entire worksheet for a single name. Do the following:
CHOOSE: Edit → Find
(*Hint:* You can also press CTRL +f to display the Find dialog box.) The Find and Replace dialog appears, as shown in Figure 7.11.

**4.** To perform a simple search:
TYPE: **Hunter** into the *Find what* text box
CLICK: Find Next command button
The cell pointer moves to "Hunter, Julie" in cell A11.

**5.** You can specify additional search options in the Find dialog box. For example, let's practice searching for cells containing a particular formatting enhancement. Do the following:
CLICK: Close command button

6. Before performing another search, let's move to the top of the worksheet. This is a good habit to get into prior to displaying the Find and Replace dialog box. Do the following:
   PRESS: CTRL + HOME

7. To find all the cells with a format matching cell D5:
   PRESS: CTRL +f to display the Find and Replace dialog box

8. In the Find and Replace dialog box:
   CLICK: Options command button
   Your screen should now appear similar to the one shown in Figure 7.12.

**Figure 7.12**

Displaying search options in the Find and Replace dialog box

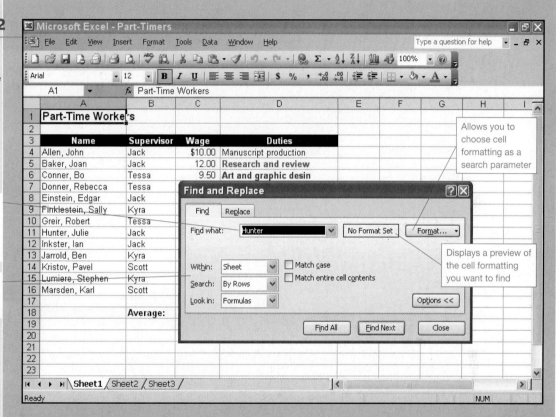

The previous search parameter remains in the *Find what* drop-down list box

Use these options to specify where and how to search

Allows you to choose cell formatting as a search parameter

Displays a preview of the cell formatting you want to find

9. Let's remove the original search parameter:
   PRESS: DELETE to remove "Hunter" from the *Find what* combo box

10. To define the new search operation:
    CLICK: down arrow attached to the Format command button
    SELECT: Choose Format From Cell
    The dialog box is temporarily hidden from view.

11. Position the eye dropper mouse pointer (⊕⧫) in cell D5, as shown below, and then click once to select its formatting. The Find and Replace dialog box reappears with a preview of the selected cell's formatting.

12. To find the next occurrence of this formatting:
    CLICK: Find Next command button
    The cell pointer moves to cell D9.

**13.** If the correct value is found, close the Find dialog box by clicking the Close command button. If you want to continue searching, click the Find Next command button. For this step:
CLICK: Find Next command button
The cell pointer now moves to cell D11.

**14.** To close the dialog box:
CLICK: Close command button

**15.** Save the workbook, and keep it open for use in the next lesson.

## 7.2.2 Replacing Data and Cell Formats

→ ## Feature

The Replace command in Excel lets you perform a global find and replace operation to update the contents of an entire workbook. Using the same process as Find, you enter an additional value to replace all occurrences of the successful match. For example, you can easily change the department names in a company directory, increase the prices in a product catalog, or change all cells appearing with boldface to italic. Replace is an excellent tool for correcting spelling mistakes and updating standard information, such as telephone area codes.

→ ## Method

To replace data in a worksheet:

• CHOOSE: Edit → Replace,

  *or*

• PRESS: CTRL +h

→ ## Practice

In this lesson you practice replacing data and cell formats in a worksheet. Ensure that you have completed the previous lesson and that the "Part-Timers" workbook is displayed.

**1.** Imagine that one of the supervisors has left the company. You've been asked to replace his name in the worksheet with the name of the newly hired supervisor. To proceed:
SELECT: cell B3
(*Hint:* Although it is not necessary, Excel performs searches faster if you place the cell pointer at the top of the desired search column. Given the small size of this workbook, there would be no noticeable speed difference in searching by column or by row.)

**2.** To replace the name "Jack" with "Andy" in column B, let's display the *Replace* tab of the Find and Replace dialog box. Do the following:
CHOOSE: Edit → Replace
Your screen should now appear similar to the one shown in Figure 7.13.

**Figure 7.13**

Find and Replace
dialog box:
*Replace* tab

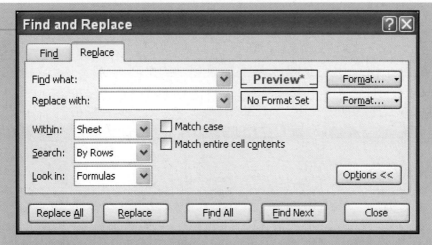

3. Let's enter the name to find:
   TYPE: **Jack** in the *Find what* drop-down list box
   PRESS: TAB

4. Now enter the name to replace:
   TYPE: **Andy** in the *Replace with* drop-down list box

5. You must now remove the formatting specification from the *Find what* row in the dialog box. Do the following:
   CLICK: down arrow attached to the Format command button for the *Find what* row
   SELECT: Clear Find Format
   The preview box for formatting should now read "No Format Set."

6. To highlight the new supervisor, let's enhance the normal formatting by applying a red color and boldface. To proceed:
   CLICK: down arrow attached to the Format command button for the *Replace with* row
   SELECT: Format
   The Replace Format dialog box (see Figure 7.14) appears, looking very similar to the Format Cells dialog box that you've used in previous chapters.

7. In the Replace Format dialog box:
   CLICK: *Font* tab
   SELECT: Bold in the *Font style* list box
   SELECT: a red color from the *Color* drop-down list box
   Your screen should now appear as shown in Figure 7.14.

Excel

**Figure 7.14**

Specifying the replacement cell format

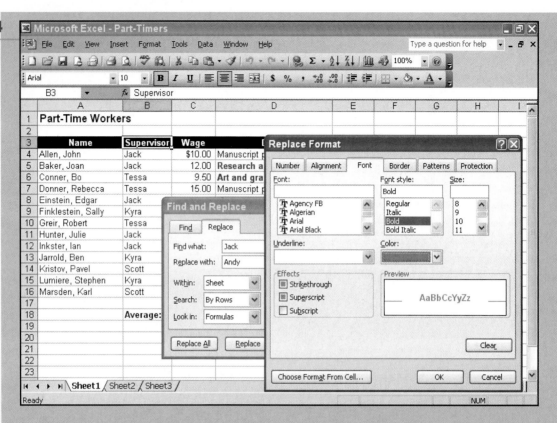

**8.** To return to the Find and Replace dialog box:
CLICK: OK command button

**9.** You may now proceed by replacing entries one at a time or all at once. For this exercise:
CLICK: Replace All command button
All of the "Jack" entries are replaced by "Andy" and the following dialog box is displayed.

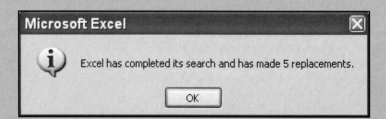

**10.** To accept the dialog box notification:
CLICK: OK command button

**11.** To close the dialog box and return to the top of the worksheet:
CLICK: Close command button
PRESS: CTRL + HOME

**12.** Save the workbook, and keep it open for use in the next lesson.

## 7.2.3 Spell-Checking a Worksheet

→ **Feature**

Excel's **AutoCorrect** feature can correct hundreds of common typographical and capitalization errors as you type. You will find this feature extremely useful if you habitually misspell particular words. AutoCorrect also helps you enter special symbols like © and ™ into a cell.

The **Spelling Checker,** a shared utility that appears in all Microsoft Office System 2003 applications, lets you perform a spelling check on a cell range, a worksheet, or an entire workbook. A spelling check scans cells containing text labels and then displays those words that do not appear in one of its dictionaries. You may then select the proper spelling from a suggested word list or retype the word. If the word is already spelled correctly, you can choose to ignore the word, add the word to a custom dictionary, or insert the word into the AutoCorrect list.

→ **Method**

To review the entries available in AutoCorrect:

* CHOOSE: Tools ➜ AutoCorrect Options

To perform a spelling check:

* CLICK: Spelling button ([✓]),

   *or*

* CHOOSE: Tools ➜ Spelling

→ **Practice**

You will now practice using AutoCorrect and spell-checking the worksheet. Ensure that the "Part-Timers" workbook is displayed.

**1.** Let's enter a misspelled word intentionally:
SELECT: cell C1
TYPE: Occassion

**2.** To demonstrate Excel's AutoCorrect feature:
PRESS: [ENTER]
The entry in cell C1 now reads "Occasion." Notice that the spelling is corrected automatically.

**3.** You can also use AutoCorrect to insert special symbols. To do so:
SELECT: cell D1
TYPE: (c)
PRESS: Space bar once
As shown below, AutoCorrect replaces "(c)" with the proper copyright symbol © when you press the Space bar. (*Note:* If you want to keep the "(c)," click the Undo button ([↺▾]) to reverse the AutoCorrect substitution.)

| | A | B | C | D |
|---|---|---|---|---|
| 1 | **Part-Time Workers** | | Occasion | © |

**4.** To continue the entry:
TYPE: Part-Time Enterprises
PRESS: [ENTER]

**5.** To review some of the other entries available in AutoCorrect:
CHOOSE: Tools ➜ AutoCorrect Options
CLICK: *AutoCorrect* tab, if not already selected

In the dialog box (Figure 7.15) that appears, there are two columns: *Replace* and *With*. AutoCorrect replaces the entry appearing in the *Replace* column with the entry in the *With* column. You can also use this dialog box to enable and disable several AutoCorrect actions.

**Figure 7.15**

AutoCorrect
dialog box:
*AutoCorrect* tab

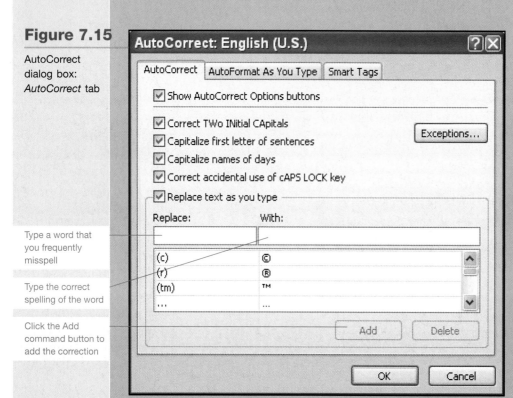

Type a word that
you frequently
misspell

Type the correct
spelling of the word

Click the Add
command button to
add the correction

**6.** To close the AutoCorrect dialog box:
CLICK: Cancel command button

**7.** To begin spell-checking the entire worksheet:
SELECT: cell A1 to start at the top of the worksheet
CLICK: Spelling button ( )

**8.** When Excel finds a misspelled word, it displays the dialog box shown in Figure 7.16 and awaits further instructions. To change the word "desin" to the correctly spelled word "design," do the following:
CLICK: Change command button
(*Note:* If this is a word that you frequently misspell, consider adding it to your AutoCorrect list by clicking the AutoCorrect command button. That way, the next time you misspell the word, Excel can correct your mistake automatically.)

**Figure 7.16**

Spelling dialog box

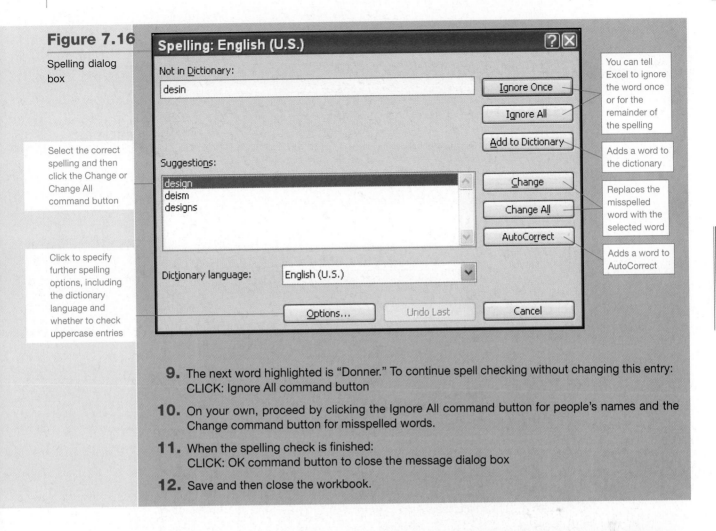

Select the correct spelling and then click the Change or Change All command button

Click to specify further spelling options, including the dictionary language and whether to check uppercase entries

You can tell Excel to ignore the word once or for the remainder of the spelling

Adds a word to the dictionary

Replaces the misspelled word with the selected word

Adds a word to AutoCorrect

9. The next word highlighted is "Donner." To continue spell checking without changing this entry:
   CLICK: Ignore All command button

10. On your own, proceed by clicking the Ignore All command button for people's names and the Change command button for misspelled words.

11. When the spelling check is finished:
    CLICK: OK command button to close the message dialog box

12. Save and then close the workbook.

 **SelfCheck**

7.2   What characters must you type to have Excel's AutoCorrect feature insert the proper trademark symbol (™)?

# 7.3 Working with Multiple-Sheet Workbooks

In this module you learn how to create and navigate a multiple-sheet workbook file. Multiple-sheet workbooks enable you to separate related information onto different pages in a single disk file. For example, a project manager can create a summary report on one worksheet and then place detailed information for each development phase on subsequent worksheets. This three-dimensional (3-D) capability enables you to easily manage and consolidate your information.

## 7.3.1 Navigating, Renaming, and Formatting Sheet Tabs

→ **Feature**

You access and navigate the sheets in a workbook using tabs that appear at the bottom of the worksheet window, as shown below. In a new workbook, Excel provides three worksheets named *Sheet1*, *Sheet2*, and *Sheet3*. Besides inserting and deleting sheets, you can rename them to display more descriptive names and format them to display using different colors. When changing the name of a sheet tab, limit your entry to thirty characters, including spaces, and avoid using the asterisk (*), question mark (?), forward slash (/), backslash (\), or colon (:).

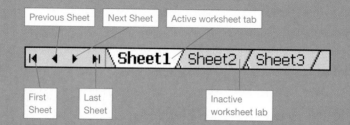

→ **Method**

To move to a visible sheet tab:

- CLICK: the desired sheet tab

To move to a hidden sheet tab:

- RIGHT-CLICK: tab scroll buttons
- SELECT: the desired sheet tab

To rename a sheet tab:

- DOUBLE-CLICK: the sheet tab
- TYPE: *a name*
- PRESS: (ENTER)

To change the tab color:

- RIGHT-CLICK: the sheet tab
- SELECT: Tab Color
- SELECT: the desired color

→ **Practice**

In this exercise you practice moving among and renaming worksheets and changing sheet tab colors. Ensure that no workbooks are open in the Excel 2003 application window.

1. Open the data file named EX0730 to display the workbook shown in Figure 7.17.

**Figure 7.17**

Opening the
EX0730
workbook

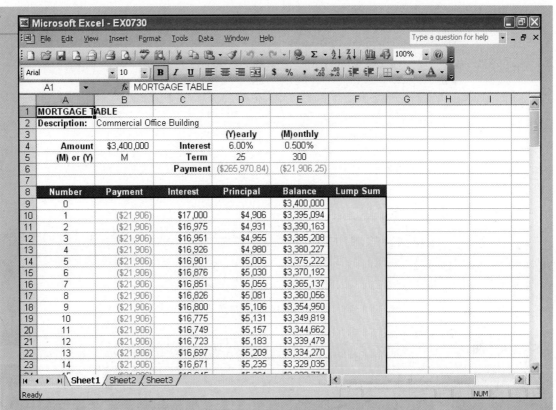

2. Save the workbook as "Loan Tables" to your personal storage location.

3. To familiarize yourself with the workbook's contents:
   CLICK: *Sheet2* tab
   CLICK: *Sheet3* tab
   Notice that the tab for the active worksheet appears with a white background.

4. To navigate among the worksheets:
   RIGHT-CLICK: one of the tab scroll buttons
   (*Hint:* The tab scroll buttons appear to the left of the sheet tabs and, when right-clicked, display the pop-up menu shown below.)

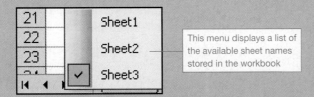

This menu displays a list of the available sheet names stored in the workbook

5. To move to the first worksheet:
   SELECT: Sheet1 in the pop-up menu

6. To rename the Sheet1 worksheet:
   DOUBLE-CLICK: *Sheet1* tab
   The text within the tab will appear highlighted, as shown below, when selected properly. (*Hint:* You can also right-click a sheet tab and select the Rename command.)

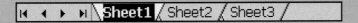

**7.** TYPE: Commercial
PRESS: (ENTER)

**8.** To rename the Sheet2 worksheet:
DOUBLE-CLICK: *Sheet2* tab
TYPE: House
PRESS: (ENTER)

**9.** To rename the Sheet3 worksheet:
DOUBLE-CLICK: *Sheet3* tab
TYPE: Townhouse
PRESS: (ENTER)
The sheet tabs should appear as shown below.

| ◄ ◄ ► ►| \ Commercial / House \ **Townhouse** / |

**10.** To change the color of the Townhouse worksheet tab:
RIGHT-CLICK: *Townhouse* tab
The right-click menu shown in Figure 7.18 appears.

**Figure 7.18**

Displaying the tab menu for the Townhouse worksheet

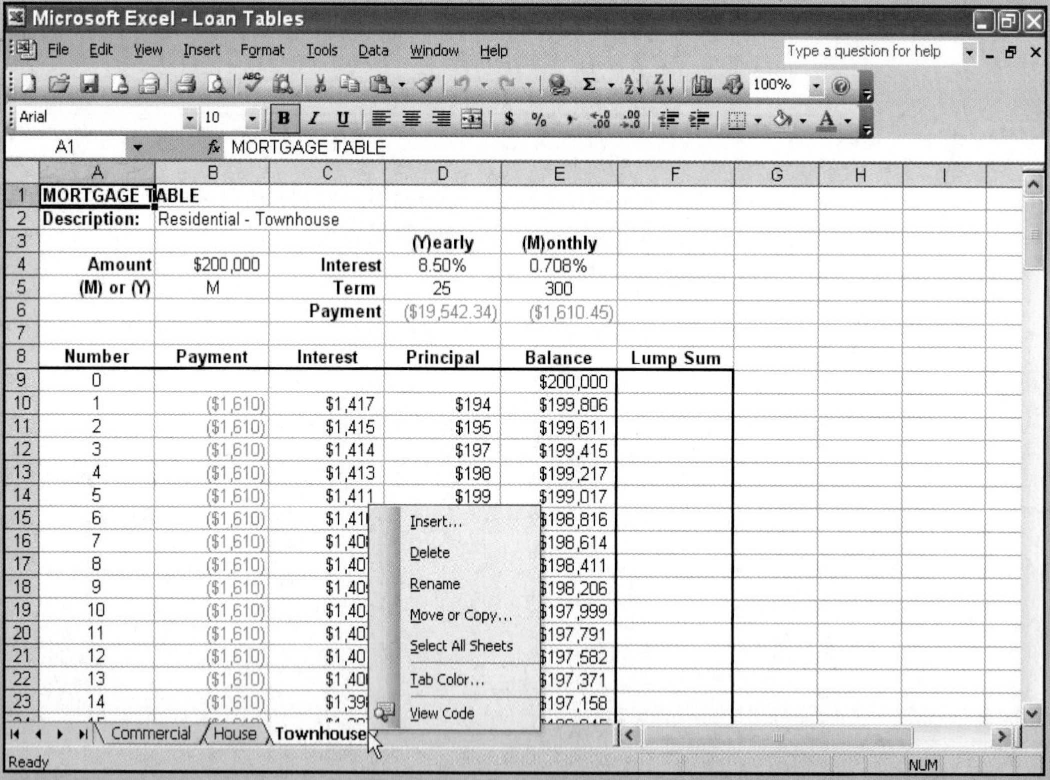

**11.** SELECT: Tab Color
The Format Tab Color dialog box, shown here, displays a palette of colors.

**12.** To complete the color selection:
SELECT: a light yellow color
CLICK: OK command button

**13.** Now let's change the color of the House worksheet tab:
RIGHT-CLICK: *House* tab
SELECT: Tab Color
SELECT: a light green color
CLICK: OK command button

**14.** On your own, change the color of the Commercial worksheet tab to a pale blue color. When finished, the Sheet tabs should appear as shown below. Notice that the active sheet tab still appears mostly white.

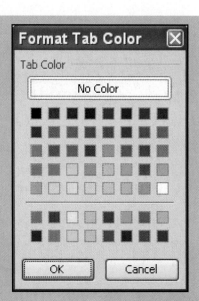

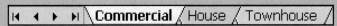

**15.** Save the workbook, and keep it open for use in the next lesson.

## 7.3.2 Inserting, Arranging, and Deleting Worksheets

### → Feature

You can insert and delete worksheets and chart sheets inside a workbook file. In addition, you can move, copy, and rearrange the order in which worksheets appear in a workbook. The collection of worksheets and chart sheets in a workbook is known as a *sheet stack*.

### → Method

To insert, delete, move, or copy a worksheet:

- RIGHT-CLICK: a sheet tab

- SELECT: Insert to insert a new worksheet,

  *or*

- SELECT: Delete to delete the current worksheet,

  *or*

- SELECT: Move or Copy to move or copy worksheets

### → Practice

You will now practice inserting, copying, moving, and deleting worksheets. Ensure that you have completed the previous lesson and that the "Loan Tables" workbook is displayed.

**1.** Before inserting and deleting worksheets, let's practice moving a sheet using the drag and drop method. Ensure that the *Commercial* tab is selected and then position the mouse pointer over its tab. Do the following:
CLICK: the left mouse button and hold it down
The mouse pointer changes shape ( ).

**2.** DRAG: *Commercial* tab to the right, as shown below, until the downward-pointing triangle appears to the right of the *Townhouse* tab

**3.** Release the mouse button when positioned correctly to complete the move operation.

**4.** On your own, move the *House* tab in between the *Townhouse* and *Commercial* tabs. The *House* tab will appear active when dropped.

**5.** To create a duplicate copy of the House worksheet:
RIGHT-CLICK: *House* tab
SELECT: Move or Copy
Your screen should appear similar to the one shown in Figure 7.19. (*Note:* The dialog box has been moved up from the sheet tabs for easier viewing.)

**Figure 7.19**

Displaying the Move or Copy dialog box for a sheet tab

Specify the target location in another workbook

Specify the target location with the current workbook

Change the operation from a Move to a Copy by selecting this check box

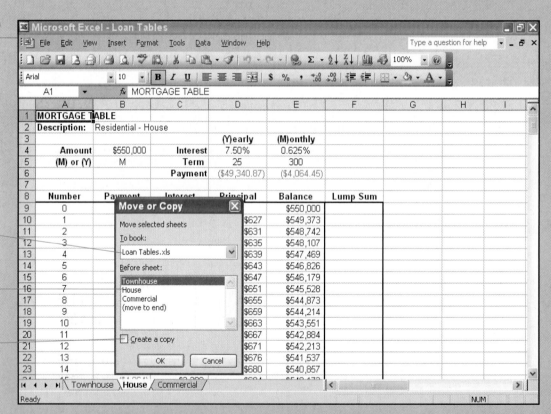

**6.** The current workbook's filename already appears in the *To book* drop-down list. To complete the copy operation:
SELECT: (move to end) in the *Before sheet* list box
SELECT: *Create a copy* check box
CLICK: OK command button
A new sheet tab appears named *House (2)*. You will remove this duplicate worksheet in the next few steps.

7. A workbook's sheet tabs share the window with the horizontal scroll bar. You can adjust how much room is devoted to each by dragging the tab split bar that appears between the two. On your own, practice dragging and releasing the tab split bar, as shown below.

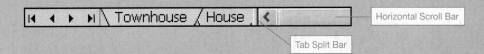

8. To return the tab split bar to its original position:
   DOUBLE-CLICK: tab split bar

9. Let's delete the House (2) worksheet. Ensure that the tab is displayed and active in the Excel 2003 application window. Then do the following:
   RIGHT-CLICK: *House (2)* tab
   SELECT: Delete
   The warning dialog box shown below appears.

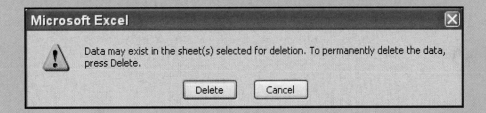

10. CLICK: Delete command button
    The worksheet is removed from the workbook.

11. To insert a worksheet:
    RIGHT-CLICK: *Commercial* tab
    SELECT: Insert
    The Insert dialog box appears (Figure 7.20), similar to the Templates dialog box used in module 1.4.1.

**Figure 7.20**

Insert dialog box:
*General* tab

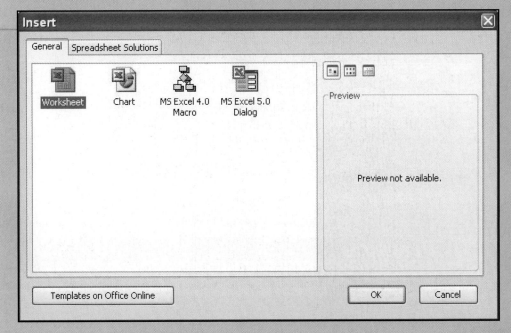

**12.** On the *General* tab of the dialog box:
SELECT: Worksheet icon
CLICK: OK command button
A blank worksheet, named *Sheet1,* appears to the left of the *Commercial* tab. (*Note:* New sheets are numbered incrementally. Therefore, new tabs will be named *Sheet2, Sheet3,* and so on.)

**13.** DRAG: *Sheet1* tab to the left of the *Townhouse* tab

**14.** Let's rename this tab for use as a summary worksheet:
DOUBLE-CLICK: *Sheet1* tab
TYPE: **Summary**
PRESS: [ENTER]
Your sheet tabs should appear similar to those shown below.

**15.** Save the workbook, and keep it open for use in the next lesson.

### 7.3.3 Creating Hyperlinks in a Worksheet

→ **Feature**

Using hyperlinks, you can connect a worksheet to other Excel workbooks, to other Office documents, or to data stored on the Internet. Your connections can be simple—linking together the worksheets in a single workbook or complex—linking a worksheet to a database stored on your company's intranet. When you click a hyperlink that appears on a worksheet, two different scenarios can result. If the hyperlink contains a URL address for your intranet or an Internet Web site, your Web browser software is launched and automatically attempts to establish a connection. On the other hand, if the hyperlink contains a reference to another workbook or Office document, the document is retrieved and displayed in its source application.

The Web may not be so famous if it were not for hyperlinks. They provide the means for "drilling down" through layers of information to find what you are looking for. With a single mouse click on a hyperlink, you can go from viewing a company's annual report to viewing its performance ratios, charts and graphs, or competitor's results. (And with another mouse click, you may even display a list of the company's majority shareholders along with links to their Web sites.)

→ **Method**

To insert a hyperlink into a worksheet:

- SELECT: a cell for which you want to insert a hyperlink
- CLICK: Insert Hyperlink button (🔳),
  *or*
- CHOOSE: Insert → Hyperlink
- TYPE: *desired prompt* in the *Text to display* text box
- SELECT: an option in the *Link to* area
- Specify the connection parameters for the hyperlink.

→ **Practice**

Let's create a simple table of contents for navigating the "Loan Tables" workbook using hyperlinks. Ensure that you have completed the previous lessons and that the "Loan Tables" workbook is displayed.

**1.** On your own, enter the information displayed in Figure 7.21 on the *Summary* worksheet. Ensure that the text labels appear in cells B3, B4, and B5.

**Figure 7.21**

Creating a table of contents

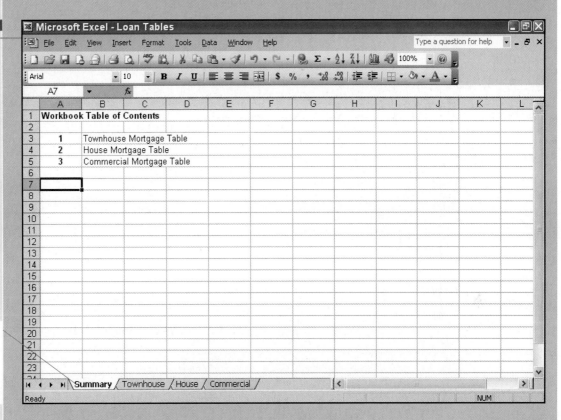

The *Summary* sheet tab will provide a table of hyperlinks to the other sheets in the workbook

**2.** SELECT: cell B3
This cell contains the text "Townhouse Mortgage Table."

**3.** To create a hyperlink using the contents of this cell:
CLICK: Insert Hyperlink button (🔖)
The Insert Hyperlink dialog box appears as shown in Figure 7.22.

**Figure 7.22**

Insert Hyperlink dialog box: Existing File or Web Page option

Select the type of link that you want to create using the *Link to* bar

Potential files that you may want to link to

4. In the *Link to* bar of the Insert Hyperlink dialog box:
   CLICK: Place in This Document button

5. To establish a hyperlink to the *Townhouse* tab:
   SELECT: Townhouse in the tree-style list box
   Notice that cell A1 is entered as the target cell reference automatically.
   The dialog box should now appear as shown in Figure 7.23.

**Figure 7.23**

Insert Hyperlink
dialog box: Place
in This Document
option

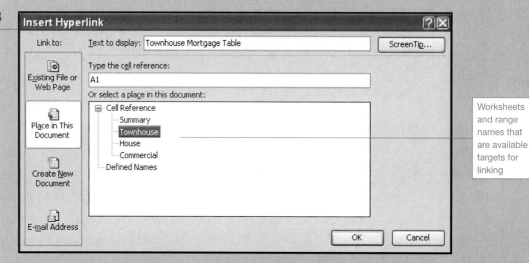

6. To complete the operation:
   CLICK: OK command button
   You will notice that the cell entry appears blue and with an underline. This is the common for-
   matting style for displaying and using hyperlinks in Web browser software.

7. To move to the *Townhouse* tab using the hyperlink, position the mouse pointer over cell B3. No-
   tice that the pointer changes shape to a hand (🖑). To initiate the hyperlink:
   CLICK: cell B3
   Cell A1 in the Townhouse worksheet is selected.

8. CLICK: *Summary* tab to return to the table of contents worksheet
   Notice that the cell entry now appears purple to show that the link has been selected at least
   once before.

9. On your own, create hyperlinks in cells B4 and B5 for the other two worksheets. Make sure that
   you test the hyperlinks before proceeding.

10. Save the workbook, and keep it open for use in the next lesson.

### 7.3.4 Grouping Worksheets for Formatting and Printing

→ ## Feature

You can group worksheets together to assist in creating and formatting identical worksheets. When
you select more than one sheet tab, **Group mode** is automatically turned on and all the commands
that you issue affect all of the selected worksheets. For example, Group mode allows you to change a
column's width in one worksheet and have that same modification made to all sheets in the workbook
file. You can also group worksheets for printing, regardless of whether the individual worksheets are
positioned next to each other in the workbook.

→ ## Method

- To activate Group mode, select multiple worksheets by clicking their tabs while holding down the `CTRL` key. (*Hint:* To select multiple contiguous sheets, hold down the `SHIFT` key.)

- To turn Group mode off, right-click on any selected tab, and select the Ungroup Sheets command from the shortcut menu.

→ ## Practice

In this exercise you practice selecting multiple worksheets and formatting them as a group. Ensure that you have completed the previous lesson and that the "Loan Tables" workbook is displayed.

**1.** In reviewing the three primary worksheets, you may have noticed that they are identical in layout and appearance. By using the same worksheet structure, you can easily format and enhance all of the worksheets as a single unit or group. To illustrate:
CLICK: *Townhouse* tab to make it active

**2.** To make all of the worksheets easier to use for novices, you will highlight the cells in which users are allowed to enter and change data. Rather than formatting each sheet separately, let's group them together and then issue the command a single time:
PRESS: `CTRL` and hold it down
CLICK: *House* tab
CLICK: *Commercial* tab
(*Note:* Remember to release the `CTRL` key.) As shown below, all three sheet tabs appear active with a white background. Also, the Title bar displays the word "[Group]" beside the workbook's filename.

| ◄ ◄ ► ►| \ Summary \ **Townhouse** / House / Commercial / |

**3.** With all three tabs selected (and active), most commands that you perform in the displayed worksheet will now be applied to the entire group of worksheets. Do the following:
SELECT: cell range from B4 to B5
PRESS: `CTRL` and hold it down
SELECT: cell range from D4 to D5
(*Note:* Remember to release the `CTRL` key.)

**4.** To change the background cell color for the selected cells:
CLICK: down arrow attached to the Fill Color button ( )
CLICK: a pale yellow color

**5.** SELECT: cell B4 to cancel the selection
Your screen should now appear similar to the one shown in Figure 7.24. Notice the three active tabs that are selected and grouped for formatting.

**Figure 7.24**

Formatting worksheets as a group

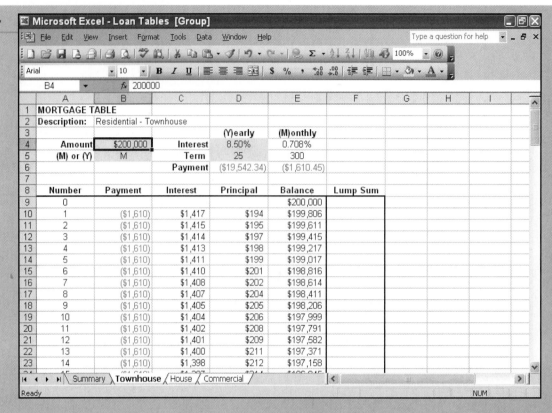

6. Let's ungroup the worksheets.
   RIGHT-CLICK: *Townhouse* tab
   SELECT: Ungroup Sheets

7. To review your work:
   CLICK: *House* tab
   CLICK: *Commercial* tab
   Notice that the background fill color has been applied to the grouped worksheets and that cell B4 is the active cell in all of them.

8. Save the workbook before proceeding.

### *In Addition* PRINTING MULTIPLE WORKSHEETS

As you would in formatting multiple worksheets, you can select a group of worksheets and then click the Print button (🖨) or choose the File → Print command. Only the worksheets that are part of the selected group are printed.

## 7.3.5 Hiding and Displaying Worksheets

→ **Feature**

There may be times when you want to hide a particular worksheet from the current user—perhaps the worksheet contains commission rates or confidential salary information. Hiding a worksheet does not limit your ability to reference its contents in formulas appearing on other worksheets in the workbook. Furthermore, you can protect a workbook's structure so that its worksheets cannot be removed, inserted, renamed, hidden, or unhidden. All of these protection features can be password-protected to ensure that they cannot be "turned off" by unauthorized users.

→ ## Method

To hide or unhide worksheets:

- CHOOSE: Format → Sheet → Hide,

  *or*

- CHOOSE: Format → Sheet → Unhide

→ ## Practice

In this exercise you practice hiding and displaying a specific worksheet in a workbook. Ensure that you have completed the previous lesson and that the "Loan Tables" workbook is displayed.

**1.** You will now hide the Commercial worksheet from displaying. To begin:
CLICK: *Commercial* tab to make it active

**2.** To hide the active worksheet:
CHOOSE: Format → Sheet → Hide
Notice that the Commercial worksheet tab no longer appears, as shown below.

|◄ ◄ ► ►|\ Summary / Townhouse \ **House** /

**3.** To redisplay the worksheet:
CHOOSE: Format → Sheet → Unhide
The Unhide dialog box shown in Figure 7.25 now appears.

**Figure 7.25**

Unhiding a
temporarily
hidden worksheet

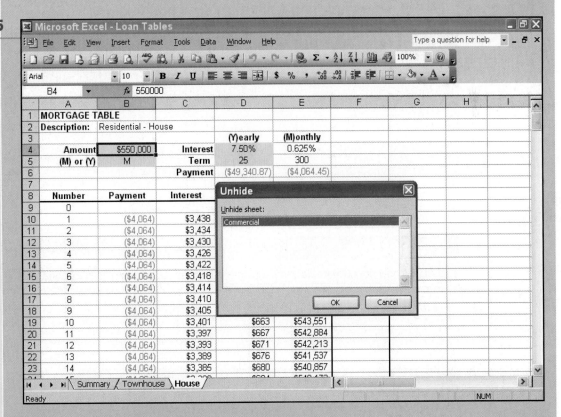

**4.** In the Unhide dialog box, ensure that the Commercial option is highlighted in the list box and then:
CLICK: OK command button
The worksheet tab reappears.

**5.** Save and then close the workbook before proceeding.

**7.3** How would you rename a chart sheet and then move it to the end of a sheet stack in a workbook?

# 7.4 Consolidating Your Data

Whether you need to combine revenues from several regions or calculate productivity statistics across several departments, Excel 2003's consolidation tools allow you to better manage, organize, and present your information. Excel enables you to **consolidate** or merge data stored in different worksheets and workbooks. There are two methods for consolidating worksheet data. First, you can enter formulas and functions that reference cells from other worksheets. Second, you can use Excel's Data → Consolidate command. In this module you learn how to consolidate data stored in a multiple-sheet workbook and in multiple workbook files.

### 7.4.1 Consolidating a Multiple-Sheet Workbook

→ **Feature**

For smaller applications, you can combine or summarize data that is stored across multiple worksheets in a single workbook. Dividing data among worksheets enables you to group and manage data logically and then merge data for performing summary calculations and creating reports.

→ **Method**

To consolidate data using a menu command:

• SELECT: the cell where you want the result to appear

• CHOOSE: Data → Consolidate

• Specify the cell ranges that you want to consolidate.

→ **Practice**

You will now consolidate data in a multiple-sheet workbook using formulas and the Data → Consolidate command. Ensure that no workbooks are open in the Excel 2003 application window.

**1.** Open the data file named EX0741 to display the workbook shown in Figure 7.26.

**Figure 7.26**

Opening the
EX0741
workbook

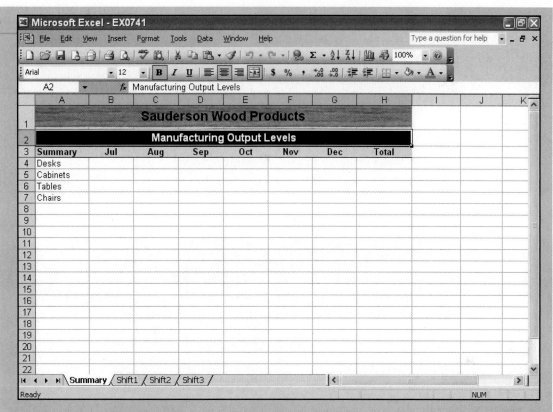

2. Save the workbook as "Sauderson" to your personal storage location.

3. Review the four worksheets that are stored in this workbook: Summary, Shift1, Shift2, and Shift3.

4. To begin, you will create a simple addition formula to consolidate the data stored on the three subsidiary worksheets. Do the following:
SELECT: cell B4 on the *Summary* tab
This is the cell where you want the consolidation result to appear.

5. To build the formula expression:
TYPE: =
CLICK: *Shift1* tab
CLICK: cell B4
Notice that **=Shift1!B4** appears in the Formula bar. The exclamation point separates the sheet name from the cell address.

6. To finish entering the formula expression:
TYPE: +
CLICK: *Shift2* tab
CLICK: cell B4
TYPE: +
CLICK: *Shift3* tab
CLICK: cell B4
The Formula bar should now read as follows:

7. To enter the formula into the cell:
PRESS: ENTER
The result, 75, appears in cell B4 on the *Summary* tab.

8. Instead of copying this formula to the remaining cells, let's practice using SUM as a consolidation function. This function works well when the structural layout of worksheets is identical. Do the following:

SELECT: cell B5 on the *Summary* tab
TYPE: =sum(
CLICK: *Shift1* tab
CLICK: cell B5
The Formula bar now reads =sum(Shift1!B5.

9. To continue:
PRESS: SHIFT and hold it down
CLICK: *Shift3* tab
TYPE: )
The Formula bar should now read as follows:

X ✓ fx =sum('Shift1:Shift3'!B5)　——　Referencing a three-dimensional range

10. To enter the formula into the cell:
PRESS: ENTER
The result, 30, appears in cell B5 on the *Summary* tab.

11. You may find using the Consolidate command easier than the previous methods. Do the following:
SELECT: cell range from B4 to H7 on the *Summary* tab
CHOOSE: Data → Consolidate
Your screen should now appear similar to the one shown in Figure 7.27.

**Figure 7.27**

Consolidate
dialog box

The two formulas
you entered
previously will be
replaced by the
results of the
Consolidate
command

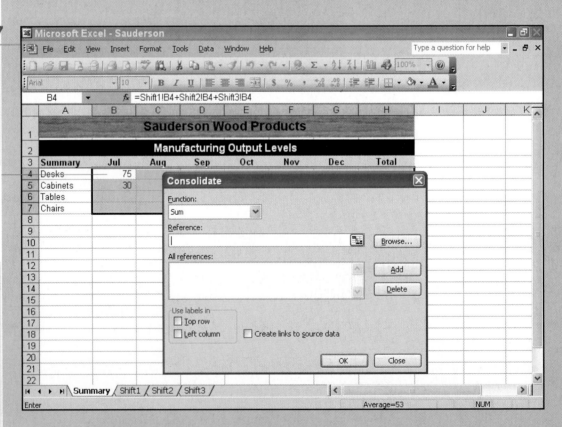

12. In the *Function* drop-down list box, make sure that the Sum function is selected, and then do the following:
CLICK: Dialog Collapse button (🔲) for the *Reference* text box

13. You must select the first cell range to include in the consolidation:
CLICK: *Shift1* tab
SELECT: cell range from B4 to H7
Your screen should appear similar to the one shown in Figure 7.28.

**Figure 7.28**

Selecting a cell range to consolidate

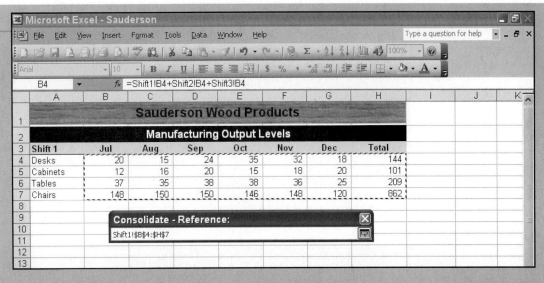

**14.** To proceed:
CLICK: Dialog Expand button (▣)
CLICK: Add command button
The cell range selected is added to the *All references* list box.

**15.** Now enter the data range for the second shift:
CLICK: Dialog Collapse button (▣)
CLICK: *Shift2* tab
Notice that the proper range is already highlighted.

**16.** CLICK: Dialog Expand button (▣)
CLICK: Add command button

**17.** And, finally, enter the data range for the third shift:
CLICK: Dialog Collapse button (▣)
CLICK: *Shift3* tab
Again, the proper range is highlighted.

**18.** CLICK: Dialog Expand button (▣)
CLICK: Add command button
The dialog box should now appear similar to the one shown in Figure 7.29.

**Figure 7.29**

Consolidating data from multiple worksheets

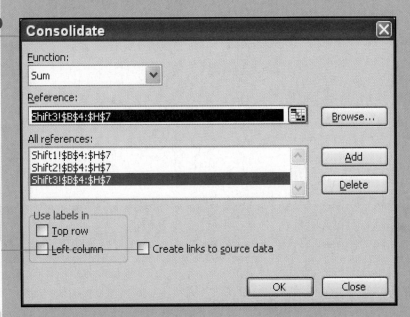

You must select this check box to enable automatic updating to occur in the workbook

**19.** If you click the OK command button, the information from the three worksheets is summed and entered into the *Summary* tab as static values. In order to keep the Summary sheet updated, you would need to perform the Consolidate command each time a value changes on a subsidiary worksheet. Instead, you can enact automatic updating:
SELECT: *Create links to source data* check box so that a ✓ appears
CLICK: OK command button

**20.** Notice that the consolidated worksheet is outlined. To display the calculation details of the consolidation:
CLICK: Row-Level 2 button ( 2 )

**21.** On your own, use the Format Painter toolbar button (🖌) to apply formatting from row 8 to rows 4, 5, and 6.

**22.** CLICK: cell A3 to position the cell pointer
Your worksheet should now appear similar to the one shown in Figure 7.30.

**Figure 7.30**

Displaying details for the *Summary* tab

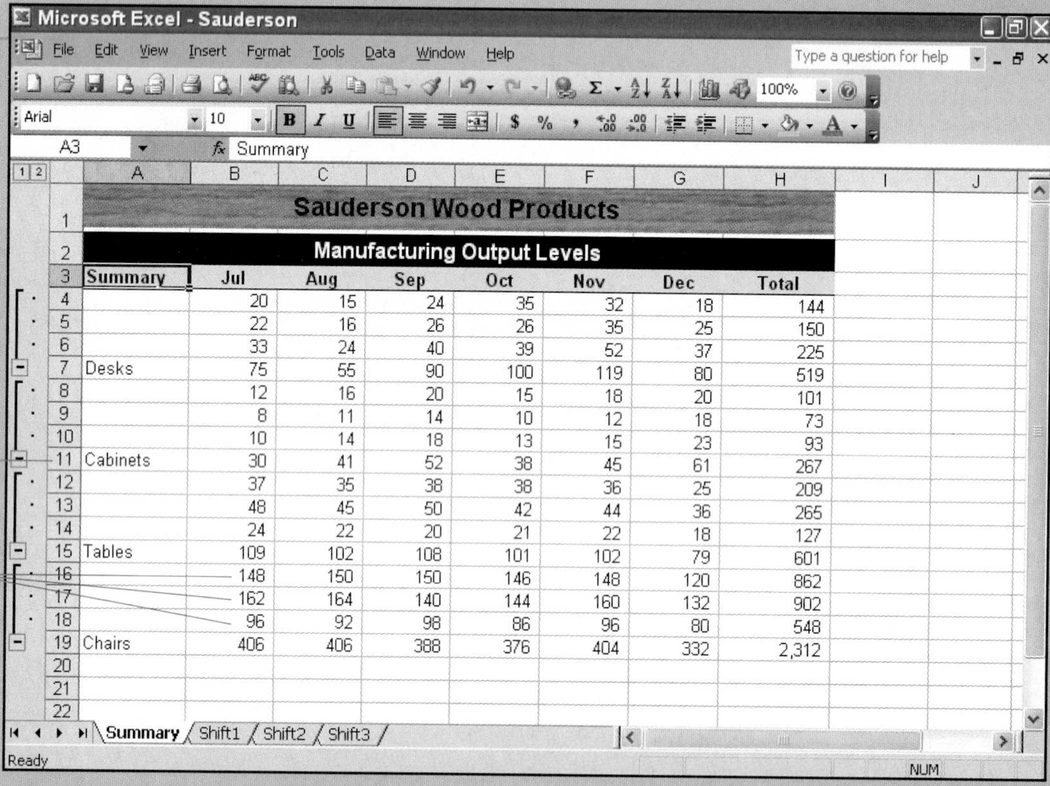

The category rows contain sub-total calculations

These rows represent values pulled from the other worksheets

**23.** On your own, change some of the values on the subsidiary worksheets and then switch to the *Summary* tab to see their effects.

**24.** Save and then close the workbook.

## 7.4.2 Consolidating Multiple Workbooks

→ **Feature**

You can link and consolidate separate workbook files into a summary workbook. Linking workbooks has two major advantages over using one large multiple-sheet workbook. First, the subsidiary workbooks are smaller in size and, therefore, easier to maintain and manage on a daily basis. Second, the subsidiary workbooks are not restricted to the same computer or network as the summary workbook. For example, each department may control its own workbook and then submit a file once a month for consolidation, perhaps on a diskette or via the Internet.

→ ## Method

To consolidate multiple workbooks, perform the following steps:

• Open the summary and subsidiary workbooks.

• Organize the workbook windows within the Excel 2003 application window.

• Enter a formula in the summary workbook that references cells in the subsidiary workbooks or choose the Data → Consolidate command.

→ ## Practice

You will now combine and summarize data that is stored in two individual workbooks. Ensure that no workbooks are open in the Excel 2003 application window.

**1.** Let's begin by opening and saving the workbooks that will be used in this lesson. Do the following:
• Open the file named EX0742A, and save it as "Group1" to your personal storage location.
• Open the file named EX0742B, and save it as "Group2" to your personal storage location.
• Open the file named EX0742C, and save it as "Groups" to your personal storage location.

**2.** To view all of the worksheets in the document area:
CHOOSE: Window → Arrange
The dialog box shown in Figure 7.31 appears.

**Figure 7.31**

Arrange Windows dialog box

Select your preference for viewing multiple workbook windows at the same time

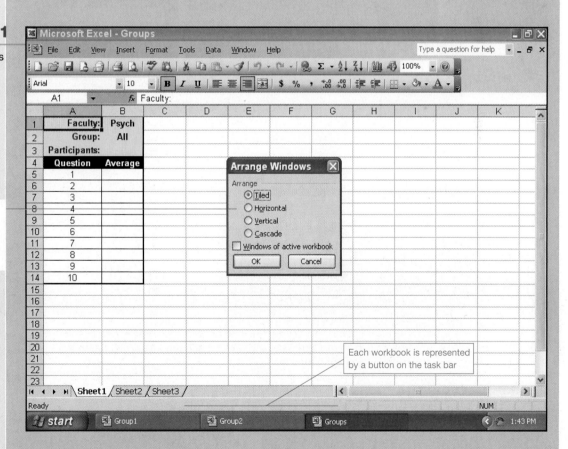

Each workbook is represented by a button on the task bar

**3.** In the Arrange Windows dialog box:
SELECT: *Tiled* option button
CLICK: OK command button
Your screen should now appear similar to the one shown in Figure 7.32.

**Figure 7.32**

Arranging
workbook
windows

The active
workbook window
appears with the
same Title bar
coloring as the
Excel 2003
application window

The inactive
workbook windows
appear with
dimmed Title bars

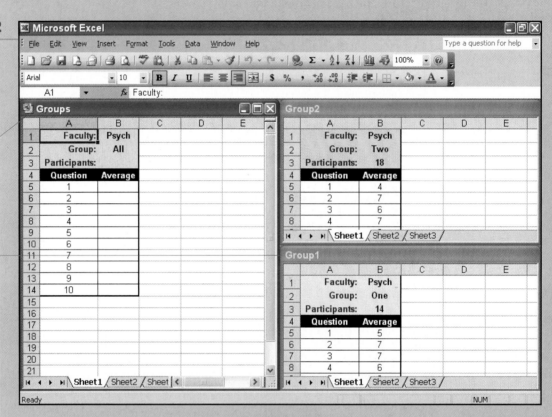

**4.** To move among the open workbooks, you position the mouse pointer on a visible part of the desired window and click once. You can also choose the workbook's name from the Window menu option. On your own, practice clicking on each window's Title bar to make it active. Notice that the cell pointer and window's scroll bars appear in the active window. When you are ready to proceed, make the Groups workbook active.

**5.** You will now enter a formula that adds together values from the Group1 and Group2 workbooks and then displays the result in cell B3 of the Groups workbook. Do the following:
SELECT: cell B3 in the Groups workbook

**6.** To enter the formula expression:
TYPE: =
CLICK: the Title bar for the Group1 workbook
CLICK: cell B3 in the Group1 workbook
The Formula bar now reads =[Group1.xls]Sheet1!$B$3. Notice that the workbook's filename is enclosed in square brackets and that the sheet name is separated from the absolute cell address using an exclamation point.

**7.** To proceed:
TYPE: +
CLICK: the Title bar for the Group2 workbook
CLICK: cell B3 in the Group2 workbook
The Formula bar should now read as follows:

✗ ✓ *fx* =[Group1.xls]Sheet1!$B$3+[Group2.xls]Sheet1!$B$3

**8.** To complete the formula:
PRESS: ENTER
The result, 32, is displayed in cell B3 of the Groups workbook.

**9.** To illustrate the dynamic nature of the link:
SELECT: Group1 workbook
SELECT: cell B3
TYPE: 24
PRESS: ENTER
Notice that the result in cell B3 of Groups has been updated to 42 automatically. (*Hint:* For this interactive linking to occur, all of the workbooks should be open.)

**10.** Let's consolidate the two subsidiary workbooks' data into the summary area for Groups. Do the following:
SELECT: Groups workbook
SELECT: cell range from B5 to B14

**11.** To calculate the average results for data stored in the two workbooks:
CHOOSE: Data → Consolidate
CLICK: down arrow attached to the *Function* drop-down list box
SELECT: Average

**12.** In the *Reference* text box, enter the data range for Group1:
CLICK: Dialog Collapse button (🔲)
SELECT: Group1 workbook
SELECT: cell range from B5 to B14
CLICK: Dialog Expand button (🔲)
CLICK: Add command button
The workbook's location, file name, sheet name, and cell range are added to the *All references* list box.

**13.** To enter the data range for Group2:
CLICK: Dialog Collapse button (🔲)
SELECT: Group2 workbook
SELECT: cell range from B5 to B14
CLICK: Dialog Expand button (🔲)
CLICK: Add command button
The Consolidate dialog box should now appear similar to the one shown in Figure 7.33.

**Figure 7.33**

Consolidating data from multiple workbooks

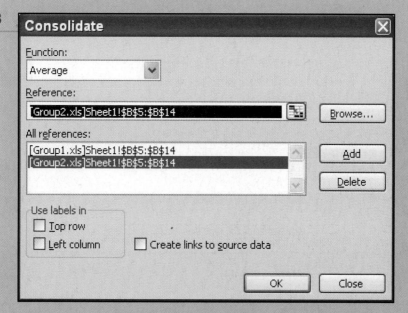

**14.** To ensure that the Groups workbook is updated to reflect changes made in its subsidiary workbooks and then proceed:
SELECT: *Create links to source data* check box
CLICK: OK command button

**15.** Excel automatically generates an outline for the Groups workbook, as shown in Figure 7.34. On your own, review the contents of the outline by expanding and contracting the Row-Level buttons ( 1 and 2 ).

**Figure 7.34**

Displaying consolidated results for the Groups workbook

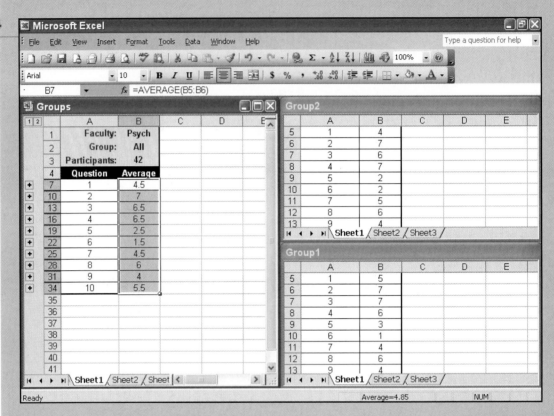

**16.** When you are ready to proceed:
CLICK: Row-Level 1 ( 1 ) button to collapse the detail

**17.** To close and save all of the workbooks at the same time:
PRESS: **SHIFT** and hold it down
CHOOSE: File → Close All
The confirmation dialog box shown below appears. (*Hint:* The Close All command only appears when the **SHIFT** key is depressed.)

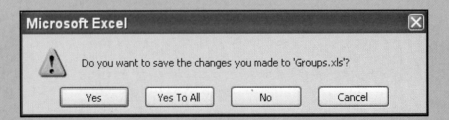

**18.** After releasing the **SHIFT** key, do the following:
CLICK: Yes to All command button
All three of the open workbooks are saved and then closed.

*In Addition* ORGANIZING YOUR WORK USING FOLDERS

Besides dividing your data into separate workbooks, you should use folders to better organize your work. Using the common Open and Save As dialog boxes, you can create, rename, and delete folders from within most Office System 2003 applications. For example, you can separate your company workbooks into Fiscal2003, Fiscal2004, and Fiscal2005 folders. Use the Tools menu (as shown below) to rename and delete existing folders.

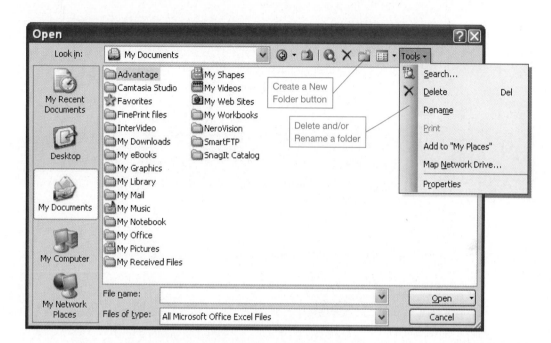

 **7.4**   Name two advantages for separating your work into multiple workbooks.

# 7.5 Documenting Your Work

Documentation seems to be far more critical when you are on the reading end of a large worksheet or an equation, as opposed to the writing end. Imagine receiving a complex workbook that you are expected to update, even though you've never seen it before. The task would be less difficult if the workbook contained instructions, explanations, and other helpful notes. A properly documented workbook shows where data may be entered, either by notation or by formatting cues, and explains what data is acceptable. From a development standpoint, another reason for documenting a workbook is to ensure that you remember the underlying logic and reasoning behind the formulas and functions entered into a worksheet. Without documentation, you may find it difficult to decipher the entries that you made months earlier. Along with a printout of the worksheet's structure, cell comments are an excellent way to document your work. In this module you learn how to insert, display, and format comments, and how to set file management properties for a workbook. You also learn how to use Excel's new Research pane for looking up information to include in your documentation.

### 7.5.1 Inserting and Deleting Comments

→ ## Feature

A **comment,** or *cell note,* is a special text box that you attach to a worksheet cell. When a cell contains a comment, a small red indicator appears in the upper right-hand corner of the cell. To display a comment, move the mouse pointer over top of the cell as you do in displaying a ToolTip for a toolbar button. You can also display comments using the View → Comments command and the Reviewing toolbar.

→ ## Method

To attach a comment text box to a cell:

• CHOOSE: Insert → Comment

To display all of the comments entered into a worksheet:

• CHOOSE: View → Comments

To edit a comment:

• RIGHT-CLICK: the cell containing the comment

• SELECT: Edit Comment

To remove a comment:

• RIGHT-CLICK: the cell containing a comment

• SELECT: Delete Comment

→ ## Practice

You will now learn how to create, edit, and remove a cell comment. Ensure that no workbooks appear in the Excel application window.

**1.** Open the data file named EX0750 to display the workbook shown in Figure 7.35. (*Note:* If necessary, maximize the workbook to fill the Excel 2003 application window.) This workbook contains a single worksheet that is used by program administrators at a small community college for program budgeting.

**Figure 7.35**

Opening the
EX0750
workbook

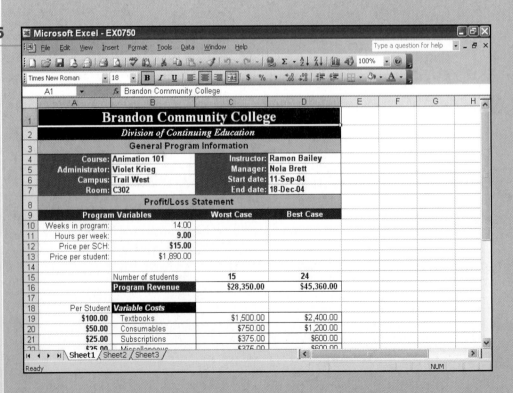

**2.** Save the workbook as "Brandon" to your personal storage location.

**3.** Review the completed worksheet. Notice that the worksheet is already documented, in that it provides formatting cues to signify where users may enter data. What is the formatting cue? (*Hint:* Look at the formulas by clicking on the cells and studying the contents of the Formula bar. What cell addresses do they reference?)

**4.** This worksheet is used by all of the program administrators in the Division of Continuing Education. Because some administrators may not be computer-literate, you need to provide some helpful instructions in the worksheet. To begin, provide an explanation on the proper method for entering date values:
SELECT: cell D6
CHOOSE: Insert → Comment
Your screen should now appear similar to the one shown in Figure 7.36. Notice that the comment text box attaches itself to the source cell using an arrow. Also, inside the upper-right corner of the cell, you should see a small red triangle, which denotes that the cell now contains a comment.

**Figure 7.36**

Inserting a new comment

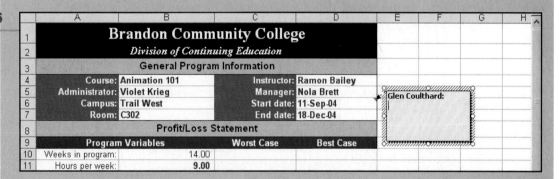

**5.** Immediately below your name or the licensee's name (which is entered automatically), type the desired comment:
TYPE: **Enter a date using the format mm/dd/yy. It will then be formatted to display as dd-mmm-yy.**
(*Note:* Do not press ENTER after typing this entry.)

**6.** To complete the insertion of the comment:
CLICK: anywhere outside the comment text box (for example, cell E1)
Notice that the comment is hidden, but the comment indicator still displays in the upper-right corner of the cell. (*Note:* If the comment text box is not hidden or you cannot see the comment indicator, choose Tools → Options and then click the *View* tab. Select the *Comment indicator only* option button from the *Comments* area and click the OK command button.)

**7.** To display the comment (as shown here), move the mouse pointer over cell D6. To hide the comment, move the mouse pointer away from cell D6.

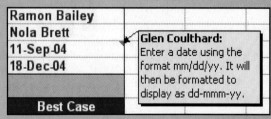

**8.** Let's add a comment for cell B11:
RIGHT-CLICK: cell B11
SELECT: Insert Comment
TYPE: **Enter the number of classroom instructional hours per week.**
CLICK: anywhere outside the comment text box

**9.** Now, add a comment for cell B12:
RIGHT-CLICK: cell B12
SELECT: Insert Comment
TYPE: **Enter the fee charged per Student Contact Hour (SCH).**
CLICK: anywhere outside the comment text box

**10.** PRESS: CTRL + HOME to move to cell A1
You should now have three comments on your worksheet.

**11.** To display all of the comments in the worksheet at the same time:
CHOOSE: View → Comments
Notice that the Reviewing toolbar appears in the Excel 2003 application window, as shown in Figure 7.37.

**Figure 7.37**

Viewing comments in a worksheet

Reviewing toolbar

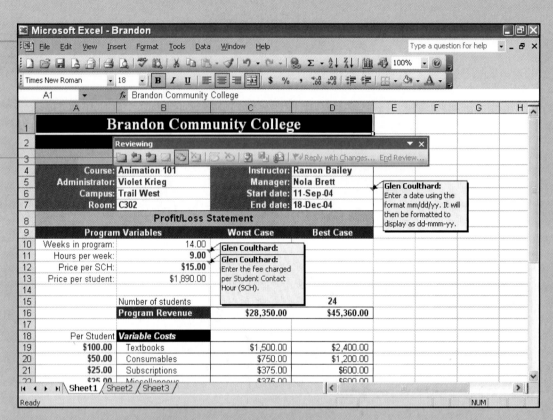

**12.** The Reviewing toolbar is useful for navigating through your comments, especially for those that are hidden or overlapped:
CLICK: Next Comment button (🔲) on the Reviewing toolbar
CLICK: Next Comment button (🔲) again
CLICK: Previous Comment button (🔲) once
Notice that these buttons let you select the text boxes, as shown by the hatched outline and selection handles around the displayed comments.

**13.** To remove a comment that you have entered:
CLICK: Next Comment button (🔲) until the comment attached to cell B12 appears
CLICK: Delete Comment button (🔲)
The comment is removed immediately from the worksheet. (*Hint:* You can also right-click a cell and select the Delete Comment command.)

**14.** To hide all of the remaining comments:
CLICK: Hide All Comments button (🔲)

**15.** To remove the Reviewing toolbar:
CLICK: its Close button (✕)
(*Hint:* If the Reviewing toolbar is docked against the application window, right-click the toolbar and then select Reviewing in order to close it.)

**16.** Let's edit the comment attached to cell B11:
RIGHT-CLICK: cell B11
SELECT: Edit Comment
The flashing I-beam cursor appears in the comment text box.

**17.** Using the arrow keys or mouse to position the cursor, edit the comment text to read "instructional **and lab** hours per week," as shown here. When finished, click on a cell outside of the comment text box.

> **Glen Coulthard:**
> Enter the number of classroom instructional and lab hours per week.

**18.** Save the workbook, and keep it open for use in the next lesson.

## 7.5.2 Formatting and Printing Comments

→ # Feature

To increase the personality and clarity of your cell comments, you can format the text entered into a text box, as well as the text box itself. For example, you can manipulate the size and position of the text box on the worksheet. You can also use formatting commands to enhance the text and make it easier to read.

→ # Method

To format a text box:

- RIGHT-CLICK: the desired cell
- SELECT: Edit → Comment
- DRAG: the hatched border of the text box to move the comment
- DRAG: the selection handles of the text box to size the comment
- RIGHT-CLICK: the hatched border of the text box
- SELECT: Format Comment
- Make the desired selections.
- CLICK: OK command button

To print comments along with the worksheet:

- CHOOSE: File → Page Setup
- CLICK: *Sheet* tab
- SELECT: "At end of sheet" or "As displayed on sheet" in the *Comments* drop-down list box
- CLICK: OK command button

→ # Practice

In this lesson you practice formatting and printing comments. Ensure that you've completed the previous lesson and that the "Brandon" workbook is displayed.

**1.** Let's start by editing an existing comment:
RIGHT-CLICK: cell D6
SELECT: Edit Comment

**2.** Now enter some additional text:
PRESS: Space bar
TYPE: **The first assignment is due on the last Friday of the month.**
CLICK: anywhere outside of the comment text box

3. To view the comment, move the mouse pointer over top of cell D6. Notice that not all of the comment text is visible. To increase the size of the comment text box, do the following:
RIGHT-CLICK: cell D6
SELECT: Edit Comment
Notice that the comment appears with a hatched outline and selection handles for moving and sizing the text box.

4. Position the mouse pointer over the selection handle in the bottom right-hand corner, and size the text box to match that shown in Figure 7.38.

**Figure 7.38**

Sizing a comment text box

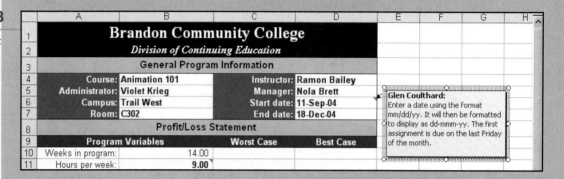

5. Using the Bold (B) and Font Color (A·) buttons on the Formatting toolbar, format the text "mm/dd/yy" to appear boldface and red. Then apply boldface and green to the text "last Friday." If required, adjust the size of the comment text box. (*Hint:* Select the desired text in the comment text box and apply the desired formatting commands.)

6. To display additional formatting options:
RIGHT-CLICK: the hatched outline border of the comment text box
SELECT: Format Comment
The Format Comment dialog box (Figure 7.39) lets you perform several formatting tasks, including selecting fonts, aligning text, and changing the line and fill color of the text box.

**Figure 7.39**

Displaying the Format Comment dialog box

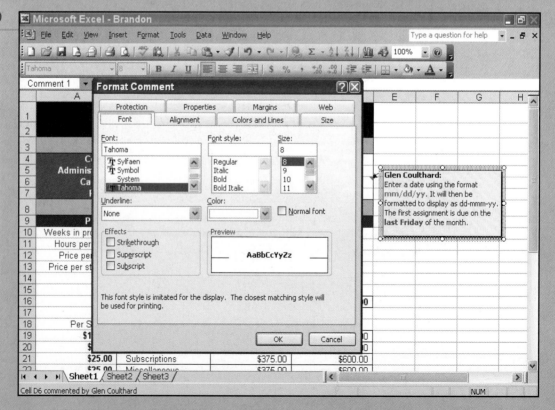

Excel

**7.** To remove the dialog box and continue:
CLICK: Cancel command button
CLICK: anywhere outside the comment text box

**8.** To view the formatted comment, move the mouse pointer over top of cell D6. Notice how much easier the text is to read and understand with the color-coded information.

**9.** You can choose to print a sheet's comments along with the worksheet (on an additional page) or as they appear in the worksheet when you choose the View → Comments command. To illustrate:
CHOOSE: File → Page Setup
CLICK: *Sheet* tab

**10.** In the *Print* area of the dialog box:
CLICK: down arrow attached to the *Comments* drop-down list box
SELECT: At end of sheet
(*Note:* To print comments as they appear in the worksheet, you must first choose the View → Comments command and then select the appropriate option from the Page Setup dialog box.)

**11.** CLICK: Print Preview to view the results

**12.** To view the comments as they will appear when printed:
CLICK: Next command button to display the second page
CLICK: Zoom command button to zoom in on the comment
Your screen should now appear similar to the one shown in Figure 7.40.

**Figure 7.40**

Previewing comments as they will look when printed

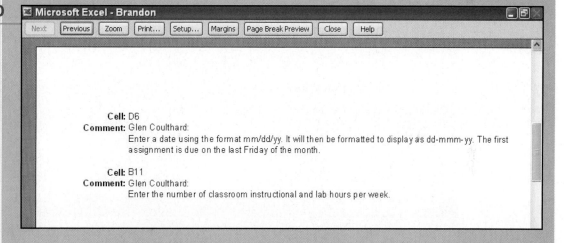

**13.** When you are finished viewing the preview:
CLICK: Close command button

**14.** Save the workbook, and keep it open for use in the next lesson.

### *In Addition* CREATING AND RESPONDING TO DISCUSSION COMMENTS

Microsoft Office Excel 2003 offers a new feature for enhanced workgroup collaboration. Web discussions are threaded (ordered alphabetically or chronologically) comments concerning a particular document or the content within a document. Since the documents may be located on a LAN, on an intranet, or on the Internet, the text comments you post are sent to and placed in a database, which is typically stored on a separate discussion server. If you have access to a discussion server, you can view these discussions in an Office System 2003 application or through the Internet Explorer Web browser.

To participate in a discussion:
CHOOSE: Tools → Online Collaboration → Web Discussions

To create a discussion comment (as shown here):
CLICK: Discussions button on the Web Discussions toolbar
CHOOSE: Insert about the Workbook

To respond to a discussion comment, click the "Show a menu of actions" button at the bottom of a discussion comment and choose Reply, Edit, or Delete. (*Note:* You can only edit or delete comments that you write.)

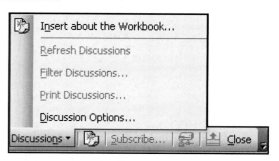

### 7.5.3 Using the Research Tool

→ **Feature**

Microsoft Office System 2003 provides a new Research Library feature that you can use to look up information, including definitions, synonyms, translations, and encyclopedia articles, from a variety of trusted sources. Integrated into Excel 2003 and other Office applications, the Research Library and its associated task pane allow you to retrieve information from corporate databases; reference books; research, business, and financial sites; and other Internet and intranet resources. Although most of these resources require you to be connected to the Internet, the benefit is that you can conduct extensive (and mostly free) research without leaving your current document or workbook!

→ **Method**

To look up information stored in your worksheet:

• RIGHT-CLICK: the cell containing the desired content

• SELECT: Look Up

To display the Research task pane and look up a word:

• CHOOSE: Tools → Research

→ **Practice**

You will now practice conducting research using the new Research Library feature. Ensure that you've completed the previous lesson and that the "Brandon" workbook is displayed.

1. Let's use the Research task pane to add some descriptive information about the course content for "Animation 101." To begin:
RIGHT-CLICK: cell B4
SELECT: Look Up
The Research task pane (shown in Figure 7.41) appears at the right side of the Excel 2003 application window. Notice that the cell contents, "Animation 101," appear in the *Search for* text box.

**Figure 7.41**

Research task pane

Enter the text for which you want to find a definition, synonym, translation, or other information

Select the specific resources that you want to use in conducting your information search

Results from your search appear in this area. Use the scroll bar to view additional information retrieved from the other resource categories

Specify the options and resource categories that you would like to use (or have paid to use) in searching for information

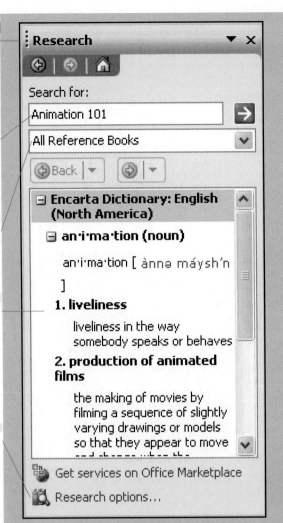

Excel

2. Before proceeding, let's view some of the other research services and resources that are available from the task pane. Do the following:
   CLICK: Research options at the bottom of the task pane
   The Research Options dialog box appears, as shown in Figure 7.42.

**Figure 7.42**

Research Options
dialog box

Research sevice
options

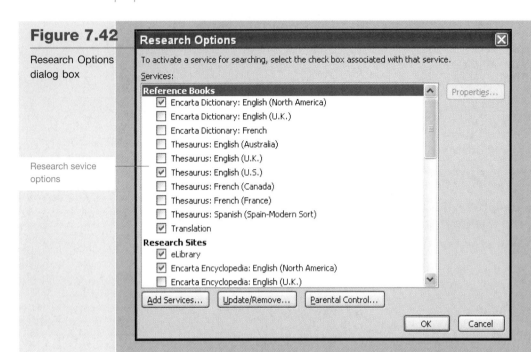

**Research Options**                                         ⊠

To activate a service for searching, select the check box associated with that service.

Services:                                                    Properties...

**Reference Books**
☑ Encarta Dictionary: English (North America)
☐ Encarta Dictionary: English (U.K.)
☐ Encarta Dictionary: French
☐ Thesaurus: English (Australia)
☐ Thesaurus: English (U.K.)
☑ Thesaurus: English (U.S.)
☐ Thesaurus: French (Canada)
☐ Thesaurus: French (France)
☐ Thesaurus: Spanish (Spain-Modern Sort)
☑ Translation
**Research Sites**
☑ eLibrary
☑ Encarta Encyclopedia: English (North America)
☐ Encarta Encyclopedia: English (U.K.)

Add Services...    Update/Remove...    Parental Control...

OK    Cancel

3. Scroll the list of research service options to see what is available. When you are ready to proceed:
   CLICK: Cancel command button

4. Assuming that you are connected to the Internet, you should see a definition(s) in the results area of the Research task pane. On your own, select the text from one of the definitions, as shown here. (*Note:* If you are not connected to the Internet, select some other appropriate text from the task pane.)

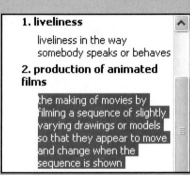

1. **liveliness**

liveliness in the way
somebody speaks or behaves

2. **production of animated films**

the making of movies by
filming a sequence of slightly
varying drawings or models
so that they appear to move
and change when the
sequence is shown

5. Once selected, copy the definition to the Clipboard:
   RIGHT-CLICK: the text selection
   SELECT: Copy

6. Move the cell pointer into the worksheet area and then:
   RIGHT-CLICK: cell B4
   SELECT: Insert Comment

7. Enter the following text comment:
   TYPE: **Excerpt taken from the Encarta Dictionary:**
   PRESS: [ENTER]
   (*Note:* You should always provide credit for any reference material that you extract from an external resource.)

8. Now paste the contents of the copied definition:
   CLICK: Paste button ([🔽]) on the Standard toolbar

9. On your own, size the cell comment to appear similar to that shown in Figure 7.43. Then click in the merged cell A1 to remove the comment from displaying. You have successfully documented your worksheet with information gleaned from the Office 2003 Research Library feature!

**Figure 7.43**

Incorporating research information into your worksheet

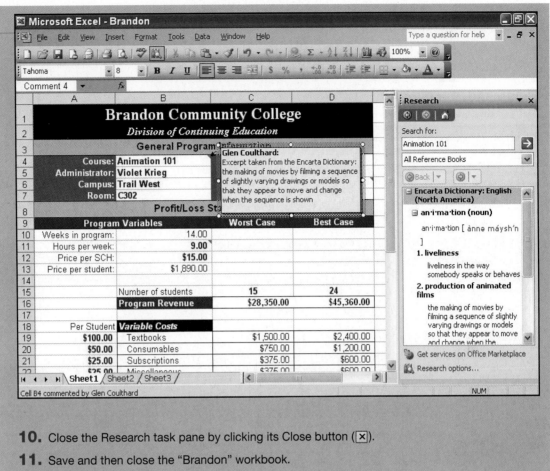

**10.** Close the Research task pane by clicking its Close button ([×]).

**11.** Save and then close the "Brandon" workbook.

---

*In Addition* SENDING A WORKBOOK VIA E-MAIL

Without leaving Excel, you can send a worksheet to another user for consolidation using electronic mail (e-mail). This feature assumes that you communicate with other users via a modem, network, or Internet connection. Once configured, click the E-mail button ([ ]) on the Standard toolbar or choose the File → Send To → Mail Recipient command. Rather than embedding the worksheet inside the mail message, you can choose to send the worksheet as an attachment to a standard mail message.

**7.5**  Can you think of any other ways to document a worksheet?

_____

_____

# Chapter
## summary

Microsoft Office Excel 2003 provides several tools specifically geared for managing large worksheets. The ability to freeze rows and columns enables the worksheet headings to remain visible as the cell pointer moves within a worksheet. Similarly, splitting the worksheet window into panes allows important information from different areas in the worksheet to be displayed at the same time. The outlining and consolidation tools are used to condense worksheet data into concise pages for viewing or printing as a summary report. Excel 2003 also provides tools, such as the find and replace commands, for editing and updating data in large worksheets. The Spelling feature is also highly regarded for creating error-free reports based on worksheet data. To assist users who are unfamiliar with your worksheets, you can provide cell notes or comments containing helpful reminders and suggestions. You can also document your worksheet using information from the Office 2003 Research Library and task pane feature.

## Command Summary

Many of the commands and procedures appearing in this chapter are summarized in the following table.

| Skill Set | To Perform This Task . . . | Do the Following . . . |
|---|---|---|
| **Modifying Workbooks** | Freeze and unfreeze rows and columns as panes on the screen | CHOOSE: Window → Freeze Panes<br>CHOOSE: Window → Unfreeze Panes |
| | Split the worksheet window into panes and then remove the split | CHOOSE: Window → Split<br>CHOOSE: Window → Remove Split |
| | Rename a worksheet or chart sheet | DOUBLE-CLICK: its sheet tab<br>TYPE: *new name* |
| | Change the color of a sheet tab | RIGHT-CLICK: its sheet tab<br>SELECT: Tab Color<br>SELECT: the desired color |
| | Insert a worksheet or chart sheet | RIGHT-CLICK: a sheet tab<br>SELECT: Insert |
| | Delete a worksheet or chart sheet | RIGHT-CLICK: its sheet tab<br>SELECT: Delete |
| | Group worksheets together | SELECT: the first sheet tab<br>PRESS: CTRL and hold it down<br>CLICK: additional tabs for inclusion |
| **Working with Cells and Cell Data** | Find data in a worksheet | CHOOSE: Edit → Find |
| | Replace data in a worksheet | CHOOSE: Edit → Replace |
| | View the AutoCorrect entries | CHOOSE: Tools → AutoCorrect |
| | Spell-check a worksheet | CLICK: Spelling button (⌨), *or*<br>CHOOSE: Tools → Spelling |
| **Summarizing Data** | Apply and remove outlining in a worksheet | CHOOSE: Data → Group and Outline → Auto Outline<br>CHOOSE: Data → Group and Outline → Clear Outline |
| **Managing Workbooks** | Consolidate data that is stored in a multiple-sheet workbook or in multiple workbooks | CHOOSE: Data → Consolidate |
| | Arrange worksheet windows in the Excel application window | CHOOSE: Window → Arrange |
| | Save and close multiple open workbook files | PRESS: SHIFT and hold it down<br>CHOOSE: File → Close All |

Excel

| Workgroup Collaboration | Define a hyperlink in a cell | SELECT: the desired cell<br>CLICK: Insert Hyperlink button ( ) |
| | Send a workbook via e-mail | CLICK: Send E-mail button ( ), *or*<br>CHOOSE: File → Send To → Mail Recipient |
| | Insert a new comment | CHOOSE: Insert → Comment |
| | Display all the comments in a worksheet, along with the Reviewing toolbar | CHOOSE: View → Comments |
| | Edit an existing comment | RIGHT-CLICK: the cell containing the comment to edit<br>SELECT: Edit Comment |
| | Delete a comment | RIGHT-CLICK: the cell containing the comment to remove<br>SELECT: Delete Comment |
| | Display the Research task pane for looking up information | CHOOSE: Tools → Research |
| | Locate supporting information for content in your worksheet | RIGHT-CLICK: the cell contents<br>SELECT: Look Up |
| Formatting and Printing | Change the page orientation and scaling | CHOOSE: File → Page Setup<br>CLICK: *Page* tab |
| | Specify print titles from the worksheet for printing | CHOOSE: File → Page Setup<br>CLICK: *Sheet* tab |
| | Insert a page break | CHOOSE: Insert → Page Break |
| | Remove a page break | CHOOSE: Insert → Remove Page Break |
| | View and set page breaks using Page Break Preview mode | CHOOSE: View → Page Break Preview<br>DRAG: the desired page break lines |
| | Return from Page Break Preview mode to normal viewing | CHOOSE: View → Normal |

## Key Terms

This section specifies page references for the key terms identified in this chapter. For a complete list of definitions, refer to the Glossary provided at the end of this learning guide.

AutoCorrect, *p. EX 377*

comment, *p. EX 402*

consolidate, *p. EX 392*

Group mode, *p. EX 388*

outlining, *p. EX 360*

panes, *p. EX 360*

print titles, *p. EX 367*

Spelling Checker, *p. EX 377*

# Chapter
quiz

## Short Answer

**1.** What is the main difference between freezing titles on a worksheet and dividing a window into panes?

**2.** How does outlining help you in working with large worksheets?

**3.** How do you replace all occurrences of one value in a worksheet with another value?

**4.** What is the purpose of the AutoCorrect feature?

**5.** How do you change the name of a sheet tab?

**6.** How do you move a tab in a workbook's sheet stack?

**7.** Name two ways you might use hyperlinks in a worksheet.

**8.** In a consolidation formula, what symbol(s) separates a worksheet's name from the cell address? A workbook's name from the sheet tab?

**9.** What are four options for arranging open workbooks in Excel 2003's application window?

**10.** When using the Data → Consolidate command, what must you do to ensure that the summary results are updated dynamically?

## True/False

**1.** _____ To unfreeze the horizontal and vertical worksheet panes, choose the Window → Undo command.

**2.** _____ You can divide a worksheet window into two, three, or four panes.

**3.** _____ Excel 2003 can outline a worksheet automatically based on the existence of summary formulas, such as the SUM function.

**4.** _____ To specify print titles in a worksheet, you enter a row range, such as **$1:$4**, into the appropriate text box.

**5.** _____ You can manipulate page breaks using the mouse when viewing the worksheet in Page Break Preview mode.

**6.** _____ To rename a sheet tab in a workbook, hold down the `CTRL` key while clicking once on the sheet tab.

**7.** _____ Chart sheets must always appear to the right of worksheets in a workbook's sheet stack.

**8.** _____ A comment is a special text box that appears when you double-click a cell.

**9.** _____ If you create a hyperlink that contains a URL address, Excel 2003 launches your Web browser software to display the link.

**10.** _____ Using the Data → Consolidate command, you can summarize data by summing or averaging the contents of various cell references.

**Excel**

## Multiple Choice

**1.** To freeze the titles appearing in rows 1 through 3 and columns A and B in a worksheet, you must first place the cell pointer in this cell prior to choosing the Freeze Panes command.

   a. B3
   b. B4
   c. C3
   d. C4

**2.** To split a worksheet window using the mouse:

   a. DRAG: horizontal or vertical scroll bars
   b. DRAG: horizontal or vertical split boxes
   c. DRAG: tab scroll buttons
   d. DRAG: tab split bar

**3.** Which of the following will display all of the detail rows in a worksheet that is outlined to three levels?

   a. CLICK: RowLevel 1 button (1)
   b. CLICK: RowLevel 3 button (3)
   c. CHOOSE: Data → Group and Outline → Outline All
   d. CHOOSE: Data → Group and Outline → Expand All

**4.** To insert a manual page break in a worksheet, position the mouse pointer and then:

   a. CHOOSE: Insert → Page Break
   b. CHOOSE: Edit → Insert Page Break
   c. CHOOSE: View → Insert Page Break
   d. PRESS: CTRL + ENTER

**5.** After you finish typing a comment into a text box, you complete the entry by doing this:

   a. CLICK: any cell in the worksheet
   b. CLICK: Save button (▤)
   c. CLICK: OK command button
   d. PRESS: ENTER

**6.** By default, a new workbook in Excel contains how many worksheets?

   a. 1
   b. 2
   c. 3
   d. 16

**7.** Which of the following is <u>not</u> a legitimate option for establishing a hyperlink?

   a. Place in This Document
   b. Existing File or Web Page
   c. E-mail Address
   d. All of the above are legitimate options.

**8.** Which of the following modes lets you apply formatting commands to more than one worksheet in a multiple-sheet workbook?

   a. Edit mode
   b. Format mode
   c. Group mode
   d. Multiple mode

**9.** To help move about the worksheets in a workbook, you right-click this set of buttons to display a menu of the sheet names.

   a. tab scroll buttons
   b. split box buttons
   c. split bar buttons
   d. toolbar buttons

**10.** Which of the following is <u>not</u> a function that is available in the Consolidate dialog box?

   a. Average
   b. Count
   c. Pmt
   d. Sum

## Hands-On
### exercises

### 1. Navigating Large Worksheets

In this exercise you practice moving the cell pointer around a large worksheet. You then apply some Excel features, such as freezing panes, to facilitate viewing and interpreting the data. Finally, you use the Find command to locate information quickly.

1. Open the data file named EX07HE01 to display the workbook shown in Figure 7.44. (*Note:* Make sure that it appears maximized in the Excel 2003 application window's work area.)

**Figure 7.44**

Opening the
EX07HE01
workbook

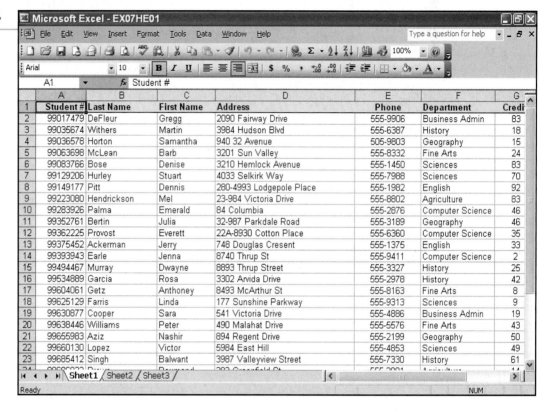

2. Save the workbook as "Student List" to your personal storage location.

3. First, let's look over the worksheet in order to become familiar with its contents. Do the following:
   PRESS: CTRL + ↓ to move to the last row in the list
   PRESS: CTRL + → to move to the last column in the last row
   PRESS: CTRL + HOME to move back to cell A1

4. Adjusting the view magnification will allow you to see more of the worksheet. To adjust the view magnification to fit a particular range:
   PRESS: CTRL + SHIFT + →
   CLICK: down arrow attached to the Zoom button ( 100% ▾ )
   SELECT: Selection
   You should now see columns A through H on the screen.

5. Let's make the data easier to read. Using the I-beam mouse pointer:
   CLICK: in the Zoom button ( 100% ▾ ) to select the zoom factor
   TYPE: **120**
   PRESS: ENTER
   The view magnification should now be 120%.

6. To ensure that the column headings and student last names are always in view, let's freeze the appropriate rows and columns:
   SELECT: cell C2
   CHOOSE: Window → Freeze Panes
   You should now notice a solid line appearing between columns B and C in the worksheet.

**7.** You can now scroll to any portion of the worksheet while keeping the row and column titles visible. To illustrate:

PRESS: CTRL + → to move to the last column in the current row

PRESS: CTRL + ↓ to move to the last row in the list

Notice that row 1 and columns A and B are always visible, as shown in Figure 7.45.

**Figure 7.45**

Freezing panes in the worksheet

| | A | B | E | F | G | H | I |
|---|---|---|---|---|---|---|---|
| 1 | Student # | Last Name | Phone | Department | Credits | GPA | |
| 14 | 99393943 | Earle | 555-9411 | Computer Science | 2 | 4.0 | |
| 15 | 99494467 | Murray | 555-3327 | History | 25 | 2.5 | |
| 16 | 99534889 | Garcia | 555-2978 | History | 42 | 3.8 | |
| 17 | 99604061 | Getz | 555-8163 | Fine Arts | 8 | 3.9 | |
| 18 | 99625129 | Farris | 555-9313 | Sciences | 9 | 4.0 | |
| 19 | 99630877 | Cooper | 555-4886 | Business Admin | 19 | 4.0 | |
| 20 | 99638446 | Williams | 555-5576 | Fine Arts | 43 | 3.0 | |
| 21 | 99655983 | Aziz | 555-2199 | Geography | 50 | 1.5 | |
| 22 | 99660130 | Lopez | 555-4853 | Sciences | 49 | 1.1 | |
| 23 | 99685412 | Singh | 555-7330 | History | 61 | 2.8 | |
| 24 | 99686022 | Brown | 555-3981 | Agriculture | 14 | 4.0 | |
| 25 | 99699395 | Flanders | 555-8821 | Geography | 15 | 4.0 | |
| 26 | 99796619 | Bows | 555-4156 | Geography | 97 | 1.5 | |
| 27 | 99813175 | Guerroro | 555-7134 | Computer Science | 18 | 3.5 | |
| 28 | 99837519 | Hamazaki | 555-1328 | Business Admin | 10 | 1.4 | |
| 29 | 99881015 | McLeish | 555-7287 | English | 30 | 3.2 | |
| 30 | 99881542 | Chan | 555-4451 | Business Admin | 69 | 3.8 | |
| 31 | 99974647 | Booth | 555-2918 | History | 21 | 2.7 | |

**8.** To remove the window panes (frozen titles):

CHOOSE: Window → Unfreeze Panes

PRESS: CTRL + HOME

**9.** To find a student's information:

PRESS: CTRL + f

TYPE: **Getz**

CLICK: Find Next command button

The cell pointer moves directly to the row containing information for Anthony Getz.

**10.** To close the Find dialog box:

CLICK: Close command button

**11.** On your own, use the Find and Replace dialog box to replace all occurrences of "Business Admin" in column F with "Commerce." When you are ready to proceed, select cell A1.

**12.** Save and then close the workbook.

step by step

## 2. Customizing a Multiple-Sheet Workbook

You will now practice working with a multiple-sheet workbook. In addition to renaming and moving the sheet tabs, you format the worksheets using Group mode.

**1.** Open the data file named EX07HE02 to display the workbook shown in Figure 7.46.

**Figure 7.46**

Opening the
EX07HE02
workbook

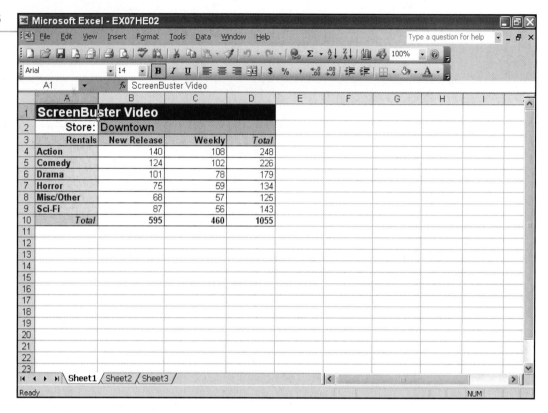

**2.** Save the workbook as "Video Outlets" to your personal storage location.

**3.** On your own, click on the three sheet tabs to familiarize yourself with the contents of the workbook. You will notice that the worksheets are identical in format and style.

**4.** To begin, let's give the sheet tabs more meaningful names:
DOUBLE-CLICK: *Sheet1* tab
TYPE: **Downtown**
PRESS: ⟨ENTER⟩

**5.** To rename the Sheet2 worksheet:
DOUBLE-CLICK: *Sheet2* tab
TYPE: **Coldstream**
PRESS: ⟨ENTER⟩

**6.** To rename the Sheet3 worksheet:
DOUBLE-CLICK: *Sheet3* tab
TYPE: **Westside**
PRESS: ⟨ENTER⟩

**7.** Let's arrange the tabs so that they appear in alphabetical order. First, select the *Coldstream* tab to make it active. Then drag it to the left until the downward-pointing triangle appears as the leftmost tab.

**8.** Now change the color of the tabs:
RIGHT-CLICK: *Coldstream* tab
SELECT: Tab Color
Your screen should now appear similar to the one shown in Figure 7.47.

**Figure 7.47**

Customizing the
sheet tabs in a
workbook

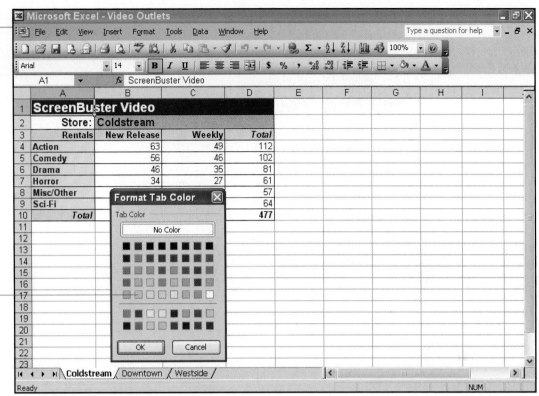

Select this color for
the *Coldstream* tab

9. In the Format Tab Color dialog box, select a light orange (salmon) color for the *Coldstream* tab. Then select a light yellow color for *Downtown* and a light green color for *Westside*. Return to the *Coldstream* worksheet before proceeding.

10. You will now use Group Mode to apply formatting to all of the worksheets. Do the following:
    PRESS: (CTRL) and hold it down
    CLICK: *Downtown* tab
    CLICK: *Westside* tab
    All three sheet tabs should appear selected with the word "[Group]" displaying in the Title bar. You can now release the (CTRL) key.

11. To format the cells containing totals:
    SELECT: cell range from D4 to D10
    PRESS: (CTRL) and hold it down
    SELECT: cell range from B10 to C10
    Make sure that you release the (CTRL) key.

12. To apply boldface and a text color to the selected cells:
    CLICK: Bold button (B) twice to toggle on boldface
    SELECT: a bright blue color from the Font Color button (A▾)
    Your screen should now appear similar to the one shown in Figure 7.48.

**Figure 7.48**

Formatting a
group of
worksheets

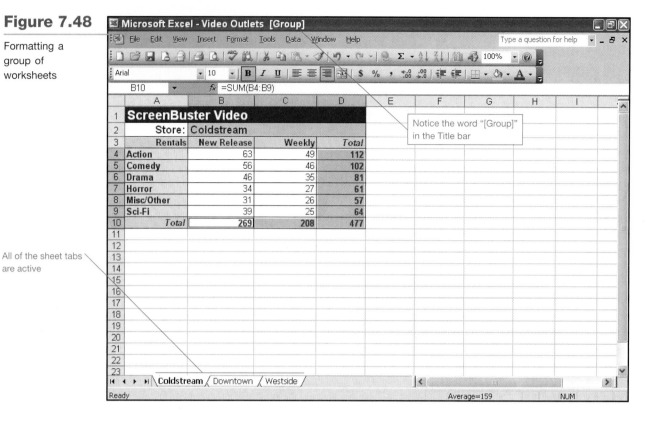

All of the sheet tabs
are active

13. SELECT: cell A2 to cancel the selection

14. Let's ungroup the worksheets.
   RIGHT-CLICK: *Coldstream* tab
   SELECT: Ungroup Sheets

15. To review the worksheets:
   CLICK: *Downtown* tab
   CLICK: *Westside* tab
   Notice that the cell formatting has been applied to the grouped worksheets and that cell A2 is the
   active cell in all of them.

16. Save and then close the "Video Outlets" workbook.

step by step          **3. Consolidating Workbooks**

In this exercise you practice combining and summarizing data that is stored in two separate workbooks.
You place the consolidated summary in a third workbook. You also specify that the summary contents
should be updated automatically when data in the other two workbooks is modified.

1. Make sure there are no workbooks open in the Excel 2003 application window. Then do the following:
   • Open the data file named EX07HE03A, and save it as "SF-Q1" to your personal storage location.
   • Open the data file named EX07HE03B, and save it as "SF-Q2" to your personal storage location.
   • Open the data file named EX07HE03C, and save it as "SF-AVG" to your personal storage
     location.

2. To arrange all of the workbooks in the document area:
   CHOOSE: Window → Arrange
   SELECT: *Tiled* option button
   CLICK: OK command button
   Your screen should now appear similar to the one shown in Figure 7.49.

**Figure 7.49**

Arranging the open workbook windows for Staples Foods

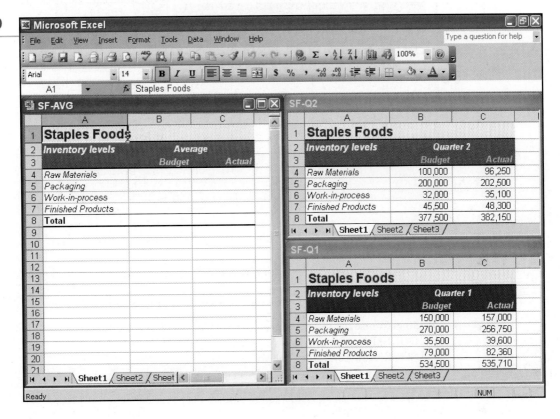

3. To calculate the average of the quarterly workbooks, do the following:
   SELECT: cell range from B4 to C8 in the "SF-AVG" workbook

4. Let's use Excel's Consolidate command:
   CHOOSE: Data → Consolidate
   SELECT: Average in the *Function* drop-down list box

5. In the *Reference* text box, enter the data range for SF-Q1:
   CLICK: Dialog Collapse button (🔲)
   CLICK: Title bar of the "SF-Q1" workbook
   SELECT: cell range from B4 to C8
   CLICK: Dialog Expand button (🔲)
   CLICK: Add command button

6. On your own, add the same cell range for the "SF-Q2" workbook to the *All references* list box. The Consolidate dialog box should appear as shown in Figure 7.50.

**Figure 7.50**

Consolidate
dialog box

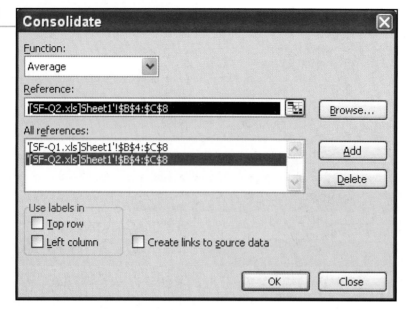

7. To ensure that the "SF-AVG" workbook is updated to reflect changes made in the two subsidiary workbooks:
   SELECT: *Create links to source data* check box
   CLICK: OK command button
   The calculated average values should now appear in the "SF-AVG" workbook.

8. To maximize the "SF-AVG" workbook and display some details:
   DOUBLE-CLICK: its Title bar
   CLICK: Row-Level 2 (2) button

9. Apply formatting from row 7 to rows 4 and 5 using the Format Painter toolbar button. Then select cell A1. Your screen should now appear similar to the one shown in Figure 7.51.

**Figure 7.51**

Displaying details
for the "SF-AVG"
workbook

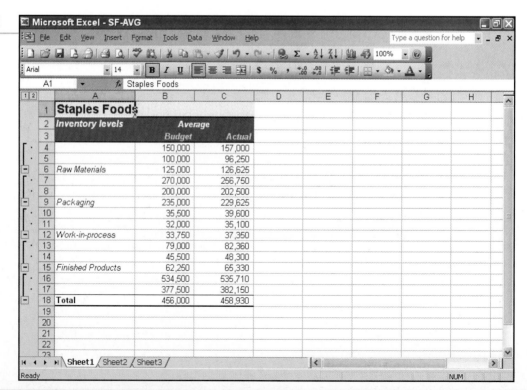

**10.** Return to viewing the summary information only.

**11.** To save and close all workbooks:
PRESS: (SHIFT) and hold it down
CHOOSE: File → Close All

**12.** When prompted by the dialog box:
CLICK: Yes To All command button

on your own

## 4. Managing Multiple Workbooks

In your role as project manager, you have been tasked with consolidating subcontractor data from two development projects into a single summary workbook. The project workbooks, EX07HE04A and EX07HE04B, should be opened and then saved as "Project1" and "Project2," respectively. You should then open the EX07HE04C workbook and save it as "ProjectSummary" to your personal storage location. When you are ready to proceed, tile the open windows to appear similar to that shown in Figure 7.52.

**Figure 7.52**

Arranging the open workbook windows

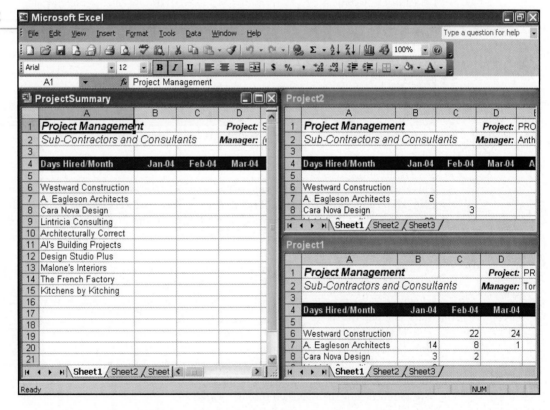

In each of the three workbooks, freeze the window panes so that column A and rows 1 through 4 are always visible. Make the "ProjectSummary" workbook active and move the cell pointer to cell B6. Enter a consolidation formula that adds together the values stored in cell B6 of the "Project1" and "Project2" workbooks. (*Note:* Do not use the Data → Consolidate command for this exercise.) Once entered, modify the formula expression in cell B6 to contain relative cell addresses rather than absolute cell addresses. (*Hint:* Remove the "$" symbols from the formula in cell B6 of the "ProjectSummary" workbook.) You may then copy the formula to the remaining cells (B6:M15) in the "ProjectSummary" workbook. Maximize the "ProjectSummary" workbook so that your screen appears similar to the one shown in Figure 7.53. When you are ready to proceed, save and then close all of the workbooks.

**Figure 7.53**

Completing the "ProjectSummary" workbook

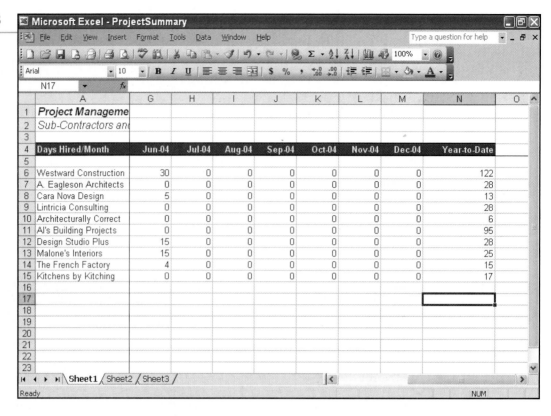

on your own

## 5. Creating a Consolidated Income Statement

This exercise lets you practice working with a multiple-sheet workbook. To begin, open the data file named EX07HE05 and maximize the window, if necessary. Save the workbook as "Division Income" to your personal storage location. After reviewing the worksheets in the workbook, rename the sheet tabs to display the division name appearing in cell A1 of each worksheet. Now change the order of the worksheets to appear as: Seaboard, Southern, and Central.

Create a copy of the Seaboard worksheet and position it as the first sheet in the workbook. Change the text in cell A1 of the new sheet to "Summary" and rename the sheet tab to display the same name. Using Group Mode, change the font in cell A1 of all the worksheets to Times New Roman. When you are finished, ungroup the sheets.

Replace the Revenue and Expense figures in the Summary worksheet with formulas that will consolidate the information from the three Division worksheets. Finally, add the comment shown here to cell B5. When you are finished, your worksheet should appear similar to the one shown in Figure 7.54. Save and then close the "Division Income" workbook.

> **Your Name:**
> Consolidated sales for the Seaboard, Southern and Central divisions.

**Figure 7.54**

Completing the "Division Income" workbook

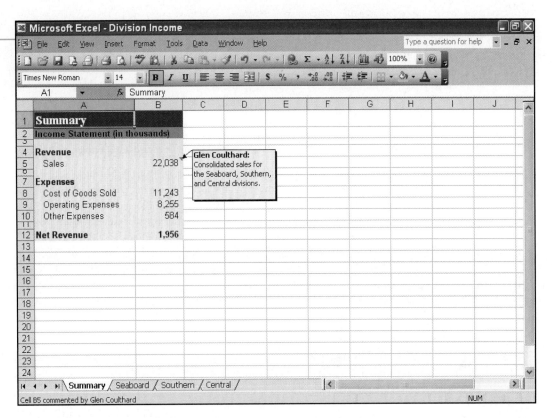

## 6. Creating a New Multiple-Sheet Workbook

The objective of this exercise is to create a new multiple-sheet workbook. The workbook should contain the following sheets: Music, Movies, and Books. For the Music worksheet, enter a title in row 1 and column headings in row 3 for Title, Artist, Year, Producer, Label, and Rating. For the Movies worksheet, enter a title and column headings for Title, Actors, Year, Director, Producer, and Rating. For the Books worksheet, enter a title and column headings for Title, Author, Year, ISBN, Publisher, and Rating. Format all of the worksheets using Group mode, and then add some sample information to the worksheets. Include data for the Rating column using a scale from 1 to 5, with 1 being poor and 5 being excellent.

Insert a new worksheet at the front of the sheet stack called Contents. Place three hyperlinks on this worksheet that navigate to the sheet tabs in the workbook when clicked. Beside each hyperlink, enter a formula that calculates and displays the average rating value (formatted to two decimals) for that particular worksheet. Then enter a summary formula beneath the hyperlink area that averages these three rating subtotal values. When you are finished, save the workbook as "My Ratings" and then close the workbook.

## CaseStudy    HOUSEHOLD DEPOT, INC.

Household Depot operates a chain of home-improvement outlets along the East Coast. In the past few years, they have opened three new stores and have recently established a central distribution warehouse to reduce inventory costs. The senior purchasing agent, Howard Bose, is responsible for monitoring the inventory levels at their distribution warehouse and must provide weekly, monthly, and quarterly summary reports to management. Being relatively experienced in using Excel 2003, Howard has created a large worksheet that contains product, inventory, and supplier information. He also has several worksheets that collect and store the data he needs to create summary reports for management. However, Howard now wants to use some of Excel 2003's productivity features to manage and summarize the data.

In the following case problems, assume the role of Howard and perform the same steps that he identifies.

1. Howard must meet today with a sales representative from Armstrong Hardware, one of the company's suppliers. To prepare for the meeting, he decides to review the Armstrong product line in a worksheet that he has developed. He opens the EX07CP01 data file and then saves it as "Armstrong" to his personal storage location. He immediately notices that the worksheet has not been updated for some time. Acme Distribution, one of Household Depot's old suppliers, is still listed on the worksheet. Howard corrects this mistake by updating all occurrences of "Acme Distribution" with their new supplier "ACE Supplies." Next, he modifies the display so that the column headings and the SKU column are always visible when scrolling. At this point, he moves the cell pointer to the bottom right-hand corner of the list using the CTRL+↓ and CTRL+→ keystrokes. The worksheet now appears similar to the one shown in Figure 7.55. Howard keeps the worksheet open for use in his next task.

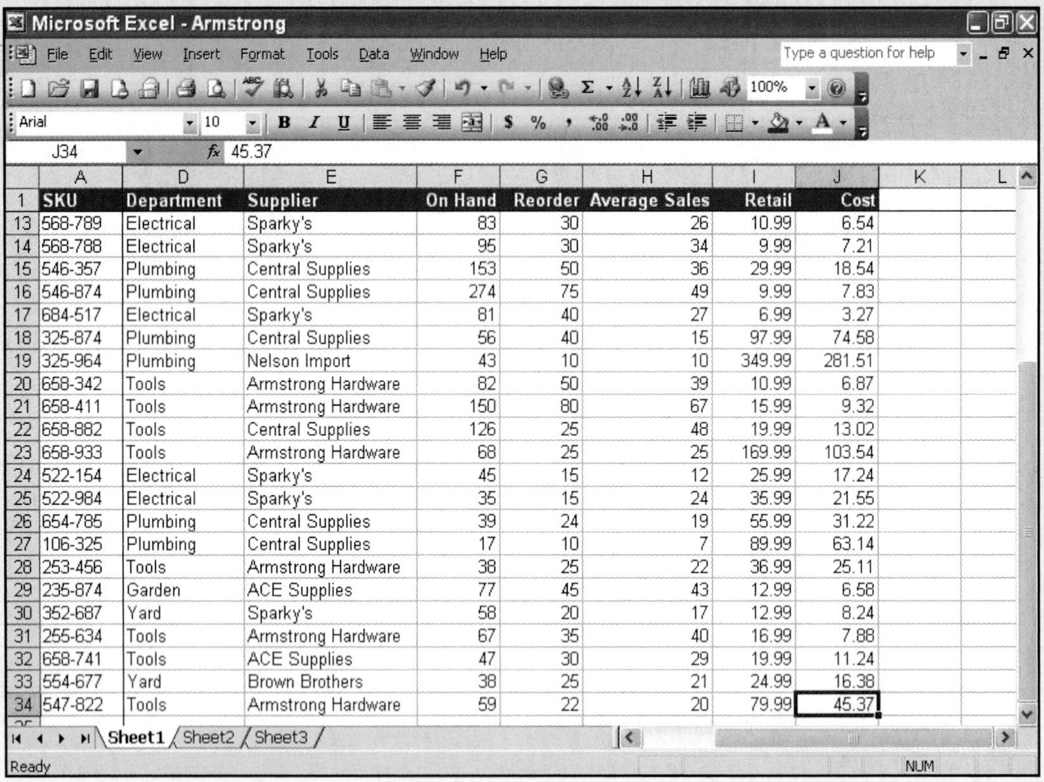


| | A | D | E | F | G | H | I | J |
|---|---|---|---|---|---|---|---|---|
| 1 | SKU | Department | Supplier | On Hand | Reorder | Average Sales | Retail | Cost |
| 13 | 568-789 | Electrical | Sparky's | 83 | 30 | 26 | 10.99 | 6.54 |
| 14 | 568-788 | Electrical | Sparky's | 95 | 30 | 34 | 9.99 | 7.21 |
| 15 | 546-357 | Plumbing | Central Supplies | 153 | 50 | 36 | 29.99 | 18.54 |
| 16 | 546-874 | Plumbing | Central Supplies | 274 | 75 | 49 | 9.99 | 7.83 |
| 17 | 684-517 | Electrical | Sparky's | 81 | 40 | 27 | 6.99 | 3.27 |
| 18 | 325-874 | Plumbing | Central Supplies | 56 | 40 | 15 | 97.99 | 74.58 |
| 19 | 325-964 | Plumbing | Nelson Import | 43 | 10 | 10 | 349.99 | 281.51 |
| 20 | 658-342 | Tools | Armstrong Hardware | 82 | 50 | 39 | 10.99 | 6.87 |
| 21 | 658-411 | Tools | Armstrong Hardware | 150 | 80 | 67 | 15.99 | 9.32 |
| 22 | 658-882 | Tools | Central Supplies | 126 | 25 | 48 | 19.99 | 13.02 |
| 23 | 658-933 | Tools | Armstrong Hardware | 68 | 25 | 25 | 169.99 | 103.54 |
| 24 | 522-154 | Electrical | Sparky's | 45 | 15 | 12 | 25.99 | 17.24 |
| 25 | 522-984 | Electrical | Sparky's | 35 | 15 | 24 | 35.99 | 21.55 |
| 26 | 654-785 | Plumbing | Central Supplies | 39 | 24 | 19 | 55.99 | 31.22 |
| 27 | 106-325 | Plumbing | Central Supplies | 17 | 10 | 7 | 89.99 | 63.14 |
| 28 | 253-456 | Tools | Armstrong Hardware | 38 | 25 | 22 | 36.99 | 25.11 |
| 29 | 235-874 | Garden | ACE Supplies | 77 | 45 | 43 | 12.99 | 6.58 |
| 30 | 352-687 | Yard | Sparky's | 58 | 20 | 17 | 12.99 | 8.24 |
| 31 | 255-634 | Tools | Armstrong Hardware | 67 | 35 | 40 | 16.99 | 7.88 |
| 32 | 658-741 | Tools | ACE Supplies | 47 | 30 | 29 | 19.99 | 11.24 |
| 33 | 554-677 | Yard | Brown Brothers | 38 | 25 | 21 | 24.99 | 16.38 |
| 34 | 547-822 | Tools | Armstrong Hardware | 59 | 22 | 20 | 79.99 | 45.37 |

**Figure 7.55**

Updating and displaying a large worksheet

**2.** Because the conference room does not have a computer, Howard must print the worksheet to take into the meeting. He unfreezes the panes and moves to cell A1. Using the Page Setup dialog box, Howard ensures that the first row of the worksheet will appear on each page of the printout. He then changes the printout to a landscape orientation and scales the size of the print upward to 140% of normal. Finally, Howard previews the worksheet printout, as shown in Figure 7.56. Satisfied that the hard copy will serve him well in the meeting, Howard prints the worksheet. He then saves and closes the workbook.

**Figure 7.56**

Previewing the
Armstrong
workbook

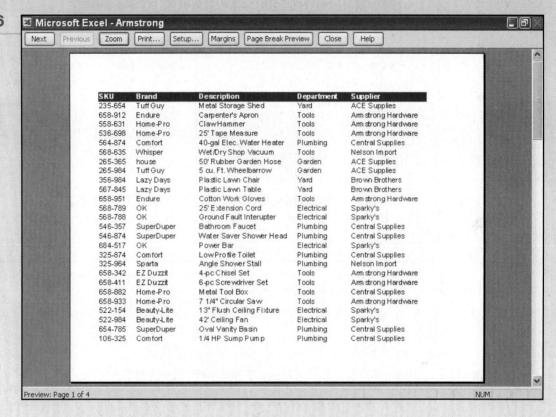

**3.** A senior vice president has asked Howard to prepare a report that summarizes inventory levels by department for the years 2003 and 2004. Furthermore, she wants to see the details for only the Garden and Yard departments. Howard realizes he can use Excel's outlining feature on an existing worksheet to produce the report.

Howard opens the data file called EX07CP03 and then saves it as "Outline Summary" to his personal storage location. After moving the cell pointer into the table area, he chooses the Auto Outline command to create an outline based on the formulas appearing in the worksheet. Next, he collapses the worksheet's rows so that the product details are hidden for all departments but "Garden" and "Yard." The worksheet appears similar to the one shown in Figure 7.57.

**Figure 7.57**

Collapsing and displaying an outline

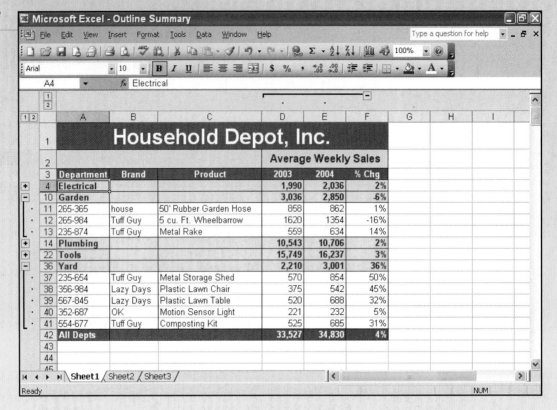

Satisfied that the worksheet displays the summarized information requested by the senior vice president, Howard prints a copy of the worksheet. As a last step, he saves and then closes the workbook.

4. Since Howard did such a nice job with the previous summary report, the executive committee has asked him to produce a weekly summary of inventory transactions for the three nonseasonal departments. To begin, Howard locates a workbook containing the necessary information. He opens the data file named EX07CP04 and then saves it as "Weekly Summary" to his personal storage location. In reviewing the workbook, Howard notices that each department appears on its own worksheet.

To make the workbook easier to use, Howard colors and renames each of the sheet tabs to display the department names. In order to create a summary worksheet, he places a copy of the Electrical worksheet at the beginning of the sheet stack. He then colors the tab and renames the worksheet "Summary." After modifying the title in cell A1, Howard creates a table of contents for hyperlinks in cells A10, A11, and A12 to the other tabs in the sheet stack.

After testing the hyperlinks, Howard decides against using the Consolidate command in favor of entering a simple SUM function. The formula that he enters in cell B3, for example, sums together values from the three departmental worksheets. After entering the formula, Howard uses the Edit → Fill → Down command to extend the calculation to cells B4 through B7 and then formats the results using the Currency style. Finally, Howard decides that he needs to make the worksheets more visually appealing. He uses Group mode to apply formatting to all four sheets simultaneously, as shown in Figure 7.58. Once finished, he ungroups the worksheets. He then saves and closes the workbook. Howard exits Microsoft Office Excel 2003.

**Figure 7.58**

Completing the "Weekly Summary" workbook

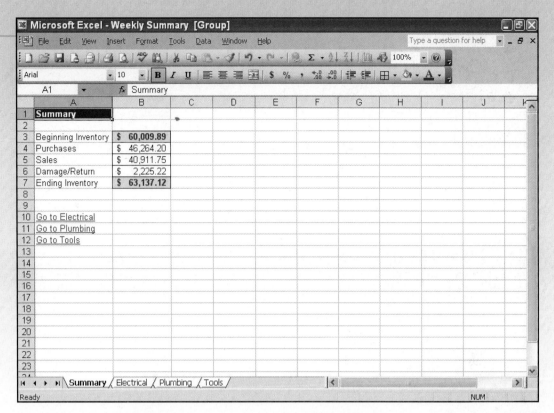

## Answers to Self-Check Questions

**7.1**  How would you divide a worksheet window into four panes? You can drag both the horizontal and vertical split boxes to create panes. Once you have finished specifying horizontal panes for example, you can then divide the worksheet window into vertical panes. You can also use the Window ➜ Split command.

**7.2**  What characters must you type to have Excel's AutoCorrect feature insert the proper trademark symbol (™)? You type **(tm)** and then press the Space bar.

**7.3**  How would you rename a chart sheet and then move it to the end of a sheet stack in a workbook? You rename and move a chart sheet just as you would a worksheet. In other words, double-click the chart sheet's tab and type a new name. Press (**ENTER**) to accept the entry. Then drag the sheet tab to the far right in the sheet stack.

**7.4**  Name two advantages for separating your work into multiple workbooks. First, the workbooks are typically smaller than a single multiple-sheet workbook. Second, the workbooks are not limited to being stored on the same computer or network.

**7.5**  Can you think of any other ways to document a worksheet? Some suggestions include:
- Enter comments in specific columns or rows, and then use the Hide command to conceal the columns or rows.
- Set aside an entire worksheet in a workbook for adding comments, notes, and explanations.
- Display and then print your worksheet formulas so that you may annotate them further on paper.

# Notes

# Microsoft® Office Excel®

## 2003

## CHAPTER 8

# Managing Worksheet Lists

### PREREQUISITES

This chapter presumes no previous database or list management experience. However, you must know how to perform basic worksheet editing commands, such as changing row heights and column widths and inserting and deleting rows. You should also have completed Chapter 7 so that you are familiar with working in large worksheets and multiple-sheet workbooks.

### LEARNING OBJECTIVES

After completing this chapter, you will be able to:

- Understand basic list terminology

- Enter and find data in a worksheet list

- Sort and filter list information

- Query and extract data from a list

- Analyze a list using database functions

- Summarize a list using subtotals

# 8.1 Creating Lists

When the electronic spreadsheet was first conceived more than twenty years ago, its applications focused on solving mathematical and statistical equations. With the widespread adoption of personal computers in the early 1980s, the spreadsheet quickly evolved from being a glorified calculator to become an essential business productivity tool, capable of creating graphic presentations and managing data. Nowadays, software is developed and marketed to solve specialized computing tasks, such as Web browsing, word processing, spreadsheet analysis, database management, computer animation, graphics production, and personal finance. Your ability to choose the "right" software for a task is as important as knowing how to use that software's commands and features.

Microsoft Office Excel 2003 is inarguably the most powerful electronic spreadsheet available. What you may not know is that you can also use Excel 2003 to efficiently manage lists of data when database management software seems like overkill. Consider the following scenario: As the sales manager for a footwear manufacturer, you need to track the unit sales and customer demographics (each customer's age and annual income) for a new line of hiking boots. Obviously a computer will help you greatly in this task, but which applications software should you choose for storing and analyzing the data? Your objective is to process or turn raw *data* into *information.* The distinction between data and information is important—information is the result of manipulating, organizing, summarizing, and presenting data in a form suitable for decision making or further analysis.

To determine whether Excel 2003 or a database management program, such as Microsoft Office Access 2003, is the more suitable software, start by answering the following questions. In your analysis, consider the ability of the program to adapt over time to your changing needs.

- *How complicated are my data management tasks?* You need to know what you want to do with the data. If you require only basic sorting and filtering capabilities, Excel handles these chores quite easily. If you require advanced querying and reporting tools, a dedicated database management program provides superior power, flexibility, and performance.

- *How much data needs to be stored?* Excel 2003 can support lists having a maximum of 256 columns and 65,535 rows.[1] In reality, your computer will experience a performance degradation that is likely unbearable prior to reaching these physical limits. Database management programs, on the other hand, allow you to work efficiently with millions of records. (*Hint:* You can always convert an Excel 2003 worksheet list into a database management program should the need for greater capacity arise.)

- *How much redundant data is expected?* For smaller applications where your focus is on analyzing numerical data, using Excel 2003 to maintain a worksheet list or **flat-file database** is a practical choice. If, however, your application's data is largely textual and repetitive in nature, you may want to consider using a **relational database.** In relational database management software, like Access 2003, you divide a list into smaller *tables* in order to reduce data duplication.

- *How important is data validation?* **Data validation** is necessary for ensuring data accuracy and completeness. Both Excel 2003 and database management programs can analyze an entry to ensure that it adheres to a specific data type (for example, text, numeric, or date) or that it falls between an acceptable range of values. If your data validation requirements are not complex, Excel 2003's features will suffice. For more advanced data validation and error checking routines, a database management program is the appropriate choice.

- *Will your application need to be controlled by programming code?* Although Excel 2003 allows you to automate a worksheet application using macros and code, database management programs provide superior programming tools for developing custom applications.

Let's assume that upon answering these questions you've chosen Excel 2003 for storing and analyzing your data. In this module you learn how to design and define a worksheet list. You also learn how to enter data, navigate a list, and find specific information using Excel 2003's Data Form tool.

---

[1] A worksheet contains 65,536 rows. After dedicating one row for the column headings, a worksheet can store up to 65,535 rows of record data.

## 8.1.1 Defining a List

→ # Feature

A worksheet **list** is a collection of related information, such as a phone book. In Excel 2003 a list is stored on a worksheet in a series of rows and columns. Each horizontal row represents an individual entry or **record** in the list, while each vertical column or **field** divides a record into manageable pieces. Like all worksheet cells, fields can contain text, numbers, dates, formulas, and functions. In the following example, notice that each student's record consists of the following fields: StudentID, Surname, Given, Quizzes, Projects, Exams, and Final. The actual record entries, beginning in row 2, appear immediately below the **field header row.** By properly separating a list into fields, you improve your options for searching, sorting, summarizing, and analyzing the data.

Field Header Row

Records

|  | A | B | C | D | E | F |
|---|---|---|---|---|---|---|
| 1 | **StudentID** | **Surname** | **Given** | **Quizzes** | **Exams** | **Final** |
| 2 | 149634 | Albertson | Sandy | 79.40% | 77.00% | 77.96% |
| 3 | 139220 | Bradley | Todd | 84.00% | 87.25% | 85.95% |
| 4 | 146882 | Davis | Cecilia | 60.50% | 65.00% | 63.20% |
| 5 | 157609 | Johnston | Wade | 89.00% | 92.50% | 91.10% |
| 6 | 138902 | Lee | Catherine | 78.00% | 84.00% | 81.60% |

People who have used worksheet lists can attest to the "90/10 rule" of good list design. It reads something like this: Spend 90 percent of your time planning and designing a list in order to spend only 10 percent of your time maintaining it. The following guidelines should help you avoid some common pitfalls of faulty planning and design.

• Be mindful of how your lists will appear when printed.

• Although not necessary, place larger lists on a separate worksheet.

• Use a one-word label to name the Sheet tab.

• Place one-word column headings (field names) in a single row.

• Format the field header row to appear differently from the data.

• Enter data immediately below the field header row.

• Do not indent cell entries using the Space Bar.

• Do not insert or leave blank columns or rows within a list.

• Do not store unrelated data on the same worksheet as a list.

After designing a worksheet list, test it by inserting a few sample entries. Remember that it is far easier to modify the structure of an empty list than it is to add and delete fields in a list containing thousands of records.

→ # Method

To define a worksheet list using the menu:

• SELECT: the range containing the desired list area

• CHOOSE: Data → List → Create List

To define a worksheet list using the right-click menu:

• RIGHT-CLICK: a cell within the desired list area

• SELECT: Create List

# → Practice

You will now practice applying the list creation guidelines and define a worksheet list for recording bill and payment transactions. Before proceeding, ensure that Excel is 2003 loaded.

**1.** In the following steps, you will first create the worksheet list shown in Figure 8.1 and then define the list using the menu. To begin, ensure that a blank worksheet appears in the Excel 2003 application window and position the cell pointer in cell A1.

**Figure 8.1**

Creating a
worksheet list for
recording bills

Field Header Row

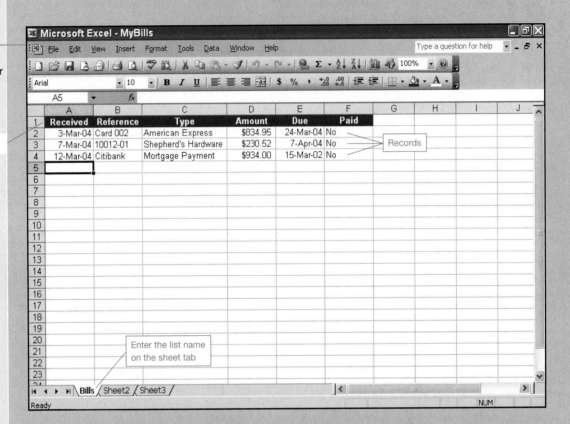

**2.** To create a worksheet list, you start by entering the column headings or field names for the field header row. Refer to Figure 8.1 and type the following text labels into row 1: **Received**, **Reference**, **Type**, **Amount**, **Due**, and **Paid**.

**3.** Now format the cell entries in row 1 to separate visually the field header row from the data:
SELECT: cell range from A1 to F1

**4.** An excellent method for setting apart your column headings is to change the background fill color and foreground font color:
CLICK: down arrow attached to the Fill Color button ([🖌▾])
SELECT: Dark Red from the drop-down list
CLICK: down arrow attached to the Font Color button ([A▾])
SELECT: White from the drop-down list

**5.** To further enhance the appearance of the headings:
CLICK: Bold button ([B])
CLICK: Center button ([≡])

**6.** With the cell range still selected, adjust the column widths:
CHOOSE: Format → Column → Width
TYPE: **10**
CLICK: OK command button
Your screen should now appear similar to the one shown in Figure 8.2.

**Figure 8.2**

Creating the field header row

|   | A | B | C | D | E | F | G |
|---|---|---|---|---|---|---|---|
| 1 | **Received** | **Reference** | **Type** | **Amount** | **Due** | **Paid** | |
| 2 | | | | | | | |
| 3 | | | | | | | |
| 4 | | | | | | | |

7. Using the mouse, increase the width of column C:
   DRAG: its right borderline in the frame area to the right until 18 appears in the ScreenTip
   (*Hint:* Remember to release the mouse button when you finish dragging the column's borderline.)

8. Let's give the sheet tab a more descriptive name:
   DOUBLE-CLICK: *Sheet1* tab
   TYPE: **Bills**
   PRESS: ENTER

9. Using Figure 8.1 as your guide, complete the data entry for rows 2 through 4.

10. You must now tell Excel 2003 that this information represents a worksheet list. To do so:
    SELECT: cell range from A1 to F4
    CHOOSE: Data → List → Create List
    Your screen should now appear similar to the one shown in Figure 8.3.

**Figure 8.3**

Create List dialog box

The range that you have selected appears in this text box automatically

Because the field header row is formatted differently, Excel 2003 identifies that the list range contains headers

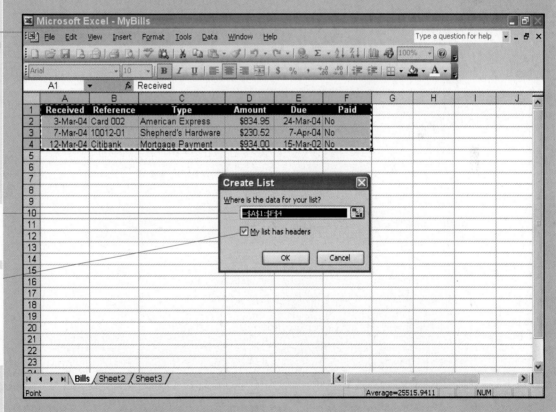

11. Ensure that the data range is correct and that the *My list has headers* check box is selected. Then:
    CLICK: OK command button
    CLICK: cell A2 to remove the selection highlighting
    Your worksheet should now appear similar to the one shown in Figure 8.4. Notice that Excel 2003 displays a List toolbar and attaches drop-down arrows to each field column header label. The more commonly used toolbar buttons are identified in the figure graphic.

**Figure 8.4**

Defining a worksheet list

The blue asterisk signifies the "insert row," where you can enter a new record's data

The blue border signifies the extent or size of the list range

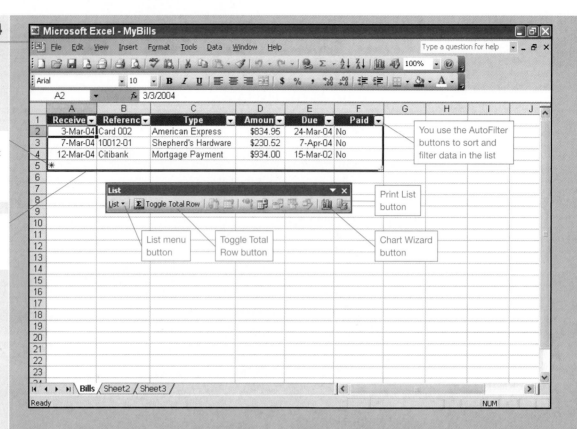

**12.** To add a new record to the list:
CLICK: cell A5 (in the insert row, with the blue asterisk)

**13.** TYPE: 14-Mar-2004 in the Received column
PRESS: ➡ to move the cell pointer to the right
Notice that the blue border around the list range automatically expands and that the blue asterisk in the insert row now moves down to row 6.

**14.** To finish entering data for the record:
TYPE: Card 087 in the Reference column
PRESS: ➡
TYPE: BC Fuel and Gas in the Type column
PRESS: ➡
TYPE: $48.50 in the Amount column
PRESS: ➡
TYPE: 14-May-2004 in the Due column
PRESS: ➡
TYPE: No in the Paid column

**15.** To reset the cell pointer:
CLICK: cell A2

**16.** Save the workbook as "My Bills" to your personal storage location, and then close the workbook.

## 8.1.2 Entering Data into a List

→ ## Feature

Previously, you entered a new record by typing cell entries directly into the worksheet list's insert row, identified by its blue asterisk in the first column of the list. To speed your work, there are several data entry shortcuts that are worth mentioning now. Similar to using the AutoComplete feature, Excel 2003 provides keyboard shortcuts for selecting cell ranges and entering data. To increase your speed and efficiency, commit this lesson's keystroke combinations to memory.

→ ## Method

- PRESS: **CTRL**+arrow keys to move quickly to beginning or end of fields and records

- PRESS: **CTRL**+* to select the active worksheet list area

- PRESS: **CTRL**+; to insert the current date

- PRESS: **CTRL**+ : to insert the current time

- PRESS: **ALT**+↓ to display a Pick From Drop-down List of values

→ ## Practice

In this lesson you will enter data using keyboard shortcuts. Ensure that no workbooks appear in the application window.

**1.** Open the data file named EX0810 to display the workbook shown in Figure 8.5. This workbook contains data for tracking your incoming and outgoing phone calls and for recording the length of each call.

**Figure 8.5**

Opening the
EX0810
workbook

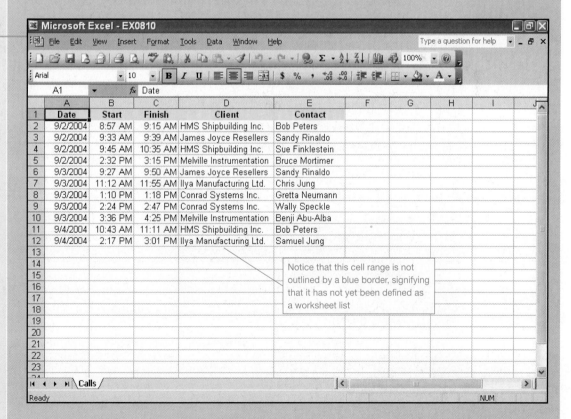

| | A | B | C | D | E |
|---|---|---|---|---|---|
| 1 | **Date** | **Start** | **Finish** | **Client** | **Contact** |
| 2 | 9/2/2004 | 8:57 AM | 9:15 AM | HMS Shipbuilding Inc. | Bob Peters |
| 3 | 9/2/2004 | 9:33 AM | 9:39 AM | James Joyce Resellers | Sandy Rinaldo |
| 4 | 9/2/2004 | 9:45 AM | 10:35 AM | HMS Shipbuilding Inc. | Sue Finklestein |
| 5 | 9/2/2004 | 2:32 PM | 3:15 PM | Melville Instrumentation | Bruce Mortimer |
| 6 | 9/3/2004 | 9:27 AM | 9:50 AM | James Joyce Resellers | Sandy Rinaldo |
| 7 | 9/3/2004 | 11:12 AM | 11:55 AM | Ilya Manufacturing Ltd. | Chris Jung |
| 8 | 9/3/2004 | 1:10 PM | 1:18 PM | Conrad Systems Inc. | Gretta Neumann |
| 9 | 9/3/2004 | 2:24 PM | 2:47 PM | Conrad Systems Inc. | Wally Speckle |
| 10 | 9/3/2004 | 3:36 PM | 4:25 PM | Melville Instrumentation | Benji Abu-Alba |
| 11 | 9/4/2004 | 10:43 AM | 11:11 AM | HMS Shipbuilding Inc. | Bob Peters |
| 12 | 9/4/2004 | 2:17 PM | 3:01 PM | Ilya Manufacturing Ltd. | Samuel Jung |

Notice that this cell range is not outlined by a blue border, signifying that it has not yet been defined as a worksheet list

**2.** Save the workbook as "Phone Log" to your personal storage location.

**3.** Ensure that the cell pointer appears in cell A1, and then do the following to practice navigating the cell range:
PRESS: CTRL + → to move to the last field
PRESS: CTRL + ↓ to move to the last record
PRESS: CTRL + ← to move to the first field
PRESS: CTRL + ↑ to move to the field header row

**4.** To select a single record:
CLICK: cell A3
PRESS: CTRL + SHIFT + →
The field entries for the record should now appear highlighted, as shown in Figure 8.6.

**Figure 8.6**

Selecting fields in a single record

| | A | B | C | D | E | F |
|---|---|---|---|---|---|---|
| 1 | **Date** | **Start** | **Finish** | **Client** | **Contact** | |
| 2 | 9/2/2004 | 8:57 AM | 9:15 AM | HMS Shipbuilding Inc. | Bob Peters | |
| 3 | 9/2/2004 | 9:33 AM | 9:39 AM | James Joyce Resellers | Sandy Rinaldo | |
| 4 | 9/2/2004 | 9:45 AM | 10:35 AM | HMS Shipbuilding Inc. | Sue Finklestein | |
| 5 | 9/2/2004 | 2:32 PM | 3:15 PM | Melville Instrumentation | Bruce Mortimer | |
| 6 | 9/3/2004 | 9:27 AM | 9:50 AM | James Joyce Resellers | Sandy Rinaldo | |
| 7 | 9/3/2004 | 11:12 AM | 11:55 AM | Ilya Manufacturing Ltd. | Chris Jung | |
| 8 | 9/3/2004 | 1:10 PM | 1:18 PM | Conrad Systems Inc. | Gretta Neumann | |
| 9 | 9/3/2004 | 2:24 PM | 2:47 PM | Conrad Systems Inc. | Wally Speckle | |
| 10 | 9/3/2004 | 3:36 PM | 4:25 PM | Melville Instrumentation | Benji Abu-Alba | |
| 11 | 9/4/2004 | 10:43 AM | 11:11 AM | HMS Shipbuilding Inc. | Bob Peters | |
| 12 | 9/4/2004 | 2:17 PM | 3:01 PM | Ilya Manufacturing Ltd. | Samuel Jung | |
| 13 | | | | | | |
| 14 | | | | | | |

**5.** To select the entire active worksheet area:
PRESS: CTRL + *
The entire list area is selected. (*Note:* The cell pointer must be positioned in the list prior to pressing this shortcut key.)

**6.** To move among the cells in the range selection:
PRESS: CTRL + . (period) several times to move from corner to corner
PRESS: ENTER a few times to move downward
PRESS: TAB a few times to move to the right
PRESS: SHIFT + ENTER a few times to move upward
PRESS: SHIFT + TAB a few times to move to the left
Notice that the range remains selected.

**7.** Let's define the selected range as a worksheet list and then add two new records to the bottom of the worksheet list:
CHOOSE: Data → List → Create List

**8.** In the Create List dialog box, ensure that the *My list has headers* check box is selected and then:
CLICK: OK command button
You should now see AutoFilter arrows attached to columns in the field header row, as shown below.

| | A | B | C | D | E |
|---|---|---|---|---|---|
| 1 | **Date** ▼ | **Start** ▼ | **Finish** ▼ | **Client** ▼ | **Contact** ▼ |
| 2 | 9/2/2004 | 8:57 AM | 9:15 AM | HMS Shipbuilding Inc. | Bob Peters |

9. On your own, move the List toolbar so you can see the majority of the list area. Then:
CLICK: cell A13 in the insert row

10. To enter the first record:
TYPE: 9/5/2004
PRESS: [ TAB ]
TYPE: 11:32 AM
PRESS: [ TAB ]
TYPE: 11:38 AM
PRESS: [ TAB ]
TYPE: Rogers Food
PRESS: [ TAB ]
TYPE: Willie Lapinshki
PRESS: [ TAB ]
Notice that the cell pointer wraps to the beginning of the next record automatically.

11. Now let's introduce some data entry shortcuts. Ensure that cell A14 is the active cell and then do the following:
PRESS: [ CTRL ]+; to insert the current date
PRESS: [ TAB ]
PRESS: [ CTRL ]+: to insert the Start time
PRESS: [ TAB ]
PRESS: [ CTRL ]+: to insert the Finish time (yes, a short call!)
PRESS: [ TAB ]

12. Let's display a data entry pick list:
PRESS: [ ALT ]+[↓] to display a Pick From Drop-down List of values
Your screen should now appear similar to the one shown in Figure 8.7.

**Figure 8.7**

Displaying a data entry pick list

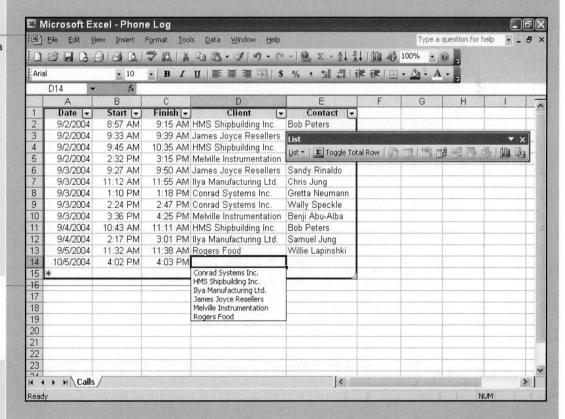

Excel 2003 scans the field column for unique entries and then displays a sorted pick list of values

**13.** SELECT: James Joyce Resellers
PRESS: [TAB]

**14.** Now display a pick list for the "Contact" field using the right-click short-cut menu:
RIGHT-CLICK: cell E14
CHOOSE: Pick From Drop-down List
SELECT: Sandy Rinaldo, as shown here
(*Hint:* You can also use the keyboard to highlight an item in a pick list and then press [ENTER] to accept the selection.)

**15.** CLICK: cell A1 to reset the cell pointer

**16.** Save the workbook and keep it open for use in the next lesson.

### 8.1.3 Navigating a List Using a Data Form

→ ## Feature

Excel 2003 provides a special tool for manipulating worksheet lists called a *data form*. A **data form** is a special dialog box that allows you to navigate, add, modify, delete, and search for records in a list. Unlike working directly with cells in the worksheet, a data form displays only a single record at a time. For this reason, some users find working with data forms easier and more manageable than navigating the worksheet list.

→ ## Method

To display the data form, select any cell within the list area and then:

• CHOOSE: Data → Form,

    *or*

• CLICK: List menu button ([List ▾])

• CHOOSE: Form

To work with a list using the data form:

• CLICK: New command button to add a record

• CLICK: Delete command button to delete the current record

• CLICK: Find Next command button to view the next record

• CLICK: Find Prev command button to view the previous record

→ ## Practice

You will now practice displaying and using the Data Form dialog box for the *Calls* worksheet list. Ensure that you've completed the previous lesson and that the "Phone Log" workbook is displayed.

**1.** To display a data form, ensure that you've selected cell A1 (or any other cell in the list area) and then:
CHOOSE: Data → Form
Excel 2003 analyzes the worksheet list, compiling the field names from the field header row and counting the total records, and then displays the Data Form dialog box (Figure 8.8). Notice that the sheet tab name, *Calls*, becomes the Title bar caption for the dialog box.

**Figure 8.8**

Data Form dialog box

Display up to 32 fields from a single record

Navigate the records in a list using this scroll bar

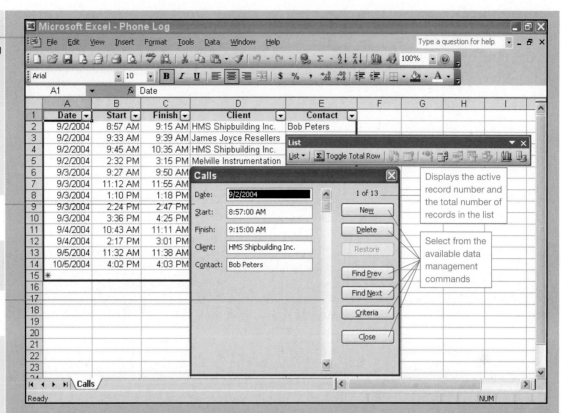

2. To navigate through the records one at a time:
CLICK: down arrow (⌄) on the scroll bar repeatedly
CLICK: up arrow (⌃) on the scroll bar repeatedly
(*Hint:* For larger lists, drag the scroll box on the scroll bar.)

3. To add a new phone conversation to the list:
CLICK: New command button
PRESS: CTRL +; to insert the current date
PRESS: TAB to move to the next field
PRESS: CTRL +: to insert the Start time
PRESS: TAB
PRESS: CTRL +: to insert the Finish time (another short call)
PRESS: TAB

4. Because Excel 2003 regards an entry such as "ABC Realty" as different from "A.B.C. Realty," you need to ensure the correct spelling and punctuation for your text entries. Furthermore, the Auto-Complete command is not available when you are working in a data form. To complete the record, enter the following data:
TYPE: **Conrad Systems Inc.**
PRESS: TAB
TYPE: **Gretta Neumann**
Except for the date and time entries, your Data Form dialog box should now appear similar to the one shown in Figure 8.9.

**Figure 8.9**

Adding a new record using the Data Form dialog box

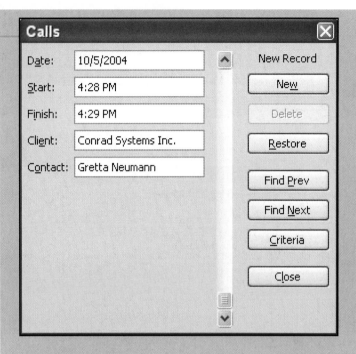

5. When you are ready to proceed:
PRESS: ENTER to save the record and continue

6. Rather than entering a new record, let's close the Data Form dialog box and return to the worksheet. Do the following:
CLICK: Close command button
Notice that the new record you added appears in row 15 at the bottom of the worksheet list. The insert row has now moved to row 16.

7. Save the workbook and keep it open for use in the next lesson.

*In Addition* DISPLAYING FORMULA RESULTS IN A DATA FORM DIALOG BOX

When a list contains a field column with formula expressions, the calculated results are displayed as read-only text labels in the Data Form dialog box. In other words, you cannot modify a cell's formula while working in the data form. Also, calculated fields are updated in the Data Form dialog box only after you press ENTER (to proceed to the next record) or click the Close command button.

### 8.1.4 Finding Data Using a Criteria Form

 **Feature**

A **criteria form** is simply an extension of a data form. When you click the Criteria command button in the Data Form dialog box, Excel 2003 switches the display to a blank form that you can use to enter search criteria. To find people named Smith, for example, type "Smith" into the field column used to store surnames and click the Find Next command button. This approach is known as **query-by-example (QBE)** because you feed the criteria form the example value(s) that you want to find.

To construct more complex criteria expressions, use Excel 2003's standard comparison operators: < (less than), <= (less than or equal to), > (greater than), >= (greater than or equal to), and <> (not equal to). For fields containing text, **wildcard characters** can also help you locate an entry, especially if you are unsure of the proper spelling. Use the question mark (?) in place of a single character and the asterisk (*) to represent a group of characters. For example, the search pattern "??S?" matches ROSI and DISK, while "Sm*" yields all entries beginning with "Sm," such as Smith and Smallwood.

→ **Method**

To use the criteria search features of the Data Form dialog box:

- Display the Data Form dialog box.

- Move to the first record at the top of the list.

- CLICK: Criteria command button

- Specify the search criteria by filling in the blank criteria form.

- CLICK: Find Next command button

→ **Practice**

You will now practice locating records in the active worksheet list. Ensure that you've completed the previous lessons and that the "Phone Log" workbook is displayed.

**1.** To display the Data Form dialog box:
CLICK: List menu button ([List ▾])
CHOOSE: Form

**2.** Before displaying the criteria form, ensure that you are viewing the first record by dragging the scroll box to the top. Then:
CLICK: Criteria command button
A blank form (Figure 8.10) appears where you can define the search criteria. Notice the resemblance to the Data Form dialog box.

**Figure 8.10**

Criteria Form dialog box

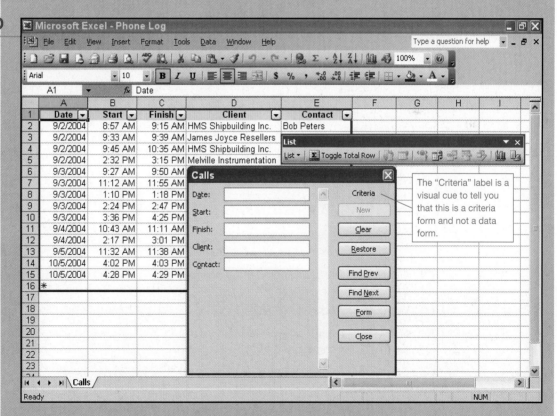

**3.** To locate the entries for Melville Instrumentation:
CLICK: in the *Client* text box to position the cursor
TYPE: **Melville**
Notice that you need not type the entire entry to search for the company.

**4.** To proceed:
CLICK: Find Next command button
The first entry for Melville, record 4, should now be displayed in the Data Form dialog box.

**5.** To search for the next occurrence of "Melville" in the Client field column, do the following:
CLICK: Find Next command button
Record 9 is displayed in the data form.

**6.** To prepare for a new search:
DRAG: scroll box on the scroll bar upward to display record 1

**7.** Now display the Criteria Form dialog box and clear the previous search criteria:
CLICK: Criteria command button
CLICK: Clear command button

**8.** To locate the calls that were made in the afternoon:
SELECT: *Start* text box
TYPE: >12:00 PM
Your screen should appear similar to the one shown in Figure 8.11.

**Figure 8.11**

Entering new
search criteria

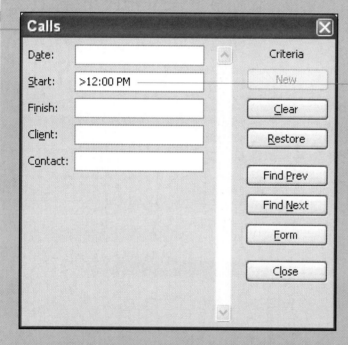

Using a comparison operator to find all records containing a time greater than 12:00 PM in the Start field column

**9.** CLICK: Find Next command button repeatedly to display all of the afternoon calls
(*Hint:* You will hear a beep when you reach the end of the worksheet list of matching records.

**10.** CLICK: Find Prev command button to work your way back up the list

**11.** When you are ready to proceed:
CLICK: Close command button

**12.** Save and keep the workbook open for use in the next lesson.

## 8.1.5 Modifying a List's Structure

→ ## Feature

A worksheet list expands as you enter new record information into the insert row of the list range. You can also insert and delete record information within the list, without affecting cell data outside of the list area. Furthermore, you can add and remove fields or columns of data, and resize the worksheet list to accommodate structural changes. Most of the commands that you will use to modify a list structure are located on the List toolbar or in the Data → List menu.

→ ## Method

To resize a worksheet list:

- DRAG: the resize handle in the bottom right-hand corner of the list range

To insert a row or column in a worksheet list:

- SELECT: the desired row or column
- CLICK: List menu button (List ▾) on the List toolbar
- CHOOSE: Insert → Row,

    or

- CHOOSE: Insert → Column

To delete a row or column in a worksheet list:

- SELECT: the desired row or column
- CLICK: List menu button (List ▾) on the List toolbar
- CHOOSE: Delete → Row,

    or

- CHOOSE: Delete → Column

→ ## Practice

You will now practice resizing a list and using the List menu button (List ▾) to insert and delete rows and columns. Ensure that you've completed the previous lessons and that the "Phone Log" workbook is displayed.

**1.** To demonstrate how the list border changes its appearance to signify whether it is active or inactive, do the following:
CLICK: cell G2
Although the border is not as thick, you can still see the blue outline around the list area. Also notice that the insert row has disappeared, along with the List toolbar.

**2.** To make the worksheet list active once again:
CLICK: cell A1
The insert row and the List toolbar are redisplayed.

**3.** Your objective over the next few steps is to insert a new field column into the worksheet list that calculates the total time spent on a call. To begin, locate the resizing handle in the bottom right-hand corner of the list and then:
DRAG: the resizing handle one column to the right

Your screen should now appear similar to that shown in Figure 8.12. (*Hint:* Excel 2003 worksheet lists have an auto-expansion feature. With auto-expansion, whatever you type into an empty row or column adjacent to the worksheet list will be incorporated into the list area automatically.)

**Figure 8.12**

Creating a new field column

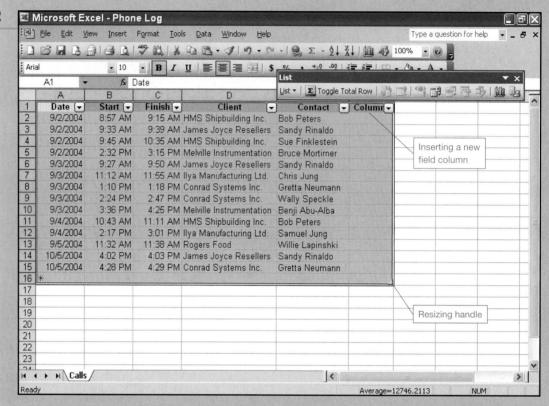

**4.** Let's rename the column:
SELECT: cell F1
TYPE: **Time**
PRESS: ENTER

**5.** To enter a calculation that calculates the time spent on a call:
SELECT: cell range F2 to F15

**6.** Ensure that the active (white) cell in the range is F2 and then:
TYPE: **=c2-b2**
PRESS: CTRL + ENTER

**7.** To format the cell entries:
CHOOSE: Format → Cells
CLICK: *Number* tab
SELECT: Time in the *Category* list box
SELECT: 37:30:55 in the *Type* list box
CLICK: OK command button
Your screen should now appear similar to the one shown in Figure 8.13.

**Figure 8.13**

Entering a calculated field

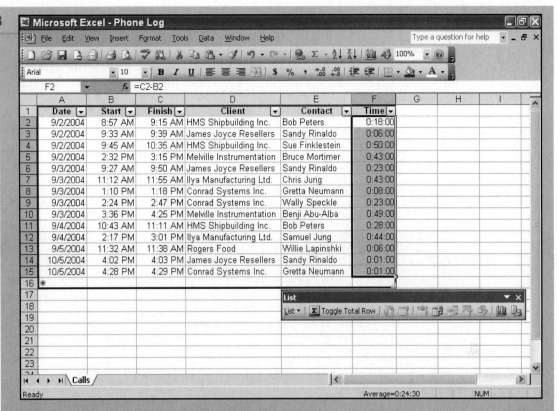

8. To remove a record within the worksheet list, you must first select a cell within the row that you wish to remove. Do the following:
CLICK: cell A8

9. To delete this record:
CLICK: List menu button (List▾) on the List toolbar
CHOOSE: Delete → Row
The record is deleted. (*Note:* Unlike the Edit → Delete Row command, this command only deletes the record information within the worksheet list. Information or data stored in the same row but outside of the list area would be unaffected.)

10. To insert a new record within the list area:
CLICK: List menu button (List▾) on the List toolbar
CHOOSE: Insert → Row
Notice that the formula calculation in column F is automatically copied to the new record's row.

11. On your own, complete the record by entering new data.

12. Save and then close the "Phone Log" workbook.

  **SelfCheck**   **8.1**   What are some advantages of adding records to a list using the Data Form dialog box? What are some disadvantages?

# 8.2 Working with Lists

A worksheet list is used as a storage area for capturing and analyzing large quantities of data. However, data does not become information until it is processed. This processing can take several forms, from arranging, organizing, and extracting data to presenting data in charts and reports. Some common techniques for manipulating list data include sorting, filtering, and summarizing. In addition to these processes, this module examines methods for efficiently and effectively printing and converting your list data.

## 8.2.1 Sorting a List

→ ## Feature

Sorting the data in a worksheet list into a particular order is often the first step in making information out of raw data. Not only does sorting allow you to better organize data, it makes it much easier to find a record by scanning a list. Excel 2003 enables you to sort a worksheet list quickly using the AutoFilter drop-down list arrows attached to each field column. You can also use the menu for conducting more advanced sort options, using up to three fields. The first field used in a sort operation is called the **primary sort key,** while the second and third fields are called **secondary sort keys.** You can choose to sort the list into ascending (0 to 9, A to Z) or descending (Z to A, 9 to 0) order. Regardless of the sort order chosen, blank entries in the sort column are always placed at the bottom of the list.

→ ## Method

To sort a list using the AutoFilter drop-down list arrow:

- CLICK: a cell within the worksheet list in order to make it active
- CLICK: a field column's AutoFilter drop-down list arrow (▾)
- SELECT: Sort Ascending,

  *or*

- SELECT: Sort Descending

To perform a simple sort using one field:

- SELECT: a cell in the field column you want sorted
- CLICK: Sort Ascending button (⬆),

  *or*

- CLICK: Sort Descending button (⬇)

To perform a complex sort using more than one field:

- CHOOSE: Data → Sort,

  *or*

- CLICK: List menu button (List ▾)
- CHOOSE: Sort

→ ## Practice

You will now practice performing single and multikey sort operations. Ensure that no workbooks appear in the application window.

1. Open the data file named EX0820 to display the workbook shown in Figure 8.14. This workbook contains a single worksheet list to store employee information.

**Figure 8.14**

Opening the
EX0820
workbook

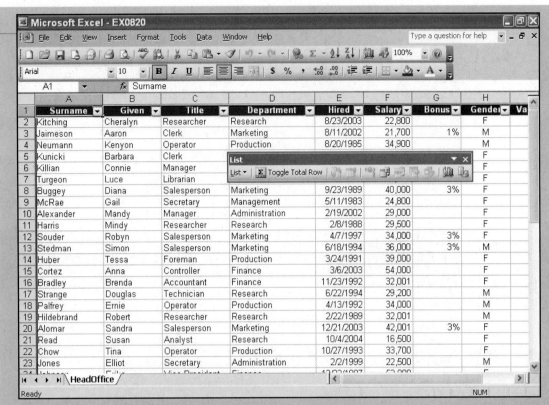

2. Save the workbook as "Personnel" to your personal storage location.

3. To sort the list into alphabetical order by surname:
   CLICK: Surname's (A1) AutoFilter drop-down list arrow (▾)
   A drop-down menu appears, as shown here.

4. To view the sort options, you may need to scroll the drop-down list upward by clicking its up arrow (▲), as shown here. Notice that the top two
   menu options are "Sort Ascending" and "Sort Descending."

5. CLICK: Sort Ascending in the AutoFilter drop-down list box
   Notice that the rows of data, called *records,* have been sorted into ascending order by employee surname.

6. Now let's group together the highest-paid individuals in the company us-
   ing the Standard toolbar. Do the following:
   SELECT: cell F2
   CLICK: Sort Descending button (⧩)
   The top two salaried positions, displayed at the top of the list, are the
   Vice President (Eric Akelaitis) and President (Bob Klimek).

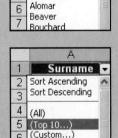

7. If you need to perform a more advanced sort operation, you can specify a multikey sort operation using the Sort dialog box. To illustrate, ensure that the cell pointer appears in the active
   worksheet list (i.e., cell F2) and then:
   CHOOSE: Data ➔ Sort
   The Sort dialog box appears, as shown in Figure 8.15.

**Figure 8.15**

Sort dialog box

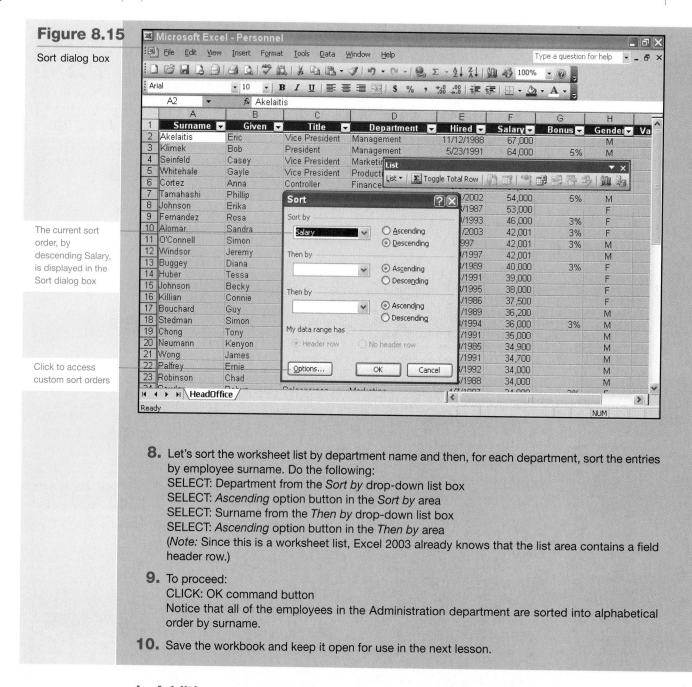

The current sort order, by descending Salary, is displayed in the Sort dialog box

Click to access custom sort orders

8. Let's sort the worksheet list by department name and then, for each department, sort the entries by employee surname. Do the following:
   SELECT: Department from the *Sort by* drop-down list box
   SELECT: *Ascending* option button in the *Sort by* area
   SELECT: Surname from the *Then by* drop-down list box
   SELECT: *Ascending* option button in the *Then by* area
   (*Note:* Since this is a worksheet list, Excel 2003 already knows that the list area contains a field header row.)

9. To proceed:
   CLICK: OK command button
   Notice that all of the employees in the Administration department are sorted into alphabetical order by surname.

10. Save the workbook and keep it open for use in the next lesson.

## *In Addition* SORTING COLUMNS IN A WORKSHEET LIST

You can use the following dialog box to rearrange the field or column order in a worksheet list. For example, you may want to rearrange the field header row so that the field names progress alphabetically from left to right. To do so, choose the Data → Sort command and then click the Options command button to display the dialog box shown here. In the *Orientation* area, select the *Sort left to right* option button, and then close the Sort Options dialog box. Choose row 1 from the *Sort by* drop-down list box and proceed with the sort operation.

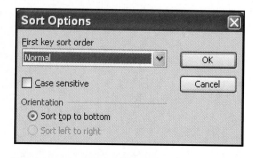

## *In Addition* USING CUSTOM SORT ORDERS

By default, Excel 2003 sorts a range into alphanumeric (A-Z; 0-9) order. You can also choose to sort a list using Excel 2003's custom sort orders. For instance, you can arrange a list into calendar order according to the weekday (Sun, Mon, Tue, . . .) or the month (Jan, Feb, Mar, . . .). To access these sort orders, choose the Data → Sort command and then click the Options command button. To create a custom list for yourself, choose Tools → Options and click on the *Custom Lists* tab, as shown below. After creating your own custom lists, apply the various sort orders to the data stored in your worksheets.

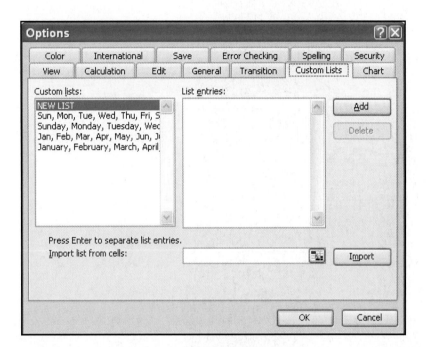

### 8.2.2  Filtering a List

→ **Feature**

A **filter** is a technique that limits the display of records in a worksheet list using a simple matching criterion. Similar to a pasta strainer that lets water through but not the pasta, a filter allows only some records to pass through for display. Filtering is an excellent way to find a subset of records to work with. To make the process faster and easier, Excel 2003 attaches the **AutoFilter** drop-down list arrows to each field column in the worksheet list. You can use these arrows to facilitate defining criteria and applying filters.

→ **Method**

To filter the data in a worksheet list:

- CLICK: a cell within the worksheet list in order to make it active
- CLICK: a field column's AutoFilter drop-down list arrow (▾)
- SELECT: a value or a custom filtering option

To toggle the display of the AutoFilter drop-down list arrows:

- CHOOSE: Data → Filter → AutoFilter

To remove the filter and display all records:

- CHOOSE: Data → Filter → Show All

→ **Practice**

You will now practice filtering a worksheet list. Ensure that the "Personnel" workbook is displayed.

**1.** When you first define a worksheet list, Excel 2003 analyzes the contents of each column, compiles a list of unique field values, and attaches a drop-down list arrow to each field name in the field header row. To use these AutoFilter arrows to apply a simple filtering criterion based on the Department column, do the following:
CLICK: Department's (D1) AutoFilter drop-down list arrow (▾)
Your screen should now appear similar to the one shown in Figure 8.16.

**Figure 8.16**

Viewing the filter options for the Department field

AutoFilter drop-down list arrows attach to each field name in the field header row

| | A | B | C | D | E | F | G | H | Va |
|---|---|---|---|---|---|---|---|---|---|
| 1 | Surname ▾ | Given ▾ | Title ▾ | Department ▾ | Hired ▾ | Salary ▾ | Bonus ▾ | Gender ▾ | |
| 2 | Alexander | Mandy | Manager | Sort Ascending | 2/19/2002 | 29,000 | | F | |
| 3 | Beaver | Geoffrey | Clerk | Sort Descending | 7/13/1988 | 19,800 | | M | |
| 4 | Fuller | Tony | Clerk | | 12/26/2002 | 17,500 | | M | |
| 5 | Jones | Elliot | Secretary | (All) | 2/2/1999 | 22,500 | | M | |
| 6 | Kunicki | Barbara | Clerk | (Top 10...) | 11/25/1993 | 17,500 | | F | |
| 7 | Turgeon | Luce | Librarian | (Custom...) | 12/13/2004 | 18,500 | | F | |
| 8 | Weirnicke | Brandi | Clerk | Administration | 4/19/1989 | 22,001 | | F | |
| 9 | Bradley | Brenda | Accountant | Finance | 11/23/1992 | 32,001 | | F | |
| 10 | Cortez | Anna | Controller | Management | 3/6/2003 | 54,000 | | F | |
| | | | | Marketing | | | | | |
| | | | | Production | | | | | |
| 11 | Johnson | Erika | Vice President | Research | 12/23/1987 | 53,000 | | F | |
| | | | | Finance | | | | | |
| 12 | Robinson | Chad | Accountant | Finance | 2/15/1988 | 34,000 | | M | |

Drop-down unique list of AutoFilter options

**2.** To view only those employees in the Marketing department:
SELECT: Marketing from the AutoFilter drop-down list
You can tell that you are now viewing a filtered subset of the list because the row numbers and AutoFilter list arrow both display in blue.

**3.** With the Department filter active, you will now limit the display to only the salespersons. To do so:
CLICK: Title's (C1) AutoFilter drop-down list arrow (▾)
SELECT: Salesperson from the drop-down list
Notice that the AutoFilter drop-down list displays only the unique Titles for personnel in the Marketing department. Your screen should now appear similar to the one shown in Figure 8.17.

**Figure 8.17**

Filtering the worksheet list

When a filter is active, row numbers appear blue

| | A | B | C | D | E | F | G | H | Va |
|---|---|---|---|---|---|---|---|---|---|
| 1 | Surname ▾ | Given ▾ | Title ▾ | Department ▾ | Hired ▾ | Salary ▾ | Bonus ▾ | Gender ▾ | |
| 18 | Alomar | Sandra | Salesperson | Marketing | 12/21/2003 | 42,001 | 3% | F | |
| 19 | Buggey | Diana | Salesperson | Marketing | 9/23/1989 | 40,000 | 3% | F | |
| 20 | Fernandez | Rosa | Salesperson | Marketing | 9/29/1993 | 46,000 | 3% | F | |
| 26 | Souder | Robyn | Salesperson | Marketing | 4/7/1997 | 34,000 | 3% | F | |
| 27 | Stedman | Simon | Salesperson | Marketing | 6/18/1994 | 36,000 | 3% | M | |
| 51 | * | | | | | | | | |
| 52 | | | | | | | | | |
| 53 | | | | | | | | | |

A blue drop-down arrow tells you that a filter has been applied

**4.** To remove the filter and redisplay all of the records:
CHOOSE: Data → Filter → Show All

5. One of the strengths of the AutoFilter command is the ability to customize the filtering options. For instance:
   CLICK: Salary's (F1) AutoFilter drop-down list arrow (▾)
   SELECT: (Top 10...) from the drop-down list
   The Top 10 AutoFilter dialog box appears, as shown below.

6. You can use the Top 10 AutoFilter dialog box to specify the number of items or the percentage of the list that you want displayed. To limit the display results, for example, to the top five salaries:
   SELECT: 5 in the middle spin box of the *Show* area
   CLICK: OK command button
   Notice that six records are displayed, due to a tie occurring at the $54,000 salary level. (*Hint:* You can also apply a sort order to a filtered list in order to rank the matching records.)

7. To remove the filter:
   CLICK: Salary's (F1) AutoFilter drop-down list arrow (▾)
   SELECT: (All) at the top of the drop-down list
   (*Hint:* This method is easier than choosing Data → Filter → Show All when only a single filter criterion has been used.)

8. Let's create a filter to display all the employees hired between 1986 and 1990. To proceed:
   CLICK: Hired's (E1) AutoFilter drop-down list arrow (▾)
   SELECT: (Custom) from the drop-down list
   The Custom AutoFilter dialog box appears.

9. You can use the Custom AutoFilter dialog box to specify ranges of values. To illustrate:
   SELECT: "is greater than or equal to" from the top-left drop-down list box
   PRESS: TAB
   TYPE: 1/1/1986 in the top-right combo box
   SELECT: "is less than or equal to" from the bottom-left drop-down list box
   PRESS: TAB
   TYPE: 12/31/1990 in the bottom-right combo box
   Your screen should now appear similar to that shown in Figure 8.18.

**Figure 8.18**

Custom AutoFilter dialog box

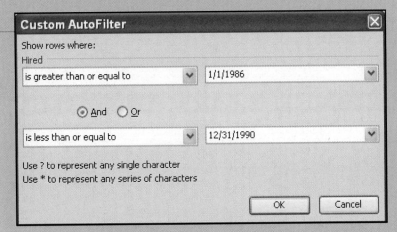

**10.** To apply the filter:
CLICK: OK command button
Only those employees hired between January 1, 1986, and December 31, 1990, are now displayed.

**11.** To sort the list into date order:
CLICK: Hired's (E1) AutoFilter drop-down list arrow (▾)
SELECT: Sort Ascending from the top of the drop-down list
Your screen should now appear similar to the one shown in Figure 8.19.

**Figure 8.19**

Applying a custom filter and sorting the results

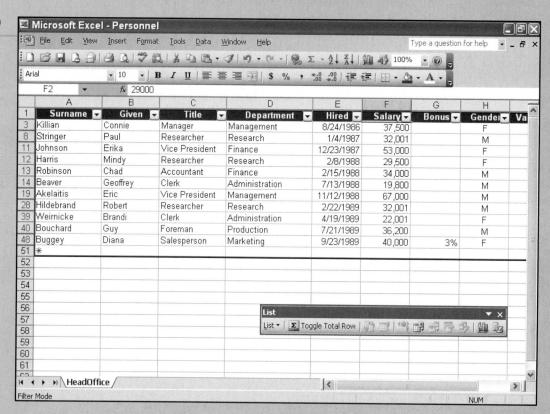

**12.** To remove the filter:
CHOOSE: Data → Filter → Show All

**13.** Save the workbook and keep it open for use in the next lesson.

### 8.2.3 Summarizing a List

→ **Feature**

There are many different ways to summarize the information in a worksheet list. The easiest method is to display results of mathematical or statistical summary functions, such as SUM, AVERAGE, and COUNT, at the bottom (or top) of the worksheet list. To facilitate the display of such results, Excel 2003 provides the Total Row, appearing at the bottom of a list range. The Total Row is specifically designed to make it easy for you to summarize the numerical and non-numerical data in a worksheet list.

→ ## Method

To display the Total Row in a worksheet list:

- CLICK: a cell within the worksheet list in order to make it active
- CLICK: Toggle Total Row button (Σ Toggle Total Row) on the List toolbar

To enter a summary calculation for a worksheet list:

- CLICK: a cell within the Total Row
- CLICK: drop-down arrow attached to the cell
- SELECT: the desired summary function from the drop-down list

→ ## Practice

In this lesson, you will use the Total Row to insert summary functions for a worksheet list. Ensure that the "Personnel" workbook is displayed.

**1.** To view all of the field columns in the worksheet list at the same time:
SELECT: cell range from A1 to J1
CLICK: drop-down arrow attached to the Zoom button (100% ▼)
SELECT: Selection

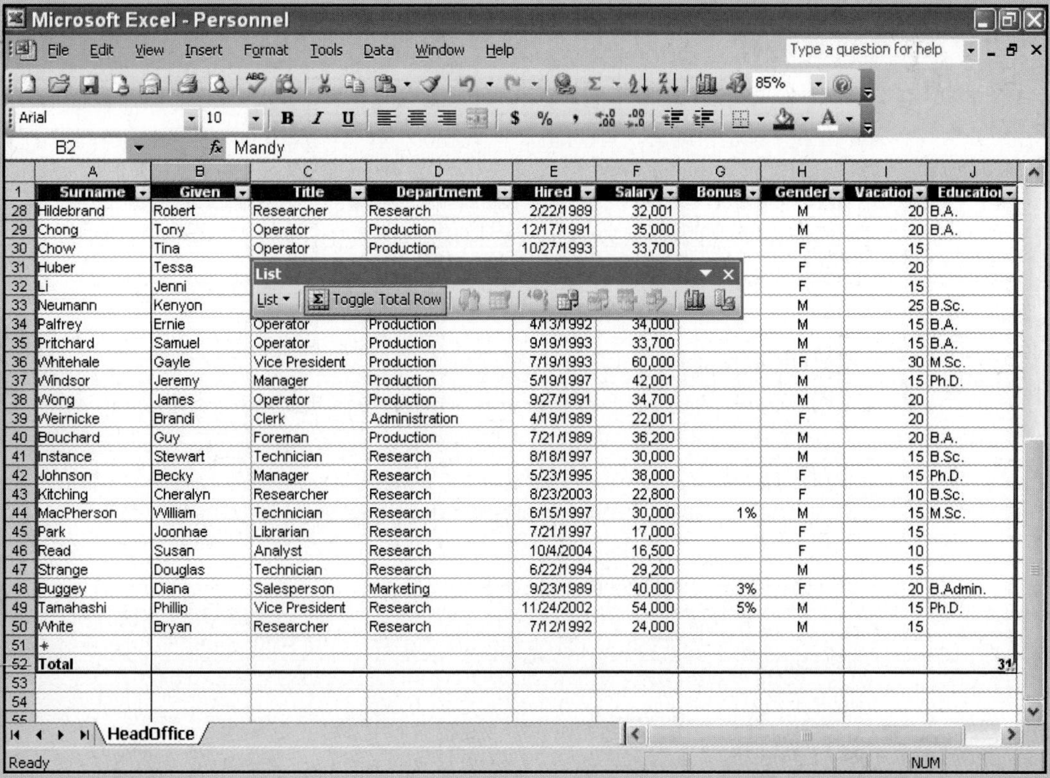

**2.** Now freeze the field header row and first column on the screen:
SELECT: cell B2
CHOOSE: Window → Freeze Panes

**3.** Using the vertical scroll bar, scroll the worksheet window so that the bottom of the list area is visible, as shown in Figure 8.20.

**4.** To display the Total Row in the worksheet list:
CLICK: Toggle Total Row button (Σ Toggle Total Row) on the List toolbar
Your screen should now appear similar to the one shown in Figure 8.20.

**Figure 8.20**

Displaying the Total Row in a worksheet list

A new row is added to the worksheet list range

**5.** To calculate the total value of salaries paid by this company:
SELECT: cell F52
A drop-down arrow should now appear attached to the active cell.

**6.** You may now select the appropriate summary function:
CLICK: drop-down arrow attached to the cell to display the menu shown here

**7.** SELECT: Sum from the drop-down list menu
The value 1,672,809 appears in cell F52.

**8.** Now display the average vacation entitlement:
CLICK: cell I52
Notice that the number 31 appears to the right in column J. Excel 2003 enters a summary function into the rightmost column of a worksheet list automatically. In this case, the COUNT function is used to count the nonblank cells in this column.

**9.** With the cell pointer in cell I52:
CLICK: drop-down arrow attached to the cell
Your screen should appear similar to that shown in Figure 8.21.

**Figure 8.21**

Displaying the drop-down list menu for cell I52

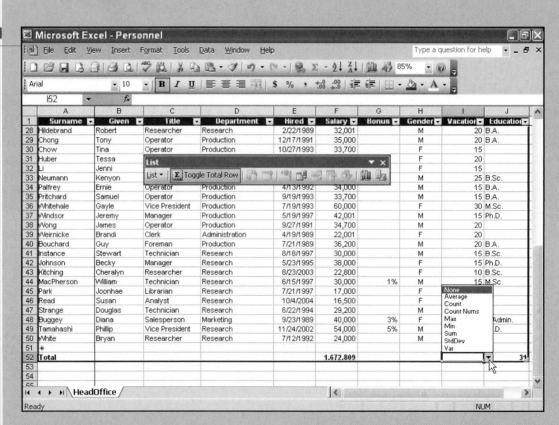

**10.** SELECT: Average from the drop-down list menu
The value 17.959184 appears in the worksheet.

**11.** To toggle the Total Row off so it no longer displays:
CLICK: Toggle Total Row button ( Σ Toggle Total Row ) on the List toolbar
The Total Row disappears and the cell pointer is now located outside of the worksheet list area in cell I52. (*Note:* If you toggle the Total Row back on, the summary functions that you have already selected will display once again.)

**12.** Save the workbook and keep it open for use in the next lesson.

### 8.2.4 Printing a List

→ ## Feature

Once you have added, modified, sorted, filtered, and otherwise manipulated the data in a worksheet list, you can prepare it for hardcopy (paper-based) presentation. Using the Print and Page Setup dialog boxes, you can insert a running header and footer, set print titles to appear at the top of each page, and send the list to the printer. You can also use Page Break Preview mode to adjust where page breaks occur in the print area. You can use the Print dialog box to print a range selection, worksheet list, the active worksheet, or the entire workbook.

→ ## Method

To print a worksheet list:

• CHOOSE: File ➜ Page Setup to adjust the print options

• CHOOSE: View ➜ Page Break Preview to adjust page breaks

• CHOOSE: File ➜ Print Preview to view the list on screen

• CHOOSE: File ➜ Print to send the results to the printer

→ ## Practice

In this lesson, you will practice setting page setup options and printing a worksheet list. Ensure that you've completed the previous lesson and the "Personnel" workbook is displayed.

**1.** Before printing the worksheet list, let's sort and then format the contents. Do the following:
SELECT: cell A2
CLICK: Sort Ascending button (🔽)

**2.** To make the list easier to read, increase the row height:
PRESS: CTRL +* to select the active list area
CHOOSE: Format ➜ Row ➜ Height
TYPE: 18
CLICK: OK command button

**3.** You can now apply an AutoFormat style without changing the previously set row height. Do the following:
CHOOSE: Format ➜ AutoFormat
SELECT: List 2 option
CLICK: Options command button
SELECT: *Width/Height* check box so that no check mark appears
CLICK: OK command button

**4.** CLICK: cell A1 to cancel the selection
Your worksheet should now appear similar to the one shown in Figure 8.22.

Figure 8.22

Formatting the
worksheet list

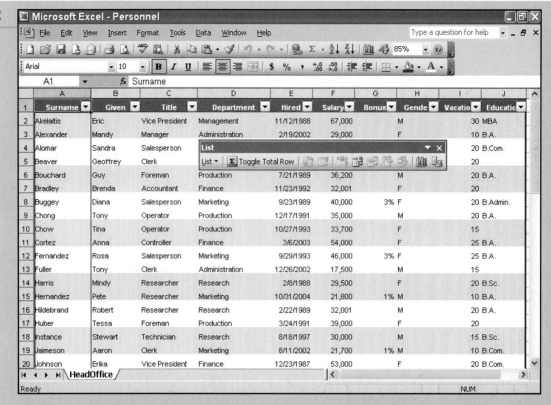

**5.** Now let's specify a landscape orientation for printing the list:
CHOOSE: File → Page Setup
CLICK: *Page* tab, if it is not already selected
SELECT: *Landscape* option button in the *Orientation* area

**6.** With the Page Setup dialog box displayed, let's select a predefined header and footer for the
report:
CLICK: *Header/Footer* tab
SELECT: HeadOffice from the *Header* drop-down list box
SELECT: Page 1 of ? from the *Footer* drop-down list box

**7.** Now specify that the field header row (row 1) should appear at the top of each printed page and
below the header:
CLICK: *Sheet* tab
CLICK: in the *Rows to repeat at top* text box in the *Print Titles* area
TYPE: 1:1

**8.** To preview the worksheet:
CLICK: Print Preview command button
Your screen should now appear similar to the one shown in Figure 8.23.

**Figure 8.23**

Previewing the worksheet list

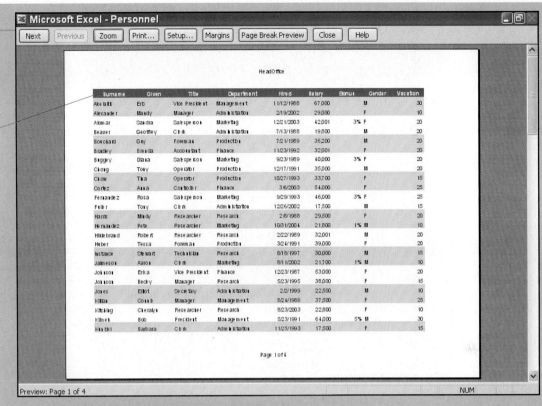

The field header row will appear at the top of each page, as specified in the *Print titles* area of the Page Setup dialog box

**9.** On your own, click the Next, Previous, and Zoom command buttons to view the multiple pages in the worksheet preview.

**10.** To proceed:
CLICK: Print command button to display the Print dialog box
SELECT: *List* option button in the *Print what* area
The Print dialog box should now appear similar to the one shown in Figure 8.24.

**Figure 8.24**

Printing the active worksheet list

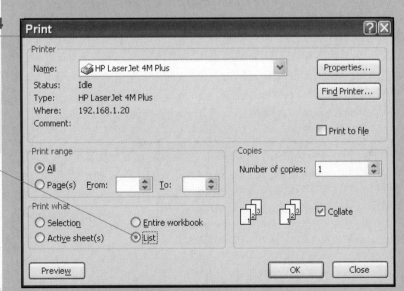

Select the *List* option button to print the active worksheet list. You can also use this area to print just the range selection, the active sheet, or the entire workbook.

**11.** If you have a printer connected to your computer:
CLICK: OK command button
(*Note:* If you do not have a printer, click the Close command button.)

**12.** Save the workbook, and keep it open for use in the next lesson.

### 8.2.5 Converting Workbooks to Different File Formats

→ **Feature**

Consider the numerous types of software programs on the market today, including Quicken for personal finance and SPSS for statistical analysis. Although many software programs require proprietary data formats, most will include the ability to import data from basic data structures. Excel 2003 enables you to save worksheet data into a variety of different formats in order to maximize transportability. For example, you may find that your worksheet list is becoming too large for Excel 2003 and you want to convert it for use in a database management program. One method is to use a "go-between" data format that acts as a common or intermediary file. If you know that both programs recognize a CSV (comma delimited) text format, you can facilitate the data transfer by converting the worksheet data to this file format prior to importing the data into the database management program. This feature is especially applicable to working with Excel 2003 worksheet lists.

→ **Method**

To convert a worksheet list into a normal range:

• CLICK: List menu button (List ▾) on the List toolbar,

   *or*

• CHOOSE: Data → List

• CHOOSE: Convert to Range

To convert worksheet data to a different file format:

• CHOOSE: File → Save As

• SELECT: a data format from the *Save as type* drop-down list box

• CLICK: Save command button

→ **Practice**

You now practice saving a worksheet's data to different file formats. Ensure that the "Personnel" workbook is displayed.

**1.** Although not necessary for saving your worksheet list into a different file format, you may find the need to remove Excel 2003's list functionality from a worksheet range. To do so, ensure that the cell pointer appears within the list area and then:
CLICK: List menu button (List ▾) on the List toolbar
CHOOSE: Convert to Range
The following dialog box is presented to you.

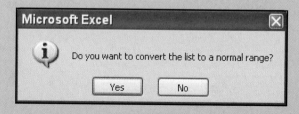

**2.** CLICK: Yes command button to remove the list functionality
Notice that the AutoFilter drop-down arrows are removed from the field header row and that the List toolbar is no longer displayed.

**3.** To convert the data within this worksheet to a different file format:
CHOOSE: File → Save As
Your screen should now appear similar to that shown in Figure 8.25.

**Figure 8.25**

Save As dialog box

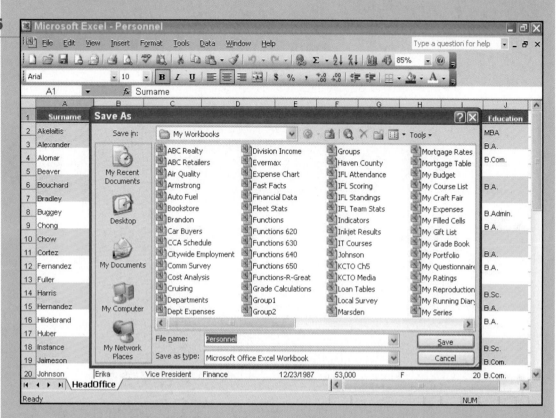

**4.** To display the different file formats that are available:
CLICK: down arrow for the *Save as type* drop-down list box
The list menu shown here is displayed. Notice the number of different formats that you can use to convert your data.

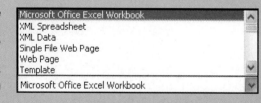

**5.** On your own, scroll through the list of available formats by clicking the scroll up ( ⌃ ) and scroll down buttons ( ⌄ ).

**6.** In the *Save as type* drop-down list box:
SELECT: CSV (Comma delimited)

**7.** CLICK: Save command button to proceed
An informational dialog box appears, as shown below.

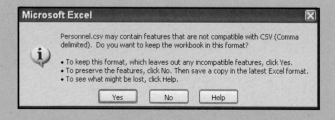

**8.** Since you already saved the workbook in Excel's 2003 format at the end of the previous lesson, let's proceed with converting the data:
CLICK: Yes command button
(*Note:* The original workbook disk file is not modified when you convert the workbook to a different file format.)

**9.** Close the workbook's window by clicking its Close button (☒). If asked to save the changes, click the Yes command button(s) until no object appears in the Excel 2003 application window.

**10.** Let's use the Windows Notepad application to view the workbook's new CSV data file format. Do the following:
CLICK: 🏁 *start* on the taskbar
CHOOSE: All Programs → Accessories → Notepad

**11.** In Notepad, use the File → Open command to display the Open dialog box. Then click the down arrow beside the *Files of type* drop-down list box in order to display all of the files.

**12.** Locate the "Personnel.csv" text file in your personal storage location.

**13.** To open the CSV (comma delimited) text file, double-click the name appearing in the list area. (*Hint:* If you cannot tell which "Personnel" file to double-click, rest the mouse pointer over each file name in the Open dialog box and read its ScreenTip.) Your screen should appear similar to the one shown in Figure 8.26.

**Figure 8.26**

Displaying a CSV (comma delimited) text file using Notepad

**14.** After reviewing the data file, close the Notepad application window by clicking its Close button (☒). You may now proceed to the next module.

## *In Addition* PUBLISHING A LIST TO A SHAREPOINT SITE

You can publish or upload a worksheet list to a SharePoint Web site in order to share data with other users. To do so, choose the Publish List command from the List menu button (List ▾) or from the Data → List command. During the uploading process, the worksheet list is converted into a SharePoint custom list. At this point, authorized users can view and maintain the data by editing and updating the online list. Excel 2003 also allows you to synchronize changes between your original worksheet list and the online SharePoint custom list. Online lists are especially important for people who work frequently in teams and need to share data amongst their workgroup.

**8.2**   How do you filter a worksheet list to display only the top 10 percent of values appearing in a field?

# 8.3 Analyzing Lists

Analyzing a list entails querying, extracting, and summarizing data. These tasks are facilitated using Excel 2003's advanced filtering techniques. In this module you learn to limit the display of records using multiple criteria, extract records to a different location in a worksheet, and summarize statistical data using a variety of database and list functions.

### 8.3.1 Querying Lists and Extracting Data

## → Feature

The AutoFilter feature enables you to filter a list by a maximum of two conditions per field. If you require additional conditions or if you want to analyze a list using Excel 2003's database functions, you must define an *advanced filter.* An **advanced criteria filter** is simply a worksheet range, usually appearing above the field header row, that provides a few blank rows for inputting search conditions. If you place conditions on the same row in the **criteria range,** the criteria are evaluated using a logical AND to combine the conditions. If your conditions appear on separate rows, the criteria are evaluated using a logical OR between the conditions. You can use an advanced criteria filter to filter a list in-place or extract records to a new location on the same worksheet.

## → Method

To set up an advanced criteria filter:

* Insert three or four blank rows above the active worksheet list.

* Copy the field header row to the top row in the new criteria range.

* Input your search conditions on the rows immediately below the criteria header row.

* CHOOSE: Data → Filter → Advanced Filter

* Specify whether to filter the list in-place or extract records to another worksheet location. Then select the required cell ranges.

* CLICK: OK command button

→ **Practice**

You will now establish a criteria range, specify search conditions, and filter the worksheet list using an advanced criteria filter. Ensure that no workbooks appear in the application window.

**1.** Open the data file named EX0830 to display the workbook shown in Figure 8.27. This workbook contains a list of media products advertised in a library resource catalog. However, the worksheet list has not yet been defined using the Create List command.

**Figure 8.27**

Opening the
EX0830
workbook

Field Header Row

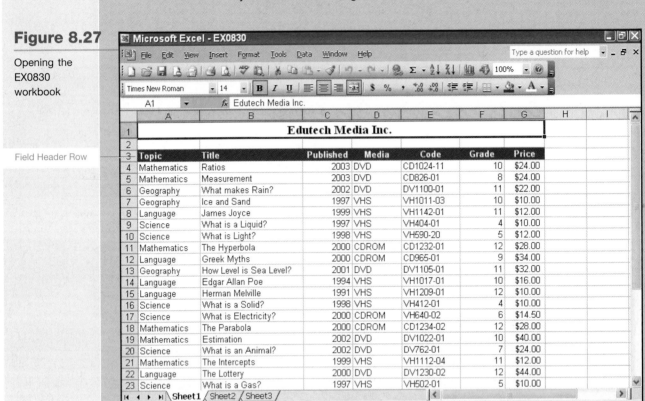

**2.** Save the workbook as "Edutech" to your personal storage location.

**3.** You must now insert four rows above the field header row. These new rows will be used for entering the criteria range, including the criteria header row and the criteria area. To begin:
SELECT: rows 3 through 6
(*Hint:* This instruction tells you to click on row 3 in the frame area and then drag the mouse pointer down to row 6. When done correctly, the cells in all four rows appear highlighted.)

**4.** To complete the insertion of new rows:
CHOOSE: Insert → Rows
(*Note:* Rows 3 to 6 remain selected after inserting the new rows.)

**5.** Next, copy the field header row from row 7 into the top row of the new criteria range. To do so:
SELECT: cell range from A7 to G7
CLICK: Copy button (⧉)
SELECT: cell A2
CLICK: Paste button (⧉▾)

**6.** To complete the copy-and-paste procedure:
PRESS: ESC to remove the bounding outline
PRESS: CTRL + HOME to move to cell A1

**7.** Let's adjust the screen view:
CLICK: down arrow attached to the Zoom button ( 100% ▾ )
SELECT: Selection in the drop-down menu
Your screen should now appear similar to the one shown in Figure 8.28.

**Figure 8.28**

Creating a criteria range

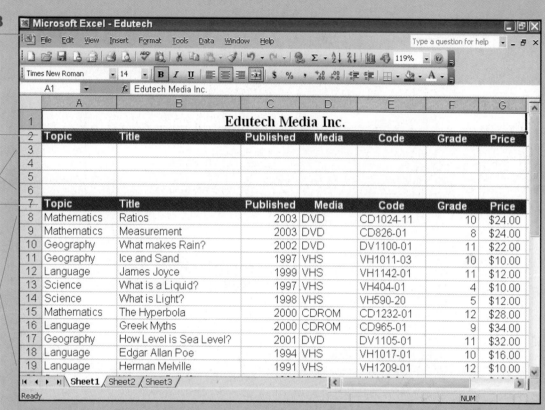

Criteria Header Row

Criteria Area

Field Header Row

List Area

**8.** Let's use the new criteria range to apply a filter for only the DVD media product. Do the following:
SELECT: cell D3
TYPE: **DVD**
PRESS: ENTER

**9.** To display the Advanced Filter dialog box:
SELECT: cell D8 (or any cell within the active list area)
CHOOSE: Data → Filter → Advanced Filter
Because a cell within the list area was selected prior to issuing the command, the *List range* text box contains the correct cell area in the Advanced Filter dialog box (Figure 8.29).

**Figure 8.29**

Advanced Filter
dialog box

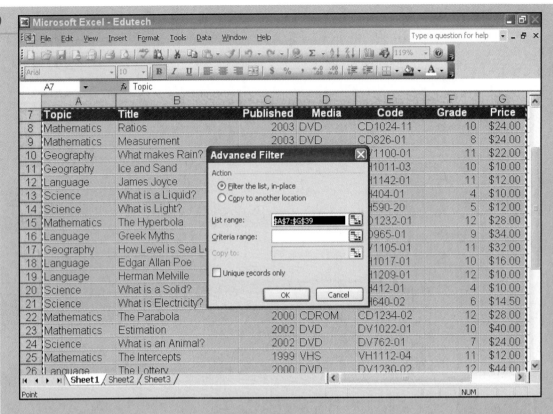

10. You can perform two types of operations using the Advanced Filter dialog box: filter the list in-place or copy records to a new location. For this step, ensure that the *Filter the list, in-place* option button is selected before proceeding.

11. To complete the filter specification:
CLICK: once in the *Criteria range* text box
CLICK: Collapse Dialog button ( ![icon] ) for the *Criteria range* text box
SELECT: cell range from A2 to G3
The dialog box should now appear as shown below.

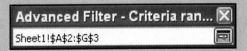

12. To return to the full-sized dialog box:
CLICK: Expand Dialog button ( ![icon] )
The entry, Sheet1!$A$2:$G$3, now appears in the text box.

13. To apply the filter:
CLICK: OK command button
Only records with the media type "DVD" now appear in the list area. Also notice that the row numbers are blue, which informs you that a filter has been applied to the list area.

14. To perform a more complex filtering operation, let's display only the DVD and CDROM media published after 2001. To begin:
SELECT: cell C3
TYPE: >2001
SELECT: cell C4
TYPE: >2001
SELECT: cell D4
TYPE: CDROM
PRESS: ENTER

Your screen should now appear similar to the one shown in Figure 8.30. Notice that ">2001" is entered on both rows of the criteria range to specify an AND condition for joining the media type and year published. Placing criteria on both rows causes an OR condition to result. In mathematical terms, the criteria may be interpreted as "(Media="DVD" AND Published>2001) OR (Media="CDROM" AND Published>2001)."

**Figure 8.30**

Entering complex search criteria

| | A | B | C | D | E | F | G |
|---|---|---|---|---|---|---|---|
| 1 | | | Edutech Media Inc. | | | | |
| 2 | Topic | Title | Published | Media | Code | Grade | Price |
| 3 | | | >2001 | DVD | | | |
| 4 | | | >2001 | CDROM | | | |
| 5 | | | | | | | |

**15.** To prepare the filter specification, ensure that the cell pointer is in the worksheet list (any cell in the range from A7 to G39), and then do the following:
CHOOSE: Data → Filter → Advanced Filter

**16.** You must now edit the range specified in the *Criteria range* text box to include the second row of criteria. Do the following:
CLICK: I-beam mouse pointer in the *Criteria range* text box and to the right of the existing entry
PRESS: **BACKSPACE**
TYPE: 4
The *Criteria range* text box should now read "$A$2:$G$4".

**17.** To apply the new filter:
CLICK: OK command button
Your screen should now appear similar to the one shown in Figure 8.31. (*Hint:* To extract data, select the *Copy to another location* option button in the Advanced Filter dialog box, and then specify the destination range on the same worksheet using the *Copy to* text box.)

**Figure 8.31**

Filtering a worksheet list

Complex Criteria using logical AND (criteria on same row but in different fields) and logical OR (criteria in different rows)

Row numbers appear in blue to signify that the list area is filtered

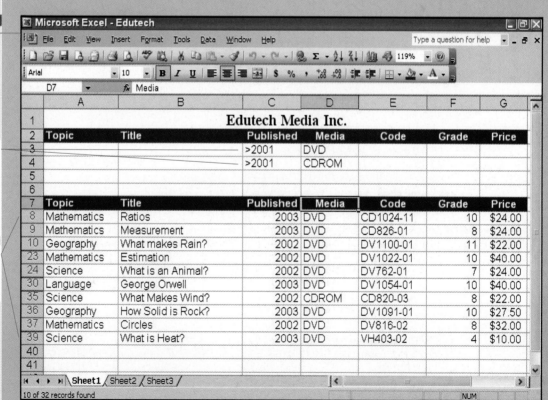

EX 468 Microsoft Office Excel 2003

**18.** To remove the filter:
CHOOSE: Data → Filter → Show All

**19.** Now let's remove the existing criteria:
SELECT: cell range from C3 to D4
PRESS: DELETE
PRESS: CTRL + HOME

**20.** Save the workbook and keep it open for use in the next lesson.

## *In Addition* APPLYING A DATE RANGE FILTER

You can apply a filter to display records published between two specific dates. To do so, place two "Date" columns in the criteria header row in order to use an AND condition. (*Hint:* The quickest way to accomplish this is to copy the desired column header and then paste it next to the rightmost field name.) Under the first column header, place the "greater than" condition (for example, >2002). Then, under the second column header and on the same row, place the "less than" condition (for example, <2004). Only those records appearing in the range are returned for display.

### 8.3.2 Using Database And List Functions

→ **Feature**

Excel 2003's database and list functions let you perform mathematical and statistical calculations, such as summing or averaging values, on selected records in a list. In other words, you can restrict the input values for a function to only those records that meet a search condition or criterion. For example, you could use database functions to display the total, average, maximum, and minimum invoice amounts for records entered during the month of January. Because most database functions begin with the letter "D," they are sometimes called *dFunctions*. Each of these functions has the same three arguments: *database* (list range), *field* (cell address or field column label in quotes), and *criteria* (criteria range).

→ **Method**

- =DAVERAGE(*list_range,field_name,criteria_range*)
- =DCOUNT(*list_range,field_name,criteria_range*)
- =DCOUNTA(*list_range,field_name,criteria_range*)
- =DMAX(*list_range,field_name,criteria_range*)
- =DMIN(*list_range,field_name,criteria_range*)
- =DSUM(*list_range,field_name,criteria_range*)

→ **Practice**

You will now practice entering some commonly used database functions. Ensure that you've completed the previous lesson and that the "Edutech" workbook is displayed.

**1.** Rather than remembering cell addresses, you will name the worksheet ranges that will be used throughout this lesson. To begin, let's name a criteria range for a single row criteria entry:
SELECT: cell range from A2 to G3
CLICK: in the Name box
TYPE: **Crit1**
PRESS: ENTER
Notice that you include the criteria header row in the range selection.

2. Now, name a criteria range for a criterion requiring two rows:
   SELECT: cell range from A2 to G4
   CLICK: in the Name box
   TYPE: **Crit2**
   PRESS: ENTER
   (*Hint:* Keep your range names as short as possible to make them easier to use and remember.)

3. To select the database list area:
   CLICK: cell A7
   PRESS: CTRL +* (which can also be written as CTRL + SHIFT +8)
   (*Note:* Once the range is selected, release the CTRL and SHIFT keys.)

4. To name the worksheet list's range:
   CLICK: in the Name box
   TYPE: **List**
   PRESS: ENTER
   Your screen should now appear similar to the one shown in Figure 8.32.

**Figure 8.32**

Selecting and naming the worksheet list

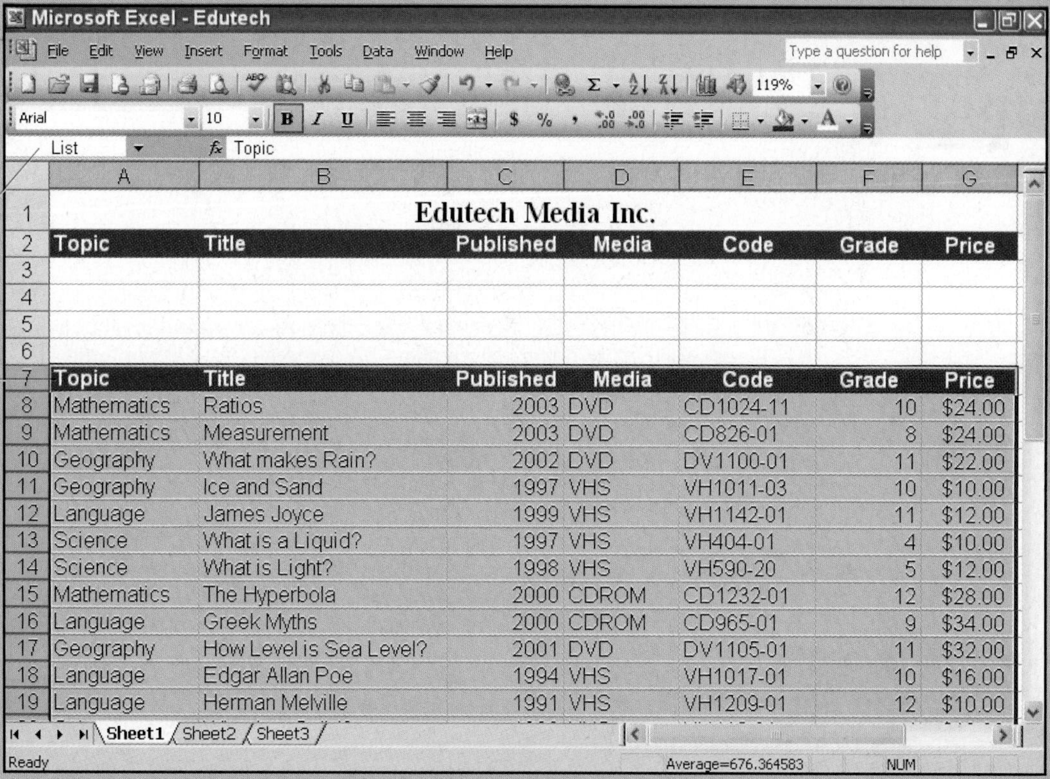

The worksheet list's range name, "List," should now appear in the Name box

The entire list range from A7 to G39 is selected prior to clicking in the Name box

5. PRESS: CTRL + HOME to return to the top of the worksheet

6. To display a summary of commonly used database functions:
   CLICK: *Sheet2* tab

7. On your own, set the zoom factor to 120% using the Zoom button ( 100% ). Your screen should appear similar to the one shown in Figure 8.33.

**Figure 8.33**

Using database functions

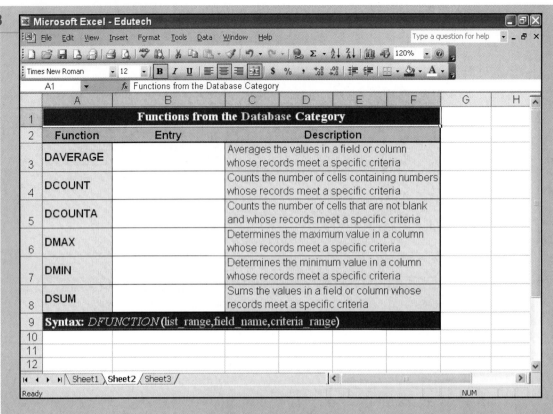

**8.** Without any criteria specified in the criteria range, any database functions that you now enter on *Sheet2* will use the entire list of values. To demonstrate, calculate the average selling price of all products in the list:
SELECT: cell B3
TYPE: =daverage(List, "Price",Crit1)
PRESS: [ENTER]
The answer, $20.59, appears in the cell. (*Note:* Field names require surrounding quotes, but range names do not.)

**9.** To find the average selling price for CDROMs, let's enter a criterion into the worksheet's criteria range. Do the following:
CLICK: *Sheet1* tab
SELECT: cell D3
TYPE: CDROM
PRESS: [ENTER]

**10.** Now return to the summary worksheet to see the results:
CLICK: *Sheet2* tab
The answer, $22.14, appears in cell B3. Notice how the function updates the result based on the contents of the criteria range.

**11.** All of your remaining calculations will now use the CDROM criterion. To count, for example, the number of records with CDROM for a media type, do the following:
SELECT: cell B5
TYPE: =dcounta(List,"Media",Crit1)
PRESS: [ENTER]
The answer, 7, appears. (*Hint:* DCOUNTA is used for counting non-numeric fields, such as Media, while DCOUNT is used to count numeric entries.)

**12.** On your own, enter dFunctions for calculating the highest and lowest "Grade" level suitable for the CDROM products. Then, using the DSUM function, calculate the sum value of the "Price" column and place the result into cell B8. Your screen should now appear similar to the one shown in Figure 8.34.

**Figure 8.34**

Entering database functions for the "Edutech" workbook

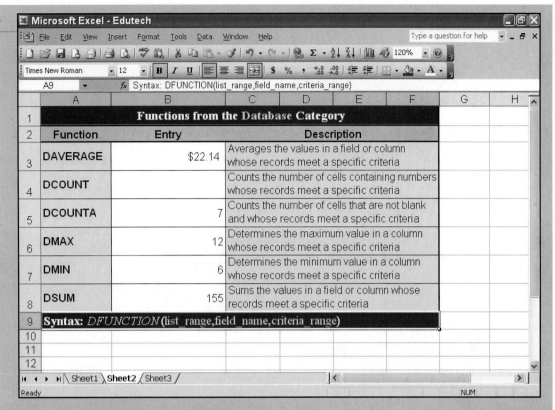

13. Now the real power of database functions will become apparent. Let's enter a new search condition into the criteria range. Do the following to remove the old criterion:
    CLICK: *Sheet1* tab
    SELECT: cell D3
    PRESS: DELETE

14. Let's summarize the records in the list that begin with the word "What" in the product title. Do the following:
    SELECT: cell B3
    TYPE: What
    PRESS: ENTER

15. Now view the results:
    CLICK: *Sheet2* tab
    There are twelve matching titles for grades 4 through 11, with an average price of $16.42.

16. On your own, modify the DMAX and DMIN functions to find the oldest and most recent publication years.

17. Now enter some new search conditions into the criteria range and then view the results.

18. Save the workbook and keep it open for use in the next lesson.

## 8.3.3 Using COUNTIF and SUMIF Functions

→ ## Feature

There are two additional functions that you may find useful in analyzing and summarizing list information: COUNTIF and SUMIF. Without using a criteria range, COUNTIF and SUMIF let you apply criteria to determine whether to include cells in a calculation. You use these functions when you need to limit calculations based on specific conditions, but you don't want to set up an advanced criteria filter.

→ **Method**

- =COUNTIF(*field_range,criteria*)
- =SUMIF(*field_range,criteria,sum_range*)

→ **Practice**

In this lesson, you will practice entering the COUNTIF and SUMIF functions. Ensure that you've completed the previous lesson and that the "Edutech" workbook is displayed.

**1.** Before proceeding, click the *Sheet1* tab in the workbook and delete any criterion values appearing in the criteria range (cells A3 to G4).

**2.** To view a summary worksheet for the COUNTIF and SUMIF functions:
CLICK: *Sheet3* tab

**3.** On your own, set the zoom factor to 120% using the Zoom button (100% ). Your screen should appear similar to the one shown in Figure 8.35.

**Figure 8.35**

Using COUNTIF and SUMIF

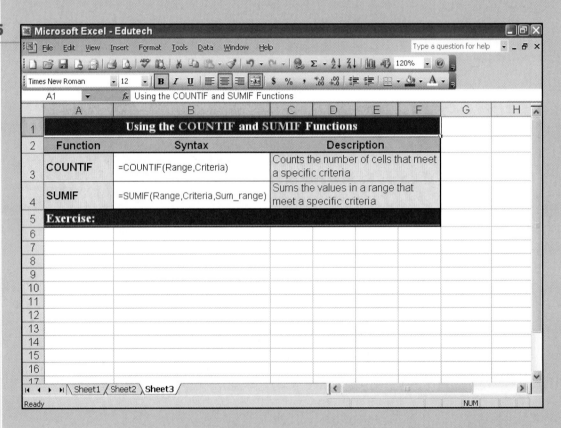

**4.** You will use the Function Arguments dialog box to enter the following functions. To begin, let's find out how many VHS media products are listed on the *Sheet1* worksheet list. Do the following:
SELECT: cell A6
TYPE: =countif(
CLICK: Insert Function button (ƒ×) in the Formula bar
The Function Arguments dialog box appears.

**5.** The first argument for COUNTIF requires the range of nonblank cells that you want to evaluate. To select the media column:
CLICK: Collapse Dialog button (🔲) for the *Range* text box
CLICK: *Sheet1* tab
SELECT: cell D8
PRESS: CTRL + SHIFT + ⬇

The dialog box should now appear as shown below. Notice that you do not select the cell containing the column name in the field header row.

**Function Arguments**

Sheet1!D8:D39

6. To return to the full-sized dialog box:
CLICK: Expand Dialog button ([🗔])

7. The second argument requires that you enter a condition to be evaluated against the values in the selected range. Do the following:
PRESS: **TAB** to move to the *Criteria* text box
TYPE: **"VHS"** (including the quotes)
The Function Arguments dialog box now displays the calculated result, as shown in Figure 8.36.

**Figure 8.36**

Function Arguments dialog box for the COUNTIF function

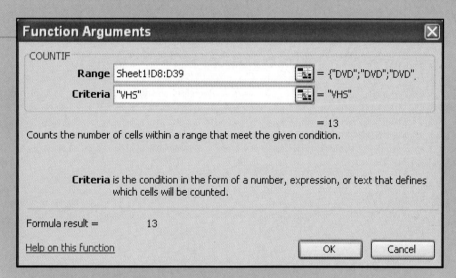

**Function Arguments**

COUNTIF

    **Range**  Sheet1!D8:D39      [🔢]  = {"DVD";"DVD";"DVD"
    **Criteria**  "VHS"            [🔢]  = "VHS"

                                      = 13
Counts the number of cells within a range that meet the given condition.

        **Criteria** is the condition in the form of a number, expression, or text that defines
              which cells will be counted.

Formula result =                13

Help on this function                                    [ OK ]      [ Cancel ]

8. To complete the function entry:
CLICK: OK command button
The answer, 13, appears in the cell.

9. Using the SUMIF function, you will now sum together the values in the "Price" column for products targeted toward students in Grade 10 and higher. Do the following:
SELECT: cell A7
TYPE: **=sumif(**
CLICK: Insert Function button ([*fx*])

10. To input the range you want to evaluate:
CLICK: Dialog Collapse button ([🔢]) for the *Range* text box
CLICK: *Sheet1* tab
SELECT: cell F8
PRESS: **CTRL**+**SHIFT**+**⬇**
The dialog box should now appear as shown below.

**Function Arguments**

Sheet1!F8:F39

**11.** To return to the full-sized dialog box:
CLICK: Expand Dialog button (▣)

**12.** Now let's enter the criterion:
PRESS: ⌨TAB⌨ to move to the *Criteria* text box
TYPE: ">=10"
(*Note:* If you forget to type the quotation marks, Excel puts them in for you.)

**13.** To input the column range to sum:
PRESS: ⌨TAB⌨ to move to the *Sum_range* text box
CLICK: Collapse Dialog button (▦) for the *Sum_range* text box
CLICK: *Sheet1* tab
SELECT: cell G8
PRESS: ⌨CTRL⌨+⌨SHIFT⌨+⌨↓⌨
The dialog box should now appear as shown below.

**Function Arguments**

Sheet1!G8:G39

**14.** To return to the full-sized dialog box:
CLICK: Expand Dialog button (▣)
The Function Arguments dialog box now displays the calculated result, as shown in Figure 8.37.

**Figure 8.37**

Function
Arguments dialog
box for the
SUMIF function

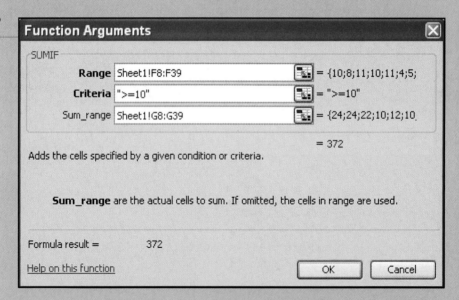

**15.** To complete the function entry:
CLICK: OK command button
The answer, 372, appears in the cell.

**16.** Save the workbook and keep it open for use in the next lesson.

### 8.3.4 Using the Conditional Sum Wizard

→ **Feature**

As demonstrated throughout this module, you can summarize information in a variety of ways. In addition to using database functions, you can calculate grand totals for rows and columns using the Total Row, AutoSum button (Σ▾), and SUM function. You are now introduced to the **Conditional Sum Wizard** add-in program. This wizard leads you step-by-step through the SUMIF function and summing values in a list that meet a specific condition.

→ **Method**

To install the Conditional Sum Wizard:

• CHOOSE: Tools → Add-Ins

To launch the Conditional Sum Wizard:

• CHOOSE: Tools → Conditional Sum

→ **Practice**

You will now practice using the Conditional Sum Wizard add-in program. Ensure that you've completed the previous lesson and that the "Edutech" workbook is displayed.

**1.** Return to the *Sheet1* worksheet and select cell A1.

**2.** The Conditional Sum Wizard is an add-in program that must be installed first before being accessed from the menu. To confirm that the wizard is available:
CHOOSE: Tools → Add-Ins
SELECT: Conditional Sum Wizard, so that a ✓ appears
The Add-Ins dialog box should appear similar to the one shown in Figure 8.38.

**Figure 8.38**

Add-Ins dialog box

3. CLICK: OK command button to proceed
(*Note:* If you have not installed this add-in feature, you will need to insert the original installation media. In this case, a dialog box will appear telling you how to proceed.)

4. To prepare for the wizard:
SELECT: cell A7 (or any other cell in the worksheet list)

5. Now launch the Conditional Sum Wizard:
CHOOSE: Tools → Conditional Sum
The first step of the Conditional Sum Wizard appears, as shown in Figure 8.39.

**Figure 8.39**

Conditional Sum
Wizard: Step 1
of 4

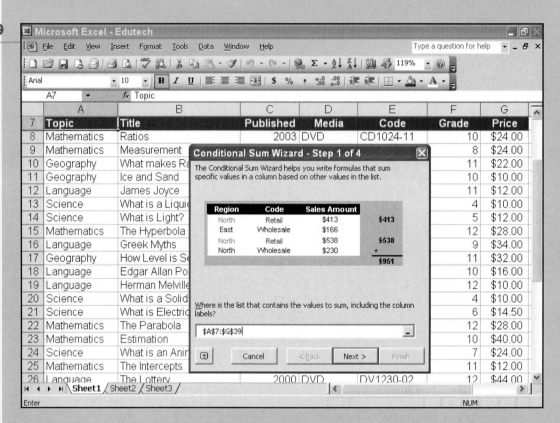

6. In the first step of the wizard, you must confirm the worksheet list range. Do the following:
CLICK: Next command button

7. In Step 2 of the wizard, specify the column that you want to sum and the conditions that must be met in selecting records. To illustrate:
SELECT: Price from the *Column to sum* drop-down list box
SELECT: Published from the *Column* to evaluate drop-down list box
SELECT: = as the *Is* operator
SELECT: 1999 from the *This value* drop-down list box
CLICK: Add Condition command button

8. To specify a second condition that must be met:
SELECT: Media from the *Column* to evaluate drop-down list box
SELECT: = as the *Is* operator
SELECT: VHS from the *This value* drop-down list box
CLICK: Add Condition command button
Your dialog box should appear similar to the one shown in Figure 8.40.

**Figure 8.40**

Conditional Sum
Wizard: Step 2
of 4

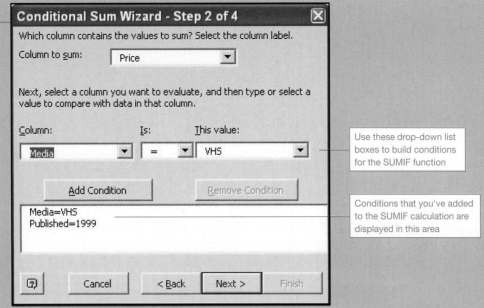

Use these drop-down list boxes to build conditions for the SUMIF function

Conditions that you've added to the SUMIF calculation are displayed in this area

**9.** To continue to the next step:
CLICK: Next command button

**10.** In this step (Figure 8.41), you must determine what to place on your worksheet. If you select only the formula, the specified conditions are **hard-coded** into the formula and the result is displayed. If you choose to also, copy the conditional values you will be able to change the conditions in the future. For this step, let's hard-code the results:
SELECT: *Copy just the formula to a single cell* option button

**Figure 8.41**

Conditional Sum
Wizard: Step 3
of 4

Select this option to insert only the formula result into the worksheet

Select this option to insert the criteria information and the formula result into the worksheet

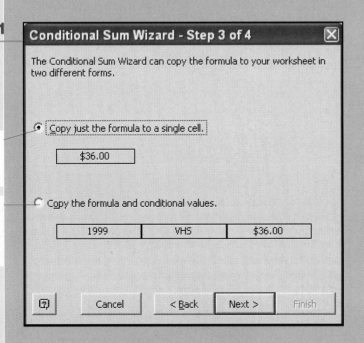

Excel

**11.** To continue to the last step:
CLICK: Next command button

**12.** You must now specify where to place the result. Let's specify an empty cell on the first worksheet. Do the following:
TYPE: **a6**
CLICK: Finish command button

**13.** PRESS: `CTRL`+`HOME` to return to the top of the worksheet
SELECT: cell A6
The answer, $36.00, appears in cell A6 of the worksheet. The Conditional Sum Wizard constructs a special type of formula for cell A6, called an *array formula*. An array formula is contained within curly braces, as shown below. You cannot edit this type of formula using normal keystrokes. To perform another conditional sum, you must launch the wizard again.

*fx* {=SUM(IF($C$8:$C$39=1999,IF($D$8:$D$39="VHS",$G$8:$G$39,0),0))}

**14.** Save and then close the workbook.

**SelfCheck**    **8.3** Using the "Edutech" list, how would you determine the average price of CDROM and DVD media published in 1999?

# 8.4  Using Subtotals and Outlines

This module describes two methods for summarizing data based on the level of worksheet detail displayed. First, creating subtotals in a worksheet automatically groups data, creates an outline, and computes summary calculations. Second, grouping and outlining data manually in a worksheet provides ultimate control over the level of column and row detail that you want to display in reports and charts. These techniques are especially helpful for organizing and summarizing data in large worksheet lists.

### 8.4.1 Creating Subtotals

→ **Feature**

Excel 2003 provides a way to create subtotals in a worksheet list using a single command. Subtotaling describes the process of grouping records together in a worksheet list and inserting new rows for computing averages, sums, minimums, and maximums. Moreover, you use subtotals in a filtered list in order to collapse the worksheet detail and display or chart only the summary information. The Data → Subtotals command creates data groupings based on the sorted column, inserts the appropriate SUBTOTAL function, and outlines the worksheet list automatically.

→ **Method**

To add subtotals to a worksheet automatically:

• Sort the list by the field for which you want to calculate subtotals.

• SELECT: any cell in the worksheet list

• CHOOSE: Data → Subtotals

• Specify the sort field that contains the groupings, the desired summary function to calculate, and the fields you want to subtotal.

→ **Practice**

You will now summarize a worksheet list with subtotal calculations. Ensure that no workbooks appear in the application window.

**1.** Open the data file named EX0840 to display the workbook shown in Figure 8.42. This workbook contains two worksheet lists, named 2003 and 2004, for tracking billable time by date, client, project, and task. Ensure that the 2003 sheet tab is selected before proceeding.

**Figure 8.42**

Opening the EX0840 workbook

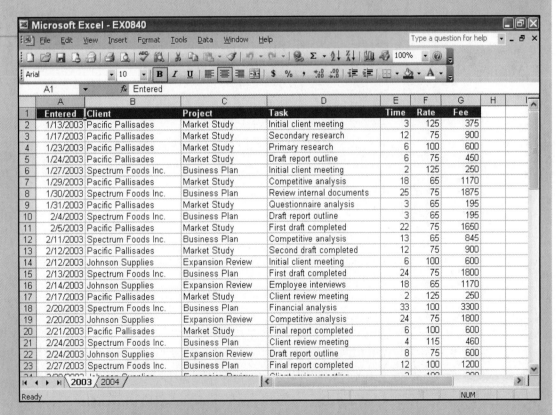

**2.** Save the workbook as "Billable" to your personal storage location.

**3.** The first step in subtotaling a list of data is to sort the data by the field for which you want to create groupings. To calculate subtotals for each client on the 2003 worksheet, for example, do the following:
SELECT: cell B2 (or any other cell in the "Client" field)
CLICK: Sort Ascending button (⥮↓)
The list's records are now sorted alphabetically by client name.

**4.** You will now create a subtotal calculation that sums the "Time" and "Fee" columns for each client. Ensure that cell B2 is selected and then:
CHOOSE: Data → Subtotals
The Subtotal dialog box appears, as shown in Figure 8.43. Notice how the entire list area, including the field header row, is selected.

**Figure 8.43**

Subtotal dialog box

Specify the field to group records by

Select a summary function to use for subtotaling

Select the fields to summarize

Specify whether to print groups on separate pages

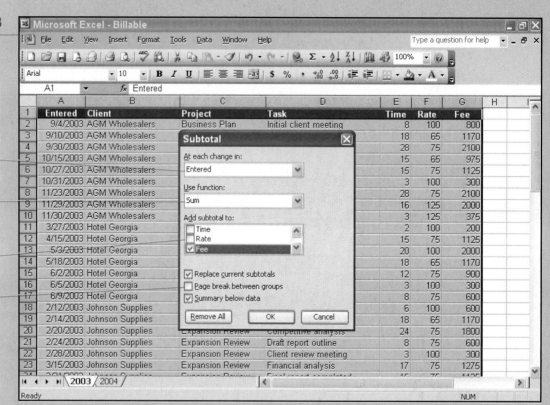

**5.** Make the following selections in the Subtotal dialog box:
SELECT: Client from the *At each change in* drop-down list box
SELECT: Sum from the *Use function* drop-down list box
SELECT: Time check box in the *Add subtotal to* list box
SELECT: Fee check box in the *Add subtotal to* list box, if not already selected
CLICK: OK command button
Subtotals are inserted for each client and the worksheet is outlined, as shown in Figure 8.44. (*Hint:* You may want to change the zoom factor for your window so that columns A through G are visible.)

**Figure 8.44**

Inserting subtotals in a worksheet list

Row-Level Buttons

Inserted subtotal row containing the SUBTOTAL function in cells E11 and G11

| 1 2 3 | | A | B | C | D | E | F | G | H |
|---|---|---|---|---|---|---|---|---|---|
| | 1 | Entered | Client | Project | Task | Time | Rate | Fee | |
| | 2 | 9/4/2003 | AGM Wholesalers | Business Plan | Initial client meeting | 8 | 100 | 800 | |
| | 3 | 9/10/2003 | AGM Wholesalers | Business Plan | Secondary research | 18 | 65 | 1170 | |
| | 4 | 9/30/2003 | AGM Wholesalers | Business Plan | Primary research | 28 | 75 | 2100 | |
| | 5 | 10/15/2003 | AGM Wholesalers | Business Plan | Competitive analysis | 15 | 65 | 975 | |
| | 6 | 10/27/2003 | AGM Wholesalers | Business Plan | First draft completed | 15 | 75 | 1125 | |
| | 7 | 10/31/2003 | AGM Wholesalers | Business Plan | Client review meeting | 3 | 100 | 300 | |
| | 8 | 11/23/2003 | AGM Wholesalers | Business Plan | Financial analysis | 28 | 75 | 2100 | |
| | 9 | 11/29/2003 | AGM Wholesalers | Business Plan | Final report completed | 16 | 125 | 2000 | |
| | 10 | 11/30/2003 | AGM Wholesalers | Business Plan | Final client review | 3 | 125 | 375 | |
| | 11 | | **AGM Wholesalers Total** | | | 134 | | 10945 | |
| | 12 | 3/27/2003 | Hotel Georgia | Valuation | Initial client meeting | 2 | 100 | 200 | |
| | 13 | 4/15/2003 | Hotel Georgia | Valuation | Primary research | 15 | 75 | 1125 | |
| | 14 | 5/3/2003 | Hotel Georgia | Valuation | Management review | 20 | 100 | 2000 | |
| | 15 | 5/18/2003 | Hotel Georgia | Valuation | Financial analysis | 18 | 65 | 1170 | |
| | 16 | 6/2/2003 | Hotel Georgia | Valuation | First draft completed | 12 | 75 | 900 | |
| | 17 | 6/5/2003 | Hotel Georgia | Valuation | Client review meeting | 3 | 100 | 300 | |
| | 18 | 6/9/2003 | Hotel Georgia | Valuation | Final report completed | 8 | 75 | 600 | |
| | 19 | | **Hotel Georgia Total** | | | 78 | | 6295 | |
| | 20 | 2/12/2003 | Johnson Supplies | Expansion Review | Initial client meeting | 6 | 100 | 600 | |
| | 21 | 2/14/2003 | Johnson Supplies | Expansion Review | Employee interviews | 18 | 65 | 1170 | |
| | 22 | 2/20/2003 | Johnson Supplies | Expansion Review | Competitive analysis | 24 | 75 | 1800 | |
| | 23 | 2/24/2003 | Johnson Supplies | Expansion Review | Draft report outline | 8 | 75 | 600 | |

**6.** To collapse the worksheet detail to view only the grand totals:
CLICK: Row-Level 1 button (1) in the top left-hand corner
From this compact summary (Figure 8.45), you can easily determine the total number of hours worked (for all clients) and the resulting billable fees.

**Figure 8.45**

Viewing the worksheet at Row-Level 1

| 1 2 3 | | A | B | C | D | E | F | G | H |
|---|---|---|---|---|---|---|---|---|---|
| | 1 | Entered | Client | Project | Task | Time | Rate | Fee | |
| | 83 | | **Grand Total** | | | 962 | | 83661 | |
| | 84 | | | | | | | | |

Total Hours Worked

Total Billable Fees

**7.** To view a subtotal report by client name:
CLICK: Row-Level 2 button (2) in the top left-hand corner
This summary (Figure 8.46) allows you to quickly determine the billable time and total fees earned for each client. You can even copy, print, and chart the results as they appear in this collapsed summary format.

**Figure 8.46**

Viewing the worksheet at Row-Level 2

| 1 2 3 | | A | B | C | D | E | F | G | H |
|---|---|---|---|---|---|---|---|---|---|
| | 1 | Entered | Client | Project | Task | Time | Rate | Fee | |
| | 11 | | **AGM Wholesalers Total** | | | 134 | | 10945 | |
| | 19 | | **Hotel Georgia Total** | | | 78 | | 6295 | |
| | 27 | | **Johnson Supplies Total** | | | 91 | | 6870 | |
| | 35 | | **La Maison Total** | | | 59 | | 4621 | |
| | 46 | | **Pacific Pallisades Total** | | | 90 | | 7090 | |
| | 54 | | **Red's Restaurant Total** | | | 89 | | 6015 | |
| | 63 | | **Spectrum Foods Inc. Total** | | | 116 | | 9925 | |
| | 82 | | **Stan Wong & Assoc. Total** | | | 305 | | 31900 | |
| | 83 | | **Grand Total** | | | 962 | | 83661 | |
| | 84 | | | | | | | | |

8. To view the detailed records for "La Maison" only:
   CLICK: Show Detail button ( + ) beside row 35 in the frame area

9. To view the cell contents for a subtotal calculation:
   SELECT: cell E35
   The function reads "SUBTOTAL(9,E28:E34)" in the Formula bar. The argument "9" tells the SUBTOTAL function to perform a SUM.

10. Let's create a new subtotals report. To do so, first remove the existing subtotal calculations from the worksheet list:
    CHOOSE: Data → Subtotals
    CLICK: Remove All command button
    The worksheet is returned to its previous state.

11. Now let's calculate the average time, rate, and fee spent on each type of project in the first half of the year. To accomplish this task, you must first prepare the list for creating the subtotals report. To begin:
    SELECT: cell C2
    CLICK: Sort Ascending button ( )

12. To limit the subtotal calculations to the first half of the year, you need to apply a filter to the list. Do the following:
    CHOOSE: Data → Filter → AutoFilter
    CLICK: down arrow attached to the Entered field (cell A1)
    SELECT: (Custom) from the AutoFilter drop-down list

13. In the Custom AutoFilter dialog box:
    SELECT: "is less than" from the top-left drop-down list box
    PRESS: TAB
    TYPE: 7/1/2003 in the top-right combo box
    Your screen should now appear similar to the one shown in Figure 8.47.

**Figure 8.47**

Filtering a list prior to subtotaling

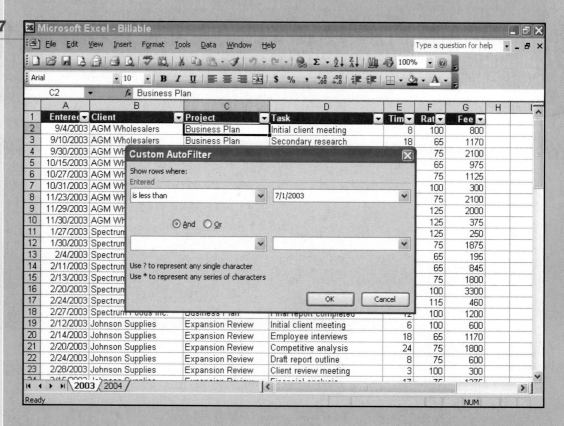

**14.** To apply the filter:
CLICK: OK command button
Only the records entered between 1/1/2003 and 6/30/2003 are now displayed in the worksheet list. (*Note:* This simple filter works for this list since only records entered in 2003 are stored in the worksheet.)

**15.** You may now insert subtotals into the filter list. Do the following:
CHOOSE: Data → Subtotals

**16.** Make the following selections in the Subtotal dialog box:
SELECT: Project from the *At each change in* drop-down list box
SELECT: Average from the *Use function* drop-down list box
SELECT: Time check box in the *Add subtotal to* list box
SELECT: Rate check box in the *Add subtotal to* list box
SELECT: Fee check box in the *Add subtotal to* list box
CLICK: OK command button
Although the subtotal rows are added to the worksheet (Figure 8.48), notice that there are no outline symbols in a filtered list.

**Figure 8.48**

Using subtotals to display averages

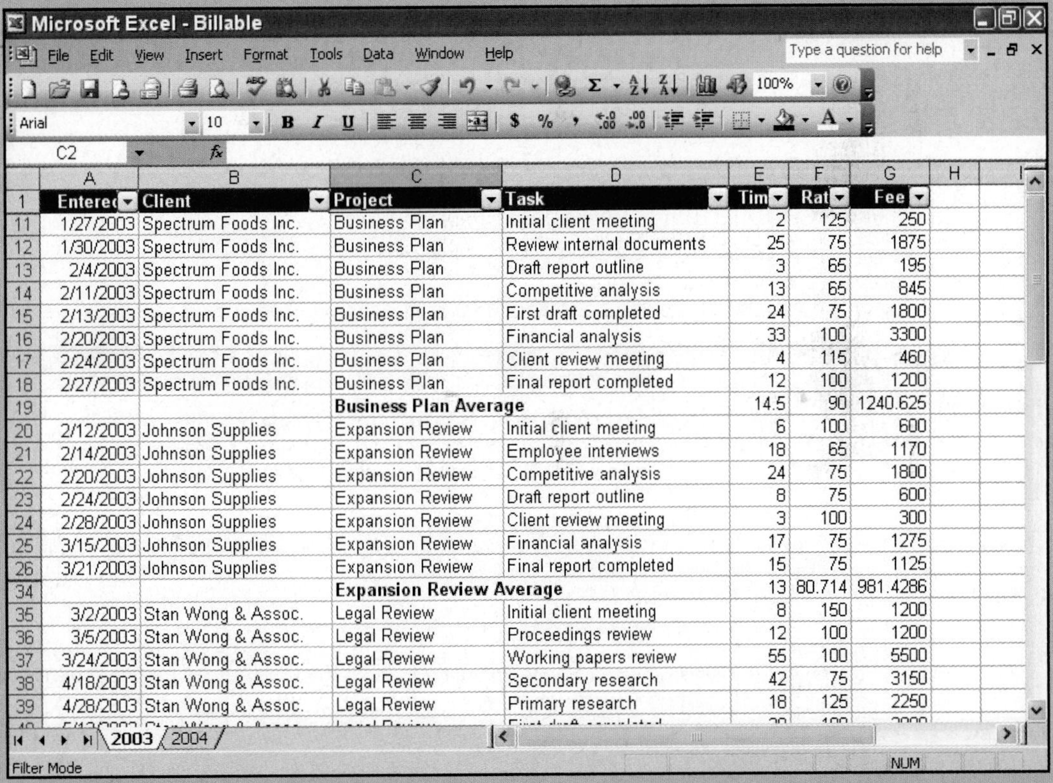


| | A | B | C | D | E | F | G |
|---|---|---|---|---|---|---|---|
| 1 | Entered | Client | Project | Task | Tim | Rat | Fee |
| 11 | 1/27/2003 | Spectrum Foods Inc. | Business Plan | Initial client meeting | 2 | 125 | 250 |
| 12 | 1/30/2003 | Spectrum Foods Inc. | Business Plan | Review internal documents | 25 | 75 | 1875 |
| 13 | 2/4/2003 | Spectrum Foods Inc. | Business Plan | Draft report outline | 3 | 65 | 195 |
| 14 | 2/11/2003 | Spectrum Foods Inc. | Business Plan | Competitive analysis | 13 | 65 | 845 |
| 15 | 2/13/2003 | Spectrum Foods Inc. | Business Plan | First draft completed | 24 | 75 | 1800 |
| 16 | 2/20/2003 | Spectrum Foods Inc. | Business Plan | Financial analysis | 33 | 100 | 3300 |
| 17 | 2/24/2003 | Spectrum Foods Inc. | Business Plan | Client review meeting | 4 | 115 | 460 |
| 18 | 2/27/2003 | Spectrum Foods Inc. | Business Plan | Final report completed | 12 | 100 | 1200 |
| 19 | | | **Business Plan Average** | | 14.5 | 90 | 1240.625 |
| 20 | 2/12/2003 | Johnson Supplies | Expansion Review | Initial client meeting | 6 | 100 | 600 |
| 21 | 2/14/2003 | Johnson Supplies | Expansion Review | Employee interviews | 18 | 65 | 1170 |
| 22 | 2/20/2003 | Johnson Supplies | Expansion Review | Competitive analysis | 24 | 75 | 1800 |
| 23 | 2/24/2003 | Johnson Supplies | Expansion Review | Draft report outline | 8 | 75 | 600 |
| 24 | 2/28/2003 | Johnson Supplies | Expansion Review | Client review meeting | 3 | 100 | 300 |
| 25 | 3/15/2003 | Johnson Supplies | Expansion Review | Financial analysis | 17 | 75 | 1275 |
| 26 | 3/21/2003 | Johnson Supplies | Expansion Review | Final report completed | 15 | 75 | 1125 |
| 34 | | | **Expansion Review Average** | | 13 | 80.714 | 981.4286 |
| 35 | 3/2/2003 | Stan Wong & Assoc. | Legal Review | Initial client meeting | 8 | 150 | 1200 |
| 36 | 3/5/2003 | Stan Wong & Assoc. | Legal Review | Proceedings review | 12 | 100 | 1200 |
| 37 | 3/24/2003 | Stan Wong & Assoc. | Legal Review | Working papers review | 55 | 100 | 5500 |
| 38 | 4/18/2003 | Stan Wong & Assoc. | Legal Review | Secondary research | 42 | 75 | 3150 |
| 39 | 4/28/2003 | Stan Wong & Assoc. | Legal Review | Primary research | 18 | 125 | 2250 |

**17.** To remove the filter:
CHOOSE: Data → Filter → AutoFilter

**18.** To remove the subtotal calculation:
CHOOSE: Data → Subtotals
CLICK: Remove All command button

**19.** PRESS: CTRL+HOME to return to cell A1

**20.** Save the workbook and keep it open for use in the next lesson.

Excel

*In Addition* CREATING NESTED SUBTOTALS

You can nest a subtotal calculation within a subtotal report by sorting the worksheet list by the fields you want to group by. Use the Data → Sort command to specify the primary and secondary sort keys. Once the list is sorted, choose the Data → Subtotals command and specify the first subtotal calculation for the primary sort key. Then choose the Data → Subtotals command again and specify the calculation for the secondary sort key. The second time the command is executed you must ensure that the *Replace current subtotals* check box is not selected.

### 8.4.2 Grouping Data Manually

→ **Feature**

Using the Data → Group and Outline → Auto Outline command, you can outline an entire worksheet automatically. However, automatic outlining is an effective technique only when a worksheet contains summary functions, such as SUM and AVERAGE. When your worksheet data is not structured using summary functions, you must create outlines manually by grouping together the desired rows and columns.

→ **Method**

To group a selection of columns or rows:

• CHOOSE: Data → Group and Outline → Group

To ungroup a selection or remove an outline:

• CHOOSE: Data → Group and Outline → Ungroup,

   *or*

• CHOOSE: Data → Group and Outline → Clear Outline

→ **Practice**

You will now practice outlining a worksheet manually. Ensure that the "Billable" workbook is displayed.

1. For worksheets that contain a lot of detail or large lists, you can use outlines to collapse or hide data. To illustrate:
   CLICK: *2004* worksheet tab

2. To prepare the worksheet list:
   SELECT: cell D2
   CLICK: Sort Ascending button (⬆↓)

3. Let's assume that you want to collapse all of the task entries for "First Draft Completed." To begin:
   SELECT: rows 10 through 14
   (*Hint:* Use the mouse to click row 10 in the row frame area, and then drag the mouse pointer down to row 14.)

4. To outline these five rows:
   CHOOSE: Data → Group and Outline → Group
   A Row-Level bar now appears to the left of the row frame area, as shown in Figure 8.49.

**Figure 8.49**

Creating a Row-
Level data
grouping

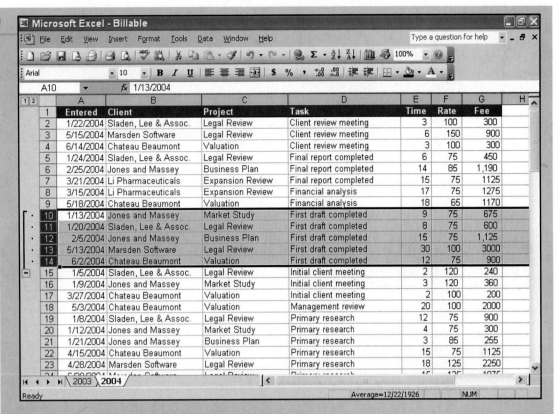

**5.** To collapse these rows from the worksheet display:
CLICK: Hide Detail button ( − ) at the bottom of the Row-Level bar
(*Hint:* Rather than grouping and collapsing rows and columns, you can use the Hide command found under the Format menu. The Unhide command is then used to redisplay the hidden rows or columns.)

**6.** To outline the Time, Rate, and Fee columns:
SELECT: columns E through G
CHOOSE: Data → Group and Outline → Group

**7.** To hide these columns from displaying:
CLICK: Hide Detail button ( − ) to the right of the Column-Level bar
The grouped rows and columns are now collapsed, as shown in Figure 8.50.

**Figure 8.50**

Collapsing manually grouped rows and columns

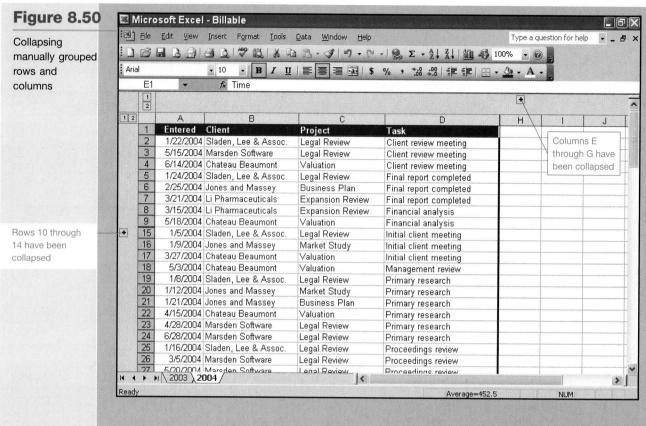

Rows 10 through 14 have been collapsed

8. To remove the manual outline groupings:
CHOOSE: Data → Group and Outline → Clear Outline
The outline symbols are removed from the worksheet and all of the list data is displayed.

9. Save and then close the "Billable" workbook.

---

**SelfCheck**

**8.4** What must you always do prior to subtotaling values in a worksheet list?

---

# Chapter
## summary

Since its introduction, Microsoft Office Excel 2003 has grown in features and in function. As a top-notch spreadsheet software, Excel 2003 can also be used effectively to manage and print lists of information. A worksheet list is a flat-file database containing a maximum of 65,535 records (rows) and 256 fields (columns). Although relational database programs, such as Microsoft Office Access 2003, have advantages over Excel in working with large or complex databases, Excel 2003 can store, summarize, and analyze numerical list data efficiently. Some of the list management tasks that you can perform in a worksheet include sorting, filtering, querying, summarizing, subtotaling, and outlining data.

## Command Summary

Many of the commands and procedures appearing in this chapter are summarized in the following table.

| Skill Set | To Perform This Task . . . | Do the Following . . . |
|---|---|---|
| Working with Cells, Cell Data, and Worksheet Lists | Creating or defining a worksheet list from a cell range | CHOOSE: Data → List → Create List |
| | Filter a worksheet list using the AutoFilter drop-down list arrows | CLICK: a field's AutoFilter drop-down list arrow<br>SELECT: a filtering value or option |
| | Display the AutoFilter drop-down list arrows for a list range | CHOOSE: Data → Filter → AutoFilter |
| | Remove a filter and display all of the records in a worksheet list | CHOOSE: Data → Filter → Show All |
| | Resize a worksheet list | DRAG: resizing handle in the bottom right-hand corner of the list range |
| | Insert a row or column in a worksheet list | CLICK: List menu button ([List ▾])<br>CHOOSE: Insert → Row, or<br>CHOOSE: Insert → Column |
| | Delete a row or column in a worksheet list | CLICK: List menu button ([List ▾])<br>CHOOSE: Delete → Row, or<br>CHOOSE: Delete → Column |
| | Convert a worksheet list into a normal range | CHOOSE: Data → List → Convert to Range |
| Summarizing Data | Display a data form to facilitate managing a worksheet list | CHOOSE: Data → Form |
| | Sort a worksheet list using the AutoFilter drop-down list arrows | CLICK: a field's AutoFilter drop-down list arrow<br>SELECT: Sort Ascending (or Sort Descending) from the list menu |
| | Sort a worksheet list into ascending or descending order using the toolbar | CLICK: Sort Ascending button ([↓]), or<br>CLICK: Sort Descending button ([↓]) |
| | Sort a worksheet list into order using more than one field or column | CHOOSE: Data → Sort |
| | Query a worksheet list using an advanced criteria filter | CHOOSE: Data → Filter → Advanced Filter |
| | Extract data from a worksheet list using an advanced criteria filter | CHOOSE: Data → Filter → Advanced Filter |
| | Create subtotals for a worksheet list | CHOOSE: Data → Subtotals |
| | Manually group data for outlining | SELECT: desired rows or columns<br>CHOOSE: Data → Group and Outline → Group |
| | Remove an outline from a worksheet | CHOOSE: Data → Group and Outline → Clear Outline |

| | | |
|---|---|---|
| **Creating and Revising Formulas** | Use database functions to summarize a list based on a set of conditions | =DFUNCTION(*list_range,field, criteria_range*) |
| | Use database functions:<br>• Average matching list values<br>• Count numerical list values<br>• Count alphabetical list values<br>• Display maximum list value<br>• Display minimum list value<br>• Add matching list values | =DAVERAGE<br>=DCOUNT<br>=DCOUNTA<br>=DMAX<br>=DMIN<br>=DSUM |
| | Use mathematical and statistical functions:<br>• Count list values matching a criterion<br>• Sum list values matching a criterion | =COUNTIF(*field_range,criteria*)<br>=SUMIF(*field_range,criteria, sum_range*) |
| **Customizing and Managing Excel** | Enable wizards and add-in programs | CHOOSE: Tools → Add-Ins |
| | Use the Conditional Sum Wizard add-in program to sum values in a list | CHOOSE: Tools → Conditional Sum |
| | Convert files to different file formats for transportability | CHOOSE: File → Save As<br>SELECT: a data format from the *Save as type* drop-down list box<br>CLICK: Save command button |

## Key Terms

This section specifies page references for the key terms identified in this chapter. For a complete list of definitions, refer to the Glossary provided at the end of this learning guide.

advanced criteria filter, *p. EX 463*

AutoFilter, *p. EX 451*

Conditional Sum Wizard, *p. EX 475*

criteria form, *p. EX 442*

criteria range, *p. EX 463*

data form, *p. EX 440*

data validation, *p. EX 432*

field, *p. EX 433*

field header row, *p. EX 433*

filter, *p. EX 451*

flat-file database, *p. EX 432*

hard-coded, *p. EX 477*

primary sort key, *p. EX 448*

query-by-example (QBE), *p. EX 442*

record, *p. EX 433*

relational database, *p. EX 432*

secondary sort keys, *p. EX 448*

wildcard character, *p. EX 442*

## Chapter
quiz

### Short Answer

1. List five questions that you should ask yourself when determining if Excel 2003 is the proper software tool for storing list information.

2. In a few short sentences, summarize the guidelines for creating a worksheet list.

3. What list management tasks can you perform using the Data Form and Criteria Form dialog boxes?

4. What are the two primary options for sorting a list?

5. What are wildcards? Provide an example of how you might use a wildcard character.

6. When would you choose an advanced criteria filter over using Excel's AutoFilter feature?

7. What is the relationship of search logic (AND, OR) in a criteria range to the row placement of the search conditions?

8. What are the two actions that you can perform using an advanced criteria filter?

9. What function does the Conditional Sum Wizard help you enter into a worksheet cell?

10. Name two summary functions that you can use to subtotal data in a worksheet.

## True/False

1. _____ A list can extend across multiple worksheets in a single workbook.

2. _____ You should choose to use a relational database program, instead of Excel 2003, when storing large amounts of repetitive textual data.

3. _____ You should format the field header row differently from the data in a worksheet list.

4. _____ The field header row for a list can consist of more than one row on the worksheet.

5. _____ The Data Form dialog box can display up to thirty-two fields from two records at the same time.

6. _____ You can sort a list according to a field's calendar data, such as January, February, March, . . . and so on.

7. _____ The COUNTIF function is one example of a database function.

8. _____ The DSUBTOTAL function is entered automatically when you choose the Data → Subtotals command.

9. _____ When you subtotal a list, Excel 2003 automatically groups and outlines the row information.

10. _____ If you have grouped together a selection of rows in a worksheet, you must first remove the row grouping before attempting to manually group columns.

## Multiple Choice

1. The two most common types of database systems include:

   a. flat-file and worksheet
   b. worksheet and rational
   c. flat-file and relational
   d. flat-file and rational

2. In a worksheet list, a row represents a:

   a. field
   b. record
   c. series
   d. list

3. In a worksheet list, a column represents a:

   a. field
   b. record
   c. series
   d. list

4. An Excel 2003 worksheet is limited to storing this many records:

   a. 8,192 including the field header row
   b. 16,834 including the field header row
   c. 65,536 including the field header row
   d. 4 GB of hard disk storage capacity

5. An Excel worksheet is limited to storing this many fields:

   a. 16
   b. 256
   c. 8,192
   d. 16,384

6. Which of the following is <u>not</u> a guideline for creating lists?

   a. Save each new list in a separate workbook file.
   b. Place concise column headings (field names) in a single row.
   c. Do not insert blank columns or rows within a list.
   d. Do not insert spaces at the beginning of cell entries.

7. Which of the following is <u>not</u> a command found in the Data Form dialog box?

   a. New

   b. Delete

   c. Sort

   d. Criteria

8. The process of restricting the display of records in a worksheet list to those matching a particular criterion is called:

   a. sifting

   b. filtering

   c. extracting

   d. restricting

9. The Conditional Sum Wizard is best described as:

   a. an add-on

   b. an add-in

   c. a macro

   d. a module

10. You can remove the subtotals for a list by choosing this command:

   a. Data → Filter → AutoFilter

   b. Data → Filter → Show All

   c. Data → Group and Outline → Clear Outline

   d. None of the above

## Hands-On

### exercises

step by step

### 1. Creating a Worksheet List

In this exercise you will practice creating a field header row, defining a worksheet list, and then formatting the results. You will then use a data form to add a new record to the list.

1. Open the data file named EX08HE01 to display the workbook shown in Figure 8.51. This worksheet contains data that has been imported from a database program. You will now modify the worksheet and define it as an Excel 2003 worksheet list.

**Figure 8.51**

Opening the EX08HE01 workbook

| | A | B | C | D | E | F | G | H |
|---|---|---|---|---|---|---|---|---|
| 1 | 99017479 | DeFleur | Gregg | 2090 Fairway Drive | 555-9906 | Business Admin | | |
| 2 | 99035674 | Withers | Martin | 3984 Hudson Blvd | 555-6387 | History | | |
| 3 | 99036578 | Horton | Samantha | 940 32 Avenue | 505-9803 | Geography | | |
| 4 | 99063698 | McLean | Barb | 3201 Sun Valley | 555-8332 | Fine Arts | | |
| 5 | 99083766 | Bose | Denise | 3210 Hemlock Avenue | 555-1450 | Sciences | | |
| 6 | 99129206 | Hurley | Stuart | 4033 Selkirk Way | 555-7988 | Sciences | | |
| 7 | 99149177 | Pitt | Dennis | 280-4993 Lodgepole Place | 555-1982 | English | | |
| 8 | 99223080 | Hendrickson | Mel | 23-984 Victoria Drive | 555-8802 | Agriculture | | |
| 9 | 99283926 | Palma | Emerald | 84 Columbia | 555-2876 | Computer Science | | |
| 10 | 99352761 | Bertin | Julia | 32-987 Parkdale Road | 555-3189 | Geography | | |
| 11 | 99362225 | Provost | Everett | 22A-8930 Cotton Place | 555-6360 | Computer Science | | |
| 12 | 99375452 | Ackerman | Jerry | 748 Douglas Cresent | 555-1375 | English | | |
| 13 | 99393943 | Earle | Jenna | 8740 Thrup St | 555-9411 | Computer Science | | |
| 14 | 99494467 | Murray | Dwayne | 8893 Thrup Street | 555-3327 | History | | |
| 15 | 99534889 | Garcia | Rosa | 3302 Arvida Drive | 555-2978 | History | | |
| 16 | 99604061 | Getz | Anthoney | 8493 McArthur St | 555-8163 | Fine Arts | | |
| 17 | 99625129 | Farris | Linda | 177 Sunshine Parkway | 555-9313 | Sciences | | |
| 18 | 99630877 | Cooper | Sara | 541 Victoria Drive | 555-4886 | Business Admin | | |
| 19 | 99638446 | Williams | Peter | 490 Malahat Drive | 555-5576 | Fine Arts | | |
| 20 | 99655983 | Aziz | Nashir | 894 Regent Drive | 555-2199 | Geography | | |
| 21 | 99660130 | Lopez | Victor | 5984 East Hill | 555-4853 | Sciences | | |
| 22 | 99685412 | Singh | Balwant | 3987 Valleyview Street | 555-7330 | History | | |
| 23 | 99686022 | Brown | Raymond | 392 Greenfield St | 555-3981 | Agriculture | | |

2. Save the workbook as "Roster List" to your personal storage location.

3. To use this worksheet as a list, you need to create a field header row above the data area. To do so:
SELECT: row 1 by clicking "1" in the row frame area
CHOOSE: Insert ➜ Rows

4. Now enter the field column labels into row 1:
SELECT: cell A1
TYPE: **RosterID**
PRESS: ⮕ to move to the next column
TYPE: **LastName**
PRESS: ⮕
TYPE: **FirstName**
PRESS: ⮕
TYPE: **Address**
PRESS: ⮕
TYPE: **Phone**
PRESS: ⮕
TYPE: **Department**
PRESS: (ENTER)

5. Finally, apply formatting to the worksheet list using an AutoFormat theme. To begin:
PRESS: (CTRL)+(HOME) to move to cell A1

6. To specify the AutoFormat specifications:
CHOOSE: Format ➜ AutoFormat
SELECT: List 3 in the preview area
CLICK: Options command button
SELECT: *Width/Height* check box so that a ✓ does not appear
CLICK: OK command button
Your worksheet should now appear with the AutoFormat formatting styles applied.

7. Now define the formatted range as a worksheet list:
RIGHT-CLICK: cell A1
SELECT: Create List

8. Ensure that the range "=$A$1:$F$31" appears in the text box and then:
CLICK: OK command button
The AutoFilter buttons should now appear next to the field column labels and a blue border surrounds the entire list area, as shown in Figure 8.52.

## Figure 8.52

Defining and
formatting a
worksheet list

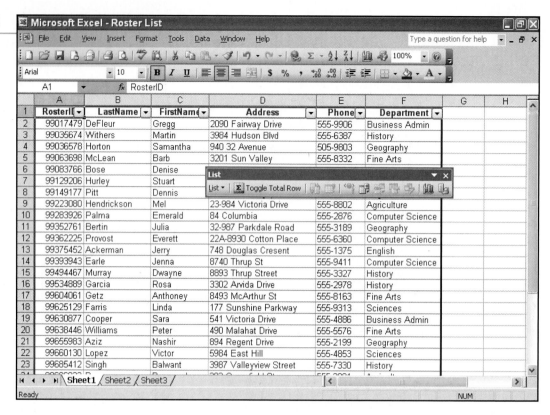

**9.** To display the Data Form dialog box for adding a new record:
CHOOSE: Data ➜ Form
The first record is displayed in the dialog box.

**10.** To add a new record to the list:
CLICK: New command button
TYPE: **99990103**
PRESS: TAB to move to the next field
TYPE: **Burnett**
PRESS: TAB
TYPE: **Tannis**
PRESS: TAB
TYPE: **1145 Fraser Street**
PRESS: TAB
TYPE: **555-6654**
PRESS: TAB
TYPE: **History**
PRESS: ENTER to save the record and continue

**11.** On your own, practice navigating through the list records using the Data Form dialog box. When
you are ready to proceed:
CLICK: Close command button

**12.** PRESS: CTRL+⬇ to move to the last record
Notice that "Tannis Burnett" now appears as the last entry.

**13.** Save and then close the "Roster List" workbook.

step by step

## 2. Sorting and Filtering a List Using AutoFilter

In this exercise, you will practice manipulating data into information in an existing worksheet list by sorting and filtering.

**1.** Open the data file named EX08HE02. Notice that the worksheet named "TopForty" contains an active list area.

**2.** Save the workbook as "Video Classics" to your personal storage location.

**3.** To sort the list into chronological order:
SELECT: cell C2 (or any other cell in the Released column)
CLICK: Sort Ascending button ()

**4.** To sort the worksheet list by values stored in two columns, use the Sort dialog box. Ensure that the cell pointer appears in the active worksheet list and then:
CHOOSE: Data → Sort

**5.** Your objective now is to sort the worksheet list by category and then, for each category, sort the titles by rank. Do the following:
SELECT: Category from the *Sort by* drop-down list box
SELECT: *Ascending* option button in the *Sort by* area
SELECT: Rank from the *Then by* drop-down list box
SELECT: *Ascending* option button in the *Then by* area
With the dialog box moved to the right of the worksheet list, your screen should appear similar to the one shown in Figure 8.53.

**Figure 8.53**

Defining a sort order using the Sort dialog box

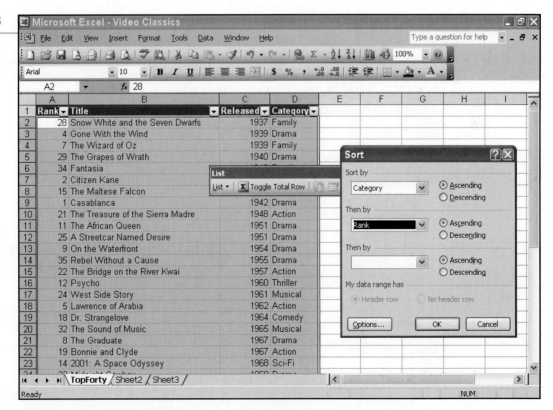

**6.** To complete the sort operation:
CLICK: OK command button
The list is now sorted using Category as the primary sort key and Rank as the secondary sort key.

**7.** Let's use the AutoFilter buttons to limit the display of movies to comedies. Do the following:
CLICK: Category's (D1) AutoFilter drop-down arrow (▾)
SELECT: Comedy from the AutoFilter drop-down list
Three records are displayed: Dr. Strangelove, M*A*S*H, and Tootsie.

**8.** To display only the dramas released before 1960, you need to define and apply a two-step filter. To begin, remove the previous filter and redisplay all of the records:
CLICK: Category's (D1) AutoFilter drop-down arrow (▾)
SELECT: (All) from the AutoFilter drop-down list
(*Hint:* You may also choose the Data ➔ Filter ➔ Show All command.)

**9.** Now display only the dramas:
CLICK: Category's (D1) AutoFilter drop-down arrow (▾)
SELECT: Drama from the AutoFilter drop-down list

**10.** To proceed, you must create a custom filter to display only the movies released before 1960. With the Category filter still active:
CLICK: Released (C1) AutoFilter drop-down arrow (▾)
SELECT: (Custom) from the drop-down list

**11.** In the Custom AutoFilter dialog box:
SELECT: "is less than" from the top-left drop-down list box
PRESS: TAB
TYPE: **1960** in the top-right combo box
CLICK: OK command button
Only the nine dramas released before 1960 are displayed, as shown in Figure 8.54.

**Figure 8.54**

Displaying a sorted and filtered list

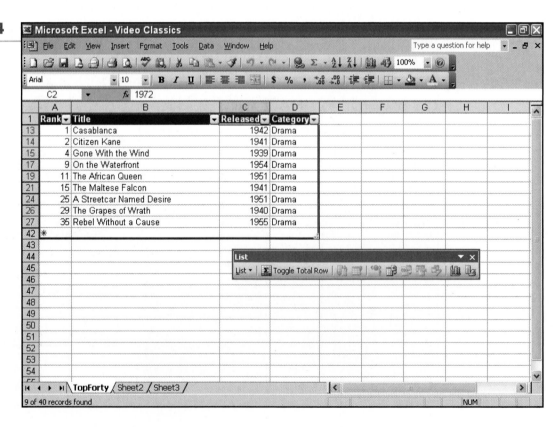

**12.** Save and then close the "Video Classics" workbook.

step by step

## 3. Creating an Advanced Query

In this exercise you practice analyzing and summarizing data in an existing worksheet list using Excel 2003's advanced filtering techniques.

1. Open the data file named EX08HE03.

2. Save the workbook as "Employee List" to your personal storage location.

3. In order to use an advanced criteria filter, you need to create a criteria range, typically positioned above the worksheet list. Let's insert three rows for the criteria range and one blank row between the criteria range and list area. To begin:
SELECT: rows 1 through 4
CHOOSE: Insert → Rows

4. Now copy the field header row from row 5 to the top of the new criteria range (row 1).

5. With the cell range still selected, use the Zoom button ( 100% ▾ ) to adjust the magnification so that only the columns containing data are visible. Then select cell A1 to remove the range highlighting, and press ( ESC ) to remove the cell marquee or rotating cell border. Your screen should appear similar to the one shown in Figure 8.55.

**Figure 8.55**

Creating a criteria range

| | A | B | C | D | E | F | G |
|---|---|---|---|---|---|---|---|
| 1 | EmployeeID | FirstName | LastName | Phone | Department | Hired | Vacation |
| 2 | | | | | | | |
| 3 | | | | | | | |
| 4 | | | | | | | |
| 5 | EmployeeID | FirstName | LastName | Phone | Department | Hired | Vacation |
| 6 | 1002 | Cecilia | Adams | 825-5661 | Management | 09/01/90 | 7 |
| 7 | 1014 | Camilla | Edsell | 882-1147 | Management | 03/11/01 | 3 |
| 8 | 1019 | Kela | Henderson | 882-9374 | Management | 02/24/87 | 6 |
| 9 | 1028 | Presley | Schuler | 654-1085 | Management | 09/04/02 | 2 |
| 10 | 1033 | Rich | Williams | 660-0767 | Management | 03/15/04 | 3 |
| 11 | 1036 | Stevey | Yap | 654-3860 | Management | 07/06/00 | 3 |
| 12 | 1045 | Gilles | Swift | 512-7411 | Warehouse | 09/07/99 | 4 |
| 13 | 1057 | Murray | Thompson | 643-7744 | Administration | 03/18/89 | 6 |
| 14 | 1094 | Moira | Walsh | 660-2895 | Management | 12/20/96 | 4 |
| 15 | 1130 | Darryl | Hamel | 321-4567 | Sales | 09/28/95 | 5 |
| 16 | 1240 | Cindy | Morgan | 654-6585 | Sales | 12/10/90 | 6 |
| 17 | 1250 | Shig | Todd | 882-3365 | Sales | 06/17/96 | 5 |
| 18 | 1254 | Kim | Tang | 315-9874 | Sales | 06/27/95 | 5 |

6. Before using the new criteria range, let's name the range:
SELECT: cell range from A1 to G2
CLICK: in the Name box
TYPE: **Crit**
PRESS: ( ENTER )

7. Let's use the criteria range to view only the warehouse employees:
   SELECT: cell E2
   TYPE: **Warehouse**
   PRESS: (ENTER)

8. Now select any cell within the active list area (such as cell A5) and then display the Advanced Filter dialog box:
   CHOOSE: Data ➜ Filter ➜ Advanced Filter
   Notice that the list area range is entered automatically.

9. To enter the criteria range and execute the filter:
   PRESS: (TAB)
   TYPE: **Crit** in the *Criteria range* text box
   CLICK: OK command button
   Eight employees are filtered through for display in the list.

10. On your own, remove the existing filter and then apply new criteria to display only the Sales employees who were hired before 1995. (*Hint:* Use **<01/01/95** as the Hired criteria.) How many records match the new criteria?

11. When you are finished, remove the filter using the Data ➜ Filter ➜ Show All command and then delete the criteria in cell F2.

12. To determine how many employees have more than five weeks vacation, let's use the COUNTIF function:
    SELECT: cell A4
    TYPE: **=countif(**
    CLICK: Insert Function button ($f_x$)
    The Function Arguments dialog box is displayed for the COUNTIF function.

13. Fill in the *Range* and *Criteria* text box arguments to evaluate the vacation entitlement in column G, as shown in Figure 8.56. When ready, click the OK command button to place the result into cell A4.

**Figure 8.56**

Function Arguments dialog box for the COUNTIF function

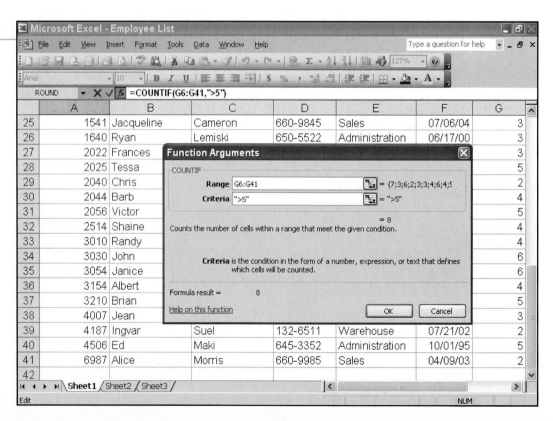

**14.** On your own, edit the formula in cell A4 to count the number of employees with greater than four weeks of vacation.

**15.** Save and then close the "Employee List" workbook.

on your own

## 4. Adding Subtotals to a Worksheet

As the new office manager for a real estate firm, you have been asked to analyze and summarize the firm's sales results by agent. You are provided with a workbook named EX08HE04, which you open and then save as "Agent Sales" to your personal storage location. After reviewing the contents of the worksheet, you are ready to proceed.

In order to best summarize the sales results by agent, you decide to use Excel 2003's Subtotal feature. You begin by sorting the list into alphabetical order by the Agents' names. You then add Subtotals to the worksheet list using the Data ➜ Subtotals command. Specifically, you display the sum values for Purchase Price and Commission for each Agent, as shown in Figure 8.57.

**Figure 8.57**

Adding subtotals to a worksheet list

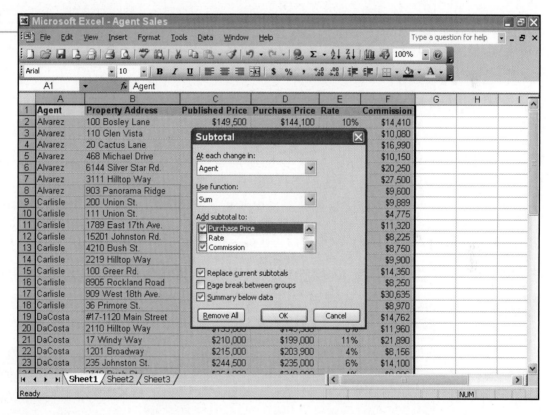

After the subtotals appear in the worksheet, you collapse the detail to the second level for all agents. You then expand the detail for DaCosta to illustrate the information that is available. You print the worksheet as it is displayed. Finally, you save and then close the "Agent Sales" workbook before proceeding.

on your own

## 5. Managing Fleet Data

LTL Fleet Systems, Inc., owns and operates twelve trucks in three locations. The company has prepared a workbook that tracks each vehicle's cost per mile (CPM). This workbook allows them to analyze and forecast operating costs (maintenance and fuel) for each period. As an intern with the company, you are responsible for performing several list management tasks using the workbook. To begin, open the EX08HE00 workbook and then save it as "LTL Fleet List" to your personal storage location. Your screen should appear similar to the one shown in Figure 8.58.

**Figure 8.58**

"LTL Fleet List" workbook

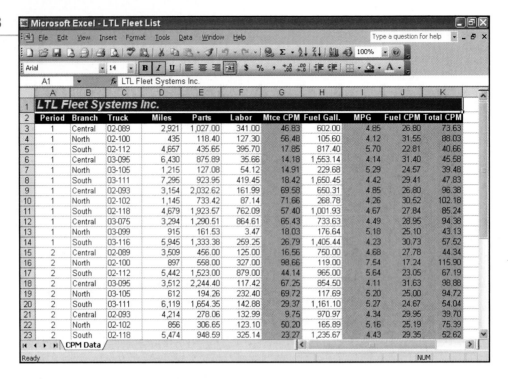

Perform the following tasks in the order in which they are presented:

• Sort the worksheet list so that the primary sort key is "Branch" and the secondary sort key is "Truck."

• Define the worksheet with a list area from cell A2 to K38.

• Apply an AutoFilter to the worksheet list so that only trucks from the North branch are displayed.

Your screen should now appear similar to the one shown in Figure 8.59.

**Figure 8.59**

Defining and filtering a worksheet list

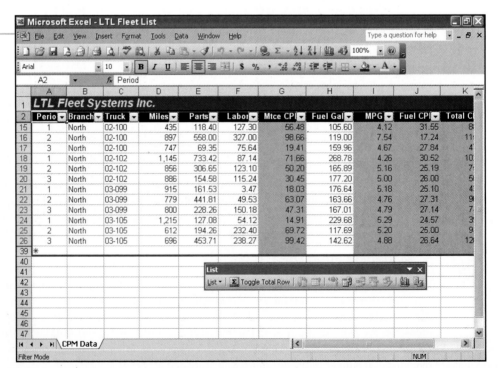

- Show all of the records in the worksheet list. (*Note:* Do not remove the AutoFilter arrows from the field header row.)

- Apply an AutoFilter to the worksheet list so that only those records with more than 6,000 miles are displayed. How many records are displayed?

- Show all of the records in the worksheet list.

- Apply an AutoFilter to the worksheet list so that only the top ten records for Total CPM (cost per mile) are displayed. Which branches are represented in the list?

When you are finished, save and then close the "LTL Fleet List" workbook.

on your own

## 6. Summarizing Fleet Data

LTL Fleet Systems, Inc., uses an Excel 2003 workbook to track operating costs for its fleet of twelve trucks. As an assistant to the president, you are responsible for generating reports from the raw data stored in the workbook. To begin, open the EX08HE00 workbook, and then save it as "LTL Reports" to your personal storage location.

Perform the following tasks in the order in which they are presented:

- To create a criteria range, select rows 2 through 5 and then choose the Insert ➜ Rows command. Copy the field header row from row 6 to row 2. Then, using the Format Painter button ( ), copy the formatting characteristics from row 7 to rows 3 through 5.

- Name the list area from A6 to K42 "List" and the criteria range from cells A2 to K3 "Crit."

- To specify a filter for trucks in the North branch that get greater than five miles to the gallon, type **North** into cell B3 and then type **>5** in cell I3. After selecting cell I6, choose Data ➜ Filter ➜ Advanced Filter command. Enter the range names into the appropriate text boxes and then select to filter the list in-place. Click the OK command button to proceed. Your screen should now appear similar to that shown in Figure 8.60.

**Figure 8.60**

Applying a criteria filter

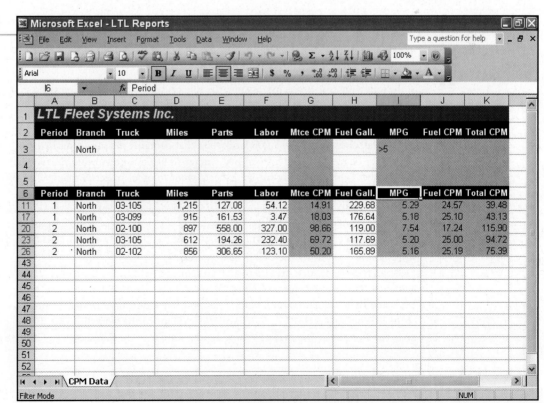

- Delete the criteria entries from row 3 and then show all of the records in the worksheet list.

- Sort the list by Branch and then by Period.

- Create a subtotals report that breaks at each change in Branch and that averages all of the numeric fields in the worksheet list. Collapse the outline to the second level, and then print the subtotals report using a landscape print orientation. Which branch has the best (lowest) Total CPM (cost per mile) average?

When you are finished, save and then close the "LTL Reports" workbook.

# CaseStudy   THE SAUDER SENTINELS

Only thirty minutes from downtown Rochester, the University of Victoria's endowment lands occupy a majority of the Point Allen peninsula. As you enter the South Gate along Marine Drive, you are treated to lush green forests to your right and the dark blue ocean waters on your left. Just beyond the expansive parking lots, the Sauder Park residences loom five stories high and are surrounded by playing fields. In one of those dormitory rooms, on a floor named First Haida, Alan Magee is busily compiling player statistics for the Sauder Sentinels hockey team. Among his responsibilities as coach and manager, Alan must submit several reports, along with a team roster that lists each player's results during the regular season, to the Intramural Sports Committee. One of the more thankless leadership tasks for Alan is the limiting of the team roster to a maximum of fifteen players. There are twenty-four players currently listed in his Excel 2003 worksheet. He now needs to analyze the data to determine the strengths and weaknesses of his players. Having read up on managing worksheet lists, Alan realizes that there are some exciting opportunities for turning the raw data into usable and useful information.

In the following case problems, assume the role of Alan and perform the same steps that he identifies.

1. Upon returning to his dorm room after a brief dinner, Alan decides to do some computer work for his team, the Sauder Sentinels. He turns on his notebook computer and then starts Microsoft Office Excel 2003. Alan opens the EX08CP00 workbook that contains the player statistics for last season and saves it as "Sauder Park" to his personal storage location. In reviewing the worksheet list, Alan realizes that he must modify the worksheet layout in order to better manipulate the list for reporting purposes.

   Alan starts by reviewing the guidelines for creating a list. Following the suggestions, he decides to change the name of the worksheet from *Sheet1* to *Roster*. Because the field header row must be contained on a single row, Alan then deletes rows 2 and 3 from the worksheet. He then defines the worksheet as a list using the Create List command.

   Upon reflection, Alan decides to add a calculated field to the list called "Points" that will add together the Goals and Assists columns. He inserts the new field between the Assists and Penalties fields and then fills the column with the appropriate addition formula. To improve the look and feel of the list, he applies the "List 2" AutoFormat theme to the worksheet list. Before proceeding, Alan saves the worksheet, which should now appear similar to the one shown in Figure 8.61.

**Figure 8.61**

Formatting the worksheet list

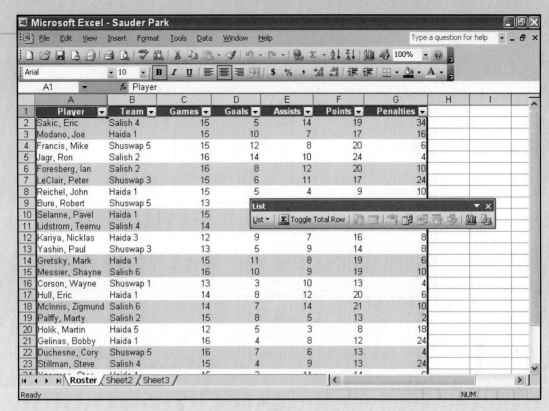

**2.** With his worksheet looking more like a list, Alan needs to perform some simple updates using the Data Form and Criteria Form dialog boxes. One of his first, and most important, updates is to include himself and his roommate in the list. Yikes, what an oversight! Using the data form, he adds the following two records:

| Player: | **Magee, Alan** | **Wengynowski, Bill** |
|---|---|---|
| Team: | **Haida 1** | **Haida 1** |
| Games: | **16** | **12** |
| Goals: | **11** | **3** |
| Assists: | **4** | **16** |
| Penalties: | **12** | **38** |

Alan must also correct a mistake that he made when initially entering the player statistics. He moves to the top of list using the Data Form dialog box. Then, using the criteria form, he enters a search criterion to locate all players from the "Salish 6" team. Upon advancing to each player (as shown in Figure 8.62), he corrects the team name to "Salish 5" and presses (ENTER). Once finished, Alan closes the dialog box and then saves the updated list. (*Note:* You can also use the Edit ➔ Replace command to perform this type of change in a worksheet.)

**Figure 8.62**

Editing records
using the Criteria
Form dialog box

3. Alan is pleased with the data that he has collected in his new list. Before committing the roster to paper, he decides to try various methods for organizing and summarizing the data. To begin, Alan uses
the Data → Sort command to sort the list by Team and then by Player. Next, he applies a custom
AutoFilter so that only those players who earned twenty points or more are displayed. He writes
down the five players' names and then removes the filter.

After converting the worksheet list back to a normal range, Alan creates a subtotal report based on
the values in the Team field. Using the SUM function, he calculates the total goals, assists, points,
and penalties earned. Once displayed, he collapses the outlined report so that it appears similar to
that shown in Figure 8.63 and then prints the result. Before proceeding to his next task, Alan
removes the subtotals from the worksheet.

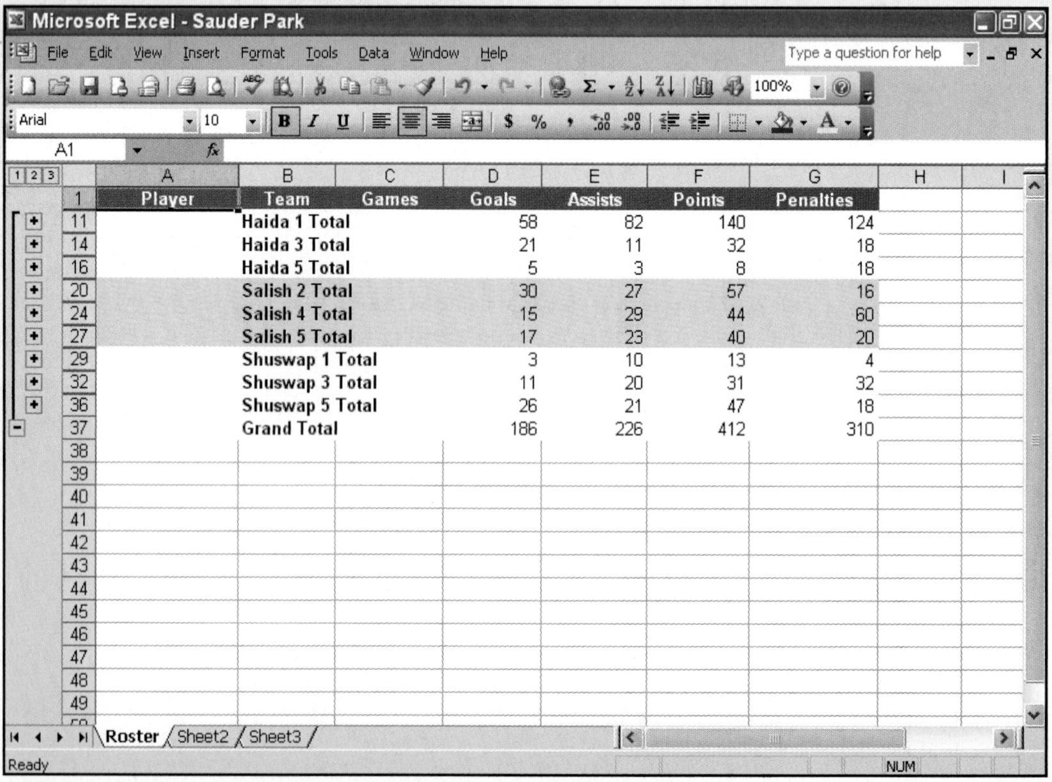

**Figure 8.63**

Subtotaling the
worksheet list

**4.** Alan decides to base his roster decision on the total points and penalty minutes accumulated during regular season play. In order to perform some analysis of the data, Alan inserts four rows above the worksheet list in order to create a criteria range. He then copies the field header row from row 5 into row 1 of the worksheet. To make life easier, Alan names the list area (cell range from A5 to G31) "List" and the criteria range (cell A1 to G2) "Crit." Lastly, Alan types **Calculations** into cell A4.

Alan enters several database functions prior to specifying the advanced filtering criteria. In cell C4, he enters the DAVERAGE function to calculate the average number of games played. In cells D4, E4, and F4, he enters the DSUM function to sum the goals, assists, and total points. In cell G4, he enters the DCOUNT function to count the number of records returned using values in the Penalties column. Then, using the "Crit" range, he enters criteria to limit the players used in the calculations to those with more than thirteen points and less than twenty penalty minutes. He then uses the Advanced Filter command to limit the display to the fifteen players meeting the criteria specification. After sorting the list alphabetically by player name, Alan prints out the worksheet (as shown in Figure 8.64) for submittal to the Intramural Sports Committee. He saves and closes the workbook and then exits Microsoft Office Excel 2003.

**Figure 8.64**

Using database functions for list analysis

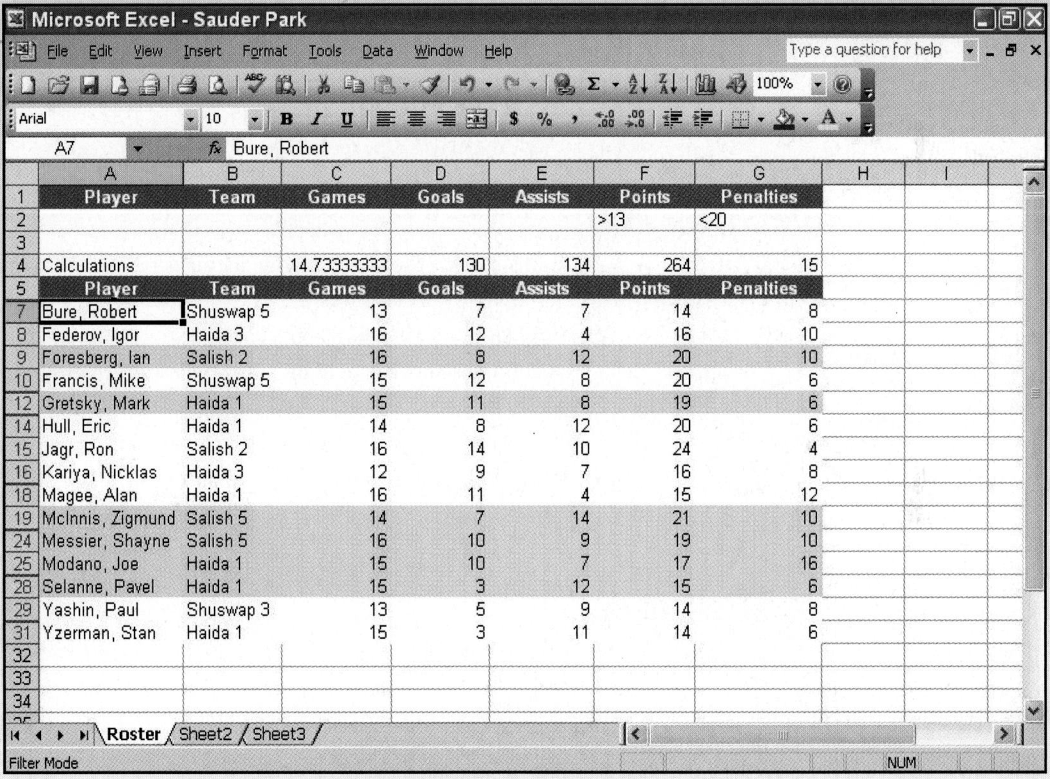

| | A | B | C | D | E | F | G | H | I |
|---|---|---|---|---|---|---|---|---|---|
| 1 | Player | Team | Games | Goals | Assists | Points | Penalties | | |
| 2 | | | | | | >13 | <20 | | |
| 3 | | | | | | | | | |
| 4 | Calculations | | 14.73333333 | 130 | 134 | 264 | 15 | | |
| 5 | Player | Team | Games | Goals | Assists | Points | Penalties | | |
| 7 | Bure, Robert | Shuswap 5 | 13 | 7 | 7 | 14 | 8 | | |
| 8 | Federov, Igor | Haida 3 | 16 | 12 | 4 | 16 | 10 | | |
| 9 | Foresberg, Ian | Salish 2 | 16 | 8 | 12 | 20 | 10 | | |
| 10 | Francis, Mike | Shuswap 5 | 15 | 12 | 8 | 20 | 6 | | |
| 12 | Gretsky, Mark | Haida 1 | 15 | 11 | 8 | 19 | 6 | | |
| 14 | Hull, Eric | Haida 1 | 14 | 8 | 12 | 20 | 6 | | |
| 15 | Jagr, Ron | Salish 2 | 16 | 14 | 10 | 24 | 4 | | |
| 16 | Kariya, Nicklas | Haida 3 | 12 | 9 | 7 | 16 | 8 | | |
| 18 | Magee, Alan | Haida 1 | 16 | 11 | 4 | 15 | 12 | | |
| 19 | McInnis, Zigmund | Salish 5 | 14 | 7 | 14 | 21 | 10 | | |
| 24 | Messier, Shayne | Salish 5 | 16 | 10 | 9 | 19 | 10 | | |
| 25 | Modano, Joe | Haida 1 | 15 | 10 | 7 | 17 | 16 | | |
| 28 | Selanne, Pavel | Haida 1 | 15 | 3 | 12 | 15 | 6 | | |
| 29 | Yashin, Paul | Shuswap 3 | 13 | 5 | 9 | 14 | 8 | | |
| 31 | Yzerman, Stan | Haida 1 | 15 | 3 | 11 | 14 | 6 | | |
| 32 | | | | | | | | | |
| 33 | | | | | | | | | |
| 34 | | | | | | | | | |

# Answers to Self-Check Questions

**8.1** What are some advantages of adding records to a list using the Data Form dialog box? What are some disadvantages?

Advantages:
- Enables you to focus on one record at a time.
- Provides for faster input of new records.
- Easier to see all fields when working with long records.

Disadvantages:
- AutoComplete command is not available in a data form.
- User can view only a single record at a time and, as a result, may duplicate an entry accidentally.

**8.2** How do you filter a worksheet list to display only the top 10 percent of values appearing in a field? Click the appropriate AutoFilter drop-down list arrow and then select the (Top 10) option from the drop-down list. In the Top 10 AutoFilter dialog box, select Top from the leftmost drop-down list box, select 10 in the middle spin box, and select Percent from the rightmost drop-down list box. Click the OK command button to apply the filter.

**8.3** Using the "Edutech" list, how would you determine the average price of CDROM and DVD media published in 1999?
On the *Sheet1* tab, set up the following criteria:

| Published | Media |
|-----------|-------|
| 1999 | CDROM |
| 1999 | DVD |

Ensure that the criteria range includes the second row. View the DAVERAGE result on the *Sheet2* tab.

**8.4** What must you always do prior to subtotaling values in a worksheet list? You must sort the field on which you want to group data.

# CHAPTER 9

## Decision-Making Using Excel

### PREREQUISITES

To successfully complete this chapter, you should know how to enter formulas and functions by typing, by pointing, and by using the Insert Function and Function Arguments dialog boxes. You must also be comfortable working with embedded charts and separate chart sheets.

### LEARNING OBJECTIVES

After reading this chapter, you will be able to:

- Describe methods for analyzing what-if scenarios

- Use Goal Seek and Solver to find the input values required to calculate a target outcome

- Use Scenario Manager to summarize assumptions and outcomes

- Forecast future results and plot a trendline in a chart

- Use one-input and two-input data tables

- Create, customize, and format PivotTable reports, PivotChart reports, and PivotTable lists

- Create custom views and save a workspace

# 9.1 Performing What-If Analysis

Microsoft Office Excel 2003 provides several powerful utilities for performing *what-if analysis*. A **what-if analysis** is a worksheet model that lets you calculate possible outcomes for a given set of assumptions. In a worksheet, assumptions are also known as **input cells** or *variables*, and are typically grouped together to speed data entry. Outcome cells contain formulas that reference the input cells either directly (as in cell D5 of the following graphic) or indirectly (as in cell D6). After changing the value stored in an input cell, Excel 2003 produces a ripple effect of recalculations for all outcome formulas dependent on that cell's value. You can use this process to test for questions such as "How will increasing the unit selling price to $10 affect the net income?" In answering this question, the input cell for "Retail Price," cell B3 in the graphic below, contains an adjustable value while the outcome formula in cell D6 calculates the "Net Income." Taken together, the values stored in a worksheet's input cells at any given time provide the set of assumptions for a single *scenario*. When you change these assumptions, you calculate a new outcome, resulting in a new scenario.

| | A | B | C | D | |
|---|---|---|---|---|---|
| 1 | **Input Cells** | | **Outcome Cells** | | |
| 2 | **Units Sold** | 12,500 | **Sales Revenue** | $121,875 | =B2*B3 |
| 3 | **Retail Price** | $9.75 | **Cost of Goods** | $73,375 | =B2*(B4+B5) |
| 4 | **Materials/Unit** | $3.67 | **Gross Margin** | $48,500 | =D2-D3 |
| 5 | **Labor/Unit** | $2.20 | **Fixed Costs** | $30,000 | =B6 |
| 6 | **Fixed Costs** | $30,000 | **Net Income** | $18,500 | =D4-D5 |

Excel 2003's most basic what-if tool is the worksheet formula itself. A formula can include constant values (such as $9.75 or 10%), cell references (B3 or B4:B6, for example), and range names. To create a new scenario, simply change the values stored in the input cells and the formulas recalculate the outcomes automatically. There are, however, additional methods provided for analyzing what-if scenarios. Your choice of method will depend on the type of problem you are attempting to solve and the amount of information you have available. In this module, you will learn to use graphical goal seeking, Excel 2003's Solver add-in program, and the Scenario Manager.

## 9.1.1 Using Goal Seeking

→ ## Feature

**Goal seeking** refers to the process of calculating the input value required to yield a desired outcome result. Lesson 6.1.3, *Finding Answers Using Goal Seek*, introduced the Goal Seek feature for manipulating a worksheet formula's outcome value. Excel 2003 also allows you to perform graphical goal seeking by manipulating a chart's data points (usually represented by bars, lines, or columns in the chart area.) If the data point that you are dragging refers to an outcome cell containing a formula, Excel 2003 displays the Goal Seek dialog box when you release the mouse button. Otherwise, the worksheet cell is updated with the value represented by the data point.

→ ## Method

To use goal seeking in a worksheet:

• CHOOSE: Tools → Goal seek

• In the *Set cell* text box, enter the cell containing the outcome formula.

- In the *To value* text box, enter the desired target value.

- In the *By changing cell* text box, enter the input cell that Excel 2003 may change to achieve the target value.

- CLICK: OK command button

To perform graphical goal seeking:

- Create and display a chart for analyzing your worksheet data.

- SELECT: the data column that you want to adjust to a target value

- DRAG: the marker at the top of the column to the desired value

- If the data column represents an outcome cell containing a formula, the Goal Seek dialog box appears.

- SELECT: the input cell to adjust in order to yield the desired result

- CLICK: OK command button

# → Practice

You will now use goal seeking to analyze payroll alternatives for a small manufacturing company. Before proceeding, start Microsoft Office Excel 2003.

**1.** Open the data file named EX0910 to display the workbook shown in Figure 9.1. This workbook contains four sheet tabs entitled *GoalSeek, GoalSeek Chart, Solver,* and *Scenarios.*

**Figure 9.1**

Opening the
EX0910
workbook

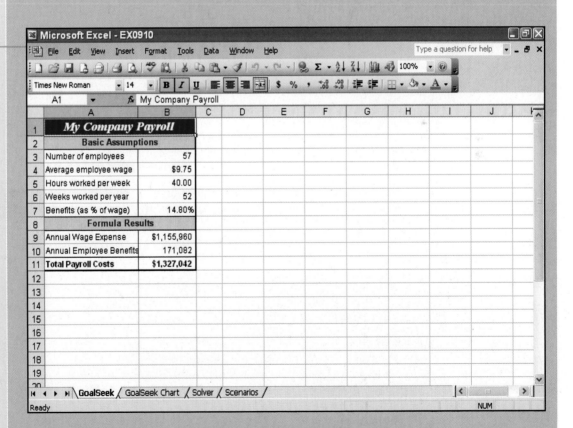

**2.** Save the workbook as "Problem Solving" to your personal storage location.

**3.** Before proceeding, ensure that the *GoalSeek* tab is selected.

**4.** To begin, position your cell pointer in the cell containing the target outcome formula:
SELECT: cell B11

**5.** To display the Goal Seek dialog box:
CHOOSE: Tools → Goal Seek
(*Note:* By selecting the outcome cell prior to launching the Goal Seek dialog box, cell B11 is entered automatically into the *Set cell* text box.)

**6.** To calculate the Benefit percentage (cell B7) required to yield total payroll costs of $1,350,000, enter the following Goal Seek arguments:
SELECT: *To value* text box
TYPE: 1350000
SELECT: *By changing cell* text box
TYPE: b7
Your dialog box should appear as shown in Figure 9.2.

**Figure 9.2**

Entering arguments in the Goal Seek dialog box

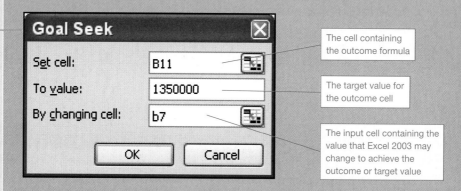

The cell containing the outcome formula

The target value for the outcome cell

The input cell containing the value that Excel 2003 may change to achieve the outcome or target value

**7.** To execute the goal seeking operation:
CLICK: OK command button

**8.** When it finds an answer, Excel 2003 updates the worksheet and then displays the Goal Seek Status dialog box (Figure 9.3). To accept the update:
CLICK: OK command button
The answer, 16.79%, now appears in cell B7 of the worksheet. This value is almost 2% greater than the original cell value of 14.80%. In other words, management can offer another 2% in benefits and still maintain a payroll budget of less than or equal to $1,350,000.

**Figure 9.3**

Goal Seek Status
dialog box

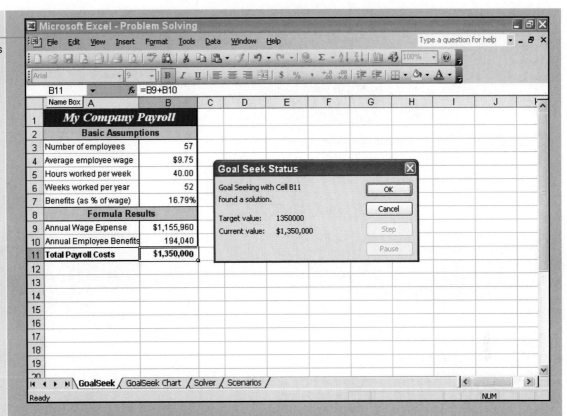

9. Save the workbook before proceeding.

10. You now use graphical goal seeking to project future payroll costs given a 0.5% cost of living adjustment. Do the following:
    CLICK: *GoalSeek Chart* tab

11. To ensure that you can see the relevant worksheet area:
    SELECT: cell range from A1 to J1
    CLICK: down arrow attached to the Zoom button ( 100% ▾ )
    CLICK: Selection from the drop-down list box
    Your screen should now appear similar to the worksheet shown in Figure 9.4.

## Figure 9.4

Displaying the
*GoalSeek Chart*
worksheet

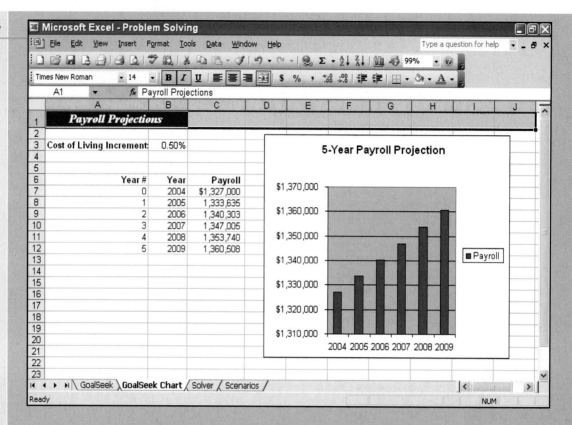

**12.** The *GoalSeek Chart* worksheet contains an input value in cell B3 for the cost of living increment. This input cell is then used to calculate the total payroll costs appearing in the cell range from C7 to C12. Using graphical goal seeking, let's find the cost of living increment that results in a payroll for Year 5 of $1.365 million.
CLICK: the data column for the year 2009
(*Hint:* To ensure that you select the correct column, position the mouse pointer over the column for year 2009. A ScreenTip appears showing the name of the data series, Payroll, and its value, $1,360,508.)

**13.** The entire data series is selected, shown by small boxes in the middle of each column. To single out the individual data column for the year 2009, do the following:
CLICK: the data column for the year 2009 a second time
Selection handles now surround the selected column and the Range Finder feature highlights the relevant worksheet cells.

**14.** As shown in Figure 9.5, position the mouse pointer over the selection handle marker appearing at the top of the selected data column. The pointer changes to a black double-headed arrow and a ScreenTip appears with the series name and value.

**Figure 9.5**

Preparing to size
a data column in
an embedded
chart

The Range Finder
selects the cell
ranges referenced
by the embedded
chart

Markers appear
when you correctly
select a single
column

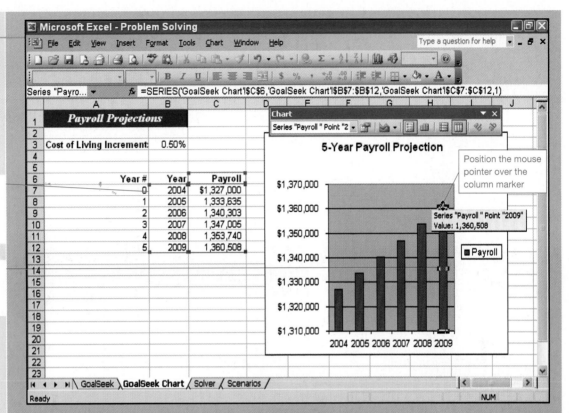

**15.** To change the value of the worksheet data plotted in this column:
DRAG: the marker at the top of the column down, until the ScreenTip displays a value of
"$1,365,000"

**16.** Because the column's worksheet cell (cell C12) contains a formula, the Goal Seek dialog box appears when you release the mouse button. From the chart, Excel 2003 completes the *Set cell* and *To value* text boxes. You need only determine the input cell to change.

**17.** To ensure that the worksheet cells are visible:
DRAG: the Goal Seek dialog box over the embedded chart or under the data area

**18.** To calculate the cost of living increment required to yield the target payroll value, ensure that the insertion point is in the *By changing cell* text box of the dialog box and then do the following:
CLICK: cell B3
CLICK: OK command button
Your screen should now appear similar to the worksheet shown in Figure 9.6.

**Figure 9.6**

Finding an answer using graphical goal seeking

Input value required to achieve the outcome or target value

Outcome or target value

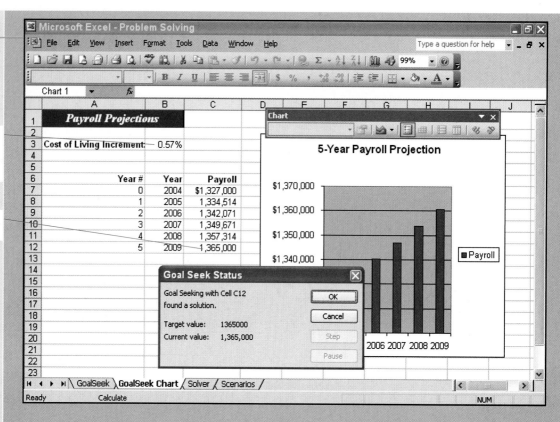

**19.** To accept the goal seek result:
CLICK: OK command button
The answer "0.57%" should now appear in cell B3.

**20.** Save the workbook and keep it open for use in the next lesson.

## 9.1.2 Using Solver

→ **Feature**

Using a mathematical technique known as *linear programming,* the Solver add-in program evaluates the most efficient solutions for problems with multiple input values and **constraints.** Solver works toward optimization by repeatedly adjusting the values appearing in a worksheet's input cells, until a potential solution is achieved. Solver can be used to calculate shift schedules for manufacturing, ingredient combinations in pharmaceutical research, and economic order quantities for purchasing. You can also use Solver to maximize profits, minimize operating costs, and make the most efficient use of resources.

→ **Method**

To use the Solver add-in program:

• CHOOSE: Tools → Solver

• In the *Set Target Cell* text box, enter the cell containing the outcome formula.

• In the *Equal To* area, choose to maximize, minimize, or set the outcome formula to a particular value.

- In the *By Changing Cells* text box, select the input cells containing the values that Excel can change to achieve the desired result.

- In the *Subject to the Constraints* list box, add constraints to which the Solver must adhere in solving the problem.

- CLICK: Solve command button

## → Practice

You will now use Solver to analyze a company's staffing requirements, given a maximum total payroll of $1.4 million. Ensure that the "Problem Solving" workbook is displayed.

**1.** CLICK: *Solver* tab in the workbook

**2.** Because Solver is an add-in program, you should verify that it has been installed on your computer:
CHOOSE: Tools → Add-Ins
SELECT: Solver Add-in check box so that a ✓ appears
Your screen should now appear similar to the worksheet shown in Figure 9.7.

**Figure 9.7**

Add-Ins dialog box with the Solver Add-in selected

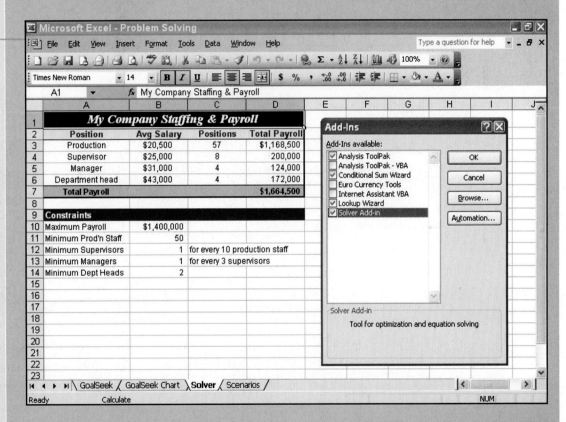

**3.** CLICK: OK command button to proceed
(*Hint:* If the Solver Add-in cannot be located, a dialog box may appear to lead you through installing the feature.)

**4.** Using Solver, find the optimal staffing levels that will keep the total payroll costs (cell D7) below $1.4 million, given the constraints provided in cells B11 through B14. To begin:
CHOOSE: Tools → Solver

**5.** To ensure that all of Solver's parameters are cleared and ready for your input:
CLICK: Reset All command button
CLICK: OK command button
The Solver Parameters dialog box should now appear similar to the one shown in Figure 9.8.

**Figure 9.8**

Solver
Parameters dialog
box

Outcome cell
containing the
formula to optimize

Input cells
containing values
that can be changed
by Solver

Constraints that
must be adhered to
by Solver when
changing values

6. In the *Set Target Cell* text box, select the cell containing the outcome formula that you want to optimize. Do the following:
CLICK: Dialog Collapse button (▣)
SELECT: cell D7
CLICK: Dialog Expand button (▣)

7. Next, specify the type of optimizing calculation to perform. Your options include finding the maximum or minimum result for an outcome formula or specifying a particular value. To enter a target value of $1.4 million for the total payroll costs:
SELECT: *Value of* option button in the *Equal To* area
TYPE: 1400000 in the adjacent text box

8. Now specify the input cells to manipulate—in this case, the number of staff positions in Column C. Do the following:
SELECT: *By Changing Cells* text box
CLICK: Dialog Collapse button (▣)
SELECT: cell range from C3 to C6
CLICK: Dialog Expand button (▣)

9. The last step is to specify constraining factors or limitations to which Solver must adhere in manipulating the input cells. To do so:
CLICK: Add command button in the *Subject to the Constraints* area
The Add Constraint dialog box appears, as shown in Figure 9.9.

**Figure 9.9**

Add Constraint
dialog box

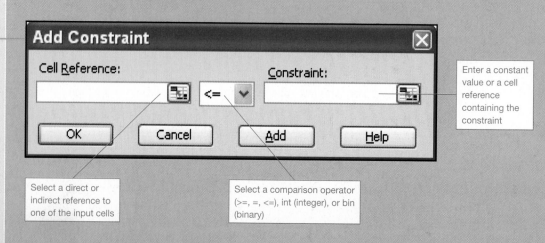

Enter a constant
value or a cell
reference
containing the
constraint

Select a direct or
indirect reference to
one of the input cells

Select a comparison operator
(>=, =, <=), int (integer), or bin
(binary)

**10.** The first constraint is that there must be a minimum number of production staff to keep the plant operating. To build this constraint:
DRAG: Add Constraint dialog box away from the data, if necessary
CLICK: cell C3 for the *Cell Reference* text box

**11.** Now select the operator to use in the constraint:
CLICK: down arrow attached to the middle drop-down list box
CLICK: >=

**12.** To complete the constraint, reference the cell that contains the minimum production staff necessary:
CLICK: cell B11 for the *Constraint* text box
(*Hint:* By entering cell reference instead of a value, you can easily modify the constraint later by entering a new value into cell B11.)

**13.** To continue adding constraints:
CLICK: Add command button
(*Note:* Although not visible, the constraint that you just built is entered into the Solver Parameters dialog box as "C3>=B11".)

**14.** Now enter a constraint that requires at least 1 supervisor for every 10 production staff members:
CLICK: cell C4 for the *Cell Reference* text box
SELECT: >=
TYPE: c3/10 into the *Constraint* text box
Your screen should now appear similar to the worksheet shown in Figure 9.10.

**Figure 9.10**

Adding constraints to Solver

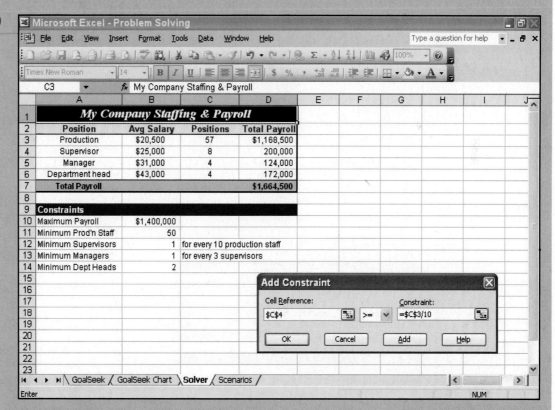

**15.** To add more constraints:
CLICK: Add command button

**16.** To indicate that there must be at least 1 manager for every 3 supervisors, do the following:
CLICK: cell C5 for the *Cell Reference* text box
SELECT: >=
TYPE: c4/3 into the *Constraint* text box
CLICK: Add command button

**17.** To indicate that there must be at least 2 department heads:
CLICK: cell C6 for the *Cell Reference* text box
SELECT: >=
CLICK: cell B14 for the *Constraint* text box
CLICK: OK command button to return to the dialog box
The Solver Parameters dialog box should now appear as shown in Figure 9.11. Notice that Solver imposes the use of absolute cell references in the *Subject to the Constraints* list area.

**Figure 9.11**

Solver
Parameters dialog
box after adding
constraints

Constraints are
added using
absolute cell
references

**18.** To calculate an answer to this problem:
CLICK: Solve command button
The worksheet is updated and the Solver Results dialog box appears (Figure 9.12).

**Figure 9.12**

Solver Results
dialog box

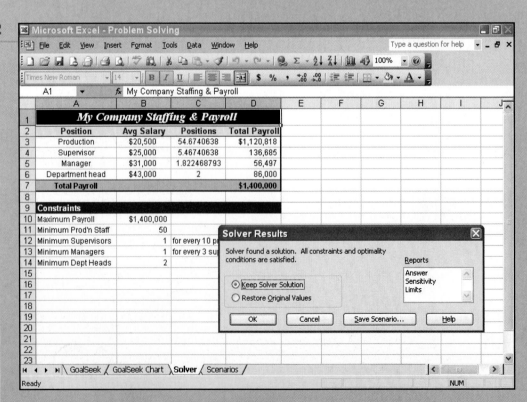

**19.** You may have noticed that Solver's results include decimal points in the Positions column (C3:C6). Assuming that you do not hire part-time managers, you must revise the constraints to specify that only integer results (whole numbers) are acceptable in cells C4 through C6. To discard the current solution:
SELECT: *Restore Original Values* option button
CLICK: OK command button
The values in the worksheet are returned to their original state.

**20.** Now let's revise the Solver parameters:
CHOOSE: Tools → Solver
Notice that all the information that you have entered into the dialog box is still available.

**21.** To add three new constraints for cells C4, C5, and C6:
CLICK: Add command button

**22.** First, ensure that the number of Supervisors is an integer value:
CLICK: cell C4 for the *Cell Reference* text box
SELECT: "int" from the middle drop-down list box
CLICK: Add command button
(*Note:* You do not enter a value into the *Constraint* text box after selecting "int" from the operators drop-down list box.)

**23.** To ensure that the number of Managers is also an integer:
CLICK: cell C5 for the *Cell Reference* text box
SELECT: "int" from the middle drop-down list box
CLICK: Add command button

**24.** Finally, ensure that the number of Department heads is also an integer:
CLICK: cell C6 for the *Cell Reference* text box
SELECT: "int" from the middle drop-down list box
CLICK: OK command button to return to the dialog box
The Solver Parameters dialog box displays these new constraints, as shown in Figure 9.13.

**Figure 9.13**

Enforcing results as integer values

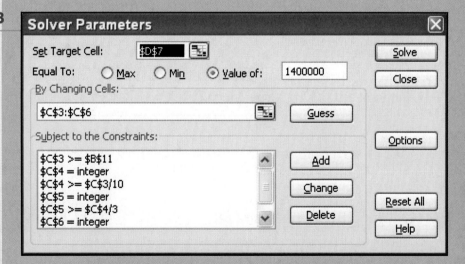

**25.** To calculate a solution that incorporates these new constraints:
CLICK: Solve command button
The solution that is displayed shows how you can restructure the company in order to remain within the targeted payroll limit.

**26.** Once you find an acceptable solution, Solver lets you create three summary reports: Answer, Sensitivity, and Limits. These reports describe the parameters of the solution, the sensitivity of the results, and a description of the limits reached. To view the Answer report:
SELECT: Answer in the *Reports* list box
CLICK: OK command button

**27.** To view the generated report:
CLICK: *Answer Report 1* tab
After scrolling down a few rows, your screen should appear similar to the worksheet shown in Figure 9.14. Notice the separation of the report-into-target (outcome) cell, adjustable (input) cells, and constraints.

**Figure 9.14**

Viewing an Answer report created by Solver

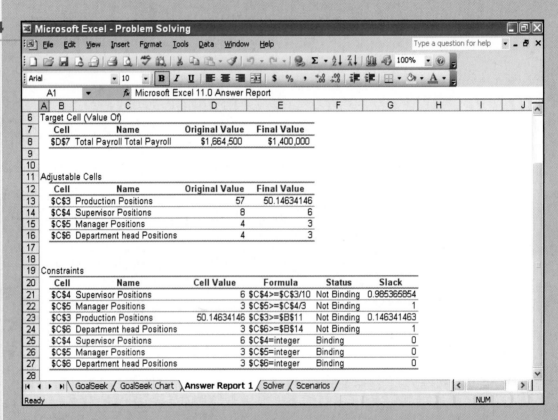

**28.** Save the workbook and keep it open for use in the next lesson.

### 9.1.3 Using Scenario Manager

→ **Feature**

A **scenario** is a set of assumptions—the values in input cells that you use to calculate a given outcome. Once formulated, you can save and manage scenarios using Excel 2003's Scenario Manager. Similar to creating and saving multiple worksheets, Scenario Manager lets you store up to 32 input values and their outcomes for each scenario. The advantage of using Scenario Manager is that you can save multiple scenarios within a single workbook and then view and summarize their results at any time. When you select a scenario for display in the Scenario Manager dialog box, Excel 2003 instantaneously updates the current worksheet with the stored input values and outcomes. You can also generate a summary report that compares various scenarios.

→ # Method

To add a new scenario:

- CHOOSE: Tools → Scenarios
- CLICK: Add command button

In the Add Scenario dialog box, enter a scenario name, specify the required input cells, and then click the OK command button.

In the Scenario Values dialog box, enter the values for each of the input cells and then click the OK command button.

- CLICK: Cancel to finish adding scenarios

To display a scenario or generate a report:

- CHOOSE: Tools → Scenarios
- SELECT: the desired scenario from the *Scenarios* list box
- CLICK: Show command button

  *or*

- CLICK: Summary command button

→ # Practice

Using Scenario Manager, you will now examine and track scenario options for limiting the total payroll costs to a specific dollar amount. Ensure that the "Problem Solving" workbook is displayed.

**1.** CLICK: *Scenarios* tab in the workbook

**2.** Let's use the Scenario Manager to review the main options in negotiating an employee contract. The union and management positions are described in the following table.

| Negotiations... | Current Status | Union Demands | Management Proposal |
|---|---|---|---|
| *Number of employees* | 57 | 57 | 55 |
| *Average hourly wage rate* | $9.75 | $11.00 | $9.45 |
| *Hours worked per week* | 40 | 38 | 40 |
| *Payroll Benefits (as %)* | 14.80% | 15.20% | 14.50% |

**3.** Before launching Scenario Manager, name the input cells that you want to keep track of:
SELECT: cell B3
CLICK: in the Name box
TYPE: **Employees**
PRESS: [ENTER]
Your screen should appear similar to the worksheet shown in Figure 9.15.

**Figure 9.15**

Displaying the *Scenarios* worksheet

Create a range name by selecting a cell and then typing in the Name box

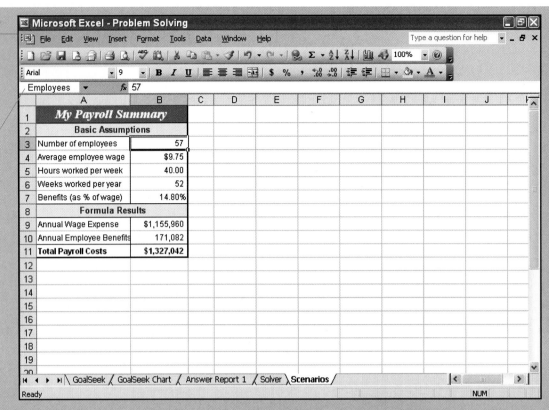

4. On your own, name cell B4 **Wage**, cell B5 **Hours**, cell B6 **Weeks**, and cell B7 **Benefits**. (*Hint:* Assigning range names makes the final summary reports generated by the Scenario Manager easier to read.)

5. CHOOSE: Tools → Scenarios
The Scenario Manager dialog box appears with a message stating that no scenarios are yet defined.

6. To add a new scenario that describes the union's demands:
CLICK: Add command button
The Add Scenario dialog box appears, as shown in Figure 9.16.

**Figure 9.16**

Add Scenario
dialog box

Enter the input cells
that you want to
modify to achieve
the desired outcome

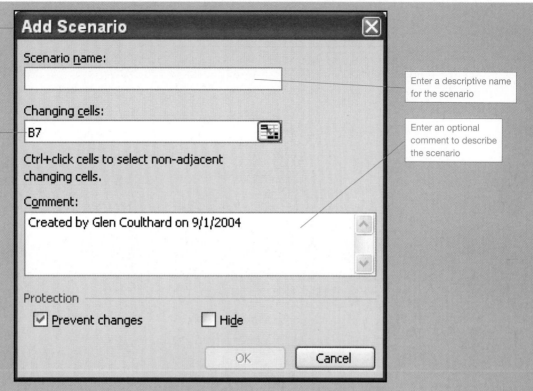

Enter a descriptive name
for the scenario

Enter an optional
comment to describe
the scenario

**7.** In the *Scenario name* text box:
TYPE: **Union**
PRESS: **TAB**

**8.** In the *Changing cells* text box, replace the current selection by entering the following range names:
TYPE: **Employees,Wage,Hours,Benefits**
(*Hint:* You can also type the cell addresses or click on the desired cells in the worksheet. Excel 2003 allows up to 32 input cells to be entered for each scenario.)

**9.** You must now define the input values for each of the changing cells:
CLICK: OK command button
The resulting Scenario Values dialog box (Figure 9.17) displays your range names as text box labels to help you enter the input values.

**Figure 9.17**

Scenario Values
dialog box

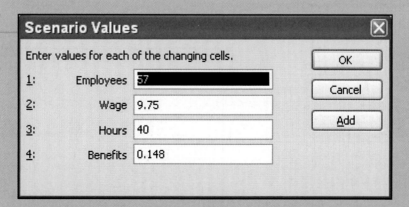

**10.** To enter the union's demands:
TYPE: **57** in the *1: Employees* text box
PRESS: TAB
TYPE: **11.00** in the *2: Wage* text box
PRESS: TAB
TYPE: **38** in the *3: Hours* text box
PRESS: TAB
TYPE: **.1520** in the *4: Benefits* text box

**11.** To create a second scenario based on management's position:
CLICK: Add command button
The Add Scenario dialog box reappears.

**12.** TYPE: **Management** in the *Scenario name* text box
CLICK: OK command button
The Scenario Values dialog box appears.

**13.** Enter the values for the management proposal:
TYPE: **55** in the *1: Employees* text box
PRESS: TAB
TYPE: **9.45** in the *2: Wage* text box
PRESS: TAB
TYPE: **40** in the *3: Hours* text box
PRESS: TAB
TYPE: **.1450** in the *4: Benefits* text box

**14.** To complete the dialog box:
CLICK: OK command button
The Scenario Manager dialog box reappears with two scenarios called "Union" and "Management."

**15.** To display the results of the union proposal:
SELECT: "Union" in the *Scenarios* list box
CLICK: Show command button
Your screen should now appear similar to the worksheet shown in Figure 9.18.

**Figure 9.18**

Showing the "Union" results

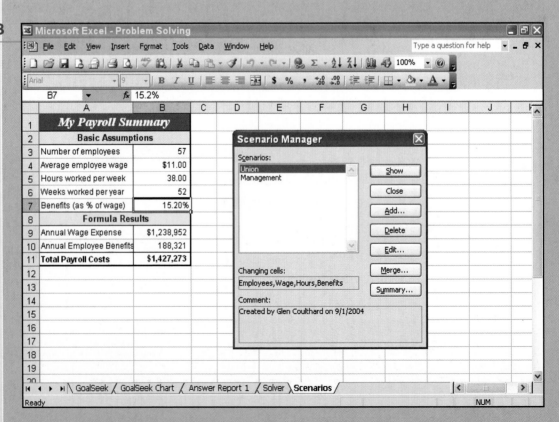

**16.** To summarize the existing scenarios using an outlined report or PivotTable report (covered later in this chapter):
CLICK: Summary command button
The Scenario Summary dialog box appears.

**17.** To create an outlined report, ensure that the *Scenario summary* option button is selected and that cell B11 appears in the *Result cells* text box. Then, do the following:
CLICK: OK command button
A new sheet is added to the workbook called *Scenario Summary* with the relevant cells displayed in an outline format (see Figure 9.19).

**Figure 9.19**

Creating a scenario summary report

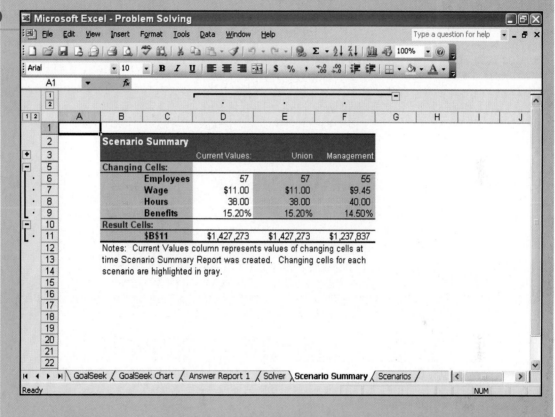

**18.** Save the workbook and keep it open for use in the next lesson.

### 9.1.4 Manipulating Scenarios

→ **Feature**

Scenarios are useful for aggregating different points of view from your friends, associates, and coworkers. For example, you can distribute a workbook to many people and then collect and merge their completed results into a set of scenarios in a single workbook. Using the Scenario Manager, you can then add, show, edit, delete, and merge these scenarios and summarize the data using an outlined report or pivot table.

→ **Method**

To edit or delete an existing scenario:

• CHOOSE: Tools → Scenarios

• SELECT: the desired scenario from the *Scenarios* list box

- CLICK: Edit command button

  *or*

- CLICK: Delete command button

To merge a scenario from another workbook:

- Open the workbook that contains the scenario you want to merge and then switch back to the current workbook.

- CHOOSE: Tools → Scenarios

- CLICK: Merge command button

In the Merge Scenarios dialog box, select the workbook, worksheet, and scenarios that you want to merge.

→ # Practice

You will now edit and merge scenarios in the current workbook. Ensure that the "Problem Solving" workbook is displayed.

**1.** CLICK: *Scenarios* tab in the workbook

**2.** Let's edit management's proposal:
CHOOSE: Tools → Scenarios

**3.** In the Scenario Manager dialog box:
SELECT: Management in the *Scenarios* list box
CLICK: Edit command button
(*Note:* To delete a scenario and start over, you can click the Delete command button instead. For this step, however, you will edit the existing the scenario.)

**4.** In the Edit Scenario dialog box:
CLICK: *Prevent changes* check box, so that no ✓ appears
Notice the comment that has been automatically added by Excel 2003, as shown in Figure 9.20.

**Figure 9.20**

Editing a scenario

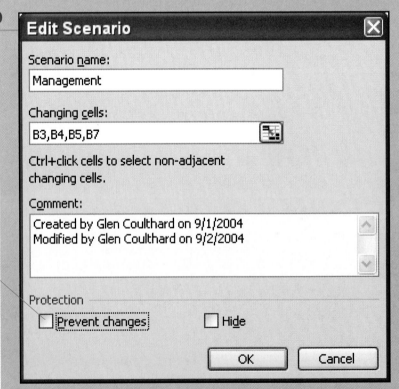

The *Prevent changes* check box only protects a scenario when the active worksheet is protected

5. To proceed:
   CLICK: OK command button

6. For the Scenario Values dialog box:
   DOUBLE-CLICK: in the *4: Benefits* text box
   TYPE: **.1425** to replace the existing value
   CLICK: OK Command button

7. CLICK: Close command to remove the Scenario Manager dialog box

8. Now let's merge an arbitrator's opinion into this workbook. Open the data file named EX0914 and save it as "Arbitration" to your personal storage location. You should now have two workbooks open.

9. Return to the "Problem Solving" workbook by clicking its button on the taskbar.

10. Launch the Scenario Manager dialog box:
    CHOOSE: Tools → Scenarios

11. To import or merge a saved scenario from another workbook into the current workbook, do the following:
    CLICK: Merge command button

12. In the Merge Scenarios dialog box:
    SELECT: Arbitration.xls in the *Book* drop-down list box
    Your screen should now appear similar to the worksheet shown in Figure 9.21.

**Figure 9.21**

Merging a
scenario

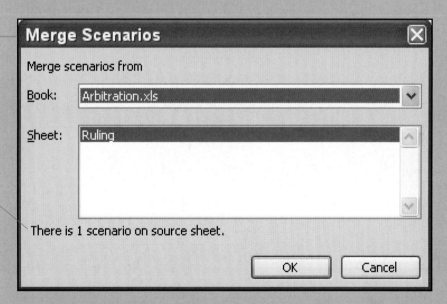

The dialog box tells
you that this
workbook contains
one saved scenario

13. CLICK: OK command button to proceed
    You should now see three scenarios (Union, Management, and Arbitrator) in the Scenario Manager dialog box.

14. To view the Arbitrator scenario:
    SELECT: "Arbitrator" in the *Scenarios* list box
    CLICK: Show command button
    The values in the worksheet are updated to reflect the input values.

15. To prepare a new summary report:
    CLICK: Summary command button

**16.** Ensure that the *Scenario summary* option button is selected and that cell B11 appears in the *Result cells* text box. Then, do the following:
CLICK: OK command button
A new sheet called *Scenario Summary 2* is added to the workbook, as shown in Figure 9.22.

**Figure 9.22**

Displaying a
summary report

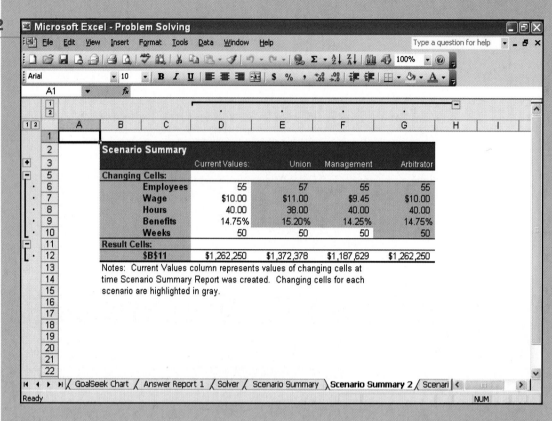

**17.** Save and then close the "Problem Solving" and "Arbitration" workbooks.

 **SelfCheck**   **9.1**   Compare and contrast Excel 2003's Goal Seek command, the Solver add-in program, and the Scenario Manager.

# 9.2 Finding Trends and Forecasting Results

Charts allow you to visually estimate trends and identify relationships among data. There are, however, more accurate methods for predicting the future than having to eyeball a line chart. Imagine, for example, that you are asked to forecast annual sales for a company that has previously achieved $100,000, $132,000, $145,000, and $173,000 over its last four years. Using Excel 2003's statistical analysis and charting tools, you may be able to extend these past results to estimate the future sales, as shown in Figure 9.23. These same analysis tools can help you to estimate inventory quantities and accounts receivable collections, project employee productivity levels, and speculate on engineering or scientific research data. (*Note:* For advanced data analysis, review the feature set available in the Analysis ToolPak add-in program.) This module introduces you to plotting trendlines and using statistical forecasting functions.

**Figure 9.23**

Predicting future
values based on
historic results

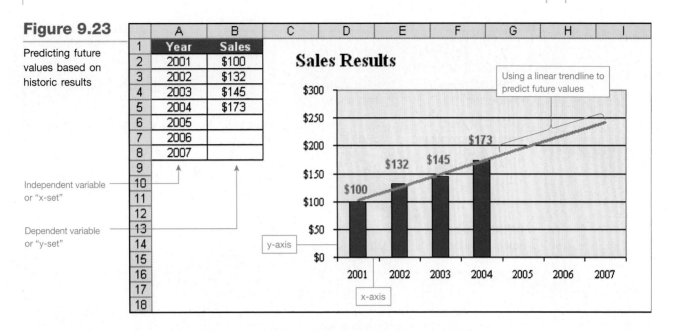

Independent variable
or "x-set"

Dependent variable
or "y-set"

## 9.2.1 Statistical Forecasting Functions

→ **Feature**

Because this is not a course in applied statistics, we will limit the discussion of Excel 2003's higher-level forecasting capabilities to the functions appearing in Table 9.1. The results calculated using these functions often require critical analysis and considerable understanding of statistical procedures and limitations. Rather than relying solely on statistical formulas, you should use these tools to aid your understanding of a problem or situation. Statistical measures can help you determine how variables are related or associated, but they do not surmise *causation*. In other words, variable X may be related to variable Y, but the existence of X does not necessarily cause Y to occur. Remember to view statistics as a helpful light on the road toward common sense!

The functions presented in this lesson help you determine how one value (called the **dependent variable**) is related to, or is associated with, another value (called the **independent variable**). The statistical method that you will employ is called *linear trend* or *linear regression* analysis. **Regression analysis** attempts to fit a straight line to a set of existing data in the hope of illustrating a relationship. Once you have determined how well a straight line fits your data, you can then use the line equation as a representative model for predicting future values. In other words, you can extend the line out further along the X-axis, as shown in Figure 9.20, to see where it ends up. The forecasting functions, described in Table 9.1, include FORECAST, GROWTH, RSQ, and TREND.

→ **Method**

=FORECAST(*new-x,y-set,x-set*)
=GROWTH(*y-set,x-set,new-x,constant*)
=RSQ(*y-set,x-set*)
=TREND(*y-set,x-set,new-x,constant*)

→ **Practice**

You will now use Excel 2003's statistical forecasting functions to project the student enrolments for a college. Ensure that no workbooks appear in the application window.

**Table 9.1**

Functions for
Forecasting

| Function... | Description... |
|---|---|
| FORECAST(*new-x, y-set,x-set*) | Uses a linear (straight-line) trend equation to predict future values based on existing or historical results. |
| GROWTH(*y-set, x-set,new-x,constant*) | Uses an exponential growth equation to predict future values based on existing or historical results. |
| RSQ(*y-set,x-set*) | Returns the **R-square** value, which is a statistical measure that shows how closely a linear line approximates the existing data. In a stable environment, the closer the R-square value is to 1.0, the closer the fit of the line. |
| TREND(*y-set,x-set, new-x,constant*) | Uses a linear trend equation to find a fit for a straight line through existing or historical results. |

1. Open the data file named EX0920 to display the workbook shown in Figure 9.24. This workbook is used to compile, analyze, and predict student enrolment for the Shuster School of Business.

**Figure 9.24**

Opening the
EX0920
workbook

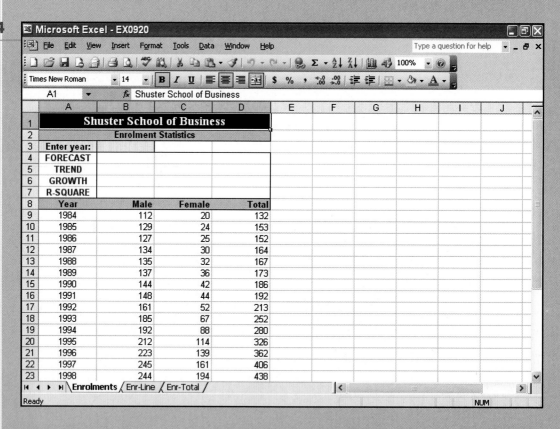

2. Save the workbook as "Shuster" to your personal storage location.

3. On your own, select each tab to review the contents of the workbook. The *Enr-Line* and *Enr-Total* chart sheets plot information from the *Enrolments* worksheet. When you are ready to proceed: CLICK: *Enrolments* tab

**4.** The *Enrolments* tab contains male and female enrolment statistics for the past 21 years. There are four named ranges in this worksheet: Year, Male, Female, and Total. To view these ranges:
CLICK: down arrow attached to the Name box
SELECT: Year

**5.** To view the other named ranges:
SELECT: Male from the Name box
SELECT: Female from the Name box
SELECT: Total from the Name box
SELECT: cell A3 before continuing

**6.** To view the enrolment statistics in the associated chart:
CLICK: *Enr-Line* tab
The chart should appear similar to the one shown in Figure 9.25. Notice that the "Male" data series shows a relatively steady increase or *linear trend* over the 21-year period. The "Female" data series, on the other hand, becomes increasingly steep and displays a tendency toward following an *exponential growth* rate.

**Figure 9.25**

Viewing the
*Enr-Line* chart

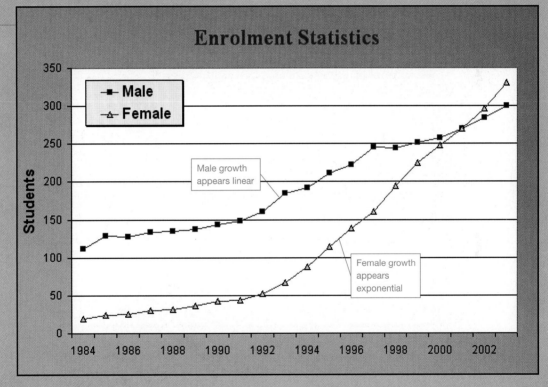

**7.** Let's return to the data:
CLICK: *Enrolments* tab

**8.** You are now charged with estimating the enrolment numbers for male students in the year 2006. To begin, let's enter the year as the independent or "x" variable:
SELECT: cell B3
TYPE: 2006
PRESS: [ENTER]
By placing this value in a cell (rather than inserting it directly into the formulas that you will develop), you will be able to re-calculate the enrolment numbers for any given year.

**9.** As illustrated in Figure 9.25, the "Male" data series is relatively constant and follows a straight pattern. Therefore, you can use the FORECAST and TREND functions, which rely on linear regression equations for fitting a straight line to the existing data. To illustrate:
SELECT: cell B4
TYPE: =forecast(
CLICK: Insert Function button (*fx*)
The Function Arguments dialog box appears.

**10.** In the *X* text box, select the cell reference containing the new independent variable (Year) for which you want the dependent variable (Male enrolment) calculated. Do the following:
TYPE: b3
PRESS: TAB

**11.** In the *Known_y's* text box, select the existing range of dependent variables (Male enrolment.) Because this range has already been assigned a name, do the following:
TYPE: Male
PRESS: TAB

**12.** In the *Known_x's* text box, select the existing range of independent variables (Year):
TYPE: Year
The dialog box should now appear similar to the one shown in Figure 9.26.

**Figure 9.26**

Function Arguments dialog box: FORECAST function

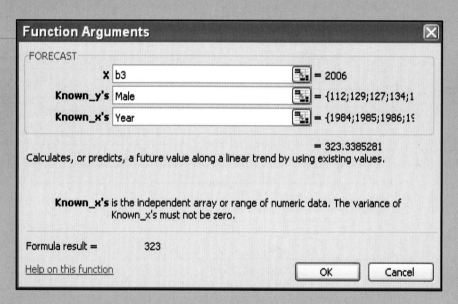

**13.** CLICK: OK command button to proceed
The answer, 323, appears. In other words, Excel extended the regression line along the X axis to predict that there will be 323 male students enrolling in the year 2006.

**14.** To see what the enrolment will be in the year 2010.
SELECT: cell B3
TYPE: 2010
PRESS: ENTER
Excel has calculated that there will be 364 male students enrolling.

**15.** The TREND function performs much the same calculation and returns similar results to the FORECAST function. For example:
SELECT: cell B5
TYPE: =trend(Male,Year,b3
Before completing the equation by typing the closing parenthesis, view the ScreenTip for the TREND function. Notice that most of the arguments are surrounded by brackets "[ ]" and that the current argument appears in boldface, as shown in Figure 9.27. Remember that the brackets "[ ]" mean that an argument is optional.

**Figure 9.27**

ScreenTip for the
TREND function

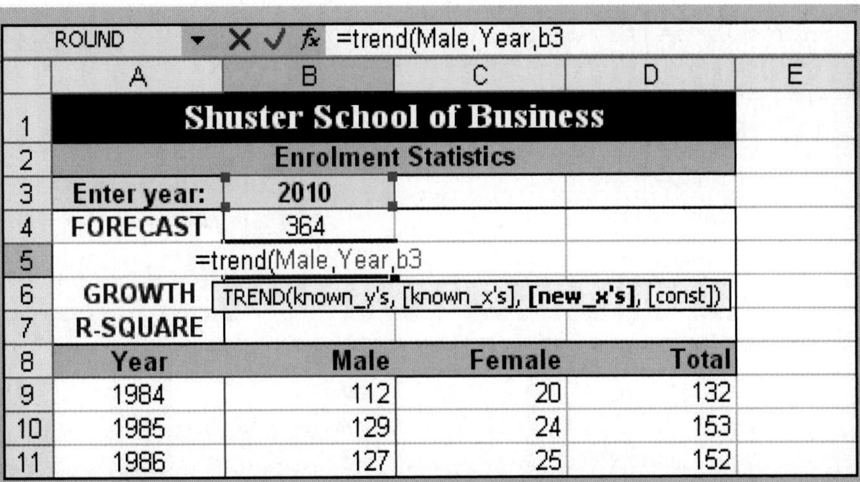

| | ROUND ▾ X ✓ *fx* =trend(Male,Year,b3 | | | |
|---|---|---|---|---|
| | A | B | C | D | E |
| 1 | **Shuster School of Business** | | | | |
| 2 | **Enrolment Statistics** | | | | |
| 3 | **Enter year:** | 2010 | | | |
| 4 | **FORECAST** | 364 | | | |
| 5 | =trend(Male,Year,b3 | | | | |
| 6 | **GROWTH** | TREND(known_y's, [known_x's], **[new_x's]**, [const]) | | | |
| 7 | **R-SQUARE** | | | | |
| 8 | **Year** | **Male** | **Female** | **Total** | |
| 9 | 1984 | 112 | 20 | 132 | |
| 10 | 1985 | 129 | 24 | 153 | |
| 11 | 1986 | 127 | 25 | 152 | |

**16.** To complete the entry:
TYPE: )
PRESS: ENTER
The same answer as displayed in cell B4 should appear. As a general rule, use the FORECAST
function to extend a data series on a worksheet (or in a chart) with projected values. Use the
TREND function to plot a straight regression line through the existing values in a data series and
to perform more complex equations.

**17.** To measure the extent to which the independent and dependent variables are truly associated,
use the RSQ function. This function calculates a statistical measure known as *R-square* and returns a value between 0 and 1. A 0.0 R-square result means that no linear relationship can be assumed. If the value is less than 0.5, a linear trend may also be suspect. If, on the other hand, the
value is 0.9950, the fitted regression line closely matches the existing values and may be a good
prediction tool for forecasting future results. Let's illustrate:
SELECT: cell B7
TYPE: =rsq(Male,Year)
PRESS: ENTER
With a result of 0.9710, you may assume that the fitted line approximates the existing data values very well.

**18.** Now let's forecast the female enrolment figures for 2003. As you may remember, the "Female"
data series showed signs of following an exponential growth trend rather than a linear trend.
Therefore, we will use the GROWTH function to predict the enrolment, rather than attempting to
fit a straight line through the data points. To begin:
SELECT: cell B3
TYPE: 2006
PRESS: ENTER

**19.** To display the Function Arguments dialog box for the GROWTH function:
SELECT: cell C6
TYPE: =growth(
CLICK: Insert Function button (*fx*)
The Function Arguments dialog box appears.

**20.** To complete the dialog box:
TYPE: **Female** in the *Known_y's* text box
PRESS: TAB
TYPE: **Year** in the *Known_x's* text box
PRESS: TAB
TYPE: **b3** in the *New_x's* text box
Your dialog box should now appear similar to the one shown in Figure 9.28.

Excel

**Figure 9.28**

Function
Arguments dialog
box: GROWTH
function

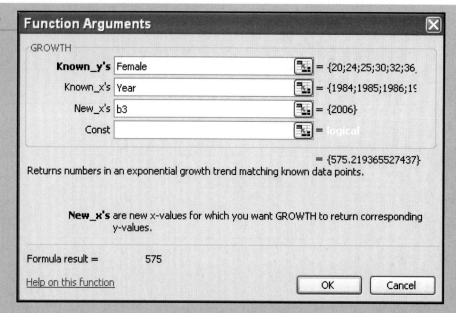

21. CLICK: OK command button
    At first glance, the answer, 575, seems quite high. Given that the 2004 value for females enrolling was a mere 337, this result raises doubts as to whether an exponential growth trend truly exists.

22. To further analyze the "Female" data series, calculate whether a linear relationship might exist between the variables. Do the following:
    SELECT: cell C7
    TYPE: =rsq(Female,Year)
    PRESS: (ENTER)
    An answer of 0.9113, while not 0.9710 as in the "Male" series, nevertheless seems quite significant. Therefore, let's try estimating the future female enrolments using a linear trend line.

23. If you study the *Enr-Line* chart (Figure 9.25), you will notice that the "Female" data series is relatively linear (straight) from 1993 to 2004. Let's use the FORECAST function and only this range of data to predict future female enrolment at the college. Do the following:
    SELECT: cell C4
    TYPE: =forecast(b3,c18:c29,a18:a29)
    PRESS: (ENTER)
    The answer, 399, appears in the cell. This number seems much more realistic than the result returned by the GROWTH function.

24. To test the R-square value for the "Female" data series, let's enter a new function into cell C7 using the past 11 years of data:
    SELECT: cell C7
    PRESS: (DELETE) to remove the existing entry

25. TYPE: =rsq(c18:c29,a18:a29)
    PRESS: (ENTER)
    Notice that the result of 0.9969 is far more significant than the previous R-square factor returned by the entire range. In other words, the past 11 years of data provide an exceptional linear regression line for use in predicting future female enrolments.

26. Save the workbook, which should now appear similar to the one shown in Figure 9.29, and keep it open for use in the next lesson.

## Figure 9.29

Entering forecasting functions in the Shuster workbook

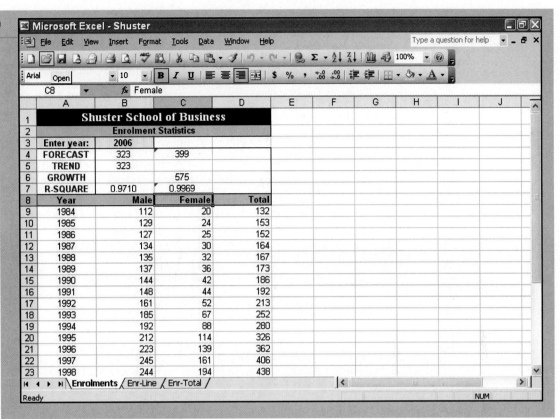

### *In Addition* USING THE FILL HANDLE TO FORECAST RESULTS

You can also use a cell range's fill handle to create a linear or growth series. When you drag a fill handle to extend a series using the right mouse button, the shortcut menu shown at the right appears. If the data represents a straight line, choose the Linear Trend command, which uses the TREND function to calculate future values in the series. If the data represents an exponential growth line, choose the Growth Trend command instead, which uses the GROWTH function to calculate the results. As you can see, many functions, features, and commands in Excel 2003 are easily accessible and closely related!

### 9.2.2 Calculating Trendlines

## Feature

In addition to forecasting and extending results for worksheet data, you can plot such trends directly in a chart. A **trendline** is simply a calculated regression or fitted line that you add to a chart in order to show a trend in an existing data series. One limitation to be aware of is that you can only add trendlines to 2-D charts, such as Area, Bar, Column, Line, and XY types. As with the previous statistical functions, you use trendlines to predict future results based on past or historical data. You can also calculate a moving average that smoothes the fluctuations in a data series and, in doing so, helps you more accurately project future results.

→ ## Method

To add a trendline to a chart:

- SELECT: the data series in the plot area for which you want to calculate and display a trendline
- CHOOSE: Chart → Add Trendline
- SELECT: the type of trendline on the *Type* tab
- SELECT: the number of periods to predict on the *Options* tab
- CLICK: OK command button

→ ## Practice

You will now add linear, growth, and moving average trendlines to existing charts in a workbook. Ensure that the "Shuster" workbook is open and that the *Enrolments* tab is selected.

**1.** CLICK: *Enr-Line* tab to display the chart

**2.** To fit a linear *Trend/Regression* line to the "Male" data series, select the desired data series in the chart. To do so:
CLICK: any data marker for the "Male" data series
(*Hint:* Series "Male" appears in the Name box when the data series is selected.)

**3.** Now select the type of trendline to add to the chart:
CHOOSE: Chart → Add Trendline
The Add Trendline dialog box appears, as shown in Figure 9.30. (*Note:* You can also display this dialog box by right-clicking a data marker and then choosing Add Trendline from the shortcut menu.)

**Figure 9.30**

Add Trendline dialog box: *Type* tab

Click the type of trendline to fit to the selected data series

Currently selected data series

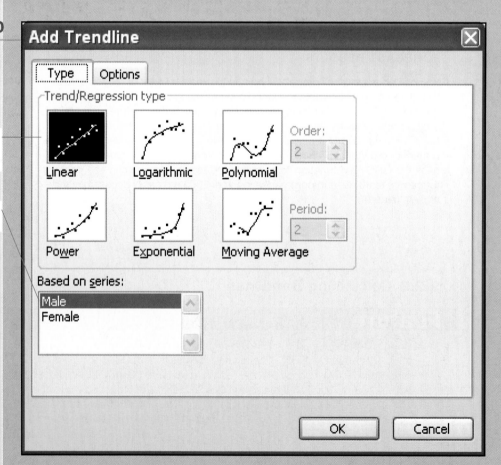

**4.** Selecting a linear trendline will produce results similar to using the TREND function in the last section. Do the following:
SELECT: *Linear* box in the *Trend/Regression type* area

**5.** To predict the future number of males enrolling at the college, you can extend the linear trend-line beyond the existing data. To do so:
CLICK: *Options* tab

**6.** In the *Forecast* area of the *Options* tab, specify an extension of three years for forecasting purposes:
SELECT: "3" *Periods* in the *Forward* spin-box
The dialog box should now appear similar to the one shown in Figure 9.31.

**Figure 9.31**

Add Trendline
dialog box:
*Options* tab

Select "3" to project
the trendline three
years into the future

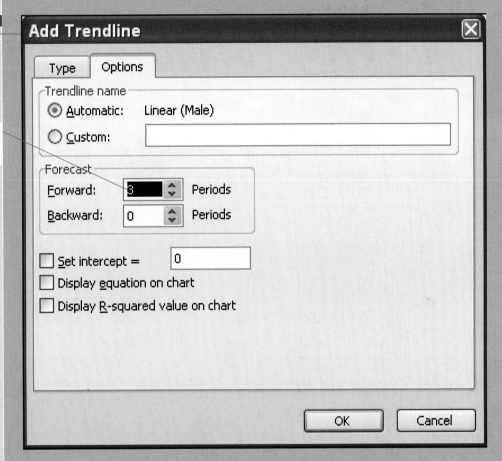

**7.** CLICK: OK command button
The chart is immediately updated with the new trendline. Notice that the line extends three periods beyond 2004.

**8.** Although in the last section we concluded that the "Female" data series was not truly exponential, let's plot an exponential growth trendline for practice. This trendline produces results similar to using the GROWTH function to predict future values. Do the following:
RIGHT-CLICK: any data marker for the "Female" data series
The right-click or shortcut menu shown in Figure 9.32 appears.

**Figure 9.32**

Adding a
trendline to a
data series

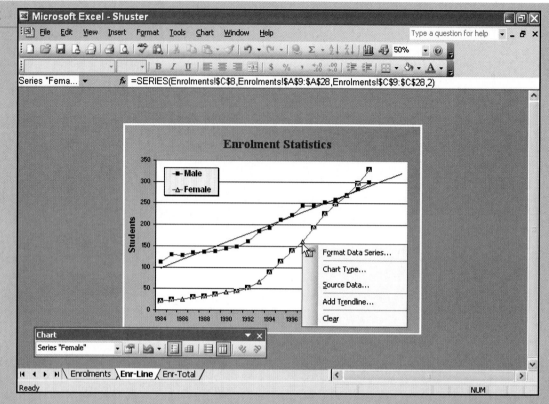

9. From the right-click menu:
   CHOOSE: Add Trendline
   SELECT: *Exponential* box in the *Trend/Regression type* area

10. To extend the exponential trendline ahead three years for predicting the number of females en-
    rolling at the college, do the following:
    CLICK: *Options* tab
    SELECT: "3" *Periods* in the *Forward* spin-box
    CLICK: OK command button

11. On your own, format the trendlines to appear in vibrant colors and with the thickest line style
    possible. (*Hint:* Format a trendline as you would any other chart element. Double-click a marker
    on the trendline to display the relevant formatting options.)

12. For better viewing results:
    CLICK: outside the chart area
    Your screen should now appear similar to the chart shown in Figure 9.33.

**Figure 9.33**

Adding trendlines to the *Enr-Line* chart

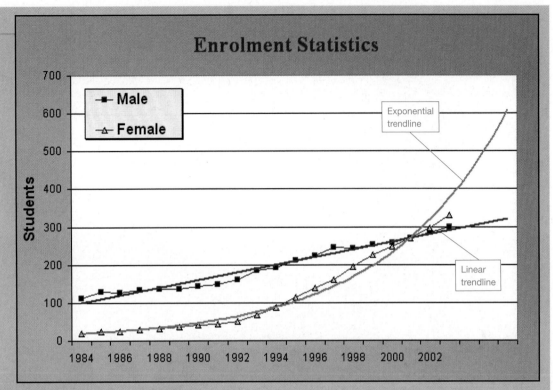

**13.** To add a moving average trendline to the "Total Enrolment" chart:
CLICK: *Enr-Total* tab
RIGHT-CLICK: anywhere in the Area (bluish-green) portion of the data series
CHOOSE: Add Trendline

**14.** In the Add Trendline dialog box:
SELECT: *Moving Average* box in the *Trend/Regression type* area
SELECT: "3" in the *Period* spin box to specify the number of prior periods to use in calculating each "averaged" data point
CLICK: OK command button
A relatively smooth line appears in the chart area (Figure 9.34), representing the moving average for total enrolment.

**Figure 9.34**

Adding a moving average trendline to the *Enr-Total* chart

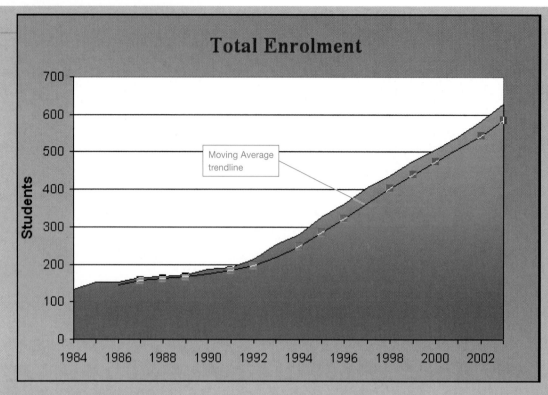

**15.** Save and then close the workbook.

## *In Addition* ANALYSIS TOOLPAK

Excel 2003 provides a special add-in program called the **Analysis ToolPak.** This add-in program provides a set of advanced data analysis tools for performing complex statistical and engineering calculations. Most of these tools introduce terminology, statistical measures, and topics that require specialized knowledge. To find out more information, refer to the Excel 2003 Help system.

**9.2** Which tools might you use to forecast the price of a mutual fund or stock in the securities market?

# 9.3 Working with Data Tables

Rather than calculating a formula using a single value from an input cell, you can calculate a table of results using a set of input values. After entering a formula as you would normally, define a substitute range of values to be used in place of the actual input cell(s). Excel 2003 will substitute these values into the formula and display the outcomes in a data table. In a **one-input data table,** a single input cell is replaced with a set of values for calculating one or more formulas. In a **two-input data table,** the contents of two input cells are replaced in a single formula. Data tables are especially useful for evaluating a formula's sensitivity to input values.

Figure 9.35 provides an example of the two types of data tables. For both data tables, the formula used in the calculation appears in cell E2. The one-input data table shows the results of substituting cell B3 with a series of interest rates (A9:A16). The two-input data table shows the results of substituting both the interest rate (cell B3) and the term (cell B4). The cell in the top left-hand corner of the one-input data table may contain a text label (cell A8) or nothing at all. The same cell in a two-input data table (cell D8), however, holds the desired formula. In Figure 9.35, a reference to cell E2 is used in cell D8 rather than an actual formula expression.

**Figure 9.35**

One-input and two-input data tables

Input cells

Contains the formula "=E2"

For a one-input table, use either a column or row arrangement; a typical column arrangement is shown here

| | A | B | C | D | E | F | G | H |
|---|---|---|---|---|---|---|---|---|
| 1 | **Loan Assumptions** | | | **Payment Calculation** | | | | Formula expression |
| 2 | Principle | $15,000 | | Monthly Pymt | $456.33 | | | |
| 3 | Rate | 6.00% | | Formula Used | =ABS(PMT(B3/12,B4*12,B2)) | | | |
| 4 | Term (yrs) | 3 | | | | | | |
| 5 | | | | | | | | |
| 6 | **One-Input Data Table** | | | **Two-Input Data Table (Rate and Term)** | | | | |
| 7 | | | | | | | | |
| 8 | **Rate** | $456.33 | | $456.33 | 3 | 5 | 10 | |
| 9 | 5.25% | $451.25 | | 5.25% | $451.25 | $284.79 | $160.94 | |
| 10 | 5.50% | $452.94 | | 5.50% | $452.94 | $286.52 | $162.79 | |
| 11 | 5.75% | $454.63 | | 5.75% | $454.63 | $288.25 | $164.65 | |
| 12 | 6.00% | $456.33 | | 6.00% | $456.33 | $289.99 | $166.53 | |
| 13 | 6.25% | $458.03 | | 6.25% | $458.03 | $291.74 | $168.42 | |
| 14 | 6.50% | $459.74 | | 6.50% | $459.74 | $293.49 | $170.32 | |
| 15 | 6.75% | $461.44 | | 6.75% | $461.44 | $295.25 | $172.24 | |
| 16 | 7.00% | $463.16 | | 7.00% | $463.16 | $297.02 | $174.16 | |
| 17 | | | | | | | | |
| 18 | | | | | | | | |

### 9.3.1 Creating a One-Input Data Table

→ **Feature**

A one-input data table summarizes how key results in a worksheet can change when you modify a single value in an input cell. These results are calculated in one or more outcome formulas that contain a direct or indirect reference to the input cell. In addition to selecting the input cell to vary, you must specify the set of values that you want substituted into the target formulas.

→ **Method**

To create a one-input data table:

- Create a set of input values for substituting into one or more formulas in the worksheet.
- SELECT: a cell range containing the set of input values, the desired formula to calculate, and an output area
- CHOOSE: Data → Table
- Specify the input cell for which to substitute the set of input values.
- CLICK: OK command button

→ **Practice**

You will now create a one-input data table for analyzing how to best reduce the payroll costs for a company. Ensure that no workbooks appear in the application window.

1. Open the data file named EX0930 to display the workbook shown in Figure 9.36. This workbook provides data for analyzing payroll alternatives in a small manufacturing company.

## Figure 9.36

Opening the
EX0930
workbook

Worksheet used for
creating a one-input
data table in this
lesson

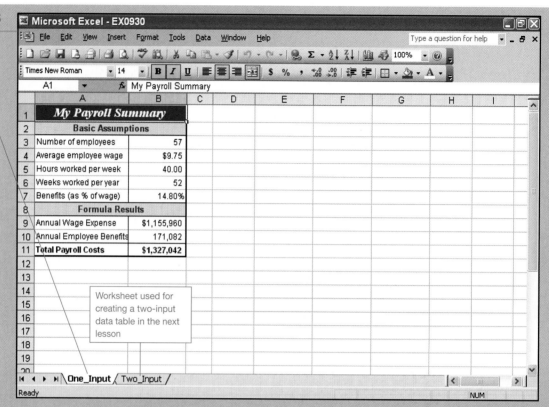

Worksheet used for
creating a two-input
data table in the next
lesson

**2.** Save the workbook as "Payroll Tables" to your personal storage location.

**3.** Before proceeding, ensure that the *One_Input* worksheet tab is selected.

**4.** Let's evaluate the financial significance of changing the number of hours worked each week. In-stead of using 40.00 (the value in cell B5), you will calculate the annual wage expense and em-ployee benefits for a variety of alternatives. To begin constructing a one-input data table, do the following:
SELECT: cell D2
TYPE: **Hours**
PRESS: ENTER

**5.** To enter the column headers:
SELECT: cell E1
TYPE: **Wages**
PRESS: →
TYPE: **Benefits**
PRESS: ENTER

**6.** Now enter the starting cells for the range of input values:
SELECT: cell D3
TYPE: **40**
PRESS: ↓
TYPE: **39**
PRESS: ENTER

**7.** To extend the data series:
SELECT: cell range from D3 to D4
DRAG: the fill handle to cell D8 or until the ScreenTip shows "35," as shown in Figure 9.37
(*Hint:* The fill handle appears as a small box in the bottom right-hand corner of the selected cell range.)

**Figure 9.37**

Preparing a one-input data table

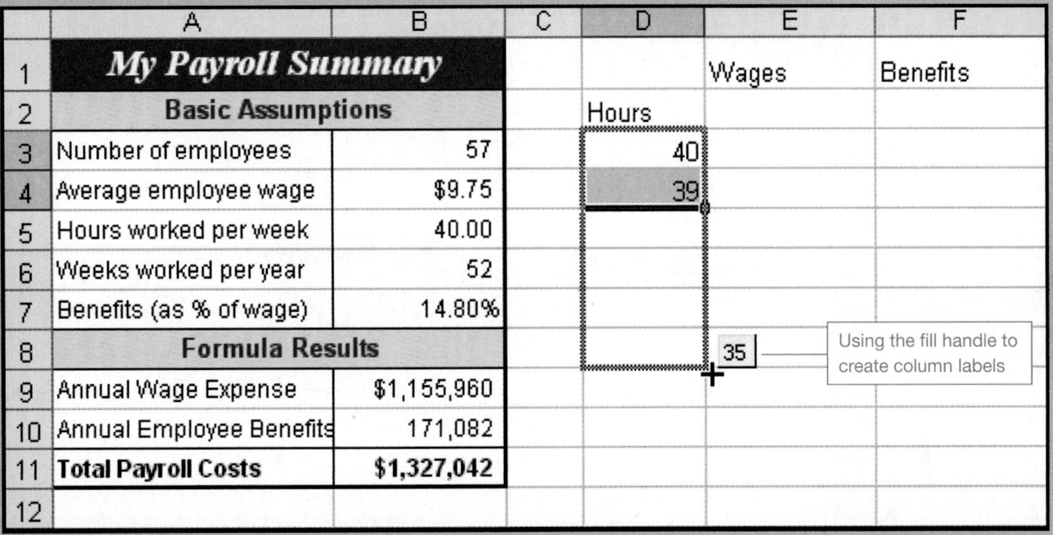

| | A | B | C | D | E | F |
|---|---|---|---|---|---|---|
| 1 | *My Payroll Summary* | | | | Wages | Benefits |
| 2 | Basic Assumptions | | | Hours | | |
| 3 | Number of employees | 57 | | 40 | | |
| 4 | Average employee wage | $9.75 | | 39 | | |
| 5 | Hours worked per week | 40.00 | | | | |
| 6 | Weeks worked per year | 52 | | | | |
| 7 | Benefits (as % of wage) | 14.80% | | | | |
| 8 | Formula Results | | | | 35 | Using the fill handle to create column labels |
| 9 | Annual Wage Expense | $1,155,960 | | | | |
| 10 | Annual Employee Benefits | 171,082 | | | | |
| 11 | Total Payroll Costs | $1,327,042 | | | | |
| 12 | | | | | | |

**8.** To specify the expression to calculate, you can enter a new formula or reference an existing formula from the worksheet. The Annual Wage Expense, cell B9, and Annual Employee Benefits, cell B10, contain formulas that reference the input cell for hours worked each week. To use these formulas in the data table:
SELECT: cell E2
TYPE: =b9
PRESS: ➡
TYPE: =b10
PRESS: ENTER
(*Note:* These two cells display the current worksheet values. They do not represent calculations performed in the data table.)

**9.** Now it is time to create the data table:
SELECT: cell range from D2 to F8
CHOOSE: Data ➔ Table
Notice that the two column headings in row 1 are not selected in this range. Your screen should appear similar to the worksheet shown in Figure 9.38.

**Figure 9.38**

Creating a one-input data table for performing two calculations

Input cells

Outcome formulas

For a one-input data table, enter either a row input cell or a column input cell but not both

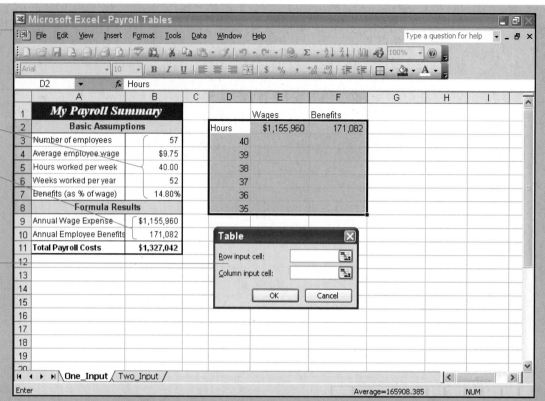

**10.** To calculate a one-input data table, select either a row or column input cell in the Table dialog box, depending on the arrangement of data in your worksheet. In this example, you will substitute a single variable (cell B5) with the set of values appearing in column D. Therefore, enter the input cell address in the *Column input cell* text box:
CLICK: in the *Column input cell* text box
CLICK: cell B5
CLICK: OK command button
After a moment, the selected cell range is filled with values.

**11.** The completed data table shows the annual wage expense (column E) and annual employee benefits (column F) for each alternative number of hours worked per week (column D). To enhance the appearance of the data table:
SELECT: cell range from E2 to F2
CLICK: Format Painter button (🖌)
SELECT: cell range from E3 to F8

**12.** To format the column and row headings, begin by selecting the cells:
SELECT: cell range from E1 to F1
PRESS: **CTRL** and hold it down
SELECT: cell range from D2 to D8
Release the **CTRL** key when you are ready to proceed.

**13.** Now apply the formatting commands:
CLICK: down arrow attached to the Fill Color button (🎨▾)
SELECT: Dark Blue from the drop-down list
CLICK: down arrow attached to the Font Color button (A▾)
SELECT: Light Yellow from the drop-down list
CLICK: Bold button (B)
CLICK: Center button (≡)

**14.** You may be wondering how Excel 2003 creates a data table. Select cell E3 and look in the Formula bar (see Figure 9.39). You will see the following expression:
{=TABLE(,B5)}
The curly braces around "=TABLE(,B5)" inform you that this is a special type of Excel formula known as an **array formula.** Using a single array formula, you can perform multiple calculations and display multiple results. In our example, the array formula calculates results in the Wages and Benefits columns for each of the alternatives listed in the Hours column. How? The array formula replaces each Hours value, from the range D3:D8 (40 to 35), into cell B5 and then uses the formulas in cells E2 and F2 to calculate the results.

**Figure 9.39**

Formatting the one-input data table

| | A | B | C | D | E | F | |
|---|---|---|---|---|---|---|---|
| | E3 ▼ | | *fx* {=TABLE(,B5)} | | | | ← Array formula |
| 1 | *My Payroll Summary* | | | | Wages | Benefits | |
| 2 | Basic Assumptions | | | Hours | $1,155,960 | 171,082 | ← Outcome formulas |
| 3 | Number of employees | 57 | | 40 | $1,155,960 | 171,082 | |
| 4 | Average employee wage | $9.75 | | 39 | $1,127,061 | 166,805 | ← Data table calculations |
| 5 | Hours worked per week | 40.00 | | 38 | $1,098,162 | 162,528 | |
| 6 | Weeks worked per year | 52 | | 37 | $1,069,263 | 158,251 | |
| 7 | Benefits (as % of wage) | 14.80% | | 36 | $1,040,364 | 153,974 | |
| 8 | Formula Results | | | 35 | $1,011,465 | 149,697 | |
| 9 | Annual Wage Expense | $1,155,960 | | | | | |
| 10 | Annual Employee Benefits | 171,082 | | | | | |
| 11 | **Total Payroll Costs** | **$1,327,042** | | | | | |
| 12 | | | | | | | |

**15.** Let's view the contents of another cell in the table:
SELECT: cell F6
Notice that the same formula also appears here. (*Note:* Because each cell in the data table is part of the entire array of results, you cannot edit the formula entries individually. You must re-create the data table whenever you want to make modifications.)

**16.** Save the workbook and keep it open for use in the next lesson.

## 9.3.2 Creating a Two-Input Data Table

→ **Feature**

A two-input data table summarizes how an outcome formula changes when you modify the values stored in two of its input cells. Unlike the one-input data table, a two-input data table only allows the results from a single formula to be displayed in the table. To create a two-input data table, place one set of input values in the leftmost column and another set in the topmost row. The upper-left corner of the table, where the input row and column intersect, holds the outcome formula (or a reference to it).

→ **Method**

To create a two-input data table:

• Create two sets (row and column) of input values for substituting into a single formula.

• Enter the formula (or a reference to it) that you want calculated in the top left-hand corner of the data table.

• SELECT: a cell range containing the input values, the desired formula to calculate, and an output area

- CHOOSE: Data → Table
- Specify the input cells for which to substitute the two sets of input values.
- CLICK: OK command button

→ # Practice

In this lesson, you will create a two-input data table to analyze what effects changing the length of the work week and the average hourly wage have on the company's total payroll costs. Ensure that the "Payroll Tables" workbook is displayed.

**1.** CLICK: *Two_Input* worksheet tab
This worksheet is identical in form and content to the *One_Input* sheet.

**2.** Similar to the last lesson, define the first set of values as the hours worked per week. This time, however, place the values in a row orientation:
SELECT: cell E2
TYPE: 40
PRESS: ➡
TYPE: 38
PRESS: ➡
TYPE: 36
PRESS: ENTER

**3.** To specify the second set of input values:
SELECT: cell D3
TYPE: 9.50
PRESS: ⬇
TYPE: 9.75
PRESS: ENTER

**4.** To extend the wage rate downward:
SELECT: cell range from D3 to D4
DRAG: the fill handle to cell D11 or until the ScreenTip shows "11.5," as shown in Figure 9.40
(*Note:* If the value series is not linear or exponential in nature, you must input each value separately, as opposed to using the fill handle.)

**Figure 9.40**

Preparing a two-input data table

| | A | B | C | D | E | F | G |
|---|---|---|---|---|---|---|---|
| 1 | *My Payroll Summary* | | | | | | |
| 2 | Basic Assumptions | | | | 40 | 38 | 36 |
| 3 | Number of employees | 57 | | 9.5 | | | |
| 4 | Average employee wage | $9.75 | | 9.75 | | | |
| 5 | Hours worked per week | 40.00 | | | | | |
| 6 | Weeks worked per year | 52 | | | | | |
| 7 | Benefits (as % of wage) | 14.80% | | | | | |
| 8 | Formula Results | | | | | | |
| 9 | Annual Wage Expense | $1,155,960 | | | | | |
| 10 | Annual Employee Benefits | 171,082 | | | | | |
| 11 | Total Payroll Costs | $1,327,042 | | | 11.5 | | |
| 12 | | | | + | | | |

**5.** Now enter a reference to the outcome formula in the top left-hand corner of the data table:
SELECT: cell D2
TYPE: =b11
PRESS: ENTER

**6.** To create the data table:
SELECT: cell range from D2 to G11
CHOOSE: Data → Table
The Table dialog box appears.

**7.** On your own, move the Table dialog box so that the input cells are visible. Then, do the following:
CLICK: in the *Row input cell* text box
CLICK: cell B5
CLICK: in the *Column input cell* text box
CLICK: cell B4

**8.** CLICK: OK command button to proceed
The values for the data table are calculated and then displayed.

**9.** On your own, format the data table to appear similar to the one shown in Figure 9.41.

**10.** Save and then close the "Payroll Tables" workbook.

**Figure 9.41**

A two-input data table

Notice that the array formula now contains arguments for both input cells

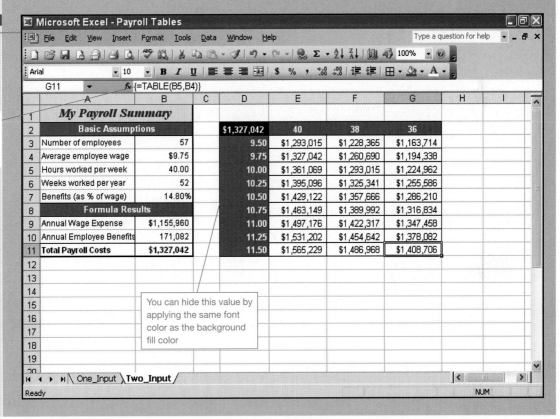

## *In Addition* SPEEDING UP THE RECALCULATION PROCESS

Data tables are recalculated along with the worksheet, even if they have not been modified. This can slow down your worksheet operations significantly. Therefore, Excel 2003 lets you turn off table recalculation using the Tools → Options command. On the *Calculations* tab of the Options dialog box, select the *Automatic except tables* option button.

**SelfCheck**

**9.3** What special type of formula is entered into a data table? Can you edit the formulas appearing in a data table's output area?

# 9.4 Working with PivotTables and PivotCharts

Microsoft Office Excel 2003 provides an extremely powerful tool, called the *PivotTable report,* for analyzing data that is stored in an Excel 2003 worksheet list or in an external data source such as an Access 2003 table. A **PivotTable report** is an interactive, but static, table that formats and displays summarized data in a worksheet. PivotTables are interactive in that, once they have been created, you can easily rearrange, filter, hide, and even *pivot* the data (rotate or transpose columns to rows and vice versa) to present alternative views. They are static because the summarized information must be refreshed manually each time you update the source data (worksheet list or Access table). You will find PivotTables most useful for presenting a concise view of a large list or table. Additionally, you can view a PivotTable's results graphically using a **PivotChart report** or publish a PivotTable to the Web. In this module, you will learn how to create, format, print, and interact with PivotTables, PivotCharts, and Web-based PivotTables.

Before creating a PivotTable report, familiarize yourself with the basic terminology and parts of a PivotTable shown in Figure 9.42 and described in Table 9.2.

## Figure 9.42

Example of a PivotTable report

| | A | B | C | D | E | F | G |
|---|---|---|---|---|---|---|---|
| 1 | Gender | (All) | | | | | |
| 2 | | | | | | | |
| 3 | Average of Salary | Education | | | | | |
| 4 | Department | B.A. | B.Admin. | B.Com. | MBA | Ph.D. | Grand Total |
| 5 | Administration | $29,000 | | | | | $29,000 |
| 6 | Finance | $54,000 | | $53,000 | | | $53,500 |
| 7 | Management | | $37,500 | $22,000 | $65,500 | | $47,625 |
| 8 | Marketing | $33,900 | $38,000 | $39,940 | | | $38,167 |
| 9 | Production | $34,725 | | | | $42,000 | $36,180 |
| 10 | Research | $32,000 | | | | $46,000 | $41,333 |
| 11 | Grand Total | $35,744 | $37,833 | $39,243 | $65,500 | $44,667 | $40,621 |
| 12 | | | | | | | |

Labels: Page field, Page field item, Column field, Column field item, Data area (cell range from B5 to G11), Data field, Row field, Row field item

**Table 9.2**

Parts of a
PivotTable Report

| Component... | Description... |
|---|---|
| Column field | A field from the worksheet list that is used to group and summarize data in a column orientation; also used to specify data for display in the PivotTable |
| Data area | Summarized results based on data stored in the worksheet list; calculated using one of Excel's mathematical or statistical built-in functions |
| Data field | Describes what you are seeing in the *data area;* displays the function and field name used in the summary calculation |
| Items | A unique value taken from a field in the worksheet list and used to group, summarize, and filter data; a subcategory of a *column field* or a *row field* |
| Page field | A field in the worksheet list that filters and displays all records or one *page field item* at a time |
| Page field item | A unique value taken from a field in the worksheet list and used to filter data for display |
| Row field | A field from the worksheet list that is used to group and summarize data in a row orientation; also used to specify data for display in the PivotTable |
| Field drop-down list | A drop-down list that appears when the down arrow attached to a field is clicked; allows you to view and select items for display in the PivotTable report. (*Note:* This feature is not shown in Figure 9.42.) |

Excel

## 9.4.1 Creating a PivotTable Report

→ **Feature**

After analyzing a specified data source, Excel 2003's **PivotTable and PivotChart Wizard** compiles the field names and unique values, or *items,* found in each particular field. You then make selections in the wizard that determine the layout of the PivotTable report and how the data will be summarized. Specifically, the data area in a PivotTable calculates results using one of Excel 2003's mathematical or statistical worksheet functions; for example, SUM, AVERAGE, MAX, MIN, COUNT, PRODUCT, STDDEV, and VAR. Once created, a PivotTable report may be formatted, customized, refreshed, printed, plotted in a chart, or saved as a Web Page.

→ **Method**

To create a PivotTable report:

- SELECT: any cell in a worksheet list (or identify an external data source)
- CHOOSE: Data → PivotTable and PivotChart Report
- In Step 1 of the wizard, confirm the desired data source and then specify the *PivotTable* option button.
- In the next step(s), select the worksheet list range, worksheet consolidation ranges, or external data source to summarize.
- In the last step, select the output location of the new PivotTable report and specify any additional layout and formatting options.
- CLICK: [ Finish ] to proceed

→ **Practice**

You will now create a PivotTable report using the PivotTable and PivotChart Wizard. Ensure that no workbooks are open in the application window.

**1.** Open the data file named EX0940 to display the workbook shown in Figure 9.43. Notice that there is only a single worksheet, entitled *HeadOffice*, stored in this workbook.

**Figure 9.43**

Opening the
EX0940
workbook

**2.** Save the workbook as "Personnel Pivots" to your personal storage location.

**3.** You will now create a PivotTable report to summarize the salary information in the *HeadOffice* worksheet list. To begin:
SELECT: cell A1 (or any cell in the worksheet list)

**4.** To launch the PivotTable and PivotChart Wizard:
CHOOSE: Data → PivotTable and PivotChart Report
Step 1 of 3 for the wizard is displayed, as shown in Figure 9.44. (*Note:* If the Office Assistant appears, click the *No, don't provide help now* option button. You can also remove the Office Assistant from the screen by right-clicking it and choosing the Hide command.)

**Figure 9.44**

PivotTable and
PivotChart
Wizard: Step 1
of 3

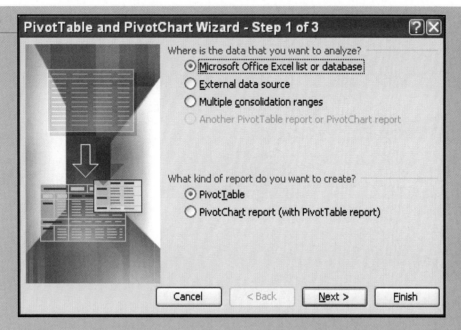

**5.** In Step 1 of the wizard, specify the data you want to summarize and the type of report that you want to create:
SELECT: *Microsoft Office Excel list or database* option button
SELECT: *PivotTable* option button
CLICK: Next>
(*Note:* These selections are the default options.)

**6.** By selecting a cell in the worksheet list range prior to launching the wizard, Step 2 is completed for you by the wizard. Ensure that the cell range "$A$1:$J$50" appears in the *Range* text box and then:
CLICK: Next>
Your screen should now appear similar to the dialog box shown in Figure 9.45.

**Figure 9.45**

PivotTable and
PivotChart
Wizard: Step 3
of 3

**7.** In Step 3, select an output location for the PivotTable, usually a new worksheet in the current workbook. If desired, you can also specify the layout structure of the PivotTable report and other options. For this exercise, let's construct the PivotTable report interactively. Do the following:
SELECT: *New worksheet* option button, if not already selected
CLICK: Finish
Your screen should now appear similar to the worksheet shown in Figure 9.46.

**8.** If the PivotTable Field List window does not appear:
CLICK: Show Field List button (⬚) in the PivotTable toolbar

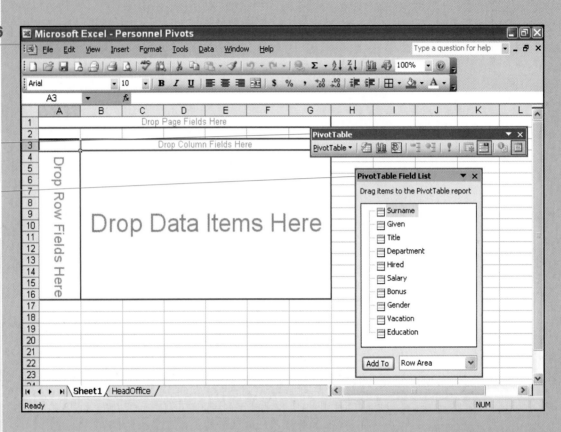

**9.** To construct the PivotTable report, you must drag the *field items* displayed in the PivotTable Field List window to the labeled areas in the worksheet. When a field item is dropped into the Pivot-Table area, it becomes a **field button.** To illustrate:
DRAG: Gender field item to the area labeled "Drop Column Fields Here," as shown in the graphic to the right
(*Note:* Make sure that you release the mouse button after reaching the desired drop location. If done properly, the Gender column field button appears in cell B3.)

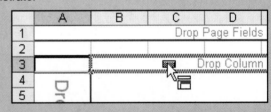

**10.** To add a row field to the PivotTable report:
DRAG: Department field item to the area labeled "Drop Row Fields Here"
The Department row field button should appear in cell A4. (*Hint:* If you drop a field item on the wrong area, drag the field button to the correct location or back to the PivotTable Field List window.)

**11.** Now let's add the most important component, the data field, which provides the summary calculation. Do the following:
DRAG: Salary field item to the area labeled "Drop Data Items Here"
Your worksheet should now appear similar to Figure 9.47. Notice that the SUM function is used by default to summarize the Salary data.

**Figure 9.47**

Adding field
items to the
PivotTable area

Data field button

Column field button

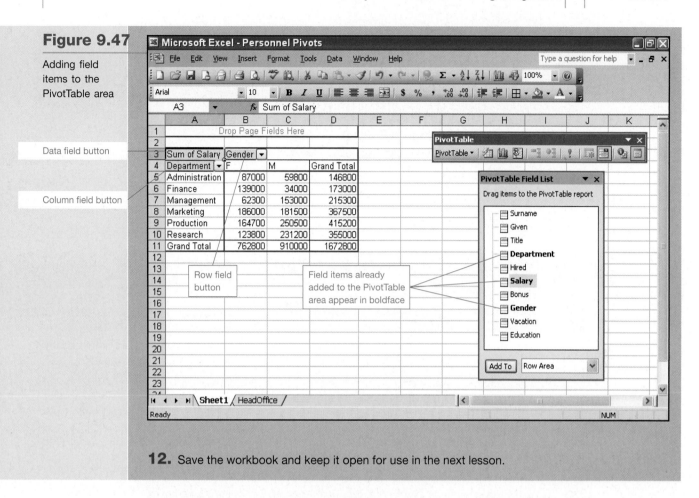

Row field
button

Field items already
added to the PivotTable
area appear in boldface

Excel

**12.** Save the workbook and keep it open for use in the next lesson.

*In Addition* CREATING A PIVOTTABLE REPORT FOR A FILTERED LIST

The PivotTable and PivotChart Wizard uses all of the data in a worksheet list when creating a Pivot-Table report. To create a PivotTable based on a filtered list, you must first extract the desired data to a new range using the Advanced Filter command. The newly extracted list then becomes the data source for creating the PivotTable report.

## 9.4.2 Customizing a PivotTable Report

→ **Feature**

There are several ways in which you can alter or enhance the appearance of a PivotTable report. For example, a *pivot table* gets its name from its ability to pivot rows and columns and, therefore, to provide alternative views of summarized information. You can alter the appearance of a report by dragging and dropping field buttons in the PivotTable. You can also enhance the appearance of a PivotTable by choosing one of Excel 2003's predefined AutoFormat styles. There are two specific categories of AutoFormat styles for PivotTables: *non-indented* and *indented.* The non-indented formats are table-oriented styles with row and column field items. (*Note:* The default style used by the PivotTable and PivotChart Wizard is a non-indented table format called "PivotTable Classic.") Indented formats are report-oriented styles that line up field items across a single row and summarize data in a column. These AutoFormat styles are useful for printing reports based on longer lists or larger data sources.

→ **Method**

To change the row and column orientation of a PivotTable report:

• DRAG: field buttons to different areas in the PivotTable

To modify the display options for a particular field:

• DOUBLE-CLICK: the desired field button

To filter data or limit the display of information:

• SELECT: an item from the page, column, or row field drop-down lists

To apply an AutoFormat style:

• CLICK: Format Report button ()

   *or*

• CLICK: [PivotTable ▾] on the PivotTable toolbar

• CHOOSE: Format Report

→ **Practice**

In this lesson, you will customize an existing PivotTable report. Ensure that you have completed the previous lesson and that the PivotTable report shown in Figure 9.47 appears on your screen.

**1.** To practice working with the interactive features of a PivotTable report, let's change the Gender column field to a page field by dragging its field button. To begin:
DRAG: Gender column field using the  mouse pointer to the PivotTable area labeled "Drop Page Fields Here"
(*Note:* Ensure that you drag the Gender column field button that is displayed on the worksheet, and not a second Gender field item from the PivotTable toolbar.)

**2.** Now add the Education field item to the column field area:
DRAG: Education field item from the toolbar to cell B3 (which appears immediately to the right of the Sum of Salary data field)
Your screen should now appear similar to the worksheet shown in Figure 9.48.

**Figure 9.48**

Customizing a PivotTable report

The Gender field button was dragged from the column field area to the page field area in the PivotTable report

Education field button

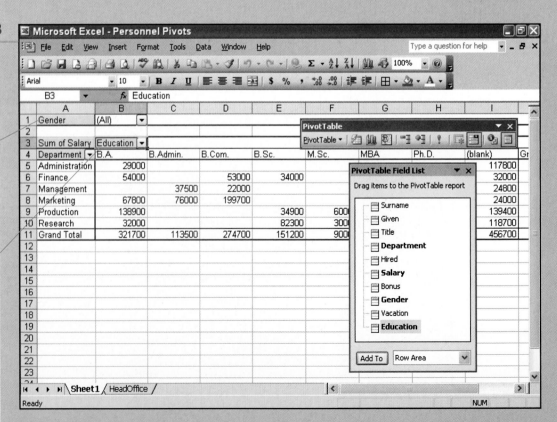

**3.** To pivot the table so that salaries are summed by Education and then subtotaled by Department, do the following:

DRAG: Education column field button below the Department row field and aligned to the left border of cell A5

(*Hint:* When you have positioned the mouse pointer properly, a faint vertical line appears along the row frame border, as shown here. Release the mouse button to drop the Education field button.)

| 3 | Sum of Salary |
|---|---|
| 4 | Department ▼ |
| 5 | Administration |
| 6 | Finance |
| 7 | Management |

**4.** Using the new PivotTable layout, you will now filter the results presented in the PivotTable using the page field. For example, to view the salary results for male employees only:

CLICK: down arrow attached to the Gender page field item

SELECT: "M" in the field drop-down list

CLICK: OK command button

Your screen should now appear similar to the worksheet shown in Figure 9.49.

**Figure 9.49**

Pivoting a PivotTable report

Filtering the PivotTable report so that only data for the male gender is included

Education is now a row field button as opposed to a column field button

| | A | B | C |
|---|---|---|---|
| 1 | Gender | M ▼ | |
| 2 | | | |
| 3 | Sum of Salary | | |
| 4 | Education ▼ | Department ▼ | Total |
| 5 | B.A. | Marketing | 21800 |
| 6 | | Production | 138900 |
| 7 | | Research | 32000 |
| 8 | B.A. Total | | 192700 |
| 9 | B.Admin. | Marketing | 36000 |
| 10 | B.Admin. Total | | 36000 |
| 11 | B.Com. | Management | 22000 |
| 12 | | Marketing | 123700 |
| 13 | B.Com. Total | | 145700 |
| 14 | B.Sc. | Finance | 34000 |
| 15 | | Production | 34900 |
| 16 | | Research | 30000 |
| 17 | B.Sc. Total | | 98900 |

**5.** To view results for male employees with a B.A. degree:

CLICK: down arrow attached to the Education row field

The Education field drop-down list appears, as shown in Figure 9.50.

**Figure 9.50**

Filtering results
by Education to
display in the
PivotTable report

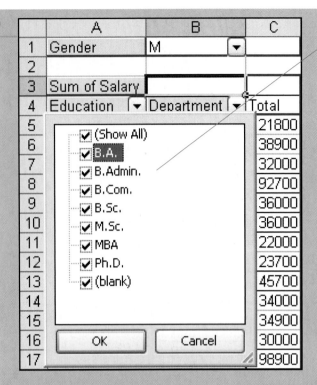

Each field button
contains a list of
unique values that you
may use to limit the
data displayed in a
PivotTable report

**6.** To remove all of the check marks and then select B.A. only:
CLICK: *(Show All)* check box to clear all the check marks (✓)
CLICK: *B.A.* check box
CLICK: OK command button
The PivotTable is immediately updated.

**7.** Using the field button drop-down list boxes, select the *(Show All)* check box for Education and
then select *(All)* for Gender. All the data should be displayed in the PivotTable report.

**8.** Now let's change the calculation from summing salaries to computing averages. Do the following:
RIGHT-CLICK: Sum of Salary data field in cell A3
CHOOSE: Field Settings from the right-click menu
The PivotTable Field dialog box shown in Figure 9.51 appears. (*Hint:* You can also double-click the
data field button to display this dialog box or click the Field Settings button (📊) on the toolbar.)

**Figure 9.51**

PivotTable Field
settings dialog
box

Select the type of
calculation to
perform in the data
area

**PivotTable Field**

Source field:    Salary

Name:    Sum of Salary

Summarize by:

Sum
Count
Average
Max
Min
Product
Count Nums

OK
Cancel
Hide
Number...
Options >>

**9.** In the PivotTable Field dialog box:
TYPE: **Average Salary** in the *Name* text box
SELECT: Average in the *Summarize by* list box

**10.** You can also specify a number format for the data area of the PivotTable report. To illustrate:
CLICK: Number command button
The Format Cells dialog box appears displaying only the *Number* tab.

**11.** To continue formatting the data area:
SELECT: Number in the *Category* list box
SELECT: 0 in the *Decimal places* spin box
SELECT: *Use 1000 Separator (,)* check box so that a ✓ appears
CLICK: OK command button to close the Format Cells dialog box

**12.** To close the PivotTable Field dialog box:
CLICK: OK command button
The PivotTable report's data area now displays the average salaries.

**13.** To pivot the table back to a row and column layout:
DRAG: Education row field button to the column field area in cell C3
Your screen should now appear similar to the worksheet shown in Figure 9.52.

**Figure 9.52**

Pivoting the
PivotTable report

Calculating
averages for the
salary data field

| | A | B | C | D |
|---|---|---|---|---|
| 1 | Gender | (All) ▼ | | |
| 2 | | | | |
| 3 | Average Salary | Education ▼ | | |
| 4 | Department ▼ | B.A. | B.Admin. | B.Com. |
| 5 | Administration | 29,000 | | |
| 6 | Finance | 54,000 | | 53,000 |
| 7 | Management | | 37,500 | 22,000 |
| 8 | Marketing | 33,900 | 38,000 | 39,940 |
| 9 | Production | 34,725 | | |
| 10 | Research | 32,000 | | |
| 11 | Grand Total | 35,744 | 37,833 | 39,243 |

The number
formatting remains
intact even after
pivoting the
PivotTable report

**14.** You will now apply one of Excel 2003's AutoFormat styles to the PivotTable. Do the following:
CLICK: PivotTable button ([PivotTable ▼]) on the PivotTable toolbar
CHOOSE: Format Report
The familiar AutoFormat dialog box appears. (*Hint:* You can also click the Format Report button
([▨]) on the PivotTable toolbar.)

**15.** On your own, scroll the list box to view the various *Report* formats and *Table* formats, as shown
in Figure 9.53.

**Figure 9.53**

AutoFormat
dialog box for
PivotTable reports

An indented Report
AutoFormat style

A non-indented
Table AutoFormat
style

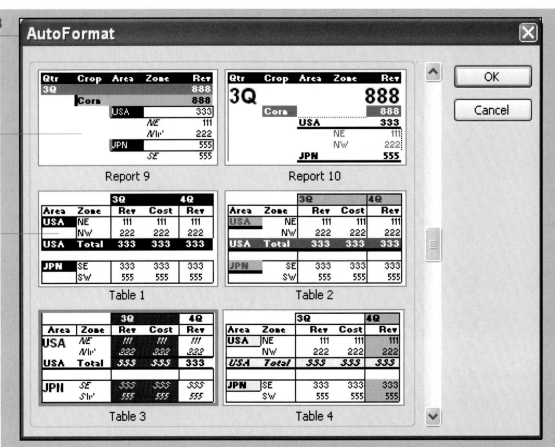

**16.** To apply an AutoFormat style:
SELECT: Report 6 in the list box
CLICK: OK command button
The PivotTable report is formatted using a row-oriented style.

**17.** PRESS: CTRL+HOME to cancel the selection
Your screen should now appear similar to the worksheet shown in Figure 9.54.

**Figure 9.54**

Displaying the
PivotTable report
using the Report
6 AutoFormat

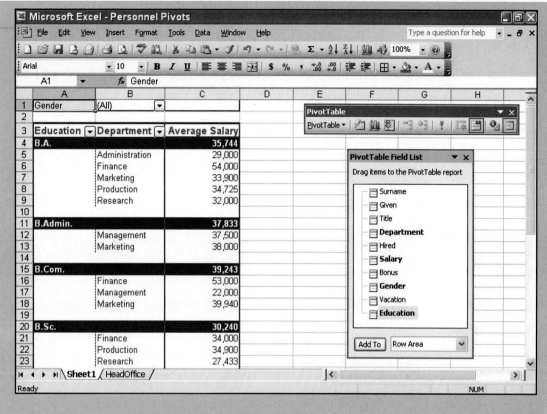

**18.** Save the workbook and keep it open for use in the next lesson.

### In Addition REFRESHING THE PIVOTTABLE REPORT

If you add, modify, or delete records in the data source (usually a worksheet list), you must refresh the PivotTable report by clicking the Refresh Data button ( ) on the PivotTable toolbar.

## 9.4.3 Printing A PivotTable Report

### → Feature

The process of printing a PivotTable report is similar to printing any large worksheet or worksheet list. In addition to selecting a specific print area, you can identify print titles to appear on each printed page. Specifically, the PivotTable Options dialog box allows you to select the PivotTables' field and item labels as print titles. You can also choose to repeat only the outer row item labels on each printed page.

### → Method

To print a PivotTable report:

**1.** CLICK: PivotTable button ( PivotTable ▾ ) in the PivotTable toolbar

**2.** CHOOSE: Table Options

**3.** SELECT: *Repeat item labels on each printed page* check box

**4.** SELECT: *Set print titles* check box

**5.** CLICK: OK command button

→ **Practice**

You will now practice printing a PivotTable report. Ensure that you have completed the previous lessons in this module.

**1.** In order to illustrate the use of print titles, the report must run across two or more pages. To ensure that this is the case:
CLICK: Select All button ( ) in the top left-hand corner of the worksheet

**2.** With the entire worksheet selected:
CHOOSE: Format → Row → Height
TYPE: **25** in the *Row height* text box
CLICK: OK command button
The PivotTable report now appears double-spaced.

**3.** PRESS: CTRL + HOME to cancel the selection

**4.** To preview how the report will appear when printed:
CLICK: Print Preview button ( )
Your screen should now appear similar to the report shown in Figure 9.55.

**Figure 9.55**

Previewing the PivotTable report

Field item labels

Page 1 of 2 is displayed

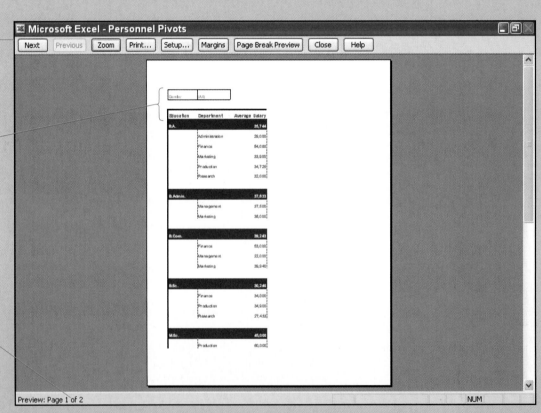

**5.** To move to the next page:
PRESS: PgDn
Notice that the field item labels are not displayed on the second page.

**6.** To return to the worksheet:
CLICK: Close command button on the toolbar

**7.** Let's specify print titles for the PivotTable report:
CLICK: PivotTable button ( PivotTable ▾ ) in the PivotTable toolbar
CHOOSE: Table Options
The PivotTable Options dialog box appears, as shown in Figure 9.56.

**Figure 9.56**

PivotTable
Options dialog
box

These two check
boxes affect how the
PivotTable report
appears when
printed

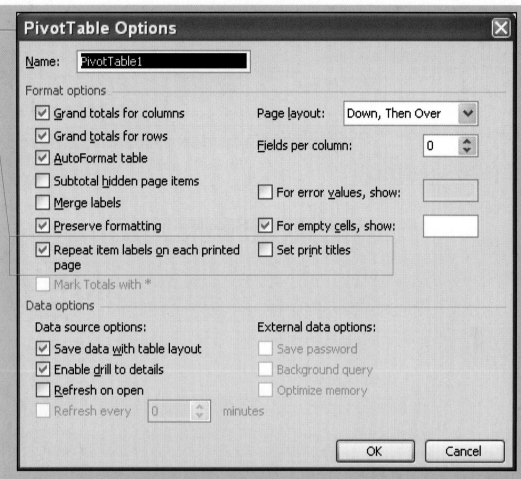

8. To specify that the field item labels appear as print titles:
   SELECT: *Set print titles* check box so that a ✓ appears
   CLICK: OK command button

9. CLICK: Print Preview button ( 🔍 )
   PRESS: **PgDn** to move to the second page
   Notice that the field item labels now appear at the top of the second page as well.

10. If you have a printer connected to your computer:
    CLICK: Print command button
    CLICK: OK command button in the Print dialog box
    (*Note:* If you do not have a printer, close the Print Preview window by clicking the Close command button.)

11. To adjust the row heights in the worksheet:
    CLICK: Select All button ( ☐ )
    CHOOSE: Format → Row → AutoFit

12. PRESS: **CTRL**+**HOME** to cancel the selection

13. Before proceeding to the next lesson, let's change the format of the PivotTable report:
    CLICK: Format Report button ( 🗐 ) on the PivotTable toolbar

14. In the AutoFormat dialog box:
    SELECT: Table 10 in the list box
    CLICK: OK command button

15. PRESS: **CTRL**+**HOME** to cancel the selection
    Your screen should appear similar to the report shown in Figure 9.57.

**Figure 9.57**

Changing the
PivotTable
report's
AutoFormat style

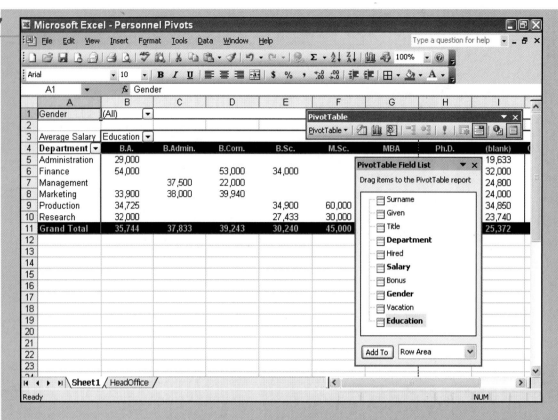

**16.** Save the workbook and keep it open for use in the next lesson.

### 9.4.4 Creating a PivotChart Report

→ **Feature**

A PivotChart report enables you to view the data summarized in a PivotTable graphically. When you choose to create a chart in the PivotTable and PivotChart Wizard, Excel 2003 first prepares an associated PivotTable to summarize the desired data and then uses the PivotTable results as the basis for plotting the chart. Not surprisingly, you can also create a PivotChart report from an existing PivotTable report. Because of this close association between the two reports, customizing or deleting a PivotTable directly affects the appearance of the PivotChart.

In addition to the regular chart elements, a PivotChart report contains field items geared toward making the chart interactive. Specifically, a PivotChart contains series fields (known as column fields in a PivotTable), category fields (known as row fields in a PivotTable), data fields, and page fields. Creating a PivotChart is an excellent way to get the benefits of charting along with the analytical power of PivotTables.

→ **Method**

To create a PivotChart report:

• SELECT: any cell in a worksheet list (or identify an external data source)

• CHOOSE: Data → PivotTable and PivotChart Report

• In Step 1, select the desired data source and then specify the *PivotChart report (with PivotTable report)* option button.

• In the next step(s), select the worksheet list range, worksheet consolidation ranges, or external data source to summarize.

• In the last step, select the output location of the new PivotChart report and specify any additional layout and formatting options.

• CLICK: Finish to proceed

→ **Practice**

In this lesson, you will create a PivotChart report from an existing PivotTable report. Ensure that you have completed the previous lessons in this module.

**1.** Creating a new PivotChart report requires launching the PivotTable and PivotChart Report Wizard. You have already created a PivotTable report, however there is a much quicker method. To begin, let's customize the PivotTable's data area to perform a SUM calculation:
DOUBLE-CLICK: Average Salary data field

**2.** In the PivotTable Field dialog box:
TYPE: **Total Salary** in the *Name* text box
SELECT: Sum in the *Summarize by* list box
CLICK: OK command button

**3.** To increase your working space, hide the PivotTable Field List window:
CLICK: Hide Field List button (□) on the PivotTable toolbar
(*Hint:* You can show and hide this window at any time by clicking this toolbar button, which is a toggle button permitting you to turn the displayed list on or off.)

**4.** Now create the PivotChart report:
CLICK: Chart Wizard button (🗠) on the PivotTable toolbar
With a single mouse click, Excel 2003 creates, formats, and displays a PivotChart report on a new chart sheet (Figure 9.58). Notice that the PivotTable and PivotChart toolbars are visible for use in formatting and customizing the new chart object. You can also manipulate the field items as you did previously in customizing a PivotTable report.

**Figure 9.58**

Creating a
PivotChart report

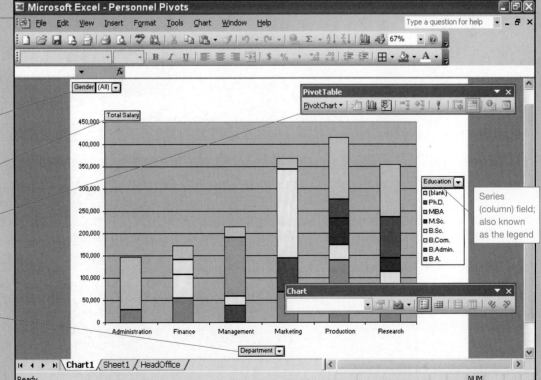

Page field

Data field

PivotChart button
replaces the
PivotTable button
on the PivotTable
toolbar

Category (row) field;
responsible for the
X-axis

Series
(column) field;
also known
as the legend

**5.** To demonstrate how the PivotChart and PivotTable reports are linked:
CLICK: *Sheet1* tab to return to the PivotTable report
CLICK: down arrow attached to the Education column field
SELECT: B.Com. check box so that no ✓ appears
SELECT: MBA check box so that no ✓ appears
SELECT: (blank) check box so that no ✓ appears
CLICK: OK command button
The PivotTable report is updated to reflect the selections.

**6.** Now let's view the PivotChart report:
CLICK: *Chart1* tab
Notice that the (blank), B.Com., and MBA series items have been removed from the legend and from the chart's plot area.

**7.** You can reinstate a series using the PivotChart report. To do so:
CLICK: down arrow attached to the Education series (or legend) field
SELECT: B.Com. check box so that a ✓ appears
Your screen should appear similar to the report shown in Figure 9.59.

**Figure 9.59**

Customizing a
PivotChart report

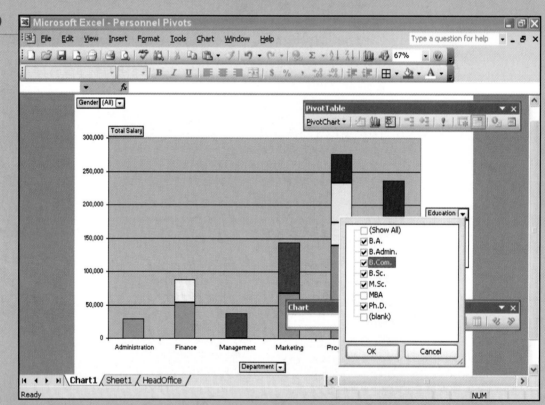

**8.** CLICK: OK command button to proceed
The PivotChart and associated PivotTable are updated immediately.

**9.** Save the workbook and keep it open for use in the next lesson.

## 9.4.5 Creating a Web-Based PivotTable

→ ## Feature

Microsoft Office Excel 2003 enables you to publish a PivotTable report to the Web for others to access using a Web browser. The two methods for creating a Web-based PivotTable are (1) without interactivity and (2) with interactivity. You can save a PivotTable report as a static and non-interactive HTML document or, using the **Microsoft Office Web Components,** display a dynamic and interactive PivotTable in a Web browser. In order to experience the full interactivity and functionality of the Office Web Components, users will need Microsoft Office 2003 installed locally and use the Microsoft Internet Explorer Web browser software.

When you save a PivotTable report as a **PivotTable list,** which is the name given to an interactive Web-based PivotTable report, most of the features and functionality remain available. However, Web-based PivotTables do not retain certain formatting enhancements. Furthermore, you must remember to click the Refresh Data button ( ) on a PivotTable list's toolbar in order to view any changes made to the source data in the workbook's PivotTable report. These limitations aside, PivotTable lists provide incredible opportunities for distributing complex analysis and summary reports to a large number of users on a corporate intranet or on the Internet.

→ ## Method

To save a PivotTable report as a non-interactive HTML table:

- SELECT: the PivotTable report to publish
- CHOOSE: File → Save as Web Page
- SELECT: *Selection: Sheet* option button in the *Save* area
- Enter a Web page name in the *File name* text box.
- CLICK: Save command button

To save a PivotTable report as an interactive PivotTable list:

- SELECT: the PivotTable report to publish
- CHOOSE: File → Save as Web Page
- CLICK: Publish command button
- SELECT: PivotTable in the *Item to publish* area
- SELECT: *Add interactivity with* check box in the *Viewing options* area
- SELECT: PivotTable functionality from the drop-down list box
- Enter a Web page name in the *File name* text box.
- CLICK: Publish command button

→ ## Practice

You will now save the PivotTable report created in this module as an interactive Web-based PivotTable list. Ensure that you have completed the previous lessons in this module.

1. To begin, display the PivotTable worksheet:
   CLICK: *Sheet1* tab

2. Now select and name the worksheet:
   DOUBLE-CLICK: *Sheet1* tab to edit the name
   TYPE: **Salary PivotTable**
   PRESS: ENTER

3. To save the PivotTable report to the Web:
   CHOOSE: File → Save as Web Page
   Your screen should appear similar to the dialog box shown in Figure 9.60.

Excel

**Figure 9.60**

Saving a
PivotTable report
as a Web page

The files listed in this
area may differ from
your screen

Enter a name for the
Web page

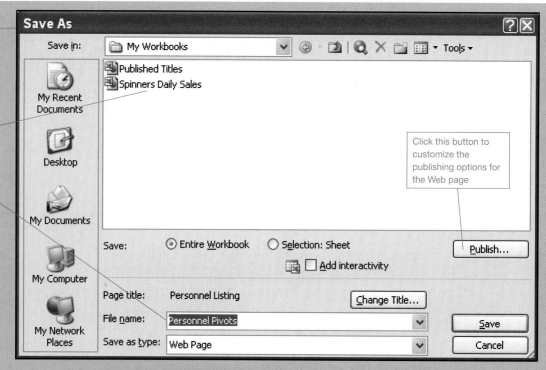

Click this button to
customize the
publishing options for
the Web page

**4.** Rather than making selections in the Save As dialog box, you can enter a name for the Web page, add interactivity using the Microsoft Office Web Components, and specify other customizing options in the Publish as Web Page dialog box (Figure 9.61). To illustrate:
CLICK: Publish command button
(*Note:* If the Office Assistant appears, click *No, don't provide help now* option button. You can hide the Office Assistant by right-clicking on it and choosing the Hide command.)

**Figure 9.61**

Publish as Web
Page dialog box

Select the item you
want to publish

Select this check
box to use the
Microsoft Office
Web Components

Select this check
box to immediately
display the result in
your Web browser
software

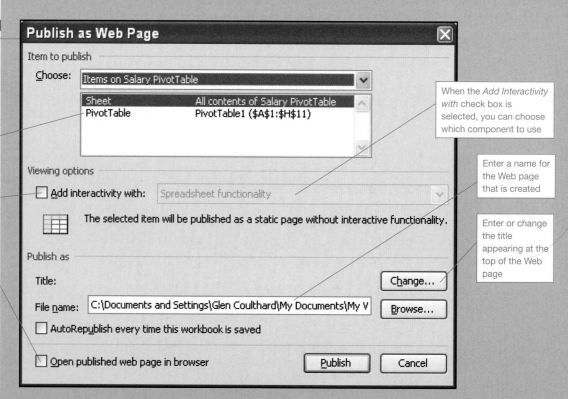

When the *Add Interactivity
with* check box is
selected, you can choose
which component to use

Enter a name for
the Web page
that is created

Enter or change
the title
appearing at the
top of the Web
page

**5.** In the Publish as Web Page dialog box:
SELECT: PivotTable in the *Item to publish* list box
SELECT: *Add interactivity with* check box
Notice that the "PivotTable functionality" appears automatically in the drop-down list box.

**6.** To provide a title for your Web page:
CLICK: Change command button

**7.** In the Set Title dialog box that appears:
TYPE: **Analysis of Personnel Salaries**
CLICK: OK command button

**8.** For this exercise, keep the default file name and then open the Web page in your default Web browser. To proceed
CLICK: *Open published web page in browser* check box so that a ✓ appears
CLICK: Publish command button
After a few moments (and assuming that you have Microsoft Internet Explorer installed), your screen should appear similar to the dialog box shown in Figure 9.62.

### Figure 9.62

Viewing a PivotTable list in a Web browser

Microsoft Office Web Component's PivotTable List toolbar

Page fields are called *filter fields* in a PivotTable list and are used for filtering data

Click the Expand (⊞) and Contract (⊟) buttons to show and hide details

The data area contains *data* or *total fields*

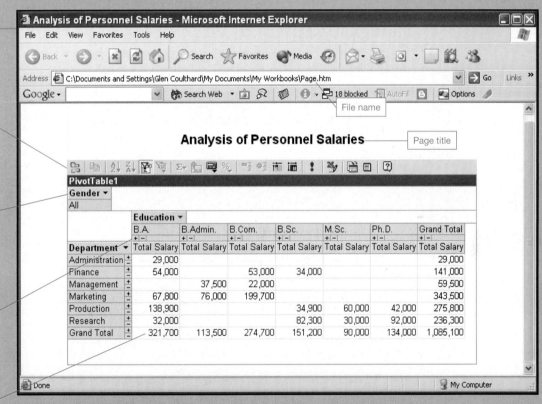

**9.** On your own, click the field arrows to display drop-down lists for Gender, Education, and Department and make a few selections. Then, manipulate the display of table information by clicking on the Expand buttons ( + ) and the Contract buttons ( − ) next to each column and row field item. Before proceeding, return the display options so that the PivotTable list appears similar to the one shown in Figure 9.62.

**10.** Let's customize the PivotTable list by adding a new data field:
CLICK: Field List button ( ▤ ) on the toolbar
The PivotTable Field List window appears, as shown in Figure 9.63.

**11.** To add the Vacation field item to the data area:
SELECT: Vacation in the PivotTable Field List window

**12.** At the bottom of the PivotTable Field List window and to the right of the Add to command button:
CLICK: down arrow attached to the drop-down list
SELECT: Data Area from the drop-down list
CLICK: Add to command button
The Vacation field is added to the data area of the PivotTable list, as shown in Figure 9.63.

**Figure 9.63**

Adding a field to the data area

The "Sum of Vacation" total field is now displayed in the detail or data area of the PivotTable list

You can click the Add to command button or use drag and drop to add field items to the PivotTable list

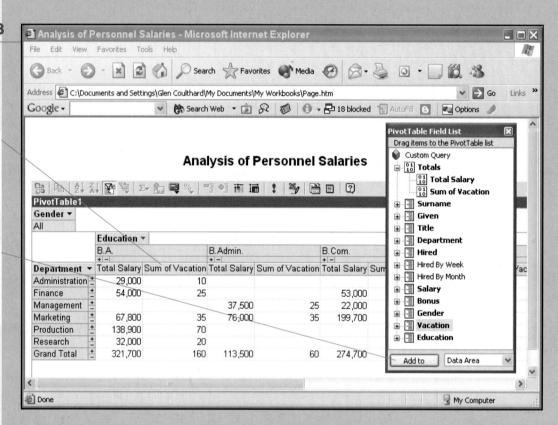

**13.** CLICK: Close button (❌) for the PivotTable Field List window

**14.** Now let's view some of the options available for customizing the PivotTable list. Do the following:
CLICK: Education filter field (not the down arrow)
The entire row of data should now appear highlighted.

**15.** To proceed:
CLICK: Commands and Options button (🖹) on the toolbar
The dialog box in Figure 9.64 appears, showing information about the Education filter field.

**Figure 9.64**

Commands and
Options dialog
box: *Format* tab

**16.** On your own, click each of the tabs in the Commands and Options dialog box to review the functional and formatting capabilities. When you are ready to proceed, click its Close button (☒).

**17.** To return to Excel 2003 and the PivotTable report, click the Close button (☒) for Microsoft Internet Explorer.

**18.** Save and then close the "Personnel Pivots" workbook.

## *In Addition* ADDING, REMOVING, AND CUSTOMIZING FIELDS IN A PIVOTTABLE LIST

PivotTable lists allow you to view and interact with PivotTable reports using Web browser software. You can customize a PivotTable list by manipulating fields using the PivotTable List toolbar, PivotTable Field List window, and the Commands and Options dialog box. For example, you can drag and drop fields from the PivotTable Field List window to the PivotTable list. Then, using the Commands and Options dialog box, you can specify formatting, sorting, and totaling options (depending on the type of field you selected.)

To add a field item to a PivotTable list:

- CLICK: Field List button (▦) on the toolbar

- SELECT: a field in the PivotTable Field List window

- SELECT: a target location (row, column, filter, data, or detail area) from the drop-down list

- CLICK: Add to command button

To remove a field item from a PivotTable list:

- RIGHT-CLICK: the desired field

- CHOOSE: Remove Field

To customize a field item in the PivotTable list:

- SELECT: the desired field

- CLICK: Commands and Options button (▤) on the toolbar

**9.4** What would happen to the summary results in the data area of a PivotTable report if some values from its source data (worksheet list) were modified?

# 9.5 Managing and Reporting Results

To many people, a *report* refers to a hard-copy printout. Besides printing a worksheet page, you can create reports in Excel 2003 by combining data stored in different worksheets and workbooks. You can then present the data as a continuous flow of thoughts and conclusions. The challenge is often separating the desired output information from your various worksheets' detailed calculations and input data. In this module, you will learn how to print multiple worksheets, create custom views, and save a custom workspace.

## 9.5.1 Printing Multiple Worksheets

### → Feature

Using a few simple steps, Excel 2003 enables you to print and preview multiple worksheets and chart sheets as a single report. From the Print dialog box, you may choose to print a cell range, the active sheet (worksheet or chart sheet), or the entire workbook. To preview and print multiple sheets, simply select the desired sheets before issuing the Print command.

### → Method

To print multiple worksheets:

- SELECT: the desired worksheets that you want to print
- CHOOSE: File → Print (or Print Preview)
- SELECT: *Active sheet(s)* option button in the *Print what* area
- CLICK: OK command button

### → Practice

You will now practice selecting multiple worksheets and issuing the Print Preview and Print commands. Ensure that no workbooks are open in the application window.

**1.** Open the data file named EX0950 to display the workbook shown in Figure 9.65. This workbook contains three worksheets and a chart sheet.

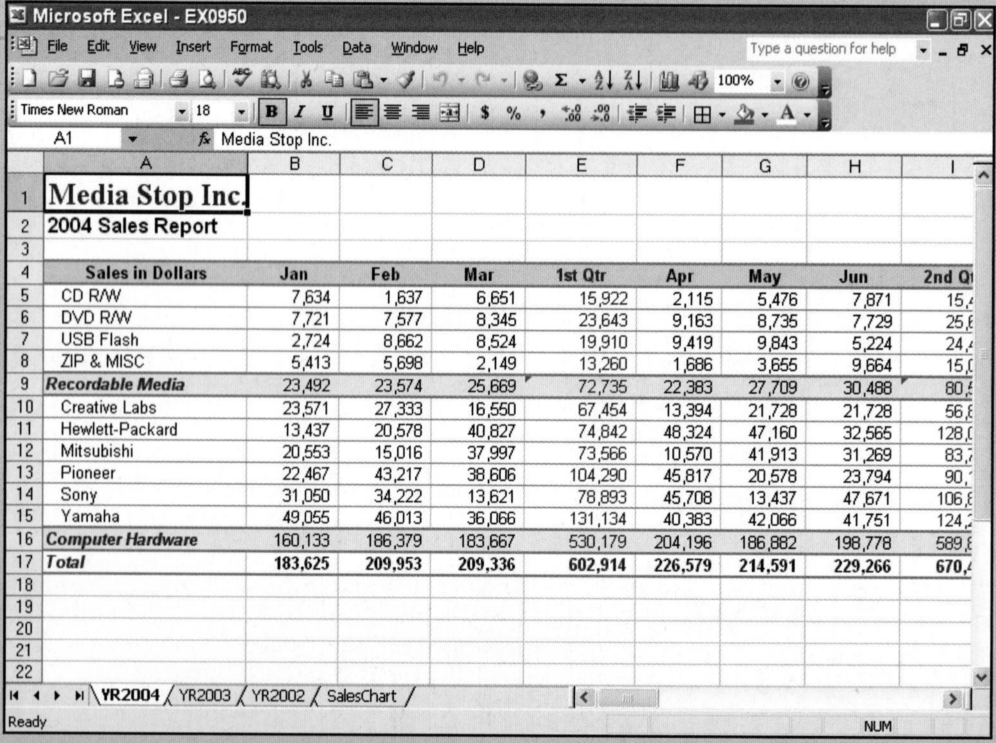

**Figure 9.65**

Opening the EX0950 workbook

**2.** Save the workbook as "Reports" to your personal storage location.

**3.** To preview the active worksheet, *YR2004,* for printing:
CLICK: Print Preview button (🔍) on the toolbar

**4.** To close the Preview window:
CLICK: Close button in the toolbar

**5.** To preview all of the worksheets and chart sheets for printing:
CHOOSE: File → Print
The Print dialog box appears, as shown in Figure 9.66.

**Figure 9.66**

Printing multiple worksheets using the Print dialog box

Select this option to specify how many pages of a multipage report to print

Use the *Print what* area to specify what portions of the workbook to print

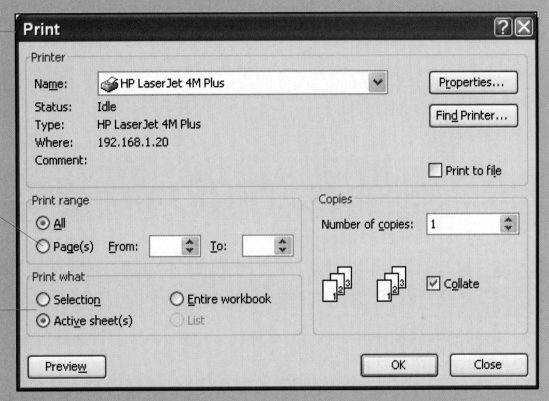

**6.** In the *Print what* area of the Print dialog box:
SELECT: *Entire workbook* option button
CLICK: Preview command button
Notice the number of pages now listed in the Status bar.

**7.** On your own, click the Next and Previous buttons on the toolbar to navigate through the pages. When you are ready to proceed:
CLICK: Close button on the toolbar

**8.** To print only the *YR2004* worksheet and the *SalesChart* chart sheet:
CLICK: *YR2004* tab
PRESS: CTRL and hold it down
CLICK: *SalesChart* tab
(*Note:* Release the CTRL key before proceeding.) The worksheet tabs should appear as shown below.

9. To prepare the two sheets for printing:
CHOOSE: File → Print
Notice that the *Active sheet(s)* option button is selected automatically.

10. To send the two sheets to the printer:
CLICK: OK command button
(*Note:* If you do not have a printer connected to your computer, click the Preview button to preview the print selection and then click the Close button to close the Preview window.)

11. To ungroup the two sheets in the workbook:
RIGHT-CLICK: *YR2004* tab
CHOOSE: Ungroup Sheets

12. Save the workbook and keep it open for use in the next lesson.

### 9.5.2 Creating Custom Views

→ **Feature**

A **custom view** is a combination of display and print options to which you can give a name and which you can save along with a workbook. You can load a custom view at any time to change the appearance of a worksheet or to prepare a workbook for printing. Some of the settings that you can store in a custom view include column widths and row heights, hidden columns and rows, frozen panes, filter options, page margins, and print orientation. Custom views also assist you in producing sophisticated or lengthy printed reports.

→ **Method**

To create a custom view:

• CHOOSE: View → Custom Views

• CLICK: Add command button

• TYPE: *a name* for the custom view

• CLICK: OK command button

→ **Practice**

You will now use custom views to save and then apply alternative print and display settings. Ensure that the "Reports" workbook is displayed and that the *YR2004* tab is the active worksheet.

1. When you need to prepare different reports that are based on the same worksheet, you can save valuable time by storing each report's view and print settings in a custom view. To begin, store the current settings in a custom view so that you may easily return to this state later:
CHOOSE: View → Custom Views
The Custom Views dialog box appears (Figure 9.67).

2. To add a new view:
CLICK: Add command button in the Custom Views dialog box
The Add View dialog box is displayed, as shown in Figure 9.67. In addition to providing an easy-to-remember name for the view, you can choose whether to store both print and display settings.

**Figure 9.67**

Displaying the
Add View dialog
box from the
Custom Views
dialog box

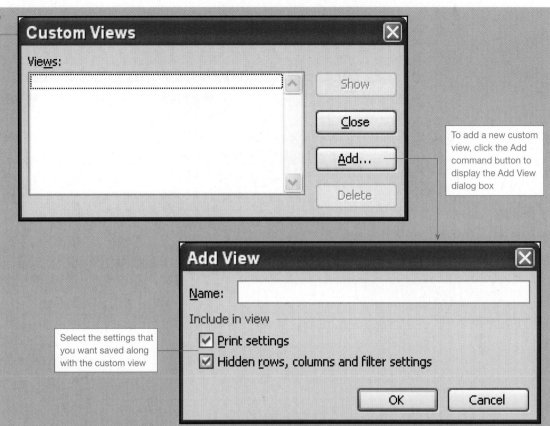

To add a new custom
view, click the Add
command button to
display the Add View
dialog box

Select the settings that
you want saved along
with the custom view

**3.** To create a view that retains the existing print and display settings:
TYPE: **Default**
CLICK: OK command button
(*Note:* A custom view affects the entire workbook, not just the active worksheet.)

**4.** With the "Default" custom view saved, you can manipulate the print and display settings without worrying about being able to later return to the original view. To prepare the worksheet for the first report, let's hide several rows and columns. To begin:
RIGHT-CLICK: row 9 in the row frame area
CHOOSE: Hide

**5.** Using the menu:
SELECT: rows 16 and 17 by dragging the mouse in the row frame area
CHOOSE: Format → Row → Hide

**6.** To hide the quarterly and grand total columns:
CLICK: column E in the frame area
PRESS: CTRL and hold it down
CLICK: columns I, M, Q, and then R in the frame area
Your screen should appear similar to the worksheet shown in Figure 9.68. (*Hint:* Click the horizontal scroll bar to view additional columns without losing the existing selections.)

**Figure 9.68**

Selecting multiple columns to hide in the worksheet

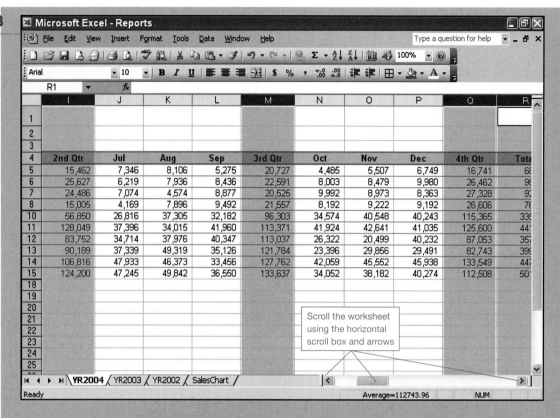

7. Release the **CTRL** key and then do the following:
   CHOOSE: Format → Column → Hide
   All of the quarterly and grand total results are now hidden.

8. To return to the top of the worksheet:
   PRESS: **CTRL**+**HOME**

9. To adjust the page setup so that the worksheet prints on a single sheet of paper in landscape orientation, do the following:
   CHOOSE: File → Page Setup
   CLICK: *Page* tab
   SELECT: *Landscape* option button in the *Orientation* area
   SELECT: *Fit to* option button
   SELECT: 1 in the *Fit to* spin box for both *page(s) wide* and *tall*

10. Now preview the print and display settings that you have selected so far:
    CLICK: Print Preview command button
    The worksheet is compressed to print on a single landscape page, as shown in Figure 9.69.

**Figure 9.69**

Previewing the display and print settings for a worksheet

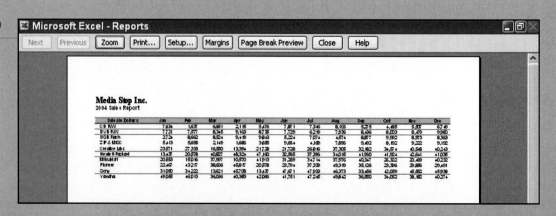

**11.** When you are finished previewing the worksheet:
CLICK: Close button on the toolbar

**12.** To save these settings as a custom view:
CHOOSE: View → Custom Views
Notice that the "Default" view appears in the list box.

**13.** Now add a new view to the current workbook:
CLICK: Add command button
TYPE: **Landscape Detail**
CLICK: OK command button
(*Note:* Ensure that both check boxes are selected prior to clicking the OK command button.)

**14.** To return to the original view:
CHOOSE: View → Custom Views
SELECT: Default in the list box, if not already selected
CLICK: Show command button
The workbook is updated to display using its original settings.

**15.** Save and then close the workbook.

### 9.5.3 Creating a Workspace

→ **Feature**

If you frequently use multiple workbooks at the same time, you can spare yourself a lot of effort by saving the arrangement of workbooks in a special file known as a **workspace.** A workspace file does not contain the actual workbooks. Instead, it stores information about which workbooks were open and how they appeared on the screen. Thereafter, you need only open the workspace file to open, size, and position all of the desired workbook windows.

→ **Method**

To create an Excel 2003 workspace file:

• Open the workbooks you want included in the workspace.

• Organize the workbook windows within the application window.

• CHOOSE: File → Save Workspace

→ **Practice**

You will now practice opening multiple workbooks, arranging the workbooks on the screen, and then saving the workspace. Ensure that no workbooks are open in the application window.

**1.** Begin by opening and then saving the workbooks that will be used in this lesson. Do the following:

• Open the file named EX0953A and save it as "Work1" to your personal storage location.

• Open the file named EX0953B and save it as "Work2" to your personal storage location.

• Open the file named EX0953C and save it as "Work3" to your personal storage location.

**2.** To view all of the workbooks in the document area of the Excel 2003 application window:
CHOOSE: Window → Arrange
SELECT: *Vertical* option button
CLICK: OK command button
Your screen should now appear similar to the workbooks shown in Figure 9.70.

**Figure 9.70**

Arranging
workbook
windows

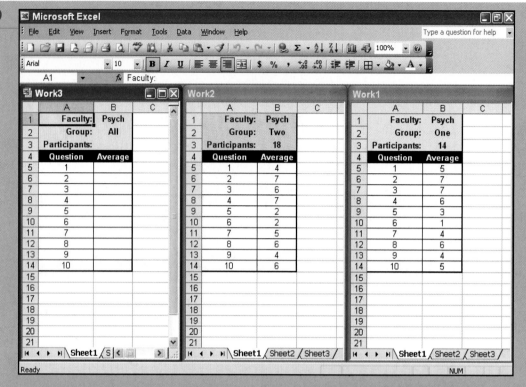

3. Rather than opening these workbooks individually and issuing the Arrange command, you can have Excel 2003 do it for you using a workspace. To illustrate:
CHOOSE: File → Save Workspace

4. In the Save Workspace dialog box (which is almost identical to the Save As dialog box):
TYPE: **My Three Workbooks** in the *File name* text box

5. Using the Save in drop-down list box or the Places bar:
SELECT: *your personal storage location*
Your screen should appear similar to the dialog box shown in Figure 9.71.

**Figure 9.71**

Save Workspace
dialog box

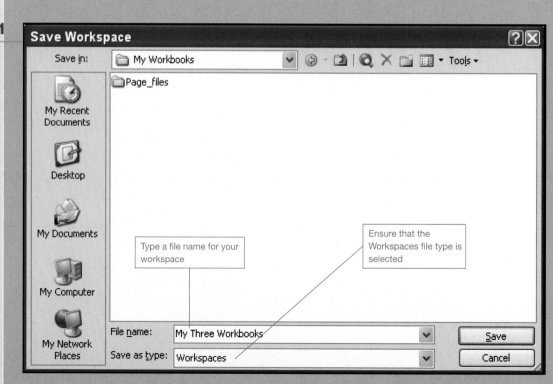

Excel

**6.** To proceed with saving the workspace:
CLICK: Save command button

**7.** You will now close all of the workbooks using a single command:
PRESS: (SHIFT) and hold it down
CHOOSE: File → Close All
(*Note:* Release the (SHIFT) key after executing the command.)

**8.** To demonstrate the utility of workspaces:
CHOOSE: File → Open
Notice that the *Files of type* drop-down list box in the Open dialog box displays "All Microsoft Excel Files," which includes workspaces. A workspace file also displays using a different icon than workbooks.

**9.** Now open the workspace:
DOUBLE-CLICK: My Three Workbooks in the list area
The three workbooks (Work1, Work2, and Work3) are opened and then arranged as displayed previously in Figure 9.70.

**10.** Close all of the workbooks before proceeding.

## *In Addition*  USING THE REPORT MANAGER ADD-IN PROGRAM

Although not yet announced for Office 2003, Microsoft Excel's **Report Manager** add-in program (available for Office XP and earlier versions) allows you to select several parts of a workbook for printing. Each part, whether an entire worksheet, custom view, or scenario, is saved as a section under a particular report name. In other words, you can create one report to print all of the worksheets in a workbook and another report to print only a few custom views. The Report Manager helps you organize these reports and also manages the print process when desired. To retrieve more information about the Report Manager add-in, visit the Microsoft Office Excel 2003 download center on the World Wide Web.

 **SelfCheck**

**9.5** How might custom views and the Report Manager feature help you compile and print reports containing both worksheets and charts?

# Chapter
### summary

*What-if analysis* is the creation of a worksheet model that allows you to systematically change values in specific cells, called input cells, and then observe the results produced by outcome formulas. An optimal worksheet model separates the input cells from the outcome formulas. Goal seeking and the Solver add-in program are tools that enable you to work backward from a target value or outcome to find the required input value(s). The Scenario Manager is another data analysis feature that is used to track and compare various combinations of input values and outcomes. To gauge the sensitivity of outcomes, one-input and two-input data tables can show you how results vary given a set of input values. Excel 2003 also provides the Analysis ToolPak add-in program for performing more advanced statistical computations.

PivotTables, PivotCharts, and PivotTable lists are exciting and powerful features in Microsoft Office Excel 2003. Primarily used for summarizing and presenting data, PivotTable reports pull the field names and data from a worksheet list and then use mathematical or statistical functions to summarize the data. The result is an interactive report that allows you to include and exclude data and to manipulate the positioning of rows and columns. With so many tools and reports available, Excel 2003 is helpful in managing alternatives. These features include the ability to create and store custom views in a workbook and to save workspace arrangements of your open workbooks.

## Command Summary
Many of the commands and procedures appearing in this chapter are summarized in the following table.

| Skill Set | To Perform This Task . . . | Do the Following . . . |
|---|---|---|
| **Analyzing Data** | Use goal seeking to find the input value required to produce an outcome | CHOOSE: Tools → Goal Seek |
| | Use graphical goal seeking to update a worksheet's input cell | SELECT: a data column in a chart<br>DRAG: the top marker up or down to adjust the associated cell value |
| | Use the Solver add-in program to calculate an optimal outcome by varying multiple input cells | CHOOSE: Tools → Solver |
| | Use Scenario Manager to add, edit, delete, show, and merge various combinations of input values and their resulting outcomes | CHOOSE: Tools → Scenarios |
| | Forecast values by creating a trendline | SELECT: a data series in a chart<br>CHOOSE: Chart → Add Trendline<br>SELECT: the type of trendline<br>SELECT: the number of periods |
| | Analyze data using one-input and two-input data tables | CHOOSE: Data → Table |
| | Create a PivotTable report | CHOOSE: Data → PivotTable and PivotChart Report<br>SELECT: *PivotTable* option button<br>Complete the steps. |
| | Format a PivotTable by applying AutoFormat styles | SELECT: a cell in the PivotTable<br>CLICK: Format Report button (⬚) on the PivotTable toolbar<br>SELECT: an AutoFormat style |
| | Display the PivotTable Options dialog box for setting print options | CLICK: PivotTable button (PivotTable ▾)<br>CHOOSE: Table Options |
| | Create a PivotTable chart | CHOOSE: Data → PivotTable and PivotChart Report<br>SELECT: *PivotChart report (with PivotTable report)* option button<br>Complete the steps. |
| | Create a PivotTable chart from a PivotTable report | SELECT: a cell in the PivotTable<br>CLICK: Chart Wizard button (⬚) on the PivotTable toolbar |
| | Create an interactive, Web-based PivotTable list | CHOOSE: File → Save as Web Page<br>CLICK: Publish command button<br>SELECT: *Add interactivity with* check box<br>SELECT: PivotTable functionality from the drop-down list box<br>CLICK: Publish command button |
| | Add fields to a PivotTable list using the Web browser | CLICK: Field List button (⬚) on the PivotTable List toolbar<br>SELECT: a field in the PivotTable Field List window<br>SELECT: a target location from the drop-down list box<br>CLICK: Add to command button |

| | | |
|---|---|---|
| **Creating and Revising Formulas** | Use statistical and forecasting functions:<br>• Use linear trend to predict future values<br>• Use exponential growth trend to predict future values<br>• Return R-square approximation measure<br>• Use linear trend to fit straight line to historical results | =FORECAST(*new-x,y-set, x-set*)<br>=GROWTH(*y-set,x-set, new-x,constant*)<br>=RSQ(*y-set,x-set*)<br><br>=TREND(*y-set,x-set, new-x,constant*) |
| **Formatting and Printing Workbooks** | Print and preview multiple worksheets and chart sheets | SELECT: the desired sheet tabs<br>CHOOSE: File → Print (or Print Preview) |
| | Create a custom view for storing print and display settings | CHOOSE: View → Custom Views<br>CLICK: Add command button |
| | Compile a report using Excel's Report Manager add-in program | CHOOSE: View → Report Manager |
| **Managing Workbooks** | Save the names and arrangement of open workbooks in the application window using a workspace | CHOOSE: File → Save Workspace |

## Key Terms

This section specifies page references for the key terms identified in this chapter. For a complete list of definitions, refer to the Glossary provided at the end of this learning guide.

Analysis ToolPak, *p. EX 538*

array formula, *p. EX 543*

constraints, *p. EX 512*

custom view, *p. EX 570*

dependent variable, *p. EX 527*

field button, *p. EX 550*

goal seeking, *p. EX 506*

independent variable, *p. EX 527*

input cells, *p. EX 506*

Microsoft Office Web Components, *p. EX 563*

one-input data table, *p. EX 538*

PivotChart report, *p. EX 546*

PivotTable and PivotChart Wizard, *p. EX 547*

PivotTable list, *p. EX 563*

PivotTable report, *p. EX 546*

R-square, *p. EX 531*

Regression analysis, *p. EX 527*

Report Manager, *p. EX 575*

scenario, *p. EX 506*

trendline, *p. EX 533*

two-input data table, *p. EX 538*

what-if analysis, *p. EX 506*

workspace, *p. EX 573*

# Chapter
## quiz

### Short Answer

**1.** List three tools for performing what-if analysis.

**2.** In what way do Goal Seek and Solver work backward when performing what-if analysis?

**3.** What are the three options in Solver for optimizing an outcome formula?

**4.** What is a constraint? Provide an example.

**5.** List the three types of reports that you can produce using Solver.

**6.** When might you want to use Scenario Manager to perform a what-if analysis?

**7.** What are the types of trendlines that you can add to a chart?

**8.** In what way is a two-input data table more limiting than a one-input data table?

**9.** What is the purpose of a page field in a PivotTable report?

**10.** What is saved in a custom view?

## True/False

**1.** _____ Outcome cells contain formulas that reference input cells either directly or indirectly.

**2.** _____ The Goal Seek feature is an example of an add-in program.

**3.** _____ You can use a chart in performing a what-if analysis.

**4.** _____ Numerous scenarios can be saved in a workbook and displayed using the Scenario Manager.

**5.** _____ Linear regression analysis attempts to fit a straight line to a set of existing data.

**6.** _____ You can add a trendline to both 2D and 3D chart types.

**7.** _____ You can display the results from multiple formulas in a one-input data table.

**8.** _____ You can display the results from multiple formulas in a two-input data table.

**9.** _____ A PivotTable report is an interactive table that continually evaluates and updates itself against a specified data source.

**10.** _____ Custom views store the print and display settings for all worksheets in a workbook.

## Multiple Choice

**1.** Which is not one of the what-if tools mentioned in this chapter?

a. Data series
b. Data tables
c. Goal Seek
d. Solver

**2.** The Goal Seek feature:

a. Presumes that you know the outcome and need the input value
b. Presumes that you know the outcome and need the constraint
c. Presumes that you know the input value and need the outcome
d. Presumes that you know the input value and need the constraint

**3.** In Goal Seek, the *By changing cell* entry refers to:

a. The cell containing the outcome formula
b. The cell containing the constraints
c. The cell containing the target value
d. The cell that you are attempting to calculate

**4.** For Solver, which of the following statements is correct?

a. Returns several results evaluated against constraints
b. Returns a single result evaluated against constraints
c. Returns a set of values, like a data table
d. Returns a PivotTable report for further analysis

**5.** The two types of reports that you can create using Scenario Manager are:

a. Ascending and descending
b. AutoFilter and AutoReport
c. Group and outline
d. Summary and PivotTable

**6.** Which of the following functions is *not* used to forecast a trend?

a. FORECAST
b. GROWTH
c. PREDICT
d. TREND

7. To smooth out the fluctuations in a chart, you should add:

   a. A moving average trendline
   b. A linear trendline
   c. An exponential trendline
   d. A logarithmic trendline

8. Which is the most accurate statement about a two-input data table?

   a. Allows two inputs and a single cell result
   b. Allows two inputs and one set of results
   c. Allows two inputs and several sets of results
   d. Allows multiple inputs and several sets of results

9. To summarize only a subset of data from a worksheet list, you can do the following

before launching the PivotTable and PivotChart Wizard:

   a. Use the AutoFilter feature to limit the display of records
   b. Use an advanced criteria filter to limit the display of records
   c. Use an advanced criteria filter to extract records to a new location
   d. You cannot create a PivotTable report based on a worksheet list.

10. In creating a custom view, you store the following:

   a. Calculation and protection settings
   b. Print and display settings
   c. Report and scenario settings
   d. Styles and formatting codes

# Hands-On
### exercises

step by step

## 1. Performing a Goal Seek

This exercise lets you practice using the Goal Seek command and graphical goal seeking to find required input values.

1. Open the data file named EX09HE01. Ensure that the workbook window is maximized to cover the entire application area, as shown in Figure 9.72.

2. Save the workbook as "Library Purchases" to your personal storage location. Before proceeding, ensure that the *Acquisitions* tab is selected.

3. Given a new acquisitions budget of $24,000, use goal seeking to find the number of books that the campus library can purchase. To begin, select the target value cell and launch the command:
SELECT: cell B12
CHOOSE: Tools → Goal Seek

4. If necessary, move the Goal Seek dialog box to the right in order to view more of the active worksheet area, as shown in Figure 9.72.

**Figure 9.72**

Executing the
Goal Seek
command

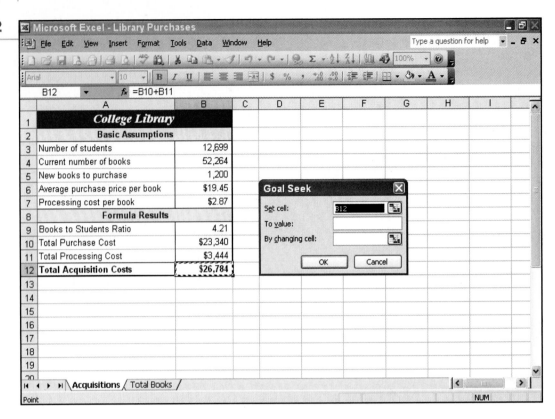

5. The *Set cell* text box now reads "B12." To set the target value:
   TYPE: **24000** in the *To value* text box
   TYPE: **b5** in the *By changing cell* text box

6. To execute the goal seeking operation:
   CLICK: OK command button

7. To accept the results and remove the Goal Seek Status dialog box:
   CLICK: OK command button
   What is the number of new books that the library can purchase?

8. You will now use graphical goal seeking to determine how student levels affect the number of new acquisitions required. To begin:
   CLICK: *Total Books* tab
   SELECT: cell range from A1 to I1
   CLICK: down arrow attached to the Zoom button ( 100% ▾ )
   CLICK: Selection in the drop-down list

9. This worksheet multiplies the "Books to Students Ratio" in cell C3 by the number of students to yield the number of Total Books required. To adjust the ratio using graphical goal seeking:
   CLICK: the data column for the year 2009 in the embedded chart
   CLICK: the data column for the year 2009 a second time
   (*Hint:* A marker should now appear at the top of the selected column and the Range Finder feature highlights the relevant worksheet cells.)

10. To change the value of the data column:
    DRAG: the marker at the top of the column upward, until the Screen tip displays a value of 76,000

11. When you release the mouse button, the Goal Seek dialog box appears (Figure 9.73.)

**Figure 9.73**

Performing graphical goal seeking

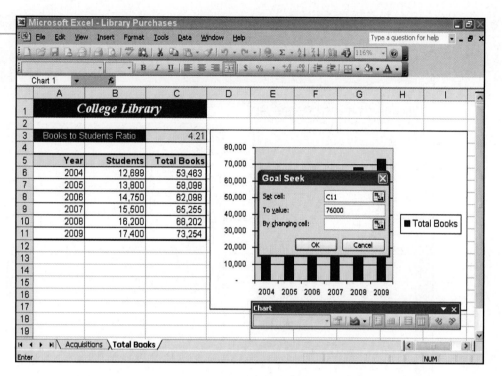

**12.** To complete the dialog box:
CLICK: cell C3 to place a reference into the *By changing cell* text box
CLICK: OK command button

**13.** To accept the Goal Seek Status dialog box:
CLICK: OK command button
What is the ratio required to yield 76,000 books by 2009?

**14.** Save and then close the "Library Purchases" workbook.

step by step

## 2. Managing Pricing Scenarios

In this exercise, you will save and manage pricing strategy scenarios using Excel 2003's Scenario Manager.

**1.** Open the data file named EX09HE02 and save the workbook as "Video Pricing" to your personal storage location.

**2.** Before launching the Scenario Manager, let's name some of the worksheet cells:
SELECT: cell B5
CLICK: in the Name box
TYPE: **NewPrice**
PRESS: (ENTER)

**3.** On your own, name cell B6 **NewRate**, cell B7 **StockPrice**, and cell B8 **StockRate**.

**4.** Launch the Scenario Manager and add the first scenario:
CHOOSE: Tools → Scenarios
CLICK: Add command button

**5.** In the Add Scenario dialog box, name the scenario and then specify the cells that you want to change:
TYPE: **Discount**
PRESS: (TAB)
TYPE: **NewPrice,NewRate,StockPrice,StockRate**
Your screen should now appear similar to Figure 9.74.

**Figure 9.74**

Adding a
scenario named
"Discount"

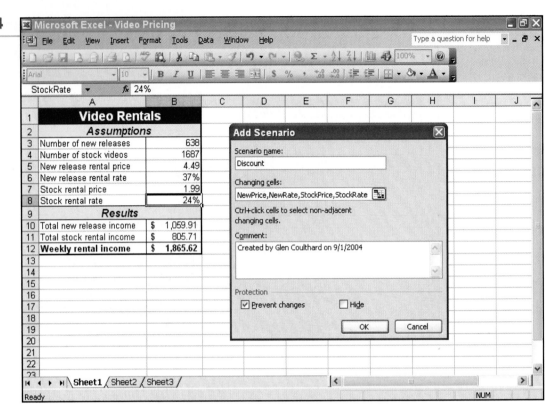

6. CLICK: OK command button

7. In the Scenario Values dialog box, enter the values for the Discount scenario:
   TYPE: **3.49** in the *1: NewPrice* text box
   PRESS: ( TAB )
   TYPE: **43%** in the *2: NewRate* text box
   PRESS: ( TAB )
   TYPE: **1.49** in the *3: StockPrice* text box
   PRESS: ( TAB )
   TYPE: **29%** in the *4: StockRate* text box

8. To create a second scenario:
   CLICK: Add command button

9. TYPE: **Premium** in the *Scenario name* text box
   CLICK: OK command button

10. Enter the values for the "Premium" scenario:
    TYPE: **4.99** in the *1: NewPrice* text box
    PRESS: ( TAB )
    TYPE: **32%** in the *2: NewRate* text box
    PRESS: ( TAB )
    TYPE: **2.49** in the *3: StockPrice* text box
    PRESS: ( TAB )
    TYPE: **21%** in the *4: StockRate* text box

11. To complete the Scenario Values dialog box and proceed:
    CLICK: OK command button
    The Scenario Manager dialog box reappears with the Discount and Premium scenarios displayed in
    the list box.

**12.** To view a summary report of the two scenarios:
CLICK: Summary command button

**13.** Ensure that the *Scenario summary* option button is selected and that cell B12 is listed in the *Result cells* text box. Then:
CLICK: OK command button
The *Scenario Summary* tab is created with a report comparing the two alternatives, as shown in Figure 9.75.

**Figure 9.75**

Scenario
Summary report

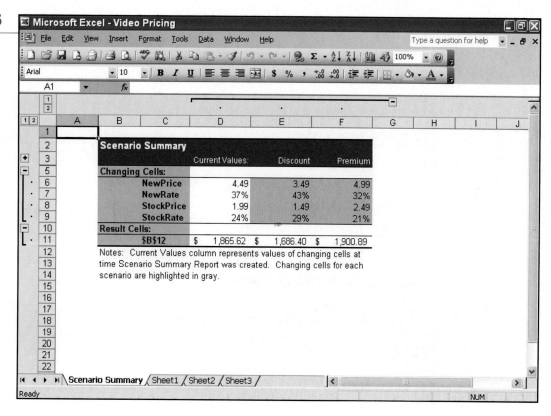

**14.** Save and then close the "Video Pricing" workbook.

step by step

## 3. Unit Costing Using Data Tables

You will now practice using a two-input data table to determine how changing the size of a production run and the type of packaging affects the total unit cost for a product.

**1.** Open the data file named EX09HE03 and save the workbook as "Unit Costs" to your personal storage location.

**2.** A two-input data table requires that you specify two sets of input values. To create the column set:
SELECT: cell D3
TYPE: **1.06**
PRESS: ⬇
TYPE: **1.05**
PRESS: (ENTER)

**3.** Using the fill handle, extend the two cells downward until the series reaches cell D9 and 1.00.

**4.** To create the row set of input values:
SELECT: cell E2
TYPE: **45,000**
PRESS: ➡
TYPE: **60,000**
PRESS: ➡
TYPE: **75,000**
PRESS: ➡
TYPE: **90,000**
PRESS: (ENTER)

**5.** Enter a reference in cell D2 to the outcome formula in cell B11. Your screen should now appear similar to the worksheet shown in Figure 9.76.

**Figure 9.76**

Preparing a worksheet for a two-input data table

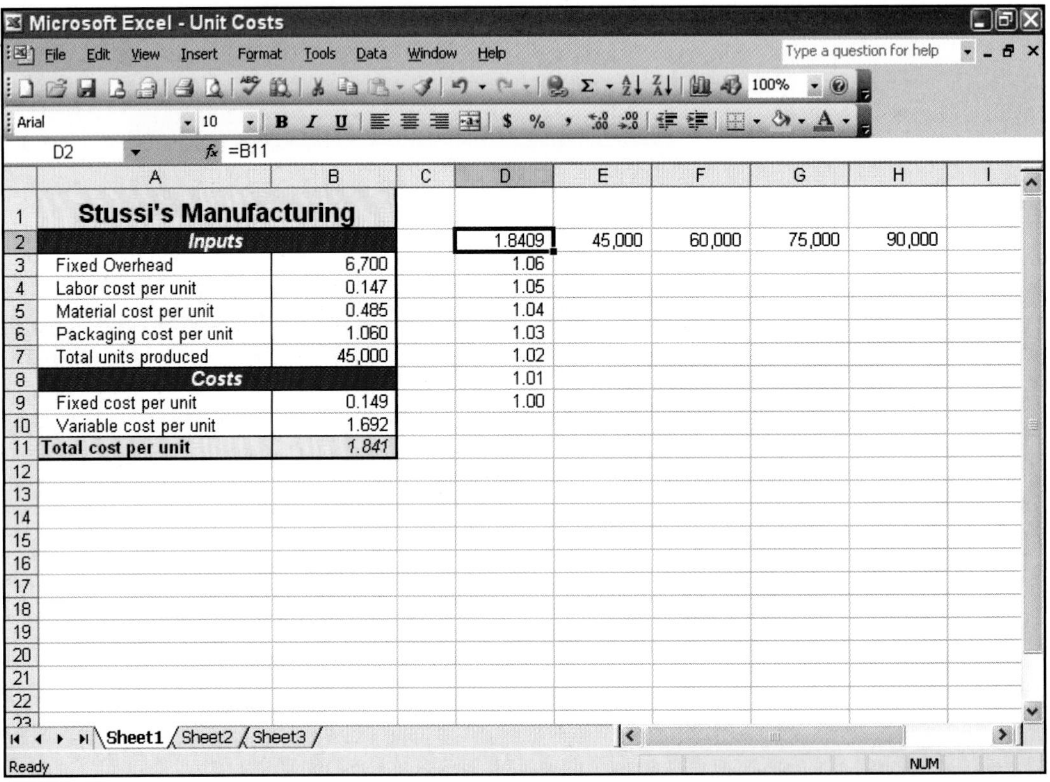

**6.** To create the data table:
SELECT: cell range from D2 to H9
CHOOSE: Data ➜ Table

**7.** In the Table dialog box that appears:
SELECT: cell B7 for the *Row input cell* text box
SELECT: cell B6 for the *Column input cell* text box
CLICK: OK command button to proceed

**8.** On your own, format the cell range from E3 to H9 to display using a number format and 3 decimal places.

**9.** Apply additional formatting, as shown in Figure 9.77, to set the column and row headings apart from the data area.

**Figure 9.77**

Formatting the
two-input data
table

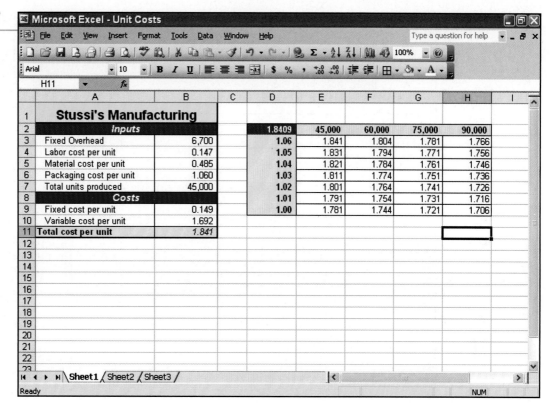

**10.** Save and then close the "Unit Costs" workbook.

on your own

## 4. Analyzing a List Using PivotTables

As the junior member of a real estate team, you have been asked to analyze agent results over the past year. After opening the source data file named EX09HE04 and saving it as "Agent Results" to your personal storage location, you are ready to begin. For fast and flexible results, you decide to use the PivotTable and PivotChart Wizard to create a PivotTable report on a new worksheet.

Perform the following tasks in the order they are presented:

- Using the PivotTable Field List window, drag the Rate field item to the "Drop Column Fields Here" area. Then, drag the Agent field item to the "Drop Row Fields Here" area. Lastly, drag the Purchase Price field item to the data area.

- Customize the "Sum of Purchase Price" data field on the worksheet to display the "Average Price," formatted as currency with no decimal places. Your screen should now appear similar to the worksheet shown in Figure 9.78.

**Figure 9.78**

Creating a
PivotTable report

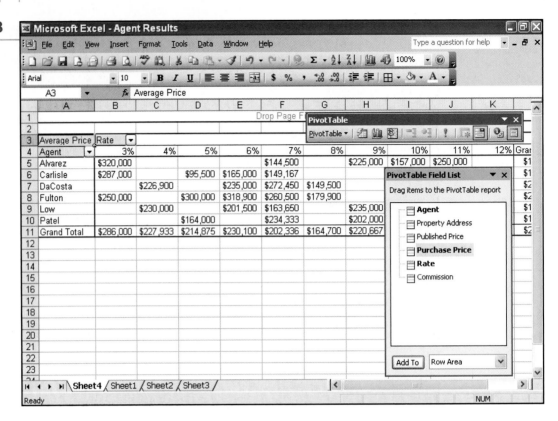

- Using the Agent row field drop-down list box, filter the table to display only the sales for agents Alvarez, Carlisle, and DaCosta.

- Using the Rate column field drop-down list box, filter the table to display only the 7% and 10% commission rates.

- Chart the PivotTable report in a PivotChart report and then close the PivotTable Field List window.

- Customize the "Average Purchase Price" data field in the chart to display the "Total Purchase Price" using the SUM function.

Your screen should now appear similar to the report shown in Figure 9.79. Print the PivotTable and PivotChart reports. Then, save and close the "Agent Results" workbook.

**Figure 9.79**

Creating a
PivotChart report

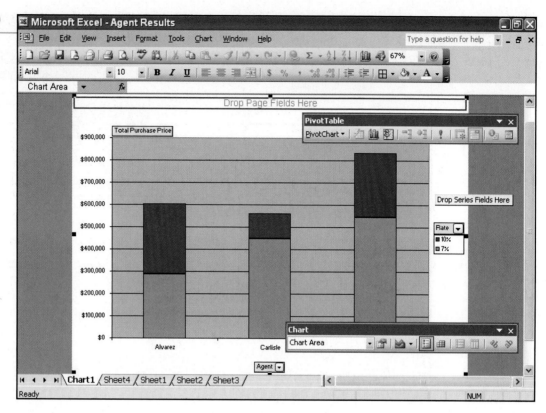

on your own

## 5. Using What-If Analysis Tools

As the Operations Manager for Gadgets Inc., you have been asked by the CEO to analyze the production data compiled by the company. To begin, open the EX09HE05 workbook and then save it as "Gadgets" to your personal storage location.

Perform the following tasks in the order they are presented:

• In the *Costing* worksheet, use goal seeking to determine how much lower the maintenance costs must be for each machine (cell B7) in order to achieve a unit cost of 30% (B18) of the selling price.

• In the *Costing* worksheet, create a one-input data table that displays how changing the maintenance cost per machine affects the average unit cost calculations. Specifically, substitute the values $150, $200, $250, $300, and $350 into cell B7 (using the Data → Table command) and calculate the set of results for the outcome formulas in cells B17 and B18. Format the results to appear similar to the worksheet shown in Figure 9.80.

**Figure 9.80**

Creating a one-input data table

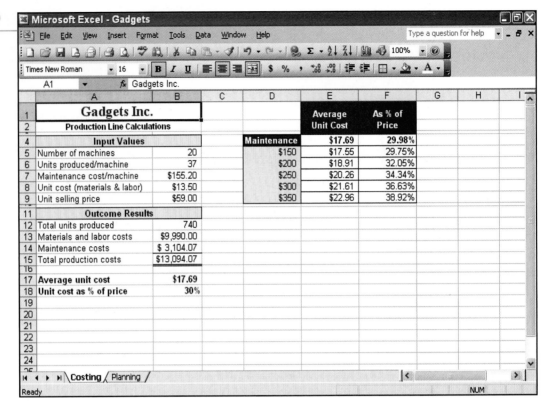

- In the *Planning* worksheet, use Solver to calculate the maximum number of items you can produce given a total cost limitation of $100,000. As for other constraints that need to be adhered to, ensure that at least 30% of the total items produced are Titanium, at least 50% are Kevlar, and at least 15% are Graphite. (*Hint:* Do not constrain your solution using the INT logical operator. In other words, allow the calculation to result in parts of units.) What is the total number of items that you can produce given this product mix and a $100,000 budget?

- Generate and print an Answer report for your solution.

When you are finished, save and then close the "Gadgets" workbook.

on your own

## 6. Creating a Web-Based PivotTable

To practice creating PivotTable and PivotChart reports, open the EX09HE06 data file and save it as "Sportmart" to your personal storage location. This workbook contains a quarterly sales forecast for a retail sporting goods store.

Perform the following tasks in the order they are presented:

- Select the worksheet list from cell A3 to G28 and then launch the PivotTable and PivotChart Wizard. Create a PivotTable report on a new worksheet.

- Using the PivotTable Field List window, drag the Sport field item to the area labeled "Drop Column Fields Here." Drag the Product field item to the area labeled "Drop Row Fields Here." Lastly, drag the YTD field item to the area labeled "Drop Data Items Here."

- Using the Sport field's drop-down list, limit the PivotTable display to the following sports: Golf, Squash, and Tennis.

- Create a PivotChart report from this refined PivotTable.

- Modify the PivotChart to display only Skiing and Hockey.

- Return to the *Sheet1* tab and redisplay all sports in the PivotTable.

- Save the PivotTable report as an interactive Web-based PivotTable list. In the Publish as Web Page dialog box, name the Web page "YTDSales.htm" and add a title of "Sportmart YTD Analysis."

- When you are ready, select the option to open the newly published PivotTable list in your Web browser, as shown in Figure 9.81.

- Practice expanding the column and row selections and working with the PivotTable list using Microsoft Internet Explorer.

- Close your Web browser and return to Microsoft Office Excel 2003.

**Figure 9.81**

Viewing a Web-based PivotTable list

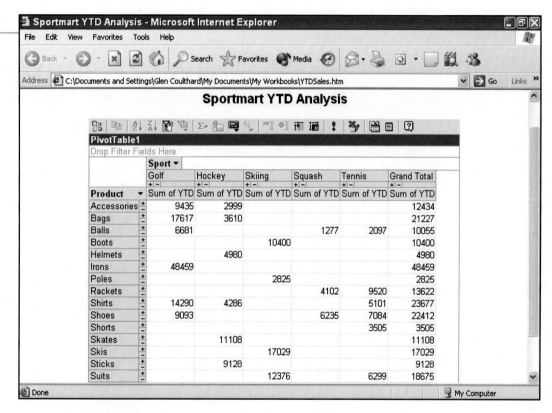

When you are finished, save and then close the "Sportmart" workbook.

# CaseStudy   SWAN LAKE NURSERY

The Swan Lake Nursery, located in the Appleby District of Bingham County, is a profitable family-owned operation. For the past several years, Swan Lake's sales have increased along with their popularity in the community. Besides possessing the best selection of flowers, plants, and trees, the staff is renowned for being honest, friendly, and knowledgeable. Although the Crane family was fearful of their employees' desire to unionize a few years earlier, everything has worked out quite well until recently. The latest round of negotiations, however, has forced the Crane family to appoint contract mediator Donna Fredriks. It is Ms. Fredriks's job to analyze the two parties' demands and then help negotiate a settlement. After gathering information from several key people, she has created a workbook and now must make use of Excel 2003's what-if tools to find the best and most acceptable solution.

In the following case problems, assume the role of Donna and perform the same steps that she identifies.

1. After another difficult day of negotiating, Donna returns to her hotel room, turns on her notebook computer, and launches Microsoft Office Excel 2003. She opens the EX09CP01 data file and then saves it as "Swan Lake" to her personal storage location. With the meeting still fresh in her mind, Donna decides to perform some further analysis on the payroll figures.

   Today's discussions around the bargaining table centered on the Crane family's refusal to implement a cost of living allowance (COLA) into their payroll calculations. The union has asked for a 3.5% allowance, while the family is standing firm at 0%. To analyze just how much an increase in the cost of living allowance will affect the company's total payroll costs, Donna creates a one-input data table on the *Payroll* worksheet. For input values, she increments the living allowance by 0.5% each year, starting at 0% in cell D3 and stopping at 3.5% in cell D10. Then, she references the worksheet formula used to calculate the total payroll costs in cell E2. After issuing the Data → Table command, Donna selects the required input cell and produces the data table. She then formats the table to appear similar to the one shown in Figure 9.82. Donna can now see the financial significance of varying the living allowance. She saves the workbook before proceeding.

2. In preparation for the next day's bargaining, Donna needs to determine how modifying the hours worked each week, along with the benefits percentage, affects the total payroll costs. To help her see the big picture, she places a two-input data table a few rows below the existing data table. For the range of hours worked each week, she enters columnar values from 40 down to 35 in one-hour steps. For the benefit percentage, she enters row values from 13.50% to 14.50% using increments of 0.25%. After generating the data table, Donna formats the results in both data tables to appear similar to the ones shown in Figure 9.82. She then remembers to save her work before proceeding.

**Figure 9.82**

Creating one-input and two-input data tables

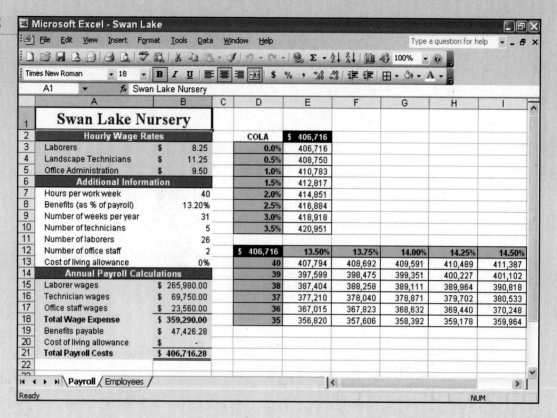

**3.** Donna decides to use the Scenario Manager to describe and then summarize the family's initial offer and the union's rebuttal. (*Hint:* Name the input cells to facilitate data entry in the Add Scenario dialog box and to make the reports more readable.) The scenarios appear as follows:

| | Swan Lake | Union |
|---|---|---|
| Hours per work week | 37.5 | 40 |
| Cost of living allowance | 1% | 3% |
| Benefits percentage | 13.4% | 13.9% |
| Number of laborers | 28 | 30 |

Once completed, Donna prepares and prints a report (see Figure 9.83) summarizing the effects that the alternative scenarios have on the total payroll costs. She then saves the workbook.

**Figure 9.83**

Scenario
Summary report

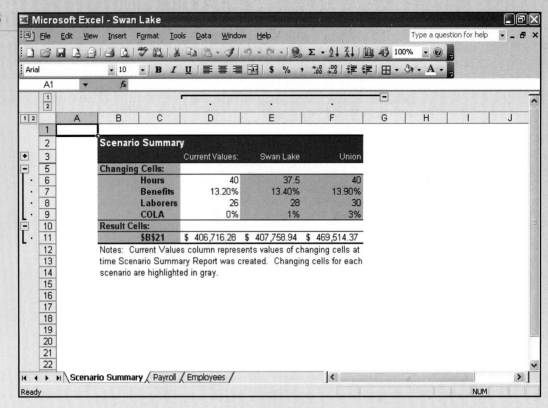

**4.** Donna now wants to summarize the employee sick and vacation days listed on the *Employees* worksheet. She determines that a PivotTable report can best calculate the average values for these figures. After proceeding through the steps in the PivotTable and PivotChart Wizard, she selects a new worksheet for creating the report. Interacting with the PivotTable on the worksheet, Donna drags the Position field item to the column field area and then the Supervisor field item to the row field area. She also adds the Station field item as a page field. For calculating results, Donna drags the Sick Days and Vac Days field items to the data area and then customizes each one to display an average value with two decimal places. (*Hint:* Right-click the desired data field and choose the Field Settings command.) Donna then uses the page field to display and print the results for the Greenhouse employees only, as shown in Figure 9.84.

**Figure 9.84**

PivotTable report for the Greenhouse employees only

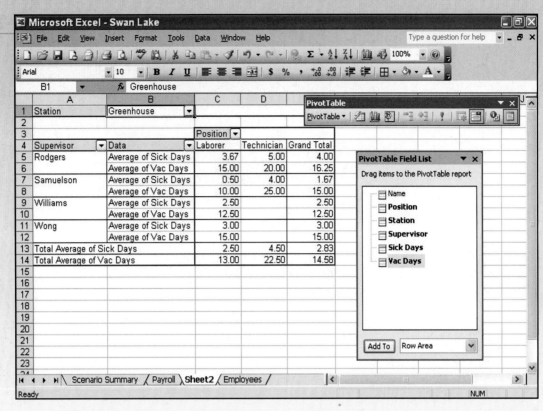

As a final step, Donna saves and closes the workbook. Exiting Excel 2003 and shutting down her computer, she finishes for the night with confidence that she has performed some solid analysis.

## Answers to Self-Check Questions

**SelfCheck**

**9.1**  Compare and contrast Excel's Goal Seek command, the Solver add-in program, and the Scenario Manager. Goal Seek lets the user specify a target value and then works backward to determine the input value required. Although similar, Solver can solve a problem requiring multiple input values. The user can also specify the constraints used to limit the input values. Scenario Manager is different from both of the previous tools in that it works forward with a set of input values to calculate outcomes. It is primarily used for storing and saving the results from various input combinations.

**9.2**  Which tools might you use to forecast the price of a mutual fund or stock in the securities market? Using historical price data, you could use Excel's statistical functions to extrapolate and project future prices. Unfortunately, the correlation between length of time and stock value is not typically linear. There are many other variables to take into consideration when attempting to forecast stock and mutual fund prices.

**9.3**  What special type of formula is entered into a data table? Can you edit the formulas appearing in a data table's output area? A data table is created using a special array formula called "TABLE." You cannot edit an array formula directly. To modify a data table, you must first delete it and then re-create it from the beginning.

**9.4** What would happen to the summary results in the data area of a PivotTable report if some values from its source data (worksheet list) were modified? There is no change in the summary results until you click the Refresh button ( ! ) on the PivotTable list toolbar.

**9.5** How might custom views and the Report Manager feature help you compile and print reports containing both worksheets and charts? Often the worksheet that provides the data for a chart includes more information than is required for a report. Therefore, you can produce a custom view that includes only relevant data for the report. Using Report Manager, you can then combine this view with the desired chart sheet.

# Microsoft®Office**Excel**®

2003

## CHAPTER 10

⊙ **Automating and Extending Excel**

## PREREQUISITES

Successful completion of this chapter requires a firm understanding of cells, formulas, functions, worksheets, and workbooks. You are also asked to import and export structured data and to work with data stored on the Web. While you need not have experience creating text, database, or Web files, a fundamental knowledge of file types and of the applications in which they are used is helpful.

## LEARNING OBJECTIVES

After reading this chapter, you will be able to:

• Retrieve data using lookup tables

• Protect a cell's contents from being changed

• Protect a workbook's structure from being changed

• Password-protect and digitally sign a workbook

• Manage workbook templates for repeated use

• Import and export data among applications

• Use Internet Explorer to view and manipulate worksheet data

• Use XML features for managing Web-based lists

# 10.1 Using Lookup Tables

Working smarter in Excel 2003 means taking advantage of helpful features that can facilitate data entry, retrieval, and analysis, not to mention workbook creation and data exchange. This module describes using *lookup tables* to retrieve data for use in displaying information and calculating formulas. A **lookup table** differs from a worksheet list in that it typically provides both row and column labels, as opposed to a single field header row. An important layout tip for lookup tables is to ensure that the value you want to use for locating data is placed in the leftmost column or topmost row of the table. Some examples of lookup tables include those used in calculating mortgage rates, sales commissions, currency exchange, and income tax. In the next two lessons, you will use the Lookup Wizard add-in program and several built-in functions to perform lookup operations.

## 10.1.1 Creating a Lookup Formula

### → Feature

A lookup operation is performed by a **lookup formula,** which typically contains one or more built-in functions and several arguments. Using a series of dialog boxes, the Lookup Wizard leads you step-by-step through constructing a lookup formula that returns the cell contents of a row and column intersection. The wizard allows you to choose between hard-coding your selections into the lookup formula or using cell references for increased flexibility. (*Note:* The Lookup Wizard is an add-in program that must first be installed using the Tools → Add-Ins command before it will appear on the Tools menu.)

### → Method

To create a lookup formula using the Lookup Wizard:

• CHOOSE: Tools → Lookup

Complete the steps in the Lookup Wizard dialog box.

### → Practice

You will now use the Lookup Wizard to help you extract information from a worksheet lookup table containing population statistics. Before proceeding, start Microsoft Office Excel 2003.

**1.** Open the data file named EX1010. This workbook provides sample data for demonstrating the Lookup Wizard and other lookup and reference functions.

**2.** Save the workbook as "Lookup Tables" to your personal storage location.

**3.** Because the Lookup Wizard is an add-in program, you should verify that it has been installed on your computer:
CHOOSE: Tools → Add-Ins
SELECT: Lookup Wizard check box so that a ✓ appears
Your screen should appear similar to the dialog box shown in Figure 10.1.

**Figure 10.1**

Add-Ins dialog
box with the
Lookup Wizard
selected

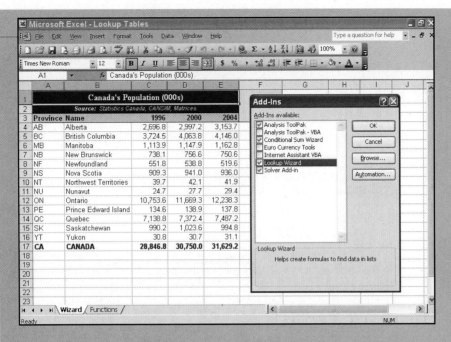

4. CLICK: OK command button to proceed
(*Hint:* If the Lookup Wizard add-in cannot be located, a dialog box may appear to lead you through installing the feature.)

5. In this exercise, you define a lookup formula that extracts population data given a province's abbreviation. To begin, select the cell range for the lookup table, including the row and column labels:
SELECT: cell range from A3 to E17

6. To launch the Lookup Wizard:
CHOOSE: Tools → Lookup
The Lookup Wizard dialog box appears, as shown in Figure 10.2.

**Figure 10.2**

Lookup Wizard
dialog box: Step
1 of 4

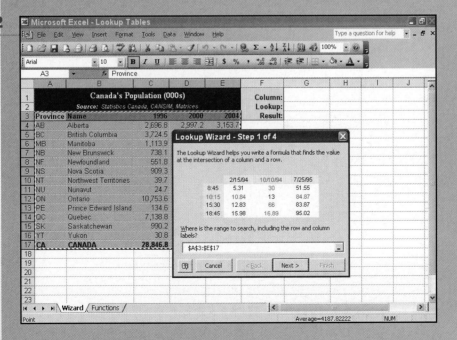

**7.** In Step 1 of 4, you enter the range of the lookup table, including the data area and the row and column labels. By selecting the range prior to launching the wizard, this step is completed for you. To proceed:
CLICK: Next>

**8.** In Step 2 of 4, you specify the column and row to search for the lookup value entered. To retrieve the 2000 population values for BC, make the following selections, as shown in Figure 10.3:
SELECT: 2000 in the *Select the column label* drop-down list box
SELECT: BC in the *Select the row label* drop-down list box

**Figure 10.3**

Lookup Wizard dialog box: Step 2 of 4

Select the column label heading for searching

Select the row label heading for searching

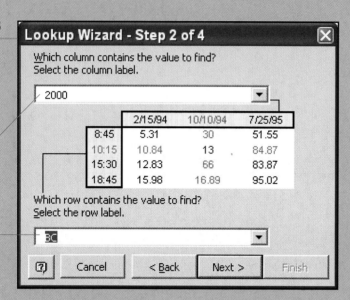

**9.** CLICK: Next> to proceed
Your screen should now appear similar to the dialog box shown in Figure 10.4.

**Figure 10.4**

Lookup Wizard dialog box: Step 3 of 4

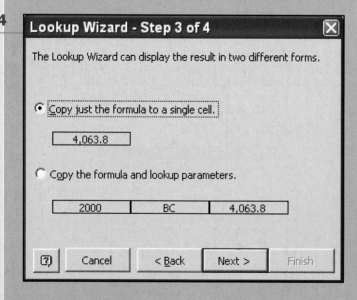

**10.** In Step 3 of 4, you specify how you want the wizard's result to appear. If you are performing a one-time lookup operation, choose the option that will place the formula in a single cell. If you want to allow for future lookups (as we do), do the following:
SELECT: *Copy the formula and lookup parameters* option button
CLICK: [ Next> ]

**11.** By selecting to copy the lookup parameters, the dialog box changes its caption to read "Step 4 of 6" to indicate that additional steps are necessary. To specify where to place each parameter, move the Lookup Wizard dialog box so that the first few rows of columns F and G are visible. Then, do the following:
CLICK: cell G1 for the column parameter (2000)
Your screen should now appear similar to the dialog box shown in Figure 10.5.

**Figure 10.5**

Lookup Wizard
dialog box: Step
4 of 6

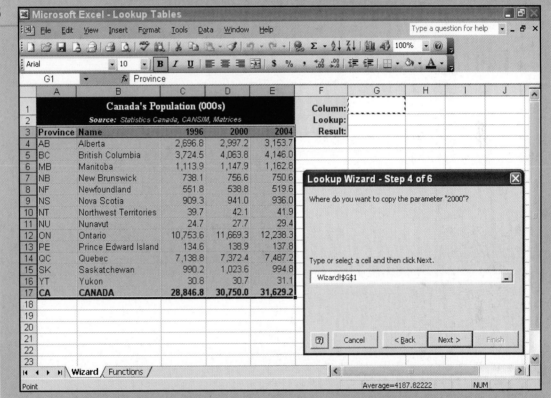

**12.** CLICK: [ Next> ] to proceed

**13.** To complete Step 5 of 6:
CLICK: cell G2 for the lookup or row parameter (BC)
CLICK: [ Next> ]

**14.** To complete Step 6 of 6:
CLICK: cell G3 for the lookup formula result
CLICK: [ Finish ]
The wizard closes and the value 4,063.8 (more than 4 million people) appears in cell G3.

**15.** To view the contents of the lookup formula:
SELECT: cell G3
PRESS: `F2` (EDIT key)
By entering Edit mode, Excel 2003's Range Finder feature activates to show you the cell ranges used in the formula (Figure 10.6).

**Figure 10.6**

Using Range Finder to view the lookup formula

Lookup formulas created using the Lookup Wizard utilize the INDEX and MATCH built-in functions

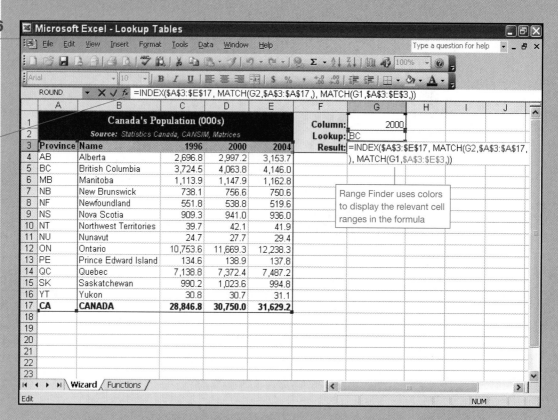

**16.** After reviewing the Formula bar and formula ranges:
PRESS: `ESC` to return to Ready mode

**17.** To find the population count for Nova Scotia in 2004:
SELECT: cell G1
TYPE: **2004**
PRESS: `↓`
TYPE: **NS**
PRESS: `ENTER`
The result, 936.0, appears immediately in cell G3. (*Hint:* The lookup formula is not case-sensitive.)

**18.** What happens if the lookup formula cannot find a value?
SELECT: cell G2
TYPE: **NY**
PRESS: [ENTER]
When the value is not located in the lookup table, cell G3 displays an error, as shown below.

This worksheet icon is called the Error Checking Options button and is accompanied by a green triangle in the upper left-hand corner of cell G3

The "#N/A" result means that a value is not available

**19.** To view the options available:
CLICK: Error Checking Options button (◈)
Your screen should appear similar to Figure 10.7.

**Figure 10.7**

Displaying the Error Checking Options button's menu

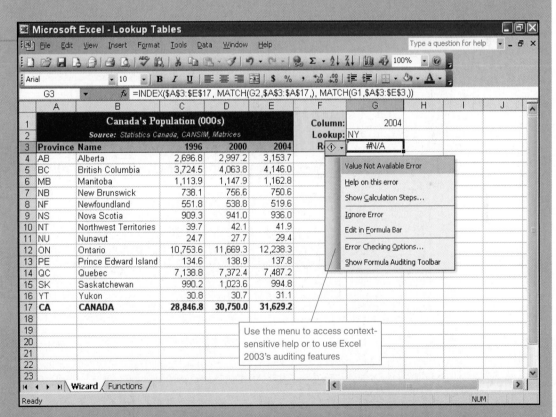

Use the menu to access context-sensitive help or to use Excel 2003's auditing features

**20.** Since you already know why the error occurred, proceed by ignoring the error. Do the following:
CHOOSE: Ignore Error
Notice that the Error Checking Options button and the cell's green triangle are both hidden.

**21.** Let's test the lookup formula one last time:
SELECT: cell G1
TYPE: **Name**
PRESS: ⬇
TYPE: **QC**
PRESS: **ENTER**
The result, Quebec, appears immediately in cell G3. (*Note:* Any column label from the lookup table can be used to find a result.)

**22.** Save the workbook and keep it open for use in the next lesson.

## 10.1.2 Using Lookup and Reference Functions

→ **Feature**

Excel 2003's Lookup & Reference functions enable you to find and extract data from a table or list. While the most popular lookup function is VLOOKUP, the INDEX, MATCH, HLOOKUP, and LOOKUP functions are also useful. Since these functions all have a similar syntax, let's use the following graphic to review the function arguments as they apply to a lookup table for calculating mortgages:

|   | A | B | C |   |
|---|---|---|---|---|
| 1 | **Mortgages** | **Variable** | **Closed** |   |
| 2 | **6 months** | 4.25% | #N/A |   |
| 3 | **1 year** | 4.50% | 4.85% |   |
| 4 | **3 years** | 5.25% | 5.65% |   |
| 5 | **5 years** | #N/A | 6.50% |   |
| 6 | **10 years** | #N/A | 7.40% |   |
| 7 |   |   |   |   |

Notice that there are explicit row and column labels in the above table. The table range, sometimes called an *array,* is the worksheet area from cell A1 to C6. For reference as function arguments, the columns in this range can be numbered 1 through 3 (columns A:C). The rows are numbered 1 through 6 (rows 1:6). The rate for a 1-year variable mortgage, therefore, is the intersection of row *(row_num)* 3 and column *(col_num)* 2, or 4.50%. The *lookup_value* refers to the value that you use to find information in the table.

→ **Method**

=INDEX(*array,row_num,col_num*)
=MATCH(*lookup_value,lookup_array,match_type*)
=HLOOKUP(*lookup_value,table_array,row_index_num,range_lookup*)
=VLOOKUP(*lookup_value,table_array,col_index_num,range_lookup*)

→ **Practice**

You will now use Excel 2003's built-in functions to perform lookup operations. Ensure that the "Lookup Tables" workbook is displayed.

**1.** CLICK: *Functions* sheet tab
Your screen should now appear similar to the worksheet shown in Figure 10.8. (*Note:* The arguments that appear in italic are optional.)

**Figure 10.8**

The Lookup &
Reference
*Functions* tab

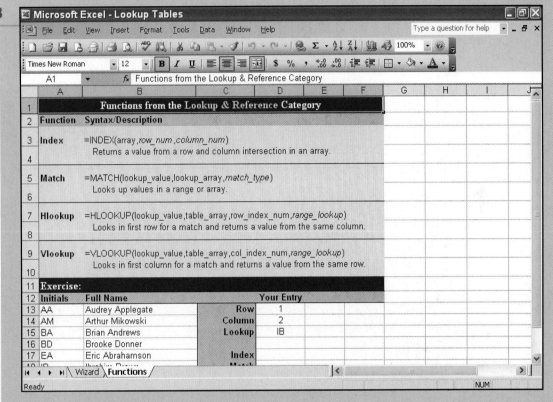

**2.** Notice that the first functions described on this worksheet, INDEX and MATCH, are the same ones used by the Lookup Wizard. Let's practice entering these functions manually. Scroll down the worksheet so that Row 11 appears at the top of your screen.

**3.** The "Exercise" area displays a table of initials and full names of individuals. In the next few steps, you will create lookup formulas to extract data from this table. To begin, let's name the lookup table:
SELECT: cell range A13 through B20
Notice that you did not select the field header row; just the leftmost column and data area.

**4.** CLICK: in the Name box
TYPE: **table**
PRESS: (ENTER)

**5.** Cells D13, D14, and D15 are input cells used for entering lookup parameters. In cell D17, you will enter the INDEX function, which returns a value from a row and column intersection:
SELECT: cell D17
TYPE: **=index(table,d13,d14**
The final parenthesis has been omitted so that the ScreenTip displays the full function list of arguments, as shown in Figure 10.9.

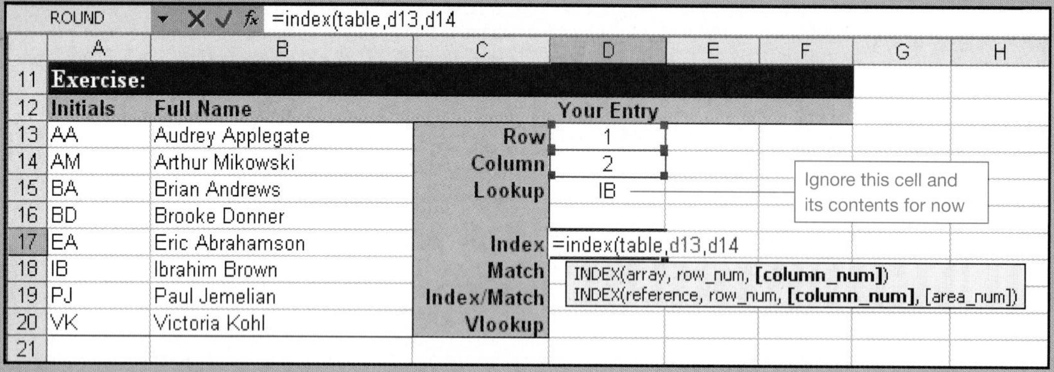

**Figure 10.9**

Entering the
INDEX function

**6.** TYPE: )
PRESS: **ENTER**
The result, Audrey Applegate, appears. The INDEX function retrieves "Audrey Applegate" at the intersection of row 1 and column 2. (*Note:* The entry in cell D15 is not relevant to this example.)

**7.** To extract another name from the table:
SELECT: D13

**8.** Now enter a new row parameter:
TYPE: 7
PRESS: **ENTER**
Paul Jemelian's name now appears in cell D17, as it exists in the seventh row of the table.

**9.** You now use the MATCH function to search a column and return a row number where a particular entry resides. To begin:
SELECT: cell D18

**10.** Let's use the Function Arguments dialog box to illustrate the MATCH function. Do the following:
TYPE: **=match(**
CLICK: Insert Function button (fx)
The Function Arguments dialog box appears immediately below the Formula bar.

**11.** To specify the value to look up:
CLICK: in the *Lookup_value* text box, unless it is already selected
CLICK: Dialog Collapse button
CLICK: cell D15
CLICK: Dialog Expand button
(*Hint:* You do not have to collapse and expand the dialog, if you simply move the dialog box in order to see the target or desired cells.)

**12.** To specify the table column, called a *Lookup_array,* to search:
CLICK: in the *Lookup_array* text box
CLICK: Dialog Collapse button (□)
SELECT: cell range A13 to A20
CLICK: Dialog Expand button (□)
Notice that the *Lookup_array* range includes only the single column where the lookup value can be found. (*Hint:* If you drag over a cell range on the worksheet without first collapsing the dialog box, it is collapsed for you automatically.)

**13.** Next, enter the type of match to perform. If you type "1" into the *Match_type* text box, the MATCH function returns a TRUE match for a value that is less than or equal to the lookup value. This is the default match type and requires a table that is sorted into ascending order. A match type of "0" returns TRUE for exact (but not case-sensitive) matches only. Do the following:
CLICK: in the *Match_type* text box
TYPE: 0
The Function Arguments dialog box should now appear as shown in Figure 10.10.

**Figure 10.10**

Function
Arguments dialog
box for MATCH

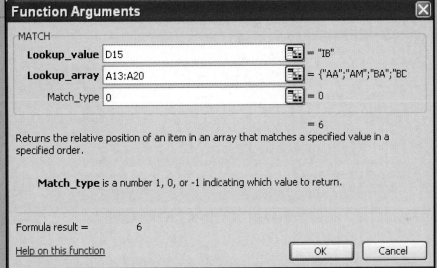

**Function Arguments**

MATCH
Lookup_value   D15                    = "IB"
Lookup_array   A13:A20                = {"AA";"AM";"BA";"BC
Match_type     0                      = 0

= 6
Returns the relative position of an item in an array that matches a specified value in a specified order.

**Match_type** is a number 1, 0, or -1 indicating which value to return.

Formula result =          6

Help on this function          OK          Cancel

**14.** CLICK: OK command button to proceed
The row number "6" should appear in the cell. In other words, the initials "IB" (in cell D15) appear in Row 6 of the range A13:A20.

**15.** By combining the INDEX and MATCH functions, you can create very powerful lookup formulas. Let's enter a formula that is similar to the one constructed by the Lookup Wizard. To begin:
SELECT: cell D19

**16.** Begin by entering the INDEX function:
TYPE: =index(
CLICK: Insert Function button (*fx*)
The Select Arguments dialog box appears, as shown in Figure 10.11.

**Figure 10.11**

Select Arguments dialog box

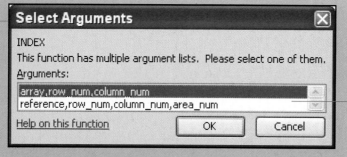

The INDEX function provides two syntax formats for returning different results. The *array* syntax returns a cell's contents, while the *reference* syntax returns a cell's address.

**17.** To return a cell's contents, choose the *array* syntax:
SELECT: array,row_num,column_num
CLICK: OK command button
The Function Arguments dialog box should now appear.

**18.** To specify the first paramenter:
TYPE: **table** in the *Array* text box
PRESS: **TAB**

**19.** Now select the row number of the matching entry:
CLICK: Dialog Collapse button (⬚) for the *Row_num* text box
CLICK: cell D18 (the result of a MATCH function)
CLICK: Dialog Expand button (⬚)

**20.** To finish the dialog box, select the column containing the value that you want returned by the function:
CLICK: in the *Column_num* text box
TYPE: **2**
Your screen should now appear similar to the dialog box shown in Figure 10.12.

**Figure 10.12**

Function Arguments dialog box for INDEX

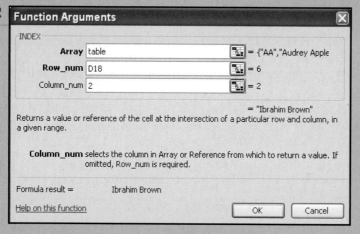

**21.** CLICK: OK command button
You should now see "Ibrahim Brown" appear in cell D19. (*Hint:* Instead of referencing cell D18, you can also nest the MATCH function inside the INDEX function to determine the row number argument. This is the approach used by the Lookup Wizard to create a lookup formula.)

**22.** Let's demonstrate this formula in action:
SELECT: cell D15

**23.** Now enter a set of initials:
TYPE: **bd**
PRESS: **ENTER**
The formulas update cell D18 to row "4" and cell D19 to "Brooke Donner." Notice that none of these functions is case-sensitive.

**24.** Before using the VLOOKUP function, you must ensure that the lookup table is sorted by the column that you want to search. Because the table is already sorted into ascending order of initials, do the following:
SELECT: cell D20

**25.** Now enter the function using the Insert Function button:
TYPE: **=vlookup(**
CLICK: Insert Function button (ƒx)
The Function Arguments dialog box appears.

**26.** To specify the value that you want to look up:
CLICK: in the *Lookup_value* text box, unless it is already selected
CLICK: Dialog Collapse button (⬚) for the *Lookup_value* text box
CLICK: cell D15
CLICK: Dialog Expand button (⬚)

**27.** To complete the Function Arguments dialog box:
CLICK: in the *Table_array* text box
TYPE: **table**
PRESS: **TAB**
TYPE: **2** in the *Col_index_num* text box
The Function Arguments dialog box should appear similar to the one shown in Figure 10.13. (*Hint:* Col_index_num 1 refers to the "Initials" column and col_index_num 2 refers to the "Full Name" column.)

**Figure 10.13**

Function Arguments dialog box for VLOOKUP

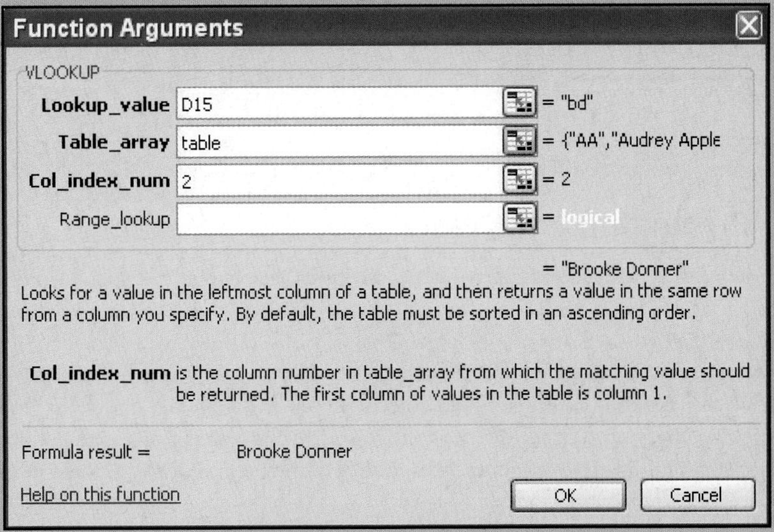

**28.** CLICK: OK command button
Although similar to using INDEX and MATCH, the VLOOKUP and HLOOKUP functions are much faster and easier to use. (*Note:* The VLOOKUP function searches down the leftmost column, *col_index_num* 1, for the *lookup_value*. When it reaches a value that is equal to or less than the *lookup_value,* it moves across the row to the column value specified by the *col_index_num* argument. The HLOOKUP function, on the other hand, searches horizontally and then, upon finding a match, moves down to the row specified by the *row_index_num*.)

**29.** On your own, test these functions using different initials in cell D15. Use both matching (i.e., EA) and non-matching (i.e., BB) values and note the different results returned for the INDEX and MATCH functions versus the VLOOKUP function. When you are ready to proceed, select the merged cell A11, as shown in Figure 10.14.

**Figure 10.14**

Completing the *Functions* tab in the Lookup Tables workbook

|  | A | B | C | D | E |
|---|---|---|---|---|---|
| 11 | **Exercise:** | | | | |
| 12 | **Initials** | **Full Name** | | **Your Entry** | |
| 13 | AA | Audrey Applegate | Row | 7 | |
| 14 | AM | Arthur Mikowski | Column | 2 | |
| 15 | BA | Brian Andrews | Lookup | ea | |
| 16 | BD | Brooke Donner | | | |
| 17 | EA | Eric Abrahamson | Index | Paul Jemelian | |
| 18 | IB | Ibrahim Brown | Match | 5 | |
| 19 | PJ | Paul Jemelian | Index/Match | Eric Abrahamson | |
| 20 | VK | Victoria Kohl | Vlookup | Eric Abrahamson | |
| 21 | | | | | |

**30.** Save and then close the "Lookup Tables" workbook.

 **SelfCheck**

**10.1** What function(s) does the Lookup Wizard use in constructing a lookup formula?

# 10.2 Protecting Your Work

If you are building worksheets that will be used by other people, you should know how to protect your work using Excel 2003's protection features. At the *file level,* you can **password-protect** a workbook so that only authorized users (people given the password) can open, view, and modify its contents. At the *workbook level,* you can protect and hide individual tabs containing worksheets, charts, and modules. Finally, at the *sheet level,* you can protect cells and objects from being modified or deleted. In this module, you will learn to use built-in protection features to save your work from prying eyes and accidental or malicious changes. You also learn to set file properties, digitally sign, and remove personal information from a workbook.

## 10.2.1 Protecting Cells, Worksheets, and Workbooks

→ **Feature**

By default, Excel 2003 locks each and every cell in a worksheet but does not activate sheet protection. Sheet-level protection is most useful for ensuring that there are no accidental deletions or modifications in a worksheet. As you now appreciate, the time spent in constructing the "perfect" formula is well worth your effort in protecting it. In addition to locking cells from overwriting entries, you can hide a cell's formula from displaying in the Formula bar. You may want to use this feature if, for example, you have a formula that calculates compensation based on classified commission rates. An added benefit to sheet-level protection is that, once a worksheet is protected, the **TAB** key lets you quickly cycle through all of the unprotected cells for user input. You can also protect a workbook's structure so that its sheets cannot be removed, inserted, renamed, hidden, or unhidden. Furthermore, all of these protection features can be password-protected to ensure that they cannot be "turned off" by unauthorized users.

→ **Method**

To protect cells:

- CHOOSE: Format → Cells
- CLICK: *Protection* tab
- SELECT: the desired options

To hide/unhide sheets:

- CHOOSE: Format → Sheet → Hide

  *or*

- CHOOSE: Format → Sheet → Unhide

To turn on/off worksheet protection:

- CHOOSE: Tools → Protection → Protect Sheet

  *or*

- CHOOSE: Tools → Protection → Unprotect Sheet

To turn on/off workbook protection:

- CHOOSE: Tools → Protection → Protect Workbook

  *or*

- CHOOSE: Tools → Protection → Unprotect Workbook

→ **Practice**

You will now practice protecting, unprotecting, and hiding the contents of cells, worksheets, and workbooks. Ensure that no workbooks are open in the application window.

**1.** Open the data file named EX1020. This workbook contains three worksheets for storing and summarizing billing data for McReady Accounting Associates.

**2.** Save the workbook as "McReady" to your personal storage location.

**3.** In this workbook, both the *Client Summary* and *Partner Summary* worksheets display pivot tables that summarize data from the *Billings* worksheet list. In fact, the only area in the workbook where data should be entered is into the *Billings* worksheet. Because all cells on a worksheet are locked by default, you must unlock the cells that will accept data before turning on protection. To begin:
CLICK: *Billings* tab
Your worksheet should appear similar to the one shown in Figure 10.15.

**Figure 10.15**

The *Billings* worksheet

Unprotect the criteria range in cells A2 to G2

Rows 4 and 5 contain database functions that need to be protected

Unprotect the worksheet list, including the rows beneath the active list area

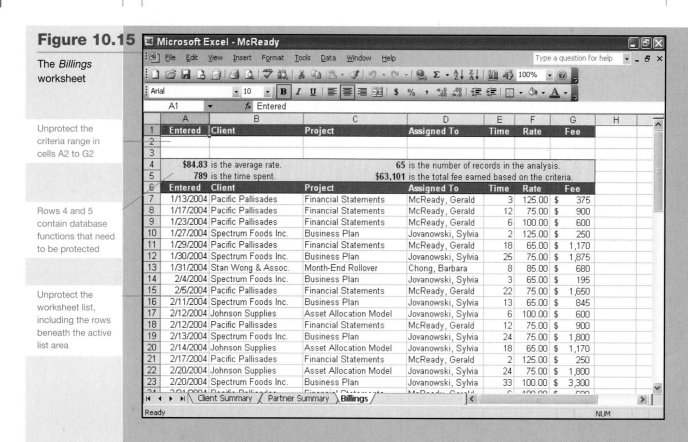

**4.** To be able to enter conditions into the criteria range, you must unprotect the cells in rows 2 and 3. To do so:

SELECT: cell range from A2 to G2
CHOOSE: Format → Cells
CLICK: *Protection* tab in the Format Cells dialog box
The dialog box in Figure 10.16 is displayed.

**Figure 10.16**

Format Cells
dialog box:
*Protection* tab

When the worksheet
is protected, you
cannot enter or edit
data in *locked* cells

When the worksheet
is protected, you
cannot view the
contents of a *hidden*
cell in the formula
bar

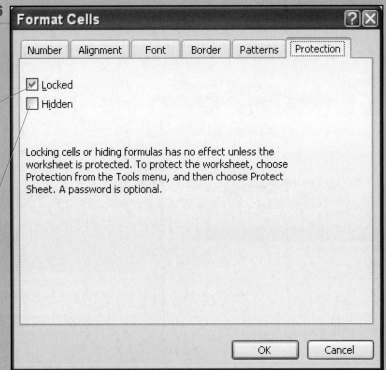

**5.** To unlock the cells in the selected range:
SELECT: *Locked* check box so that no ✓ appears
CLICK: OK command button

**6.** To be able to add or modify records in the worksheet list, you must unlock the cells in the list area. To do so:
SELECT: cell A7
PRESS: CTRL + SHIFT + ➡ to select the entire list row
PRESS: CTRL + SHIFT + ⬇ to select the entire list area
PRESS: CTRL + SHIFT + ⬇ to select the entire area below the list

**7.** Use the *Protection* tab to unlock these cells:
CHOOSE: Format ➜ Cells
SELECT: *Locked* check box so that no ✓ appears
CLICK: OK command button

**8.** To hide the database function in cell A4 from displaying in the Formula bar, do the following:
SELECT: cell A4

**9.** Now display the *Protection* tab in the Format Cells dialog box:
CHOOSE: Format ➜ Cells
CLICK: *Protection* tab in the Format Cells dialog box
SELECT: *Hidden* check box so that a ✓ appears
CLICK: OK command button
(*Note:* Notice that the expression is not hidden from displaying in the Formula bar until the protection feature is turned on in the next step.)

**10.** To turn on protection for the worksheet:
PRESS: CTRL + HOME to move to the top of the *Billings* sheet
CHOOSE: Tools → Protection → Protect Sheet
The dialog box shown in Figure 10.17 appears.

**Figure 10.17**

The Protect
Sheet dialog box

Turn protection on
or off using this
check box

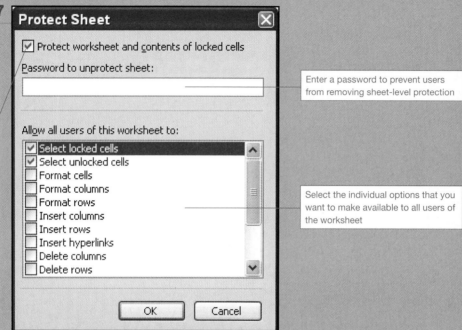

**Protect Sheet** ☒

☑ Protect worksheet and contents of locked cells

Password to unprotect sheet:

[                                            ]

Allow all users of this worksheet to:

☑ Select locked cells
☑ Select unlocked cells
☐ Format cells
☐ Format columns
☐ Format rows
☐ Insert columns
☐ Insert rows
☐ Insert hyperlinks
☐ Delete columns
☐ Delete rows

[ OK ]  [ Cancel ]

Enter a password to prevent users
from removing sheet-level protection

Select the individual options that you
want to make available to all users of
the worksheet

**11.** Ensure that the *Protect worksheet and contents of locked cells* check box is selected (as in Figure 10.17), and then:
CLICK: OK command button
Notice that there are no visible characteristics to differentiate a protected worksheet from an unprotected worksheet.

**12.** To demonstrate worksheet-level protection, attempt to overwrite a protected cell containing a formula:
SELECT: cell A4
Notice first that there is no entry in the Formula bar, because it was hidden in step 9.

**13.** TYPE: $88.00
Notice that before you can enter the "$," a warning dialog box appears (Figure 10.18). (*Note:* You are stopped from overwriting cells on the *Billings* worksheet only. Remember that you must turn on protection for each individual worksheet within a workbook.)

**Figure 10.18**

Warning dialog box displayed for protected cell

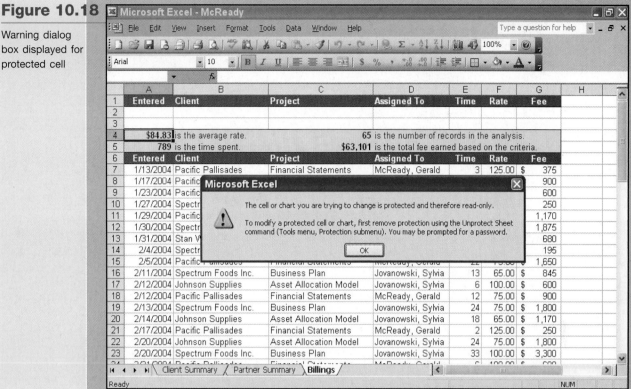

**14.** To cancel the dialog box:
CLICK: OK command button

**15.** Now attempt another entry:
SELECT: cell B2
TYPE: **Spectrum**
PRESS: ⌐ENTER¬
Because this cell is part of the criteria range that you unprotected, Excel 2003 allows the entry and automatically updates the database functions in Rows 4 and 5. (*Hint:* In a protected work-sheet, you can press ⌐TAB¬ to easily navigate among all of the unprotected cells.)

**16.** Because this workbook contains confidential performance results, the partners have decided to hide their worksheet from view. To do this:
CLICK: *Partner Summary* tab
CHOOSE: Format ➜ Sheet ➜ Hide
Notice that the sheet tab has disappeared from view.

**17.** To view the worksheet once again:
CHOOSE: Format ➜ Sheet ➜ Unhide
The dialog box shown in Figure 10.19 appears.

**Figure 10.19**

Unhide dialog
box

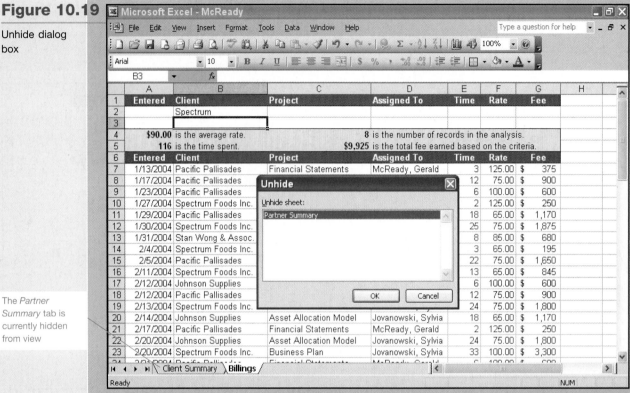

The *Partner
Summary* tab is
currently hidden
from view

18. In the Unhide dialog box:
    SELECT: *Partner Summary* worksheet (the only entry)
    CLICK: OK command button
    As you can see, this method for hiding a worksheet is not very secure, unless, of course, you en-
    able protection for the entire workbook. By protecting an entire workbook, you can effectively
    stop users from hiding, unhiding, inserting, renaming, and deleting worksheets.

19. To demonstrate workbook-level protection, let's hide the *Partner Summary* worksheet again and
    then apply the protection:
    CLICK: *Partner Summary* tab
    CHOOSE: Format → Sheet → Hide
    CHOOSE: Tools → Protection → Protect Workbook
    The dialog box shown in Figure 10.20 appears.

**Figure 10.20**

The Protect
Workbook dialog
box

Protect the individual sheets in a
workbook and/or the document
window display

Enter a password to prevent users
from removing the protection

**20.** To complete the dialog box with a password:
TYPE: **testpass01** in the *Password (optional)* text box
CLICK: OK command button

**21.** In the Confirm Password dialog box:
TYPE: **testpass01** in the *Reenter password to proceed* text box
CLICK: OK command button
(*Note:* You can enter a password using up to 255 characters.)

**22.** Now, attempt to unhide the *Partner Summary* workbook:
CHOOSE: Format → Sheet
Notice that the Unhide command appears dimmed and unavailable, along with other commands.
(*Hint:* Click the Title bar to withdraw the menu from displaying.)

**23.** Let's try to delete a worksheet:
RIGHT-CLICK: *Client Summary* sheet tab
Notice that most commands appear dimmed with the workbook protection turned on.

**24.** To remove the workbook protection:
CHOOSE: Tools → Protection → Unprotect Workbook

**25.** In the Unprotect Workbook dialog box:
TYPE: **testpass01** in the *Password* text box
CLICK: OK command button

**26.** To display the hidden sheet
CHOOSE: Format → Sheet → Unhide
SELECT: *Partner Summary* worksheet (the only entry)
CLICK: OK command button
Your screen should now appear similar to the summary shown in Figure 10.21.

**Figure 10.21**

Unhiding the
*Partner Summary*
tab

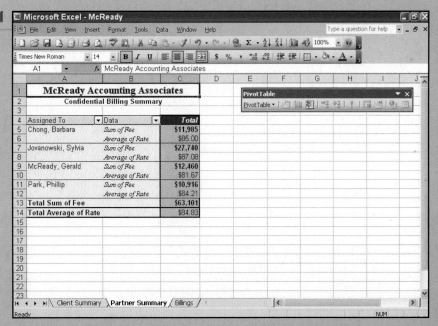

**27.** Leave the window open but do not save the workbook. Continue to the next lesson to learn about password-protecting a workbook file.

### 10.2.2 Password-Protecting a Workbook

→ **Feature**

To restrict access to a workbook file, you give it a password. A **password** is a word or name that is easy for you to remember but difficult for others to guess. The best passwords combine upper- and lower-case characters with numbers and symbols, such as *Terra4U&4Me.* An Excel 2003 password is case-sensitive and may contain up to 255 characters. You set a password for a workbook using the File → Save As command. In addition to password-protection, you can display a dialog box recommending that users open the workbook in **read-only** mode. While working in this mode, users cannot save changes back to the original workbook file; instead, they must save the modified workbook to a new file.

→ **Method**

To password-protect a workbook:

- CHOOSE: File → Save As
- CLICK: Tools ▾ in the toolbar area
- CHOOSE: General Options
- TYPE: *a password* in the *Password to open* text box

  *and/or*

- TYPE: *a password* in the *Password to modify* text box

To display a read-only recommendation:

- CHOOSE: File → Save As
- CLICK: Tools ▾ in the toolbar area
- CHOOSE: General Options
- SELECT: *Read-only recommended* check box

→ **Practice**

In this lesson, you will practice saving a workbook with a password. Ensure that the "McReady" workbook is displayed and that the *Partner Summary* tab is selected.

1. To password-protect the current workbook:
   CHOOSE: File → Save As

2. In the Save As dialog box that appears:
   CLICK: Tools ▾ in the toolbar area of the dialog box
   The menu shown here appears.

3. To specify a password:
   CHOOSE: General Options
   The Save Options dialog box is displayed, as shown in Figure 10.22.

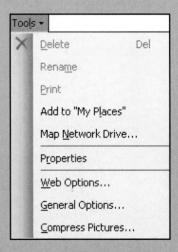

**Figure 10.22**

The Save Options dialog box

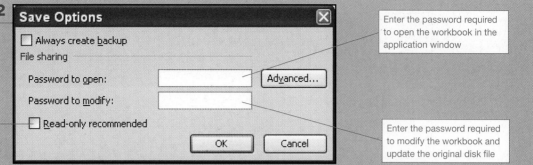

Select to display a recommendation that the user open the workbook in read-only mode

Enter the password required to open the workbook in the application window

Enter the password required to modify the workbook and update the original disk file

4. To set a password to open the workbook:
   TYPE: Terra4U&4Me in the *Password to open* text box
   CLICK: OK command button
   Your password appears as asterisks (*) or small circles (•) in the text box so that a person passing behind you cannot see your entry. (*Note:* Remember that passwords are case-sensitive and will require that you type them in exactly to retrieve the file later.)

5. You are then requested to reenter the password to make sure that you did not make a typing mistake (which is easy to do when you are shown only asterisks as you type):
   TYPE: Terra4U&4Me
   CLICK: OK command button

6. In the Save As dialog box:
   TYPE: McReady Protected in the *File name* text box
   CLICK: Save command button
   The workbook is saved to the disk with a password.

7. To test the password-protection, close the workbook:
   CHOOSE: File → Close

8. Now open the protected workbook:
   CHOOSE: File → Open
   DOUBLE-CLICK: the "McReady Protected" file name
   The Password dialog box appears, as shown in Figure 10.23. (*Note:* The Preview feature in the Open dialog box will not display the contents of a password-protected workbook.)

**Figure 10.23**

Opening a
password-
protected
workbook

Before you can view
the workbook's
contents, the
Password dialog
box appears

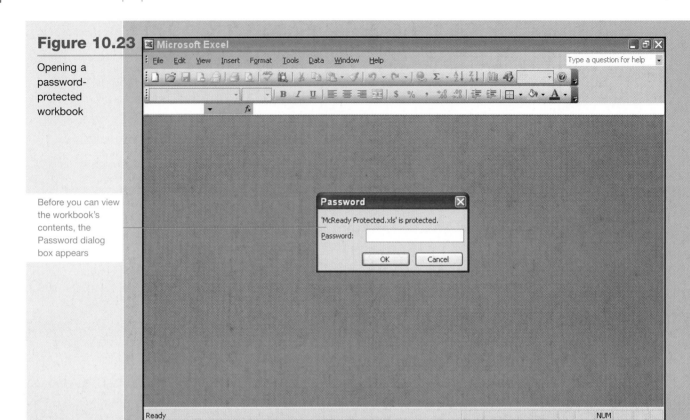

**9.** To open the workbook:
TYPE: **Terra4U&4Me**
CLICK: OK command button
If you type the entry correctly, the workbook appears. If you make a typing mistake, you must start again using the File → Open command.

**10.** To remove a password from a workbook:
CHOOSE: File → Save As
CLICK: Tools▾ in the toolbar area
CHOOSE: General Options

**11.** In the Save Options dialog box:
PRESS: **DELETE** to remove the symbols from the text box
CLICK: OK command button in the Save Options dialog box
CLICK: Save command button in the Save As dialog box
CLICK: Yes to overwrite the existing file name
Your workbook is no longer password-protected.

**12.** Keep the workbook open for use in the next lesson.

### 10.2.3 Setting Workbook Properties

→ **Feature**

Besides specifying Save Options properties, you can enter descriptive information for each workbook file. Treat this exercise as habit-forming and remember to complete the file properties page for each and every workbook you create. You and the users of your workbooks will quickly learn to appreciate this feature for managing documents created using Microsoft Office 2003 applications.

→ **Method**

To set a workbook file's properties:

• CHOOSE: File → Properties

• TYPE: the desired file properties

• CLICK: OK command button

→ **Practice**

You will now complete the file properties for a workbook. Ensure that the "McReady Protected" workbook is displayed.

**1.** To display the file properties for the "McReady Protected" workbook:
CHOOSE: File → Properties

**2.** In the Properties dialog box that appears:
CLICK: *Summary* tab (if it is not already selected)

**3.** On your own, complete the information fields appearing in Figure 10.24.

**Figure 10.24**

Filling in the File Properties for a workbook

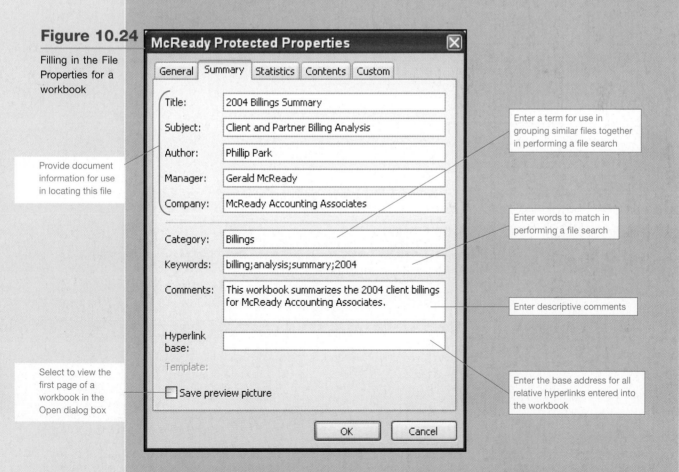

Provide document information for use in locating this file

Enter a term for use in grouping similar files together in performing a file search

Enter words to match in performing a file search

Enter descriptive comments

Enter the base address for all relative hyperlinks entered into the workbook

Select to view the first page of a workbook in the Open dialog box

**4.** CLICK: *Statistics* tab
This tab, along with the *General* tab, displays information such as when the workbook was created, last modified, and last saved.

**5.** CLICK: *Contents* tab
This tab lists the workbook's sheets and named cell ranges, as shown in Figure 10.25.

**Figure 10.25**

File Properties
dialog box:
*Content* tab

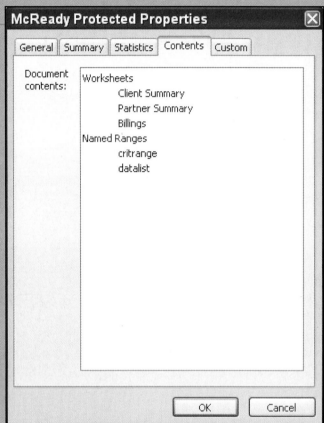

6. CLICK: *Custom* tab
This tab lets you define and manage any custom properties that you want to create for usage tracking.

7. CLICK: *General* tab
CLICK: OK command button

8. Save the "McReady Protected" workbook and keep it open for use in the next lesson.

## 10.2.4 Managing Security and Privacy

→ ## Feature

With a growing number of cases involving hacking, digital fraud, and identify theft, security and privacy are important considerations for workbook developers. Valuable information that you have stored in workbooks can be stolen or corrupted by viruses. Fortunately, Office 2003 provides tools for creating custom security settings, restricting data access, and protecting against data loss and viruses.

One of the securest methods for transmitting your workbooks via electronic mail or file transfer is to use data encryption. This Excel 2003 feature scrambles the contents of a workbook and lets you specify who is authorized to descramble (or decrypt) the file. Encryption is often used in conjunction with a digital signature, which is like an electronic identification card. A digital signature must be associated with a digital certificate, available only from an accredited list of certification authorities. Digital signatures provide you with proof that a workbook or file is indeed coming from a known and trusted source, and that it has not been altered or modified in any way. Together with password-protection, encryption and digital signatures help protect you from malicious intent. If you are concerned about privacy, you can also ask Excel 2003 to remove any personal information (for example, Author, Manager, Company, and Last Saved By) that it inserts on the Summary tab of the File Properties dialog box.

→ ## Method

To encrypt and digitally sign a workbook:

- CHOOSE: Tools → Options

- CLICK: *Security* tab

- TYPE: *a password* into the *Password to open* text box in the *File encryption settings for this workbook* area

- CLICK: Digital Signatures command button to attach a certificate to the workbook file

To remove data from a workbook file's properties:

- CHOOSE: Tools → Options

- CLICK: *Security* tab

- SELECT: *Remove personal information from file properties on save* check box, so that a ✓ appears

- CLICK: OK Command button

→ ## Practice

You will now modify some of the security settings for a workbook. Ensure that the "McReady Protected" workbook is displayed.

**1.** To begin, let's display the security options for the "McReady Protected" workbook. Do the following:
CHOOSE: Tools → Options
CLICK: *Security* tab in the Options dialog box
Your screen should now appear similar to the dialog box shown in Figure 10.26.

**Figure 10.26**

Options dialog
box: *Security* tab

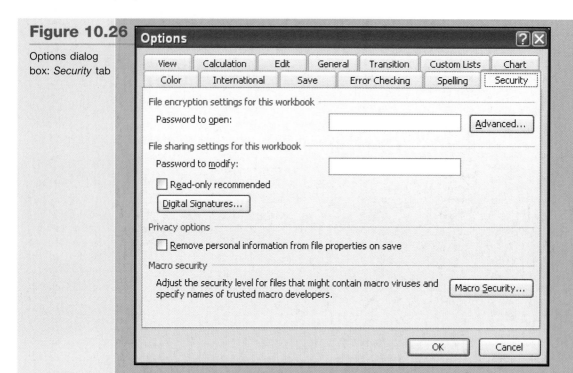

**2.** To specify a high level of encryption for this workbook:
CLICK: Advanced command button

**3.** In the Encryption Type dialog box that appears:
SELECT: RC4, Microsoft Enhanced Cryptographic Provider 1.0 in the *Choose an encryption type* list area
Your screen should appear similar to the dialog box shown in Figure 10.27.

**Figure 10.27**

Specifying an
encryption type

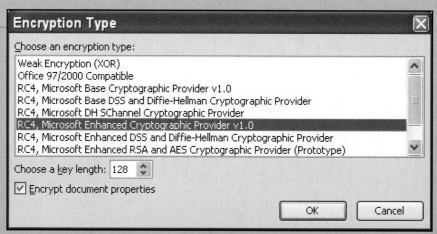

**4.** To return to the Options dialog box:
CLICK: OK command button

**5.** Now enter a password for the workbook file:
CLICK: in the *Password to open* text box
TYPE: **UrGr8**

**6.** To review your digital signing capabilities:
CLICK: Digital Signatures command button
If you have purchased a digital certificate from an accredited authority, you may click the Add command button in the Digital Signature dialog box (Figure 10.28) to sign the current workbook. If you have not purchased a digital certificate, you will not be able to digitally sign the workbook file.

**Figure 10.28**

Digital Signature
dialog box

To digitally sign this workbook, click the Add command button and then select the digital certificate that you would like to use. To purchase a certificate, visit an authorized agency such as VeriSign at www.verisign.com.

**7.** To view the certificates available on your computer:
CLICK: Add command button
The Select Certificate dialog box appears, which will list the certificate options that are available to you.

**8.** To return to the Options dialog box:
CLICK: Cancel command button in the Select Certificate dialog box
CLICK: Cancel command button in the Digital Signature dialog box

**9.** Lastly, let's protect our privacy by removing personal information from the file properties. Do the following:
CLICK: *Remove personal information from file properties on save* check box, so that a ✓ appears
CLICK: OK command button

**10.** You must retype your password:
TYPE: **UrGr8**
CLICK: OK command button

**11.** Save and then close the "McReady Protected" workbook.

**12.** On your own, open the "McReady Protected" workbook from your personal storage location using the **UrGr8** password. When you are ready to proceed, close the workbook.

Excel

 **10.2** How can you ensure that a user will not remove the worksheet protection that you have initiated?

# 10.3 Working with Templates

A **template** is a special type of workbook file that you can use as a model from which to create new workbooks. Like any workbook, templates may contain text, formulas, formatting, styles, drawing objects, and macros. By their very nature, templates are time-savers that reduce errors and promote consistency. You can use a template, for example, to create a new workbook or to present a data collection form for updating a worksheet list. You can also use a template to customize various workbook and worksheet settings, including:

- the number of sheets displayed in a new workbook

- page margins, print orientation, and headers and footers

- cell formatting characteristics and protection attributes

- cell contents, such as titles, headings, and formulas

- custom toolbars and menu commands, macros, and VBA modules

In addition to using the built-in templates provided by Microsoft, you can create your own custom templates by saving workbooks using the Template file type. Depending on where you store a template, it may display in Excel's Templates dialog box. Workbook templates that are stored in the Templates or XLStart folders display on the *General* tab of the Templates dialog box. Excel's pre-designed templates appear on the *Spreadsheet Solutions* tab. If desired, you can display your own custom tab, such as *My Templates,* in the dialog box by creating a new folder in the Templates directory. You can also access additional templates on the Microsoft Office Online Web site. In this module, you learn to create, edit, and apply workbook templates.

## 10.3.1 Creating and Applying Templates

 ## Feature

In the first chapter of this learning guide (lesson 1.4.1), you created a new workbook by opening and applying the Sales Invoice template, which appears in the *Spreadsheet Solutions* tab of the Templates dialog box. Excel 2003 provides several such built-in templates that you can use. In addition, you can download templates from Microsoft's Office Online Web site, or directly from Web sites around the world. However, the real advantage of templates is the ability to create and reuse a workbook customized to meet your personal preferences and requirements.

The custom workbook templates that you create are stored in the Templates folder. Excel 2003 also lets you create two special templates, called **AutoTemplates,** which contain the default settings for new workbooks and worksheets. Both of these templates, aptly named "Book.xlt" and "Sheet.xlt," must be stored in the XLStart folder, which is typically located at "*C:\Program Files\Microsoft Office\Office11\XLStart.*" The Book.xlt template provides the default template for all workbooks created without using a custom template. This is also the template used when you create an empty workbook by clicking the "Blank workbook" option in the New Workbook task pane. The Sheet.xlt template is accessed when you choose the Insert → Worksheet command from within a workbook. To create a worksheet template, you must ensure that the workbook file contains a single worksheet only.

## → Method

To create a new template:

- Create a workbook that you want to save as a template.
- CHOOSE: File → Save As
- SELECT: Template (*.xlt) in the *Save as type* drop-down list box
- SELECT: Templates in the *Save in* drop-down list box
- CLICK: Save command button

To apply a template in creating a new workbook:

- CHOOSE: File → New
- CLICK: *On my computer* under the *Templates* area of the New Workbook task pane
- CLICK: *General* tab in the Templates dialog box
- DOUBLE-CLICK: a template icon (📄)

To apply a template in creating a new worksheet:

- RIGHT-CLICK: an existing sheet tab
- CHOOSE: Insert
- DOUBLE-CLICK: a template icon (📄)

## → Practice

You will now create and apply your own workbook and worksheet templates. Ensure that no workbooks appear in the application window.

**1.** You begin this exercise by entering content and formatting cells in a new workbook. You will then save the workbook as a custom template so that it may be used again and again. To display a new workbook:
CHOOSE: File → New
Your screen should now appear similar to the dialog box shown in Figure 10.29.

**Figure 10.29**

Displaying the
New Workbook
task pane

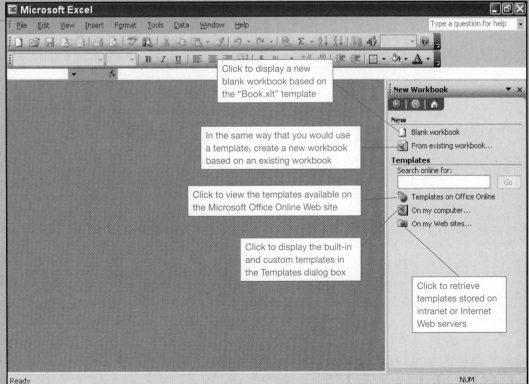

**2.** To create a new blank workbook using the task pane:
CLICK: "Blank workbook" under the *New* heading
A new workbook appears and the task pane closes.

**3.** To begin formatting, select the entire worksheet:
CLICK: Select All button (☐) appearing in the top left-hand corner of the worksheet window, to the left of column A and above row 1
(*Note:* You are only formatting the *Sheet1* worksheet in this exercise.)

**4.** To change the default font and size for the worksheet:
CLICK: down arrow attached to the Font list box (Arial ▾)
SELECT: Times New Roman
CLICK: down arrow attached to the Font Size list box (10 ▾)
SELECT: 12

**5.** CLICK: cell A1 to cancel the selection

**6.** To change the standard column width in the worksheet:
CHOOSE: Format → Column → Standard Width
TYPE: **10** in the *Standard column width* text box
CLICK: OK command button

**7.** To remove the *Sheet2* and *Sheet3* worksheets from the workbook:
CLICK: *Sheet2* tab
PRESS: CTRL and hold it down
CLICK: *Sheet3* tab

**8.** Release the CTRL key and then do the following:
RIGHT-CLICK: *Sheet3* tab
CHOOSE: Delete
Only the *Sheet1* worksheet remains in the workbook.

**9.** On your own, create and format the worksheet displayed in Figure 10.30. Name the worksheet tab **Documentation**.

**Figure 10.30**

Creating a template

Each workbook created using this template will display this information as a starting point

Each cell is formatted to display using a particular font, font size, and column width

This workbook template contains a single worksheet tab named "Documentation"

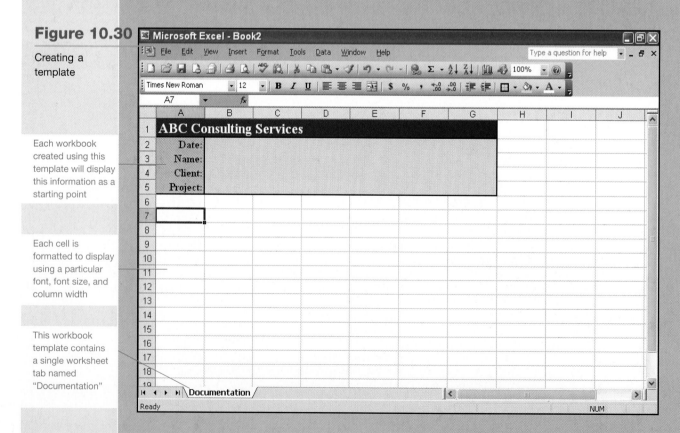

**10.** To display the current date in the workbook:
SELECT: cell B2
TYPE: =today()
PRESS: (ENTER)

**11.** Now position the cell pointer where you want it to appear when a new workbook is created. Do the following:
SELECT: cell A1

**12.** To save the workbook as a custom template:
CHOOSE: File → Save As
TYPE: **My Cover Sheet**

**13.** In the *Save as type* drop-down list box:
SELECT: Template (the characters "*.xlt" may also appear)
Notice that the *Save in* drop-down list box automatically selects and displays the Templates folder.

**14.** To view the location of the Templates folder:
CLICK: down arrow attached to the *Save in* drop-down list box
Your screen should now appear similar to Figure 10.31.

**Figure 10.31**

Viewing the location of the Templates folder

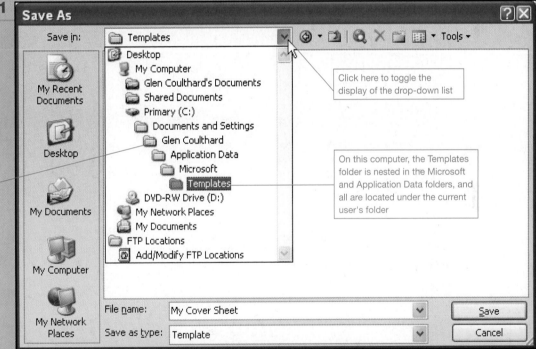

Your login or user name will appear as the name of this folder

**15.** To cancel the drop-down list box:
CLICK: down arrow attached to the *Save in* drop-down list box
(*Note:* You can also press **ESC** to cancel the display of the list box.)

**16.** You can create a custom tab on the Templates dialog box by creating a folder for your templates. To do so:
CLICK: Create New Folder button ( ) on the toolbar

**17.** In the New Folder dialog box that appears:
TYPE: **My Advantage** in the *Name* text box
CLICK: OK command button

**18.** To save the template into your new folder:
CLICK: Save command button
(*Note:* Depending on whether you are using a stand-alone computer or one that is attached to a network, you may or may not have permission to save a file to the "Templates" folder. If you do not have the required access rights, you will not be able to complete this example. In this case, save the template to your personal storage location and skip to the end of the lesson.)

**19.** Now let's see the results of your efforts:
CHOOSE: File → Close

**20.** To create a new workbook based on the "My Cover Sheet" template:
CHOOSE: File → New to display the New Workbook task pane
CLICK: "On my computer" under the *Templates* area

**21.** In the Templates dialog box (Figure 10.32):
CLICK: *My Advantage* tab
Your screen should appear similar to the dialog box shown in Figure 10.32.

**Figure 10.32**

Displaying a custom template

The template appears in the "My Advantage" folder and, therefore, on the *My Advantage* tab

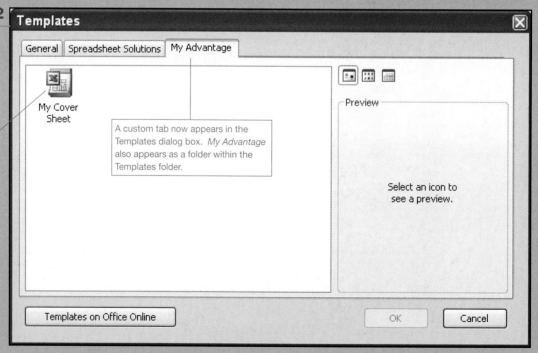

**22.** To create the workbook based on the template:
DOUBLE-CLICK: My Cover Sheet icon ()
The workbook is opened as "My Cover Sheet1."

**23.** You can now make changes to the workbook and save it under a new name. For this exercise, however, simply close the workbook without saving the changes.

**24.** You will now learn how to insert a new worksheet template into an existing workbook. Open the data file named EX1030 and save it as "My Schedule" to your personal storage location, as shown in Figure 10.33.

**Figure 10.33**

"My Schedule" workbook

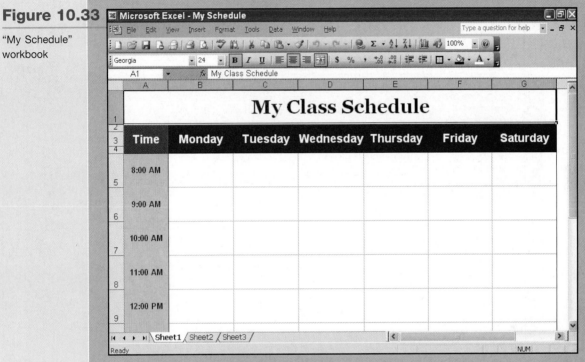

**25.** Let's add a documentation worksheet, based on the "My Cover Sheet" template, to the active workbook. Do the following:
RIGHT-CLICK: *Sheet1* tab to display the menu shown here

**26.** To proceed:
CHOOSE: Insert
An Insert dialog box, similar to the Templates dialog shown previously in Figure 10.32, appears. (*Hint:* Use the Insert → Worksheet command to add a worksheet based on the program's default settings or using the "Sheet.xlt" template. Use the right-click method above to insert a worksheet based on a custom template.)

**27.** To insert a worksheet based on the custom template:
CLICK: *My Advantage* tab, if it is not already displayed
DOUBLE-CLICK: My Cover Sheet icon ()
A new worksheet, named *Documentation,* is added to the workbook, complete with all the content and display settings stored in the template.

**28.** Save and then close the "My Schedule" workbook.

Along with other resources, Microsoft provides complimentary workbook templates on its Web site. To access these templates, display the New Workbook task pane and then click "Templates on Office On-line" under the Templates area. This command launches your Web browser software and loads the Web page for the Templates gallery, as shown in the partly scrolled window of Figure 10.34. This Web page changes frequently and your screen will appear different from the one shown in Figure 10.34. (Note: You need to have an Internet connection in order to access the Office Online Web site.) You may then explore the Web site for specific information and directions on how to download and install the templates.

**Figure 10.34**

Accessing the Microsoft Office Online templates

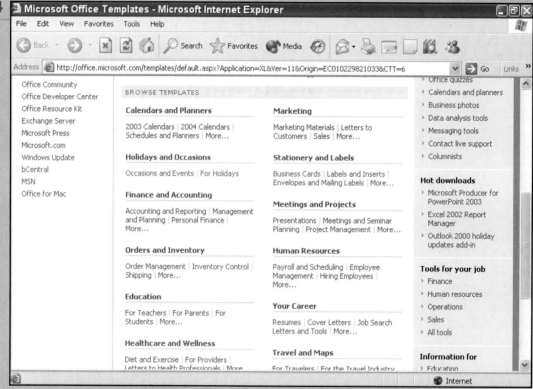

### 10.3.2 Editing Templates

→ **Feature**

As mentioned at the beginning of this session, a template is simply a special type of workbook file. Besides using a template to create a new workbook, you can modify an existing template file as you would any other workbook. Once changed, however, you must remember to save the template using the Template (*.xlt) file type. Often the most difficult part of editing templates is finding them within your computer's file system.

Depending on your computer's operating system, the Office 2003 templates that you create will be stored in different folders. For example, if you are using Windows 98, the Templates folder may be located at: *C:\Windows\Application Data\Microsoft\Templates.* If you are using Windows 2000 or XP, the folder location is located at *C:\Documents and Settings\user name\Application Data\Microsoft\Templates.* In order to browse the *user name* directory for templates, you must specify that Windows Explorer shows hidden files and folders. To do so, launch Windows Explorer and choose the Tools → Folder Options command. Then, select the *View* tab in the dialog box and select the required option in the *Advanced settings* list area. Furthermore, if you cannot remember where your template files are stored, use the Save As dialog box to display the *Save in* drop-down list for Template files, as illustrated in Figure 10.31 of the previous lesson.

→ **Method**

To modify an existing template:

- Open a template file.
- Make the desired editing changes.
- Save the file using the Template (*.xlt) file type.

→ **Practice**

You will now edit a workbook template that you create specifically for this lesson. Ensure that you have completed the previous lesson before proceeding.

**1.** Open the data file named EX1030. This workbook contains a weekly calendar that you can use to schedule your classes.

**2.** Your objective is to convert this workbook into a template:
CHOOSE: File → Save As
TYPE: **Class Schedule**

**3.** In the *Save as type* drop-down list box:
SELECT: Template
The *Save in* drop-down list box automatically selects and displays the Templates folder.

**4.** Using the Places bar and the *Save in* drop-down list box, select your personal storage location instead of the Templates folder. Then:
CLICK: Save command button

**5.** Close the workbook.

**6.** To open the Class Schedule workbook template:
CLICK: Open button (▣)
Notice that the "All Microsoft Office Excel Files" option appears in the *Files of type* drop-down list box in the Open dialog box. This option will display your workbooks and templates in the dialog box.

**7.** If necessary, use the *Look in* drop-down list box to navigate to your personal storage location. The "Class Schedule" file should appear in the list area of the Open dialog box before proceeding. Notice that its icon (▣) differs slightly from the other workbook files, as illustrated by the dialog box's Tiles view and shown in the Figure 10.35.

**Figure 10.35**

Opening a workbook template

Workbook template icon

Workbook icon

8. To open the template for editing:
DOUBLE-CLICK: "Class Schedule" in the list area

9. You will now edit this template and then save it back to the disk. To begin, select the cell range from B2 to G4.

10. Let's change the background color of this cell range:
SELECT: a black color using the Fill Color button (image)

11. To change the font size of the headings row:
SELECT: cell range from A3 to G3
SELECT: 12 from the Font Size list box (10 ▾)

12. You should always place the cell pointer in the location that you desire when opening up the workbook template. For this template:
CLICK: cell A1 (a merged cell)
Your workbook should now appear similar to the one shown in Figure 10.36.

**Figure 10.36**

Editing the Class
Schedule
template

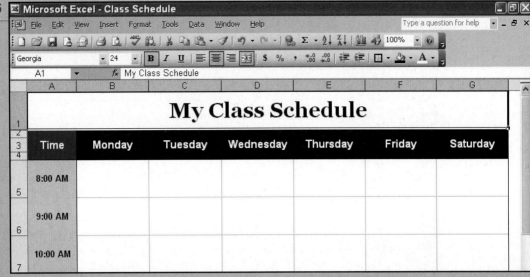

13. To save the newly revised template:

   CLICK: Save button (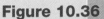)

14. Close the workbook template. There should be no workbooks open in the application window. If this template were located in the Templates folder, you could now use the modified file to create a new workbook.

### 10.3.3 Modifying Excel's Default Settings

### → Feature

In the Options dialog box, there are several opportunities available for modifying the way Excel 2003 performs on your computer system. Besides temporarily removing gridlines and row and column headers, you can permanently affect the font settings and number of worksheets that appear in new workbooks and the default location for storing your files. As you witnessed earlier in this module, Excel displays in the Templates dialog box only those templates that are saved in either the Templates folder or the XLStart folder. However, on the *General* tab of the Options dialog box, you are able to specify an additional location for your workbook templates. This feature is especially important if you are sharing workbooks and templates with other users on a network.

### → Method

To modify Excel 2003's default settings:

- CHOOSE: Tools → Options
- CLICK: *General* tab
- Select the desired options.

### → Practice

You will now use the Options dialog box to specify several default workbook settings. Ensure that you have completed the previous lesson.

1. To display a new workbook:
   CLICK: New button (⬜)

**2.** Let's display the Options dialog box:
CHOOSE: Tools → Options
CLICK: *View* tab
Your screen should appear similar to the dialog box shown in Figure 10.37. The *View* tab allows you to adjust display settings in the application and workbook windows. For example, you can toggle on and off the application window's Formula and Status bars and a workbook's gridlines, frame headers, scroll bars, and sheet tabs.

**Figure 10.37**

Options dialog box: *View* tab

Use this area to change display settings for the application window

Use this area to change display settings in the current workbook window

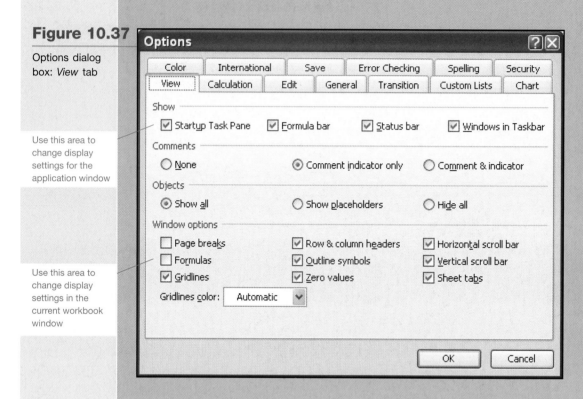

**3.** To modify the default settings for new workbooks:
CLICK: *General* tab
The dialog box shown in Figure 10.38 now appears.

**Figure 10.38**

Options dialog box: *General* tab

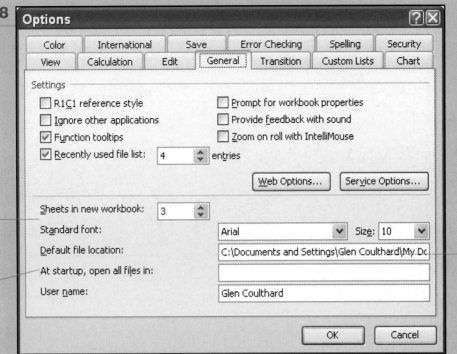

Use this area to change the default settings for new workbooks

Specify a folder location to display the templates contained in the Templates dialog box. (*Caution:* All workbooks that are stored in this folder will be opened automatically.)

Use this text box to specify the default file location for saving your workbooks

Excel

**4.** To change the number of worksheets displayed in a new workbook:
SELECT: "2" in the *Sheets in new workbook* spin box

**5.** Let's change the default font for new workbooks:
SELECT: Tahoma from the *Standard font* drop-down list box

**6.** To accept these new settings and dismiss the Options dialog box:
CLICK: OK command button
A warning dialog box appears, as shown below.

**7.** To proceed:
CLICK: OK command button

**8.** Exit and then restart Microsoft Office Excel 2003. Your screen should appear similar to the worksheet shown in Figure 10.39.

**Figure 10.39**

Restarting Excel 2003 with new default settings

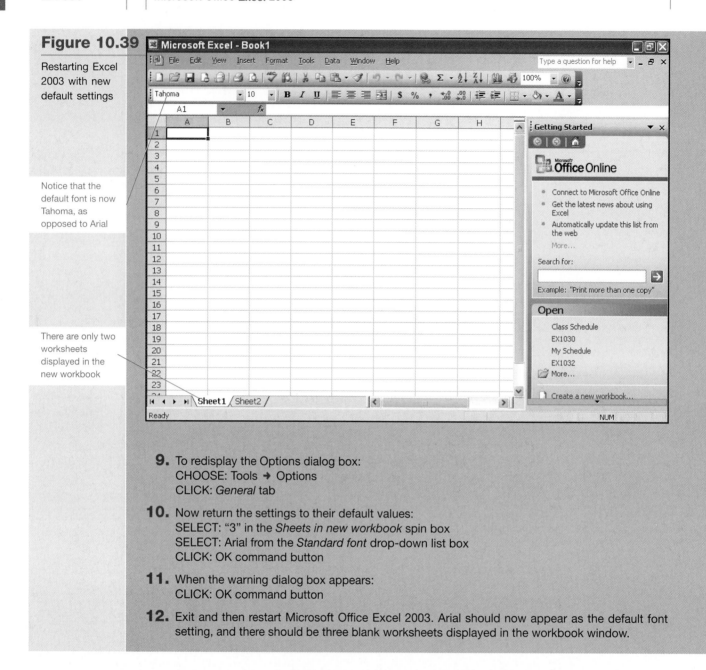

Notice that the default font is now Tahoma, as opposed to Arial

There are only two worksheets displayed in the new workbook

9. To redisplay the Options dialog box:
   CHOOSE: Tools → Options
   CLICK: *General* tab

10. Now return the settings to their default values:
    SELECT: "3" in the *Sheets in new workbook* spin box
    SELECT: Arial from the *Standard font* drop-down list box
    CLICK: OK command button

11. When the warning dialog box appears:
    CLICK: OK command button

12. Exit and then restart Microsoft Office Excel 2003. Arial should now appear as the default font setting, and there should be three blank worksheets displayed in the workbook window.

**10.3** How would you use a template to change the default font from Arial to Verdana for all new workbooks?

# 10.4 Importing and Exporting Data

With continual innovations and program updates, the only constant in the software industry is change. The sheer number of programs for performing basic computing tasks, such as word processing and data management, is astounding. While competition is good for our pocketbooks, it introduces several problems. Suppose, for example, Microsoft Office Excel 2003 is installed on your computer at home, but the university only supplies Lotus SmartSuite or StarOffice in their computer labs. As a result, you must know how to convert files between the data formats. Think about the data sharing difficulties you might face in using Excel 2003 when the remainder of your office uses an older version of Excel on the Macintosh. Clearly, the ability to import, export, and otherwise exchange data can directly impact your productivity. In this module, you learn important techniques for exporting your worksheets and importing data from text files, alternate spreadsheet formats, and other external sources. You also learn some techniques for sharing data among all of the Microsoft Office 2003 applications.

## 10.4.1 Saving and Exporting Structured Data

### → Feature

An often-overlooked method for sharing information is simply saving (exporting) data files using different file formats. Although not as flashy as working with dynamic content, exporting data is often the most efficient means for exchanging data with other users and for use in other programs. Some of the file format options available for exporting your workbooks include spreadsheet converters for Excel, Quattro Pro, and Lotus 1-2-3; database converters for Access, dBase, and SQL; and text converters for ASCII, CSV, DIF, and SYLK.

### → Method

To export data from your workbooks:

- CHOOSE: File → Save As
- SELECT: *a file format* in the *Save as type* drop-down list box
- SELECT: *a location* in the *Save in* drop-down list box
- CLICK: Save command button

### → Practice

You will now practice exporting a worksheet to a text file for display using the Notepad application. Ensure that no workbooks appear in the application window.

**1.** Open the data file named EX1041. This workbook contains a lookup table of enrolment statistics for a business school and two chart sheets.

**2.** Your objective is to convert the *Enrolments* worksheet into a text file in order to send it via email to an associate who does not own Excel. To do so:
CHOOSE: File → Save As

**3.** Using the *Save in* drop-down list box, select your personal storage location. Then, do the following:
TYPE: **Shuster** in the *File name* text box
CLICK: down arrow attached to the *Save as type* drop-down list box

**4.** After examining the file types in the drop-down list (Figure 10.40):
SELECT: Text (Tab delimited)
(*Note:* A tab delimited file uses fixed-length tabs to separate data into columns resembling a worksheet layout.)

**Figure 10.40**

Selecting an
export format for
the EX1041
workbook

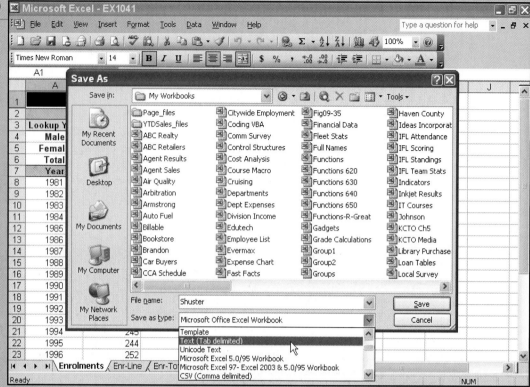

**5.** CLICK: Save command button

A warning dialog box (Figure 10.41) appears stating that only content from the active worksheet will be saved to the text file. For most formats, Excel 2003 converts only the active or displayed sheet.

**Figure 10.41**

Warning dialog
box displayed
during export to
a Text file

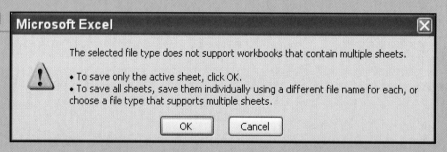

**6.** CLICK: OK command button to proceed

**7.** Another warning dialog box (Figure 10.42) appears stating that some of the features in the worksheet are not supported in the text file format. To proceed:
CLICK: Yes command button

**Figure 10.42**

Information dialog
box displayed
during export to
a Text file

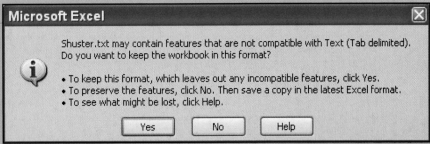

**Microsoft Excel**

Shuster.txt may contain features that are not compatible with Text (Tab delimited).
Do you want to keep the workbook in this format?

• To keep this format, which leaves out any incompatible features, click Yes.
• To preserve the features, click No. Then save a copy in the latest Excel format.
• To see what might be lost, click Help.

[ Yes ]   [ No ]   [ Help ]

**8.** To view the exported text file using the Windows Notepad:
CLICK: Start button ( *start* ) on the taskbar
CHOOSE: All Programs → Accessories → Notepad

**9.** To open the text file in Notepad:
CHOOSE: File → Open from its Menu bar

**10.** Using the *Look in* drop-down list box, select your personal storage location. Then, do the following:
DOUBLE-CLICK: Shuster in the list area
(*Note:* The file name may appear as "Shuster.txt" depending on your Windows Explorer settings.) The Notepad application window should now appear similar to the one shown in Figure 10.43. Notice that the information is lined up into columns using fixed-length tabs.

**Figure 10.43**

Displaying an
exported
worksheet using
Notepad

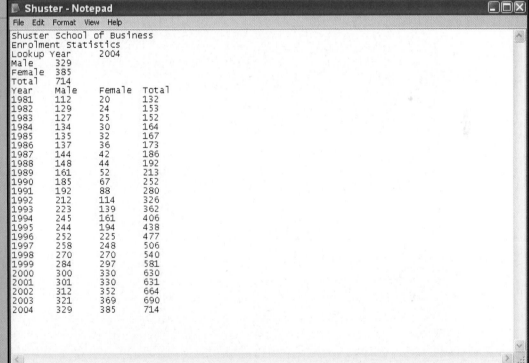

**Shuster - Notepad**

File  Edit  Format  View  Help

```
Shuster School of Business
Enrolment Statistics
Lookup Year    2004
Male    329
Female  385
Total   714
Year    Male    Female  Total
1981    112     20      132
1982    129     24      153
1983    127     25      152
1984    134     30      164
1985    135     32      167
1986    137     36      173
1987    144     42      186
1988    148     44      192
1989    161     52      213
1990    185     67      252
1991    192     88      280
1992    212     114     326
1993    223     139     362
1994    245     161     406
1995    244     194     438
1996    252     225     477
1997    258     248     506
1998    270     270     540
1999    284     297     581
2000    300     330     630
2001    301     330     631
2002    312     352     664
2003    321     369     690
2004    329     385     714
```

**11.** Close Notepad by clicking its Close button ( ✕ ).

**12.** Close the "Shuster" workbook without saving any changes.

**10.4.2** Importing Data Using File Type Converters

→ **Feature**

Similar to exporting data to different file formats, you can open or import data that is stored in text files, query files, database files, Lotus 1-2-3 and Quattro Pro spreadsheet files, and various versions of Excel workbooks. When you open a file that is recognized by Excel 2003, it uses one of its filters or converter programs to open and format the data for use in a workbook. If the file format or type is not recognized, Excel 2003 displays an error message. You must then install the converter program required for the desired file format from the Microsoft Office 2003 installation media.

→ **Method**

To import a foreign data file into an Excel 2003 workbook:

- CHOOSE: File → Open

- SELECT: *a file format* in the *Files of type* drop-down list box

- SELECT: *a location* in the *Look in* drop-down list box

- DOUBLE-CLICK: the desired file name in the list area

→ **Practice**

You will now open a spreadsheet file created in 1994 using Lotus 1-2-3 Release 4 for Windows. Ensure that no workbooks are open in the application window.

**1.** To import a file created using another application:
CHOOSE: File → Open

**2.** Using the *Look in* drop-down list box, select the Advantage student data files location. Then, do the following:
CLICK: down arrow attached to the *Files of type* drop-down list box
SELECT: Lotus 1-2-3 Files from the list
(*Note:* The entry may appear as "Lotus 1-2-3 Files (*.wk?)" in the drop-down list box. Also, you must have installed the Lotus 1-2-3 filters in order to perform the steps in this exercise.)

**3.** A single file should now appear in the Open dialog box. To open the Lotus 1-2-3 spreadsheet:
DOUBLE-CLICK: EX1042
As shown in Figure 10.44, Excel 2003 automatically converts and opens the Lotus spreadsheet as an Excel 2003 workbook containing a single worksheet entitled "A."

**Figure 10.44**

Opening a Lotus 1-2-3 spreadsheet file

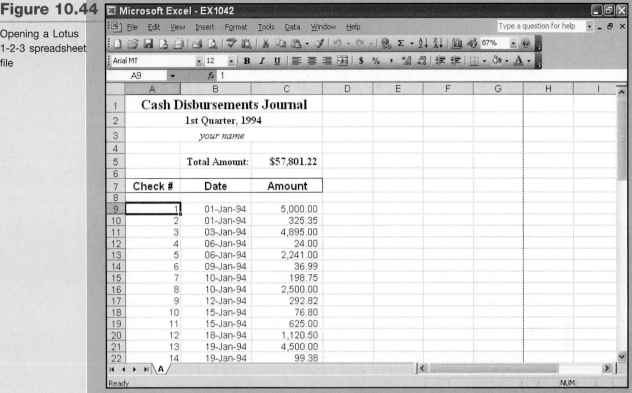

**4.** In order to manipulate and format the converted spreadsheet using Excel 2003's commands and features, you must save it using Excel's workbook file format. To do so:
CHOOSE: File → Save As

**5.** Using the *Save in* drop-down list box, select your personal storage location. Then, do the following:
TYPE: **Lotus File** in the *File name* text box

**6.** Now select the file type:
CLICK: down arrow attached to the *Save as type* drop-down list box
SELECT: Microsoft Office Excel Workbook

**7.** CLICK: Save command button

**8.** Close the "Lotus File" workbook.

### 10.4.3 Importing Data Using the Text Import Wizard

→ **Feature**

Most every application program can import and export data using the ASCII text file format. You may think of this file format as the lowest common denominator for sharing and exchanging data. For example, a text file created on a 1984 IBM PC/XT can be read by the newest Pentium processor-based and Apple Macintosh computers, and vice versa. Because text files typically contain only data, all formatting information is lost when you export your documents or database files. However, this fact results in smaller file sizes and makes it far easier for other application programs to manipulate the data. Because this method of data exchange is so common, Microsoft Office Excel 2003 provides the **Text Import Wizard** to help you convert a text file into a worksheet.

→ ## Method

To import data stored in a text file:

- CHOOSE: File → Open

- SELECT: Text Files in the *Files of type* drop-down list box

- SELECT: a location in the *Look in* drop-down list box

- DOUBLE-CLICK: the desired file name in the list area

- Proceed through the Text Import Wizard dialog boxes.

→ ## Practice

You will now use the Text Import Wizard to convert a text file into a worksheet. Ensure that no workbooks appear in the application window.

**1.** To import a text file:
CHOOSE: File → Open

**2.** Using the *Look in* drop-down list box, select the Advantage student data files location. Then, do the following:
CLICK: down arrow attached to the *Files of type* drop-down list box
SELECT: Text Files from the list
(*Note:* You must have installed the Text File filters in order to perform the steps in this exercise.)

**3.** Only text files now appear in the Open dialog box. To proceed:
DOUBLE-CLICK: EX1043

As shown in Figure 10.45, the Text Import Wizard is displayed.

**Figure 10.45**

Text Import
Wizard: Step 1
of 3

Text files exported
from other
programs typically
use commas,
quotation marks,
and tabs as
delimiters between
fields

Location of the text
file to be imported

Preview of the file
contents to be
imported

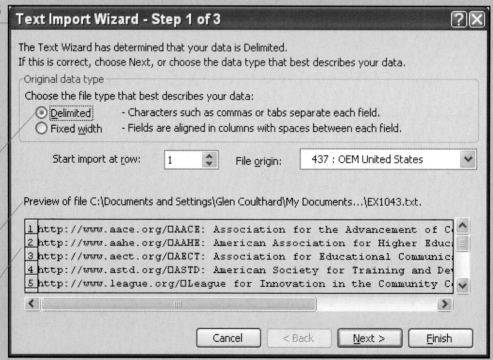

4. In Step 1 of the wizard, specify where to begin importing data and whether the data is delimited (separated by symbols or characters) or fixed width. To accept the default values:
CLICK: [Next>]

5. In Step 2 of the wizard (Figure 10.46), specify the type of **delimiter** and then confirm the preview of data in worksheet columns. Ensure that the *Tab* check box is selected in the *Delimiters* area and then:
CLICK: [Next>]

**Figure 10.46**

Text Import Wizard: Step 2 of 3

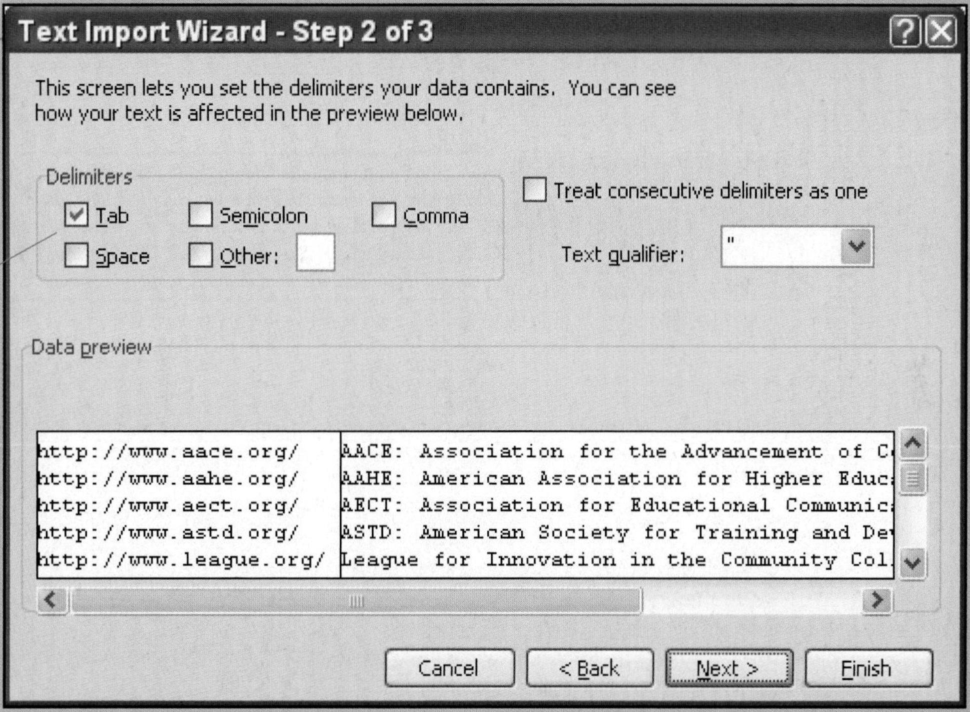

Select the delimiter used to separate the columns of data

6. In Step 3 of the wizard (Figure 10.47), specify the data format for each column identified in the previous step. For this example, just accept the default *General* format for each column:
CLICK: [Finish]

**Figure 10.47**

Text Import
Wizard: Step 3
of 3

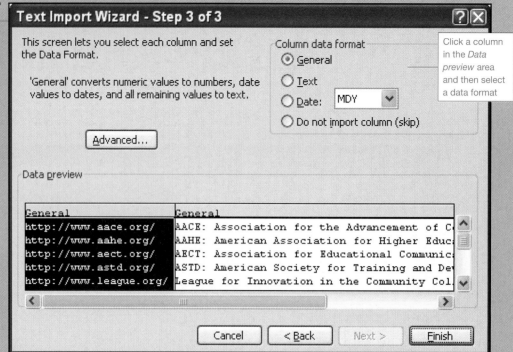

7. The text file is imported into a worksheet named EX1043 and the cell pointer is positioned in cell A1. Let's increase the column width:
CHOOSE: Format → Column → Width
TYPE: 30
PRESS: ENTER
Notice that each line in the text file is converted to a row in the worksheet.

8. You must now save the workbook using the Microsoft Office Excel Workbook file type. Do the following:
CHOOSE: File → Save As

9. Using the *Save in* drop-down list box, select your personal storage location. Then, do the following:
TYPE: **Text File** in the *File name* text box

10. Now select the file type:
CLICK: down arrow attached to the *Save as type* drop-down list box
SELECT: Microsoft Office Excel Workbook

11. CLICK: Save command button
Your screen should now appear similar to the worksheet shown in Figure 10.48.

**Figure 10.48**

Importing a text file into a workbook

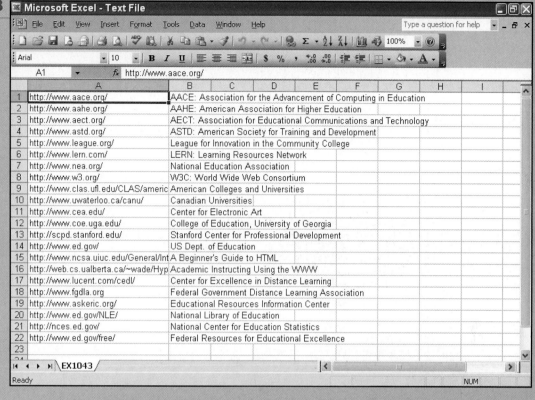

**12.** Close the "Text File" workbook.

## 10.4.4 Importing Data from External Sources

→ **Feature**

Importing data into a workbook enables you to manipulate, analyze, and summarize data without having to retype the information. The previous lessons in this module focus on converting data from one format to another. The original file is often deleted or archived in favor of using the new workbook. There will be instances, however, where you will want to access data that is maintained by another program. Especially true in database management software, large amounts of data are best stored and manipulated in one program and then summarized using the data analysis tools in Microsoft Office Excel 2003. Rather than performing a one-time conversion of a data file into a workbook, you instead establish a connection to the data that can be refreshed as data is added or updated.

→ **Method**

To connect to external data sources, such as Access 2003:

- Display a workbook to use in retrieving the data.

- Position the cell pointer in the top left-hand corner of the target or external data range.

- CHOOSE: Data → Import External Data → Import Data

- Select the desired data source.

→ **Practice**

You will now establish a connection to a Microsoft Office Access 2003 database file and then import the data that is stored in a table object. Ensure that no workbooks appear in the application window.

**1.** To begin, display a blank workbook:
CLICK: New button (🗋)
The cell pointer appears in cell A1, which will be the top left-hand corner of the new external data range.

**2.** To establish the connection with the Microsoft Access database file:
CHOOSE: Data → Import External Data → Import Data
The Select Data Source dialog box appears, as shown in Figure 10.49.

**Figure 10.49**

Select Data Source dialog box

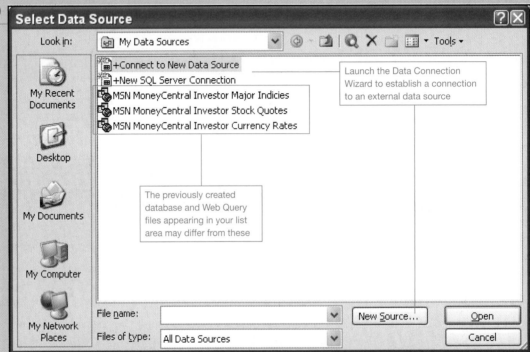

**3.** Using the *Look in* drop-down list box, select the Advantage student data files location. Then, do the following:
DOUBLE-CLICK: EX1044 (Microsoft Office Access 2003 data file)
Excel 2003 establishes the connection to the data source and then displays the Import Data dialog box (Figure 10.50).

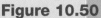

**Figure 10.50**

Import Data
dialog box

Specify the external
data range in the
worksheet

Specify options
for refreshing
(re-importing)
and formatting
the data

Edit the data connection
query parameters before
importing the data. This is
an advanced feature.

**4.** To accept the default properties:
CLICK: OK command button
Since the Microsoft Office Access 2003 data file contains a single table object only, the data is imported immediately into the workbook (Figure 10.51). Like a worksheet list, each *record* is stored in a separate row and each *field* appears in a column.

**Figure 10.51**

Importing an
Access 2003
table object

The external data
range begins at
cell A1 and
extends down and
to the right until all
records and fields
are imported

The External Data
toolbar appears,
allowing you to
quickly refresh the
data or to change
the data range
properties

| | A | B | C | D | E | F | G | H | I |
|---|---|---|---|---|---|---|---|---|---|
| 1 | BookID | ISBN | Title | AuthorSurname | AuthorGiven | Publisher | PubYear | PageCount | |
| 2 | 1 | 0399133453 | Cardinal of the Kremlin, The | Clancy | Tom | Putnam | 1988 | 543 | |
| 3 | 2 | 0425158632 | Executive Orders | Clancy | Tom | Berkley | 1997 | 328 | |
| 4 | 3 | 0440214041 | Pelican Brief, The | | hn | Dell Island | 1993 | 294 | |
| 5 | 4 | 0385472943 | Runaway Jury, The | | hn | Doubleday | 1996 | 422 | |
| 6 | 5 | 044022165X | Rainmaker, The | | John | Island | 1996 | 340 | |
| 7 | 6 | 0380718332 | All That Remains | Cornwell | Patricia | Avon | 1993 | 389 | |
| 8 | 7 | 0380717018 | Body of Evidence | Cornwell | Patricia | Avon | 1994 | 298 | |
| 9 | 8 | 039914465X | Southern Cross | Cornwell | Patricia | Putnam | 1999 | 352 | |
| 10 | 9 | 0425158616 | Cause of Death | Cornwell | Patricia | Berkley | 1997 | 368 | |
| 11 | 10 | 0553579754 | Fear Nothing | Koontz | Dean | Bantam | 1998 | 432 | |
| 12 | 11 | 0425147584 | Debt of Honor | Clancy | Tom | Berkley | 1997 | 1008 | |
| 13 | 12 | 0425161749 | Deadliest Game, The | Clancy | Tom | Penguin | 1999 | 192 | |
| 14 | 13 | 0425122123 | Clear and Present Danger | Clancy | Tom | Berkley | 1996 | 421 | |
| 15 | 14 | 0425133516 | Hunt for Red October, The | Clancy | Tom | Berkley | 1997 | 386 | |
| 16 | 15 | 0425133540 | Sum of All Fears, The | Clancy | Tom | Berkley | 1996 | 424 | |
| 17 | 16 | 0399143904 | Rainbow Six | Clancy | Tom | Putnam | 1998 | 740 | |
| 18 | 17 | 0425143325 | Without Remorse | Clancy | Tom | Berkley | 1996 | 512 | |
| 19 | 18 | 0440225701 | Street Lawyer, The | Grisham | John | Dell Island | 1999 | 416 | |
| 20 | 19 | 0440224764 | Partner, The | Grisham | John | Dell Island | 1998 | 448 | |
| 21 | 20 | 0385493800 | Testament, The | Grisham | John | Doubleday | 1999 | 480 | |
| 22 | 21 | 0440213525 | Client, The | Grisham | John | Dell Island | 1994 | 385 | |
| 23 | 22 | 0440220602 | Chamber, The | Grisham | John | Dell Island | 1995 | 392 | |

**5.** Now that you have established a data connection to the Microsoft Office Access 2003 database file, let's view some of the options for refreshing the data. Do the following:
CHOOSE: Data → Import External Data → Data Range Properties
(*Hint:* You can also click the Data Range Properties button (🖼) on the External Data toolbar.) The dialog box in Figure 10.52 appears.

**Figure 10.52**

External Data Range Properties dialog box

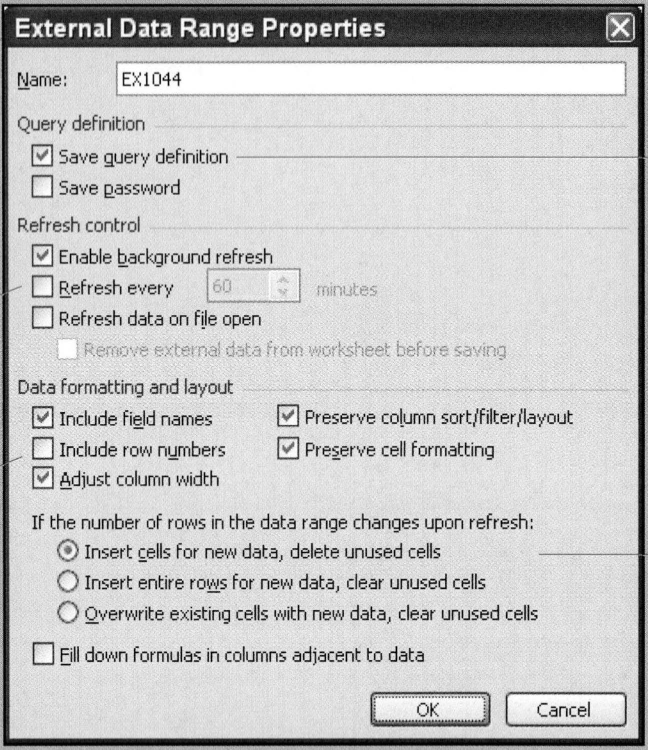

Specify when to run the query definition and refresh the data

As specified using these options, the data is imported with field names in row 1 and columns are formatted to their best-fit width

**External Data Range Properties**

Name: EX1044

Query definition
☑ Save query definition
☐ Save password

You must save the query definition so that Excel 2003 knows how to refresh the data in the worksheet

Refresh control
☑ Enable background refresh
☐ Refresh every  60  minutes
☐ Refresh data on file open
☐ Remove external data from worksheet before saving

Data formatting and layout
☑ Include field names        ☑ Preserve column sort/filter/layout
☐ Include row numbers      ☑ Preserve cell formatting
☑ Adjust column width

If the number of rows in the data range changes upon refresh:
◉ Insert cells for new data, delete unused cells
○ Insert entire rows for new data, clear unused cells
○ Overwrite existing cells with new data, clear unused cells

☐ Fill down formulas in columns adjacent to data

[ OK ]  [ Cancel ]

Use these options to specify how data is to be entered into the worksheet when refreshed

**6.** To ensure that Excel 2003 refreshes the data each time the workbook is opened, do the following:
SELECT: *Refresh the data on file open* check box so that a ✓ appears
CLICK: OK command button

**7.** Assume for the moment that the database file exists on a network server in a large company. You have gone to lunch and returned to your desk to continue working. To ensure that your worksheet still contains the latest information, let's manually refresh the data:
CHOOSE: Data → Refresh Data
(*Hint:* You can also click the Refresh Data button (❗) on the External Data toolbar.)

**8.** If the Refresh Data dialog box appears, click the OK Command button to dismiss the dialog box. Then, save the workbook as "Access File" to your personal storage location.

**9.** Close the "Access File" workbook before proceeding.

Microsoft Office Excel 2003 stores information about the data connection in a special Office Data Connection (ODC) file. This file has a file extension of ".odc" and is typically placed in a folder named My Data Sources beneath the My Documents folder. You can copy and share this file with other users. Furthermore, you can open the ODC file using Notepad or the Microsoft Internet Explorer Web browser, as shown in Figure 10.53.

**Figure 10.53**

Opening a data
connection in
Microsoft Internet
Explorer

Microsoft Office
Web Components
are used to display
the results of the
ODC data file
connection

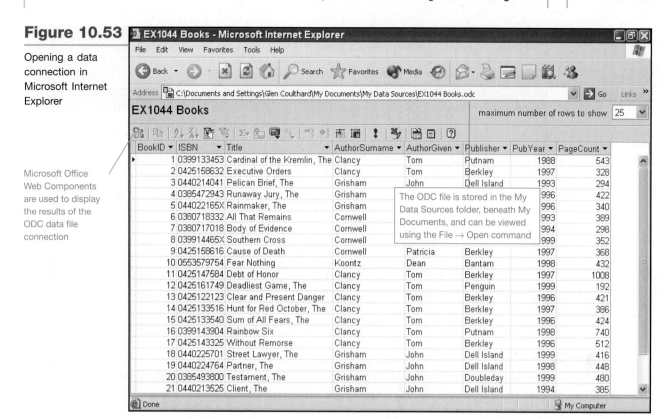

## *In Addition* USING MICROSOFT QUERY

**Microsoft Query** is a software program (Figure 10.54) bundled with Microsoft Office 2003 that helps you process and retrieve data from databases, including Access 2003 and Microsoft SQL Server. A **query** is a question that you ask of your database, such as "Who lives in Braxton County, West Virginia?" Using Microsoft Query and the Query Wizard, you create queries to connect to external data sources (databases, workbooks, and text files) and extract specific data. Microsoft Query is primarily used when you need to perform query tasks, such as filtering, sorting, or joining multiple table objects, prior to importing data into an Excel 2003 workbook. To launch the Query Wizard, choose the Data → Import External Data → New Database Query command. After being led through the Query Wizard, you are presented with the Microsoft Query application window, an example of which is shown in Figure 10.54.

**Figure 10.54**

Microsoft Query
application
window

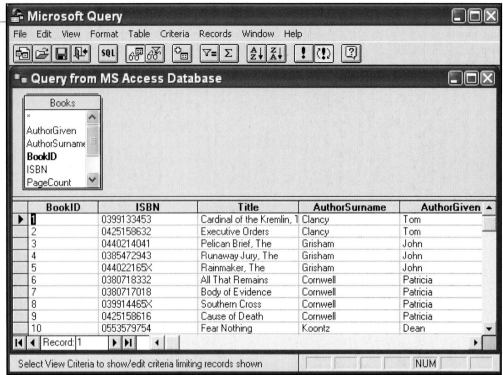

### 10.4.5 Sharing Data in Microsoft Office 2003

→ **Feature**

All of the Microsoft Office 2003 applications are designed to work together. You can include an Excel chart in a Word document, turn a Word document into a PowerPoint presentation, and generate form letters using an Access data source. There are three distinct methods for sharing data between the Office applications: *pasting*, *linking*, and *embedding*. **Pasting** data is the simplest method and refers to inserting a static representation of the source data into a destination document. In **linking**, you not only paste the data, you also establish a dynamic link between the source and destination documents. Thereafter, making changes in the source document updates the destination document automatically. **Embedding** data involves inserting a source document, called an *object*, into a destination document. Unlike pasted data, an embedded object is fully editable within the destination document. Unlike linked data, an embedded object does not retain a connection to its source document; everything is contained in the destination document.

To the person using a workbook, linked and embedded objects appear identical. The primary difference between the two objects is where the data is stored. With a linked object, the data remains in the original source document and the destination document stores only a reference to the source file. With an embedded object, the source data is stored in the destination document along with information about the application used to create the source file.

→ **Method**

To share data using the Office Clipboard:

• CHOOSE: Edit → Office Clipboard to display the task pane

• Collect up to 24 items on the Office Clipboard from the Office 2003 source application, such as Word, Excel, Access, or PowerPoint.

• Move to the Office 2003 target application.

• Paste the items individually or all at once.

• Specify the formatting, linking, and embedding options using the Paste Options button (📋 ▾).

→ **Practice**

You will now practice exchanging data with Microsoft Office Word 2003. Ensure that no workbooks appear in the application window.

**1.** Open the Microsoft Excel EX1045 data file to display the workbook shown in Figure 10.55.

**Figure 10.55**

Opening the
EX1045
workbook

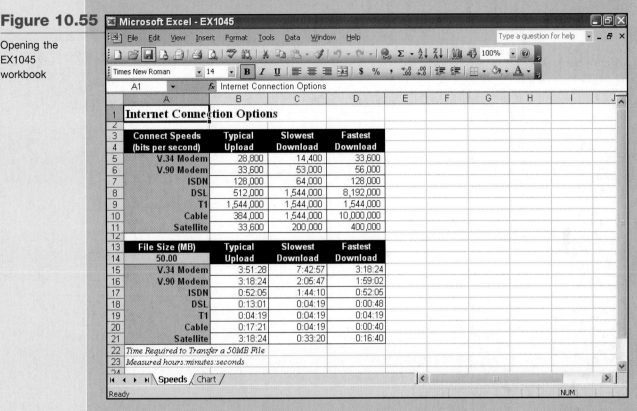

**2.** Save the workbook as "Connections" to your personal storage location.

**3.** Now load Microsoft Office Word 2003:
CLICK: Start button ( start ) on the taskbar
CHOOSE: All Programs → Microsoft Office → Microsoft Office Word 2003
(*Note:* This exercise assumes that you have Microsoft Office Word 2003 installed on your computer.) Your screen should appear similar but not identical to the application window shown in Figure 10.56.

**Figure 10.56**

Microsoft Office
Word 2003
application
window

Word 2003's Menu
bar and toolbars are
similar to those
found in Excel 2003

A blank document
appears in the work
area when Microsoft
Word is started

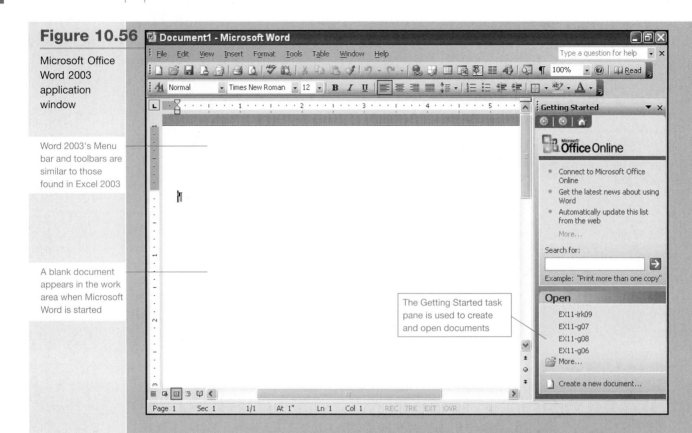

The Getting Started task
pane is used to create
and open documents

**4.** Open the Microsoft Office Word 2003 document file named EX1045, located in the Advantage student data files location, using the same methods that you would use to open a workbook in Excel 2003. (*Hint:* Click the Open button ( ) on the toolbar or click "More . . ." under the *Open* heading in the Getting Started task pane.)

**5.** Save the document as "Connect Memo" to your personal storage location.

**6.** Your objective in the next few steps is to copy information between the Connections workbook and the Connect Memo document. To begin, display and then clear the Office Clipboard in Word 2003:
CHOOSE: Edit → Office Clipboard
CLICK: Clear All button ( Clear All ) in the Clipboard task pane
(*Note:* The Clear All button will appear dim if there is nothing on the Office Clipboard.)

**7.** In the Connect Memo document, you will now select individual rows in the table and copy them to the Office Clipboard. To begin, position the right-pointing arrow mouse pointer ( ) to the left of the table's header row and click once to select it, as shown in Figure 10.57.

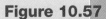

**Figure 10.57**

Selecting a table row in Word 2003

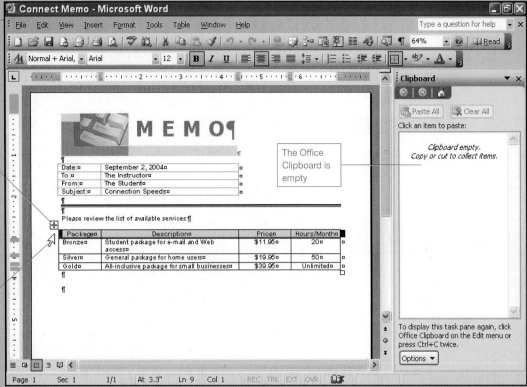

The table move handle is used to select or move the table. For this exercise, you select individual rows rather than the entire table.

Click beside a table row to select the entire row

The Office Clipboard is empty

8. With the table's header row selected:
   CLICK: Copy button (⬚)
   The copied item appears as "1 of 24" in the Clipboard task pane. Notice that the Office Clipboard icon (⬚) displays in the lower right hand corner of the taskbar to inform you that at least one of the Microsoft Office 2003 applications is using the Office Clipboard.

9. Using the same process, select two more table rows:
   SELECT: "Gold" row in the table
   CLICK: Copy button (⬚)
   SELECT: "Silver" row in the table
   CLICK: Copy button (⬚)
   Three items now appear in the Clipboard task pane.

10. Now make the Excel 2003 application window active:
    CLICK: Connections (Excel 2003 workbook) button on the taskbar

11. To display the Office Clipboard:
    CHOOSE: Edit → Office Clipboard
    Notice that the same items appear.

12. To paste all of the items into the worksheet:
    SELECT: cell F3
    CLICK: Paste All button (⬚ Paste All) in the Clipboard task pane

13. Scroll the window using the horizontal scroll bar, as shown in Figure 10.58.

## Figure 10.58

Pasting data from Word 2003 into a workbook

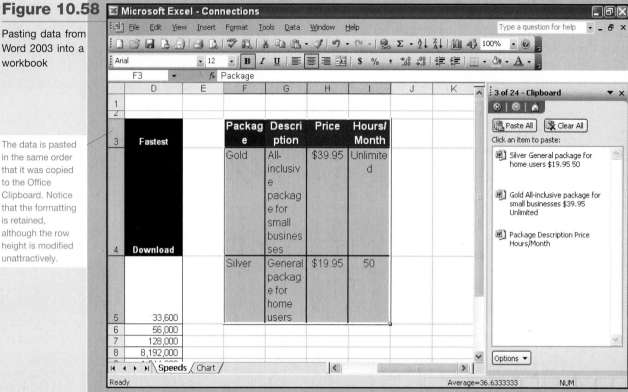

The data is pasted in the same order that it was copied to the Office Clipboard. Notice that the formatting is retained, although the row height is modified unattractively.

**14.** To format the appearance of the pasted data:
CHOOSE: Format → Cells
CLICK: *Alignment* tab
SELECT: *Wrap text* check box so that no ✓ appears
CLICK: OK command button
The row height settings are returned to their previous values.

**15.** To adjust the column widths:
CHOOSE: Format → Column → AutoFit Selection
The data now appears as it did in the Word 2003 document.

**16.** To clear the Office Clipboard and clean up the work area:
CLICK: Clear All button (🗶 Clear All) in the Clipboard task pane
CHOOSE: View → Task Pane to remove the Clipboard task pane
PRESS: CTRL + HOME to return to cell A1

**17.** Now let's practice linking data between Microsoft Office Excel 2003 and Microsoft Office Word 2003. To begin:
SELECT: cell range from A3 to D11
CLICK: Copy button (🖹)

**18.** Now make the Word 2003 application window active:
CLICK: Connect Memo (Word 2003 document) button on the taskbar

**19.** To close the Clipboard task pane in Word 2003:
CHOOSE: View → Task Pane

**20.** To move to the end of the document:
PRESS: CTRL + END

**21.** You will now paste the data and establish a dynamic link between the source document (Connections workbook) and the destination document (Connect Memo document). To begin:
CHOOSE: Edit → Paste Special from the Word 2003 menu
The Paste Special dialog box appears, as shown in Figure 10.59.

**Figure 10.59**

Paste Special
dialog box

Select this option
to establish a
dynamic link

Select the desired
format for pasting
the copied data

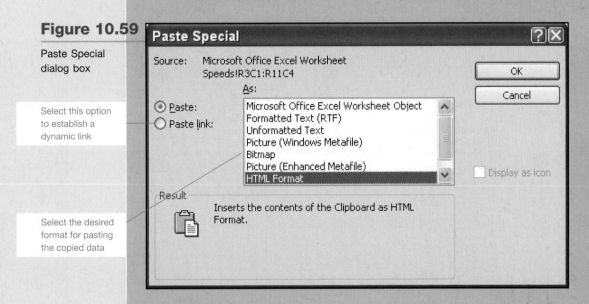

**22.** In the Paste Special dialog box:
SELECT: *Paste link* option button
SELECT: HTML Format
CLICK: OK command button

**23.** The workbook's copied cell range now appears as a linked and editable table object in the Word 2003 document. To demonstrate the linking feature, note the cell contents for the Satellite's fastest download time (400,000). Let's update this data in the workbook. Do the following:
CLICK: Connections (Excel 2003 workbook) button on the taskbar

**24.** To update a worksheet value:
PRESS: ESC to remove the bounding outline border
SELECT: cell D11
TYPE: 512,000
PRESS: ENTER

**25.** Switch back to the Word 2003 application window:
CLICK: Connect Memo (Word 2003 document) button on the taskbar
RIGHT-CLICK: any cell in the linked table
CHOOSE: Update Link
Notice that the cell entry in the Word table object is updated to display the new worksheet value, as shown in Figure 10.60. (*Hint:* This technique allows you to create dynamic reports in Microsoft Word using data stored in worksheets and charts.)

**Figure 10.60**

Modifying the contents of a linked table

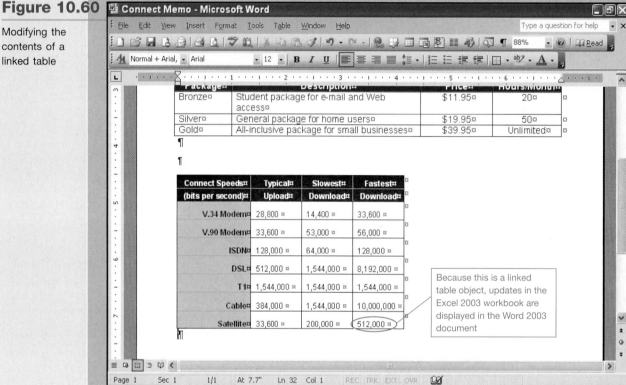

**26.** Save and then close the "Connect Memo" document. Then, exit Microsoft Office Word 2003.

**27.** Save and then close the "Connections" workbook.

### *In Addition* PERFORMING A MAIL MERGE IN MICROSOFT OFFICE WORD 2003

You can use Microsoft Office Word 2003 to perform a mail merge with data stored in a worksheet list. In Word 2003's Mail Merge Wizard, open the Excel 2003 workbook as the data source. Then, select the worksheet list using its named range or cell reference. Proceed through the wizard steps to complete the mail merge operation.

### *In Addition* EXPORTING DATA FROM MICROSOFT OFFICE ACCESS 2003

Microsoft Office Access 2003 provides a special add-in program for transferring data stored in a database file to Excel 2003. In the Access 2003 Database window, select the datasheet, form, or report that you want to export. Then, choose the Tools → Office Links → Analyze It with Microsoft Office Excel command.

Excel

**10.4** Your friend is using a specialized statistics software program to collect numerical research data. He has asked you to analyze and plot the data in a chart. Assuming that the software is not able to export data into a Microsoft Office Excel 2003 workbook, what file format should you recommend for transferring the data?

# 10.5 Working with HTML and XML

Consider the millions of documents stored on Web servers around the world. The Web offers exceptional opportunities for incorporating and referencing data in your workbooks. Microsoft Office Excel 2003 provides some powerful tools for working with Web-based data. In many cases, you can access, analyze, and integrate Web content using a few simple steps. In this module, you will work with data stored in both HTML and XML document formats.

## 10.5.1 Importing Web Data

### → Feature

Similar to importing data from databases, Excel 2003's **Web queries** allow you to retrieve data stored in HTML (Hypertext Markup Language) and XML (Extensible Markup Language) documents. You may remember that a *query* is simply a question you ask of a data source. The data source for Web queries is typically a text-based document stored on a Web server. Web queries are especially useful for up-dating worksheet cells with dynamic information, such as currency exchange rates, interest rates, weather information, and stock prices. When a query is executed, Excel 2003 connects to a Web server and retrieves the desired data.

### → Method

To create a Web query:

- CHOOSE: Data → Import External Data → New Web Query
- Enter the URL address of the HTML Web page or XML document.
- CLICK: on the arrow icons (▶) appearing beside tables
- CLICK: Save Query button ( 🖫 ) and name the query
- CLICK: Import command button

To run a Web query:

- CHOOSE: Data → Import External Data → Import Data
- SELECT: the desired query to execute
- CLICK: Open command button
- If asked, specify the worksheet location for storing the results and any parameters required to run the query.

### → Practice

You will now execute one of the example Web queries provided by Microsoft and then import a simple HTML table. Ensure that no workbooks appear in the application window. For this exercise, you must establish a live connection to the Internet before proceeding.

**1.** Before executing the example Web query, display a new workbook:
CLICK: New button ( 🗋 )

2. Save the workbook as "Stocks Web Query" to your personal storage location.

3. If you have not already done so, ensure that you have a live connection to the Internet. (*Note:* You must also have chosen to install the sample Web queries during the installation of Microsoft Office Excel 2003.)

4. To execute a Web query that will retrieve stock prices for several companies listed on the NASDAQ Exchange:
CHOOSE: Data → Import External Data → Import Data
The Select Data Source dialog box (Figure 10.61) appears, displaying some example Web queries.

**Figure 10.61**

Select Data Source dialog box

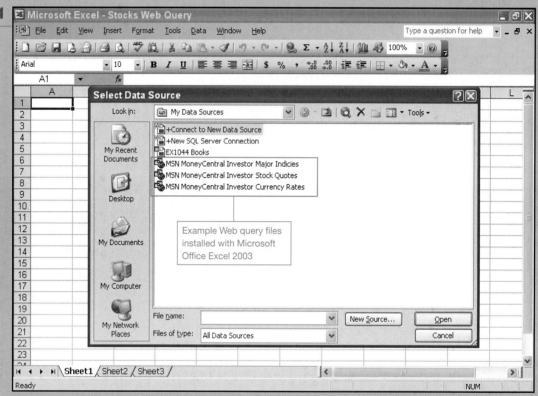

Example Web query files installed with Microsoft Office Excel 2003

5. To launch the Web query for retrieving stock prices:
SELECT: MSN MoneyCentral Investor Stock Quotes
CLICK: Open command button

6. The Import Data dialog box appears in order to confirm the target cell range. Ensure that the selected range is cell A1 and then:
CLICK: OK command button

7. In the Enter Parameter Value dialog box, enter the stock symbols that you want to retrieve from the Web. Do the following:
TYPE: **AMZN,ADBE,MSFT,SEBL**
The dialog box should appear similar to the one shown in Figure 10.62.

**Figure 10.62**

Enter Parameter
Value dialog box

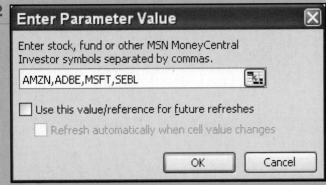

8. CLICK: OK command button to proceed
Cell A1 displays a status message while it connects to the Web server. When the desired data is retrieved, your screen should appear similar to the worksheet shown in Figure 10.63. Notice that the worksheet displays hyperlinks for quickly retrieving additional information using your Web browser.

**Figure 10.63**

Executing a Web
query to retrieve
stock prices

The four stock
symbols (AMZN,
ADBE, MSFT, and
SEBL) are
represented on
these four rows

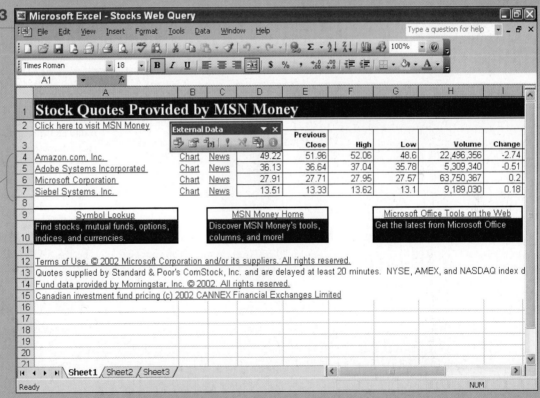

9. If the External Data toolbar is not displayed, do the following:
CHOOSE: View → Toolbars → External Data
The following toolbar appears.

**10.** To refresh the external data range with new stock quotes:
CLICK: Refresh Data button (⚠) on the toolbar
TYPE: **AAPL,CSCO,DELL,EBAY**
CLICK: OK command button
The range is updated with new stock information.

**11.** Save and then close the "Stocks Web Query" workbook. (*Note:* The configuration settings for a Web query are saved in a text file with the .IQY file extension.)

**12.** To prepare the work area, display a new workbook:
CLICK: New button (🗋)

**13.** Save the workbook as "My Web Query" to your personal storage location.

**14.** Now create a new Web query:
CHOOSE: Data → Import External Data → New Web Query
The New Web Query dialog box appears, as shown in Figure 10.64, with the default home page loaded in the browser area.

**Figure 10.64**

New Web Query dialog box

Click this arrow icon to select the entire Web page for importing

Each arrow icon represents a table area in the Web page that you may import into the workbook

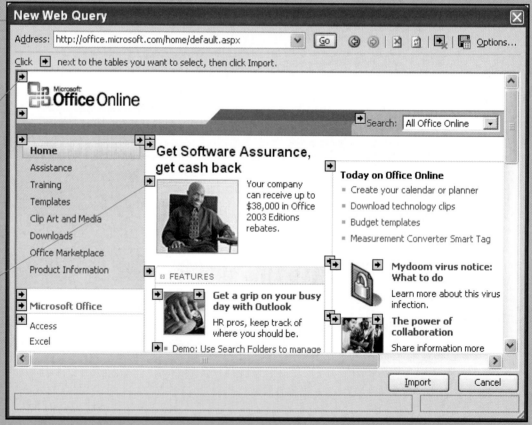

**15.** Because of the changing nature of the Web, we have provided a static HTML document named "EX1050.htm" in the Advantage student files area. To practice loading a local Web page, type the full path name in the *Address* box, as shown below. (*Note:* You will have to enter a different path name than the one shown here.)

Address: C:\Documents and Settings\Glen Coulthard\My Documents\Advantage\EX1050.htm

**16.** CLICK: Go command button
Your screen should appear similar to Figure 10.65 before proceeding.

**Figure 10.65**

Loading a local
Web page

Click this arrow icon
to select the table of
values for importing

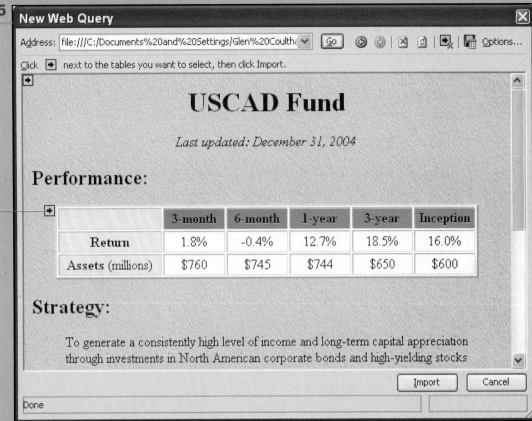

**17.** To load the table of values into your workbook:
CLICK: arrow icon (▶) beside the Performance table
(*Hint:* Refer to Figure 10.65 if you are uncertain as to which arrow icon to click. The table will appear selected and the arrow icon becomes a check mark icon (☑).)

**18.** To specify formatting options for the imported data:
CLICK: Options button ( Options... ) in the dialog box toolbar
The Web Query Options dialog box appears, as shown in Figure 10.66.

**Figure 10.66**

Web Query
Options dialog
box

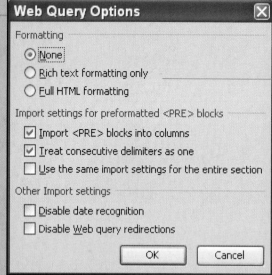

Select either of these options
to preserve formatting

**19.** To include table formatting:
SELECT: *Full HTML formatting* option button
CLICK: OK command button

**20.** Let's save the query so that it may be executed again at a later date:
CLICK: Save Query button (🖫)

**21.** In the Save Query dialog box that appears:
TYPE: **My Web Query**
CLICK: Save command button

**22.** To import the table into the worksheet:
CLICK: Import command button

**23.** When the Import Data dialog box appears:
CLICK: OK command button to accept the default selections
Your worksheet should now appear similar to the one shown in Figure 10.67.

**Figure 10.67**

Importing an
HTML table into
a worksheet

To edit the Web
query, click this
button to return to
the dialog box

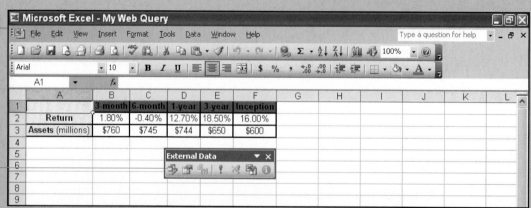

**24.** Save and then close the "My Web Query" workbook.

**25.** If necessary, close your Internet connection.

*In Addition* USING SMART TAGS TO RETRIEVE WEB INFORMATION

Microsoft Office Excel 2003 can employ *smart tags* for identifying specific data in a worksheet, such as a stock symbol, and then performing actions with the data. When the Smart Tags feature is enabled in the AutoCorrect dialog box (Figure 10.68,) Excel indicates the data it recognizes using a purple triangle in the cell's lower right corner and the Smart Tag Actions button (⊚). For stock symbols, click the button to retrieve stock quotes, news stories, and company reports from the Web. Commercial software developers also have access to the smart tags technology and may develop custom actions to facilitate importing and exporting data.

**Figure 10.68**

AutoCorrect
Options dialog
box

Select this check
box to enable the
Smart Tags feature
in your workbooks

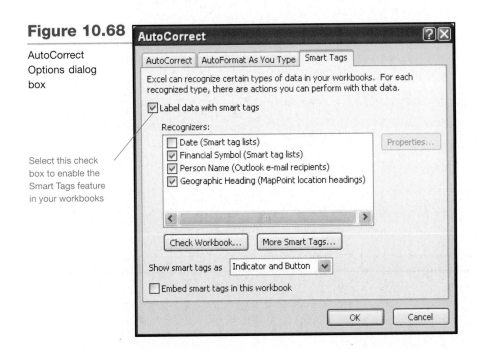

## 10.5.2 Round-Tripping with HTML

→ **Feature**

Microsoft Office Excel 2003 provides several methods for retrieving Web data for use in your workbooks. In addition to using a Web query, you can use the File → Open command to import an entire HTML document or the Copy and Paste commands to copy portions of a Web page. You can even choose to create a refreshable Web query based on the source data.

The Microsoft Office Web Components, along with Microsoft Internet Explorer, allow you to perform **HTML round-tripping**. In other words, you can save a workbook as an interactive Web page, edit the data using your Web browser, and then reopen it in Excel 2003. The **Spreadsheet component** lets you create and publish a Web page with basic spreadsheet functionality, allowing users to enter, edit, and format data using their Web browser. The **Chart component** allows you to create a graphical and dynamic view of your worksheet data. Lastly, the **PivotTable component** can filter and summarize data stored in worksheets, databases, and other external data sources. However, users must have Excel 2003 installed and use Internet Explorer 5.0 or higher in order to get the full benefit of these components.

→ **Method**

To copy Web-based HTML data into an Excel 2003 worksheet:
Display a Web document using your Web browser software.

- SELECT: the data to copy using the mouse or keyboard
- PRESS: CTRL +c to copy the data to the Clipboard
- Display Excel 2003 and select the desired worksheet.
- SELECT: the top left-hand cell of the target range
- PRESS: CTRL +v or CLICK: Paste button ( )
- CLICK: Paste Options button ( ) to select options

To publish an interactive Web page for HTML round-tripping:

- SELECT: the worksheet to publish
- CHOOSE: File → Save as Web Page
- CLICK: Publish command button
- SELECT: *Add interactivity with* check box in the *Viewing options* area
- SELECT: Spreadsheet functionality in the drop-down list box
- Enter a Web page name in the *File name* text box
- CLICK: Publish command button

→ **Practice**

After copying and pasting data from an HTML document into a workbook, practice publishing and "round-tripping" the worksheet as an interactive Web page using the Spreadsheet Office Web Component. Ensure that no workbooks appear in the application window. Other than Excel 2003, there should be no other application buttons appearing on the taskbar.

1. To begin, display a new workbook:
   CLICK: New button ( )

2. Save the workbook as "Round Trip" to your personal storage location.

3. Launch the Microsoft Internet Explorer Web browser.

4. To arrange the two application windows on the desktop:
   RIGHT-CLICK: an empty portion of the taskbar
   CHOOSE: Tile Windows Vertically
   Both windows should now be visible.

5. Now let's open a local HTML document for display. Using the Internet Explorer menu:
   CHOOSE: File → Open
   CLICK: Browse command button
   The Microsoft Internet Explorer dialog box appears.

6. Using the *Look in* drop-down list box and the Places bar, locate the Advantage student data files location. Then, open the HTML Web document named EX1050 by double-clicking its file name. Lastly:
   CLICK: OK command button
   Your screen should appear similar to the windows shown in Figure 10.69 before proceeding.

## Figure 10.69

Arranging
application
windows on the
desktop

You will select this
area of the Web
page to copy to the
Clipboard

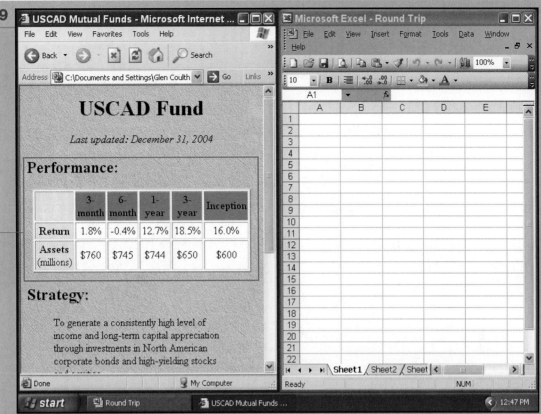

7. In the Microsoft Internet Explorer window, position the I-beam mouse pointer to the left of the
"P" in "Performance." Then:
DRAG: the mouse pointer to the bottom right-hand corner of the table
(*Note:* When you release the mouse button, the heading and table text should appear high-
lighted.)

8. You will now use the drag-and-drop method to copy the selected text from the browser window
to the workbook window. To begin, position the mouse pointer over the selected word "Performance" and then:
DRAG: the mouse pointer to cell A3 in the workbook window
(*Note:* A target range is outlined in the worksheet, and the mouse shape changes to reflect a
copy operation.)

9. When you release the mouse button, the selected data is pasted into the worksheet along with
its formatting. To cancel the range selection:
CLICK: cell A1
Your screen should now appear similar to the windows shown in Figure 10.70.

**Figure 10.70**

Copying and pasting data using the drag-and-drop method

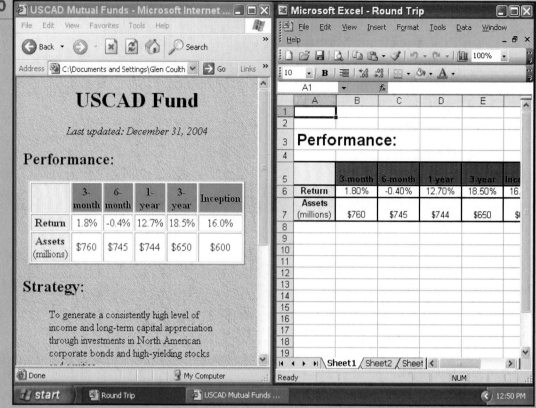

**10.** To copy the Web page title into the worksheet:
SELECT: "USCAD Fund" text in the Internet Explorer window
PRESS: CTRL +c to copy the text to the Clipboard
SELECT: cell A1 in the workbook window
PRESS: CTRL +v to paste the text

**11.** On your own, close the Microsoft Internet Explorer application window and then maximize the Excel 2003 application window.

**12.** Let's save this new worksheet as an interactive Web page using Excel 2003's Spreadsheet component. To begin:
CHOOSE: File → Save as Web Page
CLICK: Publish command button

**13.** In the Publish as Web Page dialog box:
SELECT: *Add interactivity with* check box
SELECT: Spreadsheet functionality in the drop-down list box
SELECT: *Open published web page in browser* check box
TYPE: **Web Worksheet.htm** in the *File name* text box
Your screen should appear similar to the dialog box shown in Figure 10.71.

**Figure 10.71**

Saving a worksheet as an interactive Web page

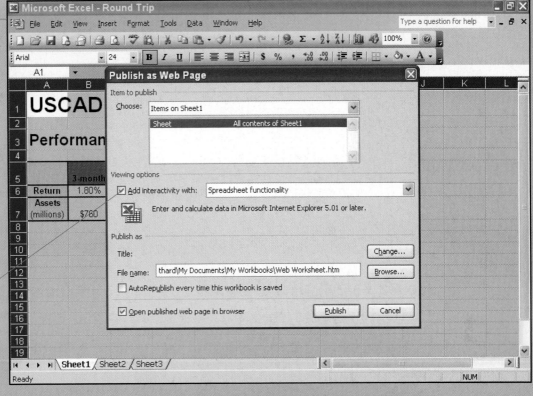

Specifying that the Web page include the Spreadsheet Office Web Component

**14.** CLICK: Publish command button

**15.** Maximize the Microsoft Internet Explorer window and then:
CHOOSE: View → Refresh from the Menu bar
The resulting Web page should appear similar to the one shown in Figure 10.72.

**Figure 10.72**

Displaying a Web page with the Spreadsheet Office Web Component

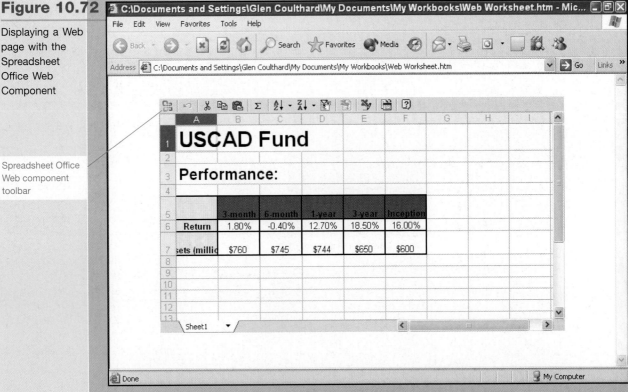

Spreadsheet Office Web component toolbar

**16.** Using the Spreadsheet component:
SELECT: cell B7 in the browser window
TYPE: 800
PRESS: ENTER

**17.** On your own, increase column A to its best-fit width by double-clicking its frame border.

**18.** Even after editing this interactive Web page, you can reopen it using Excel 2003. To illustrate:
CLICK: Export to Microsoft Office Excel button ( ) in the toolbar
The focus switches to a new Excel 2003 workbook displayed in "[Read-Only]" mode, as stated in its Title bar. You could now modify and save this worksheet locally or republish it to the Web.

**19.** To clean up our work area:
CLICK: Close button ( ) for the Excel 2003 application window
CLICK: Close button ( ) for the Microsoft Internet Explorer application window

**20.** Save and then close the "Round Trip" workbook. No workbooks should now appear in the Excel 2003 application window.

## 10.5.3 Sharing Data Using XML

→ # Feature

**Extensible Markup Language (XML)** is fast emerging as the universal data exchange format of choice for Web-based business applications. A complimentary format to HTML, XML is a meta-markup language for Web-based documents that describes structured data in a standard way. Whereas HTML provides a fixed set of tags to describe how a document is to be displayed in a Web browser, XML provides the ability to define its own tags and to describe the data inside a document. In XML, you separate the data from its presentation using style sheets based on the Extensible Style Language (XSL) and Cascading Style Sheets (CSS). Furthermore, XML uses a Document Type Definition (DTD) or an XML schema to describe the structure of data within an XML document.

A basic XML document contains data nested within element tags, as shown in the following example:

> Attribute values within an element must be enclosed in quotation marks. An element can contain one or more

XML documents have a unique first element called the *root node.*

```
<books>
  <book isbn="0-07-247262-6">
    <title>Microsoft Office Excel 2003</title>
    <author>Glen J. Coulthard</author>
  </book>
</books>
```

> Elements are case-sensitive and must be nested without overlap. Element values are located between an opening and closing tag.

In this lesson, you learn to save your workbooks using Excel 2003's XML Spreadsheet file format, which preserves a workbook's format, structure, and data using the Microsoft's XML Spreadsheet Schema (XML-SS). The topmost element in an XML-SS document is the <Workbook> element, which contains one or more <Worksheet> elements. Other elements and attributes describe styles, named ranges, tables, rows, cells, and, lastly, data. The XML-SS schema format is commonly used to analyze external data that is stored on a Web server using Excel 2003. Some features of a workbook, however, are not retained when you save it to XML-SS, including charts, drawing objects, custom views, and scenarios.

→ ## Method

To save a workbook as an XML-SS document:

- CHOOSE: File → Save As
- SELECT: XML Spreadsheet in the *Save as type* drop-down list box
- SELECT: *a location* in the *Save in* drop-down list box
- CLICK: Save command button

→ ## Practice

You will now practice saving a worksheet using the XML Spreadsheet Schema (XML-SS) file format. Ensure that no workbooks are open in the application window.

1. Open the data file named EX1053 to display the familiar workbook of "Internet Connection Options."

2. Your objective is to save the *Speeds* worksheet as an XML document, ready for publishing to a Web server. To begin:
CHOOSE: File → Save As

3. Using the *Save in* drop-down list box, select your personal storage location. Then, do the following:
TYPE: **Speeds** in the *File name* text box

4. There are two types of XML document types that you may choose from the Save As dialog box: *XML Spreadsheet* and *XML Data*. For this exercise, use the XML Spreadsheet Schema:
CLICK: down arrow attached to the *Save as type* drop-down list box
SELECT: XML Spreadsheet

5. To proceed with the export conversion:
CLICK: Save command button
A warning dialog box appears (Figure 10.73) stating that AutoShapes, drawing objects, and charts will not be saved when using the XML Spreadsheet file type.

**Figure 10.73**

Warning dialog box displayed during export to an XML Spreadsheet file

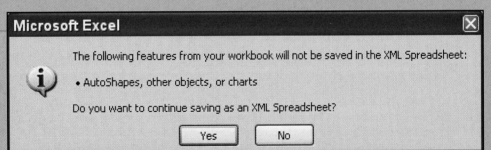

6. To accept the warning and continue:
CLICK: Yes command button

7. Close the workbook by clicking its Close button (☒).

8. To view the exported text file using the Windows Notepad:
CLICK: Start button (🏁 start) on the taskbar
CHOOSE: All Programs → Accessories → Notepad

9. To open the text file in Notepad:
   CHOOSE: File → Open from its Menu bar
10. Using the *Look in* drop-down list box and the Places bar, locate your personal storage location.
11. To open the file for display:
    SELECT: All Files in the *Files of type* drop-down list box
    DOUBLE-CLICK: Speeds in the list area
    (*Note:* The file name may appear as "Speeds.xml" depending on your Windows Explorer settings.) When maximized, the Notepad application window should appear similar to the one shown in Figure 10.74.

**Figure 10.74**

Displaying an XML Spreadsheet file

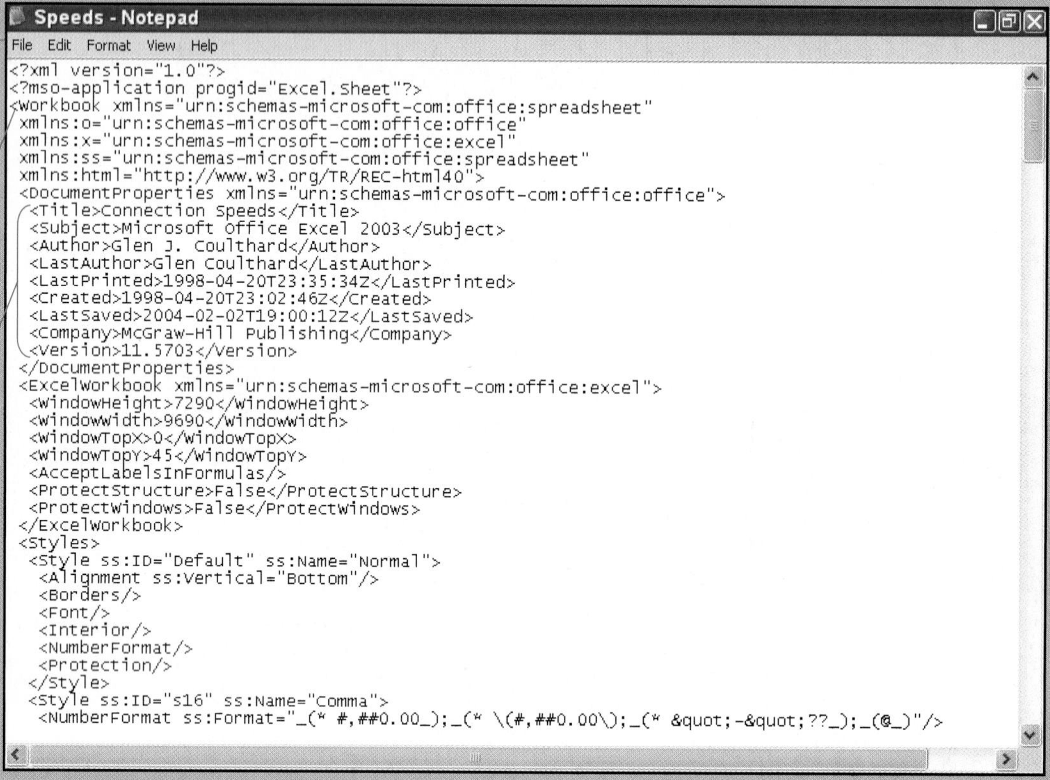

```
Speeds - Notepad
File  Edit  Format  View  Help
<?xml version="1.0"?>
<?mso-application progid="Excel.Sheet"?>
<Workbook xmlns="urn:schemas-microsoft-com:office:spreadsheet"
 xmlns:o="urn:schemas-microsoft-com:office:office"
 xmlns:x="urn:schemas-microsoft-com:office:excel"
 xmlns:ss="urn:schemas-microsoft-com:office:spreadsheet"
 xmlns:html="http://www.w3.org/TR/REC-html40">
 <DocumentProperties xmlns="urn:schemas-microsoft-com:office:office">
  <Title>Connection Speeds</Title>
  <Subject>Microsoft Office Excel 2003</Subject>
  <Author>Glen J. Coulthard</Author>
  <LastAuthor>Glen Coulthard</LastAuthor>
  <LastPrinted>1998-04-20T23:35:34Z</LastPrinted>
  <Created>1998-04-20T23:02:46Z</Created>
  <LastSaved>2004-02-02T19:00:12Z</LastSaved>
  <Company>McGraw-Hill Publishing</Company>
  <Version>11.5703</Version>
 </DocumentProperties>
 <ExcelWorkbook xmlns="urn:schemas-microsoft-com:office:excel">
  <WindowHeight>7290</WindowHeight>
  <WindowWidth>9690</WindowWidth>
  <WindowTopX>0</WindowTopX>
  <WindowTopY>45</WindowTopY>
  <AcceptLabelsInFormulas/>
  <ProtectStructure>False</ProtectStructure>
  <ProtectWindows>False</ProtectWindows>
 </ExcelWorkbook>
 <Styles>
  <Style ss:ID="Default" ss:Name="Normal">
   <Alignment ss:Vertical="Bottom"/>
   <Borders/>
   <Font/>
   <Interior/>
   <NumberFormat/>
   <Protection/>
  </Style>
  <Style ss:ID="s16" ss:Name="Comma">
   <NumberFormat ss:Format="_(* #,##0.00_);_(* \(#,##0.00\);_(* &quot;-&quot;??_);_(@_)"/>
```

The root node element is "Workbook"

Elements belonging to the DocumentProperties element

12. Close Notepad by clicking its Close button (☒).

### 10.5.4 Importing XML Data

→ **Feature**

Microsoft Office Excel 2003 lets you open an XML document and work with its data as you would any other list. As witnessed earlier in the chapter, you can use the Open command from the File menu to import data from recognized files formats. In addition to Microsoft's proprietary **XML Spreadsheet (XML-SS)** format, you can open and import data from standard XML data files. If the XML data file does not have an accompanying **XML Schema (XSD)** file to define its structure, Excel 2003 offers to create one automatically for use in the workbook. An XML Schema file is required to employ Excel 2003's extended XML feature set. Besides importing an XML document using the Open command, you can also create a Web query to retrieve the external data as you did with HTML documents in the previous lesson.

→ ## Method

To open an XML document:

- CHOOSE: File → Open

- SELECT: XML Files in the *Files of type* drop-down list box

- SELECT: *a location* in the *Look in* drop-down list box

- DOUBLE-CLICK: the desired file name in the list area
  Specify whether to open the file as an XML list or a read-only workbook or to use the XML Source task pane.

To create a Web query that opens an XML document:

- CHOOSE: Data → Import External Data → New Web Query

- Enter the URL address of the XML document.

- CLICK: on the arrow icon (🔁) appearing in the top left-hand corner

- CLICK: Save Query button (💾) and name the query

- CLICK: Import command button

→ ## Practice

You will now practice importing data from a standard XML document. Ensure that no workbooks are open in the application window.

**1.** Figure 10.75 displays the contents of the XML data file that you will import into an Excel 2003 workbook. Review the structure of the document before proceeding. (*Hint:* You can use either NotePad or Internet Explorer to open a standard XML document for display. If you use Internet Explorer, the file contents are color-coded, which makes it easier to read.) To begin importing the XML document:
CHOOSE: File → Open

**Figure 10.75**

Displaying the EX1054 XML document using Internet Explorer

The root node is "Rentals" and not "Workbook," as is the case in the XML-SS file specification

The Equipment element is repeated for each item entry or record in the XML data file

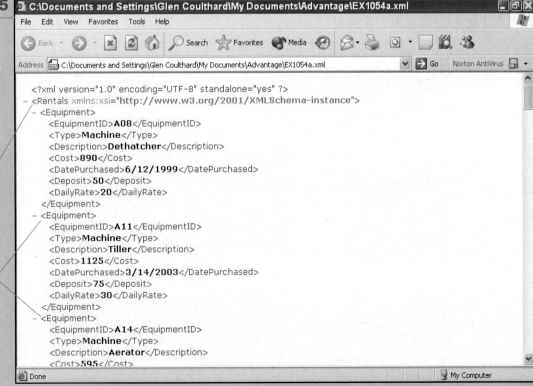

**2.** Using the *Look in* drop-down list box, select your Advantage data files location. Then, do the following:
CLICK: down arrow attached to the *Files of type* drop-down list box
SELECT: XML Files from the list

**3.** To display the desired XML document:
DOUBLE-CLICK: EX1054
The following dialog box appears.

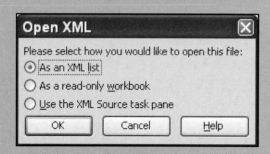

**4.** In order to have Excel 2003 import the data as an XML list:
SELECT: *As an XML list* option button, if it is not already selected
CLICK: OK command button

**5.** If the dialog box shown below is displayed, click the OK command button to have Excel 2003 create an XML Schema automatically. Otherwise, proceed to the next step.

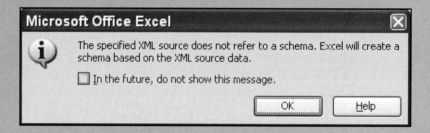

**6.** You should now see an XML list appear on your worksheet. Notice that the List toolbar is also displayed. Before proceeding, save the workbook as "XML Rentals" to your personal storage location.

**7.** Let's manipulate the data appearing in this list:
CLICK: Type column's AutoFilter button ( ⏷ ) in cell B1
CLICK: Machine in the AutoFilter drop-down list

**8.** To delete all of the "Machine" rentals:
SELECT: all rows from Row 2 through Row 27, as shown in Figure 10.76, by dragging the mouse in the row frame area

**Figure 10.76**

Selecting filtered rows in the XML list

Click the mouse pointer on Row 2 and then drag the pointer downward to row 27. All of the selected rows should appear highlighted as shown here.

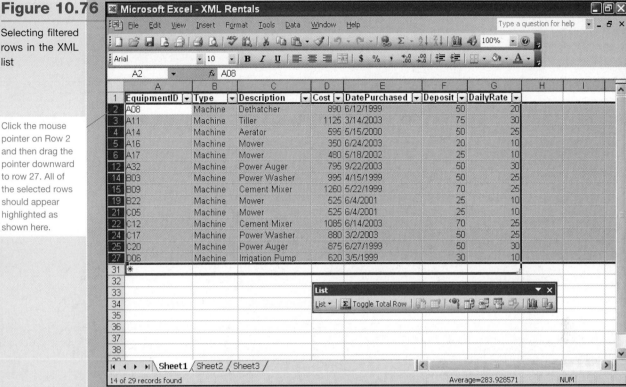

9. To delete the selected rows from the XML list:
   CHOOSE: Edit → Delete Row
   This command deletes the row data from the worksheet list, but does not affect the XML document that is stored on the disk. The original XML data remains intact and is ready to be imported once again.

10. To display the remaining data in the XML list:
    CLICK: Type column's AutoFilter button ( ▼ ) in cell B1
    CLICK: (All) in the AutoFilter drop-down list

11. CLICK: cell A1, in order to cancel the selection highlighting
    Your screen should now appear similar to the worksheet shown in Figure 10.77.

**Figure 10.77**

Displaying the remaining rows in the XML list

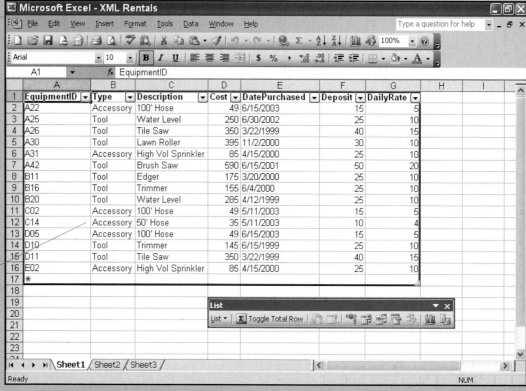

No "Machine" type entries appear in the XML list area.

**12.** Because this workbook displays data from an XML document, you can make changes and then refresh the data at any time. To demonstrate:
CLICK: Refresh XML Data button (🔁) on the List toolbar
Notice that all of the data reappears in the XML list area. The XML list in the worksheet is refreshed by importing the data stored in the XML document and overwriting the existing list.

**13.** Save and then close the "XML Rentals" workbook.

## 10.5.5 Using the XML Source Task Pane

→ **Feature**

Microsoft Office Excel 2003 introduces the new XML Source task pane to help you map worksheet cells to the data elements stored in an XML document file. The XML Source task pane requires structural information from an XML Schema file in order to work intelligently with an XML document. If an XML document does not have an accompanying XML Schema file, Excel 2003 offers to create and store the structural schema information along with your workbook. This schema information is displayed in the XML Source task pane as an XML data map. An **XML map**, whether imported from an XSD Schema file or created by Excel 2003 from an XML document, is used to create, manage, and relate mapped ranges on a worksheet with the data elements stored in an XML document. In other words, you must have an XML map defined in the workbook in order to import data from an XML document.

→ # Method

To display the XML Source task pane:

- CHOOSE: Data → XML → XML Source

  *or*

- CHOOSE: View → Task Pane
- SELECT: XML Source from the task pane navigation menu

To add, modify, or delete an XML map:

- CHOOSE: Data → XML → XML Source
- CLICK: XML Maps command button
- CLICK: Add, Rename, or Delete command buttons

→ # Practice

You will now practice working with the XML Source task pane and XML maps. You will also learn how to import an XML Schema file into a workbook. Ensure that no workbooks are open in the application window.

**1.** To illustrate how Excel 2003 can create an XML map for you, let's open an XML document:
CHOOSE: File → Open

**2.** Using the *Look in* drop-down list box, select your Advantage data files location. Then, do the following:
CLICK: down arrow attached to the *Files of type* drop-down list box
SELECT: XML Files from the list

**3.** To display the desired XML document:
DOUBLE-CLICK: EX1055a

**4.** In the Open XML dialog box:
SELECT: *As an XML list* option button, if it is not already selected
CLICK: OK command button

**5.** If an information dialog box appears, click the OK command button to have Excel 2003 create an XML Schema automatically.

**6.** Save the workbook as "XML Courses" to your personal storage location.

**7.** To display the XML Source task pane:
CHOOSE: Data → XML → XML Source
Your screen should now appear similar to the worksheet shown in Figure 10.78. Excel 2003 creates the XML map displayed in the XML Source task pane automatically. Notice that the element names in the XML map are used in (or mapped to) the field header row of the XML list area.

**Figure 10.78**

Displaying the XML Source task pane

Mapped range in the XML workbook

The XML map contains element names that are mapped into the field header and list areas

The List toolbar is used for manipulating data in both worksheet and XML list areas

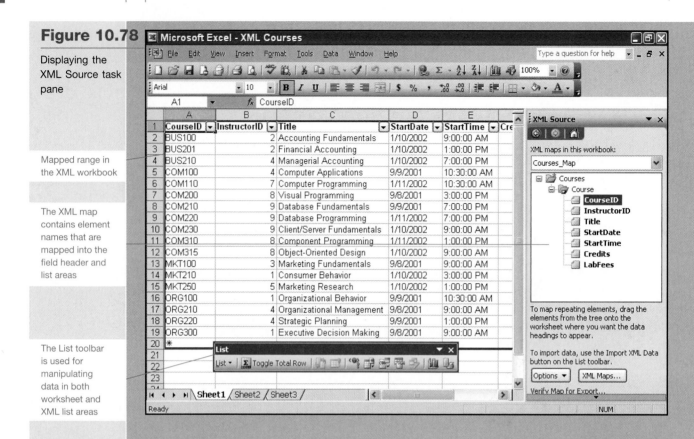

8. To rename the XML map from "Courses_Map" to "MyCourses," do the following:
   CLICK: XML Maps command button in the task pane

9. In the XML Maps dialog box:
   CLICK: Rename command button
   TYPE: **MyCourses**
   PRESS: (ENTER)
   The dialog box should now appear similar to the one shown in Figure 10.79. You will use this dialog box to add, modify, and delete XML maps in your workbook.

**Figure 10.79**

XML Maps dialog box

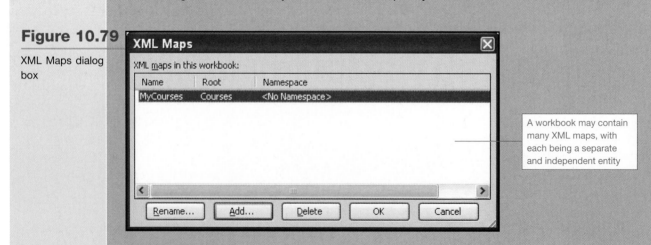

A workbook may contain many XML maps, with each being a separate and independent entity

**10.** Rather than having Excel 2003 create an XML map, you will now add a new XML map to this workbook that is based on an XML Schema file (.XSD). Similar to an XML document, an XML Schema file is a text file that may be displayed in NotePad or using Internet Explorer, as shown in Figure 10.80. To proceed:
CLICK: Add command button in the XML Maps dialog box

**Figure 10.80**

Displaying an XML Schema file (.XSD) using Internet Explorer

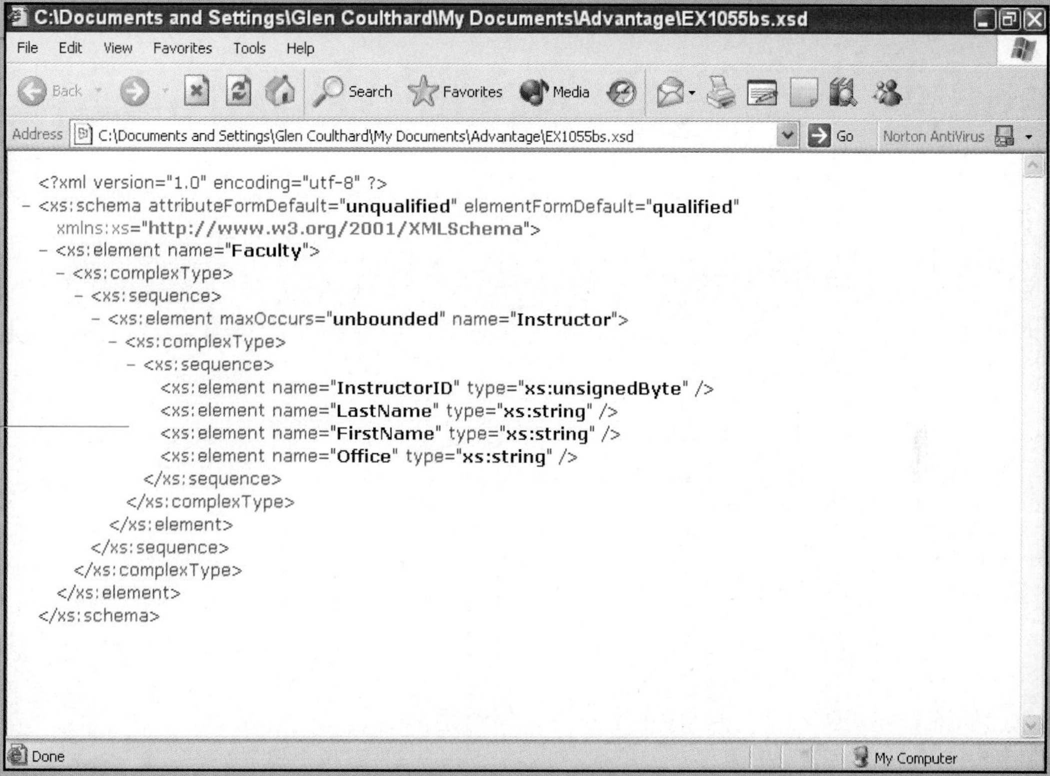

An XML Schema file contains information about the individual elements but does not contain any data

**11.** In the Select XML Source dialog box, use the *Look in* drop-down list box and select your Advantage data files location. Then, do the following:
DOUBLE-CLICK: EX1055bs in the list area
You are returned to the XML Maps dialog box.

**12.** To rename the new XML map:
CLICK: Rename command button
TYPE: **MyFaculty**
PRESS: ENTER

**13.** On your own, use the same process to add the "EX1055cs" XML Schema file to the XML Maps dialog box and then rename it to **MyRoster**, as shown in Figure 10.81.

**Figure 10.81**

Attaching three XML maps to the workbook

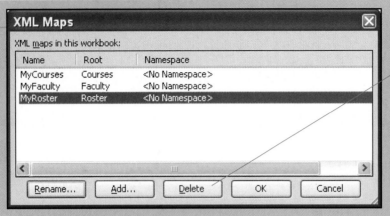

If you no longer need an XML map, select it in the list area and then click the Delete command buton

**14.** To close the XML Maps dialog box:
CLICK: OK command button
The MyRoster XML map should now appear in the XML Source task pane, as shown in Figure 10.82.

**Figure 10.82**

MyRoster XML map displayed in the XML Source task pane

The blue down arrow attached to this icon represents a "repeating element" that may display multiple data entries from an XML document

Click to define the XML view options

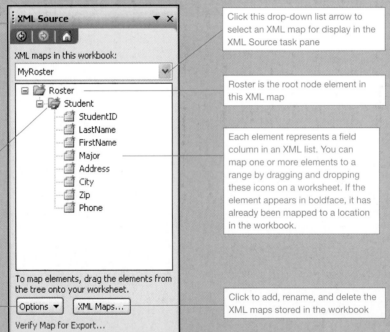

Click this drop-down list arrow to select an XML map for display in the XML Source task pane

Roster is the root node element in this XML map

Each element represents a field column in an XML list. You can map one or more elements to a range by dragging and dropping these icons on a worksheet. If the element appears in boldface, it has already been mapped to a location in the workbook.

Click to add, rename, and delete the XML maps stored in the workbook

**15.** On your own, use the drop-down list box under the *XML maps in this workbook* heading to select among the three XML maps for display in the XML Source task pane. Because the elements appearing in the MyCourses XML map have already been mapped to the worksheet, notice that these elements appear in boldface.

**16.** Before proceeding, select the MyCourses XML map for display in the XML Source task pane. Then, save the XML Courses workbook and keep it open for use in the next lesson.

## 10.5.6 Mapping and Manipulating XML Elements

→ **Feature**

Once you have defined the XML maps required to access external data in XML documents, you are ready to build your worksheets. If you import an XML document, Excel 2003 automatically creates an XML list on *Sheet1* of the workbook. Alternatively, you can manually specify which XML elements you wish to map to worksheet cells and ranges. You can then add, modify, delete, cut, and copy the elements as you would any other cell or range. In this lesson, you will learn to work with XML elements and to customize XML view options.

→ **Method**

To map XML elements to cells in a worksheet:

- CHOOSE: Data → XML → XML Source
- SELECT: element(s) in the XML Source task pane
- DRAG: element(s) to the worksheet location where you want the data to appear

To specify XML Map properties:

- CHOOSE: Data → XML → XML Map Properties

To customize XML options:

- CHOOSE: Data → XML → XML Source
- CLICK: Options button in the XML Source task pane

→ **Practice**

You will now map XML elements to cells and ranges and modify XML map properties and view options. Ensure that you have completed the previous lesson before proceeding.

1. On *Sheet1* of the XML Courses workbook:
   CLICK: cell C1 to select the "Title" field header cell
   In the XML Source task pane, notice that the "Title" element in the MyCourses XML map is also selected.

2. To select an element in the MyCourses XML map:
   CLICK: InstructorID element in the XML Source task pane
   Notice that the list area for the InstructorID column is selected, as shown in Figure 10.83.

## Figure 10.83

Selecting elements in an XML list

Clicking the "InstructorID" element in the XML Source task pane selects this range in the XML list area

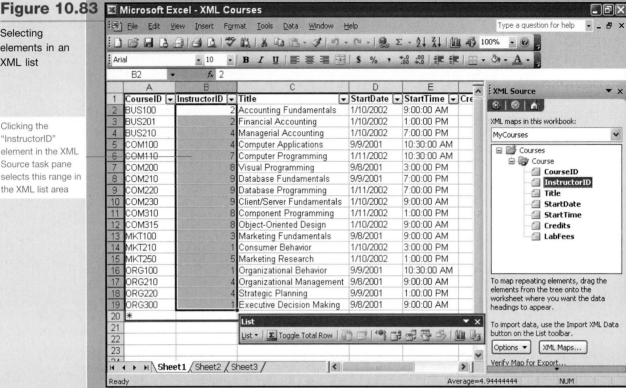

**3.** You will now remove the contents of the InstructorID column from the XML list. Do the following:
PRESS: **DELETE**
All of the data in the selected range is removed.

**4.** Because the InstructorID element is still mapped, a relationship exists between the XML list and the external XML document file. To illustrate, let's refresh the data from the original XML document:
CLICK: Refresh XML Data button (🔄) on the List toolbar
The InstructorID column is repopulated with data.

**5.** You will now remove both the data and the mapping of the InstructorID element. To begin:
PRESS: **DELETE** to remove the worksheet data

**6.** In the XML Source task pane:
RIGHT-CLICK: InstructorID element
CHOOSE: Remove element

**7.** To remove the selection highlighting:
CLICK: cell A1 in the worksheet
Notice that the InstructorID element in the XML Source task pane no longer appears in boldface.

**8.** To refresh the XML list area:
CLICK: Refresh XML Data button (🔄) on the List toolbar
Notice that the InstructorID data is not imported into the XML list area this time.

**9.** To remove the InstructorID column from the list area:
RIGHT-CLICK: column B in the column frame area
CHOOSE: Delete

**10.** To remove the Credits and Lab Fees columns:
SELECT: columns E and F in the column frame area
CHOOSE: Edit → Delete
Notice that deleting the XML list columns automatically removes the element mappings in the XML Source task pane.

**11.** To remove the selection highlighting:
CLICK: cell A1
Your screen should now appear similar to the worksheet shown in Figure 10.84.

**Figure 10.84**

Manipulating elements in the XML list area

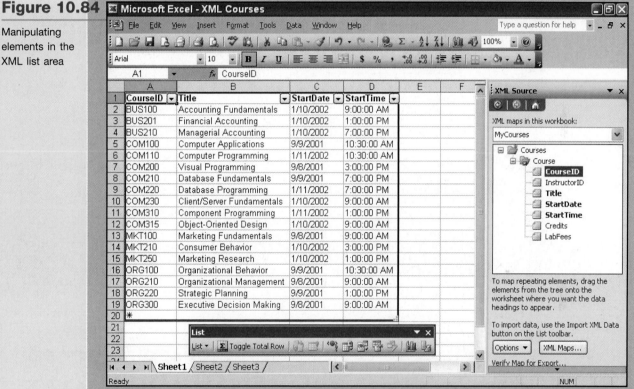

**12.** The XML map properties determine how the list data is refreshed from the external XML document, aside from other options. To display the XML map properties for MyCourses:
CHOOSE: Data → XML → XML Map Properties
Figure 10.85 identifies some of the properties available in the XML Map Properties dialog box.

**Figure 10.85**

XML Map
Properties dialog
box

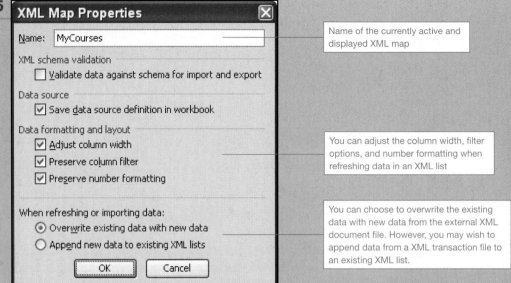

Name of the currently active and
displayed XML map

You can adjust the column width, filter
options, and number formatting when
refreshing data in an XML list

You can choose to overwrite the existing
data with new data from the external XML
document file. However, you may wish to
append data from a XML transaction file to
an existing XML list.

**13.** Let's retain the default settings and close the dialog box:
CLICK: Cancel command button

**14.** You will now build a new XML list from one of the XML Schema files imported during the last lesson. Do the following:
CLICK: *Sheet2* tab

**15.** In the *XML maps in this workbook* area of the XML Source task pane:
SELECT: MyRoster from the drop-down list box

**16.** In the elements list area of the task pane:
CLICK: LastName element
PRESS: CTRL
CLICK: FirstName element
CLICK: Major element
When you are finished selecting elements, release the CTRL key.

**17.** To create a new XML list based on the MyRoster XML map:
DRAG: the selected elements to cell B4 in the worksheet, as shown here

**18.** When you release the mouse button, the elements are placed onto the worksheet in an XML list, as shown in Figure 10.86.

**Figure 10.86**

Creating an XML list

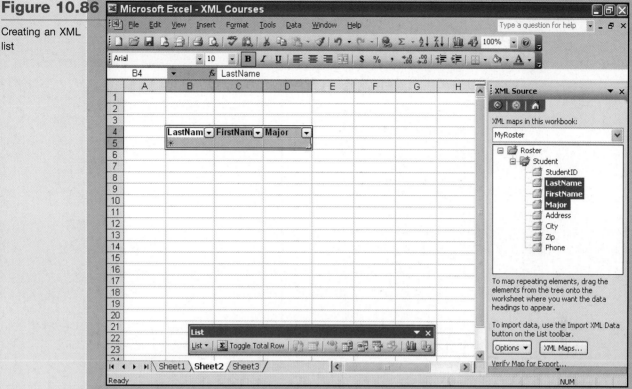

**19.** To import data from an XML document based on this XML Schema:
CLICK: Import XML Data button (⬚) on the list toolbar

**20.** Using the *Look in* drop-down list box, select your Advantage data files location. Then, do the following:
DOUBLE-CLICK: EX1055c in the list area
The XML list area is populated with data from the XML document. It is important to realize that you can cut, copy, and delete the data appearing in an XML list as you would with any other worksheet list.

**21.** To add the City element to the XML list:
CLICK: City element in the XML Source task pane
DRAG: City element to cell E4
When you release the mouse button, notice that the XML list area expands automatically to incorporate the new column, as shown in Figure 10.87.

**Figure 10.87**

Adding elements to the XML list

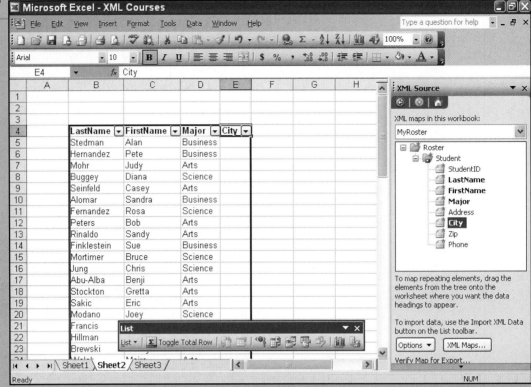

**22.** You must now refresh the XML data in order to import data for the City element. Do the following:
CLICK: Refresh XML Data button (⬚) on the List toolbar

**23.** To display some of the XML options that are available:
CLICK: Options button in the XML Source task pane
The menu shown below is displayed.

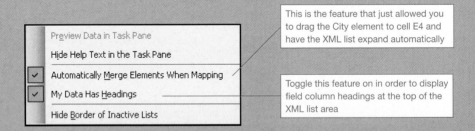

**24.** Let's retain the default settings and proceed. To remove the menu from displaying:
CLICK: cell A1 in the worksheet

**25.** You will now create one last XML list. To begin:
CLICK: *Sheet3* tab

**26.** In the *XML maps in this workbook* area of the XML Source task pane:
SELECT: MyFaculty from the drop-down list box

**27.** In the elements list area of the task pane:
CLICK: Instructor element
Notice that all of the elements beneath Instructor in the hierarchy are also selected.

**28.** DRAG: Instructor element to cell A1 in the worksheet
You have now mapped the XML Schema to the worksheet range.

**29.** To import data from an XML document based on this XML Schema:
CLICK: Import XML Data button ([🔲]) on the list toolbar

**30.** Using the *Look in* drop-down list box, select your Advantage data files location. Then, do the following:
DOUBLE-CLICK: EX1055b in the list area
The XML list area is populated with data from the XML document.

**31.** CLICK: cell A1 to remove the selection highlighting
Your screen should now appear similar to the worksheet shown in Figure 10.88.

**Figure 10.88**

Populating an XML list based on the MyFaculty XML map

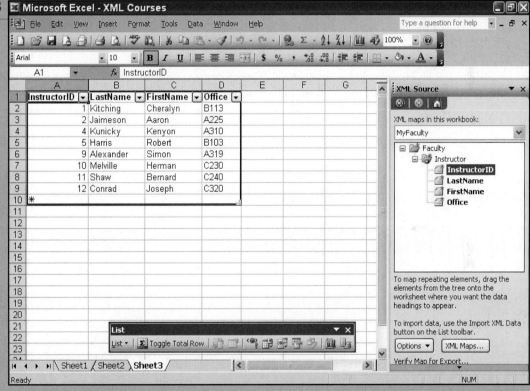

**32.** Using the Save As command, save the workbook as "XML School" to your personal storage location. Then, close the XML Source task pane and the workbook.

**10.5** Name the three Microsoft Office Web Components that allow you to create interactive Web pages using content from your workbooks.

# Chapter
### summary

There are several ways in which you can work smarter using Microsoft Office Excel 2003. First, the lookup and reference commands enable you to retrieve data quickly from lookup tables. In addition to being time-savers, lookup tables promote accuracy with data input and validation. Second, Excel 2003 provides three levels of protection (file level, workbook level, and sheet level) for ensuring workbook confidentiality and for facilitating maintenance. The File Properties dialog box also improves your ability to properly document your work. You can enter copyright information and provide helpful keywords to facilitate searching for and finding your workbooks at a later date. Third, templates are helpful time-savers that serve to ensure consistency in formatting and content. You can create personalized templates and display them on your own custom tab in the Templates dialog box.

One of the most appealing features of any application is its ability to incorporate and exchange data with other software programs. Microsoft Office Excel 2003 provides special tools for importing and exporting data. First and foremost is Excel 2003's ability to open a disparate data file and save a workbook using various file types. Special filters or converter programs provide this powerful, yet seamless, capability. The Text Import Wizard is one example of an easy-to-use tool for importing standard text files. Excel 2003 also provides the ability to import external data from leading database management programs for analysis and reporting. While the data remains stored in these databases, you can use Excel 2003's list management tools, PivotTable and PivotChart reports, and other features to summarize large amounts of data dynamically. Similarly, you can access and work with data stored on the Web in HTML and XML documents. XML is becoming the standard format for exchanging data and Microsoft Office Excel 2003 has incorporated several key features to take advantage of this technology. Specifically, the new XML Spreadsheet schema enables you to create, save, open, manipulate, and share workbook data using the XML document type. You can even import XML Schema files and then map worksheet ranges to data elements stored in an external XML document. Working with XML source files has never been easier!

## Command Summary

Many of the commands and procedures appearing in this chapter are summarized in the following table.

| Skill Set | To Perform This Task . . . | Do the Following . . . |
| --- | --- | --- |
| **Working with Ranges** | Create a lookup formula using the Lookup Wizard add-in | CHOOSE: Tools → Lookup |
| | Use lookup and reference functions: | • = INDEX(*array,row_num,col_num*) |
| | | • = MATCH(*lookup_value,lookup_array, match_type*) |
| | | • = HLOOKUP(*lookup_value, table_array,row_index_num, range_lookup*) |
| | | • = VLOOKUP(*lookup_value, table_array,col_index_num, range_lookup*) |
| **Workgroup Collaboration** | Protect/unprotect cells in a worksheet | CHOOSE: Format → Cells<br>CLICK: *Protection* tab<br>SELECT: *Locked* check box |
| | Hide/unhide sheets in a workbook | CHOOSE: Format → Sheet → Hide<br>CHOOSE: Format → Sheet → Unhide |
| | Turn on/off worksheet and workbook protection | CHOOSE: Tools → Protection |

| | | |
|---|---|---|
| | Password-protect a workbook | CHOOSE: File → Save As<br>CLICK: Tools in the toolbar area<br>CHOOSE: General Options<br>TYPE: *a password* in the *Password to open* and/or *Password to modify* text boxes |
| | Make a workbook read-only | CHOOSE: File → Save As<br>CLICK: Tools in the toolbar area<br>CHOOSE: General Options<br>SELECT: *Read-only recommended* check box |
| | Set or edit workbook properties | CHOOSE: File → Properties |
| | Remove personal information from a workbook | CHOOSE: Tools → Options<br>CLICK: *Security* tab<br>SELECT: *Remove personal information from this file* check box |
| | Attach and manage certificates and digital signatures in a workbook | CHOOSE: Tools → Options<br>CLICK: *Security* tab<br>CLICK: Digital Signatures command button |
| **Managing Workbooks** | Apply a template in creating a new workbook | CHOOSE: File → New<br>CLICK: "On my computer" under the *Templates* area of the New Workbook task pane<br>CLICK: *General* tab in the Templates dialog box<br>DOUBLE-CLICK: a template |
| | Apply a template in creating a new worksheet | RIGHT-CLICK: *any sheet tab*<br>CHOOSE: Insert<br>DOUBLE-CLICK: a template |
| | Create a workbook template | CHOOSE: File → Save As<br>SELECT: Template (*.xlt) in the *Save as type* drop-down list box<br>SELECT: Templates in the *Save in* drop-down list box<br>CLICK: Save command button |
| | Edit a workbook template | CHOOSE: File → Open<br>SELECT: Template (*.xlt) in the *Files of type* drop-down list box<br>DOUBLE-CLICK: a template |
| | Change the number of worksheets in a new workbook, along with the default font and file locations | CHOOSE: Tools → Options<br>CLICK: *General* tab |
| **Importing and Exporting Data** | Save and/or export your workbooks to other applications | CHOOSE: File → Save As<br>SELECT: *a file format* in the *Save as type* drop-down list box<br>CLICK: Save command button |
| | Import data from other applications | CHOOSE: File → Open<br>SELECT: *a file format* in the *Files of type* drop-down list box<br>DOUBLE-CLICK: the desired file |

| | | |
|---|---|---|
| | Import data from a text file using the Text Import Wizard | CHOOSE: File → Open, or<br>SELECT: Text Files in the *Files of type* drop-down list box<br>DOUBLE-CLICK: the desired file |
| | Import data from a database file or other external data source | CHOOSE: Data → Import External Data → Import Data |
| | Import data from the Internet using a Web query | CHOOSE: Data → Import External Data → New Web query<br>Enter the URL address of the HTML document to retrieve. |
| | Save an Excel 2003 worksheet as an interactive Web page using the Spreadsheet Office Web component | CHOOSE: File → Save as Web Page<br>CLICK: Publish command button<br>SELECT: *Add interactivity with* check box<br>SELECT: Spreadsheet functionality from the drop-down list box<br>CLICK: Publish command button |
| | Edit an interactive Web page using Spreadsheet Office Web component in Microsoft Excel | CLICK: Export to Microsoft Excel button ( ) on the Spreadsheet component's toolbar |
| **Organizing and Analyzing Data** | Save a workbook as an XML Spreadsheet file | CHOOSE: File → Save As<br>SELECT: XML Spreadsheet in the *Save as type* drop-down list box<br>CLICK: Save command button |
| | Open an XML Spreadsheet or standard document file | CHOOSE: File → Open<br>SELECT: XML Files in the *Files of type* drop-down list box<br>DOUBLE-CLICK: the desired file |
| | Create an XML Web query | CHOOSE: Data → Import External Data → New Web query<br>Enter the URL address of the XML document to retrieve. |
| | Display the XML Source task pane for working with an XML list | CHOOSE: Data → XML → XML Source |
| | Add, rename, or delete an XML map in a workbook | CHOOSE: Data → XML → XML Source<br>CLICK: XML Maps command button |
| | Define XML options | CHOOSE: Data → XML → XML Source<br>CLICK: Options command button |
| | Specify XML map properties | CHOOSE: Data → XML → XML Map Properties |

## Key Terms

This section specifies page references for the key terms identified in this chapter. For a complete list of definitions, refer to the Glossary provided at the end of this learning guide.

AutoTemplates, *p. EX 624*

Chart component, *p. EX 663*

delimiter, *p. EX 643*

embedding, *p. EX 650*

Extensible Markup Language (XML), *p. EX 668*

HTML round-tripping, *p. EX 663*

linking, *p. EX 650*

lookup formula, *p. EX 596*

lookup table, *p. EX 596*

Microsoft Query, *p. EX 649*

password, *p. EX 616*

password-protect, *p. EX 608*

pasting, *p. EX 650*

PivotTable component, *p. EX 663*

query, *p. EX 649*

read-only, *p. EX 616*

Spreadsheet component, *p. EX 663*

template, *p. EX 624*

Text Import Wizard, *p. EX 641*

Web queries, *p. EX 657*

XML map, *p. EX 674*

XML Schema (XSD), *p. EX 670*

XML Spreadsheet (XML-SS), *p. EX 670*

## Chapter
### q u i z

### Short Answer

1. How does a lookup table differ in structure from a worksheet list?

2. Name the five tabs displayed for workbook properties.

3. What are the three levels of protection for your work in Excel 2003?

4. Provide an example of a good workbook password. Why is it good?

5. How do templates save you time and ensure design consistency?

6. Name two types of files that Excel 2003 can use to create XML maps.

7. What is the primary difference between *opening* and *importing* an external data file?

8. Name the three methods for sharing data between Office applications.

9. How would you import a specific portion of an HTML document into a worksheet?

10. Explain the difference between an *XML document* and an *XML Spreadsheet file?*

### True/False

1. _____ The Lookup Wizard is an add-in program that must first be installed before appearing on the Tools menu.

2. _____ The Lookup Wizard constructs a lookup formula, based on your selections, using the INDEX and HLOOKUP functions.

3. _____ The *Statistics* tab in the workbook Properties dialog box displays when the workbook was created, last modified, and last saved.

**4.** _____ You can password-protect a single cell in a worksheet.

**5.** _____ You can hide an entire chart sheet in a workbook.

**6.** _____ To create a custom template, you require a special add-in program.

**7.** _____ One way to import data is to use the File ➜ Open command and then let Excel 2003 perform the necessary file format conversion.

**8.** _____ When you save a worksheet as an interactive Web page, Excel uses the Spreadsheet Office Web Component in the target document.

**9.** _____ When you copy data from an HTML table, Excel 2003 can paste the data into the worksheet but not its formatting characteristics.

**10.** _____ When you save a workbook as an XML Spreadsheet file, Excel 2003 must discard any charts or drawing objects in the workbook.

## Multiple Choice

**1.** Which of the following is _not_ a lookup and reference function described in this chapter?

  a. EXTRACT
  b. HLOOKUP
  c. MATCH
  d. VLOOKUP

**2.** Which of the following lookup and reference functions returns the row number where a particular entry resides?

  a. EXTRACT
  b. HLOOKUP
  c. MATCH
  d. VLOOKUP

**3.** On the _Summary_ tab of the workbook Properties dialog box, which of the following is _not_ an information text box?

  a. Title
  b. Author
  c. Supervisor
  d. Company

**4.** Which of the following file types defines the structure of XML data but does not contain the data itself?

  a. XML Definition file
  b. XML Document file
  c. XML Schema file
  d. XML Spreadsheet file

**5.** To specify new settings for the default workbook, create a template named:

  a. Book.xlt in the AutoTemplates folder
  b. Book.xlt in the XLStart folder
  c. Sheet.xlt in the Templates folder
  d. Workbook.xlt in the Templates folder

**6.** Custom templates are typically stored in the following folder:

  a. AutoTemplates
  b. Spreadsheet Solutions
  c. Templates
  d. XLStart

**7.** When you attempt to open a text file, Excel 2003 launches the following wizard automatically:

  a. AutoFilter Wizard
  b. File Format Wizard
  c. Import External Data Wizard
  d. Text Import Wizard

**8.** To successfully run a Web query against a Web server, you must first:

  a. Install Web browser software
  b. Establish an active connection to the Internet
  c. Install the Microsoft Office Web Components
  d. Install the Web query add-in program

**9.** An XML element that has been mapped to a worksheet cell or range is displayed in the XML Source task pane with the following attribute:

  a. Boldface
  b. Red color
  c. Italic
  d. Underlined

**10.** XML documents have a unique first element called the:

  a. Root node
  b. Attribute node
  c. Schema node
  d. Topmost node

## Hands-On
### exercises

step by step

### 1. Retrieving Data Using VLOOKUP

In this exercise, you practice retrieving data from lookup tables using formulas and functions. Before proceeding, ensure that there are no workbooks displayed in the Excel 2003 application window.

**1.** Open the data file named EX10HE01 to display the workbook shown in Figure 10.89. (*Note:* Depending on your system settings, the date's year value in cell B4 may appear as "04" instead of "2004.")

**Figure 10.89**

Opening the
EX10HE01
workbook

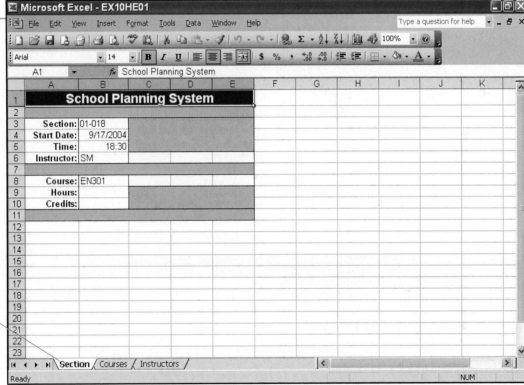

This workbook
contains three
worksheets:
Section, Courses,
and Instructors

**2.** Save the workbook as "Section Form" to your personal storage location.

**3.** After familiarizing yourself with the *Section* worksheet, name the lookup table appearing on the *Courses* worksheet:
CLICK: *Courses* tab
SELECT: cell range from A2 to E26
CLICK: in the Name box
TYPE: **courses**
PRESS: (ENTER)

**4.** In order to use the VLOOKUP function, you must make sure that the table is sorted by the lookup or search column:
CLICK: cell A2
CLICK: Sort Ascending button (↓)

**5.** Now name the lookup table on the *Instructors* worksheet:
CLICK: *Instructors* tab
SELECT: cell range from A2 to C21
CLICK: in the Name box
TYPE: **instructors**
PRESS: (ENTER)

**6.** To sort the lookup table:
CLICK: cell A2
CLICK: Sort Ascending button ([↓])

**7.** You will now enter lookup formulas into the *Section* worksheet. To begin:
CLICK: *Section* tab
SELECT: cell C8
TYPE: **=vlookup(**
CLICK: Insert Function button ([*fx*])
The Function Arguments dialog box appears.

**8.** To specify the lookup value:
CLICK: Dialog Collapse button ([⬚]) for the *Lookup_value* text box
CLICK: cell B8
CLICK: Dialog Expand button ([⬚])

**9.** To complete the Function Arguments dialog box:
SELECT: *Table_array* text box
TYPE: **courses**
PRESS: (TAB)
TYPE: **2** in the *Col_index_num* text box
The dialog box should now appear similar to the one shown in Figure 10.90.

**Figure 10.90**

Function Arguments dialog box for VLOOKUP

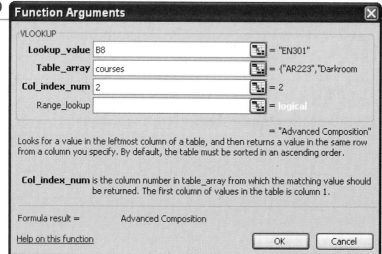

**10.** CLICK: OK command button to proceed
The result, "Advanced Composition," appears in cell C8.

**11.** Now enter the VLOOKUP function into some additional cells using the typing method. Do the following:
SELECT: cell B9
TYPE: **=vlookup(b8,courses,4)**
PRESS: (ENTER)

12. On your own, enter a formula into cell B10 that will return the number of credits for the desired course. Use either of the methods that were demonstrated in the previous steps. (*Hint:* The information is in column 5 of the lookup table.)

13. To test the lookup formulas:
SELECT: cell B8
TYPE: **AR355**
PRESS: (ENTER)
The course title, hours, and credits are updated to reflect the new value in cell B8.

14. The next formula entry returns the instructor's name in the format "Last Name, First Name" using the initials entered into cell B6 as the lookup value. To begin:
SELECT: cell C6

15. Enter the lookup formula:
TYPE: **=vlookup(b6,instructors,3)&", "& vlookup(b6,instructors,2)**
Your screen should now appear similar to the worksheet shown in Figure 10.91. Notice that this formula uses the VLOOKUP function twice as well as the concatenation operator (&).

**Figure 10.91**

Entering a concatenation formula using VLOOKUP

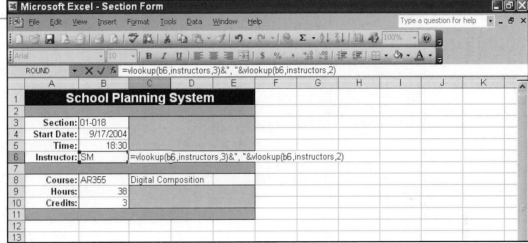

16. PRESS: (ENTER) to complete the formula entry
The entry, "Molina, Steffi" appears in cell C6.

17. To test that this formula is working properly:
SELECT: cell B6
TYPE: **EB**
PRESS: (ENTER)
The entry, "Bonham, Earl" appears in cell C6.

18. Save and then close the "Section Form" workbook.

step by step

## 2. Protecting a Workbook

In this exercise, you will edit an existing workbook by protecting its worksheet cells and then applying a password.

1. Open the data file named EX10HE02 and then save it as "Video Unprotected" to your personal storage location.

**2.** Begin by unlocking the cells where you will want to enter data:
SELECT: cell range from B5 to B7
PRESS: **CTRL** and hold it down
SELECT: cell range from B11 to B12
When the two cell ranges are selected (as shown in Figure 10.92), release the **CTRL** key.

**3.** CHOOSE: Format → Cells
CLICK: *Protection* tab
Your screen should now appear similar to the worksheet shown in Figure 10.92.

**Figure 10.92**

Format Cells
dialog box:
*Protection* tab

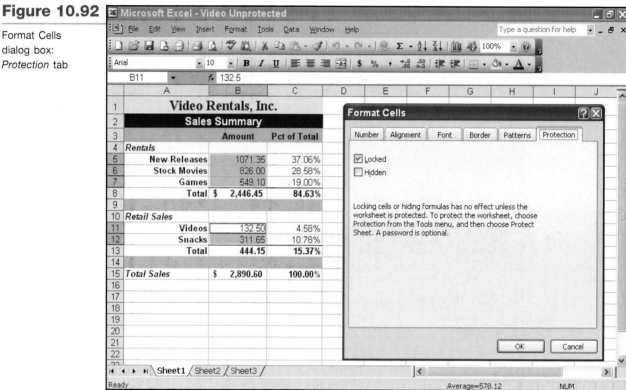

**4.** To unlock the cells in the selected range:
SELECT: *Locked* check box so that no ✓ appears
CLICK: OK command button

**5.** To turn on protection for the worksheet:
PRESS: **CTRL**+**HOME** to move to the top of the worksheet
CHOOSE: Tools → Protection → Protect Sheet

**6.** Ensure that the *Protect worksheet and contents of locked cells* check box is selected, and then:
CLICK: OK command button

**7.** To demonstrate the worksheet-level protection:
SELECT: cell B8
TYPE: **2500**
Notice that a warning dialog box appears when you type the first character.

**8.** To cancel the dialog box:
CLICK: OK command button

9. SELECT: cell B5
   TYPE: **1500**
   PRESS: (ENTER)
   Because the cell has been unprotected, you can input a new value into this cell.

10. To save the file with a password:
    CHOOSE: File → Save As

11. In the Save As dialog box:
    CLICK: Tools ▾ in the toolbar area of the dialog box
    CHOOSE: General Options

12. In the Save Options dialog box (Figure 10.93), type a password to open the workbook:
    TYPE: **Vid2See**
    CLICK: OK command button

**Figure 10.93**

Save Options
dialog box

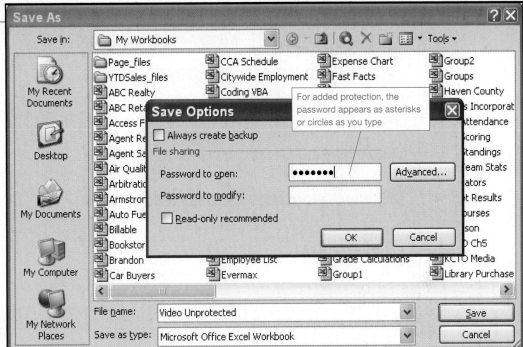

13. In the Confirm Password dialog box:
    TYPE: **Vid2See**
    CLICK: OK command button

14. In the Save As dialog box:
    TYPE: **Video Protected** in the *File name* text box
    CLICK: Save command button
    The workbook is saved to the disk with a password.

15. Close the workbook.

step by step

## 3. Creating a Production Template

You will now practice converting an existing workbook into a template that can be used to enter daily production information.

1. Open the data file named EX10HE03 and then save it as "Production Stats" to your personal storage location.

2. Replace the contents of cell D2 with a function that displays the current date.

3. Select the cell range from B4 to E8, as shown in Figure 10.94.

**Figure 10.94**

Selecting a cell range in the Production Stats workbook

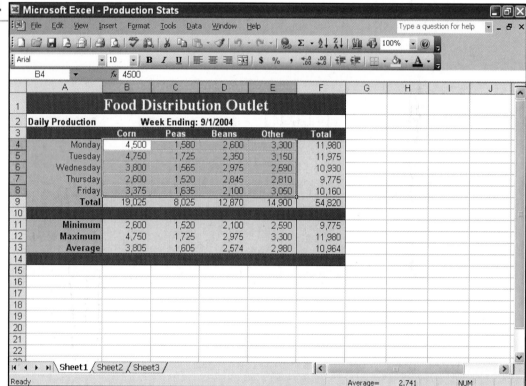

4. Use the *Protection* tab in the Format Cells dialog box to unlock the cells from B4 to E8.

5. Delete the contents of the selected cells.

6. Notice that the error value "#DIV/0" displays in row 13. To correct this "divide by zero" error, enter the following conditional formula:
   SELECT: cell B13
   TYPE: =if(sum(b4:b8) >0,average(b4:b8),0)
   PRESS: **ENTER**

7. Use the AutoFill handle to extend the new formula across to cell E13.

8. Using the File ➜ Properties command, open the worksheet's Properties dialog box and enter the following in the *Category* text box:
   TYPE: **Production Department Forms**
   CLICK: OK command button

9. Move the cell pointer to the top of the worksheet and turn on protection for the entire sheet. Do not enter a password.

**10.** Save the workbook as a template in the "Templates" folder and then close the new template file.

**11.** To test the template, use the File ➜ New command and New Workbook task pane to display the Templates dialog box, as shown in Figure 10.95.

**Figure 10.95**

Templates dialog box

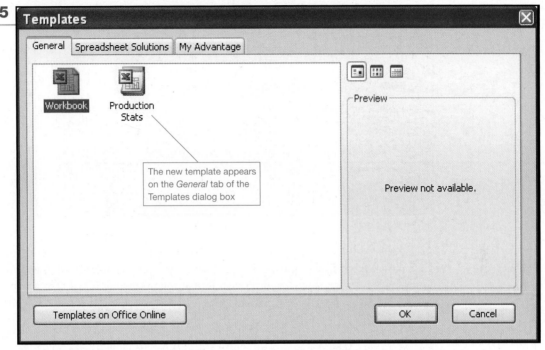

The new template appears on the *General* tab of the Templates dialog box

**12.** Create a new workbook based on the "Production Stats" template.

**13.** On your own, enter data into some of the unprotected cells. Verify that only these cells accept data.

**14.** Save the workbook as "Production Stats1" to your personal storage location. Then, close the workbook.

on your own

## 4. Converting a Text File

An associate in your real estate firm has asked you to convert a text file that she downloaded from the Internet into an Excel 2003 workbook. Given your recent experience importing and exporting different file types, you readily agree and begin to prepare for the task ahead. To begin, ensure that there are no workbooks in the application window.

Using the Open dialog box, locate the EX10HE04 text file in the Advantage student data files location. Then, use the Text Import Wizard shown in Figure 10.96 to import the file using the Delimited option. Notice in the preview area of Figure 10.96 that the first line in the text file displays a title. Therefore, in Step 1 of the wizard, specify that you want to start the import at row 2. Then, for the remaining steps in the wizard, accept the default selections.

**Figure 10.96**

Text Import
Wizard dialog
box: Step 1 of 3

Once the data has been imported from the text file, save the workbook as "Jan Sales" to your personal storage location. (*Hint:* Ensure that you change the file type to Microsoft Office Excel Workbook.) Apply the "Colorful 2" AutoFormat style and currency formatting to columns C and D to improve the appearance of the worksheet. Then, create a worksheet list from the data. Using the AutoFilter drop-down list arrow (▼), sort the list into ascending order by the Date Purchased column and then filter the results for those "Purchase Price" values exceeding $200,000. When you select cell A1 to remove the selection highlighting, your screen should appear similar to the worksheet shown in Figure 10.97. Save and then close the "Jan Sales" workbook.

**Figure 10.97**

Importing a text
file and then
formatting the
worksheet list

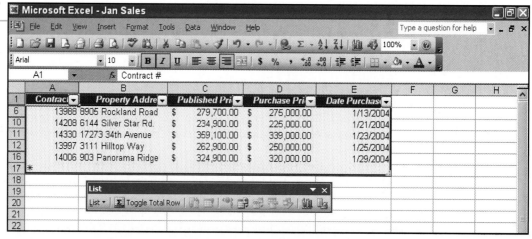

**on your own**

### 5. Constructing an Employee Discount Purchase Form

You now practice creating formulas using lookup tables. To begin, open the data file named EX10HE05. Then, save the workbook as "Discount Form" to your personal storage location. This workbook contains two worksheets, named *Purchase* and *Table*. Review the two worksheets before proceeding. Notice that the discount percentage to which an employee is entitled depends solely on his or her department.

Perform the following tasks in the order they are presented:

- On the *Table* tab, name the range for the lookup table "dept."

- On the *Purchase* tab, enter your name into cell B3.

- In cell B4, enter **PR** to denote the Production department.

- In cell C4, enter a lookup formula that uses the abbreviated code in cell B4 to display the department's full name from the *Table* worksheet.

- In cell B7, enter a lookup formula that uses the abbreviated code in cell B4 to display the discount percentage available to the employee. Once completed, the formula in cell B8 of the *Purchase* worksheet recalculates the "Amount Due."

- Change the department code in cell B4 to **AC**. Make sure that cells C4 and B7 are updated automatically, as shown in Figure 10.98.

- Unlock cells B3, B4, and B6 using the *Protection* tab in the Format Cells dialog box. Then, turn on worksheet protection so that users can only change the values appearing in the three unlocked cells.

**Figure 10.98**

Using a lookup table in a form

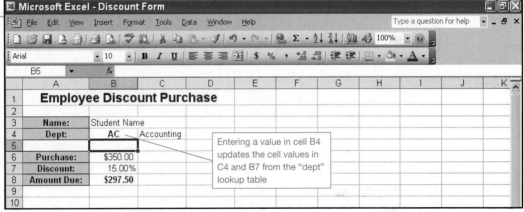

As a last step, save and then close the "Discount Form" workbook.

on your own

## 6. Importing an XML Document

In this exercise, you will import an XML document that is stored on your local hard disk into a workbook. Assume that the XML document is maintained and updated by another application. Therefore, you need to establish a dynamic connection to the document rather than just open and convert its contents into a worksheet.

Perform the following tasks in the order they are presented:

- Open the EX10HE06 XML document from the Advantage student data files location as an XML list.

- Allow Excel 2003 to create the XML map and schema definition.

- Save the new workbook as "XML Grades" to your personal storage location.

- Display the XML Source task pane.

- Delete the ID column from the XML list.

- Select cell A1 to remove the selection highlighting.

- Rename the XML map from "EX10HE06" to "Grades."

- Display the "Top 10" list items, according to Grade.

Your screen should now appear similar to the worksheet shown in Figure 10.99. Save and then close the workbook. Then, close the XML Source task pane so that no windows appear open in the Excel 2003 application window.

**Figure 10.99**

The "XML Grades" workbook

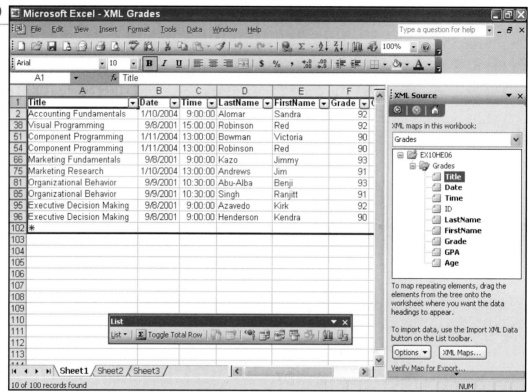

# CaseStudy    FAST TRAINING, INC.

Jack Griffey is the general manager of FAST Training, Inc. (FAST). Specializing in teaching Microsoft Office applications, FAST offers scheduled classes for the general public and customizes in-house seminars for their corporate clients. While Jack's personal computer savvy is somewhat lacking, he makes sure to hire only experienced trainers who are Microsoft certified. He is also revered for his work in the community and for donating manuals and learning guides for older software products to local charity groups. To this end, Jack has identified several suppliers of the both new and older training products and has now begun creating a workbook for generating purchase orders. His goal is to hand over the completed workbook to his assistant, Claire Beecham, to use as needed. Unfortunately, Claire's Excel skills are rather modest and Jack must ensure that she knows exactly where and how to enter data. He also wants to ensure that the worksheets (and especially the formulas that he has entered) are not vulnerable to editing mistakes. With information gleaned from this chapter, Jack is now ready to complete the purchase order workbook.

In the following case problems, assume the role of Jack and perform the same steps that he identifies.

1. With a few spare minutes on his hands, Jack decides to work on his purchase order application. He opens the EX10CP01 workbook and then saves it as "FAST Ordering" to his personal storage location. Jack wants to create lookup formulas to display information on the *Order* worksheet that is retrieved from the *Suppliers* and *Titles* worksheets. His first step, however, is to finish preparing the lookup tables on these sheet tabs. He clicks the *Suppliers* tab and reviews the data therein. His focus then switches to the empty *Titles* tab. Early in the day, Claire downloaded an HTML document from a supplier's Web site listing some of their available titles. Jack now wants to import the data from the Web page into the *Titles* worksheet.

To begin, Jack uses the Data → Import External Data command to create a new Web query. He enters the name of the HTML document (EX10CP01.htm) into the *Address* box, as shown below, and then clicks the Go command button. (*Note:* You will have to substitute the directory path where you have stored the Advantage student data files.)

The HTML document is loaded into the New Web Query dialog box. When he clicks the arrow icon (▶) appearing beside the book table, it changes to a check mark icon (✔) and the table appears selected. Jack clicks the Import command button. He then accepts the starting point of cell A1 and clicks the OK command button in the Import Data dialog box to finish the process. Jack selects cell A1 and then sorts the list into ascending order by ISBN. He completes the worksheet by applying the "List 2" AutoFormat style, as shown in Figure 10.100.

**Figure 10.100**

Importing an HTML table into a worksheet

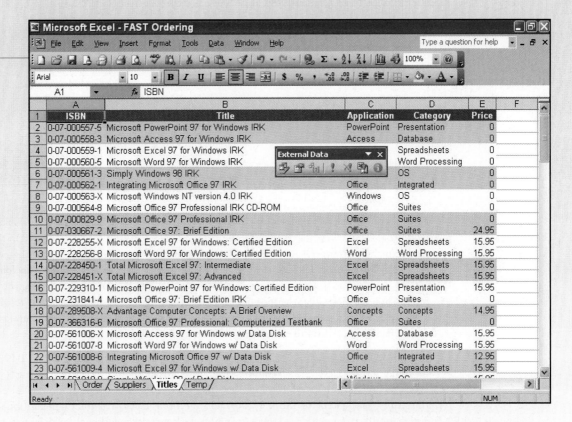

**2.** Claire enters Jacks office to notify him that the supplier from which she downloaded the HTML document has just sent her a list of additional titles via e-mail. She has saved the information to a text file named EX10CP02.txt. Jack thanks her and decides to import the new data onto the *Temp* worksheet. First, he moves the cell pointer to cell A1 on the *Temp* worksheet and then chooses the File ➜ Open command. He locates the text file in the Advantage student data files location and double-clicks the file to open it. The Text Import Wizard is displayed.

In Step 1 of the Text Import Wizard, Jack tells the wizard to start importing data at row 1 in the text file. He then proceeds to import the delimited data using a *General* column format. The data appears in a new workbook. Jack copies and pastes the data into the *Temp* worksheet. He then sorts the list by ISBN and applies a "List 3" AutoFormat style, as shown in Figure 10.101. After saving the workbook for safekeeping, he displays the EX10CP02 workbook and then closes it without saving the changes.

**Figure 10.101**

Importing a text file and pasting data into a worksheet

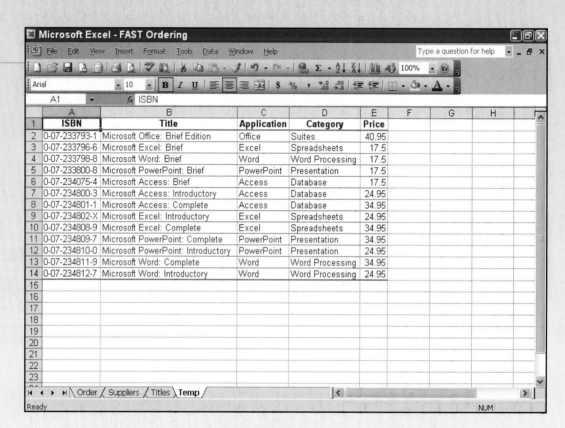

**3.** Before entering the lookup formulas in the *Order* worksheet, Jack names the three lookup tables in the workbook. On the *Temp* tab, he names the range from cell A2 to E14 **NewTitles**. On the *Titles* tab, he names the range from cell A2 to E121 **OldTitles**. On the *Suppliers* tab, he names the range from cell A2 to I13 **Suppliers**. He then selects the *Order* worksheet for display. Based on the lookup value in cell B4, Jack enters VLOOKUP formulas into cells B5, B6, B7, D3, and D4 using the Suppliers range name. He notes that the formula in cell B7 requires him to concatenate the results of three separate lookup formulas using the ampersand (&) character. After entering the lookup formulas, Jack types FIRST into cell B4 to ensure that the lookup formulas update the worksheet cells correctly.

Using data from the "OldTitles" lookup table, Jack enters formulas into cells B9, B10, B11, and B12 for filling in the "Description" column. Then he enters similar formulas into cells D9, D10, D11, and D12. The lookup value for searching the table of book titles appears in column A for each row. To test the results, Jack enters the ISBN **0-256-26004-4** into cell A9. The total purchase amount is updated automatically, along with the lookup formulas. Jack saves the workbook, which appears similar to the one shown in Figure 10.102, before proceeding.

**Figure 10.102**

Entering lookup formulas into a worksheet

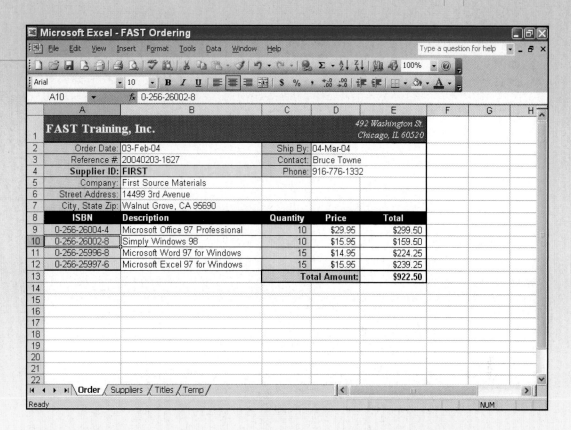

4. To avoid someone entering data over the formulas in the *Order* worksheet, Jack unlocks only the yellow data entry cells. He then applies sheet-level protection. Finally, he saves the workbook with password-protection, using the password "L8Latte" and replacing the original file. After closing the workbook, Jack exits Microsoft Office Excel 2003 and begins to think about exporting the lookup tables to a Microsoft Office Access 2003 database. Maybe another time, he muses.

## Answers to Self-Check Questions

**10.1** What function(s) does the Lookup Wizard use in constructing a lookup formula? The INDEX and MATCH lookup and reference functions.

**10.2** How can you ensure that a user will not remove the worksheet protection that you have initiated? To ensure that the protection is not removed, use a password when protecting the worksheet.

**10.3** How would you use a template to change the default font from Arial to Verdana for all new workbooks? To update the default settings for a workbook, create a template named "Book.xlt" with the desired font and then save it in the XLStart folder. To update the default settings for a worksheet, create a template named "Sheet.xlt" and then save it in the XLStart folder.

**10.4** Your friend is using a specialized statistics software program to collect numerical research data. He has asked you to analyze and chart the data. Assuming that the software is not able to export data into an Excel 2003 workbook, what file format should you recommend for transferring the data? An ASCII Text file format is the most common format used in data exchange. Almost every software program can export and import ASCII text files. Furthermore, the Text Import Wizard facility of Excel 2003 greatly facilitates the import process.

**10.5** Name the three Microsoft Office Web Components that allow you to create interactive Web pages using content from your workbooks. The Spreadsheet, Chart, and PivotTable components enable you to add interactivity to Web pages created from an Excel 2003 workbook.

# Microsoft® Office Excel®

## 2003

## CHAPTER 11

 # Developing Applications Using Excel

## PREREQUISITES

This chapter assumes competency in designing and constructing a worksheet in Microsoft Office Excel 2003. Specifically, a good understanding of formulas and functions is required for completing the modules on validating data and auditing a worksheet. You should also be familiar with accessing commands from the Menu bar and toolbars.

## LEARNING OBJECTIVES

After reading this chapter, you will be able to:

• Explain the features and limitations of working with shared workbooks

• Validate and format data that is input by the user

• Identify common cell indicators and use smart tags

• Audit a worksheet for cell references and incorrect or non-conforming values and formulas

• Automate everyday procedures by recording and running macros

• Use the Visual Basic Editor to modify and print recorded macros

• Streamline the Menu bar and toolbars to your specific work habits and patterns

# 11.1 Planning a Workbook Application

To be successful as a spreadsheet developer, you should place yourself in the users' position and strive to meet their expectations. Before you enter even the first label on a worksheet, understand your target audience and identify their basic *input* and *output* requirements. The **users** for your workbook application are the people who will enter and manipulate the data, analyze calculated results, and make decisions based on its reports and charts. They are also, most likely, the people paying your salary!

When starting a workbook application, follow some basic planning guidelines and proceed through the following stages in the development life cycle: *Analyze, Design, Develop, Implement,* and *Evaluate,* and then loop back to *Analyze.* At each stage, gather feedback from your users to ensure that they approve of your work and want you to continue. It is always wise to involve your users (to a certain extent anyway) in the development process because they are more likely to assume ownership of the completed application if they have been consulted throughout. Make your users an integral part of the development cycle.

### Planning Guidelines for Workbook Applications

➤ Know your audience and define the workbook objectives.

➤ Design the workbook based on the input and output requirements.

➤ Develop worksheets by entering the known data, creating formulas for analyzing and summarizing the data, validating the input data, and then automating common procedures and tasks.

➤ Audit, test, and evaluate the workbook for completeness and accuracy.

➤ Document the workbook, including labels, cell comments, instructions, and troubleshooting scenarios.

## 11.1.1 Creating a Shared Workbook

→ **Feature**

When might you need to develop a workbook application for other people to use? One situation arises when you assume responsibility for maintaining a workbook, while others are responsible for drawing conclusions or making strategic decisions from its reports. In this case, the presentation of the printed output is as important as the workbook structure. Another common situation is when you must create a **shared workbook** that will be stored on a *network file server.* Microsoft Office Excel 2003 provides several tools that will allow two or more users in a networked office environment to access and edit the same workbook, such as a worksheet list, simultaneously. If other users on the network are editing the same workbook, Excel 2003 allows you to view their changes when you save the workbook. If there are any conflicts, such as another user changing data in the same cell as yourself, a dialog box appears giving you the option to save your changes or leave the existing modifications intact. Excel 2003 saves a custom view of the workbook for each user, so that all personal display and print settings, including filters, are reapplied the next time the shared workbook is opened.

It is important to note that the original author of a workbook establishes its shared properties and then stores it on a network server that is accessible to a specific group of users. In working with shared workbooks, you are limited from performing certain worksheet operations that may negatively affect other users. To name a few of these restrictions: You cannot delete worksheets, apply conditional formats, group or outline data, create data tables, create PivotTable reports, or use tools from the Drawing toolbar. Given these restrictions, you can see that the original author is largely responsible for entering and formatting data in a shared workbook.

→ ## Method

To share a workbook:

- CHOOSE: Tools → Share Workbook
- CLICK: *Editing* tab
- SELECT: *Allow changes by more than one user . . .* check box
- CLICK: OK command button
- Save the workbook to a network location that allows multiple users to access it at the same time.

To specify options for tracking and updating changes in a shared workbook:

- CLICK: *Advanced* tab in the Share Workbook dialog box
- Specify how long to track changes in the *Track changes* area.
- Specify when to display changes in the *Update changes* area.
- Specify how to deal with change conflicts in the *Conflicting changes between users* area.
- Specify what settings to save in the custom view in the *Include in personal view* area.
- CLICK: OK command button

→ ## Practice

In this lesson, you will open an existing workbook and then share the workbook for network access. Before proceeding, start Microsoft Office Excel 2003.

**1.** Open the data file named EX1110 to display the workbook shown in Figure 11.1. This workbook contains one worksheet form and two worksheet lists.

**Figure 11.1**

Opening the
EX1110
workbook

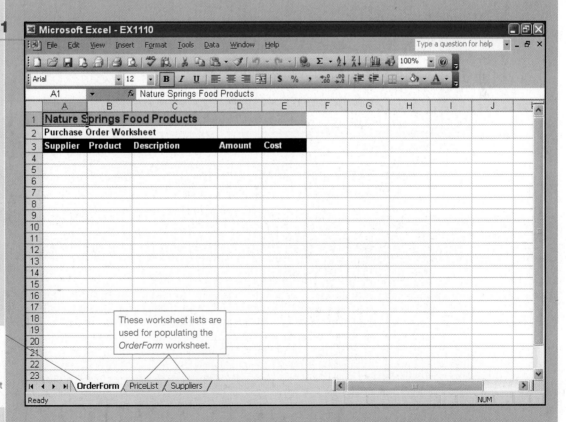

The *OrderForm* worksheet draws data from the *PriceList* and *Suppliers* worksheet lists.

These worksheet lists are used for populating the *OrderForm* worksheet.

**2.** Save the workbook as "Nature Springs" to your personal storage location.

**3.** To allow multiple users to access this workbook on a network server, you need to share it. Do the following:
CHOOSE: Tools → Share Workbook

**4.** On the *Editing* tab of the Share Workbook dialog box:
SELECT: *Allow changes by more than one user . . .* check box

**5.** To specify further options:
CLICK: *Advanced* tab
Your screen should now appear similar to the dialog box shown in Figure 11.2.

**Figure 11.2**

Share Workbook
dialog box:
*Advanced* tab

Select whether to
store a change
history for the
workbook
(recommended).

Select the interval
frequency for
displaying changes
made by other
users.

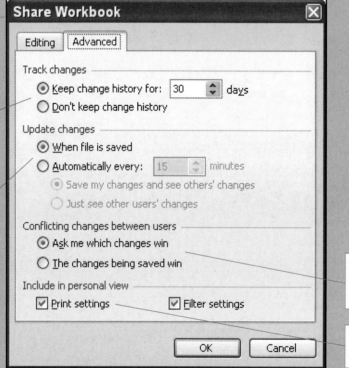

Specify the method for
dealing with change
conflicts between
users.

Specify the settings to
save in the custom
view for each user.

**6.** To track the changes made in the workbook for two weeks:
SELECT: 14 days using the *Keep change history for* spin box

**7.** Leave the remaining default settings selected, as shown in Figure 11.2. Then, to complete the dialog box:
CLICK: OK command button

**8.** When prompted to save the workbook:
CLICK: OK command button
Notice that the word "Shared" now appears between square brackets in the Title bar. (*Note:* At this point, you would use Windows Explorer or another file management tool to transfer or copy the workbook file to a shared location on a network file server. For this module, however, you continue to save the workbook to your personal storage location.)

## 11.1.2 Tracking Changes to a Workbook

→ **Feature**

Shared workbooks are accessible by anyone who has the appropriate network connection and security permissions. For example, product catalogs, price lists, inventory records, and personnel schedules can be stored in workbooks on a central computer and then accessed by all employees in the organization. Although allowing multiple users to modify the same workbook at the same time seems ludicrous, Microsoft Office Excel 2003 actually keeps track of all content changes that are made, including when they are made and by whom. Change tracking does not, however, keep track of formatting changes. In fact, each user's changes are displayed using a unique color for easy identification. Unlike the Undo command for reversing mistakes, Excel 2003's change tracking feature allows you to manage, accept, reject, and merge changes from many users.

By default, Excel 2003 keeps 30 days of change history stored in a shared workbook but you can modify this interval to your own needs. The more information retained, the greater the file size and, therefore, the longer it will take to open and save the workbook. Besides adjusting the change tracking features, you should also specify sheet-level protection. This setting will protect cells containing formulas and prevent users from modifying the workbook's shared and change-tracking status.

→ **Method**

To compile a historical listing of changes:

- CHOOSE: Tools → Track Changes → Highlight Changes
- SELECT: *Track changes while editing* check box
- Specify which changes to highlight and how to display them.
- CLICK: OK command button

To review and then accept or reject the changes one at a time:

- CHOOSE: Tools → Track Changes → Accept or Reject Changes
- Specify which changes to review.
- CLICK: OK command button
- Specify whether to accept or reject each change that appears in the dialog box by clicking the associated command button.

→ **Practice**

Using the shared workbook from the previous lesson, you will now practice setting options for highlighting, accepting, and rejecting changes. Ensure that you have completed the previous lesson and that the "Nature Springs" workbook is displayed.

**1.** Display the *PriceList* worksheet by clicking its sheet tab.

**2.** To ensure that your changes are highlighted in the worksheet:
CHOOSE: Tools → Track Changes → Highlight Changes
Your screen should now appear similar to the dialog box shown in Figure 11.3.

**Figure 11.3**

Highlight
Changes dialog
box

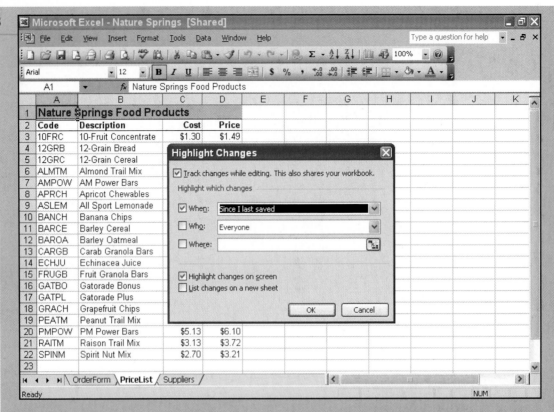

3. Ensure that the *Track changes while editing* check box is selected, as shown in Figure 11.3, and then:
   CLICK: OK command button

4. If a warning dialog box appears stating that no changes were found:
   CLICK: OK command button

5. To adjust a product's cost:
   SELECT: cell C3
   TYPE: 1.52
   PRESS: ENTER
   Notice that a blue triangle, called a *cell indicator,* now appears in the top left-hand corner of the modified cell. Additionally, the row number and column letter in the frame area are highlighted for the modified cell.

6. Move the cell pointer over cell C3 until a ScreenTip appears. Along with the author and date of the change, the comment displays the original and new cell values, as shown in Figure 11.4.

**Figure 11.4**

Tracking changes
in a shared
workbook

A ScreenTip,
colored row
number and
column letter,
triangular cell
indicator, and a cell
outline highlight the
changed cell.

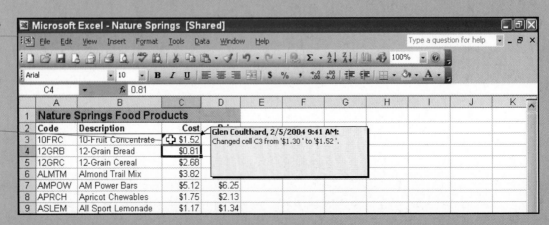

7. Now make another change:
   SELECT: cell D6
   TYPE: 5.10
   PRESS: ENTER
   Notice that the triangular cell indicator appears and that the cell is outlined by a blue border.

8. To save the changes that you have made to the workbook:
   CLICK: Save button (🖫)
   (*Note:* Because the workbook has not been modified by anyone else, the change is accepted without conflict. Notice that the triangle cell indicator and highlighting have been removed from the two cells.)

9. To customize the way Excel 2003 tracks changes:
   CHOOSE: Tools → Track Changes → Highlight Changes

10. To highlight all the changes that are made in the workbook, remove the check marks (✓) from the three filter options. Do the following:
    SELECT: *When* check box so that no ✓ appears
    (*Note:* The triangle cell indicator and highlighting for the two changed cells will now reappear on the *Pricelist* worksheet.)

11. To list the changes in a new *History* worksheet:
    SELECT: *List changes on a new sheet* check box so that a ✓ appears
    CLICK: OK command button
    A new worksheet, named *History,* appears (Figure 11.5) with a listing of the changes that have been made to the workbook.

**Figure 11.5**

*History* worksheet showing tracked changes

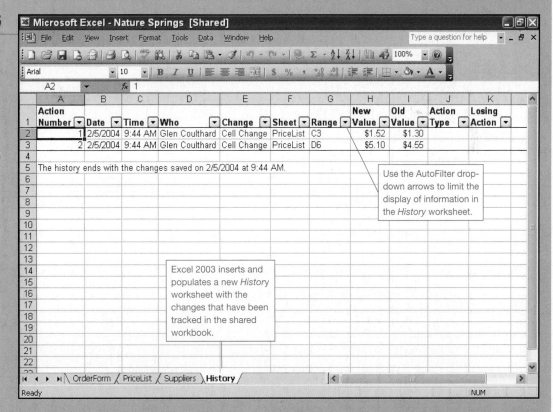

12. After viewing the entries in the *History* worksheet, return to the *PriceList* worksheet:
    CLICK: *PriceList* sheet tab

13. Now let's review the changes made in the workbook one at a time:
    CHOOSE: Tools → Track Changes → Accept or Reject Changes
    The dialog box shown in Figure 11.6 appears.

**Figure 11.6**

Select Changes
to Accept or
Reject dialog box

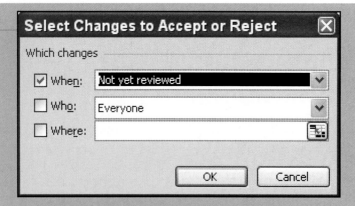

**14.** To view all of the changes:
SELECT: *When* check box so that no ✓ appears
CLICK: OK command button
The first change (cell C3) is highlighted and the Accept or Reject Changes dialog box appears
(Figure 11.7).

**Figure 11.7**

Accept or Reject
Changes dialog
box

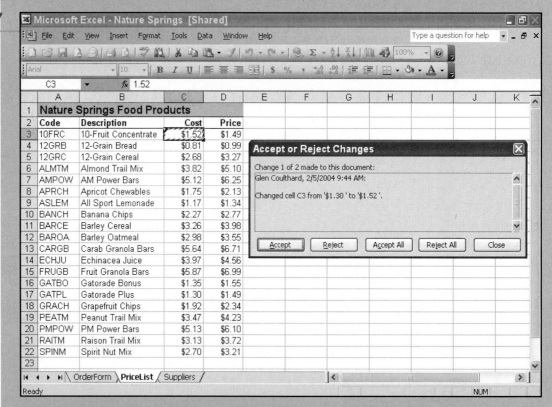

**15.** To reject the first change:
CLICK: Reject command button
The original value is reinstated in cell C3 and the next change (cell D6) is highlighted in the work-
sheet.

**16.** To accept the second change:
CLICK: Accept command button

**17.** Save and then close the "Nature Springs" workbook.

### 11.1.3 Merging Workbook Revisions

→ ## Feature

Accessing a shared workbook on a network server does not always fit well with the situation. Assume, for instance, that you need to take a shared workbook with you to a client's office. After saving the workbook file to a notebook computer, you proceed to update its contents with new data. Now assume that your company has twenty salespeople all performing similar tasks. Fortunately, Microsoft Office Excel 2003 has anticipated such distributed activities in the workplace. For this very reason, Excel 2003 facilitates the process of comparing and merging multiple workbooks into a single comprehensive workbook.

→ ## Method

To merge multiple workbooks:

• Open the workbook into which the changes will be merged.

• CHOOSE: Tools → Compare and Merge Workbooks

• Select the files to merge into the current workbook.

• CLICK: OK command button

→ ## Practice

You will now practice merging changes from three workbooks into a master shared workbook. Ensure that there are no workbooks open in the application window.

**1.** Open the data file named EX1113. Notice the word "Shared" in the Title bar.

**2.** Save the workbook as "Nature Springs PriceList" to your personal storage location.

**3.** You will now merge the changes made in three separate copies of this workbook into the "Nature Springs PriceList" workbook. To begin:
CHOOSE: Tools → Compare and Merge Workbooks
The Select Files to Merge Into Current Workbook dialog box appears.

**4.** Using the *Look in* drop-down list box, select the Advantage student data files location. Then, do the following:
CLICK: EX1113A in the list area
PRESS: CTRL and hold it down
CLICK: EX1113B
CLICK: EX1113C
Your dialog box should appear similar to the one shown in Figure 11.8. (*Note:* Release the CTRL key when the files are selected.)

**Figure 11.8**

Selecting multiple workbook files to compare and merge

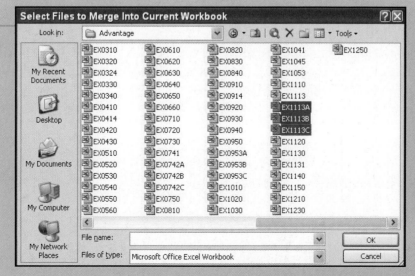

5. CLICK: OK command button to proceed

6. Now review the changes that were made:
CHOOSE: Tools → Track Changes → Accept or Reject Changes
CLICK: OK command button
The first cell change appears in cell C21, as shown in Figure 11.9. As recorded in the Accept or Reject Changes dialog box, the original value ($3.13) was changed first by another user to $2.98 and then by user "Glen Coulthard" to $2.99. (*Note:* The modification in cell C6 may appear first on your screen.)

**Figure 11.9**

Reviewing tracked changes after merging workbooks

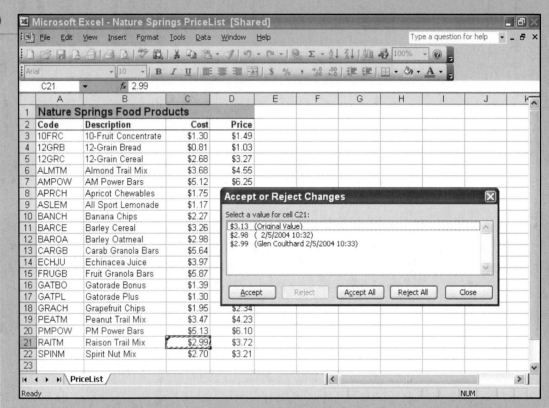

7. To select the modification by user "Glen Coulthard" as correct:
SELECT: $2.99 (Glen Coulthard 2/5/2004 10:33) in the list area
CLICK: Accept command button

8. To accept one of the changes in cell C6:
SELECT: $3.66 ( 2/5/2004 10:32)
CLICK: Accept command button

9. To reject the next two changes:
CLICK: Reject command button to accept the change in cell D11
CLICK: Reject command button to accept the change in cell D13

10. To accept all of the remaining changes:
CLICK: Accept All command button

11. To view a worksheet list of the changes:
CHOOSE: Tools → Track Changes → Highlight Changes

12. In the Highlight Changes dialog box:
SELECT: *When* check box so that no ✓ appears
SELECT: *List changes on a new sheet* check box so that a ✓ appears
CLICK: OK command button
Your screen should now appear similar to the worksheet shown in Figure 11.10.

**Figure 11.10**

Displaying the *History* tracking worksheet

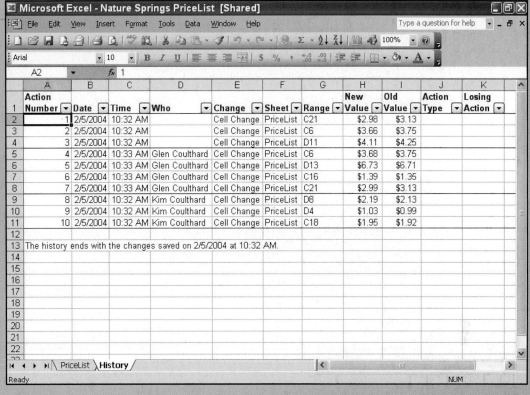

**13.** Save and then close the workbook.

 **SelfCheck**

**11.1** Provide an example of a workbook that would lend itself to being shared, especially for history tracking and merging in a workgroup environment.

# 11.2 Validating Data

Validating data that is entered into a worksheet ensures the reliability and accuracy of a workbook application. In addition to displaying drop-down lists of values, Excel 2003's data validation feature provides helpful prompts and can even warn users when incorrect entries are made. As a workbook developer, it is your job to determine what data is valid by setting a numeric or date range or by comparing an entry to a list of acceptable values. This module presents several techniques for ensuring the completeness and accuracy of data.

## 11.2.1 Applying Conditional Formatting

→ **Feature**

Excel 2003's **conditional formatting** feature allows you to change a cell's appearance (fill color, font color, border, typeface, and font style) based on its value or on a particular condition. Moreover, you can evaluate up to three separate conditions, with each having a different set of formatting options to apply. Conditional formatting is most useful when you need to quickly identify cell values that stray from a standard result, incorporate visual cues based on performance, categorize or group data in worksheet lists, or create your own AutoFormats.

→ ## Method

To apply conditional formatting to the worksheet:

• SELECT: the cell range for conditional formatting

• CHOOSE: Format → Conditional Formatting

• Specify the condition(s) that you want to evaluate.

• SELECT: the formatting to apply if the condition is met

• CLICK: OK command button

→ ## Practice

You will now practice setting conditions and applying formatting options using Excel 2003's conditional formatting feature. Ensure that no workbooks appear in the application window.

**1.** Open the data file named EX1120 to display the workbook shown in Figure 11.11. This workbook contains two worksheets: *Inventory* and *Employees*.

**Figure 11.11**

Opening the EX1120 workbook

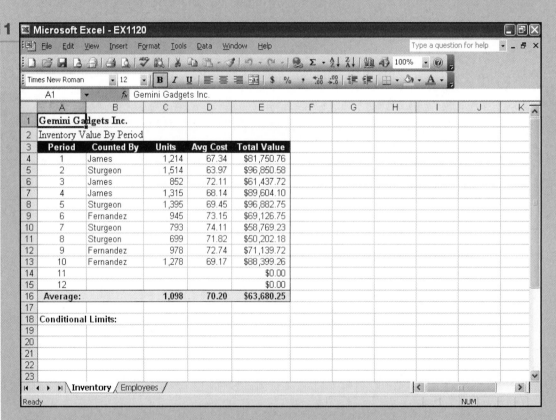

**2.** Save the workbook as "Validate Gemini" to your personal storage location.

**3.** Assume that the Vice President of Operations has asked you to bring to her attention any period where the total inventory value exceeds $85,000. Let's use conditional formatting to facilitate the flagging of these periods. Ensure that the *Inventory* worksheet is selected. Then:
SELECT: cell range from E4 to E15

**4.** CHOOSE: Format → Conditional Formatting
The Conditional Formatting dialog box appears, as shown in Figure 11.12.

**Figure 11.12**

Conditional
Formatting dialog
box

Specify a condition
by first selecting
"Cell Value Is" or
"Formula Is."

Preview the formatting
options selected.

Specify up to three
conditions.

Select the formatting to apply
if the current condition
evaluates to true.

Excel

**5.** There are two methods for specifying conditions. First, select the "Cell Value Is" option when the value that you want to format is also part of the condition to evaluate. For example, you can compare values in the selected range to a constant value or to the contents of a cell. Second, select the "Formula Is" option to test cell values other than the cell that you want to format. This option lets you compare values with an evaluated expression. In this exercise, you know the value, $85,000, that you want to evaluate against the selected range. Therefore:
SELECT: "Cell Value Is" from the leftmost drop-down list box
SELECT: "greater than" from the next drop-down list box
TYPE: 85000 into the rightmost text box

**6.** For all the values in the selected cell range where this condition evaluates to true, you can now specify the formatting attributes:
CLICK: Format command button
The familiar Format Cells dialog box appears.

**7.** On the *Font* tab of the dialog box:
SELECT: Bold from the *Font style* list box
SELECT: Blue from the *Color* drop-down list box
CLICK: OK command button
Your dialog box should now appear similar to the one shown in Figure 11.13.

**Figure 11.13**

Specifying a
condition based
on a cell value

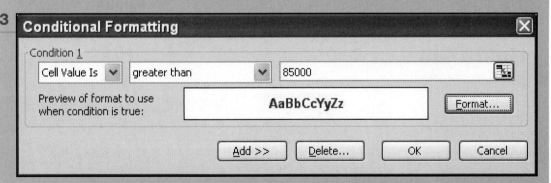

**8.** To complete the Conditional Formatting dialog box:
CLICK: OK command button

**9.** To better see the results:
SELECT: cell E3
Notice the four entries in column E that appear boldface and blue.

**10.** To apply conditional formatting to the Period column based on values appearing in two other columns, you must select a "Formula Is" condition and use the AND function. In this example, you place the limiting values in cells to provide greater flexibility. To begin:
SELECT: cell C18
TYPE: 1200
SELECT: cell D18
TYPE: 68
PRESS: ENTER

**11.** On your own, use the Name box to name cell C18 **MaxUnits** and cell D18 **MaxCost**.

**12.** Your objective is to format a cell in the Period column when its Units value exceeds 1,200 (Max-Units) *and* its Avg Cost value exceeds $68.00 (MaxCost). This task requires two conditions (a logical AND) to be true before the formatting options are applied. To begin:
SELECT: cell range from A4 to A15
CHOOSE: Format → Conditional Formatting

**13.** In the Conditional Formatting dialog box:
SELECT: "Formula Is" from the leftmost drop-down list box

**14.** Enter the formula expression using the AND built-in function:
CLICK: in the adjacent text box
TYPE: **=and(c4>MaxUnits,d4>MaxCost)**
(*Hint:* This condition evaluates to true only if both arguments are true. The first cell address in each argument (c4 and d4) is relative and relates to the first row in the selected range. The named ranges are absolute references to cells C18 and C19 on the worksheet.)

**15.** To specify the formatting options to apply:
CLICK: Format command button
SELECT: Bold from the *Font style* list box
SELECT: White from the *Color* drop-down list box

**16.** Now specify a background color for the cell:
CLICK: *Patterns* tab in the Format Cells dialog box
SELECT: a dark red color in the *Color* area
CLICK: OK command button
Your screen should now appear similar to the dialog box shown in Figure 11.14.

**Figure 11.14**

Specifying a
condition based
on a formula

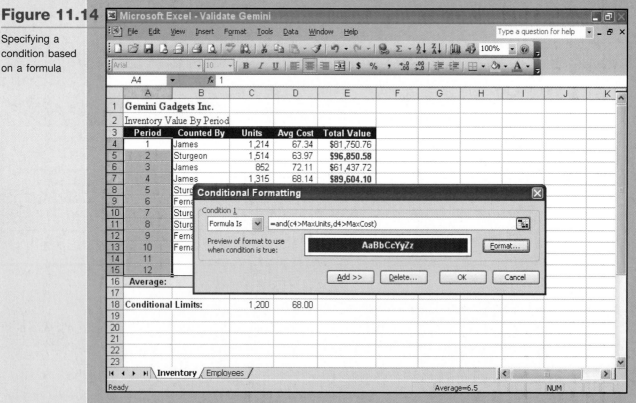

**17.** To complete the dialog box:
CLICK: OK command button

**18.** To view the results:
SELECT: cell A3
Notice that three cells are highlighted in column A of the worksheet. Check the row values to ensure that both the units are greater than 1,200 and the average cost is greater than $68.00.

**19.** To demonstrate the flexibility of using named ranges in specifying conditions:
SELECT: cell C18
TYPE: 800
PRESS: ENTER
Several cells are now highlighted in the worksheet, as shown in Figure 11.15.

**Figure 11.15**

Applying
conditional
formatting to a
worksheet

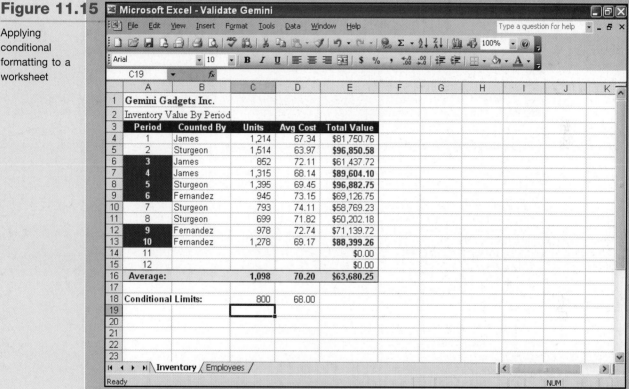

**20.** Save the workbook and keep it open for use in the next lesson.

## 11.2.2 Applying and Removing Validation Rules

## → Feature

Excel 2003's conditional formatting and data validation capabilities work very well together. You can specify acceptable entries in a worksheet list and then format the cells based on a user's selections. In addition to restricting the possible contents of a cell, list validation actually speeds data entry. You can also specify that entries be within a given range of dates or values and limit the number of characters that are typed in a cell. The input and error messages are also appreciated additions when you must create a workbook for other users. Especially for novice users, data validation provides assurances that the data being entered into a worksheet is correct.

→ ## Method

To apply a validation rule to a cell or cell range:

- SELECT: the cell range for data validation
- CHOOSE: Data → Validation
- Specify the validation rules using the *Settings* tab.
- Create a custom ScreenTip message using the *Input Message* tab.
- Create a custom error message using the *Error Alert* tab.
- CLICK: OK command button

To remove a validation rule:

- SELECT: the cell range containing data validation
- CHOOSE: Data → Validation
- CLICK: Clear All command button
- CLICK: OK command button

→ ## Practice

You will now use Excel 2003's data validation features to limit a user from inputting incorrect data. Ensure that you have completed the previous lesson and that the "Validate Gemini" workbook is displayed.

**1.** Let's limit the input of data in the Units column to accept only values less than 2,000. To begin:
SELECT: cell range from C4 to C15

**2.** To define data validation rules:
CHOOSE: Data → Validation
(*Hint:* Validation rules only apply to input cells. You cannot specify a validation rule for a cell containing a formula.)

**3.** On the *Settings* tab of the Data Validation dialog box, specify the acceptable values or validation rules (Figure 11.16). Do the following:
SELECT: Custom from the *Allow* drop-down list box
TYPE: =c4<2000 in the *Formula* text box
Notice that the active cell's relative address (c4) is used so that the data validation criteria will apply to the entire highlighted range.

**Figure 11.16**

Data Validation
dialog box:
*Settings* tab

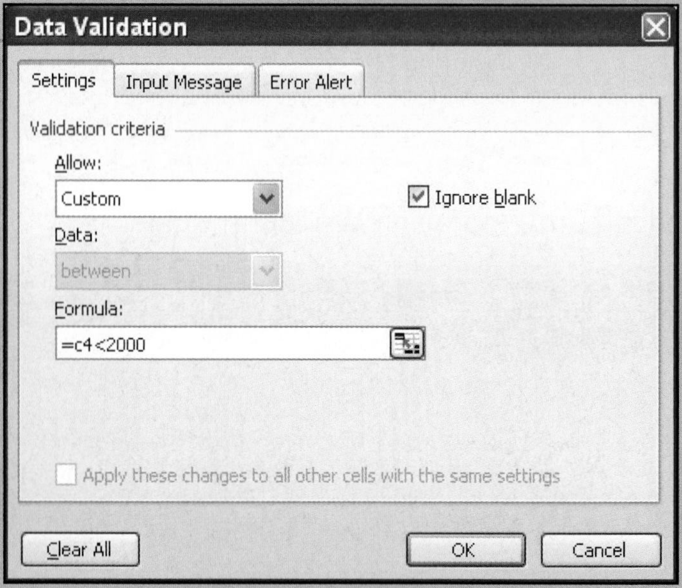

**4.** On the *Input Message* tab, specify a helpful ScreenTip message to display when the user selects one of the highlighted cells:
CLICK: *Input Message* tab
TYPE: **Maximum Inventory Notice** in the *Title* text box
PRESS: TAB
TYPE: **There is only room for 2,000 units in the warehouse.**
The dialog box should now appear similar to the one shown in Figure 11.17.

**Figure 11.17**

Data Validation
dialog box: *Input
Message* tab

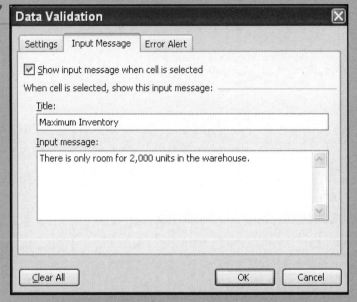

**5.** On the *Error Alert* tab (Figure 11.18), customize the warning dialog box that is displayed for non-conforming entries:
CLICK: *Error Alert* tab
SELECT: Warning from the *Style* drop-down list box
TYPE: **Maximum Inventory Notice** in the *Title* text box
PRESS: TAB
TYPE: **Please enter a value that is less than the warehouse capacity of 2,000 units.**

**Figure 11.18**

Data Validation
dialog box: *Error
Alert* tab

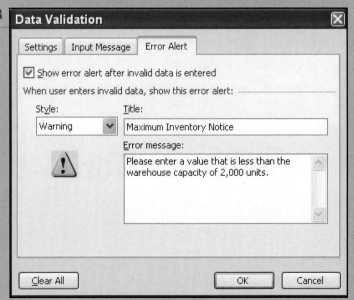

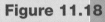

**6.** To complete the dialog box:
CLICK: OK command button
Because the validated range is still selected, a ScreenTip appears in the worksheet area under active cell.

**7.** To remove the ScreenTip from displaying:
SELECT: cell C3

**8.** Now let's test the data validation rule:
SELECT: cell C14
TYPE: 2100
PRESS: ENTER
A warning dialog box appears with the custom message you entered earlier. Your screen should now appear similar to the dialog box shown in Figure 11.19.

**Figure 11.19**

Displaying a custom warning message

Displays the text entered on the *Error Alert* tab of the Data Validation dialog box.

Displays the text entered on the *Input Message* tab of the Data Validation dialog box.

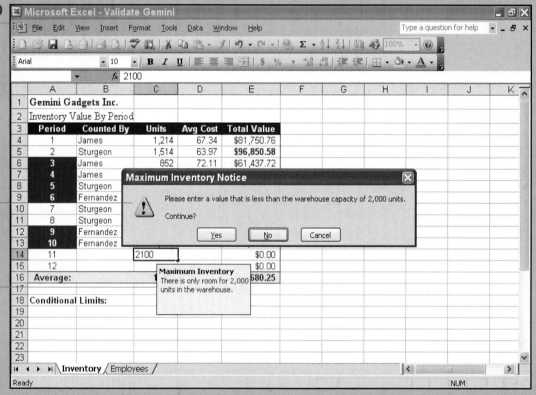

**9.** CLICK: No command button to proceed

**10.** You may now enter a compliant value:
TYPE: 1900
PRESS: ENTER
The entry is accepted and the cell pointer moves to the cell.

**11.** Let's demonstrate how to remove a validation rule from a range:
SELECT: cell range from C4 to C9
CHOOSE: Data → Validation

**12.** In the Data Validation dialog box:
CLICK: Clear All command button to remove all of the settings

**13.** CLICK: OK command button to proceed
Notice that the ScreenTip no longer appears.

**14.** On your own, click between cell C9 and C10. Notice that the validation rule is no longer applied to cell C9.

**15.** Save the workbook and keep it open for use in the next lesson.

### 11.2.3 Finding and Copying Validation Rules

→ **Feature**

Defining and applying data validation rules is an important part of creating workbooks for other people to use. In fact, applying data validation rules to cells often takes place immediately after you finish creating a workbook. You then establish worksheet protection, share the workbook for multiple users to access, save the workbook to a network file server, and maintain your work. This lesson illustrates some helpful features for finding and then copying and pasting data validation rules.

→ **Method**

To locate cells containing data validation settings:

- CHOOSE: Edit → Go To
- CLICK: Special command button
- SELECT: *Data validation* option button
- SELECT: *All* option button for *Data validation*
- CLICK: OK command button
- PRESS: TAB and SHIFT + TAB to cycle through the selected cells

To copy and paste data validation settings:

- SELECT: the source cell with the desired data validation settings
- CLICK: Copy button (⬚)
- SELECT: the target cell
- CHOOSE: Edit → Paste Special
- SELECT: *Validation* option button in the *Paste* area
- CLICK: OK command button

→ **Practice**

You will now use some special commands for finding, copying, and pasting data validation rules. Ensure that the "Validate Gemini" workbook is displayed.

**1.** To begin, move to cell A1.

**2.** To find cells containing a validation rule:
CHOOSE: Edit → Go To
CLICK: Special command button
The Go To Special dialog box appears, as shown in Figure 11.20.

Excel

**Figure 11.20**

Go To Special
dialog box

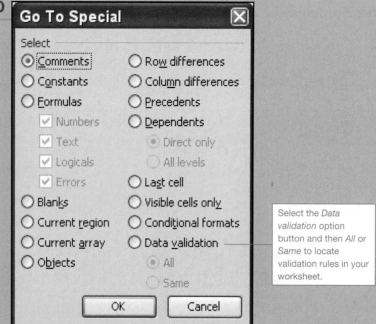

Select the *Data validation* option button and then *All* or *Same* to locate validation rules in your worksheet.

**3.** In the Go To Special dialog box:
SELECT: *Data validation* option button
SELECT: *All* option button
CLICK: OK command button
The cell range from C10 to C15 is identified as containing data validation rules and the range is selected.

**4.** Now let's copy a cell's validation rule to the Clipboard:
SELECT: cell C10
CLICK: Copy button (🖻)

**5.** To apply the copied cell's validation rule to another cell range:
SELECT: cell range from C4 to C9
CHOOSE: Edit → Paste Special
Your screen should now appear similar to the dialog box shown in Figure 11.21.

**Figure 11.21**

Paste Special
dialog box

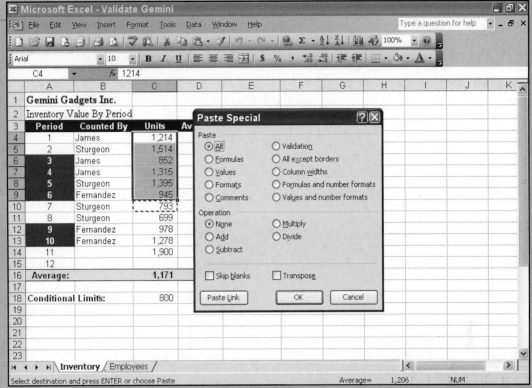

**6.** In the Paste Special dialog box:
SELECT: *Validation* option button in the *Paste* area
CLICK: OK command button

**7.** PRESS: `ESC` to remove the bounding outline

**8.** On your own, click the cells in the range from C4 to C15. Notice that the validation rule is now applied to all the cells in the range.

**9.** Save the workbook and keep it open for use in the next lesson.

## 11.2.4 Using Dynamic Ranges for Data Validation

→ # Feature

Matching a list or range of existing values is an excellent way to validate data. By referencing a *dynamic cell range* on the worksheet, you can provide a changing list of acceptable values. A **dynamic cell range** is one that grows and shrinks automatically as you enter and remove data. You create a dynamic cell range using the INDIRECT and COUNTA functions. The INDIRECT function returns a usable cell reference from a text string, while the COUNTA function counts the number of non-blank cells in a range. In this lesson, you learn how to specify more advanced (and useful) data validation criteria using formula comparisons.

→ # Method

=INDIRECT(*character_string*)
=COUNTA(*cell reference*)

# Practice

You will now use data validation to limit the entry of values to only those records appearing in a worksheet list. Ensure that the "Validate Gemini" workbook is displayed.

**1.** To specify a pick list for entering employees into the Counted By column, you will reference a dynamic cell range on the *Employees* worksheet. To view this worksheet:
CLICK: *Employees* sheet tab
Notice that the first record in the worksheet list appears on row 2 and that the employee last names appear in column C.

**2.** Because the *Employees* worksheet will expand as new employees are hired, you must create a dynamic range reference for the pick list. To begin, display the Define Name dialog box:
CHOOSE: Insert → Name → Define

**3.** Now enter a name for the dynamic range:
TYPE: **EmpNames** in the *Names in workbook* text box

**4.** Select the existing text in the *Refers to* text box at the bottom of the Define Name dialog box. Then, do the following:
TYPE: =indirect("Employees!$C$2:$C$"& counta(Employees!$C:$C))
(*Hint:* Enter this expression on a single line as shown in Figure 11.22.) This formula combines the text "Employees!$C$2:$C$" with the total number of used rows in the *Employees* worksheet, which is calculated using the COUNTA function. The INDIRECT function then converts the resulting text string to a usable cell range address. As employees are added and deleted, the total number of rows will increase and decrease and so will the defined range.

**Figure 11.22**

Creating a dynamic range reference

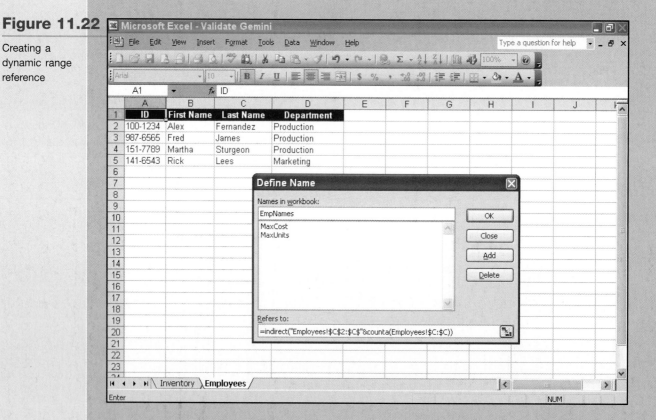

**5.** To complete the range name definition:
CLICK: OK command button

**6.** You can now use the range name as the source for a validation list. Do the following:
CLICK: *Inventory* sheet tab
SELECT: cell range from B4 to B15

**7.** To specify the validation rule:
CHOOSE: Data → Validation
CLICK: *Settings* tab

**8.** To use the dynamic range in a validation rule:
SELECT: List from the *Allow* drop-down list box
TYPE: =EmpNames into the *Source* text box
Notice that an equal sign (=) precedes the range name reference, as shown in Figure 11.23.

**Figure 11.23**

Using a dynamic range in a validation rule

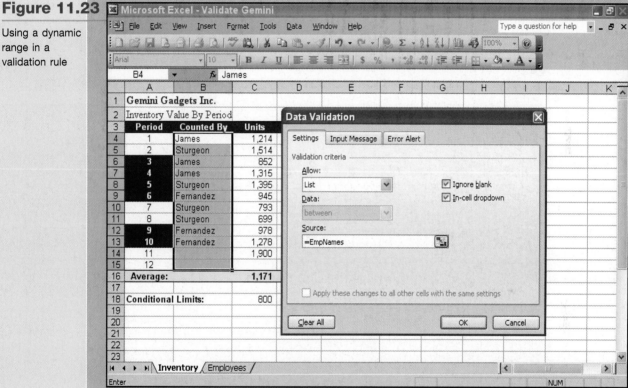

**9.** CLICK: OK command button to proceed

**10.** To test the new validation scenario:
SELECT: cell B14
CLICK: drop-down list arrow attached to the cell
The drop-down list at the right should appear.

**11.** SELECT: "Sturgeon" from the list
Notice that all of the last names from the *Employees* tab are displayed in the list as valid and acceptable entries.

**12.** On your own, enter your name into the next available row on the *Employees* worksheet. Then sort the employee list by last name:
SELECT: cell C1
CLICK: Sort Ascending button ( )

**13.** Use the validation pick list to select your name for input into cell B15 on the *Inventory* worksheet.

**14.** Save and then close the "Validate Gemini" workbook.

**11.2** How could you check whether a customer account code is valid when entering invoice data into a worksheet template?

# 11.3 Auditing a Worksheet

To **audit** a worksheet means to review it for incorrect or suspect entries and formulas. Although conditional formatting and data validation provide some measure of error checking, mistakes can still occur when you construct and use a worksheet. For these instances, Excel 2003 offers several auditing features to assist you in tracking down rogue cells. Microsoft Office Excel 2003 also provides cell indicators and option buttons to assist you in performing error checking. In this module, you learn to use various auditing tools to find errors and graphically display cell dependencies.

## 11.3.1 Identifying Cell Indicators, Option Buttons, and Smart Tags

### → Feature

As you work in Microsoft Office Excel 2003, you may notice triangles and worksheet icons or option buttons appearing in and around cells as you perform data entry and other actions. Color-coded triangles appear in the corners of cells and indicate errors, comments, and smart tags. A green triangle in the upper-left corner of a cell warns you of a possible formula error. Moving the mouse pointer into the cell displays the Error Checking Options button (⬦), which is also known as the Trace Error button. A red triangle in the upper-right corner of cell informs you that a comment is attached. When you move the mouse pointer over the cell, text is displayed in a comment box. A purple triangle in the lower-right corner represents a *smart tag*—data that is recognized by Microsoft Office Excel 2003 for tagging, such as a stock symbol. Office 2003's **smart tags** enable you to perform tasks, such as retrieving information from the Internet, that would normally require multiple actions to execute. Move the mouse pointer over the smart tag to display the Smart Tag Actions button (⬛). Then, click the button to display a context-sensitive menu of actions that you can perform.

There are other options buttons that you may encounter. The Paste Options (📋), AutoFill Options (🔲), and Insert Options (🖊) buttons appear next to pasted, filled, or inserted selections. Depending on the task, these buttons provide commands for formatting and filling the selection. The AutoCorrect Options button (🖼), on the other hand, first appears as a small blue box next to a cell. When you point to it, the button appears to display a list of menu commands for reversing an AutoCorrect entry or for toggling the feature on and off.

### → Method

When a triangle indicator appears:

• Select the cell or move the mouse pointer over the cell to display the options button.

• CLICK: the options button

• CHOOSE: the desired command

To turn on the smart tags feature:

• CHOOSE: Tools → AutoCorrect Options

• CLICK: *Smart Tags* tab in the AutoCorrect dialog box

• SELECT: *Label data with smart tags* check box so that a ✓ appears

• SELECT: the data you want to recognize in the *Recognizers* list box

→ **Practice**

You will now practice using cell indicators, option buttons, and smart tags. Ensure that no workbooks appear in the application window.

**1.** Open the data file named EX1131 to display the workbook shown in Figure 11.24.

**Figure 11.24**

Opening the EX1131 workbook

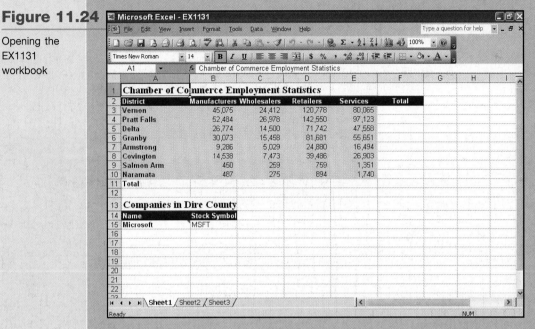

**2.** Save the workbook as "Dire County" to your personal storage location.

**3.** To demonstrate the display and use of option buttons, you will now edit this worksheet:
SELECT: cell F3
CLICK: AutoSum button ([Σ ▾])
PRESS: **ENTER**
The result, 270,330, appears in cell F3.

**4.** Now use the cell's fill handle to copy the formula down to row 10:
SELECT: cell F3
DRAG: its fill handle down to cell F10
When you release the mouse button, the range is filled with formula results and the AutoFill Options button appears, as shown here.

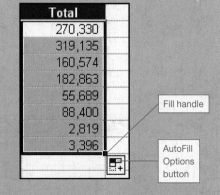

**5.** To display the menu choices for filling a range using the fill handle:
CLICK: AutoFill Options button
The menu shown below appears. By selecting the Fill Formatting Only command, you can use the fill handle to copy only the formatting of a selected range, similar to using the Format Painter toolbar button. The Fill Without Formatting command copies a cell's contents but not the formatting.

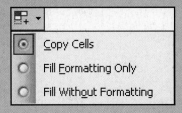

**6.** Since the default menu choice "Copy Cells" is the desired effect, let's cancel the menu from displaying:
CLICK: AutoFill Options button again

**7.** Use the AutoSum feature to sum the entire bottom row:
SELECT: cell range from B11 to F11
CLICK: AutoSum button ($\Sigma$ ·)

**8.** Let's insert an entry above "Vernon" in row 3. To begin:
SELECT: row 3 by clicking its number in the row frame area

**9.** CHOOSE: Insert → Rows
Microsoft Office Excel 2003 assumes that the formatting from row 2 should be applied to the new row, as shown in Figure 11.25. However, it also displays the Insert Options button in case this is not the desired effect.

**Figure 11.25**

Using the Insert Option button

When you insert a new row, the formatting from the topmost row is applied to the new row. The Insert Options button appears to speed the process of changing this formatting assumption.

| | A | B | C | D | E | F | G | H | I |
|---|---|---|---|---|---|---|---|---|---|
| 1 | **Chamber of Commerce Employment Statistics** | | | | | | | | |
| 2 | **District** | **Manufacturers** | **Wholesalers** | **Retailers** | **Services** | **Total** | | | |
| 3 | | | | | | | | | |
| 4 | Vernon | 45,075 | 24,412 | 120,778 | 80,065 | 270,330 | | | |
| 5 | Pratt Falls | 52,484 | 26,978 | 142,550 | 97,123 | 319,135 | | | |
| 6 | Delta | 26,774 | 14,500 | 71,742 | 47,558 | 160,574 | | | |
| 7 | Granby | 30,073 | 15,458 | 81,681 | 55,651 | 182,863 | | | |
| 8 | Armstrong | 9,286 | 5,029 | 24,880 | 16,494 | 55,689 | | | |
| 9 | Covington | 14,538 | 7,473 | 39,486 | 26,903 | 88,400 | | | |
| 10 | Salmon Arm | 450 | 259 | 759 | 1,351 | 2,819 | | | |
| 11 | Naramata | 487 | 275 | 894 | 1,740 | 3,396 | | | |
| 12 | Total | 179,167 | 94,384 | 482,770 | 326,885 | 1,083,206 | | | |
| 13 | | | | | | | | | |
| 14 | **Companies in Dire County** | | | | | | | | |
| 15 | **Name** | **Stock Symbol** | | | | | | | |
| 16 | Microsoft | MSFT | | | | | | | |
| 17 | | | | | | | | | |
| 18 | | | | | | | | | |
| 19 | | | | | | | | | |
| 20 | | | | | | | | | |
| 21 | | | | | | | | | |
| 22 | | | | | | | | | |

Sheet1 / Sheet2 / Sheet3 /

**10.** To change the formatting to match the green district rows:
CLICK: Insert Options button to display the menu shown below
CHOOSE: Format Same As Below

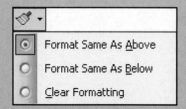

- ● Format Same As Above
- ○ Format Same As Below
- ○ Clear Formatting

**11.** To cancel the row selection:
CLICK: cell A18

**12.** You may have noticed a red cell indicator attached to cell A16. To display its comment, move the mouse pointer over the cell. (*Hint:* For lessons on creating, editing, and formatting comments, refer to module 7.5 in Chapter 7 of this guide.)

**13.** By default, the smart tags feature is turned off in Microsoft Office Excel 2003. To turn on the smart tags feature:
CHOOSE: Tools → AutoCorrect Options
CLICK: *Smart Tags* tab
Your screen should now appear similar to the dialog box shown in Figure 11.26.

**Figure 11.26**

Auto correct dialog box: *Smart Tags* tab

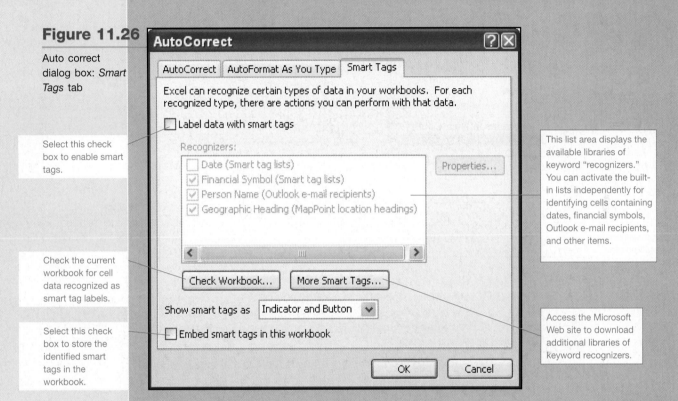

Select this check box to enable smart tags.

Check the current workbook for cell data recognized as smart tag labels.

Select this check box to store the identified smart tags in the workbook.

This list area displays the available libraries of keyword "recognizers." You can activate the built-in lists independently for identifying cells containing dates, financial symbols, Outlook e-mail recipients, and other items.

Access the Microsoft Web site to download additional libraries of keyword recognizers.

**14.** Turn on the smart tags feature and ensure that the identified smart tags are saved in the workbook:
SELECT: *Label data with smart tags* check box
SELECT: *Embed smart tags in this workbook* check box

**15.** Now check the workbook for existing smart tags:
CLICK: Check Workbook command button

**16.** You are returned to the worksheet and a confirmation dialog box is displayed. Do the following:
CLICK: OK command button to proceed
Notice that cell B16 displays a purple smart tag cell indicator.

**17.** To display the menu of choices for the identified smart tag, position the mouse pointer over cell B16 and then:
CLICK: its Smart Tag Actions button (⊙)
Your screen should now appear similar to the worksheet shown in Figure 11.27.

**Figure 11.27**

Displaying the
Smart Tag
Actions menu

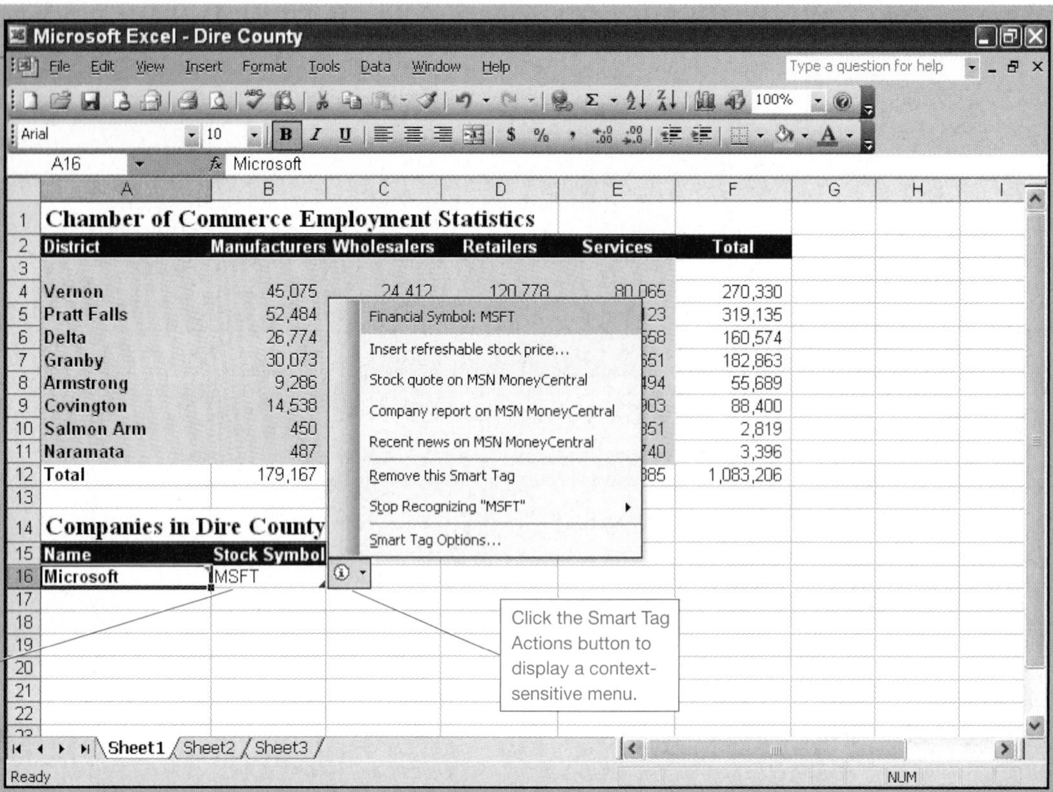

Click the Smart Tag
Actions button to
display a context-
sensitive menu.

"MSFT" is
recognized as a
stock symbol and
labeled with a smart
tag cell indicator.

**18.** Establish a connection to the Internet and then:
CHOOSE: Insert refreshable stock price from the popup menu
(*Note:* If you do not have Internet access, click the Smart Tag Actions button again to remove the
menu and proceed to step 20.)

**19.** In the Insert Stock Price dialog box that appears, ensure that the *On a new sheet* option button
is selected and then:
CLICK: OK command button
Your screen should now appear similar, but not identical, to the worksheet shown in Figure
11.28. You can refresh the stock information using the External Data toolbar or customize the
External Data Range Properties to specify a time interval for refreshing the data automatically.
(*Hint:* Refer to Chapter 10 for more information on importing data from external sources and the
Web.)

**Figure 11.28**

Retrieving stock information from the Web using a smart tag

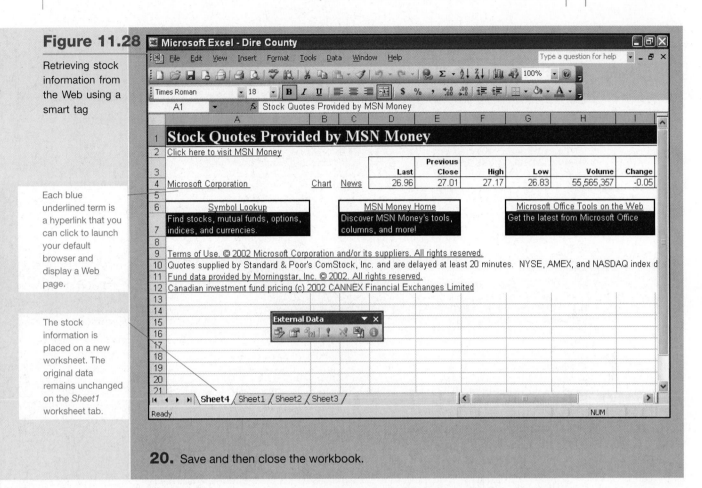

Each blue underlined term is a hyperlink that you can click to launch your default browser and display a Web page.

The stock information is placed on a new worksheet. The original data remains unchanged on the *Sheet1* worksheet tab.

**20.** Save and then close the workbook.

Displaying a refreshable stock quote is only one example of retrieving external data using the *MSN Money-Central Financial Symbol* smart tags. Assuming that you have an Internet connection, you can perform a variety of actions, such as displaying recent news stories in your Web browser and retrieving a detailed Web page of company information. You can also use smart tags to copy and paste contact information, such as addresses and phone numbers, between Microsoft Office 2003 applications and your Outlook Contacts address book. Additionally, independent developers are creating custom smart tag libraries to facilitate information retrieval from intranet and Internet servers worldwide.

### *In Addition* WHERE CAN I FIND MORE SMART TAGS?

You can get additional smart tags by visiting Microsoft's Web site. On the *Smart Tags* tab of the Auto-Correct dialog box, click the More Smart Tags command button to launch the default Web browser. A Web page appears with links to third party companies that have prepared custom libraries of recognizers. At the time of this writing, some of the featured libraries include Expedia smart tags for generating travel searches from destination names, ESPN smart tags for retrieving statistics for baseball teams and their players, and vertical solutions for the insurance and investment services industries.

## 11.3.2 Locating Invalid Data Using the Formula Auditing Toolbar

→ **Feature**

The Formula Auditing toolbar provides access to several helpful auditing tools. Especially useful when you have specified data validation rules, the Formula Auditing toolbar can pinpoint non-conforming cells by placing red circles around them on the worksheet. You can also use Excel 2003's auditing features to graphically display and trace the relationships between cells and formulas in an unprotected worksheet. These tools are indispensable for troubleshooting and resolving errors.

→ **Method**

To use the Formula Auditing toolbar with data validation:

• CHOOSE: Tools → Formula Auditing → Show Formula Auditing Toolbar

• CLICK: Circle Invalid Data button (⊞) to highlight values that do not comply with the validation rules

• CLICK: Clear Validation Circles button (⊞) to remove the red validation circles from the worksheet

→ **Practice**

You will now use the Formula Auditing toolbar to perform error checking and highlight those values that do not comply with the specified validation rules. Ensure that no workbooks appear in the application window.

**1.** Open the data file named EX1130 to display the workbook shown in Figure 11.29. This workbook contains two worksheets: *Inventory* and *Production*. On the *Inventory* worksheet, conditional formatting and data validation rules have been imposed for the Units and Avg Cost columns, according to the maximum limits presented in row 18.

**Figure 11.29**

Opening the
EX1130
workbook

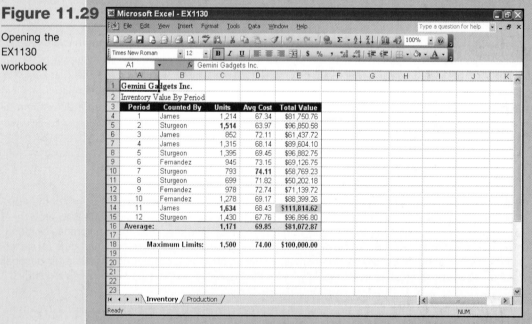

**2.** Save the workbook as "Audit Gemini" to your personal storage location.

**3.** To display the Formula Auditing toolbar:
CHOOSE: Tools → Formula Auditing → Show Formula Auditing Toolbar
Figure 11.30 labels each of the buttons in the Formula Auditing toolbar.

**Figure 11.30**

Formula Auditing
toolbar

**4.** You will now execute a command that highlights the entries that do not comply with the validation rules specified in the worksheet. On the Formula Auditing toolbar:
CLICK: Circle Invalid Data button (⊞)
Red circles are drawn around the cells that contain values greater than the maximum values specified in row 18. Your screen should now appear similar to the worksheet shown in Figure 11.31.

**Figure 11.31**

Auditing a
worksheet for
noncomplying
values

Because this value
does not comply
with the data
validation rule
specified, it
appears highlighted
using a red auditing
circle.

| | A | B | C | D | E |
|---|---|---|---|---|---|
| 1 | Gemini Gadgets Inc. | | | | |
| 2 | Inventory Value By Period | | | | |
| 3 | Period | Counted By | Units | Avg Cost | Total Value |
| 4 | 1 | James | 1,214 | 67.34 | $81,750.76 |
| 5 | 2 | Sturgeon | 1,514 | 63.97 | $96,850.58 |
| 6 | 3 | James | 852 | 72.11 | $61,437.72 |
| 7 | 4 | James | 1,315 | 68.14 | $89,604.10 |
| 8 | 5 | Sturgeon | 1,395 | 69.45 | $96,882.75 |
| 9 | 6 | Fernandez | 945 | 73.15 | $69,126.75 |
| 10 | 7 | Sturgeon | 793 | 74.11 | $58,769.23 |
| 11 | 8 | Sturgeon | 699 | 71.82 | $50,202.18 |
| 12 | 9 | Fernandez | 978 | 72.74 | $71,139.72 |
| 13 | 10 | Fernandez | 1,278 | 69.17 | $88,399.26 |
| 14 | 11 | James | 1,634 | 68.43 | $111,814.62 |
| 15 | 12 | Sturgeon | 1,430 | 67.76 | $96,896.80 |
| 16 | Average: | | 1,171 | 69.85 | $81,072.87 |
| 17 | | | | | |
| 18 | | Maximum Limits: | 1,500 | 74.00 | $100,000.00 |

Formula Auditing toolbar

**5.** Together with conditional formatting, the red circles overlaid on the worksheet enable you to pin-
point the noncomplying cell values. Let's correct one of the errant values:
SELECT: cell C14
TYPE: **1400**
PRESS: **ENTER**
The conditional formatting and the red circle disappear.

**6.** Now let's adjust the maximum limit:
SELECT: cell C18
TYPE: **1200**
PRESS: **ENTER**
The conditional formatting is dynamically refreshed, but the auditing circles are not.

**7.** To reapply the auditing circles:
CLICK: Circle Invalid Data button (⊞)

**8.** To remove the circles from the worksheet:
CLICK: Clear Validation Circles button (⊞)

**9.** To remove the Formula Auditing toolbar:
CLICK: its Close button (✕)

**10.** Save the workbook and keep it open for use in the next lesson.

### 11.3.3 Tracing Precedents and Dependents

→ **Feature**

Auditing a worksheet refers to the process of finding errors and identifying relationships between cells in a worksheet. For example, searching for the cells that are referred to in a specific formula is called **tracing precedents**. Searching for the formulas that reference a particular cell is called **tracing dependents**. During an audit, blue lines, called **tracer arrows**, are displayed on the worksheet showing the cell relationships. Excel 2003 also displays red tracer arrows to help you find cell locations that contain error values. These tracer arrows point from the cell causing the error to the cell containing the error.

→ **Method**

To trace precedents:

- CHOOSE: Tools → Formula Auditing → Trace Precedents

  *or*

- CLICK: Trace Precedents button (⊞) on the Formula Auditing toolbar

To trace dependents:

- CHOOSE: Tools → Formula Auditing → Trace Dependents

  *or*

- CLICK: Trace Dependents button (⊞) on the Formula Auditing toolbar

To remove tracer arrows from the worksheet:

- CLICK: Remove Precedent Arrows button (⊞) to remove only the precedent tracer arrows
- CLICK: Remove Dependent Arrows button (⊞) to remove only the dependent tracer arrows
- CLICK: Remove All Arrows button (⊞) to remove all tracer arrows

→ **Practice**

You will now practice tracing cell precedents and cell dependents using the Formula Auditing toolbar. Ensure that the "Audit Gemini" workbook is displayed.

**1.** To begin, display the *Production* worksheet and review the contents:
CLICK: *Production* sheet tab
(*Note:* The S:P column of calculations (column F) display a Sales-to-Production ratio.)

**2.** The cells that supply data to a formula are called *precedents*. To trace precedents, you must first select a cell containing a formula:
SELECT: cell F4

**3.** Now display the Formula Auditing toolbar:
CHOOSE: Tools → Formula Auditing → Show Formula Auditing Toolbar

**4.** To trace the formula's precedents:
CLICK: Trace Precedents button (⊞) on the Formula Auditing toolbar
As shown in Figure 11.32, a blue tracer arrow (there are actually two tracer arrows overlaid one on top of the other) appears with two end points (circles) denoting the source cells for the formula calculation.

**Figure 11.32**

Tracing
precedents for a
formula

Each circle endpoint
shows a cell that
provides precedent
information for the
selected formula.

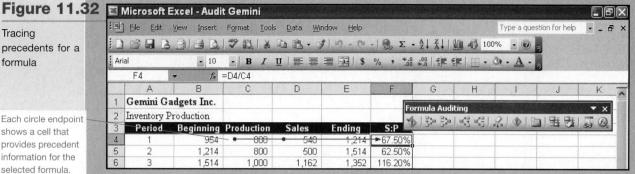

5. To begin a new tracing exercise, select another cell containing a formula. Do the following:
SELECT: cell E6

6. To identify the formula's immediate precedents:
CLICK: Trace Precedents button ()
Notice that three cells are required in the formula calculation.

7. To identify any associated precedents, you can click the Trace Precedent button two times for the same cell. To illustrate:
CLICK: Trace Precedents button () again
Notice that another blue tracer arrow appears from E5 to B6. In other words, cell B6 is reliant on cell E5 for its value. Your screen should now appear similar to the worksheet shown in Figure 11.33.

**Figure 11.33**

Tracing
immediate and
associated
precedents

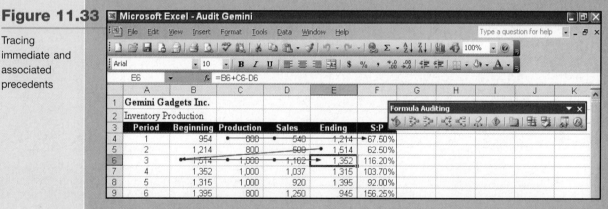

8. To remove the tracer arrows one at a time, you can click the Remove Precedent Arrows button (). To remove all tracer arrows:
CLICK: Remove All Arrows button ()

9. The formulas that reference other cells are called *dependents*. To trace dependents, first select a cell that is referenced in a formula:
SELECT: cell C13

10. To trace the cell's dependents (the cells dependent on its value):
CLICK: Trace Dependents button ()
Following the blue tracer arrows shown in Figure 11.34, notice that the cell is used in three formula calculations.

## Figure 11.34

Tracing dependents in a worksheet

Each arrowhead endpoint shows a cell that is dependent on the selected cell for information.

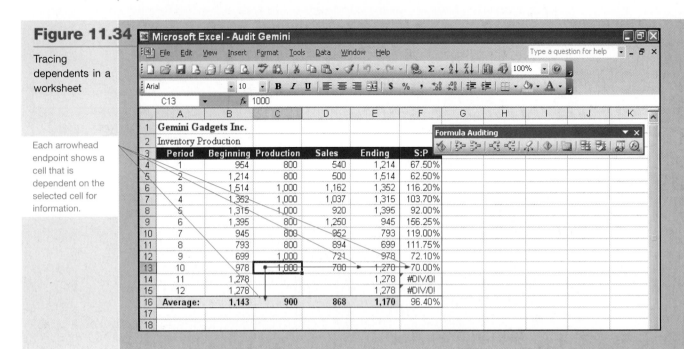

11. To remove all of the tracer arrows and the Formula Auditing toolbar:
 CLICK: Remove All Arrows button ([🔲])
 CLICK: Close button ([✕]) on the Formula Auditing toolbar

12. Save the workbook and keep it open for use in the next lesson.

## 11.3.4 Locating Errors in Formulas

### → Feature

Like a grammar checker, the formula error checker follows specific rules in checking a cell's contents for calculation errors. The most obvious error arises when a formula evaluates to an error value, such as #DIV/0!, N/A, #NAME?, or #VALUE!. A less obvious error arises when numbers are stored as text and not values, usually a result of importing data from an external data source. Besides examining formulas for inconsistent or omitted cell references, the error checker notes cell references that are empty. Finally, the error checker notes whether a cell containing a formula is locked and protected or unlocked. If an error is found, a green triangle indicator appears in the upper-left corner of a cell and the Error Checking Options button ([◈]) appears when the mouse pointer moves over the cell. Regardless of your current position in a worksheet, the **Watch Window**, which is more accurately a toolbar, allows you to display the values and formulas stored in one or more cells.

### → Method

To perform error-checking on a worksheet:

• CHOOSE: Tools → Error Checking

 or

• CLICK: Error Checking button ([◈]) on the Formula Auditing toolbar

To view formula dependencies using tracer arrows:

• CHOOSE: Tools → Formula Auditing → Trace Error

 or

• CLICK: Trace Error button ([◈]) on the Formula Auditing toolbar

To evaluate a formula and locate errors:

• CHOOSE: Tools → Formula Auditing → Evaluate Formula

  *or*

• CLICK: Evaluate Formula button (⬚) on the Formula Auditing toolbar

To toggle the display of the Watch Window:

• CHOOSE: Tools → Formula Auditing → Show/Hide Watch Window

  *or*

• CLICK: Show Watch Window button (⬚) on the Formula Auditing toolbar

→ **Practice**

You will now practice tracing errors using the Formula Auditing toolbar. Ensure that the "Audit Gemini" workbook is displayed.

**1.** PRESS: CTRL + HOME to move to the top of the worksheet

**2.** You may have noticed that two green cell indicators appear in cells F14 and F15. These indicators inform you that errors exist in the cells. To begin error-checking the worksheet:
CHOOSE: Tools → Error Checking
The error-checking command immediately selects cell F14 and displays the dialog box shown in Figure 11.35. (*Hint:* For similar functionality, select a cell with a green indicator and then click the Error Checking Options button (⬚) that appears.)

**Figure 11.35**

Error Checking dialog box

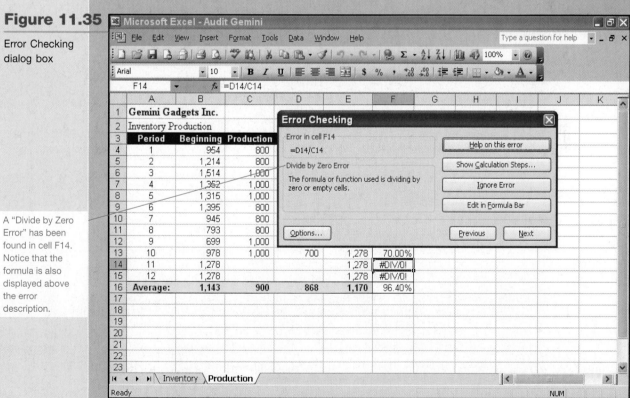

A "Divide by Zero Error" has been found in cell F14. Notice that the formula is also displayed above the error description.

**3.** To evaluate the formula and locate the error:
CLICK: Show Calculation Steps command button
The Evaluate Formula dialog box appears, as shown in Figure 11.36.

**Figure 11.36**

Evaluate Formula dialog box

The next expression to be evaluated is shown in the *Evaluation* area.

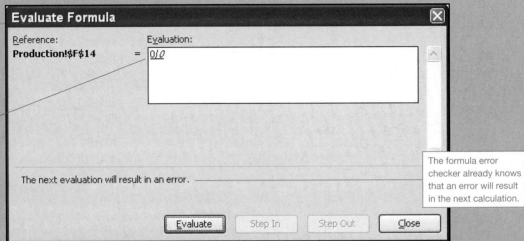

Evaluate Formula

Reference:                    Evaluation:
**Production!$F$14**      =  0/0

The formula error checker already knows that an error will result in the next calculation.

The next evaluation will result in an error.

[Evaluate]   [Step In]   [Step Out]   [Close]

**4.** CLICK: Evaluate command button to proceed
As expected, the #DIV/0! error results from the calculation and is displayed in the Evaluate Formula dialog box.

**5.** To proceed:
CLICK: Close command button

**6.** In the Error Checking dialog box:
CLICK: [Next >] to move to the next error
Notice that the same error is displayed in the dialog box for cell F15.

**7.** If the error is an expected result, you can click the Ignore Error command button to ignore the errors and proceed. If, however, you need to fix the error, click the Edit in Formula Bar command button in order to make your modifications. For additional practice, let's close the Error Checking dialog box and proceed manually:
CLICK: Close button (✕) on the dialog box

**8.** SELECT: cell F14
Notice the Error Checking Options button (⬦) that appears. (*Hint:* If you hover the mouse pointer over the button, a ScreenTip displays the possible error.)

**9.** When you find a cell containing an error, use the Trace Error command to draw tracer arrows to the active cell from the cells causing the error. For example, let's trace the origin of the "#DIV/0!" error appearing in the current worksheet:
CHOOSE: Tools → Formula Auditing → Trace Error
The two cells involved in the calculation are highlighted. (*Hint:* You can also display the Formula Auditing toolbar and then click the Trace Error button (⬦) to show the dependencies.)

**10.** For additional information, you will now use Excel 2003's Watch Window—an excellent tool for debugging errors. To begin:
CHOOSE: Tools → Formula Auditing → Show Formula Auditing Toolbar

**11.** Now open the Watch Window:
CLICK: Show Watch Window button (⬚)

**12.** To add two formulas to the Watch Window:
RIGHT-CLICK: cell F14
CHOOSE: Add Watch
RIGHT-CLICK: cell F15
CHOOSE: Add Watch
(*Note:* You can also click the Add Watch command button in the Watch Window and then specify the cells containing formulas to watch.)

**13.** On your own, drag the borderlines in the column frame area so that the Watch Window appears similar to the one shown in Figure 11.37.

**Figure 11.37**

Displaying the Watch Window

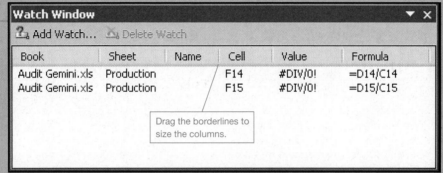

**14.** Now edit some cells in the worksheet:
SELECT: cell C15
TYPE: 800
PRESS: ➡
TYPE: 600
PRESS: ENTER
As shown in Figure 11.38, the Watch Window is updated to display the formula and its calculated result. Notice that the cell indicator no longer appears in cell F15.

**Figure 11.38**

Tracing calculation errors using the Watch Window

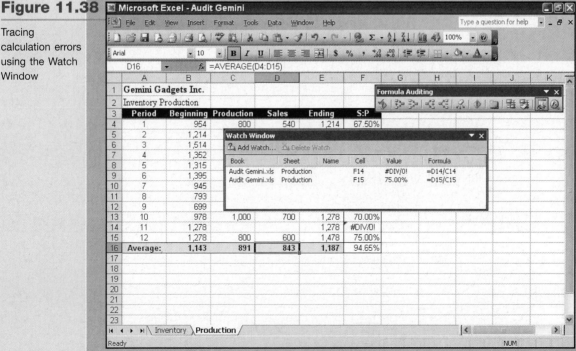

**15.** To remove the formula from the Watch Window:
RIGHT-CLICK: cell F15
CHOOSE: Delete Watch
(*Note:* You can also select the formula in the Watch Window and click the Delete Watch command button in its toolbar.)

**16.** To clean up the work area:
CLICK: Close button (☒) for the Watch Window
CLICK: Close button (☒) on the Formula Auditing toolbar

**17.** Save the workbook and keep it open for use in the next lesson.

### 11.3.5 Preventing Calculation Errors

→ **Feature**

Excel 2003 provides several "IS" functions that you may use to test for the existence of labels, values, and errors in a worksheet. For example, when you need to ensure that a number appears in a cell before performing a calculation, use the ISBLANK and ISNUMBER functions to test for the existence and data type of an entry. When you need to suppress the display of errors in a worksheet, use the ISERROR function to ensure that a formula's result is acceptable. For best results, consider nesting the IS functions within an IF function, so that you can provide alternative actions or helpful messages for the user.

→ **Method**

=ISBLANK(*cell_address* or *value*)
=ISERROR(*cell_address* or *value*)
=ISNUMBER(*cell_address* or *value*)
=ISTEXT(*cell_address* or *value*)

→ **Practice**

You will now practice nesting an IS function inside an IF function to suppress errors in a worksheet. Ensure that the "Audit Gemini" workbook is displayed.

**1.** To demonstrate how you can catch errors before they occur, let's enter a replacement formula for one of the cells in the S:P column:
SELECT: cell F14
Notice that the formula reads "=D14/C14" in the Formula bar.

**2.** Your objective is to display the acronym "TBA" for "To Be Announced," in place of the error message "#DIV/0!." To begin:
TYPE: **=if(**

**3.** To display the Function Arguments dialog box:
CLICK: Insert Function button (*fx*)

**4.** In the *Logical_test* text box:
TYPE: **iserror(d14/c14)**
PRESS: **TAB**
This function returns "TRUE" if an error results from the expression argument in the parentheses.

**5.** To complete the Formula Palette:
TYPE: **"TBA"** (including the quotation marks)
PRESS: **TAB**
TYPE: **d14/c14**
PRESS: **TAB**
(*Note:* Press the final **TAB** only to display the result of the "d14/c14" expression in the dialog box.) The Function Arguments dialog box should now appear similar to the one shown in Figure 11.39.

**Figure 11.39**

Nesting an
ISERROR
function within an
IF function

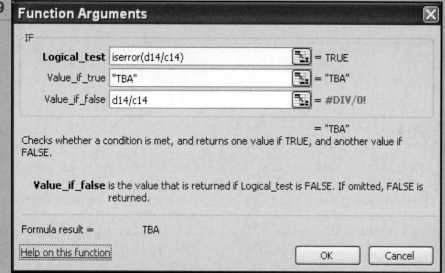

6. CLICK: OK command button to proceed
   The acronym "TBA" now appears in the cell.

7. To test the new function:
   SELECT: cell C14
   TYPE: **750**
   PRESS: ➡
   TYPE: **500**
   PRESS: [ENTER]
   The formula result in cell F14 is now 66.67%.

8. You may have noticed that the green cell indicator still appears in cell F14. In order to ignore this error, display the error checking options:
   SELECT: cell F14
   CLICK: Error Checking Options button (⟨◇⟩)
   The menu shown below should now appear. Notice that the commands are similar to the options available in the Error Checking dialog box.

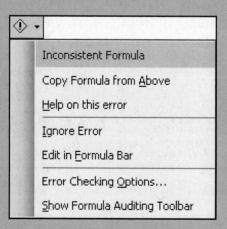

9. The menu appears with the title "Inconsistent Formula." Since we already know that this formula is inconsistent:
   CHOOSE: Ignore Error
   The cell indicator no longer appears in the cell.

10. Save and then close the "Audit Gemini" workbook.

**11.3** What result occurs by clicking the Trace Precedents button (⊞) or the Trace Dependents button (⊞) twice on the Formula Auditing toolbar?

# 11.4 Automating a Workbook

Many spreadsheet tasks are repetitive, such as enhancing cell ranges, creating summary reports, or printing worksheets. Fortunately, Excel 2003 has assigned most of these monotonous tasks to toolbar buttons and "Auto" commands. However, there are still tasks that you will have to perform over and over again that are not included as buttons on a toolbar. For these activities, Excel 2003 allows you to store and play back keystrokes and commands. In addition to saving you an enormous amount of time, these stored instructions, called **macros,** also improve the consistency and accuracy of repetitive procedures. Using a macro, you can execute a sequence of instructions by simply clicking a button, pressing a key combination, or selecting a name from a list box.

By incorporating macros into your workbook applications, you make it easier to use for yourself and for others. Any procedures you perform repeatedly are perfectly suited for macros. A few examples might include consolidating data from multiple workbooks; inserting your company logo and address at the top of a worksheet; and performing a year-end roll-over of accounting data. Instead of having to remember all of the steps required to perform such procedures, with macros you only have to remember a few simple keystrokes or which button to click. Furthermore, you can use macros to automate complicated or time-consuming procedures for personnel who are not familiar with using spreadsheets. This module leads you through recording and editing simple macros.

## 11.4.1 Recording a Macro

→ **Feature**

Microsoft Office Excel 2003 and the other Office 2003 applications share a common programming language, called **Visual Basic for Applications (VBA),** for writing macros. If the word "programming" makes you a little nervous, you can relax. Excel 2003's **Macro Recorder** enables you to create simple macros without knowing anything about VBA or programming. The Macro Recorder records your actions, such as choosing menu commands or clicking toolbar buttons, and then writes the required VBA programming code for you. If a macro is not performing to your satisfaction, you simply record it again or edit the macro's generated code.

Before starting the macro recording process, it's best to plan the steps that you want to store in the macro. It is also important to consider where you might want to use the macro again. If the steps are specific to a workbook, then store the macro in the workbook. If, on the other hand, the steps are generic and can be used with any number of workbooks, store the macro in a special Excel 2003 workbook file called the **Personal Macro Workbook.** The Personal Macro Workbook is located in the XLStart folder and is managed privately by Excel 2003 (you do not have to create, open, or close it). This workbook provides a common storage area for macros that you want to make available to all your workbooks.

→ **Method**

To record a new macro:

- CHOOSE: Tools → Macro → Record New Macro
- Enter a name, shortcut key, and description in the Record Macro dialog box.
- SELECT: a location from the *Store macro in* drop-down list box
- CLICK: OK command button to start recording
- Perform the steps that you want to record.
- CLICK: Stop button (▫) to end recording

## → Practice

You will now create a simple macro that enters a company's name and address into a worksheet cell range. Ensure that no workbooks appear in the application window.

**1.** Display a new workbook using the New button (⬜) on the toolbar. The cell pointer should be positioned in cell A1 before proceeding.

**2.** Save the workbook as "First Macros" to your personal storage location.

**3.** To create a new macro:
CHOOSE: Tools → Macro → Record New Macro
The Record Macro dialog box appears, as shown in Figure 11.40.

**Figure 11.40**

Record Macro dialog box

Provide a descriptive one-word name for the macro.

Provide a shortcut key for executing the macro quickly.

Select a storage location for the macro. Where you store a macro determines its availability to other workbooks.

Enter a description specifying the purpose of the macro. Excel 2003 enters a description like this one automatically.

**4.** An acceptable macro name begins with a letter and does not contain any spaces. To name your new macro:
TYPE: **BusInfo** in the *Macro name* text box
PRESS: **TAB**

**5.** To specify a keyboard shortcut for executing the macro:
TYPE: **q** in the *Shortcut key* text box
PRESS: **TAB**
(*Note:* The shortcut key is case-sensitive! In other words, Excel 2003 makes a distinction between **CTRL**+q and **CTRL**+Q. Also, be careful not to select commonly used key combinations like **CTRL**+x, **CTRL**+c, and **CTRL**+v, which are Windows' Cut, Copy, and Paste shortcuts.)

**6.** Assuming that the macro will only be used in this workbook, leave the default "This Workbook" selection in the *Store macro in* drop-down list box. Then, proceed to entering a description of the macro:
PRESS: **TAB**

**7.** To add text to the existing description:
PRESS: **END** to move to the end of the line
TYPE: .
PRESS: Space bar
TYPE: **This macro enters and formats my business name and address.**
Your dialog box should now appear similar to the one shown in Figure 11.41.

**Figure 11.41**

Completing the
Record Macro
dialog box

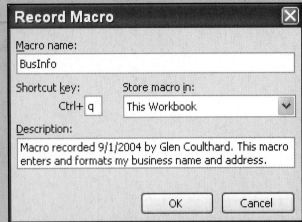

8. CLICK: OK command button to start recording
   Notice that the word "Recording" appears in the Status bar and that the Stop
   Recording toolbar (shown here) floats above the application window.

9. The Relative Reference button (⊞) on the Stop Recording toolbar controls how Excel 2003
   records cell movements. In its default (unselected) position, Excel 2003 records the exact or absolute cell references, such as $A$1, that you select in the worksheet. When selected, Excel
   2003 records cell movements relative to the active or starting cell. Because you will want to use
   the following macro anywhere in the worksheet, let's turn on relative cell addressing:
   CLICK: Relative Reference button (⊞)

10. Enter a fictitious business name and address:
    TYPE: **Polson Pet Emporium**
    PRESS: ⊡
    TYPE: **1000 Main Street**
    PRESS: ⊡
    TYPE: **Ferndale, CA 94105**
    PRESS: (ENTER)

11. Now format the information that you just entered:
    SELECT: cell range from A1 to A3
    CHOOSE: Format → Cells

12. In the Format Cells dialog box:
    CLICK: *Font* tab
    SELECT: Times New Roman from the *Font* list box
    SELECT: Bold from the *Font style* list box
    SELECT: 14 from the *Size* list box
    SELECT: Dark Blue from the *Color* drop-down list box
    Your screen should now appear similar to the dialog box shown in Figure 11.42.

## Figure 11.42

Recording cell
formatting
commands

Stop Recording
toolbar

"Recording" status

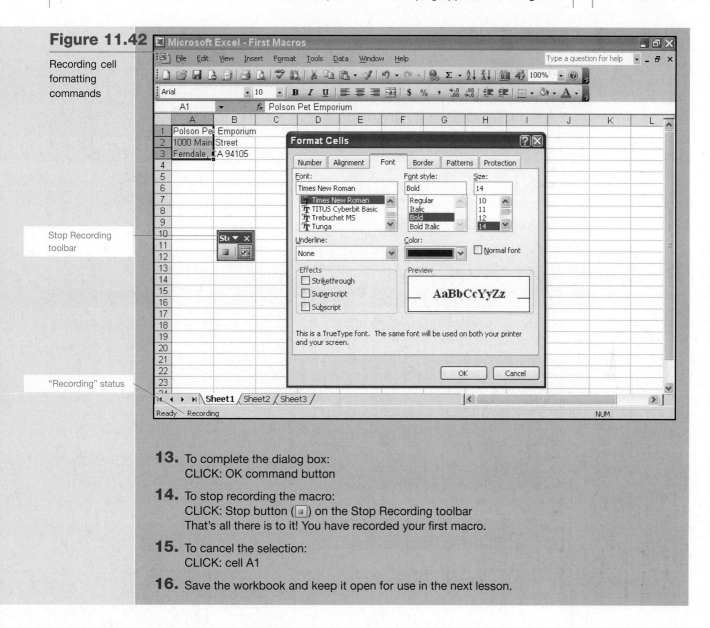

**13.** To complete the dialog box:
CLICK: OK command button

**14.** To stop recording the macro:
CLICK: Stop button (■) on the Stop Recording toolbar
That's all there is to it! You have recorded your first macro.

**15.** To cancel the selection:
CLICK: cell A1

**16.** Save the workbook and keep it open for use in the next lesson.

### *In Addition* CREATING AN AUTOMATIC MACRO

An automatic macro or **automacro** is a special type of macro that executes without your interaction. Instead, it is initiated by something that happens in Excel 2003. Although you create an automacro as you would any other macro, the name that you give the macro determines how it operates. The most commonly used automacro, named "Auto_Open," runs automatically when you open a workbook. If, for whatever reason, you want to stop the Auto_Open macro from executing, hold down the (SHIFT) key when opening the workbook.

## 11.4.2 Playing Back a Macro

### → Feature

Excel 2003 provides a number of different methods for running, or executing, your macros. You can execute a macro by selecting its name from a dialog box, by pressing a key combination, by clicking a toolbar or command button, or by selecting a custom command from the menu. Macros can also run automatically when you perform procedures such as opening a workbook or selecting a worksheet.

### → Method

To execute or run a macro:

- CHOOSE: Tools → Macro → Macros
- SELECT: *a macro* in the list box
- CLICK: Run command button

### → Practice

In this lesson, you practice running the macro that you recorded in the previous lesson. Ensure that you have completed the previous lesson and that the "First Macros" workbook is displayed.

**1.** To demonstrate the macro that you previously recorded, first position the cell pointer:
SELECT: cell A6

**2.** CHOOSE: Tools → Macro → Macros
The Macro dialog box appears, as shown in Figure 11.43. (*Hint:* As a shortcut, you can display the Macro dialog box by pressing **ALT** + **F8** .)

**Figure 11.43**

Macro dialog box

All of the macros stored in the *Macros in* selection appear in this list box.

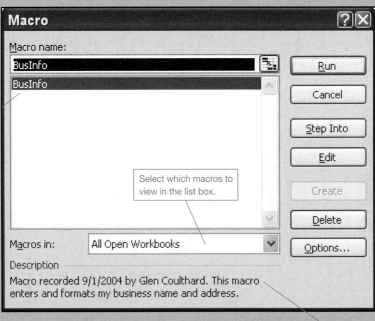

Select which macros to view in the list box.

A description of the currently selected macro is displayed.

**3.** To run the macro you recorded in the last lesson, ensure that the BusInfo macro is selected in the list area and then:
CLICK: Run command button
(*Note:* You can also double-click the macro name in the list box.) Notice that the business name and address are entered into the cell range from A6 to A8, as shown in Figure 11.44.

**Figure 11.44**

Executing a macro to enter a business name and address

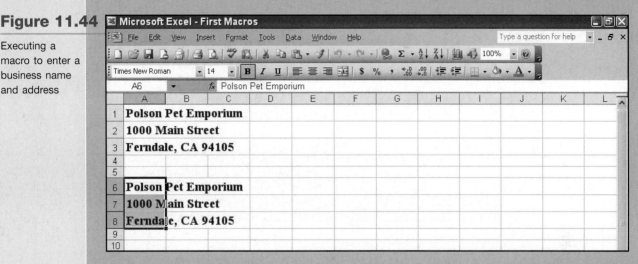

**4.** Let's select a new worksheet and position the cell pointer:
CLICK: *Sheet2* tab
SELECT: cell D4

**5.** Now use the shortcut key to run the macro:
PRESS: CTRL +q
Notice that the macro enters the information at the active cell's location, because you selected relative cell addressing when you recorded the macro. (*Hint:* Especially important for longer and more complex macros, Excel 2003 provides the ESC key as a panic button to interrupt or halt a macro's execution before it finishes processing.)

**6.** Save and then close the "First Macros" workbook.

### 11.4.3 Protecting Yourself from Macro Viruses

→ **Feature**

A **virus** is a program that is created with the intention of doing harm to your computer. Viruses can infect other programs, delete files, or worse, turn your hard disk into an unsalvageable mess. A **macro virus** is a special type of virus that lives inside a macro. Unlike other viruses, macro viruses do not infect programs; they infect documents, such as workbooks. This type of virus is not any different from a macro that you might create; however, its intent is harmful rather than helpful. Because macros are stored in templates and workbooks, macro viruses are easily spread, often unknowingly. To protect against common viruses, purchase or download a virus-protection program and run it regularly. You should also be familiar with Microsoft Office Excel 2003's macro security features, as discussed in this lesson.

→ ## Method

To adjust your macro security settings:

- CHOOSE: Tools → Macro → Security
- Select the desired security level (*High, Medium,* or *Low*)
- CLICK: OK command button

→ ## Practice

You will now practice specifying security levels and opening workbooks containing macros. Ensure that you have completed the previous lessons and that no workbooks are displayed in the application window.

**1.** To specify a security level for opening workbooks containing macros, select an option in the macro settings Security dialog box. To begin:
CHOOSE: Tools → Macro → Security
The Security dialog box appears, as shown in Figure 11.45.

**Figure 11.45**

Security dialog box: *Security Level* tab

Most users will specify the "Medium" security setting if they also have antivirus software installed on their system. If you do not have a virus scanner, consider selecting the High or Very High security.

This computer has a virus scanner installed.

For more information about security settings, trusted publishers, and digital signing, click the Help button in the Title bar.

**2.** In order to perform the exercises in this workbook, you will need to specify a *Medium* level of security. Read the four options in the dialog box and then:
SELECT: *Medium* option button
CLICK: OK command button

**3.** Open the data file named EX1140. Because this workbook contains macros and you have specified a *Medium* security level, Excel 2003 displays the warning dialog box shown in Figure 11.46. (*Note:* The *Medium* level of security allows you to choose whether to open a workbook with its macros enabled or disabled. If you trust the source of the workbook, open it with macros enabled. However, if you do not know who created the workbook, open it first with its macros disabled in order to review the contents safely.)

**Figure 11.46**

Opening a
workbook
containing
macros

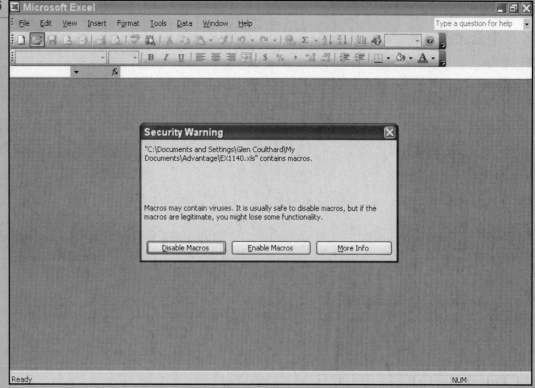

**4.** To open the Advantage student data file with its macros enabled:
CLICK: Enable Macros command button

**5.** Save the workbook as "Simple Macros" to your personal storage location. Although the three worksheets appear to be empty, there are macros stored in the workbook file.

**6.** To test two of the macros stored in this workbook:
PRESS: ALT + F8
DOUBLE-CLICK: BusName in the *Macro name* list box
PRESS: ALT + F8
DOUBLE-CLICK: BusAddress in the *Macro name* list box

**7.** To enter the company slogan:
SELECT: cell A4
PRESS: ALT + F8
DOUBLE-CLICK: BusSlogan in the *Macro name* list box
Your screen should now appear similar to the worksheet shown in Figure 11.47.

**Figure 11.47**

Opening a
workbook and
running macros

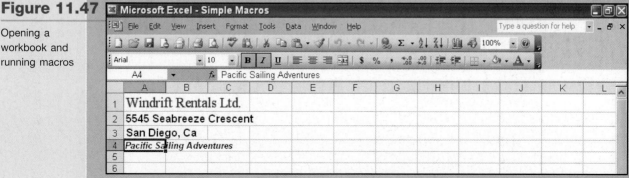

**8.** Save the workbook and keep it open for use in the next lesson.

### 11.4.4 Editing a Recorded Macro

→ ## Feature

The Macro Recorder is an excellent tool for quickly storing sequences of instructions that can be played back immediately. But there will be times when you need to edit your macros. You may have chosen a wrong command during the recording process; you may need to change some data that you entered; you may want to expand the macro with a few additional steps; you may even want to consolidate several smaller macros into one comprehensive routine. Rather than rerecording a macro, you can easily modify the macro's code using the **Visual Basic Editor.** The Editor, which is covered in greater detail in Chapter 12, is a special utility that enables you to create, edit, and print macros.

Be aware that VBA uses the terms *macro* and *procedure* interchangeably and together (for example, *macro procedure.*) As a general rule, use "macro" to refer to the actions captured by the Macro Recorder and translated into VBA. Macros are stored as "Sub" procedures in a VBA **module.** A VBA **project file** can contain multiple modules, and it is always associated with a specific workbook or with the Personal Macro Workbook. In this lesson, you learn to edit VBA code that has been written by the Macro Recorder and stored in a VBA module.

→ ## Method

To edit an existing macro:

- CHOOSE: Tools → Macro → Macros
- SELECT: *a macro* in the list box
- CLICK: Edit command button
- Make the desired modifications.
- CHOOSE: File → Close and Return to Microsoft Excel

→ ## Practice

You will now practice editing a macro using the Visual Basic Editor. Ensure that you have completed the previous lesson and that the "Simple Macros" workbook is displayed.

**1.** In order to edit a macro, you must first display its VBA programming code in the Visual Basic Editor. Do the following:
CHOOSE: Tools → Macro → Macros

**2.** In the Macro dialog box:
SELECT: BusAddress in the list box, if it is not already selected
CLICK: Edit command button
The Visual Basic Editor (Figure 11.48) is launched and the macro's Code window is displayed in the work area.

**3.** Maximize the Visual Basic Editor window.

**4.** Before proceeding, drag the Code window's sizing corner and Title bar so that it appears similar to Figure 11.48. (*Note:* For this lesson, focus on the contents of the Code window rather than the other elements in the Visual Basic Editor.)

## Figure 11.48

Displaying macro code in the Visual Basic Editor

Code window

The Code window contains the VBA programming code.

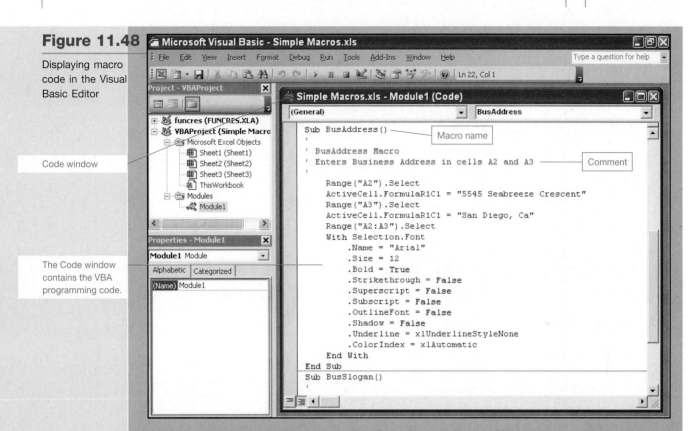

```
Microsoft Visual Basic - Simple Macros.xls

File  Edit  View  Insert  Format  Debug  Run  Tools  Add-Ins  Window  Help        Type a question for help

Ln 22, Col 1
```

Project - VBAProject

- funcres (FUNCRES.XLA)
- VBAProject (Simple Macro
  - Microsoft Excel Objects
    - Sheet1 (Sheet1)
    - Sheet2 (Sheet2)
    - Sheet3 (Sheet3)
    - ThisWorkbook
  - Modules
    - Module1

Properties - Module1

Module1 Module

Alphabetic | Categorized

(Name) Module1

```
Simple Macros.xls - Module1 (Code)

(General)                                          BusAddress

Sub BusAddress()                    Macro name
'
' BusAddress Macro
' Enters Business Address in cells A2 and A3        Comment
'
    Range("A2").Select
    ActiveCell.FormulaR1C1 = "5545 Seabreeze Crescent"
    Range("A3").Select
    ActiveCell.FormulaR1C1 = "San Diego, Ca"
    Range("A2:A3").Select
    With Selection.Font
        .Name = "Arial"
        .Size = 12
        .Bold = True
        .Strikethrough = False
        .Superscript = False
        .Subscript = False
        .OutlineFont = False
        .Shadow = False
        .Underline = xlUnderlineStyleNone
        .ColorIndex = xlAutomatic
    End With
End Sub
Sub BusSlogan()
'
```

Excel

**5.** You can edit a macro's code similar to how you would edit text in a word processor. For instance, you can insert, delete, cut, copy, and paste code segments using familiar keyboard shortcuts and menu commands. To illustrate, let's change the address information:
DOUBLE-CLICK: "Seabreeze" in the macro code
TYPE: **Oceanside**
DOUBLE-CLICK: "Crescent" in the same code line
TYPE: **Avenue**

**6.** On your own, edit the text "San Diego, Ca" to read "San Mateo, CA." Then, change the ".Size =" value to 10 and the ".Bold =" value to False. The Code window should now appear similar to the one shown in Figure 11.49.

**Figure 11.49**

Editing VBA programming code

```
Simple Macros.xls - Module1 (Code)

(General)                              BusAddress

    Sub BusAddress()
    '
    ' BusAddress Macro
    ' Enters Business Address in cells A2 and A3
    '
        Range("A2").Select
        ActiveCell.FormulaR1C1 = "5545 Oceanside Avenue"
        Range("A3").Select
        ActiveCell.FormulaR1C1 = "San Mateo, CA"
        Range("A2:A3").Select
        With Selection.Font
            .Name = "Arial"
            .Size = 10
            .Bold = False
            .Strikethrough = False
            .Superscript = False
            .Subscript = False
            .OutlineFont = False
            .Shadow = False
            .Underline = xlUnderlineStyleNone
            .ColorIndex = xlAutomatic
        End With
    End Sub
    Sub BusSlogan()
    '
```

**7.** To see the results of this simple modification:
CHOOSE: File → Close and Return to Microsoft Excel
(*Note:* This command closes the Visual Basic Editor and returns you to the workbook. Your changes are not saved permanently, however, until you save the workbook.)

**8.** To practice executing the BusName and BusAddress macros:
CLICK: *Sheet2* tab

**9.** Now display the Macro dialog box and pick the macros to run:
PRESS: ALT + F8
DOUBLE-CLICK: BusName in the *Macro name* list box
PRESS: ALT + F8
DOUBLE-CLICK: BusAddress in the *Macro name* list box
Notice that the new address information is entered, as shown here. This exercise demonstrates how quickly you can make changes to a recorded macro.

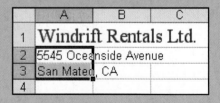

**10.** Save the workbook and keep it open for use in the next lesson.

### *In Addition* COMBINING MACROS

Often, when you are first learning about macros, the command sequences you record are very short and manageable. Later on, you may want to create a single macro to perform all the tasks that you have stored in smaller macros. One macro-editing technique involves using the Copy and Paste commands to combine smaller macros into one larger macro. Another method is to create a new macro whose function is to run the other macros. If you have created a macro that will be used by several other macro procedures, use the second method so that you need only maintain the code in a single location. For other situations, however, the copy and paste method may be faster and easier.

### 11.4.5 Printing Your Macros

→ ## Feature

Printing your macros can be especially helpful when you need to jot down a few handwritten notes describing a particular block of code or fax a copy to an associate for review. Perhaps you just want to edit a macro while riding the bus or train to work or school. A printout will also provide you with a hard copy backup of your work, in case you accidentally lose the electronic version.

→ ## Method

To print your VBA programming code:

- Display the macro procedures in the Visual Basic Editor.
- CHOOSE: File → Print
- SELECT: *Current Module* option button in the *Range* area
- SELECT: *Code* check box in the *Print What* area
- CLICK: OK command button

→ ## Practice

You will now practice printing out the macros stored in a workbook. Ensure that you have completed the previous lesson and that the "Simple Macros" workbook is displayed.

**1.** To display the Visual Basic Editor:
CHOOSE: Tools → Macro → Visual Basic Editor

**2.** The Code window displays all of the procedures stored in the "Module1" module. On your own, use the vertical scroll bar in the Code window to view the VBA programming code stored in the module for the BusName, BusAddress, and BusSlogan procedures.

**3.** To print the currently displayed module:
CHOOSE: File → Print
The dialog box shown in Figure 11.50 appears.

**Figure 11.50**

Print dialog box in the Visual Basic Editor

Specify whether to print the selected code, the entire module, or all the modules in the current project.

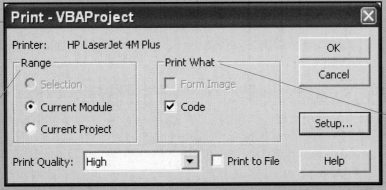

When printing a custom form, you can specify whether to print its image in addition to its code.

**4.** If you have a printer connected to your computer, ensure that the *Current Module* option button is selected and then:
CLICK: OK command button
(*Note:* If you do not have a printer, you can skip to the next step by clicking the Cancel command button.)

**5.** To close the Visual Basic Editor and return to the workbook:
CHOOSE: File → Close and Return to Microsoft Excel

**6.** Save and then close the "Simple Macros" workbook.

**11.4** Aside from running the macro, how would you determine whether absolute or relative cell referencing was being used?

# 11.5 Customizing Menus and Toolbars

When Microsoft Office Excel 2003 is first installed on your system, the Menu bar, shortcut menus, and toolbars are set up in a default configuration. As you gain experience with Excel 2003 and create macros for automating everyday procedures, you may want to customize the application window to your preferred way of working. Fortunately, Excel 2003's environment is extremely flexible and easily changed. You can change the number of worksheets that are displayed in a new workbook. You can even modify the existing interface elements, such as the Menu bar, and create entirely new menu options and toolbars. Whatever your requirements, your overall objective should be to make it easier to access the commands and procedures you use most often.

## 11.5.1 Modifying the Menu Bar

### → Feature

Microsoft Office Excel 2003 provides personalized menus and toolbars for dynamically presenting the commands you use most often. In the first chapter of this book, you turned this feature off so that all of Excel 2003's default commands would appear in the Menu bar. You can further customize the menus by adding, arranging, and removing commands. For example, rather than selecting macros from the Macro dialog box, you can create new menu commands that run specific macros. This feature can make the macros you create very accessible, especially to new users.

### → Method

To modify the Menu bar:

- CHOOSE: Tools → Customize
- CLICK: *Commands* tab
- SELECT: a category in the *Categories* list box
- DRAG: a command from the *Commands* list box to the desired location on an existing menu
- CLICK: Close command button

### → Practice

You will now learn to modify the Menu bar by assigning a macro to a custom menu item. Ensure that no workbooks appear in the application window.

**1.** Open the data file named EX1150 and enable the macros by clicking the Enable Macros command button.

**2.** Save the workbook as "My Workplace" to your personal storage location. This workbook contains the same macros (BusName, BusAddress, and BusSlogan) used in the previous module.

**3.** You will now modify Excel 2003's menu system to contain options for running the three macros. Do the following:
CHOOSE: Tools → Customize
CLICK: *Commands* tab
The Customize dialog box shown in Figure 11.51 appears. Whenever this dialog box is displayed, all of the toolbar buttons and menu commands in the application window are disabled to allow for editing.

**Figure 11.51**

Customize dialog
box: *Commands*
tab

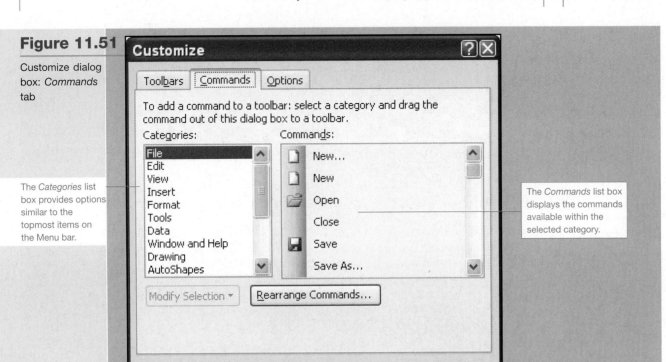

The *Categories* list
box provides options
similar to the
topmost items on
the Menu bar.

The *Commands* list box
displays the commands
available within the
selected category.

Excel

4. Your objective is to add a custom menu item to the bottom of the Insert menu and then assign a macro to the item. To begin:
   SELECT: Macros in the *Categories* list box (near the bottom)
   SELECT: Custom Menu Item in the *Commands* list box

5. To insert the new menu item:
   DRAG: Custom Menu Item from the *Commands* list box up to the Menu bar and over the Insert menu name and then to the bottom of the menu, as shown in Figure 11.52

**Figure 11.52**

Adding a new
item to the menu

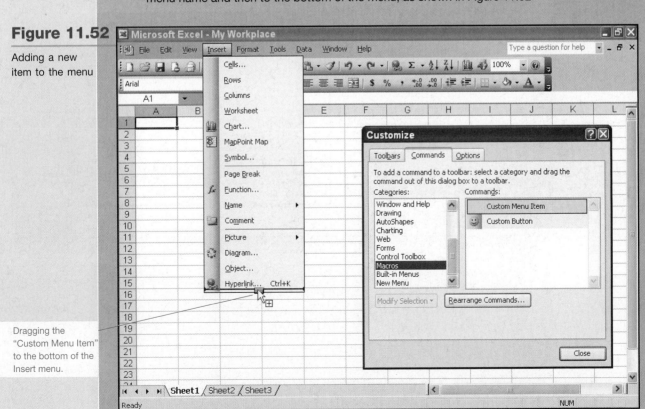

Dragging the
"Custom Menu Item"
to the bottom of the
Insert menu.

**6.** When you release the mouse button, a new menu item appears at the bottom of the Insert pull-down menu called Custom Menu Item. To edit the new menu item:
RIGHT-CLICK: Custom Menu Item in the Insert menu to display the menu shown here

**7.** To change the menu item's name:
CHOOSE: Name (by clicking on the word "Name" so that the existing menu text appears highlighted)
TYPE: **Insert Business Name**
(*Note:* Do not press `ENTER`.)

**8.** You must now assign the macro that you want to execute when the new menu item is selected. To do so:
CHOOSE: Assign Macro
The Assign Macro dialog box appears, as shown in Figure 11.53.
(*Note:* If the Insert menu is covering the display of the dialog box, drag the Assign Macro dialog box to a new location by its Title bar.)

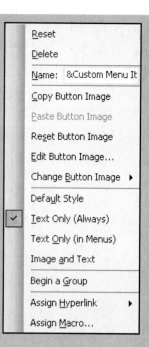

**Figure 11.53**

Assigning a macro to the new "Insert Business Name" menu item

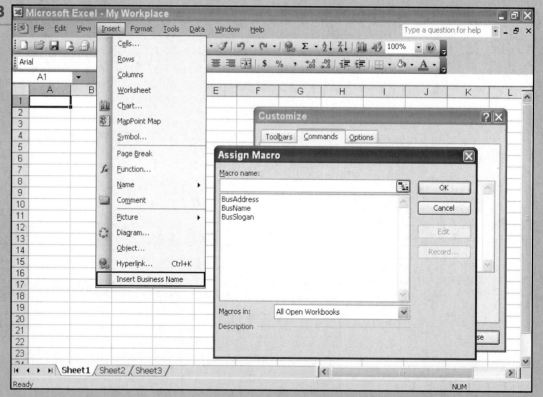

**9.** To specify the macro to run:
SELECT: BusName in the *Macro name* list box
CLICK: OK command button

**10.** Now close the Customize dialog box:
CLICK: Close command button

**11.** To test the new menu item:
CHOOSE: Insert → Insert Business Name
You should now see "Windrift Rentals Ltd." in cell A1.

**12.** You will now learn how to remove a menu item. Do the following:
CHOOSE: Tools → Customize

**13.** You can now edit the menu items directly:
CLICK: Insert in the Excel 2003 Menu bar
DRAG: Insert Business Name menu item below or away from the menu and then drop it on the worksheet, as shown here

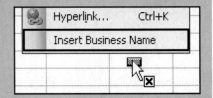

**14.** CLICK: Close command button in the Customize dialog box

**15.** Save the workbook and keep it open for use in the next lesson.

### 11.5.2 Manipulating Toolbars

## → Feature

Toolbars allow you to organize multiple commands and features into compact and conveniently located button strips. The Standard toolbar itself gives you single-click access to more than 20 commands. In addition to dozens of useful built-in toolbars, Excel 2003 allows you to create custom toolbars that are suited to your personal needs and preferences. You can add existing menus and buttons to a custom toolbar or create new buttons that run macros. In fact, a toolbar can contain buttons, menus, drop-down list boxes, and a variety of other interface controls.

Did you know that Excel 2003's menu is actually a special toolbar called the *Worksheet Menu Bar*? Like all toolbars, you can display the Worksheet Menu Bar docked alongside the application window or *floating* in its own window, complete with a Title bar and Close button ( ✕ ). There are four docking areas for toolbars, alongside the top and bottom horizontal walls and the left and right vertical walls.

## → Method

To float a toolbar

- DRAG: the toolbar by its move handle away from its docked position

To dock a toolbar:

- DRAG: the toolbar by its Title bar to one of the walls in the application window

To display or hide a toolbar:

- CHOOSE: View → Toolbars

## → Practice

In this lesson, you will practice manipulating the display and appearance of toolbars. Ensure that the "My Workplace" workbook is displayed.

**1.** Toolbars are easily moved and sized in the Microsoft Office Excel 2003 application window. To float the Standard toolbar:
DRAG: its move handle ( ), appearing at the far left of the Standard toolbar, toward the center of the worksheet

**2.** When you release the mouse button, the Standard toolbar appears in its own window, as shown in Figure 11.54.

**Figure 11.54**

Floating the
Standard toolbar

The move handle
for the Formatting
toolbar

The Standard
toolbar appears as
a floating window
with a Title bar and
Close button.

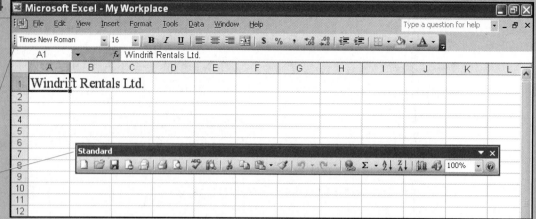

3. To size the toolbar, position the mouse pointer over the Standard toolbar's right-hand border until the pointer changes shape to a horizontal double-headed arrow. Then, drag the toolbar's border to about half its width, as shown below.

4. On your own, drag the Standard toolbar by its Title bar back to its original position between the Menu bar and the Formatting toolbar. (*Hint:* You can also double-click its Title bar to reposition the toolbar.)

5. To view the most commonly used toolbars:
CHOOSE: View → Toolbars
The toolbars that are active and displayed in the application window are shown with a check mark in the menu.

6. To activate a new toolbar:
CHOOSE: Picture
The Picture toolbar appears in the same location where it was last activated.

7. You can also display a toolbar using the right-click menu:
RIGHT-CLICK: any button on the Picture toolbar
CHOOSE: Drawing

8. If it is not already there, dock the Drawing toolbar to the bottom of the application window, as shown in Figure 11.55.

**Figure 11.55**

Displaying and hiding toolbars

Worksheet Menu Bar

Standard toolbar

Formatting toolbar

Picture toolbar

Drawing toolbar

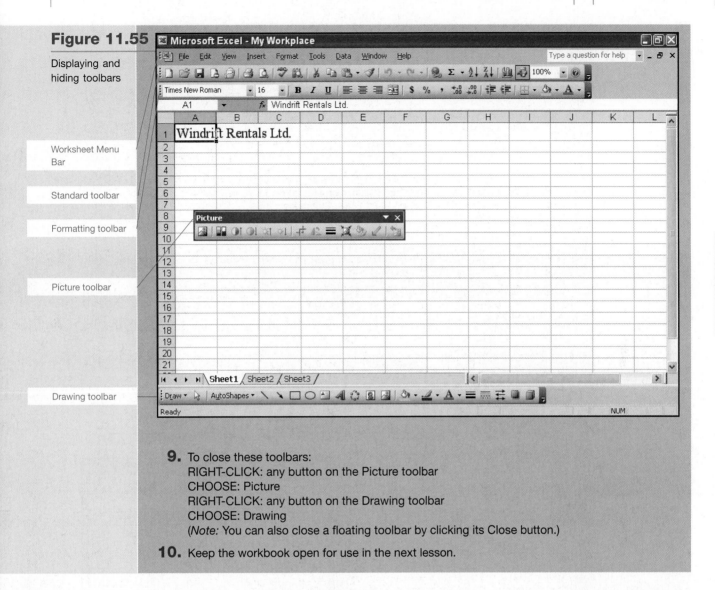

9. To close these toolbars:
   RIGHT-CLICK: any button on the Picture toolbar
   CHOOSE: Picture
   RIGHT-CLICK: any button on the Drawing toolbar
   CHOOSE: Drawing
   (*Note:* You can also close a floating toolbar by clicking its Close button.)

10. Keep the workbook open for use in the next lesson.

## 11.5.3 Customizing a Toolbar

→ **Feature**

Besides having the ability to control where toolbars are positioned in the application window, you can modify the location of buttons in a toolbar, size buttons, add and delete buttons, and create new buttons that are assigned to macros. Rearranging buttons on a toolbar offers limited improvement. However, removing buttons that you do not use and replacing them with frequently used commands can increase your productivity.

→ **Method**

To customize a toolbar:

• CHOOSE: Tools → Customize

• CLICK: *Toolbars* tab

• DRAG: buttons and commands within a toolbar to change the order, away from a toolbar to delete them, or onto a toolbar to add them

• RIGHT-CLICK: a toolbar button to display editing commands

• CLICK: Close command button

→ **Practice**

You will now learn how to modify the contents of a toolbar. Ensure that the "My Workplace" workbook is displayed.

**1.** To customize a toolbar:
CHOOSE: Tools → Customize
CLICK: *Toolbars* tab
(*Hint:* You can also right-click any button on any toolbar and then choose the Customize command from the shortcut menu.)

**2.** As mentioned previously, when the Customize dialog box is displayed, all of the toolbar buttons and menu commands are disabled. Therefore, you can move and remove buttons on a toolbar by simply clicking and dragging them. To illustrate:
CLICK: Bold button (B) on the Formatting toolbar
The button should now appear highlighted with a thick black border.

**3.** DRAG: Bold button (B) away from the toolbar and into the worksheet area, as shown in Figure 11.56
When you release the mouse button, the button is removed from the toolbar. (Do not be concerned about making changes to the toolbars, you can reset them to their default appearance at any time.)

**Figure 11.56**

Removing a button from the Formatting toolbar

Dragging the Bold button from the Formatting toolbar into the worksheet.

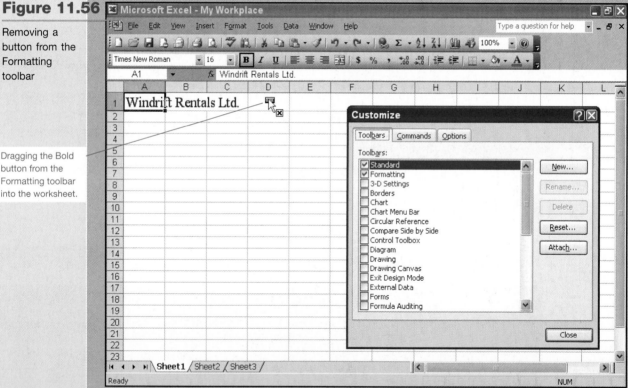

**4.** To add a new command button to the Standard toolbar:
CLICK: *Commands* tab

**5.** Pick the desired option from the list boxes:
SELECT: File in the *Categories* list box
*or*
SELECT: Publish as Web Page in the *Commands* list box

**6.** DRAG: Publish as Web Page option from the Customize dialog box and position it to the left of the Print button (🖨), as shown in Figure 11.57

**Figure 11.57**

Adding a button to the Standard toolbar

Dragging the "Publish as Web Page" option to the left of the Print button.

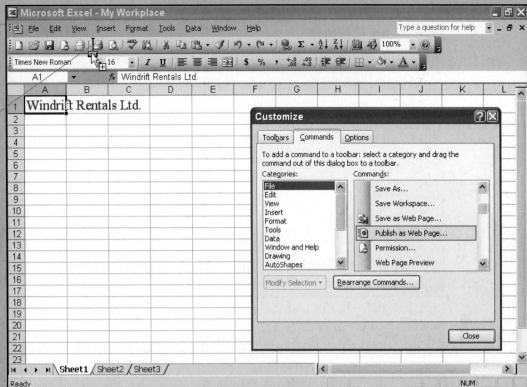

7. To reset the Standard toolbar to its default appearance:
   CLICK: *Toolbars* tab
   SELECT: Standard in the *Toolbars* list box by clicking on its name
   CLICK: Reset command button

8. In the warning dialog box that is displayed:
   CLICK: OK command button
   Notice that the Publish as Web Page button () is removed.

9. To reset the Formatting toolbar:
   SELECT: Formatting in the *Toolbars* list box by clicking on its name
   CLICK: Reset command button

10. To accept the warning dialog box:
    CLICK: OK command button
    Notice that the Bold button (![B]) is redisplayed.

11. To finish customizing the toolbars:
    CLICK: Close command button in the Customize dialog box

12. Save the workbook and keep it open for use in the next lesson.

## 11.5.4  Creating a New Toolbar

→ **Feature**

There may be circumstances in which creating a new toolbar is easier than modifying the existing ones. For example, you should not change Excel 2003's default toolbar settings if there are less experienced users who might be confused by such modifications. Creating a toolbar with your personal command favorites gives you the versatility you need without creating problems for others. Assigning your recorded macros to toolbar buttons can also increase your productivity.

## Method

To create a new toolbar:

- CHOOSE: Tools → Customize
- CLICK: *Toolbars* tab
- CLICK: New command button
- TYPE: *name* for the toolbar
- DRAG: the desired commands and buttons to the empty toolbar palette

To assign a macro to a toolbar button:

- RIGHT-CLICK: the desired button
- CHOOSE: Assign Macro
- SELECT: *a macro* in the list box
- CLICK: OK command button

## Practice

In this lesson, you will create a custom toolbar and then populate it with a custom button that runs an assigned macro. Ensure that the "My Workplace" workbook is displayed.

**1.** To create a new toolbar:
CHOOSE: Tools → Customize
CLICK: *Toolbars* tab
CLICK: New command button

**2.** In the New Toolbar dialog box:
TYPE: **My Macros**
CLICK: OK command button
A small empty toolbar window is displayed, as shown below.

Drag buttons and commands to this empty area in the new toolbar.

**3.** You can now add a button to the toolbar:
CLICK: *Commands* tab
SELECT: Macros in the *Categories* list box
DRAG: Custom Button from the *Commands* list box to the new toolbar, as shown below

Drag the "Custom Button" option to the new toolbar.

**4.** To assign a macro to the new toolbar button:
RIGHT-CLICK: Custom Button (☺)
CHOOSE: Name (so that the existing text appears highlighted)
TYPE: **Insert Business Name**
(*Note:* Do not press **ENTER** after typing the button's name.)

**5.** CHOOSE: Assign Macro
The Assign Macro dialog box appears.

**6.** To specify the macro to run when the button is clicked:
SELECT: BusName in the *Macro name* list box
CLICK: OK command button

**7.** Now select a new icon for the toolbar button:
RIGHT-CLICK: Insert Business Name button (⬚)
CHOOSE: Change Button Image
Your screen should now appear similar to the dialog box shown in Figure 11.58.

**Figure 11.58**

Changing a
toolbar button's
image

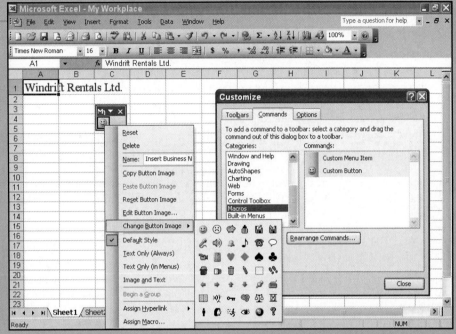

**8.** In the Change Button Image cascading palette:
SELECT: Keyboard image (⌨)
Your toolbar should now appear similar to the one below.

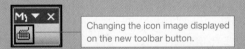
Changing the icon image displayed
on the new toolbar button.

**9.** To complete the new toolbar:
CLICK: Close button in the Customize dialog box

**10.** To test the new toolbar button:
CLICK: *Sheet2* tab
CLICK: Insert Business Name button (⌨) on the My Macros toolbar
(*Note:* To share a custom toolbar with an associate, you must add the toolbar to the workbook by clicking the Attach command button in the Customize dialog box.)

**11.** Close the toolbar by clicking its Close button (✖).

**12.** Now let's delete the toolbar:
CHOOSE: Tools → Customize
CLICK: *Toolbars* tab

**13.** SELECT: My Macros in the *Toolbars* list box
CLICK: Delete command button

**14.** When the warning dialog box appears:
CLICK: OK command button to proceed

**15.** Close the Customize dialog box.

**16.** Save and then close the "My Workplace" workbook.

**11.5** How would you create an option on the Menu bar that contained all of your macros?

# Chapter
## summary

Microsoft Office Excel 2003 provides tools to develop and maintain workbook applications for teams and workgroups. Shared workbooks, for example, allow multiple people to revise a single workbook simultaneously. Shared workbooks are commonly stored on a private network file server. Excel 2003 provides several additional features to facilitate collaborative efforts, including revision tracking and the ability to merge workbooks. When creating workbooks for other people to use, you must be especially cautious of errors and other complications. Excel 2003 provides important features to assist you in creating error-free workbooks. First, validation rules enable you to restrict the data entered in a cell or cell range to meet a certain condition. If you do not actually need to restrict entries, you can use conditional formatting to simply display visual cues in your worksheets. The Formula Auditing toolbar and related error checking commands, like tracing cell precedents and dependents, help you to locate and solve errors in formulas and functions.

Also important in developing workbook applications are the concepts of consistency and ease of use. To this end, Excel 2003 provides the Macro Recorder for recording a series of command instructions in a macro. Typically saved with the workbook, macros are used to automate repetitive or routine tasks. You can edit your recorded macros using the Visual Basic Editor. Finally, Excel 2003 enables you to create and customize menus and toolbars in the application window. This feature is especially important for personalizing your workspace. You can also provide easy access to your recorded macros by assigning them to toolbar buttons or menu items that you create.

## Command Summary

Many of the commands and procedures appearing in this chapter are summarized in the following table.

| Skill Set | To Perform This Task . . . | Do the Following . . . |
|---|---|---|
| **Workgroup Collaboration** | Create a shared workbook | CHOOSE: Tools → Share Workbook<br>CLICK: *Editing* tab<br>SELECT: *Allow changes by more than one user* . . . check box |
| | Specify options for tracking changes and resolving conflicts between users | CHOOSE: Tools → Share Workbook<br>CLICK: *Advanced* tab<br>SELECT: the desired options |
| | Compile a historical listing of changes | CHOOSE: Tools → Track Changes → Highlight Changes<br>SELECT: *Track changes while editing* check box |
| | Review the highlighted changes and accept or reject them | CHOOSE: Tools → Changes → Accept or Reject Changes |
| | Merge workbooks and their modifications | CHOOSE: Tools → Compare and Merge Workbooks |
| **Formatting Numbers** | Apply conditional formatting to cell ranges | CHOOSE: Format → Conditional Formatting |

| Summarizing Data | Specify data validation rules for inputting information | CHOOSE: Data → Validation |
|---|---|---|
| **Creating and Revising Formulas** | Create a dynamic cell range using named ranges:<br><br>Prevent calculation errors using formula expressions: | • =INDIRECT(*character_string*)<br>• =COUNTA(*cell reference*)<br><br>• =ISBLANK(*cell reference* or *value*)<br>• =ISERROR(*cell reference* or *value*)<br>• =ISNUMBER(*cell reference* or *value*)<br>• =ISTEXT(*cell reference* or *value*) |
| **Auditing Worksheets** | Display the Formula Auditing toolbar | CHOOSE: Tools → Formula Auditing → Show Formula Auditing Toolbar |
| | Toggle highlighting on and off for invalid data on the worksheet | CLICK: Circle Invalid Data button (▦) on the Formula Auditing toolbar<br>CLICK: Clear Validation Circles button (▦) on the Formula Auditing toolbar |
| | Trace precedents (locate the cells used in a specific formula) | CLICK: Trace Precedents button (▦) on the Formula Auditing toolbar |
| | Trace dependents (locate the formulas that reference a specific cell) | CLICK: Trace Dependents button (▦) on the Formula Auditing toolbar |
| | Locate errors in the worksheet | CHOOSE: Tools → Error Checking, or CLICK: Error Checking button (▦) on the Formula Auditing toolbar |
| | Trace errors in the worksheet | CLICK: Trace Error button (▦) on the Formula Auditing toolbar |
| | Remove all tracer arrows from a worksheet | CLICK: Remove All Arrows button (▦) on the Formula Auditing toolbar |
| | Evaluate a formula and locate errors | CLICK: Evaluate Formula button (▦) on the Formula Auditing toolbar |
| | Display the Watch Window | CLICK: Show Watch Window button (▦) on the Formula Auditing toolbar |
| **Customizing Excel 2003** | Record a new macro | CHOOSE: Tools → Macro → Record New Macro |
| | Run a macro | CHOOSE: Tools → Macro → Macros<br>SELECT: *a macro*<br>CLICK: Run command button |
| | Edit a macro using the Visual Basic Editor | CHOOSE: Tools → Macro → Macros<br>SELECT: *a macro*<br>CLICK: Edit command button |
| | Set the macro security level | CHOOSE: Tools → Macro → Security |
| | Customize the Menu bar by adding and removing items | CHOOSE: Tools → Customize<br>CLICK: *Commands* tab |

Excel

| Toggle the display of a toolbar on and off | CHOOSE: View → Toolbars
CHOOSE: *the desired toolbar* |
| Customize a toolbar by adding and removing buttons | CHOOSE: Tools → Customize
CLICK: *Toolbars* tab |
| Assign a macro to a command button, toolbar button, or menu item during customizing | RIGHT-CLICK: *the button or item*
CHOOSE: Assign Macro
DOUBLE-CLICK: *a macro* |

## Key Terms

This section specifies page references for the key terms identified in this chapter. For a complete list of definitions, refer to the Glossary provided at the end of this learning guide.

audit, *p. EX 728*

automacro, *p. EX 747*

conditional formatting, *p. EX 715*

dynamic cell range, *p. EX 725*

Macro Recorder, *p. EX 744*

macro virus, *p. EX 749*

macros, *p. EX 744*

module, *p. EX 752*

Personal Macro Workbook, *p. EX 744*

project file, *p. EX 752*

shared workbook, *p. EX 706*

smart tags, *p. EX 728*

tracer arrows, *p. EX 736*

tracing dependents, *p. EX 736*

tracing precedents, *p. EX 736*

users, *p. EX 706*

virus, *p. EX 749*

Visual Basic Editor, *p. EX 752*

Visual Basic for Applications (VBA), *p. EX 744*

Watch Window, *p. EX 738*

## Chapter
### q u i z

### Short Answer

1. Name the five stages in the workbook development life cycle.

2. What would you do to prepare a workbook for placement onto a workgroup's network server?

3. How does conditional formatting complement data validation?

4. How could you determine whether existing values in a worksheet conform to newly specified data validation rules?

5. What is a macro? Where are they stored?

6. What is an automacro? Provide an example.

7. Why might you want to edit an existing macro?

8. How do macros and macro viruses differ?

9. How do you protect yourself against macro viruses?

10. How do you assign a macro to a toolbar button?

## True/False

1. _____ You can track changes in a stand-alone, non-shared workbook.

2. _____ You can validate text, numeric, and date values entered into a cell.

3. _____ The red validation circle that appears over an invalid entry can be moved out of the way like any other object on the Draw layer.

4. _____ A good understanding of the Visual Basic programming language is required to create macros in Excel 2003.

5. _____ Macro names can include spaces but not wildcard characters.

6. _____ The Macro Recorder allows you to record both absolute and relative cell references.

7. _____ Macros that are stored in the Personal Macro Workbook are available for use in all of your workbooks.

8. _____ Macro viruses can be stored in workbook template files, as well as in workbooks.

9. _____ When a custom toolbar button that has been assigned a macro is removed from a toolbar, the underlying macro is also deleted.

10. _____ Excel 2003's built-in toolbars, such as the Standard toolbar, cannot be modified.

## Multiple Choice

1. Which of the following cannot be performed on a shared workbook?

   a. Editing a cell's contents
   b. Saving the workbook
   c. Deleting a worksheet
   d. Printing a cell range

2. Which of the following statements about conditional formatting is *false?*

   a. You can format an area using fonts, shading, and border attributes.
   b. You can evaluate a condition only for cells containing numbers.
   c. You can specify up to three conditions.
   d. You can specify formatting options for each condition.

3. The two methods for entering conditions in the Conditional Formatting dialog box include:

   a. Cell Value Is; Cell Label Is
   b. Cell Label Is; Date Range Is
   c. Cell Value Is; Formula Is
   d. Cell Value Is; Calculation Is

4. Which of the following is *not* a valid criterion for data validation?

   a. A range of dates
   b. A list of values
   c. The contents of a cell range
   d. All of the above are valid criteria

5. Which of the following is a proper dynamic cell range formula?

   a. =INDIRECT("$C$1:$C$"&COUNTA ($C:$C))
   b. =INDISCREET("$C$1:$C$"&COUNTA($C:$C))
   c. =INDIRECT($C$1:$C$&COUNTA($C:$C))
   d. =ISDIRECT($C$1:$C$&COUNTA($C:$C))

6. The _____ makes it easy to create macros in Excel 2003.

   a. Macro Assembler
   b. Macro Editor
   c. Macro Recorder
   d. Macro Wizard

**7.** The _____ is a special utility program that enables you to create, edit, modify, and print macros in Excel 2003.

    **a.** Macro Assembler
    **b.** Macro Editor
    **c.** Macro Recorder
    **d.** Visual Basic Editor

**8.** The two buttons available in the Stop Recording toolbar are:

    **a.** Stop Recording; Pause Recording
    **b.** Stop Recording; Relative Reference
    **c.** Pause Recording; Absolute Reference
    **d.** Stop Recording; Save Recording

**9.** Excel 2003's menu is actually a special toolbar called the:

    **a.** Spreadsheet Menu Bar
    **b.** Standard Menu Bar
    **c.** Workbook Menu Bar
    **d.** Worksheet Menu Bar

**10.** To add a new command button to the Standard toolbar, drag an option from this tab in the Customize dialog box:

    **a.** *Toolbars* tab
    **b.** *Commands* tab
    **c.** *Menu* tab
    **d.** *Options* tab

# Hands-On
### exercises

step by step   

## 1. Validating marks

This exercise lets you practice using data validation to restrict the marks that are entered into a gradebook. You will then apply conditional formatting to the worksheet in order to highlight the failing grades.

  **1.** Open the data file named EX11HE01.

  **2.** Save the workbook file as "Valid Marks" to your personal storage location.

  **3.** Let's begin by making sure that the percentage values entered into the Quizzes column are between 0 and 100. To begin:
    SELECT: cell range from B5 to B16

  **4.** To create the data validation rule:
    CHOOSE: Data ➜ Validation
    CLICK: *Settings* tab

  **5.** In the Data Validation dialog box, specify an acceptable value range:
    SELECT: "Whole number" from the *Allow* drop-down list box
    SELECT: "between" from the *Data* drop-down list box
    SELECT: *Minimum* text box
    TYPE: **0**
    PRESS: ( **TAB** )
    TYPE: **100**
    Your screen should now appear similar to the dialog box shown in Figure 11.59.

**Figure 11.59**

Specifying a data validation rule

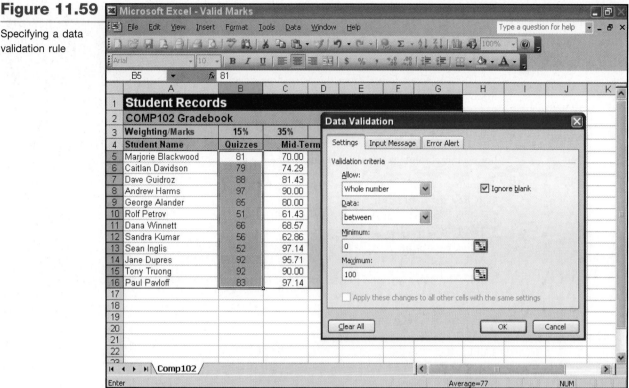

6. To create a custom error message:
   CLICK: *Error Alert* tab
   SELECT: "Stop" from the *Style* drop-down list box
   SELECT: *Title* text box
   TYPE: **Gradebook**
   PRESS: (TAB)
   TYPE: **The score for quizzes cannot be greater than 100%**
   CLICK: OK command button

7. To test the data validation rule:
   SELECT: cell B5
   TYPE: **115**
   PRESS: (ENTER)
   The custom error message appears in a dialog box.

8. To correct the entry:
   CLICK: Retry command button.
   TYPE: **55**
   PRESS: (ENTER)

9. Now let's add a data validation rule that restricts the marks entered into the Mid-Term and Final Exam columns. Your objective is to ensure that the marks do not exceed the total marks available, as provided in cells D3 and F3 respectively. To begin:
   SELECT: cell range from D5 to D16
   PRESS: (CTRL) and hold it down
   SELECT: cell range from F5 to F16
   Both ranges should now appear highlighted. Notice that the active cell is cell F5.

10. To create the data validation rule:
    CHOOSE: Data → Validation
    CLICK: *Settings* tab

11. Now specify the validation rule:
    SELECT: "Whole number" from the *Allow* drop-down list box
    SELECT: "less than or equal to" from the *Data* drop-down list box
    SELECT: *Maximum* text box
    TYPE: **=f$3**
    The column letter is relative so that the condition will apply to both columns. The row number, however, is absolute so that the selected range is compared to the values in cells D3 and F3 only.

12. To create a custom error message:
    CLICK: *Error Alert* tab
    CHOOSE: "Stop" from the *Style* drop-down list box
    SELECT: *Title* text box
    TYPE: **Gradebook**
    PRESS: ( **TAB** )
    TYPE: **The mark entered is greater than the total available marks for the test**
    CLICK: OK command button

13. To test the data validation rule:
    SELECT: cell F8
    TYPE: **73**
    PRESS: ( **ENTER** )
    SELECT: cell D8
    TYPE: **73**
    PRESS: ( **ENTER** )
    As shown in Figure 11.60, the custom error message is displayed because 73 is greater than 70.

**Figure 11.60**

Custom error alert displayed in a dialog box

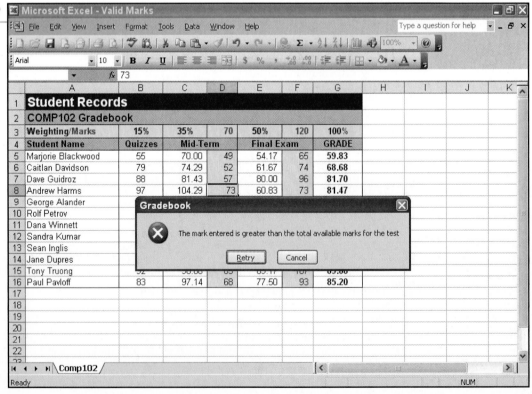

14. To continue:
CLICK: Cancel command button

15. Now let's apply conditional formatting to the Grade column:
SELECT: cell range from G5 to G16
CHOOSE: Format → Conditional Formatting

16. To specify a condition that will identify unacceptable grades:
SELECT: "Cell Value Is" from the leftmost drop-down list box
SELECT: "less than" from the next drop-down list box
TYPE: **60** in the rightmost text box

17. To specify the formatting characteristics to apply when the condition evaluates to true:
CLICK: Format command button
CLICK: *Font* tab, if it is not already selected
SELECT: Bold in the *Font style* list box
SELECT: Red from the *Color* drop-down list box
CLICK: OK command button in the Format Cells dialog box
The dialog box should now appear similar to the one shown in Figure 11.61.

**Figure 11.61**

Conditional Formatting dialog box

18. In the Conditional Formatting dialog box:
CLICK: OK command button

19. To cancel the selection:
PRESS: (CTRL)+(HOME)
How many students have a final grade below 60 percent?

20. Save and then close the "Valid Marks" workbook.

step by step

## 2. Titling a Worksheet

Using the Macro Recorder, you will now create a macro that inserts a row, enters a worksheet title, and then formats the entry.

1. Open the data file named EX11HE02.

2. Save the workbook as "Video Macro" to your personal storage location.

3. To begin recording a new macro:
CHOOSE: Tools → Macro → Record New Macro

4. Complete the Record Macro dialog box as follows:
TYPE: **InsertTitle** in the *Macro name* text box
PRESS: (TAB)
TYPE: **t** in the *Shortcut key* text box
Your screen should appear similar to the dialog box shown in Figure 11.62.

**Figure 11.62**

Record Macro
dialog box

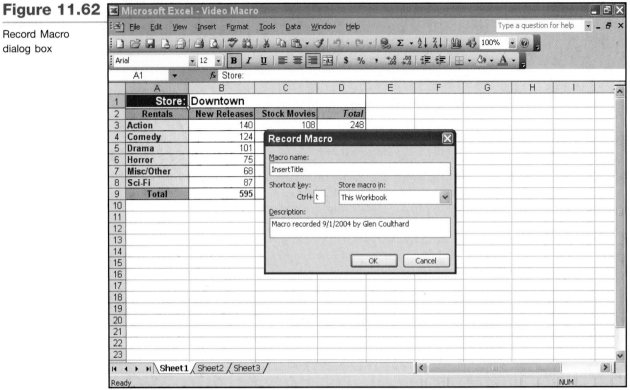

5. In the Record Macro dialog box:
   CLICK: OK command button to proceed

6. Now perform the actions that you want stored in the Insert Title macro. To begin, let's make sure the macro always starts in the cell A1:
   PRESS: (CTRL)+(HOME)

7. Next, insert a new row and adjust the height:
   CHOOSE: Insert → Rows
   CHOOSE: Format → Row → Height
   TYPE: **20**
   CLICK: OK command button

8. You can now insert and center the title. Do the following:
   TYPE: **Smackers Video Stop**
   PRESS: (ENTER)
   SELECT: cell range from A1 to D1
   CLICK: Merge and Center button (⊞)

9. To apply formatting to the title:
   CLICK: down arrow attached to the Font Size list box (10 ▼)
   SELECT: 16
   CLICK: Bold button (**B**)
   CLICK: down arrow attached to the Fill Color button (🎨▼)
   SELECT: Dark Blue from the drop-down list
   CLICK: down arrow attached to the Font Color button (A▼)
   SELECT: White from the drop-down list
   Your worksheet should appear similar to the one shown in Figure 11.63.

## Figure 11.63

Recording steps
for a macro

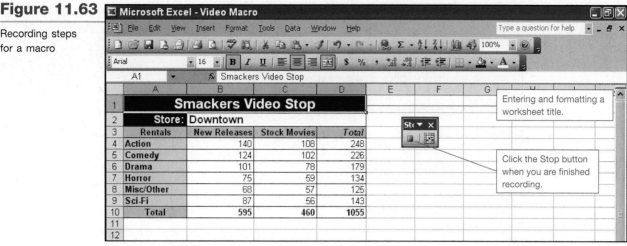

10. To stop recording the macro:
    CLICK: Stop button (■)

11. Now let's play back the macro to see if it produces the expected results. First, switch to the next
    worksheet:
    CLICK: *Sheet2* tab
    SELECT: cell A9
    (*Note:* By starting in cell A9, you will be able to see the effect of pressing **CTRL**+**HOME** at the start
    of the macro.)

12. To run the macro:
    CHOOSE: Tools → Macro → Macros
    SELECT: InsertTitle in the list box
    CLICK: Run command button
    The formatted title is entered into row 1 of the *Sheet2* worksheet.

13. Now let's play back the macro using the keyboard shortcut:
    CLICK: *Sheet3* tab

14. To run the macro:
    PRESS: **CTRL**+**t**
    The formatted title is entered into the *Sheet3* worksheet.

15. Save and then close the "Video Macro" workbook.

**step by step**

## 3. Auditing a Worksheet

You will now practice using the Formula Auditing toolbar to find invalid data and formula errors in a
worksheet.

1. Open the data file named EX11HE03.

2. Save the workbook as "Production Audit" to your personal storage location.

3. Before using the Formula Auditing toolbar to track down invalid data, you must define the data
   validation rules for the worksheet. To begin:
   SELECT: cell range from B4 to B8
   CHOOSE: Data → Validation
   CLICK: *Settings* tab

4. Add a data validation rule that restricts entries in the selected range to a whole number that is less
   than or equal to 4700, as shown in Figure 11.64.

**Figure 11.64**

Data Validation
dialog box

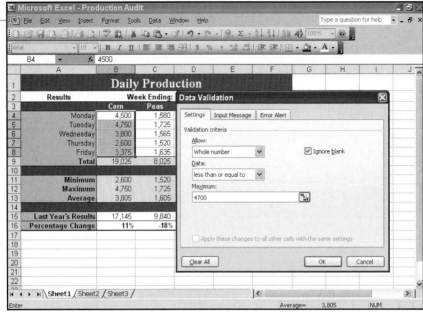

5. Using the same approach, add data validation rules that limit the daily production levels for the remaining input columns. The maximum levels are 1600 for Peas, 2800 for Beans, and 3300 for all Other products.

6. Select cell A1 and then display the Formula Auditing toolbar.

7. To highlight the input values that violate the data validation rules:
CLICK: Circle Invalid Data button (⊞)
Several red validation circles appear in the worksheet area.

8. Next, use the trace precedents feature to review each Percentage Change calculation in the bottom row of the worksheet. Your screen should now appear similar to the worksheet shown in Figure 11.65. Notice that the formula's precedents in cell F16 differ from the other calculations.

**Figure 11.65**

Auditing a
production
worksheet

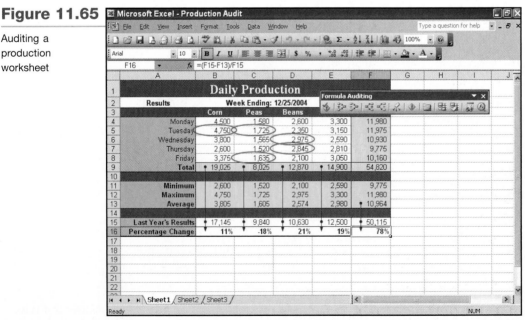

**9.** Using the other formulas in row 16 as your guide, correct the formula entry in cell F16 and then re-display its tracer arrows.

**10.** Apply the trace precedents feature again to see the next level of cell relationships.

**11.** When you are finished, remove all of the tracer arrows, clear the red validation circles, and remove the Formula Auditing toolbar from displaying.

**12.** Save and then close the "Production Audit" workbook.

on your own

## 4. Highlighting Results

Because of your well-known experience with Excel 2003, you have been asked by your colleagues to record a macro that will highlight worksheet information. After reviewing the specifics of the request, you decide to add a new toolbar to the workbook with a custom button for launching the macro. In order to begin, open the data file named EX11HE04 and save it as "Realtor Macros" to your personal storage location.

Perform the following tasks:

- Using the Macro Recorder, create a macro named "Emphasize" that uses relative referencing and is executed by pressing **CTRL**+e. The macro should apply a light blue fill color with a border outline to a cell and display its contents using a dark blue and boldface font style.

- Test the macro using the shortcut key on cell F6.

- Create a new toolbar called "My Faves" and then name and designate a custom macro button to run the "Emphasize" macro. Lastly, change its image to display a red diamond shape, as shown in Figure 11.66.

**Figure 11.66**

Assigning a macro to a new toolbar button

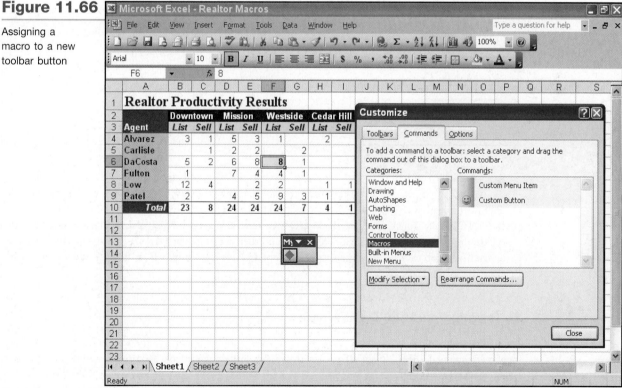

After closing the Customize dialog box, make sure that the new toolbar button works properly by emphasizing cell J5. Hide the custom "My Faves" toolbar by clicking its Close button ( ). In order to clean up your work area, delete the "My Faves" toolbar using the Customize dialog box. Then, save and close the "Realtor Macros" workbook.

on your own

### 5. Creating a Titling Macro

In this exercise, you will create, edit, and print a macro. Starting with a new workbook, use the Macro Recorder to create a new macro called "AddTitle" that is stored in the current workbook. Record the following actions in the new macro:

- Enter your school or business name into cell A1.

- Enter your school or business address into cells A2 and A3.

- Format the information using a Times New Roman font, 14 point font size, boldface style, and a dark blue color.

- Enter the **=today()** function into cell A4.

- Format cell A4 to display the date using the "March 14, 2001" format.

- Format the cell using a Times New Roman font, 12 point font size, and a teal color. Your worksheet should appear similar to the one shown in Figure 11.67, although your information will differ.

**Figure 11.67**

Entering and
formatting a title

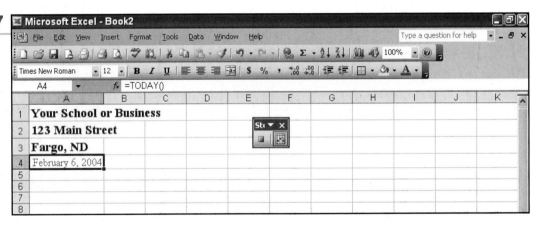

After you have finished recording the steps, move to the *Sheet2* tab and execute the macro. Then, view the macro code in the Visual Basic Editor. (*Hint:* To display the proper Code window, you may need to double-click "Module1" in the Project window.) Once displayed, change the code line containing the "=TODAY()" function to use the "=NOW()" function instead. Next, change the font size for cells A1 through A3 to 18 points. Print the macro and then return to the worksheet. Execute the function on the *Sheet3* tab to make sure that it works properly. Save the workbook as "Titling Macro" and then close the workbook.

on your own

### 6. Creating an Auto_Open Macro

Display a new workbook in the Excel 2003 application window. Then, use the Macro Recorder to create a new macro named "Auto_Open" that is stored in the current workbook. Record the following actions in the new macro:

- Make the Picture toolbar visible.

- Make the Drawing toolbar visible.

- Using the Tools ➜ Options command, turn off the gridlines and row and column headers.

After you stop recording, position the toolbars where you would like them to appear in the window. Then, hide the Picture and Drawing toolbars. Lastly, turn on the gridlines and row and column headers.

You may now save the workbook as "OpenTools" to your personal storage location. On your own, test the Auto_Open macro by closing the workbook and then reopening it. (*Note:* You must enable the macros.) When you are ready to proceed, hide the toolbars once again and then close the workbook without saving the changes.

# CaseStudy   SCHUETZ & SONS, INC.

Having just completed his studies at Florida State, Joseph Schuetz is the third son to join his father's accounting firm in Jacksonville. As the youngest member of the firm, Joseph's initial duties revolve around making life easier for the other partners—his older brothers. In fact, his first official assignment, which came directly from his father, is to review the firm's use of electronic spreadsheets. In addition to recommending how the firm can improve their efficiency and productivity, Joseph must perform the tedious task of checking the validity and accuracy of some existing workbooks.

Upon reviewing the workflow for one such account, Adam's Books, Joseph selects one of their more time-consuming tasks to audit and automate. Each month, Adam's in-house accountants send over a month-end workbook. One of his brothers then checks the formulas and retypes all of the information into a new worksheet; they are novice users and they are not confident enough of their Excel 2003 skills to do it any other way. By automating this task, Joseph feels that he can demonstrate to his family how Excel 2003 can help the firm become more productive.

In the following case problems, assume the role of Joseph and perform the same steps that he identifies.

**1.** Joseph settles quietly into his cubicle and launches Microsoft Office Excel 2003. Although several accountants in the office have Excel 2003 on their computers, they are using it merely as an expensive calculator rather than a full-featured analysis and productivity tool. Knowing the powerful features of Excel 2003, Joseph decides to display a new workbook file and create some macros that he will be able to use in all of the workbooks he creates. From his computer course in college, Joseph remembers that he has to store all of these macros in the Personal Macro Workbook.

The first macro that Joseph records is called "Letterhead;" it places the firm's name and address centered between columns A and F at the top of the worksheet. Specifically, the firm's name "Schuetz & Sons, Inc." appears in row 1, the street address "Suite 400, 1010 Granville Street" appears in row 2, and the remainder of the address "Jacksonville, Florida" appears in row 3. Joseph formats the information to match the company letterhead, which uses a Times New Roman typeface, 18-point font size and a boldface style for the name, and a 14-point font size and an italic style for the address. He tests the macro on the *Sheet2* tab to ensure that it is working properly, as shown in Figure 11.68.

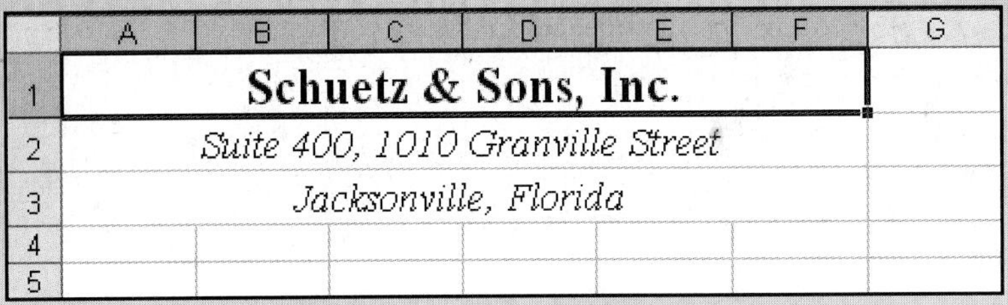

**Figure 11.68**

Viewing the
results of the
Letterhead macro

| | A | B | C | D | E | F | G |
|---|---|---|---|---|---|---|---|
| 1 | | | Schuetz & Sons, Inc. | | | | |
| 2 | | Suite 400, 1010 Granville Street | | | | | |
| 3 | | Jacksonville, Florida | | | | | |
| 4 | | | | | | | |
| 5 | | | | | | | |

**2.** Realizing that macros are exactly what his father was asking for in terms of enhancing productivity, Joseph continues recording a few more instructions. The next macro that he adds to his Personal Macro Workbook is called "PageSet." This macro specifies page layout specifications for printing a worksheet report in landscape orientation on 81/2 by 11-inch paper. This macro also sets the margins to 1.25 inches on all sides and centers the page horizontally. Lastly, Joseph inserts a custom footer at the bottom of the page that centers the text "Prepared by Joseph Schuetz" on the printout. After closing the Page Setup dialog box, Joseph stops recording the macro.

To view his new page setup, Joseph previews the worksheet by clicking the Print Preview button ( ) on the Standard toolbar. As shown in Figure 11.69, he then clicks the Margins command button at the top of the Preview window. To further test the macros, he closes the Preview window and selects the *Sheet3* tab. Joseph first runs the Letterhead macro and then the PageSet macro. To see the results once again, he clicks the Print Preview button ( ). Joseph is quite satisfied with the results and closes the Preview window. Remembering that all of the macros are stored in the Personal Macro Workbook, Joseph closes the workbook file without saving the changes.

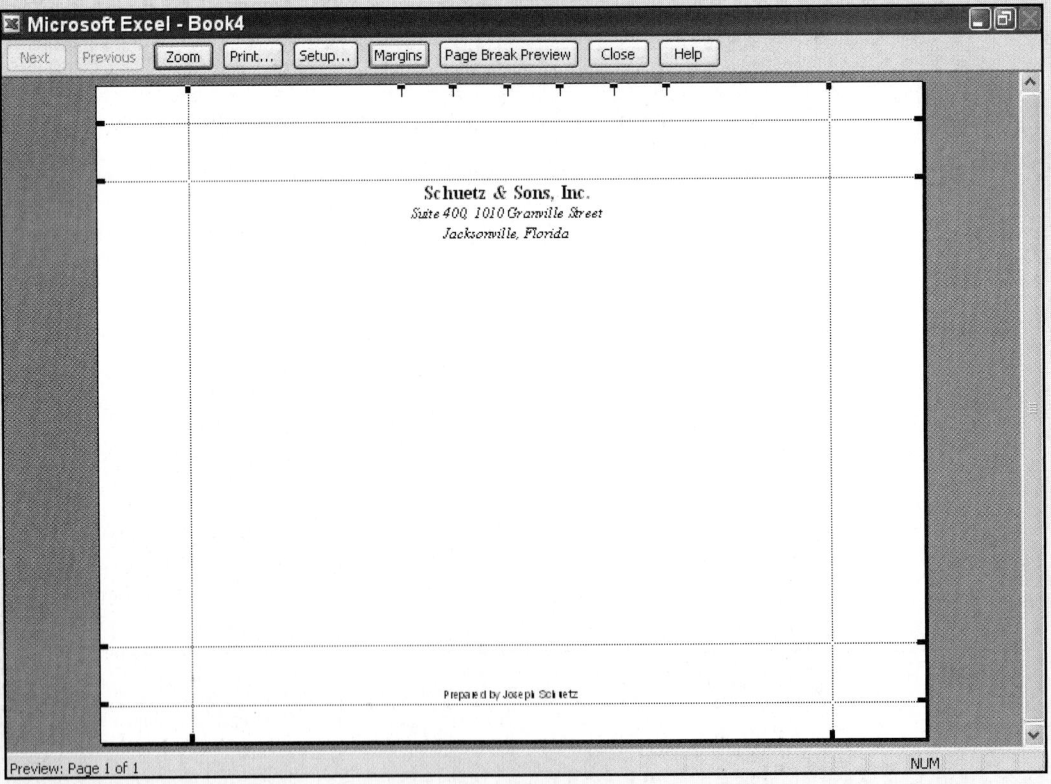

**Figure 11.69**

Viewing the
results of the
PageSet macro

3. To begin his workbook review for Adam's Books, Joseph opens the EX11CP00 workbook and saves it as "Adam's Audit" to his personal storage location. Having spoken with Mr. Adam earlier that morning, Joseph knows to highlight those products in the cell range B3:E12 with sales exceeding $10,000. He uses Excel 2003's conditional formatting feature to apply a dark teal green color and a boldface font style to these values in the worksheet area. Then, using Excel 2003's data validation feature, Joseph ensures that each store enters a valid sales figure (a whole number greater than zero) for each product.

Now Joseph needs to figure out which products are included in the "Core Microsoft Office System" line item versus the "Other Microsoft Applications" line item in rows 14 and 15. After displaying the Formula Auditing toolbar, he traces the formulas in cells B14 and C15 to their precedents, as shown in Figure 11.70. Armed with a better understanding of the worksheet, Joseph removes the tracer arrows and hides the Formula Auditing toolbar. He then saves and closes the "Adam's Audit" workbook.

**Figure 11.70**

Tracing precedents in the "Adam's Audit" workbook

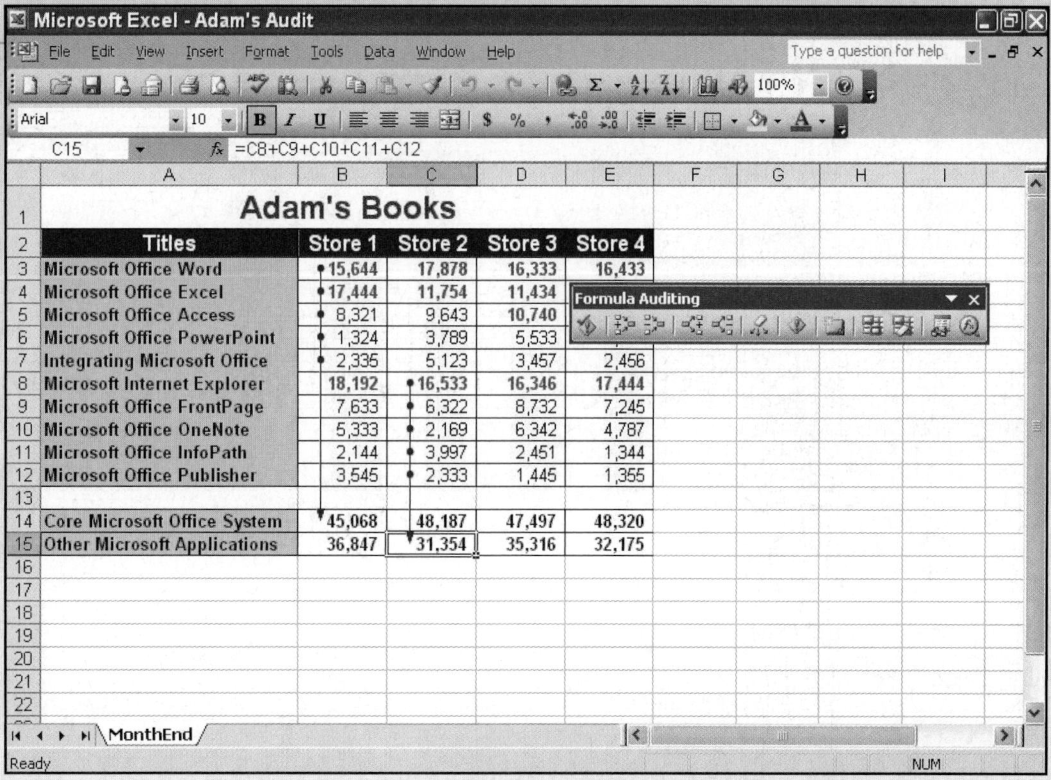

4. Joseph is now ready to tackle automating the month-end process for Adam's Books. He displays a new workbook, removes the *Sheet2* and *Sheet3* worksheet tabs, and then saves the workbook as "Adam's Amalgamated" to his personal storage location. This workbook will be used to import data from the other workbooks that are sent at the end of each month. Joseph must create a macro that will insert a new worksheet in "Adam's Amalgamated" and then copy the data from the monthly workbook. To begin, Joseph starts the Macro Recorder, names the macro "GetMonthEnd," and chooses to store the macro in this workbook only. Having run through the steps he needs to follow, Joseph performs the following tasks:

- Insert a new worksheet

- Rename the worksheet tab "Import"

- Open the EX11CP00 data file ("Adam's MonthEnd" workbook)

- Copy the cell range from A2 to E12 to the Clipboard

- Display the "Adam's Amalgamated" workbook

- Select cell A1 on the *Import* tab

- Paste the Clipboard contents into the workbook

- Size the columns on the *Import* tab to display the best fit

- Select cell A1 on the *Import* tab

Your screen should now appear similar to the worksheet shown in Figure 11.71. Joseph stops the macro recording at this point and then renames the *Import* tab to appear as *July*. He also displays and then closes the EX11CP00 data file without saving the changes.

## Figure 11.71

Creating an
import macro
routine

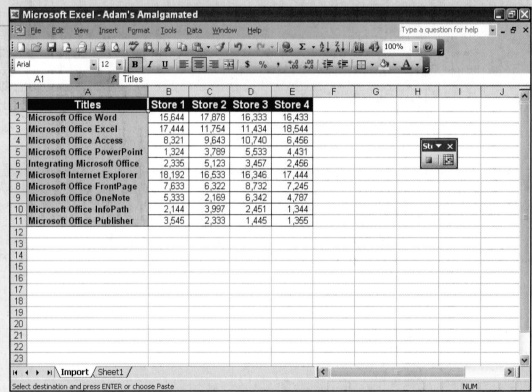

To make sure that the macro works as planned, Joseph tests the macro by choosing it from the Macro dialog box. He is surprised when he receives an error dialog box but knows enough about editing macros to attempt to fix the code. He clicks the Debug command button to launch the Visual Basic Editor and then maximizes the Code window to appear similar to the one shown in Figure 11.72.

**Figure 11.72**

Editing the absolute references in a macro

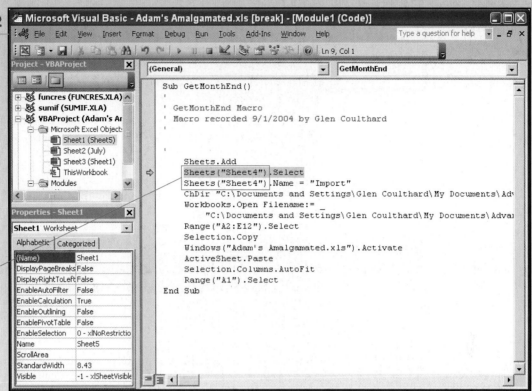

Change these two code lines to read ActiveSheet instead of Sheets("Sheet4").

Joseph realizes that he must replace the absolute Sheets("Sheet4") reference in favor of using the "ActiveSheet" object. With the modifications complete, Joseph clicks the Reset button (▪) in the Visual Basic Editor's toolbar and returns to the workbook. He successfully tests the macro and then saves and closes the "Adam's Amalgamated" workbook. After exiting Excel 2003 without saving the changes to the Personal Macro Workbook, Joseph starts daydreaming about becoming the youngest partner in the firm's history!

(*Note:* Before exiting Excel 2003, you can delete the macros created and stored in the Personal Macro Workbook. However, before Excel 2003 will allow you to delete these macros, you must first unhide a special workbook called "PERSONAL.xls." To do so, choose the Window ➜ Unhide command and double-click the workbook name in the list box. Then, choose the Tools ➜ Macro ➜ Macros command and remove the macros by clicking the Delete command button. Lastly, close the "PERSONAL.xls" workbook, saving the changes when prompted, and exit Microsoft Office Excel 2003.)

# Answers to Self-Check Questions

**SelfCheck**

**11.1** Provide an example of a workbook that would lend itself to being shared, especially for history tracking and merging in a workgroup environment. This answer will vary. Some examples of shared workbooks include price lists, inventory records, customer worksheet lists, accounting workbooks, and personnel schedules.

**11.2** How could you check whether a customer account code is valid when entering invoice data into a worksheet template? To check whether a customer account code is valid, use the Data Validation dialog box. You can compare, for example, the customer account code to a list of acceptable values appearing in a worksheet list.

**11.3** What result occurs by clicking the Trace Precedents button ([icon]) or the Trace Dependents button ([icon]) twice on the Formula Auditing toolbar? When you click either button a second time, additional tracer arrows appear on the worksheet to display the next level of cell relationships.

**11.4** Aside from running the macro, how would you determine whether absolute or relative cell referencing was being used? You can examine the macro's programming code in the Code window of the Visual Basic Editor.

**11.5** How would you create an option on the Menu bar that contained all of your macros? To begin, open the Customize dialog box, click the *Commands* tab, and then select the New Menu item at the bottom of the Categories list box. Drag the selection from the *Commands* list box to the Menu bar. Then, using the right-click menu, change the name to something more appropriate like "My Macros." You can now drag the Custom Menu Item selection from the Macros category to appear in the new menu. Assign a macro and rename the new menu item. Repeat this step for each of the macros you want to add to the menu.

# Microsoft®Office**Excel**®

## 2003

### CHAPTER 12

## Introducing Visual Basic for Applications

**PREREQUISITES**

To successfully complete this chapter, you must know how to record and play macros. You should also be able to launch the Visual Basic Editor and perform simple editing tasks in the Code window. Although no previous programming knowledge is required, this chapter presumes competence in all areas of worksheet creation, editing, and formatting.

LEARNING
**OBJECTIVES**

After reading this chapter, you will be able to:

• Use Visual Basic for Applications (VBA) within Microsoft Office Excel 2003

• Describe the elements of the VBA integrated development environment

• Define terms such as *objects, properties, methods, variables,* and *constants*

• Write program code using the Editor

• Develop procedures that select and format cells, input data, make decisions, and perform looping operations

• Place controls, such as command buttons and drop-down list boxes, on a worksheet

# 12.1 Introducing the VBA Environment

Microsoft Visual Basic for Applications (VBA) is the shared and fully integrated macro development environment available in Microsoft Office System 2003. Aside from its familial status in Office, VBA is itself an independent software program, and you may find it included in other application software, such as AutoCAD and Microsoft Visio. VBA provides a subset of the features found in the Microsoft Visual Basic programming language. While Visual Basic creates stand-alone applications, VBA must be run within a host application such as Microsoft Office Excel 2003. Another version of Visual Basic, called **VB Script** (short for *Visual Basic Scripting Edition*), provides lesser capabilities but allows you to program and support Web content. As VBA requires a host application, VB Script requires a Web browser to interpret its code. Many users, however, associate and equate VB Script programs with virus attachments, given their history of abuse by hackers. With Microsoft **Visual Studio Tools for Office** (VSTO), you can create and use managed code within the Visual Studio environment and tap into the powerful features of the .NET (pronounced *Dot Net*) Framework. Initially, however, VSTO is available only for Word 2003 and Excel 2003. With Visual Studio .Net's growing popularity, you may soon need only a single programming language and environment to control many different application software programs!

The object-oriented programming model used in VBA is called **event-driven programming**, which places an application's *objects* at the center of attention and allows you to specify how those objects look and behave. Using VBA, for example, you can create a dialog box that displays text boxes, option buttons, and command buttons. Each one of these elements, including the dialog box itself, is an *object* that you may instruct how to react to a particular *event*. When you click a command button in the dialog box, a "click-event" message is sent to the object. If the object contains a program written to respond to such an event, the code is run and the instructions carried out. An **event** can be initiated by the user, as in clicking a button, or by the software program, as in performing an automated or scheduled backup.

VBA is specifically designed to work with application software like Office 2003. For users of Microsoft Office Excel 2003, the potential power behind VBA lies in the fact that all of the major Office applications *expose,* or make available, their objects to VBA. In other words, an application's objects, such as Word's documents, Excel's workbooks, and Access' forms and reports, can be used by any other application. You can use VBA, for example, to launch Word 2003, load a document template, collect data using a form, convert the document to a slide, and then display it on-screen—and all from within Excel 2003!

## 12.1.1 Touring the Visual Basic Editor

→ **Feature**

The Visual Basic Editor provides the programming tools that you use in **coding** and editing procedures. Because the Editor window exists separate of its host application (Excel 2003), you can tile both application windows on the desktop, make changes to your code in the Editor window, and view the results immediately within Excel. Within the Editor window, you can display, hide, and dock several informative and functional windows, including the **Project Explorer window** (or Project window), **Properties window,** and **Code window.** These windows make up the main elements of the VBA environment. Table 12.1 describes the windows that may appear in the Visual Basic Editor.

**Table 12.1**

Windows in the Visual Basic Editor

| Window... | Description... |
|---|---|
| **Project Explorer Window** | Displays a hierarchical list of the objects, code modules, user forms, and other files associated with a VBA project; you can display more than one project at a time in this window |
| **Properties Window** | Displays the characteristics and settings for the selected object; if you select multiple objects, only the common properties are displayed |

| Window... | Description... |
|---|---|
| Code Window | Used to display, write, edit, debug, and print macros and other procedures; you can display multiple Code windows at the same time in the Editor window |
| Immediate Window | Used to modify the environment or test code before placing it into a procedure; type a programming statement into the window and press ENTER to execute it immediately |
| Locals Window | Displays the current procedure's variables, along with their values and data types; you can edit the value of a variable in this window |
| Watch Window | Displays the values of watch expressions that you have set in order to observe the behavior of variables or debug program statements |

→ **Method**

To display the various components of the Visual Basic Editor:

- CHOOSE: View → Project Explorer
- CHOOSE: View → Properties Window
- CHOOSE: View → Code
- CHOOSE: View → Immediate Window
- CHOOSE: View → Locals Window
- CHOOSE: View → Watch Window

→ **Practice**

You will now practice customizing and viewing the windows displayed in the Visual Basic Editor. Before proceeding, start Microsoft Office Excel 2003.

1. Open the data file named EX1210 and enable the macros. The workbook appears empty.

2. Save the workbook as "VBA Tour" to your personal storage location.

3. To demonstrate the macro stored in this workbook:
   SELECT: cell B2
   PRESS: CTRL +e
   A formatted title appears in the worksheet, as shown in Figure 12.1.

**Figure 12.1**

Executing a macro

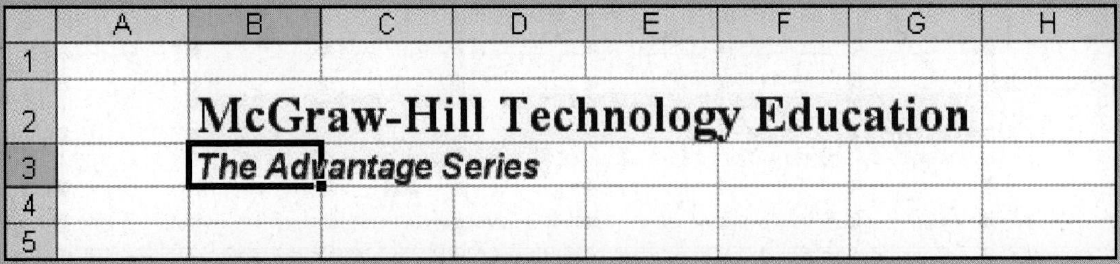

| | A | B | C | D | E | F | G | H |
|---|---|---|---|---|---|---|---|---|
| 1 | | | | | | | | |
| 2 | | McGraw-Hill Technology Education | | | | | | |
| 3 | | *The Advantage Series* | | | | | | |
| 4 | | | | | | | | |
| 5 | | | | | | | | |

**4.** To display this macro in the Visual Basic Editor:
CHOOSE: Tools → Macro → Macros
SELECT: SpeedEntry in the *Macro name* list box
CLICK: Edit command button
The Editor application window appears. (*Note:* The Editor remembers the window layout from the last time you worked in the application window. Therefore, you may see the Code window or other windows docked with the Editor window.)

**5.** Size and move the Code window to appear similar to the one shown in Figure 12.2. (*Hint:* If the Code window appears maximized, restore it to a window by clicking its Restore button (⊡) in the top right-hand corner.)

**Figure 12.2**

The Visual Basic Editor

Project Explorer window

Code window

Properties window

Work area

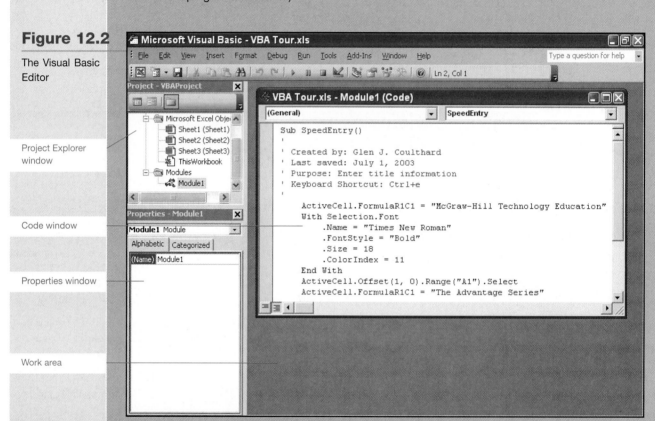

**6.** To display the Immediate window:
CHOOSE: View → Immediate Window
The Immediate window is displayed, usually docked at the bottom of the Visual Basic Editor window.

**7.** On your own, click the Close buttons (✗) on the Immediate window, Code window, Properties window, and Project Explorer window. The Visual Basic Editor's application window should now appear empty.

**8.** A VBA *project file* is the container that stores all of the code modules, user forms or custom dialog boxes, and other objects related to a single workbook. For each open workbook in Excel 2003, including the Personal Macro Workbook, a project file is displayed in the Project Explorer window. You do not need to create or save a project file—each project is saved automatically when you save its associated workbook. To display the Project Explorer window (Figure 12.3):
CLICK: Project Explorer button (🗐) on the toolbar

**Figure 12.3**

Project Explorer
window

Project file for the
"VBA Tour"
workbook

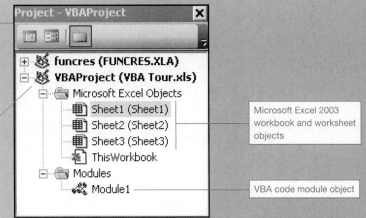

Microsoft Excel 2003
workbook and worksheet
objects

VBA code module object

**9.** The Properties window (Figure 12.4) displays the characteristics that you may set for an object. The window itself is divided vertically with the leftmost column displaying the property name and the rightmost column displaying its current value. Use the Properties window to specify values for an object at **design time,** before the user runs the macro and interacts with the object (referred to as **run time.**) To display the Properties window for a worksheet object:
SELECT: Sheet1 object in the Project Explorer window
CLICK: Properties Window button ([🔲])

**Figure 12.4**

Properties
window

Click a tab to
display the
properties in
alphabetical order
or grouped by
category.

Select a property
by clicking its
name.

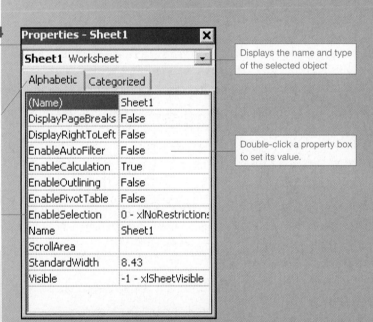

Displays the name and type
of the selected object

Double-click a property box
to set its value.

**10.** You can move, or undock, the windows displayed in the Editor window using the same methods you use to float toolbars. However, re-docking and arranging these windows can be tricky. To practice sizing the windows, position the mouse pointer over the Properties window's top border until it changes shape (⬍). Then, drag the window border to the middle of the work area. On your own, practice changing the height and width of the docked windows by dragging their borders back and forth.

Excel

**11.** The Code window (Figure 12.5) displays the macro procedures stored in a module. You can view one procedure at a time by clicking the Procedure View button ( ≡ ) at the bottom of the Code window, or you can view multiple procedures at the same time by clicking the Full Module View button ( ≣ ). To navigate the procedures listed in a Code window, scroll the window or make a selection from the Object and Procedure drop-down list boxes. To display the Code window:
DOUBLE-CLICK: Module1 in the Project Explorer window

**Figure 12.5**

Code window

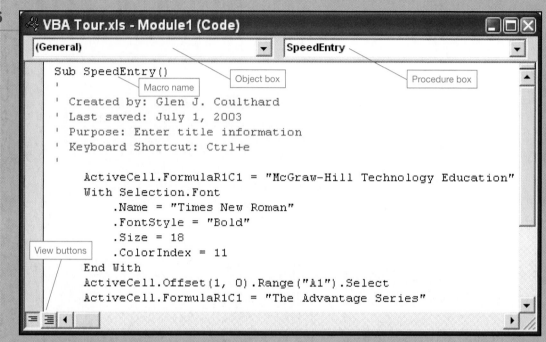

**12.** To view another Code window:
SELECT: Sheet1 object in the Project Explorer window
CLICK: View Code button ( ▣ ) in the Project Explorer toolbar
An empty Code window is displayed.

**13.** To tile the Code windows in the work area:
CHOOSE: Window → Tile Horizontally
The two Code windows should now appear tiled in the work area, as shown in Figure 12.6. Use tiling when you need to position the Code windows for copying or moving code. Notice that only the Code windows are tiled; the docked windows are unaffected.

**Figure 12.6**

Tiling Code
windows in the
Visual Basic
Editor

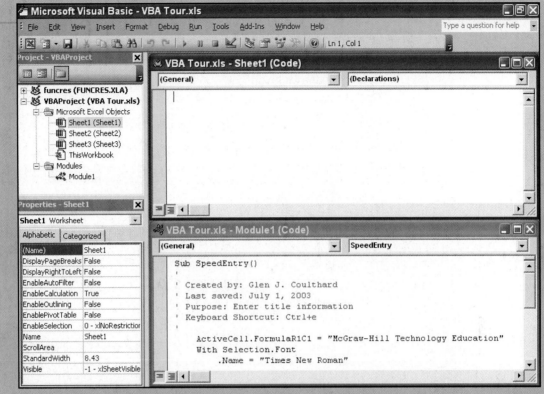

**14.** To cascade the windows so that the Module1 Code window appears on top:
    CLICK: Title bar for the Module1 Code window (bottom window)
    CHOOSE: Window → Cascade

**15.** Close the two Code windows by clicking their Close buttons (✕). The work area in the Visual Basic Editor should now appear empty.

**16.** To switch to the Excel 2003 workbook and then back again:
    CLICK: View Microsoft Excel button (🖾) on the toolbar
    CLICK: Microsoft Visual Basic button on the taskbar

**17.** To close the Editor and return to Excel 2003:
    CHOOSE: File → Close and Return to Microsoft Excel

**18.** Keep the workbook open for use in the next lesson.

## 12.1.2 Stepping Through a Macro

→ **Feature**

One of the best methods for learning VBA is to examine the code generated by the Macro Recorder. To this end, you can step through a macro's code line by line to determine what it is doing. This process, known as **debugging,** is typically used to check code for errors. In addition to finding where a macro goes awry, debugging tools and the Editor windows can help you learn how to code procedures using VBA.

As with any programming language, VBA does not tolerate spelling errors when you type code (except in comments, which are ignored during execution anyway). Each program statement must follow a specific **syntax,** or programming rule. If the syntax is not followed precisely, the code will not work correctly. Fortunately, spelling and syntax errors are relatively easy to locate and correct. But sometimes the error is not so obvious. Some errors, called *logical errors* or *calculation errors,* require a more thoughtful approach. In these cases, analyzing your code by *stepping* through it line by line is the best way to resolve conflicts and fix errors.

→ **Method**

To debug your code one step at a time:

- CHOOSE: Tools → Macro → Macros
- SELECT: *a macro* in the list box
- CLICK: Step Into command button
- PRESS: F8 to execute the highlighted line of code in the Editor
- CLICK: Reset button (⬛) to stop stepping through a macro

→ **Practice**

You will now step through a macro procedure using the Editor's debugging tools. Ensure that the "VBA Tour" workbook is displayed.

**1.** Display the *Sheet2* worksheet:
CLICK: *Sheet2* tab
SELECT: cell A1, if it is not already selected

**2.** To begin stepping through the SpeedEntry macro:
CHOOSE: Tools → Macro → Macros
SELECT: SpeedEntry in the *Macro name* list box
CLICK: Step Into command button
The Module1 Code window is opened for display in the Editor, as shown in Figure 12.7. Also, notice the word "[break]," which means "stopped temporarily," in the Title bar of the Visual Basic Editor.

**Figure 12.7**

Stepping through
code in the Editor

The yellow arrow
and code
highlighting indicate
the line to be
executed next.

Margin Indicator bar

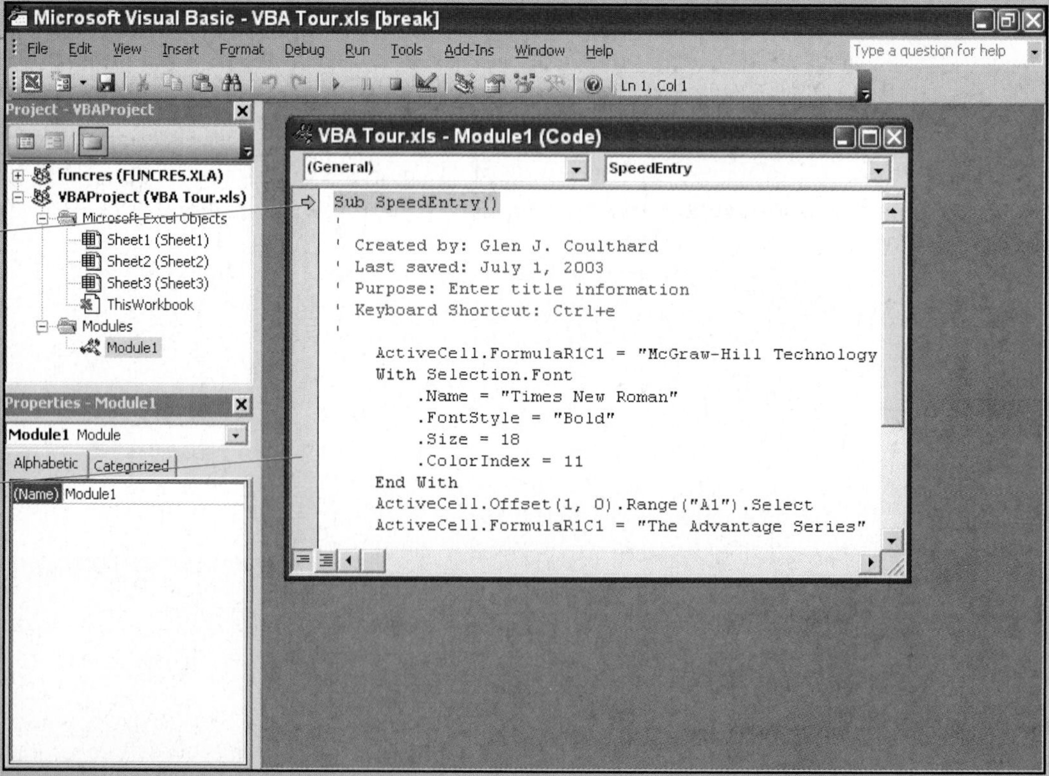

**3.** To continue processing the macro code:
PRESS: [F8]
Notice that the arrow and highlighting jump to the first line of code appearing after the comments, which appear green and preceded by apostrophes.

**4.** To execute the highlighted line of code:
PRESS: [F8]

**5.** To concurrently see what is happening in the workbook, you can tile both application windows on your desktop, or you can use the taskbar to switch between the two windows. Do the following:
CLICK: Microsoft Excel–VBA Tour button on the taskbar
Notice that the text "McGraw-Hill Technology Education" is entered into cell A1.

**6.** To return to the Editor window:
CLICK: Microsoft Visual Basic button on the taskbar

**7.** On your own, step through the remaining lines of code in the Editor window. Switch to the workbook after every three or four lines to see the effect of the code.

**8.** With the highlight on the "End Sub" instruction:
PRESS: [F8] to conclude the "stepping" process
The yellow arrow and highlight disappear. If you want to stop stepping through a macro before it reaches the "End Sub" instruction, click the Reset button (▣) on the Editor's Standard toolbar.

**9.** To close the Editor and return to Excel 2003:
CHOOSE: File → Close and Return to Microsoft Excel
You should now see the familiar formatted text in cells A1 and A2.

**10.** Keep the workbook open for use in the next lesson.

### *In Addition* HANDLING ERRORS GRACEFULLY

There are three types of errors that can occur in VBA: syntax errors, run-time errors, and logical errors. A *syntax error* occurs when you misspell a keyword or enter arguments in an incorrect order. A *run-time error* occurs when the procedure cannot deal with a particular circumstance, such as the user entering "0" as the divisor in a calculation. A *logical error* is a human error whereby the procedure does not do what it is supposed to do. In programming, you need to anticipate most of these errors and, at the least, code special routines (called *error handlers*) to deal with the run-time errors.

## 12.1.3 Using Breakpoints

→ **Feature**

Imagine that you have just added a few new lines of code to an existing macro. You know that the old code works fine and would now like to test only the new code. Instead of stepping through the entire macro, you can set a **breakpoint** in your code. When you subsequently execute the macro, the Editor will stop executing at the breakpoint and display the Code window. At this point, you can begin stepping through each line of the new code.

→ **Method**

To set and use a breakpoint:

• Position the insertion point in the code line that you want to test.

• CHOOSE: Debug → Toggle Breakpoint

  *or*

• CLICK: beside the code line in the Margin Indicator bar

- Run the macro.

- PRESS: **F8** to execute the highlighted line of code

- CLICK: Reset button (▣) to stop stepping through a macro

→ **Practice**

You will now practice setting a breakpoint in an existing macro. Ensure that the "VBA Tour" workbook is displayed.

**1.** Display the *Sheet3* worksheet:
CLICK: *Sheet3* tab
SELECT: cell A1, if it is not already selected

**2.** To display the Editor window using a keyboard shortcut:
PRESS: **ALT**+**F11**
The Editor is displayed with the Module1 Code window.

**3.** To set a breakpoint on a specific line:
CLICK: in the Margin Indicator bar beside the line containing "The Advantage Series"
The Code window should now appear similar to the one shown in Figure 12.8. (*Hint:* If you make an incorrect selection, click the red circle to toggle off the breakpoint and then try again.)

**Figure 12.8**

Setting a breakpoint

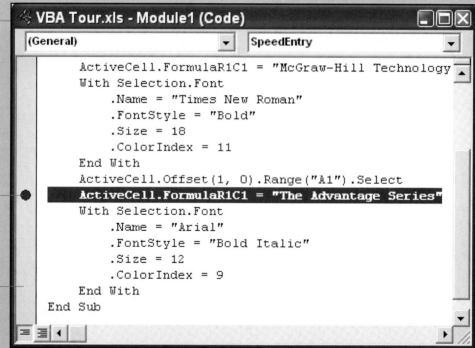

The red circle and highlighting indicate that a breakpoint has been set.

Margin Indicator bar

**4.** To run the macro:
CLICK: Microsoft Excel–VBA Tour button on the taskbar
PRESS: **CTRL**+e
The macro begins execution and, when the breakpoint is reached, the Editor window appears with the code line highlighted as shown below.

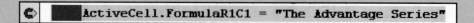

**5.** To check the workbook results up to this point in the macro:
CLICK: Microsoft Excel–VBA Tour button on the taskbar
Notice that only the first text line has been entered.

**6.** Rather than proceed with stepping through the macro, let's stop it at this point in its execution:
CLICK: Microsoft Visual Basic button on the taskbar
CLICK: Reset button (■)

**7.** To return to the workbook:
CHOOSE: File → Close and Return to Microsoft Excel

**8.** Save and then close the "VBA Tour" workbook.

**SelfCheck**   **12.1** Which window would you display in the Visual Basic Editor if you wanted to set the design-time properties for an object?

## 12.2 Understanding the VBA Language

The Macro Recorder translates keystrokes and command selections into VBA programming code, which are then stored as a "Sub" procedure in a standard module. There will be times, however, when you will need to develop a program that is not simply a sequential series of captured keystrokes. For these situations, you must code your own procedures. Although VBA programming is relatively easy to learn, you still need to understand fundamental programming concepts to write efficient code. This module focuses on coding your own VBA procedures.

### Macros and Other Procedures

Let's review the anatomy of the VBA code appearing in Figure 12.9. In the first line, the statement **Sub CompanyName()** is known as the *declaration line* because it declares the existence of the CompanyName Sub procedure to VBA. To execute this procedure, double-click "CompanyName" in the Macro dialog box. All of the macros that you create using the Macro Recorder are stored as Sub procedures. (*Note:* Sub is an example of a **keyword,** a word reserved by VBA for a specific purpose. By default, all keywords appear blue in the Code window.) Like functions, the empty parentheses that appear after the procedure name are used for *arguments,* or information that is fed into the procedure when it is executed. The end of the macro procedure is marked by the **End Sub** keyword.

**Figure 12.9**

Sub procedure named "CompanyName"

Comments appear green in the Code window and are preceded by an apostrophe.

Keywords appear blue among the program statements.

```
Sub CompanyName()                    The declaration line specifies the
                                     name and type of the procedure.
'
'  Author:   Glen J. Coulthard
'  Purpose: Types and formats a title
'
   ActiveCell.FormulaR1C1 = "My Company Name"
   With Selection.Font
      .Name = "Times New Roman"
      .Size = 18
      .Bold = True
   End With


End Sub
```

## Comments

Following the declaration line, you will typically see comments describing the macro's purpose and any relevant authoring information, such as the date it was created and the developer's name. Comments must be preceded by an apostrophe and are displayed in green, by default. Comments are ignored entirely during execution of the macro and, therefore, you may place these explanatory notes throughout your code. You can even place a comment on the same line as a program statement, as long as it appears after the statement and is preceded by an apostrophe. When you are working with complex or lengthy macros, documenting your code with comments will make the macro easier to understand and maintain.

## Objects

Objects are the fundamental building blocks of VBA. Each application in Office 2003 has its own "native" **object model,** which is the conceptual or hierarchical map to the functionality exposed by the application. Figure 12.10 displays the Help window for the Microsoft Office Excel 2003 Objects topic. Notice the color distinction made between boxes representing *objects* (blue) versus those representing *objects and collections* (yellow). A **collection** is most easily defined as a group of objects. For example, all of the worksheets in an open workbook make up a collection of worksheets. Each individual worksheet in a collection is also an object. Your ability to program effectively will be augmented by a more-than-casual familiarity with Excel 2003's object model.

**Figure 12.10**

Excel 2003's Object Model, as displayed in the Editor's Help system

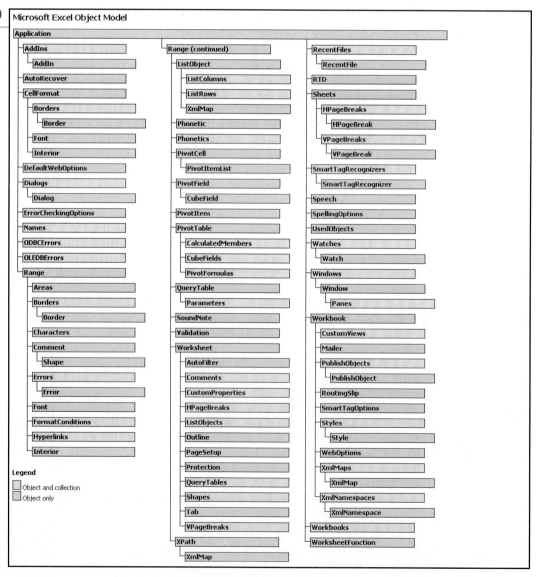

## Properties and Methods

If an object, such as a workbook or worksheet, is a noun, then its properties are adjectives and its methods are verbs. Each object has its own unique collection of properties and methods. Whereas a **property** has to do with a characteristic of an object, such as its color or size, a **method** has to do with the actions an object can perform. Put another way, you describe an object using its properties and you make it do something using its methods. A **program statement,** therefore, is a combination of VBA keywords, objects, properties, methods, and operators that together perform a valid instruction. In writing program statements, reference an object's property using the form *objectname.property.* Similarly, you can affect an object's method using the statement *objectname.method.* As you can see, a period is used to separate an object from its property or method. The period is also used to separate objects within a hierarchy, such as **Worksheets("Sheet1").Range("A1")**. Later in this module, you will practice entering these types of program statements.

## Variables

A **variable** is a temporary storage location in your computer's memory where you can collect data from the user or retain results from calculations. You may name a variable using up to 255 characters, as long as it begins with a letter and does not include any spaces or restricted symbols (!, #, and $, for example.) A common naming convention is to use lowercase for the first letter and then capitalize the start of each additional word, such as "netSurTax."

Once you have decided upon a name, you can explicitly declare the existence of the variable by typing the keyword "Dim" followed by the variable's name. For example, the code **Dim myAge** creates a new variable of the *variant* data type called "myAge." A variable's data type determines the kind of data that the variable can hold. Some common data types include byte (values from 0 to 255), currency (values with up to four decimal places), date, integer (values from –32,768 to 32,767), object, and string (text). The default **variant** data type allows you to store any kind of data, but it is less efficient and consumes more memory than most other data types.

VBA allows you to specify a data type using the "As" keyword in a "Dim" statement. For example, the code **Dim mySalary As Currency** defines a variable to hold a currency value. The next step is to place data into the variable using the assignment operator (=), which differs slightly from the equal sign. Whereas an equal sign tests for both sides of an equation being equal, the assignment operator assigns the value on the right to the variable on the left. Figure 12.11 illustrates how three variables are defined using Dim statements and then assigned values.

**Figure 12.11**

Declaring and assigning values to variables

Declaring variables and data types

Assigning values to variables

```
Sub CalcTotalBill()
'
' Author:  Glen J. Coulthard
' Purpose: Calculates sales tax and totals a bill
'
    Dim subTotal As Currency
    Dim salesTax As Currency
    Dim totAmount As Currency

    subTotal = 145.97
    salesTax = subTotal * 0.07
    totAmount = subTotal + salesTax

End Sub
```

Another important concept regarding variables is **scope.** Variables that are declared within a procedure are only visible to that procedure. These variables, called *private variables,* have a *procedure-level* scope. For example, the variables declared in Figure 12.11 are limited to being used in the "CalcTotalBill" procedure. Once the procedure is completed, the variables are wiped from memory. To make your variables accessible to all procedures in a module, you must place their declaration statements at the top of the module and outside any single procedure. Variables declared in this way have a *module-level* scope. You can also make your variables accessible to all procedures in all modules by labeling them with a *public* scope. To do so, simply place the **Public** keyword before a variable's **Dim** statement.

### *In Addition* USING OPTION EXPLICIT

If you assign a value to a variable that you have not declared using Dim, VBA creates the variable for you. Although a nice gesture, this feature allows you to misspell a variable name in your code without knowing it. For example, imagine that you have declared a variable named "totSales" but assign a value mistakenly to "totalSales" in your code. VBA creates a second variable, assigns the value, and continues processing. As you can imagine, this "feature" can result in serious calculation errors. To guard yourself against this type of error, add the Option Explicit statement to the declaration area of your code. Thereafter, VBA warns you when you attempt to use a variable that has not been explicitly declared using the Dim statement.

### Constants

**Constants** are values that do not often change. Like a variable, you can assign a value to a constant, such as a company name, at *design time.* However, unlike a variable, you cannot change its value while the code is being executed (during *run time.*) Constants allow you to give easily remembered names to values and then use those names throughout your code. In this way, if you need to change a company's name, you need only do it once in the constant's declaration statement. To declare a constant, precede the constant's name with the keyword "Const." For example, the code **Const COMMISSION = 0.05** creates a new constant containing the value 0.05 for 5%. Notice that constants are typically declared using uppercase letters for their names. In addition to defining your own constants, there are many built-in constants provided by both VBA and Excel 2003.

### 12.2.1 Writing VBA Code

## Feature

To begin coding in the Visual Basic Editor, you insert a procedure in a module using the Insert ➜ Procedure command. The types of procedures that you may define include a **Function procedure,** which you use to perform a calculation and then return or assign a value to a variable, a **Sub procedure,** which you use to perform a series of instructions, or a **Property procedure,** which you use to create or apply a user-defined property. In this lesson, you will learn how to write a Sub procedure.

Working in the Code window, you will find that there are several useful tricks for coding procedures. For example, you can use the line continuation character ( _; a space and underscore) at the end of a line in order to continue a single program statement onto the next line. Use of the line continuation character can dramatically improve the readability of your code. Additionally, when you type the name of an object followed by a period, a pop-up list box appears with all the available properties and methods for the object. After running your code, you can place the mouse pointer over a variable name and its value will appear automatically in a ScreenTip!

→ ## Method

To start coding in the Visual Basic Editor window:

- CHOOSE: Insert → Procedure
- TYPE: *a name* for the procedure in the *Name* text box
- SELECT: *a procedure type* option button in the *Type* area
- CLICK: OK command button

→ ## Practice

You will now practice inserting and coding a Sub procedure that will toggle specific worksheet display settings on and off. Ensure that no workbooks appear in the application window.

**1.** Display a new workbook using the New button (⬜) on the toolbar. The cell pointer should be positioned in cell A1 before proceeding.

**2.** Save the workbook as "Coding VBA" to your personal storage location.

**3.** To launch the Visual Basic Editor:
PRESS: ALT + F11

**4.** Ensure that the Project Explorer and Properties windows are displayed. Then, insert a new module for writing code:
CHOOSE: Insert → Module
The standard "Module1" module is added to the workbook's project file and the Code window is displayed.

**5.** To rename the module to something less generic, edit the Name property in the Properties window:
DOUBLE-CLICK: "Module1" in the *(Name)* property box
TYPE: **MyCode**
PRESS: ENTER
The Properties window should appear similar to one shown below. Notice also that the Title bar in the Code window is also updated.

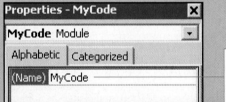

To change the name of a module, double-click its value in the Properties window and then type a new name.

**6.** Now insert a new Sub procedure into the MyCode module:
CLICK: anywhere in the Code window to make it active
CHOOSE: Insert → Procedure
Your screen should appear similar to the Code window shown in Figure 12.12.

**Figure 12.12**

Adding a
procedure to a
module

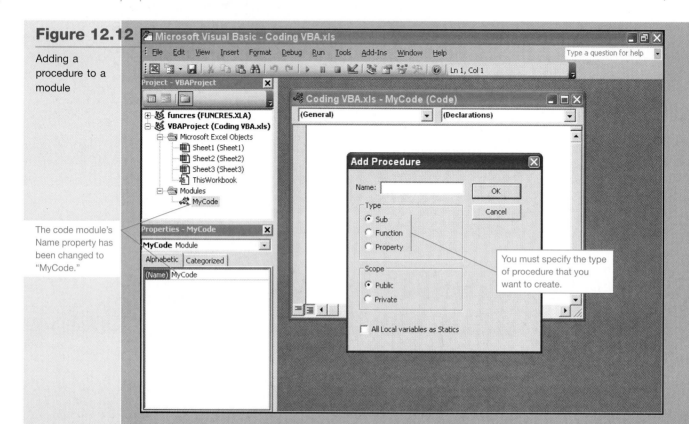

The code module's
Name property has
been changed to
"MyCode."

**7.** In the Add Procedure dialog box:
TYPE: **ToggleDisplay** in the *Name* text box
SELECT: *Sub* option button in the *Type* area
SELECT: *Public* option button in the *Scope* area
CLICK: OK command button
You should now see **Public Sub ToggleDisplay( )** in the declaration line. (*Hint:* If you want the procedure to appear in the Macro dialog box, you must specify "Public" in the *Scope* area.)

**8.** Begin the procedure with a comment:
TYPE: **'Purpose: To toggle display settings**
PRESS: **ENTER** twice
The line will appear in green to denote a comment.

**9.** When you need to set multiple properties for a single object, use the "With" structure to specify the object for which the subsequent statements apply. Thereafter, you will need only enter the property names for the object (until "End With" is reached). The **With** statement saves you from having to type an object's name repeatedly. To illustrate, you will now use the With statement to set properties for the ActiveWindow object. Do the following:
TYPE: **With ActiveWindow**
PRESS: **ENTER**
PRESS: **TAB**
Notice that the With keyword turned blue when you pressed **ENTER**. Also, indenting a code line using **TAB** within a structure is a common practice that improves the readability of your code.

**10.** Typically, a property is set using the syntax *objectname.property = newsetting*. For example, to turn off the active worksheet's gridlines, use the statement **DisplayGridlines = False.** However, we want to toggle the gridlines on or off, depending on its current state. Therefore, you must select the opposite value from the current display setting. (If the gridlines are displayed, turn them off; if they are off, turn them back on.) To toggle a property setting, use the "Not" keyword to reverse the current setting. To illustrate:

TYPE: .
Notice that a pop-up list box appears (as shown in Figure 12.13) with all the properties and methods relating to the ActiveWindow object.

**Figure 12.13**

Using the AutoList feature to enter code

When you type a period in the With structure, the Editor displays a list of the properties and methods that apply to the object.

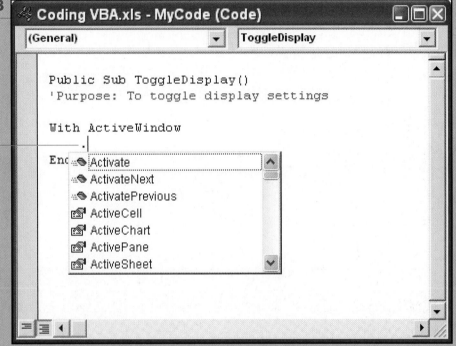

11. To select the DisplayGridlines property:
TYPE: **displayg**
PRESS: **TAB**
Notice that the entire property name is inserted into your code.

12. Now enter the assignment operator (=) followed by the new value:
TYPE: **=not .displaygridlines**
PRESS: **ENTER**
Notice that the line is formatted to display keywords in blue and property names in mixed case. Also, spaces are inserted in the code line to improve its readability.

13. To toggle the row and column headings on and off:
TYPE: **.displayh**
PRESS: **TAB**
The property "DisplayHeadings" is inserted into the Code window.

14. To complete the statement:
TYPE: **=not .displayh**
PRESS: **TAB**
PRESS: **ENTER**

15. Now let's end the procedure:
PRESS: **BACKSPACE** to align with the "With" keyword
TYPE: **end with**
PRESS: **ENTER**
Your Code window should contain the program statements shown in Figure 12.14.

**Figure 12.14**

The
ToggleDisplay
Sub procedure

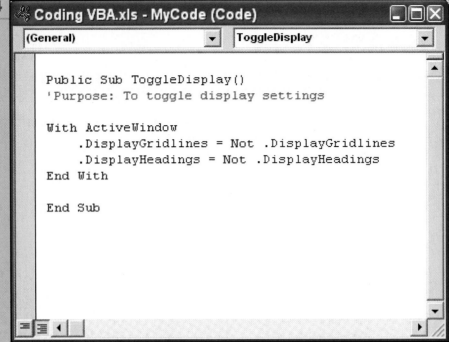

```
Coding VBA.xls - MyCode (Code)

(General)                          ToggleDisplay

Public Sub ToggleDisplay()
'Purpose: To toggle display settings

With ActiveWindow
    .DisplayGridlines = Not .DisplayGridlines
    .DisplayHeadings = Not .DisplayHeadings
End With

End Sub
```

**16.** To run the procedure:
CLICK: Run Sub/UserForm button (▶) on the Editor's toolbar

**17.** Switch to Excel 2003 using the taskbar. The window has been updated to display no gridlines or row and column headings, as shown in Figure 12.15. To proceed, switch back to the Visual Basic Editor.

**Figure 12.15**

Running the
ToggleDisplay
Sub procedure

The display of
gridlines and row
and column
headings is toggled
off.

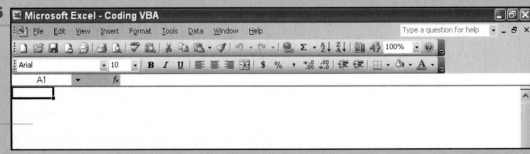

**18.** To toggle the display settings back on:
CLICK: Run Sub/UserForm button (▶)

**19.** Switch to Excel 2003 using the taskbar. Notice that the window is updated to display gridlines and row and column headings once again.

**20.** Save the workbook and keep it open for use in the next lesson.

## 12.2.2 Working with Excel Objects

→ ## Feature

Your ability to effectively program Microsoft Office Excel 2003 using VBA code is directly related to your knowledge of Excel 2003's object model. Imagine the difficulty you would have programming a VBA solution if you did not know how to open a workbook or select a cell range. Like the ActiveWindow object introduced in the last lesson, Table 12.2 describes several Excel 2003 objects that you should know how to reference using code.

**Table 12.2**

Common Excel Object References

| Excel Object... | Description... |
|---|---|
| Application | Refers to Excel 2003; used to control the application window and to perform several commands including recalculating workbooks and quitting Excel 2003 |
| Workbook | Refers to a workbook, which is a member of the *Workbooks* collection; used to create, open, print, save, and close a workbook file |
| ActiveWorkbook | Refers to the currently active workbook; the *ThisWorkbook* object refers to the workbook containing the VBA code that is currently running |
| Worksheet | Refers to a worksheet, which is a member of both the *Worksheets* and *Sheets* collections; used to activate, calculate, display, hide, print, copy, move, and delete a worksheet |
| ActiveSheet | Refers to the currently displayed or active worksheet or chart sheet |
| Range | Refers to a single cell, a group of cells, a column, a row, or a 3-D range; used to enter and edit data, select cells, and format, cut, copy, and delete a cell's contents |
| Cells | Refers to a single cell with a collection of cells; a worksheet property that is used to perform editing and formatting operations on a single cell at a time |
| ActiveCell | Refers to a single cell, returned as a *Range* object; used to refer to the current cell pointer location |

→ ## Method

On an active worksheet, you can reference a cell using an absolute cell address, a relative cell location, or a range name. The most common way to refer to a cell range is using the *A1 notation,* such as "A5:B8." For example, both **Range("A5:B8").Select** and **Range("A5","B8").Select** highlight the cell range from A5 through B8. You can also reference several rows **[Range("1:5")]**, columns **[Range("A:C")]**, or ranges **[Range("A1:A5, B1:B5, C1:C5")]** at a time.

As a shortcut, VBA allows you to drop the "Range" keyword and place the range name or cell reference inside square brackets. For example, the code **[A5:B8]** refers to the same cell range as the statement **Range("A5:B8")**. A common method for referencing a cell relative to another cell is using the "Offset" property. If, for example, the current cell is B4, the statement **ActiveCell.Offset(2,4)** refers to cell E3, which is two rows down and four columns to the right. Realize that these are only a few of the methods for referencing cell ranges on a worksheet!

Excel

→ **Practice**

In this lesson, you will learn how to reference and input information into a worksheet. Ensure that you have completed the previous lesson and that the "Coding VBA" workbook is displayed.

**1.** To begin, position the cell pointer in cell A1 of the *Sheet1* worksheet. Then, do the following:
TYPE: **Operating System**
PRESS: ⬇
TYPE: **Memory Free**
PRESS: ⬇
TYPE: **Memory Used**
PRESS: **ENTER**

**2.** On your own, size column A to 20 characters wide and column B to 10 characters wide, as shown in Figure 12.16.

**Figure 12.16**

Preparing the
worksheet

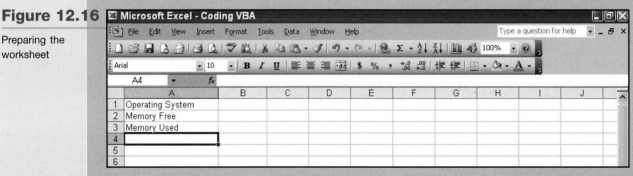

**3.** Your objective is to create a procedure that will access the Excel 2003 Application object and gather the desired information for input beside each label in column A. To begin:
PRESS: **ALT** + **F11**

**4.** To insert a Sub procedure into the current module:
CHOOSE: Insert → Procedure
TYPE: **AppInfo** in the *Name* text box
SELECT: *Sub* option button in the *Type* area
SELECT: *Public* option button in the *Scope* area
CLICK: OK command button

**5.** Maximize the Code window by clicking its Maximize button (□). Your screen should appear similar to the Code window shown in Figure 12.17.

**Figure 12.17**

Maximizing the
Code window

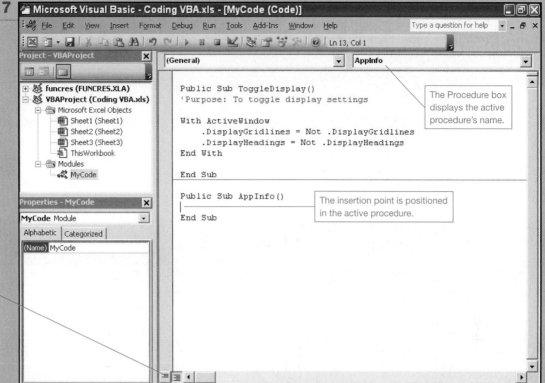

Click the Procedure
View button to view
the active
procedure only.

---

**6.** To limit the Code window to displaying the new AppInfo procedure:
CLICK: Procedure View button ( ≡ )

**7.** Let's add a brief comment:
TYPE: **'Purpose: Gathers system information**
PRESS: **ENTER** twice

**8.** This procedure requires variables to store the information that will be entered into the worksheet.
To begin, add a comment for this portion of the procedure:
TYPE: **'Declare the variables**
PRESS: **ENTER**

**9.** Now enter the first variable declaration statement:
TYPE: **dim osName as str**
The AutoList feature provides a list of possible entries.

**10.** To accept "String" and proceed:
PRESS: **TAB**
PRESS: **ENTER**
Notice the capitalization used in entering the declaration statement versus the code that results
when you press **ENTER**.

**11.** Now enter the remaining variable declarations:
TYPE: **dim memFree as long**
PRESS: **ENTER**
TYPE: **dim memUsed as long**
PRESS: **ENTER** twice

**12.** To assign values to these variables, you will access properties of the Application object. First,
enter a comment describing this portion of the procedure:
TYPE: **'Assign values to the variables**
PRESS: **ENTER**

**13.** Now enter the first assignment statement:
TYPE: **osname = application.op**
The AutoList moves to "OperatingSystem" property, as shown in Figure 12.18.

**Figure 12.18**

Displaying the
Application
object's AutoList
window

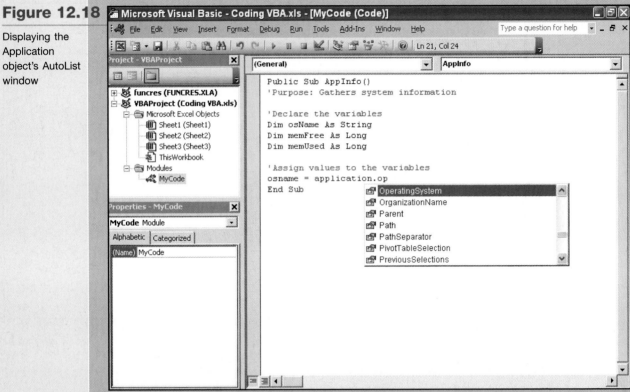

**14.** PRESS: `TAB` to complete the property name
PRESS: `ENTER`
Notice that "osname" changes to "osName" when you press `ENTER`. This automatic capitalization informs you that VBA recognizes "osName" as a declared variable.

**15.** To assign a value to the memFree variable:
TYPE: **memfree = Application.MemoryFree**
PRESS: `ENTER`

**16.** To assign a value to the memUsed variable:
TYPE: **memused = Application.MemoryUsed**
PRESS: `ENTER` twice

**17.** You will now enter the contents of these three variables into the appropriate cells in column B of the *Sheet1* worksheet. Because the macro is to work only in the active workbook and only on the active worksheet, you need not explicitly reference these objects when selecting cells. Let's begin by entering a comment:
TYPE: **'Enter variable values into the worksheet**
PRESS: `ENTER`

**18.** There are several ways to input data into the worksheet. In this step, you will assign a variable's value to the **Value** property of a cell. To do so:
TYPE: **[B1].value = osname**
PRESS: `ENTER`
TYPE: **[B2].value = memfree**
PRESS: `ENTER`

TYPE: **[B3].value = memused**
PRESS: **ENTER** twice
(*Hint:* Some people argue that using the "Range("B1")" notation is more easily read and deciphered than "[B1]." You must decide which method you prefer.)

**19.** To reset the cell pointer to cell A1:
TYPE: **[A1].Select**
PRESS: **TAB**
TYPE: **`Reset the cell pointer**
PRESS: **ENTER**
Notice that you can enter a comment on the same line as the code. Your screen should now appear similar to the Code window shown in Figure 12.19.

**Figure 12.19**

Completing the
AppInfo Sub
procedure

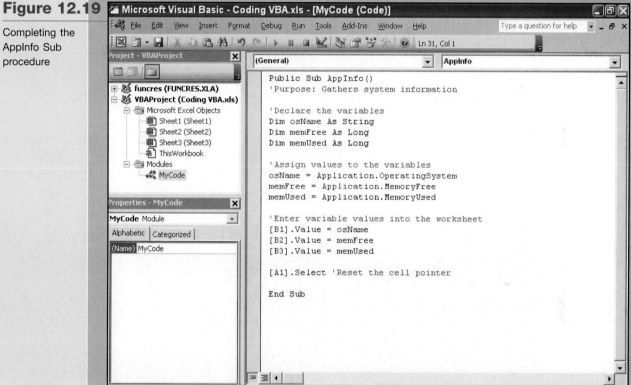

**20.** To test the completed procedure:
CLICK: Run Sub/UserForm button ( ▶ )
CLICK: Microsoft Excel button in the taskbar
Notice that the desired information appears in the proper cells and that cell A1 is selected, an example of which is shown below. (*Hint:* Rather than requiring the worksheet labels to be present in the worksheet, you could define them as constants and insert them programmatically into the appropriate cells.)

| | A | B | C | D |
|---|---|---|---|---|
| 1 | Operating System | Windows (32-bit) NT 5.01 | | |
| 2 | Memory Free | 1048576 | | |
| 3 | Memory Used | 1467380 | | |
| 4 | | | | |

Your information will
differ from the values
appearing here.

**21.** To run this procedure again using the menu:
SELECT: cell range B1 to B3
PRESS: `DELETE`

**22.** Now display the Macro dialog box:
CHOOSE: Tools → Macro → Macros
DOUBLE-CLICK: AppInfo in the *Macro name* list box
This step merely reminds you that the procedures you code manually will also appear in the Macro dialog box.

**23.** Save and then close the "Coding VBA" workbook.

 **SelfCheck**

**12.2** What purpose does the With statement serve in VBA code?

_____

# 12.3 Controlling Your Procedures

One of the greatest benefits of writing your own procedures is the ability to control how, when, and what code executes. VBA provides several **control structures** that allow you to test conditions for processing and to perform *looping* operations, which run the same lines of code repeatedly. These structures let you work within a dynamic environment, engage the user, and make processing decisions within your code. In this module, you are introduced to the most commonly used VBA control structures.

### 12.3.1 Making Decisions with If . . . Then

→ **Feature**

Most programming languages provide the ability to test a true/false, yes/no, or on/off decision. In VBA, a conditional expression is used to evaluate a question about a property or a variable's value. If the expression evaluates to true, the program branches to process the "if true" or Then code. If false, the program branches to the "if false" or Else code; only if desired though, since this portion is optional. You can enter an **If . . . Then** *branching* structure on a single line or across multiple lines in the Code window.

→ **Method**

```
If condition Then
    statements to execute
Else
    statements to execute
End If
```

→ **Practice**

You will now practice branching using the If . . . Then control structure. Ensure that no workbooks appear in the application window.

**1.** Open the EX1230 data file to display the workbook shown in Figure 12.20. This workbook contains two worksheets. The *Branch* worksheet contains loan payment and grade calculators and is used in this lesson and the next. The *Loop* worksheet contains a worksheet list and is used for the last two lessons in this module.

**Figure 12.20**

Opening the
EX1230
workbook

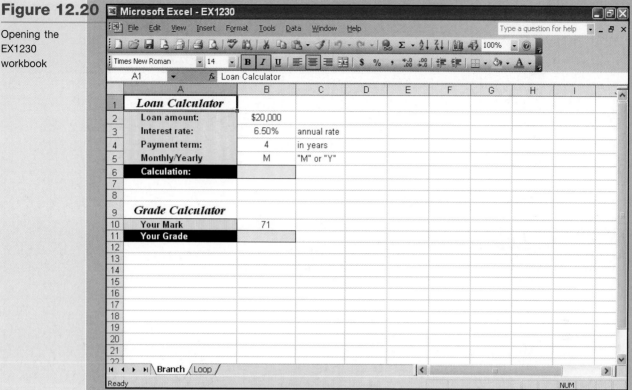

2. Save the workbook as "Control Structures" to your personal storage location.

3. Your objective is to code a procedure that evaluates the contents of cell B5 and then inserts the correct calculation formula into cell B6. In other words, the user can enter "M" or "Y" to change the payment calculation from a monthly formula to a yearly formula. To begin, name the cell ranges in the worksheet:
SELECT: cell B2
CLICK: in the Name box
TYPE: **Principal**
PRESS: **ENTER**

4. On your own, name cell B3 **Rate**, cell B4 **Term**, cell B5 **Type**, and cell B6 **CalcFormula**.

5. To begin coding the procedure, display the Visual Basic Editor:
PRESS: **ALT** + **F11**

6. Insert a code module and then define a public Sub procedure:
CHOOSE: Insert → Module
CHOOSE: Insert → Procedure
TYPE: **CalcPayment** in the *Name* text box
CLICK: OK command button
Your screen should now appear similar to the Code window shown in Figure 12.21. (*Note:* Make sure that the Code window is maximized in the work area.)

**Figure 12.21**

Creating the
CalcPayment Sub
procedure

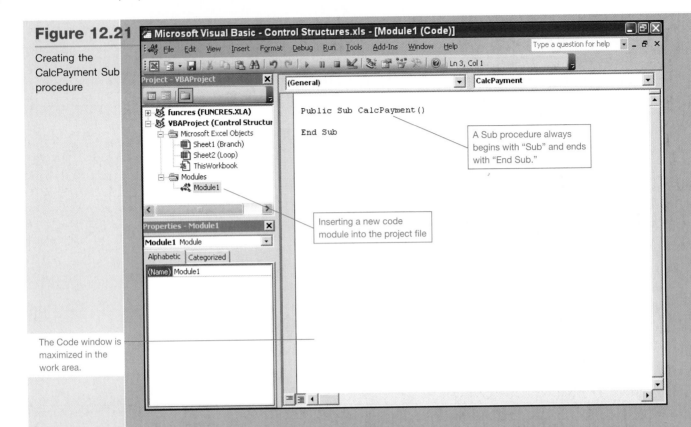

The Code window is
maximized in the
work area.

**7.** Let's enter a comment describing the new procedure:
TYPE: **'Purpose: Enters a PMT function based on a worksheet value**
PRESS: [ENTER]

**8.** When you want to refer to one of Excel 2003's objects throughout your code, define it using a special object variable. This way, you need only type the variable's name instead of the entire object reference time after time. For example, let's declare an object variable to use in referencing the cell named "Type" on the *Branch* worksheet:
TYPE: **dim rType as range**
PRESS: [ENTER]
Notice that the variable's data type is a Range object. (*Note:* For clarity in coding instructions, we will write the entire code line. If you prefer, you can use the AutoList feature to help complete each entry.)

**9.** For an object variable like Range, you must use the **Set** statement to assign a value. To illustrate:
TYPE: **set rType = ActiveWorkbook. Sheets("Branch") . [Type]**
PRESS: [ENTER] twice
Notice that you can place a range name within the square brackets, in the same way that you can use a cell reference such as "[B5]."

**10.** Before constructing the conditional expression, ensure that the *Branch* worksheet tab is active when this procedure executes. To do so:
TYPE: **ActiveWorkbook. Sheets("Branch"). Activate**
PRESS: [ENTER]

**11.** You must now create a condition that tests whether or not the "Type" cell (now referenced by the "rType" variable) contains the uppercase equivalent to the letter "M." If so, the monthly calculation will be entered into the CalcFormula cell. To proceed:
TYPE: **if ucase$ (rType.value) = "M" then**
PRESS: [ENTER]
PRESS: [TAB]
The **VBA UCase$** function converts a text string to uppercase.

**12.** Now enter the code to perform if the condition evaluates to true:
TYPE: **'Perform this code if Type contains "M"**
PRESS: ENTER
TYPE: **[CalcFormula] . Formula = "=pmt (rate/12,term*12, principal)"**
PRESS: ENTER
(*Hint:* The program statement must appear on a single code line, unless a line continuation character is used.)

**13.** To specify the code to perform if the condition evaluates to false, enter the "Else" statement:
PRESS: BACKSPACE
TYPE: **else**
PRESS: ENTER
PRESS: TAB

**14.** On your own, complete the procedure as displayed in Figure 12.22.

**Figure 12.22**

The completed CalcPayment Sub procedure

```
(General)                                      CalcPayment

Public Sub CalcPayment()
'Purpose: Enters a PMT function based on a worksheet value
Dim rType As Range
Set rType = ActiveWorkbook.Sheets("Branch").[Type]

ActiveWorkbook.Sheets("Branch").Activate
If UCase$(rType.Value) = "M" Then
    'Perform this code if Type contains "M"
    [CalcFormula].Formula = "=pmt(rate/12,term*12,principal)"
Else
    'Perform this code if Type does not contain "M"
    [CalcFormula].Formula = "=pmt(rate,term,principal)"
End If

End Sub
```

**15.** You are now ready to run the procedure. Switch to Microsoft Excel–Control Structures using the taskbar. Then, do the following:
CHOOSE: Tools → Macro → Macros
DOUBLE-CLICK: CalcPayment in the *Macro name* list box
The calculation result, ($474.30), appears in cell B6.

**16.** To calculate the yearly payment amount:
SELECT: cell B5
TYPE: **Y**
PRESS: ENTER

**17.** Now run the macro again:
CHOOSE: Tools → Macro → Macros
DOUBLE-CLICK: CalcPayment in the *Macro name* list box
The calculation result, ($5,838.05), is displayed.

**18.** Save the workbook and keep it open for use in the next lesson.

## *In Addition* IIF FUNCTION

VBA's IIF function, also called an "inline IF" function, allows you to evaluate an expression and return a true or false value using a single line of code. The syntax is **IIF(condition,if_True,if_False)**. For more information, refer to the Visual Basic Help system.

### 12.3.2 Making Decisions with Select . . . Case

→ **Feature**

When you need to evaluate a condition for more than one or two results, use the **Select Case** decision structure. Like the If . . . Then structure, the Select Case branches your procedure based on a value or condition. When you find yourself writing too many If statements, it is time to use this structure instead.

→ **Method**

Select Case *expression*
Case *value1*
    *statements to execute*
Case *value2*
    *statements to execute*
Case Else
    *statements to execute*
End Select

→ **Practice**

You will now practice branching using the Select Case control structure. Ensure that you have completed the previous lesson and that the "Control Structures" workbook is displayed.

1. Your objective is to code a procedure that assigns a letter grade to an exam mark programmatically. To begin, switch to Microsoft Visual Basic using the taskbar.

2. To insert a public Sub procedure:
   CHOOSE: Insert → Procedure
   TYPE: **CalcGrade** in the *Name* text box
   CLICK: OK command button

3. To view only the new procedure in the Code window:
   CLICK: Procedure View button (≡)

4. Let's begin by entering a comment:
   TYPE: **'Purpose: Calculates a letter grade given an exam mark**
   PRESS: ENTER

5. To declare and set object variables for the cells containing the exam mark and letter grade, do the following:
   TYPE: **dim rMark as range**
   PRESS: ENTER
   TYPE: **dim rGrade as range**
   PRESS: ENTER
   TYPE: **set rmark = ActiveWorkbook.Sheets("Branch").[B10]**
   PRESS: ENTER
   TYPE: **set rgrade = ActiveWorkbook.Sheets("Branch").[B11]**
   PRESS: ENTER twice
   Your screen should now appear similar to the Code window shown in Figure 12.23.

**Figure 12.23**

Entering variable
declarations

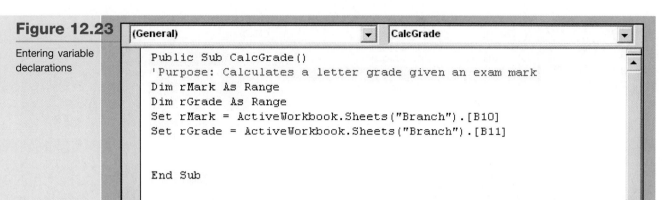

```
(General)                              ▼    CalcGrade                    ▼

Public Sub CalcGrade()
'Purpose: Calculates a letter grade given an exam mark
Dim rMark As Range
Dim rGrade As Range
Set rMark = ActiveWorkbook.Sheets("Branch").[B10]
Set rGrade = ActiveWorkbook.Sheets("Branch").[B11]


End Sub
```

**6.** As before, you should activate the *Branch* worksheet:
TYPE: **ActiveWorkbook.Sheets("Branch").Activate**
PRESS: `ENTER`

**7.** Now enter the Select Case structure that will provide the letter grade for the exam mark. Do the following:
TYPE: **select case rmark.value**
PRESS: `ENTER`
PRESS: `TAB`
This statement specifies the comparison value for the following case statements.

**8.** Because you will need to specify a range (as opposed to a single value) for exam marks, use the **Is** keyword in each Case statement. For example:
TYPE: **case is < 50**
PRESS: `ENTER`
This statement evaluates whether the "rMark.Value" is less than 50. If so, the statement below it will execute and the procedure ends. (*Hint:* You must order the Case statements carefully. When one statement evaluates to true, no other statements in the structure are evaluated.)

**9.** To specify the code to execute when the first Case statement is correct:
PRESS: `TAB` to indent the line
TYPE: **rgrade.value = "F"**
PRESS: `ENTER`
PRESS: `BACKSPACE`

**10.** On your own, complete the procedure as displayed in the Editor window shown in Figure 12.24.

**Figure 12.24**

The completed
CalcGrade Sub
procedure

| (General) ▼ | CalcGrade ▼ |
| --- | --- |

```vba
Public Sub CalcGrade()
'Purpose: Calculates a letter grade given an exam mark
Dim rMark As Range
Dim rGrade As Range
Set rMark = ActiveWorkbook.Sheets("Branch").[B10]
Set rGrade = ActiveWorkbook.Sheets("Branch").[B11]

ActiveWorkbook.Sheets("Branch").Activate
Select Case rMark.Value
    Case Is < 50
        rGrade.Value = "F"
    Case Is < 60
        rGrade.Value = "D"
    Case Is < 70
        rGrade.Value = "C"
    Case Is < 85
        rGrade.Value = "B"
    Case Is <= 100
        rGrade.Value = "A"
    Case Else
        rGrade.Value = "N/A"
End Select

End Sub
```

**11.** To run the procedure, switch to Microsoft Excel–Control Structures using the taskbar. Then, do the following:
CHOOSE: Tools → Macro → Macros
DOUBLE-CLICK: CalcGrade in the *Macro name* list box
The letter "B" appears in cell B11.

**12.** On your own, enter a couple of different letter grades and then run the macro again to test the results.

**13.** Save the workbook and keep it open for use in the next lesson.

## 12.3.3 Looping with For . . . Next

→ **Feature**

Rather than making a decision and branching a procedure, you may want to perform the same program statements over and over again. This process is called *looping,* and VBA provides two commonly used structures: **For . . . Next** and **Do While . . . Loop.** You will use the For . . . Next loop to execute a series of instructions a specified number of times. If you need to exit a **For . . . Next** loop early, you can place the **Exit For** statement inside an If . . . Then structure that tests for a condition within the loop.

→ ## Method

To perform a standard loop:

**For** *counter* = *start* **To** *end*
   *statements to execute*
**Next** *counter*

To loop through a collection of objects:

**For Each** *item* **In** *collection*
   *statements to execute*
**Next** *item*

→ ## Practice

You will now practice looping with the For . . . Next control structure. Ensure that you have completed the previous lessons and that the "Control Structures" workbook is displayed.

**1.** To begin, make the *Loop* worksheet (Figure 12.25) active and then switch to Visual Basic using the taskbar.

**Figure 12.25**

The *Loop* worksheet in the Control Structures workbook

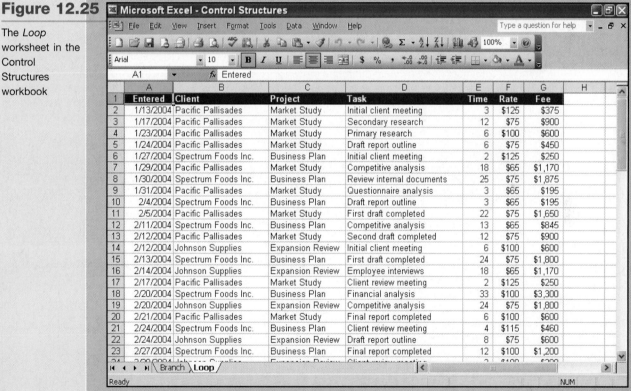

**2.** Your objective is to apply boldface to all cells in the Task column that contain the words "First Draft Completed." Although you can easily employ Excel 2003's Conditional Formatting feature to achieve this objective, this example illustrates the For Each . . . Next structure in VBA. To insert a new public Sub procedure:
CHOOSE: Insert → Procedure
TYPE: **BoldTask** in the *Name* text box
CLICK: OK command button

**3.** Start by entering a comment:
TYPE: **'Purpose: Applies boldface to specific entries**
PRESS: **ENTER**

**4.** To declare the variables that you will use in this procedure:
TYPE: **dim rTasks as range**
PRESS: `ENTER`
TYPE: **dim rRegion as range**
PRESS: `ENTER`
TYPE: **dim iRows as integer**
PRESS: `ENTER` twice
The rTasks variable will hold the range of cells in the Task column for processing; the rRegion variable will store the entire active area of the worksheet in a Range object; and the iRows variable will contain an integer value representing the total number of rows in the active area.

**5.** You will now assign values to the variables:
TYPE: **'Assign values to variables**
PRESS: `ENTER`
TYPE: **set rRegion = Sheets("Loop").[A1].CurrentRegion**
PRESS: `ENTER`
This statement places the currently used worksheet range into the object variable named rRegion.

**6.** Because the worksheet area is dynamic and will expand as new records are added, you must calculate the total number of rows in the active worksheet. Do the following:
TYPE: **iRows = rRegion.rows.count**
PRESS: `ENTER`
The iRows variable now contains an integer value matching the number of rows in the active area (rRegion) of the worksheet list.

**7.** You must now calculate the range for which to evaluate in the loop. In this example, you will want to select the entire cell range from D2 to the bottom of the active list area. You begin with cell D2 since you do not want to evaluate the values in the field header row. To specify the last value in the range, you will concatenate the column letter "D" with the number of total rows stored in the iRows variable. To illustrate:
TYPE: **set rTasks = Sheets("Loop").Range("D2","D"&iRows)**
PRESS: `ENTER` twice
If the number of rows in the active area is 80, this statement places the range from cell D2 to D80 into the object variable named rTasks. Your Code window should now appear similar to the one shown in Figure 12.26.

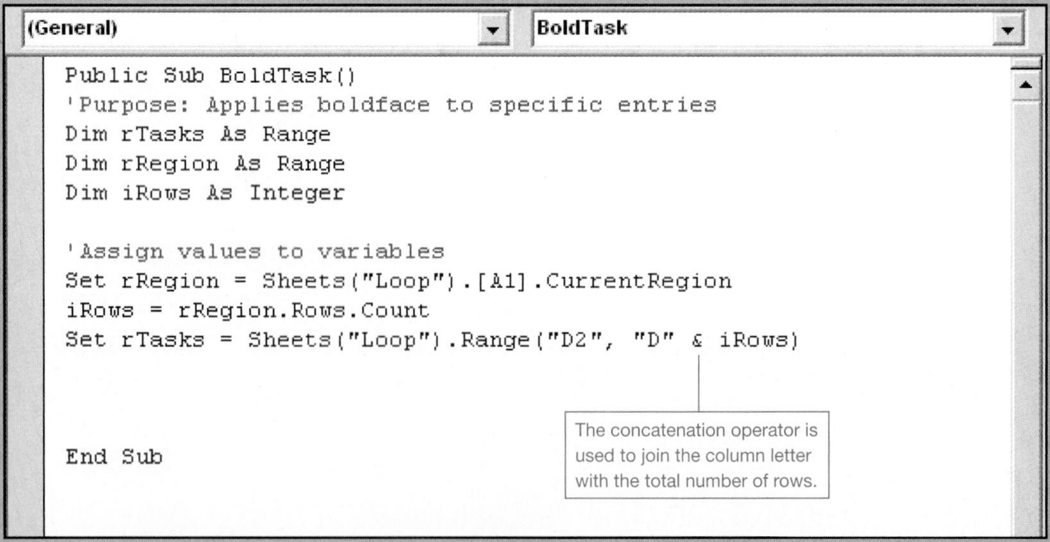

**Figure 12.26**

Declaring
variables and
assigning values

| (General) | ▼ | BoldTask | ▼ |

```
Public Sub BoldTask()
'Purpose: Applies boldface to specific entries
Dim rTasks As Range
Dim rRegion As Range
Dim iRows As Integer

'Assign values to variables
Set rRegion = Sheets("Loop").[A1].CurrentRegion
iRows = rRegion.Rows.Count
Set rTasks = Sheets("Loop").Range("D2", "D" & iRows)




End Sub
```

The concatenation operator is
used to join the column letter
with the total number of rows.

Excel

8. You now enter the For Each . . . Next structure using the variable "c" as an item counter. Do the following:
   TYPE: **'Perform looping operation**
   PRESS: ENTER
   TYPE: **for each c in rTasks.cells**
   PRESS: ENTER
   PRESS: TAB
   This structure will loop through each item ("c" stands for "cell," but you can use any letter) in the Cells collection for the range specified in the rTasks variable.

9. To continue, enter a conditional expression to test whether the current cell contains the desired text. Do the following:
   TYPE: **if lcase$(c.value) = "first draft completed" then**
   PRESS: ENTER
   PRESS: TAB
   Notice that the **LCase$** function is used to convert the cell values to lowercase prior to a comparison being made. Also, note that the contents of the "c.value" statement changes for each cell that is evaluated.

10. Complete the nested If . . . Then structure:
    TYPE: **c.font.bold = True**
    PRESS: ENTER
    PRESS: BACKSPACE
    TYPE: **end if**
    PRESS: ENTER
    PRESS: BACKSPACE

11. You now complete the For Each . . . Next structure:
    TYPE: **next c**
    PRESS: ENTER
    This statement continues processing by moving to the next cell in the Cells collection. Your screen should appear similar to the Code window shown in Figure 12.27.

**Figure 12.27**

The completed BoldTask Sub procedure

| (General) | ▼ | BoldTask | ▼ |

```
Public Sub BoldTask()
'Purpose: Applies boldface to specific entries
Dim rTasks As Range
Dim rRegion As Range
Dim iRows As Integer

'Assign values to variables
Set rRegion = Sheets("Loop").[A1].CurrentRegion
iRows = rRegion.Rows.Count
Set rTasks = Sheets("Loop").Range("D2", "D" & iRows)

'Perform looping operation
For Each c In rTasks.Cells
    If LCase$(c.Value) = "first draft completed" Then
        c.Font.Bold = True
    End If
Next c


End Sub
```

The "c" represents each cell in the rTasks range object.

**12.** To test the procedure, switch to Excel 2003 using the Microsoft Excel–Control Structures button on the taskbar. Ensure that the cell pointer appears in cell A1 of the *Loop* worksheet.

**13.** From the Menu bar:
CHOOSE: Tools → Macro → Macros
DOUBLE-CLICK: BoldTask in the *Macro name* list box
Notice that the cells in column D that contain "First draft completed" now appear in boldface.

**14.** Save the workbook and keep it open for use in the next lesson.

### 12.3.4 Looping with Do . . . While

→ **Feature**

Unlike the For . . . Next structure that executes a set number of times, a Do While . . . Loop structure executes a series of instructions each time a condition evaluates to true. When the condition proves false, the loop is completed and you proceed to the next program statement after the structure. If you need to exit a Do While loop early, place the **Exit Do** statement inside an If . . . Then structure within the loop.

→ **Method**

**Do While** *condition*
    *statements to execute*
**Loop**

→ **Practice**

You will now practice looping with the Do . . . While control structure. Ensure that you have completed the previous lessons and that the "Control Structures" workbook is displayed.

**1.** Switch to Microsoft Visual Basic using the taskbar.

**2.** Your objective is to apply boldface to all January dates in the Entered column of the *Loop* worksheet. To insert a new public Sub procedure:
CHOOSE: Insert → Procedure
TYPE: **BoldJan** in the *Name* text box
CLICK: OK command button

**3.** Start by entering a comment:
TYPE: **'Purpose: Applies boldface to January, 2004 dates only**
PRESS: ENTER

**4.** Declare the variables:
TYPE: **dim rowNum as integer**
PRESS: ENTER
TYPE: **dim colNum as integer**
PRESS: ENTER
TYPE: **dim currCell as range**
PRESS: ENTER twice

**5.** Now set up the variables:
TYPE: **'Assign values to the variables**
PRESS: ENTER
TYPE: **rowNum = 2**
PRESS: ENTER
TYPE: **colNum = 1**
PRESS: ENTER
TYPE: **set currCell = Sheets("Loop").Cells(rownum,colnum)**
PRESS: ENTER twice

This last assignment statement sets the currCell variable to cell A2, which is in row 2 and column 1 of the worksheet. Your screen should appear similar to the Code window shown in Figure 12.28.

**Figure 12.28**

Declaring variables and assigning values

```
(General)                                    BoldJan

Public Sub BoldJan()
'Purpose: Applies boldface to January, 2004 dates only
Dim rowNum As Integer
Dim colNum As Integer
Dim currCell As Range

'Assign values to the variables
rowNum = 2
colNum = 1
Set currCell = Sheets("Loop").Cells(rowNum, colNum)


End Sub
```

**6.** You will now use a Do While . . . Loop structure to ensure that only date values prior to February 1$^{st}$, 2004, are processed inside the loop. (*Note:* This example requires that the column is sorted in ascending date order.) To proceed:
TYPE: **'Perform looping operation**
PRESS: ENTER
TYPE: **do while currCell.value < #2/1/2004#**
PRESS: ENTER
PRESS: TAB
Notice that the date value must be surrounded by number signs in VBA.

**7.** To enhance a cell that meets the condition:
TYPE: **currCell.font.bold = true**
PRESS: ENTER

**8.** Next, you must increment the values in the loop in order to evaluate the next cell's contents. Do the following:
TYPE: **rownum = rownum + 1**
PRESS: ENTER
TYPE: **set currCell = ActiveSheet.Cells(rownum,colnum)**
PRESS: ENTER
PRESS: BACKSPACE
These statements are extremely important. Without them, the loop will evaluate the original condition again and again, continuing endlessly.

**9.** To complete the loop:
TYPE: **loop**
PRESS: ENTER
Your screen should now appear similar to the Code window shown in Figure 12.29.

**Figure 12.29**

The completed BoldJan Sub procedure

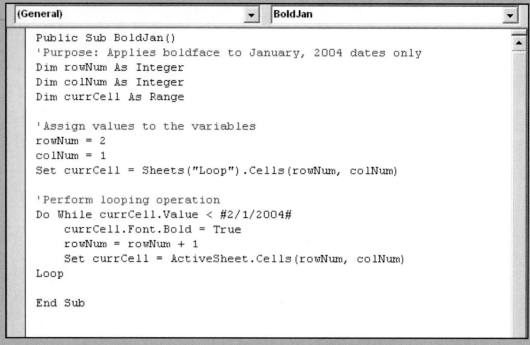

```
(General)                              ▼   BoldJan                              ▼

Public Sub BoldJan()
'Purpose: Applies boldface to January, 2004 dates only
Dim rowNum As Integer
Dim colNum As Integer
Dim currCell As Range

'Assign values to the variables
rowNum = 2
colNum = 1
Set currCell = Sheets("Loop").Cells(rowNum, colNum)

'Perform looping operation
Do While currCell.Value < #2/1/2004#
    currCell.Font.Bold = True
    rowNum = rowNum + 1
    Set currCell = ActiveSheet.Cells(rowNum, colNum)
Loop

End Sub
```

**10.** To test the procedure:
CLICK: Run Sub/UserForm button (▶)

**11.** Now switch to Microsoft Excel using the taskbar and review the entries in the Entered column of the *Loop* worksheet. Notice that only the cells containing January 2004 dates appear in boldface.

**12.** Save and then close the "Control Structures" workbook.

 **SelfCheck**

**12.3** What type of control structure might you implement if you were applying tax rates based on various income levels?

# 12.4 Interacting with the User

A successful program creates and fosters a positive user experience and trust in the system. For some users, the black box approach of having workbook tasks and procedures running silently in the background is disconcerting. They appreciate knowing more about what is happening and being able to control execution or, at the very least, provide input. There are other times when a program requires user input or direction in order to continue processing. VBA provides two functions, **MsgBox** and **InputBox,** for use in programming user interaction. These functions enable you to display and collect information using built-in dialog box forms.

## 12.4.1 Using the MsgBox Function

→ **Feature**

The **MsgBox** function is used to display a built-in form, complete with command buttons and icons, for the purpose of providing information to the user. The MsgBox function also allows you to evaluate a user's response (for example, which command button he or she clicked.) If the message box is for display purposes only, enter the "MsgBox" statement in the Code window followed by the text that you want displayed. A single OK command button will appear in the message box. If you want to make a processing decision based on which command button is clicked by the user, assign the return value from the function to a variable. You may then use a branching control structure to determine the code to be processed after the message box.

→ **Method**

MsgBox "prompt"
*or*
returnVar = MsgBox*(prompt,buttons,title)*

→ **Practice**

You will now use the MsgBox function to provide user feedback. Ensure that no workbooks appear in the application window.

**1.** Display a new workbook using the New button (▣) on the toolbar. The cell pointer should be positioned in cell A1 before proceeding.

**2.** Save the workbook as "User Boxes" to your personal storage location.

**3.** To launch the Visual Basic Editor:
PRESS: ALT + F11

**4.** Now insert a new module:
CHOOSE: Insert → Module

**5.** Rather than using the Insert → Procedure command, you can define a new Sub procedure by typing in the Code window. To demonstrate:
TYPE: **sub DisplayMessage()**
PRESS: ENTER
Notice that the Editor adds the "End Sub" code line automatically.

**6.** Enter a comment:
TYPE: **'Purpose: Displays a message box**
PRESS: ENTER

**7.** To enter a simple MsgBox function:
TYPE: **msgbox "Welcome to my application"**
PRESS: ENTER

**8.** To test the new procedure:
CLICK: Run Sub/UserForm button (▸)
A dialog box should now appear over the worksheet, as shown in Figure 12.30.

**Figure 12.30**

Displaying a message box

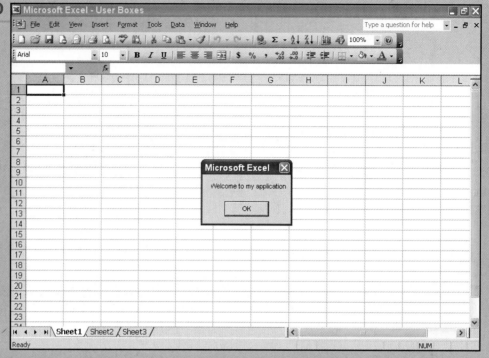

9. To remove the dialog box from displaying:
CLICK: OK command button
You are returned to the Visual Basic Editor. Because the **MsgBox** statement did not include any arguments, the dialog box simply displays a text string and the default OK command button.

10. Now let's create a message box with some added functionality. Delete the "MsgBox" code line that currently appears in the Code window and then position the insertion point immediately below the comment.

11. You can use the **MsgBox** function to return a value signifying the command button that the user clicked. In this exercise, an integer variable, called *returnNum*, is defined to hold the return value (see Table 12.3) of the clicked button. You can also use variables and built-in constants for the arguments required by the function. To begin:
TYPE: **dim msgText as string, msgTitle as string**
PRESS: **ENTER**
TYPE: **dim msgButtons as integer, returnNum as integer**
PRESS: **ENTER** twice
Notice that you can define more than one variable on a code line.

**Table 12.3**

Message Box Return Values

| Button Constant... | Value Returned... | Button Clicked... |
|---|---|---|
| vbOK | 1 | OK command button |
| vbCancel | 2 | Cancel command button |
| vbAbort | 3 | Abort command button |
| vbRetry | 4 | Retry command button |
| vbIgnore | 5 | Ignore command button |
| vbYes | 6 | Yes command button |
| vbNo | 7 | No command button |

**12.** Let's assign some values for the function arguments:
TYPE: **msgText = "Are you having fun yet?"**
PRESS: ENTER
TYPE: **msgButtons = vbYesNoCancel + vbQuestion**
PRESS: ENTER
TYPE: **msgTitle = "Question Sample"**
PRESS: ENTER twice
You can now use these variables within a program statement. (*Note:* The constants vbYesNo-Cancel and vbQuestion dictate the command buttons and icon to display in the message box. Refer to the Visual Basic Help system for more information on these constants.)

**13.** To create the message box function:
TYPE: **returnNum = msgbox(msgText,msgButtons,msgTitle)**
PRESS: ENTER
Depending on whether the user clicks the Yes, No, or Cancel buttons, the returnNum variable will store 6, 7, or 2, respectively (Table 12.3).

**14.** To determine whether the function is working, let's use an informational message box to display the variable's value:
TYPE: **msgbox "You pressed " & returnNum**
PRESS: ENTER
Notice that the variable name is concatenated to the end of the text string using the ampersand (&) character. Your screen should now appear similar to the Code window shown in Figure 12.31.

**Figure 12.31**

The completed
DisplayMessage
Sub procedure

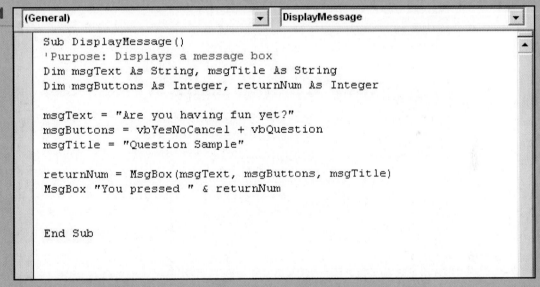

```
(General)                              ▼   DisplayMessage                      ▼

Sub DisplayMessage()
'Purpose: Displays a message box
Dim msgText As String, msgTitle As String
Dim msgButtons As Integer, returnNum As Integer

msgText = "Are you having fun yet?"
msgButtons = vbYesNoCancel + vbQuestion
msgTitle = "Question Sample"

returnNum = MsgBox(msgText, msgButtons, msgTitle)
MsgBox "You pressed " & returnNum


End Sub
```

**15.** To test the procedure:
CLICK: Run Sub/UserForm button ( ▶ )
The dialog box shown in Figure 12.32 appears. The callouts show the variable names that are used to generate the displayed information.

**16.** CLICK: Yes command button to proceed
As shown in Figure 12.32, another message box is displayed with the text "You pressed 6," which is the return value for the Yes command button. Using an **If . . . Then** or **Select Case** structure, you could perform conditional processing based on the button clicked (value returned).

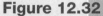
**Figure 12.32**

Running the
DisplayMessage
Sub procedure

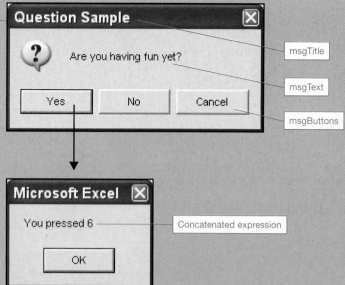

17. To remove the dialog box:
    CLICK: OK command button
    You are returned to the Visual Basic Editor application window.

18. Keep the Visual Basic Editor window open for use in the next lesson.

## 12.4.2 Using the InputBox Function

→ **Feature**

The **InputBox** function is used to display a built-in form for the purpose of gathering simple pieces of information from the user. Typically, the data entered into an input box is stored in a variable for later processing or for entry directly into a cell range. The *prompt* argument in the function syntax refers to the message that you want displayed and the *title* argument refers to the Title bar caption. The *default* argument provides the default value that will display in the input box. Other arguments for the Input-Box function are available for screen positioning, if you do not wish to have it centered in the window.

→ **Method**

returnVar = InputBox(*prompt,title,default*)

→ **Practice**

You will now practice creating and displaying an input dialog box. Ensure that you have completed the previous lesson and that the Visual Basic Editor window is displayed.

1. To create a new Sub procedure in the Code window:
   PRESS: CTRL + END to move to the bottom of the window
   PRESS: ENTER twice

2. Your objective is to create an input box that asks the user his or her age and then calculates the year that he or she were born. To begin:
   TYPE: sub YearBorn()
   PRESS: ENTER
   TYPE: 'Purpose: Calculates a birth year
   PRESS: ENTER

**3.** To view only the new procedure in the Code window:
CLICK: Procedure View button (☰)

**4.** Declare variables to hold the function arguments, the user's input, and the calculated answer:
TYPE: **dim inpText as string, inpTitle as string**
PRESS: ENTER
TYPE: **dim userAge as variant**
PRESS: ENTER
TYPE: **dim calcYear as integer**
PRESS: ENTER twice
(*Note:* Because the InputBox function returns a string, userAge is declared as a variant to hold either a string or a value.)

**5.** To set values for the arguments and display the input box:
TYPE: **inpText = "How old are you this year?"**
PRESS: ENTER
TYPE: **inpTitle = "Calculate Birth Year"**
PRESS: ENTER
TYPE: **userAge = inputbox(inpText, inpTitle)**
PRESS: ENTER twice
Your screen should now appear similar to the Code window shown in Figure 12.33.

**Figure 12.33**

Declaring
variables and
assigning values

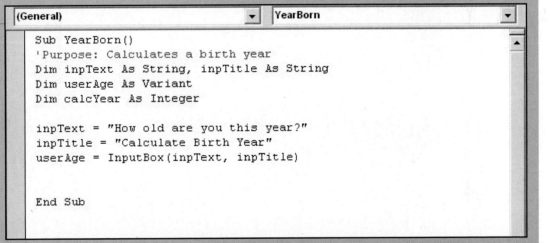

```
(General)                                    ▼    YearBorn                        ▼

    Sub YearBorn()
    'Purpose: Calculates a birth year
    Dim inpText As String, inpTitle As String
    Dim userAge As Variant
    Dim calcYear As Integer

    inpText = "How old are you this year?"
    inpTitle = "Calculate Birth Year"
    userAge = InputBox(inpText, inpTitle)



    End Sub
```

**6.** Once the user enters his or her age into the input dialog box, check to ensure that the entry is numeric and then calculate his or her birth year:
TYPE: **if isnumeric(userAge) then**
PRESS: ENTER
PRESS: TAB
TYPE: **calcYear = year(now()) – userAge**
PRESS: ENTER

**7.** Now concatenate the result with a message string:
TYPE: **msgbox "You were born in " & calcYear**
PRESS: ENTER
PRESS: BACKSPACE
This calculation takes the current year and subtracts the age that was entered by the user. The message box then displays the answer.

**8.** If the user enters a string value or fails to make an entry, the following code is performed:
TYPE: **Else**
PRESS: ENTER
PRESS: TAB
TYPE: **msgbox "Please enter a value."**
PRESS: ENTER
PRESS: BACKSPACE

**9.** To complete the If . . . Then structure:
TYPE: **end if**
PRESS: **ENTER**
Your screen should now appear similar to the Code window shown in Figure 12.34.

**Figure 12.34**

The completed
YearBorn Sub
procedure

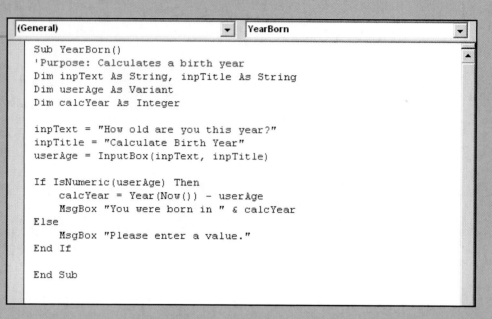

```
(General)                                    ▼   YearBorn                          ▼

    Sub YearBorn()
    'Purpose: Calculates a birth year
    Dim inpText As String, inpTitle As String
    Dim userAge As Variant
    Dim calcYear As Integer

    inpText = "How old are you this year?"
    inpTitle = "Calculate Birth Year"
    userAge = InputBox(inpText, inpTitle)

    If IsNumeric(userAge) Then
        calcYear = Year(Now()) - userAge
        MsgBox "You were born in " & calcYear
    Else
        MsgBox "Please enter a value."
    End If

    End Sub
```

**10.** To test the procedure:
CLICK: Run Sub/UserForm button (▶)
The form shown in Figure 12.35 is displayed to accept input from the user.

**11.** In the text box provided:
TYPE: *your age (for example, 24)*
CLICK: OK command button (or press **ENTER**)
A message box (Figure 12.35) appears with the year that you were born. (*Hint:* Instead of using a message box for display, you can place the value into a cell. Refer to the previous modules for more information on placing variable values into worksheet cells.)

**Figure 12.35**

Running the
YearBorn Sub
procedure

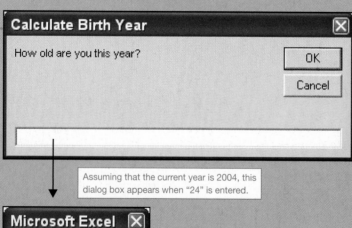

Assuming that the current year is 2004, this
dialog box appears when "24" is entered.

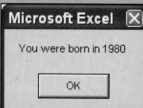

**12.** To remove the dialog box:
CLICK: OK command button
You are returned to the Visual Basic Editor.

**13.** To return to the Excel 2003 workbook:
CHOOSE: File → Close and Return to Microsoft Excel

**14.** Save and then close the "User Boxes" workbook.

**12.4** In displaying a message box that contains the Yes and No command buttons, how do you evaluate in your code which button is clicked by the user?

# 12.5 Working with Controls

Like all of the Microsoft Office System 2003 applications, Excel 2003 provides full support for *ActiveX controls*. Formerly known as OLE controls, **ActiveX controls** are prebuilt, reusable software components, such as command buttons and drop-down list boxes, that you can use to add interface elements and functionality to your workbooks. You can place these controls directly on a worksheet or display them in a custom user form. There are thousands of ActiveX controls, produced by Microsoft and third-party developers, that you can take advantage of in Excel 2003.

## 12.5.1 Placing a Command Button on the Worksheet

→ ## Feature

The **Control Toolbox** is a special toolbar containing ActiveX controls, such as list boxes and command buttons, that you may add to your worksheets. What makes these professionally programmed controls especially attractive is that they can be linked to cells in a worksheet. For example, you can populate a drop-down list box control with data from a worksheet list and then use the selection in calculating a formula. You can also enhance the functionality of an ActiveX control by coding responses to specific events. For example, you can execute a procedure each time a control is clicked or its value is changed. There are many opportunities for using ActiveX controls in designing advanced workbook applications.

→ ## Method

To add an ActiveX control to a worksheet:

• RIGHT-CLICK: any toolbar button

• CHOOSE: Control Toolbox to display the Control Toolbox

• CLICK: the desired control in the toolbox

• DRAG: in the worksheet where you want the control to appear, using ⌐ALT⌐ to align the control with the cell grid on the worksheet

• Move and size the control as you would a graphic object on the draw layer of the worksheet.

→ **Practice**

You will now practice adding worksheet controls and switching from run-time mode to design-time mode. Ensure that no workbooks appear in the application window.

**1.** Open the data file named EX1250 and enable the macros. This workbook, shown in Figure 12.36, contains a *Form* worksheet that employees may use to submit automobile mileage claims and a *Lists* worksheet containing two list areas named "MonthNames" and "EmpTable."

**Figure 12.36**

Opening the
EX1250
workbook

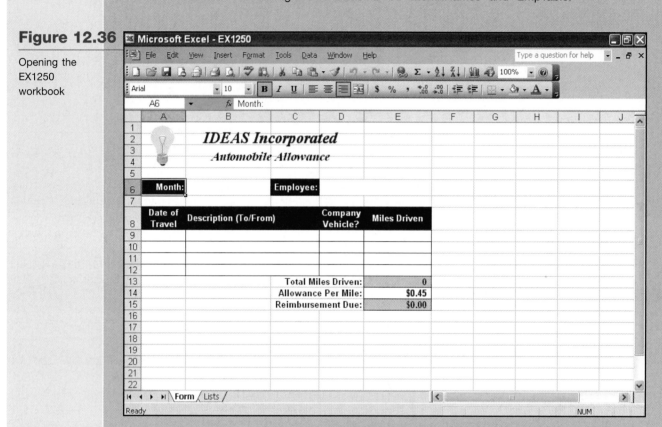

**2.** Save the workbook as "Ideas Incorporated" to your personal storage location.

**3.** Using the Control Toolbox (shown in Figure 12.37), you will now add a command button that runs a macro for inserting new rows into the *Form* worksheet. To begin:
RIGHT-CLICK: a button on any visible toolbar
CHOOSE: Control Toolbox

**Figure 12.37**

Control Toolbox
toolbar

**4.** To review the Control Toolbox, place the mouse pointer over each button. A ToolTip appears describing the button.

**5.** The Design Mode button (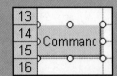) in the Control Toolbox allows you to switch between *design-time* and *run-time* modes. After you click a button in the Control Toolbox, the Design Mode button will appear active (pressed in). In this mode, you can manipulate (move, size, and set properties for) controls on the worksheet. When you want to return to run-time mode, click the Design Mode button again. To illustrate:
CLICK: Command Button control ( ) in the Toolbox

**6.** To place the command button over cells A14 and A15, first move the cross-hair mouse pointer to the top left-hand corner of cell A14. You will now use the **ALT** key to align the control with the cells. Do the following:
PRESS: **ALT** and hold it down
DRAG: mouse pointer toward the bottom right-hand corner of cell A15

**7.** When the control outline covers the cells, release the mouse button and **ALT** key. A command button control should now appear selected (surrounded by white selection handles) on the worksheet, as shown here. (*Note:* Remember that you are working in Design mode.)

**8.** To assign a macro to run when the command button is clicked:
RIGHT-CLICK: command button control
CHOOSE: Properties

**9.** Move and size the Properties window to appear as shown in Figure 12.38.

**Figure 12.38**

Inserting a command button control

Displaying the Properties window for the selected control

The Command Button ActiveX control is selected in Design mode.

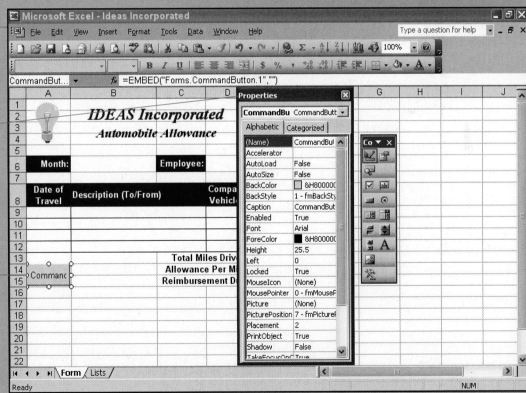

**10.** To specify the text that will appear on the face of the command button:
DOUBLE-CLICK: Caption property in the left-hand column
TYPE: **New Line**
PRESS: **ENTER**
The command button's text now reads "New Line."

**11.** Close the Properties window by clicking its Close button (⊠).

**12.** To specify the macro procedure to execute when the command button is clicked, you must enter the code into its Click event:
RIGHT-CLICK: command button control
CHOOSE: View Code
The Visual Basic Editor is launched and the Click event for the command button appears in the Code window.

**13.** To run an existing macro named "InsertLine," do the following:
TYPE: **insertline**
PRESS: (ENTER)
(*Note:* After you press (ENTER), the code appears in mixed case, denoting that Excel 2003 recognizes "insertline" as a macro procedure.) Your screen should now appear similar to the code window shown in Figure 12.39.

**Figure 12.39**

Running a macro procedure in the command button's Click event

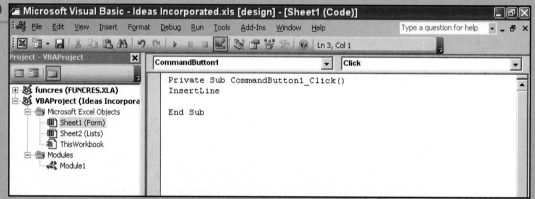

**14.** To return to Excel 2003 and exit Design mode:
CHOOSE: File → Close and Return to Microsoft Excel
CLICK: Exit Design Mode button (⊠) on the Control Toolbox toolbar

**15.** SELECT: cell E13
Notice that the formula reads " = SUM(E9:E12)" in the Formula bar.

**16.** To test the command button control:
CLICK: New Line command button
A new line is entered in the form and the formula changes to "=SUM(E9:E13)."

**17.** Let's try the control one more time:
CLICK: New Line command button
Notice that the command button moves down each time a row is inserted into the form, as shown in Figure 12.40.

**Figure 12.40**

Running the macro procedure from the command button

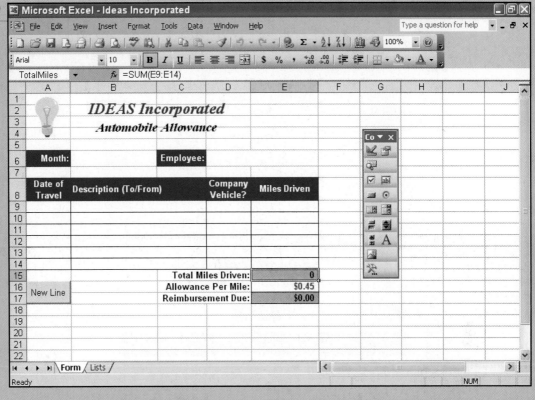

**18.** Save the workbook and keep it open for use in the next lesson.

## *In Addition* CREATING A USER FORM

In the Visual Basic Editor, you can use ActiveX controls to create custom user forms for your workbook applications. In addition to being a controllable VBA object itself, a user form can display a menu, toolbars, command buttons, text boxes, list boxes, and other dialog box elements. User forms are especially useful for displaying introductory splash screens with your company or school logo, helpful information or instructions, warnings, or data input screens. For more information, refer to the Visual Basic Help system.

## 12.5.2 Linking Controls and Cells

→ ## Feature

In addition to executing macro procedures, you can use ActiveX controls to display and collect information. Using the combo box control, for example, you can display values from a worksheet list and then place the selected value into a linked cell (as well as storing the data internally as a property setting). Besides responding to events, linking controls and cells provides a new level of interactivity for your workbook applications.

→ ## Method

To link a control with worksheet data:

• RIGHT-CLICK: the desired control

• CHOOSE: Properties

• Set the desired properties for the control.

→ **Practice**

You will now add a combo box to the worksheet for displaying information. Ensure that you have completed the previous lesson and that the "Ideas Incorporated" workbook and Control Toolbox are displayed.

**1.** You will now add a drop-down list box to the worksheet that displays values stored in a worksheet list. To add a combo box control:
CLICK: Combo Box control (▤) in the Toolbox

**2.** Move the cross-hair mouse pointer to the top left-hand corner of cell B6. Then, do the following:
PRESS: ALT and hold it down
DRAG: mouse pointer toward the bottom right-hand corner of the cell

**3.** When the control outline covers the entire cell area, release the mouse button ALT and key. A combo box control should now appear selected on the worksheet, as shown in Figure 12.41.

**Figure 12.41**

Placing a combo box on the worksheet

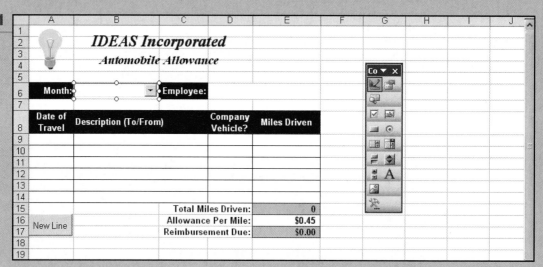

**4.** Now add the month names for display in the drop-down list:
RIGHT-CLICK: combo box control
CHOOSE: Properties

**5.** Locate the "ListFillRange" property in the Properties window. This property accepts a cell reference or range name for loading worksheet data into the combo box control. To set this property:
DOUBLE-CLICK: ListFillRange property in the left column
TYPE: **MonthNames** (a defined range name in the workbook)
PRESS: ENTER

**6.** Locate the "LinkedCell" property in the Properties window. This property enables you to permanently store the selected value in the worksheet. For example:
DOUBLE-CLICK: LinkedCell property in the left column
TYPE: **B7**
PRESS: ENTER

**7.** Close the Properties window by clicking its Close button (✕).

**8.** To test the combo box control:
CLICK: Exit Design Mode button (▣)

**9.** To select a value from the combo box control:
CLICK: down arrow attached to the combo box
Your screen should now appear similar to the worksheet shown in Figure 12.42.

**Figure 12.42**

Testing a combo box control

Values displayed in this combo box control are stored in the MonthNames range on the *Lists* worksheet.

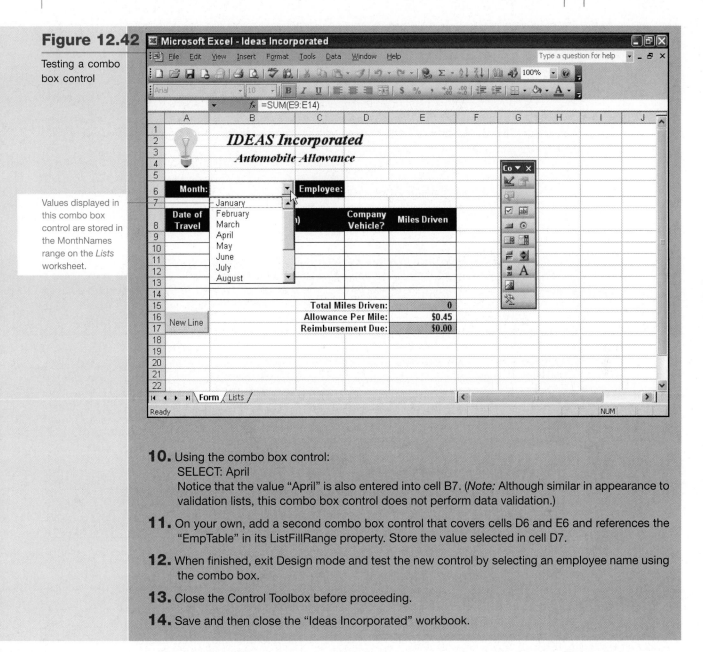

**10.** Using the combo box control:
SELECT: April
Notice that the value "April" is also entered into cell B7. (*Note:* Although similar in appearance to validation lists, this combo box control does not perform data validation.)

**11.** On your own, add a second combo box control that covers cells D6 and E6 and references the "EmpTable" in its ListFillRange property. Store the value selected in cell D7.

**12.** When finished, exit Design mode and test the new control by selecting an employee name using the combo box.

**13.** Close the Control Toolbox before proceeding.

**14.** Save and then close the "Ideas Incorporated" workbook.

## *In Addition* EXPLORING ADDITIONAL PROPERTIES FOR ACTIVEX CONTROLS

Rather than placing a selected value from a combo box control into a cell, you can specify another value from a different column in the worksheet list. In the Properties window for the combo box control, for example, use the ColumnCount property to tell Excel 2003 in which column the desired value is stored. There are many such properties that you may access for enhancing the functionality of ActiveX controls.

### 12.5.3 Deploying Your Applications

→ **Feature**

Once you have finished creating and testing a workbook application, you must determine how to distribute it to your users for installation onto their systems. For smaller applications, you can send the required workbook or workbooks on floppy diskettes. You can also compress or zip the files for online distribution over the Internet. If, however, your workbook application is better suited to being delivered as a set of macros, you can package it as a *custom add-in* program or as a *COM add-in* program. A **custom add-in** is application-specific and, therefore, will only work in Excel 2003. A **COM add-in** is an add-in architecture that allows you to create a single solution to run on all Office 2003 applications.

→ **Method**

To create an Excel 2003 custom add-in program, save the workbook using the Microsoft Office Excel Add-In (*.xla) file type to the \*username*\Application Data\Microsoft\Addins folder. When you save a workbook as a custom add-in, its worksheets and macros are hidden. To use the code stored in an add-in, choose the Tools → Add-Ins command and then browse for and select the desired add-in file. At this point, the macro procedures and functions are made available. If you are concerned that other users will modify or plagiarize your code, choose the Tools → VBAProject Properties command in the Editor. Then, click the *Protection* tab and select the *Lock project for viewing* check box. To have the add-in loaded automatically each time Excel 2003 is launched, place the add-in in the XLStart folder. Be aware, however, that add-ins consume memory and remain loaded until you explicitly unload them. For this reason, you may want to load your add-ins programmatically and only when they are needed. Refer to the **Add-ins** collection and the **Installed** property in the Visual Basic Help system for further information.

 **SelfCheck**

**12.5** How do you attach a previously recorded macro to a command button placed on the worksheet?

## Chapter summary

Visual Basic for Applications (VBA) is a programming tool that you can use to develop application-specific macros for Microsoft Office System 2003. Going beyond recording and editing macros, VBA provides an integrated development environment that gives you the ability to programmatically control all of the Microsoft Office 2003 applications. The primary components of the VBA environment include the Visual Basic Editor window, Project Explorer window, and Properties window. Using VBA, you are able to code procedures that manipulate windows, select and format cells, and evaluate data in a worksheet. Like its full-featured sibling, the Visual Basic programming language, you can use control structures to program decisions into your code (branching) and to run the same code multiple times (looping). You can also enhance your programs by adding interactive capabilities, displaying message and input boxes, and inserting ActiveX controls onto worksheets. VBA is a powerful tool for automating common tasks in your workbook applications.

## Command Summary

Many of the commands and procedures appearing in this chapter are summarized in the following table.

| Skill Set | To Perform This Task . . . | Do the Following . . . |
|---|---|---|
| **Working in the Visual Basic Editor** | Display the Project Explorer window | CHOOSE: View → Project Explorer |
| | Display the Properties window | CHOOSE: View → Properties window |
| | Display the Code window | CHOOSE: View → Code |
| | Insert a new code module | CHOOSE: Insert → Module |
| | Create a new procedure | CHOOSE: Insert → Procedure |
| | Toggle between Procedure view and Module view in the Code window | CLICK: Procedure View button (▤) <br> CLICK: Full Module View button (▤) |
| | Close the Editor and return to Microsoft Excel | CHOOSE: File → Close and Return to Microsoft Excel |
| | Run a procedure in the Editor | CLICK: Run Sub/UserForm button (▶) |
| **Debugging a Macro** | Step through a procedure line by line | CHOOSE: Tools → Macro → Macros <br> SELECT: *a macro* in the list box <br> CLICK: Step Into command button <br> PRESS: **F8** to proceed |
| | Toggle breakpoints on and off in the Code window | CLICK: in the Margin Indicator bar, or <br> CHOOSE: Debug → Toggle Breakpoint |
| **Referencing Excel Objects in VBA** | Refer to the active window, workbook, sheet, and cell | Use **ActiveWindow**, **ActiveWorkbook**, **ActiveSheet**, and **ActiveCell** respectively |
| | Activate a worksheet | **Worksheets("Sheetname").Activate** |
| | Select a cell range | **Range("A1:G7").Select, or [A1:G7].Select** |
| | Select a cell | **[A1:A1].Activate** |
| **Coding VBA** | Enter a comment in the Code window | TYPE: ' (an apostrophe) <br> TYPE: *the comment* |
| | Define a variable or constant and then assign a value | **Dim varName As DataType** <br> **varName = value** |
| | Declare an object variable and then assign a reference | **Dim objName As ObjectType** <br> **Set objName = ObjectReference** |
| | Set multiple properties for a single object | **With . . . End With** structure |
| | Perform a branching procedure | **If . . . Then** control structure, or <br> **Select Case** control structure |
| | Perform a looping procedure | **For . . . Next** control structure, or <br> **For Each . . . Next** control structure, or <br> **Do While . . . Loop** control structure |
| | Code a message box for displaying information | **MsgBox** *"prompt"*, or <br> **MsgBox**(*prompt,buttons,title*) |
| | Code an input box for gathering information | **InputBox**(*prompt,title,default*) |

Excel

| Working with ActiveX Controls | Display the Control Toolbox | RIGHT-CLICK: *any toolbar button* CHOOSE: Control Toolbox |
|---|---|---|
| | Add a control to a worksheet | CLICK: *the desired control* in the Control Toolbox DRAG: cross-hair mouse pointer on the worksheet to place the control |
| | Specify properties for a control | RIGHT-CLICK: *the desired control* CHOOSE: Properties |
| | Insert VBA code into a control | RIGHT-CLICK: *the desired control* CHOOSE: View Code |
| | Change from Design-time mode to Run-time mode | CLICK: Exit Design Mode button (◪) |

## Key Terms

This section specifies page references for the key terms identified in this chapter. For a complete list of definitions, refer to the Glossary provided at the end of this learning guide.

ActiveX controls, *p. EX 827*

breakpoint, *p. EX 793*

Code window, *p. EX 786*

coding, *p. EX 786*

collection, *p. EX 796*

COM add-in, *p. EX 834*

constants, *p. EX 798*

control structures, *p. EX 808*

Control Toolbox, *p. EX 827*

custom add-in, *p. EX 834*

debugging, *p. EX 791*

design time, *p. EX 789*

event, *p. EX 786*

event-driven programming, *p. EX 786*

Function procedure, *p. EX 798*

InputBox, *p. EX 824*

keyword, *p. EX 795*

method, *p. EX 797*

object model, *p. EX 796*

program statement, *p. EX 797*

Project Explorer window, *p. EX 786*

Properties window, *p. EX 786*

property, *p. EX 797*

Property procedure, *p. EX 798*

run time, *p. EX 789*

scope, *p. EX 798*

Sub procedure, *p. EX 798*

syntax, *p. EX 791*

variable, *p. EX 797*

variant, *p. EX 797*

VB Script, *p. EX 786*

Visual Studio Tools for Office, *p. EX 786*

## Chapter
quiz

### Short Answer

**1.** Describe the relationship between an *object* and a *property*.

**2.** Describe the relationship between an *object* and a *method*.

**3.** Provide an example of an *event* in Excel 2003.

**4.** What information is provided in the Properties window?

5. Explain the difference between *design time* and *run time.*

6. Explain the difference between a *variable* and a *constant.*

7. Why should you specify a variable's data type in its declaration?

8. When do you use a *branching* control structure?

9. When do you use a *looping* control structure?

10. What does the value returned by the MsgBox function represent?

## True/False

1. _____ Unlike Visual Basic, VBA requires a host application, such as Excel 2003, in which to execute procedures.

2. _____ The Visual Basic Editor contains the Project Explorer window, Properties window, and Code windows.

3. _____ The Immediate window is used to display the current procedure's variable values and to review immediate watch expressions.

4. _____ Every new workbook contains a "Module1" module by default.

5. _____ You use the Properties window to change property settings for an object at run time.

6. _____ You can place a comment on the same line as a program statement.

7. _____ A Select Case control structure is an example of a branching structure.

8. _____ A For Each . . . Next control structure is an example of a branching structure.

9. _____ Declaring a variable without the **As** keyword results in the variable being assigned a *String* data type by default.

10. _____ Each ActiveX control added to a worksheet is itself a programmable object.

## Multiple Choice

1. Which of the following applications lets you create stand-alone executable (.EXE) programs?

   a. Visual Basic
   b. Visual Basic for Applications
   c. Visual Basic Scripting Edition
   d. None of the above

2. Which of the following would you access to change the color of an object?

   a. Method
   b. Property
   c. Event
   d. Collection

3. Which of the following would you access to change the name of an object?

   a. Method
   b. Property
   c. Event
   d. Collection

4. The macros that you create using the Macro Recorder are of this procedure type:

   a. Function procedure
   b. Property procedure
   c. Sub procedure
   d. Variant procedure

5. A comment is always preceded by this symbol:

   a. '
   b. "
   c. \
   d. _

6. This term is used to describe the conceptual map or hierarchy of objects that are exposed by an application.

   a. Object loop
   b. Object model
   c. Object constant
   d. Object layer

**7.** In VBA code, you reference an object's property setting using the following syntax:

   a. ***Objectname.Property***
   b. ***Property.Objectname***
   c. ***Set Objectname.Property***
   d. ***Dim Objectname.Property***

**8.** In VBA code, you select the cell range from B3 to D9 on the active worksheet using the following syntax:

   a. **Range("B3:D9")**
   b. **Range(Cells(B3,D9))**
   c. **Range[B3:D9]**
   d. All of the above

**9.** In VBA code, you activate a worksheet named "Stats" using the following syntax:

   a. **Worksheet("Stats").Activate**
   b. **Worksheets(Stats).Activate**
   c. **Worksheets("Stats").Activate**
   d. None of the above

**10.** To add ActiveX controls to a worksheet, you must first display this component:

   a. ActiveX Wizard
   b. Control Wizard
   c. Control Toolbar
   d. Control Toolbox

## Hands-On
### exercises

step by step

### 1. Coding a Simple Procedure

This exercise lets you practice writing a new VBA procedure. In coding the procedure, you use an If . . . Then control structure to make an entry into the worksheet based on the contents of another cell.

   **1.** Open the data file named EX12HE01 to display the workbook shown in Figure 12.43.

**Figure 12.43**

Opening the EX12HE01 workbook

| | A | B | C | D | E | F | G | H |
|---|---|---|---|---|---|---|---|---|
| 1 | Course | Description | Minimum | Maximum | Enrolled | Waiting | Action | |
| 2 | EN301 | Advanced Composition | 12 | 20 | 20 | 2 | | |
| 3 | IT271 | Advanced HTML | 12 | 20 | 18 | | | |
| 4 | EN144 | American Literary Classics | 10 | 20 | 16 | 3 | | |
| 5 | IT098 | Computer Fundamentals | 12 | 20 | 20 | | | |
| 6 | IT420 | Computer Security Issues | 12 | 20 | 20 | 1 | | |
| 7 | BU050 | Conflict Resolution | 10 | 20 | 15 | | | |
| 8 | LN011 | Conversational Spanish | 12 | 20 | 14 | | | |
| 9 | AR223 | Darkroom Basics | 6 | 12 | 5 | | | |
| 10 | IT350 | Database Design | 10 | 20 | 14 | | | |
| 11 | AR355 | Digital Composition | 6 | 12 | 12 | 5 | | |
| 12 | BU099 | First-time Supervisor | 10 | 20 | 7 | | | |
| 13 | AR265 | History of Typography | 12 | 20 | 9 | | | |
| 14 | IT365 | Interface Design | 12 | 20 | 20 | 4 | | |

Microsoft Excel - EX12HE01

File  Edit  View  Insert  Format  Tools  Data  Window  Help

Arial    10    A1    Course

Sheet1 / Sheet2 / Sheet3 /

Ready    NUM

2. Save the workbook as "Course Macro" to your personal storage location.

3. To display the Visual Basic Editor:
   PRESS: ALT + F11

4. Ensure that both the Project Explorer and Properties windows are displayed in the Visual Basic Editor application window.

5. In the Editor window, insert a new module and define a procedure:
   CHOOSE: Insert → Module
   CHOOSE: Insert → Procedure

6. In the Add Procedure dialog box, enter a name for the procedure:
   TYPE: **CourseAction** in the *Name* text box
   SELECT: *Sub* option button in the *Type* area
   SELECT: *Public* option button in the *Scope* area
   CLICK: OK command button
   Your screen should now appear similar to the code window shown in Figure 12.44.

**Figure 12.44**

Inserting a module and Sub procedure

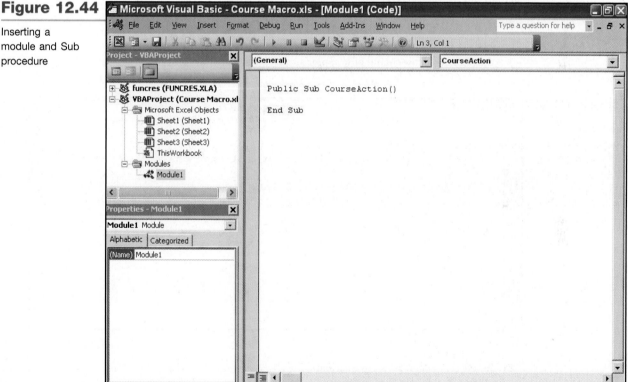

7. To begin the procedure, let's enter a comment:
   TYPE: **'Purpose: Add a section if waiting list exceeds 2**
   PRESS: ENTER twice

8. Use an If . . . Then control structure to evaluate whether the cell immediately left of the current cell contains a value greater than 2. Enter the following code:
   TYPE: **If ActiveCell.Offset(0, -1)  >  2 Then**
   PRESS: ENTER
   (*Hint:* You need not be overly concerned with capitalization or spacing between keywords, arguments, and other parameters on a code line. When you press ENTER, the Editor will reformat the line to meet standard conventions and for readability.)

**9.** To specify the code to process if the condition is *true:*
PRESS: (TAB)
TYPE: **ActiveCell.Value = "Add Section"**
PRESS: (ENTER)

**10.** Now let's apply formatting to the text:
TYPE: **With Selection**
PRESS: (ENTER)
PRESS: (TAB)
TYPE: **.Font.Bold = True**
PRESS: (ENTER)
TYPE: **.Font.ColorIndex = 10**
PRESS: (ENTER)
PRESS: (BACKSPACE)
TYPE: **End With**
PRESS: (ENTER)
This code applies boldfacing to the text and selects a green font color.

**11.** To end the control structure:
PRESS: (BACKSPACE)
TYPE: **End If**
PRESS: (ENTER)
Your Code window should now appear similar to the one shown in Figure 12.45.

**Figure 12.45**

The completed
CourseAction
Sub procedure

| (General) ▾ | CourseAction ▾ |
|---|---|

```
Public Sub CourseAction()
'Purpose: Add a section if waiting list exceeds 2

If ActiveCell.Offset(0, -1) > 2 Then
    ActiveCell.Value = "Add Section"
    With Selection
        .Font.Bold = True
        .Font.ColorIndex = 10
    End With
End If

End Sub
```

**12.** To test the code, close the Visual Basic Editor:
CHOOSE: File → Close and Return to Microsoft Excel

**13.** Now perform the macro:
SELECT: cell G2
CHOOSE: Tools → Macro → Macros
DOUBLE-CLICK: CourseAction in the *Macro name* list box
Nothing happens because the value in cell F2 is not greater than 2.

**14.** Let's try a different cell:
SELECT: cell G4
PRESS: (ALT)+(F8) to display the Macro dialog box
DOUBLE-CLICK: CourseAction in the *Macro name* list box
This time the text "Add Section" is added to the cell and formatted.

**15.** Save and then close the "Course Macro" workbook.

step by step

## 2. Coding An Interactive Procedure

In this exercise, you will create a procedure that marks up a wholesale cost to yield a retail price. To enhance the procedure, you will use the InputBox function to retrieve the markup percentage from the user.

**1.** Open the data file named EX12HE02 to display the workbook shown in Figure 12.46.

**Figure 12.46**

Opening the
EX12HE02
workbook

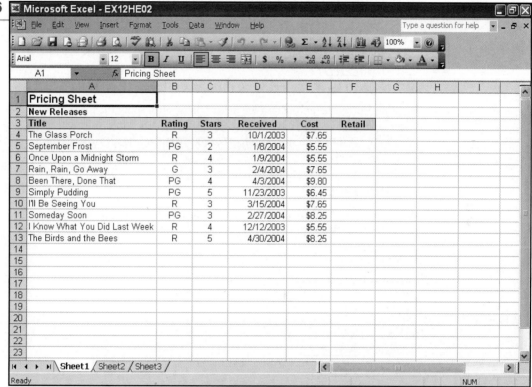

**2.** Save the workbook as "Retail Markup" to your personal storage location.

**3.** To create a new procedure, launch the Visual Basic Editor:
PRESS: ( ALT )+( F11 )

**4.** In the Editor window:
CHOOSE: Insert → Module
TYPE: **Sub MarkUp**
PRESS: ( ENTER )
The Editor automatically provides the parentheses and the End Sub program statement.

**5.** Enter a descriptive comment and define some variables:
TYPE: **'Purpose: Prompts user for a markup and calculates retail price**
PRESS: ( ENTER )
TYPE: **dim markUpPercent as variant**
PRESS: ( ENTER )
TYPE: **dim retailPrice as currency**
PRESS: ( ENTER )
TYPE: **dim msgPrompt as string, msgTitle as string**
PRESS: ( ENTER ) twice

**6.** You will now use the InputBox function to prompt for a markup amount. Enter the following code:
TYPE: **msgPrompt = "Please enter a markup without the percent symbol"**
PRESS: (ENTER)
TYPE: **msgTitle = "Calculate Markup"**
PRESS: (ENTER)
TYPE: **markUpPercent = inputBox(msgPrompt,msgTitle,60)**
PRESS: (ENTER) twice
(*Note:* The value 60 in the inputBox statement displays a default markup value of 60% in the dialog box.)

**7.** Let's use the **IsNumeric** function to ensure that a valid amount is entered:
TYPE: **if isNumeric(markUpPercent) then**
PRESS: (ENTER)
PRESS: (TAB)

**8.** When the value returned by the input box is valid, apply the markup percent to calculate the retail price and then enter the result into the cell. Enter the following code:
TYPE: **retailPrice = activecell.offset(0,-1)\*(1+(markUpPercent/100))**
PRESS: (ENTER)
TYPE: **activecell.value = retailPrice**
PRESS: (ENTER)

**9.** If the user did not enter a valid number, display a warning message:
PRESS: (BACKSPACE)
TYPE: **else**
PRESS: (ENTER)
PRESS: (TAB)
TYPE: **msgbox "Please enter a valid markup"**
PRESS: (ENTER)

**10.** To complete the If . . . Then structure:
PRESS: (BACKSPACE)
TYPE: **end if**
PRESS: (ENTER)
Your screen should now appear similar to the code window shown in Figure 12.47.

**Figure 12.47**

The completed MarkUp Sub procedure

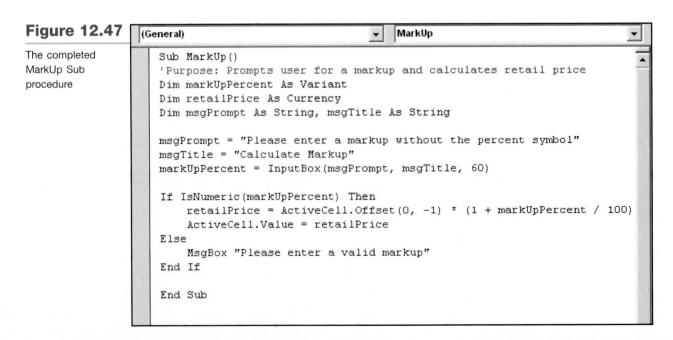

```
(General)                                    MarkUp

Sub MarkUp()
'Purpose: Prompts user for a markup and calculates retail price
Dim markUpPercent As Variant
Dim retailPrice As Currency
Dim msgPrompt As String, msgTitle As String

msgPrompt = "Please enter a markup without the percent symbol"
msgTitle = "Calculate Markup"
markUpPercent = InputBox(msgPrompt, msgTitle, 60)

If IsNumeric(markUpPercent) Then
    retailPrice = ActiveCell.Offset(0, -1) * (1 + markUpPercent / 100)
    ActiveCell.Value = retailPrice
Else
    MsgBox "Please enter a valid markup"
End If

End Sub
```

11. To test the procedure:
CHOOSE: File ➔ Close and Return to the Microsoft Excel
SELECT: cell F4
PRESS: [ALT]+[F8]
DOUBLE-CLICK: MarkUp in the *Macro name* list box
The Calculate Markup input box appears with the default value 60 displayed.

12. Let's specify a new markup percentage:
TYPE: **50**
CLICK: OK command button
The calculated retail price, $11.48, is inserted into the cell.

13. On your own, select cell F5 and run the MarkUp procedure again. This time enter a markup percentage of 35 in the dialog box. What is the calculated retail price?

14. Save and then close the "Retail Markup" workbook.

step by step

## 3. Coding a Looping Procedure

You will now practice creating a procedure that uses a looping structure to insert the main activity for each working day. Inside the loop, the procedure uses a Select Case control structure to determine the text to insert into the current cell.

1. Open the data file named EX12HE03.

2. Save the workbook as "Looping Macro" to your personal storage location.

3. To begin, display the Visual Basic Editor, insert a code module, and then define a new Sub procedure named **SetWeek**.

4. In the Code window for the SetWeek procedure, enter the program statements displayed in Figure 12.48.

**Figure 12.48**

The completed SetWeek Sub procedure

| (General) ▼ | SetWeek ▼ |
| --- | --- |

```
Public Sub SetWeek()
'Purpose: Enters values into the worksheet
Dim dayNumber As Integer

'Loops through five workdays
For dayNumber = 1 To 5

    'Inserts activity depending on the day
    Select Case dayNumber
        Case 1
            ActiveCell.Value = "Receiving"
        Case 2
            ActiveCell.Value = "Production"
        Case 3
            ActiveCell.Value = "Production"
        Case 4
            ActiveCell.Value = "Shipping"
        Case 5
            ActiveCell.Value = "Inventory"
    End Select

    'Moves to the next cell
    ActiveCell.Offset(0, 1).Select
Next dayNumber

End Sub
```

5. Examine the code that you just entered. An integer variable named "dayNumber" is defined and then used to control the For . . . Next loop. Inside the loop, a Select Case statement evaluates the value of the "dayNumber" variable and determines the text to insert into the current cell. The last step in the loop is to move the cell pointer one cell to the right in preparation for the next loop iteration.

6. To test the procedure, switch to Excel 2003 using the taskbar and select cell B3.

7. Make the Visual Basic Editor window active and run the procedure. Now switch back to the workbook to view the results. Notice that the values are entered into row 3 of the worksheet.

8. To make the procedure easier to run, add a custom toolbar named "Scheduling" to the workbook. Then, add a custom menu item to the toolbar that runs the SetWeek procedure. When completed, select cell B4 and use the new toolbar button to run the procedure. Your screen should appear similar to the worksheet shown in Figure 12.49.

**Figure 12.49**

Running the SetWeek Sub procedure

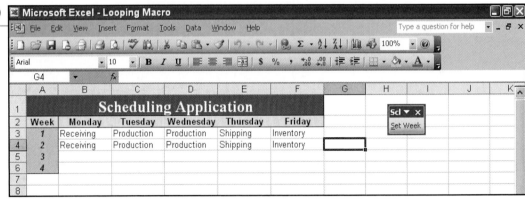

9. Close the toolbar by clicking its Close button (⊠).

10. Save and then close the "Looping Macro" workbook.

on your own

## 4. Coding Worksheet Selections

For this exercise, you will add an ActiveX command button control to a worksheet and then code a VBA procedure that will run when the button is clicked. To begin, open the data file named EX12HE04 and then save it as "Realty Coding" to your personal storage location.

Perform the following tasks:

- Using the Control Toolbox, add a command button control to cover cell F1 in the worksheet. (*Hint:* Use ⎡ALT⎤ to place the control.)

- Change the (Name) property to **cmdHighlight** and set the Caption property to **Highlight**. Your screen should now appear similar the worksheet shown in to Figure 12.50.

**Figure 12.50**

Adding a
command button
to the worksheet

The name of the
selected command
button control
appears in the
Name box.

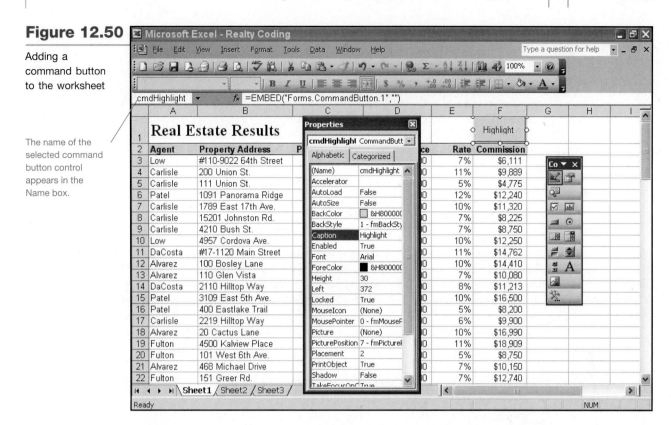

- Close the Properties window.

- View the code for the cmdHighlight command button control. In the Code window, enter the
  program statements displayed in Figure 12.51.

**Figure 12.51**

Coding the
cmdHighlight_Click
event

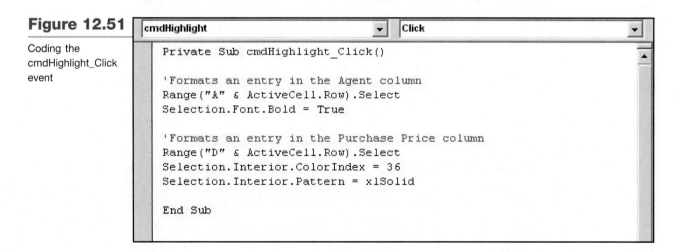

```
Private Sub cmdHighlight_Click()

    'Formats an entry in the Agent column
    Range("A" & ActiveCell.Row).Select
    Selection.Font.Bold = True

    'Formats an entry in the Purchase Price column
    Range("D" & ActiveCell.Row).Select
    Selection.Interior.ColorIndex = 36
    Selection.Interior.Pattern = xlSolid

End Sub
```

- Close the Visual Basic Editor and return to Excel 2003. Then, exit Design Mode and close the Control
  Toolbox.

- Test the command button control by selecting cell E5 in the list area and clicking the "Highlight"
  command button. Cells A5 and D5 should now appear formatted.

After testing the macro on a few other rows, save and then close the "Realty Coding" workbook.

on your own

### 5. Concatenating Column Values

To practice writing a new VBA procedure, open the data file named EX12HE05 and save it as "Full Names" to your personal storage location. The *Names* worksheet provides a list of 29 names that will expand or contract as individuals are added or removed. Your objective is to create a VBA procedure that concatenates or joins the entries in the first two columns into a third column called "Full Name." Have the procedure automatically travel down the column performing concatenations, and then stop on the last name entered. After running, testing, and debugging the procedure, print the code module. Then, save and close the workbook.

on your own

### 6. Selecting Cells and Ranges

To practice writing VBA procedures, display a new workbook and then save it as "Selections" to your personal storage location. You learned several methods for referencing and selecting cells in this chapter. To practice these methods, create three variables of the "String" data type to hold the top left-hand cell address, the bottom right-hand cell address, and the worksheet name, respectively. Create input cells on the worksheet to accept these values and then assign their contents to the variables in your code. For example, if **A5**, **B6**, and **Sheet3** were entered, the range from cell A5 through B6 on the *Sheet3* worksheet would appear highlighted after the procedure executes. After running, testing, and debugging the procedure, print the code module. Then, save and close the workbook.

## CaseStudy    LUCKY CLOVER VIDEO OUTLET

Lori Shanahan has dreamt about owning her own business since she can remember. On her twentieth birthday, her dreams became reality when her aunt purchased a small corner grocery and video rental outlet. Promising that the video rental business would be hers if she managed it properly, her aunt announced the gift to Lori at a family dinner celebration. Lori had recently completed her Business Administration diegree, which included courses in Microsoft Office System 2003, but she was uncertain of the demands involved in running a video rental operation. From the previous owners, she received an Excel 2003 workbook that outlined the movie titles that were available and some summary rental information from the past year. After reviewing the workbook, Lori realized that there were several opportunities for automating the month-end reporting procedures. Specifically, Lori wants to use a VBA procedure to automate the process of summarizing the rentals by type and to reset the monthly tracking worksheet in preparation for a new month. With the Visual Basic Help system at standby, Lori is ready to tackle this challenging venture.

In the following case problems, assume the role of Lori and perform the same steps that she identifies.

**1.** In the comfort of her office, Lori opens the EX12CP00 data file and saves it as "Lucky Clover" to her personal storage location. She reviews the three sheet tabs in the workbook: *Monthly,* which contains the daily rentals for a single month and is shown in Figure 12.52; *Summary,* which summarizes the number of rentals by type or genre; and *Titles,* which provides an inventory of the movie titles that are available. She decides to focus on the *Monthly* tab, which currently lists the rentals for November, 2004. Lori notices that the cells in the "Genre" column contain VLOOKUP formulas. These formulas search a named range called "inventory" to retrieve and enter the correct genre automatically when a title is typed into column B. Lori's first task is to count the values in the Genre column and place the results in the next available row on the *Summary* tab.

**Figure 12.52**

Lucky Clover workbook: *Monthly* tab

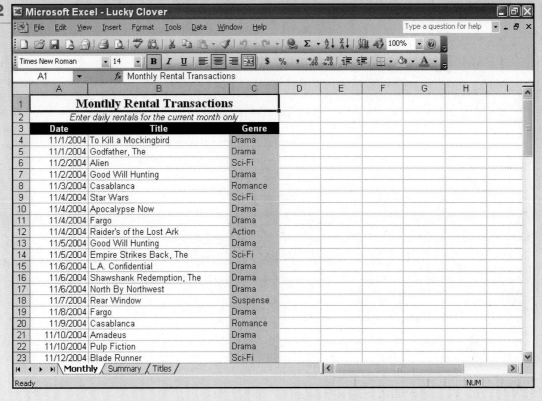

She spends the next few moments planning how to summarize the monthly information. Her planning notes are as follow:

- Sort the daily rentals on the *Monthly* worksheet by genre

- Move down the Genre column, counting the number of titles that were rented, and store the total count for each genre in a variable

- Place the contents of each variable into the appropriate cell on the *Summary* worksheet

- Clear the *Monthly* worksheet in preparation for a new month

On a piece of paper or in a word processor, write down your initial thoughts on the commands, variables, objects, and control structures that you might need to use and reference in order to meet the above objectives. When finished, proceed to the next step.

**2.** Lori decides to store the entire operation in a single procedure. To begin, she inserts a new module and then creates a Sub procedure called "RollOver" using the Visual Basic Editor. At the top of the RollOver procedure, Lori enters a comment stating her intentions for the new procedure. She then declares five integer variables to hold a count of the titles rented from each genre. She names the variables: **iAction**, **iDrama**, **iRomance**, **iSciFi**, and **iSuspense**. She then declares two integer variables named **rowNum** and **totRows** that will contain the current row number and the total rows in the active worksheet. In addition, Lori defines a variant variable named **vGenre** and two Range object variables named **rMonthly** and **rSummary**.

Before entering any more code, Lori closes the Project Explorer and Properties windows so that the Code window is maximized in the Editor. Her first program statement, placed immediately after the variable declarations and a comment line, activates the "Monthly" worksheet in the active workbook. Because the number of rentals for each month will change, she must select a dynamic data range in preparation for sorting. After reviewing some sample code in the Visual Basic Help system, she enters the following program statement in the Code window.

**Set rMonthly = Range([a4].address,[a4].End(xlDown).offset(0,2).address)**

(*Hint:* Besides using the Help system, Lori could have recorded the following keystrokes using the Macro Recorder to find out how to enter this program statement.) Notice that the statement uses cell A4 as the first argument in the range. It then calculates the bottom right-hand cell address using the ☐END☐+☐↓☐ keystroke to select the last entry in column A. The Offset property is then used to return the cell address for column C.

Lori proceeds by coding the Sort method for the rMonthly range. In order to sort the range by the values in the "Genre" column, she enters the following statement: **rMonthly.Sort rMonthly.Columns("C")**. The Editor window now appears similar to the one shown in Figure 12.53. She runs the procedure and reviews the Excel 2003 worksheet to ensure that the procedure works as expected. Pleased with the results, Lori returns to the Visual Basic Editor.

**Figure 12.53**

Coding the
RollOver Sub
procedure

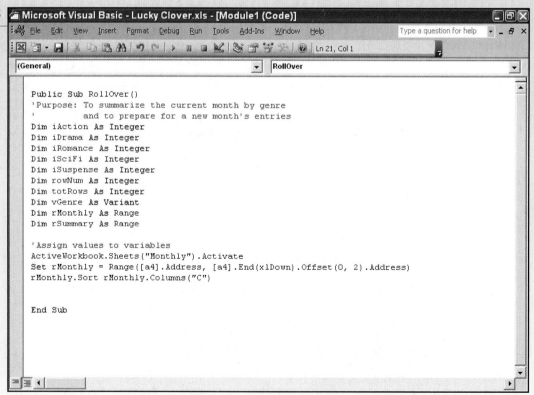

```
Public Sub RollOver()
'Purpose: To summarize the current month by genre
'         and to prepare for a new month's entries
Dim iAction As Integer
Dim iDrama As Integer
Dim iRomance As Integer
Dim iSciFi As Integer
Dim iSuspense As Integer
Dim rowNum As Integer
Dim totRows As Integer
Dim vGenre As Variant
Dim rMonthly As Range
Dim rSummary As Range

'Assign values to variables
ActiveWorkbook.Sheets("Monthly").Activate
Set rMonthly = Range([a4].Address, [a4].End(xlDown).Offset(0, 2).Address)
rMonthly.Sort rMonthly.Columns("C")



End Sub
```

**3.** In order to calculate the information required for the *Summary* tab, Lori must code a looping structure that accumulates the number of rentals for each genre. She will store the results in the variables declared at the top of the procedure. To begin, Lori inserts a blank line and then types the code appearing in Figure 12.54. (Notice the liberal use of comments, the For . . . Next structure, and the Select Case structure in this code block.)

**Figure 12.54**

Coding the
looping structure
for the Rollover
Sub procedure

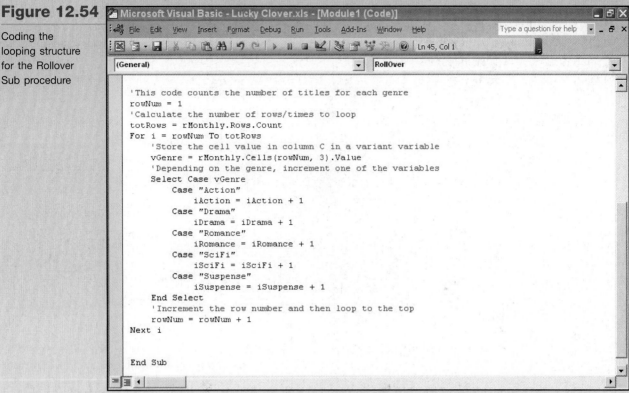

```
'This code counts the number of titles for each genre
rowNum = 1
'Calculate the number of rows/times to loop
totRows = rMonthly.Rows.Count
For i = rowNum To totRows
    'Store the cell value in column C in a variant variable
    vGenre = rMonthly.Cells(rowNum, 3).Value
    'Depending on the genre, increment one of the variables
    Select Case vGenre
        Case "Action"
            iAction = iAction + 1
        Case "Drama"
            iDrama = iDrama + 1
        Case "Romance"
            iRomance = iRomance + 1
        Case "SciFi"
            iSciFi = iSciFi + 1
        Case "Suspense"
            iSuspense = iSuspense + 1
    End Select
    'Increment the row number and then loop to the top
    rowNum = rowNum + 1
Next i


End Sub
```

**4.** Nearing completion, Lori writes the code for entering the accumulated values into the *Summary* worksheet. She then clears the contents of the *Monthly* worksheet using the VBA **ClearContents** method.
The completed code is displayed in Figure 12.55.

**Figure 12.55**

Completing the
RollOver Sub
procedure

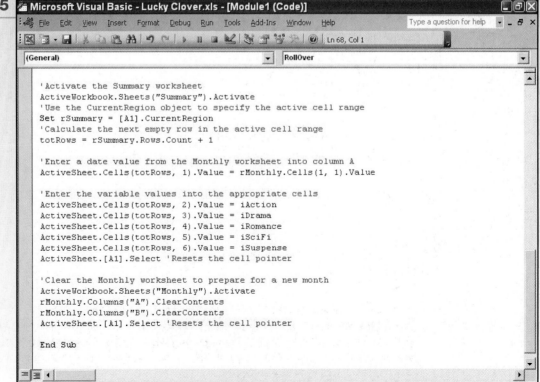

```
'Activate the Summary worksheet
ActiveWorkbook.Sheets("Summary").Activate
'Use the CurrentRegion object to specify the active cell range
Set rSummary = [A1].CurrentRegion
'Calculate the next empty row in the active cell range
totRows = rSummary.Rows.Count + 1

'Enter a date value from the Monthly worksheet into column A
ActiveSheet.Cells(totRows, 1).Value = rMonthly.Cells(1, 1).Value

'Enter the variable values into the appropriate cells
ActiveSheet.Cells(totRows, 2).Value = iAction
ActiveSheet.Cells(totRows, 3).Value = iDrama
ActiveSheet.Cells(totRows, 4).Value = iRomance
ActiveSheet.Cells(totRows, 5).Value = iSciFi
ActiveSheet.Cells(totRows, 6).Value = iSuspense
ActiveSheet.[A1].Select 'Resets the cell pointer

'Clear the Monthly worksheet to prepare for a new month
ActiveWorkbook.Sheets("Monthly").Activate
rMonthly.Columns("A").ClearContents
rMonthly.Columns("B").ClearContents
ActiveSheet.[A1].Select 'Resets the cell pointer


End Sub
```

Lori runs the procedure, reviews the results, and then prints the code module. Pleased with her new RollOver procedure, she saves and closes the "Lucky Clover" workbook. After exiting Excel 2003, she leaves her office and begins restocking the shelves with the returned rentals. Unfortunately, her day is not over yet!

## Answers to Self-Check Questions

**12.1** Which window would you display in the Visual Basic Editor if you wanted to set the design-time properties for an object? The Properties window allows you to set the design-time properties for an object.

**12.2** What purpose does the With statement serve in VBA code? The With statement saves you from having to type the object name repeatedly when setting multiple properties or coding multiple statements.

**12.3** What type of control structure might you implement if you were applying tax rates based on various income levels? The Select Case structure provides the greatest flexibility for making calculation decisions based on various income levels.

**12.4** In displaying a message box that contains the Yes and No command buttons, how do you evaluate in your code which button is clicked by the user? First, store the return value of the button clicked in a variable. Then, evaluate the variable using a branching control structure to determine which code to process after the message box is accepted.

**12.5** How do you attach a previously recorded macro to a command button placed on the worksheet? In Design mode, open the Code window for the command button control and then enter the procedure name to execute in the control's Click event.

| | Skill Sets and Skills | Information for Vendors of Approved Courseware | Advantage Lesson |
|---|---|---|---|
| **XL03E-1** | **Organizing and Analyzing Data** | | |
| XL03E-1-1 | Use subtotals | Adding subtotals to worksheet data | 8.4.1 |
| XL03E-1-2 | Define and apply advanced filters | Creating and applying advanced filters | 8.2.2; 8.3.1 |
| XL03E-1-3 | Group and outline data | Grouping and outlining data | 7.1.3; 8.4.2 |
| XL03E-1-4 | Use data validation | Adding data validation criteria to cells | 11.2 |
| XL03E-1-5 | Create and modify list ranges | Creating and modifying list ranges | 8.1.1; 8.1.5 |
| XL03E-1-6 | Add, show, close, edit, merge and summarize scenarios | Managing scenarios | 9.1.3/9.1.4 |
| XL03E-1-7 | Perform data analysis using automated tools | Projecting values using analysis tools (e.g., *Analysis ToolPak*) Performing What-If analysis Using the Solver add-in | 9.2<br>9.1<br>9.1.2 |
| XL03E-1-8 | Create PivotTable and PivotChart reports | Creating PivotTable Reports and PivotChart Reports | 9.4 |
| XL03E-1-9 | Use Lookup and Reference functions | Using Lookup and Reference functions (e.g., *HLOOKUP, VLOOKUP*) | 10.1 |
| XL03E-1-10 | Use Database functions | Creating and editing Database functions (e.g., *DSUM, DAVERAGE*) | 8.3 |
| XL03E-1-11 | Trace formula precedents, dependents and errors | Tracing formula precedents Tracing formula dependents Tracing formula errors | 11.3.3<br>11.3.3<br>11.3.4 |
| XL03E-1-12 | Locate invalid data and formulas | Using Error Checking Circling invalid data | 11.3.2<br>11.3.2 |
| XL03E-1-13 | Watch and evaluate formulas | Using Evaluate formulas Using cell Watch | 11.3.4<br>11.3.4 |
| XL03E-1-14 | Define, modify and use named ranges | Naming one or more cell ranges Using a named range reference in a formula | 4.1.1; 4.1.2<br>4.1; 4.2 |
| XL03E-1-15 | Structure workbooks using XML | Adding, modifying and deleting maps Managing elements and attributes in XML workbooks (e.g., adding, modifying, deleting, cutting, copying) Defining XML options (e.g., applying XML view options) | 10.5; 10.5.4-6<br>10.5; 10.5.4-6<br>10.5; 10.5.4-6 |
| **XL03E-2** | **Formatting Data and Content** | | |
| XL03E-2-1 | Create and modify custom data formats | Creating and applying custom number formats | 5.2.2 |
| XL03E-2-2 | Use conditional formatting | Using conditional formatting | 11.2.1 |
| XL03E-2-3 | Format and resize graphics | Using cropping and rotating tools Controlling image contrast and brightness Scaling and resizing graphics | 5.3; 5.4<br>5.4.3<br>5.3; 5.4 |

| XL03E-2-4 | Format charts and diagrams | Applying formats to charts and diagrams (e.g., data series, plot area) | 5.6 |
|---|---|---|---|
| **XL03E-3** | **Collaborating** | | |
| XL03E-3-1 | Protect cells, worksheets, and workbooks | Adding protection to cells, worksheets and workbooks | 10.2.1 |
| XL03E-3-2 | Apply workbook security settings | Using digital signatures to authenticate workbooks<br>Setting passwords<br>Setting macro settings | 10.2.4<br><br>10.2.2; 10.2.4<br>11.4.3 |
| XL03E-3-3 | Share workbooks | Creating and modifying shared workbooks | 11.1.1 |
| XL03E-3-4 | Merge workbooks | Merging multiple versions of the same workbook | 11.1.3 |
| XL03E-3-5 | Track, accept, and reject changes to workbooks | Tracking changes<br>Accepting and rejecting changes | 11.1.2<br>11.1.2 |
| **XL03E-4** | **Managing Data and Workbooks** | | |
| XL03E-4-1 | Import data to Excel | Bringing information into Excel from external sources<br>Linking to Web page data | 10.4<br><br>10.5.1 |
| XL03E-4-2 | Export data from Excel | Exporting structured data from Excel | 8.2.5; 10.4.1 |
| XL03E-4-3 | Publish and edit Web worksheets and workbooks | Publishing Web based worksheets | 3.3.2; 10.5.2 |
| XL03E-4-4 | Create and edit templates | Creating a workbook template<br>Creating a new workbook based upon a user-defined template<br>Editing a workbook template | 10.3.1<br>10.3.1; 10.3.2<br><br>10.3.2 |
| XL03E-4-5 | Consolidate data | Consolidating data from two or more worksheets | 7.4 |
| XL03E-4-6 | Define and modify workbook properties | Managing workbook properties (e.g., summary data) | 10.2.4 |
| **XL03E-5** | **Customizing Excel** | | |
| XL03E-5-1 | Customize toolbars and menus | Adding and removing buttons from toolbars<br>Adding custom menus | 11.5.3; 11.5.4<br><br>11.5.1 |
| XL03E-5-2 | Create, edit, and run macros | Creating macros<br>Editing macros using the Visual Basic Editor<br>Running macros | 11.4.1; 12.1<br>11.4.4; 12.1-4<br><br>11.4.2; 12.1-4 |
| XL03E-5-3 | Modify Excel default settings | Modifying default font settings<br>Setting the default number of worksheets<br>Changing the default file location for templates | 10.3.3<br>10.3.3<br><br>10.3.3 |

# Answers

to self-check questions

**1.1** How do you turn the adaptive menus feature on or off? Choose the Tools, Customize command and then check the **Always show full menus** check box to turn the adaptive menus feature off. Remove the check to turn the feature back on.

**1.2** Explain why a phone number is not considered a numeric value in an Excel worksheet. Although it contains numbers, a phone number is never used to perform mathematical calculations.

**1.3** Why is worksheet editing such a valuable skill? Most worksheets in use today are revisions and updates of older worksheets. As a novice user, you often spend more time updating existing worksheets than constructing new ones.

**1.4** In the Open and Save As dialog boxes, how do the List and Details views differ? Name two other views that are accessible from the Views button. The List view uses a multicolumn format. The Details view displays one file per row. Furthermore, the Details view displays other information, including the file size, type, and modification date. The other views that appear on the drop-down menu include: Thumbnails, Tiles, Icons, Properties, Preview, and WebView.

**2.1** Which of the "Auto" features enables you to sum a range of values and display the result in the Status bar? AutoCalculate

**2.2** Which method would you use to copy several nonadjacent (not beside one another) values for placement into a single worksheet column? The Office Clipboard would provide the fastest method. After displaying the Clipboard task pane, clear the Clipboard and then collect up to 24 items in the desired sequence. You would then move to the target range and paste these items into a single column using the Paste All button (Paste All).

**2.3** Why must you be careful when deleting rows or columns? You must be careful because if you delete the entire row or column, you may inadvertently delete data that exists further down a column or further across a row. Ensure that a row or column is indeed empty before deleting it.

**3.1** What is the basic difference between using the Underline button (U) and the Borders button? When you apply an underline to a cell, only the words in the cell appear underlined. When you apply a border underline to a cell, the entire cell is underlined. Also, borders may be applied to each side of a cell, such as top, bottom, left, and right.

**3.2** How might you ensure that related worksheets and workbooks are formatted consistently? Use the same predefined AutoFormat style to format data in all of the worksheets.

**3.3** How does the Print Preview display mode differ from the Web Page Preview display mode? Print Preview appears in the Excel application window and displays the workbook as it will appear when printed. Web Page Preview uses the computer's default Web browser to display an HTML rendering of the current worksheet.

**3.4** How would you create a custom footer that displayed your name against the left page border and your company's name against the right page border? In the Page Setup dialog box, click the Custom Footer command button on the *Header/Footer* tab. Then, enter your name into the left text box and your company's name into the right text box of the Footer dialog box.

**4.1** Why is "AD2002" an unacceptable name for a cell range? You cannot name a cell range using an actual cell reference on the worksheet.

**4.2** When might you use the Function Arguments dialog box or Insert Function dialog box to enter a function into the worksheet? If you need help entering the arguments in the correct order or if you cannot remember a function's name or proper syntax, you can use these tools to refresh your memory or to assist you in completing the task.

**4.3** What must you do when selecting the print range for a worksheet that contains an embedded chart? Because charts do not appear in cells on a worksheet, you must be sure to select the print range to include these graphic objects. For example, select the cells that appear underneath the embedded chart that you want to print.

**5.1** What are the two ways that you can indent a cell entry? To indent a cell's contents, (1) use the *Alignment* tab of the Format Cells dialog box or (2) click the Increase Indent (⬚) button on the toolbar.

**5.2** Using the Style dialog box, how would you change the default font for an entire workbook to be 12-point, Times New Roman? You can modify the Normal style for the workbook using the Format, Style command. Click the Modify command button in the Style dialog box and then make the required changes in the Format Cells dialog box. After you return to the worksheet, all cells based on the Normal style will appear formatted.

**5.3** How would you place a "STOP" sign on a worksheet using the techniques described in this module? Click the AutoShapes button on the Drawing toolbar and then select an Octagon shape from the Basic Shapes menu. After placing the object onto the draw layer, apply a red fill color. Then add and center the text "STOP" inside the object and format the word to appear white and boldface.

**5.4** Name four types of media files that you can search for using the Clip Art task pane. The four media types shown in Figure 5.28 are Clip Art, Photographs, Movies, and Sounds.

**5.5** What must you remember when selecting nonadjacent ranges in preparation for the Chart Wizard or to add to a chart's plot area? You must ensure that the ranges are the same shape and size.

**5.6** What might you do differently in formatting a chart for printing as opposed to formatting a chart for displaying online? When formatting a chart for printing, you must concern yourself with the quality of output the printer is capable of. Therefore, you may use patterns and shading levels instead of colors. For online or computer-based presentations, the use of colors in charts works well to differentiate the various elements.

**6.1** Provide two reasons for nesting a calculation in a formula expression.
1. to force the calculation to perform before another calculation, as dictated by the operator order of precedence
2. to make a formula expression easier to read and understand

**6.2** Name two methods for calculating and displaying the day of the week (e.g., Wednesday).
1. Use the WEEKDAY function, and then translate the return value (1 to 7) to the appropriate weekday value.
2. Use the Format command to apply a custom number format using either the "ddd" or "dddd" option.

**6.3** What are the results of the functions INT(4.55) and ROUND(4.55,0)?
• INT(4.55) returns the number 4.
• ROUND(4.55,0) returns the number 5.

**6.4** Cell A1 contains a person's area code and phone number in the form (789)555-1234. What expression would you enter in cell A2 to extract only the phone number for display? Here is one formula expression that solves the stated problem:
**=RIGHT(A1,LEN(A1)-SEARCH(")",A1))**

**6.5** How might you incorporate the IF function to calculate a mortgage payment in which the interest rate changed depending on the term chosen? You would use a nested IF function, with a logical test on the term period, to calculate the *Rate* argument for the PMT function.

**7.1** How would you divide a worksheet window into four panes? You can drag both the horizontal and vertical split boxes to create panes. Once you have finished specifying horizontal panes for example, you can then divide the worksheet window into vertical panes. You can also use the Window → Split command.

**7.2** What characters must you type to have Excel's AutoCorrect feature insert the proper trademark symbol (™)? You type **(tm)** and then press the Space bar.

**7.3** How would you rename a chart sheet and then move it to the end of a sheet stack in a workbook? You rename and move a chart sheet just as you would a worksheet. In other words, double-click the chart sheet's tab and type a new name. Press **ENTER** to accept the entry. Then drag the sheet tab to the far right in the sheet stack.

**7.4** Name two advantages for separating your work into multiple workbooks. First, the workbooks are typically smaller than a single multiple-sheet workbook. Second, the workbooks are not limited to being stored on the same computer or network.

**7.5** Can you think of any other ways to document a worksheet? Some suggestions include:
• Enter comments in specific columns or rows, and then use the Hide command to conceal the columns or rows.
• Set aside an entire worksheet in a workbook for adding comments, notes, and explanations.
• Display and then print your worksheet formulas so that you may annotate them further on paper.

**8.1**  What are some advantages of adding records to a list using the Data Form dialog box? What are some disadvantages?
Advantages:
- Enables you to focus on one record at a time.
- Provides for faster input of new records.
- Easier to see all fields when working with long records.

Disadvantages:
- AutoComplete command is not available in a data form.
- User can view only a single record at a time and, as a result, may duplicate an entry accidentally.

**8.2**  How do you filter a worksheet list to display only the top 10 percent of values appearing in a field? Click the appropriate AutoFilter drop-down list arrow and then select the (Top 10) option from the drop-down list. In the Top 10 AutoFilter dialog box, select Top from the leftmost drop-down list box, select 10 in the middle spin box, and select Percent from the rightmost drop-down list box. Click the OK command button to apply the filter.

**8.3**  Using the "Edutech" list, how would you determine the average price of CDROM and DVD media published in 1999?
On the *Sheet1* tab, set up the following criteria:

| Published | Media |
|-----------|-------|
| 1999      | CDROM |
| 1999      | DVD   |

Ensure that the criteria range includes the second row. View the DAVERAGE result on the *Sheet2* tab.

**8.4**  What must you always do prior to subtotaling values in a worksheet list? You must sort the field on which you want to group data.

**9.1**  Compare and contrast Excel's Goal Seek command, the Solver add-in program, and the Scenario Manager. Goal Seek lets the user specify a target value and then works backward to determine the input value required. Although similar, Solver can solve a problem requiring multiple input values. The user can also specify the constraints used to limit the input values. Scenario Manager is different from both of the previous tools in that it works forward with a set of input values to calculate outcomes. It is primarily used for storing and saving the results from various input combinations.

**9.2**  Which tools might you use to forecast the price of a mutual fund or stock in the securities market? Using historical price data, you could use Excel's statistical functions to extrapolate and project future prices. Unfortunately, the correlation between length of time and stock value is not typically linear. There are many other variables to take into consideration when attempting to forecast stock and mutual fund prices.

**9.3**  What special type of formula is entered into a data table? Can you edit the formulas appearing in a data table's output area? A data table is created using a special array formula called "TABLE." You cannot edit an array formula directly. To modify a data table, you must first delete it and then re-create it from the beginning.

**9.4**  What would happen to the summary results in the data area of a PivotTable report if some values from its source data (worksheet list) were modified? There is no change in the summary results until you click the Refresh button (![icon]) on the PivotTable list toolbar.

**9.5** How might custom views and the Report Manager feature help you compile and print reports containing both worksheets and charts? Often the worksheet that provides the data for a chart includes more information than is required for a report. Therefore, you can produce a custom view that includes only relevant data for the report. Using Report Manager, you can then combine this view with the desired chart sheet.

**10.1** What function(s) does the Lookup Wizard use in constructing a lookup formula? The INDEX and MATCH lookup and reference functions.

**10.2** How can you ensure that a user will not remove the worksheet protection that you have initiated? To ensure that the protection is not removed, use a password when protecting the worksheet.

**10.3** How would you use a template to change the default font from Arial to Verdana for all new workbooks? To update the default settings for a workbook, create a template named "Book.xlt" with the desired font and then save it in the XLStart folder. To update the default settings for a worksheet, create a template named "Sheet.xlt" and then save it in the XLStart folder.

**10.4** Your friend is using a specialized statistics software program to collect numerical research data. He has asked you to analyze and chart the data. Assuming that the software is not able to export data into an Excel 2003 workbook, what file format should you recommend for transferring the data? An ASCII Text file format is the most common format used in data exchange. Almost every software program can export and import ASCII text files. Furthermore, the Text Import Wizard facility of Excel 2003 greatly facilitates the import process.

**10.5** Name the three Microsoft Office Web Components that allow you to create interactive Web pages using content from your workbooks. The Spreadsheet, Chart, and PivotTable components enable you to add interactivity to Web pages created from an Excel 2003 workbook.

**11.1** Provide an example of a workbook that would lend itself to being shared, especially for history tracking and merging in a workgroup environment. This answer will vary. Some examples of shared workbooks include price lists, inventory records, customer worksheet lists, accounting workbooks, and personnel schedules.

**11.2** How could you check whether a customer account code is valid when entering invoice data into a worksheet template? To check whether a customer account code is valid, use the Data Validation dialog box. You can compare, for example, the customer account code to a list of acceptable values appearing in a worksheet list.

**11.3** What result occurs by clicking the Trace Precedents button (⊞) or the Trace Dependents button (⊞) twice on the Formula Auditing toolbar? When you click either button a second time, additional tracer arrows appear on the worksheet to display the next level of cell relationships.

**11.4** Aside from running the macro, how would you determine whether absolute or relative cell referencing was being used? You can examine the macro's programming code in the Code window of the Visual Basic Editor.

**11.5** How would you create an option on the Menu bar that contained all of your macros? To begin, open the Customize dialog box, click the *Commands* tab, and then select the New Menu item at the bottom of the Categories list box. Drag the selection from the *Commands* list box to the Menu bar. Then, using the right-click menu, change the name to something more appropriate like "My Macros." You can now drag the Custom Menu Item selection from the Macros category to appear in the new menu. Assign a macro and rename the new menu item. Repeat this step for each of the macros you want to add to the menu.

**12.1** Which window would you display in the Visual Basic Editor if you wanted to set the design-time properties for an object? The Properties window allows you to set the design-time properties for an object.

**12.2** What purpose does the With statement serve in VBA code? The With statement saves you from having to type the object name repeatedly when setting multiple properties or coding multiple statements.

**12.3** What type of control structure might you implement if you were applying tax rates based on various income levels? The Select Case structure provides the greatest flexibility for making calculation decisions based on various income levels.

**12.4** In displaying a message box that contains the Yes and No command buttons, how do you evaluate in your code which button is clicked by the user? First, store the return value of the button clicked in a variable. Then, evaluate the variable using a branching control structure to determine which code to process after the message box is accepted.

**12.5** How do you attach a previously recorded macro to a command button placed on the worksheet? In Design mode, open the Code window for the command button control and then enter the procedure name to execute in the control's Click event.

# Glossary

**Absolute cell address:** Cell reference in a worksheet that does not adjust when copied to other cells; you make a cell address absolute by placing dollar signs ($) before the column letter and row number, such as $C$4

**ActiveX controls:** Re-usable program components or objects that provide some functionality; for example, calendar applications, Internet connectivity, and interface elements

**Adaptive menus:** The dynamic menu bars and toolbars that are personalized to the way you work; Office 2003 watches the tasks that you perform in an application and then displays only those commands and buttons that you use most often

**Advanced criteria filter:** A filtering command and process that uses conditions stored in a criteria range to limit the display of records in a list or to extract records to a new location in the same worksheet

**Analysis ToolPak:** An Excel 2003 add-in program; provides specialized data analysis tools for performing statistical and engineering analyses, such as calculating ANOVA tables, performing Fourier Analysis, and extrapolating regression equations

**Annuity:** A series of equal cash payments made over a given period of time

**Application window:** In Windows, each running application program appears in its own application window; these windows may be sized and moved anywhere on the Windows desktop

**Arguments:** The parameters used in entering a function according to its *syntax;* may include text, numbers, formulas, functions, and cell references

**Array formula:** A single formula that produces multiple results or that accommodates a group of arguments in a row or column orientation

**Audit:** In Excel 2003, the process of reviewing a workbook, worksheet, range, or cell for incorrect entries, non-conforming values, formula references, and other information

**AutoCalculate:** A software feature that sums the selected range of cells and displays the result in the Status bar

**AutoComplete:** A software feature that assists you in entering data into a worksheet by filling in letters from existing entries in the column as you type

**AutoCorrect:** A software feature that corrects common typing and spelling mistakes automatically as you type; it also enables you to enter complex symbols quickly and easily

**AutoFill:** A software feature that enables you to copy and extend a formula or data series automatically in a worksheet

**AutoFilter:** A software feature that makes it quick and easy for you to select, filter, and display records from a worksheet list

**AutoFit:** A software feature that calculates the optimal row height or column width based on existing data in the worksheet

**AutoFormat:** A software feature that applies professionally designed formatting styles to your documents

**Automacro:** A macro that runs automatically when a specific event occurs, such as opening a workbook

**AutoShapes:** Ready-made graphic objects that you can add to your worksheet using the Drawing toolbar and then format and customize to suit your needs

**AutoSum:** A software feature that automatically inserts a formula for adding values from a surrounding row or column of cells

**AutoTemplates:** Special *template* workbooks that contain the default settings for new workbooks (Book.xlt) and worksheets (Sheet.xlt); these templates are stored in the XLStart folder

**Bar chart:** A chart that compares one data element to another data element using horizontal bars; similar to a *column chart*

**Breakpoint:** In VBA code, a user-defined stopping point that interrupts a macro's execution and displays the Visual Basic Editor

**Cell:** The intersection of a column and a row

**Cell address:** The location of a cell on a worksheet given by the intersection of a column and a row; columns are labeled using letters; rows are numbered; a cell address combines the column letter with the row number (for example, B9 or DF134)

**Cell alignment:** The positioning of data entered into a worksheet cell in relation to the cell borders

**Cell layer:** The layer for worksheet cells; this layer holds data, calculated expressions, formatting attributes, and other information

**Cell pointer:** The cursor on a worksheet that points to a cell; moved using the arrow keys or the mouse

**Cell range:** One or more cells in a worksheet that together form a rectangle

**Character strings:** Any combination of letters, symbols, and numerals that is not a numerical or date value

**Chart component:** A Microsoft Office Web Component; an ActiveX object that provides basic interactive charting capabilities using the Microsoft Internet Explorer Web browser

**Chart sheet:** A sheet tab or page within a workbook file that is used to create, modify, and display a chart graphic

**Chart Wizard:** A linear step progression of dialog boxes that leads you through creating a chart in Excel 2003

**Clip Organizer:** A shared application in Microsoft Office that lets you manage clip art images, pictures, sounds, animation, and video clips and insert them into a worksheet's draw layer

**Code window:** In the Visual Basic Editor, the window containing the macro procedure code; used for *coding* and *debugging* program statements

**Coding:** Developing and writing code manually from scratch

**Collection:** Object type that acts as a container for a set of similar objects

**Column chart:** A chart that compares one data element with another data element and can show variations over a period of time

**COM add-in:** An add-in program, based on the Component Object Model (COM), that is created using Microsoft Office 2003 or Visual Basic; COM add-in programs can be run in any Office 2003 application

**Comment:** A special text box that is attached to a cell and used to display helpful information; you display a cell's comment by moving the mouse pointer over the cell containing a comment indicator, a small red triangle in the upper-right corner of the cell

**Concatenate:** In Excel 2003, joining together characters from separate cells or strings using the ampersand (&) operator to form a single cell entry; combining characters to form a string

**Conditional formatting:** A software feature that gives you the ability to change a cell's formatting based on its contents or based on the results of a formula calculation

**Conditional Sum Wizard:** An Excel 2003 add-in program; a series of dialog boxes that lead you through summing a worksheet range based on specific conditions being met

**Consolidate:** The process of combining smaller worksheet files into a single summary worksheet, making it easier to manage large amounts of data

**Constant:** Any number, date, or text value that is entered directly into a cell, as an operand in a formula, or as an argument in a function; an unchanging value that the user cannot adjust or modify; opposite of a *variable*

**Constraints:** Logical conditions or business rules that you define in the Solver add-in program to limit a resource's value or availability

**Control structures:** Group of program statements that allows you to make decisions and direct the flow of executed instructions; two common control structures are "branching" and "looping"

**Control Toolbox:** A special type of toolbar that contains *ActiveX controls* that you may add to your worksheet or custom *user forms*

**Criteria form:** A special dialog box that displays an empty data form that you use to enter search criteria; you can use the criteria form to find *records*

**Criteria range:** The worksheet range used in an advanced criteria filter, or as an argument in a database function, for inputting search conditions; the first row always contains the criteria header row—select fields from the field header row; the rows beneath the criteria header contain the conditions that match entries or evaluate to true and false

**Custom add-in:** An application-specific add-in program containing macro procedures and other VBA code that you may hide, protect, and distribute for use with your workbook applications

**Custom format:** A combination of formatting codes that when placed in a particular sequence enhance the display of numeric and date values; you construct and store custom formats on the *Number* tab of the Format Cells dialog box

**Custom view:** A combination of print and display settings that are named and stored with the workbook in which they were created

**Data form:** A special dialog box that displays one record at a time from the active worksheet list; you can use the data form to add, modify, and delete a *record*

**Data validation:** A term used to describe the process of evaluating data once it has been entered into a software program; using a set of rules, which may contain a range of acceptable values, the evaluation results in the entry either being accepted or rejected

**Debugging:** A programming term that means locating errors in your VBA code and correcting those errors

**Delimiter:** A symbol or character, such as a tab or quotation mark, that is used to separate fields or columns of information in a text file

**Dependent variable:** A worksheet value that is used in testing for a hypothesized relationship with another worksheet value called the *independent variable;* having proven a relationship exists, you can use regression analysis to forecast the value of a dependent variable for a given independent variable

**Design time:** The period during which a program is created or modified in the Visual Basic Editor or ActiveX controls are added to a worksheet

**Document window:** In Excel 2003, each open *workbook* appears in its own document window; these windows may be sized and moved anywhere within the application window

**Drag and drop:** A software feature that allows you to copy and move information by dragging information from one location to another using the mouse

**Draw layer:** The invisible surface that exists above the *cell layer* and holds inserted or embedded graphic objects and charts

**Dynamic cell range:** A named range that uses the INDEX and COUNTA functions to expand and contract the referenced area automatically as information is entered or removed

**Embedded chart:** A chart that is placed on the draw layer of a worksheet

**Embedding:** A way of sharing data and exchanging information; refers to the process of inserting an object into a destination document

**Event:** An action or reaction that occurs in Windows programming; you can code unique responses to events, such as performing a procedure whenever a button is clicked

**Event-driven programming:** Coding a program to respond to events that may occur, such as clicking a button; uses *objects, properties,* and *methods* to describe elements, attributes, and actions

**Extensible Markup Language (XML):** A standardized meta-markup language used for defining, maintaining, and exchanging structured data using Web-based documents; Microsoft provides an XML Spreadsheet schema specification that defines a special XML file format for storing and manipulating workbook data

**Field:** A piece of information in a *record,* such as a person's last name in a phone book listing; in Excel 2003, a field is represented by a column in the worksheet list

**Field buttons:** In working with PivotTables and Pivot-Charts, the buttons (taken from the column or field headings in the data source) that represent the data stored in a particular field

**Field header row:** The top row in a worksheet list that contains the field names or column headings; describes the contents of each column; usually row 1, but not necessarily so

**Fill handle:** The small black square that is located in the bottom right-hand corner of a cell or cell range; you use the fill handle to create a series or to copy cell information

**Filter:** The process or method of temporarily restricting the display of records in a worksheet list to those that match a particular search specification

**Flat-file database:** A two-dimensional, stand-alone database that is composed of rows and columns; Excel 2003 provides flat-file database capabilities through the use of worksheet lists

**Font(s):** All the characters of one size in a particular *typeface;* includes numbers, punctuation marks, and upper- and lowercase letters

**Footer(s):** Descriptive information (such as page number and date) that appears at the bottom of each page of a document

**Format Painter:** A software feature that enables you to copy only the formatting attributes and styles from one location to another

**Formula:** A mathematical expression that typically defines the relationships among various cells in a worksheet or table

**Formula Palette:** The dialog box, appearing beneath the Formula bar, that provides assistance for entering a function's *arguments* using the correct syntax

**Function procedure:** In VBA, a procedure that typically performs a calculation and returns a value to the calling program

**Functions:** Built-in shortcuts that can be used in formulas to perform calculations

**Future value:** The value in future dollars of a series of equal cash payments

**Goal seeking:** The process of stating a desired outcome and then working backward to solve the input values necessary to produce the outcome

**Graphic file:** A computer graphic, created by an artist or scanned from an existing picture, that you can insert into your worksheets

**Gridlines:** The lines on a worksheet that assist the user in lining up the cell pointer with a particular column letter or row number

**Group mode:** In Excel 2003, a special mode for working with multiple-sheet workbooks; enables you to perform commands on a single sheet and have those commands reflected in all other sheets in the file

**Hard-coded:** A formula or module that contains a constant value rather than using a cell reference, range name, or implicit intersection (as in natural language formulas)

**Header(s):** Descriptive information (such as page number and data) that appears at the top of each page of a document.

**HTML:** An acronym for Hypertext Markup Language, which is the standardized markup language used in creating documents for display on the World Wide Web

**HTML round-tripping:** The back and forth publishing and editing of content between Office 2003 applications and the Microsoft Internet Explorer Web browser; after creating and saving a workbook as an interactive Web page using the *Spreadsheet component,* the process of editing and then exporting the spreadsheet from Internet Explorer back to Excel 2003 for further editing

**Hyperlink:** In terms of Internet technologies, a text string or graphics that when clicked takes you to another location, either within the same document or to a separate document stored on your computer, an intranet resource, or onto the Internet

**In-cell editing:** In Excel 2003, the feature that enables you to revise text labels, numbers, dates, and other entries directly within a cell; to activate in-cell editing, you double-click a cell

**Independent variable:** A worksheet value that is used in testing for a hypothesized relationship with another worksheet value called the *dependent variable;* having proven a relationship exists, you can use regression analysis to forecast the value of a dependent variable for a given independent variable

**Input cells:** Worksheet cells in which you store dynamic and variable data; input cells contain the values that are referenced by outcome formulas in a worksheet model

**Integer value:** The value of a number to the left of the decimal point; for example, the integer of 123.987 is 123

**Internet:** A worldwide network of computer networks that are interconnected by standard telephone lines, fiber optics, and satellites

**Intranet:** A private local or wide area network that uses Internet protocols and technologies to share information within an institution or corporation

**Keyword:** A reserved word that holds special meaning for the VBA compiler and, therefore, cannot be used as a variable or constant name

**Legend:** A key for deciphering the data series appearing in the plot area of a chart

**Line chart:** A chart that plots trends or shows changes over a period of time

**Linking:** A way of sharing data and exchanging information; refers to the process of copying data from a source document into a destination document and establishing a dynamic link between the two

**List:** A defined worksheet range containing column headings as *fields* and row entries as *records;* useful for storing and manipulating large amounts of data

**Lookup formula:** A formula expression that uses one of Excel's built-in lookup functions (LOOKUP, VLOOKUP, HLOOKUP, MATCH, or INDEX) to retrieve a value from a lookup table

**Lookup table:** A worksheet range, bounded by row and column labels, that you can use to look up information in a table format

**Macro Recorder:** A special tool that you use to record, translate, and store keystrokes as VBA code in a programming module

**Macro virus:** A malicious program that attaches itself to a document or template and performs instructions that may damage files on your computer

**Macros:** Programs that you create to automate repetitive procedures

**Margins:** Space between the edge of the paper and the top, bottom, left, and right edges of the printed document

**Method:** The actions that can be performed on or by an object, such as activate, open, and close

**Microsoft Map:** A shared application in Microsoft Office that enables you to create and plot an embedded map from geographic data stored in a worksheet

**Microsoft Office Web Components:** Component objects of executable program code that allow you to view and interact with Microsoft Office 2003 data using the Microsoft Internet Explorer Web browser software

**Microsoft Query:** A software program that allows you to develop queries for retrieving data from external database files

**Mixed cell address:** Cell reference in a worksheet that includes both *relative* and *absolute cell references;* for example, the address C$4 provides a "relative" column letter and an "absolute" row number

**Module:** In the *Visual Basic Editor,* a module is a container for storing and organizing VBA macros and procedures

**Name box:** The text box appearing at the left-hand side of the Formula bar that displays the current cell address and that enables you to navigate quickly to any cell location in the worksheet

**Natural language formula:** In Excel 2003, a type of *formula* that allows you to use the column and row labels within a worksheet in building a mathematical expression

**Nesting:** Using a formula or function as an operand or argument in another formula or function; placing a formula within an expression using parentheses, such as (2+3)*4; a formula or function can contain up to seven levels of nested expressions

**Normal view:** In Excel 2003, the standard view mode used for creating a workbook; you can adjust a zoom factor for viewing more or less of a worksheet in this mode

**Object model:** A conceptual map for the hierarchical chain of objects that are exposed by an application

**Objects:** Any type of data , such as a graphic image or WordArt, that has been pasted or embedded into a worksheet

**Office Clipboard:** A program, in Office 2003, that allows you to copy and move information within or among Office 2003 applications; unlike the Windows Clipboard, the Office Clipboard can store up to twenty-four items and then paste them all at once

**One-input data table:** A worksheet table that displays the results from one or more outcome formulas as a set of values is substituted into a single input cell

**Operand:** In Excel 2003, a constant value, range name, or cell address that you use in building formula expressions

**Operator:** In Excel 2003, a symbol used to determine what calculations to perform on operands; Excel 2003 provides four types—arithmetic, comparison or logical, text, and reference

**Order of precedence:** The sequential order in which formula expressions are evaluated is determined by the use of parentheses and the operator *order of precedence*

**Outlining:** In Excel 2003, the process of grouping data together on a worksheet in order to hide (collapse) or display (expand) detailed information

**Page Break Preview:** In Excel 2003, the preview mode used prior to printing in order to adjust the print area and page breaks that occur in a workbook

**Panes:** When a worksheet window has been divided into separate areas using the Window Ë Freeze Panes command or the Window Ë Split command, these areas are called *window panes* or *panes;* a worksheet can have a maximum of four panes at any one time

**Parsing:** In Excel 2003, dividing a single cell entry or text string across multiple cells; extracting a character or characters from a string; to parse data in Excel 2003, you use functions from the Text category

**Password:** A series of characters that you can use as a lock and key to restrict access to a workbook; the best passwords combine letters, numbers, and special symbols, which makes them difficult to guess

**Password-protect:** The process of restricting access to information using an easily remembered word or group of characters that will prove difficult for others to guess

**Personal Macro Workbook:** A special Excel 2003 workbook, stored in the XLStart folder, used for storing macros that you want made available for use in all workbooks

**Pie chart:** A chart that shows the proportions of individual components compared to the whole

**PivotChart report:** An interactive chart sheet, based on an associated *PivotTable report,* that summarizes and displays data graphically.

**PivotTable and PivotChart Wizard:** A series of dialog boxes that lead you through creating a *PivotTable report* or *PivotChart report*

**PivotTable component:** A Microsoft Office Web Component; an ActiveX object that enables the presentation of an interactive PivotTable list using the Microsoft Internet Explorer Web browser

**PivotTable list:** A PivotTable report that is saved as an interactive Web page, incorporating the Microsoft Office Web Components, for display using the Microsoft Internet Explorer Web browser software

**PivotTable report:** An interactive worksheet table that summarizes data stored in a worksheet list or an external data source using Excel 2003's summary functions, such as SUM, AVERAGE, MIN, MAX, and COUNT

**Places bar:** The strip of icon buttons appearing in the Open and Save As dialog boxes that allow you to display the most common areas for retrieving and storing files using a single mouse click

**Plot area:** The area for plotting values in a chart; contains the axes and data series

**Present value:** The value in present-day dollars of a series of equal cash payments made sometime in the future

**Primary sort key:** The field or column used to sort the contents of a worksheet list; also called the primary sort order

**Print Preview:** In Excel 2003, the preview mode used to view a workbook in a full-page WYSIWYG display prior to printing; you can use Print Preview to move through pages, zoom in and out on areas of a worksheet, and adjust page margins and column widths

**Print titles:** Row and column data that is stored in a worksheet and used to display repeating header information across page breaks for printed output

**Program statement:** A line of code combining objects, properties, methods, variables, constants, symbols, and/or other elements to perform a task

**Project Explorer window:** In the Visual Basic Editor, the window that displays the open project files, including workbook objects, modules, and user forms

**Project file:** In the *Visual Basic Editor,* a project file is a container for storing and organizing related or associated workbook, worksheet, and module objects; each workbook typically has its own project file, as does the *Personal Macro Workbook*

**Properties window:** In the Visual Basic Editor, the window that displays property settings for the selected object(s); you can change an object's properties at *design time* using this window

**Property procedure:** In VBA, a procedure that you use to create or apply a user-defined property

**Property:** A characteristic or attribute of an object, such as its name or color

**Query:** A question that you ask of the contents of a worksheet list or database file

**Query-by-example (QBE):** The process of querying a worksheet list in a visual mode by specifying criteria in an empty criteria form

**R-square:** A statistical measure of the extent to which two variables are associated; in statistics, this measure is also referred to as the *coefficient of determination*

**Random number:** In Excel 2003, a value between 0 and 1 that results by chance but with equal probability of any other value between 0 and 1

**Range Finder:** An Excel 2003 feature that color-codes the cell or range references in a formula expression for easy reference and error-checking

**Read-only:** A mode that you use or specify for opening a workbook; in read-only mode, you can only save changes that you make to a workbook under a new file name; you cannot replace or "save over" an existing workbook

**Range name:** A name that is given to a range of cells in the worksheet. This name can then be used in formulas and functions to refer to the cell range

**Redo command:** A command that makes it possible to reverse the effects of an Undo command

**Record:** An individual item or entry, such as a person's name, address, and phone number, in a phone book listing; in Excel 2003, represented by a row in the worksheet list

**Regression analysis:** The process of calculating an equation that fits a straight line to a set of historical data points; used in forecasting future values based on past results

**Relational database:** A collection of individual table objects that are related to one another through a common field for the purpose of sharing information and reducing data redundancy; one example of relational database management software is Microsoft Office Access 2003

**Relative cell address:** Default cell reference in a worksheet that automatically adjusts when copied to other cells

**Report Manager:** An Excel 2003 add-in program; used to print a variety of worksheets, *custom views,* and *scenarios* as a single report; you can name and store a report's specifications within a workbook

**Rounded value:** The value of a number rounded to a specific number of decimal places; for example, the number 2.378 rounded to a single decimal returns the number 2.4

**Run time:** During program execution; as the program code is being run

**Scanner:** A hardware device that converts an existing paper-based image, such as a photograph or drawing, into a computer image that is stored digitally on the disk

**Scatter plot chart:** A chart that shows how one or more data elements relate to another data element; also called *XY charts*

**Scenario:** In Excel, a set of assumptions and outcomes that can be saved, documented, and summarized by the Excel 2003 Scenario Manager

**Scope:** The level of visibility in which a procedure or variable operates; a variable's scope or visibility may be at the procedure-level (private), module-level, or macro-level (public)

**Secondary sort key:** The field or column used to sort the contents of an already sorted worksheet list; also called the secondary sort order

**Series:** A sequence of numbers or dates that follows a mathematical or date pattern

**Shared workbook:** A workbook that you expressly share for use in a workgroup or networked environment; workbooks that allow editing functions to be performed by multiple *users* simultaneously

**Sizing handles:** The white boxes or circles that appear around an object that is selected on the *draw layer;* you use the sizing handles to increase or decrease the size of an object

**Smart tags:** An extension of the AutoCorrect feature that attempts to match the contents of a cell with pre-defined "recognizer" keywords; when a match is made, the contents are underlined and the Smart Tag Actions button (⬚) appears next to the cell; click the button to perform context sensitive tasks, such as retrieving stock information from the Web given a stock symbol

**Spelling Checker:** A shared proofing tool in Microsoft Office 2003 that you use to check your workbooks for typing errors and spelling mistakes

**Spreadsheet component:** A Microsoft Office Web Component; an ActiveX object that provides basic interactive spreadsheet functionality using the Microsoft Internet Explorer Web browser

**Style:** A set of formatting specifications that are named and stored with the workbook in which they were created

**Sub procedure:** In VBA, the default procedure type that is used to perform a series of instructions and to effect change on its environment

**Syntax:** The rules, structure, and order of *arguments* used in entering a formula or function

**Task Pane:** A toolbar-like window providing quick access to frequently used commands; by default, the Task Pane appears docked to the right side of the application window, but it may be displayed and hidden using the View menu command

**Template:** A workbook or document that has been saved to a special file and location so that it may be used again and again as a model for creating new documents

**Text Import Wizard:** A series of dialog boxes that lead you through importing and converting a text file to an Excel 2003 worksheet

**Tracer arrows:** The lines that appear on the worksheet when performing an *audit;* blue tracer arrows identify cell relationships, while red tracer arrows show cells producing errors

**Tracing dependents:** When performing an *audit,* the process of identifying formulas that reference a particular cell; the cells containing formulas are known as dependents

**Tracing precedents:** When performing an *audit,* the process of identifying the cells that are used in a formula to calculate a result; the cells containing data are known as precedents

**Trendline:** In an Excel 2003 chart, a line that overlays a data series in an attempt to show a linear, exponential, or other statistical trend

**Two-input data table:** A worksheet table that displays the results from a single outcome formula as two sets of values are substituted into two input cells

**Typeface(s):** The shape and appearance of characters; there are two categories of typefaces: serif and sans serif; serif type (for example, Times Roman) is more decorative and, some say, easier to read than sans serif type (for example, Arial)

**Undo command:** A command that makes it possible to reverse up to the past sixteen commands or actions performed

**Users:** The target audience for a workbook application; the people who will be working with the workbook on a daily basis

**Variable:** A temporary value or storage location in memory for data that can be adjusted and modified

**Variant:** The default data type in VBA that allows you to store any kind of data

**VB Script:** Short for *Visual Basic Scripting Edition;* a subset of Visual Basic functionality created specifically for programming Web content

**Virus:** Program that is created with the intention of doing harm to a computer system

**Visual Basic Editor:** A special utility program for creating, editing, and managing VBA macros and procedures. See *Visual Basic for Applications (VBA)*

**Visual Basic for Applications (VBA):** A subset of the Microsoft Visual Basic programming language that is shared by Microsoft Office 2003 applications, including Excel, for developing macros

**Visual Studio Tools for Office:** A technology that allows Office developers to use Visual Studio .NET (Visual Basic .NET or Visual C# .NET) and the .NET Framework to write code for Word 2003 and Excel 2003 applications; Visual Studio Tools for Office may prove to be the successor to Office VBA programming

**Watch Window:** A window displayed during the auditing of a worksheet that enables you to view a cell's formula and its calculated result

**Web queries:** A set of instructions stored in a text file that allow you to query and interact with Internet Web servers in real-time; used to gain access to and import "live" data from the Web into your local workbooks

**What-if analysis:** The process of changing values in a worksheet model in order to observe the results produced by outcome formulas that are directly or indirectly dependent on the values being changed

**Wildcard characters:** Special symbols that are used to represent other alphanumeric characters in search and filter operations; in Excel 2003, you can use the ? (question mark) to represent any single character and the * (asterisk) to represent any group of characters

**Windows Clipboard:** A program in Windows that allows you to copy and move information within an application or among applications; the system or Windows Clipboard temporarily stores the information in memory before you paste the data in a new location

**Wizard:** A program or process whereby a series of dialog boxes lead you step by step through performing a procedure

**WordArt:** A shared application in Microsoft Office that lets you manipulate and apply special effects to text and then insert the text into a worksheet

**Workbook:** The disk file that contains the *worksheets* and *chart sheets* that you create in Excel 2003

**Worksheet:** A sheet tab or page within a workbook file that is used to create, modify, and display a worksheet grid of columns and rows

**Workspace:** A disk file that stores the names, locations, window positions, and window sizes of open workbooks in the Excel 2003 application window

**World Wide Web:** A visual interface to the Internet based on *hyperlinks;* using Web browser software, you click on hyperlinks to navigate resources on the Internet

**X-axis:** The horizontal, or category, axis that shows the categories for which the chart is making comparisons

**XML:** See *Extensible Markup Language (XML)*

**XY charts:** Charts that show how one or more data elements relate to another data element; also called *scatter plot diagrams*

**Y-axis:** The vertical or value axis in a two-dimensional chart that shows the value or measurement unit for making comparisons among the various categories

# Appendix

## Microsoft Office
## Quick Reference

### Getting Started with Windows

Microsoft Windows is an operating system intended for use on desktop and notebook computers. An *operating system* is a collection of software programs that manage, coordinate, and in a sense, bring life to the computer hardware (the physical components of a computer). Every computer must have an operating system to control its basic input and output operations, such as receiving commands from the keyboard or mouse (input) and displaying information to the screen (output). An operating system is also responsible for managing the storage areas of the computer, namely, hard disks and floppy disks, and for connecting to networks and the Internet. Without an operating system, you cannot communicate with your computer.

### Starting Windows

→ ## Feature

Microsoft Windows provides a graphical environment for working in your application software, such as Microsoft Office. In Windows, you display your work in one or more *windows* on the desktop. You interact with content in these windows using the keyboard, mouse, voice command, or other input device.

→ ## Method

- Turn on your computer and monitor.

- If you are attached to a network, enter your assigned user name and password.

→ ## Practice

In this lesson you start your computer and load Windows.

**1.** Turn on your computer and monitor.

**2.** After a few seconds, a dialog box may appear asking you to enter your *User name* and *Password*. Enter this information now or ask your instructor for further instructions. (*Note:* If this dialog box doesn't display on your computer, proceed to the next step.)

**3.** The entire screen area is referred to as your *desktop*. If there are any windows open on your desktop, do the following:
CLICK: Close button () in the top right-hand corner of each open window
Your Windows desktop should now appear similar, but not identical, to the one shown in Figure 1. Think of the Windows desktop as a virtual desktop where you view your work in progress. In addition, graphical *icons,* such as "My Computer," represent the tools on your desktop that you use most. Some icons allow you to launch applications. Other icons allow you to access and display the contents of storage areas. Since the Windows desktop represents your personal working area, it is likely that your desktop will look different from the one shown in Figure 1.

## Figure 1

The Windows desktop

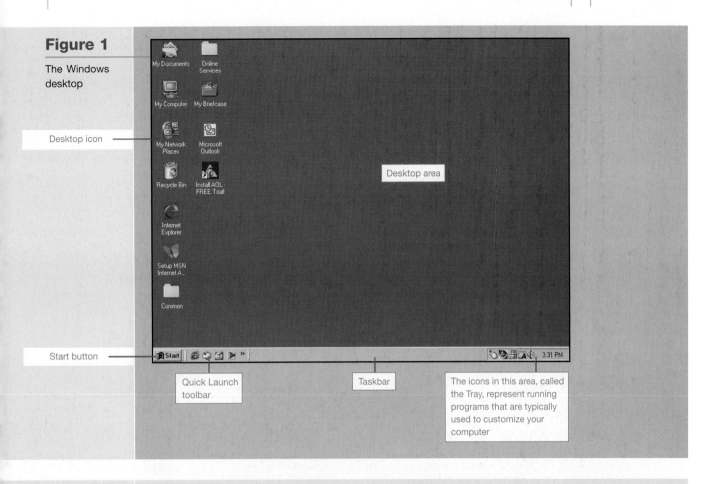

Desktop icon

Desktop area

Start button

Quick Launch toolbar

Taskbar

The icons in this area, called the Tray, represent running programs that are typically used to customize your computer

## Using the Mouse

### → Feature

A **mouse** is an input device that is rolled about on a physical desktop to direct a pointer on your computer's display screen. To work effectively in Windows, you must know how to use the mouse.

### → Method

The most common mouse actions in Windows are:

- **Point**        Slide the mouse on your desk to position the tip of the mouse pointer over the desired object on the screen.

- **Click**        Press down and release the left mouse button quickly. This action, often referred to as *single-clicking*, is typically used for selecting items.

- **Right-click**        Press down and release the right mouse button quickly. Right-clicking the mouse pointer on an object, such as an icon, displays a context-sensitive menu, if available.

- **Double-click**  Press down and release the left mouse button twice in rapid succession. This action is typically used for opening items or programs.

- **Drag**        Press down and hold the left mouse button as you move the mouse pointer across the screen. When the mouse pointer reaches the desired location, release the mouse button. Dragging is used to move objects or windows or to create shortcuts for objects.

→ **Practice**

In this lesson you practice pointing, clicking, right-clicking, and double-clicking with the mouse.
*Setup:* Having loaded Windows, ensure that your Windows desktop appears similar to the one shown in Figure 1.

**1.** The default shape for the mouse pointer looks like a left-pointing diagonal arrow. As you work in Windows, the mouse pointer will change shape as you move it over different parts of the screen or when an application performs a certain task. Each mouse pointer shape has its own purpose and may provide you with important information. There are four primary mouse pointer shapes you should be aware of:

| | | |
|---|---|---|
| ▨ | **left arrow** | Used to select objects, choose menu commands, and access buttons on the taskbar and application toolbars. |
| ⧖ | **hourglass** | Informs you that Windows is busy and requests that you wait. |
| I | **I-beam** | Used to edit text and to position the insertion point (also called a *cursor*). |
| 🖑 | **hand** | In the Help window, the hand is used to select topics and definitions. When browsing your computer or the Web, the hand is used to select a hyperlink that launches an application or takes you to a new document or bookmark. |

**2.** To practice clicking with the mouse:
CLICK: "My Computer" icon (▨) on your desktop
The "My Computer" icon should now appear shaded. This shading indicates that the object is now selected.

**3.** To deselect the "My Computer" icon:
CLICK: on a blank area of the desktop

**4.** To practice right-clicking, do the following:
RIGHT-CLICK: on a blank area of the desktop
A context-sensitive menu is displayed, as shown here. In this learning guide, we refer to menus that you display by right-clicking as *right-click menus*.

**5.** To remove the right-click menu:
CLICK: on a blank area of the desktop

**6.** To practice double-clicking, do the following:
DOUBLE-CLICK: "My Computer" icon (▨) on your desktop
A window should have opened, similar to the one shown in Figure 2.

**7.** Keep this window open for use in the next lesson.

| Arrange Icons By | ▶ |
|---|---|
| Refresh | |
| Paste | |
| Paste Shortcut | |
| Undo Copy | Ctrl+Z |
| New | ▶ |
| Properties | |

**Figure 2**

The "My Computer" window

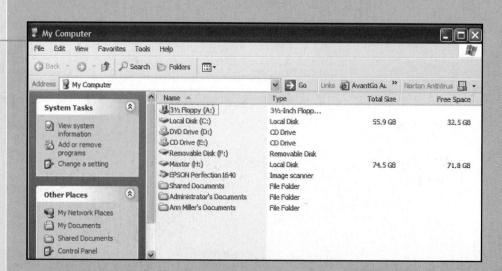

## Using Dialog Boxes

→ **Feature**

In Windows applications, dialog boxes are also used to display messages or to ask for the confirmation of commands. In a dialog box, you indicate the options you want to use and then click the OK command button when you're finished. Dialog boxes are sometimes composed of multiple tabs that allow you to access additional pages within the dialog box by simply clicking on the named tab.

→ **Method**

A dialog box uses the following types of controls or components for collecting information:

| Name | Example | Action |
|---|---|---|
| Check box | Effects: Strikethrough, Double strikethrough, Superscript, Subscript | Click an option to turn it on or off. A check mark (✔) appears in the box when the option is turned on. |
| Command button | OK / Cancel | Click a command button to execute an action. Click OK to accept your selections or click Cancel to exit the dialog box. |
| Combo or drop-down list box | Whole document | Make a choice from the list that appears when you click the down arrow next to the box; only the currently selected option is visible. |
| List box | Font: Times New Roman, Times New Roman Special G1, Times New Roman Special G2, TimeScrDLig, TimeScrDMed | Make a choice from the scrollable list box; several choices, if not all, are always visible. |
| Option button | Page range: All, Current page, Selection, Pages: | Select an exclusive option from a group of related options. |
| Slide box | Screen resolution: Less — More, 1280 by 1024 pixels | Drag the slider bar to make a selection, like using a radio's volume control. |
| Spin box | By: 6 | Click the up and down arrows to the right of the text box until the number you want appears. |
| Tab | Font, Character Spacing, Text Effects | Click a named tab to access other pages in the dialog box. |
| Text box | Category: | Click inside the text box and then type the desired information. |

→ **Practice**

In this lesson you practice using a dialog box.

*Setup:* Ensure that the "My Computer" window is open on the desktop.

**1.** To practice using a dialog box, let's open the Folder Options dialog box. In this step you choose the Tools option by clicking it once in the Menu bar.
CHOOSE: Tools (as shown here)

**2.** From the Tools menu, you will now choose the Folder Options by clicking it in the drop-down menu. Do the following:
CHOOSE: Folder Options from the Tools menu

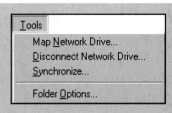

## Figure 3

Folder Options
dialog box:
*General* tab

The contents of
the *General* tab are
displaying.

The Folder Options dialog box appears, as shown in Figure 3. Depending on the version of Windows you are using, this dialog box displays four tabs: *General, View, File Types,* and *Offline Files.*

**3.** To leave the dialog box without making a selection:
CLICK: Cancel command button

## Shutting Down Windows

→ **Feature**

In Windows, the task of exiting Windows is referred to as "shutting down" the computer. You should always follow the suggested steps in this lesson before turning off the computer's power. Otherwise, you run the risk of losing your data.

→ **Method**

- CLICK: Start button ( *start* )
- CLICK: Turn Off Computer from the bottom of the Start menu
- CLICK: Turn Off

→ **Practice**

In this lesson you display the Shut Down Windows dialog box.

**1.** CLICK: *start*
CLICK: Turn Off Computer from the bottom of the Start menu

## Figure 4

Turn off computer
Windows dialog
box

The Turn off computer dialog box should now display (Figure 4). Depending on your version of Windows, the dialog box may appear different on your computer.

**2.** Three options are available; these are explained in Table 1.

**3.** To leave the dialog box without shutting down your computer:
CLICK: Cancel command button

## Table 1

Windows Shut
Down Options

| Command... | When to Use... |
|---|---|
| Stand By | Use this to conserve power. Your computer will appear to shut down, but it is actually still running and all open documents and windows are restored when you press the power switch on your computer. |
| Turn Off | Use this option when you are done with the current work session and want to turn off your computer. After choosing this option, your computer will shut down. |
| Restart | Use this option when you want to continue working in Windows but want to "reboot" your computer. If your system locks up, you may find it necessary to restart your computer. |

## Getting Help in Microsoft Office

Microsoft Office provides several context-sensitive help features and a comprehensive library of online documentation. Like many developers trying to minimize the retail price of software and maximize profits, Microsoft has stopped shipping volumes of print-based documentation in favor of online and Web-based Help options. This module describes several methods for finding answers to your questions.

### Using the Ask a Question Text Box

→ **Feature**

The Ask a Question text box is located on the right side of the Menu bar and provides quick access to your application's Help system. This text box is a convenient starting point for finding answers to your questions. Furthermore, it is available across all of the Microsoft Office applications.

→ **Method**

- CLICK: in the Ask a Question text box
- TYPE: a question or topic
- PRESS: [ENTER]

→ **Practice**

In this lesson you use the Ask a Question box to access an application's Help system.

**1.** Let's begin by loading an Office XP application. To load Microsoft Word, do the following:
CLICK: Start button ( start )

CHOOSE: Programs in the displayed menu
CHOOSE: Microsoft Word from the list of programs
The Microsoft Word application window should appear.

**2.** Locate the Ask a Question text box on the right side of the Menu bar (Figure 5).

**3.** To find out how to write a formal letter using Word, do the following:
CLICK: in the Ask a Question text box
TYPE: **create a letter**

**Figure 5**

Microsoft Word
application
window

PRESS: (**ENTER**)
A list of choices should now appear in the Search Results Task Pane, as shown
in Figure 6.

**Figure 6**

Search Results

Each of these items
is formatted as a
hyperlink that you
can click to access
Word's Help system.

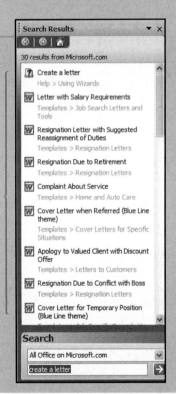

**Figure 7**

Create a letter
help

**4.** To display information for
a specific topic:
CLICK: "Create a letter"
topic. Your window should
now appear similar to the
one shown in Figure 7.

**5.** Close the Help window.
CLICK: Close () button

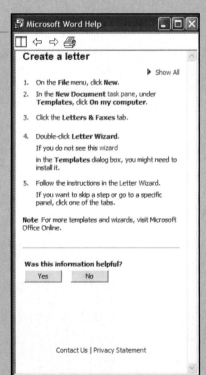

## Using the Help Window

→ **Feature**

You can think of the Help window as the front door to your application's vast help resources. The Help
window provides various methods of searching for information easily and quickly. The *Table of Contents* task pane displays a list of help topics organized as a hierarchy of books and pages.

→ # Method

To access the Help window:

• CHOOSE: Help → Microsoft Word Help from the Menu bar
(*Note:* For this command to work, you must have previously deactivated the Office Assistant, a procedure we describe in the next lesson.)

→ # Practice

In this lesson you use the Help window.

*Setup:* Ensure that the Microsoft Word Help window is displaying. Your screen should appear similar to the one shown in Figure 8.

**Figure 8**

Help Task Pane

**Figure 9**

Help window

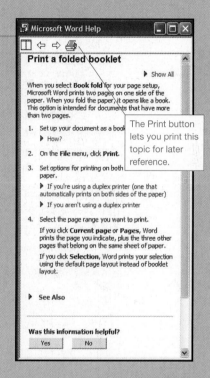

**1.** Note that the *Contents* tab is selected and that the "Creating a Document Quickly Using Wizard" category is expanded. Let's expand a different topic.
DOUBLE-CLICK: "Getting Started with Microsoft Word" topic
A topic and a few additional categories should now be displaying.

**2.** To display information about what's new in Microsoft Word:
CLICK: "What's new in Microsoft Word" topic
Your screen should now appear similar to the one shown in Figure 8.

**3.** Now, let's practice using the *Table of Contents.*
CLICK: Table of Contents hyperlink

**4.** To retrieve help information on the Printing command:
CLICK: Printing hyperlink
In this case, there are several print-related topics to choose from.

**5.** To display information about the "Print a folded booklet" topic:
CLICK: "Print a folded booklet" in the topics list
The Help window should now appear similar to the one shown in Figure 9.

**6.** To close the Help window:
CLICK: its Close button (⊠)

## Using the Office Assistant

→ **Feature**

The Office Assistant watches your keystrokes and mouse clicks as you work and offers suggestions and shortcuts to make you more productive and efficient. For example, in Word, if the Assistant sees that you're creating a letter, it will provide a list of Help topics and tips for creating the letter. You can choose to hide or turn off the Assistant, or otherwise customize it to meet your needs.

→ **Method**

To hide or show the Office Assistant:

- CHOOSE: Help → Hide the Office Assistant,

  *or*

- CHOOSE: Help → Show the Office Assistant

To obtain help from the Office Assistant:

- CLICK: the Office Assistant character to display the question window
- TYPE: a description of what you would like to do
- CLICK: Search

To deactivate the Office Assistant:

- RIGHT-CLICK: the Office Assistant character
- SELECT: *Hide*

→ **Practice**

In this lesson you practice using the Office Assistant.

*Setup:* Ensure that Microsoft Word is loaded.

**1.** If the Office Assistant character isn't displaying, do the following:
CHOOSE: Help → Show the Office Assistant
An Office Assistant character should be displaying, as shown to the right. Because you can select alternate Office Assistant characters, the character on your computer might not be the same as ours.

**2.** To display a question window:
CLICK: the Office Assistant character
The Office Assistant and associated question window might now look like the one shown in Figure 10. Similar to using the Ask a Question text box, described earlier, you type your question in the tip window and then press **ENTER** or click the Search button. A list of suggested topics will display.

**Figure 10**

Office Assistant and associated tip window

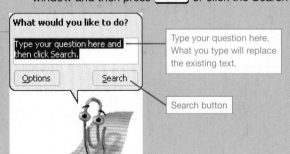

**3.** To remove the tip window:
CLICK: in your document
The insertion point is blinking at the very beginning of your document.

**4.** To close Microsoft Word:
CLICK: Close button (☒) appearing in the top right-hand corner

---

***In Addition*** GETTING HELP ON THE WEB

You can obtain additional help from the Web by choosing Help → Office on Microsoft.com from your application's Menu bar.

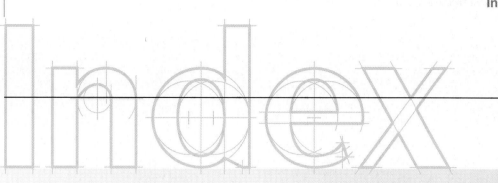

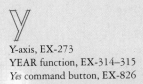